WINN L. ROSCH
HARDWARE BIBLE,
SIXTH EDITION

Winn L. Rosch Hardware Bible, Sixth Edition

International Standard Book Number: 0-7897-2859-1

Library of Congress Catalog Card Number: 2002095010

Printed in the United States of America

First Printing: March 2003

06   05   04   03   4   3   2   1

Trademarks

Warning and Disclaimer

Associate Publisher
Greg Wiegand

Acquisitions Editor
Angelina Ward

Development Editor
Howard Jones

Managing Editor
Charlotte Clapp

Project Editors
Carol Bowers
Tonya Simpson

Copy Editor
Bart Reed

Indexer
Ginny Bess

Proofreader
Kevin Ober

Technical Editors
Rima Regas
Tyler Regas

Team Coordinator
Sharry Lee Gregory

Interior Designer
Anne Jones

Cover Designer
Anne Jones

Page Layout
Stacey Richwine-DeRome

Contents at a Glance

Table of Contents

Foreword

What a time for a book about computers! Machines are faster than ever, with some systems clocking in at more than three gigahertz. Yet, amazingly, they cost less than ever before, too. You can buy a new personal computer for less than $300—at least if you turn over rocks for the best prices and look for a free operating system (which is sort of like buying a car and curb-surfing for tires).

But there's another side to the story. Engineers shudder in corners hoping their jobs will exist next week. High-tech manufacturers jump as high as they can in a not-always-successful effort to keep their nostrils above the rising waters of ruin. How can you make sense of this out-of-kilter world?

One way is by reading the book you hold in your hand. It's designed to help you understand all the technologies that underlie the modern personal computer and all its peripherals that help make it useful. Although you won't be able to design a computer when you're finished (that is, unless you already knew how to when you started), you will know what it takes to design one, how computers work, and how you can work better with them—and get them to do more for you. It doesn't matter if you regard a screwdriver as a tool, an instrument of torture, or a new curiosity you've never before encountered. Even if you have no technical background whatsoever, this book will guide you to a level of understanding that will let you buy, use, and upgrade your computer with confidence. At the same time, you'll find all the technical information that you need to do a school report or business presentation on nearly any current computer topic.

If this book has any weakness, it's that I don't know what the future holds. If I did, I might still have a retirement plan—but that's another story. What I know—and what this book relates—is what's happening in the present.

To put it plainly, we're in a time of change. No one seriously doubts that the entire computer industry is changing radically. It has matured and shifted from growth mode to a sustaining mode. Both businesses and homes are stuffed nearly to capacity with personal computers.

On the other hand, computers have become an essential part of our lives. Rather than exotic and revered machines serving as centerpieces to hobbies and business plans, the computer is something you use every day for chores as mundane as looking up an address, typing a school report, or printing a picture of the kids. As much as computers are used for business, they're also used for fun—for making movies or playing games that test the limits of both your imagination and current technology.

But that's not the end of it. New technologies continue to sweep through the industry. Both still and video cameras have gone digital. Wireless networking is sweeping through both businesses and homes, along with some novel wired systems that use your existing telephone or electrical wiring. Direct digital connections to the Internet—stuff with names like digital subscriber lines and cable modems—are now in the mainstream. The digital versatile disc is in nearly everyone's home, and your computer can now burn your own DVDs. The universal serial bus connection system has matured, and its latest incarnation, version 2.0, will make it the choice for most computer peripherals. Speeds of everything, from those USB ports to microprocessors and disk drives, is going in only one direction: up.

This new edition of the *Hardware Bible* covers all these new developments to help you keep up with the changes in the personal computer industry. Indeed, the industry has been dominated by such changes—dramatic movements from one technology to another, from one generation to the next. Each has marked a major stage in its evolution, and each has brought a new, invigorating era of innovation—and a new edition of this book.

One such change was the move between computer buses. When the last edition of the *Hardware Bible* appeared, the computer industry was finally moving to throw off one of its last links with its origins, now more than two decades old: Industry Standard Architecture (ISA). The innovation of Peripheral Component Interconnect (PCI), with its improved performance and ease of configuration, made mainstream computers possible. Without it, for example, you could never edit video on a desktop computer; burning your own CDs would be chancy; and computer games would be stuck somewhere between *Pong* and *PacMan*.

We are at the very beginning of another period of change. You'll see the rising forces inside this book—Intel's new Itanium processor and AMD's response, the Opteron. The Itanium breaks with the Intel architecture that makes Windows possible. It will require a new Windows, and new software. The Opteron hedges its bets and gives the potential for new 64-bit performance but with backward-looking compatibility that has been so essential at helping us across cusps.

In either case, the transition to 64-bit computing will have an effect that you can see. Edit a snapshot, and big changes will happen fast, almost instantly. You won't grow old making a home movie. Easy animation will be something anyone can do as easily as making a business card from a template.

This new edition of the *Hardware Bible* looks forward to the next generation of computing while retaining its past roots. The good news is that the only thing I've eliminated from this Sixth Edition is redundancy. Nothing has fallen on the cutting room floor. Achieving the contradictory ends of including everything while trimming length is possible thanks to the Web. I've tried to exploit both print and the Internet to put each to work at what it does best.

This book is designed in conjunction with the *Hardware Bible* Web site at www.hardwarebible. com. At the Web site, you'll find additional material—in fact, more than is in the physical book—to enhance the printed edition. In particular, you'll find updates too recent to be printed, as well as discussions of older technologies that are no longer relevant to today's computers, more detailed explanations of the operation of interfaces, and interesting things to know that didn't quite mesh with the narrative of this book.

The selection process was based on making this book something you can readily read. After all, what good is a book if you don't want to read it? To prevent the Web site from interfering with your reading experience, we're not going to flag every tiny instance where you can find more details on the Web site—you'd get the reading equivalent of driving down a rutted road too fast with doubtful shock absorbers. In other words, this book is designed to be a standalone book; you can read it without reference to the Web.

Go to the Web, and it becomes *better*. You get more. But you can select what you want, when you want. The Web site is keyed to individual chapters, but an overall slick navigation system will help you target what you want. Later in this foreword I've included a listing of the supplementary files posted at the time the printed book was published (more than 140 files), along with the chapters they are meant to accompany. As new technologies develop in the computer industry, the Web site will add them.

To preserve the reference value of the *Hardware Bible*, the Web site also includes a reference to all the popular industry connectors and the signals assigned to each pin. I called it Connectorama. You'll also find many of the tables deemed too ungainly or of too little general interest to include in the printed version of the text.

What a time for a book about computers, indeed! In this age of change and exciting new technologies, it's the perfect time for a book. I've tried to make this edition of the *Hardware Bible* the perfect book for the times.

WLR, 12 December 2002

Electronic Addenda

The following supplemental files, grouped by the chapters they are meant to accompany, can be found on the official *Hardware Bible* Web site at www.hardwarebible.com.

Chapter 1
PC History

Chapter 2
Legacy Labeling Standards

Chapter 4
Microprocessor Operating Modes

Chapter 5
Microprocessors of the Past

Non-PC Microprocessors

Chapter 6
Early Commercial Chipsets

Chapter 7
BIOS Identification

BIOS Performance Penalties

BIOS Suppliers

Error Codes

Plug and Play Step-by-Step

About the Author

Winn L. Rosch has written about personal computers since 1981 and has penned nearly 1,500 articles about them—a mixture of reviews, how-to guides, and background pieces explaining new technologies—published in newspapers, magazines, and on the Web. He holds three patents on computer technologies and has won two awards for his writing. He has served as a contributing editor to more than half a dozen computer magazines (including *PC Magazine*) and as a technology reporter (now columnist) for the *Plain Dealer* in Cleveland, Ohio's largest newspaper. His books and articles have been reprinted in several languages (among them French, German, Greek, Italian, Japanese, Portuguese, and Spanish).

Besides writing, Rosch is an attorney licensed to practice in Ohio and holds a Juris Doctor degree. A member of the Ohio State Bar Association, he has served on the association's computer law committee. In other lifetimes, Rosch has worked as a photojournalist, electronic journalist, and broadcast engineer. When deadlines don't loom too close, Rosch has been known to ambush people to collect their images on photographic film, some of whose faces result in oil paintings.

Although Rosch has abandoned his efforts at creating a perpetual motion machine (it kept him up at night), he is now putting the finishing touches on his latest creation, the world's first perpetual stillness machine.

Dedication

For Tess, our first edition together.

We Want to Hear from You!

As the reader of this book, *you* are our most important critic and commentator. We value your opinion and want to know what we're doing right, what we could do better, what areas you'd like to see us publish in, and any other words of wisdom you're willing to pass our way.

As an associate publisher for Que, I welcome your comments. You can email or write me directly to let me know what you did or didn't like about this book—as well as what we can do to make our books better.

Please note that I cannot help you with technical problems related to the *topic* of this book. We do have a User Services group, however, where I will forward specific technical questions related to the book.

When you write, please be sure to include this book's title and author as well as your name, email address, and phone number. I will carefully review your comments and share them with the author and editors who worked on the book.

Email: feedback@quepublishing.com

Mail: Greg Wiegand
            Que Publishing
            201 West 103rd Street
            Indianapolis, IN 46290 USA

For more information about this book or another Que title, visit our Web site at www.quepublishing.com. Type the ISBN (excluding hyphens) or the title of a book in the Search field to find the page you're looking for.

PART I
Introduction

Before venturing off on some quest, most people find it handy to know what they are looking for. Imagine King Arthur's knights off looking for the Holy Grail and returning with an old fishing net, a lipstick-stained Starbucks cup, an empty wine bottle, and so on—with each knight claiming he had found the one true holy relic from the Last Supper. Without guidance as to what a "grail" really is, each could easily justify his find and claim success in his quest. Certainly such a free-form search would have changed the face of literature, but anyone depending on the magical powers of the Grail would likely be disappointed.

Although you're more likely to succeed in a quest to learn about computers than Arthur's knights were in finding the Grail, knowing what you're after will truly help you know when you've got it.

The title of this book, taken in its most general sense, might imply that it's all about nuts and bolts, but we're going to deal with a more specific kind of hardware—the type that goes into computer systems and the devices that computer systems go into. Of course, we *will* talk about real nuts and bolts—both the ones you use to put computers together and the figurative kind. However, our aim here is understanding the digital hardware that defines our lives and the age in which we live.

The first step on our quest will be defining what a computer really is, what it does, and how it relates to us. Imagine King Arthur holding up a placard and pointing to it saying, "This is what the Grail you seek looks like." According to legend, he actually had it easier—the Grail appeared to all the knights of the Round Table in a vision, so they all got a peek at the real thing before they donned their armor. Odds are you own or have access to a computer already, so you're ahead of the knights. Not only have you already seen one, you've also likely touched one.

If you have a computer handy, try it. Touch your computer. Get a tingly feeling? If you did, there's probably something wrong with the grounding of your electrical supply. Otherwise, you probably feel like you've followed someone's guidance and have done something that, after thinking about it, is pretty stupid. You probably don't feel you know anything more about computers than you did before you made this touch. That's because, unlike the Grail, the humble computer isn't going to fill you with mystical knowledge. Therefore, you know right away that the computer is nothing mystical, nothing you have to hold in awe. More than that, you need never touch a computer and feel stupid again. You've already done that.

Let's begin our quest and peer inside to see what a computer really is…intelligently.

Computers

Pinning down the meaning of a word is devilishly difficult, particularly when it's used by a sideshow huckster, lawyer, or some other professional liar. Definitions vary not only with who is speaking, but also when. Language evolves and meanings shift. Words often go to extremes, shifting meanings even to opposites—cold becomes hot, bad becomes good, and rap becomes popular.

Computer is one of those shifty words. Exactly what makes up a computer depends on who you are and when you're talking about. Today a computer is something you can hold in your hand or at least lift with your hands. Thirty years ago, you would have needed a hand from a friend or two to roll a computer machine around. Sixty years ago, a computer could have given you a hand.

Computers in History

Strictly speaking, a computer is something that computes, which is not a particularly informative definition. In the vagueness of the term, however, you'll find an interesting bit of history. The word *computer* does not necessarily mean an electronic machine or a machine at all. If you were a researcher a hundred years ago and you wanted to take a break from heavy-duty math work, such as creating a tide table, you might have taken your computer out to lunch. Scientists engaged in difficult mathematics often employed a bevy of computers—men and women with pencils, papers, and green eye-shades who computed the numbers they needed.

Up until the end of World War II, a *computer* was a person who computed. She might use a pencil (a pen if she were particularly confident of her results), a slide rule, or even a mechanical *calculator*. Poke a few numbers in, pull a crank, and the calculator machine printed an answer in purple ink on paper tape—at least if the questions involved simple arithmetic, such as addition. If this person did a lot of calculations, the black ink of the numbers soon faded to a pale gray, and he grew calluses on his fingertips and cranking hand.

The early machines for mathematics were once all known as *calculators*, no matter how elaborate—and they could be quite elaborate. Charles Babbage, a 19th-century English country gentleman with a bold idea and too much time on his hands, conceived the idea of a machine that would replace the human computers used to calculate values in navigational tables. Babbage foresaw his mechanical computer-replacement as having three advantages over number-crunchers who wielded pencil and paper: The machine would eliminate mistakes, it would be faster, and it would be cheaper. He was right about all but the last, and for that reason he never saw the most intricate machines he designed actually built. Moreover, he never called his unbuilt machines "computers." His names for them were the *Difference Engine* and the *Analytical Engine*. Even though Babbage's machines are considered the forerunners of today's computers—sometimes even considered the *first* computers by people who believe they know such things—they really weren't known as "computers" in Babbage's time. The word was still reserved for the humans who actually did the work.

The word *computer* was first applied to machines after electricity replaced blood as the working medium inside them. In the early part of the 20th century, researchers struggled with the same sort of problems as those in Babbage's time, and they solved them the same way. In the 10 years from 1937 to 1947, scientists created the first devices that are classed as true computers, starting with an electrically powered mechanical machine and ending with an all-electronic device powered by an immense number of vacuum tubes, which required an equally immense amount of good fortune for them to all work long enough to carry out a calculation. Nobody called them computers just yet, however.

The first of these machines—a mechanical computer of which Babbage would have been proud—was the IBM-financed Automatic Sequence Controlled Calculator, which is often called Harvard Mark I. The five-ton design included 750,000 parts, including switches, relays, and rotating shafts and clutches. It stretched out for 50 feet and was eight feet tall. It sounded, according to an observer of the time, like a roomful of ladies knitting.

Many of the fundamentals of today's computers first took form in the partly electronic, partly mechanical machine devised by John Vincent Atanasoff at Iowa State College (now University). His ideas and a prototype built with the aid of graduate student Clifford Berry have become a legend known as the Atanasoff Berry Computer (with the acronym

ABC), the first electronic digital computer—although it was never contemporaneously called a "computer." Iowa State called the device "the world's fastest calculator" as late as 1942.

In Britain, crypto-analysts developed a vacuum-tube (*valve* in Britain) device they called Colossus that some people now call the first electronic computer—usually British folk who don't want you to forget that the English can be clever, too. But the rest of the world never called Colossus a computer—or anything else—because it was top secret until the end of the century.

The present usage of the word *computer* goes back only to June 5, 1943, when ENIAC (the most complex vacuum tube-based device ever made) was first proposed as a collaboration between the United States Army and the University of Pennsylvania. The original agreement on that date first used the description that became its name, as well as the name for all subsequent machines: the Electronic Numerical Integrator and *Computer*.

Three years and $486,804.22 later, the machine made its first computation at the university. The 30-ton behemoth, and its offspring, captured the imagination of the world, and the term *computer* shifted from flesh-and-blood human calculators to machines. In Hollywood, such thinking machines grew even bigger and took over the world, at least in 1950s science fiction movies. In business, ENIAC's offspring, the Univac, took over billing for utilities and gave a new name to bookkeeping foul-ups and bureaucratic incompetence: computer error. Also, scientists tried to figure out how to squeeze a room-sized computer into a space capsule, into which they could barely shoehorn a space-suited human being.

The scientists pretty much figured things out—they created the microprocessor, which led to the age of microcircuits—but not until after a few scientific diversions, including sending men to the moon. Oddly enough, although modern microelectronic circuitry is credited as an offshoot of the space program (shrinking things down and making them lighter was important to an industry in which lifting each ounce cost thousands of dollars), in the history of technology, the moon landing (1969) comes two years before the invention of the microprocessor (1971).

Once the microprocessor hit, however, tinkerers figured how to make small computers cheap enough that everyone could afford one. Computers became personal.

Computers in Today's World

The glitz is gone. Computers no longer rule Hollywood. Robots and aliens (and alien robots in particular) are now the big villains set to rule the world. Businesses no longer seek the fastest computers but instead strive for slowness—that is, slowing down the time between buying and replacing machines.

Computers are now as disposable as old newspaper. We all have one—or will soon. But their advantages hark back to Babbage's claims for his unrealized Analytical Engine. They are accurate, error-free, fast, and cheap—particularly when you compare using a computer for calculations with doing the same work by hand. Got an aspirin?

The one claim that we won't award to the modern computer is being smarter than human calculators. Computers aren't smarter than you are, even if one can balance a checkbook and you can't. Certainly the computer has a better head for numbers than you do. After all, computers are specifically designed to work with numbers. For people, numbers are—at best—an afterthought, at least if you're not an accountant. People have bigger worries, such as finding food, shelter, and sex. Computers have us to take care of those details for them (maybe not the sex) so that they can concentrate on calculating.

Computers are good at calculating—and they're fast. Even today's cheapest personal computers can figure the product of two 40-bit numbers billions of times in the fraction of a second it takes one of us human beings even to realize we have two 40-bit numbers to multiply.

Scientists and engineers like to make comparisons between the intelligence of their computers (usually the fastest computer ever built, which changes month to month) and the thinking ability of animate creatures, typically something like "an insect brain." Most scientists know it's all balderdash, but they make these claims because it gets them big headlines. No mere bug can multiply two 40-bit numbers—or even wants to.

Computers are more accurate because they are designed that way. Using digital logic, their thinking automatically wipes out any noise that can confuse their calculations. By elaborating on the math with error-checking, they can quickly detect and prevent most mistakes. They don't think at all like you and I do. They have to be told exactly what to do, led by the hand through the process of finding an answer by a set of instructions we call a *program*.

Computers also have better memories than people. Again, they are designed that way. One of our human advantages is that we can adapt and shift the way we deal with things thanks to our malleable memories. Remember Mom's cooking? Computers have long-term memories designed for just the opposite purpose—to remember everything, down to the last detail, without error and without limit. Even Deep Blue, the computer that finally beat a flesh-and-blood chess Grand Master, would quickly succumb to the elements if left outside. Although able to calculate billions of chess moves in seconds, it lacks the human sense to come in out of the rain. And the feet.

What we call "computer intelligence" is something far different from what we call "intelligence" in humans. That's actually good, because even experts can't agree on what human intelligence is, or even how humans think. Things are much more straightforward for computers. We know how they think as well as how to measure how well they do their jobs.

Computer Intelligence

Biomechanical engineers are changing the way people think about insect intelligence. In an effort to develop machines that walk like insects, they have discovered that form doesn't dictate function, and function doesn't dictate form. The two are intimately linked.

Although some researchers have worked hard to develop machines that walk like insects by adding more and more intelligence, others have gone back to the drawing board with a more mechanical approach. By mimicking the structure of the insect body, they have been able to make mechanical insects that duplicate the gait of your typical six-legged bug. These mechanical insects can even change their gait and crawl over obstacles, all using no more intelligence than an electric motor. In other words, biomechanical engineers have discovered that the intelligence is in the design, not the insect.

Comparing the thinking power of the 12 neurons in an insect's brain with the power of a computer becomes a question of design. The insect is designed for eating garbage and buzzing around your head. Although you might feed your computer a diet of garbage, it's really designed for executing programs that calculate answers for you, thus letting you communicate and otherwise waste your time. Any comparison between bug and computer is necessarily unfair. It must inevitably put one or the other on alien turf. The computer is easily outclassed by anything that walks, but walking bugs won't help you solve crossword puzzles.

With that perspective, you can begin to see the problems with comparing computer and human intelligence. Although they sometimes perform the same tasks—for example, playing chess—they have wildly different designs. A human can forage in the jungle (African or Manhattan), whereas a computer can only sit around and rust. A computer can turn one pixel on your monitor green at 7:15 a.m. on August 15, 2012, whereas you might not even bother waking up for the event.

Computers earn our awe because they can calculate faster and remember better. Even the most complex computer applications—video games, photo editors, and digital animators—all reduce down to these two capabilities.

Calculating involves making decisions and following instructions. People are able to and often do both, so comparing computers to people is only natural. However, whereas it might take you 10 minutes to decide between chocolate and vanilla, a computer makes a decision in about a billionth of a second. If you had to make all the decisions your computer does to load a copy of Microsoft Windows, multicellular organisms could evolve, rise up from the sea, mutate into dinosaurs and human beings, and then grow wings and fly to nearby planets before you finished. So it stands to reason that computers are smarter, right?

As with insects, the playing field is not quite level. Your decision isn't as simple as it looks. It's not a single issue: Your stomach is clamoring for chocolate, but your brain knows that with just one taste, a zit will grow on your nose and make you look like a rhinoceros. And there are those other flavors to tempt you, too. You might just have several billion conflicts to resolve before you can select a cone, plain or sugar, and fill it full of…did you want ice cream or frozen yogurt, by the way?

No doubt some of us follow instructions better than others. Computers, on the other hand, can't help but follow their instructions. They are much better at it, patiently going through the list step by step. But again, that doesn't make them smarter than you. On the contrary, if you follow instructions to the letter, you're apt to end up in trouble. Say you've found the map to Blackbeard's treasure, and you stand, shovel in hand, at the lip of a precipice. If the map says to take 10 paces forward, you're smart enough to know better. A computer confronted with the same sort of problem would plummet from its own digital precipice. It doesn't look ahead (well, some new machines have a limited ability to sneak a peek at coming instructions), and it doesn't know enough to stop short of trouble.

Computers have excellent memory. But unlike a person, a computer's memory isn't relational. Try to remember the name of an old friend, and you might race through every name you know in alphabetical order. Or you might remember he had big ears, and instantly the name "Ross" might pop into your mind. You've related your friend's name with a distinguishing feature.

By itself, a computer's memory is more like a carved stone tablet—permanent, unchanging, and exacting. A computer has to know precisely what it's looking for in order to find it. For example, a computer can find a record of your 2002 adjusted gross income quite easily, but it can't come up with Ross's name based on the fact that he has big ears. On the other hand, you, as a mere human, have about zero chance of remembering the 2002 adjusted gross incomes of 10,000 people—something even a 10-year-old personal computer can tackle adroitly.

The point is not to call either you or your computer dumb but rather to make you see the differences in the way you both work. The computer's capabilities compliment your own. That's what makes them so wonderfully useful. They can't compete with people in the brain function department, except in the imaginations of science fiction writers.

So What Is a Computer?

In today's world and using today's technology, a computer is an electronic device that uses digital logic under the direction of a program for carrying out calculations and making decisions based on those calculations. By this essential definition, a computer has four elements to its construction: electronics, digital logic, programming, and calculating/decision-making.

That's a mouthful of a definition, and one that's pretty hard to swallow, at least in one piece. To help you understand what all this means, let's take a closer look at each of the elements of this definition.

Electronics

The technology that makes the circuits of a computer work is called *electronics*. Dig into this word, and you'll find that it comes from *electrons*, the lightweight particles carrying a negative charge that comprise one of the fundamental constituents of atoms. The flow of electrons through metals is what we normally think of as electricity, a word taken from the Greek word for amber, *elektrum*. Static electricity, the stuff that creates sparks when you touch a metal doorknob after shuffling across a carpet on a dry winter day, was once most readily produced by rubbing amber with a silk cloth. So, the stuff that makes computers work is named after what's essentially petrified pine tree sap.

Electronics is a technology that alters the flow of charges through electrical circuits. In the more than two centuries since Benjamin Franklin started toying with kites and keys, scientists have learned how to use electricity to do all sorts of useful things, with two of the most important being to operate motors and burn light bulbs. Motors can use electricity to move and change real-world objects. Lights not only help you see but also see what an electrical circuit is doing.

For the record, this electricity stuff is essential for building a computer. Babbage showed how it could be done with cams, levers, gears, and an old crank (which might have been Babbage himself). If you, like Babbage, have too much time on your hands, you could build a computer for yourself that runs hydraulically or with steam. In fact, scientists hope to build computers that toy with quantum states.

However, electricity and electronics have several big advantages for running a computer over nearly everything else (except that quantum stuff, and that's why scientists are interested in it). Electricity moves quickly, at nearly the speed of light. Electrical devices are easy to interface with (or connect to) the real world. Think of those motors and electric lights. They operate in the real world, and an electrical computer can change the currents that run these motors and lights. Moreover, engineers have mastered the fabrication of electrical circuits of all sizes, down to those so small you can't see them, even if you can see the results of their work on your computer screen. And above all, electrical circuits are familiar with off-the-shelf parts readily available, so you can easily tinker with electrical devices and build them economically. And that's the bottom line. Just as celebrities are famous primarily for being famous, electronics are used a lot because they are used a lot.

Digital

Most of the circuits inside a computer use a special subset of electronic technology called *digital electronics*. The most important characteristic of the digital signals in these circuits is that they usually have only two states, which are most often described as on and off (or one and zero). Some special digital systems have more than two states, but they are more than you need to understand right now.

Usually the states are defined as the difference between two voltage levels, typically zero and some standard voltage, or between a positive and negative voltage value. The important part about the states of digital electronics is not what they are but what is between them—nothing. Certainly you can find a whole world of numbers between zero and one—fractions come to mind—but with digital technology the important fact is not whether there could be something between the digital states, but that anything other than the two digital states gets completely *ignored*. In essence, digital technology says if something is not a zero it is a one. It cannot be anything else.

Think about it, defining the world this way *could* make sense. For example, an object is either a horse or it is not a horse. Take a close look. It has hooves, four legs, a mane, and a tail, so you call it a horse. If it has six legs and a horny shell and, by the way, you just stepped on it, it is probably not a horse. Yes, we could get on sketchy ground with things such as horseflies, but nit-picking like that is just noise, which is exactly what the two digital states ignore.

This noise-free either/or design is what makes digital technology so important. Noise is normally a problem with electrical signals. The little bit of electricity in the air leaks into the electrical signals flowing through wires. The unwanted signal becomes noise, something that interferes with the signal you want to use. With enough noise, the signal becomes unusable. Think of trying to converse over the telephone with a television playing in the background. At some point, turning the TV up too much makes it impossible to hold a phone conversation. The noise level is simply too high.

Digital signals, however, allow circuits to ignore the noise. For computers, that's wonderful, because every little bit of added noise could confuse results. Adding two plus two would equal four plus some noise—perhaps just a little, but a little might be the difference between being solvent and having your checking account overdrawn. Noise-free digital technology helps ensure the accuracy of computer calculations.

But sometimes things can get tricky. Say you encounter a beast with hooves, four legs, a mane, a tail, and black-and-white stripes. That's a horse of a different color—a creature that most zoologists would call a *zebra* and spend hours telling you why it's *not* a horse. The lesson here (besides being careful about befriending didactic zoologists) is that how you define the difference between the two digital states is critical. You have to draw the line somewhere. Once you do—that is, once you decide whether a zebra is a horse or not—it fits the two-state binary logic system.

Logic

Logic is what we use to make sense of digital technology. Logic is a way of solving problems, so you can consider it a way of thinking. For computers, "logically" describes exactly how they think. Computers use a special system of logic that defines rules for making decisions based, roughly, on the same sort of deductive reasoning used by Sherlock Holmes, some great Greek philosophers, and even you (although you might not be aware of it—and might not always use it).

Traditional logic uses combinations of statements to reach a conclusion. Here is an example of logical reasoning:

1. Dragons eat people.
2. I am a people.
3. There is a dragon waiting outside my door.

Conclusion: If I go outside, I will be eaten.

This sort of reasoning works even when you believe more in superstition than science, as the example shows.

Computer circuitry is designed to follow the rules of a formal logic system and will always follow the rules exactly. That's one reason why people sometimes believe computers are infallible. But computers make no judgments about whether the statements they operate on are true or false. As long as they get logically consistent statements (that is, the statements don't contradict one another), they will reach the correct conclusions those statements imply.

Computers are not like editors, who question the content of the information they are given. To a computer, proposition 1, "Dragons eat people," is accepted unquestioningly. Computers don't consider whether a race of vegetarian dragons might be running about.

Computers don't judge the information they process because they don't really process information. They process symbols represented by electrical signals. People translate information into symbols that computers can process. The process of translation can be long and difficult. You do some of it by typing, and you know how hard that is—translating thoughts into words, then words into keystrokes.

Computers work logically on the symbols. For the computer, these symbols take electronic form. After all, electrical signals are the only things that they can deal with. Some symbols indicate the dragon, for example. They are the *data*. Other symbols indicate what to do with the data—the logical operations to carry out. All are represented electronically inside the computer.

Engineers figured out ways of shifting much of the translation work from you to the computer. Consequently, most of the processing power of a computer is used to translate information from one form to another, from something compatible with human beings into an electronic form that can be processed by the logic of the computer. Yes, someone has to write logic to make the translation—and that's what computer programming is all about.

Programmability

A computer is *programmable*, which means that it follows a program. A program is a set of instructions that tells the computer how to carry out a specific task. In that way, a program is like a recipe for chocolate chip cookies (a metaphor we'll visit again) that tells, step by step, how to mix ingredients together and then burn the cookies.

Programmability is important because it determines what a computer does. Change the program the computer follows, and it will start performing a new, different task. The function of the computer is consequently determined by the program.

That's how computers differ from nearly all machines that came before them. Other machines are designed for a specific purpose: A car carries you from here to there; an electric drill makes holes in boards and whatever else gets in the way; a toaster makes toast from bread. But a computer? It can be a film editor, a dictation machine, a sound recorder, or a simple calculator. The program tells it what to do.

Calculating and Decision-Making

The real work that goes on inside your computer bears no resemblance to what you ask it to do. Programs translate human-oriented tasks into what the computer actually does. And what the computer does is amazingly simple: It reacts to and changes patterns of bits, data, and logic symbols.

Most of the time the bit-patterns the computer deals with represent numbers. In fact, any pattern of binary bits—the digital ones and zeroes that are the computer's fodder—translates directly into a binary number. The computer manipulates these bit-patterns or binary numbers to come up with its answers. In effect, it is calculating with binary numbers.

The computer's calculations involve addition, subtraction, multiplication, division, and a number of other operations you wouldn't consider arithmetic, such as logic operations (*and*, *or*, and *not*) and strange tasks such as moving bits in a binary code left and right.

More importantly, the computer can compare two binary codes and do something based on that comparison. In effect, it decides whether one code is bigger (or smaller, or whatever) than another code and acts on that decision.

Work your way up through this discussion, and you'll see that those codes aren't necessarily numbers. They could be translations of human concerns and problems—or just translations of letters of the alphabet. In any case, the computer can decide what to do with the results, even if it doesn't understand the ideas behind the symbols it manipulates.

The whole of the operation of the computer is simply one decision after another, one operation after another, as instructed by the computer's program, which is a translation of human ideas into a logic system that uses binary code that can be carried out by electronic signals.

So what is a computer? You have one answer—one that more than anything else tells you that there is no easy answer to what a computer is. In fact, it takes an entire book to explain most of the details, the ins and outs of a computer. This book.

Functions and Components

Going through a long-winded description of what a computer is doesn't seem to make sense when you can *see* what a computer is, sitting right in front of you. It's a box, a keyboard, and a screen with a headache attached.

Rather than looking at a strictly formal definition of a computer, it's probably more useful to learn what it is with a more practical approach: Examine the machine in front of you. After all, you can see the parts and how they fit together.

If you have a desktop computer or a tower, you've got a big box with an empty slot or two on the front and a bunch of jacks and connectors on the back. A notebook scatters the slots and jacks all around its edges, but in either style of case you get essentially the same repertory. And, if you look closely in either case, you'll see that all the parts are held together with a few screws. With a flashlight in hand, you might be able to squint through the slots and see some of the internal parts. Get daring and twist out the screws, and you'll get a much better view. But there will still be something you cannot see—what those parts do.

The functions of the components of a computer are not at all obvious based on what they look like. Although some machines make the functions of their parts quite obvious—the wheels of a car pretty much shout their function—with a computer, the function of each part is hidden in a snarled mass of digital electronic circuitry and accompanying programs. Take, for example, arguably the most important part of any modern computer, the microprocessor. Its inner workings must be protected inside a hermetically sealed case because air would destroy the delicate crystalline circuits inside. Even if the microprocessor were encased in glass, however, you could never see the electricity flowing through it or the logic operations it performs in creating your computer's thoughts. About the only electricity you can normally see is lightning, and you probably hope you'll never see *that* inside your computer.

Even though all the good stuff inside a computer is essentially invisible, examining the individual parts that deal with the stuff you can't see is key to understanding how the whole thing works. This microscope-to-the-parts strategy makes sense for economic as well as explanatory reasons. You buy a computer as a collection of parts, even if you pay one price and get one big box. One reason is that not all computers are the same, a fact that should be obvious as soon as you pull out your credit card. You can buy a brand new (though technologically old) computer for barely more than $100 today, or you can pay fifty times more. Even though you might not notice a difference between them when you run Microsoft Word—scary as it sounds, that's often true for reasons you'll understand before you finish this book—manufacturers and retailers can easily justify the difference. One machine can handle some tasks (obviously other than running Word) more adroitly than the other. The underlying reason for this difference is a matter of the component parts from which the two machines are made.

Electronic devices, whether computers, digital cameras, or portable radios, are all built from tiny electronic parts such as resistors, capacitors, transistors, and integrated circuits. Each of these changes the flow of electronics in some small, simple way, and figuring out how to connect them together to accomplish some tiny task is how electrical engineers earn their salaries. But combine these tiny assemblies together at the next level (another task for engineers), and the result is a module or computer component with a definite, defined task. Each is a subassembly like the various parts of a car or refrigerator. A car has a motor, wheels, steering system, doors, and windows. A refrigerator has a motor, a compressor, cooling coils, a box, doors, and insulation. Similarly, every computer is built from an array of components, such as a microprocessor, power supply, and flashing lights.

Each of these individual components has a well-defined function. For example, in your car, the motor, transmission, axle, and wheels make the car move along the highway, providing the *motive* function. In the refrigerator, the motor, compressor, and coils make up the *cooling* function.

Of course, the car has other functions in addition to its motive function. For example, the body, windows, and seats provide a *passenger-carrying* function, much as a refrigerator has a *food-holding* function. Although at first thought such secondary functions might seem incidental to the overall concept of the car or refrigerator, these functions are actually essential parts that help define what a car or refrigerator is. After all, you wouldn't have much of a car if it couldn't go anywhere or hold people. Nor would a refrigerator be as useful if it couldn't keep cool or hold food.

Similarly, the computer has several functions that define what it is and what it does. Although some of the functions might seem incidental to the concept of a computer as a thinking (or calculating) machine, all are essential for making a modern computer the useful device that it is.

The typical modern personal computer has four major functions. These include thinking, communicating, remembering, and listening and monitoring, all tied together by an electronic and mechanical infrastructure. Of course, this division is somewhat arbitrary. Some people might, for example, combine thinking and remembering, and others (say people who sell security software) might add additional functions, such as security. But this five-way split has one big advantage over any other: It's how I've chosen to arrange this book.

Each of these functions requires one or more hardware components to carry it out. For example, thinking is not merely a matter for microprocessors. It requires memory in which to execute programs, a chipset to link the microprocessor's circuits to the rest of the computer, and some semi-permanent software in the form of the BIOS to bring everything to life. Memory involves not only the chips that we think of as computer memory but also devices for longer-term memory, which include hard disks and other mass storage devices that keep a computer from forgetting even after you switch its power off.

We'll start our computer tour by taking a look at these functions and subdividing them into the components your computer uses to carry them out.

Processing

The function that defines the computer is its ability to calculate and make decisions. Without the ability to make decisions, a computer could not follow a program more complex than a simple sequence. If your computer lacked the ability to calculate, you might as well have a footstool next to your desk or a dumbbell in your briefcase. These abilities give the computer its electronic thinking power—or more importantly, help the computer enhance your own thinking power.

Several components make up the thinking function of a computer. The most important is the *microprocessor*, but by itself a microprocessor couldn't function. It would be like a brain without a spine and blood supply. For the computer, such support functions are handled by a *chipset*. In addition, the computer needs the equivalent of instinct in animals and humans, the primitive behaviors that help it survive even without learning. For the computer, the equivalent of instinct is the *BIOS*, a set of factory-installed, essentially unchangeable programs that give the computer its basic functions and, some say, personality.

Microprocessor

The most important of the electronic components on the motherboard is the micro-processor. It does the actual thinking inside the computer. The power of a computer—how fast it can accomplish a given job, such as resizing a digital photo—depends on the model of microprocessor inside the computer as well as how fast that microprocessor operates (the speed is measured in the familiar megahertz or gigahertz). The kind of microprocessor also determines what software language it understands. For example, Windows computers and Macintosh computers use microprocessors from different families that understand different software languages.

As fits its role, the microprocessor usually is the largest single *integrated circuit* in a computer. It makes more connections, so it has the biggest socket and usually holds the dominant position on the main circuit board. It is the centerpiece of every computer. In fact, the microprocessor is the most complicated device yet devised by human beings, so complex that earlier designs couldn't fit all the silicon microcircuitry into a single chip. Many older microprocessors (such as the Pentium II series) were modules that combined several smaller integrated circuit chips into a big assembly that included a main microprocessor, a coprocessor, a cache controller, and cache memory. Today, however, everything for an advanced microprocessor such as the Pentium 4 fits on a single silicon chip about one-inch square.

Chipset

The *chipset* of a computer provides vital support functions to its microprocessor. The chipset creates signals that are the lifeblood of the microprocessor, such as the clock or oscillator that sets the pace of its logic operations. In addition, the chipset links the micro-processor to the rest of the computer, both the memory and external functions, through input/output ports. The chipset also provides the vital link to your computer's expansion bus that enables you to add new capabilities to its repertory. The chipset is so important that in most computers it affects the performance and operation of the system as much as does its microprocessor. In fact, for some knowledgeable buyers, the choice of chipset is a major purchasing criterion that distinguishes one computer from another.

At one time, a chipset was a collection of dozens of individual electronic components. In today's computers, however, manufacturers have combined all the traditional functions of this essential support circuitry into a few large integrated circuits. In computers, in fact, the entire chipset has been squeezed into a single package. Typically the integrated circuit or circuits that make up the chipset are squares of black epoxy sitting on the main computer circuit board, usually the largest individual electronic components there, except for the microprocessor.

BIOS

Just as animals rely on instincts to survive in the real world before they can learn from their experiences, a computer has a built-in program that tells it what to do before you load any software. This program is called the *Basic Input/Output System* because it tells the computer's microprocessor how to get input from the outside world and send output there. The BIOS defines how a computer acts and behaves before you load software. In modern computers, the BIOS has several additional functions, all essential to making the computers get started and work.

Unlike the microprocessor and chipset, the BIOS is mostly ephemeral: It is a program, a list of software codes. It takes physical form because it permanently resides in a special kind of memory chip, one that retains its memory without the need for electricity. This way, the BIOS program is always remembered, ready to be used as soon as the computer gets switched on. The chip holding the BIOS typically is a large flash memory chip. Its most distinguishing feature is its label, however. Because it holds software, the BIOS chip is usually emblazoned with a copyright notice just like other software products.

Communicating

The real useful work that computers do involves not just you but also the outside world. Your computer must be able to communicate to put its intelligence to work. When your computer communicates with other systems far away, the process is often called *telecommunications*. When your computer connects with other computers over a network, engineers call the communication capability *connectivity*. When your computer plugs into printers and other nearby peripherals, engineers say your computer is doing what it's supposed to—there's no fancy word for it. No matter. Thanks to the communication capabilities of your computer, it can link to any of a number of hardware peripherals through its network jacks and input/output ports. Better still, through modems and the Internet, it can connect with nearly any computer in the world.

Expansion Buses

Computers need to communicate with any of a number of peripherals, some of which reside *inside* the computer's case. The primary link to these internal components is the *expansion bus*.

As the name implies, the *expansion bus* of a computer allows you to expand its capabilities by sliding in accessory boards (cleverly termed *expansion boards*). For this to work, the expansion bus sets up an internal communication channel inside your computer. *Expansion slots* are spaces inside the computer that provide special sockets or connectors to plug in the capabilities and functions locked in the circuitry of the expansion boards.

In a desktop computer, the expansion bus usually is a row of three or more long connectors on the main circuit board near the back of the computer's case. Depending on the overall design of the computer, one or more of these slots will be filled with expansion boards in the basic factory configuration. In a notebook computer, expansion slots are different, meant to accept modules the size of credit cards that deliver the same functions as expansion boards.

Interfaces

Interfaces provide a communication channel that lets your computer exchange information with a variety of devices, primarily storage systems (discussed later in the chapter). The interface translates the signals inside your computer into a form that's more suited to traveling outside the confines of its main circuit boards. You've probably heard people speak about the most familiar interfaces, such as ATA (also called IDE) and SCSI, acronyms that describe connections used by hard and optical disk drives.

The interface takes the form of a connector. The ATA interface is usually built in to the main circuit board of all modern computers. A cable links this connector to one on a disk drive. The SCSI interface usually resides on a separate circuit board that fits into the expansion bus of your computer.

Input/Output Ports

Your computer links to its peripherals through its input and output ports. Every computer needs some way of acquiring information and putting it to work. Input/output ports are the primary routes for this information exchange.

In the past, the standard equipment of most computers was simple and almost preordained—one serial port and one parallel port, typically as part of their motherboard circuitry. Modern standards are phasing out these ports, so we'll consider them (for purposes of this book) *legacy* ports. Today, new and wonderful port standards are proliferating faster than dandelions in a new lawn. Hard-wired serial connections are moving to the new Universal Serial Bus (USB), whereas the Infrared Data Association (IrDA) system and oddly named Bluetooth provide wireless links. Digital video connections use FireWire, also called IEEE 1394. Even the simple parallel port has become an external expansion bus capable of linking dozens of devices to a single jack.

The ports are the jacks or connectors you'll find on the back of most desktop computers or scattered around the edges of notebook machines. They come in various sizes and shapes, meant to match special connectors unambiguously.

Local Area Networks

Any time you link two or more computers together, you've created a network. Keep the machines all in one place—one home, one business, one *site* in today's jargon—and you have a local area network (LAN). Spread them across the country, world, or universe with telephone, cable, or satellite links and you get a wide area network (WAN). A network is both a wiring system and a software system. The wires connect computers together; the software is the language for passing messages around.

Most networks use some kind of wire to connect computers, although *wireles* networks are becoming popular, especially in homes where their short range is no problem and their lack of wires a great advantage.

Telecommunications

To extend the reach of your computer beyond your home or office, you usually must rely on the international telephone system to provide the connection. Because short-sighted engineers a hundred years ago never considered that you'd want to connect your computer to your telephone, they built the phone system to use an entirely different kind of signal than your computer uses. Consequently, when you want to connect with other computers and information sources such as the Internet through the international telephone system, you need a *modem* to adapt your computer's data to a form compatible with the telephone system's.

In a quest for faster transfers than the ancient technology of the classic telephone circuit can provide, however, data communications are shifting to newer systems, including digital telephone services (such as DSL), high-speed cable connections, and direct digital links with satellites. Each of these requires its own variety of connecting device—not strictly speaking a "modem" but called that for consistency's sake. Which you need depends on the speed you want and the connections available to you.

Internet

The Internet is properly described as a "network of networks." In concept, it links all the computers in the world together so that they can share information (but more often games and pornography). The World Wide Web is essentially the commercial side of the Internet. Once you link up with the Web, your computer is no longer merely the box on your desk. It becomes part of a single, massive international computer system with a single goal: transferring money out of your bank account. Even so, it retains all the features and abilities you expect from a computer—an Internet connection only makes it even more powerful.

The Internet is more an idea than a physical form. Picture it as a spider web anchored to each and every computer in the world.

Remembering

No matter how smart you are, you wouldn't *know* anything if you couldn't remember. Thoughts and ideas would go in one neuron and out another, forever lost in the entropy of the universe. You know things because you can call back thoughts and ideas, to work on them again or just talk about them. A computer, too, needs some way of retaining its thoughts. Like you, it needs both short-term memory for holding ideas while it works on them and long-term memory to store all the facts and old ideas that, by chance, it might need another day.

The short-term memory of computers is often called simply *memory*. The long-term memory is often termed *mass storage* and involves several technologies. *Hard disk drives* hold the ideas you put into the computer, both commercial programs and your own original data. *Floppy disks* and *optical drives* (CDs and DVDs for the most part) store the ideas of others than you want your computer to access. *Tape drives* provide a safety net, keeping a duplicate copy of your computer's most important ideas.

Memory

Just as you need your hands and workbench to hold tools and raw materials to make things, your computer's microprocessor needs a place to hold the data it works on and the tools to do its work. *Memory*, which is often described by the more specific term *RAM* (which means Random Access Memory), serves as the microprocessor's workbench. The amount and architecture of the memory of a system determines how it can be programmed and, to some extent, the level of complexity of the problems it can work on. Modern software often requires that you install a specific minimum of memory—a minimum measured in megabytes—to execute properly. With modern operating systems, more memory often equates to faster overall system performance.

In today's computers, memory usually comes in subassemblies called *memory modules* that plug into special sockets on the main circuit board of your computer. Most computers have three or more of these sockets in a group, one or more of which is filled with a memory module as standard equipment.

Hard Disk Drives

Long-term memory is where you store thoughts and ideas that, although you don't need them immediately, you need to know—stuff like your shoe size, which doesn't come up in everyday conversation (at least not among normal adults) but becomes a handy factoid when musing through a mail-order catalog. Your computer's hard disk holds such factoids along with all the other stuff it needs to know but not at this exact moment—such as the instructions for programs you're not using, financial records you hope the auditor will ignore, term papers you someday hope to publish as best-selling fiction, and even extra designs for wallpaper for your computer screen. Your computer's hard disk lets you call on any of those stored facts on a microsecond's notice.

Most hard disks take the form of a sealed box, typically silver and black with a green circuit board dotted with tiny electrical components on the bottom. A hard disk connects to the main circuit board of your computer through that *interface* we talked about earlier via a short, wide, and flat set of wires, called a *ribbon cable* because it looks like a ribbon (although an admittedly strange gray ribbed ribbon).

Floppy Disk Drives

Once upon a time, some computers lacked hard disk drives and instead used *floppy disk drives* ("once upon a time" being in the unbelievable past, a little before Cinderella cleaned out fireplaces). Inexpensive, exchangeable, and technically unchallenging, the floppy disk served as a data interchange system for years because it was based on well-proven technologies and was mass produced by the millions.

Today, the floppy disk drive is found on nearly every computer, but functionally it's about as useful to your computer as an appendix. (Granted, an appendix won't fit into a drive slot, but you get the idea.) In today's world the floppy disk is slow and holds too little information, so it is gradually disappearing from computers, replaced in function by any of a variety of optical drives.

The computers that still have floppy disk drives usually wear them proudly, out in front. On desktop systems, it's usually the uppermost drive in the case. From the outside you see only a long, black slot about three-and-a-half inches wide with a rectangular button near one corner. Notebook computers put their floppy disk drives, if they have one, wherever they fit—usually hidden in the side of the computer under the keyboard.

Optical Drives

Getting new memories into your computer is the primary job served by optical drives. They store programs and data in a convenient form—small discs—that's standardized so that you can exchange the discs (and memories) between computers. (Note that due to a strange quirk of design and origin, magnetic drives use "disks" whereas optical drives use "discs.")

Optical discs currently come in two flavors: Compact Discs and Digital Versatile Discs. These are the CDs and DVDs you slide into your home entertainment system. In either form, discs are cheap and easy to copy, so software publishers have made the CD-ROM their preferred means of getting their products to you, with DVDs slowly replacing CD-ROMs because of their higher capacity. You can create your own optical disks with a suitable drive to store either data for your computer or music and video for your entertainment systems.

A CD-ROM or DVD drive is usually the other drive on the front of your desktop computer, bigger than the floppy and featuring a volume control and headphone jack (should you want to slide a music CD into the drive). You'll know what it is as soon as you press the eject button and the tray rolls out. On a notebook computer, manufacturers stuff their optical drives wherever they fit, usually on the side near the back of the computer.

Tape Drives

Tape is for backup, pure and simple. It provides an inexpensive place to put your data just in case—just in case some light-fingered freelancer decides to separate your computer from your desktop; just in case the fire department hoses to death everything in your office that the fire and smoke failed to destroy; just in case you empty your Recycle Bin moments before discovering you accidentally deleted all your exculpatory tax records; just in case an errant asteroid ambles through your roof. Having an extra copy of your important data helps you recover from such disasters as well as those that are even less likely to happen.

Tape drives are optional on personal computers. They add enough cost that people would rather risk their data. On larger computers (the servers used in business), tape drives are more common because the cost of restoring data is so high, probably thousands of times the cost of a drive, that their use is justified.

Listening and Monitoring

If you want your computer to do anything useful, you have to be able to tell it what to do. Although some computers actually do listen to you speak using voice-recognition technology, most systems depend on traditional control systems, the keyboard, and the mouse to put you in command. In addition, many applications require that you fill your computer with data—keystrokes, images, and sounds. Your computer acquires this information by electronically listening to any of several *input devices*—scanners, digital cameras, sound board samplers, and so on.

Your window into the mind of your computer that lets you monitor what it does is its display system, itself a combination of a graphics adapter or video board and a monitor or flat-panel display. The display system gives your computer the means to tell you what it is thinking and to show you your data in the form that you best understand—be it numbers, words, or pictures. The two halves of the display system work hand in hand. The graphics adapter uses the digital signals inside your computer to build an electronic map of what the final image should look like, storing the data for every dot on your monitor in memory. Electronics generate the image that appears on your monitor screen.

Keyboard

The keyboard remains the most efficient way to enter text into applications, faster than even the most advanced voice-recognition systems, which let you talk to your computer. Scientists believe that keyboarding is a more direct route from your brain. Speaking requires more work, and the mechanics of sounding your voice take more time. But the keyboard lets you do more than mere typing. It is the primary command-and-control center for your computer.

The keyboard is probably the most identifiable part of any computer. You can't miss an array of over 100 buttons meant to be individually activated by your fingers. They come built into notebook computers, tethered on short cords to most desktop systems, and warped and bent in magnificent curves meant to soothe tired hands.

Pointing Devices

Although computers once recognized only text—for which a keyboard sufficed—today's computers work with pictures (what computer-people call *graphics*). The keyboard is notoriously poor at picking out pieces of pictures, but the mouse—more correctly termed a *pointing device* to include mouse-derived devices such as trackballs and the proprietary devices used by notebook computers—readily relays graphic instructions to your computer. Not only can the pointing device point, but it also lets you draw, sketch, and paint.

The most familiar pointing device is the hand-size mouse that you move around your desktop to cause a *mouse pointer* to move analogously on the screen. But some people prefer upside-down mice called *trackballs* for rolling the pointer around. Notebook computers use specialized pointing devices called *pointing sticks* (IBM's TrackPoint is the premier example) or *touchpads*, which let you move around the desktop by scratching your finger across a plastic pad.

Scanners

The range of input devices naturally grows to embrace whatever kind of information you want to get into your computer. Say you have on-paper images you want to capture—drawings your kids made in first grade, your likeness on a poster from the post office, portraits of presidents on small sheets of paper—so that you can get into your graphics program to clean them up. Engineers developed the *scanner* to do just that. A scanner dissects the image into bits of graphic information like little dots that your computer can manipulate and store digitally.

Although engineers have developed an entire zoo of scanners to suit different kinds of original material (for example, photos or documents), most of today's scanners prefer to look at flat sheets. They take the form of flat boxes with glass plates on top, on which you lay printed images that you want to capture to your computer.

Digital Cameras

Scanners work when you have an image already fixed on paper, but when you want to get something you see in the real world into computer-compatible form, you need a *digital camera*. As with a scanner, a digital camera reduces an image—in this case, a scene you see in the real world—into tiny dots that your computer can store as digital data. The digital camera is a completely self-contained system for capturing and saving real-world images. It works with and without a computer, but the full power of the digital camera is realized best when you can edit its images with software on your computer.

A digital camera looks and works much like old-time film cameras with a lens in front and a viewfinder to help you frame the scenes you want to save. Some digital cameras are as simple as old box cameras—press a button and let the camera do the rest. Others have more controls than a small space shuttle, letting you unleash your full creative powers.

Display Systems

Your computer's thoughts, like your own, are invisible. Making your thoughts visible to others is what language and art are all about. The computer's equivalent is the *graphics adapter*. This component takes the digital thoughts of your computer and turns them into an electronic image, essentially a picture saved in the computer's electronic memory.

Once a graphics adapter has an image in this form—be it a page of text or a picture of an oasis—a *monitor* (sometimes called a *display*) connected to your computer makes the actual image that you can see. Monitors are essentially television sets built to military specifications. They produce sharper, higher-quality images than any television (including a new digital, high-resolution models) can hope to show.

Almost any monitor will let you work with your desktop computer (the monitor is built in to notebook machines), but the quality of the monitor attached to your computer determines the quality of the image you see and, often, of the work you do. Although no monitor can make anything look better than what's in the signals from your graphics adapter, a bad monitor can make them look much worse and limit both the range of colors and the resolution (or sharpness) of the images.

In most desktop computers, the graphics adapter is an expansion board, often the only one that comes as factory equipment, although notebook computers and many desktop systems have their graphics adapter functionality built in to the circuitry of the main circuit boards. Modern monitors for desktop computers come in two types: Cathode-ray tube (CRT) monitors use picture tubes like old-fashioned television sets and are big boxes that sit on your desk and, often, crowd everything off. Flat-panel monitors use liquid-crystal displays (LCDs) that run cooler and take up less room than CRTs (but cost substantially more). Either type is tethered to a desktop computer by a short cable. Notebook computers universally have built-in flat-panel displays.

Audio

A pretty picture is not enough in today's world. You need a total experience, one that involves both pictures and sound. After all, silent films went out of date in 1927. Consequently, every computer now has a sound system. In business computers, it's often nothing more than a beeper to warn you when you've pressed the wrong key. In most of today's computers, however, the sound system is on par with those in theaters (only not as loud). They can generate any sound you can hear and make it appear to be anywhere in the room.

Speakers are the most obvious part of any sound system, if just because you've got to find a place for two or three more boxes on your office desk. The real sound-generating capability of a computer comes from its sound board, however, which either slides into an expansion slot in the computer or is built into its main circuitry.

Printers

The electronic thoughts of a computer are notoriously evanescent. Pull the plug and your work disappears. Moreover, monitors are frustratingly difficult to pass around and post through the mail when you want to show off your latest digital art creation. *Hard copy* (the printout on paper) solves this problem. A printer is the device of choice for making hard copy from your computer's thoughts.

Printers come in many varieties. The most common are laser printers and inkjet printers. Either is a box with two paper trays that connects to your computer with a short cord. Lasers make fast, cheap, black-and-white pages. Inkjets are low-cost printers that excel at printing color but do so at a higher price per page because of their use of expensive inks.

Fax

Fax combines both the telecommunications capability of a modem with the hard-copy output of a printer. In effect, a fax machine becomes a remote printer for your computer—a system that allows your computer to print remotely to anywhere in the world you can get a telephone connection.

Today, fax is an invisible part of nearly every modem. If you can get online through a dial-up connection with your computer, you can fax. In most cases, you need nothing more than the modem already in your computer. The only addition required is invisible software.

Infrastructure

Infrastructure is what holds your computer together. It is the overall form of your computer, the substrate that it is built upon, and the essential supplies required to make it run. The substrate of the modern computer is the motherboard (or system board or main board) coupled with the expansion boards plugged into it. The case provides the basic form of the computer. And the one essential service required by any modern computer is power, the electricity used in the computer's logic operations.

Motherboards

The centerpiece of the system unit is the motherboard. All the other circuitry of the system unit is usually part of the motherboard or plugs directly into it. The electronic components on the motherboard carry out most of the function of the machine—running programs, making calculations, and even arranging the bits that will display on the screen. Because the motherboard defines each computer's functions and capabilities and because every computer is different, it only stands to reason that every motherboard is different, too. Not exactly. Many different computers have the same motherboard designs inside. And oftentimes a single computer model might have any of several different motherboards, depending on when it came down the production line (and what motherboard the manufacturer got the best deal on).

The motherboard is the main circuit board in nearly every computer—desktop or laptop. Usually it lines the bottom of the case like thick, green shelf-paper decorated with lines and blobs that could be a Martian roadmap.

Expansion Boards

Expansion boards are the physical form of the expansion devices that connect to your computer through its expansion slots. They are simply circuit boards that are smaller than the motherboard.

However, they are not just any circuit boards. Expansion boards must follow strict standards as to size, signals, power consumption, and software interface to ensure that they will work inside any given computer. Although at one time nearly all computers used Industry Standard Architecture (ISA) for their expansion boards, the modern replacement is Peripheral Component Interconnect (PCI). Some desktop computers don't allow the use of expansion boards at all. Notebook machines use PC cards instead.

Power

Every computer requires a continuous supply of carefully conditioned direct current at low voltage, well below that available at your wall outlet. Although batteries can provide this power for portable computers, desktop units require power supplies to convert house current into computer current. Similarly, power supplies charge and substitute for portable computer batteries.

Bringing power to your computer also imports danger, however, and your computer requires protection from glitches on the power line. *Surge suppressors* and *backup power systems* help to ensure that your computer gets the proper electrical diet.

The power supply in most desktop computers is locked for your protection in a steel box inside your computer's case. It keeps your hands out of harm's way if you dig into your computer to add an expansion board or other accessory. Notebook computers put much of the function of the power supply into their external "bricks" that plug directly into a wall outlet. The output of the brick is at a voltage that's safe should you accidentally encounter it (and safe for your notebook computer, as well).

Cases

The case is what most people think of as the entire computer, ignoring all the essential parts attached by cables and often the individual components inside. The main box goes by a special name, *system unit*, because it is the heart of the system. Some people call it the CPU (central processing unit), although that term is also (and confusingly) used for the microprocessor inside. The system unit houses the main circuitry of the computer and provides spaces called *bays* for internal disk drives as well as a place for the jacks (or outlets) that link the computer to the rest of its accouterments, including the keyboard, monitor, and peripherals. A notebook computer combines all these external components into one unit, but it's usually called simply the "computer" rather than system unit or CPU.

The case is more than a box. It's also a protective shell that keeps the dangers of the real world away from the delicate electronics of the computer. What's more, it protects the world from interference from the signals of the computer. The case is also part of a cooling system (which may include one or more fans) that keeps the electronics inside cool for longer life.

The case of a modern computer can take many forms—from small-footprint desktop computers to maxi-tower computers, from compact sub-notebook computers (or even handheld computers) to huge, almost unportable desktop-replacement notebook computers. In desktop systems, the size more than anything else determines how many accessories you can add to your system—and how much of your home or office you have to give up to technology. Weight, more than size, is the limiting physical factor for notebook computers. How much you want to carry often determines how many features you get.

Software

You probably think you already know what software is. It's that CD a friend gives you with the latest game to run on your computer. Were life only so simple (and copyright laws so liberal) that you could live happily ever after with such beliefs.

Life, alas, is not so simple, and neither is software. The disc isn't software. Software is nothing you can hold in your hand. Rather, it's the hardware that stores the software. The real software is made from the same stuff as dreams, as evanescent as an inspiration, as elusive as the meaning of the current copyright laws. Software is nothing but a set of ideas, ideas that (one hopes) express a way to do something. Those ideas are written in a code the same way our words and sentences code our thoughts. The codes take the form of symbols, which may appear on paper or be represented as pulses in electrical circuits. No matter. The code is only the representation of the ideas, and the ideas are really the software.

So much for the philosophy of software. Not many people think about software that way. Most approach it more practically. Software is something your computer needs. You might say your computer needs software to run its programs, but that's like saying you need food to eat dinner. The food *is* dinner. The software is the programs.

Ouch. No matter how bad that sounds, that's the way most people think. As a practical matter, they're getting close to the truth, but software is more than programs even at a practical level. Software is more than the box you buy and little silver disc that comes inside it. Software is not a singular thing. It is an entire technology that embraces not only what you see when you run your computer but also a multitude of invisible happenings hiding beneath the surface. A modern computer runs several software programs simultaneously, even when you think you're using just one, or even when you don't think anything is running at all. These programs operate at different levels, each one taking care of its own specific job, invisibly linking to the others to give you the illusion you're working with a single, smooth-running machine.

What shows on your monitor is only the most obvious of all this software—the *applications*, the programs such as *Microsoft Office* and *Grand Theft Auto 3* that you actually buy and load onto your computer, the ones that boldly emblazon their names on your screen every time you launch them. But there's more. Related to applications are the *utilities* you use to keep your computer in top running order, protect yourself from disasters, and automate repetitive chores. Down deeper is the *operating system*, which links your applications and utilities together to the actual hardware of your computer. At or below the operating system level, you use *programming languages* to tell your computer what to do. You can write applications, utilities, or even your own operating system with the right programming language.

Definitions

Software earns its name for what it is not. It is not hardware. Whatever is not hard is soft, and thus the derivation of the name. Hardware came first—simply because the hard reality of machines and tools existed long before anyone thought of computers or of the concept of programming. Hardware happily resides on page 551 of the 1965 dictionary I keep in my office—you know, nuts, bolts, and stuff like that. Software is nowhere to be found. (Why I keep a 1965 dictionary in my office is another matter entirely.)

Software comprises abstract ideas. In computers, the term embraces not only the application programs you buy and the other kinds of software listed earlier but also the information or data used by those programs.

Programs are the more useful parts of software because programs do the actual work. The program tells your computer what to do—how to act, how to use the data it has, how to react to your commands, how to be a computer at all. Data just slow things down.

Although important, a program is actually a simple thing. Broken down to its constituent parts, a computer program is nothing but a list of commands to tell your hardware what to do. Like a recipe, the program is a step-by-step procedure that, to the uninitiated, seems to be written in a secret code. In fact, the program *is* written in a code called the *programming language*, and the resultant list of instructions is usually called *code* by its programmers.

Applications

The programs you buy in the box off your dealer's shelves, in person or through the Web, the ones you run to do actual work on your computer, are its *applications*. The word is actually short for *application software*. These are programs with a purpose, programs you apply to get something done. They are the dominant beasts of computing, the top of the food chain, the colorful boxes in the store, the software you actually pay for. Everything else in your computer system, hardware and software alike, exists merely to make your applications work. Your applications determine what you need in your computer simply because they won't run—or run well—if you don't supply them with what they want.

Today's typical application comes on one or more CDs and is comprised of megabytes, possibly hundreds of megabytes, of digital stuff that you dutifully copy to your hard disk during the installation process. Hidden inside these megabytes is the actual function of the program, the part of the code that does what you buy the software for—be it to translate keystrokes into documents, calculate your bank balance, brighten your photographs, or turn MP3 files into music. The part of the program that actually works on the data you want to process is called an *algorithm*, the mathematical formula of the task converted into program code. An algorithm is just a way for doing something written down as instructions so you can do it again.

The hard-core computing work performed by major applications—the work of the algorithms inside them—is typically both simple and repetitive. For example, a tough statistical analysis may involve only a few lines of calculations, although the simple calculations will often be repeated again and again. Changing the color of a photo is no more than a simple algorithm executed over and over for each dot in the image.

That's why computers exist at all. They are simply good at repeatedly carrying out the simple mathematical operations of the algorithms without complaining.

If you were to tear apart a program to see how it works—what computer scientists call *disassembling* the program—you'd make a shocking discovery. The algorithm makes up little of the code of a program. Most of the multimegabyte bulk you buy is meant to hide the algorithm from you, like the fillers and flavoring added to some potent but noxious medicine.

Before the days of graphical operating systems, as exemplified by Microsoft's ubiquitous Windows family, the bulk of the code of most software applications was devoted to making the rigorous requirements of the computer hardware more palatable to your human ideas, aspirations, and whims. The part of the software that serves as the bridge between your human understanding and the computer's needs is called the *user interface*. It can be anything from a typewritten question mark that demands you type some response to a multicolor graphic menu luring your mouse to point and click.

Windows simplifies the programmers' task by providing most of the user interface functions from your applications. Now, most of the bulk of an application is devoted to mating not with your computer but with Windows. The effect is the same. It just takes more megabytes to get there.

No matter whether your application must build its own user interface or rely on the one provided by Windows, the most important job of most modern software is simply translation. The program converts your commands, instructions, and desires into a form digestible by your operating system and computer. In particular, the user interface translates the words you type and the motion of your arm pointing your mouse into computer code.

This translation function, like the Windows user interface, is consistent across most applications. All programs work with the same kind of human input and produce the same kind of computer codes. The big differences between modern applications are the algorithms central to the tasks to be carried out. Application software often is divided into several broad classes based on these tasks. Table 3.1 lists the traditional division of functions or major classifications of computer application software.

TABLE 3.1   Basic Types of Computer Application Software

Class of Software	Function
Web browsers	Entering and interacting with Web sites and servers to buy, sell, research your favorite interests, and just while away evenings, afternoons, and the rest of your life
E-mail programs	Sending and receiving instant messages from friends, associates, and solicitors in your neighborhood and around the world
Word processors	Getting your words write for print or electronic publishing
Spreadsheets	The accountant's ledger made automatic to calculate arrays of numbers
Databases	A filing system with instant access and the ability to automatically sort itself
Drawing and painting programs	Creating and editing images such as blueprints and cartoon cels that can be filed and edited with electronic ease
Multimedia software	Playing MP3 and WAV files for music, showing AVI or MOV video files, playing games, or displaying images and sound like a movie theatre under the control of an absolute dictator (you)

The lines between many of these applications are blurry. For example, many people find that spreadsheets serve all their database needs, and most spreadsheets now incorporate their own graphics for charting results.

Suites

Several software publishers completely confound the distinctions by combining most of these application functions into a single package that includes database, graphics, spread-sheet, and word processing functionalities. These combinations are termed *application suites*. Ideally, they offer several advantages. Because many functions (and particularly the user interface) are shared between applications, large portions of code need not be dupli-cated, as would be the case with standalone applications. Because the programs work together, they better know and understand one another's resource requirements, which means you should encounter fewer conflicts and memory shortfalls. Because they are all packaged together, you stand to get a better price from the publisher.

Today there's another name for the application suite: *Microsoft Office*. Although at one time at least three major suites competed for space on your desktop, the other offerings have, for the most part, faded away. You can still buy Corel WordPerfect Office or Lotus SmartSuite, although almost no one does. (In fact, most copies of Office are sold to busi-nesses. Most individuals get it bundled along with a new computer.) Office has become popular because it offers a single-box solution that fills the needs of most people, handling more tasks with more depth than they ordinarily need. The current version, Office XP, dominates the market because Microsoft sells it to computer makers at a favorable price (and, some say, with more than a little coercion).

Utilities

Even when you're working toward a specific goal, you often have to make some side trips. Although they seem unrelated to where you're going, they are as much a necessary part of the journey as any other. You may run a billion-dollar pickle-packing empire from your office, but you might never get your business negotiations done were it not for the regular housekeeping that keeps the place clean enough for visiting dignitaries to walk around without slipping on pickle juice on the floor.

The situation is the same with software. Although you need applications to get your work done, you need to take care of basic housekeeping functions to keep your system running in top condition and working most efficiently. The programs that handle the necessary auxiliary functions are called *utility software*.

From the name alone you know that utilities do something useful, which in itself sets them apart from much of the software on today's market. Of course, the usefulness of any tool depends on the job you have to do—a pastry chef has little need for the hammer that so well serves the carpenter or computer technician—and most utilities are crafted for some similar, specific need. For example, common computer utilities keep your disk organized and running at top speed, prevent disasters by detecting disk problems and viruses, and save your sanity should you accidentally erase a file.

The most important of these functions are included with today's computer operating systems, either integrated into the operating system itself or as individual programs that are part of the operating system package. Others you buy separately, at least until Microsoft buys out the company that offers them.

Common utilities include backup, disk defragmenting, font management, file compression, and scheduling—all of which were once individual programs from different publishers but now come packaged in Windows. Antivirus and version-tracking programs are utilities available from separately from Windows.

Modern utilities are essentially individual programs that load like ordinary applications when you call on them. The only difference between them and other applications is what they do. Utilities are meant to maintain your system rather than come up with answers or generate output.

Applets

An *applet* is a small software application that's usually dedicated to a single simple purpose. It may function as a standalone program you launch like an ordinary application, or it may run from within another application. Typically the applet performs a housekeeping function much like a utility, but the function of an applet is devoted to supporting an overriding application rather than your computer in general. That said, some system utilities may take the form of applets, too. Applets are mostly distinguished from other software by their size and the scope of their functions.

When you download a page from the Web that does something exciting on the screen (which means it shows you something other than text that just lays there), it's likely you've invisibly downloaded an applet from the Internet. Applets let you or distant programmers add animation and screen effects to Web pages.

Other applets are often included with or as part of application software packages (for example, the "wizard" that leads you through the installation process). Some are included with operating systems such as Windows. In fact, the chief distinction between an applet and a full application may be little more than the fact that you don't buy applets separately and never have.

Operating Systems

The basic level of software with which you will work on your computer is the operating system. It's what you see when you don't have an application or utility program running. But an operating system is much more than what you see on the screen.

As the name implies, the operating system tells your computer how to operate, how to carry on its most basic functions. Early operating systems were designed simply to control how you read from and wrote to files on disks and were hence termed *disk operating systems* (which is why the original computer operating system was called DOS). Today's operating systems add a wealth of functions for controlling every possible computer peripheral from keyboard (and mouse) to monitor screen.

The operating system in today's computers has evolved from simply providing a means of controlling disk storage into a complex web of interacting programs that perform several functions. The most important of these is linking the various elements of your computer system together. These linked elements include your computer hardware, your programs, and you. In computer language, the operating system is said to provide a common hardware interface, a common programming interface, and a common user interface.

An *interface*, by the way, is the point where two things connect together—for example, the human interface is where you, the human being, interact with your computer. The hardware interface is where your computer hardware links to its software. The programming interface is where programs link to the operating system. And the user interface is where you, as the user, link to the operating system. Interfaces can combine and blend together. For example, the user interface of your operating system is part of the human interface of your computer.

Of the operating system's many interfaces only one, the user interface, is visible to you. The user interface is the place where you interact with your computer at its most basic level. Sometimes this part of the operating system is called the user shell. In today's operating systems, the shell is simply another program, and you can substitute one shell for another. Although with Windows most people stick with the shell that Microsoft gives them, you don't have to. People who use Unix or Linux often pick their own favorite shell.

In the way they change the appearance of your operating system, shells are like the *skins* used by some applications—for example, the skins that give your MP3 player software the look of an old-fashioned Wurlitzer jukebox.

In effect, the shell is a starting point to get your applications running, and it's the home base that you return to between applications. The shell is the program that paints the desktop on the screen and lets you choose the applications you want to run.

Behind the shell, the *Application Program Interface* (or API) of the operating system gives programmers a uniform set of *calls*, key words that instruct the operating system to execute a built-in program routine that carries out some predefined function. For example, the API of Windows enables programmers to link their applications to the operating system to take advantage of its user interface. A program can call a routine from the operating system that draws a menu box on the screen.

Using the API offers programmers the benefit of having the complicated aspects of common program procedures already written and ready to go. Programmers don't have to waste their time on the minutiae of moving every bit on your monitor screen or other common operations. The use of a common base of code also eliminates duplication, which makes today's overweight applications a bit more svelte. Moreover, because all applications use basically the same code, they have a consistent look and work in a consistent manner. This prevents your computer from looking like the accidental amalgamation of the late-night work of thousands of slightly aberrant engineers that it is.

At the other side of the API, the operating system links your applications to the underlying computer hardware through the hardware interface. Once we take a look at what that hardware might be, we'll take a look how the operating system makes the connection in the following section, titled "Hardware Interfaces."

Outside of the shell of the user interface, you see and directly interact with little of an operating system. The bulk of the operating system program code works invisibly (and continuously). And that's the way it's designed to be.

Operating systems must match your hardware to work on a given computer. The software instructions must be able to operate your computer. Consequently, Apple computers and Intel-based computers use different operating systems. Similarly, programs must match the underlying operating system, so you must be sure that any given program you select is compatible with your operating system.

Today, four families of operating system are popular with personal computers.

Windows 9*X*

The Windows 9*X* family includes Windows 95, Windows 98, and Windows Millennium Edition (Me). These operating systems are built on a core of the original 16-bit DOS (dating back to 1981) and are meant to run only on Intel microprocessors and chips that are completely compatible with Intel architecture.

Microsoft announced Windows at a news conference in New York on November 10, 1983. But development of the graphic environment (as it was then classified) proved more troublesome than Microsoft anticipated, and the first version of the "16-bit version" of Windows did not reach store shelves as Windows 1.0 until November 20, 1985. The last major release of 16-bit Windows was Windows Me, which was first put on sale on September 14, 2000.

Because DOS was originally written in a time before running several programs at once was common, Microsoft's programmers had to add on this ability and provide the power to isolate each program from one another. In fact, they kludged together DOS, graphics, and multitasking control into what most programmers regard as a gnarled mess of code. Little wonder, then, that these 16-bit versions of Windows have a reputation for unreliability and are most suited to home computer users. You wouldn't want your life to depend on them.

Windows NT

The 32-bit Windows family includes Windows NT, Windows 2000, and Windows XP, in all its versions. When the core of this operating systems was originally conceived as Window NT, Microsoft's programmers decided to scrap all of the original Windows and start over. Instead of DOS they used OS/2, an operating system jointly developed by Microsoft and IBM, as its core. Microsoft called the first release of the new operating system Windows NT 3.1, cleverly skipping over early version numbers to make the new NT seem like a continuation of the then-current 16-bit Windows version, 3.1. According to Microsoft, Windows NT 3.1 was officially released to manufacturing on July 27, 1993. The same 32-bit core, although extensively refined, is still in use in current versions of Windows XP.

Instead of recycling old 16-bit code, Microsoft's programmers started off with the 32-bit code native to the 386 microprocessor that was current at the time (and is still used by today's latest Pentium 4 microprocessors). Although Microsoft attempted to craft versions of Windows NT to run on processors other than those using Intel architecture, no such adaptation has proven successful, and the operating system runs exclusively on Intel-architecture microprocessors.

From the very beginning, Microsoft conceived Windows NT as a multitasking operating system, so its engineers built in features that ensure the isolation of each application it runs. The result was a robust operating system that had but one problem—it lacked complete compatibility with old, DOS-based programs. Over the years, this compatibility became both less necessary (as fewer people ran DOS applications) and better, as Microsoft's engineers refined their code. Most professionals regard Windows XP as a robust operating system on par with any other, suitable for running critical applications.

Unix

Unix is not a single operating system but several incompatible families that share a common command structure. Originally written at Bell Labs to run on a 16-bit Digital

Equipment Company PDP-7 computer, Unix has been successfully adapted to nearly every microprocessor family and includes 8-, 16-, 32-, and 64-bit versions under various names.

Unix traces its roots to 1969, but according to Dennis M. Ritchie, one of its principal developers (along with Ken Thompson), its development was not announced to the world until 1974. From the beginning, Unix was designed to be a time-sharing, multiuser system for mainframe-style computers. It proved so elegant and robust that it has been adapted to nearly every microprocessor platform, and it runs on everything from desktop computers to huge clusters of servers.

Nearly every major hardware platform has a proprietary version of Unix available to it. Some of these include AIX for IBM computers, Solaris for Sun Microsystems machines, and even OS X, the latest Apple Macintosh operating system. Note that programs written for one version of Unix will likely not run on other hardware than for which it was intended. It has become a sort of universal language among many computer professionals.

Linux

Unlike other operating systems, Linux can be traced back to a single individual creator, Linus Torvalds, who wrote its kernel, the core of the operating system that integrates its most basic functions, in 1991 while a student at the University of Helsinki. He sent early versions around for testing and comment as early as September of that year, but a workable version (numbered 0.11) didn't become available until December. Version 1.0, regarded as the first truly stable (and therefore usable) version of Linux came in March, 1994. Torvalds himself recommends pronouncing the name of the operating system with a short-i sound (say *Lynn*-ucks).

The most notable aspect of Linux is that it is "open source." That is, Torvalds has shared the source code—the lines of program code he actually wrote—of his operating system with the world, whereas most software publishers keep their source code secret. This open-source model, as it is called, lets other programmers help refine and develop the operating system. It also results in what is essentially a free, although copyrighted, operating system.

Contrary to popular opinion, Linux is not a variety of Unix. It looks and works like Unix—the commands and structure are the same—but its kernel is entirely different. Programs written for Unix will not run under Linux (although if you have the source code, these programs can be relatively easily converted between the two operating systems). Programmers have adapted Linux to many hardware platforms, including those based on Intel microprocessors.

The open-source status of Linux, along with its reputation for reliability and robustness (inherited without justification from Unix), have made it popular. In other words, it's like

Unix and it's free, so it has become the choice for many Web servers and small business systems. On the other hand, the strength it gains from its similarity to Unix is also a weakness. It is difficult for most people to install, and it lacks the wide software support of Windows.

Programming Languages

A computer program—whether it's an applet, utility, application, or operating system—is nothing more than a list of instructions for the brain inside your computer, the microprocessor, to carry out. A microprocessor instruction, in turn, is a specific pattern of bits, a digital code. Your computer sends the list of instructions making up a program to its microprocessor one at a time. Upon receiving each instruction, the microprocessor looks up what function the code says to do, then it carries out the appropriate action.

Microprocessors by themselves only react to patterns of electrical signals. Reduced to its purest form, the computer program is information that finds its final representation as the ever-changing pattern of signals applied to the pins of the microprocessor. That electrical pattern is difficult for most people to think about, so the ideas in the program are traditionally represented in a form more meaningful to human beings. That representation of instructions in human-recognizable form is called a *programming language*.

As with a human language, a programming language is a set of symbols and the syntax for putting them together. Instead of human words or letters, the symbols of the programming language correspond to patterns of bits that signal a microprocessor exactly as letters of the alphabet represent sounds that you might speak. Of course, with the same back-to-the-real-basics reasoning, an orange is a collection of quarks squatting together with reasonable stability in the center of your fruit bowl.

The metaphor is apt. The primary constituents of an orange—whether you consider them quarks, atoms, or molecules—are essentially interchangeable, even indistinguishable. By itself, every one is meaningless. Only when they are taken together do they make something worthwhile (at least from a human perspective): the orange. The overall pattern, not the individual pieces, is what's important.

Letters and words work the same way. A box full of vowels wouldn't mean anything to anyone not engaged in a heated game of *Wheel of Fortune*. Match the vowels with consonants and arrange them properly, and you might make words of irreplaceable value to humanity: the works of Shakespeare, Einstein's expression of general relativity, or the formula for Coca-Cola. The meaning is not in the pieces but their patterns.

The same holds true for computer programs. The individual commands are not as important as the pattern they make when they are put together. Only the pattern is truly meaningful.

You make the pattern of a computer program by writing a list of commands for a micro-processor to carry out. At this level, programming is like writing reminder notes for a not-too-bright person—first socks, then shoes.

This step-by-step command system is perfect for control freaks but otherwise is more than most people want to tangle with. Even simple computer operations require dozens of microprocessor operations, so writing complete lists of commands in this form can be more than many programmers—let alone normal human beings—want to deal with. To make life and writing programs more understandable, engineers developed *higher-level programming languages*.

A higher-level language uses a vocabulary that's more familiar to people than patterns of bits, often commands that look something like ordinary words. A special program trans-lates each higher-level command into a sequence of bit-patterns that tells the micro-processor what to do.

Machine Language

Every microprocessor understand its own repertoire of instructions, just as a dog might understands a few spoken commands. Whereas your pooch might sit down and roll over when you ask it to, your processor can add, subtract, and move bit-patterns around as well as change them. Every family of microprocessor has a set of instructions that it can recog-nize and carry out: the necessary understanding designed into the internal circuitry of each microprocessor chip.

The entire group of commands that a given model of microprocessor understands and can react to is called that microprocessor's *instruction set* or its *command set*. Different micro-processor families recognize different instruction sets, so the commands meant for one chip family would be gibberish to another. For example, the Intel family of microproces-sors understands one command set; the IBM/Motorola PowerPC family of chips recog-nizes an entirely different command set. That's the basic reason why programs written for the Apple Macintosh (which is based on PowerPC microprocessors) won't work on com-puters that use Intel microprocessors.

That native language a microprocessor understands, including the instruction set and the rules for using it, is called *machine language*. The bit-patterns of electrical signals in machine language can be expressed directly as a series of ones and zeros, such as 0010110. Note that this pattern directly corresponds to a binary (or base-two) number. As with any binary number, the machine language code of an instruction can be translated into other numerical systems as well. Most commonly, machine language instructions are expressed in hexadecimal form (base-16 number system). For example, the 0010110 subtraction instruction becomes 16(hex). (The "(hex)" indicates the number is in hexadecimal nota-tion, that is, base 16.)

Assembly Language

Machine language is great if you're a machine. People, however, don't usually think in terms of bit-patterns or pure numbers. Although some otherwise normal human beings can and do program in machine language, the rigors of dealing with the obscure codes takes more than a little getting used to. After weeks, months, or years of machine language programming, you begin to learn which numbers do what. That's great if you want to dedicate your life to talking to machines, but not so good if you have better things to do with your time.

For human beings, a better representation of machine language codes involves mnemonics rather than strictly numerical codes. Descriptive word fragments can be assigned to each machine language code so that 16(hex) might translate into SUB (for subtraction). *Assembly language* takes this additional step, enabling programmers to write in more memorable symbols.

Once a program is written in assembly language, it must be converted into the machine language code understood by the microprocessor. A special program, called an *assembler*, handles the necessary conversion. Most assemblers do even more to make the programmer's life more manageable. For example, they enable blocks of instructions to be linked together into a block called a *subroutine*, which can later be called into action by using its name instead of repeating the same block of instructions again and again.

Most of assembly language involves directly operating the microprocessor using the mnemonic equivalents of its machine language instructions. Consequently, programmers must be able to think in the same step-by-step manner as the microprocessor. Every action that the microprocessor does must be handled in its lowest terms. Assembly language is consequently known as a *low-level language* because programmers write at the most basic level.

High-Level Languages

Just as an assembler can convert the mnemonics and subroutines of assembly language into machine language, a computer program can go one step further by translating more human-like instructions into the multiple machine language instructions needed to carry them out. In effect, each language instruction becomes a subroutine in itself.

The breaking of the one-to-one correspondence between language instruction and machine language code puts this kind of programming one level of abstraction farther from the microprocessor. That's the job of the high-level languages. Instead of dealing with each movement of a byte of information, high-level languages enable the programmer to deal with problems as decimal numbers, words, or graphic elements. The language program takes each of these high-level instructions and converts it into a long series of digital code microprocessor commands in machine language.

High-level languages can be classified into two types: interpreted and compiled. Batch languages are a special kind of interpreted language.

Interpreted Languages

An interpreted language is translated from human to machine form each time it is run by a program called an *interpreter*. People who need immediate gratification like interpreted programs because they can be run immediately, without intervening steps. If the computer encounters a programming error, it can be fixed, and the program can be tested again immediately. On the other hand, the computer must make its interpretation each time the program is run, performing the same act again and again. This repetition wastes the computer's time. More importantly, because the computer is doing two things at once—both executing the program and interpreting it at the same time—it runs more slowly.

Today the most important interpreted computer language is *Java*, the tongue of the Web created by Sun Microsystems. Your computer downloads a list of Java commands and converts them into executable form inside your computer. Your computer then runs the Java code to put make some obnoxious advertisement dance and flash across your screen.

The interpreted design of Java helps make it universal. The Java code contains instructions that any computer can carry out, regardless of its operating system. The Java interpreter inside your computer converts the universal code into the specific machine language instructions your computer and its operating system understand.

Before Java, the most popular interpreted language was BASIC, an acronym for the Beginner's All-purpose Symbolic Instruction Set. BASIC was the first language for personal computers and was the foundation upon which the Microsoft Corporation was built.

In classic form, using an interpreted language involved two steps. First, you would start the language interpreter program, which gave you a new environment to work in, complete with its own system of commands and prompts. Once in that environment, you then executed your program, typically starting it with a "Run" instruction. More modern interpreted systems such as Java hide the actual interpreter from you. The Java program appears to run automatically by itself, although in reality the interpreter is hidden in your Internet browser or operating system. Microsoft's Visual Basic gets its interpreter support from a runtime module, which must be available to your computer's operating system for Visual Basic programs to run.

Compiled Languages

Compiled languages execute like a program written in assembler, but the code is written in a more human-like form. A program written with a compiled language gets translated from high-level symbols into machine language just once. The resultant machine language is then stored and called into action each time you run the program. The act of converting the program from the English-like compiled language into machine language is called *compiling the program.* To do this you use a language program called a *compiler*. The original, English-like version of the program, the words and symbols actually written by the programmer, is called the *source code*. The resultant machine language makes up the program's *object code*.

Compiling a complex program can be a long operation, taking minutes, even hours. Once the program is compiled, however, it runs quickly because the computer needs only to run the resultant machine language instructions instead of having to run a program interpreter at the same time. Most of the time, you run a compiled program directly from the DOS prompt or by clicking an icon. The operating system loads and executes the program without further ado. Examples of compiled languages include today's most popular computer programming language, C++, as well as other tongues left over from earlier days of programming—COBOL, Fortran, and Pascal.

Object-oriented languages are special compiled languages designed so that programmers can write complex programs as separate modules termed *objects*. A programmer writes an object for a specific, common task and gives it a name. To carry out the function assigned to an object, the programmer need only put its name in the program without reiterating all the object's code. A program may use the same object in many places and at many different times. Moreover, a programmer can put a copy of an object into different programs without the need to rewrite and test the basic code, which speeds up the creation of complex programs. C++ is object oriented.

Optimizing compilers do the same thing as ordinary compilers, but do it better. By adding an extra step (or more) to the program compiling process, the optimizing compiler checks to ensure that program instructions are arranged in the most efficient order possible to take advantage of all the capabilities of the computer's processor. In effect, the optimizing compiler does the work that would otherwise require the concentration of an assembly language programmer.

Libraries

Inventing the wheel was difficult and probably took human beings something like a million years—a long time to have your car sitting up on blocks. Reinventing the wheel is easier because you can steal your design from a pattern you already know. But it's far, far easier to simply go out and buy a wheel.

Writing program code for a specific but common task often is equivalent to reinventing your own wheel. You're stuck with stringing together a long list of program commands, just like all the other people writing programs have to do. Your biggest consolation is that you need to do it only once. You can then reuse the same set of instructions the next time you have to write a program that needs the same function.

For really common functions, you don't have to do that. Rather than reinventing the wheel, you can buy one. Today's programming languages include collections of common functions called *libraries* so that you don't have to bother with reinventing anything. You only need pick the prepackaged code you want from the library and incorporate it into your program. The language compiler links the appropriate libraries to your program so that you only need to refer to a function by a code name. The functions in the library become an extension to the language, called a *meta-language*.

Development Environments

Even when using libraries, you're still stuck with writing a program in the old-fashioned way—a list of instructions. That's an effective but tedious way of building a program. The computer's strength is taking over tedious tasks, so you'd think you could use some of that power to help you write programs more easily. In fact, you might expect someone to write a program to help you write programs.

A *development environment* is exactly that kind of program, one that lets you drag and drop items from menus to build the interfaces for your own applications. The environment includes not only all the routines of the library, but also its own, easy-to-use interface for putting the code in those libraries to work. Most environments let you create programs by interactively choosing the features you want—drop-down menus, dialog boxes, and even entire animated screens—and match them with operations. The environment watches what you do, remembers everything, and then kicks in a *code generator*, which creates the series of programming language commands that achieves the same end. One example of a development environment is Microsoft Visual Studio.

Working with a development environment is a breeze compared to traditional programming. For example, instead of writing all the commands to pop a dialog box on the screen, you click a menu and choose the kind of box you want. After the box obediently pops on the screen, you can choose the elements you want inside it from another menu, using your mouse to drag buttons and labels around inside the box. When you're happy with the results, the program grinds out the code. In a few minutes you can accomplish what it might have taken you days to write by hand.

Batch Languages

A *batch language* allows you to submit a program directly to your operating system for execution. That is, the batch language is a set of operating system commands that your computer executes sequentially as a program. The resultant batch program works like an interpreted language in that each step gets evaluated and executed only as it appears in the program.

Applications often include their own batch languages. These, too, are merely lists of commands for the application to carry out in the order you've listed them to perform some common, everyday function. Communications programs use this type of programming to automatically log in to the service of your choice and even retrieve files. Databases use their own sort of programming to automatically generate reports that you regularly need. The process of transcribing your list of commands is usually termed *scripting*. The commands that you can put in your program scripts are sometimes called the *scripting language*.

Scripting actually *is* programming. The only difference is the language. Because you use commands that are second nature to you (at least after you've learned to use the program) and follow the syntax that you've already learned running the program, the process seems more natural than writing in a programming language. That means if you've ever written a script to log on to the Internet or have modified an existing script, you're a programmer already. Give yourself a gold star.

Hardware Interfaces

Linking hardware to software has always been one of the biggest challenges facing those charged with designing computer systems—not just individual computers but whole families of computers, those able to run the same programs. The solution has almost invariably been to wed the two together by layering on software, so much so that the fastest processors struggle when confronted by relatively simple tasks. An almost unbelievable amount of computer power gets devoted to moving bytes from software to hardware through a maze of program code, all in the name of making the widest variety of hardware imaginable work with a universal (at least if Microsoft has its way) operating system.

The underlying problem is the same as in any mating ritual. Software is from Venus, and hardware is from Mars (or, to ruin the allusion for sake of accuracy, Vulcan). Software is the programmer's labor of love, an ephemeral spirit that can only be represented. Hardware is the physical reality, the stuff pounded out in Vulcan's forge—enduring, unchanging, and often priced like gold. (And, yes, for all you Trekkers out there, it *is* always logical.) Bringing the two together is a challenge that even self-help books would find hard to manage. Yet every computer not only faces that formidable task but also tackles it with aplomb, although maybe not as fast as you'd like.

Here's the challenge: In the basic computer, every instruction in a program gets targeted on the microprocessor. Consequently, the instructions can control only the microprocessor and don't themselves reach beyond. The circuitry of the rest of the computer and the peripherals connected to it all must get their commands and data relayed to them by the microprocessor. Somehow the microprocessor must be able to send signals to these devices. Today the pathway of command is rarely direct. Rather, the chain of command is a hierarchy, one that often takes on aspects of a bureaucracy.

Control Hierarchy

Perhaps the best way to get to know how software controls hardware is to look at how your system executes a simple command. Let's start with a common situation.

Because your patience is so sorely tested by reading the electronic version of this book using your Web browser, *Internet Scapegoat*, you decide to quit and go on to do something really useful, such as playing FreeCell. Your hand wraps around your mouse, you scoot it up to the big black × at the upper-right corner of the screen, and you click your left mouse button. Your hardware has made a link with software.

Your click is a physical act, one that closes the contacts of a switch inside the mouse, squirting a brief pulse of electricity through its circuitry. The mouse hardware reacts by sending a message out the mouse wire to your computer. The mouse port of your computer detects the message and warns your computer by sending a special attention signal called a *hardware interrupt* squarely at your microprocessor.

At the same time, the mouse driver has been counting pulses sent out by your mouse that indicate its motion. The mouse driver counts each pulse and puts the results into the memory of your computer. It uses these values to find where to put the mouse pointer on the screen.

The interrupt causes your computer to run a software interrupt routine contained in the mouse *driver software*. The driver, in turn, signals to Windows that you've clicked the button. Windows checks in memory for the value the mouse driver has stored there for the position of the mouse pointer. This value tells Windows where the mouse pointer is to determine how to react to your button press. When it discovers you've targeted the ×, Windows sends a message to the program associated with it—in this case, your browser.

The browsers reacts, muttering to itself the digital equivalent of "He must be insane," and it immediately decides to pop up a dialog box that asks whether you really, really want to quit such a quality program as the browser. The dialog box routine is part of the program itself, but it builds the box and its contents from graphics subroutines that are part of the Windows operating system. The browser activates the subroutines through the Windows application interface.

Windows itself does not draw the box. Rather it acts as a translator, converting the box request into a series of commands to draw it. It then sends these commands to its graphics driver. The driver determines what commands to use so that the video board will understand what to do. The driver then passes those commands to another driver, the one associated with the video board.

The video board's driver routes the command to the proper hardware ports through which the video board accepts instructions. The driver sends a series of commands that causes the processor on the video board (a graphics accelerator) to compute where it must change pixels to make the lines constituting the box. Once the graphic accelerator finishes the computations, it changes the bytes that correspond to the areas on the screen where the line will appear in a special memory area on the video board called the *frame buffer*.

Another part of the video board, the *rasterizer*, scans through the frame buffer and sends the data it finds there to the port leading to your monitor, converting it into a serial data stream for the journey. Using synchronizing signals sent from the video board as a guide, the monitor takes the data from the data stream and illuminates the proper pixels on the screen to form the pattern of the dialog box.

When you awake from your boredom-inspired daze, you finally see the warning box pop up on the screen and react.

The journey is tortuous, but when all goes right, it takes a smaller fraction of a second than it does for you to become aware of what you've done. And when all doesn't go right, another tortuous chain of events will likely result, often one involving flying computers, picture windows, and shards of glass on the front lawn.

Keys to making this chain of command function are the application program interface, the driver software, and the device interfaces of the hardware itself. Sometimes a special part of your computer, the *BIOS*, also gets involved. Let's take a deeper look at each of these links.

Application Program Interface

A quick recap: An interface is where two distinct entities come together. The most important of the software interfaces in the Windows environment is the *application program interface* or API.

Rather than a physical thing, the API is a standard set of rules for exchanging commands and data. The Windows API comprises a set of word-like commands termed *program calls*. Each of these causes Windows to take a particular action. For example, the command DrawBox could tell Windows to draw a box on the screen, as in the preceding example.

To pass along data associated with the command—in the example, how large the box should be and where to put it on the screen—many calls require your program to send along *parameters*. Each parameter is ordinary data that is strictly formatted to meet the expectation of Windows. That is, the order of the parameters is predefined, and the range permitted for the data is similarly constrained.

Each software interface in the Windows system uses a similar system of calls and parameter passing. Gaining familiarity with the full repertory of the API is one of the biggest challenges facing programmers.

Device Drivers

Device drivers are matchmakers. A device driver takes a set of standardized commands from the operating system and matches them to the capabilities of the device that the driver controls. Typically the device that gets controlled is a piece of hardware, but, as our example shows, one driver may control another driver that controls the hardware.

Just about every class of peripheral has some special function shared with no other device. Printers need to switch ribbon colors; graphics boards need to put dots onscreen at high resolution; sound boards need to blast fortissimo arpeggios; video capture boards must grab frames; and mice have to do whatever mice do. Different manufacturers often have widely different ideas about the best way to handle even the most fundamental functions. No programmer or even collaborative program can ever hope to know all the possibilities. It's even unlikely that you could fit all the possibilities into an operating system written in code that would fit onto a stack of disks you could carry. There are just too many possibilities.

Drivers make the connection, translating generalized commands made for any hardware into those used by the specific device in your computer. Instead of packing every control or command you might potentially need, the driver implements only those that are appropriate for a specific type, brand, and model of product that you actually connect up to your computer. Without the driver, your operating system could not communicate with your computer.

Device drivers give you a further advantage. You can change them almost as often as you change your mind. If you discover a bug in one driver—say sending an uppercase *F* to your printer causes it to form-feed through a full ream of paper before coming to a panting stop—you can slide in an updated driver that fixes the problem. You don't have to replace the device or alter your software. In some cases, new drivers extend the features of your existing peripherals because programmer didn't have enough time or inspiration to add everything to the initial release.

The way you and your system handles drivers depends on your operating system. Older operating systems (such as DOS and old versions of Windows) load all their drivers when they start and stick with them all while you use your computer. Windows 95 and newer versions treat drivers dynamically, loading them only when they are needed. Not only does this design save memory, because you only need to load the drivers that are actually in use, it also lets you add and remove devices while you're using your computer. For example, when you plug in a USB scanner, Windows can determine what make and model of scanner you have and then load the driver appropriate for it.

Although today drivers load invisibly and automatically, things were not always so easy. The driver needs to know what system resources your hardware uses for its communications. These resources are the values you set through the Windows Add Hardware

Wizard (click the Resources tab in Device Manager to see them). With old-fashioned drivers, hardware, and operating systems, you had to physically adjust settings on the hardware to assign resources and then configure the driver to match what you configured. It wasn't pretty, often wasn't easy, and was the most common reason people could not get hardware to work—usually because they created the problem themselves. Now Windows creates the problems automatically.

BIOS

The *Basic Input/Output System*, mentioned earlier as giving a personality to your computer, has many other functions. One of the original design intentions of the BIOS was to help match your computer's hardware to its software. To that end, the BIOS was meant to act as a special driver software included with your computer so that it can boot up right after you take it out of the box.

Part of the BIOS is program code for drivers that's permanently or semi-permanently recorded in special memory chips. The code acts like the hardware interface of an operating system but at a lower level—it is a hardware interface that's independent of the operating system.

Programs or operating systems send commands to the BIOS, and the BIOS sends out the instructions to the hardware using the proper resource values. It lies waiting in your computer, ready for use.

The original goal of the BIOS was to make computer software "platform independent," meaning that programs don't care what kind of computer they're running on. Although that seems a trivial concern in these days of dynamic-loading drivers, it was only a dream decades ago when computers were invented. In those dark-old days, programmers had to write commands aimed specifically at the hardware of the computer. Change the hardware—plug in a different printer—and the software wouldn't work. The BIOS, like today's driver software, was meant to wallpaper over the difference in hardware.

The idea, although a good one, didn't work. Programmers avoided the BIOS in older computers because it added an extra software layer that slowed things down. But the BIOS really fell from favor when Microsoft introduced modern Windows. The old hardware-based BIOS couldn't keep up with changes in technology. Moreover, using software drivers allowed hardware engineers to use more memory for the needed program code.

The BIOS persists in modern computers as a common means of accessing hardware before the operating system loads. The BIOS code of every computer today still includes the equivalent of driver software to handle accessing floppy disk drives, the keyboard, printers, video, and parallel and serial port operation.

Device Interfaces

Regardless of whether software uses device drivers, looks through the BIOS, or accesses hardware directly, the final link to hardware may be made in one of two ways, set by the hardware design: input/output mapping and memory mapping. *Input/output mapping* relies on sending instructions and data through ports. *Memory mapping* requires passing data through memory addresses. Ports and addresses are similar in concept but different in operation.

Input/Output Mapping

A *port* is an address but not a physical location. The port is a logical construct that operates as an addressing system separate from the address bus of the microprocessor, even though it uses the same address lines. If you imagine normal memory addresses as a set of pigeon holes for holding bytes, input/output ports act like a second set of pigeon holes on the other side of the room. To distinguish which set of holes to use, the microprocessor controls a flag signal on its bus called *memory I/O*. In one condition, it tells the rest of the computer that the signals on the address bus indicate a memory location; in its other state, the signals indicate an input/output port.

The microprocessor's internal mechanism for sending data to a port also differs from memory access. One instruction, *move*, allows the microprocessor to move bytes from any of its registers to any memory location. Some microprocessor operations can even be performed in immediate mode, directly on the values stored at memory locations.

Ports, however, use a pair of instructions: *In* to read from a port, and *Out* to write to a port. The values read can only be transferred into one specific register of the microprocessor (called the *accumulator*) and can only be written from that register. The accumulator has other functions as well. Immediate operations on values held at port locations is impossible, which means a value stored in a port cannot be changed by the microprocessor. It must load the port value into the accumulator, alter it, and then reload the new value back into the port.

Memory Mapping

The essence of memory mapping is *sharing*. The microprocessor and the hardware device it controls share access to a specific range of memory addresses. To send data to the device, your microprocessor simply moves the information into the memory locations exactly as if it were storing something for later recall. The hardware device can then read those same locations to obtain the data.

Memory-mapped devices, of course, need direct access to your computer's memory bus. Through this connection, they can gain speed and operate as fast as the memory system and its bus connection allow. In addition, the microprocessor can directly manipulate the data at the memory location used by the connection, thus eliminating the multistep load/change/reload process required by I/O mapping.

The most familiar memory-mapped device is your computer's display. Most graphic systems allow the microprocessor to directly address the frame buffer that holds the image that appears on your monitor screen. This design allows the video system to operate at the highest possible speed.

The addresses used for memory mapping must be off limits to the range in which the operating system loads your programs. If a program should transgress on the area used for the hardware connection, it can inadvertently change the data there—nearly always with bad results. Moreover, the addresses used by the interface cannot serve any other function, so they take away from the maximum memory addressable by a computer. Although such deductions are insignificant with today's computers, it was a significant shortcoming for old systems that were limited to a maximum of 1 to 16 megabytes. Because these shortcomings have diminished over the years, memory mapping has gained popularity in interfacing.

Addressing

To the microprocessor, the difference between ports and memory is one of perception: Memory is a direct extension of the chip. Ports are the external world. Writing to I/O ports is consequently more cumbersome and usually requires more time and microprocessor cycles.

I/O ports give the microprocessor and computer designer greater flexibility, and they give you a headache when you want to install multimedia accessories.

Implicit in the concept of addressing, whether memory or port addresses, is proper delivery. You expect a letter carrier to bring your mail to your address and not deliver it to someone else's mailbox. Similarly, computers and their software assume that deliveries of data and instructions will always go where they are supposed to. To ensure proper delivery, addresses must be correct and unambiguous. If someone types a wrong digit on a mailing label, it will likely get lost in the postal system.

In order to use port or memory addresses properly, your software needs to know the proper addresses used by your peripherals. Many hardware functions have fixed or standardized addresses that are the same in every computer. For example, the memory addresses used by video boards are standardized (at least in basic operating modes), and the ports used by most hard disk drives are similarly standardized. Programmers can write the addresses used by this fixed-address hardware into their programs and not worry whether their data will get where it's going.

The layered BIOS approach was originally designed to eliminate the need for writing explicit hardware addresses in programs. Drivers accomplish a similar function. They are written with the necessary hardware addresses built in.

Resource Allocation

The basic hardware devices got assigned addresses and memory ranges early in the history of the computer and for compatibility reasons have never changed. These fixed values include those of serial and parallel ports, keyboards, disk drives, and the frame buffer that stores the monitor image. Add-in devices and more recent enhancements to the traditional devices require their own assignments of system resources. Unfortunately, beyond the original hardware assignments there are no standards for the rest of the resources. Manufacturers consequently pick values of their own choices for new products. More often than you'd like, several products may use the same address values.

Manufacturers attempt to avoid conflicts by allowing a number of options for the addresses used by their equipment. In days gone by, you had to select among the choices offered by manufacturers using switches or jumpers. Modern expansion products still require resource allocation but use a software-controlled scheme called *Plug-and-Play* to set the values, usually without your intervention or knowledge.

Although a useful computer requires all three—software, hardware, and the glue to hold them together—hardware plays the enabling role. Without it, the computer doesn't exist. It *is* the computer. The rest of this book will examine the individual components of that hardware as well as related technologies that enable your computer to be the powerful tool it is.

PART 2
Processing

The difference between a computer and a television set at first seems obvious—one has a keyboard and the other doesn't. Take a look at the modern remote control, however, and you'll see the difference is more subtle. It's something that's going on behind the screens. When you sit around watching the television, you're gradually putting down roots as a couch potato or some less respected vegetable, but when you sit at the computer, it watches *you*. It wants to know what you want. It listens to your thoughts, relayed through the keyboard, to carry out your commands—calculating, organizing, alphabetizing, filing away, drawing, and editing. No other machine takes information from you and handles it so adroitly. That's the computer's power as a data-processing machine, a thinking machine.

As a physical entity, the processing part of a desktop computer is inside the big box you may call the system unit, CPU (for *central processing unit*), or simply "the computer." But the processing part of the computer only takes up a fraction of the space occupied by the system unit. All the essential processing power of the computer fits into a handful of circuit components—the microprocessor, the chipset, and the BIOS. Each has its own function in bringing the processing power of the computer to life, and each is substantially different in concept, design, and operation.

The microprocessor, the chipset, and the BIOS—and the rest of the computer as well—are themselves built the same. Each is a tiny slice of nearly pure silicon that has been carefully fabricated into a digital electronic circuit. Because all three processing components of a computer have this same silicon/electrical foundation—indeed, all of today's electronic devices share these same design elements—we'll talk about the underlying technologies that make the processing of a computer possible before looking at the individual components themselves.

Digital Electronics

First and foremost, the computer is a thinking machine—and that implies all sorts of preposterous nonsense. The thinking machine could be a devious device, hatching plots against you as it sits on your desk. A thinking machine must work the same unfathomable way as the human mind, something so complicated that in thousands of years of attempts by the best geniuses, no one has yet satisfactorily explained how it works. A thinking machine has a brain, so you might suppose that opening it up and working inside it is brain surgery, and the electronic patient is likely to suffer irreversible damage at the hands of an unskilled operator.

But computers don't think—at least not in the same way you and I do or Albert Einstein did. The computer has no emotions or motivations. The impulses traveling through it are no odd mixture of chemicals and electrical activity, of activation and repression. The computer deals in simple pulses of electricity, well understood and carefully controlled. The intimate workings of the computer are probably better understood than the seemingly simple flame that inhabits the internal combustion engine inside your car. Nothing mysterious lurks inside the thinking machine called the computer.

What gives those electrical pulses their thinking power is a powerful logic system that allows electrical states to represent propositions and combinations of them. Engineers and philosophers tailored this logic system to precisely match the capabilities of a computer while, at the same time, approximating the way you think and express yourself—or at least how *they* thought you would think and express yourself. When you work with a computer, you bend your thoughts to fit into this clever logical system; then the computer manipulates your ideas with the speed and precision of digital electronics.

This logic system doesn't deal with full-fledged ideas such as life, liberty, and the pursuit of happiness. It works at a much smaller level, dealing with concepts no more complex than whether a light switch is on or off. But stacking those tiny logical operations together in more and more complex combinations, building them layer after layer, you can approach an approximation of human language with which to control the thoughts of the computer. This language-like control system is the computer program, the software that makes the computer work.

The logic and electronics of computer circuitry are intimately combined. Engineers designed the electronics of computers exactly to suit the needs of binary logic. Through that design, your computer comes to life.

Electronic Design

Computers are thought fearsome because they are based on electrical circuits. Electricity can be dangerous, as the anyone struck by lightning will attest. But inside the computer, the danger is low. At its worst, it measures 12 volts, which makes the inside of a computer as safe as playing with an electric train. Nothing that's readily accessible inside the computer will shock you, straighten your hair, or shorten your life.

Personal computers could not exist—at least in their current, wildly successful form— were it not for two concepts: binary logic and digital circuitry. The binary approach reduces data to its most minimalist form, essentially an information quantum. A binary data bit simply indicates whether something is or is not. Binary logic provides rules for manipulating those bits to allow them to represent and act like real-world information we care about, such as numbers, names, and images. The binary approach involves both *digitization* (using binary data to represent information) and *Boolean algebra* (the rules for carrying out the manipulations of binary data).

The electrical circuits mimic the logic electrically. Binary logic involves two states, which a computer's digital logic circuitry mimics with two voltage levels.

The logic isn't only what the computer works with; it's also what controls the computer. The same voltages used to represent values in binary logic act as signals that control the circuits. That means the signals flowing through the computer can control the computer—and the computer can control the signals. In other words, the computer can control itself. This design gives the computer its power.

Digital Logic Circuitry

The essence of the digital logic that underlies the operation of the microprocessor and motherboard is the ability to use one electrical signal to control another.

Certainly there are a myriad of ways of using one electrical signal to control another, as any student of Rube Goldberg can attest. As interesting and amusing as interspersing cats, bellows, and bowling balls in the flow of control may be, most engineers have opted for a more direct system that uses a more direct means based on time-proved electrical technologies.

In modern digital logic circuitry, the basis of this control is *amplification*, the process of using a small current to control a larger current (or a small voltage to control a larger voltage). The large current (or voltage) exactly mimics the controlling current (or voltage) but is stronger or amplified. In that every change in the large signal is exactly analogous to each one in the small signal, devices that amplify in this way are called *analog*. The intensity of the control signal can represent continuously variable information—for example, a sound level in stereo equipment. The electrical signal in this kind of equipment is therefore an analogy to the sound that it represents.

In the early years of the evolution of electronic technology, improving this analog amplification process was the primary goal of engineers. After all, without amplification, signals eventually deteriorated into nothingness. The advent of digital information and the earliest computers made them use the power of amplification differently.

The limiting case of amplification occurs when the control signal causes the larger signal to go from its lowest value, typically zero, to its highest value. In other words, the large signal goes off and on—switches—under control of the smaller signal. The two states of the output signal (on and off) can be used as part of a binary code that represents information. For example, the switch could be used to produce a series of seven pulses to represent the number 7. Because information can be coded as groups of such numbers (digits), electrical devices that use this switching technology are described as *digital*. Note that this switching directly corresponds to other, more direct control of on/off information, such as pounding on a telegraph key, a concept we'll return to in later chapters.

Strictly speaking, an electronic digital system works with signals called *high* and *low*, corresponding to a digital one and zero. In formal logic systems, these same values are often termed *true* and *false*. In general, a digital one or logical true corresponds to an electronic high. Sometimes, however, special digital codes reverse this relationship.

In practical electrical circuits, the high and low signals only roughly correspond to on and off. Standard digital logic systems define both the high and low signals as ranges of voltages. High is a voltage range near the maximum voltage accepted by the system, and low is a voltage range near (but not necessarily exactly at or including) zero. A wide range of undefined voltages spreads between the two, lower than the lowest edge of high but higher than the highest edge of low. The digital system ignores the voltages in the undefined range. Figure 4.1 shows how the ranges of voltages interrelate.

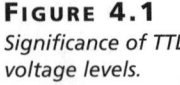

FIGURE 4.1

Significance of TTL voltage levels.

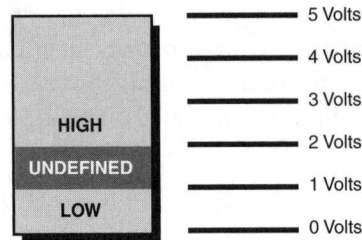

Perhaps the most widely known standard is called *TTL* (for transistor-transistor logic). In the TTL system, which is still common inside computer equipment, a logical low is any voltage below 0.8 volts. A logical high is any level above 2.0 volts. The range between 0.8 and 2.0 volts is undefined.

As modern computers shift to lower voltages, the top level of the logical high shifts downward—for example, from the old standard of 5.0 volts to the 3.3 volts of the latest computer equipment (and even lower voltages of new power-conserving microprocessors)—but the relationship between the high and low voltages, along with the undefined range in between, remains the same. Modern systems usually retain the same low and undefined ranges—they just lop the top off the figure showing the TTL voltage levels.

Electronics

Modern electronics are filled with mysterious acronyms and even stranger-sounding names. Computer are filled with circuits made from these things, unfamiliar terms such as CMOS and NMOS, semiconductors, and integrated circuits. A bit of historical perspective will show you what the names means and where (and how) the technologies they describe originated.

Over the years, electrical engineers have developed a number of ways one signal can control another. The first approach to the electrical control of electrical flow evolved from the rattling telegraph key. When a telegrapher jammed down on his key to make dots and dashes, he actually closed an electrical circuit, which sent a voltage down the telegraph line. At the far end of the connection, this signal powered an electromagnet that snapped against a piece of iron to create the dot and dash sound.

In 1835 Joseph Henry saw that the electromagnet could be adapted to operate a switch rather than just pull on a hunk of iron. The electromagnetically actuated switch allowed a feeble current to switch on a more powerful current. The resulting device, the *electrical relay*, was key to the development of the long-distance telegraph. When telegraph signals got too weak from traveling a great distance, a relay could revitalize them.

In operation, a relay is just a switch that's controlled by an electromagnet. Activating the electromagnet with a small current moves a set of contacts that switch the flow of a larger current. The relay doesn't care whether the control current starts off in the same box as the relay or from a continent away. As simple in concept as the relay is, its ability to use one signal to control another proved very powerful—powerful enough that relays served as the foundation of some of the first computers (or electrical calculators), such as Bell Lab's 1946 Mark V computer. Relays are still used in modern electrical equipment.

Vacuum Tubes

The vacuum tube improved on the relay design for computers by eliminating the mechanical part of the remote-action switch. Using electronics only, a tube could switch and perform logic operations faster, thousands of times faster, than relays.

Vacuum tubes developed out of Thomas Edison's 1879 invention of the incandescent light bulb. After the public demonstration of the bulb, Edison continued to work with and improve it. Along the way, he made a discovery in 1883 (which some historians credit as Edison's sole original contribution to pure scientific research) of what has come to be called the *Edison Effect*. Edison noted he could make a current flow through the vacuum in the bulb from the filament to a metal plate he had introduced inside.

The Edison Effect remained a curiosity until 1904 when John Ambrose Fleming created the *diode* vacuum tube. Fleming found that electrons would flow from the negatively charged hot filament of the light bulb to a positively charged cold collector plate, but not in the other direction. Fleming made an electrical one-way street that could operate as a *rectifier* to change alternating current into direct current or as a *detector* that pulled modulation from carrier waves (by stripping off the carrier wave's alternating cycles).

In 1907 Lee De Forest created the Audion, now known as the triode tube. De Forest introduced an element of control to the bulb-cum-diode. He interposed a control grid between the hot filament (the cathode) and the cold plate (the anode). De Forest found that he could control the electron flow by varying the voltage he applied to the control grid.

The grid allowed the Audion to harness the power of the attraction of unlike electrical charges and the repulsion of like charges, enabling a small charge to control the flow of electrons through the vacuum inside the tube. In the Audion, as with the relay, a small voltage could control a much larger voltage. De Forest created the first electronic amplifier, the basis of all modern electronics.

The advantage of the vacuum tube over the relay in controlling signals is speed. The relay operates at mechanical rates, perhaps a few thousand operations per second. The vacuum tube can switch millions of times per second. The first recognizable computers (such as ENIAC) were built from thousands of tubes, each configured as a digital logic gate.

Semiconductors

Using tube-based electronics in computers is fraught with problems. First is the space-heater effect: Tubes have to glow like light bulbs to work, and they generate heat along the way, enough to smelt rather than process data. And, like light bulbs, tubes burn out. Large tube-based computers required daily shutdown and maintenance as well as several technicians on the payroll. ENIAC was reported to have a mean time between failures of 5.6 hours.

In addition, tube circuits are big. ENIAC filled a room, yet the house-sized computers of 1950s vintage science fiction would easily be outclassed in computing power by today's desktop machines. In the typical tube-based computer design, one logic gate required one tube that took up considerably more space than a single microprocessor with tens of millions of logic gates. Moreover, physical size isn't only a matter of housing. The bigger the computer, the longer it takes its thoughts to travel through its circuits—even at the speed of light—and the more slowly it thinks.

Making today's practical computers took another true breakthrough in electronics: the *transistor*, first created at Bell Laboratories in 1947 and announced in 1948 by the team of John Bardeen, Walter Brattain, and William Shockley. A tiny fleck of germanium (later, silicon) formed into three layers, the transistor was endowed with the capability to let one electrical current applied to one layer alter the flow of another, larger current between the other two layers. Unlike the vacuum tube, the transistor needed no hot electrons because the current flowed entirely through a solid material—the germanium or silicon—hence, the common name for tubeless technology, *solid-state electronics*.

Germanium and silicon are special materials—actually, metals—called *semiconductors*. The term describes how these materials resist the flow of electrical currents. A true electrical conductor (such as the copper in wires) hardly resists the flow of electricity, whereas a non-conductor (or *insulator*, such as the plastic wrapped around the wires) almost totally prevents the flow of electricity. Semiconductors allow some—but not much—electricity to flow.

By itself, being a poor but not awful electrical conductor is as remarkable as lukewarm water. However, infusing atoms of impurities into the semiconductor's microscopic lattice structure dramatically alters the electrical characteristics of the material and makes solid-state electronics possible.

This process of adding impurities is called *doping*. Some impurities add extra electrons (carriers of negative charges) to the crystal. A semiconductor doped to be rich in electrons is called an *N-type semiconductor*. Other impurities in the lattice leave holes where electrons would ordinarily be, and these holes act as positive charge carriers. A semiconductor doped to be rich in holes is called a *P-type semiconductor*.

Electricity easily flows across the junction between the two materials when an N-type semiconductor on one side passes electrons to the holes in a P-type semiconductor on the other side. The empty holes willingly accept the electrons. They just fit right in. But electricity doesn't flow well in the opposite direction, however. If the P-type semiconductor's holes ferry electrons to the N-type material at the junction, the N-type semiconductor will refuse delivery. It already has all the electrons it needs. It has no place to put any more. In other words, electricity flows only in one direction through the semiconductor junction, just as it flows only one way through a vacuum-tube diode.

The original transistor incorporated three layers with two junctions between dissimilar materials, stacked in layers as N-P-N or P-N-P. Each layer has its own name: The top is the *emitter*, the middle of the sandwich is the *gate*, and the bottom is the *collector*. (The structure of a transistor isn't usually a three-layer cake with top and bottom, but that's effectively how it works.)

Ordinarily no electricity could pass through such a stack from emitter to collector because the two junctions in the middle are oriented in opposite directions. One blocks electrical flow one way, and the second blocks the flow in the other direction.

The neat trick that makes a transistor work is changing the voltage on the middle layer. Say you have a P-N-P transistor. Your wire dumps electrons into the holes in the P-layer, and they travel to the junction with the N-layer. The N-layer is full of electrons, so it won't let the current flow further. But if you drain off some of those electrons through the gate, current can flow through the junction—and it can keep flowing through the next junction as well. It only takes a small current to drain electrons from the gate to permit a large current to flow from emitter to collector.

The design of transistor circuits is more complicated than our simple example. Electrical flow through the transistor depends on the complex relationships between voltages on its junctions, and the electricity doesn't necessarily have to flow from emitter to collector. In fact, the junction transistor design, although essential to the first transistors, is rarely used in computer circuits today. But the junction transistor best illustrates the core principles of all solid-state electronics.

Modern computer circuits mostly rely on a kind of transistor in which the electrical current flow through a narrow channel of semiconductor material is controlled by a voltage applied to a gate (which surrounds the channel) made from metal oxide. The most common variety of these transistors is made from N-type material and results in a technology called *NMOS*, an acronym for N-channel Metal Oxide Semiconductor. A related technology combines both N-channel and P-channel devices and is called *CMOS* (Complementary Metal Oxide Semiconductor) because the N-and P-type materials are complements (opposites) of one another. These names—CMOS particularly—pop up occasionally in discussions of electronic circuits.

The typical microprocessor once was built from NMOS technology. Although NMOS designs are distinguished by their simplicity and small size (even on a microchip level), they have a severe shortcoming: They constantly use electricity whenever their gates are turned on. Because about half of the tens or hundreds of thousands of gates in a microprocessor are switched on at any given time, an NMOS chip can draw a lot of current. This current flow creates heat and wastes power, making NMOS unsuitable for miniaturized computers (which can be difficult to cool) and battery-operated equipment, such as notebook computers.

Some earlier and most contemporary microprocessors now use CMOS designs. CMOS is inherently more complex than NMOS because each gate requires more transistors, at least a pair per gate. But this complexity brings a benefit: When one transistor in a CMOS gate is turned on, its complementary partner is switched off, thus minimizing the current flow through the complementary pair that make up the circuit. When a CMOS gate is idle, just maintaining its state, it requires almost no power. During a state change, the current flow is large but brief. Consequently, the faster the CMOS gate changes state, the more current that flows through it and the more heat it generates. In other words, the faster a CMOS circuit operates, the hotter it becomes. This speed-induced temperature rise is one of the limits on the operating speed of many microprocessors.

CMOS technology can duplicate every logic function made with NMOS but with a substantial saving of electricity. On the other hand, manufacturing costs somewhat more because of the added circuit complexity.

Integrated Circuits

The transistor overcomes several of the problems with using tubes to make a computer. Transistors are smaller than tubes and give off less heat because they don't need to glow to work. But every logic gate still requires one or more transistors (as well as several other electronic components) to build. If you allocated a mere square inch to every logic gate, the number of logic gates in a personal computer microprocessor such as the Pentium 4 (about fifty million) would require a circuit board on the order of 600 square feet.

At the very end of the 1950s, Robert N. Noyce at Fairchild Instrument and Jack S. Kilby of Texas Instruments independently came up with the same brilliant idea of putting multiple semiconductor devices into a single package. Transistors are typically grown as crystals from thin-cut slices of silicon called *wafers*. Typically, thousands of transistors are grown at the same time on the same wafer. Instead of carving the wafer into separate transistors, the engineer linked them together (integrated them) to create a complete electronic circuit all on one wafer. Kilby linked the devices with micro-wires; Noyce envisioned fabricating the interconnecting circuits between devices on the silicon itself. The resulting electronic device, for which Noyce applied for a patent on July 30, 1959, became known as the *integrated circuit*, or IC. Such devices now are often called *chips* because of their construction from a single small piece of silicon—a chip off the old crystal. Integrated circuit technology has been adapted to both analog and digital circuitry. Their grandest development, however, is the microprocessor.

Partly because of the Noyce invention, Fairchild flourished as a semiconductor manufacturer throughout the 1960s. The company was acquired by Schlumberger Ltd. in 1979, which sold it to National Semiconductor in 1987. In 1996, National spun off Fairchild as an independent manufacturer once again, and the developer of the integrated circuit continues to operate as an independent business, Fairchild Semiconductor Corporation, based in South Portland, Maine.

The IC has several advantages over circuits built from individual (or discrete) transistors, most resulting from miniaturization. Most importantly, integration reduces the amount of packaging. Instead of one metal or plastic transistor case per logic gate, multiple gates (even millions of them) can be combined into one chip package.

Because the current inside the chip need not interact with external circuits, the chips can be made arbitrarily small, enabling the circuits to be made smaller, too. In fact, today the limit on the size of elements inside an integrated circuit is mostly determined by fabrication technology; internal circuitry is as small as today's manufacturing equipment can make it affordably. The latest Intel microprocessors, which use integrated circuit technology, incorporate the equivalent of over 50 million transistors using interconnections that measure less than 0.13 of a micron (millionths of a meter) across.

In the past, a hierarchy of names was given to ICs depending on the size of circuit elements. Ordinary ICs were the coarsest in construction. Large-scale integration (LSI) put between 500 and 20,000 circuit elements together; very large-scale integration (VLSI) put more than 20,000 circuit elements onto a single chip. All microprocessors use VLSI technology, although the most recent products have become so complex (Intel's Pentium 4, for example, has the equivalent of about 50 million transistors inside) that a new term has been coined for them, ultra large-scale integration (ULSI).

Moore's Law

The development of the microprocessor often is summed up by quoting Moore's Law, which sounds authoritative and predicts an exponential acceleration in computer power. At least that's how Moore's Law is most often described when you stumble over it in books and magazines. The most common interpretation occurring these days is that Moore's Law holds that computer power doubles every 18 months.

In truth, you'll never find the law concisely quoted anywhere. That's because it's a slippery thing. It doesn't say what most people think. As originally formulated, it doesn't even apply to microprocessors. That's because Gordon E. Moore actually created his "law" well before the microprocessor was invented. In its original form, Moore's Law describes only how quickly the number of transistors in integrated circuits was growing.

What became known as Moore's Law was first published in the industry journal *Electronics* on April 19, 1965, in a paper titled "Cramming More Components into Integrated Circuits," written when Moore was director of the research and development laboratories at Fairchild Semiconductor. His observation—and what Moore's Law really says—was that the number of transistors in the most complex circuits tended to double every year. Moore's conclusion was that by 1975, ten years after he was writing, economics would force semiconductor makers to squeeze as many as 65,000 transistors onto a single silicon chip.

Although Moore's fundamental premise, that integrated circuit complexity increases exponentially, was accurate (although not entirely obvious at the time), the actual numbers given in Moore's predictions in the paper missed the mark. He was quite optimistic. For example, over the 31-year history of the microprocessor from 4004 to Pentium 4, the transistor count has increased by a factor of 18,667 (from 2250 to 42 million). That's approximately a doubling every *two* years.

That's more of a difference than you might think. At Moore's rate, a microprocessor today would have over four trillion transistors inside. Even the 18-month doubling rate so often quoted would put about 32 billion transistors in every chip. In either case, you're talking *real* computer power.

Over the years, people have gradually adapted Moore's Law to better suit the facts—in other words, Moore's Law doesn't predict how many transistors will be in future circuits. It only describes how circuit complexity has increased.

The future of the "law" is cloudier still. A constant doubling of transistor count requires ever-accelerating spending on circuit design research, which was possible during the 20 years of the personal computer boom but may suffer as the rapid growth of the industry falters. Moreover, the law—or even a linear increase in the number of transistors on a chip—ultimately bumps into fundamental limits imposed by the laws of physics. At some point the increase in complexity of integrated circuits, taken to extreme, will require circuit elements smaller than atoms or quarks, which most physicists believe is not possible.

Printed Circuits

An integrated circuit is like a gear of a complex machine. By itself it does nothing. It must be connected to the rest of the mechanism to perform its appointed task. The integrated circuit needs a means to acquire and send out the logic and electrical signals it manipulates. In other words, each integrated circuit in a computer must be logically and electrically connected—essentially that means linked by wires.

In early electrical devices, wires in fact provided the necessary link. Each wire carried one signal from one point to another, creating a technology called *point-to-point wiring*. Because people routinely soldered together these point-to-point connections by hand using a soldering iron, they were sometimes called *hand-wired*. This was a workable, if not particularly cost-effective, technology in the days of tubes, when even a simple circuit spanned a few inches of physical space. Today, point-to-point wiring is virtually inconceivable because a computer crams the equivalent of half a million tube circuits into a few square inches of space. Connecting them with old-fashioned wiring would take a careful hand and some very fine wire. The time required to cut, strip, and solder in place each wire would make building a single computer a lifetime endeavor.

Long before the introduction of the first computer, engineers found a better way of wiring together electrical devices—the *printed circuit board*. The term is sometimes confusingly shortened to *computer board*, even when the board is part of some other, non-computer device. Today, printed circuit boards are the standard from which nearly all electronic devices are made. The "board" in the name "motherboard" results from the assembly being a printed circuit board.

Fabrication

Printed circuit board technology allows all the wiring for an entire circuit assembly to be fabricated together in a quick process that can be entirely mechanized. The wires themselves are reduced to copper traces, a pattern of copper foil bonded to the substrate that makes up the support structure of the printed circuit board. In computers, this substrate is usually green composite material called *glass-epoxy*, because it has a woven glass fiber base that's filled and reinforced with an epoxy plastic. Less-critical electronic devices (read "cheap") substitute a simple brownish substrate of phenolic plastic for the glass-epoxy.

The simplest printed circuit boards start life as a sheet of thin copper foil bonded to a substrate. The copper is coated with a compound called *photo-resist*, a light-sensitive material. When exposed to light, the photo-resist becomes resistant to the effects of compounds, such as nitric acid, that strongly react with copper. A negative image of the desired final circuit pattern is placed over the photo-resist covered copper and exposed to a strong light source. This process is akin to making a print of a photograph. The exposed board is then immersed in an *etchant*, one of those nasty compounds that etch or eat away the copper that is not protected by the light-exposed photo-resist. The result is a pattern of copper on the substrate corresponding to the photographic original. The copper traces can then be used to connect the various electronic components that will make up the final circuit. All the wiring on a circuit board is thus fabricated in a single step.

When the electronic design on a printed circuit board is too complex to be successfully fabricated on one side of the substrate, engineers can switch to a slightly more complex technology to make two-sided boards. The traces on each side are separately exposed but etched during the same bath in etchant. In general, the circuit traces on one side of the board run parallel in one direction, and the traces on the other side run generally perpendicular. The two sides get connected together by components inserted through the board or through *plated-through holes*, holes drilled through the board and then filled with solder to provide an electrical connection

To accommodate even more complex designs, engineers have designed *multilayer circuit boards*. These are essentially two or more thin double-sided boards tightly glued together into a single assembly. Most computer system boards use multilayer technology, both to accommodate complex designs and to improve signals characteristics. Sometimes a layer is left nearly covered with copper to shield the signal in the layers from interacting with one another. These shielding layers are typically held at ground potential and are consequently called *ground planes*.

One of the biggest problems with the multilayer design (besides the difficulty in fabrication) is the difficulty in repair. Abnormally flexing a multilayer board can break one of the traces hidden in the center of the board. No reasonable amount of work can repair such damage.

Pin-in-Hole Technology

Two technologies are in wide use for attaching components to the printed circuit board. The older technology is called *pin-in-hole*. Electric drills bore holes in the circuit board at the points where the electronic components are to attach. Machines (usually) push the leads (wires that come out of the electronic components) into and through the circuit board holes and bend them slightly so that they hold firmly in place. The components are then permanently fixed in place with solder, which forms both a physical and electrical connection. Figure 4.2 shows the installation of a pin-in-hole electronic component.

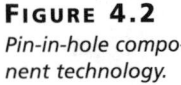

FIGURE 4.2
*Pin-in-hole compo-
nent technology.*

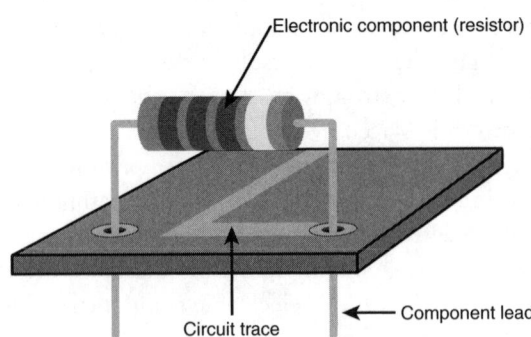

Electronic component (resistor)

Circuit trace

Component lead

Most mass-produced pin-in-hole boards use *wave-soldering* to attach pin-in-hole components. In wave-soldering, a conveyer belt slides the entire board over a pool of molten solder (a tin and lead alloy), and a wave on the solder pool extends up to the board, coating the leads and the circuit traces. When cool, the solder holds all the components firmly in place.

Workers can also push pin-in-hole components into circuit boards and solder them individually in place by hand. Although hand fabrication is time consuming and expensive, it can be effective when a manufacturer requires only a small number of boards. Automatic machinery cuts labor costs and speeds production on long runs; assembly workers typically make prototypes and small production runs or provide the sole means of assembly for tiny companies that can afford neither automatic machinery nor farming out their circuit board work.

Surface Mount Technology

The newer method of attaching components, called *surface-mount technology*, promises greater miniaturization and lower costs than pin-in-hole. Instead of holes to secure them, surface-mount components are glued to circuit boards using solder flux or paste, which temporarily holds them in place. After all the components are affixed to a circuit board in their proper places, the entire board assembly runs through a temperature-controlled oven, which melts the solder paste and firmly solders each component to the board. Figure 4.3 illustrates surface-mount construction.

FIGURE 4.3

Surface mount circuit board construction.

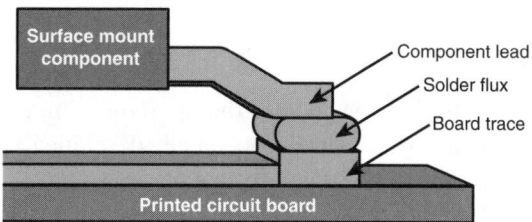

Surface mount components are smaller than their pin-in-hole kin because they don't need leads. Manufacturing is simpler because there's no need to drill holes in the circuit boards. Without the need for large leads, the packages of the surface-mount components can be smaller, so more components will fit in a given space with surface mount technology.

On the downside, surface mount fabrication doesn't lend itself to small production runs or prototyping. It can also be a headache for repair workers. They have to squint and peer at components that are often too small to be handled without tweezers and a lot of luck. Moreover, many surface-mount boards also incorporate some pin-in-hole components, so they still need drilling and wave-soldering.

Logic Design

Reduced to its fundamental principles, the workings of a modern silicon-based micro-processor are not difficult to understand. They are simply the electronic equivalent of a knee-jerk. Every time you hit the microprocessor with an electronic hammer blow (the proper digital input), it reacts by doing a specific something. Like a knee-jerk reflex, the microprocessor's reaction is always the same. When hammered by the same input and conditions, it kicks out the same function.

The complexity of the microprocessor and what it does arises from the wealth of inputs it can react to and the interaction between successive inputs. Although the microprocessor's function is precisely defined by its input, the output from that function varies with what the microprocessor has to work on, and that depends on previous inputs. For example, the result of you carrying out a specific command—"Simon says lift your left leg"—will differ dramatically depending on whether the previous command was "Simon says sit down" or "Simon says lift your right leg."

The rules for controlling the knee-jerks inside a computer are the rules of logic, and not just any logic. Computers use a special symbolic logic system that was created about a century and a half ago in the belief that human thinking could be mechanized much as the production of goods had been mechanized in the Industrial Revolution.

Boolean Logic

As people began to learn to think again after the Dark Ages, they began exploring mathematics, first in the Arabian world, then Europe. They developed a rigorous, objective system—one that was reassuring in its ability to replicate results. Carry out the same operation on the same numbers, and you always got the same answer. Mathematics delivered a certainty that was absent from the rest of the world, one in which dragons inhabited the unknown areas of maps and people had no conception that micro-organisms might cause disease.

Applying the same rigor and structure, scientific methods first pioneered by the Greeks were rediscovered. The objective scientific method found truth, the answers that eluded the world of superstition. Science led to an understanding of the world, new processes, new machines, and medicine.

In Victorian England, philosophers wondered whether the same objectivity and rigor could be applied to all of human thought. A mathematician, George Boole, first proposed applying the rigorous approach of algebra to logical decision-making. In 1847, Boole founded the system of modern symbolic logic that we now term *Boolean logic* (alternately,

Boolean algebra). In his system, Boole reduced propositions to symbols and formal opera-tors that followed the strict rules of mathematics. Using his rigorous approach, logical propositions could be proven with the same certainty as mathematical equations.

Philosophers, including Ludwig Wittgenstein and Bertrand Russell, further developed the concept of symbolic logic and showed that anything that could be known could be expressed in its symbols. By translating what you knew and wanted to know into symbols, you could apply the rules of Boolean logic and find an answer. Knowledge was reduced to a mechanical process, and that made it the province of machines.

In concept, Babbage's Analytical Engine could have deployed Boole's symbolic logic and become the first thinking machine. However, neither the logic nor the hardware was up to the task at the time. But when fast calculations became possible, Boolean logic proved key to programming the computers that carried out the tasks.

Logic Gates

Giving an electrical circuit the power to make a decision isn't as hard as you might think. Start with that same remote signaling of the telegraph but add a mechanical arm that links it to a light switch on your wall. As the telegraph pounds, the light flashes on and off. Certainly you'll have done a lot of work for a little return, in that the electricity could be used to directly light the bulb. There are other possibilities, however, that produce intriguing results. You could, for example, pair two weak telegraph arms so that their joint effort would be required to throw the switch to turn on the light. Or you could link the two telegraphs so that a signal on either one would switch on the light. Or you could install the switch backwards so that when the telegraph is activated, the light would go out instead of come on.

These three telegraph-based design examples actually provide the basis for three different types of computer circuits, called *logic gates* (the AND, OR, and NOT gates, respectively). These electrical circuits are called *gates* because they regulate the flow of electricity, allow-ing it to pass through or cutting it off, much as a gate in a fence allows or impedes your own progress. These logic gates endow the electrical assembly with decision-making power. In the light example, the decision is necessarily simple: when to switch on the light. But these same simple gates can be formed into elaborate combinations that make up a computer that can make complex logical decisions.

The three logic gates can perform the function of all the operators in Boolean logic. They form the basis of the decision-making capabilities of the computer as well as other logic circuitry. You'll encounter other kinds of gates, such as NAND (short for "Not AND"), NOR (short for "Not OR"), and XOR (for "Exclusive OR"), but you can build any one of the others from the basic three: AND, OR, and NOT.

In computer circuits, each gate requires at least one transistor. A microprocessor with ten million transistors may have nearly that many gates.

Memory

These same gates also can be arranged to form memory. Start with the familiar telegraph. Instead of operating the current for a light bulb, however, reroute the wires from the switch so that they, too, link to the telegraph's electromagnet. In other words, when the telegraph moves, it throws a switch that supplies itself with electricity. Once the telegraph is supplying itself with electricity, it will stay on using that power even if you switch off the original power that first made the switch. In effect, this simple system *remembers* whether it has once been activated. You can go back at any time and see if someone has ever sent a signal to the telegraph memory system.

This basic form of memory has one shortcoming: It's elephantine and never forgets. Resetting this memory system requires manually switching off both the control voltage and the main voltage source.

A more useful form of memory takes two control signals: One switches it on, the other switches it off. In simplest form, each cell of this kind of memory is made from two latches connected at cross-purposes so that switching one latch on cuts the other off. Because one signal sets this memory to hold data and the other one resets it, this circuit is sometimes called *set-reset memory*. A more common term is *flip-flop* because it alternately flips between its two states. In computer circuits, this kind of memory is often simply called a *latch*. Although the main memory of your computer uses a type of memory that works on a different electrical principal, latch memory remains important in circuit design.

Instructions

Although the millions of gates in a microprocessor are so tiny that you can't even discern them with an optical microscope (you need at least an electron microscope), they act exactly like elemental, telegraph-based circuits. They use electrical signals to control other signals. The signals are just more complicated, reflecting the more elaborate nature of the computer.

Today's microprocessors don't use a single signal to control their operations, rather, they use complex combinations of signals. Each microprocessor command is coded as a pattern of signals, the presence or absence of an electrical signal at one of the pins of the micro-processor's package. The signal at each pin represents one bit of digital information.

The designers of a microprocessor give certain patterns of these bit-signals specific meanings. Each pattern is a command called a *microprocessor instruction* that tells the micro-processor to carry out a specific operation. The bit pattern 0010110, for example, is the instruction that tells an Intel 8086-family microprocessor to subtract in a very explicit manner. Other instructions tell the microprocessor to add, multiply, divide, move bits or bytes around, change individual bits, or just wait around for another instruction.

Microprocessor designers can add instructions to do just about anything—from matrix calculations to brewing coffee (that is, if the designers wanted to, if the instructions actually did something useful, and if they had unlimited time and resources to engineer the chip). Practical concerns such as keeping the design work and the chip manageable constrain the range of commands given to a microprocessor.

The entire repertoire of commands that a given microprocessor model understands and can react to is called that microprocessor's *instruction set* or its *command set*. The designer of the microprocessor chooses which pattern to assign to a given function. As a result, different microprocessor designs recognize different instruction sets, just as different board games have different rules.

Despite their pragmatic limits, microprocessor instruction sets can be incredibly rich and diverse, and the individual instructions incredibly specific. The designers of the original 8086-style microprocessor, for example, felt that a simple command to subtract was not enough by itself. They believed that the microprocessor also needed to know what to subtract from what and what it should do with the result. Consequently, they added a rich variety of subtraction instructions to the 8086 family of chips that persists into today's Athlon and Pentium 4 chips. Each different subtraction instruction tells the microprocessor to take numbers from different places and find the difference in a slightly different manner.

Some microprocessor instructions require a series of steps to be carried out. These multi-step commands are sometimes called *complex instructions* because of their composite nature. Although a complex instruction looks like a simple command, it may involve much work. A simple instruction would be something such as "pound a nail." A complex instruction may be as far ranging as "frame a house." Simple subtraction or addition of two numbers may actually involve dozens of steps, including the conversion of the numbers from decimal to the binary (ones and zeros) notation that the microprocessor understands. For instance, the previous sample subtraction instruction tells one kind of microprocessor that it should subtract a number in memory from another number in the microprocessor's accumulator, a place that's favored for calculations in today's most popular microprocessors.

Registers

Before the microprocessor can work on numbers or any other data, it first must know what numbers to work on. The most straightforward method of giving the chip the variables it needs would seem to be supplying more coded signals at the same time the instruction is given. You could dump in the numbers 6 and 3 along with the subtract instruction, just as you would load laundry detergent along with shirts and sheets into your washing machine. This simple method has its shortcomings, however. Somehow the proper numbers must be routed to the right microprocessor inputs. The microprocessor needs to know whether to subtract 6 from 3 or 3 from 6 (the difference could be significant, particularly when you're balancing your checkbook).

Just as you distinguish the numbers in a subtraction problem by where you put them in the equation (6–3 versus 3–6), a microprocessor distinguishes the numbers on which it works by their position (where they are found). Two memory addresses might suffice were it not for the way most microprocessors are designed. They have only one pathway to memory, so they can effectively "see" only one memory value at a time. So instead, a microprocessor loads at least one number to an internal storage area called a *register*. It can then simultaneously reach both the number in memory and the value in its internal register. Alternatively (and more commonly today), both values on which the microprocessor is to work can be loaded into separate internal registers.

Part of the function of each microprocessor instruction is to tell the chip which registers to use for data and where to put the answers it comes up with. Other instructions tell the chip to load numbers into its registers to be worked on later or to move information from a register someplace else (for instance, to memory or an output port).

A register functions both as memory and a workbench. It holds bit-patterns until they can be worked on or sent out of the chip. The register is also connected with the processing circuits of the microprocessor so that the changes ordered by instructions actually appear in the register. Most microprocessors typically have several registers, some dedicated to specific functions (such as remembering which step in a function the chip is currently carrying out; this register is called a *counter* or *instruction pointer*) and some designed for general purposes. At one time, the *accumulator* was the only register in a microprocessor that could manage calculations. In modern microprocessors, all registers are more nearly equal (in some of the latest designs, all registers are equal, even interchangeable), so the accumulator is now little more than a colorful term left over from a bygone era.

Not only do microprocessors have differing numbers of registers, but the registers may also be of different sizes. Registers are measured by the number of bits that they can work with at one time. A 16-bit microprocessor, for example, should have one or more registers that each holds 16 bits of data at a time. Today's microprocessors have 32- or 64-bit registers.

Adding more registers to a microprocessor does not make it inherently faster. When a microprocessor lacks advanced features such as pipelining or superscalar technology (discussed later in this chapter), it can perform only one operation at a time. More than two registers would seem superfluous. After all, most math operations involve only two numbers at a time (or can be reduced to a series of two-number operations). Even with old-technology microprocessors, however, having more registers helps the software writer create more efficient programs. With more places to put data, a program needs to move information in and out of the microprocessor less often, which can potentially save several program steps and clock cycles.

Modern microprocessor designs, particularly those influenced by the latest research into design efficiency, demand more registers. Because microprocessors run much faster than memory, every time the microprocessor has to go to memory, it must slow down. Therefore, minimizing memory accessing helps improve performance. Keeping data in registers instead of memory speeds things up.

The *width* of the registers also has a substantial effect on the performance of a microprocessor. The more bits assigned to each register, the more information that the microprocessor can process in every cycle. Consequently, a 64-bit register in the next generation of microprocessor chips holds the potential of calculating eight times as fast as an 8-bit register of a first generation microprocessor—all else being equal.

Programs

A computer program is nothing more than a list of instructions. The computer goes through the instruction list of the program step by step, executing each one in turn. Each builds on the previous instructions to carry out a complex function. The program is essentially a recipe for a microprocessor or the step-by-step instructions in a how-to manual.

The challenge for the programmer is to figure out into which steps to break a complex job and to arrange those steps in the best possible order. It can be a big job. Although a program can be as simple as a single step (say, stop), a modern program or software package may comprise millions or tens of millions of steps. They are quite literally too complex for a single human being to understand—or write. They are joint efforts. Not just the work of many people, but the work of people and machines using development environments to divide up the work and take advantage of routines and libraries created by other teams. A modern software package is the result of years of work in putting together simple microprocessor instructions.

One of the most important concepts in the use of modern personal computers is *multitasking*, the ability to run multiple programs at the same time, shifting your focus from one to another. You can, for example, type a term paper on L. Frank Baum and the real meaning of the *Wizard of Oz* using your word processor while your MP3 program churns out a techno version of "Over the Rainbow" through your computer's speakers. Today, you take that kind of thing for granted. But thinking about it, this doesn't make sense in the context of computer programs being simple lists of instructions and your microprocessor executing the instructions, one by one, in order. How can a computer do two things at the same time?

The answer is easy. It cannot. Computers do, in fact, process instructions as a single list. Computers can, however, switch between lists of instructions. They can execute a series of instructions from one list, shift to another list for a time, and then shift back to the first list. You get the illusion that the computer is doing several things at the same time because it shifts between instruction lists very quickly, dozens of times a second. Just as the separate frames of an animated cartoon blur together into an illusion of continuous motion, the computer switches so fast you cannot perceive the changes.

Multitasking is not an ability of a microprocessor. Even when you're doing six things at once on your computer, the microprocessor is still doing one thing at a time. It just runs all those instructions. The mediator of the multitasking is your operating system, basically a master program. It keeps track of every program (and subprogram) that's running—including itself—and decides which gets a given moment of the microprocessor's time for executing instructions.

Interrupts

Give a computer a program, and it's like a runaway freight train. Nothing can stop it. It keeps churning through instructions until it reaches the last one. That's great if what you want is the answer, whenever it may arrive. But if you have a task that needs immediate attention—say a block of data has just arrived from the Internet—you don't want to wait forever for one program to end before you can start another.

To add immediacy and interactivity to microprocessors, chip designers incorporate a feature called the *interrupt*. An interrupt is basically a signal to the microprocessor to stop what it is doing and turn its attention to something else. Intel microprocessors understand two kinds of interrupts: software and hardware.

A *software interrupt* is simply a special instruction in a program that's controlling the microprocessor. Instead of adding, subtracting, or whatever, the software interrupt causes program execution to temporarily shift to another section of code in memory.

A *hardware interrupt* causes the same effect but is controlled by special signals outside of the normal data stream. The only problem is that the microprocessors recognize far fewer interrupts than would be useful—only two interrupt signal lines are provided. One of these is a special case, the Non-Maskable Interrupt. The other line is shared by all system interrupts. The support hardware of your computer multiplies the number of hardware interrupts so that all devices that need them have the ability to interrupt the microprocessor.

Clocked Logic

Microprocessors do not carry out instructions as soon as the instruction code signals reach the pins that connect the microprocessor to your computer's circuitry. If chips did react immediately, they would quickly become confused. Electrical signals cannot change state instantly; they always go through a brief, though measurable, transition period—a period of indeterminate voltage level during which the signals would probably perplex a microprocessor into a crash. Moreover, all signals do not necessarily change at the same rate, so when some signals reach the right values, others may still be at odd values. As a result, a microprocessor must live through long periods of confusion during which its signals are at best meaningless, at worst dangerous.

To prevent the microprocessor from reacting to these invalid signals, the chip waits for an indication that it has a valid command to carry out. It waits until it gets a "Simon says" signal. In today's computers, this indication is provided by the system clock. The clock sends out regular voltage pulses, the electronic equivalent of the ticking of a grandfather's clock. The microprocessor checks the instructions given to it each time it receives a clock pulse, providing it is not already busy carrying out another instruction.

Early microprocessors were unable to carry out even one instruction every clock cycle. Vintage microprocessors may require as many as 100 discrete steps (and clock pulses) to carry out a single instruction. The number of cycles required to carry out instructions varies with the instruction and the microprocessor design. Some instructions take a few cycles, others dozens. Moreover, some microprocessors are more efficient than others in carrying out their instructions. The trend today is to minimize and equalize the number of clock cycles needed to carry out a typical instruction.

When you want to squeeze every last bit of performance from a computer, you can sometimes tinker with its timing settings. You can up the pace at which its circuits operate, thus making the system faster. This technique also forces circuits to operate at speeds higher than they were intended, thus compromising the reliability of the computer's operations. Tinkers don't worry about such things, believing that most circuits have such a wide safety margin that a little boost will do no harm. The results of their work may delight them— they might eke 10 percent or more extra performance from a computer—but these results might also surprise them when the system operates erratically and shuts down randomly. This game is called *overclocking* because it forces the microprocessor in the computer to operate at a clock speed that's over its ratings.

Overclocking also takes a more insidious form. Unscrupulous semiconductor dealers sometimes buy microprocessors (or memory chips or other speed-rated devices) and change their labels to reflect higher-speed potentials (for example, buying a 2.2GHz Pentium 4 and altering its markings to say 2.53GHz). A little white paint increases the market value of some chips by hundreds of dollars. It also creates a product that is likely to be operated out of its reliable range. Intel introduced internal chip serial numbers with the Pentium III to help prevent this form of fraud. From the unalterable serial number of the chip, the circuitry of a computer can figure out the factory-issue speed rating of the chip and automatically adjust itself to the proper speed.

Microprocessors

Microprocessors are the most complicated devices ever created by human beings. But don't despair. A microprocessor is complicated the same way a castle you might build from Legos is complicated. You can easily understand each of the individual parts of a microprocessor and how they fit together, just as you might build a fort or castle from a legion of blocks of assorted shapes. The metaphor is more apt than you might think. Engineers, in fact, design microprocessors as a set of functional blocks—not physical blocks like Legos, but blocks of electronic circuits that perform specific functions. And they don't fit them together on the floor of a giant playroom. Most of their work is mental, a lot of it performed on computers. Yes, you need a computer to design a computer these days. Using a computer is faster; it can give engineers insight by showing them ideas they could only before imagine, and it doesn't leave a mess of blocks on the floor that Mom makes them clean up.

In creating a microprocessor, a team of engineers may work on each one of the blocks that makes up the final chip, and the work of one team may be almost entirely unfathomable by another team. That's okay, because all that teams need to know about the parts besides their own is what those other parts do and how they fit together, not how they are made. All the complex details—the logic gates from which each block is built—are irrelevant to anyone not designing that block. It's like those Legos. You might know a Lego block is made from molecules of plastic, but you don't need to know about the carbon backbones and the side-chains that make up each molecule to put the blocks together.

Legos come in different shapes. The functional blocks of a microprocessor have different functions. We'll start our look at microprocessors by defining what those functions are. Then we'll leave the playroom behind and look at how you make a microprocessor operate by examining the instructions that it uses. This detour is more important than you might think. Much of the design work in creating a series of microprocessors goes into deciding exactly what instructions it must carry out—which instructions are most useful for solving problems and doing it quickest. From there, we'll look at how engineers have used their imaginations to design ever-faster microprocessors and at the tricks they use to coax more speed for each new generation of chip.

Microprocessor designers can't just play with theory in creating microprocessors. They have to deal with real-world issues. Somehow, machines must make the chips. Once they are made, they have to operate—and keep operating. Hard reality puts some tight constraints on microprocessor design. If engineers aren't careful, microprocessors can become miniature incinerators, burning themselves up. We'll take a look at some of these real-world issues that guide microprocessor design—including electricity, heat, and packaging, all of which work together (and at times, against the design engineer).

Next, we'll look at real microprocessors, the chips you can actually buy. We'll start with a brief history lesson to put today's commercial offerings in perspective. And, finally, we'll look at the chips in today's (and tomorrow's) computers to see which is meant for what purpose—and which is best for your own computer.

Background

Every modern microprocessor starts with the basics—clocked-logic digital circuitry. The chip has millions of separate gates combined into three basic function blocks: the input/output unit (or I/O unit), the control unit, and the arithmetic/logic unit (ALU). The last two are sometimes jointly called the *central processing unit* (CPU), although the same term often is used as a synonym for the entire microprocessor. Some chipmakers further subdivide these units, give them other names, or include more than one of each in a particular microprocessor. In any case, the functions of these three units are an inherent part of any chip. The differences are mostly a matter of nomenclature, because you can understand the entire operation of any microprocessor as a product of these three functions.

All three parts of the microprocessor interact together. In all but the simplest microprocessor designs, the I/O unit is under the control of the control unit, and the operation of the control unit may be determined by the results of calculations of the arithmetic/logic unit CPU. The combination of the three parts determines the power and performance of the microprocessor.

Each part of the microprocessor also has its own effect on the processing speed of the system. The control unit operates the microprocessor's internal clock, which determines the rate at which the chip operates. The I/O unit determines the bus width of the microprocessor, which influences how quickly data and instructions can be moved in and out of the microprocessor. And the registers in the arithmetic/control unit determine how much data the microprocessor can operate on at one time.

Input/Output Unit

The input/output unit links the microprocessor to the rest of the circuitry of the computer, passing along program instructions and data to the registers of the control unit and arithmetic/logic unit. The I/O unit matches the signal levels and timing of the microprocessor's internal solid-state circuitry to the requirements of the other components inside the computer. The internal circuits of a microprocessor, for example, are designed to be stingy with electricity so that they can operate faster and cooler. These delicate internal circuits cannot handle the higher currents needed to link to external components. Consequently, each signal leaving the microprocessor goes through a signal buffer in the I/O unit that boosts its current capacity.

The input/output unit can be as simple as a few buffers, or it may involve many complex functions. In the latest Intel microprocessors used in some of the most powerful computers, the I/O unit includes cache memory and clock-doubling or -tripling logic to match the high operating speed of the microprocessor to slower external memory.

The microprocessors used in computers have two kinds of external connections to their input/output units: those connections that indicate the address of memory locations to or from which the microprocessor will send or receive data or instructions, and those connections that convey the meaning of the data or instructions. The former is called the *address bus* of the microprocessor; the latter, the *data bus*.

The number of bits in the data bus of a microprocessor directly influences how quickly it can move information. The more bits that a chip can use at a time, the faster it is. The first microprocessors had data buses only four bits wide. Pentium chips use a 32-bit data bus, as do the related Athlon, Celeron, and Duron chips. Itanium and Opteron chips have 64-bit data buses.

The number of bits available on the address bus influences how much memory a microprocessor can address. A microprocessor with 16 address lines, for example, can directly work with 2^{16} addresses; that's 65,536 (or 64K) different memory locations. The different microprocessors used in various computers span a range of address bus widths from 32 to 64 or more bits.

The range of bit addresses used by a microprocessor and the physical number of address lines of the chip no longer correspond. That's because people and microprocessors look at memory differently. Although people tend to think of memory in terms of bytes, each comprising eight bits, microprocessors now deal in larger chunks of data, corresponding to the number of bits in their data buses. For example, a Pentium chip chews into data 32 bits at a time, so it doesn't need to look to individual bytes. It swallows them four at a time. Chipmakers consequently omit the address lines needed to distinguish chunks of memory smaller than their data buses. This bit of frugality saves the number of connections the chip needs to make with the computer's circuitry, an issue that becomes important once you see (as you will later) that the modern microprocessor requires several hundred external connections—each prone to failure.

Control Unit

The *control unit* of a microprocessor is a clocked logic circuit that, as its name implies, controls the operation of the entire chip. Unlike more common integrated circuits, whose function is fixed by hardware design, the control unit is more flexible. The control unit follows the instructions contained in an external program and tells the arithmetic/logic unit what to do. The control unit receives instructions from the I/O unit, translates them into a form that can be understood by the arithmetic/logic unit, and keeps track of which step of the program is being executed.

With the increasing complexity of microprocessors, the control unit has become more sophisticated. In the basic Pentium, for example, the control unit must decide how to route signals between what amounts to two separate processing units called *pipelines*. In other advanced microprocessors, the function of the control unit is split among other functional blocks, such as those that specialize in evaluating and handling branches in the stream of instructions.

Arithmetic/Logic Unit

The arithmetic/logic unit handles all the decision-making operations (the mathematical computations and logic functions) performed by the microprocessor. The unit takes the instructions decoded by the control unit and either carries them out directly or executes the appropriate microcode (see the section titled "Microcode" later in this chapter) to modify the data contained in its registers. The results are passed back out of the microprocessor through the I/O unit.

The first microprocessors had but one ALU. Modern chips may have several, which commonly are classed into two types. The basic form is the *integer unit*, one that carries out only the simplest mathematical operations. More powerful microprocessors also include one or more *floating-point units*, which handle advanced math operations (such as trigonometric and transcendental functions), typically at greater precision.

Floating-Point Unit

Although functionally a floating-point unit is part of the arithmetic/logic unit, engineers often discuss it separately because the floating-point unit is designed to process only *floating-point numbers* and not to take care of ordinary math or logic operations.

Floating-point describes a way of expressing values, not a mathematically defined type of number such as an integer, rational, or real number. The essence of a floating-point number is that its decimal point "floats" between a predefined number of significant digits rather than being fixed in place the way dollar values always have two decimal places.

Mathematically speaking, a floating-point number has three parts: a *sign*, which indicates whether the number is greater or less than zero; a *significant* (sometimes called a *mantissa*), which comprises all the digits that are mathematically meaningful; and an *exponent*, which determines the order of magnitude of the significant (essentially the location to which the decimal point floats). Think of a floating-point number as being like those represented by scientific notation. But whereas scientists are apt to deal in base-10 (the exponents in scientific notation are powers of 10), floating-point units think of numbers digitally in base-2 (all ones and zeros in powers of two).

As a practical matter, the form of floating-point numbers used in computer calculations follows standards laid down by the Institute of Electrical and Electronic Engineers (IEEE). The IEEE formats take values that can be represented in binary form using 80 bits. Although 80 bits seems somewhat arbitrary in a computer world that's based on powers of two and a steady doubling of register size from 8 to 16 to 32 to 64 bits, it's exactly the right size to accommodate 64 bits of the significant, with 15 bits leftover to hold an exponent value and an extra bit for the sign of the number held in the register. Although the IEEE standard allows for 32-bit and 64-bit floating-point values, most floating-point units are designed to accommodate the full 80-bit values. The floating-point unit (FPU) carries out all its calculations using the full 80 bits of the chip's registers, unlike the integer unit, which can independently manipulate its registers in byte-wide pieces.

The floating-point units of Intel-architecture processors have eight of these 80-bit registers in which to perform their calculations. Instructions in your programs tell the microprocessor whether to use its ordinary integer ALU or its floating-point unit to carry out a mathematical operation. The different instructions are important because the eight 80-bit registers in Intel floating-point units also differ from integer units in the way they are addressed. Commands for integer unit registers are directly routed to the appropriate register as if sent by a switchboard. Floating-point unit registers are arranged in a *stack*, sort of an elevator system. Values are pushed onto the stack, and with each new number the old one goes down one level. *Stack machines* are generally regarded as lean and mean computers. Their design is austere and streamlined, which helps them run more quickly. The same holds true for stack-oriented floating-point units.

Until the advent of the Pentium, a floating-point unit was not a guaranteed part of a microprocessor. Some 486 and all previous chips omitted floating-point circuitry. The floating-point circuitry simply added too much to the complexity of the chip, at least for the state of fabrication technology at that time. To cut costs, chipmakers simply left the floating-point unit as an option.

When it was necessary to accelerate numeric operations, the earliest microprocessors used in computers allowed you to add an additional, optional chip to your computer to accelerate the calculation of floating-point values. These external floating-point units were termed *math coprocessors*.

The floating-point units of modern microprocessors have evolved beyond mere number-crunching. They have been optimized to reflect the applications for which computers most often crunch floating-point numbers—graphics and multimedia (calculating dots, shapes, colors, depth, and action on your screen display).

Instruction Sets

Instructions are the basic units for telling a microprocessor what to do. Internally, the circuitry of the microprocessor has to carry out hundreds, thousands, or even millions of logic operations to carry out one instruction. The instruction, in effect, triggers a cascade of logical operations. How this cascade is controlled marks the great divide in microprocessor and computer design.

The first electronic computers used a *hard-wired* design. An instruction simply activated the circuits appropriate for carrying out all the steps required. This design has its advantages. It optimizes the speed of the system because the direct hard-wire connection adds nothing to slow down the system. Simplicity means speed, and the hard-wired approach is the simplest. Moreover, the hard-wired design was the practical and obvious choice. After all, computers were so new that no one had thought up any alternative.

However, the hard-wired computer design has a significant drawback. It ties the hardware and software together into a single unit. Any change in the hardware must be reflected in the software. A modification to the computer means that programs have to be modified. A new computer design may require that programs be entirely rewritten from the ground up.

Microcode

The inspiration for breaking away from the hard-wired approach was the need for flexibility in instruction sets. Throughout most of the history of computing, determining exactly what instructions should make up a machine's instruction set was more an art than a science. IBM's first commercial computers, the 701 and 702, were designed more from intuition than from any study of which instructions programmers would need to use. Each machine was tailored to a specific application. The 701 ran instructions thought to serve scientific users; the 702 had instructions aimed at business and commercial applications.

When IBM tried to unite its many application-specific computers into a single, more general-purpose line, these instruction sets were combined so that one machine could satisfy all needs. The result was, of course, a wide, varied, and complex set of instructions. The new machine, the IBM 360 (introduced in 1964), was unlike previous computers in that it was created not as hardware but as an *architecture*. IBM developed specifications and rules for how the machine would operate but enabled the actual machine to be created from any hardware implementation designers found most expedient. In other words, IBM defined the instructions that the 360 would use but not the circuitry that would carry them out. Previous computers used instructions that directly controlled the underlying hardware. To adapt the instructions defined by the architecture to the actual hardware that made up the machine, IBM adopted an idea called *microcode*, originally conceived by Maurice Wilkes at Cambridge University.

In the microcode design, an instruction causes a computer to execute a small program to carry out the logic instructions required by the instruction. The collection of small programs for all the instructions the computer understands is its *microcode*.

Although the additional layer of microcode made machines more complex, it added a great deal of design flexibility. Engineers could incorporate whatever new technologies they wanted inside the computer, yet still run the same software with the same instructions originally written for older designs. In other words, microcode enabled new hardware designs and computer systems to have backward compatibility with earlier machines.

After the introduction of the IBM 360, nearly all mainframe computers used microcode. When the microprocessors came along, they followed the same design philosophy, using microcode to match instructions to hardware. Using this design, a microprocessor actually has a smaller microprocessor inside it, which is sometimes called a *nanoprocessor*, running the microcode.

This microcode-and-nanoprocessor approach makes creating a complex microprocessor easier. The powerful data-processing circuitry of the chip can be designed independently of the instructions it must carry out. The manner in which the chip handles its complex instructions can be fine-tuned even after the architecture of the main circuits are laid into place. Bugs in the design can be fixed relatively quickly by altering the microcode, which is an easy operation compared to the alternative of developing a new design for the whole chip (a task that's not trivial when millions of transistors are involved). The rich instruction set fostered by microcode also makes writing software for the microprocessor (and computers built from it) easier, thus reducing the number of instructions needed for each operation.

Microcode has a big disadvantage, however. It makes computers and microprocessors more complicated. In a microprocessor, the nanoprocessor must go through several of its own microcode instructions to carry out every instruction you send to the microprocessor. More steps means more processing time taken for each instruction. Extra processing time means slower operation. Engineers found that microcode had its own way to compensate for its performance penalty—complex instructions.

Using microcode, computer designers could easily give an architecture a rich repertoire of instructions that carry out elaborate functions. A single, complex instruction might do the job of half a dozen or more simpler instructions. Although each instruction would take longer to execute because of the microcode, programs would need fewer instructions overall. Moreover, adding more instructions could boost speed. One result of this microcode "more is merrier" instruction approach is that typical computer microprocessors have seven different subtraction commands.

RISC

Although long the mainstay of computer and microprocessor design, microcode is not necessary. While system architects were staying up nights concocting ever more powerful and obscure instructions, a counter force was gathering. Starting in the 1970s, the microcode approach came under attack by researchers who claimed it takes a greater toll on performance than its benefits justify.

By eliminating microcode, this design camp believed, simpler instructions could be executed at speeds so much higher that no degree of instruction complexity could compensate. By necessity, such hard-wired machines would offer only a few instructions because the complexity of their hard-wired circuitry would increase dramatically with every additional instruction added. Practical designs are best made with small instruction sets.

John Cocke at IBM's Yorktown Research Laboratory analyzed the usage of instructions by computers and discovered that most of the work done by computers involves relatively few instructions. Given a computer with a set of 200 instructions, for example, two-thirds of its processing involves using as few as 10 of the total instructions. Cocke went on to design a computer that was based on a few instructions that could be executed quickly. He is credited with inventing the *Reduced Instruction Set Computer* (RISC) in 1974. The term *RISC* itself is credited to David Peterson, who used it in a course in microprocessor design at the University of California at Berkeley in 1980.

The first chip to bear the label and to take advantage of Cocke's discoveries was RISC-I, a laboratory design that was completed in 1982. To distinguish this new design approach from traditional microprocessors, microcode-based systems with large instruction sets have come to be known as *Complex Instruction Set Computers (CISC)*.

Cocke's research showed that most of the computing was done by basic instructions, not by the more powerful, complex, and specialized instructions. Further research at Berkeley and Stanford Universities demonstrated that there were even instances in which a sequence of simple instructions could perform a complex task faster than a single complex instruction could. The result of this research is often summarized as the *80/20 Rule*, meaning that about 20 percent of a computer's instructions do about 80 percent of the work. The aim of the RISC design is to optimize a computer's performance for that 20 percent of instructions, speeding up their execution as much as possible. The remaining 80 percent of the commands could be duplicated, when necessary, by combinations of the quick 20 percent. Analysis and practical experience has shown that the 20 percent could be made so much faster that the overhead required to emulate the remaining 80 percent was no handicap at all.

To enable a microprocessor to carry out all the required functions with a handful of instructions requires a rethinking of the programming process. Instead of simply translating human instructions into machine-readable form, the compilers used by RISC processors attempt to find the optimum instructions to use. The compiler takes a more in-depth look at the requested operations and finds the best way to handle them. The result was the creation of *optimizing compilers* discussed in Chapter 3, "Software."

If effect, the RISC design shifts a lot of the processing from the microprocessor to the compiler—a lot of the work in running a program gets taken care of before the program actually runs. Of course, the compiler does more work and takes longer to run, but that's a fair tradeoff—a program needs to be compiled only once but runs many, many times when the streamlined execution really pays off.

RISC microprocessors have several distinguishing characteristics. Most instructions execute in a single clock cycle—or even faster with advanced microprocessor designs with several execution pathways. All the instructions are the same length with similar syntax. The processor itself does not use microcode; instead, the small repertory of instructions is hard-wired into the chip. RISC instructions operate only on data in the registers of the chip, not in memory, making what is called a *load-store* design. The design of the chip itself is relatively simple, with comparatively few logic gates that are themselves constructed from simple, almost cookie-cutter designs. And most of the hard work is shifted from the microprocessor itself to the compiler.

Micro-Ops

Both CISC and RISC have a compelling design rationale and performance, desirable enough that engineers working on one kind of chip often looked over the shoulders of those working in the other camp. As a result, they developed hybrid chips embodying elements of both the CISC and RISC design. All the latest processors—from the Pentium Pro to the

Pentium 4, Athlon, and Duron as well—have RISC cores mated with complex instruction sets.

The basic technique involves converting the classic Intel instructions into RISC-style instructions to be processed by the internal chip circuitry. Intel calls the internal RISC-like instructions *micro-ops*. The term is often abbreviated as *uops* (strictly speaking, the initial *u* should be the Greek letter *mu*, which is an abbreviation for *micro*) and pronounced *you-ops*. Other companies use slightly different terminology.

By design, the micro-ops sidestep the primary shortcomings of the Intel instruction set by making the encoding of all commands more uniform, converting all instructions to the same length for processing, and eliminating arithmetic operations that directly change memory by loading memory data into registers before processing.

The translation to RISC-like instructions allows the microprocessor to function internally as a RISC engine. The code conversion occurs in hardware, completely invisible to your applications and out of the control of programmers. In other words, it shifts back from the RISC shift to doing the work in the compiler. There's a good reason for this backward shift: It lets the RISC code deal with existing programs—those compiled before the RISC designs were created.

Single Instruction, Multiple Data

In a quest to improve the performance of Intel microprocessors on common multimedia tasks, Intel's hardware and software engineers analyzed the operations multimedia programs most often required. They then sought the most efficient way to enable their chips to carry out these operations. They essentially worked to enhance the signal-processing capabilities of their general-purpose microprocessors so that they would be competitive with dedicated processors, such as digital signal processor (DSP) chips. They called the technology they developed *Single Instruction, Multiple Data (SIMD)*. In effect a new class of microprocessor instructions, SIMD is the enabling element of Intel's MultiMedia Extensions (MMX) to its microprocessor command set. Intel further developed this technology to add its Streaming SIMD Extensions (SSE, once known as the *Katmai New Instructions*) to its Pentium III microprocessors to enhance their 3D processing power. The Pentium 4 further enhances SSE with more multimedia instructions to create what Intel calls *SSE2*.

As the name implies, SIMD allows one microprocessor instruction to operate across several bytes or words (or even larger blocks of data). In the MMX scheme of things, the SIMD instructions are matched to the 64-bit data buses of Intel's Pentium and newer microprocessors. All data, whether it originates as bytes, words, or 16-bit double-words, gets packed into 64-bit form. Eight bytes, four words, or two double-words get packed into a single 64-bit package that, in turn, gets loaded into a 64-bit register in the microprocessor. One microprocessor instruction then manipulates the entire 64-bit block.

Although the approach at first appears counterintuitive, it improves the handling of common graphic and audio data. In video processor applications, for example, it can trim the number of microprocessor clock cycles for some operations by 50 percent or more.

Very Long Instruction Words

Just as RISC started flowing into the product mainstream, a new idea started designers thinking in the opposite direction. Very long instruction word (VLIW) technology at first appears to run against the RISC stream by using long, complex instructions. In reality, VLIW is a refinement of RISC meant to better take advantage of superscalar microprocessors. Each very long instruction word is made from several RISC instructions. In a typical implementation, eight 32-bit RISC instructions combine to make one instruction word.

Ordinarily, combining RISC instructions would add little to overall speed. As with RISC, the secret of VLIW technology is in the software—the compiler that produces the final program code. The instructions in the long word are chosen so that they execute at the same time (or as close to it as possible) in parallel processing units in the superscalar microprocessor. The compiler chooses and arranges instructions to match the needs of the superscalar processor as best as possible, essentially taking the optimizing compiler one step further. In essence, the VLIW system takes advantage of preprocessing in the compiler to make the final code and microprocessor more efficient.

VLIW technology also takes advantage of the wider bus connections of the latest generation of microprocessors. Existing chips link to their support circuitry with 64-bit buses. Many have 128-bit internal buses. The 256-bit very long instruction words push a little further yet enable a microprocessor to load several cycles of work in a single memory cycle. Transmeta's Crusoe processor uses VLIW technology.

Performance-Enhancing Architectures

Functionally, the first microprocessors operated a lot like meat grinders. You put something in such as meat scraps, turned a crank, and something new and wonderful came out—a sausage. Microprocessors started with data and instructions and yielded answers, but operationally they were as simple and direct as turning a crank. Every operation carried out by the microprocessor clicked with a turn of the crank—one clock cycle, one operation.

Such a design is straightforward and almost elegant. But its wonderful simplicity imposes a heavy constraint. The computer's clock becomes an unforgiving jailor, locking up the performance of the microprocessor. A chip with this turn-the-crank design is locked to the clock speed and can never improve its performance beyond one operation per clock cycle. The situation is worse than that. The use of microcode almost ensures that at least some instructions will require multiple clock cycles.

One way to speed up the execution of instructions is to reduce the number of internal steps the microprocessor must take for execution. That idea was the guiding principle behind the first RISC microprocessors and what made them so interesting to chip designers. Actually, however, step reduction can take one of two forms: making the microprocessor more complex so that steps can be combined or making the instructions simpler so that fewer steps are required. Both approaches have been used successfully by microprocessor designers—the former as CISC microprocessors, the latter as RISC.

Ideally, it would seem, executing one instruction every clock cycle would be the best anyone could hope for, the ultimate design goal. With conventional microprocessor designs, that would be true. But engineers have found another way to trim the clock cycles required by each instruction—by processing more than one instruction at the same time.

Two basic approaches to processing more instructions at once are pipelining and superscalar architecture. All modern microprocessors take advantage of these technologies as well as several other architectural refinements that help them carry out more instructions for every cycle of the system clock.

Clock Speed

The operating speed of a microprocessor is usually called its *clock speed*, which describes the frequency at which the core logic of the chip operates. Clock speed is usually measured in megahertz (one million hertz or clock cycles per second) or gigahertz (a billion hertz). All else being equal, a higher number in megahertz means a faster microprocessor.

Faster does not necessarily mean the microprocessor will compute an answer more quickly, however. Different microprocessor designs can execute instructions more efficiently because there's no one-to-one correspondence between instruction processing and clock speed. In fact, each new generation of microprocessor has been able to execute more instructions per clock cycle, so a new microprocessor can carry out more instructions at a given megahertz rating. At the same megahertz rating, a Pentium 4 is faster than a Pentium III. Why? Because of pipelining, superscalar architecture, and other design features.

Sometimes microprocessor-makers take advantage of this fact and claim that megahertz doesn't matter. For example, AMD's Athlon processors carry out more instructions per clock cycle than Intel's Pentium III, so AMD stopped using megahertz numbers to describe its chips. Instead, it substituted model designations that hinted at the speed of a comparable Pentium chips. An Athlon XP 2200+ processes data as quickly as a Pentium 4 at 2200MHz chip, although the Athlon chip actually operates at less than 2000MHz. With the introduction of its Itanium series of processors, Intel also made assertions that megahertz doesn't matter because Itanium chips have clock speeds substantially lower than Pentium chips.

A further complication is software overhead. Microprocessor speed doesn't affect the performance of Windows or its applications very much. That's because the performance of Windows depends on the speed of your hard disk, video system, memory system, and other system resources as well as your microprocessor. Although a Windows system using a 2GHz processor will appear faster than a system with a 1GHz processor, it won't be anywhere near twice as fast.

In other words, the megahertz rating of a microprocessor gives only rough guidance in comparing microprocessor performance in real-world applications. Faster is better, but a comparison of megahertz (or gigahertz) numbers does not necessarily express the relationship between the performance of two chips or computer systems.

Pipelining

In older microprocessor designs, a chip works single-mindedly. It reads an instruction from memory, carries it out, step by step, and then advances to the next instruction. Each step requires at least one tick of the microprocessor's clock. *Pipelining* enables a microprocessor to read an instruction, start to process it, and then, before finishing with the first instruction, read another instruction. Because every instruction requires several steps, each in a different part of the chip, several instructions can be worked on at once and passed along through the chip like a bucket brigade (or its more efficient alternative, the *pipeline*). Intel's Pentium chips, for example, have four levels of pipelining. Up to four different instructions may be undergoing different phases of execution at the same time inside the chip. When operating at its best, pipelining reduces the multiple-step/multiple-clock-cycle processing of an instruction to a single clock cycle.

Pipelining is very powerful, but it is also demanding. The pipeline must be carefully organized, and the parallel paths kept carefully in step. It's sort of like a chorus singing a canon such as Fréré Jacques—one missed beat and the harmony falls apart. If one of the execution stages delays, all the rest delay as well. The demands of pipelining push microprocessor designers to make all instructions execute in the same number of clock cycles. That way, keeping the pipeline in step is easier.

In general, the more stages to a pipeline, the greater acceleration it can offer. Intel has added superlatives to the pipeline name to convey the enhancement. *Super-pipelining* is Intel's term for breaking the basic pipeline stages into several steps, resulting in a 12-stage design used for its Pentium Pro through Pentium III chips. Later, Intel further sliced the stages to create the current Pentium 4 chip with 20 stages, a design Intel calls *hyper-pipelining*.

Real-world programs conspire against lengthy pipelines, however. Nearly all programs branch. That is, their execution can take alternate paths down different instruction streams, depending on the results of calculations and decision-making. A pipeline can load up with instructions of one program branch before it discovers that another branch is the one the program is supposed to follow. In that case, the entire contents of the pipeline must be dumped and the whole thing loaded up again. The result is a lot of logical wheel-spinning and wasted time. The bigger the pipeline, the more time that's wasted. The waste resulting from branching begins to outweigh the benefits of bigger pipelines in the vicinity of five stages.

Branch Prediction

Today's most powerful microprocessors are adopting a technology called *branch prediction logic* to deal with this problem. The microprocessor makes its best guess at which branch a program will take as it is filling up the pipeline. It then executes these most likely instructions. Because the chip is guessing at what to do, this technology is sometimes called *speculative execution*.

When the microprocessor's guesses turn out to be correct, the chip benefits from the multiple-pipeline stages and is able to run through more instructions than clock cycles. When the chip's guess turns out wrong, however, it must discard the results obtained under speculation and execute the correct code. The chip marks the data in later pipeline stages as invalid and discards it. Although the chip doesn't lose time—the program would have executed in the same order anyway—it does lose the extra boost bequeathed by the pipeline.

Speculative Execution

To further increase performance, more modern microprocessors use *speculative execution*. That is, the chip may carry out an instruction in a predicted branch before it confirms whether it has properly predicted the branch. If the chip's prediction is correct, the instruction has already been executed, so the chip wastes no time. If the prediction was incorrect, the chip will have to execute a different instruction, which it would have to have done anyhow, so it suffers no penalty.

Superscalar Architectures

The steps in a program normally are listed sequentially, but they don't always need to be carried out exactly in order. Just as tough problems can be broken into easier pieces, program code can be divided as well. If, for example, you want to know the larger of two rooms, you have to compute the volume of each and then make your comparison. If you had two brains, you could compute the two volumes simultaneously. A superscalar microprocessor design does essentially that. By providing two or more execution paths for programs, it can process two or more program parts simultaneously. Of course, the chip needs enough innate intelligence to determine which problems can be split up and how to do it. The Pentium, for example, has two parallel, pipelined execution paths.

The first superscalar computer design was the Control Data Corporation 6600 mainframe, introduced in 1964. Designed specifically for intense scientific applications, the initial 6600 machines were built from eight functional units and were the fastest computers in the world at the time of their introduction.

Superscalar architecture gets its name because it goes beyond the incremental increase in speed made possible by scaling down microprocessor technology. An improvement to the scale of a microprocessor design would reduce the size of the microcircuitry on the silicon chip. The size reduction shortens the distance signals must travel and lowers the amount of heat generated by the circuit (because the elements are smaller and need less current to effect changes). Some microprocessor designs lend themselves to scaling down. Superscalar designs get a more substantial performance increase by incorporating a more dramatic change in circuit complexity.

Using pipelining and superscalar architecture cycle-saving techniques has cut the number of clock cycles required for the execution of a typical microprocessor instruction dramatically. Early microprocessors needed, on average, several cycles for each instruction. Today's chips can often carry out multiple instructions in a single clock cycle. Engineers describe pipelined, superscalar chips by the number of instructions they can *retire* per clock cycle. They look at the number of instructions that are completed, because this best describes how much work the chip has (or can) actually accomplish.

Out-of-Order Execution

No matter how well the logic of a superscalar microprocessor divides up a program, each pipeline is unlikely to get an equal share of the work. One or another pipeline will grind away while another finishes in an instant. Certainly the chip logic can shove another instruction down the free pipeline (if another instruction is ready). But if the next instruction depends on the results of the one before it, and that instruction is the one stuck grinding away in the other pipeline, the free pipeline stalls. It is available for work but can do no work, thus potential processor power gets wasted.

Like a good Type-A employee who always looks for something to do, microprocessors can do the same. They can check the program for the next instruction that doesn't depend on previous work that's not finished and work on the new instruction. This sort of ambitious approach to programs is termed *out-of-order execution*, and it helps microprocessors take full advantage of superscalar designs.

This sort of ambitious microprocessor faces a problem, however. It is no longer running the program in the order it was written, and the results might be other than the programmer had intended. Consequently, microprocessors capable of out-of-order execution don't immediately post the results from their processing into their registers. The work gets carried out invisibly and the results of the instructions that are processed out of order are held in a buffer until the chip has finished the processing of all the previous instructions. The chip puts the results back into the proper order, checking to be sure that the out-of-order execution has not caused any anomalies, before posting the results to its registers. To the program and the rest of the outside world, the results appear in the microprocessor's registers as if they had been processed in normal order, only faster.

Register Renaming

Out-of-order execution often runs into its own problems. Two independently executable instructions may refer to or change the same register. In the original program, one would carry out its operation, then the other would do its work later. During superscalar out-of-order execution, the two instructions may want to work on the register simultaneously. Because that conflict would inevitably lead to confusing results and errors, an ordinary superscalar microprocessor would have to ensure the two instructions referencing the same register executed sequentially instead of in parallel, thus eliminating the advantage of its superscalar design.

To avoid such problems, advanced microprocessors use *register renaming*. Instead of a small number of registers with fixed names, they use a larger bank of registers that can be named dynamically. The circuitry in each chip converts the references made by an instruction to a specific register name to point instead to its choice of physical register. In effect, the program asks for the EAX register, and the chip says, "Sure," and gives the program a register it calls EAX. If another part of the program asks for EAX, the chip pulls out a different register and tells the program that this one is EAX, too. The program takes the microprocessor's word for it, and the microprocessor doesn't worry because it has several million transistors to sort things out in the end.

And it takes several million transistors because the chip must track all references to registers. It does this to ensure that when one program instruction depends on the result in a given register, it has the right register and results dished up to it.

Explicitly Parallel Instruction Computing

With Intel's shift to 64-bit architecture for its most powerful line of microprocessors (aimed, for now, at the server market), the company introduced a new instruction set to compliment the new architecture. Called *Explicitly Parallel Instruction Computing (EPIC)*, the design follows the precepts of RISC architecture by putting the hard work into software (the compiler), while retaining the advantages of longer instructions used by SIMD and VLIW technologies.

The difference between EPIC and older Intel chips is that the compiler takes a swipe at each program and determines where parallel processes can occur. It then optimizes the program code to sort out separate streams of execution that can be routed to different microprocessor pipelines and carried out concurrently. This not only relieves the chip from working to figure out how to divide up the instruction stream, but it also allows the software to more thoroughly analyze the code rather than trying to do it on the fly.

By analyzing and dividing the instruction streams before they are submitted to the microprocessor, EPIC trims the need and use of speculative execution and branch prediction. The compiler can look ahead in the program, so it doesn't have to speculate or predict. It knows how best to carry out a complex program.

Front-Side Bus

The instruction stream is not the only bottleneck in a modern computer. The core logic of most microprocessors operates much faster than other parts of most computers, including the memory and support circuitry. The microprocessor links to the rest of the computer through a connection called the *system bus* or the *front-side bus*. The speed at which the system bus operates sets a maximum limit on how fast the microprocessor can send data to other circuits (including memory) in the computer.

When the microprocessor needs to retrieve data or an instruction from memory, it must wait for this to come across the system bus. The slower the bus, the longer the microprocessor has to wait. More importantly, the greater the mismatch between microprocessor speed and system bus speed, the more clock cycles the microprocessor needs to wait. Applications that involve repeated calculations on large blocks of data—graphics and video in particular—are apt to require the most access to the system bus to retrieve data from memory. These applications are most likely to suffer from a slow system bus.

The first commercial microprocessors of the current generation operated their system buses at 66MHz. Through the years, manufacturers have boosted this speed and increased the speed at which the microprocessor can communicate with the rest of the computer. Chips now use clock speeds of 100MHz or 133MHz for their system buses.

With the Pentium 4, Intel added a further refinement to the system bus. Using a technology called *quad-pumping*, Intel forces four data bits onto each clock cycle of the system bus. A quad-pumped system bus operating at 100MHz can actually move 400Mb of data in a second. A quad-pumped system bus running at 133MHz achieves a 533Mbps data rate.

The performance of the system bus is often described in its *bandwidth*, the number of total bytes of data that can move through the bus in one second. The data buses of all current computers are 64 bits wide—that's 8 bytes. Multiplying the clock speed or data rate of the bus by its width yields its bandwidth. A 100MHz system bus therefore has an 800MBps (mega*bytes* per second) bandwidth. A 400MHz bus has a 3.2GBps bandwidth.

Intel usually locks the system bus speed to the clock speed of the microprocessor. This synchronous operation optimizes the transfer rate between the bus and the microprocessor. It also explains some of the odd frequencies at which some microprocessors are designed to operate (for example, 1.33GHz or 2.56GHz). Sometimes the system bus operates at a speed that's not an even divisor of the microprocessor speed—for example, the microprocessor clock speed may be 4.5, 5, or 5.5 times the system bus speed. Such a mismatch can slow down system performance, although such mismatches are minimized by effective microprocessor caching (see the upcoming section "Caching" for more information).

Translation Look-Aside Buffers

Modern pipelined, superscalar microprocessors need to access memory quickly, and they often repeatedly go to the same address in the execution of a program. To speed up such operations, most newer microprocessors include a quick lookup list of the pages in memory that the chip has addressed most recently. This list is termed a *translation look-aside* and is a small block of fast memory inside the microprocessor that stores a table that cross-references the virtual addresses in programs with the corresponding real addresses in physical memory that the program has most recently used. The microprocessor can take a quick glance away from its normal address-translation pipeline, effectively "looking aside," to fetch the addresses it needs.

The translation look-aside buffer (TLB) appears to be very small in relation to the memory of most computers. Typically, a TLB may be 64 to 256 entries. Each entry, however, refers to an entire page of memory, which with today's Intel microprocessors, totals four kilobytes. The amount of memory that the microprocessor can quickly address by checking the TLB is the *TLB address space*, which is the product of the number of entries in the TLB and the page size. A 256-entry TLB can provide fast access to a megabyte of memory (256 entries times 4KB per page).

Caching

The most important means of matching today's fast microprocessors to the speeds of affordable memory, which is inevitably slower, is *memory caching*. A memory cache interposes a block of fast memory—typically high-speed static RAM—between the microprocessor and the bulk of primary storage. A special circuit called a *cache controller* (which current designs make into an essential part of the microprocessor) attempts to keep the cache filled with the data or instructions that the microprocessor is most likely to need next. If the information the microprocessor requests next is held within the cache, it can be retrieved without waiting.

This fastest possible operation is called a *cache hit*. If the needed data is not in the cache memory, it is retrieved from outside the cache, typically from ordinary RAM at ordinary RAM speed. The result is called a *cache miss*.

Not all memory caches are created equal. Memory caches differ in many ways: size, logical arrangement, location, and operation.

Cache Level

Caches are sometimes described by their logical and electrical proximity to the microprocessor's core logic. The closest physically and electrically to the microprocessor's core logic is the *primary cache*, also called a *Level One cache*. A *secondary cache* (or *Level Two cache*) fits between the primary cache and main memory. The secondary cache usually is larger than the primary cache but operates at a lower speed (to make its larger mass of memory more affordable). Rarely is a *tertiary cache* (or *Level Three cache*) interposed between the secondary cache and memory.

In modern microprocessor designs, both the primary and secondary caches are part of the microprocessor itself. Older designs put the secondary cache in a separate part of a microprocessor module or in external memory.

Primary and secondary caches differ in the way they connect with the core logic of the microprocessor. A primary cache invariably operates at the full speed of the microprocessor's core logic with the widest possible bit-width connection between the core logic and the cache. Secondary caches often operate at a rate slower than the chip's core logic, although all current chips operate the secondary cache at full core speed.

Cache Size

A major factor that determines how successful the cache will be is how much information it contains. The larger the cache, the more data that is in it and the more likely any needed byte will be there when you system calls for it. Obviously, the best cache is one that's as large as, and duplicates, the entirety of system memory. Of course, a cache that big is also absurd. You could use the cache as primary memory and forget the rest. The smallest cache would be a byte, also an absurd situation because it guarantees the next read is not in the cache. Chipmakers try to make caches as large as possible within the constraints of fabricating microprocessors affordably.

Today's primary caches are typically 64 or 128KB. Secondary caches range from 128 to 512KB for chips for desktop and mobile applications and up to 2MB for server-oriented microprocessors.

Instruction and Data Caches

Modern microprocessors subdivide their primary caches into separate instruction and data caches, typically with each assigned one-half the total cache memory. This separation allows for a more efficient microprocessor design. Microprocessors handle instructions and data differently and may even send them down different pipelines. Moreover, instructions and data typically use memory differently—instructions are sequential whereas data can be completely random. Separating the two allows designers to optimize the cache design for each.

Write-Through and Write-Back Caches

Caches also differ in the way they treat writing to memory. Most caches make no attempt to speed up write operations. Instead, they push write commands through the cache immediately, writing to cache and main memory (with normal wait-state delays) at the same time. This *write-through cache* design is the safe approach because it guarantees that main memory and cache are constantly in agreement. Most Intel microprocessors through the current versions of the Pentium use write-through technology.

The faster alternative is the *write-back cache*, which allows the microprocessor to write changes to its cache memory and then immediately go back about its work. The cache controller eventually writes the changed data back to main memory as time allows.

Cache Mapping

The logical configuration of a cache involves how the memory in the cache is arranged and how it is addressed (that is, how the microprocessor determines whether needed information is available inside the cache). The major choices are direct-mapped, full associative, and set-associative.

The direct-mapped cache divides the fast memory of the cache into small units, called *lines* (corresponding to the lines of storage used by Intel 32-bit microprocessors, which allow addressing in 16-byte multiples, blocks of 128 bits), each of which is identified by an index bit. Main memory is divided into blocks the size of the cache, and the lines in the cache correspond to the locations within such a memory block. Each line can be drawn from a different memory block, but only from the location corresponding to the location in the cache. Which block the line is drawn from is identified by a tag. For the cache controller—the electronics that ride herd on the cache—determining whether a given byte is stored in a direct-mapped cache is easy. It just checks the tag for a given index value.

The problem with the direct-mapped cache is that if a program regularly moves between addresses with the same indexes in different blocks of memory, the cache needs to be continually refreshed—which means cache misses. Although such operation is uncommon in single-tasking systems, it can occur often during multitasking and slow down the direct-mapped cache.

The opposite design approach is the full-associative cache. In this design, each line of the cache can correspond to (or be associated with) any part of main memory. Lines of bytes from diverse locations throughout main memory can be piled cheek-by-jowl in the cache. The major shortcoming of the full-associative approach is that the cache controller must check the addresses of every line in the cache to determine whether a memory request from the microprocessor is a hit or miss. The more lines there are to check, the more time it takes. A lot of checking can make cache memory respond more slowly than main memory.

A compromise between direct-mapped and full-associative caches is the set-associative cache, which essentially divides up the total cache memory into several smaller direct-mapped areas. The cache is described as the number of *ways* into which it is divided. A four-way set-associative cache, therefore, resembles four smaller direct-mapped caches. This arrangement overcomes the problem of moving between blocks with the same indexes. Consequently, the set-associative cache has more performance potential than a direct-mapped cache. Unfortunately, it is also more complex, making the technology more expensive to implement. Moreover, the more "ways" there are to a cache, the longer the cache controller must search to determine whether needed information is in the cache. This ultimately slows down the cache, mitigating the advantage of splitting it into sets. Most computer-makers find a four-way set-associative cache to be the optimum compromise between performance and complexity.

Electrical Characteristics

At its heart, a microprocessor is an electronic device. This electronic foundation has important ramifications in the construction and operation of chips. The "free lunch" principle (that is, there is none) tells us that every operation has its cost. Even the quick electronic thinking of a microprocessor takes a toll. The thinking involves the switching of the state of tiny transistors, and each state change consumes a bit of electrical power, which gets converted to heat. The transistors are so small that the process generates a minuscule amount of heat, but with millions of them in a single chip, the heat adds up. Modern microprocessors generate so much heat that keeping them cool is a major concern in their design.

Thermal Constraints

Heat is the enemy of the semiconductor because it can destroy the delicate crystal structure of a chip. If a chip gets too hot, it will be irrevocably destroyed. Packing circuits tightly concentrates the heat they generate, and the small size of the individual circuit components makes them more vulnerable to damage.

Heat can cause problems more subtle than simple destruction. Because the conductivity of semiconductor circuits also varies with temperature, the effective switching speed of transistors and logic gates also changes when chips get too hot or too cold. Although this temperature-induced speed change does not alter how fast a microprocessor can compute (the chip must stay locked to the system clock at all times), it can affect the relative timing between signals inside the microprocessor. Should the timing get too far off, a microprocessor might make a mistake, with the inevitable result of crashing your system. All chips have rated temperature ranges within which they are guaranteed to operate without such timing errors.

Because chips generate more heat as speed increases, they can produce heat faster than it can radiate away. This heat buildup can alter the timing of the internal signals of the chip so drastically that the microprocessor will stop working and—as if you couldn't guess—cause your system to crash. To avoid such problems, computer manufacturers often attach heatsinks to microprocessors and other semiconductor components to aid in their cooling.

A *heatsink* is simply a metal extrusion that increases the surface area from which heat can radiate from a microprocessor or other heat-generating circuit element. Most heatsinks have several fins (rows of pins) or some geometry that increases its surface area. Heatsinks are usually made from aluminum because that metal is one of the better thermal conductors, enabling the heat from the microprocessor to quickly spread across the heatsink.

Heatsinks provide *passive cooling* (*passive* because cooling requires no power-using mechanism). Heatsinks work by convection, transferring heat to the air that circulates past the heatsink. Air circulates around the heatsink because the warmed air rises away from the heatsink and cooler air flows in to replace it.

In contrast, *active cooling* involves some kind of mechanical or electrical assistance to remove heat. The most common form of active cooling is a fan, which blows a greater volume of air past the heatsink than would be possible with convection alone. Nearly all modern microprocessors require a fan for active cooling, typically built into the chip's heatsink.

The makers of notebook computers face another challenge in efficiently managing the cooling of their computers. Using a fan to cool a notebook system is problematic. The fan consumes substantial energy, which trims battery life. Moreover, the heat generated by the fan motor itself can be a significant part of the thermal load of the system. Most designers of notebook machines have turned to more innovative passive thermal controls, such as heat pipes and using the entire chassis of the computer as a heatsink.

Operating Voltages

In desktop computers, overheating rather than excess electrical consumption is the major power concern. Even the most wasteful of microprocessors uses far less power than an ordinary light bulb. The most that any computer-compatible microprocessor consumes is about nine watts, hardly more than a night light and of little concern when the power grid supplying your computer has megawatts at its disposal.

If you switch to battery power, however, every last milliwatt is important. The more power used by a computer, the shorter the time its battery can power the system or the heavier the battery it will need to achieve a given life between charges. Every degree a microprocessor raises its case temperature clips minutes from its battery runtime.

Battery-powered notebooks and sub-notebook computers consequently caused micro-processor engineers to do a quick about-face. Whereas once they were content to use bigger and bigger heatsinks, fans, and refrigerators to keep their chips cool, today they focus on reducing temperatures and wasted power at the source.

One way to cut power requirements is to make the design elements of a chip smaller. Smaller digital circuits require less power. But shrinking chips is not an option; micro-processors are invariably designed to be as small as possible with the prevailing technology.

To further trim the power required by microprocessors to make them more amenable to battery operation, engineers have come up with two new design twists: low-voltage operation and system-management mode. Although founded on separate ideas, both are often used together to minimize microprocessor power consumption. All new microprocessor designs incorporate both technologies.

Since the very beginning of the transistor-transistor logic family of digital circuits (the design technology that later blossomed into the microprocessor), digital logic has operated with a supply voltage of 5 volts. That level is essentially arbitrary. Almost any voltage would work. But 5-volt technology offers some practical advantages. It's low enough to be both safe and frugal with power needs but high enough to avoid noise and allow for several diode drops, the inevitable reduction of voltage that occurs when a current flows across a semiconductor junction.

Every semiconductor junction, which essentially forms a diode, reduces or drops the voltage flowing through it. Silicon junctions impose a diode drop of about 0.7 volts, and there may be one or more such junctions in a logic gate. Other materials impose smaller drops—that of germanium, for example, is 0.4 volts—but the drop is unavoidable.

There's nothing magical about using 5 volts. Reducing the voltage used by logic circuits dramatically reduces power consumption because power consumption in electrical circuits increases by the square of the voltage. That is, doubling the voltage of a circuit increases the power it uses by fourfold. Reducing the voltage by one-half reduces power consumption by three-quarters (providing, of course, that the circuit will continue to operate at the lower voltage).

All current microprocessor designs operate at about 2 volts or less. The Pentium 4 operates at just over 1.3 volts with minor variations, depending on the clock frequency of the chip. For example, the 2.53GHz version requires 1.325 volts. Microprocessors designed for mobile applications typically operate at about 1.1 volts; some as low as 0.95 volt.

To minimize power consumption, Intel sets the operating voltage of the core logic of its chips as low as possible—some, such as Intel's ultra-low-voltage Mobile Pentium III-M, to just under 1 volt. The integral secondary caches of these chips (which are fabricated separately from the core logic) usually require their own, often higher, voltage supply. In fact, operating voltage has become so critical that Intel devotes several pins of its Pentium II and later microprocessors to encoding the voltage needs of the chip, and the host computer must adjust its supply to the chip to precisely meet those needs.

Most bus architectures and most of today's memory modules operate at the 3.3 volt level. Future designs will push that level lower. Rambus memory systems, for example, operate at 2.5 volts (see Chapter 6, "Chipsets," for more information).

Power Management

Trimming the power need of a microprocessor both reduces the heat the chip generates and increases how long it can run off a battery supply, an important consideration for portable computers. Reducing the voltage and power use of the chip is one way of keeping the heat down and the battery running, but chipmakers have discovered they can save even more power through frugality. The chips use power only when they have to, thus managing their power consumption.

Chipmakers have two basic power-management strategies: shutting off circuits when they are not needed and slowing down the microprocessor when high performance is not required.

The earliest form of power-savings built into microprocessors was part of system management mode (SMM), which allowed the circuitry of the chip to be shut off. In terms of clock speed, the chip went from full speed to zero. Initially, chips switched off after a period of system inactivity and woke up to full speed when triggered by an appropriate interrupt.

More advanced systems cycled the microprocessor between on and off states as they required processing power. The chief difficulty with this design is that nothing gets done when the chip isn't processing. This kind of power management only works when you're not looking (not exactly a salesman's dream) and is a benefit you should never be able to see. Intel gives this technique the name *QuickStart* and claims that it can save enough energy between your keystrokes to significantly reduce overall power consumption by briefly cutting the microprocessor's electrical needs by 95 percent. Intel introduced QuickStart in the Mobile Pentium II processor, although it has not widely publicized the technology.

In the last few years, chipmakers have approached the power problem with more advanced power-saving systems that take an intermediary approach. One way is to reduce microprocessor power when it doesn't need it for particular operations. Intel slightly reduces the voltage applied to its core logic based on the activity of the processor. Called *Intel Mobile Voltage Positio*ning (IMVP), this technology can reduce the thermal design power—which means the heat produced by the microprocessor—by about 8.5 percent. According to Intel, this reduction is equivalent to reducing the speed of a 750MHz Mobile Pentium III by 100MHz.

Another technique for saving power is to reduce the performance of a microprocessor when its top speed is not required by your applications. Instead of entirely switching off the microprocessor, the chipmakers reduce its performance to trim power consumption. Each of the three current major microprocessor manufacturers puts its own spin on this performance-as-needed technology, labeling it with a clever trademark. Intel offers *SpeedStep*, AMD offers *PowerNow!*, and Transmeta offers *LongRun*. Although at heart all three are conceptually much the same, in operation you'll find distinct differences between them.

Intel SpeedStep

Internal mobile microprocessor power savings started with SpeedStep, introduced by Intel on January 18, 2000, with the Mobile Pentium III microprocessors, operating at 600MHz and 650MHz. To save power, these chips can be configured to reduce their operating speed when running on battery power to 500MHz. All Mobile Pentium III and Mobile Pentium 4 chips since that date have incorporated SpeedStep into their designs. Mobile Celeron processors do not use SpeedStep.

The triggering event is a reduction of power to the chip. For example, the initial Mobile Pentium III chips go from the 1.7 volts that is required for operating at their top speeds to 1.35 volts. As noted earlier, the M-series step down from 1.4 to 1.15 volts, the low-voltage M-series from 1.35 to 1.1 volts, and the ultra-low-voltage chips from 1.1 to 0.975 volts. Note that a 15-percent reduction in voltage in itself reduces power consumption by about 29 percent, with a further reduction that's proportional to the speed decrease. The 600MHz Pentium III, for example, cuts its power consumption an additional 17 percent thanks to voltage reduction when slipping down from 600MHz to 500MHz.

Intel calls the two modes *Maximum Performance Mode* (for high speed) and *Battery Optimized Mode* (for low speed). According to Intel, switching between speeds requires about one two-thousandths of a second. The M-series of Mobile Pentium III adds an additional step to provide an intermediary level of performance when operating on battery. Intel calls this technology *Enhanced SpeedStep*. Table 5.1 lists the SpeedStep capabilities of many Intel chips.

TABLE 5.1   The Effect of SpeedStep in Intel Mobile Pentium-III Microprocessors

Pentium III

Original speed (MHz)	500	600	650	700	750	850	900	1000
After SpeedStep reduction (MHz)	300	500	500	500	550	750	700	700

Ultra-Low-Voltage Pentium III-M

Original speed (MHz)	700
After SpeedStep reduction (MHz)	300

Low-Voltage Pentium III-M

Original speed (MHz)	733	750	800
After SpeedStep reduction (MHz)	466	450	533

Pentium III-M

Original speed (MHz)	800A	866	933	1000	1060	1130	1200
After SpeedStep reduction (MHz)	500	667	733	733	733	733	800

AMD PowerNow!

Advanced Micro Devices devised its own power-saving technology, called *PowerNow!*, for its mobile processors. The AMD technology differs from Intel's SpeedStep by providing up to 32 levels of speed reduction and power savings. Note that 32 levels is the design limit. Actual implementations of the technology from AMD have far fewer levels. All current AMD mobile processors—both the Mobile Athlon and Mobile Duron lines—use PowerNow! technology.

PowerNow! operates in one of three modes:

- **Hi-Performance**. This mode runs the microprocessor at full speed and full voltage so that the chip maximizes its processing power.

- **Battery Saver**. This mode runs the chip at a lower speed using a lower voltage to conserve battery power, exactly as a SpeedStep chip would, but with multiple levels. The speed and voltage are determined by the chip's requirements and programming of the BIOS (which triggers the change).

- **Automatic**. This mode makes the changes in voltage and clock speed dynamic, responding to the needs of the system. When an application requires maximum processing power, the chip runs at full speed. As the need for processing declines, the chip adjusts its performance to match. Current implementations allow for four discrete speeds at various operating voltages. Automatic mode is the best compromise for normal operation of portable computers.

The actual means of varying the clock frequency involves dynamic control of the clock multiplier inside the AMD chip. The external oscillator or clock frequency the computer supplies the microprocessor does not change, regardless of the performance demand. In the case of the initial chip to use PowerNow! (the Mobile K6-2+ chip, operating at 550MHz), its actual operating speed could vary from 200MHz to 550MHz in a system that takes full advantage of the technology.

Control of PowerNow! starts with the operating system (which is almost always Windows). Windows monitors processor usage, and when it dips below a predetermined level, such as 50 percent, Windows signals the PowerNow! system to cut back the clock multiplier inside the microprocessor and then signals a programmable voltage regulator to trim the voltage going to the chip. Note that even with PowerNow!, the chip's supply voltage must be adjusted externally to the chip to achieve the greatest power savings.

If the operating system detects that the available processing power is still underused, it signals to cut back another step. Similarly, should processing needs reach above a predetermined level (say, 90 percent of the available ability), the operating system signals PowerNow! to kick up performance (and voltage) by a notch.

Transmeta LongRun

Transmeta calls its proprietary power-saving technology *LongRun*. It is a feature of both current Crusoe processors, the TM5500 and TM5800. In concept, LongRun is much like AMD's PowerNow! The chief difference is control. Because of the design of Transmeta's Crusoe processors, Windows instructions are irrelevant to their power usage—Crusoe chips translate the Windows instructions into their own format. To gauge its power needs, the Crusoe chip monitors the flow of its own native instructions and adjusts its speed to match the processing needs of that code stream. In other words, the Crusoe chip does its own monitoring and decision-making regarding power savings without regard to Windows power-conservation information.

According to Transmeta, LongRun allows its microprocessors to adjust their power consumption by changing their clock frequency on the fly, just as PowerNow! does, as well as to adjust their operating voltage. The processor core steps down processor speed in 33MHz increments, and each step holds the potential of reducing chip voltage. For example, trimming the speed of a chip from 667MHz to 633MHz also allows for reducing the operating voltage from 1.65 to 1.60 volts.

Packaging

The working part of a microprocessor is exactly what the nickname "chip" implies: a small flake of a silicon crystal no larger than a postage stamp. Although silicon is a fairly robust material with moderate physical strength, it is sensitive to chemical contamination. After all, semiconductors are grown in precisely controlled atmospheres, the chemical content of which affects the operating properties of the final chip. To prevent oxygen and contaminants in the atmosphere from adversely affecting the precision-engineered silicon, the chip itself must be sealed away. The first semiconductors, transistors, were hermetically sealed in tiny metal cans.

The art and science of semiconductor packaging has advanced since those early days. Modern integrated circuits (ICs) are often surrounded in epoxy plastic, an inexpensive material that can be easily molded to the proper shape. Unfortunately, microprocessors can get very hot, sometimes too hot for plastics to safely contain. Most powerful modern microprocessors are consequently cased in ceramic materials that are fused together at high temperatures. Older, cooler chips reside in plastic. The most recent trend in chip packaging is the development of inexpensive tape-based packages optimized for automated assembly of circuit boards.

The most primitive of microprocessors (that is, those of the early generation that had neither substantial signal nor power requirements) fit in the same style housing popular for other integrated circuits—the infamous dual inline pin (DIP) package. The packages grew more pins—or *legs*, as engineers sometimes call them—to accommodate the ever-increasing number of signals in data and address buses.

The DIP package is far from ideal for a number of reasons. Adding more connections, for example, makes for an ungainly chip. A centipede microprocessor would be a beast measuring a full five inches long. Not only would such a critter be hard to fit onto a reasonably sized circuit board, it would require that signals travel substantially farther to reach the end pins than those in the center. At modern operating frequencies, that difference in distance can amount to a substantial fraction of a clock cycle, potentially putting the pins out of sync.

Modern chip packages are compact squares that avoid these problems. Engineers developed several separate styles to accommodate the needs of the latest microprocessors.

The most common is the *pin grid array* (PGA), a square package that varies in size with the number of pins that it must accommodate (typically about two inches square). The first PGA chips had 68 pins. Pentium 4 chips in PGA packages have up to 478.

No matter their number, the pins are spaced as if they were laid out on a checkerboard, making the "grid array" of the package name (see Figure 5.1).

To fit the larger number of pins used by wider-bus microprocessors into a reasonable space, Intel rearranged the pins of some processors (notably the Pentium Pro), staggering them so that they can fit closer together. The result is a *staggered pin grid array* (SPGA) package, as shown in Figure 5.2.

FIGURE 5.1
Pin-grid array socket (with PGA chip).

FIGURE 5.2
A Multi-Cavity Module (MCM) SPGA package.

Pins take up space and add to the cost of fabrication, so chipmakers have developed a number of pinless packages. The first of these to find general use was the Leadless Chip Carrier (LCC) socket. Instead of pins, this style of package has contact pads on one of its surfaces. The pads are plated with gold to avoid corrosion or oxidation that would impede the flow of the minute electrical signals used by the chip (see Figure 5.3). The pads are designed to contact special springy mating contacts in a special socket. Once installed, the chip itself may be hidden in the socket, under a heat sink, or perhaps only the top of the chip may be visible, framed by the four sides of the socket.

FIGURE 5.3
Leadless Chip Carrier microprocessor, top and bottom views.

A related design, the *Plastic Leaded Chip Carrier (PLCC)*, substitutes epoxy plastic for the ceramic materials ordinarily used for encasing chips. Plastic is less expensive and easier to work with. Some microprocessors with low thermal output sometimes use a housing designed to be soldered down—the *Plastic Quad Flat Package (PQFP)*, sometimes called simply the *quad flat pack* because the chips are flat (they fit flat against the circuit board) and they have four sides (making them a quadrilateral, as shown in Figure 5.4).

The *Tape Carrier Package* takes the advantage of the quad flat pack a step further, reducing the chip to what looks like a pregnant bulge in the middle of a piece of photographic film (see Figure 5.5).

FIGURE 5.4
Plastic Quad Flat Package microprocessor.

FIGURE 5.5
Tape Carrier Package microprocessor.

Another way to deal with the problem of pins is to reduce them to vestigial bumps, substituting precision-formed globs of solder that can mate with socket contacts. Alternately, the globs can be soldered directly to a circuit board using surface-mount technology. Because the solder contacts start out as tiny balls but use a variation on the PGA layout, the package is termed *solder-ball grid array*. (Note that *solder* is often omitted from the name, thus yielding the abbreviation BGA.)

When Intel's engineers first decided to add secondary caches to the company's microprocessors, they used a separately housed slice of silicon for the cache. Initially Intel put the CPU and cache chips in separate chambers in one big, black chip. The design, called the *Multi-Cavity Module* (MCM), was used only for the Pentium Pro chip.

Next, Intel shifted to putting the CPU and cache on a small circuit board inside a cartridge, initially called the *Single Edge Contact cartridge* or *SEC cartridge* (which Intel often abbreviates *SECC*) when it was used for the Pentium II chip. Figure 5.6 shows the Pentium II microprocessor SEC cartridge.

Intel used a functionally similar but physically different design for its Pentium II Xeon chips and a similar cartridge but slightly different bus design for the Pentium III.

To cut the cost of the cartridge for the inexpensive Celeron line, Intel eliminated the case around the chip to make the Singe-Edge Processor (SEP) package (see Figure 5.7).

FIGURE 5.6

The SEC cartridge as used in the Intel Pentium II.

FIGURE 5.7

The SEP package as used by the Intel Celeron micro-processor.

When Intel developed the capability to put the CPU and secondary cache on a single piece of silicon, called a *die*, the need for cartridges disappeared. Both later Celeron and Pentium III had *on-die* caches and were packaged both as cartridges and as individual chips in PGA and similar packages. With the Pentium 4, the circle was complete. Intel offers the latest Pentiums only in compact chip-style packages.

The package that the chip is housed in has no effect on its performance. It can, however, be important when you want to replace or upgrade your microprocessor with a new chip or upgrade card. Many of these enhancement products require that you replace your system's microprocessor with a new chip or adapter cable that links to a circuit board. If you want the upgrade or a replacement part to fit on your motherboard, you may have to specify which package your computer uses for its microprocessor.

Ordinarily you don't have to deal with microprocessor sockets unless you're curious and want to pull out the chip, hold it in your hand, and watch a static discharge turn a $300 circuit into epoxy-encapsulated sand. Choose to upgrade your computer to a new and better microprocessor, and you'll tangle with the details of socketry, particularly if you want to improve your Pentium.

Intel recognizes nine different microprocessor sockets for its processors, from the 486 to the Pentium Pro. In 1999, it added a new socket for some incarnations of the Pentium II Celeron. Other Pentium II and Pentium III chips, packaged as modules or cartridges, mate with slots instead of sockets. Table 5.2 summarizes these socket types, the chips that use them, and the upgrades appropriate to them.

TABLE 5.2   Slots and Sockets for Intel Microprocessors

Socket/Slot Number	Pins	Layout	Voltage	Microprocessor	OverDrives
Sockets for Older Intel Microprocessors and Upgrades					
0	168	Inline	5V	486DX	DX2, DX4
1	169	Inline	5V	486DX, 486SX	DX2, DX4
2	238	Inline	5V	486DX, 486SX, DX2	DX2, DX4, Pentium
3	237	Inline	3V or 5V	486DX, 486SX, DX2, DX4	DX2, DX4, Pentium
4	273	Inline	5V	60MHz or 66MHz Pentium	Pentium
5	320	Staggered	3V	Other Pentium	Pentium
6	235	Inline	3V	DX4	Pentium
7	321	Staggered	3V	Other Pentium	Pentium
8	387	Staggered	3V	Pentium Pro	Pentium Pro
Slots for Intel Architecture Microprocessors					
1	242	Inline	3V	Pentium II, Celeron	
2	330	Inline	3V	Xeon	
A (EV6)	NA	Inline	3V	AMD K7	
M	NA	Inline	3V	Merced	
SC242	242	Inline	3V	Pentium III, Celeron	

History

No matter the designation or origin, all microprocessors in today's Windows-based computers share a unique characteristic and heritage. All are direct descendents of the very first microprocessor. The instruction set used by all current computer microprocessors is rooted in the instructions selected for that first-ever chip. Even the fastest of today's Pentium 4 chips has, hidden in its millions of transistors, the capability of acting exactly like that first chip.

In a way, that's good because this backward-looking design assures us that each new generation of microprocessor remains compatible with its predecessors. When a new chip arrives, manufacturers can plug it into a computer and give you reasonable expectations that all your old software will still work. But holding to the historical standard also heaps extra baggage on chip designs that holds back performance. By switching to a radically new design, engineers could create a faster, simpler microprocessor—one that could run circles around any of today's chips, but, alas, one that can't use any of your current programs or operating systems.

Initial Development

The history of the microprocessor stretches back to a 1969 request to Intel by a now-defunct Japanese calculator company, Busicom. The original plan was to build a series of calculators, each one different and each requiring a custom integrated circuit. Using conventional IC technology, the project would have required the design of 12 different chips. The small volumes of each design would have made development costs prohibitive.

Intel engineer Mercian E. (Ted) Hoff had a better idea, one that could slash the necessary design work. Instead of a collection of individually tailored circuits, he envisioned creating one general-purpose device that would satisfy the needs of all the calculators. Hoff laid out an integrated circuit with 2,300 transistors using 10-micron design rules with four-bit registers and a four-bit data bus. Using a 12-bit multiplexed addressing system, it was able to address 640 bytes of memory for storing subproducts and results.

Most amazing of all, once fabricated, the chip worked. It became the first general-purpose microprocessor, which Intel put on sale as the 4004 on November 15, 1971.

The chip was a success. Not only did it usher in the age of low-cost calculators, it also gave designers a single solid-state programmable device for the first time. Instead of designing the digital decision-making circuits in products from scratch, developers could buy an off-the-shelf component and tailor it to their needs simply by writing the appropriate program.

With the microprocessor's ability to handle numbers proven, the logical next step was to enable chips to deal with a broader range of data, including text characters. The 4004's narrow four-bit design was sufficient for encoding only numbers and basic operations—a total of 16 symbols. The registers would need to be wider to accommodate a wider repertory. Rather than simply bump up the registers a couple of bits, Intel's engineers chose to go double and design a full eight-bit microprocessor with eight-bit registers and an eight-bit data bus. In addition, this endowed the chip with the ability to address a full 16KB of memory using 14 multiplexed address lines. The result, which required a total of 3450 transistors, was the Intel 8008, introduced in April 1972.

Intel continued development (as did other integrated circuit manufacturers) and, in April 1974, created a rather more drastic revision, the 8080, which required nearly twice as many transistors (6,000) as the earlier chip. Unlike the 8008, the new 8080 chip was planned from the start for byte-size data. Intel gave the 8080 a 16-bit address bus that could handle a full 64KB of memory and a richer command set, one that embraced all the commands of the 8008 but went further. This set a pattern for Intel microprocessors: Every increase in power and range of command set enlarged on what had gone before rather than replacing it, thus ensuring backward compatibility (at least to some degree) of the software. To this day, the Intel-architecture chips used in personal computers can run program code written using 8080 instructions. From the 8080 on, the story of the microprocessor is simply one of improvements in fabrication technology and increasingly complex designs.

With each new generation of microprocessor, manufacturers relied on improving technology in circuit design and fabrication to increase the number and size of the registers in each microprocessor, broadening the data and address buses to match. When that strategy stalled, they moved to superscalar designs with multiple pipelines. Improvements in semiconductor fabrication technology made the increasing complexity of modern microprocessor designs both practical and affordable. In the three decades since the introduction of the first microprocessor, the linear dimensions of semiconductor circuits have decreased to 1/50th their original size, from 10-micron design rules to 0.13 micron, which means microprocessor-makers can squeeze 6,000 transistors where only one fit originally. This size reduction also facilitates higher speeds. Today's microprocessors run nearly 25,000 times faster than the first chip out of the Intel foundry, 2.5GHz in comparison to the 108KHz of the first 4004 chip.

Personal Computer Influence

The success of the personal computer marked a major turning point in microprocessor design. Before the PC, microprocessor engineers designed what they regarded as the best possible chips. Afterward, they focused their efforts on making chips for PCs. This change came between what is now regarded as the first generation of Intel microprocessors and the third generation, in the years 1981 to 1987.

8086 Family

The engineers who designed the IBM Personal Computer chose to use a chip from the Intel 8086 family. Intel introduced the 8086 chip in 1978 as an improvement over its first chips. Intel's engineers doubled the size of the registers in its 8080 to create a chip with 16-bit registers and about 10 times the performance. The 16-bit design carried through completely, also doubling the size of the data bus of earlier chips to 16 bits to move information in and out twice as fast.

In addition, Intel broadened the address bus from 16-bit to 20-bits to allow the 8086 to directly address up to one megabyte of RAM. Intel divided this memory into 64KB segments to make programming and the transition to the new chip easier. A single 16-bit register could address any byte in a given segment. Another, separate register indicated which of the segments that address was in.

A year after the introduction of the 8086, Intel introduced the 8088. The new chip was identical to the 8086 in every way—16-bit registers, 20 address lines, and the same command set—except one. Its data bus was reduced to eight bits, enabling the 8088 to exploit readily available eight-bit support hardware. At that, the 8088 broke no new ground and should have been little more than a footnote in the history of the microprocessor. However, its compromise design that mated 16-bit power with cheap 8-bit support chips made the 8088 IBM's choice for its first personal computer. With that, the 8088 entered history as the second most important product in the development of the microprocessor, after the ground-breaking 4004.

286 Family

After the release of the 8086, Intel's engineers began to work on a successor chip with even more power. Designated the 80286, the new chip was to feature several times the speed and 16 times more addressable memory than its predecessors. Inherent in its design was the capability of multitasking, with new instructions for managing tasks and a new operating mode, called *protected mode*, that made its full 16MB of memory fodder for advanced operating systems.

The 80286 chip itself was introduced in 1982, but its first major (and most important) application didn't come until 1984 with the introduction of IBM's Personal Computer AT. Unfortunately, this development work began before the PC arrived, and few of the new features were compatible with the personal computer design. The DOS operating system for PCs and all the software that ran under it could not take advantage of the chip's new protected mode—which effectively put most of the new chip's memory off limits to PC programs.

With all its innovations ignored by PCs, the only thing the 80286 had going for it was its higher clock speed, which yielded better computer performance. Initially released running at 6MHz, computers powered by the 80286 quickly climbed to 8MHz, and then 10MHz. Versions operating at 12.5MHz, 16MHz, 20MHz, and ultimately 24MHz were eventually marketed.

The 80286 proved to be an important chip for Intel, although not because of any enduring success. It taught the company's engineers two lessons. First was the new importance of the personal computer to Intel's microprocessor market. Second was licensing. Although the 80286 was designed by Intel, the company licensed the design to several manufacturers, including AMD, Harris Semiconductor, IBM, and Siemens. Intel granted these licenses not only for income but also to assure the chip buyers that they had alternate sources of supply for the 80286, just in case Intel went out of business. At the time,

Intel was a relatively new company, one of many struggling chipmakers. With the success of the PC and its future ensured, however, Intel would never again license its designs so freely.

Even before the 80286 made it to the marketplace, Intel's engineers were working on its successor, a chip designed with the power of hindsight. By then they could see the importance that the personal computer's primeval DOS operating system had on the microprocessor market, so they designed to match DOS instead of some vaguely conceived successor. They also added in enough power to make the chip a fearsome competitor.

386 Family

The next chip, the third generation of Intel design, was the 80386. Two features distinguish it from the 80286: a full 32-bit design, for both data and addressing, and the new Virtual 8086 mode. The first gave the third generation unprecedented power. The second made that power useful.

Moreover, Intel learned to tailor the basic microprocessor design to specific niches in the marketplace. In addition to the mainstream microprocessor, the company saw the need to introduce an "entry level" chip, which would enable computer makers to sell lower-cost systems, and a version designed particularly for the needs of battery-powered portable computers. Intel renamed the mainstream 80386 as the 386DX, designated an entry-level chip the 386SX (introduced in 1988), and reengineered the same logic core for low-power applications as the 386SL (introduced in 1990).

The only difference between the 386DX and 386SX was that the latter had a 16-bit external data bus whereas the former had a 32-bit external bus. Internally, however, both chips had full 32-bit registers. The origin of the D/S nomenclature is easily explained. The external bus of the 386DX handled *double* words (32 bits), and that of the 386SX, *single* words (16 bits).

Intel knew it had a winner and severely restricted its licensing of the 386 design. IBM (Intel's biggest customer at the time) got a license only by promising not to sell chips. It could only market the 386-based microprocessors it built inside complete computers or on fully assembled motherboards. AMD won its license to duplicate the 386 in court based on technology-sharing agreements with Intel dating before even the 80286 had been announced. Another company, Chip and Technologies, reverse-engineered the 386 to build clones, but these were introduced too late—well after Intel advanced to its fourth generation of chips—to see much market success.

Age of Refinement

The 386 established Intel Architecture in essentially its final form. Later chips differ only in details. They have no new modes. Although Intel has added new instructions to the basic 386 command set, almost any commercial software written today will run on any Intel processor all the way back to the 386—but not likely any earlier processor, if the software is Windows based. The 386 design had proven itself and had become the foundation for a multibillion-dollar software industry. The one area for improvement was performance. Today's programs may run on a 386-based machine, but they are likely to run *very* slowly. Current chips are about 100 times faster than any 386.

486 Family

The next major processor after the 386 was, as you might expect, the 486. Even Intel conceded its new chip was basically an improved 386. The most significant difference was that Intel added three features that could boost processing speed by working *around* handicaps in circuitry external to the microprocessor. These innovations included an integral Level One cache that helped compensate for slow memory systems, pipelining within the microprocessor to get more processing power from low clock speeds, and an integral floating-point unit that eliminated the handicap of an external connection. As this generation matured, Intel added one further refinement that let the microprocessor race ahead of laggardly support circuits—splitting the chip so that its core logic and external bus interface could operate at different speeds.

Intel introduced the first of this new generation in 1989 in the form of a chip then designated 80486, continuing with its traditional nomenclature. When the company added other models derived from this basic design, it renamed the then-flagship chip as the 486DX and distinguished lower-priced models by substituting the SX suffix and low-power designs for portable computers using the SL designation, as it had with the third generation. Other manufacturers followed suit, using the 486 designation for their similar products—and often the D/S indicators for top-of-the-line and economy models.

In the 486 family, however, the D/S split does not distinguish the width of the data bus. The designations had become disconnected from their origins. In the 486 family, Intel economized on the SX version by eliminating the integral floating-point unit. The savings from this strategy was substantial—without the floating-point circuitry, the 486SX required only about half the silicon of the full-fledged chip, making it cheaper to make. In the first runs of the 486SX, however, the difference was more marketing. The SX chips were identical to the DX chips except that their floating-point circuitry was either defective or deliberately disabled to make a less capable processor.

As far as hardware basics are concerned, the 486 series retained the principal features of the earlier generation of processors. Chips in both the third and fourth generations have three operating modes (real, protected, and virtual 8086), full 32-bit registers, and a 32-bit address bus enabling up to 4GB of memory to be directly addressed. Both support virtual memory that extends their addressing to 64TB. Both have built-in memory-management units that can remap memory in 4KB pages.

But the hardware of the 486 also differs substantially from the 386 (or any previous Intel microprocessor). The pipelining in the core logic allows the chip to work on parts of several instructions at the same time. At times the 486 could carry out one instruction every clock cycle. Tighter silicon design rules (smaller details etched into the actual silicon that makes up the chip) gave the 486 more speed potential than preceding chips. The small but robust 8KB integral primary cache helped the 486 work around the memory wait states that plagued faster 386-based computers.

The streamlined hardware design (particularly pipelining) meant that the 486-level microprocessors could think faster than 386 chips when the two operated at the same clock speed. On most applications, the 486 proved about twice as fast as a 386 at the same clock rate, so a 20MHz 486 delivered about the same program throughput as a 40MHz 386.

Pentium Family

In March 1993, Intel introduced its first superscalar microprocessor, the first chip to bear the designation *Pentium*. At the time the computer industry expected Intel to continue its naming tradition and label the new chip the 80586. In fact, the competition was banking on it. Many had already decided to use that numerical designation for their next generation of products. Intel, however, wanted to distinguish its new chip from any potential clones and establish its own recognizable brand on the marketplace. Getting trademark protection for the 586 designation was unlikely. A federal court had earlier ruled that the 386 numeric designation was generic—that is, it described a type of product rather than something exclusive to a particular manufacturer—so trademark status was not available for it. Intel coined the word *Pentium* because it could get trademark protection. It also implied the number 5, signifying fifth generation, much as "586" would have.

Intel has used the Pentium name quite broadly as the designation for mainstream (or desktop performance) microprocessors, but even in its initial usage the singular Pentium designation obscured changes in silicon circuitry. Two very different chips wear the plain designation "Pentium." The original Pentium began its life under the code name *P5* and was the designated successor to the 486DX. Characterized by 5-volt operation, low operating speeds, and high power consumption, the Intel made the P5 available only at three speeds: 60MHz, 66MHz, and 90MHz. Later, Intel refined the initial Pentium design as the *P54C* (another internal code name), with tighter design rules and lower voltage operation. These innovations raised the speed potential of the design, and commercial chips gradually stepped up from 100MHz to 200MHz. The same basic design underlies the Pentium OverDrive (or P24T) processor used for upgrading 486-based PCs.

In January 1997, Intel enhanced the Pentium instruction set to better handle multimedia applications and created *Pentium Processor with MMX Technology* (code-named *P55C* during development). These chips also incorporated a larger on-chip primary memory cache, 32KB.

To put the latest in Pentium power in the field. Intel reengineered the Pentium with MMX Technology chip for low-power operation to make the *Mobile Pentium with MMX Technology* chip, also released in January 1997. Unlike the deskbound version, the addressing capability of the mobile chip was enhanced by four more lines to allow direct access to 64GB of physical memory.

Mature Design

The Pentium was Intel's last CISC design. Other manufacturers were adapting RISC designs to handle the Intel instruction set and achieving results that put Intel on notice. The company responded with its own RISC-based design in 1995 that became the standard Intel core logic until the introduction of the Pentium 4 in the year 2000. Intel developed this logic core under the code name *P6*, and it has appeared in a wide variety of chips, including those bearing the names Pentium Pro, Pentium II, Celeron, Xeon, and Pentium III.

That's not to say all these chips are the same. Although the entire series uses essentially the same execution units, the floating-point unit continued to evolve throughout the series. The Pentium Pro incorporates a traditional floating-point unit. That of the Pentium II is enhanced to handle the MMX instruction set. The Pentium III adds Streaming SIMD Extensions. In addition, Intel altered the memory cache and bus of these chips to match the requirements of particular market segments to distinguish the Celeron and Xeon lines from the plain Pentium series.

The basic P6 design uses its own internal circuits to translate classic Intel instructions into micro-ops that can be processed in a RISC-based core, which has been tuned using all the RISC design tricks to massage extra processing speed from the code. Intel called this design *Dynamic Execution*. In the standard language of RISC processors, Dynamic Execution merely indicates a combination of out-of-order instruction execution and the underlying technologies that enable its operation (branch prediction, register renaming, and so on).

The P6 pipeline has 12 stages, divided into three sections: an in-order fetch/decode stage, an out-of-order execution/dispatch stage, and an in-order retirement stage. The design is superscalar, incorporating two integer units and one floating-point unit.

Pentium Pro

One look and there's no mistaking the Pentium Pro. Instead of a neat square chip, it's a rectangular giant. Intel gives this package the name *Multi-Chip Module* (MCM). It is also termed a *dual-cavity PGA* (pin-grid array) package because it holds two distinct slices of silicon, the microprocessor core and secondary cache memory. This was Intel's first chip with an integral secondary cache. Notably, this design results in more pins than any previous Intel microprocessor and a new socket requirement, Socket 8 (discussed earlier).

The main processor chip of the Pentium Pro uses the equivalent of 5.5 million transistors. About 4.5 million of them are devoted to the actual processor itself. The other million provide the circuitry of the chip's primary cache, which provides a total of 16KB storage bifurcated into separate 8KB sections for program instructions and data. Compared to true RISC processors, the Pentium Pro uses about twice as many transistors. The circuitry that translates instructions into RISC-compatible micro-ops requires the additional transistor logic.

The integral secondary RAM cache fits onto a separate slice of silicon in the other cavity of the MCM. Its circuitry involves another 15.5 million transistors for 256KB of storage and operates at the same speed as the core logic of the rest of the Pentium Pro.

The secondary cache connects with the microprocessor core logic through a dedicated 64-bit bus, termed a *back-side bus*, that is separate and distinct from the 64-bit *front-side bus* that connects to main memory. The back-side bus operates at the full internal speed of the microprocessor, whereas the front-side bus operates at a fraction of the internal speed of the microprocessor.

The Pentium Pro bus design superficially appears identical to that of the Pentium with 32-bit addressing, a 64-bit data path, and a maximum clock rate of 66MHz. Below the surface, however, Intel enhanced the design by shifting to a *split-transaction protocol*. Whereas the Pentium (and, indeed, all previous Intel processors) handled memory accessing as a two-step process (on one clock cycle the chip sends an address out the bus, and reads the data at the next clock cycle), the Pentium Pro can put an address on the bus at the same time it reads data from a previously posted address. Because the address and data buses use separate lines, these two operations can occur simultaneously. In effect, the throughput of the bus can nearly double without an increase in its clock speed.

The internal bus interface logic of the Pentium Pro is designed for multiprocessor systems. Up to four Pentium Pro chips can be directly connected together, pin for pin, without any additional support circuitry. The computer's chipset arbitrates the combination.

Pentium II

The chief distinctions of the Pentium II are its addition of MMX technology and new package called the *Single Edge Contact* cartridge, or *SEC cartridge*. The socket it plugs into is termed Slot 1.

One underlying reason for the cartridge-style design is to accommodate the Pentium II's larger secondary cache, which is not integral to the chip package but rather co-mounted on the circuit board inside the cartridge. The 512KB of static cache memory connect through a 64-bit back-side bus. Note that the secondary cache memory of a Pentium II operates at one-half the speed of the core logic of the chip itself. This reduced speed is, of course, a handicap. It was a design expediency. It lowers the cost of the technology, allowing Intel to use off-the-shelf cache memory (from another manufacturer, at least initially) in a lower-cost package. The Pentium II secondary cache design has another limitation. Although the Pentium II can address up to 64GB of memory, its cache can track only 512MB. The Pentium II also has a 32KB primary cache that's split with 16KB assigned to data and 16KB to instructions. Table 5.3 summarizes the Intel Pentium II line.

TABLE 5.3   Introduction Dates and Speeds of Intel Pentium II Microprocessors

Speed	Introduction Date	Cache Size	Front-Side Bus Speed	Instruction Set	Design Rules
233	May 7, 1997	512KB	66MHz	IA32	0.35 micron
266	May 7, 1997	512KB	66MHz	IA32	0.35 micron
300	May 7, 1997	512KB	66MHz	IA32	0.35 micron
333	January 26, 1997	512KB	66MHz	IA32	0.25 micron
350	April 15, 1998	512KB	66MHz	IA32	0.25 micron
400	April 15, 1998	512KB	66MHz	IA32	0.25 micron
450	August 24, 1998	512KB	66MHz	IA32	0.25 micron

Mobile Pentium II

To bring the power of the Pentium II processor to notebook computers, Intel reengineered the desktop chip to reduce its power consumption and altered its packaging to fit slim systems. The resulting chip—the *Mobile Pentium II*, introduced on April 2, 1997—preserved the full power of the Pentium II while sacrificing only its multiprocessor support. The power savings comes from two changes. The core logic of the Mobile Pentium II is specifically designed for low-voltage operation and has been engineered to work well with higher external voltages. It also incorporates an enriched set of power-management modes, including a new QuickStart mode that essentially shuts down the chip, except for the logic that monitors for bus activity by the PCI bridge chip, and allows the chip to wake up when it's needed. This design, because it does not monitor for other processor activity, prevents the Mobile Pentium II from being used in multiprocessor applications. The Mobile Pentium II can also switch off its cache clock during its sleep or QuickStart states.

Initially, the Mobile Pentium II shared the same P6 core logic design and cache design with the desktop Pentium II (full-speed 32KB primary cache and half-speed 512KB secondary cache inside its mini-cartridge package). However, as fabrication technology improved, Intel was able to integrate the secondary cache on the same die as the processor core, and on January 25, 1999, the company introduced a new version of the Mobile Pentium II with an integral 256KB cache operating at full core speed. Unlike the Pentium

II, the mobile chip has the ratio between its core and bus clocks fixed at the factory to operate with a 66MHz front-side bus. Table 5.4 lists the introduction dates and basic characteristics of the Mobile Pentium II models.

TABLE 5.4   Introduction Dates and Speed of Intel Mobile Pentium II Microprocessors

Speed	Introduction Date	Cache Size	Front-Side Bus Speed	Design Rules
233MHz	April 2, 1998	512KB	66MHz	0.25 micron
266MHz	April 2, 1998	512KB	66MHz	0.25 micron
266MHz	January 25, 1999	256KB	66MHz	0.25 micron
300MHz	September 9, 1998	512KB	66MHz	0.25 micron
300MHz	January 25, 1999	256KB	66MHz	0.25 micron
333MHz	January 25, 1999	256KB	66MHz	0.25 micron
366MHz	January 25, 1999	256KB	66MHz	0.25 micron
400MHz	June 14, 1999	256KB	66MHz	0.25 micron

Pentium II Celeron

Introduced on March 4, 1998, the *Pentium II Celeron* was Intel's entry-level processor derived from the Pentium II. Although it had the same processor core as what was at the time Intel's premier chip (the second-generation Pentium II with 0.45-micron design rules), Intel trimmed the cost of building the chip by eliminating the integral 512KB secondary (Level Two) memory cache installed in the Pentium II cartridge. The company also opted to lower the packaging cost of the chip by omitting the metal outer shell of the full Pentium II and instead leaving the Celeron's circuit board substrate bare. In addition, the cartridge-based Celeron package lacked the thermal plate of the Pentium II and the latches that secure it to the slot. Intel terms the Celeron a *Single Edge Processor Package* to distinguish it from the Single Edge Contact cartridge used by the Pentium II.

In 1999, Intel introduced a new, lower-cost package for the Celeron, a plastic pin-grid array (PPGA) shell that looks like a first generation Pentium on steroids. It has 370 pins and mates with Intel's PGA370 socket. The chip itself measures just under two inches square (nominally 49.5 millimeters) and about three millimeters thick, not counting the pins, which hang down another three millimeters or so (the actual specification is 3.05 to 3.30 millimeters).

When the Celeron chip was initially introduced, the absence of a cache made such a hit on the performance that Intel was forced by market pressure to revise its design. In August, 1998, the company added a 128KB cache operating at one-half core speed to the Celeron. Code names distinguished the two chips: The first Celeron was code-named

Covington during development; the revised chip was code-named *Mendocino*. Intel further increased the cache to 256KB on October 2, 2001, with the introduction of a 1.2GHz Celeron variant.

Intel also distinguished the Celeron from its more expensive processor lines by limiting its front-side bus speed to 66MHz. All Celerons sold before January 3, 2001 were limited to that speed. With the introduction of the 800MHz Celeron, Intel kicked the chip's front-side bus up to 100MHz. With the introduction of a 1.7GHz Celeron on May 2, 2002, Intel started quad-clocking the chip's front-side bus, yielding an effective data rate of 400MHz.

Intel also limited the memory addressing of the Celeron to 4GB of physical RAM by omitting the four highest address bus signals used by the Pentiums II and III from the Celeron pin-out. The Celeron does not support multiprocessor operation, and, until Intel introduced the Streaming SIMD Extensions to the 1.2GHz version, the Celeron understood only the MMX extension to the Intel instruction set.

Table 5.5 lists the features and introduction dates of various Celeron models.

TABLE 5.5   Introduction Dates and Specifications of Intel Pentium II Celeron Microprocessors

Speed	Introduction Date	Cache Size	Front-Side Bus	Instruction Set	Design Rules
266	March 4, 1998	None	66MHz	MMX	0.35 micron
300	June 8, 1998	None	66MHz	MMX	0.35 micron
300A	August 24, 1998	128KB	66MHz	MMX	0.25 micron
333	August 24, 1998	128KB	66MHz	MMX	0.25 micron
366	January 4, 1999	128KB	66MHz	MMX	0.25 micron
400	January 4, 1999	128KB	66MHz	MMX	0.25 micron
433	March 22, 1999	128KB	66MHz	MMX	0.25 micron
450	August 2, 1999	128KB	66MHz	MMX	0.25 micron
566	March 29, 2000	128KB	66MHz	MMX	0.25 micron
600	March 29, 2000	128KB	66MHz	MMX	0.18 micron
633	June 26, 2000	128KB	66MHz	MMX	0.18 micron
667	June 26, 2000	128KB	66MHz	MMX	0.18 micron
700	June 26, 2000	128KB	66MHz	MMX	0.18 micron
733	November 13, 2000	128KB	66MHz	MMX	0.18 micron

continues

TABLE 5.5   Continued

Speed	Introduction Date	Cache Size	Front-Side Bus	Instruction Set	Design Rules
750	November 13, 2000	128KB	66MHz	MMX	0.18 micron
800	January 3, 2001	128KB	100MHz	MMX	0.18 micron
850	May 21, 2001	128KB	100MHz	MMX	0.18 micron
900	July 2, 2001	128KB	100MHz	MMX	0.18 micron
950	August 31, 2001	128KB	100MHz	MMX	0.18 micron
1000	August 31, 2001	128KB	100MHz	MMX	0.18 micron
1100	August 31, 2001	128KB	100MHz	MMX	0.18 micron
1200	October 2, 2001	256KB	100MHz	SSE	0.13 micron
1300	January 3, 2002	256KB	100MHz	SSE	0.13 micron
1400	May 15, 2002	256KB	100MHz	SSE	0.13 micron
1700	May 15, 2002	256KB	400MHz	SSE2	0.13 micron
1800	June 12, 2002	256KB	400MHz	SSE2	0.13 micron

Pentium II Xeon

In 1998, Intel sought to distinguish its higher performance microprocessors from its economy line. In the process, the company created the *Xeon*, a refined Pentium II microprocessor core enhanced by a higher-speed memory cache, one that operated at the same clock rate as the core logic of the chip.

At heart, the Xeon is a full 32-bit microprocessor with a 64-bit data bus, as with all Pentium-series processors. Its address bus provides for direct access to up to 64GB of RAM. The internal logic of the chip allows for up to four Xeons to be linked together without external circuitry to form powerful multiprocessor systems.

A sixth generation processor, the Xeon is a Pentium Pro derivative by way of the standard Pentium II. It incorporates two 12-stage pipelines to make what Intel terms *Dynamic Execution micro-architecture*.

The Xeon incorporates two levels of caching. One is integral to the logic core itself, a primary 32KB cache split 16KB for instructions, 16KB for data. In addition, a separate secondary cache is part of the Xeon processor module but is mounted separately from the core logic on the cartridge substrate. This integral-but-separate design allows flexibility in configuring the Xeon. Current chips are available equipped with either 512KB or 1MB of L2 cache, and the architecture and slot design allow for secondary caches of up to 2MB. This integral cache runs at the full core speed of the microprocessor.

This design required a new interface, tagged *Slot 2* by Intel.

Initially the core operating speed of the Xeon started where the Pentium II left off (at the time, 400MHz) and followed the Pentium II up to 450MHz.

The front-side bus of the Xeon was initially designed for 100MHz operation, although higher speeds are possible and expected. A set of contacts on the SEC cartridge allows the motherboard to adjust the multiplier that determines the ratio between front-side bus and core logic speed.

The independence of the logic core and cache is emphasized by the power requirements of the Xeon. Each section requires its own voltage level. The design of the Xeon allows Intel flexibility in the power requirements of the chip through a special coding scheme. A set of pins indicates the core voltage and the cache voltage required by the chip, and the chip expects the motherboard to determine the requirements of the board and deliver the required voltages. The Xeon design allows for core voltages as low as 1.8 volts or as high as 2.1 volts (the level required by the first chips). Cache voltage requirements may reach as high as 2.8 volts. Nominally, the Xeon is a 2-volt chip.

Overall, the Xeon is optimized for workstations and servers and features built-in provide support for up to four identical chips in a single computer. Table 5.6 summarizes the original Xeon product line.

TABLE 5.6   Introduction Dates and Specification of Intel Pentium II Xeon Microprocessors

Speed	Introduction Date	Cache Size	Front-Side Bus Speed	Instruction Set	Design Rules
400MHz	June 29, 1998	512KB	100MHz	IA32	0.25 micron
400MHz	June 29, 1998	1MB	100MHz	IA32	0.25 micron
450MHz	October 6, 1998	512KB	100MHz	IA32	0.25 micron
450MHz	January 5, 1999	512KB	100MHz	IA32	0.25 micron
450MHz	January 5, 1999	1MB	100MHz	IA32	0.25 micron
450MHz	January 5, 1999	2MB	100MHz	IA32	0.25 micron

Pentium II OverDrive

To give an upgrade path for systems originally equipped with the Pentium Pro processor, Intel developed a new OverDrive line of direct-replacement upgrades. These *Pentium II OverDrive* chips fit the same zero-insertion force Socket 8 used by the Pentium Pro, so you can slide one chip out and put the other in. Dual-processor systems can use two OverDrive upgrades. Intel warns that some systems may require a BIOS upgrade to accommodate the OverDrive upgrade.

The upgrade offers the revised design of the Pentium II (which means better 16-bit operation) as well as higher clock speeds. The chip also can earn an edge over ordinary Pentium II chips operating at the same speeds—the 512KB secondary cache in the OverDrive chip operates at full core logic speed, not half speed as in the Pentium II.

Current Products

Although more than a dozen companies make microprocessors, any new personal computer you buy will likely be based on a chip from one of only three companies: Advanced Micro Devices, Intel, or Transmeta. Intel, the largest semiconductor-maker in the world, makes the majority of computer processors—about 80 percent in the first quarter of the year 2002, according to Mercury Research. In the same period, AMD sold 18.2 percent of the chips destined for personal computers.

Intel earned its enviable position by not only inventing the microprocessor but also by a quirk of fate. IBM chose one of its chips for its first Personal Computer in 1981, the machine that all modern personal computers have been patterned after. Computers must use Intel chips or chips designed to match the Intel Architecture to be able to run today's most popular software. Because microprocessors are so complicated, designing and building them requires a huge investment, which prevents new competitors from edging into the market.

Intel Microprocessors

Currently Intel sells microprocessors under several brand names. The most popular is the Pentium 4, which Intel claims as its best-selling microprocessor, ever. But the Pentium 4 is not a single chip design. Rather, it's a trade name. Intel has marketed two distinctly different chip designs as Pentium 4. More confusing still, Intel markets the same core logic under more than one name. At one time, the Pentium, Celeron, and Xeon all used essentially the same internal design. The names designated the market segment Intel hoped to carve for the respective chips—Celeron for the price-sensitive low end of the personal computer marketplace, Pentium for the mainstream, and Xeon for the pricey, high-end server marketplace. Although Intel did tailor some features to justify its market positioning of the chips, they nevertheless shared the same circuitry deep inside.

Today, that situation has changed. Intel now designs Xeon chips separately, and Celerons often retain older designs and technologies longer than mainstream Pentiums. The market position assigned the microprocessor names remains the same. Intel offers Celeron chips for the budget conscious. It sacrifices the last bit of performance to make computers more affordable. Pentium processors are meant for the mainstream (most computer purchasers) and deliver full performance for single-user computers. Xeons are specialized microprocessors designed primarily for high-powered server systems. Intel has added a further name, Itanium, to its trademark lineup. The Itanium uses a new architecture (usually termed *IA64*, shorthand for *64-bit Intel Architecture*) that is not directly compatible with software meant for other Intel chips.

The important lesson is that the names you see on the market are only brand names and do not reflect what's inside a chip. Some people avoid confusion by using the code name the manufacturer called a given microprocessor design during its development. These code names allow consumers to distinguish the Northwood processor from the Willamette, both of which are sold as Pentium 4. The Northwood is a newer design with higher-speed potentials. Table 5.7 lists many of Intel's microprocessor code names.

TABLE 5.7   Intel Microprocessor Code Names

Code Name	Corresponding Brand Name
Klamath	Original Pentium II
Deschutes	Improved Pentium II (100MHz bus)
Katmai	Original Pentium III (0.25 micron)
Coppermine	Pentium III (0.18 micron)
Willamette	Original Pentium 4 (0.18 micron)
Northwood	Pentium 4 (0.13 micron)
Foster	Pentium 4 Xeon (0.18 micron)
Prestonia	Pentium 4 Xeon (0.13 micron)
Nocona	Proposed Pentium 4 Xeon (0.09 micron)
Gallatin	Multiprocessor Prestonia (0.13 micron)
Merced	Original Itanium (0.18 micron)
McKinley	Itanium 2 (0.18 micron)
Madison	Proposed Itanium 2 (0.13 micron)
Deerfield	Proposed Desktop Itanium 2
Banias	Proposed high-performance IA-32 portable chip

Pentium III

Announced in January and officially released on February 26, 1999, the Pentium III was the swan song for Intel's P6 processor core, developed for the Pentium Pro. Code-named *Katmai* during its development, the Pentium III chip is most notable for adding SSE to the Intel microprocessor repertory. SSE is a compound acronym for Streaming SIMD Extensions (SIMD itself being an acronym for Single Instruction, Multiple Data). SIMD technology allows one microprocessor instruction to operate across several bytes or words (or even larger blocks of data). In the Pentium III, SSE (formerly known as the *Katmai New Instructions* or *KNI*) is a set of 70 new SIMD codes for microprocessor instructions that allows programs to specify elaborate three-dimensional processing functions with a single command.

Unlike the MMX extensions, which added no new registers to the basic Pentium design and instead simply redesignated the floating-point unit registers for multimedia functions, Intel's Streaming SIMD Extensions add new registers to Intel architecture, pushing the total number of transistors inside the core logic of the chip above 9.5 million.

At heart, the Pentium III uses the same core logic as its Pentium II and Pentium Pro fore-bears, amended to handle its larger instruction set. The enhancements chiefly involve the floating-point unit, which does double-duty processing multimedia instructions. In other words, the Pentium III does not mark a new generation of microprocessor technology or performance. Even Intel noted that on programs that do not take advantage of the Streaming SIMD Extensions of the Pentium III, the chips deliver performance that's about the same as a Pentium II.

Although the initial fabrication used 0.25-micron technology, Intel rapidly shifted to 0.18-micron technology with the Coppermine design. The result is that the circuitry of the chip takes less silicon (making fabrication less expensive), requires less power, and is able to operate at higher speeds. The initial Pentium III releases, and all versions through at least the 600MHz chip, operate with a 100MHz memory bus. Many of the new chips using the Coppermine core ratchet the maximum memory speed to 133MHz using Rambus memory technology, although some retain a 100MHz maximum memory speed.

In going to the new Coppermine design, Intel replaced earlier Pentium III chips with 0.25-micron design features, in particular those at the 450, 533, 550, and 600MHz speeds. The newer chips are designed with the suffix *E*. In addition, to distinguish chips with 133MHz front-side bus capability (when 100MHz versions of the chip were once offered), Intel added a *B* suffix to the designation of 533 and 600MHz chips that are capable of running their memory buses at the higher 133MHz speed.

The Pentium III was the first Intel processor to cross the line at a 1GHz clock speed with a chip released on March 8, 2000. The series ended its development run at 1.13GHz on July 31, 2000, although Intel continued to manufacturer the chip into 2002.

The Pentium III was designed to plug into the same Slot 1 as the Pentium II, however, the Pentium III now comes in three distinct packages. One, the SEC cartridge, is familiar from the Pentium II. Pentium III is also available in the SEC cartridge 2 (or SECC2). In all aspects, the SECC2 is identical to the SEC cartridge and plugs into the same slot (Slot 1, which Intel has renamed SC242), but the SECC2 package lacks the thermal plate of the earlier design. Instead, the SECC2 is designed to mate with an external heatsink, and, because of the lack of the thermal plate, it will make a better thermal connection for more effective cooling. (Well, it makes sense when Intel explains it.) In addition, the 450 and 550E are available in a new package design termed *FC-PGA* (for *Flip-Chip Pin Grid Array*), which is more compact and less expensive than the cartridge design.

As with the Pentium II, the 0.25-micron versions of the Pentium III have a 32KB integral primary cache and include a 512KB secondary cache on the same substrate but not in the same hermetic package at the core CPU. The secondary cache runs at half the chip speed. The newer 0.18-micron versions have a smaller, 256KB secondary cache but operate it at full chip speed and locate it on the same silicon as the core logic. In addition, Intel has broadened the data path between the core logic and the cache to enhance performance (Intel calls this *Advanced Transfer Cache* technology). According to Intel, these improvements give the newer Coppermine-based (0.18-micron) Pentium III chips a 25-percent performance advantage over older Pentium III chips operating at the same clock speed. The entire Pentium III line supports multiprocessing with up to two chips.

The most controversial aspect of the Pentium III lineup is its internal serial number. Hard-coded into the chip, this number is unique to each individual microprocessor. Originally Intel foresaw that a single command—including a query from a distant Web site—would cause the chip to send out its serial number for positive identification (of the chip, of the computer it is in, and of the person owning or using the computer). Intel believed the feature would improve Internet security, not to mention allowing the company to track its products and detect counterfeits. Consumer groups saw the "feature" as in invasion of privacy, and under threat of boycott Intel changed its policy. Where formerly the Pentium III would default to making the identification information available, after the first production run of the new chip, the identification would default to off and require a specific software command to make the serial number accessible. Whether the chip serial number is available becomes a setup feature of the BIOS in PCs using the Pentium III chip, although a software command can override that setting. In other words, someone can always interrogate your PC to discover your Pentium III's serial number. Therefore, you might want to watch what you say online when you run with the Pentium III. Table 5.8 summarizes the history of the Pentium III.

TABLE 5.8   Introduction Dates and Specification of Intel Pentium III Microprocessors

Speed	Introduction Date	Cache Size	Front-Side Bus Speed	Instruction Set	Design Rules
450	February 26, 1999	512KB	100MHz	SSE	0.25 micron
500	February 26, 1999	512KB	100MHz	SSE	0.25 micron
500	October 25, 1999	256KB	100MHz	SSE	0.18 micron
533	October 25, 1999	256KB	133MHz	SSE	0.18 micron
550	May 17, 1999	512KB	100MHz	SSE	0.25 micron
550	October 25, 1999	256KB	100MHz	SSE	0.18 micron
600	August 2, 1999	512KB	100MHz	SSE	0.25 micron
600E	October 25, 1999	256KB	100MHz	SSE	0.18 micron
600EB	October 25, 1999	256KB	133MHz	SSE	0.18 micron
650	October 25, 1999	256KB	100MHz	SSE	0.18 micron
667	October 25, 1999	256KB	133MHz	SSE	0.18 micron
700	October 25, 1999	256KB	100MHz	SSE	0.18 micron
733	October 25, 1999	256KB	133MHz	SSE	0.18 micron
750	December 20, 1999	256KB	100MHz	SSE	0.18 micron
800	December 20, 1999	256KB	133MHz	SSE	0.18 micron
850	March 20, 2000	256KB	100MHz	SSE	0.18 micron
866	March 20, 2000	256KB	133MHz	SSE	0.18 micron
933	May 24, 2000	256KB	133MHz	SSE	0.18 micron
1000	March 8, 2000	256KB	133MHz	SSE	0.18 micron
1130	July 31, 2000	256KB	133MHz	SSE	0.18 micron

Pentium III Xeon

To add its Streaming SIMD Extensions to its server products, on March 17, 1999, Intel introduced the Pentium III Xeon. As with the Pentium III itself, the new instructions are the chief change, but they are complemented by a shift to finer technology. As a result, the initial new Xeons start with a speed of 500MHz. At this speed, Intel offers the chip with either a 512KB, 1MB, or 2MB integral secondary cache operating at core speed. The new Slot 2 chips also incorporate the hardware serial number feature of the Pentium III chip.

Developed under the code name *Tanner*, the Pentium III Xeon improved upon the original (Pentium II) Xeon with additions to the core logic to handle Intel's Streaming SIMD Extensions. Aimed at the same workstation market as the original Xeon, the Pentium III Xeon is distinguished from the ordinary Pentium III by its larger integral cache, its Slot 2 packaging, and its wider multiprocessor support—the Pentium III Xeon design allows for servers with up to eight processors.

When Intel introduced its Coppermine 0.18-micron technology on October 25, 1999, it unveiled three new Pentium III Xeon versions with speed ratings up to 733MHz. Except for packaging, however, these new Xeons differed little from the ordinary Pentium III line. As with the mainstream processors, the Xeons supported a maximum of two processors per system and had cache designs identical to the ordinary Pentium III with a 256KB secondary cache operating at full processor speed using wide-bus Advanced Transfer Cache technology. In May of 2000, Intel added Xeons with larger, 1MB and 2MB caches as well as higher-speed models with 256KB caches. Table 5.9 lists the characteristics of all of Intel's Pentium III Xeon chips.

TABLE 5.9   Introduction Dates and Specification of Intel Pentium III Xeon Microprocessors

Speed	Introduction Date	Cache Size	Front-Side Bus Speed	Instruction Set	Design Rules
500MHz	March 17, 1999	512KB	100MHz	SSE	0.25 micron
500MHz	March 17, 1999	1MB	100MHz	SSE	0.25 micron
500MHz	March 17, 1999	2MB	100MHz	SSE	0.25 micron
550MHz	March 17, 1999	512KB	100MHz	SSE	0.25 micron
550MHz	March 17, 1999	1MB	100MHz	SSE	0.25 micron
550MHz	March 17, 1999	2MB	100MHz	SSE	0.25 micron
600MHz	October 25, 1999	256KB	133MHz	SSE	0.18 micron
667MHz	October 25, 1999	256KB	133MHz	SSE	0.18 micron
700MHz	May 22, 2000	1MB	100MHz	SSE	0.18 micron
700MHz	May 22, 2000	2MB	100MHz	SSE	0.18 micron
733MHz	October 25, 1999	256KB	133MHz	SSE	0.18 micron
800MHz	January 12, 2000	256KB	133MHz	SSE	0.18 micron
866MHz	April 10, 2000	256KB	133MHz	SSE	0.18 micron
900MHz	March 21, 2001	2MB	100MHz	SSE	0.18 micron
933MHz	May 24, 2000	256KB	133MHz	SSE	0.18 micron

Intel Pentium 4

Officially introduced on November 20, 2000, the Pentium 4 is Intel's newest and most powerful microprocessor core for personal computers. According to Intel, the key advance made by the new chip is its use of NetBurst micro-architecture, which can be roughly explained as a better way of translating program instructions into the micro-ops that the chip actually carries out. NetBurst is the first truly new Intel core logic design since the introduction of the P6 (Pentium Pro) in 1995.

Part of the innovation is an enhancement to the instruction set; another part is an improvement to the underlying hardware. All told, the first Pentium 4 design required the equivalent of 42 million transistors.

Chips designated *Pentium 4* actually use one of two designs. Intel code-named the early chips *Willamette* and used 0.18-micron design rules in their fabrication. At initial release, these chips operated at 1.4GHz and 1.5GHz, but Intel soon upped their clock speeds. At the time, Intel and AMD were in a horserace for the fastest microprocessor, and the title shifted between the Athlon and Pentium 4 with each new chip release.

In 2002, Intel shifted to 0.13-micron design rules with a new processor code designed under the name *Northwood*. This shift resulted in a physically smaller chip that also allows more space for cache memory—whereas the Willamette chips boasts 256KB of on-chip Level Two cache operating at full core speed, the Northwood design doubles that to 512KB. The difference is in size only. Both chips have a 256-bit-wide connection with the caches, which use an eight-way set-associative design.

Of particular note, the Pentium 4 uses a different system bus from that of the Pentium III chip. As a practical matter, that means the Pentium 4 requires different chipsets and motherboards from those of the Pentium III. Although this is ordinarily the concern of the computer manufacturer, the new design has important benefits. It adds extra speed to the system (memory) bus by shifting data up to four times faster than older designs using a technology Intel calls *Source-Synchronous Transfer*. In effect, this signaling system packs four bits of information into each clock cycle, so a bus with a 133MHz nominal clock speed can shift data at an effective rate of 533MHz. The address bus is double-clocked, signaling twice in each clock cycle, yielding an effective rate of 266MHz. In that the Pentium 4, like earlier Pentiums, has a 64-bit-wide data bus, that speed allows the Pentium 4 to move information at a peak rate of 4.3GBps (that is, 8 bytes times 533MHz).

Only Northwood chips rated at 2.26GHz, 2.4GHz, and 2.53GHz have 533MHz system buses. Other Northwood chips, as well as all Willamette versions, use a 400MHz system bus (that is, a quadruple-clocked 100MHz bus). Note that chips operating at 2.4GHz may have either a 400MHz or 533MHz system bus. The system bus speed is set in the system design and cannot be varied through hardware or software.

The Pentium 4 has three execution units. The two integer arithmetic/logic units (ALUs) comprise what Intel calls a *rapid execution engine*. They are "rapid" because they operate at twice the speed of the rest of the core logic (that is, 5.06GHz in a 2.53GHz chip), executing up to two instructions in each clock cycle. The registers in each ALU are 32 bits wide.

Unlike previous Intel floating-point units, the registers in the Pentium 4 FPU are 128 bits wide. The chief benefit of these wider registers is in carrying out multimedia instructions using a further enhancement on Intel's Streaming SIMD Extensions (SSE), a set of 144 new instructions (mainly aimed at moving bytes in and out of the 128-bit registers but also including double-precision floating-point and memory-management instructions) called SSE2.

Intel lengthened the pipelines pumping instructions into the execution units to 20 stages, the longest of any microprocessor currently in production. Intel calls this design *hyperpipelined technology*.

One way Intel pushes more performance from the Pentium 4 is by double-clocking the integer units in the chip. They operate at twice the external clock frequency applied to the chip (that is, at 3GHz in the 1.5GHz Pentium 4 chip). Balancing the increased speed is a 400MHz system bus throughput as well as an improved primary cache and integral 256KB secondary cache. Intel connects this secondary cache to the rest of the chip through a new 256-bit-wide bus, double the size of those in previous chips.

Intel also coins the term *hyperpipelining* to describe the Pentium 4. The term refers to Intel's doubling the depth of the instruction pipeline, as compared to the previous line-leader, the Pentium III. One (but not all) of the pipelines in the Pentium 4 stretches out for 20 stages. Intel claims that the new NetBurst micro-architecture enabled the successful development of the long pipeline because it minimizes the penalties associated with mis-predicting instruction branches.

The Pentium 4 recognizes the same instruction set as previous Intel microprocessors, including the Streaming SIMD Extensions introduced with the Pentium III, but the Pentium 4 adds 144 more instructions to the list. The result is termed by Intel *SSE2*. The chip has the same basic data and address bus structure as the Pentium III, allowing it to access up to 64GB of physical memory eight bytes (64-bits) at a time.

Table 5.10 summarizes the Intel Pentium 4 line.

TABLE 5.10   Introduction Dates and Specification of Intel Pentium 4 Microprocessors

Speed (MHz)	Introduction Date	Cache Size	Front-Side Bus Speed	Instruction Set	Design Rules
1400	November 20, 2000	256KB	400MHz	SSE2	0.18 micron
1500	November 20, 2000	256KB	400MHz	SSE2	0.18 micron
1600	July 2, 2001	256KB	400MHz	SSE2	0.18 micron
1700	April 23, 2001	256KB	400MHz	SSE2	0.18 micron
1800	July 2, 2001	256KB	400MHz	SSE2	0.18 micron
1900	August 27, 2001	256KB	400MHz	SSE2	0.18 micron
2000	August 27, 2001	256KB	400MHz	SSE2	0.18 micron
2000	August 27, 2001	512KB	400MHz	SSE2	0.13 micron
2200	January 7, 2002	512KB	400MHz	SSE2	0.13 micron
2260	May 6, 2002	512KB	533MHz	SSE2	0.13 micron
2400	April 2, 2002	512KB	400MHz	SSE2	0.13 micron
2400	May 6, 2002	512KB	533MHz	SSE2	0.13 micron
2530	May 6, 2002	512KB	533MHz	SSE2	0.13 micron
2660	August 26, 2002	512KB	533MHz	SSE2	0,13 micron
2800	August 26, 2002	512KB	533MHz	SSE2	0.13 micron
3060	November 14, 2002	512KB	533MHz	SSE2	0.13 micron

Xeon (Pentium 4)

On May 21, 2001, Intel released the first of its Xeon microprocessors built using the NetBurst core logic of the Pentium 4 microprocessor. To optimize the chip for use in computer servers, the company increased the secondary cache size of the chip, up to 2MB of on-chip cache. For multiprocessor systems, Intel later derived a separate chip, the Xeon MP processor, for servers with two to four microprocessors. The chief difference between the MP chip and the base Xeon chip is the former chip's caching—a three-level design. The primary cache is 8KB, the secondary cache is 256KB, and the tertiary cache is either 512KB or 1MB.

Table 5.11 summarizes the Pentium 4 Xeon, including Xeon MP processors.

TABLE 5.11   Summary of Intel Pentium 4 Xeon and Xeon MP Microprocessors

Processor	Clock Speed	Introduction Date	Technology
Xeon	2.8GHz	September 11, 2002	0.13 micron
Xeon	2.6GHz	September 11, 2002	0.13 micron

Current Products

Processor	Clock Speed	Introduction Date	Technology
Xeon	2.4GHz	April 23, 2002	0.13 micron
Xeon	2.2GHz	February 25, 2002	0.13 micron
Xeon	2.0GHz	February 25, 2002	0.13 micron
Xeon	2.0GHz	September 25, 2001	0.13 micron
Xeon	1.8GHz	February 25, 2002	0.13 micron
Xeon	1.7GHz	May 21, 2001	0.13 micron
Xeon	1.5GHz	May 21, 2001	0.13 micron
Xeon	1.4GHz	May 21, 2001	0.13 micron
Xeon MP	1.6GHz	March 12, 2002	0.13 micron
Xeon MP	1.5GHz	March 12, 2002	0.13 micron
Xeon MP	1.4GHz	March 12, 2002	0.13 micron

Mobile Processors

The diversity of models that Intel puts on the desktop is exceeded only by the number of microprocessors it makes for portable computers. The current lineup includes four major models, each of which includes chips meant to operate on three different voltage levels, in a wide range of frequencies. The choices include Mobile Celeron, Mobile Pentium III (soon to fall from the product line, as of this writing), Mobile Pentium III-M, and Mobile Pentium 4-M. Each has its target market, with Celeron at the low end, Pentium 4 at the highest, and the various Pentium III chips for everything in between. Each chip shares essentially the same core as the desktop chip bearing the same designation. But mobile chips have added circuitry for power management and, in some models, different packaging.

Microprocessors for portable computers differ from those meant for desktop systems in three ways: operating power, power management, and performance. The last is a result of the first and, in normal operation, the second.

To help portable computers run longer from a single charge of their batteries, Intel and other microprocessor manufacturers reduce the voltage at which their chips operate. Intel, in fact, produces chips in three voltage ranges, which it calls very (or sometimes, *ultra*) low voltage, low voltage, and nothing. Very-low-voltage chips operate as low as 0.95 volts. Low-voltage chips dip down to about 1.1. Low-voltage operation necessitates lower-speed operation, which limits performance. Of the chips that Intel produces in all three power levels, the very-low-voltage chips inevitably have the slowest megahertz rating.

Power management aids in the same end—prolonging battery life—and incidentally prevents your laptop computer from singeing you should you operate it on your lap. Some machines still get uncomfortably hot.

Mobile Celeron

Intel aims its Mobile Celeron at the budget market. The chips are not only restricted to lower clock speeds than their Pentium siblings, but most Mobile Celeron chips lack Intel's SpeedStep power-saving technology. The Mobile Celeron perpetually lags Intel's desktop processors in other performance indexes. For example, much like the desktop Celerons, the mobile chips usually are one step out-of-date in front-side bus speed. Although Intel has bumped its top memory bus speed to 533MHz, it only endows the latest versions of the Mobile Celeron with the older quad-pumped 400MHz rating. Most Mobile Celerons still have 100MHz front-side buses.

Much like the desktop line, the first Mobile Celeron was a modest alteration of the Pentium II. Introduced on January 25, 1999, it used the same core logic but with a different cache design, a 128KB cache on the chip substrate operating at full core speed. Otherwise, the chip followed the Pentium II design and followed it up in speed, from 266MHz up to 466MHz, using the same 66MHz front-side bus as the desktop chips and the same 0.25-micro design rules. It differs chiefly by operating at a lower, power-saving voltage, 1.6 volts.

On February 14, 2000, Intel revised the Mobile Celeron design to take advantage of the Pentium III core and its 0.18-micro design rules. The newer Mobile Celerons gained two advantages: the higher, 100MHz front-side bus speed and the Streaming SIMD Extensions to the instruction set. In addition to a faster chip (at 500MHz), Intel also introduced a 450MHz chip, slower than the quickest of the old Mobile Celeron design but able to take advantage of the higher bus speed. Intel continued to upgrade this core up to a speed of 933MHz, introduced on October 1, 2001.

When Intel move the Mobile Celeron line to 0.13-micron technology, the company cut the core voltage of the chips down to 1.45 volts while pushing up its top clock speed to 1.2GHz. The smaller design rules left more space on the chip's silicon, which Intel utilized for an enhanced secondary cache, pushing it to 256KB.

On June 24, 2002, Intel switched the Mobile Celeron core once again, bringing in a design derived from the Pentium 4. The new core allowed Intel to trim the chip's operating voltage once again, down to 1.3 volts. In addition, new versions of the Mobile Celeron boast the quad-pumped 400MHz front-side bus speed of the Pentium 4 as well as its enhanced Streaming SIMD Extensions 2 instruction set.

Table 5.12 summarizes the life history of Intel's Mobile Celeron product line.

TABLE 5.12   Summary of Intel Mobile Celeron Features

Speed	Introduction Date	Cache	Front-Side Bus Speed	Design Rules	Core Voltage	Instruction Set
266MHz	January 25, 1999	128KB	66MHz	0.25 micron	1.6 volts	MMX
300MHz	January 25, 1999	128KB	66MHz	0.25 micron	1.6 volts	MMX
333MHz	April 5, 1999	128KB	66MHz	0.25 micron	1.6 volts	MMX
366MHz	May 17, 1999	128KB	66MHz	0.25 micron	1.6 volts	MMX
400MHz	June 14, 1999	128KB	66MHz	0.18 micron	1.6 volts	MMX
433MHz	September 15, 1999	128KB	66MHz	0.25 micron	1.9 volts	MMX
450MHz	February 14, 2000	128KB	100MHz	0.18 micron	1.6 volts	SSE
466MHz	September 15, 1999	128KB	66MHz	0.25 micron	1.9 volts	MMX
500MHz	February 14, 2000	128KB	100MHz	0.18 micron	1.6 volts	SSE
550MHz	April 24, 2000	128KB	100MHz	0.18 micron	1.6 volts	SSE
600MHz	June 19, 2000	128KB	100MHz	0.18 micron	1.6 volts	SSE
650MHz	June 19, 2000	128KB	100MHz	0.18 micron	1.6 volts	SSE
700MHz	September 25, 2000	128KB	100MHz	0.18 micron	1.6 volts	SSE
733MHz	October 1, 2001	128KB	100MHz	0.18 micron	1.7 volts	SSE
750MHz	March 19, 2001	128KB	100MHz	0.18 micron	1.6 volts	SSE
800MHz	May 21, 2001	128KB	100MHz	0.18 micron	1.6 volts	SSE
800AMHz	October 1, 2001	128KB	100MHz	0.18 micron	1.7 volts	SSE
850MHz	July 2, 2001	128KB	100MHz	0.18 micron	1.6 volts	SSE
866MHz	October 1, 2001	128KB	100MHz	0.18 micron	1.7 volts	SSE
900MHz	October 1, 2001	128KB	100MHz	0.18 micron	1.7 volts	SSE
933MHz	October 1, 2001	128KB	100MHz	0.18 micron	1.7 volts	SSE
1000MHz	April 17, 2002	256KB	133MHz	0.13 micron	1.4 volts	SSE
1060MHz	January 21, 2002	256KB	133MHz	0.13 micron	1.45 volts	SSE
1130MHz	January 21, 2002	256KB	133MHz	0.13 micron	1.45 volts	SSE
1200MHz	January 21, 2002	256KB	133MHz	0.13 micron	1.45 volts	SSE
1330MHz	June 24, 2002	256KB	133MHz	0.13 micron	1.5 volts	SSE
1400MHz	June 24, 2002	256KB	400MHz	0.13 micron	1.3 volts	SSE2
1500MHz	June 24, 2002	256KB	400MHz	0.13 micron	1.3 volts	SSE2

Mobile Pentium III

For about a year, Intel's most powerful mobile chips wore the Pentium III designation. As the name implies, they were derived from the desktop series with several features added to optimize them for mobile applications and, incidentally, to bring the number of transistors on their single slice of silicon to 28 million. Table 5.13 summarizes the Mobile Pentium III product line.

TABLE 5.13   Summary of Intel Mobile Pentium III Features

Core Speed	Introduction Date	Cache Size	Front-Side Bus Speed	Design Rules	Operating Voltage	Instruction Set
400MHz	October 25, 1999	256KB	100MHz	0.18 micron	1.35 volts	SSE
450MHz	October 25, 1999	256KB	100MHz	0.18 micron	1.6 volts	SSE
500MHz	October 25, 1999	256KB	100MHz	0.18 micron	1.6 volts	SSE
600MHz	January 18, 2000	256KB	100MHz	0.18 micron	1.6 volts	SSE
650MHz	January 18, 2000	256KB	100MHz	0.18 micron	1.6 volts	SSE
700MHz	April 24, 2000	256KB	100MHz	0.18 micron	1.6 volts	SSE
750MHz	June 19, 2000	256KB	100MHz	0.18 micron	1.35 volts	SSE
800MHz	September 25, 2000	256KB	100MHz	0.18 micron	1.35 volts	SSE
850MHz	September 25, 2000	256KB	100MHz	0.18 micron	1.35 volts	SSE
900MHz	March 19, 2001	256KB	100MHz	0.18 micron	1.35 volts	SSE
1.0GHz	March 19, 2001	256KB	100MHz	0.18 micron	1.35 volts	SSE

Mobile Pentium III-M

When Intel shifted to new fabrication, the company altered the core logic design of the Pentium III. Although the basic design remained the same, the tighter design rules allowed for higher-speed operation. In addition, Intel improved the power management of the Mobile Pentium III with Enhanced SpeedStep technology, which allows the chip to shift down in speed in increments to conserve power. Table 5.14 summarizes the Mobile Pentium III-M lineup.

TABLE 5.14   Summary of Intel Mobile Pentium III-M Features

Core Speed	Introduction Date	Cache Size	Front-Side Bus Speed	Design Rules	Operating Voltage	Instruction Set
866MHz	July 30, 2001	512KB	133MHz	0.13 micron	1.15 volts	SSE
933MHz	July 30, 2001	512KB	133MHz	0.13 micron	1.15 volts	SSE
1000MHz	July 30, 2001	512KB	133MHz	0.13 micron	1.4 volts	SSE

Core Speed	Introduction Date	Cache Size	Front-Side Bus Speed	Design Rules	Operating Voltage	Instruction Set
1060MHz	July 30, 2001	512KB	133MHz	0.13 micron	1.4 volts	SSE
1130MHz	July 30, 2001	512KB	133MHz	0.13 micron	1.4 volts	SSE
1200MHz	October 1, 2001	512KB	133MHz	0.13 micron	1.4 volts	SSE

Mobile Pentium 4-M

Intel's highest performance mobile chip is the Mobile Pentium 4-M. Based on the same core logic as the line-leading Pentium 4, the mobile chip is enhanced with additional power-management features and lower-voltage operation. Table 5.15 summarizes the Pentium 4-M lineup.

TABLE 5.15   Summary of Intel Mobile Pentium 4-M Features

Core Speed	Introduction Date	Cache Size	Front-Side Bus Speed	Design Rules	Operating Voltage	Instruction Set
1400MHz	April 23, 2002	512KB	400MHz	0.13 micron	1.3 volts	SSE2
1500MHz	April 23, 2002	512KB	400MHz	0.13 micron	1.3 volts	SSE2
1600MHz	March 4, 2002	512KB	400MHz	0.13 micron	1.3 volts	SSE2
1700MHz	March 4, 2002	512KB	400MHz	0.13 micron	1.3 volts	SSE2
1800MHz	April 23, 2002	512KB	400MHz	0.13 micron	1.3 volts	SSE2
1900MHz	June 24, 2002	512KB	400MHz	0.13 micron	1.3 volts	SSE2
2000MHz	June 24, 2002	512KB	400MHz	0.13 micron	1.3 volts	SSE2
2200MHz	September 26, 2002	512KB	400MHz	0.13 micron	1.3 volts	SSE2

Low-Voltage Microprocessors

For use in computers with strict power budgets—either because the manufacturer decided to devote little space to batteries or because the maker opted for extremely long runtimes—Intel has developed several lines of low-voltage microprocessors. These mobile chips have operating voltages substantially lower than the mainstream chips. Such low-voltage chips have been produced in three major mobile processor lines: the Mobile Celeron, the Mobile Pentium III, and the Mobile Pentium III-M.

Ultra-Low-Voltage Microprocessors

For systems in which power consumption is absolutely critical, Intel has offered versions of its various mobile chips designed for ultra-low-voltage operation. *Ultra*, like beauty, is in the eye of the beholder—these chips often operate at voltages only a fraction lower than ordinary low-voltage chips. The lower operating voltage limits the top speed of these chips; they are substantially slower than the ordinary low-voltage chips at the time of their introduction. But again, they are meant for systems where long battery life is more important than performance. Table 5.16 summarizes Intel's ultra-low-voltage microprocessors.

TABLE 5.16   Summary of Intel Low-Voltage Mobile Microprocessor Features

Designation	Core Speed	Introduction Date	Cache Size	Front-Side Bus Speed	Design Rules	Operating Voltage	Instruction Set
Mobile Celeron	500MHz	January 30, 2001	128KB	100MHz	0.18 micron	1.1 volts	MMX
Mobile Celeron	600MHz	May 21, 2001	128KB	100MHz	0.18 micron	1.1 volts	MMX
Mobile Celeron	650MHz	January 21, 2002	256KB	133MHz	0.13 micron	1.1 volts	SSE
Mobile Pentium III	500MHz	January 30, 2001	256KB	100MHz	0.18 micron	1.1 volts	SSE
Mobile Pentium III	600MHz	May 21, 2001	256KB	100MHz	0.18 micron	1.1 volts	SSE
Mobile Pentium III	750MHz	January 21, 2002	512KB	133MHz	0.13 micron	1.1 volts	SSE
Mobile Pentium III 512KB	700MHz	November 13, 2001	512KB	100MHz	0.13 micron	1.1 volts	SSE
Mobile Pentium III-M	800MHz	April 17, 2002	512KB	133MHz	0.13 micron	1.15 volts	SSE
Mobile Pentium III-M	800MHz	April 17, 2002	512KB	100MHz	0.13 micron	1.15 volts	SSE

Itanium

Intel's Itanium microprocessor line marks an extreme shift for Intel, entirely breaking with the Intel Architecture of the past—which means that the Itanium cannot run programs or operating systems designed for other Intel chips. Instead of using the old Intel design dating back to the 4004, the Itanium introduces Intel's Explicitly Parallel Instruction Computing architecture, which is based on the Precision Architecture originally developed by Hewlett-Packard Corporation for its line of RISC chips. In short, that means everything you know about Intel processors doesn't apply to the Itanium, especially the performance you should expect from the megahertz ratings of the chips. Itanium chips look slow on paper but perform fast in computers.

The original Itanium was code-named *Merced* and was introduced in mid-2001, with an announcement from Intel on May 29, 2001, that systems soon would be shipping. The original Itanium was sold in two speeds: 733MHz and 800MHz. Equipped with a 266MHz system bus (double-clocked 133MHz), the Itanium further enhanced performance with a three-level on-chip cache design with 32KB in its primary cache, 96KB in its secondary cache, and 2MB or 4MB in its tertiary cache (depending on chip model). All aspects of the chip feature a full 64-bit bus width, both data and address lines. Meant for high-performance servers, the Itanium allows for up to 512 processors in a single computer.

Introduced on July 8, 2002, the Itanium 2 (code-named *McKinley*) pushed up the clock speed of the same basic design as the original Itanium by shifting down the design rules to 0.13 micron. Intel increased the secondary cache of the Itanium 2 to 256KB and allowed for tertiary caches of 1.5MB or 3MB. The refined design also increased the system bus speed to 400MHz (actually, a double-clocked 200MHz bus) with a bus width of 128 bits. Initially, Itanium 2 chips were offered at speeds of 900MHz and 1.0GHz. Table 5.17 summarizes the Itanium line.

TABLE 5.17   Summary of Intel Itanium Product Line

Model	Introduction	Clock Speed	Primary Cache	Secondary Cache	Tertiary Cache	System Bus	Design Rules
Itanium	May 29, 2001	733MHz	32KB	96KB	2MB	266MHz	0.18 micron
Itanium	May 29, 2001	733MHz	32KB	96KB	4MB	266MHz	0.18 micron
Itanium	May 29, 2001	800MHz	32KB	96KB	2MB	266MHz	0.18 micron
Itanium	May 29, 2001	800MHz	32KB	96KB	4MB	266MHz	0.18 micron
Itanium 2	July 8, 2002	900MHz	32KB	256KB	1.5MB	400MHz	0.13 micron
Itanium 2	July 8, 2002	900MHz	32KB	256KB	3MB	400MHz	0.13 micron
Itanium 2	July 8, 2002	1000MHz	32KB	256KB	1.5MB	400MHz	0.13 micron
Itanium 2	July 8, 2002	1000MHz	32KB	256KB	3MB	400MHz	0.13 micron

Advanced Micro Devices Microprocessors

Advanced Micro Devices currently fields two lines of microprocessor. Duron chips correspond to Intel's Celeron line, targeting the budget-minded consumer. Athlon chips are mainstream, full-performance microprocessors. Around the end of the year 2002, AMD will add the Opteron name to its product line. Meant to compete with the performance of Intel's Itanium, the Opteron will differ with a design meant to run today's software as well or better than current Intel processors. Opteron will become the new top-end of the AMD lineup.

Athlon

AMD's answer to the Pentium III and its P6 core was the Athlon. The Athlon is built on a RISC core with three integer pipelines (compared to the two inside the Pentium III), three floating-point pipelines (versus one in the Pentium III), and three instruction decoders (compared one in the Pentium III). The design permits the Athlon to achieve up to nine operations per clock cycle, compared to five for the Pentium III. AMD designed the floating-point units specifically for multimedia and endowed them with both the MMX (under Intel license) and 3DNow! instruction sets.

Program code being what it is—not very amendable to superscalar processing—the Athlon's advantage proved more modest in reality. Most people gave the Athlon a slight edge on the Pentium III, megahertz for megahertz. The Athlon chip was more than powerful enough to challenge Intel for leadership in processing power. For more than a year, AMD and Intel ran a speed race for the fastest processor, with AMD occasionally edging ahead even in pure megahertz.

The Athlon has several other features that help to boost its performance. It has both primary (L1) and secondary (L2) caches on-chip, operating at the full speed rating of the core logic. A full 128KB is devoted to the primary cache, half for instructions and half for data, and 256KB is devoted to the secondary cache, for a total (the figure that AMD usually quotes) of 384KB of cache. The secondary cache connects to the chip through a 64-bit back-side bus operating at the core speed of the chip.

The system bus of the Athlon also edged past that used by Intel for the Pentium III. At introduction, the Athlon allowed for a 200MHz system bus (and 133MHz memory). Later, in March, 2001, the system bus interface was bumped up to 266MHz. This bus operates asynchronously with the core logic, so AMD never bothered with some of the odd speeds Intel used for its chips. The instruction set of the Athlon includes an enhanced form of AMD's 3DNow! The Athlon recognizes 45 3D instructions, compared to 21 for AMD's previous-generation K6-III chip.

The design of the Athlon requires more than 22 million transistors. As with other chips in its generation, it has registers 32 bits wide but connects to its primary cache through a 128-bit bus and to the system through a 64-bit data bus. It can directly address up to 8TB of memory through an address bus that's effectively 43-bits wide.

AMD has introduced several variations on the Athlon name—the basic Athlon, the Athlon 4 (to parallel the introduction of the Pentium 4), and the Athlon XP (paralleling Microsoft's introduction of Windows XP). The difference between the Athlon and Athlon 4 are in name alone. The basic core of all these Athlons is the same. Only the speed rating has increased with time. With the XP designation, however, AMD added Intel's Streaming SIMD Extensions to the instruction set of the chip, giving it better multimedia performance.

The Athlon comes in cartridge form and slides into AMD's Slot A. Based on the EV6 bus design developed by Digital Equipment Corporation (now part of Compaq) for the Alpha chip (a microprocessor originally meant for minicomputers but now being phased out), the new socket is physically the same as Intel's Slot 1, but the signals are different and the AMD chip is incompatible with slots for Intel processors.

AMD fabricated its initial Athlon chips using 0.25-micron design rules. In November, 1999, the company shifted to new fabrication facilities that enabled it to build the Athlon with 0.18-micron design rules.

Table 5.18 summarizes the features of the AMD Athlon line.

TABLE 5.18   Summary of AMD Athlon Microprocessor Features

Processor	Model orMHz	Introduction Date	Front-Side Bus Speed	Cache Size	Design Rules
Athlon XP	2100+	March 13, 2002	266MHz	128KB/256KB	0.18 micron
Athlon XP	2000+	January 7, 2002	266MHz	128KB/256KB	0.18 micron
Athlon XP	1900+	November 5, 2001	266MHz	128KB/256KB	0.18 micron
Athlon XP	1800+	October 9, 2001	266MHz	128KB/256KB	0.18 micron
Athlon XP	1700+	October 9, 2001	266MHz	128KB/256KB	0.18 micron
Athlon XP	1600+	October 9, 2001	266MHz	128KB/256KB	0.18 micron
Athlon XP	1500+	October 9, 2001	266MHz	128KB/256KB	0.18 micron
Athlon	1400	June 6, 2001	266MHz	128KB/256KB	0.18 micron
Athlon	1330	March 21, 2001	266MHz	128KB/256KB	0.18 micron
Athlon	1300	March 21, 2001	266MHz	128KB/256KB	0.18 micron
Athlon	1200	October 17, 2000	200MHz	128KB/256KB	0.18 micron
Athlon	1100	August 14, 2000	200MHz	128KB/256KB	0.18 micron
Athlon	1000	March 6, 2000	200MHz	128KB/256KB	0.18 micron
Athlon	950	March 6, 2000	200MHz	128KB/256KB	0.18 micron
Athlon	900	March 6, 2000	200MHz	128KB/256KB	0.18 micron
Athlon	850	February 11, 2000	200MHz	128KB/256KB	0.18 micron
Athlon	800	January 6, 2000	200MHz	128KB/256KB	0.18 micron
Athlon	750	November 29, 1999	200MHz	128KB/256KB	0.18 micron
Athlon	700	October 4, 1999	200MHz	128KB/256KB	0.25 micron

continues

			Front-Side		
Processor	Model or MHz	Introduction Date	Bus Speed	Cache Size	Design Rules
Athlon	650	August 9, 1999	200MHz	128KB/256KB	0.25 micron
Athlon	600	June 23, 1999	200MHz	128KB/256KB	0.25 micron
Athlon	550	June 23, 1999	200MHz	128KB/256KB	0.25 micron
Athlon	500	June 23, 1999	200MHz	128KB/256KB	0.25 micron

TABLE 5.18   Continued

Athlon MP

For multiprocessor applications, AMD adapted the core logic of the Athlon chip with bus control circuitry meant for high-bandwidth transfers. These chips are specifically aimed at servers rather than desktop computers. Table 5.19 summarizes the AMD offerings.

TABLE 5.19   Summary of AMD Athlon MP Features

Processor	Introduction Date	FSB Speed	Technology
Athlon MP 2000+	March 13, 2002	266MHz	0.18 micron
Athlon MP 1900+	December 12, 2001	266MHz	0.18 micron
Athlon MP 1800+	October 15, 2001	266MHz	0.18 micron
Athlon MP 1600+	October 15, 2001	266MHz	0.18 micron
Athlon MP 1500+	October 15, 2001	266MHz	0.18 micron

Duron

To take on Intel's budget-priced Celeron chips, AMD slimmed down the Athlon to make a lower-priced product. Although based on the same logic core as the Athlon, the Duron skimps on cache. Although it retains the same 128KB primary cache, split with half handling data and half instructions, the secondary cache is cut to 64KB. As with the Athlon, however, both caches operate at full core logic speed. The smaller secondary cache reduces the size of the silicon die required to make the chip, allowing more Durons than Athlons to be fabricated from each silicon wafer, thus cutting manufacturing cost.

The basic architecture of the Duron core matches the Athlon with three integer pipelines, three floating-point pipelines (which also process both 3DNow! and Intel's MMX instruction sets), and three instruction/address decoders. Duron chips even share the same 0.18-micron technology used by the higher-priced Athlon. For now, however, Durons are restricted to lower speeds than the Athlon line and have not benefited from AMD's higher-speed 266MHz system bus. All Durons use a 200MHz bus.

During development AMD used the code name *Spitfire* for the Duron. The company explains the official name of the chip as "derived from the Latin root *durare*, meaning 'to last' and *on*, meaning 'unit.'" The root is the same as the English word *durability*. Table 5.20 summarizes the characteristics of the AMD Duron line.

TABLE 5.20   Summary of AMD Duron Microprocessor Features

Processor	Speed (MHz)	Introduction	Front-Side Bus Speed	Cache Size (L1/L2)	Technology
Duron	1300	January 21, 2002	200MHz	128KB/64KB	0.18 micron
Duron	1200	November 15, 2001	200MHz	128KB/64KB	0.18 micron
Duron	1100	October 1, 2001	200MHz	128KB/64KB	0.18 micron
Duron	950	June 6, 2001	200MHz	128KB/64KB	0.18 micron
Duron	900	April 2, 2001	200MHz	128KB/64KB	0.18 micron
Duron	850	January 8, 2001	200MHz	128KB/64KB	0.18 micron
Duron	800	October 17, 2000	200MHz	128KB/64KB	0.18 micron
Duron	750	September 5, 2000	200MHz	128KB/64KB	0.18 micron
Duron	700	June 19, 2000	200MHz	128KB/64KB	0.18 micron
Duron	650	June 19, 2000	200MHz	128KB/64KB	0.18 micron
Duron	600	June 19, 2000	200MHz	128KB/64KB	0.18 micron

Mobile Processors

As with its desktop processors, AMD has two lines of chips for portable computers, the Athlon and Duron, for the high and low ends of the market, respectively. Unlike Intel, AMD puts essentially the same processors as used on the desktop in mobile packages. The AMD chips operate at the same low voltages as chips specifically designed for mobile applications, and AMD's desktop (and therefore, mobile) products all use its power-saving PowerNow! technology.

The one difference: AMD shifted to 0.13-micron technology for its portable Athlon XP while the desktop chip stuck with 0.18-micron technology. Table 5.21 summarizes AMD's Mobile Athlon product line.

TABLE 5.21   Summary of AMD Mobile Athlon Microprocessor Features

Processor	Model orMHz	Introduction Date	FSB Speed	Cache Size (L1/L2)	Technology
Mobile Athlon XP	1800+	July 15, 2002	266MHz	128KB/256KB	0.13 micron
Mobile Athlon XP	1700+	April 17, 2002	266MHz	128KB/256KB	0.13 micron
Mobile Athlon XP	1600+	April 17, 2002	266MHz	128KB/256KB	0.13 micron
Mobile Athlon XP	1500+	April 17, 2002	266MHz	128KB/256KB	0.13 micron
Mobile Athlon XP	1400+	April 17, 2002	266MHz	128KB/256KB	0.13 micron
Mobile Athlon 4	1600+	March 13, 2002	266MHz	128KB/256KB	0.18 micron
Mobile Athlon 4	1500+	January 28, 2002	266MHz	128KB/256KB	0.18 micron
Mobile Athlon 4	1200	November 12, 2001	200MHz	128KB/256KB	0.18 micron
Mobile Athlon 4	1100	August 20, 2001	200MHz	128KB/256KB	0.18 micron
Mobile Athlon 4	1000	May 14, 2001	200MHz	128KB/256KB	0.18 micron
Mobile Athlon 4	950	May 14, 2001	200MHz	128KB/256KB	0.18 micron
Mobile Athlon 4	900	May 14, 2001	200MHz	128KB/256KB	0.18 micron
Mobile Athlon 4	850	May 14, 2001	200MHz	128KB/256KB	0.18 micron

As with desktop chips, the chief difference between AMD's Mobile Athlon and Mobile Duron is the size of the secondary cache—only 64KB in the Duron chips. Table 5.22 summarizes the Mobile Duron line.

TABLE 5.22   Summary of AMD Mobile Duron Microprocessor Features

Processor	MHz	Introduction Date	FSB Speed	Cache Size (L1/L2)	Technology
Mobile Duron	1200	January 30, 2002	200MHz	128KB/64KB	0.18 micron
Mobile Duron	1100	January 30, 2002	200MHz	128KB/64KB	0.18 micron
Mobile Duron	1000	December 17, 2001	200MHz	128KB/64KB	0.18 micron
Mobile Duron	950	November 12, 2001	200MHz	128KB/64KB	0.18 micron
Mobile Duron	850	May 14, 2001	200MHz	128KB/64KB	0.18 micron
Mobile Duron	800	May 14, 2001	200MHz	128KB/64KB	0.18 micron
Mobile Duron	700	January 15, 2001	200MHz	128KB/64KB	0.18 micron
Mobile Duron	600	January 15, 2001	200MHz	128KB/64KB	0.18 micron

Opteron

AMD chose the name *Opteron* for what it calls its eighth generation of microprocessors, for which it has used the code-name *Hammer* during development. The Opteron represents the first 64-bit implementation of Intel architecture, something Intel has neglected to develop.

The Opteron design extends the registers of Pentium-style computers to a full 64-bits wide. It's a forthright extension of the current Intel architecture, and AMD makes the transition the same way Intel extended the original 16-bit bus of the 8086-style chips to 32 bits for the 386 series. The new, wide registers are a superset of the 32-bit registers. In the Opteron's compatibility mode, 16-bit instructions simply use the least significant 16 bits of the wide registers, 32-bit instructions use the least significant 32 bits, and 64-bit instructions use the entire register width. As a result, the Opteron can run any Intel code at any time without the need for emulators or coprocessors. Taking advantage of the full 64-bit power of the Opteron will, of course, require new programs written with the new 64-bit instructions.

The Opteron design also changes the structure of the processor core, rearranging the pipelines and processing units. The Opteron design uses three separate decode pipelines that feed a packing stage that links all three pipelines to more efficiently divide operations between them. The pipelines then feed into another stage of decoding, then eight stages of scheduling. At that point, the pipelines route integer and floating-point operations to individual processors. AMD quotes a total pipeline of 12 stages for integers and 17 for floating-point operations. The floating-point unit understands everything from MMX through 3DNow! to Intel's latest SSE2.

As important as the core logic is, AMD has made vast improvements on the I/O of the Opteron. Major changes come in two areas. AMD builds the memory controller into the Opteron, so the chip requires no separate memory control hub. The interface uses DDR memory through two 128-bit-wide channels. Each channel can handle four memory modules, initially those rated for PC1600 operation, although the Opteron design allows for memory as fast as PC2700. According to AMD, building the memory interface into the Opteron reduces latency (waiting time), the advantage of which is an increase with every step up in clock speed.

The system bus of the Opteron uses the HyperTranport interface with a 16-bit channel operating at an effective data rate of 1.6Gbps, giving the chip a peak I/O bandwidth of 3.2Gbps.

Transmeta Microprocessors

Strictly speaking, the Crusoe processors from Transmeta Corporation are not Intel architecture chips. They use an entirely different instruction set from Intel chips, and by themselves could run a Windows program on a dare. Transmeta's not-so-secret weapon is what it calls *Code Morphing software*, a program that runs on the Crusoe chip and translates Intel's instruction set into its own. In effect, the Crusoe chip is the core logic of a modern Intel Architecture stripped of its hardware code translation.

The core is a *very long instruction word* processor, one that uses instructions that can be either 64 or 128 bits long. The core has two pipelines—an integer pipeline with seven stages and a floating-point pipeline with 10. Transmeta keeps the control logic for the core logic simple. It does not allow out-of-order execution, and instruction scheduling is handled by software.

Transmeta provides both a 64KB primary instruction cache and a 64KB primary data cache. The Crusoe comes with either of two sizes of secondary cache. The TMS5500 uses a 256KB secondary cache, and the TMS5800 has a 512KB secondary cache. At the time this was written, the chips were available with speed ratings of 667, 700, 733, 800, 867, and 900MHz.

To help the chip mimic Intel processors, the Crusoe family has a translation look-aside buffer that uses the same protection bits and address-mapping as Intel processors. The Crusoe hardware generates the same condition codes as Intel chips, and their floating-point units use the same 80-bit format as Intel's basic FPU design (but not the 128-bit registers used by SSE2 instructions).

The result of this design is a very compact microprocessor that does what it does very quickly while using very little power. Transmeta has concentrated its marketing on the low power needs of the Crusoe chips, and they are used almost exclusively in portable computers. A less charitable way of looking at the Crusoe is that its smaller silicon needs make for a chip that's far less expensive to manufacturer and easier to design. That's not quite fair because developing the Code Morphing software is as expensive as designing silicon logic. Moreover, the current Crusoe chips take advantage of small silicon needs of their small logic cores, adding more features onto the same die. The current Crusoe models include the north bridge circuits of a conventional chipset on the same silicon as the core logic. The Crusoe chip includes the system bus, memory, and PCI bus interfaces, making portable computer designs potentially more compact. Current Crusoe versions support both SDR and DDR memory with system bus speeds up to 133MHz.

Another way to look at Code Morphing is to consider it as a *software emulator*, a program that runs on a chip to mimic another. Emulators are often used at the system level to allow programs meant for one computer to run on another. The chief distinctions between Code Morphing and traditional emulation is that Code Morphing works at the chip level, and the Crusoe chip keeps the necessary translation routines in firmware stored in read-only memory (ROM) chips.

According to Transmeta, Code Morphing also helps the Crusoe chip to be faster, enabling it to keep up with modern superscalar chips. The Code Morphing software doesn't translate each Intel instruction on the fly. Instead, it translates a series of instructions, potentially even full subroutines. It retains the results as if in a cache so that if it encounters the same set of Intel instructions again, it can look up the code to use rather than translating it again. The effect doesn't become apparent, according to Transmeta, until the Intel-based routine has been executed several times. The tasks typically involved with running a modern computer—the Windows graphic routines, software drivers, and so on—should benefit greatly from this technology. In reality, Crusoe processors don't test well, but they deliver adequate performance for the sub-notebook computers that are their primary application.

Chipsets

Buy a microprocessor, and it's just an inert lump that sits in its static-free box, super-powered silicon with extreme potential but no motivation. It's sort of like a Hollywood hunk proto-star before he takes acting classes. Even out of the box, the most powerful microprocessor is hardly impressive—or effective. It can't do anything on its own. Although it serves as the centerpiece of a computer, it is not the computer itself. It needs help.

The electronics inside a personal computer that flesh out its circuitry and make it work are called *support circuits*. At one time, support circuits made up everything in a computer except for the microprocessor. Today, most of the support functions needed to make a computer work take the form of a few large integrated circuits called a *chipset*. Support circuits handle only a few low-level functions to take care of the needs of the chipset.

In current designs, the chipset is second in importance only to the microprocessor in making your computer work—and making your computer a computer. Your computer's chipset is the foundation of its motherboard, and a computer-maker's choice of chipsets determines the overall capabilities of your computer. The microprocessor embodies its potential. The chipset makes it a reality.

Although the chipset used by a computer is rarely mentioned in advertisements and specification sheets, its influence is pervasive. Among other issues, the chipset determines the type and number of microprocessors that can be installed in the system; the maximum memory a system can address; the memory technology used by the system (SDR, DDR, or Rambus); whether the system can detect memory errors; the speed of the memory bus; the size and kind of secondary memory cache; the type, speed, and operating mode of the expansion bus; whether you can plug a video board into an Accelerated Graphics Port in your computer; the mass-storage interfaces available on the motherboard and the speed at which they operate; the ports available on your mother-board; and whether your computer has a built-in network adapter. That's a lot of power packed into a few chips—and a good reason for wondering what you have in your computer.

Background

The functions needed to make a microprocessor into a computer reads like a laundry list for a three-ring circus—long and exotic, with a trace of the unexpected. A fully opera-tional computer requires a clock or oscillator to generate the signals that lock the circuits together; a memory mastermind that ensures each byte goes to the proper place and stays there; a traffic cop for the expansion bus and other interconnecting circuitry to control the flow of data in and out of the chip and the rest of the system; office-assistant circuits for taking care of the daily routines and lifting the responsibility for minor chores from the microprocessor; and, in most modern computers, communications, video, and audio circuitry that let you and the computer deal with one another like rational beings.

Every computer manufactured since the first amphibians crawled from the primeval swamp has required these functions, although in the earliest computers they did not take the form of a chipset. The micro-miniaturization technology was nascent, and the need for combining so many functions in so small a package was negligible. Instead, computer engineers built the required functions from a variety of discrete circuits—small, general-purpose integrated circuits such as logic gates—and a few functional blocks, which are larger integrated circuits designed to a particular purpose but not necessarily one that had anything to do with computers. These garden-variety circuits, together termed *support chips*, were combined to build all the necessary computer functions into the first computer. The modern chipset not only combines these support functions onto a single silicon slice but also adds features beyond the dreams of the first computer's designers—things such as USB ports, surround-sound systems, and power-management circuits. This all-in-one design makes for simpler and far cheaper computers.

Trivial as it seems, encapsulating a piece of silicon in an epoxy plastic package is one of the more expensive parts of making chips. For chipmakers, it's much more expensive than adding more functions to the silicon itself. The more functions the chipmaker puts on a single chip, the less each function costs. Those savings dribble down to computer-makers and, eventually, you. Moreover, designing a computer motherboard with discrete support circuitry was a true engineering challenge because it required a deep understanding of the electronic function of all the elements of a computer. Using a chipset, a computer engi-neer need only be concerned with the signals going in and out of a few components. The chipset might be a magical black box for all the designer cares. In fact, in many cases the only skill required to design a computer from a chipset is the ability to navigate from a roadmap. Most chipset manufacturers provide circuit designs for motherboards to aid in the evaluation of their products. Many motherboard manufacturers (all too many, perhaps) simply take the chipset-maker's evaluation design and turn it into a commercial product.

You can trace the chipset genealogy all the way back to the first computer. This heritage results from the simple need for compatibility. Today's computers mimic the function of the earliest computers—and IBM's original Personal Computer of 1981 in particular—so that they can all run the same software. Although seemingly anachronistic in an age when those who can remember the first computer also harbor memories of Desotos and dinosaurs, even the most current chipsets must precisely mimic the actions of early computers so that the oldest software will still operate properly in new computers—provided, of course, all the other required support is also present. After all, some Neanderthal will set switchboards glowing from I-95 to the Silicon Valley with threats of lawsuits and aspersions about the parenthood of chipset designers when the DOS utilities he downloaded in 1982 won't run on his new Pentium 4.

Functions

No matter how simple or elaborate the chipset in a modern computer, it has three chief functions. It must act as a *system controller* that holds together the entire computer, giving all the support the microprocessor needs to be a true computer system. As a *memory controller*, it links the microprocessor to the memory system, establishes the main memory and cache architectures, and ensures the reliability of the data stashed away in RAM chips. And to extend the reach of the microprocessor to other system components, it must act as a *peripheral controller* and operate input/output ports and disk interfaces.

How these functions get divided among silicon chips and the terminology describing the chips has itself evolved.

When computers first took their current form, incorporating the PCI system for linking components together, engineers lumped the system and memory functions together as a unit they called the *north bridge*. Intel sometimes uses the term *host bridge* to indicate the same function. The peripheral control functions make up the *south bridge*, sometimes called the *I/O bridge*. The circuits that controlled the expansion bus often were grouped together with the north bridge or as a separate chip termed the *PCI bridge*.

Intel has reworked its design and nomenclature to make the main liaison with the microprocessor into the *memory controller hub*. This chip includes the essential support functions of the north bridge. It provides a wide, fast data pathway to memory and to the system's video circuitry.

The *I/O controller hub* takes over all the other interface functions of the chipset, including control of the expansion bus, all disks, all ports, and sound and power management. The host controller provides a high-speed connection between the I/O controller hub and the microprocessor.

The memory control hub links to the microprocessor through its system bus, sometimes termed the *front side bus*, which provides the highest speed linkup available to peripheral circuits. The logic inside the memory control hub translates the microprocessor's address requests, pumped down the system bus as address cycles, into the form used by the memory in the system. Because memory modules differ in their bus connections, the memory hub controller circuitry determines what kind of memory can connect to the system. Some memory hub controllers, for example, link only to Rambus memory, whereas others may use double data-rate (DDR) modules.

Although the connection with graphics circuitry naturally is a part of the input/output system of a computer, the modern chipset design puts the link in the memory hub controller. Video displays involve moving around large blocks of memory, and the memory host controller provides the highest-speed connection with the microprocessor, speeding video access and screen updates. In addition, the design of the current video interconnection standard, accelerated graphics port (AGP), uses a *memory aperture* to transfer bytes between the microprocessor and the frame buffer (the memory that stores the image on the display screen). Accessing this aperture is easiest and most direct through the memory controller.

The I/O hub controller generates all the signals used for controlling the microprocessor and the operation of the computer. It doesn't tell the microprocessor what instructions to execute. Rather, it sets the speed of the system by governing the various clocks in the computer, it manages the microprocessor's power usage (as well as that of the rest of the computer), and it tells the microprocessor when to interrupt one task and switch to another or give a piece of hardware immediate attention. These are all system-control functions, once the province of a dedicated system controller chip.

In addition, the I/O hub controller provides both the internal and external links to the rest of the computer and its peripherals, its true input/output function. It controls the computer's expansion bus (which not only generates the signals for the expansion slots for add-in cards but also provides the high-speed hark disk interface), all the ports (including USB), and network connections. Audio circuitry is sometimes built in to the I/O hub controller, again linking through the expansion bus circuitry.

Memory Control

Memory speed is one of the most important factors in determining the speed of a computer. If a microprocessor cannot get the data and program code it needs, it has to wait.

Using the right kind of memory and controlling it effectively are both issues governed by the chipset.

Handling memory for today's chipsets is actually easier than a few years ago. When computer-makers first stated using memory caches to improve system performance, they thrust the responsibility for managing the cache on the chipset. But with the current generation of microprocessors, cache management has been integrated with the microprocessor. The chipset only needs to provide the microprocessors access to main memory through its system bus.

Addressing

To a microprocessor, accessing memory couldn't be simpler. It just needs to activate the proper combination of address lines to indicate a storage location and then read its contents or write a new value. The address is a simple binary code that uses the available address lines, essentially a 64-bit code with a Pentium-level microprocessor.

Unfortunately, the 64-bit code of the microprocessor is completely unintelligible to memory chips and modules. Semiconductor-makers design their memory chips so that they will fit any application, regardless of the addressing of the microprocessor or even whether they link to a microprocessor. Chips, with a few megabytes of storage at most, have no need for gigabyte addressability. They need only a sufficient number of addresses to put their entire contents—and nothing more—online.

Translating between the addresses and storage format used by a microprocessor and the format used by memory chips and modules is the job of the *memory decoder*. This chip (or, in the case of chipsets, function) determines not only the logical arrangement of memory, but also how much and what kind of memory a computer can use.

The memory functions of modern chipsets determine the basic timing of the memory system, controlling which signals in the memory system are active at each instant for any given function. The ability to adjust these timing values determines the memory technology that a computer can use. For example, early chipsets timed their signals to match Synchronous Dynamic Random Access Memory (SDRAM) memory chips. High-performance chipsets need to address Rambus memory and double-data rate memory, which use not only a different addressing system but also an entirely different access technology.

In addition, the chipset determines how much memory a computer can possibly handle. Although a current microprocessor such as the Pentium 4 can physically address up to 64GB of memory, modern chipsets do not support the full range of microprocessor addresses. Most current Intel chipsets, for example, address only up to 2GB of physical memory. Not that Intel's engineers want to slight you—they have not purposely short-changed you. The paltry memory capacity is a result of physical limits of the high-speed memory buses. The distance that the signals can travel at today's memory speed is severely limited, which constrains how many memory packages can fit near enough to the chipset. Intel actually provides two channels on its Rambus chipsets, doubling the capacity that otherwise would be available through a Rambus connection.

Refreshing

Most memory chips that use current technologies require periodic refreshing of their storage. That is, the tiny charge they store tends to drain away. Refreshing recharges each memory cell. Although memory chips handle the process of recharging themselves, they need to coordinate the refresh operation with the rest of the computer. Your computer cannot access the bits in storage while they are being refreshed.

The chipset is in charge of signaling memory when to refresh. Typically the chipset sends a signal to your system's memory at a preset interval that's chosen by the computer's designer. With SDRAM memory and current chipsets, the refresh interval is usually 15.6 microseconds.

Memory can also *self-refresh*, triggering its own refresh when necessary. Self-refresh becomes desirable when a system powers down to one of its sleep modes, during which memory access is suspended along with microprocessor operation, and even the major portions of the chipset switch off. Operating in this way, self-refresh preserves the contents of memory while reducing the power required for the chipset.

Error Handling

Computers, for which the integrity of their data is paramount, use memory systems with error detection or error correction. The chipset manages the error-detection and error-correction processes.

Early personal computers relied on simple error detection, in which your computer warned when an error changed the contents of memory (unfortunately "warning" usually meant shutting down your computer). Current systems use an *error-correction code* (ECC), extra information added to that sent into memory through which the change of a stored bit can be precisely identified and repaired. The chipset adds the ECC to the data sent to memory, an extra eight bits for every eight bytes of data stored. When the chipset later reads back those eight bytes, it checks the ECC before passing the bytes on to your microprocessor. If a single bit is in error, the ECC identifies it, and the chipset restores the correct bit. If an error occurs in more than one bit, the offending bits cannot be repaired, but the chipset can warn that they have changed.

ECC is a programmable feature of most chipsets. Depending on the design of your computer, it can be permanently set on or off at the factory, or you may be able to switch it on and off through your system's advanced setup procedure. Simply switching ECC on doesn't automatically make your computer's memory more secure. An ECC system requires that your computer have special ECC memory modules installed.

System Control

The basic function of a chipset is to turn a chip into a computer, to add what a microprocessor needs to be an entire computer system. Not just any computer. You expect your computer to match the prevailing industry standards so that it can run as wide a variety of software as possible. You don't want surprises, such as your screen freezing when you try to install an application recommended by a friend. No matter what program you buy, borrow, or steal, you want it to find all the features it needs in your computer.

To assure you this level of compatibility, nearly all the functions of the system controller in a computer chipset are well defined and for the most part standardized. In nearly all computers, the most basic of these functions use the same means of access and control—the ports and memory locations match those used by the very first computers. You might, after all, want to load an old DOS program to balance your checkbook. Some people actually do it, dredging up programs that put roughshod white characters on a black screen, flashing a white block cursor at them that demand they type a command. A few people even attempt to balance their checkbooks.

Some features of the modern chipset exactly mimic the handful of discrete logic circuits that were put together to make the very first personal computer, cobwebs and all. Although many of these features are ignored by modern hardware and software, they continue as a vestigial part of all systems, sort of like an appendix.

Timing Circuits

Although anarchy has much to recommend should you believe in individual freedom or sell firearms, it's an anathema to computer circuits. Today's data-processing designs depend on organization and controlled cooperation—factors that make timing critical. The meaning of each pulse passing through a computer depends to a large degree on time relationships. Signals must be passed between circuits at just the right moment for the entire system to work properly.

Timing is critical in computers because of their clocked logic. The circuit element that sends out timing pulses to keep everything synchronized is called a *clock*. Today's computers don't have just one clock, however. They have several, each for a specific purpose. Among these are the system clock, the bus clock, the video clock, and even a real-time clock.

The *system clock* is the conductor who beats the time that all the circuits follow, sending out special timing pulses at precisely controlled intervals. The clock, however, must get its cues from somewhere, either its own internal sense of timing or some kind of metronome. Most clocks in electronic circuits derive their beats from oscillators.

Oscillators

An electronic circuit that accurately and continuously beats time is termed an *oscillator*. Most oscillators work on a simple feedback principle. Like the microphone that picks up its own sounds from public address speakers too near or turned up too high, the oscillator, too, listens to what it says. As with the acoustic-feedback squeal that the public address system complains with, the oscillator, too, generates it own howl. Because the feedback circuit is much shorter, however, the signal need not travel as far and the resulting frequency is higher, perhaps by several thousand-fold.

The oscillator takes its output as its input, then amplifies the signal, sends it to its output, where it goes back to the input again in an endless and out-of-control loop. The oscillator is tamed by adding impediments to the feedback loop, through special electronic components added between the oscillator's output and its input. The feedback and its frequency can thus be brought under control.

In nearly all computers a carefully crafted crystal of quartz is used as this frequency-control element. Quartz is one of many piezoelectric compounds. Piezoelectric materials have an interesting property—if you bend a piezoelectric crystal, it generates a tiny voltage. What's more, if you apply a voltage to it in the right way, the piezoelectric material bends.

Quartz crystals do exactly that. But beyond this simple stimulus/response relationship, quartz crystals offer another important property. By stringently controlling the size and shape of a quartz crystal, it can be made to resonate at a specific frequency. The frequency of this resonance is extremely stable and very reliable—so much so that it can help an electric watch keep time to within seconds a month. Although computers don't need the absolute precision of a quartz watch to operate their logic circuits properly, the fundamental stability of the quartz oscillator guarantees that the computer operates at a clock frequency within the design limits always available to it.

The various clocks in a computer can operate separately, or they may be locked together. Most computers link these frequencies together, synchronizing them. They may all originate in a single oscillator and use special circuits such as *frequency dividers*, which reduce the oscillation rate by a selectable factor, or *frequency multipliers*, which increase it. For example, a computer may have a 133MHz oscillator that directly controls the memory system. A frequency divider may reduce that to one-quarter the rate to run the PCI bus, and another divider may reduce it by 24 to produce the clock for the ISA legacy bus, should the computer have one.

To go the other way, a frequency multiplier can boost the oscillator frequency to a higher value, doubling the 133MHz clock to 266MHz or raising it to some other multiple.

Because all the frequencies created through frequency division and multiplication originate in a single clock signal, they are automatically synchronized. Even the most minute variations in the original clock are reflected in all those derived from it.

Some sections of computers operate asynchronously using their own clocks. For example, the scan rate used by your computer's video system usually is derived from a separate oscillator on the video board. In fact, some video boards have multiple oscillators for different scan rates. Some computers may even have separate clocks for their basic system board functions and run their buses asynchronously from their memory and microprocessor. For keeping track of the date, most computers have dedicated real-time clocks that are essentially a digital Timex grafted into its chipset.

Although engineers can build the various oscillators needed in a computer into the chipset—only the crystal in its large metal can must reside outside—the current design trend is to generate the needed frequencies outside the chipset. Separate circuits provide the needed oscillators and send their signals to the chipset (and elsewhere in the computer) to keep everything operating at the right rates.

System Clocks

Current Intel chipsets use eight different clock frequencies in their everyday operation. They are used for everything from sampling sounds to passing bytes through your computer's ports.

What Intel calls the *oscillator clock* operates at an odd-sounding 14.31818MHz rate. This strange frequency is a carryover from the first personal computer, locked to four times the 3.58MHz subcarrier frequency used to put color in images in analog television signals. The engineers who created the original computer thought compatibility with televisions would be an important design element of the computer—they thought you might use one instead of a dedicated monitor. Rather than anticipating multimedia, they were looking for a cheap way of putting computer images onscreen. When the computer was released, no inexpensive color computer monitors were available (or necessary because color graphic software was almost nonexistent). Making computers work with color televisions seemed an expedient way of creating computer graphics.

The TV-as-monitor never really caught on, but the 14.31818MHz frequency persists, but not for motherboard television circuits. Instead, the chipset locks onto this frequency and slices it down to 1.19MHz to serve as the timebase for the computer's timer/counter circuit.

Because the chipset serves as the PCI bus controller, it also needs a precision reference from which to generate the timing signals used by the PCI bus. The *PCI clock* provides what's needed: a 33MHz signal. In addition, current Intel chipsets also need another clock for the PCI bus, *CLK66*, which operates at 66MHz. These two signals are usually derived from the same timebase, keeping them exactly synchronized. Typically a 66MHz may be divided down to 33MHz.

New chipsets require a *USB clock*, an oscillator that provides the operating frequency for the Universal Serial Bus (USB) port circuitry in the chipset, to develop the signals that let you connect peripherals to your computer. This clock operates at 48MHz. It can be divided down to 12MHz for USB 1.1 signals or multiplied up to 480MHz for USB 2.0.

Intel's current chipsets have built-in audio capabilities, designed to follow the AC97 audio standard. The chipsets use the *AC97 Bit Clock* as a timebase for digital audio sampling. The required clock operating frequency is 12.288MHz. It is usually supplied by the audio codec (coder/decoder), which performs the digital-to-analog and analog-to-digital conversion on the purely digital audio signals used by the chipset. A single source for this frequency ensures that the chipset and codec stay synchronized.

The Advanced Programmable Interrupt Controller (APIC) system used by the PCI bus sends messages on its own bus conductors. The *APIC clock* provides a clocking signal (its rising edge indicates when data on the APIC bus is valid). According to Intel's specifications, its chipsets accept APIC clocks operating at up to 33.3MHz (for example, a signal derived from the PCI bus clock).

The *SMBus clock* is one of the standard signals of the System Management Bus. All SMBus interfaces use two signals for carrying data: a data signal and the clock signal. The chipset provides this standard clock signal to properly pace the data and indicate when it is valid.

Current Intel chipsets integrate a standard Ethernet local area network controller into their circuitry, designed to work with an external module called *LAN Connect*, which provides both the physical interface for the network as well as a clock signal for the chipset's LAN circuitry. The *LAN I/F clock* operates at one-half the frequency of the network carrier, either 5 or 50MHz under current standards.

Real-Time Clock

The first computers tracked time only when they were awake and running, simply counting the ticks of their timers. Every time you booted up, your computer asked you the time to set its clock. To lift that heavy chore from your shoulders, all personal computers built since 1984 have a built-in real-time clock among their support circuits. It's like your computer is wearing its own wristwatch (but, all too often, not as accurate).

All these built-in real-time clocks trace their heritage back to a specific clock circuit, the Motorola MC146818, essentially an arbitrary choice that IBM's engineers made in designing the personal computer AT. No computer has used the MC146818 chip in over a decade, but chipsets usually include circuitry patterned after the MC146818 to achieve full compatibility with older computers.

The real-time clocks have their own timebases, typically an oscillator built into the chip, one that's independent from the other clocks in a computer. The oscillator (and even the entire clock) may be external to the chipset. Intel's current design puts all the real-time-clock circuitry, including the oscillator, inside the chipset. To be operational it requires only a handful of discrete components and a crystal tuned to a frequency of 32.768 KHz. A battery supplies current to this clock circuitry (and only this clock circuitry) when your computer is switched off—to keep accurate time, this clock must run constantly.

The battery often is not enough to ensure the accuracy of the real-time clock. Although it should be as accurate as a digital watch (its circuitry is nothing more than a digital watch in a different form), many tell time as imaginatively as a four-year old child. One reason is that although a quartz oscillator is excellent at maintaining a constant frequency, that frequency may not be the one required to keep time correctly. Some computers have trimmers for adjusting the frequency of their real-time clocks, but their manufacturers sometimes don't think to adjust them properly.

In many computers, a trimmer (an adjustable capacitor), in series with a quartz crystal, allows the manufacturer—or anyone with a screwdriver—to alter the resonate frequency of the oscillator. Giving the trimmer a tweak can bring the real-time clock closer to reality—or further into the twilight zone. (You can find the trimmer by looking for the short cylinder with a slotted shaft in the center near the clock crystal, which is usually the only one in a computer with a kilohertz rather than megahertz rating.) There are many other solutions to clock inaccuracy. The best is to regularly run a program that synchronizes your clock with that of the National Institute of Standards and Technology's atomic clock, the official U.S. time standard. You can download this time-setting program from the NIST Web site at `tf.nist.gov/timefreq/service/its.htm`.

The real-time clocks in many computers are also sensitive to the battery voltage. When the CMOS backup battery is nearing failure, the real-time clock may go wildly awry. If your computer keeps good time for a while (months or years) and then suddenly wakes up hours or days off, try replacing your computer's CMOS backup battery.

The real-time clock chip first installed in early computers also had a built-in alarm function, which has been carried into the real-time clocks of new computers. As with the rest of the real-time clock, the alarm function runs from the battery supply so it can operate while your computer is switched off. This alarm can thus generate an interrupt at the appropriate time to start or stop a program or process. In some systems, it can even cause your computer to switch at a preset time. Throw a WAV file of the national anthem in your startup folder, and you'll have a truly patriotic alarm clock.

The clock circuitry also includes 128 bytes of low-power CMOS memory that is used to store configuration information. This is discussed in the next chapter.

Timers

In addition to the clock in your computer—both the oscillators and the real-time clock—you'll find *timers*. Digitally speaking, computer timers are simply counters. They count pulses received by an oscillator and then perform some action when they achieve a preset value. These timers serve two important functions. They maintain the real time for your computer separately from the dedicated real-time clock, and they signal the time to refresh memory. Also, they generate the sounds that come from the tiny speakers of computers that lack multimedia pretensions.

The original IBM personal computer used a simple timer chip for these functions, specifically chip type 8253. Although this chip would be as foreign in a modern computer as a smudge pot or buggy whip, modern chipsets emulate an updated version of that timer chip, the 8254. The system timer counts pulses from the 1.19MHz clock (that the chipset derives from the 14.31818MHz system clock) and divides them down to the actual frequencies it needs (for example, to make a beep of the right pitch).

The timer works simply. You load one of its registers with a number, and it counts to that number. When it reaches the number, it outputs a pulse and starts all over again. Load a 8254 register with 2, and it sends out a pulse at half the frequency of the input. Load it with 1000, and the output becomes 1/1000th the input. In this mode, the chip (real or emulated) can generate an interrupt at any of a wide range of user-defined intervals. Because the highest value you can load into its 16-bit register is 2^{16} or 65,536, the longest single interval it can count is about .055 seconds (that is, the 1.19MHz input signal divided by 65,536).

The timer circuitry actually had six operating modes, all of which are carried through on modern computers. Table 6.1 lists these modes.

TABLE 6.1　Operating Modes of the 8253 Timer/Counter Chip

Name	Operation
Interrupt on Terminal Count	The timer is loaded with a value and counts down from that value to zero, one counter per clock pulse.
Hardware Retriggerable One-Shot	A trigger pulse causes timer output to go low; when the counter reaches zero, the output goes high and stays high until reset. The process repeats every time it's triggered. The pulse length is set by writing a control word and initial count to chip before the first cycle.
Rate Generator	The timer divides incoming frequency by the value of the initial count loaded into it.

Name	Operation
Square Wave	Produces a series of square waves with a period (measured in clock pulses) equal to the value loaded into the timer.
Software Retriggerable Strobe	The timer counts down the number of clock cycles loaded into it; then it pulses its output. Software starts the next cycle.
Hardware Retriggerable Strobe	The timer counts down the number of clock cycles loaded into it; then it pulses its output. A hardware-generated pulse initiates the next cycle.

The real-time signal of the timer counts out its longest possible increment, generating pulses at a rate of 18.2 per second. The pulses cause the real-time interrupt, which the computer counts to keep track of the time. These interrupts can also be used by programs that need to regularly investigate what the computer is doing; for instance, checking the hour to see whether it's time to dial up a distant computer.

The speaker section of the timer system works the same way, only it generates a square wave that is routed through an amplifier to the internal speaker of the computer to make primitive sounds. Programs can modify any of its settings to change the pitch of the tone, and with clever programming, its timbre.

In modern computers, the memory controller in the chipset rather than the system timer handles refresh operations. Otherwise, the timer functions are much the same as they were with the first computers, and the same signals are available to programmers.

Interrupt Control

Timers and strange oscillator frequencies aren't the only place where computers show their primitive heritage. Modern machines also carry over the old interrupt and direct memory access systems of the first personal computers, and it's the chipset's job to emulate these old functions. Most are left over from the design of the original PC expansion bus that became enshrined as Industry Standard Architecture. Although the newest computers don't have any ISA slots, they need to incorporate the ISA functions for full compatibility with old software.

The hardware interrupts that signal microprocessors to shift their attention originate outside the chip. In the first personal computers, a *programmable interrupt controller* funneled requests for interrupts from hardware devices to the microprocessor. The first personal computer design used a type 8259A interrupt controller chip that accepted eight hardware interrupt signals. The needs of even basic computers quickly swallowed up those eight interrupts, so the engineers who designed the next generation of computers added a second 8259A chip. The interrupts from the new chip cascade into one interrupt input of the old one. That is, the new chip consolidates the signals of eight interrupts and sends them to one of the interrupt inputs of the chip used in the original design. The eight new interrupts, combined with the seven remaining on the old chip, yield a total of 15 available hardware interrupts.

The PCI bus does not use this interrupt structure, substituting a newer design that uses a four-wire system with serialized interrupts (discussed in Chapter 9, "Expansion Buses").

The PCI system uses four interrupt lines, and the function of each is left up to the designer of each individual expansion board. The PCI specification puts no limits on how these interrupt signals are used (the software driver that services the board determines that) but specifies level-sensitive interrupts so that the four signals can be reliably shared. However, all computers that maintain an ISA legacy bus—which currently includes nearly all computers—mimic this design for compatibility reasons. Several legacy functions, such as the keyboard controller, legacy ports, real-time clock, and IDE disk drives still use these interrupts.

In this legacy scheme, each interrupt is assigned a priority, the more important one getting attention before those of lesser importance. In the original computer scheme of things with eight interrupts, the lower the number assigned to an interrupt, the most priority it got. The two-stage design in current systems, however, abridges the rule.

In the current cascade design, the second interrupt controller links to the input of the first controller that was assigned to interrupt 2 (IRQ2). Consequently, *every* interrupt on the second controller (that is, numbers 8 through 15) has a higher priority than those on the first controller that are numbered higher than 2. The hardware-based priorities of interrupts in current computers therefore ranges as listed in Table 6.2, along with the functions that usually use those interrupts.

TABLE 6.2   The Priorities of Interrupts

Interrupt Number	Priority	Function
IRQ0	1	Timer output 0
IRQ1	2	Keyboard (buffer full)
IRQ2	Unusable	Cascade from IRQ9
IRQ3	11	Serial port 2, serial port 4, SDLC communications, BSC communications, cluster adapter, network (alternate), 3278/79 (alternate)
IRQ4	12	Serial port 1, serial port 3, SDLC communications, BSC communications, voice communications adapter
IRQ5	13	Parallel port 2, audio

Interrupt Number	Priority	Function
IRQ6	14	Floppy disk controller
IRQ7	15	Parallel port 1, cluster adapter (alternate)
IRQ8	3	Real-time clock
IRQ9	4	Software redirected to INT 0A(hex), video, network, 3278/79 adapter
IRQ10	5	Reserved
IRQ11	6	Reserved
IRQ12	7	Reserved, built-in mouse
IRQ13	8	Coprocessor
IRQ14	9	Primary hard disk controller (IDE)
IRQ15	10	Secondary hard disk controller

The original Plug-and-Play configuration system altered how computers assign interrupt numbers, making the assignments automatically without regard to the traditional values. In these systems, interrupt values and the resulting priorities get assigned dynamically when the computer configures itself. The values depend on the combination of hardware devices installed in the such systems. Although the standardized step-by-step nature of Plug-and-Play and its Advanced Configuration and Power Interface (ACPI) successor usually assign the same interrupt value to the same devices in a given computer each time that computer boots up, it doesn't have to. Interrupt values *could* (but usually do not) change day to day.

A few interrupt assignments are inviolable. In all systems, four interrupts can never be used for expansion devices. These include IRQ0, used by the timer/counter; IRQ1, used by the keyboard controller; IRQ2, the cascade point for the upper interrupts (which is redirected to IRQ9); and IRQ8, used by the real-time clock. In addition, all modern computers have microprocessors with integral floating-point units (FPUs) or accept external FPUs, both of which use IRQ13.

If you want to know what's what, you can check interrupt assignment through Windows. To view the actual interrupt usage of your computer, you need to consult the Device Manager, available through the System icon in Control Panel. In Device Manager, select View, Resources from the drop-down menu or (under Windows 95, 98, and Me) the View Resources tab. Select your computer on the Device menu and click the Properties button. Click the Interrupt Request menu selection or radio button (depending on your version of Windows), and you'll see a list of the actual interrupt assignments in use in your computer, akin what's shown in Figure 6.1.

FIGURE 6.1

Windows Device Manager showing actual interrupt assignments.

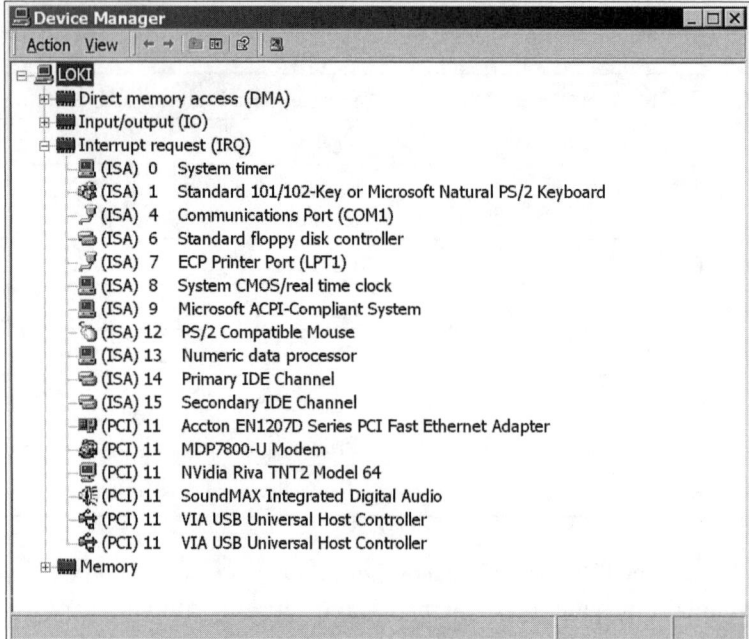

Although 15 interrupts seem like a lot, this number is nowhere near enough to give every device in a modern computer its own interrupt. Fortunately, engineers found ways to let devices share interrupts. Although interrupt sharing is possible even with the older computer designs, interrupt sharing works best when the expansion bus and its support circuitry are designed from the start for sharing. The PCI system was; ISA was not.

When an interrupt is shared, each device that's sharing a given interrupt uses the same hardware interrupt request line to signal to the microprocessor. The interrupt-handling software or firmware then directs the microprocessor for the action to take to service the device making the interrupt. The interrupt handler distinguishes between the various devices sharing the interrupt to ensure only the right routine gets carried out.

Although software or firmware actually sorts out the sharing of interrupts, a computer expansion bus needs to be properly designed to make the sharing reliable. Old bus designs such as the ISA legacy bus use *edge-triggered* interrupts, a technique that is particularly prone to sharing problems. Modern systems use a different technology, *level-sensitive* interrupts, which avoids some of the pitfalls of the older technique.

An edge-triggered interrupt signals the interrupt condition as the transition of the voltage on the interrupt line from one state to another. Only the change—the edge of the waveform—is significant. The interrupt signal needs only to be a pulse, after which the interrupt line returns to its idle state. A problem arises if a second device sends another pulse down the interrupt line before the first has been fully processed. The system may lose track of the interrupts it is serving.

A level-sensitive interrupt signals the interrupt condition by shifting the voltage on the interrupt request line (for example, from low to high). It then maintains that shifted condition throughout the processing of the interrupt. It effectively ties up the interrupt line during the processing of the interrupt so that no other device can get attention through that interrupt line. Although it would seem that one device would hog the interrupt line and not share with anyone, the presence of the signal on the line effectively warns other devices to wait before sending out their own interrupt requests. This way, interrupts are less likely to be confused.

Direct Memory Access

The best way to speed up system performance is to relieve the host microprocessor of all its housekeeping chores. Among the more time consuming is moving blocks of memory around inside the computer; for instance, shifting bytes from a hard disk (where they are stored) through its controller into main memory (where the microprocessor can use them). Today's system designs allow computers to delegate this chore to support chips and expansion boards (for example, through bus mastering). Before such innovations, when the microprocessor was in total control of the computer, engineers developed Direct Memory Access (DMA) technology to relieve the load on the microprocessor by allowing a special device called the *DMA controller* to manage some device-to-memory transfers.

DMA was an integral part of the ISA bus design. Even though PCI lacks DMA features (and soon computers will entirely lack ISA slots), DMA technology survives in motherboard circuitry and the ATA disk interface. Consequently, the DMA function has been carried through into modern chipsets.

DMA functions through the DMA controller. This specialized chip only needs to know the base location of where bytes are to be moved from, the address to where they should go, and the number of bytes to move. Once it has received that information from the microprocessor, the DMA controller takes command and does all the dirty work itself. DMA operations can be used to move data between I/O devices and memory. Although DMA operations could in theory also expedite the transfer of data between memory locations, this mode of operation was not implemented in computers.

The current DMA system offers seven channels, based on the design of the IBM personal computer AT, which used a pair of type 8237A DMA controller chips. As with the interrupt system, the prototype DMA system emulated by modern chipsets used two four-channel DMA controllers, one cascaded into the other. Each DMA channel is 16 bits wide. Table 6.3 summarizes the functions commonly assigned to the seven DMA channels.

TABLE 6.3   DMA Assignments of a Modern Motherboard

DMA Channel	Data Width	Function
0	8 or 16 bits	Audio
1	8 or 16 bits	Audio or LAN
2	8 or 16 bits	Floppy disk
3	8 or 16 bits	ECP/EPP port
4	16 bits	Cascade channel
5	16 bits	Not assigned
6	16 bits	Not assigned
7	16 bits	ISA IDE

You can check the DMA assignment of your computer much as you do interrupts, through the Device Manager. Simply select DMA from the drop-down menu or radio button instead of Interrupts. You should see your computer's current DMA assignments, listed much like Figure 6.2.

FIGURE 6.2

Windows Device Manager showing DMA usage.

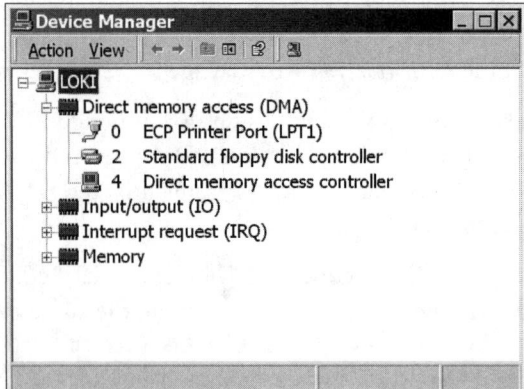

In general, individual tasks use only one DMA channel at a time. When you run multiple tasks at the same time, nothing changes under Windows 95, 98, or Me, because they serialize I/O. That means those operating systems handle only one I/O task at a time and switch between them. Only a single path for data is available. In rare instances, however, a path may have a DMA channel at both ends (which puts two channels into operation simultaneously). Windows NT and 2000 know no such limits and can run multiple I/O tasks and use multiple DMA channels.

Bus Interface

In early computers, the expansion bus was nothing more than an extension of the connections on the microprocessor. In modern designs, the bus is a free-standing entity with its own *bus controller* separate from the microprocessor. In fact, the microprocessor connects to the bus as if it were just another expansion device. All modern chipsets use this latter design to control the expansion bus. Not only does the chipset take on the management of the PCI bus, but it also uses this decentralized control system for the legacy ISA bus, should one be used in your computer. The chipset takes over the role of the microprocessor in the traditional ISA system. In fact, the entire ISA bus gets treated as if it were just another PCI device.

The *PCI bridge* in the chipset handles all the functions of the PCI bus. Circuitry built in to the PCI bridge, independent of the host microprocessor, operates as a *DMA master.* When a program or the operating system requests a DMA transfer, the DMA master intercepts the signal. It translates the commands bound for the 8237A DMA controller in older computers into signals compatible with the PCI design. These signals are routed through the PCI bus to a DMA slave, which may in turn be connected to the ISA compatibility bus, PCMCIA bus, disk drives, or I/O ports in the system. The DMA slave interprets the instructions from the DMA master and carries them out as if it were an ordinary DMA controller.

In other words, to your software the DMA master looks like a pair of 8237A DMA controller chips. Your hardware sees the DMA slave as an 8237A that's in control. The signal translations to make this mimicry possible are built in to the PCI bridges in the chipset.

Power Management

To economize on power to meet Energy Star standards or prolong the period of operation on a single battery charge, most chipsets—especially those designed for notebook computers—incorporate power-management abilities. These include both manual power control, which lets you slow your computer or suspend its operation, and automatic control, which reduces power similarly when it detects system inactivity lasting for more than a predetermined period.

Typically, when a chipset switches to standby state, it will instruct the microprocessor to shift to its low-power mode, spin down the hard disk, and switch off the monitor. In standby mode, the chipset itself stays in operation to monitor for alarms, communications requests (answering the phone or receiving a fax), and network accesses. In suspend mode, the chipset itself shuts down until you reactivate it, and your computer goes into a vegetative state.

By design, most new chipsets conform to a variety of standards. They take advantage of the System Management Mode of recent Intel microprocessors and use interrupts to direct the power conservation.

Peripheral Control

If your computer didn't have a keyboard, it might be less intimidating, but you probably wouldn't find it very useful. You might make do, drawing pictures with your mouse or trying to teach it to recognize your handwriting, but some devices are so integral to using a computer that you naturally expect them to be a part of it. The list of these mandatory components includes the keyboard (naturally), a mouse, a hard disk, a CD drive, ports, and a display system. Each of these devices requires its own connection system or interface. In early computers, each interface used a separate expansion board that plugged into a slot in the computer. Worse than that, you often had to do the plugging.

You probably don't like the sound of such a system, and computer manufacturers liked it even less. Individual boards were expensive and, with most people likely not as capable as you in plugging in boards, not very reliable. Clever engineers found a clever way to avoid both the problems and expenses. They built the required interfaces into the chipset. At one time, all these functions were built into a single chip called the *peripheral controller*, an apt description of its purpose. Intel's current chipset design scheme puts all the peripheral control functions inside the I/O controller hub.

As with the system-control functions, most of the peripheral interface functions are well-defined standards that have been in use for years. The time-proven functions usually cause few problems in the design, selection, or operation of a chipset. Some interfaces have a more recent ancestry, and if anything will cause a problem with a chipset, they will. For example, the PCI bus and ATA-133 disk interface (described in Chapter 10, "Interfaces") are newcomers when compared to the decade-old keyboard interface or even-older ISA bus. When a chipset shows teething pains, they usually arise in the circuits relating to these newer functions.

Hard Disk Interface

Most modern chipsets include all the circuitry needed to connect a hard disk to a computer, typically following an enhancement of the AT Attachment standard, such as UDMA. Although this interface is a straightforward extension of the classic ISA bus, it requires a host of control ports for its operation, all provided for in the chipset. Most chipsets now connect the ISA bus through their PCI bridges, which may or may not be an intrinsic part of the south bridge.

The chipset thus determines which modes of the AT Attachment interface your computer supports. Intel's current chipsets, for example, support all ATA modes up to and including ATA/100. They do *not* support ATA/133, so computers based on Intel chipsets cannot take full advantage of the highest speeds of the latest ATA (IDE) hard disk drives.

Floppy Disk Controller

Chipsets often include a variety of other functions to make the computer designer's life easier. These can include everything from controls for indicator lights for the front panel to floppy disk controllers. Nearly all chipsets incorporate circuitry that mimics the NEC 765 floppy disk controller used by nearly all adapter boards.

In that the basic floppy disk interface dates back to the dark days of the first computers, it is a technological dinosaur. Computer-makers desperately want to eliminate it in favor of more modern (and faster) interface alternatives. Some software, however, attempts to control the floppy disk by reaching deep into the hardware and manipulating the floppy controller directly through its powers. To maintain backward compatibility with new floppy interfaces, the chipset must still mimic this original controller and translate commands meant for it to the new interface.

Keyboard Controller

One additional support chip is necessary in every computer: a keyboard decoder. This special-purpose chip (an Intel 8042 in most computers, an equivalent chip, or part of a chipset that emulates an 8042) links the keyboard to the motherboard. The primary function of the keyboard decoder is to translate the serial data that the keyboard sends out into the parallel form that can be used by your computer. As it receives each character from the keyboard, the keyboard decoder generates an interrupt to make your computer aware you have typed a character. The keyboard decoder also verifies that the character was correctly received (by performing a parity check) and translates the scan code of each character. The keyboard decoder automatically requests the keyboard to retransmit characters that arrive with parity errors.

USB-based keyboards promise the elimination of the keyboard controller. These pass packets of predigested keyboard data through the USB port of your computer instead of through a dedicated keyboard controller. In modern system design, the keyboard controller is therefore a legacy device and may be eliminated from new systems over the next few years.

Input/Output Ports

The peripheral control circuitry of the chipset also powers most peripheral ports. Today's computers usually have legacy serial and parallel ports in addition to two or more USB connections. As with much else of the chipset design, the legacy ports mimic old designs made from discrete logic components. For example, most chipsets emulate 16550 universal asynchronous receiver/transmitters (UARTs) to operate their serial ports.

WINN L. ROSCH
HARDWARE BIBLE,
SIXTH EDITION

CHAPTER

7

BIOS

Think of the Basic Input/Output System of your computer as its crazy Aunt Maud, locked away from public eyes in a cobwebby garret. Except for the occasional deranged laughter that rings through the halls, you might never know she was there, and you don't think about her again until the next reel of the B-movie that makes up your life.

As with your own old Aunt Maud, your computer's BIOS is something that you want to forget but is always there, lingering in the background, popping into sight only at the least convenient times. Despite its idiosyncrasies and age, despite the embarrassment it causes, the BIOS is something your computer can't live without. It defines what your computer is and keeps it in line, just as Aunt Maud defines what your family really is and her antics keep you in line (or at least tangled up in obscure legal proceedings). You'd really like to be rid of Aunt Maud, but only she knows the secret of your family's jewels, a secret someday you hope you'll wrest from her.

The BIOS of your computer lingers around like that unwelcome relative, but it also holds the secrets of your computer. You can lock it up, even build a wall around it, but it will always be there. When you switch on your computer, it laughs at you from the monitor screen, appearing in the rags and tatters of text mode before your system jumps off into modern high-resolution color. Most of what you do on your computer now sidesteps the BIOS, so you'd think you could do without it. You might never suspect that behind the scenes the BIOS of your computer tests your system, assures you that everything is okay when you start your system, helps you set up your computer so that it runs at its best, and gracefully steps out of the way when you no longer need it.

Although modern operating systems such as Windows do their best to hide the BIOS and take its place, it always lurks in the background like crazy old Aunt Maud locked in the garret. Just as Aunt Maud may ruin a dinner party when she suddenly pops up babbling about a talking moose, your BIOS bursts onto the scene when you least expect it and ruins your fun (for example, hiding half of your new hard disk).

However, your Aunt Maud might just not be as crazy as she seems, watching over you quietly from her garret, hiding in the background but working in her own mysterious ways to make sure your life goes well.

Background

Although mostly invisible and oft forgotten, your computer's BIOS is nevertheless one of its most important and enabling parts. The BIOS is, in fact, the one essential constituent that distinguishes one computer from another, even when they both share the same microprocessor, motherboard, and support hardware.

Firmware

Strictly speaking, however, the BIOS isn't hardware at all, even though it is an essential part of your computer's hardware. The BIOS is special program code—in a word, *software*—that's permanently (or nearly so) encapsulated in ROM chips or, as is most often the case with newer computers, Flash memory. Because of the two-sided aspects of the BIOS, existing in the netherworld between hardware and software, it and other pieces of program code encapsulated in ROM or Flash memory are often termed *firmware*.

The importance of the BIOS arises from its function. The BIOS tests your computer every time you turn it on. It may even allocate your system's resources for you automatically, making all the adjustments necessary to accommodate new hardware. The BIOS also determines the compatibility of your computer with both hardware and software and can even determine how flexible your computer is in setup and use.

Firmware can do more. If some enterprising computer-maker wanted to, it could put the entire operating system and application software into firmware. Some portable computers actually came close—early Hewlett-Packard Omnibook sub-notebook computers packed Windows and part of Microsoft Office into their ROMs. Of course, these machines are not very useful any more. The Windows inside is version 3.0, which points out the disadvantage of putting too much into firmware—updates are cumbersome and the code-storage requirements of today's software would fill more chips than you could comfortably carry. The storage available in a computer's ROM gives engineers kilobytes to work with, not the gigabytes today's systems demand for storage of their software.

Today, firmware plays only a subsidiary role in most computers. All modern operating systems enhance the basic BIOS firmware with additional instructions loaded from disk like ordinary software—typically such enhancements totally replace the BIOS firmware. This new code supplied by the operating system performs some of the same functions as the traditional BIOS firmware, linking your computer's hardware to the software programs that you run. But every computer still requires at least a vestigial piece of BIOS firmware, if just to enable enough of your system to run so that it can load the operating system. Although the BIOS plays a less active role in every operation of your computer, it is essential to getting your computer going, and it remains an essential part of every new computer and future machines still waiting on the engineer's drawing board.

Functions

The BIOS code of most computers has a number of separate and distinct functions. The BIOS of a typical computer has routines that test the computer, blocks of data that give the machine its personality, special program routines that allow software to take control of the computer's hardware so that it can more smoothly mesh with the electronics of the system, and even a complete system (in some computers) for determining which expansion boards and peripherals you have installed and ensuring that they do not conflict in their requests for input/output ports and memory assignments. Although all these functions get stored in the same memory chips, the program code of each function is essentially independent of the rest. Each function is a separate module, and the name *BIOS* refers to the entire group of modules.

This list of functions is not an exhaustive list of what a BIOS *could* do. It represents only what the makers of current computers use the BIOS for. In fact, there's little limit on what BIOS code can do. Apple has long (since 1984) put most of the graphics of its Macintosh systems in its BIOS, and IBM for years encapsulated a small programming language in the BIOSs of its first computers.

The classic definition of the computer BIOS is the firmware that gives the computer its *personality*. This definition refers only to one functional module of the computer—the one that's invariably replaced by operating system code. The nebulous term *personality* described how the computer performed its basic functions, those necessary to make it a real computer. Although this definition included a number of different factors, including how quickly and smoothly various operations were completed, the term *personality* mostly distinguished computers from Apple Macintoshes.

Most of the personality of the computer has moved from its BIOS to the operating system, loaded entirely from disk storage into RAM. The BIOS now plays a subsidiary role. Chiefly it is in charge of getting your computer going and running things until your hard disk can disgorge the hundreds of megabytes of operating system code and software can take over control of your computer.

In most computers, the first thing the BIOS tells the microprocessor to do is to run through all the known components of the system—the microprocessor, memory, keyboard, and so on—and to test to determine whether they are operating properly. After the system is sure of its own integrity, it checks to see whether you have installed any expansion boards that hold additional BIOS code. If you have, the microprocessor checks the code and carries out any instructions it finds. A modern computer may even check to see whether any new expansion boards are plugged in without being set up properly. The BIOS code might then configure the expansion board so that it functions properly in your computer.

When the microprocessor runs out of add-in peripherals, it begins the actual bootup process, which engineers call the *Initial Program Load* (IPL). The BIOS code tells the microprocessor to jump to a section of code that tells the chip how to read the first sector of your floppy or hard disk. Program code then takes over from the BIOS and tells the microprocessor how to load the operating system from the disk to start the computer running.

Exactly what the BIOS does after the operating system loads depends on the operating system. The first computer operating system, DOS, worked in conjunction with the BIOS. DOS relied on the BIOS firmware, which includes several sets of routines that programs can call to carry out everyday functions, such as typing characters on the screen or to a printer, reading keystrokes, and timing events. Because of this basic library, programmers writing for DOS could create their grand designs without worrying about the tiny details.

With Windows, however, the BIOS gets pushed out of the way. After the BIOS has assured the operating integrity of your system, Windows takes over. First, the operating system starts loading its own boot code. Then, it installs drivers that take over the various interface functions of the BIOS, one by one.

The operating system replaces the BIOS interface routines for several reasons. Because software drivers load into RAM, they are not limited in the amount of space available for their code. Software drivers also extend the capabilities, whereas the BIOS limits them. Using only the BIOS, your computer cannot do anything that the BIOS does not know about. It enables you to use the wide variety of peripherals you're apt to connect to your computer. Moreover, because the BIOS is designed to run at bootup when your computer is in real mode, it uses only real-mode code, with all the limitations that implies (in particular, a total address space of 1MB). Software drivers can (and nowadays invariably do) run in protected mode. Not only can they access more memory, but protected mode drivers can be written in 32-bit code that executes faster on modern microprocessors.

Initialization Functions

The BIOS starts to work as soon as you switch your system on. When all modern Intel microprocessors start to work, they immediately set themselves up in real mode and look at a special memory location that is exactly 16 bytes short of the top of the 1MB real-mode addressing range—absolute address 0FFFF0(hex). This location holds a special program instruction, a jump that points to another address where the BIOS code actually begins.

The term *cold boot* describes the process of starting your computer and loading its operating system by turning the power on. If your computer is running, you cold boot by first switching it off and then back on.

Warm boot describes the process of restarting your computer and loading its operating system anew after it has already been running and has booted up at least once before. You start a warm boot by giving the infamous "three-finger salute" by pressing the Ctrl, Alt, and Delete keys at the same time.

Finally, *hot boot* describes what you get when you slide a piece of footwear into your oven in a mistaken attempt at the preparation of filet of sole. The term is not used to describe the computer bootup process.

At the operating system level, a cold boot and a warm boot are essentially the same. Your computer starts from the beginning and loads the operating system from scratch. A warm boot or switching your computer off for a cold boot signals the microprocessor to reset itself to its "turn-on" condition, erasing the contents of its registers. The microprocessor then loads or reloads the operating system.

The important difference between a cold and warm boot is not what happens to your operating system but the effect on your computer's internal circuits. A cold boot automatically restores all the circuits in your computer to their original, default condition, whether they are on the motherboard or the expansion boards, because it cuts off their electrical supply. It also wipes away everything in its memory for a fresh start. A warm boot does not affect the supply of electricity to your computer's circuitry, so memory and the boards installed in your computer are not wiped clean, although some of the contents get over-written as your operating system reloads.

Because a warm boot does not automatically restore all the expansion boards in your computer to their initial conditions, it sometimes does not solve software problems. For example, your modem may not release the telephone line (hang up) at the end of your Internet session. A warm boot may leave the modem connected, but a cold boot will ensure the modem disconnects and releases your telephone line.

Unless the boards in your computer follow the Plug-and-Play standard that specifies a standard reset condition, your computer has no way of telling the state of each board in your computer after a warm boot. It makes no attempt to find out and just takes what it gets. Ordinarily such blind acceptance is not a problem. If, however, some odd state of an expansion board caused your computer to crash, a warm boot will not solve the problem. For example, sometimes video boards will come up in odd states with strange screen displays after a crash that's followed by a warm boot. Cold-booting your computer again usually eliminates such problems.

Your computer also behaves differently during the cold- and warm-booting processes. During a cold boot, your computer runs through its Power-On Self Test (POST) procedure to test all its circuitry. During a warm boot, your computer sidesteps POST under the assumption that it has already booted up once, so its circuitry must be working properly.

Your computer must somehow distinguish between a cold and warm boot to decide whether to run its POST diagnostics. To sort things out, your computer uses its normal memory, which it does not wipe out during a warm boot. Each time your computer boots up, it plants a special two-byte signature in memory. When your system boots, it looks for the signature. If it find the signature, it knows it has been booted at least once since you turned on the power, so it does not need to run through POST. When it fails to find the signature, it runs its diagnostics as part of the cold-boot process. Note that if something in your system changes the signature bytes—as crashing programs sometimes do—your computer will run through a cold boot even though you haven't turned it off.

The signature bytes have the value 1234(hex). Because they are stored in Intel *little endian format* (that is, the least significant byte comes first), they appear in memory as the sequence 34 12.

Programs can also initiate a warm or cold boot simply by jumping to the appropriate section of BIOS code. However, because some expansion boards don't automatically reset when your computer runs through the cold-boot BIOS code, anomalies may persist after such a program-initiated cold boot. For example, your video board may place itself into an odd state, and a complete reset may not unlock it. For this reason, some programs instruct you to turn your computer off and back on during the installation process to guarantee all the hardware in your system properly resets.

Power-On Self Test

Every time your computer switches on, the BIOS immediately takes command. Its first duty is to run through a series of diagnostic routines (system checks) called the *Power-On Self Test routine*, or *POST*. This ensures every part of your computer's hardware is functioning properly before you trust your time and data to it. One by one, the POST routine checks the circuits of your system board and memory, the keyboard, your disks, and each expansion board. After the BIOS makes sure the system is operating properly, it initializes the electronics so that they are ready for the first program to load.

Error Codes

The BIOS tests are relatively simple. The BIOS sends data to a port or register and then looks to see the results. If it receives expected results, the BIOS assumes all is well. If it finds a problem, however, it reports the failure as well as it can. If the display system is working, it posts an error-code number on your monitor screen. (The limited amount of memory available prevents the BIOS from storing an elaborate—that is, *understandable*—message for all the hundreds of possible error conditions.) If your computer is so ill that the display system will not even work, the BIOS sends out a coded series of beeps through your system's loudspeaker.

Many BIOSs also write the code numbers of the ongoing tests to input/output port 80(hex). Special diagnostic boards that plug into a vacant expansion slot can monitor this test procedure and show the test progress and failure. Repair technicians often use such diagnostic boards when servicing systems.

Beep Codes

Displaying an error code on your monitor screen presupposes that at least part of your computer (and a major part at that) is operating properly—namely, the display system. If your video board or monitor is not functioning and you don't have a diagnostic board, the error code display is useless. Consequently, most BIOSs also generate error identifications that are independent of the display system.

Instead of visual displays, they use audible error codes played through the small speaker system that is standard equipment in all computers. Because the speaker system links to your computer at a rudimentary level—only a single amplifier chip stands between the speaker and its associated input/output port—the basic computer speaker will always function except during the most dire failures, such as a nonworking microprocessor. (Note that this basic computer speaker is separate from the sound board or multimedia sound system present in most new computers.) These audible error messages take the form of beeps from the system speaker. Consequently, they are usually termed *beep codes*.

As computers have become more complex, the systems of beep codes have become correspondingly elaborate. Some sound more elaborate than a Mayday call from a sinking ocean liner. Ever BIOS-maker uses its own coding scheme for these aural error warnings. Usually a single short beep means your computer is okay; anything else warns of an error.

Should your computer start with a continuous beep that won't stop until you switch the power off, your computer has a major problem, most likely with its power or logic system. Oftentimes a defective expansion board or an improperly inserted expansion board will

elicit such an unending beep. It can also result from a bad microprocessor or other motherboard problem. If you encounter a beep that won't end, check your expansion boards
first. Ensure that all are seated properly and then remove them one by one or *en masse*
until the beep quiets down. (Be sure to switch off your computer before you add or
remove an expansion board.)

BIOS Extensions

After the actual testing of your computer and its associated circuitry is complete, its BIOS
begins to execute initialization routines that configure the various options inside your
computer. Exactly what happens next depends on the design of the BIOS. A conventional
BIOS merely looks for add-in BIOS routines, initializes devices using the routines already
in the BIOS, and starts the disk bootup.

Every computer assumes that many of its peripherals are loaded with specific data values
when it starts up. That is, all the default operating values are loaded by the BIOS, so your
timer knows what to time and the speaker knows the frequency at which to beep. The serial ports are set to their default speed. A Plug-and-Play system like those of nearly all new
computers runs through a more structured initialization process that amounts to completely setting up system resources each time the computer boots. The "Plug-and-Play"
section, later in this chapter, gives a step-by-step outline of this BIOS boot procedure.

By design, the basic computer BIOS knows how to search beyond the confines of the system board. It knows how to locate the extra instructions and data that get added in with
some expansion boards. Although some computers require you to replace the BIOS
firmware with new chips to add new features, the computer BIOS was designed to be
extendible. That is, the full extent of the BIOS is not forever cast in the silicon of the
firmware. The extendible BIOS is capable of accepting additional code as its own, creating
one integrated whole. Rather than replacing the BIOS chips, this extendibility means that
you can add more firmware containing it own BIOS routines to your computer. The
BIOS incorporates the new routines into itself.

The key to making the BIOS extendible is itself an extra firmware routine that enables the
BIOS to look for add-in code. During the initialization process, the BIOS code reads
through the address range looking for code stored on add-in boards. If it finds a valid section of code, it adds those instructions to the BIOS repertory. New interrupt routines may
be added, for instance, or the function of existing routines may be changed.

The routine to extend the BIOS works as follows: Following the actual testing portion of
the Power-On Self Test, after basic system board functions have been initialized (for
example, the interrupt vectors have been loaded into RAM), the resident BIOS code
instructs the computer to check through its ROM memory for the occurrence of the special preamble bytes that mark the beginning of add-in BIOS routines. The original IBM

BIOS searches for these preamble bytes in the absolute address range 0C8000(hex) to 0F4000(hex); newer BIOSs check the range from 0C0000(hex) to 0EFFFF(hex). Either of these subsets of the full, reserved, high memory range—that is, 0A0000(hex) to 0FFFFF(hex)—exclude the areas used by video memory and the BIOS itself to prevent confusing data with preamble bytes.

If the BIOS finds the special preamble bytes, it verifies that the subsequent section of code is a legitimate BIOS extension by performing a form of cyclical redundancy check on the specified number of 512 byte blocks. The values of each byte in the block are totaled using Modulo 0100(hex) addition—the effect is the same as dividing the sum of all the bytes by 4096. A remainder of zero indicates that the extension BIOS contains valid code.

The preamble bytes take a specific form. Two bytes indicate the beginning of an extension code section—055(hex) followed by 0AA(hex). Immediately following the two-byte preamble bytes is a third byte that quantifies the length of the additional BIOS. The number represents the number of blocks, 512-bytes long, needed to hold the extra code. Plug-and-Play peripherals have a more structured header that follows the preamble bytes.

After a valid section of code is identified, system control (BIOS program execution) jumps to the fourth byte in the extension BIOS and performs any functions specified there in machine language. Typically, these instructions tell the BIOS how to install the extra code. Finally, when the instructions in the extension BIOS have been completed, control returns to the resident BIOS. The system then continues to search for additional blocks of extension BIOS. When it finally completes its search by reaching the absolute address 0F4000(hex), it starts the process of booting up your computer from disk.

The ROM or Flash memory chips containing this extra BIOS code do not have to be present on the system board. The memory locations used also are accessible on the expansion bus. This feature allows new chips that add to the BIOS to be part of expansion boards that slide into the computer. The code necessary to control the expansion accessory loads automatically whenever the system boots up.

Multiple sections of this add-on code fit into any computer, limited only by the address range available. One complication is that no two sections of code can occupy the same memory area. As a result, the makers of conventional ISA expansion boards typically incorporate jumpers, DIP switches, or EEPROM memory on their products to allow you to reassign the addresses used by their BIOS extensions and avoid conflicts. Plug-and-Play designs have made this conflict resolution automatic during the setup process.

Initial Program Load

Once the BIOS of your computer has completed all its tests, checked for additional BIOS code, and set up all the devices it knows about, it yields control over to your operating system. In older computers, the operating system simply takes over and brings your computer to life. In a Plug-and-Play system, the operating system continues the initialization of the devices inside and connected to your computer. In effect, the Plug-and-Play system completes the BIOS configuration process.

In either case, whether your BIOS completes the initialization of your system or transfers control to the operating system to complete the process, somehow your operating system must load. Your computer must know enough about your disks—floppy, hard, and CD-ROM—to be able to find the operating system and get its code running. The process of getting the operating system started is called the *Initial Program Load* (IPL).

The IPL procedure originally was a design expedient. When the first computer was created, ROM chips, like all other parts of computers, were expensive. The computer's designers opted to use as little ROM as possible to get the system started. They added a short code routine at the end of the BIOS test procedure that told the BIOS to read the first sector from your computer's floppy disk (the only drive in the first personal computers). This first sector is sometimes called the *boot sector* because of its function.

In modern computers, the BIOS is smart enough to look to your hard disk as well as floppy drive, and sometimes even to your CD-ROM drive, to find a boot sector. Many BIOSs allow you to select which of these are searched for and in what order. If the BIOS finds executable code there, it loads that code into memory and executes it. If it finds no executable code or no available disk, the BIOS complains and does nothing because it doesn't know how to do anything else.

The small amount of code used by the IPL routine is unforgiving. It searches only the first physical sector on your disks. It looks for sectors rather than clusters or allocation units because at this point it doesn't know what operating system you have and how it organizes disk storage. The BIOS must know how to find the first physical sector on the disk; consequently it requires a BIOS extension associated with the disk to tell it how to make the required access. A disk drive that uses only a software device driver will be invisible to the BIOS and the IPL routines, and consequently such a disk cannot boot the system.

The code in the boot sector is also short and to the point because it has to fit into the confines of a single sector. This code tells your computer how to find the rest of the operating system. Once it locates the main operating system, the boot sector code starts loading that code into memory and yields control to it. The operating system takes command and completes the process of booting your computer.

Plug-and-Play

One of the gravest shortcomings of legacy computers—old computers built in pre-Pentium days—was that their ISA expansion bus lacked automatic configuration procedures. You were left to adjust settings and configure software yourself. And each of the dozens of settings you had to make brought its own potential for error. Putting even one jumper in the wrong place or throwing the wrong switch was often sufficient to turn two thousand dollars of computer into a noisy desk ornament.

To eliminate such setup problems and shift the tedious job of system configuration to someone (or something) better equipped to deal with it, the computer industry developed the *Plug-and-Play initiative.* The idea was to make your computer responsible for configuring itself. After all, computers specialize in taking over jobs that you find tedious. The goal was to create computers with no switches, no jumpers, and no headaches. So far, they've achieved two out of three, a pretty good average.

The straightforward goal belies the arduous journey in reaching today's reasonably successful automatic configuration systems. Making Plug-and-Play work required changes in every computer's BIOS, expansion bus, expansion boards, and operating system. The universal adoption of Plug-and-Play was a lengthy transition, one dragged on as compliant products slowly coursed into the market.

Background
The idea behind the Plug-and-Play initiative was to shift responsibility for remembering and assigning setup options from you to your computer system. After all, your computer likely has a better memory than you do, and it doesn't mind running through a checkup procedure however many times as is needed.

The first stab at a Plug-and-Play specification appeared with the original Intel/Microsoft specification for ISA on May 28, 1993. That effort inspired other companies to join in. Related standards are being developed to extend Plug-and-Play to other troubling configuration processes, particularly SCSI expansion. Compaq Computer Corporation and Phoenix Technologies joined Intel to develop a BIOS specification for Plug-and-Play, first released November 1, 1993.

Toshiba joined Intel and Microsoft to come up with a system to move power-management responsibilities to the operating system. Because configuring the host system was an important part of power management, they extended their specification to embrace setting up all computer accessories, not just power, with one of its foundations being the Plug-and-Play specification. They called the result the *Advanced Configuration and Power Interface* (ACPI), first published in December 1996. The next major revision of the specification was Revision 2.0, published on July 27, 2000, as a 450-page tome covering the intimate details of the design of new computers. A minor revision on March 31, 2002, brought the standard up to its current version, Revision 2.0a.

ACPI is neither a hardware nor software specification. Rather, it details the interface between the two. That makes it not only function like the BIOS, but the specification also details how the BIOS works with hardware and software to configure your computer. Although it is not a BIOS in itself, the specification details how your computer's BIOS must operate. To wear a Windows logo, new computers must conform to the current ACPI version.

ACPI doesn't replace Plug-and-Play but instead builds upon it. The basic Plug-and-Play system still takes care of configuring your system, but ACPI gives it new commands and versatility. The automatic configuration process is still termed Plug-and-Play (or, by those who have less faith in its reliability, Plug-and-*Pray*).

For automatic configuration to work properly, it requires all three elements of the system written to its standards—the computer and its BIOS, the operating system, and the expansion boards and peripherals attached to the computer. Any older device that does not conform to the various Plug-and-Play standards is considered to be a *legacy* device. The Plug-and-Play system attempts to accommodate legacy devices, but it cannot resolve all conflicts between them. Developers see the ultimate solution as being *attrition*. As time goes by, old noncompliant products will fade from the market. To accelerate the demise of legacy products, Intel and Microsoft have written support for ISA out of their most recent system standards, although many people still insist on at least one ISA slot in their newest computers.

Expansion Board Support

The basic Plug-and-Play procedure is a three-step process that lends itself to automation: First, the Plug-and-Play BIOS directs your system to check what resources each expansion device needs. Next, the BIOS coordinates the assignments to avoid conflicts. Finally, it tells your system and software which choices it has made.

The configuration process calls upon specific hardware features of ACPI-compliant expansion boards. Most importantly, each board is able to deactivate itself so that it does not respond to the normal control signals inside your computer. The board disconnects itself from all system resources so that when it is inactive it cannot possibly cause conflicts.

In addition, each ACPI-compliant board has several new onboard registers that are reached through a standardized set of three I/O port addresses so that the BIOS or operating system can control the configuration of the board. These ports are designated Address, Write Data, and Read Data.

The Address port functions as a pointer that expands the number of control registers directly accessible to your system without stealing more system resources. Loading a register number in the Address port makes that register available for reading or writing through the Write Data and Read Data ports.

The ACPI specification explicitly defines eight card control registers and reserves two large ranges—one of 24 registers for future elaboration of the standard and the other a

16-port range that board-makers can assign to their own purposes. In addition, the specification allows cards to be configured as multiple logical devices, and it assigns ports for their control. The Address port allows the Write Data port to select which of the logical devices is active and the resources used by each.

ACPI-compliant expansion boards act in one of two ways, depending on whether they are needed for booting the system. Boards that are required for bootup (that is, display adapters and disk controllers) start up active. That is, they come online exactly like conventional expansion boards using the resources assigned them as power-on defaults. They will grab the resources that they need, participate in the normal Power-On Self Test procedure, and let you operate your computer normally. They may also cause the same old resource allocation problems, as will any conventional expansion boards that don't support Plug-and-Play or ACPI. The other Plug-and-Play devices (those not needed in booting your computer) automatically deactivate themselves when your system comes on, waiting to be told what configuration to use by your operating system.

ACPI-compliant boards not required during bootup normally start up inactive. They do nothing until specifically activated, typically by the ACPI-compliant operating system.

Every ACPI-compliant board has specific circuitry for managing its configuration. This circuitry operates independently from the normal functions of the board. Unlike the functional circuits on the board that can be disconnected from the bus interface, the Plug-and-Play circuits always monitor the signals on the bus. However, the Plug-and-Play circuitry operates in one of four states—Wait for Key, Isolation, Configuration, and Sleep—without regard for whether the functional circuitry is active or inactive.

Boot Operation

All ACPI-compliant boards, whether active or inactive, boot up in their Wait for Key state, in which they refuse to respond until they receive an explicit command called an *initiation key*. This key is not a simple password but rather a precisely defined 32-step interaction between the host system and each board. All 32 steps must be completed successfully before the board can be set up.

Once a board has been singled out with the initiation key, the BIOS can interrogate it individually and determine whether it is required for booting up the system and what system resources it requires. The BIOS allocates the needed resources to boot devices. If a board is not required to boot the system, however, the BIOS bows out, leaving resource assignment to the operating system. The BIOS only needs to get the system going well enough that the operating system can load and take over.

Plug-and-Play boards on the legacy ISA bus use a different process. They are isolated using *card select numbers*, assigned by the BIOS. Once each board is uniquely identified, it can be automatically configured by the BIOS (if it is required for booting the system) or by the operating system.

Onboard ROM

The ACPI configuration process and the ability to isolate individual boards hold advantages beyond automatic resource allocation. The greatly enlarge the potential capacity of storing firmware on each board.

In pre–Plug-and-Play days, the BIOS scanned each expansion board for additional BIOS code. That code had to fit in a tight range of addresses, and the code contained on each board could not overlap. Using Plug-and-Play technology, the BIOS scans each board in isolation, so conflicts between boards are not a problem.

The Plug-and-Play BIOS scans for additional code exactly like a pre–Plug-and-Play BIOS, looking for the special add-in ROM signature—the two-byte code 055(hex) followed by 0AA(hex)—that indicates a block of add-in BIOS code follows. The firmware on Plug-and-Play boards adds a pointer that immediately follows this signature to indicate the location of an expansion header in the BIOS code or a chain of several headers. Each header is identified by a special four-byte preamble—024(hex), 050(hex), 06E(hex), or 050(hex)—that corresponds to the ASCII characters $PnP.

The ACPI scheme allows the ROM on each expansion board to hold interface and driver code for multiple operating systems, each coded by its own expansion header. An operating system can identify the code that applies specifically to it by reading the headers.

The ACPI specification allows each board-maker a generous apportionment of the available memory and port addresses. Each board can use up to four noncontiguous ranges of memory base addresses for BIOS code and up to eight noncontiguous base addresses for input/output ports. In addition, a board can use from zero to two separate interrupt levels and up to two DMA channels. Each manufacturer determines the number of resources that a given board can use. Which it uses, however, is a matter left to the board-maker.

As this is written, the current ACPI specification is version 2.0a, and it runs over 500 pages long. You can download a copy from a Web site devoted to it, www.acpi.info.

Interface Functions

Although the primary role for the BIOS today is to get your computer started, it retains the name it earned from its function as the software-to-hardware interface of your machine. It is a control system that operates at the lowest possible level (the most basic) at which the input and output of your computer are designed to link to programs. In effect, it is like a remote control for a television set. The BIOS allows your software to press buttons at a distance from the hardware, just as you control the channel of your TV from your easy chair—and without prying open the set and ratcheting its tuning circuits. In operation, the BIOS is a universal remote control. It lets you push the same buttons, regardless of the model or brand of television at which you point it.

The original purpose of this one-step-removed BIOS design was to allow computer hardware to be revised and updated without the need to change software correspondingly. It helps guarantee the backward compatibility of computers. The extra BIOS step is needed, because all computers have many hardware elements that are located at specific addresses in memory or within the range of certain input/output ports. Other computer components may have registers of their own, used in their control, that also are addressed at specific locations. Because of the number of separate components inside any computer, the potential number of possible variations in the location of these features is limitless. Software that attempts to control any of this hardware must properly reach out to these registers. As long as all computers are crafted exactly the same, with the same ports used for exactly the same hardware with exactly the same registers, no problems should occur. But if a computer designer wants to change the hardware to a technology that delivers better performance or greater reliability, he may be stymied by the old addresses. Software may expect to reach the old design at one set of ports, whereas the new-and-improved design may be memory-mapped and not use ports at all. In this case, the old software would not know how to reach the new hardware, and the new design simply would not work.

The BIOS gives the software a link. The software reaches into the BIOS for the hardware function it wants. Then the BIOS dips down into the hardware. If the design of a computer system is changed radically, only the BIOS needs to be changed to reflect the new way of getting at the features of the computer. The changed BIOS still works the same way as the software, so all older programs run exactly as they did before the change. In effect, the new system design requires a new route to get to an old destination—a detour. The new BIOS is an updated roadmap that shows only the detour.

Certainly today's driver software easily accomplishes this function of the BIOS. Back in the days when the computer was first created, however, there were no drivers. The original computer BIOS didn't even have provisions for adding extra hardware, and the first operating system had no intrinsic provisions for adding drivers. Not knowing what was to come of the personal computer, IBM put its reliance on BIOS technology in its first computers and reserved the right to alter the hardware at will. The company made no guarantee that any of the ports or registers of the computer would be the same in any later computer.

In effect, IBM created the computer in a well-ordered dream world in which programs would never need to directly address hardware. Instead, each program would call up a software routine in the BIOS, which would have the addressing part of the instruction permanently set in its code. Later computers with different hardware arrangements would use BIOS routines that worked like the old ones and were indistinguishable from the old ones when used by application software. The addresses inside the routines would be changed, however, to match the updated hardware. The same software could work, then, with a wide variety of hardware designs, giving the designer and manufacturer the flexibility to upgrade the entirety of system hardware, if necessary.

Compatibility

In the days when your computer's operating system worked cooperatively with the BIOS instead of co-opting its function, BIOS compatibility was a major issue in buying a new computer. A computer had to have a BIOS functionally equivalent to that of an IBM personal computer to work reliably with the software of the day. Consequently, after the IBM BIOS made its debut, it became the most copied set of software routines in the world. The computer BIOS laid out all the entry points used by subsequent IBM BIOSs and most compatible BIOSs as well. It also defined the functions that could—and must—be expected in any BIOS as well as established the way that the BIOS works. The BIOS that IBM developed for its 1984 Personal Computer AT still defines the minimum level of compatibility for *all* computers.

Today, computer-makers can buy a compatible BIOS off the shelf from any of several sources. It wasn't always that easy. Achieving off-the-shelf BIOS compatibility was one of the great sagas of computer history.

Because the copyright laws forbade any copying of someone else's work, compatible BIOSs had to be written "clean." That is, the programmers were kept from ever viewing the source code or having any knowledge of the routines it contained. Instead, they worked from a list of instructions and the functions that the BIOS carries out when given each specific instruction. In other words, they looked at the BIOS they wanted to copy as a black box that takes an input and gives an output. The programmers then deduced the instructions for the inside of the box that would give the desired results.

Working in this way was time consuming and expensive. Few computer companies had the resources to do it all themselves. Compaq was the first to successfully tackle the job. The vast majority of compatible computer manufacturers bought the necessary BIOS firmware from specialist firms. The first to offer compatible BIOSs was Phoenix Technologies. Now computer-makers also select BIOS chips from American Megatrends, Inc., Award Software, and Mr. BIOS.

Because each BIOS vendor must develop its own product separately, the exact code used by each BIOS version is different. Functionally, however, they all look the same to your software (including your operating system).

At the other side of the interface—where the BIOS links to your computer's hardware—BIOSs can be quite different. By design, every BIOS is created to match the specific hardware in the computer in which it operates. That is part of its job—uniting different hardware designs so that they work interchangeably with all software. Every BIOS is customized for the computer it controls. Typically, computer motherboard manufacturers modify a generic BIOS from one of the BIOS-makers to suit their own purposes.

Because each BIOS is customized for a particular model of computer, no generic BIOS can hope to work properly in a given computer. BIOSs are not interchangeable. Moreover, should you want to change or upgrade your computer's BIOS for any reason—either through buying new chips or downloading code for Flash memory—you need to get one that matches the exact model of computer you own.

Software Interrupts

The BIOS design created for the first computers does its linking through a system of software interrupts. To gain access to the underlying hardware, a program sends out an *interrupt*, which is a special instruction to the microprocessor. The software interrupt causes the microprocessor to stop what it is doing and start a new routine. It does this by suspending the execution of the code on which it is working, saving its place, and then executing the program code of the BIOS routine.

The various functions the BIOS carries out are termed *interrupt service routines* or *interrupt handlers*. To call a given interrupt handler, a calling program needs to be able to find the program code that carries out the function. The design of the computer BIOS allows the system to put these interrupt handlers at any convenient address. So that a calling program can find the proper routine, the BIOS reserves part of your computer's memory for a map called a *BIOS interrupt vector table*. This map consists of a long list of 32-bit addresses, with one address corresponding to each interrupt handler. These addresses point to the first byte of the program code for carrying out the interrupt and are called *interrupt vectors*. The microprocessor reads the value of the vector and starts executing the code located at the value stored in the vector.

The table of interrupt vectors begins at the very start of the microprocessor's memory, address 00000(hex). Each vector comprises four bytes, and all vectors are stored in increasing order. Table 7.1 summarizes the principal BIOS interrupt vectors and the associated functions.

TABLE 7.1   BIOS Interrupt Vector Table

Absolute Address (Hex)	Interrupt Value	Function	Hardware Interrupt
0000:0000	00H	Divide-by-zero interrupt header	
0000:0004	01H	Single-step interrupt handler	

continues

TABLE 7.1 Continued

Absolute Address (Hex)	Interrupt Value	Function	Hardware Interrupt
0000:0008	02H	Non-maskable interrupt	
0000:000C	03H	Breakpoint	
0000:0010	04H	Arithmetic overflow handler	
0000:0014	05H	Print screen	
0000:0018	06H	Reserved	
0000:001C	07H	Reserved	
0000:0020	08H	Timer interrupt (18.21590/sec)	
0000:0024	09H	Keyboard service	
0000:0028	0AH	VGA retrace (AT slave)	IRQ2
0000:002C	0BH	Serial port 2	IRQ3
0000:0030	0CH	Serial port 1	IRQ4
0000:0034	0DH	Hard disk	IRQ5
0000:0038	0EH	Floppy disk	IRQ6
0000:003C	0FH	Parallel port	IRQ7
0000:0040	10H	Video services	
0000:0044	11H	Equipment check	
0000:0048	12H	Memory size check	
0000:004C	13H	Floppy and hard disk I/O	
0000:0050	14H	RS-232 service	
0000:0054	15H	System services	
0000:0058	16H	Keyboard	
0000:005C	17H	Printer I/O	
0000:0060	18H	Basic ROM entry point (startup)	
0000:0064	19H	Initial Program Load (IPL)	
0000:0068	1AH	Time of day	
0000:006C	1BH	Keyboard break	
0000:0070	1CH	User timer	
0000:0074	1DH	Monitor ROM pointer	

Absolute Address (Hex)	Interrupt Value	Function	Hardware Interrupt
0000:0078	1EH	Disk control table pointer	
0000:007C	1FH	Character generator pattern table pointer	
0000:0080	20H	DOS terminate program	
0000:0084	21H	DOS function calls	
0000:0088	22H	DOS terminate address	
0000:008C	23H	DOS Ctrl+Break exit address	
0000:0090	24H	DOS fatal error exit address	
0000:0094	25H	DOS absolute disk read	
0000:0098	26H	DOS absolute disk write	
0000:009C	27H	DOS Terminate and Stay Resident	
0000:00A0	28H	DOS idle loop	
0000:00A4	29H	DOS console device raw output handler	
0000:00A8	2AH	DOS network communications	
0000:00AC	2BH–2DH	Reserved	
0000:00B8	2EH	DOS execute command	
0000:00BC	2FH	DOS print spool control	
0000:00C0	30H-31H	DOS internal use	
0000:00C8	32H	Reserved	
0000:00CC	33H	Mouse driver calls	
0000:00D0	34H–3EH	Reserved	
0000:00FC	3FH	LINK (internal use)	
0000:0100	40H	Floppy and hard disk handler	
0000:0104	41H	Pointer to hard disk parameters	
0000:0108	42H	EGA video vector screen BIOS entry	
0000:010C	43H	EGA initialization parameters	
0000:0100	44H	EGA graphics character patterns	
0000:0114	45H	Reserved	
0000:0118	46H	Pointer to second fixed disk parameters	
0000:011C	47H	Reserved	

continues

TABLE 7.1   Continued

Absolute Address (Hex)	Interrupt Value	Function	Hardware Interrupt
0000:0120	48H	PCjr cordless keyboard	
0000:0124	49H	PCjr non-keyboard scan code table	
0000:0128	4AH	Alarm routine	
0000:012C	4BH–4FH	Reserved	
0000:0140	50H	Periodic alarm from timer	
0000:0144	51H–59H	Reserved	
0000:0168	5AH	Cluster adapter BIOS-entry address	
0000:016C	5BH	Cluster boot	
0000:0170	5CH	NetBIOS entry point	
0000:0174	5DH–5FH	Reserved	
0000:0180	60H–66H	User program interrupts	
0000:019C	67H	Expanded memory manager routines	
0000:01A0	68H–6BH	Unused	
0000:01B0	6CH	System resume vector	
0000:01B4	6DH–6FH	Unused	
0000:01C0	70H	Real-time clock	IRQ8
0000:01C4	71H	LAN adapter (IRQ2 replacement)	IRQ9
0000:01C8	72H	Reserved	IRQ10
0000:01CC	73H	Reserved	IRQ11
0000:01D0	74H	Mouse	IRQ12
0000:01D4	75H	80287 NMI error	IRQ13
0000:01D8	76H	Hard disk controller	IRQ14
0000:01DC	77H	Reserved	IRQ15
0000:01E0	78H–7FH	Unused	
0000:0200	80H–85H	BASIC	
0000:0218	86H	NetBIOS	
0000:021C	87H–F0H	BASIC	
0000:03C4	F1H–FFH	Reserved for program interrupts	

The interrupt vectors are stored in the RAM of your computer so that the values in the table can be changed. For example, a program or software driver may want to alter or update a BIOS routine to take advantage of a special feature of new hardware you install in your computer. The BIOS code itself loads default values for many of these interrupt vectors into the appropriate RAM locations with the vectors pointing at the routines stored in your computer's ROM.

Sometimes programs add extra routines to a given BIOS function, a process called *chaining interrupts*. To chain an interrupt, a program looks at the interrupt vector it wants to chain to and remembers its value. It then substitutes the starting location of the program code that it wants to add to the old routine. It then modifies its own code to make the execution of its routines jump to the old interrupt when the processing of the new code finishes. In this way, the new routine added in the interrupt chain executes first and then starts the original interrupt handler.

Parameter Passing

Because fewer interrupts are available than tasks you might want the BIOS to handle, different functions are available for many of the interrupts. These separate functions are identified through a technique called *parameter passing*. An interrupt needing service from the BIOS—the calling program—passes a number identifying the command to be carried out to the BIOS as a *parameter*, a value held in one or more of the registers at the time the software interrupt is issued.

The calling program decides what function it wants the BIOS to carry out, loads the parameter value into the proper register, and issues the interrupt. The BIOS code examines the register to determine what function the programs wants.

This same technique may be used to pass information between the calling program and the BIOS. The data to be passed along is simply loaded into one register and the parameter identifying the command into another. To pass new data back to the calling program, the BIOS loads the data into a register, which the calling program can then read.

Using registers to move data into a BIOS routine has its shortcomings. The functions and parameters are limited to those that are common among computers. There's little room for programs to add their own interrupts. Moreover, the scant number of registers in Intel microprocessors limits the number of parameters that can be passed to and from a function. Most routines use a single byte of data.

To move larger blocks of data, some BIOS routines and most programs use memory. A calling program stores the values it wants to pass to a subroutine in a block of RAM addresses. It then passes to the subroutine the location of the data, and the subroutine digs into the data, changing what it requires, and leaves the block for later access by the program. Although programs and subroutines identify the block of memory by its address, programming languages let you use names for the data. The program chooses the block of addresses to associate with the name and looks to those addresses whenever the programmer uses that name. Similarly, program subroutines may be named, and the program uses the names to find the block of memory holding the microprocessor instructions that comprise the subroutine.

Entry Points

The various code routines in each BIOS start and end at addresses assigned to the BIOS function in the computer memory map. The address at which each routine starts is called that routine's *entry point*. The entry point of a BIOS function is completely different from the interrupt that calls that function. When the BIOS in your computer sets itself up—either before or during the actual bootup—it loads the addresses of the entry points into a table in memory that becomes the interrupt vectors. In theory, an entry point can be at any location for any BIOS function—it needs only to be loaded into the slot in the BIOS interrupt vector table to be properly recognized. Unfortunately, some program writers decided to call BIOS routines by their entry points instead of using interrupts, because the direct approach is faster. Consequently, a few applications require that some entry points be at specific physical BIOS addresses. If the entry point of a BIOS differs from what the program expects, the result is likely to be a system crash.

IBM has maintained the same entry points with all its BIOSs, and many compatible BIOSs use exactly the same addresses. A few do not, however. In general, the BIOSs with varying entry points have been written as programming modules that can be combined in various ways to suit the needs of a computer designer. What these modular BIOSs add in flexibility, they lose in compatibility.

Unlike programs that write directly to system hardware, however, programs that require specific BIOS entry points are rare. With the popularity of compatible computers and modular BIOSs, they are sure to become more rare. Modern software, nevertheless, is getting away from a dependency on complete compatibility down to the level of specific entry points. In fact, many programs avoid the BIOS entirely.

The chief beneficiaries of the BIOS are individual programmers who need to create code quickly. In many cases, using BIOS routines can simplify the writing of a program. Certain system operations always are available and can be accessed easily through software. They are reasonably well documented and understood, removing many of the programmer's concerns.

Linking to Hardware

Controlling the hardware of your computer requires that your system be able to pass commands and data to that hardware. For example, if you have a modem, you need to send the modem commands to dial numbers and change speeds. Once you're communicating, you have to send bytes, even megabytes, of data to the modem and receive more bytes in return.

The BIOS routines may use memory or I/O ports to pass the commands and data to hardware devices. When a device uses a block of memory to exchange information, it is termed *memory mapped*. When it uses I/O ports, it is termed *I/O mapped*.

Memory mapping works exactly as described in the previous section on parameter passing. The BIOS routine and hardware device share a common range of memory addresses they use for passing bytes back and forth. Programs use BIOS routines instead of physical addresses to reach memory-mapped devices, giving the hardware designer the freedom to move the memory window used by a given device. The designer needs only to change the interrupt handler to match the address he chooses.

I/O mapping uses input/output ports to exchange data. An input/output port of a microprocessor is a special range of addresses that is isolated from main memory and has special access instructions.

In the Intel scheme of things, microprocessors have a range of 65,536 input/output ports (compared to over four billion discrete memory addresses). However, due to an aberration in the design of the first expansion boards for computers, only 1024 are commonly assigned to devices that plug into standard computer expansion slots. To cut costs of the first expansion boards, engineers designed boards to decode only 10 of the 16 address lines.

Although newer buses can take advantage of the full range of input/output ports, expansion boards can quickly consume the available ports, or two boards may attempt to use the same port. Such conflicts between boards is the most common reason why expansion boards fail to operate properly. Sometimes installing an expansion board creates a port conflict that prevents the rest of the system from working at all. Table 7.2 lists some of the common conflicts that arise in I/O port assignments.

TABLE 7.2 Common I/O Port Assignments and Potential Conflicts

Device	Range Used	Conflict
Color video boards	3D0–3DF	3C0
COM1	3F8–3FF	3E0

continues

TABLE 7.2   Continued

Device	Range Used	Conflict
COM2	2F8–2FF	2E0
COM3	3E8–3EF	3E0
COM4	2E8–2EF	2E0
Expansion unit	210–217	200
Floppy controller	3F0–3F7	3E0
Game controller	200–20F	200
LPT1	3BC–3BF	3A0
LPT2	378–37F	360
LPT3	278–27F	260
MDA, monochrome video	3B0–3BF	3A0
Microsoft bus mouse, primary	23C–23F	
Microsoft bus mouse, alternate	238–23B	
Primary bi-sync card	3A0–3A9	3A0
Secondary bi-sync card	380–38C	380
SoundBlaster speaker default	220–223	220
SoundBlaster control	388–389	
VGA	3C0–3CF	3C0

If you're running Windows on your computer, you can view the actual I/O port assignments used by your computer. To view these assignments, consult the Device Manager by selecting the System icon in Control Panel. Select your computer on the Device menu and click the Properties button. From the View Resources menu that pops on your screen, select the Input/Output (I/O) radio button. You'll see a screen akin Figure 7.1, listing all the input/output ports in use and the hardware using them.

Through Plug-and-Play and the manual options of the Add Hardware process, Windows generally will make the proper assignments of I/O ports. If you want to reserve one or more I/O ports so that devices you install later cannot steal them, click the Reserve Resources tab and enter the ports you want to reserve.

New expansion buses such as PCI provide access to the full range of I/O ports, thus reducing the chance of conflicts. Plug-and-Play expansion boards are supposed to automatically resolve port conflicts entirely. Eventually, worries about I/O conflicts should disappear. For most computers, however, *eventually* has not yet arrived.

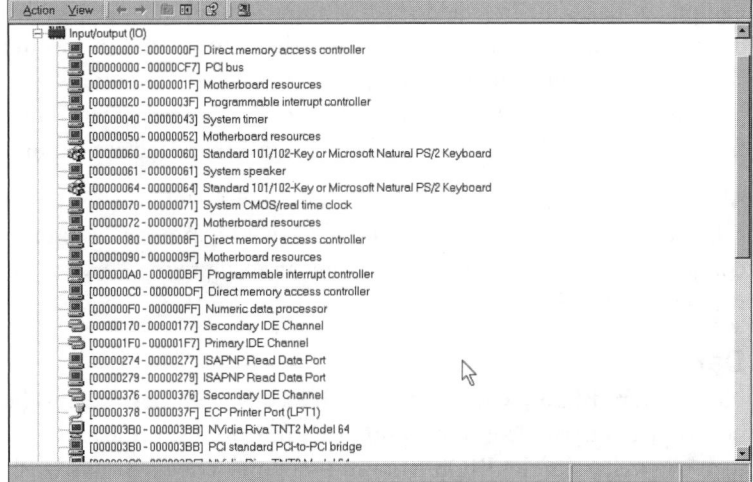

FIGURE 7.1

The Windows Device Manager showing I/O port usage.

Storage Functions

Because the BIOS comes in the physical form of ROM chips, its storage functions should not be surprising. For example, the BIOS stores its own name and the date it was written inside its own code. But the BIOS also incorporates storage functions that go beyond the bytes encapsulated in its ROM silicon. Although physically separate from the BIOS chips themselves, the setup memory of your computer is controlled by BIOS functions and is often considered with—and even as part of—the BIOS. This memory records vital details about your computer hardware so that you don't have to set up each expansion board and disk drive every time you switch on your computer. In addition, the BIOS tells your computer to reserve several small blocks of memory for dynamic data that your computer and its operating system use for tracking several system functions.

Legacy Data

As with any computer program, the BIOS code uses data for its operations and produces data as its result. The BIOS stores some of this data to be used as a reference by your programs. The BIOS acquires some of this information as it sets up the system. By storing it all in one place, the BIOS eliminates the need for every program to waste its time looking up common features. Other data is encoded as part of the BIOS itself so that programs can determine what kind of computer—and what kind of BIOS—they have to work with.

BIOS Data Area

During the initialization process, the BIOS searches through the system for specific features. It checks the number and kinds of ports installed, the type of display adapter (monochrome or color), and other options. Included among the data that it stores are equipment flags, the base addresses of input/output adapters, keyboard characters, and operating modes. The BIOS then stores this information in specific memory locations so that your programs can check to see which features are available or being used. For example, the BIOS looks for serial ports at specific addresses (see Chapter 11, "Ports"). As it finds them, the BIOS records the base address that each serial port uses.

All this self-descriptive information about your system is stored in a special part of RAM called the *BIOS data area*. Located just above the interrupt vectors, the BIOS data area comprises 256 bytes of memory, starting at absolute memory location 000400(hex) and running to 0004FF(hex).

Date

Nearly every BIOS identifies itself with a copyright message and (usually) a version number so that you can determine who made it. (More specifically, the copyright message protects the writers of the BIOS from other people copying their work.) This identification information may appear anywhere within the BIOS code range.

In addition, the revision date of your BIOS helps you identify how recently its code was updated. As computers have expanded their capabilities, BIOSs have been revised to enable new operations. Sometimes older BIOSs will not work with new peripherals. For example, many BIOSs from before 1998 don't let you use all the space on hard disks larger than 8GB. Older BIOSs may impose even more severe limits.

You can determine the date of your BIOS in several ways. The most convenient include catching the bootup screen of your computer, which usually displays the date and revision number of the BIOS, and using a diagnostic utility. Microsoft Diagnostics, supplied with most versions of Windows, will show you the detail of your computer's BIOS—its date and manufacturer. This program is located in the Command subfolder of your Windows folder as MSD.EXE. You can either click its icon or run it from the MS-DOS prompt by typing **MSD** and then pressing Enter. Click the Computer button, and it will list some of the BIOS details of your computer, as shown in Figure 7.2.

Note that Microsoft has not updated the diagnostic program for years, so the most recent microprocessor it will recognize is a 486DX! The System Information program found under System Tools in Accessories from the Programs option at the Start button is Microsoft's preferred tool. It shows your system in exquisite, even painful, detail, but it offers no direct display of your system's BIOS date.

System Identification Bytes

The original computer BIOS included a byte of data to identify the kind of computer in which the BIOS was installed. Programs that might react differently depending on the processor or other aspects of the computer could use this byte to identify the hardware

and adjust themselves accordingly. At least that was the idea of the IBM engineers who
came up with it in 1981.

FIGURE 7.2
*Microsoft Diagnostics
showing system
details.*

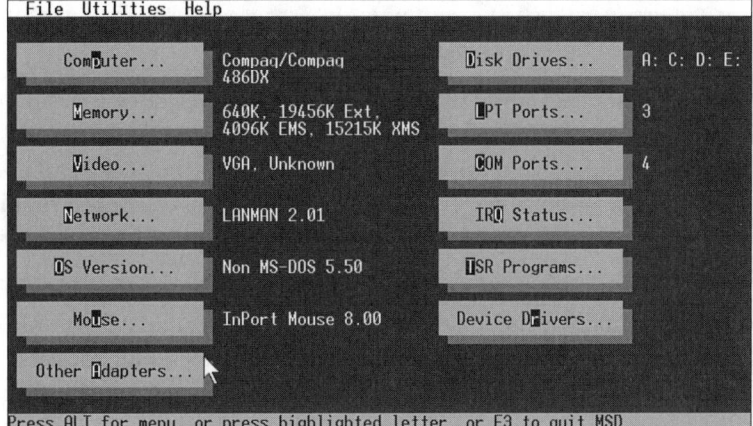

The scheme had its problems, however. Allowing for a single byte soon seemed short-
sighted, so this memory area was expanded to two bytes, starting with the IBM XT Model
286, introduced in 1985. The overall storage area was termed the *system identification bytes*,
and in IBM nomenclature, it was divided into the *model byte* and the *submodel byte*. A third
byte was reserved to indicate any major revision to the system.

IBM created an elaborate table of designations for the various computer models it offered.
Unfortunately, the company made no provision to coordinate the use of this storage area
for other manufacturers. Consequently, the rest of the industry used designations marking
their IBM equivalent. Because all systems since 1984 follow the architecture of the IBM
AT system, nearly all computers now define themselves as using the AT code. In other
words, the system identification bytes store essentially meaningless data.

The model byte is located at absolute memory address 0FFFFE(hex) and is FC(hex) in
nearly all current computers. The submodel byte follows it with a value of 01(hex). The
revision byte follows next and is usually zero.

The BIOS also has its own individual identification encoded into its bytes. Although it
may be nothing more than a copyright notice, each BIOS has some code identifying its
origins. Most BIOS makes have their own codes to identify the version of the BIOS,
which revision it is, and even the model of computer for which it is meant.

Disk Parameter Tables

One of the more important entries in the BIOS data area is the *disk parameter table*. Most
computers store the parameters used by user-defined hard disks, typically reflected as hard
disk type 47 in the setup program, in the BIOS data area. The most common memory

location for this information is absolute address 0000:0300. Some BIOSs give you the option of locating the disk parameter table in an alternate location, typically DOS memory. In any case, interrupt vector 41(hex) points to the location of the disk parameter table for the first hard disk in a computer. Interrupt vector 46(hex) points to the location of the parameters of the second hard disk.

In general, the best location for your disk parameter table is absolute address 0000:0300. However, some peripherals, such as older sound cards and network adapters, use this address for their own purposes. Conflicts between the peripheral and your hard disk may render either or both inoperable. Relocating the disk parameter table through a BIOS setting solves the problem.

You may encounter two kinds of disk parameter tables. A standard *fixed disk parameter table* (FDPT) contains a single description of the vital parameters of the associated hard disk, listing the number of cylinders, heads, and sectors used by the disk. An *enhanced fixed disk parameter table* (EDPT) has two entries: the logical cylinder-head-sector values and the physical cylinder-head-sector values. The logical values reflect the way your computer sees and accesses the disk. The physical values reflect the actual number of cylinders, heads, and sectors used by the disk.

The standard FDPT is sufficient only for smaller disks, those with both fewer than 1024 cylinders and a capacity less than 504MB. Due to the design of the standard FDPT, only ten bits are allowed for storing the number of cylinders, so numbers larger than 1024 cannot be encoded. The EDPT defaults to 16 heads for all disks, allowing four more bits for storing the number of cylinders.

Your computer deals with any disk by the logical values in the EDPT. Programmers check the value stored here using software interrupt 13(hex).

DOS Tables

DOS stores many of the parameters it uses for managing your computer and its programs in a series of tables. To achieve the utmost in compatibility, DOS locates these tables at the lowest available reaches of conventional memory. Among the data stored here are file handle identifications (FILES), the last referenced disk data (BUFFERS), file control information (FCBS), drive tables (LASTDRIVE), and system operating information (STACK).

Most memory managers allow you to relocate this data into XMS memory to free up more space in the conventional area. Although this technique is commonplace and well tested, you will sometimes encounter compatibility problems, such as a crash of your system. For example, early incarnations of most network operating systems expect to find this data in conventional memory (along with COMMAND.COM itself). The only way to avoid this problem is to avoid the network, avoid DOS, or refrain from relocating this data with your memory manager—the last usually being the most viable option. You'll want to avoid relocating any of these DOS tables if your system exhibits compatibility problems or its network redirector behaves oddly.

ACPI Tables

One of the chief responsibilities of an ACPI-compliant BIOS is to set up the ACPI tables that describe the interfaces to the hardware installed in the system. The operating system can then read the tables to determine not only the resources required by a specific board but also the code with initialization routines or arbitrary operation sequences needed to make the hardware function. The ACPI tables may contain not only data but also program code in *p-code*, the programming code or the language of the ACPI system.

The ACPI specification describes a programming language, called the *ACPI Source Language* (ASL), in which engineers can write their code for their device interfaces. ASL is then compiled into *ACPI Machine Language* (AML), the object code that is actually stored in the ACPI tables. The ACPI-compatible operating system reads the AML as a set of program instructions.

The BIOS sets up the tables during the boot process. It reads the data for each table from the devices it scans and then stores each table separately in system memory. It makes one master table, called the *root system description table*, which holds the location of each of the separate data tables.

The BIOS itself does nothing with the data it puts in these tables. It is only an agent that moves the data from device to memory. The ACPI-compliant operating system uses the data or p-code contained in the tables.

To enable the operating system to find the root system description table, the BIOS plants a pointer in the Extended BIOS data area of memory. The operating system identifies this *root system description pointer* by looking for the character sequence "RSD PTR" (including the trailing space) in the Extended BIOS data area. The pointer stores the base address of the root system description table from which the operating system can find the rest of the tables.

System Configuration

In order to properly test a computer, the BIOS needs to know exactly what it is testing—what peripherals are installed, how much memory it must look through, and whether you have installed a coprocessor. In order to boot a computer, the BIOS needs to know exactly what kind of disk is connected to it. In order for you to see what is going on when your system boots up, the BIOS needs to know what kind of display system you have.

In some cases, the BIOS code itself can be written to search out and find the vital information it needs to get your system going. Such a search is not always accurate, nor is it easy to write the proper search method into a few kilobytes of BIOS code. Even if the proper program could be written and packed into ROM, you probably do not want to sit around and wait—and wait—while the BIOS probes into every nook and cranny to see if something is there.

To let the BIOS (and the rest of the computer) know what options are installed in a given system, all computers record vital setup information that can be referenced quickly. The storage system for this data—that is, system setup memory—has one requirement: It must be nonvolatile. Other than that, the storage format and method are flexible because the BIOS isolates them from the rest of your software. The BIOS looks up this system data and transfers it to the BIOS data area for reference by your programs.

This flexibility has given designers freedom to use a number of storage technologies for this setup information. Among the most popular have been physical memory (switches), nonvolatile electronic memory, and magnetic (disk) memory. Since the AT was introduced a decade and a half ago, however, the basic form of this setup memory used by most computers has been the same—a few bytes of CMOS memory kept fresh (that is, continuously operating) by battery power.

CMOS

When the world and computers were young, all the differences between computers could be coded by one or two banks of DIP switches. But as the options began to pile up, the switch proved to be more a problem than a panacea. A reasonable number of switches couldn't allow for the number of options possible in a modern computer. Another problem with switches is that they are prone to mechanical problems—both of their own making and otherwise. Switch contacts naturally go bad, and they can be helped along the path of their own destruction by people who attempt to adjust them with pencils (the graphite that scrapes off the point is conductive and can short out the switches). People often set switches wrong and wonder what is awry.

Background

IBM developed a better scheme for the AT. Vital system parameters would be stored in a special, small block of battery-backed CMOS memory, a total of 64 bytes, in the form of a special chip, a Motorola MC146818, which also held a real-time clock. The lower 14 of those bytes are used by the real-time clock to hold the current time and an alarm time, leaving 40 bytes for storage of setup information. Locations were assigned for storing information about floppy and hard disks, the presence of a coprocessor, the amount of installed memory, and the type of display system (monochrome or color). Because CMOS memory is volatile, every system has a battery of some kind to keep this memory fresh and the real-time clock running. (See Chapter 31, "Power.")

Most computers followed the basic IBM scheme, minimally augmenting it to reflect the increasing capabilities of their systems. Although the MC146818 chip rarely appears in computers anymore, its functions are carried over into new support chips. For example, clock modules from Dallas Semiconductor incorporate all the functions of the Motorola chip, a built-in lithium battery, and more. The only major change in CMOS storage that has been made is the almost universal adoption (under the aegis of Microsoft) of the Plug-and-Play system.

Basic Memory Assignments

The basic CMOS data remains the same regardless of the manufacturer of the computer, and the various bytes of data are stored in the same rigidly structured format. Table 7.3 summarizes the basic storage assignments that are common across nearly all modern computers.

TABLE 7.3   CMOS Memory Byte Assignments

Byte	Assignment	Purpose
00	Seconds	Real-time clock
01	Second alarm	Real-time clock
02	Minutes	Real-time clock
03	Minute Alarm	Real-time clock
04	Hours	Real-time clock
05	Hours Alarm	Real-time clock
06	Day of the week	Real-time clock
07	Date of the month	Real-time clock
08	Month	Real-time clock
09	Year	Real-time clock
10	Status Register A	Real-time clock
11	Status Register B	Real-time clock
12	Status Register C	Real-time clock
13	Status Register D	Real-time clock
0A	Status Register A	
0B	Status Register B	
0C	Status Register C	

continues

TABLE 7.3 Continued

Byte	Assignment	Purpose
0D	Status Register D	
0F	Shutdown Status	
10	Diskette Drive Type	
11	Reserved	
12	Hard Disk Type	
13	Reserved	
14	Equipment Type	
15	Low Base Memory	
16	High Base Memory	
17	Low Expansion Memory	
18	High Expansion Memory	
19	Reserved	
1A	Reserved	
1B	Reserved	
1C	Reserved	
1D	Reserved	
1E	Reserved	
20	Reserved	
21	Reserved	
22	Reserved	
23	Reserved	
24	Reserved	
25	Reserved	
26	Reserved	
27	Reserved	
28	Reserved	
29	Reserved	
2A	Reserved	
2B	Reserved	

Byte	Assignment	Purpose
2C	Reserved	
2D	CMOS checksum	
2E	CMOS checksum	
30	Low expansion memory	
31	High expansion memory	
32	Date century	
33	Information flags	
34	Reserved	
35	Reserved	
36	Reserved	
37	Reserved	
38	Reserved	
39	Reserved	
3A	Reserved	
3B	Reserved	
3C	Reserved	
3D	Reserved	
3E	Reserved	
3F	Reserved	

Although the CMOS that holds this data is conventional memory, it is not in the direct reach of your computer's microprocessor. Unlike normal system memory, this CMOS setup memory was I/O mapped. That is, its contents were accessed through two input/output ports. Port 070(hex) indicates the memory byte you want to access, and port 071(hex) provides the pathway to the indicated byte. Reading or writing a byte of CMOS setup memory requires two steps. First, you write to port 070(hex) with the byte location in the CMOS range you want to read or write. Reading port 071(hex) tells you the value stored at the location you have chosen. Writing to port 071(hex) changes the byte value at the appointed location.

The contents of most of the storage locations in this CMOS setup memory are monitored by storing a checksum in bytes 02E and 02F(hex). If the checksum does not agree with the modular total of the monitored bytes, your system reports a CMOS memory error. The diagnostic status byte, 00E(hex), indicates the gross nature of the error and additionally reports whether battery power has failed. If all systems are go, this byte has a zero value; any bit set indicates a specific error (with two bits reserved).

Newer computers have elaborated on this CMOS storage scheme, adding more bytes to hold the status of other system features. In function and operation, however, all follow the pattern set by the AT.

Resetting CMOS

The chief reason you're advised not to tinker with the advanced settings of your computer's BIOS is that the control they afford allows you to set your computer up so that it does not work. For example, if you err by setting too few wait states for the memory you have installed in your computer, you may encounter a memory error as soon as your computer switches on and checks its BIOS settings. You won't have an opportunity to jump back into setup to fix the problem. You'll be stuck with a dead computer and have no way of bringing it back to life.

Well, not quite. Most computer BIOSs have factory defaults that are set conservatively enough that the machine will operate with whatever you've installed. The only trick is to restore the factory defaults.

Switch or Jumper Reset

Many computers have jumpers or a DIP switch that forces the reset. Check the documentation of your computer or motherboard to see if this option is available to you. Typically you'll find this information using the index of your instruction manual and looking under "factory defaults" or "BIOS defaults."

The exact procedure usually takes one of two forms, depending on the design of your computer. The easiest requires only that you move a jumper or slide a DIP switch and then turn your computer back on. The position of the switch or jumper doesn't matter. All that counts is that you move it. The most complicated procedure isn't much more difficult. You move the jumper or slide the switch, wait a few minutes, and then move it back. The delay allows the tiny amount of power that's locked in the CMOS circuitry to drain away.

Power Deprivation

The alternate procedure for resetting your CMOS works for nearly every computer and is based on the same power-depravation principle. You only need to deprive your computer's CMOS of its battery power so that the contents of its memory evaporate. Exactly how to deprive your CMOS of its lifeblood electricity depends on the design of your system.

If your computer's motherboard uses an external battery, simply unplug it from the motherboard. If your computer uses a replaceable disc-style battery in a matching battery holder, pop the battery out. In either case, allow ten minutes for the residual power in the CMOS to drain away before reconnecting or reinstalling the battery.

Some motherboards use permanently installed rechargeable nickel-cadmium batteries instead of replaceable cells. Usually these computers have some provision for electrically disconnecting the battery power from the CMOS (a jumper or switch, as noted in the preceding section). A few computer motherboards make no provision for disconnecting their nickel-cadmium batteries (also known as *ni-cads*). If you have such a computer and have put your BIOS in a nonfunctional configuration, as a last resort you can sometimes force a reset to the factory defaults by discharging the battery. The battery will recharge the next time you operate your computer.

Never short out a nickel-cadmium battery to discharge it. The low resistance of ni-cad cells produces high currents (even with small batteries), sufficient to melt circuit board traces and even set your computer on fire. Instead of shorting out the battery, discharge it through a resistor. A half-watt, 39-ohm resistor will safely discharge a ni-cad cell in about half an hour without danger to you or your computer. Alternately, you can use a six-volt lamp, such as one designed for battery-powered lanterns, as a battery load. The lamp will show you the progress of the discharge, glowing brightly at first and dimming as the battery's charge gets drained away. Connect either the resistor or the lamp directly between the terminals of the battery using clip leads.

Advanced Setup

After you press the right combination of keys to bring up your computer's setup menu, you are usually allowed to jump to Advanced Setup. This extension of Setup allows you to alter vital system operating parameters that are controlled by the motherboard chipset. The Advanced Setup procedure alters additional, often proprietary, storage in CMOS and, sometimes, in other parts of your computer. Typically, Advanced Setup is a second menu (or series of menus) accessed through the initial Setup menu.

Altering the options can have a dramatic effect on the performance of your computer. Importune tinkering often can lead to having a machine that will not work. Performance becomes zero. On the other hand, you can sometimes optimize your system to take best advantage of the options you've installed (for example, to coax the best possible performance from the memory system or highest transfer rate from your expansion bus).

The range of features controlled by advanced setup varies with both the BIOS and the chipset inside your computer. Most chipsets give you a wide range of options to wade through. However, one of the most popular, Intel's Triton chipset, provides very limited control range. For example, the only way to alter the ISA bus speed is to change jumper or DIP switch settings, and you cannot alter cache timing at all.

Some of the options available with different chipsets and BIOSs are detailed in the following subsections.

Parity Check

Some systems permit you to switch off memory parity checking, thus disabling error detection. Taking this option prevents your system from halting when memory parity errors are detected. You are well advised to leave parity checking enabled except when attempting to find elusive memory problems. Because this option is meaningful only for computers that have parity-checked memory, it offers you no savings as would a system that used 8-bit SIMMs instead of parity-checked 9-bit SIMMs. Your system is likely to halt when a parity-error occurs in program code, but the crash is less controlled than an error-warning message. Files may be destroyed. If the error occurs within data, you may never know when your information is inaccurate.

Memory Testing

Testing the prodigious amounts of RAM in a modern computer can take a long time, indeed, adding a minute or more to the cold boot sequence. To minimize the wear and tear on your patience, many BIOSs allow you to defeat the entire memory test sequence or specific portions of it. With the claims of extreme reliability for today's memory systems, you may want to consider switching off your computer's memory test.

Commonly you'll find an option called Above 1MB Memory Check that allows you to switch off memory testing beyond the base megabyte in your computer. Selecting this option will cut your bootup time from a few minutes to a few dozen seconds. Checking the base megabyte of memory in your computer usually is not an option because your computer needs error-free real-mode memory for running the setup program.

Some systems give you the option of adding an audible click or beep each time a memory block of a megabyte or so is tested. The sound is simply reassurance that your computer is successfully coursing through its lengthy memory test. Some people find this sound obnoxious rather than reassuring, and the Memory Test Click Sound setup option allows them to silence their systems.

Numeric Processor Testing

The BIOSs of some older computers offer the option of defeating the numeric processor test. Although you might be tempted to forgo this test to accelerate the boot process, you may be surprised at its effect. Many BIOSs assume that if you tell them not to test the numeric processor, you don't have one. They set a flag that tells your applications you don't have a coprocessor installed, so your software won't use the coprocessor even if one is installed—even as part of your microprocessor.

Computers based on the 386 and 486 microprocessors may also give you the option of selecting a Weitek coprocessor. You must select this option to enable your software to take advantage of the Weitek chip.

Cache Operation

Some systems require that you set the size of secondary (external) memory cache you have installed. You'll want to change this setting only if you install additional SRAM chips to increase the size of your computer's memory cache.

Some BIOSs allow you to switch on or off the cache. Some allow the individual control of the internal (primary) cache inside your microprocessor and the external (secondary) cache. The only time you should switch off your system's caches is when you want to pin down software problems or diagnose hardware errors.

Wait States

This setting controls the number of wait states injected during memory accesses. Typically, you have a choice of zero, one, two, or possibly three wait states. Some systems allow the separate setting of read and write wait states. Choosing fewer wait states makes your computer faster, but choosing too few to accommodate the speed of your system's memory leads to memory errors. Set this value too low and your computer may not boot at all. If you are a die-hard tinkerer and want to explore the potentials of this setting, adjust it downward one step at a time. Then run your computer for a while to check its reliability. Toying with this may also familiarize you with the location of the CMOS reset jumper.

Bus Clock

Many ISA systems allow you to adjust the clock speed of their expansion buses so that you can eke the most performance from your old expansion boards. Some systems give you a choice of clock speeds in megahertz; others express the speed in terms of the microprocessor clock (for example, CLOCKIN/4 implies one-quarter the microprocessor clock speed—8.25MHz with a 33MHz system). Higher speeds (lower divisors) can deliver more performance, but rates above about 12MHz may sacrifice reliability. In VL Bus and PCI systems, the bus clock setting has less effect on overall performance because the devices that need the most bus bandwidth (that is, a faster bus speed) will be connected to the higher-speed local bus. The clock speed of the local bus is not affected by the bus clock setting.

ROM Shadowing

Manufacturers may provide any of a number of options to enable or disable the shadowing of ROM code in fast RAM memory. Some merely allow the simple enable/disable choice. Others allow you to control ROM elements separately. One variety of BIOS lets you individually enable/disable system ROM and expansion ROM. System ROM means the BIOS code on your motherboard; expansion ROM is the code on expansion boards, which typically includes your video card and hard disk host adapter. Another variety of BIOS gives the choice of system, video, or adapter. A fourth BIOS type lets you choose whether to shadow ROM memory by address range, letting you select enabling or disabling by 16K, 32K, or 64K blocks.

In general, you should shadow only those memory ranges actually in use by ROM. Shadowing unused ranges wastes memory. Shadowing memory ranges used for buffers by network adapters or ancient expanded memory (EMS) boards may actually degrade system performance or cause compatibility problems.

Remember, shadowing only helps the performance of applications that use BIOS code in ROM, which for the most part means only DOS. If you primarily run any version of Windows or OS/2 that makes little use of the BIOS, shadowing yields no performance improvement and may cause compatibility problems. You will probably want to switch off shadowing when using any modern operating system.

Experimenting with shadowing can also lead to a system that does not boot. It is best to enable one block or shadowing feature at a time and then run your system to observe the result.

Concurrent Refresh

Most early computers must devote 10 percent or more of their active time to refreshing memory. Newer systems are able to refresh memory concurrently (that is, while they are performing normal tasks). Concurrent refreshing ekes more performance from your system, so it is the preferred operating mode. Some BIOS-makers call this kind of memory refresh *hidden refresh*. Normally your computer will deliver better performance with concurrent refresh. Some older RAM designs (used mostly in 386 and older computers) cannot handle concurrent refreshing and may cause memory errors when this feature is enabled.

Page Interleave

Some systems with two or four identical banks of RAM chips or memory modules can operate in an interleaved fashion (that is, alternating banks in back-to-back memory requests). Statistically, interleaving can cut wait states by nearly half. Although the effect is less pronounced in modern cached systems, enabling page interleave (when supported with sufficient memory) can improve performance.

Page Mode

Page mode memory chips and modules also can trim wait states. Page mode SIMMs can make repeated accesses to one memory page without wait states. If you equip your system with page mode memory and enable this option, you should get better performance.

Virus Protection

With all the concern in the industry about computer viruses, some BIOS-makers have added their own form of protection, a warning message that appears when software attempts to write to the boot sector of your hard disk. When the protection is switched on, you're given the option of canceling the write operation to prevent infection. Because some operating systems, such as the OS/2 Boot Manager, rewrite boot sector data when you switch between boot modes, you can't simply obstruct all boot sector write operations.

The protection afforded by this system is limited in two ways. It potentially stops only boot sector viruses. It does not stop those that afflict the active operating system files. Also, it protects only hard disks controlled through the computer BIOS. SCSI disks that rely on separate BIOS code in your SCSI host adapter are not protected.

Typematic Rate

Many BIOSs allow you to alter the way the keyboard reacts to your keystrokes, repeating them if you hold a key down. This feature, called *typematic*, is fully discussed in Chapter 20, "Keyboards."

Many BIOSs have an overall toggle, typically termed *Typematic Programming*, that enables or disables the settings for the typematic feature. You must enable typematic programming to alter other typematic settings. In addition, your keyboard must allow its typematic feature to be programmed. You can control the typematic feature through Windows 95 and 98 no matter what kind of keyboard you have or the BIOS typematic settings.

If a BIOS and keyboard support typematic programming, you can generally alter two aspects of this feature. Typematic Rate Delay specifies how long you must hold down a key before the typematic feature kicks in and characters start repeating. This setting is generally specified in milliseconds. Typematic Rate controls how quickly the characters repeat after the initial delay. This value is usually specified as a number of characters per second that will appear on your screen and in your text.

Num Lock

Some BIOSs let you configure the toggle state of some keyboard keys. The most common option is the setting of the Num Lock key. Most systems default to booting up with Num Lock switched off. This option lets you have your system boot with Num Lock on so you can go right to work crunching numbers. This option is an aid primarily for systems with old 84-key keyboards that lack a separate cursor pad. MS-DOS 6.0 and later enable you to accomplish the same effect as this option by adding the line NUMLOCK=ON to your CONFIG.SYS file.

Boot Device or Sequence

By design, computers normally try to boot from the floppy disk first, and only if they find no disk in the floppy drive do they attempt to boot from the hard disk. This strategy helps you get going when something happens to your hard disk so that it's no longer bootable. On the downside, it slows the boot process and forces you to wait for the buzz of the first floppy drive access. It also requires you keep disks out of your floppy drive until after your computer boots up.

Although neither of these shortcomings is fatal, they can be bothersome. Consequently, some BIOS-makers give you the option of setting the order that the BIOS searches for a bootable disk drive. Depending on the computer and BIOS-maker, several options are possible.

Some BIOS-makers enable you to directly specify the *boot order* of your computer's disk drives. Typically your options will be listed as "A:, C:" or "C:, A:." Sometimes only the first drive letter will be listed. Specify A: to make your system attempt first to boot from floppy or C: to skip the floppy and try your hard disk first.

Other BIOSs have the option Floppy Seek at Bootup, which lets you toggle between Yes or No. If you select No, the BIOS will ignore the floppy disk drive when attempting to boot your computer, even if it has a valid system disk in it. You can take advantage of this option to prevent inexperienced users from booting your computer from their own, possibly virus-infected, floppy disks.

Recent systems also give you the option Auto Boot Sequence, or Smart Boot. This is an attempt at the best of both worlds. Most of the time the intelligence of this technique is limited to sampling the floppy disk drive to determine whether it contains a disk, booting from it if the disk is a system disk, and ignoring the drive and booting from hard disk if the disk in the floppy drive is not a system disk or no disk is there at all.

Passwords

Many BIOSs have built-in password protection so that you can limit who uses your computer. The setup program typically gives you the option to enable or disable password protection. When you enable protection, the system stores your password in its CMOS memory. If the battery that backs up your CMOS gets low, you'll lose password protection until you replace the battery.

Tuning for Performance

Extra speed is hidden in each of the major components of your computer—the microprocessor, the memory, and your chipset. It takes the form of component tolerances and safety factors, a little bit more than the ratings that every electronic part is good for. By pushing a little harder, you can gain more power from your computer. Although you won't double your system's overall speed, you could gain several percent, enough to give you an edge in game-playing or quicken your daily grind.

Fine-tuning your BIOS is the key to unlocking the extra speed potential of your computer. A suitable BIOS will allow you to tweak the configuration of your motherboard chipset and alter microprocessor and memory timing. Each adjustment promises an extra dollop of speed.

Unfortunately, the tenability of BIOSs varies widely. Large computer companies—Compaq, Dell, Hewlett-Packard, IBM, Sony, and Toshiba—give you control only over a handful of setup parameters that enable you to customize security, add a few peripherals, and configure ports. They don't let you try to eke more performance from your computer because, well, they figure you're likely to screw up. Set the wrong value for a vital parameter, and your computer will stop working and the manufacturer will get a support call—and may have to send out a technician to get your machine running again. By not giving you such intimate control, the manufacturer saves on support.

Smaller computer-makers—say, the one operating in the garage next door—get a competitive edge by using motherboards with tunable BIOSs. They can tweak in more performance than the bigger computer-makers and give you a faster system. Most makers of motherboards not affiliated with one of the big computer companies have learned that they gain a competitive edge with power users by giving them complete setup flexibility. The pioneer among these companies was Abit, which developed its extremely tweakable SoftBIOS in 1994. Through it and its successors, you can adjust nearly every controllable parameter of your motherboard's chipset. Not only can you adjust the clock speed of the microprocessor to edge up performance by overclocking, you can shave cycles off the inevitable waits for memory refresh and access. With some systems, you can even adjust the voltage supplied to the microprocessor, monitor the environment inside your computer, and set limits on its operation.

Most computer-makers—and the major brands in particular—are conservative in the demands they make on computer components, such as the microprocessor and memory. They prefer to err on the cautious side because it minimizes the need for support. Moreover, they make no allowances for the differences between individual components. You may be lucky and get memory that's rated at 133MHz but will function fine at 150MHz. No motherboard-maker wants to take on the burden of testing the limits of each component when preparing a product. But you can do the testing yourself and set your computer to take advantage of the full potential of its major components.

Realistically speaking, the major manufacturers' caution is justifiable. The gains from fine-tuning your BIOS setup are modest, typically a few percentage points. If you're the slightest bit greedy and push your chipset too hard, you can render your computer completely unusable and even destroy the data stored on your hard disk. Go too far, and you can even kiss off an investment in $1000 silicon when your microprocessor melts down into worthless sand.

Play it safe. Backup anything that's important on your system before you begin. Familiarize yourself with your motherboard and locate its CMOS reset (if it has one). Also, check for jumper or switch settings for the basic microprocessor and bus operating parameters. Some BIOSs, although they allege to give you complete control through the setup, actually require hardware settings of some vital parameters. Your BIOS may or may not be able to override these hardware settings. If in the process of trying to set the chip speed through your BIOS your system does not cooperate, double-check your motherboard manual for hardware adjustments.

Clock Speeds

The obvious way to eke more speed from a system is to up the microprocessor speed, an enhancement usually termed *overclocking* because it requires operating the chip over and beyond the clock speed rating set by its manufacturer. Kick up the microprocessor's clock, and you can expect a corresponding linear increase in performance.

Raising memory speed also influences the overall performance of your system. The effect can be dramatic because memory performance has not kept in step with microprocessor speed. All modern computer memory systems operate at a fraction of microprocessor speed, requiring the microprocessor to slow down or wait for memory access. On-chip memory caching reduces, but does not eliminate, the waiting.

Optimizing the performance of your computer requires considering both the speed at which you operate the microprocessor and the speed at which you operate memory. Not only do you need to consider adjusting both, but in most systems you will also be forced to adjust both. The two speeds interact, and their control is often linked.

Most BIOS setup systems do not give you the option of simply changing the microprocessor clock speed because of the design of the chips themselves. Most microprocessors accept a single external clock frequency, which controls the operation of the front side bus or memory bus. The microprocessor speed is derived from this value through a *multiplier*. Consequently, if you do not vary the multiplier, microprocessor and memory speed settings interact. Up the memory speed and you'll raise the microprocessor speed.

The multiplier guarantees that the jump in microprocessor speed will be substantially higher than the memory speed increase (it multiplies the effect—what did you expect?), and you may soon run past the microprocessor's inherent speed limit.

Depending on the actual memory modules installed in your computer, your system's memory system may be more or less tolerant of speed adjustments, as is your microprocessor, even after allowing for the effect of the multiplier. Consequently, you may need to adjust both the clock speed setting and multiplier setting to achieve optimum perfor-mance from your system.

A further clocking issue is that the design of some motherboards links the PCI expansion bus clock to the front side bus (memory) clock. Although the PCI bus is designed to allow asynchronous operation (it need not be linked to memory speed), many systems do forge such a connection. This linkup can be problematic because PCI devices can be the most speed sensitive in your system. Typical expansion boards—modems, network interface cards (NICs), and SCSI disk controllers—often develop problems when you raise the PCI bus from its nominal 33MHz speed past about 37MHz.

Cycle Shaving

In addition to adjusting the clock speed of memory, many BIOSs allow you to adjust inti-mate aspects of memory timing (for example, the number of clock cycles required for the operation of the memory system). Most of the available settings control the number of cycles of delay between memory control signals. The opportunities for fine-tuning are amazing—you could spend weeks testing the potential combinations of adjustments.

Such attempts will likely be fraught with problems, however. Most adjustments will yield nonworking systems. Moreover, many of them interact, and most make no discernable dif-ference in system performance.

The most worthwhile memory parameter to experiment with is the Column Address Strobe latency, or *CAS latency*. This setting adjusts the number of clock cycles the system waits in between reading bits in the same memory column. A lower value means less wait-ing and thus a faster computer.

Typical CAS latency values in Pentium III-class and Athlon systems range from two to four cycles. Some BIOSs may even allow half-cycle values (for example, 2.5 cycles).

From a technical standpoint, adjusting CAS latency rather than clock speed holds an advantage of a different type. Changing the CAS latency does not raise the operating speed of any part of the computer. Hence, it should not add to the heat stress of any com-puter component and should not affect the life of your computer's circuits.

System Integrity

Pushing any component beyond its rating runs the risk that the component will no longer operate. A single malfunctioning component can lead to your computer no longer boot-ing. But just because your computer boots after you make a BIOS adjustment that affects performance does not mean all is well. You still run the risk that one or more of the parts inside your computer are on the edge of failing. As a result, your computer may boot, but may not operate reliably.

Memory errors are among the most likely problems to arise from pushing memory speed up. Although server memory often has built-in error correction to ward against memory problems, most modern workstations, desktops, and notebook computers lack even parity-checking memory that warns of memory errors (by halting the system). These unprotected systems can develop memory errors without warning, and these errors can ripple though your system until it crashes. In other words, adjust memory speed cautiously, and don't depend on a souped-up system until you've given it time to prove itself.

Microprocessors, too, become unreliable if operated at speeds that are too high. Some BIOSs, however, allow you to help your microprocessor cope with high clock speeds by increasing the core voltage. Higher voltages allow the chip to operate faster without sacrificing data integrity. If you increase your microprocessor speed significantly, you may want to increase its core voltage to ensure its reliable operation. The corollary also applies. If you increase the core voltage of your microprocessor, you should be able to increase the chip's clock frequency more than would have otherwise been possible.

You won't find guidance as to the relationship between voltage and potential speed increases anywhere. Chip-makers test only at design voltages and frequencies. Motherboard-makers defer to the chip-makers, warning only that you should keep within the range specified by the chip-maker. Your only choice is to try and see.

Before adjusting microprocessor core voltage, be sure that you have adequate cooling for your chip. Microprocessor power use—and therefore heat output—increases to the square of the increase in voltage. Consequently, a small voltage increase can quickly lead to the overheating of your microprocessor and, potentially, its self-immolation.

BIOS-makers provide some help with this issue, however. Among the settings for most BIOSs affording voltage control are temperature sensors that allow you to monitor both chip temperature and the temperature inside your computer's case. Some allow for warning when temperatures exceed the limits you set. You may be able to set a shutdown temperature for your microprocessor.

Even these shutdown temperature settings don't guarantee the safety of your expensive silicon, however. The temperature probes measure the microprocessor's external temperature, not the temperature at the semiconductor junctions where damage actually occurs. If you grossly increase the voltage to the microprocessor, the junction temperature can skyrocket into the meltdown range well before any external chip sensor detects a significant temperature change. In other words, step cautiously. If you are tempted to try increasing chip core voltage, do so in small increments—and carefully monitor chip temperature after each change.

Other Options

Speeding up clocks and shaving cycles aren't the only ways you can potentially pluck more performance from your system through BIOS adjustments. Many BIOSs afford you some opportunity to optimize the waits inherent in bus access. In addition, nearly all modern BIOSs allow you to shadow the BIOS code itself.

Although these adjustments sound promising, in reality they do little to improve the overall speed of your system. For example, the real purpose of the bus recovery time adjustments is to help achieve compatibility with older expansion boards. Both the 8-bit I/O recovery time and 16-bit I/O recovery time settings present in the BIOSs of systems with both PCI and ISA expansion buses let you *slow down* the system to accommodate marginal expansion boards connected through the legacy or ISA bus. Although increasing the recovery time, usually measured in bus cycles, may allow you to use older ISA expansion boards, decreasing it will not affect normal system performance.

BIOS shadowing copies the BIOS firmware from ROM to RAM. In theory, it enables your system to read the BIOS code from RAM (32-bit or 64-bit) memory instead of 8- or 16-bit ROM memory. This should speed up BIOS-mediated operations substantially. However, modern operating systems, including Linux and all varieties of Windows from 95 through XP, sidestep the BIOS by using drivers that take direct control of system hardware. Shadowing will not affect the performance of programs run under any of these modern operating systems. In other words, shadowing is a carryover from the days of DOS that's essentially irrelevant to modern computers. Leaving BIOS shadowing *off* will help ensure system stability and slightly increase available memory.

Video shadowing is similarly ineffectual in accelerating today's software. Windows uses its own drivers that directly access video hardware, so video shadowing does not affect normal system performance.

Some BIOSs also offer adjustments for your system's memory cache. Depending on the BIOS, you may have individual control of both Level 1 (L1) and Level 2 (L2) caches, which are sometimes termed *primary* and *secondary*, or more confusingly, *internal* and *external* (confusing because both the L1 and L2 caches are internal with many microprocessors, such as current Athlon, Duron, Pentium III, and Pentium 4 chips). Your BIOS may also allow you to selectively switch off the microprocessor read cache or write cache.

No matter. In any case, the only potential here is for slowing down your system by turning the cache off. These cache controls are not designed to adjust performance. Rather, they are useful only for troubleshooting or preventing problems with software. But programs that have problems with the cache are probably programs you shouldn't be running.

Tuning your system with its BIOS is inevitably a trial-and-error experience. You are investing your time to make tests more rigorous than those made by chip manufacturers so that you can run all of your computer's components as close to the edge as possible.

Upgrades

At one time, engineers viewed the BIOS as a great sculpture or other great work of art, fixed forever in time, perfect and immutable. The BIOS code would be written in read-only memory chips that could not be altered, at least by mere mortals without electrical engineering degrees. But human frailties and rapidly changing technologies forced them to change their minds. They made mistakes in writing some BIOSs that only became apparent after they were shipped off to consumers in finished computers. Or, a few months after they had finished work on their BIOSs—and after computers using them found their ways into consumers' hands—someone decided it would be great if hard disks could store twice as much as the BIOS made allowances for. The only way to make up for the shortcoming of the permanent BIOS was to replace the memory chips, a task most people face with the same calm ease as disarming a tactical nuclear weapon.

Consequently, today most computers come with their BIOS code written in Flash ROM chips, which can be rewritten with relative safety and without even removing the lid from your computer system. If your BIOS needs an upgrade, either to fix an error or to accommodate a new technology, you can usually download a new BIOS from the Web site of the computer's manufacturer.

Updating a Flash BIOS usually involves two files: a binary file that contains the actual BIOS code, and a special program called a *loader*. The loader activates the motherboard circuitry required to write to the BIOS chips and then transfers the contents of the binary BIOS file to the chips. The loader's job is one of the most delicate in the operation of a computer because if it makes a mistake, your system may be rendered inoperable. It might not be able to boot up and rerun the loader. Consequently, for your security, some system-makers require you take elaborate precautions before you try making a BIOS upgrade. For example, the manufacturer may require you to use both the battery and AC power supplies of a notebook computer to make a BIOS update.

To prevent a BIOS upgrade from accidentally rendering your computer inoperable, many computers include *boot block protection*. This feature simply protects or prevents the block of the Flash ROM used for the essential bootup code—the code necessary to let your system read a floppy disk—from being erased during the upgrade. The protected code is sufficient to get your floppy going so that you can try upgrading your BIOS once again (or if the new BIOS itself is the problem, restore your old BIOS).

Because motherboard circuitry varies among different computer brands and models, the BIOS loader made for one system may not work with another. Unless you're advised otherwise by your computer's manufacturer or a BIOS-maker, you should assume that you need a matched pair of files—the BIOS code and loader—to make a BIOS upgrade. In general a loader will warn if it is not meant for your particular system, but don't depend on such a warning to avoid incompatibilities. A loader that makes a mistake can mean your computer must go back to the factory for new BIOS chips before it will boot again.

Along with fixing problems, upgrading a flash BIOS can sometimes cause them, too. BIOS-makers usually design their flash BIOS loaders to reset your computer's setup parameters to the factory defaults so your system gets a fresh start with its new BIOS. If you've customized your system before making the upgrade (for example, adjusting the energy conservation options of a notebook machine), you'll have to re-establish your settings after the upgrade. Sometimes you may find that the load process has altered the date set in CMOS. Operating your system without checking and resetting the date can cause problems with programs sensitive to the relationship between the current time and file date codes. For example, your backup system or disk maintenance program may not work properly after you've upgraded your BIOS if you don't properly restore your system clock.

PART 3
Communications

Let's say I have a box containing all the knowledge in the world. How much would you pay me for it? Oh, one more thing. It's a sealed box and nothing you can do will open it. Nothing, not now or ever. It has no hinges or even a lid. You can't saw the top off or even bore a hole through one of the sides. It resists all acids, nuclear explosions, even Superman's X-ray eyes. It is just an unopenable, sealed box that I absolutely guarantee you is filled with the answers to all your questions and all those of everyone else in the world. And it's a nifty box, oak-oiled a nice, rich brown.

I'd guess you might offer a few dollars, whatever its decorative value. You might even eye it for seating if you didn't have a chair (though I have to admit that the box is not all that big—and it sounds pretty empty at that). Basically, the value of all that knowledge is nothing if you can't get at it and use it.

What would your computer be worth to you if you couldn't get your answers out? If you couldn't connect with the Internet? If you couldn't plug in a CD writer or even a printer? I'd wager not much. It's even an uncomfortable flop as a chair.

Fortunately, your computer is not resistant to a handsaw or electric drill. You can even open it up with a screwdriver. Better still, you can simply plug in a cable or two and connect up with another computer, a network, the Internet, or an Erector set. Your computer is a superlative communications machine. That's what gives it its value—unless you really are using yours as a chair.

A computer communicates in many ways, both outside and inside its box. Moving information around electronically takes a lot of ingenuity and some pretty amazing technologies. Your system's microprocessor must organize its thoughts, make them into messages that it can send out through its ports or down the wires that make up its expansion bus. It needs to know how to talk and, more importantly, how to listen. It needs to put the signals in a form that other computers and add-on devices (*peripherals*) can understand—a form that can travel a few inches across a circuit board, tens of thousands of miles through thin copper wires, or as blips of light in a fiber-optic cable. And it has to do all that without making a mistake.

The next seven chapters outline how your computer communicates. We'll start out with the concepts that underlie all computer (and, for that matter, electronic) communications. From there, we'll step into the real world and examine how your system talks to itself, sending messages inside its own case to other devices you might install there. We'll look at the interfaces it uses to send messages—the computer's equivalent of a telephone handset that it speaks and listens through. Then we'll examine how it connects to external devices, all the accessories and peripherals you plug in. From there, we'll examine the technologies that allow you to connect to the most important peripherals of all—other computers—both in your home or office on a network, and elsewhere in the world through the Internet.

There's a lot to explore, so you might as well put your feet up. After all, a computer may not work well as a chair, but it can be a pretty good footstool.

Channels and Coding

Communications is all about language and, unfortunately, understanding computer communications requires learning another language, one that explains the technology that allows us to send messages, music, and even pictures electronically.

We're going to talk about *channels*, which are nothing more than the paths your electronic messages take. A communication channel is like a television channel. More than that, a television channel *is* a communication channel—a designated pathway for the television signal to get from the broadcasting station to your antenna and television set.

Different channels require technologies for moving information. Paper mail is a communication channel that requires you to use ink and paper (maybe a pencil in a pinch). Electronic communication requires that you translate your message into electronic form.

You cannot directly read an electronic message, no more than you could read it were it written in a secret code. In fact, when your message becomes electronic, it is written in a nonsecret code. Although human beings cannot read it, computers can, because some aspects of the signal correspond to the information in your message, exactly as code letters correspond to the text of a secret message.

As background for understanding how computer communications work, we're first going to look at the characteristics and limitations of the channels that your computer might use. Then we'll take a look at some of the ways that signals get coded so they can be passed through those channels—first as expansion *buses* inside your computer, then as *serial* and *parallel* communication channels between computers. Note that this coding of data is an important technology that has wide applications. It's useful not only in communications but also data storage.

Signal Characteristics

Communications simply means getting information—be it your dulcet voice, a sheaf of your most intimate thoughts, or digital data—from one place to another. It could involve yelling into the wind, smoke signals, express riders on horseback, telegraph keys, laser beams, or whatever technology currently holds favor. Even before people learned to speak, they gestured and grunted to communicate with one another. Although today many people don't do much more than that, we do have a modern array of technologies for moving our thoughts and feelings from one point to another to share with others or for posterity. Computers change neither the need for, nor purpose of, communications. Instead, they offer alternatives and challenges.

Thanks to computer technology, you can move not only your words but also images— both still and moving—at the speed of light. Anything that can be reduced to digital form moves along with computer signals. But the challenge is getting what you want to communicate into digital form, a challenge we won't face until we delve into Part 5, "Human Interface."

Even in digital form, communications can be a challenge.

Channels

If you were Emperor of the Universe, you could solve one of the biggest challenges in communications simply by forbidding anyone else to send messages. You would have every frequency in the airwaves and all the signal capacity of every wire and optic cable available to you. You wouldn't have to worry about interference because should someone interfere with your communications, you could just play the Red Queen and shout "Off with their heads!" Alas, if your not Emperor of the Universe, someone may take a dim view of your hogging the airwaves and severing the heads of friends and family. Worse yet, you're forced to do the most unnatural of acts—actually sharing your means of communication.

Our somewhat civilized societies have created a way to make sharing more orderly if not fair—dividing the space available for communications into channels. Each television and radio station, for example, gets a range of frequencies in which to locate its signals.

But a communications channel is something more general. It is any path through which you can send your signals. For example, when you make a telephone connection, you've established a channel.

Although there are regulatory systems to ensure that channels get fairly shared, all channels are not created equal. Some have room for more signals or more information than others. The channel used by a telephone allows only a small trickle of information to flow (which is why telephone calls sound so tinny). A fiber optic cable, on the other hand, has an immense space for information, so much that it is usually sliced into several hundred or thousand channels.

Bandwidth

The primary limit on any communications channel is its *bandwidth*, the chief constraint on the data rate through that channel. Bandwidth merely specifies a range of frequencies from the lowest to the highest that the channel can carry or present in the signal. It's like your stereo system. Turn the bass (the low frequencies) and the treble (the high frequencies) all the way down, and you've limited the bandwidth to the middle frequencies. It doesn't sound very good because you're missing part of the signal—you've reduced its bandwidth.

Bandwidth is one way of describing the maximum amount of information that the channel can carry. Bandwidth is expressed differently for analog and digital circuits. In analog technology, the bandwidth of a circuit is the difference between the lowest and highest frequencies that can pass through the channel. Engineers measure analog bandwidth in kilohertz or megahertz. In a digital circuit, the bandwidth is the amount of information that can pass through the channel. Engineers measure digital bandwidth in bits, kilobits, or megabits per second. The kilohertz of an analog bandwidth and the kilobits per second of digital bandwidth for the same circuit are not necessarily the same and often differ greatly.

Nature conspires with the laws of physics to limit the bandwidth of most communications channels. Although an ideal wire should be able to carry any and every frequency, real wires cannot. Electrical signals are social busybodies of the physical world. They interact with themselves, other signals, and nearly everything else in the world—and all these interactions limit bandwidth. The longer the wire, the more chance there is for interaction, and the lower the bandwidth the wire allows. Certain physical characteristics of wires cause degradations in their high frequency transmission capabilities. The capacitance between conductors in a cable pair, for instance, increasingly degrades signals as their frequencies rise, finally reaching a point that a high frequency signal might not be able to traverse more than a few centimeters of wire. Amplifiers or repeaters, which boost signals so that they can travel longer distances, often cannot handle very low or very high frequencies, thus imposing more limits.

Even fiber optic cables, which have bandwidths dozens of times that of copper wires, also degrade signals with distance—pulses of light blur a bit as they travel through the fiber, until equipment can no longer pick digital bits from the blur.

Emissions Limitations

Even the wires inside computers have bandwidth limitations, although they are infrequently explicitly discussed as such. Every wire, even the copper traces on circuit boards (which act as wires), not only carries electricity but also acts as a miniature radio antenna. It's unavoidable physics—moving electricity *always* creates a magnetic field that can radiate away as radio waves.

The closer the length of a wire matches the wavelength of an electrical signal, the better it acts as an antenna. Because radio waves are really long at low frequencies (at one megahertz, the wavelength is about 1000 feet long), radio emissions are not much of a problem at low frequencies. But today's computers push frequencies into the gigahertz range, and their short wavelengths make ordinary wires and circuit traces into pretty good antennas. Engineers designing modern computers have to be radio engineers as well as electrical engineers.

Good designs cause fewer emissions. For example, engineers can arrange circuits so the signals they emit tend to cancel out. But the best way to minimize problems is to keep frequencies lower.

Lower frequencies, of course, limit bandwidth. But when you're working inside a computer, there's an easy way around that—increase the number of channels by using several in parallel. That expedient is the basis for the *bus*, a collection of several signals traveling in parallel, both electrically and physically. A computer expansion bus uses 8, 16, 32, or 64 separate signal pathways, thus lowering the operating frequency to a fraction of that required by putting all the data into a single, serial channel.

Standards-Based Limitations

The airwaves also have a wide bandwidth, and they are not bothered by radiation issues. After all, the signals in the airwaves *are* radiation. Nor are they bothered by signal degradation (except at certain frequencies where physical objects can block signals). But because radio signals tend to go everywhere, bandwidth through the airwaves is limited by the old bugaboo of sharing. To permit as many people to share the airwaves as possible, channels are assigned to arbitrarily defined frequency bands.

Sharing also applies to wire- and cable-based communications. Most telephone channels, for example, have an artificial bandwidth limitation imposed by the telephone company. To get the greatest financial potential from the capacity of their transmissions cables, microwave systems, and satellites, telephone carriers normally limit the bandwidth of telephone signals to a narrow slice of the full human voice range. That's why phone calls have their unmistakable sound. By restricting the bandwidth of each call, the telephone company can stack many calls on top of one another using an electronic technique called *multiplexing*. This strategy allows a single pair of wires to carry hundreds of simultaneous conversations.

The real issue is not how signals get constrained by bandwidth, but rather the effect of bandwidth on the signal. Bandwidth constrains the ability of a channel to carry information. The narrower the bandwidth, the less information that gets through. It doesn't matter whether the signal is analog or digital, your voice, a television picture, or computer data. The bandwidth of the channel will constrain the actual information of any signal passing through the channel.

Bandwidth limits appear wherever signals must go. Even the signals flowing from one part of a circuit to another inside a computer are constrained by bandwidth limits.

Modulation

Computers and the standard international communications systems grew up independently, each with its own technological basis. Computers began their commercial lives as digital devices because of the wonderful ability of digital signals to resist errors. Communications systems started on a foundation of analog technology. Their primary focus began as the transmission of the human voice, which was most easily communicated in analog form with the primitive technologies then available. Since the early days of computers and communications, the two technologies have become intimately intertwined: Computers have become communications engines, and most communications are now routed by computers. Despite this convergence, however, the two technologies remain stuck with their incompatible foundations—computers are digital and human communications are analog.

The technology that allows modems to send digital signals through the analog communications circuits is called *modulation*. The modulation process creates analog signals that contain all the digital information of the original digital computer code but which can be transmitted through the analog circuits, such as the voice-only channels of the telephone system.

Someday the incompatibility between the computer and communications worlds will end, perhaps sooner than you might think. In the year 2000, computer data overtook the human voice as the leading use of long-distance communications. Even before that, nearly all long distance voice circuits had been converted to use digital signals. But these changes haven't eliminated the need for using modulation technology. Dial-up telephone lines remain the way most people connect their computers to the Internet, and local loops (the wires from the telephone company central office to your home) remain stubbornly analog. Moreover, many types of communications media (for example, radio waves) require modulation technology to carry digital (and even voice and music) signals.

The modulation process begins with a constant signal called the *carrier*, which carries or bears the load of the digital information. The digital data in some ways modifies the carrier, changing some aspect of it in such a way the change can be later detected in receiving equipment. The changes to the carrier—the information content of the signal—are the *modulation*, and the data is said to "modulate the carrier."

Demodulation is the signal-recovery process, the opposite of modulation. During demodulation, the carrier is stripped away and the encoded information is returned to its original form. Although logically just the compliment of modulation, demodulation usually involves entirely different circuits and operating principles.

In most modulation systems, the carrier is a steady-state signal of constant amplitude (strength), frequency, and coherent phase—the electrical equivalent of a pure tone. Because it is unchanging, the carrier itself is devoid of content and information. It's the equivalent of one, unchanging digital bit. The carrier is simply a package, like a milk carton for holding information. Although you need both the carrier and milk carton to move its contents from one place to another, the package doesn't affect the contents and is essentially irrelevant to the product. You throw it away once you've got the product where you want it.

The most common piece of equipment you connect to your computer that uses modulation is the modem. In fact, the very name *modem* is derived from this term and the reciprocal circuit—the demodulator—that's used in reception. Modem is a foreshortening of the words *modulator* and *demodulator*.

A modem modulates an analog signal that can travel through the telephone system with the digital direct current signals produced by your computer. The modem also demodulates incoming signals, stripping off the analog component and passing the digital information to your computer. The resulting modulated carrier wave remains an analog signal that, usually, whisks easily through the telephone system.

Radio systems also rely on modulation. They apply voice, video, or data information to a carrier wave. Radio works because engineers created receivers, which can tune to the frequency of the carrier and exclude other frequencies, so you can tune in to only the signal (and modulation) you want to receive. Note that most commonly, radio systems use analog signals to modulate their carriers. The modulation need not be digital.

The modulation process has two requirements. The first is the continued compatibility with the communications medium so that the signal is still useful. The second is the ability to separate the modulation from the carrier so that you can recover the original signal.

Just as AM and FM radio stations use different modulation methods to achieve the same end, designers of communications systems can select from several modulation technologies to encode digital data in a form compatible with analog transmission systems. The different forms of modulation are distinguished by the characteristics of the carrier wave that are changed in response to changes in data to encode information. The three primary characteristics of a carrier wave that designers might elect to vary for modulation are its amplitude, its frequency, and its phase. Pulse modulation is actually a digital signal that emulates an analog signal and can be handled by communications systems as it if it were one.

Carrier Wave Modulation

The easiest way to understand the technique of modulation is to look at its simplest form, *carrier wave* modulation, which is often abbreviated as CW, particularly by radio broadcasters.

As noted previously, a digital signal, when stripped to its essential quality, is nothing more than a series of bits of information that can be encoded in any of a variety of forms. We use zeros and ones to express digital values on paper. In digital circuits, the same bits take the form of the high and low direct current voltages, the same ones that are incompatible with the telephone system. However, we can just as easily convert digital bits into the presence or absence of a signal that can travel through the telephone system (or that can be broadcast as a radio wave). The compatible signal is, of course, the carrier wave. By switching the carrier wave off and on, we can encode digital zeroes and ones with it.

The resulting CW signal looks like interrupted bursts of round sine waves, as shown in Figure 8.1.

FIGURE 8.1
Carrier wave modula-
tion.

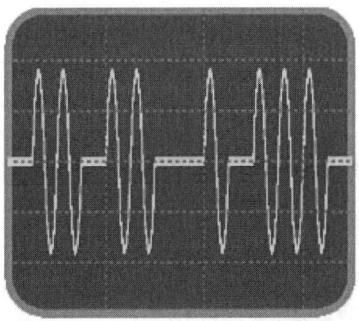

The figure shows the most straightforward way to visualize the conversion between digital and analog, assigning one full wave of the carrier to represent a digital one (1) and the absence of a wave to represent a zero (0). In most practical simple carrier waves systems, however, each bit occupies the space of several waves. The system codes the digital information not as pulses per se, but as time. A bit lasts a given period regardless of the number of cycles occurring within that period, making the frequency of the carrier wave irrelevant to the information content.

Although CW modulation has its shortcomings, particularly in wire-based communications, it retains a practical application in radio transmission. It is used in the simplest radio transmission methods, typically for sending messages in Morse code.

One of the biggest drawbacks of carrier wave modulation is ambiguity. Any interruption in the signal may be misinterpreted as a digital zero. In telephone systems, the problem is particularly pernicious. Equipment has no way of discerning whether a long gap between bursts of carrier wave is actually significant data or a break in or end of the message.

Frequency Shift Keying

A more reliable way of signaling digital information is to use separate and distinct frequencies for each digital state. For example, a digital 1 would cause the carrier wave to change to a higher frequency, much as it causes a higher voltage, and a digital 0 would shift the signal to a lower frequency. Two different frequencies and the shifts between them could then encode binary data for transmission across an analog system. This form of modulation is called *frequency shift keying*, or FSK, because information is encoded in (think of it being "keyed to") the shifting of frequency.

The "keying" part of the name is actually left over from the days of the telegraph when this form of modulation was used for transmitting Morse code. The frequency shift came with the banging of the telegraph key.

In practical FSK systems, the two shifting frequencies are the modulation that is applied to a separate (and usually much higher) carrier wave. When no modulation is present, only the carrier wave at its fundamental frequency appears. With modulation, the overall signal jumps between two different frequencies. Figure 8.2 shows what an FSK modulation looks like electrically.

FIGURE 8.2
Frequency shift keying.

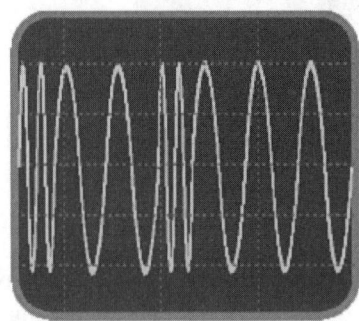

Frequency shift keying unambiguously distinguishes between proper code and a loss of signal. In FSK, a carrier remains present even when no code is being actively transmitted. FSK is thus more reliable than CW and more widely used in communications systems. The very earliest of computer modems (those following the Bell 103 standard) used ordinary FSK to put digital signals on analog telephone lines.

Amplitude Modulation

Carrier wave modulation is actually a special case of *amplitude modulation*. Amplitude is the strength of the signal or the loudness of a tone carried through a transmission medium, such as the telephone wire. Varying the strength of the carrier in response to modulation to transmit information is called *amplitude modulation*. Instead of simply being switched on and off, as with carrier wave modulation, in amplitude modulation the carrier tone gets louder or softer in response to the modulating signal. Figure 8.3 shows what an amplitude modulated signal looks like electrically.

FIGURE 8.3
Amplitude modulation—signal strength (vertical) versus time (horizontal).

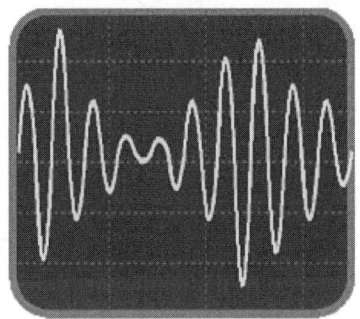

Amplitude modulation is most commonly used by radio and television broadcasters to transmit analog signals because the carrier can be modulated in a continuous manner, matching the raw analog signal. Although amplitude modulation carries talk and music to your AM radio and the picture to your (nondigital) television set, engineers also exploit amplitude modulation for digital transmissions. They can, for example, assign one amplitude to indicate a logical 1 and another amplitude to indicate a logical 0.

Pure amplitude modulation has one big weakness. The loudness of a signal is the characteristic most likely to vary during transmission. Extraneous signals add to the carrier and mimic modulation. Noise in the communication channel line mimics amplitude modulation and might be confused with data.

Frequency Modulation

Just as amplitude modulation is a refinement of CW, frequency shift keying is a special case of the more general technology called *frequency modulation*. In the classic frequency modulation system used by FM radio, variations in the loudness of sound modulate a carrier wave by changing its frequency. When music on an FM station gets louder, for example, the radio station's carrier frequency shifts its frequency more. In effect, FM translates changes in modulation amplitude into changes in carrier frequency. The modulation does not alter the level of the carrier wave. As a result, an FM signal electrically looks like a train of wide and narrow waves of constant height, as shown in Figure 8.4.

FIGURE 8.4
Frequency modula-
tion—signal strength
(vertical) versus time
(horizontal).

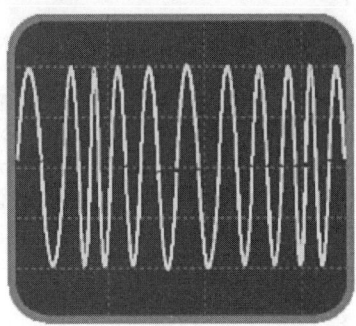

In a pure FM system, the strength or amplitude of the signal is irrelevant. This characteristic makes FM almost immune to noise. Interference and noise signals add into the desired signal and alter its strength, but FM demodulators ignore these amplitude changes. That's why lightning storms and motors don't interfere with FM radios. This same immunity from noise and variations in amplitude makes frequency modulation a more reliable, if more complex, transmission method for digital data.

Phase Modulation

Another variation on the theme of frequency modulation is *phase modulation*. This technology works by altering the phase relationship between the waves in the signal. An unmodulated carrier is a train wave in a constant phase relationship. That is, the waves follow one after another precisely in step. The peaks and troughs of the train of waves flow in constant intervals. If one wave were delayed for exactly one wavelength, it would fit exactly atop the next one.

By delaying the peak of one wave so that it occurs later than it should, you can break the constant phase relationship between the waves in the train without altering the overall amplitude or frequency of the wave train. In other words, you shift the onset of a subsequent wave compared to those that precede it. At the same time, you will create a detectable state change called a *phase shift*. You can then code digital bits as the presence or absence of a phase shift.

Signals are said to be "in phase" when the peaks and troughs of one align exactly with another. When signals are 180 degrees "out of phase," the peaks of one signal align with the troughs of the other. Figure 8.5 shows a 180-degree phase shift of a carrier wave. Note that the two waveforms shown start "in phase" and then, after a phase shift, end up being 180 degrees out of phase.

FIGURE 8.5

Phase modulation showing a 180-degree phase shift.

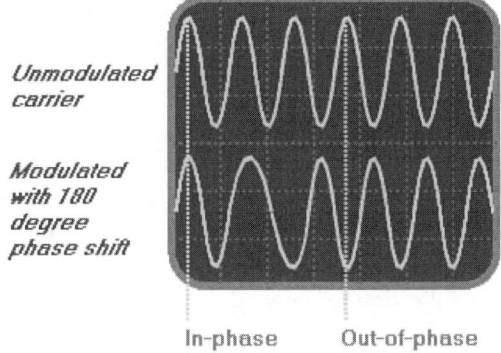

Unmodulated carrier

Modulated with 180 degree phase shift

In-phase   Out-of-phase

If you examine the shapes of waves that result from a phase shift, you'll see that phase modulation is a special case of FM. Delaying a wave lengthens the time between its peak and that of the preceding wave. As a result, the frequency of the signal shifts downward during the change, although over the long term the frequency of the signal appears to remain constant.

One particular type of phase modulation. called *quadrature modulation*. alters the phase of the signal solely in increments of 90 degrees. That is, the shift between waves occurs at a phase angle of 0, 90, 180, or 270 degrees. The "quad" in the name of this modulation method refers to the four possible phase delays.

Pulse Modulation

Pulse modulation is actually a digital signal made up from discrete pulses of energy. The pulses have an underlying characteristic frequency—essentially their data clock—that is the equivalent of a carrier wave. In fact, to analog circuits, some forms of pulse modulation are demodulated as if they were analog signals. For example, add in some extra pulses, and you change the apparent frequency of the clock/carrier, thus creating frequency modulation. Change the duty cycle of the pulses (make the "on" part of the pulse last longer or shorter), and the analog strength of the carrier varies, thus creating analog modulation.

But you can also alter the pulses in a strictly digital manner, changing the bit-pattern to convey information. The signal then is completely digital, yet it still acts like it is an ordinary modulated carrier wave because it retains its periodic clock signal.

Pulse frequency modulation (PFM) is the simplest form of most pulse modulation. Using PFM, the modulator changes the number of pulses in a given period to indicate the strength of the underlying analog signal. More pulses means a higher frequency, so the frequency changes in correspondence with the amplitude of the analog signal. The result can be detected as ordinary frequency modulation.

Pulse width modulation (PWM) varies the width of each pulse to correspond to the strength of the underlying analog signal. This is just another way of saying that PWM alters the duty cycle of the pulses. The changes in signal strength with modulation translate into ordinary amplitude modulation.

Pulse code modulation (PCM) is the most complex form of pulse modulation, and it is purely digital. PCM uses a digital number or code to indicate the strength of the underlying analog signal. For example, the voltage of the signal is translated into a number, and the digital signal represents that number in binary code. This form of digital modulation is familiar from its wide application in digital audio equipment such as CD players.

Pulse position modulation (PPM) uses the temporal position of a pulse within a clock period to indicate a discrete value. For example, the length of one clock period may be divided into four equal segments. A pulse can occur in one, and only one, of these chip segments, and which chip the pulse appears in (its position inside the symbol duration or clock period) encodes its value. For example, the four segments may be numbered 0, 1, 2, and 3. If the pulse appears in segment 2, that clock period carries a value of 2.

Figure 8.6 shows the pulse position for the four valid code values using the PPM scheme developed for the IrDA interface.

FIGURE 8.6

Pulse positions for the four valid code values of 4PPM under IrDA.

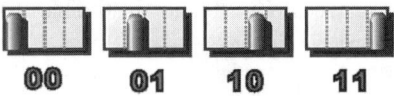

Complex Modulation

The various modulation techniques are not mutually exclusive. Engineers have found ways of pushing more data through a given communication channel by combining two or more techniques to create *complex modulation* schemes.

In broadcasting, complex modulation is not widely used. There's not much point to it. In data communications, however, it allows engineers to develop systems in which a signal can have any of several states in a clock period. Each state, called a *symbol* by engineers, can encode one or more bits of data. The more states, the more bits that each symbol can encode using a technique called *group-coding*, which is discussed later in the section with the same name.

Parallel Channels

A *parallel connection* is one with multiple signals traveling down separate wires, side by side. For computers, this is the natural way of dealing with communications. Everything about a microprocessor is parallel. Its registers look at data bits in parallel—32 or more at a time. The chip sucks information into its circuitry the same way—32, 64, or even 128 bits at a time. It's only natural. The chip works on multiple bits with every tick of the system clock, so you want to fill it with data the same way (and at the same rate).

When it comes time for the chip to communicate—both with the rest of the computer and with the outside world—it's only natural to use the same kind of connection, one that can pass multiple data bits in parallel. Moreover, by providing a number of data paths, a parallel channel has the potential for moving more information in a given time. Parallel channels can be faster.

With this design philosophy in mind, engineers have developed parallel communication channels of two types. Expansion *buses* provide a wide, parallel path for data inside the computer. The familiar Peripheral Component Interconnect (PCI) bus is such a design. Parallel communications *ports* serve to connect the computer with other equipment. The parallel printer port is the exemplar of this technology.

Of the two, ports are simpler. They just have less to do. They connect external devices to the computer, and they only need to move information back and forth. They sacrifice the last bit of versatility for practicality. Expansion buses must do more. In addition to providing a route for a stream of data, they also must provide random access to that data. They must operate at higher speeds, as well, as close to the clock speed of the microprocessor as can be successfully engineered and operated. They need more signals and a more complex design to carry out all their functions.

Some designs, however, straddle the difference. SCSI offers external parallel connections like a port but also works a bit like an expansion bus. The common hard disk interface, AT Attachment (or IDE), is part of an expansion bus, but it doesn't allow direct addressing. All, however, use parallel channels to move their information.

Ports

The concept behind a parallel port is simply to extend the signals of the computer to another device. When microprocessors had data buses only eight bits wide, providing an external connection with the same number of bits was the logical thing to do. Of course, when microprocessors had data buses only eight bits wide, the circuitry needed in order to convert signals to another form was prohibitively expensive, especially when you need to convert the signal when it leaves the computer and convert it back to parallel form at the receiving device, even a device as simple as a printer. Of course, when microprocessors had eight-bit data buses, Mammoths still strode the earth (or so it seems).

Many people use the term *port* to refer to external connections on their computers. A port is a jack into which you plug a cable. By extension, the name refers to the connection system (and standard) used to make the port work. Take a similar design and restrict it to use inside the computer, and it becomes an *interface*, such as the common disk interfaces. By these definitions, the Small Computer System Interface (SCSI) is schizophrenic. It has a split personality and works either way. In truth, the terms *port* and *interface* have many overlapping meanings.

In the modern world, parallel connections have fallen by the wayside for use as ports. One reason is that it has become cheaper to design circuits to convert signal formats. In addition, the cost of equipping signal paths to ward off interference increases with every added path, so cables for high-speed parallel connections become prohibitively expensive. Consequently, most new port designs use serial rather than parallel technology. But parallel designs remain a good starting point in any discussion of communications because they are inherently simpler, working with computer data in its native form.

Even the most basic parallel connection raises several design issues. Just having a parallel connection is not sufficient. Besides moving data from point to point, a parallel channel must be able to control the flow of data, both pacing the flow of bits and ensuring that information won't be dumped where it cannot be used. These issues will arise in the design of every communications system.

Data Lines

The connections that carry data across a parallel channel are termed *data lines*. They are nothing more than wires that conduct electrical signals from one end of the connection to the other. In most parallel channels, the data lines carry ordinary digital signals, on-or-off pulses, without modulation.

The fundamental factor in describing a parallel connection is therefore the number of data lines it provides. More is always better, but more also means increased complexity and cost. As a practical matter, most parallel channels use eight data lines. More usually is unwieldy, and fewer would be pointless. The only standard connection system to use more than eight is *Wide SCSI*, which doubles the channel width to 16 bits to correspondingly double its speed potential.

Although today's most popular standards use only enough data lines to convey data, sometimes engineers add an extra line for each eight called a *parity-check* line. Parity-checking provides a means to detect errors that might occur during communication.

Parity-checking uses a simple algorithm for finding errors. The sending equipment adds together the bits on the data lines without regard to their significance. That is, it checks which lines carry a digital one (1) and which carry a digital zero (0). It adds all the ones together. If the sum is an odd number, it makes the parity-check line a one. If the sum is even, it makes the parity-check line a zero. In that way, the sum of all the lines—data lines and parity-check lines—is always an even number. The receiving equipment repeats the summing. If it comes up with an odd number, it knows the value of one of the data lines (or the parity-check line) has changed, indicating an error has occurred.

Timing

The signals on a parallel channel use the same clocked logic as the signals inside a computer. Accordingly, there are times when the signals on the data lines are not valid—for example, when they are changing or have changed but are not yet stable. As with the signals inside the computer system, the parallel channel uses a clock to indicate when the signals on the data lines represent valid data and when they do not.

The expedient design, in keeping with the rest of the design of the parallel channel, is to include an extra signal (and a wire to carry it) that provides the necessary clock pulses. Most parallel channels use a dedicated clock line to carry the pulses of the required timing signal.

Flow Control

The metaphor often used for a communications channel is that of a pipe. With nothing more to the design than data lines and a clock, that pipe would be open ended, like a waterline with the spigot stuck on. Data would gush out of it until the equipment drowned in a sea of bits. Left too long, a whole room might fill up with errant data; perhaps buildings would explode and scatter bits all over creation.

To prevent that kind of disaster, a parallel channel needs some means of moderating the flow of data, a giant hand to operate a digital spigot. With a parallel connection, the natural means of controlling data flow is yet another signal.

Some parallel channels have several such flow-control signals. In a two-way communications system, both ends of the connection may need to signal when they can no longer accept data. Additional flow-control signals might indicate specific reasons *why* no more data can be accepted. For example, one line in a parallel port might signal that the printer has run out of paper.

Buses

The computer *expansion bus* shows digital communications at its most basic—if you want to move digital signals away from a microprocessor, just make the wires longer. The first expansion bus shows this principle in action. The IBM Personal Computer expansion bus, which evolved into the Industry Standard Architecture (a defining characteristic of personal computers for nearly 15 years), was really nothing more than the connections to the microprocessor extended to reach further inside the computer.

Modern expansion buses go further—in technology rather than distance. Although they still stay within the confines of a computer's case, they have evolved into elaborate switching and control systems to help move data faster. One of the reasons for this change in design arises from limitations imposed by the communications channel of the bus itself. In addition, the modern bus has evolved as a communications system independent of the microprocessor in the computer. By looking at the bus as a communications system unto itself, engineers have added both versatility and speed. The next generation of expansion buses will be almost indistinguishable from long-distance data communications systems, sharing nearly all their technologies, except for being shorter and faster.

Background

The concept of a bus is simple: If you have to move more information than a single wire can hold, use several. A bus is comprised of several electrical connections linking circuits carrying related signals in parallel. The similarity in the name with the vehicle that carries passengers across and between cities is hardly coincidental. Just as many riders fit in one vehicle, the bus, many signals travel together in an electrical bus. As with a highway bus, an electrical bus often makes multiple stops on its way to its destination. Because all the signals on a bus are related, a bus comprises a single communication channel.

The most familiar bus in computer systems is the *expansion bus*. As the name implies, it is an electrical bus that gives you a way to expand the potential of your computer by attaching additional electrical devices to it. The additional devices are often termed *peripherals* or, because many people prefer to reserve that term for external accessories, simply *expansion boards*.

A simple bus links circuits, but today's expansion bus is complicated by many issues. Each expansion bus design represents a complex set of design choices confined by practical constraints. Designers make many of the choices by necessity; others they pick pragmatically. The evolution of the modern expansion bus has been mostly a matter of building upon the ideas that came before (or stealing the best ideas of the predecessors). The result in today's computers is a high-performance *Peripheral Component Interconnect*, or PCI, upgrade system that minimizes (but has yet to eliminate) setup woes.

The range of bus functions and resources is wide. The most important of these is providing a data pathway that links the various components of your computer together. It must provide both the channel through which the data moves and a means of ensuring the data gets where it is meant to go. In addition, the expansion bus must provide special signals to synchronize the thoughts of the add-in circuitry with those of the rest of the computer. Newer bus designs (for example, PCI, but not the old Industry Standard Architecture, or ISA, of the last generation of personal computers) also include a means of delegating system control to add-in products and tricks for squeezing extra speed from data transfers.

Although not part of the electrical operation of the expansion bus, the physical dimensions of the boards and other components are also governed by agreed-on expansion bus specifications, which we will look at in Chapter 30, "Expansion Boards." Moreover, today's bus standards go far beyond merely specifying signals. They also dictate transfer protocols and integrated, often automated, configuration systems.

How these various bus features work—and how well they work—depends on the specific features of each bus design. In turn, the expansion bus design exerts a major influence on the overall performance of the computer it serves. Bus characteristics also determine what you can add to your computer—how many expansion boards, how much memory, and what other system components—as well as how easy your system is to set up. The following sections examine the features and functions of all expansion buses, the differences among them, and the effects of those differences in the performance and expandability of your computer.

Data Lines

Although the information could be transferred inside a computer either by serial or parallel means, the expansion buses inside computers use parallel data transfers. The choice of the parallel design is a natural. All commercial microprocessors have parallel connections for their data transfers. The reason for this choice in microprocessors and buses is exactly the same: Parallel transfers are faster. Having multiple connections means that the system can move multiple bits every clock cycle. The more bits the bus can pass in a single cycle, the faster it will move information. Wider buses—those with more parallel connections—are faster, all else being equal.

Ideally, the expansion bus should provide a data path that matches that of the microprocessor. That way, an entire digital *quad-word* used by today's Pentium-class microprocessors (a full 64 bits) can stream across the bus without the need for data conversions. When the bus is narrower than a device that sends or receives the signals, the data must be repackaged for transmission—the computer might have to break a quad-word into four sequential words or eight bytes to fit an old 16- or 8-bit bus. Besides the obvious penalty of requiring multiple bus cycles to move the data the microprocessor needs, a narrow bus also makes system design more complex. Circuitry to handle the required data repackaging complicates both motherboards and expansion boards.

On the other hand, increasing the number of data connections also complicates the design of a computer, if just because of the extra space and materials required. Finding the optimal number of connections for a given application consequently is a tradeoff between speed (which requires more connections) and complexity (which increases with connection count and thus speed).

In modern computers with multiple expansion buses, each bus usually has a different number of data connections, reflecting the speed requirements of each bus. The bus with the highest performance demands—the memory bus—has the most connections. The bus with the least performance demands—the compatibility bus—has the fewest.

Address Lines

As long as a program knows what to do with data, a bus can transfer information without reference to memory addresses. Having address information available, however, increases the flexibility of the bus. For example, making addressing available on the bus enables you to add normal system memory on expansion boards. Addressing allows memory-mapped information transfers and random access to information. It allows data bytes to be routed to the exact location at which they will be used or stored. Imagine the delight of the dead letter office of the Post Office and the ever-increasing stack of stationery accumulating there if everyone decided that appending addresses to envelopes was superfluous. Similarly, expansion boards must be able to address origins and destinations for data. The easiest method of doing this is to provide address lines on the expansion bus corresponding to those of the microprocessor.

The number of address lines used by a bus determines the maximum memory range addressable by the bus. It's a purely digital issue—two to the power of the number of address lines yields the maximum discrete address values that the bus can indicate. A bus with eight address lines can address 256 locations (two to the eighth power); with 16 address lines, it can identify 65,536 locations (that is, two to the sixteenth power.)

Engineers have a few tricks to trim the number of address lines they need. For example, modern microprocessors have no need to address every individual byte. They swallow data in 32- or 64-bit chunks (that is, double-words or quad-words). They do not have to be able to address memory any more specifically than every fourth or eighth byte. When they do need to retrieve a single byte, they just grab a whole double-word or quad-word at once and sort out what they need internally. Consequently, most 32-bit expansion buses designed to accommodate these chips commonly delete the two least-significant address bits.

Some bus designs eliminate the need for address lines entirely by using *multiplexing*. Instead of separate address lines for addresses and data, they combine the functions on the same connections. Some multiplexed designs use a special signal that, when present, indicates the bits appearing on the combined address and data lines are data. In the absence of the signal, the bits on the lines represent an address. The system alternates between addresses and data, first giving the location to put information and then sending the information itself. In wide-bus systems, this multiplexing technique can drastically cut the number of connections required. A full 64-bit system might have 64 address lines and 64 data lines—a total of 128 connections for moving information. When multiplexed, the same system could get by with 65 connections—64 combined address/data lines and one signal to discriminate which is which.

Most systems require an address for every transfer of data across the bus. That is, for each 32-bit transfer through a 32-bit bus, the system requires an address to indicate where that information goes. Some buses allow for a *burst mode*, in which a block of data going to sequential addresses travels without indicating each address. Typically, a burst-mode transfer requires a starting address, the transfer of data words one after another, and some indication the burst has ended. A burst mode can nearly double the speed of data transfer across the bus.

Timing

Buses need timing or clock signals for two reasons. The bus may be called upon to distribute timing systems throughout a computer to keep all the circuits synchronized. In addition, the data traveling on the bus itself requires clocking—the clock signal indicates when the data (or addresses, or both) on the bus is valid.

The same signal can be used for clocking the bus data and synchronizing other circuits. Such a bus is termed *synchronous* because it is synchronized. Alternatively, the bus may have two (or more) separate clock signals for different purposes. Buses in which the clock for data on the bus is not synchronized with the system clock are termed *asynchronous* buses.

Flow Control

Buses require flow control for the same reason as ports—to prevent peripherals from being swamped with a tidal wave of data or to keep a peripheral from flooding the rest of the system. To avoid data losses when a speed disparity arises between peripherals and the host, most buses include flow-control signals. In the simplest form, the peripheral sends a special "not ready" signal across the bus, warning the host to wait until the peripheral catches up. Switching off the "not ready" signal indicates to the host to dump more data on the peripheral.

System Control

Buses often carry signals for purposes other than moving data. For example, computer expansion buses may carry separate lines to indicate each interrupt or request for a DMA transfer. Alternatively, buses can use signals like those of parallel ports to indicate system faults or warnings.

Most buses have a *reset* signal that tells the peripherals to initialize themselves and reset their circuits to the same state they would have when initially powering up. Buses may also have special signals that indicate the number of data lines containing valid data during a transfer. Another signal may indicate whether the address lines hold a memory address or an I/O port address.

Bus-Mastering

In the early days of computers, the entire operation of the expansion bus was controlled by the microprocessor in the host computer. The bus was directly connected to the microprocessor; in fact, the bus was little more than an extension of the connections on the chip itself. A bus connected directly to the microprocessor data and address lines is termed a *local bus* because it is meant to service only the components in the close vicinity of the microprocessor itself. Most modern buses now use a separate bus controller that manages the transfers across the bus.

Many bus designs allow for decentralized control, where any device connected to the bus (or any device in a particular class of devices) may take command. This design allows each device to manage its own transfers, thus eliminating any bottlenecks that can occur with a single, centralized controller. The device that takes control of the bus is usually termed a *bus master*. The device that it transfers data to is the *bus slave*. The bus master is dynamic. Almost any device may be in control of the bus at any given moment. Only the device in control is the master of the bus. However, in some systems where not every device can control the bus, the devices that are *capable* of mastering the bus are termed "bus masters," even when they are not in control—or even installed on the system, for that matter.

If multiple devices try to take control of the bus at the same time, the result is confusion (or worse, a loss of data). All buses that allow mastering consequently must have some scheme that determines when and which master can take control of the bus, a process called *bus arbitration*. Each bus design uses its own protocol for controlling the arbitration process. This protocol can be software, typically using a set of commands set across the bus like data, or hardware, using special dedicated control lines in the bus. Most practical bus designs use a hardware signaling scheme.

In the typical hardware-based arbitration system, a potential master indicates its need to take control of the bus by sending an attention signal on a special bus line. If several devices want to take control at the same time, an algorithm determines which competing master is granted control, how long that control persists, and when after losing control it can be granted the same master again.

In software-based systems, the potential bus master device sends a request to its host's bus-control logic. The host grants control by sending a special software command in return.

The design of the arbitration system usually has two competing goals: fairness and priority. *Fairness* ensures that one device cannot monopolize the bus, and that within a given period every device is given a crack at bus control. For example, some designs require that once a master has gotten control of the bus, it will not get a grant of control again until all other masters also seeking control have been served. *Priority* allows the system to act somewhat unfairly, to give more of the bus to devices that need it more. Some bus designs forever fix the priorities of certain devices; others allow priorities of some or all masters to be programmed.

Power Distribution

Although all electrical devices need some source of electricity to operate, no immutable law requires an expansion bus to provide that power. For example, when you plug a printer into your computer, you also usually plug the printer into a wall outlet. Similarly, peripherals could have their own sources of needed electricity. Providing that power on the bus makes the lives of engineers much easier. They don't have to worry about the design requirements, metaphysics, or costs of adding power sources such as solar panels, magnetohydrodynamic generators, or cold fusion reactors to their products.

Non-Bussed Signals

Buses are so named because their signals are "bused" together; but sometimes engineers design buses with separate, dedicated signals to individual devices. Most systems use only a single device-specific signal on a dedicated pin (the same pin at each device location, but a different device-specific signal on the pin for each peripheral). This device-specific signaling is used chiefly during power-on testing and setup. By activating this signal, one device can be singled out for individual control. For example, in computer expansion buses, a single, non-bussed signal allows each peripheral to be individually activated for testing, and the peripheral (or its separately controllable parts) can be switched off if defective. Device-specific signals also are used to poll peripherals individually about their resource usage so that port and memory conflicts can be automatically managed by the host system.

Bridges

The modern computer with multiple buses—often operating with different widths and speeds—poses a problem for the system designer: how to link those buses together. Make a poor link-up, and performance will suffer on *all* the buses.

A device that connects two buses together is called a *bridge*. The bridge takes care of all the details of the transfer, converting data formats and protocols automatically without the need for special programming or additional hardware.

A bridge can span buses that are similar or different. A PCI-based computer can readily incorporate any bus for which bridge hardware is available. For example, in a typical PCI system, bridges will link three dissimilar buses—the microprocessor bus, the high-speed PCI bus, and an ISA compatibility bus—and may additionally tie in another, similar PCI bus to yield a greater number of expansion opportunities.

The interconnected buses logically link together in the form of a family tree, spreading out as it radiates downward. The buses closer to the single original bus at the top are termed *upstream*. Those in the lower generations more distant from the progenitor bus are termed *downstream*. Bridge design allows data to flow from any location on the family tree to any other. However, because each bridge imposes a delay for its internal processing, called *latency*, a transfer that must pass across many bridges suffers performance penalties. The penalties increase the farther downstream the bus is located.

To avoid latency problems, when computers have multiple PCI buses, they are usually arranged in a *peer bus* configuration. That is, instead of one bridge being connected to another, the two or three bridges powering the expansion buses in the computer are connected to a common point—either the PCI controller or the most upstream bridge.

Serial Channels

The one great strength of a bus—its wealth of signal pathways—can be its greatest disadvantage. For every digital signal you want to move, you've got to arrange for 8, 16, even 64 separate connections, and each one must be protected from interference. Simple cables become wide, complex, and expensive. Plugs and jacks sprout connections like a Tyrannosaurus Rex's mouth does teeth—and can be just as vicious. You also need to work out every day at the gym just to plug one in. Moreover, most communications channels provide a single data path, much a matter of history as convenience. For conventional communications such as the telephone, a single pathway (a single pair of wires) suffices for each channel.

The simplicity of a single data pathway has another allure for engineers. It's easier for them to design a channel with a single pathway for high speeds than it is to design a channel with multiple pathways. In terms of the amount of information they can squeeze through a channel, a single fast pathway can move more information than multiple slower paths.

The problem faced by engineers is how to convert a bus signal into one compatible with a single pathway (say, a telephone connection). As with most communications problems, the issue is one of coding information. A parallel connection like a bus encodes information as the pattern of signals on the bus when the clock cycles. Information is a snapshot of the bits on the bus, a pattern stretched across space at one instant of time. The bits form a line in physical space—a row of digital ones and zeroes.

The solution is simple: Reverse the dimensions. Let the data stretch out into a long row, not in the physical dimension but instead across time. Instead of the code being a pattern that stretches across space, it becomes a code that spans time. Instead of the *parallel position* of the digital bits coding the information, their *serial order* in a time sequence codes the data. This earns its name "serial" because the individual bits of information are transferred in a long series. Encoding and moving information in which the position of bits in time conveys importance is called *serial technology*, and the pathway is a called a *serial channel*.

Clocking

The most straightforward way of communicating (or storing) data is to assign a digital code so that the presence of a signal (for instance, turning on a five-volt signal) indicates a digital value of one, and another signal (say, zero volts) indicates the other digital value, zero. That's what digital is all about, after all.

However, such a signaling system doesn't work very well to communicate or store digital values, especially when the values are arranged in a serial string. The problem is timing. With serial data, timing is important in sorting out bits, and a straight one-for-one coding system doesn't help with timing.

The problem becomes apparent when you string a dozen or so bits of the same value in a row. Electrically, such a signal looks like a prolonged period of high or low voltage, depending on whether the signal is a digital one or zero. Some circuit has to sort out how many bits on one value this prolonged voltage shift represents. If the "prolonged" voltage lasts only a bit or two, figuring out how many bits is pretty easy. The length of a two-bit string differs from a three-bit string by 50 percent. If you time the duration of the shift, the accuracy of your timing needs only to be accurate to a bit less than 50 percent for you to properly sort out the bits. But string 100 bits in a row, and a mistake of 2 percent in timing can mean the loss or, worse, misinterpretation of two bits of information.

An easy way to sort out the bits is to provide a separate timing signal, a clock, that defines when each bit begins and ends. A separate clock is standard operating procedure for clocked logic circuits, anyway. That's why they are called *clock logic*. You can similarly provide a clock signal in communication circuits. Just add a separate clock signal.

However, a separate clock would take a separate channel, another communication circuit, with all its added complication. Consequently, engineers have developed ways of eliminating the need for a separate clock.

Synchronous communications require the sending and receiving system—for our purposes, the computer and printer—to synchronize their actions. They share a common timebase, a serial *clock*. This clock signal is passed between the two systems either as a separate signal or by using the pulses of data in the data stream to define it. The serial transmitter and receiver can unambiguously identify each bit in the data stream by its relationship to the shared clock. Because each uses exactly the same clock, they can make the match based on timing alone.

In *asynchronous communications*, the transmitter and receiver use separate clocks. Although the two clocks are supposed to be running at the same speed, they don't necessarily tell the same time. They are like your wristwatch and the clock on the town square. One or the other may be a few minutes faster, even though both operate at essentially the same speed: a day has 24 hours for both.

An asynchronous communications system also relies on the timing of pulses to define the digital code. But they cannot look to their clocks as infallible guidance. A small error in timing can shift a bit a few positions (say, from the least-significant place to the most significant), which can drastically affect the meaning of the digital message.

If you've ever had a clock that kept bad time—for example, the CMOS clock inside your computer—you probably noticed that time errors are cumulative. They add up. If your clock is a minute off today, it will be two minutes off tomorrow. The more time that elapses, the more the difference between two clocks will be apparent. The corollary is also true: If you make a comparison over a short enough period, you won't notice a shift between two clocks even if they are running at quite different speeds.

Asynchronous communications banks on this fine slicing of time. By keeping intervals short, they can make two unsynchronized clocks act as if they were synchronized. The otherwise unsynchronized signals can identify the time relationships in the bits of a serial code.

Isochronous communications involve time-critical data. Your computer uses information that is transferred isochronously in real time. That is, the data is meant for immediate display, typically in a continuous stream. The most common examples are video image data that must be displayed at the proper rate for smooth full-motion video and digital audio data that produces sound. Isochronous transmissions may be made using any signaling scheme—be it synchronous or asynchronous. They usually differ from ordinary data transfers in that the system tolerates data errors. It compromises accuracy for the proper timing of information. Whereas error-correction in a conventional data transfer may require the retransmission of packets containing errors, an isochronous transmission lets the errors pass through uncorrected. The underlying philosophy is that a bad pixel in an image is less objectionable than image frames that jerk because the flow of the data stream stops for the retransmission of bad packets.

Bit-Coding

In putting bits on a data line, a simple question arises: What is a bit, anyway? Sure, we know what of bit of information is—it's the smallest possible piece of information. However, in a communications system, the issue is what represents each bit. It could be a pulse of electricity, but it could equally be a piece of copper in the wire or a wildebeest or a green-and-purple flying saucer with twin chrome air horns. Although some of these codes might not be practical, they would be interesting.

Certainly the code will have to be an electrical signal of some sort. After all, that's what we can move through wires. But what's a bit? What makes a digital one and what makes a digital zero?

The obvious thing to do is make the two states of the voltage on the communication wire correspond to the two digital states. In that way, the system signals a digital one as the presence of a voltage and a zero as its absence.

To fit with the requirements of a serial data stream, each bit gets assigned a timed position in the data stream called a *bit-cell*. In most basic form, if a bit appears in the cell, it indicates a digital one; if not, it's a zero.

Easy enough. But such a design is prone to problems. A long string of digital ones would result in a constant voltage. In asynchronous systems, that's a problem because equipment can easily lose track of individual bits. For example, when two "ones" travel one after another, the clock only needs to be accurate to 50 percent of the bit-length to properly decipher both. With a hundred "ones" in a series, even a 1 percent inaccuracy will lose a bit or more of data.

RTZ

To help keep the data properly clocked, most digital signals work by switching each bit both on and off in each bit-cell. To indicate a digital one, the most basic of such systems will switch on a voltage and then switch it off before the end of the bit-cell. Because the signaling voltage rises and then falls back to zero in each data cell, this form of bit-coding is called *Return-to-Zero* coding, abbreviated RTZ.

RZI

Related to RTZ is *Return-to-Zero Inverted* coding, abbreviated RZI. The only difference is a result of the *I* in the designation, the *inversion*, which simply means that a pulse of electricity encodes a digital zero instead of a digital one. The voltage on the line is constant except when interrupted by a pulse of data.

NRZ

Although RTZ and RZI bit-coding are simple, they are not efficient. They effectively double the frequency of the data signal, thus increasing the required bandwidth for a given rate of data transmission by a factor of two. That's plain wasteful.

Engineers found a better way. Instead of encoding bits as a voltage level, they opted to code data as the *change* in voltage. When a bit appears in the data stream, NRZ coding shifts the voltage from whatever it is to its opposite. A bit could be a transition from zero to high voltage or the transition back the other way, from high voltage to zero. The signal then remains at that level until the next bit comes along. Because each bit does not cause the signal to fall back to zero voltage, this system is called *No Return-to-Zero* bit-coding.

NRZI

A related form of signaling is *No Return-to-Zero Inverted* bit-coding. The inversion is before the coding. That is, a lack of a data bit in a bit-cell causes the coded signal voltage to change. If data appears in the bit-cell, no change occurs in the encoded signal. Note that a zero in the code stream triggers each transition in the resulting NRZI code. A long period of no data on an NRZI-encoded channel (a continuous stream of logical zeros) results in a on-off pattern of voltages on the signal wires. This signal is essentially a square wave, which looks exactly like a clock signal. Figure 8.7 shows how the transitions in an NRZI signal encode data bits.

FIGURE 8.7
NRZI coding scheme used by USB.

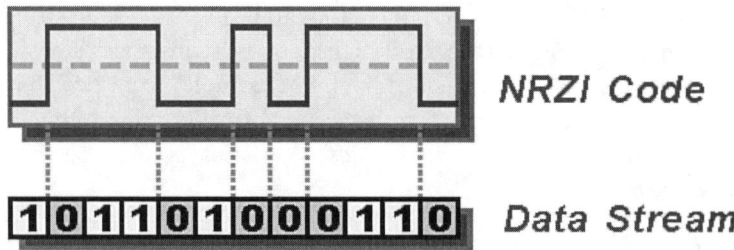

The NRZI signal is useful because it is self-clocking. That is, it allows the receiving system to regenerate the clock directly from the signal. For example, the square wave of a stream of zeros acts as the clock signal. The receiver adjusts its timing to fit this interval. It keeps timing even when a logical one in the signal results in no transition. When a new transition occurs, the timer resets itself, making whatever small adjustment might be necessary to compensate for timing differences at the sending and receiving ends.

Bit-Stuffing

No matter the coding scheme, including NRZI, long periods of an unchanging signal can still occur. With an NRZ signal, a string of zeros results in no signal. In NRZI, it takes a string of digital ones, but it can happen nevertheless. And if it does, the result can be clock problems and data errors.

For example, two back-to-back bit-cells of constant voltage can be properly decoded even if the data clock is 50 percent off. But with 100 back-to-back data cells of constant voltage, even being 1 percent off will result in an error. It all depends on the data.

That's not a good situation to be in. Sometimes the data you are sending will automatically cause errors. An engineer designing such a system might as well hang up his hat and jump from the locomotive.

But engineers are more clever than that. They have developed a novel way to cope with any signal and ensure that constant voltage will never occur: break up the stream of data that causes the uninterrupted voltage by adding extra bits that can be stripped out of the signal later. Adding these removable extraneous bits results in a technology called *bit-stuffing*.

Bit-stuffing can use any of a variety of algorithms to add extra bits. For example, bit-stuffing as used by the Universal Serial Port standard injects a zero after every continuous stream of six logical ones. Consequently, a transition is guaranteed to occur at least every seven clock cycles. When the receiver in a USB system detects a lack of transitions for six cycles and then receives the transition of the seventh, it knows it has received a *stuffed bit*. It resets its timer and discards the stuffed bit and then counts the voltage transition (or lack of it) occurring at the next clock cycle to be the next data bit.

Group-Coding

Bit-coding is a true cipher in that it uses one symbol to code another—a bit of data is one symbol, and the voltage on the communication line (or its change) is a different one. Nothing about enciphering says, however, that one bit must equal one symbol. In fact, encoding groups of bits as individual symbols is not only possible but also often a better strategy. For obvious reasons, this technology is called *group-coding*.

Can't think of a situation where one symbol equals multiple bits would work? Think about the alphabet. The ASCII code—ASCII is short for the American Standard Code for Information Interchange—that's used for encoding letters of the alphabet in binary form is exactly that. The letter *H*, for example, corresponds to the binary code 00101000 in ASCII.

Certain properties of data communications systems and data storage systems make group-coding the most efficient way of moving and storing information. Group-coding can increase the speed of a communications system, and it can increase the capacity of a storage system.

One way that group-coding can increase data communication speed is when the communications medium allows you to use more than the two binary states to encode bits. For example, if a telephone line is stable, predictable, and reliable enough, you might be able to distinguish four different voltage levels on the line instead of just two (on and off). You could use the four states each as an individual symbol to encode bit-patterns. This example allows for an easy code in which numbers encode the binary value, as shown in Table 8.1.

TABLE 8.1   A Simple Example of Symbol Encoding Using Binary Bit Patterns

Symbol	Bit-Pattern
0	00
1	01
2	10
3	11

Although this encoding process seems trivial, it actually doubles the speed of the communication channel. Send the symbols down the line at the highest speed it allows. When you decode the symbols, you get twice as many bits. This kind of group-coding makes high-speed modems possible.

In the language of telecommunications, the speed at which symbols move through a communications medium is measured in units of *baud*. One baud is a communications rate of one symbol per second. The term *baud* was named after J.M.E. Baudot, a French telegraphy expert. His full name (Baudot) is used to describe a five-bit digital code used in teletype systems.

The relationship between the number of bits that can be coded for each baud and the number of signal symbols required is geometric. The number of required symbols skyrockets as you try to code more data in every baud, as shown in Table 8.2.

TABLE 8.2   Signals States Required to Encode Bits

Number of States	Bits per Baud
2	1
4	2
16	4
64	8
256	16

Although it can be more efficient, this form of group-coding has a big disadvantage. It makes the transmitted data more vulnerable to error. An error in one bad baud causes multiple bits of raw data to be wrong. Moreover, the more symbols you use in any communication medium, the more similar they are to one another. The smaller the differences between symbols, the more likely errors will result from smaller disruptions to the signal. With modems, this drawback translates into the need for the best possible connection.

Engineers use a similar group-coding technique when they want to optimize the storage capacity of a medium. As with communications systems, storage systems suffer bandwidth limitations. The electronics of a rotating storage system such as a hard disk drive (see Chapter 17, "Magnetic Storage") are tuned to operate at a particular frequency, which is set by the speed the disk spins and how tightly bits can be packed on the disk. The packing of bits is a physical characteristic of the storage medium, which is made from particles of a finite size. Instead of electrical signals, hard disks use magnetic fields to encode information. More specifically, the basic storage unit is the *flux transition*, the change in direction of the magnetic field. Flux transitions occur only between particles (or agglomerations of particles). A medium can store no more data than the number of flux transitions its magnetic particles can make.

The first disk systems recorded a series of regularly spaced flux transitions to form a clock. An extra flux transition between two clock bits indicated a one in digital data. No added flux transition between bits indicated a zero. This system essentially imposed an NRZ signal on the clock and was called *frequency modulation* because it detected data as the change in frequency of the flux transitions. It was also called *single-density recording*.

The FM system wastes half of the flux transitions on the disk because of the need for the clock signal. By eliminating the clock and using a coding system even more like NRZ, disk capacities could be doubled. This technique, called *Modified Frequency Modulation recording* (MFM) or double-density recording was once the most widely used coding system for computer hard disks and is still used by many computer floppy disk drives. Instead of clock bits, digital ones are stored as a flux transition and zeros as the lack of a transition within a given period. To prevent flux reversals from occurring too far apart, MFM differs from pure NRZ coding by adding an extra flux reversal between consecutive zeros.

Modern disks use a variety of group-codings called *Run Length Limited* (RLL). The symbols used for coding data in RLL are bit-patterns, but patterns that are different from the data to be recorded. The RLL patterns actually use more bits than the original data. RLL increases data density by the careful choice of which bit-patterns to use.

RLL works by using a flux transition to indicate not individual bits but the change from zero to one or from one to zero. If two ones occur in a row, there's no flux transition. If eight ones occur in a row, there is still no flux transition. Similarly, two or eight zeros in a row result in no flux transition. The trick in RLL is to choose bit-patterns that only have long series of ones or zeros in them, resulting in fewer flux transitions.

The first common RLL system was called *2,7 RLL* because it used a set of symbols, each 16-bits long, chosen so that no symbol in the code had fewer than two identical bits and more than seven. Of the 65,564 possible 16-bit symbols, the 256 with the bit-patterns best fitting the 2,7 RLL requirements encode the 256 possible byte values of the original data. In other words, the RLL coding system picks only the bit-patterns that allow the highest storage density from a wide-ranging group of potential symbols. The 16-bit code patterns that do not enforce the 2,7 rule are made illegal and never appear in the data stream that goes to the magnetic storage device. Although each symbol involves twice as many bits as the original data, the flux transitions used by the code occur closer together, resulting in a 50 percent increase in the capacity of the storage system.

Other RLL systems, sometimes called *Advanced RLL*, work the same way but use different code symbols. One system uses a different code that changes the bit-pattern so that the number of sequential zeros is between three and nine. This system, known for obvious reasons as *3,9 RLL* or Advanced RLL, still uses an 8-to-16 bit code translation, but it ensures that digital ones will never be closer than every four bits. As a result, it allows data to be packed into flux transitions four times denser. The net gain is that information can be stored about twice as densely with 3,9 RLL as ordinary double-density recording techniques.

Frames

The basic element of digital information in a serial communications system is the *data frame*. Think of this as a time frame, the frame bracketing the information like a frame surrounds a window. The bits of the digital code are assigned their value in accord with their position in the frame. In a synchronous serial communications system, the frame contains the bits of a digital code word. In asynchronous serial communications, the frame also contains a word of data, but it has a greater significance. It is also the time interval in which the clocks of the sending and receiving systems are assumed to be synchronized.

When an asynchronous receiver detects the start of a frame, it resets its clock and then uses its clock to define the significance of each bit in the digital code within the frame. At the start of the next frame, it resets its clock and starts timing the bits again.

The only problem with this system is that an asynchronous receiver needs to know when a frame begins and ends. Synchronous receivers can always look to the clock to know, but the asynchronous system has no such luxury. The trick to making asynchronous communications work is unambiguously defining the frame. Today's asynchronous systems use *start bits* to mark the beginning of a frame and *stop bits* to mark its end. In the middle are a group of *data bits*.

The start bit helps the asynchronous receiver find data in a sea of noise. In some systems, the start bit is given a special identity. In most asynchronous systems, it is twice the length of the other bits inside the frame. In others, the appearance of the bit itself is sufficient. After all, without data, you would expect no pulses. When any pulse pops up, you might expect it to be a start bit.

Each frame ends with one or more stop bits. They assure the receiver that the data in the frame is complete. Most asynchronous communication systems allow for one, one and a half, or two stop bits. Most systems use one because that length makes each frame shorter (which, in turn, means that it takes a shorter time to transmit).

The number of data bits in a frame varies widely. In most asynchronous systems, there will be from five to eight bits of data in each frame. If you plan to use a serial port to connect a modern serial device to your computer, your choices will usually be to use either seven bits or eight bits, the latter being the most popular.

In addition, the data bits in the frame may be augmented by error-correction information called a *parity bit*, which fits between the last bit of data and the stop bit. In modern serial systems, any of five varieties of parity bits are sometimes used: odd, even, space, mark, and none.

The value of the parity bit is keyed to the data bits. The serial transmitter counts the number of digital ones in the data bits and determines whether this total is odd or even. In the odd parity scheme, the transmitter will turn on the parity bit (making it a digital one) only if the total number of digital ones in the data bits is odd. In even priority systems, the parity bit is set as one only if the data bits contain an even number of digital ones. In mark parity, the parity bit is always a mark, a digital one. In space parity, the parity bit is always a space, a digital zero. With no parity, no parity bit is included in the digital frames, and the stop bits immediately follow the data bits.

By convention, the bits of serial data in each frame are sent least-significant bit first. Subsequent bits follow in order of increasing significance. Figure 8.8 illustrates the contents of a single data frame that uses eight data bits and a single stop bit.

FIGURE 8.8

A serial data frame with eight data bits and one stop bit.

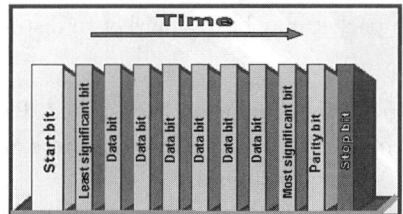

A frame corresponds to a single character. Taken alone, that's not a whole lot of information. A single character rarely suffices for anything except answering multiple-choice tests. To make something meaningful, you combine a sequence of characters together to form words and sentences.

The serial communications equivalent of a sentence is a *packet*. A packet is a standardized group of characters, or frame, that makes up the smallest unit that conveys information through the communications system.

As the name implies, a packet is a container for a message, such as a diplomatic packet or envelope. The packet holds the data. In addition, in most packetized systems, the packet also includes an address and, often, a description of its contents. Packets may also include extra data to ensure the integrity of their contents (for example, an error-detection or error-correction scheme of some sort). Figure 8.9 shows the constituents of a typical data packet.

FIGURE 8.9
Constituents of a typical data packet.

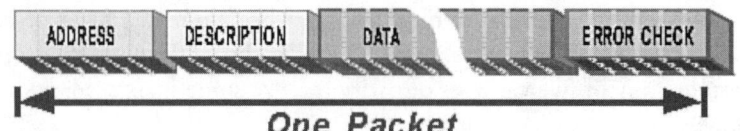

The exact constituents of a packet depend on the communication protocol. In general, however, all packets have much the same construction. They begin with a symbol or character string that allows systems listening in to the communication channel to recognize the bit-pattern that follows as a packet.

Each packet bears an address that tells where it is bound. Devices listening in on the communication channel check the address. If it does not match their own or does not indicate that the packet is being broadcast to all devices—in other words, the packet wears an address equivalent to "occupant"—the device ignores the rest of the packet. Communications equipment is courteous enough not to listen in on messages meant for someone else.

Most packets include some kind of identifying information that tells the recipient what to do with the data. For example, a packet may bear a market to distinguish commands from ordinary data.

The bulk of the packet is made from the data being transmitted. Packets vary in size, and hence, the amount of data that they may contain. Although there are no hard-and-fast limits, most packets range from 256 to 2048 bytes.

Error-Handling

Of course, a perfect world would also have fairies and other benevolent spirits to help usher the data along and protect it from all the evil imps and energies lurking about trying to debase and disgrace the singular purity of serial transfer.

The world is, alas, not perfect, and the world of computers is even less so. Many misfortunes can befall the vulnerable serial data bit as it crawls through its connection. One of the bits of a full byte of data may go astray, leaving a piece of data with a smaller value on arrival as it had at departure—a problem akin to shipping alcohol by a courier service operated by dipsomaniacs. With the vacancy in the data stream, all the other bits will slip up a place and assume new values. Or the opposite case—in the spirit of electronic camaraderie, an otherwise well-meaning signal might adopt a stray bit like a child takes on a kitten, only to later discover the miracle of pregnancy and a progeny of errors that ripple through the communications stream, pushing all the bits backward. In either case, the prognosis is not good. With this elementary form of serial communications, one mistaken bit either way, and every byte that follows will be in error.

Establishing reliable serial communications means overcoming these bit-error problems and many others as well. Thanks to some digital ingenuity, however, serial communications work and work well—well enough that you and your computer can depend on them. Because no communication channel is error free, most packets include error-detection or error-correction information. The principle behind error detection is simple: Include duplicate or redundant information that you can compare to the original. Because communication errors are random, they are unlikely to affect both of two copies of the transmitted data. Compare two copies sent along and if they do not match, you can be sure one of them changed during transmission and became corrupted.

Many communications systems don't rely on complex error-correction algorithms as are used in storage and high-quality memory systems. Communications systems have a luxury storage systems do not: They can get a second chance. If an error occurs in transmission, the system can try again—and again—until an error-free copy gets through.

As a function of communication protocol, packets are part of the software standard used by the communication system. Even so, they are essential to making the hardware—the entire communication system—work properly and reliably.

Control

In a perfect world, a single circuit—nothing more than two wires, a signal line, and a ground—would be all that was necessary to move this serial signal from the one place to another without further ado. But such a serial connection would be like a fire hose squirting out a big, fat stream of bits without rhyme, reason, or nozzle. There's nothing to control the flow of data. If the receiving end of the serial channel can't keep up with the sending end, data might flood out every which way and drown the poor recipient.

Laugh if you want, but controlling the flow of data is a major issue of the designers of serial communications systems. Engineers working on the problem have come up with not one but several solutions. Some add an extra connection just for controlling the data flow, a technology called *hardware flow control*. Some reserve special character values in the data stream to produce *software flow control*. And some take a further step and redefine the flow of data into digestible chunks and provide a software-based control system built in to these chunks. This system, quickly becoming the most popular, is termed *packetized communications*.

One difference between these three technologies is range related. Hardware flow control, with its need for extra physical connections, naturally limits its application to short ranges, typically connections between computers and peripherals. Adding the extra wires for control is a small burden when they only need to go a few feet. But the cost and complexity of those wires quickly gets out of hand when distances stretch to miles and signals must go through switching or routing centers. Software flow control works with any range because it requires only a single data pathway. However, because it relies on some of the characters in the data stream and only a few characters can be reserved without compromising the capacity of the channel, it works best only in one-on-one communications. That is, software flow control works best between two devices. Packetized communication, however, has greater versatility. By putting control information into packets, a packet-based system can handle signals meant for a nearly unlimited number of devices. Hence, packetized communications work to link together entire networks.

Hardware and software flow controls are usually reserved for local, direct connections. The most important application for these techniques of flow control is in serial ports, simple links between your computer and its peripherals. single In these applications, flow control is often termed *handshaking*.

In its most basic form, hardware handshaking adds one signal from the receiving device back to the sending device. This signal has two states: on and off. One state says, "I am ready and willing to accept data from you." The other state says, "Whoa! I can't take another byte." Often these two signals are called *ready* and *busy*. The receiving device is in control. When it sends the ready signal, the sending device knows it can send data and does, if it has any ready. When the recipient sends the busy signal back, the sending device stops and waits for the next ready signal.

Software handshaking uses special characters in the data stream to indicate whether they should transfer data. The device receiving data normally sends out one character to indicate it can accept data and a different character to indicate it is busy and cannot accommodate more. In the most common connection system to use software handshaking—the legacy serial port—either of the two characters pairs, XON/XOFF or ETX/ACK, is often used.

In the XON/XOFF scheme, the XOFF character sent from a receiving device to the sending device says to hold off sending data. This character is also sometimes called DC1 and has an ASCII value of 19 or 013(hex). It is sometimes called *Control-S*. When the receiving device is ready to receive data again, it sends out XON, also known as *DC3*, to the sender. This character has an ASCII value of 17 or 011(hex). It is sometimes called *Control-Q*.

ETX/ACK works similarly. ETX, which is an abbreviation for *end text*, says to hold off on sending more text. This character has an ASCII value of 3 (decimal or hexadecimal) and is sometimes called *Control-C*. ACK, short for *acknowledge*, says to resume sending data. It has an ASCII value of 6 (decimal or hexadecimal) and is sometimes called *Control-F*.

There's no issue as to whether hardware or software flow control is better. Both work, and that's all that's necessary. The important issue is what kind of flow control is used in asingle given system. Both ends must use the same handshaking, even the same characters.

Expansion Buses

Given an old house, closets packed tighter than the economy section of a Boeing 737, and a charge card, most people will broach the idea of adding to their homes. After all, when you need more room, nothing seems more natural than building an addition. If you have more ambition than second thoughts, the most humble bungalow can become a manse of overwhelming grandeur with a mortgage to match.

Making the same magic on your computer might not seem as natural, but it is. Adding to your computer is easier than adding to your house—and less likely to lead to bankruptcy and divorce—because, unlike a house, computers are *designed* to be added to. They sprout connectors and ports like a Chia pet does hair.

Computers are different, however, in that the best way to add to them is not on the outside. Odd as it may seem, you can effectively increase the power and capabilities of most computers by expanding them on the inside.

The design feature key to this interior growth is the *expansion bus*. By plugging a card into your computer's expansion bus, you can make the machine into almost anything you want it to be—within reason, of course. You can't expect to turn your computer into a flying boat, but a video production system, international communications center, cryptographic analyzer, and medical instrument interface are all easily within the power of your expansion bus. Even if your aim is more modest, you'll need to become familiar with this bus. All the most common options for customizing your computer—modems, network interface cards, and television tuners—plug into it. Even if your computer has a modem, sound, and video built in to its motherboard, forever fixed and irremovable, these features invisibly connect to the computer's expansion bus.

The expansion bus is your computer's electrical umbilical cord, a direct connection with the computer's logical circulatory system that enables whatever expansion brainchild you have to link to your system. The purpose of the expansion bus is straightforward: It enables you to plug things into the machine and, hopefully, enhance the computer's operation.

Background

Expansion buses are much more than the simple electrical connections you make when plugging in a lamp. Through the bus circuits, your computer transfers not only electricity but also information. Like all the data your computer must deal with, that information is defined by a special coding in the sequence and pattern of digital bits.

The bus connection must flawlessly transfer that data. To prevent mistakes, every bus design also includes extra signals to control the flow of that information, adjust its rate to accommodate the speed limits of your computer and its expansion accessories, and adjust the digital pattern itself to match design variations. Each different bus design takes it own approach to the signals required for control and translation. Some use extra hardware signals to control transfers across the bus. Others use extensive signaling systems that package information into blocks or packets and route them across the bus by adding addresses and identification bytes to these blocks.

Expansion bus standards define how your computer and the cards you add to it negotiate their data transfers. As a result, the standard that your computer's bus follows is a primary determinant of what enhancement products work with it. Nearly all of today's computers follow a single standard, the oft-mentioned *Peripheral Component Interconnect (PCI)*, which ensures that the most popular computer cards will work inside them.

Older computers often had two expansion buses: a high-speed bus (inevitably PCI) that was the preferred expansion connection and a compatibility bus to accommodate older add-in devices that frugal-minded computer owners refused to discard. The compatibility bus followed the Industry Standard Architecture design, often called the *PC bus*. In addition, most new computers have an accelerated graphics port (AGP) for their video cards. Although AGP is a high-speed variation on PCI, it is not compatible with ordinary expansion cards. PCI replaced ISA because of speed. PCI was about eight times faster than ISA. But time has taken its toll, and engineers are now eyeing higher-performance alternatives to PCI. Some of these, such as PCI-X, are straightforward extrapolations on the basic PCI design. Others, such as HyperTransport and InfiniBand, represent new ways of thinking about the interconnections inside a computer.

Notebook computers have their own style of expansion buses that use PC Cards rather than the slide-in circuit boards used by PCI. This design follows the standards set by the Personal Computer Memory Card International Association (PCMCIA). The basic

PC Card design allows for performance and operation patterned after the old ISA design, but the CardBus design expands on PC Card with PCI-style bus connections that are backward compatible. That means a CardBus slot will accept either a CardBus or PC Card expansion card (with one exception—fat "Type 3" cards won't fit in ordinary skinny slots), so your old cards will happily work even in the newest of computers.

Unlike those of desktop computers, the expansion buses of notebook machines are externally accessible—you don't have to open up the computer to slide in a card. External upgrades are, in fact, a necessity for notebook computers in that cracking open the case of a portable computer is about as messy as opening an egg and, for most people, an equally irreversible process. In addition, both the PC Card and CardBus standards allow for hot-swapping. That is, you can plug in a card or unplug it while the electricity is on to your computer and the machine is running. The expansion slots inside desktop computers generally do not allow for hot-swapping.

Expansion board technology is mature, at least for now. The necessary standards are in place and stable. You can take it for granted that you can slide a PCI expansion board in a PCI slot and have it automatically configure itself and operate in your computer. You can even select from a wealth of PC Card and CardBus modules for your notebook computer—all without any concern about compatibility. Although those statements sound so obvious as to be trivial, reaching this point has been a long journey marked by pragmatism and insight, cooperation and argument, and even battles between industry giants. At least 11 major standards for computer expansion have been the result, as summarized in Table 9.1.

TABLE 9.1 Comparison of Expansion Bus Standards

Name	Date	Bus Width	Clock Speed	Addressing
PC bus	1981	8 bits	4.77MHz	1MB
ISA	1984	16 bits	8MHz	16MB
Micro Channel	1987	16/32 bits	10MHz	16MB/4GB
EISA	1988	32 bits	8MHz	4GB
VL bus	1992	32/64 bits	50MHz	4GB
PCI	1992	32/64 bits	33MHz	4GB
PCIX	1998	32/64 bits	66 or 133MHz	4GB
PC Card	1990	16 bits	8MHz	64MB
CardBus	1994	32 bits	33MHz	4GB
InfiniBand	2000	12 bits	2500MHz	Packetized
HyperTransport	2001	32 bits	1600MHz	Packetized

The *PC bus*, so called because it was the expansion bus used by the first IBM personal computer, was little more than an extension of the connections from the 8088 microprocessor, with a few control signals thrown in. The *AT bus* was IBM's extrapolation on the PC bus, adding the signals needed to match the 80286 microprocessor used in the IBM personal computer AT (for Advanced Technology). Compaq Corporation altered the design by moving memory to a separate bus when the company introduced its Deskpro 386 in 1987. This basic design was made into an official standard by the Institute of Electrical and Electronic Engineers as *Industry Standard Architecture*. *Micro Channel Architecture* represented IBM's take on a new, revolutionary bus design, but did not survive poor marketing. *EISA*, short for *Enhanced ISA*, was an industry response to Micro Channel, which found little acceptance. Neither of the new buses (Micro Channel nor EISA) made a visible improvement on performance. The *VESA Local Bus* (or *VL Bus*, created by the Video Electronics Standards Association) did offer a visible improvement because it allowed for faster video displays. It was a promising new bus standard, but it was out-promoted (and out-developed) by Intel's *Peripheral Component Interconnect* (PCI), which became the most popular expansion bus ever used by the computer industry.

Peripheral Component Interconnect

No one might have predicted that Peripheral Component Interconnect would become the most popular expansion bus in the world when Intel Corporation introduced it in July 1992. PCI was long awaited as a high-speed expansion bus specification, but the initial announcement proved to be more and less than the industry hoped for. The first PCI standard defined mandatory design rules, including hardware guidelines to help ensure proper circuit operation of motherboards at high speeds with a minimum of design complications. It showed how to link together computer circuits—including the expansion bus—for high-speed operation but failed to provide a standard for the actual signals and connections that would make it a real expansion bus.

The design first took the form of a true expansion bus with Intel's development of PCI Release 2.0 in May 1993, which added the missing pieces to create a full 64-bit expansion bus. Although it got off to a rocky start when the initial chipsets for empowering it proved flawed, computer-makers have almost universally announced support. The standard has been revised many times since then. By the time this book appears, Version 3.0 should be the reigning standard.

Architectural Overview

The original explicit purpose of the PCI design was to make the lives of those who engineer chipsets and motherboards easier. It wasn't so much an expansion bus as an interconnection system, hence its pompous name (Peripheral Component is just a haughty way of saying *chip*, and Interconnect means simply *link*). And that is what PCI is meant to be—a fast and easy chip link.

Even when PCI was without pretensions of being a bus standard, its streamlined linking capabilities held promise for revolutionizing computer designs. Whereas each new Intel microprocessor family required the makers of chipsets and motherboards to completely redesign their products with every new generation of microprocessor, PCI promised a common standard, one independent of the microprocessor generation or family. As originally envisioned, PCI would allow designers to link together entire universes of processors, coprocessors, and support chips without glue logic—the pesky profusion of chips needed to match the signals between different integrated circuits—using a connection whose speed was unfettered by frequency (and clock) limits. All computer chips that follow the PCI standard can be connected together on a circuit board without the need for glue logic. In itself, this could lower computer prices by making designs more economical while increasing reliability by minimizing the number of circuit components.

A key tenant of the PCI design is processor independence; that is, its circuits and signals are not tied to the requirements of a specific microprocessor or family. Even though the standard was developed by Intel, the PCI design is not limited to Intel microprocessors. In fact, Apple's PowerMac computers use PCI.

Bus Speed

PCI can operate synchronously or asynchronously. In the former case, the speed of operation of the PCI bus is dependent on the host microprocessor's clock and PCI components are synchronized with the host microprocessor. Typically the PCI bus will operate at a fraction of the external interface of the host microprocessor. With today's high microprocessor speeds, however, the bus speed often is synchronized to the system bus or frontside bus, which may operate at 66, 100, or 133MHz. (The 400 and 533MHz buses used by the latest Pentium 4 chips actually run at 100 and 133MHz, respectively, and ship multiple bytes per clock cycle to achieve their high data rates.) The PCI bus can operate at speeds up to 66MHz under the revised PCI 2.2 (and later) standards. PCI-bus derivations, such as PCI-Express, use this higher speed.

PCI is designed to maintain data integrity at operating speeds down to 0 Hz, a dead stop. Although it won't pass data at 0 Hz, the design allows notebook computers to freely shift to standby mode or suspend mode.

Although all PCI peripherals should be able to operate at 33MHz, the PCI design allows you to connect slower peripherals. To accommodate PCI devices that cannot operate at the full speed of the PCI bus, the design incorporates three flow-control signals that indicate when a given peripheral or board is ready to send or receive data. One of these signals halts the current transaction. Consequently, PCI transactions can take place at a rate far lower than the maximum 33MHz bus speed implies.

The PCI design provides for expansion connectors extending the bus off the motherboard, but it limits such expansion to a maximum of three connectors (none are required by the standard). As with VL bus, this limit is imposed by the high operating frequency of the PCI bus. More connectors would increase bus capacitance and make full-speed operation less reliable.

To attain reliable operation at high speeds without the need for terminations (as required by the SCSI bus), Intel chose a reflected rather than direct signaling system for PCI. To activate a bus signal, a device raises (or lowers) the signal on the bus only to half its required activation level. As with any bus, the high-frequency signals meant for the slots propagate down the bus lines and are reflected back by the unterminated ends of the conductors. The reflected signal combines with the original signal, doubling its value up to the required activation voltage.

The basic PCI interface requires only 47 discrete connections for slave boards (or devices), with two more on bus-mastering boards. To accommodate multiple power supply and ground signals and blanked off spaces to key the connectors for proper insertion, the physical 32-bit PCI bus connector actually includes 124 pins. Every active signal on the PCI bus is adjacent to (either next to or on the opposite side of the board from) a power supply or ground signal to minimize extraneous radiation.

Multiplexing

Although the number of connections used by the PCI system sounds high, Intel actually had to resort to a powerful trick to keep the number of bus pins manageable. The address and data signals on the PCI bus are time-multiplexed on the same 32 pins. That is, the address and data signals share the same bus connections (AD00 through AD31). On the one clock cycle, the combined address/data lines carry the address values and set up the location to move information to or from. On the next cycle, the same lines switch to carrying the actual data.

This address/data cycling of the bus does not slow the bus. Even in nonmultiplexed designs, the address lines are used on one bus cycle and then the data lines are used on the next. Moreover, PCI has its own burst mode that eliminates the need for alteration between address and data cycles. PCI also can operate in its own burst mode. During burst mode transfers, a single address cycle can be followed by multiple data cycles that access sequential memory locations.

PCI achieves its multiplexing using a special bus signal called *Cycle Frame* (FRAME#). The appearance of the Cycle Frame signal identifies the beginning of a transfer cycle and indicates the address/data bus holds a valid address. The Cycle Frame signal is then held active for the duration of the data transfer.

Burst Mode

During burst mode transfers, a single address cycle can be followed by multiple data cycles that access sequential memory locations, limited only by the needs of other devices to use the bus and other system functions (such as memory refresh). The burst can continue as long as the Cycle Frame signal remains active. With each clock cycle that Cycle Frame is high, new data is placed on the bus. If Cycle Frame is active only for one data cycle, an ordinary transfer takes place. When it stays active across multiple data cycles, a burst occurs.

This burst mode underlies the 132MBps throughput claimed for the 32-bit PCI design. (With the 64-bit extension, PCI claims a peak transfer rate of 264MBps.) Of course, PCI attains that rate only during the burst. The initial address cycle steals away a bit of time and lowers the data rate (the penalty for which declines with the increasing length of the burst). System overhead, however, holds down the ultimate throughput.

PCI need not use all 32 (or 64) bits of the bus's data lines. Four Byte Enable signals (C/BE0# through C/BE3#) are used to indicate which of the four-byte-wide blocks of PCI's 32-bit signals contain valid data. In 64-bit systems, another four signals (C/BE4# through C/BE7#) indicate the additional active byte lanes.

To accommodate devices that cannot operate at the full speed of the PCI bus, the design incorporates three flow-control signals: Initiator Ready (IRDY#, at pin B35), Target Ready (TRDY#, at pin A36), and Stop (STOP#, at pin A38). Target Ready is activated to indicate that a bus device is ready to supply data during a read cycle or accept it during a write cycle. When Initiator Ready is activated, it signals that a bus master is ready to complete an ongoing transaction. A Stop signal is sent from a target device to a master to stop the current transaction.

Data Integrity Signals

To ensure the integrity of information traversing the bus, the PCI specification makes mandatory the parity-checking of both the address and data cycles. One bit (signal PAR) is used to confirm parity across 32 address/data lines and the four associated Byte Enable signals. A second parity signal is used in 64-bit implementations. The parity signal lags the data it verifies by one cycle, and its state is set so that the sum of it, the address/data values, and the Byte Enable values are a logical high (1).

If a parity error is detected during a data transfer, the bus controller asserts the Parity Error signal (PERR#). The action taken on error detection (for example, resending data) depends on how the system is configured. Another signal, System Error (SERR#) handles address parity and other errors.

Parity-checking of the data bus becomes particularly important as the bus width and speed grow. Every increase in bus complexity also raises the chance of errors creeping in. Parity-checking prevents such problems from affecting the information transferred across the bus.

Serialized Interrupts

Because of the design of the PCI system, the lack of the old IRQ signals poses a problem. Under standard PCI architecture, the compatibility expansion bus (ISA) links to the host microprocessor through the PCI bus and its host bridge. The IRQ signals cannot be passed directly through this channel because the PCI specification does not define them. To accommodate the old IRQ system under PCI architecture, several chipset and computer makers, including Compaq, Cirrus Logic, National Semiconductor, OPTi, Standard Microsystems, Texas Instruments, and VLSI Technology, developed a standard they called *Serialized IRQ Support for PCI Systems.*

The serialized IRQ system relies on a special signal called *IRQSER* that encodes all available interrupts as pulses in a series. One long series of pulses, called an *IRQSER cycle*, sends data about the state of all interrupts in the system across the PCI channel.

The IRQSER cycle begins with an extended pulse of the IRQSER signal, lasting from four to eight cycles of the PCI clock (each of which is nominally 33MHz but may be slower in systems with slower bus clocks). After a delay of two PCI clock cycles, the IRQSER cycle is divided into frames, each of which is three PCI clock cycles long. Each frame encodes the state of one interrupt—if the IRQSER signal pulses during the first third of the frame, it indicates the interrupt assigned to that frame is active. Table 9.2 lists which interrupts are assigned to each frame position.

TABLE 9.2 PCI Serialized Interrupt Frame Encoding

Interrupt Encoded	Frame Position	Clocks Past Start
IRQ0	1	2
IRQ1	2	5
SMI#	3	8
IRQ3	4	11
IRQ4	5	14
IRQ5	6	17
IRQ6	7	20
IRQ7	8	23
IRQ8	9	26

Peripheral Component Interconnect

Interrupt Encoded	Frame Position	Clocks Past Start
IRQ9	10	29
IRQ10	11	32
IRQ11	12	35
IRQ12	13	38
IRQ13	14	41
IRQ14	15	44
IRQ15	16	47
IOCHCK#	17	50
INTA#	18	53
INTB#	19	56
INTC#	20	59
INTD#	21	62
Unassigned	22 to 32	65 to 95

In addition to the 16 IRQ signals used by the old interrupt system, the PCI serialized interrupt scheme also carries data about the state of the system management interrupt (SMI#) and the I/O check (IOCHCK#) signals as well as the four native PCI interrupts and 10 unassigned values that may be used by system designers. According to the serialized interrupt scheme, support for the last 14 frames is optional.

The IRQSER cycle ends with a Stop signal, a pulse of the IRQSER signal that lasts two or three PCI clocks, depending on the operating mode of the serialized interrupt system.

The PCI serialized interrupt system is only a means of data transportation. It carries the information across the PCI bus and delivers it to the microprocessor and its support circuitry. The information about the old IRQ signals gets delivered to a conventional 8259A interrupt controller or its equivalent in the microprocessor support chipset. Once at the controller, the interrupts are handled conventionally.

Although the PCI interrupt-sharing scheme helps eliminate setup problems, some systems demonstrate their own difficulties. For example, some computers force the video and audio systems to share interrupts. Any video routine that generates an interrupt, such as scrolling a window, will briefly halt the playing of audio. The audio effects can be unlistenable. The cure is to reassign one of the interrupts, if your system allows it.

Bus-Mastering and Arbitration

The basic PCI design supports arbitrated bus-mastering like that of other advanced expansion buses, but PCI has its own bus command language (a four-bit code) and supports secondary cache memory.

In operation, a bus master board sends a signal to its host to request control of the bus and starts to transfer when it receives a confirmation. Each PCI board gets its own slot-specific signals to request bus control and receive confirmation that control has been granted. This approach allows great flexibility in assigning the priorities, even the arbitration protocol, of the complete computer system. The designer of a PCI-based computer can adapt the arbitration procedure to suit his needs rather than having to adapt to the ideas of the obscure engineers who conceived the original bus specification.

Bus mastering across the PCI bus is achieved with two special signals: Request (REQ#) and Grant (GNT#). A master asserts its Request signal when it wants to take control of the bus. In return, the central resource (Intel's name for the circuitry shared by all bus devices on the motherboard, including the bus control logic) sends a Grant signal to the master to give it permission to take control. Each PCI device gets its own dedicated Request and Grant signal.

As a self-contained expansion bus, PCI naturally provides for hardware interrupts. PCI includes four level-sensitive interrupts (INTA# through INTD#, at pins A6, B7, A7, and B8, respectively) that enable interrupt sharing. The specification does not itself define what the interrupts are or how they are to be shared. Even the relationship between the four signals is left to the designer (for example, each can indicate its own interrupt, or they can define up to 16 separate interrupts as binary values). Typically, these details are implemented in a device driver for the PCI board. The interrupt lines are not synchronized to the other bus signals and may therefore be activated at any time during a bus cycle.

Low-Voltage Evolution

As the world shifts to lower-power systems and lower-voltage operation, PCI has been adapted to fit. Although the early incarnations of the standard provided for 3.3-volt operation in addition to the then-standard 5-volt level, the acceptance of the lower voltage standard became official only with PCI version 2.3. Version 3.0 (not yet released at the time of this writing) takes the next step and eliminates the 5-volt connector from the standard.

Slot Limits

High frequencies, radiation, and other electrical effects also conspire to limit the number of expansion slots that can be attached in a given bus system. These limits become especially apparent with local bus systems that operate at high clock speeds. All current local bus standards limit to three the number of high-speed devices that can be connected to a single bus.

Note that the limit is measured in devices and not slots. Many local bus systems use a local bus connection for their motherboard-based display systems. These circuits count as one local bus device, so computers with local bus video on the motherboard can offer at most two local bus expansion slots.

The three-device limit results from speed considerations. The larger the bus, the higher the capacitance between its circuits (because they have a longer distance over which to interact). Every connector adds more capacitance. As speed increases, circuit capacitance increasingly degrades its signals. The only way to overcome the capacitive losses is to start with more signals. To keep local bus signals at reasonable levels and yet maintain high speeds, the standards enforce the three-device limit.

A single computer can accommodate multiple PCI expansion buses bridged together to allow more than three slots. Each of these sub-buses then uses its own bus-control circuitry. From an expansion standpoint—or from the standpoint of an expansion board—splitting the system into multiple buses makes no difference. The signals get where they are supposed to, and that's all that counts. The only worries are for the engineer who has to design the system to begin with—and even that is no big deal. The chipset takes care of most expansion bus issues.

Hot-Plugging

Standard PCI cards do not allow for hot-plugging. That is, you cannot and should not remove or insert a PCI expansion board into a connector in a running computer. Try it, and you risk damage to both the board and the computer.

In some applications, however, hot-plugging is desirable. For example, in fault-tolerant computers you can replace defective boards without shutting down the host system. You can also add new boards to a system while it is operating.

To facilitate using PCI expansion boards in such circumstances, engineers developed a variation on the PCI standard called *PCI Hot Plug* and published a specification that defines the requirements for expansion cards, computers, and their software to make it all work. The specification, now available as revision 1.1, is a supplement to the ordinary PCI Specification.

Unless you have all three—the board, computer, and software—you should not attempt hot-plugging with PCI boards. Products that meet the standard are identifiable by a special PCI Hot Plug logo.

Setup

PCI builds upon the Plug-and-Play system to automatically configure itself and the devices connected to it without the need to set jumpers or DIP switches. Under the PCI specification, expansion boards include Plug-and-Play registers to store configuration information that can be tapped into for automatic configuration. The PCI setup system requires 256 registers. This configuration space is tightly defined by the PCI specification to ensure compatibility. A special signal, Initialization Device Select (IDSEL), dedicated to each slot activates the configuration read and write operations as required by the Plug-and-Play system.

PCI-X

In the late 1990s, engineers at Compaq, Hewlett-Packard, and IBM realized that microprocessor speeds were quickly outrunning the throughput capabilities of the PCI bus, so they began to develop a new, higher-speed alternative aimed particularly at servers. Working jointly, they developed a new bus specification, which they submitted to the PCI Special Interest group in September 1998. After evaluating the specification for a year, in September 1999, the PCI SIG adopted the specification and published it as the official *PCI-X Version 1.0* standard.

The PCI-X design not only increases the potential bus speed of PCI but also adds a new kind of transfer that makes the higher speeds practical. On July 23, 2002, PCI-X Version 2.0 was released to provide a further upgrade path built upon PCI-X technology. Table 9.3 compares the speed and bandwidth available under various existing and proposed PCI and PCI-X specifications.

TABLE 9.3   PCI and PCI-X Implementations Compared

Specification	Bus Width	Bus Speed	Maximum Peak Bandwidth
PCI .2.2	32 bits	33MHz	133Mbps
PCI 2.2	64 bits	33MHz	266Mbps
PCI 2.2	64 bits	66MHz	533Mbps
PCI-X 1.0	64 bits	133MHz	1066Mbps
PCI-X 2.0	64 bits	266MHz	2133Mbps
PCI-X 2.0	64 bits	533MHz	4266Mbps

The PCI-X design follows the PCI specification in regard to signal assignments on the bus. It supports both 32-bit and 64-bit bus designs. In fact, a PCI card will function normally in a PCI-X expansion slot, and a PCI-X expansion board will work in a standard PCI slot, although at less than its full potential speed.

The speed of the PCI-X expansion bus is not always the 133MHz of the specifications. It depends on how many slots are connected in a single circuit with the bus controller and what's in the slots. To accommodate ordinary PCI boards, for example, all interconnected PCI-X slots automatically slow to the highest speed the PCI board will accept—typically 33MHz. In addition, motherboard layouts limit the high-frequency capabilities of any bus design. Under PCI-X, only a single slot is possible at 133MHz. Two-slot designs require retarding the bus to 100MHz. With four slots, the practical top speed falls to 66MHz. The higher speeds possible under PCI-X 2.0 keep the clock at 133MHz but switch to double-clocking or quad-clocking the data to achieve higher transfer rates.

To reach even the 133MHz rate (and more reliable operation at 66MHz), PCI-X adds a new twist to the bus design, known as *register-to-register transfers*. On the PCI bus, cards read data directly from the bus, but the timing of signals on the bus leaves only a short window for valid data. At 33MHz, a PCI card has a window of about 7 milliseconds to read from the bus; at 66MHz, only about 3 milliseconds is available. In contrast, PCI-X uses a register to latch the signals on the bus. When a signal appears on the bus, the PCI-X registers lock down that value until data appears during the next clock cycle. A PCI-X card therefore has a full clock cycle to read the data—about 15 milliseconds at 66MHz and about 7.5 milliseconds at 133MHz.

Although register-to-register transfers make higher bus speeds feasible, at any given speed they actually slow the throughput of the bus by adding one cycle of delay to each transfer. Because transfers require multiple clock cycles, however, the penalty is not great, especially for bursts of data. But PCI-X incorporates several improvements in transfer efficiency that help make the real-world throughput of the PCI-X bus actually higher than PCI at the same speed.

One such addition is *attribute phase*, an additional phase in data transfers that allows devices to send each other a 36-bit attribute field that adds a detailed description to the transfer. The field contains a *transaction byte count* that describes the total size of the transfer to permit more efficient use of bursts. Transfers can be designated to allow *relaxed ordering* so that transactions do not have to be completed in the order they are requested. For example, a transfer of time-critical data can zoom around previously requested transfers. Relaxed ordering can keep video streaming without interruption. Transactions that are flagged as *non-cache coherent* in the attribute field tell the system that it need not waste time snooping through its cache for changes if the transfer won't affect the cache. By applying a *sequence number* in the attribute field, bus transfers in the same sequence can be managed together, which can improve the efficiency in caching algorithms.

In addition to the attribute phase, PCI-X allows for *split transactions*. If a device starts a bus transaction but delays in finishing it, the bus controller can use the intervening idle time for other transactions. The PCI-X bus also eliminates wait states (except for the inevitable lag at the beginning of a transaction) through split transactions by disconnecting idle devices from the bus to free up bandwidth. All PCI-X transactions are one standard size that matches the 128-bit cache line used by Intel microprocessors, permitting more efficient operation of the cache. When all the new features are taken together, the net result is that PCI-X throughput may be 10 percent or more higher than using standard PCI technology.

Because PCI-X is designed for servers, the integrity of data and the system are paramount concerns. Although PCI allows for parity-checking transfers across the bus, its error-handling mechanism is both simple and inelegant—an error would shut down the host system. PCI-X allows for more graceful recovery. For example, the controller can request that an erroneous transmission be repeated, it can reinitialize the device that erred or disable it entirely, or it can notify the operator that the error occurred.

PCI-X cards can operate at either 5.0 or 3.3 volts. However, high-speed operation is allowed only at the lower operating voltage. The PCI-X design allows for 128 bus segments in a given computer system. A segment runs from the PCI-X controller to a PCI-X bridge or between the bridge and an actual expansion bus encompassing one to four slots, so a single PCI-X system can handle any practical number of devices.

PCI Express

According to the PCI Special Interest Group, the designated successor to today's PCI-X (and PCI) expansion buses is PCI Express. Under development for years as 3GIO (indicating it was to be the third generation input/output bus design), PCI Express represents a radical change from previous expansion bus architectures. Instead of using relatively low-speed parallel data lines, it opts for high-speed serial signaling. Instead of operating as a bus, it uses a switched design for point-to-point communications between devices—each gets the full bandwidth of the system during transfers. Instead of special signals for service functions such as interrupts, it uses a packet-based system to exchange both data and commands. The PCI-SIG announced the first PCI Express specification at the same time as PCI-X 2.0, on July 23, 2002.

In its initial implementation, PCI Express uses a four-wire interconnection system, two wires each (a balanced pair) for separate sending and receiving channels. Each channel operates at a speed of 2.5GHz, which yields a peak throughput of 200MBps (ignoring packet overhead). The system uses the 8b/10b encoding scheme, which embeds the clock in the data stream so that no additional clock signal is required. The initial design contemplates future increases in speed, up to 10GHz, the theoretic maximum speed that can be achieved in standard copper circuits.

To accommodate devices that require higher data rates, PCI Express allows for multiple *lanes* within a single channel. In effect, each lane is a parallel signal path between two devices with its own four-wire connection. The PCI Express hardware divides the data between the multiple lanes for transmission and reconstructs it at the other end of the connection. The PCI Express specifications allow for channels with 1, 2, 4, 8, 12, 16, or 32 lanes (effectively boosting the speed of the connection by the equivalent factor). A 32-lane system at today's 2.5GHz bus speed would deliver throughput of 6400MBps.

The switched design is integral to the high-speed operation of PCI Express. It eliminates most of the electrical problems inherent in a bus, such as changes in termination and the unpredictable loading that occur as different cards are installed. Each PCI Express expansion connector links a single circuit designed for high-speed operation, so sliding a card into one slot affects no other. The wiring from each PCI Express connector runs directly back to a single centralized switch that selects which device has access to the system functions, much like a bus controller in older PCI designs. This switch can be either a stand-alone circuit or a part of the host computer's chipset.

All data and commands for PCI Express devices are contained in packets, which incorporate error correction to ensure the integrity of transfers. Even interrupts are packetized using the *Messaged Signal Interrupt* system introduced with PCI version 2.2, the implementation of which is optional for ordinary PCI but mandatory for PCI Express. The packets used by PCI Express use both 32-bit and extended 64-bit addressing.

The primary concern in creating PCI Express was to accommodate the conflicting needs of compatibility while keeping up with advancing technology. Consequently, the designers chose a layered approach with the top software layers designed to match current PCI protocols, while the lowest layer, the physical, permits multiple variations.

In the PCI Express scheme, there are five layers, designated as follows:

- **Config/OS**—Handles configuration at the operating system level based on the current PCI Plug-and-Play specifications for initializing, enumerating, and configuring expansion devices.
- **S/W**—This is the main software layer, which uses the same drivers as the standard PCI bus. This is the main layer that interacts with the host operating system.
- **Transaction**—This is a packet-based protocol for passing data between the devices. This layer handles the send and receive functions.
- **Data Link**—This layer ensures the integrity of the transfers with full error-checking using a cyclic redundancy check (CRC) code.
- **Physical**—This is the PCI Express hardware itself.

The top two layers, Config/OS and S/W, require no change from ordinary PCI. In other words, the high-speed innovations of PCI Express are invisible to the host computer's operating system.

As to the actual hardware, PCI Express retains the standard PCI board design and dimensions. It envisions dual-standard boards that have both conventional and high-speed PCI Express connections. Such dual-standard boards are restricted to one or two lanes on a extra edge connector that's collinear with the standard PCI expansion connector but mounted between it and the back of the computer. Devices requiring a greater number of lanes need a new PCI Express connector system.

Standards and Coordination

The PCI, PCI-X, and PCI Express standards are managed and maintained by the PCI Special Interest Group. The latest revision of each specification is available from the following address:

> PCI Special Interest Group
> 2575 NE Kathryn St. #17
> Hillsboro, OR 97124
>
> Fax: 503-693-8344
> Web site: http://www.pcisig.com

InfiniBand

At one time, engineers (who are as unlikely to gamble as the parish priest) put their money on *InfiniBand Architecture* as the likely successor to PCI and PCI-X as the next interconnection standard for servers and, eventually, individual computers. The standard had wide industry backing and proven advantages in moving data around inside computers. Its success seemed all but assured by its mixed parentage that pulled together factions once as friendly as the Montagues and Capulets. But as this is written, some industry insiders believe that the introduction of a new PCI variation, PCI Express, may usurp the role originally reserved for InfiniBand.

InfiniBand Architecture (also known as *IBA*) marks a major design change. It hardly resembles what's come to be known as an expansion bus. Instead of being loaded with clocks and control signals as well as data links, InfiniBand more resembles a network wire. It's stripped down to nothing but the connections carrying the data signals and, if necessary, some power lines to run peripherals. As with a network connection, InfiniBand packages data into packets. The control signals usually carried over that forest of extra bus connections are put into packets, too. Moreover, InfiniBand has no shared bus but rather operates as a switched fabric. In fact, InfiniBand sounds more like a network than an expansion system. In truth, it's both. And it also operates as an interconnection system that links together motherboard components.

Designed to overcome many of the inherent limitations of PCI and all other bus designs, IBA uses data-switching technology instead of a shared bus. Not only does this design increase the potential speed of each connection because the bandwidth is never shared, it also allows more effective management of individual connected devices and almost unlimited scalability. That is, it has no device limit (as does PCI) but allows you to link together as many peripherals as you want, both as expansion boards inside a computer and as external devices.

As with PCI, InfiniBand starts as an interconnection system to link components together on motherboards. But the specification doesn't stop there. It defines a complete system that includes expansion boards and an entire network.

The initial implementation of InfiniBand operates with a base frequency of 2.5GHz. Because it is a packetized communication system, it suffers from some signaling overhead. As a result, the maximum throughput of an InfiniBand circuit is 250MBps or 2.0Gbps. The speed is limited by necessity. Affordable wiring systems simply cannot handle higher rates.

To achieve better performance, InfiniBand defines a multicircuit communication system. In effect, it allows a sort of parallel channel capable of boosting performance by a factor of 12.

InfiniBand is a radical change for system expansion, as different from PCI as PCI was from ISA. Good as it is, however, don't expect to find an InfiniBand expansion bus in new personal computers. As an expansion bus, it is expensive, designed foremost for servers. You'll find the physical dimensions for InfiniBand expansion in Chapter 30, "Expansion Boards."

As an interconnection system for motherboard circuits, however, InfiniBand will find its way into personal computers, along with the next generation of Intel microprocessors, those that use 64-bit architecture.

History

The shortcomings of PCI architecture were apparent to engineers almost by the time the computer industry adopted the standard. It was quicker than ISA but not all that swift. Within a few years, high-bandwidth applications outgrew the PCI design, resulting in the AGP design for video subsystems (and eventually 2x, 4x, and 8x versions of AGP).

To the engineers working on InfiniBand, PCI-X was only a band-aid to the bandwidth problems suffered by high-powered systems. Most major manufacturers were already aware that PCI-X shared the same shortcomings as PCI, burdened with its heritage of interrupts and hardware-mediated flow control. Increasing the PCI speed exacerbated the problems rather than curing them.

Two separate groups sought to create a radically different expansion system to supercede PCI. One group sought a standard that would be able to link all the devices in a company without limit and without regard to cost. The group working on this initiative called it *Future I/O*. Another group sought a lower-cost alternative that would break through the barriers of the PCI design inside individual computers. This group called its initiative *Next Generation I/O*.

On August 31, 2000, the two groups announced they had joined together to work on a single new standard, which became InfiniBand. To create and support the new standard, the two groups formed the InfiniBand Trade Association (ITA) with seven founding members serving as the organization's steering committee. These included Compaq, Dell, Hewlett-Packard, IBM, Intel, Microsoft, and Sun Microsystems. Other companies from the FI/O and NGI/O initiatives joined as sponsoring members, including 3Com, Adaptec, Cisco, Fujitsu-Siemens, Hitachi, Lucent, NEC, and Nortel Networks. On November 30, 2000, the ITA announced that three new members joined—Agilent Technologies Inc., Brocade Communications Systems Inc., and EMC Corporation.

The group released the initial version of the InfiniBand Architecture specification (version 1.0) on October 23, 2000. The current version, 1.0.a, was released on June 19, 2001. The two-volume specification is distributed in electronic form without cost from the InfiniBand Trade Association Web site, `www.infinibandta.com`.

Communications

In traditional terms, InfiniBand is a serial communication system. Unlike other expansion designs, it is not a bus but rather a *switched fabric*. That means it weaves together devices that must communicate together, providing each one with a full-bandwidth channel. InfiniBand works more like the telephone system than a traditional bus. A controller routes the high-speed InfiniBand signals to the appropriate device. In technical terms, it is a point-to-point interconnection system.

InfiniBand moves information as packets across its channel. As with other packet-based designs, each block of data contains addressing, control signals, and information. InfiniBand uses a packet design based on the Internet Protocol so that engineers will have an easier time designing links between InfiniBand and external networks (including, of course, the Internet itself).

All InfiniBand connections use the same signaling rate, 2.5GHz. Because of the packet structure and advanced data coding used by the system, this signaling rate amounts to an actual throughput of about 500MBps. The InfiniBand system achieves even higher throughputs by moving to a form of parallel technology, moving its signals through 4 or

12 separate connections simultaneously. Table 9.4 summarizes the three current transfer speeds of the InfiniBand Architecture.

TABLE 9.4 InfiniBand Peak Throughput Versus Bus Width

Peak Throughput	Signaling Rate	Wire Pairs
500MBps	2.5GHz	1
2GBps	2.5GHz	4
6GBps	2.5GHz	12

These connections are full-duplex, so devices can transfer information at the same data rate in either direction. The signals are differential (the system uses two wires for each of its signals) to help minimize noise and interference at the high frequencies it uses.

The InfiniBand design allows the system to use copper traces on a printed circuit board like a conventional expansion bus. In addition, the same signaling scheme works on copper wires like a conventional networking system or through optical fiber.

As with modern interconnection designs, InfiniBand uses intelligent controllers that handle most of the work of passing information around so that it requires a minimum of intervention from the host computer and its operating system. The controller packages the data into packets, adds all the necessary routing and control information to each one, and sends them on their way. The host computer or other device need only send raw data to the controller, so it loses a minimal share of its processing power in data transfers.

The InfiniBand design is inherently modular. Its design enables you to add devices up to the limit of a switch or to add more switches to increase its capacity without limit. Individual switches create subnetworks, which exchange data through routers, much like a conventional network.

Structure

InfiniBand is a system area network (SAN), which simply means a network that lives inside a computer system. It can also reach outside the computer to act as a real network. In any of its applications—internal network, expansion system, or true local network— InfiniBand uses the same signaling scheme and same protocol. In fact, it uses Internet Protocol, version 6 (IPv6), the next generation of the protocol currently used by the Internet, for addressing and routing data.

In InfiniBand terminology, a complete IBA system is a *network*. The individual endpoints that connect to hardware devices, such as microprocessors and output devices, are called *nodes*. The wiring and other hardware that ties the network together make up the IBA *fabric*.

The hardware link between a device and the InfiniBand network that makes up a node is a *channel adapter*. The channel adapter translates the logic signals of the device connected to it into the form that will be passed along the InfiniBand fabric. For example, a channel adapter may convert 32-bit parallel data into a serial data stream spread across four differential channels. It also includes enough intelligence to manage communications, providing functions similar to the handshaking of a conventional serial connection.

InfiniBand uses two types of channel adapters: the *Host Channel Adapter* (HCA) and the *Target Channel Adapter* (TCA). As the name implies, the HCA resides in the host computer. More specifically, it is typically built in to the north bridge in the computer's chipset to take full advantage of the host's performance. (Traditionally, Ethernet would link to a system through its south bridge and suffer the speed restrictions of the host's expansion bus circuitry.) The distinction serves only to identify the two ends of a communications channel; the HCA is a microprocessor or similar device. The TCA is an input/output device such as a connection to a storage system. Either the HCA or the TCA can originate and control the flow of data.

The InfiniBand fabric separates the system from conventional expansion buses. Instead of using a bus structure to connect multiple devices into the expansion system, the InfiniBand fabric uses a *switch*, which sets up a direct channel from one device to another. Switching signals rather than busing them together ensures higher speed—every device has available to it the full bandwidth of the system. The switch design also improves reliability. Because multiple connections are not shared, a problem in one device or channel does not affect others. Based on the address information in the header of each packet, the switch directs the packet toward its destination, a journey that may pass through several switches.

A switch directs packets only within an InfiniBand network (or within a device such as a server). The IPv6 nature of InfiniBand's packets allows easy interfacing of an individual InfiniBand network with external networks (which may, in turn, be linked to other InfiniBand systems). A *router* serves as the connection between an InfiniBand network and another network.

The physical connections within the InfiniBand network (between channel adapters, switches, and routers) are termed *links* in IBA parlance. The fabric of an InfiniBand network may also include one or more *repeaters* that clean up and boost the signals in a link to allow greater range.

In a simple InfiniBand system, two nodes connect through links to a switch. The links and the switch are the fabric of the network. A complex InfiniBand system may involve multiple switches, routers, and repeaters knitted into a far-reaching web.

Standards and Coordination

The InfiniBand specification is managed and maintained by the InfiniBand Trade Association. The latest revision of the specification is available from the following address:

InfiniBand Trade Association

5440 SW Westgate Drive, Suite 217

Portland, OR 97221

Telephone: 503-291-2565

Fax: 503-297-1090

E-mail: administration@infinibandta.org

Web site: www.infinibandta.org

HyperTransport

The fastest way to send signals inside a computer is via HyperTransport, but HyperTransport is not an expansion bus. It isn't a bus at all. Strictly defined, it is a point-to-point communications system. The HyperTransport specification makes no provision for removable expansion boards. However, HyperTransport is destined to play a major role in the expansion of high-performance computers because it ties the circuitry of the computer together. For example, it can link the microprocessor to the bus control circuitry, serving as a bridge between the north and south bridges in the motherboard chipset. It may also link the video system to the north bridge. Anywhere signals need to move their quickest, HyperTransport can move them.

Quick? HyperTransport tops out with a claimed peak data rate of 12.8GBps. That's well beyond the bandwidth of today's microprocessor memory buses, the fastest connections currently in use. It easily eclipses the InfiniBand Architecture connection system, which peaks out at 2GBps.

But that's it. Unlike InfiniBand, which does everything from host expansion boards to connect to the World Wide Web, HyperTransport is nothing but fast. It is limited to the confines of a single circuit board, albeit a board that may span several square feet of real estate. As far as your operating system or applications are concerned, HyperTransport is invisible. It works without any change in a computer's software and requires no special drivers or other attention at all.

On the other hand, fast is enough. HyperTransport breaks the interconnection bottle-necks in common system designs. A system with HyperTransport may be several times faster than one without it on chores that reach beyond the microprocessor and its memory.

History

HyperTransport was the brainchild of Advanced Micro Devices (AMD). The Texas chip-maker created the interconnection design to complement its highest performance micro-processors, initially codenamed *Hammer*.

Originally named *Lightning Data Transport*, the design gained the HyperTransport name when AMD shared its design with other companies (primarily the designers of peripher-als) who were facing similar bandwidth problems. On July 23, 2001, AMD and a handful of other interested companies created the HyperTransport Technology Consortium to further standardize, develop, and promote the interface. The charter members of the HyperTransport Consortium included Advanced Micro Devices, API NetWorks, Apple Computers, PMC-Sierra, Cisco Systems, NVidia, and Sun Microsystems.

The Consortium publishes an official HyperTransport I/O Link Specification, which is currently available for download without charge from the group's Web site at www.hypertransport.org. The current version of the specification is 1.03 and was released on October 10, 2001.

Performance

In terms of data transport speed, HyperTransport is the fastest interface currently in use. Its top speed is nearly 100 times quicker than the standard PCI expansion bus and three times faster than the InfiniBand specification currently allows. Grand as those numbers look, they are also misleading. Both InfiniBand and HyperTransport are duplex interfaces, which means they can transfer data in two directions simultaneously. Optimistic engineers calculate throughput by adding the two duplex channels together. Information actually moves from one device to another through the InfiniBand and HyperTransport interfaces at half the maximum rate shown, at most. Overhead required by the packet-based inter-faces eats up more of the actual throughput performance.

Not all HyperTransport systems operate at these hyperspeeds. Most run more slowly. In any electronic design, higher speeds make parts layout more critical and add increased worries about interference. Consequently, HyperTransport operates at a variety of speeds. The current specification allows for six discrete speeds, only the fastest of which reaches the maximum value.

The speed of a HyperTransport connection is measured in the number of bits transferred through a single data path in a second. The actual clock speed of the connection on the HyperTransport bus is 800MHz. The link achieves its higher bit-rates by transferring two bits per clock cycle, much as double data-rate memory does. One transfer is keyed to each the rise and fall of the clock signal. The six speeds are 400, 600, 800, 1000, 1200, and 1600Mbps.

In addition, HyperTransport uses several connections in parallel for each of its links. It achieves its maximum data rate only through its widest connection with 32 parallel circuits. The design also supports bus widths of 16, 8, 4, and 2 bits.

Table 9.5 lists the link speeds as well as the maximum bus throughputs in megabytes per second at each of the allowed bus widths.

TABLE 9.5 HyperTransport Peak Throughput As a Function of Bus Width and Speed

	HyperTransport Link Width (In Bits)				
Link Speed in Mbps	*2*	*4*	*8*	*16*	*32*
400	100	200	400	800	1600
600	150	300	600	1200	2400
800	200	400	800	1600	3200
1000	250	500	1000	2000	4000
1200	300	600	1200	2400	4800
1600	400	800	1600	3200	6400

Certainly, a wider bus gives a performance edge, but the wider connections also rapidly increase in complexity because of the structure of the interface.

Structure

HyperTransport is a point-to-point communications system. Functionally, it is equivalent to a wire with two ends. The signals on the HyperTransport channel cannot be shared with multiple devices. However, a device can have several HyperTransport channels leading to several different peripheral devices.

The basic HyperTransport design is a duplex communications system based on differential signals. *Duplex* means that HyperTransport uses separate channels for sending and receiving data. *Differential* means that HyperTransport uses two wires for each signal, sending the same digital code down both wires at the same time but with the polarity of the two signals opposite. The system registers the difference between the two signals. Any noise picked up along the way should, in theory, be the same on the two lines because they are so close together, so it does not register on the differential receiver.

HyperTransport uses multiple sets of differential wire pairs for each communications channel. In its most basic form, HyperTransport uses two pairs for sending and two for receiving, effectively creating two parallel paths in the channel. That is, the most basic form of HyperTransport moves data two bits at a time. The HyperTransport specification allows for channel widths of 2, 4, 8, 16, or 32 parallel paths to move data the correspond-ing number of bits at a time. Of course, the more data paths in a channel, the faster the channel can move data. The two ends of the connection negotiate the width of the chan-nel when they power up, and the negotiated width remains set until the next power up or reset. The channel width cannot change dynamically.

The HyperTransport specification allows for asymmetrical channels. That is, the specifi-cation allows for systems that might have a 32-bit data path in one direction but only 2 bits in return.

Although HyperTransport moves data in packets, it also uses several control lines to help reduce software overhead and maintain the integrity of the network. A clock signal (CLK) indicates when data on the channel is valid and may be read. Channels 2-, 4-, or 8-bits wide have single clock signals; 16-bit channels have two synchronized clock signals; 32-bit channels have four clock signals. A control signal (CTL) indicates whether the bits on the data lines are actually data or control information. Activating this signal indicates the data on the channel is control information. The line can be activated even during a data packet, allowing control information to take immediate control. A separate signal (POWEROK) ensures the integrity of the connection, indicating that the power to the system and the clock are operating properly. A reset signal (RESET#) does exactly what you'd expect—it resets the system so that it reloads its configuration.

For compatibility with power-managed computers based on Intel architecture, the HyperTransport interface also includes two signals to allow a connection to be set up again after the system goes into standby or hibernate mode. The LDTSTOP# signal, when present, enables the data link. When it shifts off, the link is disabled. The host sys-tem or a device can request the link be reenabled (which also reconfigures the link) with the LDTREQ# signal. Table 9.6 summarizes the signals in a HyperTransport link.

TABLE 9.6   HyperTransport Bus Signals

Mnemonic	Function	Width
CAD	Command, address, and data lines	2, 4, 8, 16, or 32
CTL	Control	1
CLK	Clock	1, 2, or 4
PWROK	Power and clock okay	1
RESET#	Reset chain	1
LDTSTOP#	Enable/disable link	1
LDTREQ#	Request link enable	1

The design of the HyperTransport mechanical bus is meant to minimize the number of connections used because more connections need more power, generate more heat, and reduce the overall reliability of the system. Even so, a HyperTransport channel requires a large number of connections—each CAD bit requires four conductors, a two-wire differential pair for each of the two duplex signals. A 32-bit HyperTransport channel therefore requires 128 conductors for its CAD signals. At a minimum, the six control signals, which are single ended, require six more conductors, increasing to nine in a 32-bit system because of the four differential clock signals.

Each differential pair uses a variation on the *low-voltage differential signaling* (LVDS) standard. The differential voltage shift between the pairs of a signal is only 600 millivolts.

Standards and Coordination

The HyperTransport specification is maintained by the HyperTransport Technology Consortium, which can be reached at the following addresses:

HyperTransport Technology Consortium

1030 E. El Camino Real #447

Sunnyvale, CA 94087

Phone: 800-538-8450 (Ext. 47739)

E-mail: info@hypertransport.org

Web site: www.hypertransport.org

PCMCIA

While the desktop remains a battlefield for bus designers, notebook computer–makers have selected a single standard to rally around: PC Card, promulgated by the Personal Computer Memory Card International Association (PCMCIA). Moreover, the PC Card bus is flexible and cooperative. Because it is operating system and device independent, you can plug the same PC Card peripheral into a computer, Mac, Newton, or whatever the next generation holds in store. The PC Card expansion system can cohabitate in a computer with a desktop bus such as ISA or PCI. What's more, it will work in devices that aren't even computers—from calculators to hair curlers, from CAD workstations to auto-everything cameras. Someday you may even find a PC Card lurking in your toaster oven or your music synthesizer.

The PC Card system is self-configuring, so you do not have to deal with DIP switches, fiddle with jumpers, or search for a reference diskette. PC Card differs from other bus standards in that it allows for external expansion—you don't have to open up your computer to add a PC Card.

The design is so robust that you can insert or remove a PC Card with the power on without worrying that you will damage it, your computer, or the data stored on the card. In other words, PC Cards are designed for *hot-swapping*. The system is designed to notify your operating system what you've done, so it can reallocate its resources as you switch cards. The operating system sets up its own rules and may complain if you switch cards without first warning it, although the resulting damage accrues mostly to your pride.

The engineers who created the PC Card standard originally envisioned only a system that put memory in credit-card format—hence the name, *Personal Computer Memory Card International Association*. The U.S.-based association drew on the work of the *Japan Electronics and Information Technology Industries Association*, which had previously developed four memory-only card specifications.

They saw PC Card as an easy way to put programs into portable computers without the need for disk drives. Since then the standard has grown to embrace nearly any expansion option—modems, network interface cards, SCSI host adapters, video subsystems, all the way to hard disk drives. Along the way, the PCMCIA and JEITIA standards merged, so one specification now governs PC Cards worldwide.

The first release of the PC Card standard allowed only for memory and came in September 1990. In September 1991, it was updated to Release 2.0 to include storage and input/output devices as well as thicker cards. After some minor changes, the standard jumped to Release 5.0 in February 1995. The big jump in numbering (from Release 2.1 to Release 5.0) put the PCMCIA and JEITIA number schemes on equal footing—the specification was number 5.0 for both. Since that event, the numbering of the standard as issued by both organizations has tracked, culminating in the current standard, Release 8.0, published in April 2001. Note, too, the specification title changed from PCMCIA Release 2.1 to PC Card Release 5.0. Table 9.7 summarizes the history of the PCMCIA standard.

TABLE 9.7   History of the PCMCIA/JEITIA/PC Card Standard

Version	Introduction Date	Features
PCMCIA 1.0	June 1990	First PCMCIA Standard, JEITIA Version 4.0; memory only.
PCMCIA 2.0	September 1991	I/O interface added; socket services introduced.
PCMCIA 2.01	November 1992	PC Card ATA specification; card services introduced.
PCMCIA 2.1	July 1993	Card and socket services enhanced.
PC Card 5.0	February 1995	Compatibility enhancements; low-voltage added, CardBus introduced; power management.
PC Card 6.0	March 1997	Zoomed video; hot dock; streamlined configuration.

Version	Introduction Date	Features
PC Card 6.1	April 1998	Small PC Card form factor added; Win32 bindings.
PC Card 7.0	February 1999	Windows NT bindings; memory paging.
PC Card 7.1	March 2000	OpenCable custom interface; DMA references removed.
PC Card 7.2	November 2000	New maximum current requirements; new guidelines.
PC Card 8.0	April 2001	New low-voltage support; 3-watt maximum per card limit.

The PCMCIA/JEITIA specifications cover every aspect of the cards you slide into your computer (or other device—the standard envisions you using the same cards in other kinds of electronic gear). It details the size and shape of cards, how they are protected, how they are connected (including the physical connector), the firmware the cards use to identify themselves, and the software your computer wields to recognize and use the cards. Moreover, the specifications don't describe a hard-and-fast hardware interface. The same connector and software system can embrace a wide variety of different purposes and interfaces. The PC Card was only the first of the interconnection schemes documented by the PCMCIA/JEITIA specifications. By redefining the signals on the PC Card connector, a high-speed 32-bit expansion bus called *CardBus*, a dedicated high-speed video system called *Zoomed Video*, and a cable television–oriented video system called *OpenCable* all fit within the system.

All types of PC Cards use the same 68-pin connector, whose contacts are arranged in two parallel rows of 34 pins. The lines are spaced at 1.27 mm (0.050-inch) intervals between rows and between adjacent pins in the same row. Male pins on the card engage a single molded socket on the host. We'll look at the PCMCIA packages in more detail in Chapter 30.

To ensure proper powering up of the card, the pins are arranged so that the power and ground connections are longer (3.6 mm) than the signal leads (3.2 mm). Because of their greater length, power leads engage first so that potentially damaging signals are not applied to unpowered circuits. The two pins (36 and 67) that signal that the card has been inserted all the way are shorter (2.6 mm) than the signal leads.

PC Card

The original and still most popular of the PCMCIA card specifications is PC Card. Based on the ISA design, the standard expansion bus at the time the specifications were written, PC Card is a 16-bit interface. Unlike modern expansion buses, it lacks such advanced features as bus-mastering. However, the PC Card standard is more than the old bus. It is a system designed specifically for removable cards that includes both hardware and software support.

The hardware side of the standard sets its limits so high that engineers are unlikely to bump into them. For example, it allows for a single system to use from 1 to 255 PCMCIA adapters (that is, circuits that match the signals of PC Cards to the host). Up to 16 separate PC Card sockets can be connected to each adapter, so under the PCMCIA specifications you could potentially plug up to 4080 PC Cards into one system. Most computers shortchange you a bit on that—typically you get only one or two slots.

The memory and I/O registers of each PC Card are individually mapped into a window in the address range of the host device. The entire memory on a PC Card can be mapped into a single large window (for simple memory expansion, for example), or it can be paged through one or more windows. The PC Card itself determines the access method through configuration information it stores in its own memory.

Signals and Operation

The PCMCIA specifications allow for three PC Card variations: memory-only (which essentially conforms to the Release 1.0 standard), I/O cards, and multimedia cards.

When a PCMCIA connector hosts PC Cards, all but 10 pins of the standard 68 share common functions between the memory and I/O-style cards. Four memory card signals are differently defined for I/O cards (pins 16, 33, 62, and 63); three memory card signals are modified for I/O functions (pins 18, 52, and 61); and three pins reserved on memory cards are used by I/O cards (pins 44, 45, and 60).

The PC Card specifications allow for card implementations that use either 8- or 16-bit data buses. In memory operations, two Card Enable signals (pins 7 and 42) set the bus width; pin 7 enables even-numbered address bytes; and pin 42 enables odd bytes. All bytes can be read by an 8-bit system by activating pin 7 but not 42 and toggling the lowest address line (A0, pin 29) to step to the next byte.

Memory Control

The original PC Card specifications allow the use of 26 address lines, which permitted direct addressing of up to 64MB of data. The memory areas on each card are independent. That is, each PC Card can define its own 64MB address range as its *common memory*. In addition to common memory, each card has a second 64MB address space devoted to attribute memory, which holds the card's setup information. The typical PC Card devotes only a few kilobytes of this range to actual CIS storage.

Activating the Register Select signal (pin 61) shifts the 26 address lines normally used to address common memory to specifying locations in attribute memory instead. The address space assigned to attribute memory need not correspond to a block of memory separate from common memory. To avoid the need for two distinct memory systems, a PC Card can be designed so that activating the Register Select signal simply points to a block of common memory devoted to storing setup information. All PC Cards limit access to attribute memory to an eight-bit link using the eight least-significant data lines.

To accommodate more storage, the specifications provide *address extension registers*, a bank-switching system that enables the computer host to page through much larger memory areas on PC Cards. A number of different address extension register options are permitted, all the way up to 16 bits, which extends the total card common memory to four terabytes (4TB, which is 2 to the 42nd power—that is, 26 addresses and 65,536 possible pages).

Memory cards that use EPROM memory often require higher-than-normal voltages to reprogram their chips. Pins 18 and 52 on the PCMCIA interface provide these voltages when needed.

Data Transfers

To open or close access to data read from a PC Card, the host computer activates a signal on the card's Output Enable line (pin 9). A Ready/Busy line (pin 16) on memory cards allows the card to signal when it is busy processing and cannot accept a data-transfer operation. The same pin is used on I/O cards to make interrupt requests to the host system. During setup, however, an I/O card can redefine pin 16 back to its Ready/Busy function. Since Release 2.0, memory or I/O PC Cards also can delay the completion of an operation in progress—in effect, slowing the host to accommodate the time needs of the card—by activating an Extend Bus Cycle signal on pin 59.

The Write Protect pin (pin 33) relays the status of the write-protect switch on memory cards to the computer host. On I/O cards, this pin indicates that a given I/O port has a 16-bit width.

The same 26 lines used for addressing common and attribute memory serve as port-selection addresses on I/O cards. Two pins, I/O read (44) and I/O write (45), signal that the address pins will be used for identifying ports and whether the operation is a read or a write.

Unlike memory addresses, however, the I/O facilities available to all PC Cards in a system share "only" one 67,108,864-byte (64MB) range of port addresses. Although small compared to total memory addressing, this allotment of I/O ports is indeed generous. When the specification was first contrived, the most popular computer expansion bus (the AT bus) allowed only 64KB of I/O ports, of which some systems recognized a mere 16KB. Whether ports are 8 or 16 bit is indicated by the signal on pin 33.

I/O PC Cards each have a single interrupt request signal. The signal is mapped to one of the computer interrupt lines by the computer host. In other words, the PC Card generates a generic interrupt, and it is the responsibility of the host computer's software and operation system to route each interrupt to the appropriate channel.

Configuration

The PC Card specifications provide for automatic setup of each card. When the host computer activates the Reset signal on pin 58 of the PCMCIA socket, the card returns to its preinitialization settings, with I/O cards returning to their power-on memory card emulation. The host can then read from the card's memory to identify it and run the appropriate configuration software.

When a PC Card is plugged into a slot, the host computer's PCMCIA adapter circuitry initially assumes that it is a memory card. The card defines itself as an I/O card through its onboard CIS data, which the host computer reads upon initializing the PC Card. Multimedia cards similarly identify themselves through their software and automatically reconfigure the PC Card to accept their special signals.

Audio

An audio output line also is available from I/O PC Cards. This connection is not intended for high-quality sound, however, because it allows only binary digital (on/off) signals (much like the basic speaker in early desktop computers). The audio lines of all PC Cards in a system are linked together by an XOR (exclusive OR) logic gate fed to a single common loudspeaker, equivalent to the sound system of a primitive computer lacking a sound board. Under the CardBus standard (discussed later in this chapter) the same socket supports high-quality digital audio.

Power

Pins 62 and 63 on memory cards output two battery status signals. Pin 63 indicates the status of the battery: When activated, the battery is in good condition; when not activated, it indicates that the battery needs to be replaced. Pin 62 refines this to indicate that the battery level is sufficient to maintain card memory without errors; if this signal is not activated, it indicates that the integrity of on-card memory may already be compromised by low battery power.

Although the PCMCIA specifications were originally written to accommodate only the 5-volt TTL signaling that was the industry standard at the time of their conception, the standard has evolved. It now supports cards using 3.3-volt signaling and makes provisions for future lower operating voltages. Cards are protected so you cannot harm a card or your computer by mismatching voltages.

Software Interface

The PC Card specifications require layers of software to ensure its compatibility across device architectures. Most computers, for example, require two layers of software drivers—Socket Services and Card Services—to match the card slots in addition to whatever drivers an individual card requires (for example, a modem requires a modem driver).

As with other hardware advances, Windows 95 helped out the PC Card. Support for the expansion standard is built in to the operating system (as well as Windows 98). Although Windows NT (through version 4.0) lacks integral PC Card support, Windows 2000 embraced the standard. Most systems accept cards after you slide them in, automatically installing the required software. Unusual or obscure boards usually require only that you install drivers for their manufacturer-specific features using the built-in Windows installation process.

Socket Services

To link the PC Card to an Intel-architecture computer host, PCMCIA has defined a software interface called *Socket Services*. By using a set of function calls under interrupt 1A (which Socket Services shares with the CMOS real-time clock), software can access PC Card features without specific knowledge of the underlying hardware. In other words, Socket Services make access to the PC Card hardware independent, much like the BIOS of a computer. In fact, Socket Services are designed so that they can be built in to the computer BIOS. However, Socket Services also can be implemented in the form of a device driver so that PCMCIA functionality can be added to existing computers.

Using Socket Services, the host establishes the windows used by the PC Card for access. Memory or registers then can be directly addressed by the host. Alternatively, individual or multiple bytes can be read or written through Socket Services function calls.

Card Services

With Release 2.01, PCMCIA approved a Card Services standard that defines a program interface for accessing PC Cards. This standard establishes a set of program calls that link to those Socket Services independent of the host operating system. Like the Socket Services associated with interrupt 1A, Card Services can either be implemented as a driver or be built in as part of an operating system. (Protected-mode operating systems such as OS/2 and Windows NT require the latter implementation.)

Setup

For an advanced PC Card system to work effectively, each PC Card must be able to identify itself and its characteristics to its computer host. Specifically, it must be able to tell the computer how much storage it contains; the device type (solid-state memory, disk, I/O devices, or other peripherals); the format of the data; the speed capabilities of the card; and any of a multitude of other variables about how the card operates.

Card Identification Structure

Asking you to enter all the required data every time you install a PC Card would be both inconvenient and dangerous. Considerable typing would be required, and a single errant keystroke could forever erase the data off the card. Therefore, PCMCIA developed a self-contained system through which the basic card setup information can be passed to the host regardless of either the data structure of the on-card storage or the operating system of the host.

Called the *Card Identification Structure (CIS)* or *metaformat* of the card, the PCMCIA configuration system works through a succession of compatibility layers to establish the necessary link between the PC Card and its host. As with the hardware interface, each layer of CIS is increasingly device specific.

Only the first layer, the Basic Compatibility Layer, is mandatory. This layer indicates how the card's storage is organized. Only two kinds of information are relevant here: the data structures used by the layer itself and such standard and physical device information as the number of heads, cylinders, and sectors of a physical or emulated disk. Since Release 5.0, each card must bear a Card Information Structure so it can identify itself to the host system.

Data Recording Format Layer

The next layer up is the Data Recording Format Layer, which specifies how the stored data is organized at the block level. Four data formats are supported under Release 2.0: unchecked blocks, blocks with checksum error correction, blocks with cyclic redundancy error checking, and unblocked data that does not correspond to disk organization (for example, random access to the data, such as is permitted for memory).

Data Organization Layer

The third CIS layer, the *Data Organization Layer*, specifies how information is logically organized on the card; that is, it specifies the operating system format to which the data conforms. PCMCIA recognizes four possibilities: DOS, Microsoft's Flash File System for Flash RAM, PCMCIA's own Execute-in-Place (XIP) ROM image, and application-specific organization. Microsoft's Flash File System is an operating system specifically designed for the constraints of Flash memory. It minimizes rewriting specific memory areas to extend the limited life of the medium and to allow for speedy updates of required block writes.

System-Specific Standards

The fourth CIS layer is assigned to system-specific standards that comply with particular operating environments. For example, the Execute-in-Place (XIP) standard defines how programs encoded on ROM cards are to be read and executed.

XIP is PCMCIA's own specification that allows program code in read-only memory to execute without being first loaded into main system (read/write) memory. Application-specific organization allows card developers to create data organizations unique to their products so as to implement special features.

Attribute Memory

The setup information for all these layers is stored in a reserved area on the PC Card called *attribute memory*. This area is isolated from the card's ordinary storage, which under

PCMCIA 2.1 is called *common memory*. The CIS information is structured as a linked chain of data blocks called *tuples*, each of which can be up to 128 bytes long. To give all systems a common starting point to search for CIS data, the first tuple of the metaformat is located at the first address in attribute memory. This ensures that the data is within the addressing range of even those primitive microprocessors that can address only 1MB of RAM. Because the CIS system must work in any computer or other host, it assumes that memory can be accessed only in byte widths.

The first two bytes of each tuple, as well as the format of many predefined tuples, are strictly defined. The first byte encodes the function of the tuple and the parameters it describes. The second byte links to the next tuple in the chain (if any); it specifies the number of data bytes in the tuple, which, of course, indicates where the next tuple begins. The PCMCIA 2.1 specifications define the options available for many common tuples. PC Card manufacturers are free to add their own tuples to store data for setting up cards that contain proprietary features.

As the storage and expansion needs of computers and other electronic devices continue to evolve, the PCMCIA PC Card standard will likely follow in lockstep. Undoubtedly it is the computer expansion system of the future—and the first truly universal data-interchange system.

CardBus

To bring the PC Card into the 32-bit world, PCMCIA adapted the highly regarded PCI expansion bus to the credit-card format to create the *CardBus* in November 1994, formalized in Release 5.0. Just as PC Card is a miniaturized version of ISA, CardBus shrinks down PCI while yielding the same high data-transfer rates, with one important exception: Due to limitations in the connector design, CardBus extends only to a 32-bit bus width, whereas the PCI standard allows for 64-bit buses. Although CardBus is not truly a PCI system—it is designed to be a platform-independent 32-bit system—it is functionally equivalent to PCI and uses the PCI protocol for bus operations.

Under CardBus, effectively all the active signals on the 68-pin PCMCIA connector are redefined. Only the grounds, fixed voltages, and card-identification pins are unchanged.

To accommodate the full 32-bit addressing range and 32-bit data buses of the PCI bus, the CardBus system multiplexes the two onto the same 32 connections of the PC Card, just as they are in the full-size PCI implementation. In addition, the CardBus standard boosts the signaling rate to match that of PCI, up to 33MHz, while allowing lower-speed operation as well (all the way down to zero).

Besides a wider, faster bus and PCI-based protocol, CardBus adds several new features to the PC Card repertory. CardBus supports arbitration and bus-mastering with multiple bus masters, again patterned after PCI. A CardBus device can take command of its own transfers to the host system and free the host computer's microprocessor from the chore.

CardBus also incorporates a new *pulse width modulation* (PWM) audio mode. This mode allows a CardBus device to transfer audio in digital form across a single bus line. As with all digital audio, the PWM signal is a series of pulses; however, the length of each pulse rather than a coded pattern determines its audio equivalent. PWM mode allows the CardBus device to transfer multiple high-quality audio signals in real time.

All CardBus cards operate at 3.3 volts, in keeping with the trend toward lower-voltage operation in both desktop and notebook computers. The CardBus cards take advantage of the PC Card voltage keying system so that you cannot insert a CardBus product into a PC Card slot that supports only 5-volt operation (and thereby damaging the card, your computer, or both).

The low operating voltage helps ensure minimal power drain on the computer host. The configuration system, too, was designed with power in mind. When a CardBus product starts, only a limited part of its circuitry gets powered up, only enough to allow the host computer to read the Card Identification Structure. The host can then determine what kind of card it is, how much power it requires, and whether it has enough resources to operate the card. Only when the host computer determines the compatibility of the CardBus product and accepts it, does full power flow into the card. Besides allowing the host system to reject products that might otherwise drain its energy resources, the stepped startup procedure also prevents a surge in power demand when the host computer boots up.

One primary design intention with CardBus was continuity with the PC Card standard. PCMCIA wanted CardBus and PC Cards to be as compatible with one another as possible.

One incompatibility cannot be breeched. Because CardBus supports only 3.3-volt operation, its slots are off-limits to 5-volt-only PC Cards. The voltage key prevents you from inserting 5-volt PC Cards into CardBus slots. Except for the voltage issue, the two types of slots accept cards made to either standard. That is, all 3.3-volt PC Cards fit in and work with CardBus slots.

The primary challenge in making CardBus backward compatible with PC Card was fitting all the necessary 32 bits of addressing and 32 bits of data signaling onto a 68-pin connector while still having enough connections for support functions. The simple design expedient was the same as used by PCI—*multiplexing*. CardBus connections do double-duty, handling both address and data signals, cutting the number of pins required in half and making a 32-bit bus on a 68-pin card viable.

Zoomed Video

For higher-quality sound or video applications, the PC Card standard defines special multimedia cards. When the PC Card software in your computer recognizes a multimedia card, it redefines many of the connections in the card connector to switch it into operating as a *Zoomed Video* port.

Specifically in multimedia mode, 21 address signals and three control signals get replaced by four audio and 19 video signals as well as a new control signal. The video signals are meant to write directly to the frame buffer of the host computer, allowing a PC Card to generate quick displays. In effect, whatever device is on the PC Card with Zoomed Video has direct access to your notebook computer's screen. It can push pixels without the delays inherent in bus transfers.

In addition, a Zoomed Video connection also gives a PC Card a direct connection to the audio system in the host computer. The card provides pulse code modulation (PCM) digital audio directly to a codec in the host computer, which in turn links to the sound system.

The PC Card connection is only part of the Zoomed Video system. The host computer must also be designed to give access to its frame buffer from the port connector.

Despite its appealing name, Zoomed Video does not make the ordinary displays on your computer screen any faster. The only time it helps the display speed is when you have a graphics accelerator or other high-performance video device that installs on a PC Card or CardBus card.

Standards and Coordination

One key to the PC Card's success is that it is not a proprietary standard foisted on the industry by a single company or small coterie. The design is the product of a group called the Personal Computer Memory Card International Association (PCMCIA), which has more than 220 members involved in all aspects of the computer and electronics industry. CardBus continues in that tradition and is similarly maintained. The various PCMCIA standards are completely open, and all specifications are available to anyone requesting them from the organization. (The charge for the latest specification release was not set at the time of this writing, but it is estimated to be between $200 and $300.)

Rather than operate completely independently, PCMCIA cooperates with other standard-setting organizations. For example, by working jointly with the Japan Electronic Industry Technology Association (JEITA) in December 1989, PCMCIA was able to ensure that the standards it developed would be truly international in scope. Today, each organization sends a delegation to the meetings of the other.

Besides the efforts at extending PCMCIA to future technologies, such as 32-bit data paths and bus-mastering, PCMCIA is also developing standards for incorporating specific device types into the system. Already the group has fully described the needs for XIP, which allows programs to execute from their storage locations on PC Cards instead of needing to be loaded as if from disk into normal system RAM. PCMCIA has also developed standards for linking AT Attachment–style IDE hard disks into PC Card sockets.

To obtain more information about PCMCIA products and standards, contact the following address:

Personal Computer Memory Card International Association
1030 East Duane Avenue, Suite G
Sunnyvale, CA 94086

Phone: 408-720-0107
Fax: 408-720-9416
Web site: www.pc-card.com

Interfaces

If you could pry one of the expansion bus connectors off the motherboard of your computer and solder a length of cable to it, you'd probably ruin your computer. But you'd also make the equivalent of a mass storage interface. This may be educational, but don't try it at home. Not only will it be expensive and wasteful (of your computer), but unnecessary. Some clever engineers have already done it for you.

In fact, the most popular interface for hard disk, CD, and DVD drives, is nothing more than a pried-off expansion board connector. The AT Attachment interface earned its name by putting the AT expansion bus connector on a short cable that plugged into hard disk drives. The interface has matured somewhat since then—it's about 16 times faster, has developed its own language, and trimmed off a lot of fat. But deep down, underneath all the gloss and the layers of specifications, is the heart of the AT expansion bus.

At that, AT Attachment is almost the perfect interface. It brings devices both electrically and logically closer to your computer's circuitry than any other connection system. And that's exactly what the interface is supposed to do—connect individual devices to your computer.

AT Attachment isn't the only popular interface, however. It has a number of rivals and predecessors. If you have a high-performance computer and disk system, you're likely to covet its closet rival, SCSI, for its speed and versatility—or even ATA's designated successor, Serial ATA, which promises to be the fastest yet lowest cost interface developed so far.

At the other end of the spectrum, your computer likely also has the slowest interface in common use still stuffed within its circuitry—

a floppy disk interface. You probably don't need an engineering degree to figure out what it does. It runs the floppy disk drive that is the one remaining (or at least the most prominent) vestige of the technology of the first personal computer in modern machines. It's the equivalent of you wearing your grandmother's locket around your neck.

AT Attachment

The dominant hard disk interface for the computer has become the AT Attachment design—a natural outcome considering that the interface is based on the ISA expansion bus, at one time the most widely used computer bus. Despite its wide application, you still might never have heard of the AT Attachment name. It goes under more aliases than a candidate for the Ten Most Wanted list. The most familiar of its alternate monikers is IDE, which stands for *Integrated Drive Electronics* and is a term that correctly describes a technology rather than a specific interface. Nevertheless, the name IDE gets used indiscriminately by people in the computer industry for the AT Attachment design. Sometimes engineers call ATA the *AT interface*, which strictly speaking it is not.

Although engineers created ATA in its original form for low-cost small-capacity drives, it has grown along with the needs of modern computers, keeping in step with the need for both higher capacities and faster access to information. In fact, today's ATA interface can handle more capacity than any disk drive foreseeable in your lifetime. And its speed far exceeds the capabilities of any current disk drive mechanism.

But AT Attachment isn't a single interface. During its long evolution since its introduction in 1991 (several preliminary versions were used by products before then and after 1985, when engineers first began work on what eventually became the standard), it has undergone several stages of refinement. Every year or two, a new version of the standard gets approved. The current version is ATA-6, although ATA-7 is already in the works. Table 10.1 briefly summarizes the history of the AT Attachment standard.

TABLE 10.1   The ATA Standards

Standard	Year Introduced	Maximum Capacity	Maximum Speed
ATA	1994	504MB (CHS only)	4.17Mbps
ATA-2	1996	137.5GB	11.3Mbps
ATA-3	1997	137.5GB	16.7Mbps
ATA-4	1998	137.5GB	33.3Mbps
ATA-5	2000	137.5GB	66.6Mbps
ATA-6	2002	16PB	133Mbps
ATA-7	Proposed	16PB	133Mbps

Performance

Much of the development of ATA has been focused on improving its performance to keep it in step with disk drive and computer technology. The designers of the interface have done an admirable job, not only keeping it ahead of current technology but also pushing far beyond it. Today's hard disk drive mechanisms are limited by physical and design factors to far lower speeds than the ATA interface can deliver.

As engineers refined the ATA standard, they increased performance by adding new *transfer modes* to the operating features of the drive. Each new drive usually supports the fastest mode defined at the time it is made as well as all the older, slower modes. The host computer, its operating system, and the drive negotiate the fastest transfer mode that all understand to use for their transfers. That way, you always get the fastest possible performance from your disk drive. Moreover, even the newest drives can work with old computers (or old drives can work with new computers).

The current ATA standard recognizes 11 transfer modes, each with its own performance limit. Table 10.2 summarizes the principal transfer modes of the AT Attachment standard.

TABLE 10.2   AT Attachment Transfer Modes and Speeds

Transfer Mode	Cycle Time (Nanoseconds)	Speed (Mbps)	Standard
PIO mode 0	600	1.67	ATA
PIO mode 1	383	2.61	ATA
PIO mode 2	240	4.17	ATA
PIO mode 3	180	11.1	ATA-2
PIO mode 4	120	16.7	ATA-3
DMA, single-word, mode 0	960	1.04	ATA
DMA, single-word, mode 1	480	2.08	ATA
DMA, single-word, mode 2	240	4.17	ATA
DMA, multi-word, mode 0	480	4.17	ATA
DMA, multi-word, mode 1	150	13.3	ATA-2
DMA, multi-word, mode 2	120	16.7	ATA-3
UltraDMA, mode 0	235	16	ATA-4
UltraDMA, mode 1	160	24	ATA-4
UltraDMA, mode 2	120	33.3	ATA-4
UltraDMA, mode 3	90	45	ATA-5

continues

TABLE 10.2 Continued

Transfer Mode	Cycle Time (Nanoseconds)	Speed (Mbps)	Standard
UltraDMA, mode 4	60	66.6	ATA-5
UltraDMA, mode 5	40	100	ATA-6
UltraDMA, mode 6	30	133	ATA-7

AT Attachment supports two broad classes of transfers: Programmed Input/Output (PIO) and Direct Memory Access (DMA). Under the more recent iterations of the ATA standard, DMA is further divided into Single-Word DMA, Multi-Word DMA, and UltraDMA (once called *synchronous DMA*) modes. With today's computers, UDMA modes are preferred for their higher performance.

The difference between PIO and DMA modes is how they use the resources in your computer. The DMA modes provide an opportunity for improved overall system performance through bus-mastering, but the full potential of this benefit requires matching hardware and software in your computer. The fastest modes match only with the most recent computers.

Programmed Input/Output puts your microprocessor to work. The microprocessor in your system directly controls every byte that moves through the interface. The microprocessor directly writes values from its registers or memory to a special I/O port, which transfers the data to the control circuitry of the interface. PIO transfers can be of one of two types: blind and flow-control.

Blind transfers don't give the AT Attachment drive full control of the transfers. It has no information about the ability of the microprocessor host to accept data. In effect, it is blind to the capabilities of the host. By design, any error the system makes will be on the conservative side to maximize the reliability of the system. Because sometimes only a part of the full bandwidth of your computer is available for making disk transfers, blind transfers throttle back to the worst case. Consequently, AT Attachment operates blind transfers at a slow rate regardless of the host computer's ability to capture the data. It moves bytes at the lower, throttled rate even when 100 percent of the bandwidth is available.

Flow-control transfers use a form of handshaking to ensure that disk transfers take advantage of all the available bandwidth. Specifically, controlled transfers use the I/O Channel Ready (IORDY) line in the AT Attachment interface to signal to the computer host when the drive needs to make a high-speed transfer. Using the IORDY line, the drive can call for maximum drive bandwidth support and increase its transfer rate.

The current ATA specifications allow for five modes of PIO transfers, as listed in Table 10.3. Modes 0, 1, and 2 use blind transfers. Modes 3 and 4 use flow control.

TABLE 10.3 AT Attachment Programmed I/O Modes

Transfer Mode	Cycle Time (Nanoseconds)	Speed (Mbps)
PIO mode 0	600	1.67
PIO mode 1	383	2.61
PIO mode 2	240	4.17
PIO mode 3	180	11.1
PIO mode 4	120	16.7

The AT Attachment standard allows for Direct Memory Access transfers, which in turn allow for bypassing the host computer's microprocessor and moving data directly to memory. But their real speed comes from the reduced cycle times, bursting blocks of data, and bus-mastering. Moreover, when the host operating system does not serialize input/output functions, DMA transfers allow a degree of parallel processing. The host microprocessor can engage in other activities while the DMA transfer progresses. Versions of Windows based on DOS (including Windows 95, 98, and Me) serialize their I/O functions, so they do not gain this benefit. Unix, Windows NT, Windows 2000, and Windows XP can achieve gains from this transfer strategy.

AT Attachment allows both single- and multi-word DMA transfers. *Single-word DMA transfers* move one word at a time. The host sets up the transfer, selects the data to be transferred, and then makes the transfer. The next word repeats the process. The ATA specifications acknowledge three single-word DMA modes, as listed in Table 10.4. But the one-word-at-a-time transfers incur substantial unnecessary overhead, so these modes are classified as obsolete.

TABLE 10.4 AT Attachment Single-Word DMA Transfer Modes and Speeds

Transfer Mode	Cycle Time (Nanoseconds)	Speed (Mbps)	Standard
DMA, single-word, mode 0	960	1.04	ATA
DMA, single-word mode 1,	480	2.08	ATA
DMA, single-word, mode 2	240	4.17	ATA

Multi-word DMA transfers replace single-word modes under more recent standards, delivering improved performance by operating as a burst mode. After the host sets up the transfer, it selects the starting and ending words for the transfer; then the interface moves the entire block of data from start to end with no further intervention. Table 10.5 lists these ATA multi-word DMA modes.

TABLE 10.5   AT Attachment Multi-Word DMA Transfer Modes and Speeds

Transfer Mode	Cycle Time (Nanoseconds)	Speed (Mbps)	Standard
DMA, multi-word, mode 0	480	4.17	ATA
DMA, multi-word, mode 1	150	13.3	ATA-2
DMA, multi-word, mode 2	120	16.7	ATA-3

The *UltraDMA* modes combine two performance-enhancing technologies. The most straightforward boost comes from quickening the clock or reducing cycle time and taking advantage of bus-mastering technology. By shifting control of the bus to the drive system, the UDMA modes can quicken the pace of transfers.

In addition, UltraDMA doubles-up transfers. Normally a DMA transfer is made on one edge of the clock cycle—typically on the leading or rising edge when the cycle begins—so one transfer occurs during each clock tick. An UltraDMA system can transfer data on both the rising and the falling edge of each clock cycle—that's two transfers for every clock tick, an effective doubling of throughput. To make this system work reliably, the ATA designers shifted from asynchronous transfers to synchronous transfers. The transmitting device (the computer when writing data; the disk drive when reading) generates the clock and synchronizes the data pulses to the clock. Because one device controls both the clock and the data, it can control them better.

In order for the disk drive to take control of the timing, it must act as a bus master, so this technology is sometimes termed *bus master DMA*. In addition, error protection is built in to the transfer protocol using a cyclical redundancy check (CRC) algorithm. The CRC applies only to the cable transfer, not the data stored on disk.

Plain UltraDMA takes advantage of the 16.6MHz clocking speed available in ATA PIO mode 4 but enhances it with double-clocking. Other UltraDMA modes use faster clocks to achieve higher peak data rates. These UltraDMA modes are often referred to by their peak transfer rates, so UltraDMA mode 4 is commonly termed ATA/66 or UDMA/66; mode 5, ATA/100 or UDMA/100; and mode 6, ATA/133 or UDMA/133.

Ordinarily you don't have to worry about the transfer mode used by an ATA drive system. Your computer should automatically use the fastest mode available without your intervention—or knowledge.

Addressing and Capacity

The AT Attachment interface can limit the storage you connect to your computer because of limitations in addressing data in various ATA versions. Although a drive may physically be able to store hundreds of gigabytes, that capacity might not be useful because the interface used by the drive does not allow all the bytes to be addressed. In effect, the bytes on the drive beyond the addressing limit imposed by the interface have unlisted numbers, and no amount of begging or cajoling the operator will get you through to them.

Addressing limitations have constrained the usable capacity of AT Attachment drives almost since their inception. As the need for greater addressing reach has appeared, designers have added new addressing modes to the ATA standard. The latest move finally pushes the upper limit beyond any currently feasible drive capacity.

CHS Addressing

When engineers first conceived ATA, they based its addressing system on physical attributes of the hard disk the interface was to control. They assigned blocks of storage based on the heads, tracks, and sectors of the disk drive. This addressing system is sometimes called *CHS addressing* for Cylinder (the techie term for *track*), Head, Sector addressing.

Somewhat arbitrarily, the engineers allowed for addressing disks with 16 separate heads or disk surfaces, each of which may have up to 65,536 tracks spread across it. Each track could contain up to 255 sectors of 512 bytes each—all generous figures for the state of technology at the time. Multiply these numbers, and you'll see the that CHS scheme allowed for a capacity limit of 136,902,082,560 bytes or 127.5GB (in the days when a *large* hard disk measured 40MB).

Most people round that capacity number to 128GB, even though it's a bit less, because of the limit of 255 rather than 256 sectors per track. (For historical reasons, drive-makers start numbering sectors with one rather than zero.) The scheme should have worked until the year 2002, when the drive-makers introduced the first 130GB drive, the first to exceed the CHS imposed limit.

Unfortunately, in practical application, the BIOSs of older computers severely constrained ATA addressing. All software that relies on interrupt 13(hex) code routines in your computer's BIOS must abide by the BIOS's own disk addressing system. The BIOS routines originally developed in 1982 for the IBM personal computer XT allowed for disks with up to 255 heads or disk surfaces (IBM started number heads with one so the limit is 255 rather than 256), each with up to 1024 tracks on them. Each track can hold up to 63 sectors. This somewhat different geometry allowed for a small total capacity—8,422,686,720 bytes or 7.8GB—when using standard 512-byte sectors. Most sources round this figure up to 8GB.

A problem arises when the two limits of these two geometries get combined. The largest value that the system can handle for any of the three drive parameters is the smaller of the limits set by the two standards. Table 10.6 summarizes the interaction between the BIOS and ATA limits.

TABLE 10.6 ATA and Interrupt 13(hex) Addressing Limits

Feature	ATA Limit	BIOS Limit	Combined Limit
Heads	16	255	16
Tracks	65,536	1024	1024
Sectors	255	63	63
Total sectors	267,386,880	16,450,560	1,032,192
Capacity	127.5GB	7.8GB	0.5GB

The result is that ATA disks that are addressed through the interrupt 13 facilities of the BIOS of a computer cannot address more than 63 sectors per track (the BIOS limit), 16 heads (the ATA limit), and 1024 tracks (the BIOS limit again). With 512-byte sectors, the top capacity is 528,482,304 bytes (about 504MB). Bytes beyond this limit simply cannot be addressed through the standard interrupt 13(hex) routines of the standard computer BIOS.

CHS Translation

Because the AT Attachment design as a system-level interface allows the inner workings of the ATA device to be hidden from your computer, manufacturers are free to alter the geometry of the drive as long as they make it look like something recognizable to your computer. The number of physical heads, tracks, and sectors inside the drive are usually totally different from the number of heads, tracks, and sectors your computer uses to address the sectors on the disk. The drive *translates* the incoming addresses to its own, internal physical addresses when it seeks out a sector.

Engineers broke through the 504MB limit by adding *CHS translation* to the BIOSs of computers. The BIOS translates commands from your software and operating system to its own CHS addressing system with the 8GB capacity limit. CHS translation is more a band-aid than solution and, thanks to revisions in the ATA specification, is not needed by modern drives (which are larger than the 8GB limit, anyway).

Logical Block Addressing

The ATA-2 specification introduced an alternate way of organizing disks called *logical block addressing* (LBA). It sidesteps the BIOS and substitutes 28-bit logical block addresses for disk sectors. Each sector on the drive is assigned a unique logical address that would be used by the BIOS to reach its contents. The full 28-bit addressing scheme allows for 268,435,456 sectors—about 137.5GB. The choice of a 28-bit scheme was essentially arbitrary—it simply matched the CHS limit well, allowing slightly more capacity.

Of course, this scheme was foreign to BIOSs and operating systems. BIOSs written after the development of LBA technology accommodate it by translating LBA addresses into

CHS addresses (sound familiar?). Operating systems require drivers to understand the technology (which are included with all modern versions of Windows). Problems with some BIOSs limited the capacity of hard disk that could be addressed (sometimes to as small as 2 or 3GB, but more often to 8GB) because the BIOS translated LBA addresses into CHS addresses with all their limitations.

48-bit Addressing

As the ATA standard bearers, known formally as the *ANSI T13 Technical Committee*, were preparing the fifth version of their specification, they decided to put to rest capacity limits once and forever—at least for the foreseeable future. With the ATA-6 specification, they added a new addressing system that accommodated logical block addresses 48 bits long, equivalent to about a million times more on-disk capacity (a total of 144,115,188,075,855,360 bytes). In more convenient language, that's 144 quadrillion bytes, or 144 petabytes (PB).

The new addressing scheme uses the same registers as the older 28-bit addressing system. It doubles the width of the registers used for LBA addresses by layering them. (Technically speaking, the registers act as a two-byte First In/First Out buffer.) For example, the operating system first writes the most significant bits of the LBA of a sector and then writes again to load the least significant bits of the LBA.

Just adding more bits is not sufficient to make a new addressing system work, of course. The addressing revision also includes new commands to access and use the longer addresses. At the same time, the committee elected to increase the largest possible transfer per command from 256 sectors to 65,536 sectors, allowing new drives to swallow and disgorge up to 32MB with a single command. The ATA system accommodates such large transfers by doubling the width of the sector count register by layering it in the same way as the LBA registers.

An operating system that's aware of the ATA-6 specifications can determine whether a drive uses 48-bit addressing using the ATA Identify Device command. For compatibility, all drives with 48-bit addressing also support 28-bit addressing, although only part of their capacity may be available using it.

Unfortunately, 48-bit addressing doesn't entirely eliminate addressing limits on disk capacity. It just shifts them back to the operating system. Most operating systems are designed for handling only 32-bit addresses, so most (including most versions of Linux and the entire Windows family) cannot handle capacities larger than 2.19 terabytes (trillion bytes, abbreviated *TB*).

Other Features

Although speed and capacity issues highlight most discussions of disk interfaces, the AT Attachment standard covers other issues as well. The ATA Packet Interface allows you to connect other devices such as CD and DVD drives to an interface that was originally designed just to handle hard disks. Power management under the ATA rubric makes your computer more energy efficient—and lets you keep computing on your notebook computer even after a mixture of fog and pilots lost in the lounge leaves you waiting at the airport gate long after any of your hopes of making your connection have departed. Built-in security features protect you from prying eyes and your data from errant erasures. And the automatic drive-identification capabilities of ATA makes setting up a computer a simpler chore, one that makes lengthy lists of drive parameters as happily behind you as a visit from in-laws who have finally finished an overly prolonged visit.

ATA Packet Interface

As it was originally conceived, the AT interface lacked facilities to control everything that a CD or DVD drive needed to do, such as play audio and video or simply change disks. It was designed for hard disks that never change and merely absorb and disgorge data. When it comes to ordinary data, however, CD-ROMs are simpler still—they only discharge data.

To accommodate other kinds of storage media, the T13 committee added the *AT Attachment Packet Interface* (ATAPI) to the ATA specifications. The committee based the command set on those used by the SCSI system but otherwise kept the scheme completely compatible with existing ATA hardware and drivers. They did not entirely duplicate SCSI, however. Although ATAPI uses many of the same block and command definitions described by SCSI, it does not use many of the other features of SCSI protocol, such as messaging, bus sharing with multiple computers, disconnect/reconnect, and linking and queuing of commands.

ATAPI changes nothing on the computer side of the AT connection, and it does not affect the design or operation of ATA hard disk drives. It just gives the makers of other storage devices and programmers guidance as to how to link their products to computers in a standard way.

Normally, an ATA hard disk gets its commands through eight registers called the *Task File*, which passes along all the commands and parameters needed to operate the disk. Unfortunately, these eight registers are not sufficient for the needed CD or DVD control. ATAPI adds one new command, the Packet Command, that initiates a mode in which multiple writes to the Task File will send packets of commands to the CD or DVD drive. Most ATAPI command packets contain 12 bytes, although the standard also defines 16-byte packets for compatibility with future devices.

The first of the 12 bytes in the ATAPI Command Packet (byte 0) is an operation code that defines the command itself. The initial ATAPI specification defined 29 operation codes. The third through sixth byte (bytes 2–5) of each packet hold the logical block address of the data to be used if the command involves the use of data. The logical addresses start with zero as the first block and increase sequentially up to the last block. The eight and ninth bytes (bytes 7 and 8) of the packet define the length of the transfer, parameter list, or allocation involved in the command. Special extended commands add an extra byte for indicating this length. The remaining bytes in the packet were not originally defined but are left reserved for future implementations.

Power Management

In computers where electrical consumption is a critical issue (for example, battery powered notebook machines), the hard disk is one of the major drains of power. Most disk drives meant for portable machines help conserve power by allowing their electrical use to be trimmed when the drive's fastest response is unnecessary. The T13 committee added power-management commands to the specification starting with ATA-3. This design adds four power modes, which allow frugal computers to economize as the occasions arise:

- **Active mode**. This mode means normal operation for a disk drive. All functions of the drive are available, the drive electronics are fully operational, and the disk platters are spinning. The drive can react immediately to any command, including a seek to move its head to read or write data. The only delay is that imposed in normal disk access. The price for this fast access is that this mode consumes the most power, particularly during seeks.

- **Idle mode**. This mode is provided more for safety than power savings. The head may move away from the active data area of the disk, but otherwise the drive is fully operational. A seek command sends the head instantly scurrying to the appointed sector with little additional delay. Because the drive does not transfer data in idle mode, the part of its electronics associated with decoding, deserializing, and transferring data from (or to) the disk can be shut down. The part of the electronics that processes commands stays alive, ready to receive instructions from your computer and carry them out.

- **Standby mode**. This mode saves power by stopping the spin of the platters and shutting down the spindle motor to eliminate that power drain. The electronics of the drive are left in essentially the same state as idle mode. Only as much of the circuitry is kept awake as is needed to receive commands and activate the rest of the drive when requested. Because the drive must spin up to its normal operating speed before it can read or write data, this mode imposes a delay on all data-handling operations. Typically this delay will be on the order of ten seconds, although the ATA standard allows for a delay of up to 30 seconds.

- **Sleep mode**. This mode totally shuts down the hard disk and its electronics. The drive does not listen for commands and cannot act on commands sent to it. The only way of leaving sleep mode is by sending a hardware or software reset command. The reset causes the drive to enter its normal power-up mode as determined by its manufacturer. Sleep mode reduces the power consumption of a drive nearly to zero but incurs the longest delay in accessing data. Not only must the drive spin up its platter, but the rest of the system must also take its normal course through its reset action.

Table 10.7 summarizes and distinguishes the four power-management modes of the ATA specification.

TABLE 10.7   AT Attachment Power Management Modes

Mode	Electronics	Motor (Spin)	Response	Power Savings
Active	On	On	Instant	None
Idle	Partially off	On	Instant	Small
Standby	Partially off	Off	Delay	Substantial
Sleep	Off	Off	Delay	Complete

AT Attachment drives with the power-management option also include a built-in *standby timer* that can shift the drive into its lower-power standby mode after the drive has been inactive for a preset period. This changeover is a function of the drive and occurs automatically without the intervention of the host computer. The host computer can, however, switch off the standby timer so that the drive does not shift to standby automatically. The host computer can then take full command of the power mode of the drive.

To switch the drive from active mode to a lower-power mode, the host computer sends the drive a power-management command. Any drive-access command automatically forces the drive back into active mode. In addition, the AT Attachment standard includes a Check Power Mode command that allows the host computer at any time to determine in which mode the drive is currently operating.

Security

Starting with ATA-3, the T13 committee added device-level password security to limit access to disk storage. Although you set the ATA drive access password through your computer, the drive stores the password on its own media and it uses the same password, even if you unplug the drive from one computer and attach it to another. Consequently, if you activate its password security system and someone later steals your drive, this person cannot access the data stored on the drive.

Depending on the secrecy of your data, you can set security to one of two levels: normal or maximum. The chief ramification of your choice is what happens should you forget your password. Choose normal security, and the drive-maker can recover your data for you. When you set your drive for maximum security, even the drive-maker cannot retrieve your data.

The AT Attachment standard allows for two kinds of passwords:

- **User passwords**. These passwords you set yourself to limit access to your drive. The command structure used by the AT Attachment standard allows for passwords up to 32 bytes long. The standard provides a common means of setting these passwords and gaining access to the drive that operates at the interface level. Normally, you'll deal with a password through your BIOS, operating system, or application software, which links to the drive security system through the ATA interface.

- **Master passwords**. These passwords are set at the factory. They are not normally used in the everyday operation of the drive but rather allow for recovery of data by the drive-maker should you forget your password. If you've set your drive for normal security, the drive-maker can use its master password to access your data or inactivate the old password so you can change your password to something that you *can* remember. When you set security to maximum, the master password only allows the drive-maker to *erase* your drive and restore it to its original condition—blank with no password set. Your files will be gone forever.

Under the ATA security system, your drive operates in one of three modes:

- **Unlocked mode**. This is the normal operating mode of the disk drive. The drive carries out all commands sent to it. It can read and write to any of the data areas on the disk. You can also add or change your password in unlocked mode.

  A new drive will normally arrive in unlocked mode. It will operate as unlocked until you set a user password. Thereafter, the drive will always start operating in the locked mode and remain in locked mode until it receives a valid user or master password. Normally, the drive will accept five tries at sending it a password. It will then reject subsequent password attempts until it has been reset.

- **Locked mode**. This mode prevents you from accessing or changing any data that's stored on the disk. In locked mode, the drive automatically aborts all read and write commands without executing them. The drive carries out normally all commands that do not access or alter the data stored on the disk (for example, to enter a low-power mode).

- **Frozen mode**. This mode prevents the security features of the drive from being altered. The drive carries out all normal read and write operations but will not change its security level or password. If you value your data, frozen mode will be your standard operating mode so that no one can change your drive password should you leave your computer unattended.

Device Identification

Each device includes 512 bytes of storage for identifying information. Device-makers are free to locate this storage anywhere they want. It can be stored on a nonremovable storage medium, such as a hard disk, or in EEPROM or Flash memory.

Regardless of its location, the AT Attachment standard includes a standard command for reading this identifying block. Using this command, your computer can interrogate the device to find out what it is and automatically configure itself for optimum operation, including maximizing its data-transfer rate. Included are the device parameters, the features supported (including transfer modes and thus speeds), the model number, and the serial number of the drive.

Logical Interface

The AT Attachment interface logically links to the rest of your computer through a series of registers. The standard does not constrain the port addresses used by these registers. Their location is set by the BIOS writer and chipset designer of your computer. The registers are generally inside the motherboard chipset, and the BIOS must be written to match. Add-in host adapters include their own registers and matching add-on BIOS.

Applications and operating systems that use the BIOS never need know the location of these ports. Software drivers for operating systems that bypass the BIOS must be written with the proper register addresses.

Most chipset-makers use the same range of addresses for the I/O ports used in communicating with their AT Attachment interfaces. Consequently, a single set of register addresses has become a *de facto* standard in nearly all computers. Table 10.8 lists these register addresses.

TABLE 10.8   AT Attachment Primary Port Host System Registers

Register	Read Function	Write Function
01F0h	Read data	Write data (16 bits)
01F1h	Error register	Set features data
01F2h	Status of sector count	Write sector count
01F3h	Starting sector	Write sector
01F4h	Cylinder low location	Write cylinder low location
01F5h	Cylinder high location	Write cylinder high location
01F6h	Head/device selection	Write device/head selection
01F7h	Device status	Device command
03F6h	Alternate status	Device control
03F7h	Drive address	(Read only)

A single ATA connection is meant to handle the control of two drives. Most modern host adapters include a *secondary port*—another connector to plug in a cable for two more ATA devices. The logical location of the ports used by both the primary and secondary AT Attachment host adapters is not fixed and can be set at any of several ranges of values that the hardware manufacturer chooses. The chosen I/O port addresses only need to be reflected in the BIOS routines for interrupt 13(hex) service and the software drivers used to control the board. Nevertheless, most manufacturers use the same ports and interrupts for their primary and secondary AT Attachment ports.

Signals and Operation

The hardware side of the AT Attachment interface is based on the Industry Standard Architecture (ISA) bus, but it is not the complete bus. For example, hard disk drives are not normally memory-mapped devices, so there's no need to give a hard disk control of the addressing signals (24 of them) of the ISA bus. Instead, the registers of the interface connect to the input/output address space of the ISA bus, and only those signals used in addressing the ATA registers need to be used.

In addition, AT Attachment uses a 16-bit data bus (although it allows for drives that only use eight) as well as a variety of control signals. These include signals to request reading or writing data, to make DMA transfers, to check the results of running diagnostics, and to indicate which of the two drives that can be connected to an AT interface port is to perform a given function. ATA also allows for a "spindle sync" signal so that two drives can spin synchronously, as is required for some implementations of drive arrays.

Connectors

An AT Attachment interface uses any of three connectors for its interface. The most common has 40 pins to accommodate its addressing, data, and control signals. As shown in Figure 10.1, one pin is sometime removed and the connector shell is notched. The connector has a tab corresponding to the notch. Together the tab/notch and missing pin key the connector against improper insertion.

FIGURE 10.1

The 40-pin ATA connector.

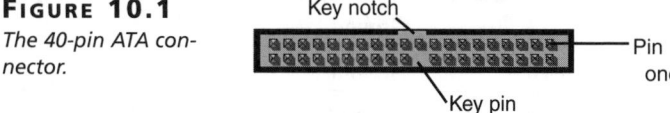

The 44-pin connector used by 2.5-inch drives adds the three essential power connections as well as a coding pin. A 50-pin connector additionally allows four vendor-unique pin assignments, which are typically used for indicating master or slave status for a given drive. (Two pin spaces are skipped.) Figure 10.2 shows how the power and vendor-unique pins are arrayed on a 50-pin connector.

FIGURE 10.2

The 50-pin ATA connector (of which the 44-pin connector is a subset).

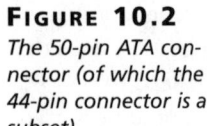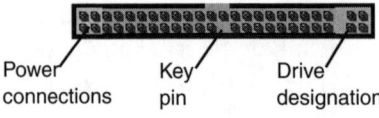

Power connections   Key pin   Drive designation

Regardless of the connector used by a drive, the function assigned each pin remains the same. Table 10.9 lists the signal assignments of the interface.

TABLE 10.9 AT Attachment Signal Assignments

Pin	Function	Pin	Function
A	Vendor Unique	B	Vendor unique
C	Vendor Unique	D	Vendor unique
E	(Key pin)	F	(Key pin)
1	RESET-	2	Ground
3	Data line 7	4	Data line 8
5	Data line 6	6	Data line 9
7	Data line 5	8	Data line 10
9	Data line 4	10	Data line 11
11	Data line 3	12	Data line 12
13	Data line 2	14	Data line 13
15	Data line 1	16	Data line 14
17	Data line 0	18	Data line 15
19	Ground	20	(Key pin)
21	DMARQ	22	Ground
23	DIOW-	24	Ground
25	DIOR-	26	Ground
27	IORDY	28	PSYNC:CSEL
29	DMACK-	30	Ground
31	INTRQ	32	IOCS16-
33	DA1	34	PDIAG-
35	DAO	36	DA2
37	CS1FX-	38	CS3FX-

Pin	Function	Pin	Function
39	DASP-	40	Ground
41*	+5V (Logic)	42*	+5V (Motor)
43*	Ground (Return)	44*	Type- (0=ATA)

Note: Pins 41 through 44 are used in 44-pin connectors only.

ATA drives that are built in to PC Cards or CardBus cards use the 68-pin connection of the associated PCMCIA standards. These are essentially bus connections and are covered in Chapter 9, "Expansion Buses."

Signals

Seven of the connections of the AT Attachment interface (numbers 2, 19, 22, 24, 26, 30, and 40) are grounds, scattered among the signals to provide some degree of isolation of one signal from another. Sixteen pins (3 through 18) are devoted to ATA's 16-bit data bus.

Beside the 16-bit connection system used by all of today's devices, the AT Attachment specification allows for eight-bit connections through the interface. Such narrow-bus systems use only the odd numbered eight pins in the standard sequence.

The remaining 16 pins of the standard 40-pin connector are assigned various signal-control functions, such as those to manage reading or writing data, make DMA transfers, and coordinate the operation of two drives.

The AT Attachment signals primarily concerned with controlling the transfer of data across the interface are given their own dedicated connections. Commands to the drives and the responses from the drives (including error indications) are passed through 17 eight-bit registers.

The two drives permitted under the AT Attachment standard share the connection and receive all signals across the interface indiscriminately. To signal which drive should act on a given command, the AT Attachment uses a special control register. The same register also determines the head, track, and sector that is to be used at any given time.

Seven signals are used to select among the registers. The registers are divided into two groups: Control Block Registers and Command Registers, indicated by two interface signals. Activating the Drive Chip Select 0 signal (pin 37) selects the Control Block registers. Activating the Drive Chip Select 1 signal (pin 38) selects the Command Block Registers. When the Drive I/O Write signal (pin 23) is active, the registers that accept commands from the host are accessible through the interface data lines. When the Drive I/O Read signal (pin 25) is active, the registers indicate drive status through the data lines.

Drive Address Bus 0 through 2 are located on pins 35, 33, and 36 and control which register is currently selected and accessible through the data lines. The AT Attachment standard defines two read and one write control-block registers as well as seven read and seven write command-block registers. Of these, one write command-block register selects the active drive and head (up to 16 heads are allowed). Two registers select the drive track (allowing up to 65,536 tracks on a single drive), another register selects the sector to start reading from or writing to, and another register selects the number of the track to be read or written. The read registers indicate which drive and head are active and which track and head are being scanned. Other registers provide status information and define errors that occur during drive operation.

The number of register bits available sets the logical limits on device size: up to 16 heads, 65,536 tracks, and 256 sectors per track. Because many computers are incapable of handling more than 1024 tracks, the maximum practical capacity of an AT Attachment drive is 2,147,483,648 bytes (2GB).

During active data transfers, separate signals are used as strobes to indicate that the data going to or coming from the drive or values in the control registers are valid and can be used. The falling edge of the Drive I/O Read signal (pin 25) indicates to the host that valid data read from the disk is on the bus. The falling edge of the Drive I/O Write signal (pin 23) indicates that data on the bus to be written on-disk is valid.

The Drive 16-bit I/O signal (pin 32) indicates whether the read or write transfer comprises 8 or 16 bits. The signal is active to indicate 16-bit transfers.

Normally, AT Attachment transfers are accomplished through programmed I/O, the standard mode of operation using the standard AT hard disk BIOS. However, the AT Attachment standard optionally supports Direct Memory Access (DMA) transfers. Two signals control handshaking during DMA data moves. The drive signals that it is ready to read data and transfer it in DMA mode by asserting the DMA Request signal (pin 21). The computer host acknowledges that it is ready to accept that data with the DMA Acknowledge signal (pin 29). If the host cannot accept all the data at once, it removes the DMA Acknowledge signal until it is ready to receive more.

In DMA write operations, the host computer uses DMA Acknowledge to indicate that it has data available, and the active drive uses DMA Request for handshaking to control the flow of data. The Drive I/O Read and Write signals indicate in which direction the data should flow (as a disk read or write).

An AT Attachment disk drive can interrupt the host computer to gain immediate attention by activating the Drive Interrupt signal (pin 31). On programmed I/O transfers, the drive generates an interrupt at the beginning of each block of data (typically a sector) to be transferred. On DMA transfers, the interrupt is used only to indicate that the command has been completed. (The interrupt used is determined by the host's circuitry.)

A drive can signal to the host computer that it is *not* ready to process a read or write request using the I/O Channel Ready signal (pin 27). Normally, this signal is activated; the drive switches it off when it cannot immediately respond to a request to transfer data.

The Drive Reset signal (pin 1) causes the drive to return to its normal power-on state, ignoring transfers in progress and losing the contents of its registers (returning them to their default values). Normally, the drive is activated briefly (for at least 25 microseconds) when the host computer is turned on so that it will initialize itself. Activating this signal thereafter will cancel the command in progress and reinitialize the drive.

The Passed Diagnostics signal (pin 34) is used by the slave drive to indicate to its host that it is running its diagnostics. The *Passed* part of the name does not mean that the diagnostics are completed successfully but that the results are ready to be passed along to the host system. Actual results (and the command to actually execute diagnostics) are given through the AT Attachment registers.

The Spindle Sync/Cable Select signal (pin 28) can be used at the drive manufacturer's option to make the drives spin synchronously (as is required by some drive-array technologies) or to set drive identification as master or slave by the cable rather than using a jumper or switch on the drive. When used as a spindle-synchronizing signal, the master drive generates a periodic pulse (typically once each revolution of the disk, although the actual timing is left to the drive manufacturer), and the slave uses this signal to lock its spin to the master. When this connection is used as a cable-select signal, supplying a ground on pin 28 causes a drive to function as the master (drive 0); leaving the connection open causes the connected drive to act as the slave (drive 1).

A single signal, termed *Drive Active/Drive 1 Present*, located on pin 39, indicates that one of the drives is active (for example, to illuminate the drive activity indicator on the system front panel). The same pin is used by the host signal to determine whether one or two AT Attachment drives are installed when the power is switched on. The drive assigned as the slave is given a 400-millisecond period during system startup to put a signal on this pin to indicate its availability; after waiting 450 milliseconds to give the slave drive time to signal, the master drive puts its signal on the pin to indicate its presence to the host computer. It switches its signal off and converts the function of the signal to drive activity when the drive accepts its first command from the host computer or after waiting 31 seconds, whichever comes first.

Compatibility

As a general rule, all ATA drives support the standard under which they were made as well as all earlier versions of the ATA standard. That is, you can plug the most recent ATA drive into the ATA connector of a vintage computer and have reasonable expectations that it will work. Similarly, you can blow the cobwebs out of drives that conform to earlier ATA standards, plug one into the newest computer, and have it work. (You may have to manually configure your system to accept an old drive by entering parameters into its setup program.)

Plugging a fast drive into a slow system yields a slow drive, however. The interface is not magic and is constrained by the oldest technology in the system. Plug the latest ATA/133 drive into a old computer and you may get a drive the works only in PIO modes. Worse, if your system doesn't recognize logical block addressing, only a fraction of the total capacity of the drive may be accessible.

In general, you can mix drives with different speed ratings on a single cable. Because ATA handles each transaction individually, the drives should operate at the highest speed at which they are individually capable in the given system.

Wiring

Two different cables are used by the AT Attachment interface. The basic cable is a flat ribbon with 40 conductors and three connectors, all the same. The typical cable puts two connectors close together at one end and a single connector at the other. Sometimes a computer-maker "cheaps out" and only puts two connectors on the cable, so you can connect only one drive (the other end plugs into your motherboard or a host adapter).

The chief problem with the cable design is that it works only for speeds up to 33MHz (that is, ATA/33 or UDMA/33). Higher-speed transfer modes require a more sophisticated 80-conductor cable. The signals in the cable are essentially the same, but every other conductor in the cable is held at ground potential. That way, there is always a ground between two active signals on the cable. The ground effectively shields the two active signals from one another. The ground wires are all linked together in the cable connector. ATA/66 and above interfaces can sense this cable. If they do not find it, they will restrict the transfer speed to 33MHz or less, regardless of the capabilities of the drives you install. Figure 10.3 illustrates the difference between the two cable types.

FIGURE 10.3

ATA connections for speeds greater than 33MHz require 80-conductor cables (left) instead of the 40-conductor cables (right) that suffice for 33MHz and slower speeds.

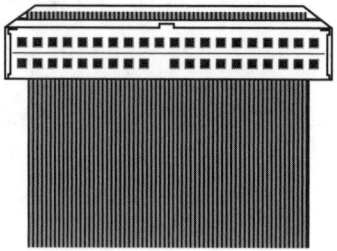

All connectors on an ATA cable are supposed to be keyed (with a missing pin 20) and on the shell of the connectors. In addition, the ATA cable is marked with a red or blue stripe on the edge corresponding to pin 1 on the connector.

Single Drive

All three connectors on an ATA cable are the same, so in theory you should be able to plug any connector into any drive or the host adapter. That's not the best practice, however. Convenience dictates that you plug the connector spaced farthest from the rest at one end of the cable into your host adapter. Use the two more closely spaced connectors for disk drives.

In a one-drive system, plug the connector at the other end of the cable into the drive and leave the middle connector unconnected. This properly terminates the cable. Otherwise, a fraction of the signal travels down the loose stub and reflects off the unterminated end. The reflected signal travels back and mixes with the signal at the middle drive connector. Because of the time it takes the signal to travel back and forth through the stub, the reflected signal is not a mirror image of the signal at the connector. The signal at the connector will have changed during the travel time. As a result, the combination of the new and reflected signals will be something unpredictable. Figure 10.4 shows how to terminate a single drive properly.

FIGURE 10.4

Recommended wiring of a single AT Attachment drive.

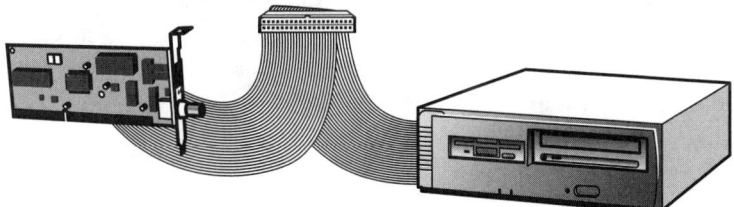

Two Drives

Connecting two drives to an AT Attachment cable eliminates the electrical concerns. One drive necessarily will be at the end of the cable and terminate it properly. It doesn't matter which drive connects to which connector—master or slave, big or small, old or new. The connectors are electrically identical.

Three or Four Drives

Most AT interface host adapters enable you to connect more than two drives by providing two distinct interfaces: primary and secondary. Some systems insist you use the primary connection for the drive that boots your computer. Others are more flexible.

In any case, treat both the primary and secondary as an individual ATA interface with its own cable. Always use the last connectors on the cable first, then the connector in the middle of the cable for the second drive. Most dual-interface systems will allow you to connect a single drive to each interface—two drives, two cables, two interfaces.

Master/Slave Designation

The AT Attachment system distinguishes the two drives attached to a single cable by making one the *master* and the other the *slave*. The chief distinction is, as a default, the master gets assigned a drive letter first (it gets the letter closer to the front of the alphabet), and the master is usually preferred as the boot drive (although many BIOSs will let you select which drive to boot your system).

All AT Attachment drives have the potential for being masters or slaves. The function of each drive is determined by jumper settings on the drive. These are usually called *drive select* jumpers or simply indicated with DS near the contact on the drive's electronic circuit board. Different manufacturers use various designation schemes. A jumper on the pins marked with the "DS," for example, indicates a master. Other manufacturers might use position-sensitive system. A jumper in one position indicates the drive will act as the master, and the jumper in another position indicates it will be a slave. Most drives have a *cable select* setting, although few computer-makers implement this feature (by which the cable does, in fact, indicate whether the drive is master or slave).

Only one master and one slave are permitted in a single AT Attachment connection, so each of the two drives in a single AT Attachment chain must have its master/slave jumpers properly set for the system to work. Moreover, most computers will not boot with only a slave drive. Most drives are shipped "jumpered" for operation as the master, so you only have to adjust the second AT Attachment drive you add to your computer—but be sure to check.

Sanctioning Organization

The ATA standards are published and maintained by the American National Standards Institute, Inc., 11 West 42nd Street, New York, New York, 10036. The more recent versions of the ATA standards have been prepared by the T13 technical committee of Accredited Standards Committee NCITS. The committee maintains a Web site that publishes the working documents and drafts of prospective standards at www.t13.org. The final approved standards are available in final form only from ANSI.

Serial ATA

Over the last decade and a half, engineers have used several tricks to extend the life of the ATA interface, such as altering timing and developing new wiring systems. And they've succeeded beyond anything that could have been expected at the introduction of the interface. Today's ATA is potentially 25 times faster than the original. Hard disk drives have yet to exploit the full potential of its latest improvements. But disk developers know they won't be able to stretch ATA out another 25 times. Nor do they want to. The design has several weaknesses (not all of which are technical).

Looking to the future, on the 15th of February, 2000, Intel, along with several drive-makers including APT, Dell, IBM, Maxtor, and Seagate Technology, announced a radically new conception of ATA that they called Serial ATA. Through an industry association called the Serial ATA Working Group, they published a final specification on August 29, 2001. Although the group expects getting the official imprimatur of a standards organization is still a year off, several companies are already manufacturing to the standard. Seagate demonstrated the first Serial ATA drive in June 2002.

The name indicates the basic concept. Today's ATA is a parallel interface that uses 16 separate data connections. Serial ATA will use a single data channel operating at a much higher speed—at least 20 times the clock rate of current parallel ATA systems.

The initial specification for Serial ATA calls for an initial peak transfer rate of 150MBps, a little more than a 10-percent improvement over the current top speed for conventional parallel ATA, 133MBps. But parallel ATA has no future, according to the Serial ATA Working Group. It's unlikely that the speed of the parallel interface could be doubled. The Serial ATA specification, on the other hand, provides a growth path to double and quadruple that initial rate to peak rates of 300MBps and 600MBps. According to the Serial ATA Working Group, that speed potential should be enough to satisfy speed needs for the next decade.

To serialize data on the Serial ATA channel, the system uses conventional 8b/10b encoding (that is, it encodes bytes in ten-bit data groups). To reduce interference levels, it also uses a combination of spread spectrum clock and data scrambling to minimize repetitive bit-patterns in the data stream. The group-coding overhead (ten bits to the byte) results in a 1.5GHz signaling rate on the Serial ATA channel. The higher-speed versions of Serial ATA will push the signaling rate to 3.0 and then 6.0GHz.

The wiring uses four pairs of wires for two balanced signaling pairs—one to the device and one from the device—for full-duplex communications. The total voltage swing between the wires in each pair is only 250 millivolts.

Serial ATA uses a point-to-point connections scheme. That is, only one device connects to each Serial ATA port. Drives will not daisy-chain as they do with today's parallel ATA systems. To accommodate multiple devices, a host computer needs multiple ports. The typical installation will follow current ATA practice and deliver four ports per computer system—two primary and two secondary ports.

For computer-makers, one of the chief allures of the Serial ATA system is the smaller cable that it used to connect the drive to the computer. Instead of a wide 40- or 80-conductor ribbon cable, Serial ATA will likely use a four-conductor cable with compact connectors, similar to those of USB and FireWire. Such a design will eliminate some of the clutter inside computers. Beside aesthetics, the compact cable will also improve the cooling of the host computer and will likely reduce interference.

Serial ATA retains the ATA designation despite the radical wiring change because it retains full software compatibility with the ATA system. Drives will use the same commands as parallel ATA. Consequently, Serial ATA will work with today's operating systems and software.

On the other hand, Serial ATA will be incompatible with today's parallel ATA drives and controllers at the hardware level. You simply won't be able to plug one directly into the other, although manufacturers may produce adapters to mate one to the other.

The Serial ATA Working Group maintains a Web site at `www.serialata.org`.

SCSI Parallel Interface

Pronounced *scuzzy* by much of the computer industry (and much less often *sexy* by its most fervent advocates), SCSI is a system-level interface that provides what is essentially a complete expansion bus into which to plug peripherals. SCSI isn't simply a connection that links a device or two to your computer. Rather, it functions like a sub-bus. SCSI devices can exchange data between themselves without the intervention of the host computer's microprocessor. In fact, they can act across the SCSI bus even while other transfers are shifting across the host computer's normal expansion bus.

SCSI is even older than ATA. In fact, it's effectively the oldest interface still in use in personal computers. Originally simply a means to add hard disk drives to minicomputers, SCSI has evolved into a complete interconnection system that can link hard disk drives, CD-ROM players, scanners, and even arrays of hard disks to any kind of computer.

The basic SCSI hardware interface is a parallel connection on a multiconductor cable called the *SCSI Parallel Interface* (SPI). In original form, the SCSI interface comprised an eight-bit bus with a ninth parity bit for error detection and a maximum clock speed of 5MHz. Since then, four versions of the SPI system have been developed, the most recent of which (SPI-4) pushes the width of the bus to 16 bits (not counting parity) and the peak data rate to 320MBps.

More a place to plug in hard disks, SPI has become an expansion bus that can link up to 15 devices of various types to your computer through a single-port connection. All the devices function independently, under the control of the host system through the host adapter that provides the SCSI port.

Standards

The original SCSI standard evolved from another interface called *SASI*, the Shugart Associates Standard Interface, developed in 1981 by hard-disk pioneer Shugart Associates working with NCR Corporation. Together they developed SCSI as an eight-bit parallel connection between host computers and disk drives. Later that year, the X3T9 committee of the American National Standards Institute used the SASI specification as the foundation for its work on a parallel interface standard. That standard, now known as *SCSI-1*, was formally approved in 1986.

Even before the ANSI acceptance of SCSI, manufacturers were wary of the shortcomings in the original specification. In 1985 device manufacturers approached the group working on the standard with proposals to increase the mandatory requirements of the SCSI standard. Because the standard was already near completion and the industry was impatient, ANSI adopted SCSI while at the same time forming a new group to develop a set of commands for SCSI with broader application, eventually published (though not as an official standard) as the *Common Command Set*.

Because the Common Command Set was not a mandatory part of SCSI, each device manufacturer made its own interpretation of it. As a result, individual SCSI devices often required their own driver software, and many combinations of SCSI devices simply wouldn't work together at all.

SCSI-2

In 1991, a revision of SCSI was introduced to help fix some of the problems in mating SCSI devices, as well as to increase the speed of SCSI transfers. Referred to as *SCSI-2*, the new standard integrated the newly developed Common Command Set with several optional hardware enhancements.

Through the Common Command Set, SCSI-2 embraces communications as well as other storage devices. It incorporates specific command sets for read-only and erasable optical devices, in addition to CD-ROM. Other commands control devices that can change the medium on which they store data (for example, cartridges), such as optical jukeboxes. SCSI-2 also includes commands for printers (carried over from the original SCSI), scanners, and communications equipment.

Hardware improvements included the broadening of the eight-bit SCSI data bus to Wide SCSI, which doubled the bus width to 16 bits. In addition, the top speed of SCSI transfers was doubled with the addition of Fast SCSI. With an eight-bit bus width, Fast SCSI pushed transfer rates up to 10MBps; Wide and Fast SCSI could peak at 20MBps. Wide SCSI also expanded the number of possible devices connected to a single host adapter channel from 7 to 15.

SCSI-3

Almost immediately after the SCSI-2 standard was approved, the industry began work on its successor, SCSI-3, to refine the standard further. Although not formally approved at the time this was written, SCSI-3 has been out in draft for long enough that most manufacturers have incorporated its requirements into their designs. For the purposes of this discussion, SCSI-3 is considered the current standard.

Rather than a single standard, SCSI-3 has become an umbrella that covers a multitude of individual hardware and protocol standards. Notably, it divorces software from hardware so that the Common Command Set and the various cabling systems go their separate directions. At that, SCSI itself becomes a command protocol, and the various interconnection standards control how you wire your peripherals together.

At the hardware level, SCSI-3 brought with it the first generation of the SCSI Parallel Interface, along with three other interconnection systems. *Serial Storage Architecture* currently delivers two channels of 20MBps transfer rate for full-duplex operation (a device can transmit and receive simultaneously at that data rate). *P1394* gives a 100MBps serial system that plugs together like a set of stereo components. *Fibre Channel Arbitrated Loop* provides a 100MBps system that uses simple plug-in connections for the disk drive and a bridge to optical fiber with even higher speeds. These hardware standards give SCSI-3 enough headroom to take peripheral connections into the next generation—and the next incarnation of SCSI.

After the introduction of the SCSI-3, the parallel interface was independently revised as SPI 2 through 5 (currently). Table 10.10 summarizes some of the various SCSI standards, their official designations, and the popular names of the speed modes included under them.

TABLE 10.10   SCSI Standard Documents

Common Name	Official Standard	Technology
SCSI-2	ANSI X3:131:1994	CCS and hardware
SCSI-3	ANSI X3:270:1996	Architecture
SCSI-3	ANSI X3:301:1997	Primary commands
SPI-2	ANSI X3:302:1998	Ultra2 SCSI
SPI-3	ANSI NCITS:336:2000	Ultra3 SCSI, Ultra160 SCSI-m
SPI-4	Draft T10 Project 1365D	Ultra320 SCSI
SPI-5	Draft T10 Project 1528D	Ultra640 SCSI

Clocking

SCSI Parallel Interface allows for both asynchronous and synchronous transfers. *Asynchronous transfers* allow data to be sent at irregular intervals using start and stop bits to mark the beginning and end of data bytes. *Synchronous transfers* use system timing to define data bytes. Because synchronous transfers require less overhead—fewer bits need to be transferred and less processing of the data is required—they can be faster. The first

implementation of synchronous SCSI is sometimes called *Fast SCSI*, usually with a designation of the bus clock speed.

Asynchronous SCSI

Asynchronous SCSI operates as a handshaking system. First, a device issues a request (signaling REQ) and waits for an acknowledgment (ACK) to be sure its request was received
before doing anything else. In every step and every byte of the transfer, this two-step
process must take place. Actual transfers require four steps: First, one device sends the
REQ and it is answered by ACK. The first device turns off its REQ and waits for the
other device to switch off its ACK before the first device can go on to the next byte.

Each of these handshakes must travel down the SCSI cable, so the signal must go back
and forth through the cable twice for each transfer. Although electrical signals are fast,
they travel at a finite and measurable speed, about one-third the speed of light in a vacuum. In typical SCSI cables, it takes a signal about 5.25 nanoseconds to move one meter.
This travel time is termed the *propagation delay*, and it is the primary constraint on the
speed of asynchronous SCSI transfers in long cables. The longer the cable, the longer the
delay.

Although the original SCSI standard puts a speed limit of 1.25MBps on asynchronous
transfers, that rate applies only to the longest permitted cables, 25 meters. Shorter cables
can achieve higher rates using asynchronous transfers.

The overhead involved in transferring each byte across the parallel SCSI bus using asynchronous signaling is about 160 nanoseconds. Adding in the propagation delay sets the
minimum cycle time and maximum transfer rate of the connection.

Synchronous SCSI

Synchronous SCSI requires an acknowledgment for each request sent, but it allows the
acknowledgment to be delayed. Consequently, a device can send packets one after another
without enduring the propagation delays required in interlocked handshaking.
Synchronous SCSI operates at a speed determined by its cycle time without regard to
propagation delay. In other words, the speed of synchronous SCSI is independent of cable
length.

The first clock speed specified for synchronous transfers was 5MHz. Through the years,
the standard has raised this speed, with each improvement doubling the speed of its predecessor. Each improvement also earned a distinctive name. *Fast SCSI* boosts the clock
speed to 10MHz. *Ultra SCSI* kicks it up another increment to 20MHz. *Ultra2 SCSI* doubles the speed again to 40MHz. *Ultra160 SCSI* doubles it again, to 80MHz. Today's
fastest, *Ultra320 SCSI*, leaves the bus speed alone but double-clocks the data so that transfers are made on both the rising and falling edge of each clock cycle. Therefore, data
moves at twice the clock speed.

The most recent SPI standards also permit *double-clocking*, the transfer of two data bits on every clock pulse—one on the rising edge, one on the falling edge. In fact, double-clocking is necessary to achieve the highest peak rates for all the most recent SPI standards. Double-clocking was introduced with the SPI-3 specification.

Bus Width

The current SCSI parallel interface standards allow the use of either an 8- or 16-bit data bus, with the latter moving data twice as fast as the former. The 16-bit version usually is called *Wide SCSI*. Under early SCSI standards, a wider, 32-bit bus was also allowed, although it was never commercially implemented. The SPI-3 standard declared the 32-bit bus obsolete.

Under the SCSI-3 standard, Wide SCSI is an optional implementation. However, the wide bus is mandatory for Ultra160 and Ultra320 SCSI connections.

Table 10.11 lists the nomenclature and speed limits (more correctly, *peak transfer rates*) of today's common parallel SCSI connection systems.

TABLE 10.11   Comparison of SCSI Parallel Interface Performance Specifications

Interface Name	Bus Width	Bus Speed	Peak Transfer Rate
Plain SCSI (SCSI-2)	8 bits	5MHz	5MBps
Fast SCSI	8 bits	10MHz	10MBps
Wide SCSI	16 bits	5MHz	10MBps
Fast Wide SCSI	16 bits	10MHz	20MBps
Ultra SCSI	8 bits	20MHz	20MBps
Ultra Wide SCSI	16 bits	20MHz	40MBps
Ultra2 SCSI	8 bits	40MHz	40MBps
Ultra2 Wide SCSI	16 bits	40MHz	80MBps
Ultra160/m SCSI	16 bits	40MHz	160MBps
Ultra320	16 bits	80MHz	320MBps

Capacity and Addressing

SCSI devices store data in the form of blocks. Each block is assigned an address, and a host indicates which block to read or write by its address. The size of each block and the number of available addresses constrain the capacity of any given device.

The original SCSI command structure provided 21 bits for identifying block addresses, sufficient for 2,097,152 blocks. With hard disk drives that used blocks of standard 512-byte sectors, this addressing scheme allowed for drives storing up to 1GB.

The SCSI-2 refinement allows for a full three bytes (24 bits) for encoding block addresses by taking advantage of three bits reserved under the earlier implementation. SCSI host adapters designed to that standard can access up to 16,777,216 blocks, which with sector-size blocks limits capacity to 8GB, or 8,589,934,592 bytes. Larger drives could be accommodated by defining blocks as multiple sectors.

Increasing block size is a band-aid solution, one that only covers up an underlying problem. Consequently, the current SCSI Block Commands now include a second form of read, write, and related commands that allocate four bytes (32 bits) for block addresses. Using the new commands, the system can address up to 4,294,967,296 blocks, enough to handle devices storing 2TB (2,199,023,255,552 bytes) of data.

Note that some early SCSI host adapters suffered addressing limits imposed by design choices made by their manufacturers. In particular, many old host adapters made before about 1995 may limit addressing to 1GB or less. In other words, large-capacity SCSI devices may not work properly with older host adapters.

Signaling

SCSI systems can use any of three kinds of signaling: single-ended and two forms of differential signaling. Early generations of SCSI devices used single-ended signals, as do many modern low-cost and/or low-speed devices. Differential signaling allows for higher speed and is mandatory under the fastest SPI standards.

Single-ended SCSI uses an unbalanced (or *single-ended*) electrical signal—a single wire for each signal, with all signals in the bus using a single common ground return. Differential SCSI uses balanced (or *differential*) signals. Each signal on the SCSI bus has its own return line that is isolated from the reference ground. Differential SCSI signals use twisted-pair wiring. Most SCSI implementations have been single-ended because they require half the pins, cheaper wire, and simpler electronics than do differential SCSI implementations.

As with all single-ended electrical systems, single-ended SCSI is more prone to picking up noise and interference than differential SCSI. As a result, the specifications for SCSI systems that use single-ended signals limit cable lengths to no more than 6 meters (just under 20 feet). Differential SCSI allows for bus lengths up to 25 meters (about 82 feet). You must have at least one-third meter (about 12 inches) of cable between SCSI devices, so the shortest possible SCSI cable is that length. External SCSI cables should be shielded.

The voltages on the single-ended SCSI vary a bit with speed. The levels used are summarized in Table 10.12.

TABLE 10.12	Single-Ended SCSI Signaling Levels	
Signal Type	*Logic Zero*	*Logic One*
Fast-5	2.0 to 5.25 VDC	0 to 0.8 VDC
Fast-10	2.0 to 5.25 VDC	0 to 0.8 VDC
Fast-20	1.9 VDC maximum	1.0 VDC maximum

Instead of centering the logic signals on zero volts, differential SCSI signals are designed so that the currents flowing during logic transitions exactly cancel out each other in the two signal conductors. When one of the two differential signal lines transitions from low to high, the other goes from high to low. Even though both high and low are positive values, the current flows cancel. The current flow generates the magnetic field that limits performance as well as generates interference.

The first differential signaling system used by the SCSI system was quite tolerant of high common-mode voltages (for instance, noise). Called *High-Voltage Differential* (HVD) SCSI, the difference between low and high signals was required to be one volt or more. The maximum voltage for a low signal is 1.7 volts; the minimum for a high signal is 2.7 volts. The common mode voltage, which is the same on both the positive and negative signals lines, can range from −7 to +12 volts.

The SPI-3 standard declares HVD signals obsolete. They should no longer be used in new SCSI devices.

The SPI-2 specification introduced another differential signaling scheme that ensured the appearance of only lower voltages on the SCSI lines, making the system compatible with single-ended signaling. Called *Low-Voltage Differential* (LVD) SCSI signaling, this scheme is optional for speeds of 20MHz and under and mandatory for clock speeds of 40MHz and higher, including Ultra2 SCSI, Ultra160 SCSI, and Ultra320 SCSI.

Wiring

Because SCSI is a bus, its wiring is essentially simple. The pins of the connectors on one device are directly linked to the pins of the same position (and function). You can run a straight cable (no twists or crossovers) from the host adapter to one SCSI device, then on to the next. Unfortunately, reality interferes with this idealized connection system. All the variations of the parallel interface need to be taken into account. As a result, the mechanics of the actual cabling vary with bus speed and width, whether your SCSI connections are strictly inside your computer, external to it, or both.

SCSI also saddles you with two other worries: device identification and termination. The proper operation of a SCSI system requires that you get both of these setup chores right.

SCSI Identification

As a bus, all devices are simultaneously connected and receive all transmissions (commands and data). Commands are routed to individual SCSI devices by identifying them by their SCSI address. Standard SCSI systems use eight dedicated lines in the SCSI cable for identifying devices. Each device uses one line, allowing eight unambiguous addresses that translate into SCSI identification (SCSI ID) numbers. In eight-bit SCSI systems, these are usually designated in standard Arabic numerals as SCSI ID numbers 0 through 7. Wide SCSI systems expand the identification possibilities to 0 through 15. In either case, one number (usually the highest) is reserved for the SCSI host adapter. The other addresses, 0 through 6 or 0 through 14, can be assigned to any device connected anywhere in the SCSI chain. Each address is assigned a priority to the device using it, with the host adapter having the highest address (7 or 15) and therefore the top priority. The device with a SCSI ID of 0 always has the lowest priority.

In the latest SCSI systems that operate under the Plug-and-Play aegis, you don't have to worry about these numbers. The *SCAM* system (which stands for *SCSI Configured Automagically*) does exactly what its name implies—it queries each SCSI device and assigns nonconflicting ID numbers to each one it finds. For SCAM to work, of course, your host adapter, operating system, and SCSI devices must comply with the standard. Note, by the way, the *magically* part of the name was applied in the initial standard, although some less inspired engineers are apt to interpret the name to be SCSI Configured *Automatically*.

If you have an older host adapter and a mess of old SCSI devices, you'll be left to configure them without prestidigitation. And that's where the complication of SCSI begins. Except for the arbitrary address of 7 assigned to the host adapter (or 15 in Wide SCSI systems), you assign the addresses that each SCSI device uses. The most basic rule is simple: Each SCSI ID number must be unique, so never assign the same ID number to two or more devices in the same SCSI chain.

In the formal SCSI scheme of things, you can assign any number to any device, as long as you configure your software properly. The SCSI specification does not reserve any particular number for any device. As a practical matter, you cannot be so cavalier about the ID numbers that you use for different devices. One concern is matching your software. A SCSI driver may require that you indicate the SCSI address that you assign to your CD-ROM player. The software for the CD-ROM player may demand that you assign a particular address to the player in order for it to work.

If there is any one guide to follow, it is the model set by Adaptec, the largest maker of SCSI host adapters. To provide some consistency for its host adapters that emulate Western Digital WD1002 controllers so they can boot your computer, Adaptec chose rather pragmatically that you *must* assign your boot hard disk drive (if it is a SCSI drive) ID number 0. Newer SCSI systems allow you to choose the ID number for the boot device.

The SCSI ID controls the arbitration priority of the device to which it is assigned. In the SCSI scheme, device ID 0, oddly enough, receives the *lowest* priority in arbitration. Device 7, usually the host adapter, receives the highest priority. In Wide SCSI systems with a 16-bit bus, the priority system is a bit more complex, but device 7 maintains the greatest priority. Table 10.13 summarizes the relationship between device ID and arbitration priority on the Wide SCSI bus.

TABLE 10.13   Wide SCSI Arbitration Priorities by Device ID

SCSI ID	Priority
0	8
1	7
2	6
3	5
4	4
5	3
6	2
7	1
8	16
9	15
10	14
11	13
12	12
13	11
14	10
15	9

Early host adapters had built-in BIOSs that enabled the boot drive and one additional drive to link to your computer without an additional software driver. In order for your second drive to be recognized when using this kind of controller, the second hard disk must have ID number 1. Many of the latest SCSI host adapters include an advanced BIOS capable of recognizing up to seven hard disk drives, giving you the freedom to assign them any ID, *providing you give the boot device ID 0.* The BIOS recognizes disk drives (and dispenses drive letters) according to the order of the ID you assign. The lower numbers get the first drive letters.

Some host adapters put one more restriction on your freedom in assigning device IDs. If you cannot get a device to be properly recognized in a SCSI system based on an older host adapter, you may need to check the host adapter manual to see if it enforces any restrictions on SCSI ID assignment.

Internal SCSI devices such as hard disks typically have several jumpers or switches on each device that set its SCSI ID. The location of these selectors varies, but they're usually easy to find. Look for a set of jumpers with some form of the legend "ID" silk-screened on the circuit board. Older drives often offer a row of seven jumper pairs numbered 0 through 6, with one jumper spanning a single pair. With these, setting the ID is easy. Move the jumper to the ID number you want. Other drive manufacturers use a binary code to set the ID, so you'll face a set of three header pin pairs that require from zero to three jumpers, depending on the ID you want.

Newer drives typically use a binary code for assigning the ID number. Four pairs of pins allow the choice of any ID from 0 to 15. Figure 10.5 gives an example of this binary coding scheme.

FIGURE 10.5
SCSI ID binary code shown as jumper positions.

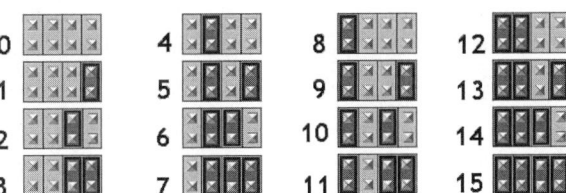

Drives vary in the location and labeling of these identification pins, so you should check with the instructions supplied with a given drive or the drive-maker's Web site for guidance in setting the ID number you want.

External SCSI devices commonly use two forms of selector switches for choosing the SCSI ID number assigned to the device: pushbutton and rotary switches. Figure 10.6 illustrates both of these selectors.

FIGURE 10.6
The pushbutton (left) and rotary selector switches for setting the SCSI ID.

Pushbutton selectors allow you to ratchet up and down the series of identification numbers by pressing two push-tabs on the selector. Some switches cycle around and around without stopping; others limit their movement from 0 to 7. You only need to push the appropriate button until you see the SCSI ID you want in the small adjacent window.

Rotary switches select the SCSI ID numbers like an old-fashioned television channel selector, the miniature equivalent of the rotating knob. Most of these rotary switches require a small screwdriver to adjust, preventing them from getting inadvertently changed by bumping the back of the SCSI device.

Note that nothing in the design of the SCSI Parallel Interface precludes two computers sharing one chain of SCSI devices *except* for SCSI identification numbers. Because each device in a single chain must have a unique ID, two host adapters assigned SCSI ID 7 cannot coexist. If you can alter the ID number assigned to the SCSI host adapter in either computer, however, you can connect both in a single SCSI chain. Either computer will be able to access the various devices. In theory, the two computers could transfer files between one another as well, but most SCSI software makes no provision for such installations.

Cable Connections

Once you've manually configured your SCSI devices with the proper ID numbers (or left matters to the Fates under SCAM), you have to connect them all together. The SCSI system uses a straightforward daisy-chain wiring system—each device connects to the next one down the line.

The exact mechanics of the wiring system depends on whether you have internal or external SCSI devices or a mixture of both.

Internal Devices

An internal SCSI system is like a flexible expansion bus. Instead of connectors to a printed circuit board, the bus takes the form of a ribbon cable, and the expansion connectors are plugs on the cable. One end of the cable plugs into your SCSI host adapter. Each drive attaches to one of the plugs in the cable.

All plugs on the cable have identical signals, so you can use any convenient connector for any SCSI device. The devices and host adapter use SCSI ID numbers to sort out which commands and data go where.

For best operation, always plug a device into the last connector at the end of the cable. When this device is terminated (explained later in this chapter), it prevents signal reflections from the end of the wire that might interfere with the operation of the SCSI system.

Modern SCSI devices may use 50-, 68-, or 80-pin connectors. The last two (and one form of the first) are molded in a vague "D" shape that acts as a key, so you cannot plug in a drive improperly. Older 50-pin connectors sometimes are not keyed and can pose orientation problems.

As with nearly all ribbon cable systems, a red (or sometimes blue) stripe on one edge of the cable used by SCSI devices marks the polarity of the cable. The stripe corresponds to pin 1 of the SCSI connector. Most internal 50-pin SCSI connectors and receptacles are also keyed with a tab and corresponding notch in the middle of one long edge of the connector and receptacle. When you look into the holes of the cable-mounted female SCSI connector with the keying tab on top, pin 1 (and the red stripe) appears on the left, as shown in Figure 10.7.

FIGURE 10.7

The keying of an internal SCSI cable connector.

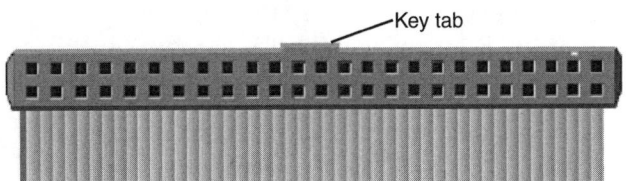

Key tab

The SCSI cable in systems with 50-pin and 68-pin connectors links both control and data signals. However, it does not provide power to the individual internal SCSI devices. Each SCSI device will also require you to plug in its own power connector. The 80-pin SCA system includes power in its connections.

Drives that use the 80-pin system are designed for hot-swapping. You can plug them in at any time, even when your computer is running. The other connection systems require that you switch off your computer before you plug in a drive.

External Devices

External SCSI cabling is somewhat different from that of internal devices. Using the external SCSI cabling system, you run a cable from the host adapter to the first device in the external SCSI chain. For the next device, you plug another cable into the first device and then plug the other end of the cable into a second device. Just continue in the same manner, adding another cable for each additional device.

Most external SCSI devices have two SCSI connectors to facilitate their daisy-chain connection. It doesn't matter which of the two connectors on the SCSI device you use to attach each cable. Functionally, both connectors are the same; each is equally adept at handling incoming and outgoing signals.

The empty jack on the last device gets a terminator (unless the device has other provisions for termination). The complete wiring system is a daisy-chain as shown in Figure 10.8.

Wider bus SCSI systems may require *two* cables to link each device in the chain. The cables run in parallel following the same daisy-chain path as a single cable SCSI system.

FIGURE 10.8
External wiring of the
SCSI Parallel Interface.

As long as the SCSI system is properly terminated, cable length is not supposed to matter, providing that each of the cables is between 18 inches (one-half meter) and six feet (two meters) long. High-frequency electrical signals such as those used by SCSI sometimes act differently from what the rules predict, so the length and placement of the cables may affect SCSI operation. Rearranging the cables in a recalcitrant system can sometimes bring the entire SCSI chain to life.

After you finish connecting your SCSI cables, be sure to snap in place the retaining clips or wires on each SCSI connector to be sure that each connector is held securely in place. This mechanical locking is particularly important with SCSI connections because the wiring works like old-fashioned Christmas lights—if one goes out, they all go out. Not only will whatever SCSI device that has a loose connector be out of touch, all other devices after the loose connector in the chain also will lose communication. Moreover, because the chain will no longer be terminated properly, even the devices earlier in the chain may not work reliably. Locking the wire on each SCSI connector will help ensure that none of the connectors accidentally gets loosened.

Mixed Devices

When your SCSI system has a mixture of internal and external devices, the wiring is exactly as you would expect—a mixture of both of the preceding schemes. Most SCSI host adapters have connectors that allow you to link both internal and external devices at the same time. The individual rules for internal and external wiring apply to the respective parts of the system. The only change is in terminating the system, as discussed in the next section.

Terminations

Eventually all SCSI daisy-chains must come to an end. You will have one last device to which you have no more peripherals to connect. To prevent spurious signals bouncing back and forth across the SCSI cable chain, the SCSI standard requires that you properly terminate the entire SCSI system. The SCAM system can automatically activate the proper terminations in a SCSI system. For manually settings, the SCSI-2 standard allows for two methods of terminating SCSI buses.

Alternative 1 is the old-fashioned (original SCSI) method of passive terminations using only resistors. Alternative 2 uses active terminations, which means the terminator uses a voltage regulator to ensure the voltage on the SCSI line remains constant.

In classic SCSI implementations, the three most popular physical means of providing a SCSI termination are internally with resistor packs, externally with dummy termination plugs, and using switches. SCSI-2 systems with active terminations usually use switches.

Resistor packs are components attached directly to circuit boards. Unlike the other interfaces, SCSI devices typically use three resistor packs (instead of one) for their terminations. Most computer-based SCSI host adapters and hard disks come with termination resistors already installed on them.

You can easily identify terminating resistors as three identical components about an inch long, one-quarter to three-eighths of an inch high, and hardly an eighth inch thick. Most commonly, these resistor packs are red, brownish yellow, or black and shiny, and they are located adjacent to the SCSI connector on the SCSI device or host adapter. When necessary, you remove these terminations simply by pulling them out of their sockets on the circuit board. Figure 10.9 shows two of the most common styles of terminating resistor packs—those in DIP and SIP cases.

FIGURE 10.9
Passive terminators (SIP shown on left, DIP on right).

External SCSI terminators are plugs that look like short extensions to the SCSI jacks on the back of SCSI devices. One end of the terminator plugs into one of the jacks on your SCSI device, and the other end of the dummy plug yields another jack that can be attached to another SCSI cable. Some external terminators, however, lack the second jack on the back. Generally, the absence of a second connector is no problem because the dummy plug should be attached only to the last device in the SCSI chain.

Switches, the third variety of termination, may be found on both external and internal drives. Sometimes a single switch handles the entire termination, but occasionally a SCSI drive will have three banks of DIP switches that all must be flipped to the same position to select whether the termination is active. These switches are sometimes found on the SCSI device or on the case of an external unit.

A few external SCSI devices rely on the terminators on the drive inside their cases for their terminations. For these, you must take apart the device to adjust the terminators.

According to the SCSI specification, the first and last device in a SCSI chain must be terminated. The first device is almost always the SCSI host adapter in your computer. If you install a single internal hard disk to the host adapter, it is the other end of the chain and requires termination. Similarly, a single external hard disk also requires termination.

With multiple devices connected to a single host adapter, the termination issue becomes complex. Generally, the host adapter will be one end of the SCSI chain, except when you have both internal and external devices connected to it. Then, and only then, should you remove the terminations from your host adapter. In that case, the device nearest the end of the internal SCSI cable should be terminated, as should the external device at the end of the daisy-chain of cables (the only external device that likely has a connector without a cable plugged into it). Remove or switch off the terminators on all other devices.

Maximum Cable Length

SCSI host adapter maker Adaptec provides these rules of thumb as recommendations for the maximum cable length under various SCSI standards, speeds, and number of connected devices. Table 10.14 lists these recommendations.

TABLE 10.14   Maximum Recommended SCSI Cable Lengths

SCSI Standard	Bus Clock	Devices	Maximum Cable Length	
			Meters	Feet
SCSI	5MHz	<7	6	16
Fast SCSI	10MHz	<7	3	9
Fast/Wide SCSI	10MHz	<15	3	9
Ultra SCSI	20MHz	>4	1.5	4.5
Ultra SCSI	20MHz	<4	3	9
Ultra2 SCSI	40MHz	>2	12	36

The general rule underlying these recommendations is to divide 30 by the bus clock to derive the maximum recommended cable length in meters. The rule does not apply to Ultra2 SCSI because of the special low-voltage differential signals used under that standard.

Cables

In the current SCSI scheme of things, only two different cable types are used. These are designated the A cable and the P cable.

The *A cable* has 50 conductors and serves for all eight-bit SPI systems, both single-ended and differential. Similarly, the 68-conductor *P cable* serves wide signaling systems.

The purpose assigned each conductor in the cable varies with the type of signaling used and the connector system. The allowed variety is wide. In fact, the cable is a minor concern compared to connector considerations.

Connectors

More than any other standard computer wiring system, SCSI suffers from a plague of connectors. Not only do internal and external devices use different connector styles, but both also come in a wide variety. Beside separate internal and external connector styles, the system also suffers from generational differences.

The SPI-3 specifications acknowledge eight connector systems—four nonshielded alternatives for internal devices and four shielded systems for external devices. In the past, computer-makers have used other designs to suit their particular requirements. Table 10.15 summarizes the SPI connector options.

TABLE 10.15   SCSI Versions and Cabling Requirements

Implement-ation	Bus Width	Cable Config-uration	Pin Count	Maximum Transfer Rate	Devices Supported	Notes
SCSI-1	8	A	50	5	8	Asynchronous
SCSI-2	8	A	50	10	8	Fast
SCSI-2	16	A+B	50+68	20	8	Fast + Wide
SCSI-2	32	A+B	50+68	40	8	Fast + Wide
SCSI-3	8	A	50	10	8	Fast
SCSI-3	16	P	68	20	16	Fast + Wide
SCSI-3	32	P+Q	68+68	40	32	Fast + Wide

The oldest SCSI devices use 50-pin connectors. More recent devices use 68-pin connectors that support wide as well as narrow SCSI implementations. Many hard disk drives use 80-pin connectors (also called *SCA* for *Single Connector Attachment*) that integrate power as well as the SCSI signal onto a single connector, allowing for the easier hot-swapping of devices—in particular, the hard disks used in massive disk arrays (see Chapter 17, "Magnetic Storage").

For the most part, a SCSI connector is like a shoe. If it fits, use it. All too often, however, your SCSI device comes equipped with a connector that looks weirdly different from the one on the cable you're trying to snap onto it. You can prevent problems by checking the connector type used by the SCSI cables in your computer and matching any device you buy to your cabling. SCSI devices—hard disk drives in particular—often have several connector options. When buying a new drive, choose the one that fits. Adapters are also available for matching unlike connectors. Within the limitations noted in the next section, an adapter is often sufficient to get any SCSI device to link up with any host adapter.

50-pin Internal Connectors

The initial incarnation of the SCSI interface was the basic 50-contact pin connector used on the first SCSI drives. Officially, this system is termed the *nonshielded connector alternative 2*.

Basically a glorified header, this connector featured two parallel rows of pins in a rectangular array, the centers of the pins separated at increments of 0.1 inch, both horizontally and vertically. Figure 10.7 shows the male connector of this type as you would find it on the rear of a SCSI device.

At one time, nearly all SCSI devices that used the eight-bit implementation of the standard used this connector. However, both SPI-2 and SPI-3 offer another 50-pin non-shielded design that's more compact and more consistent with current circuit design practices.

Termed the *nonshielded connector alternative 1*, this design also uses two parallel rows of pins. As with the older connector, the rows are spaced on 0.1-inch centers, but the individual pins in each row are spaced at only half that distance, 0.05 inch. The female receptacle is molded with a vague "D" shape. The male connector has a matching extended D-shaped perimeter that protects the pins. Drives use the female connector as a jack. Figure 10.10 shows this connector.

FIGURE 10.10

The 50-pin non-shielded connector alternative 1.

Although both nonshielded connector alternatives 1 and 2 have 50 pins, the functions assigned each pin differ between the two alternatives. In fact, there are four variations: single-ended alternative 1, single-ended alternative 2, differential alternative 1, and differential alternative 2. You cannot tell the four options apart by merely looking at the connector. You must check the specifications of the drive to determine the signal type it uses.

50-pin External Connectors

The most common form of external SCSI connectors has 50 pins arranged in two rows of 25 and looks like an enlarged Centronics printer connector. This connector is termed the *shielded connector alternative 2* under SPI-2 and SPI-3. It is still the most common 50-pin connector used by external SCSI devices and is shown in Figure 10.11.

The shielded connector alternative 1 also offers 50-pins to external devices. It uses the same layout and signal system as the alternative 1 nonshielded connector, except the mating portions of the connector are metal shields. Figure 10.12 shows this connector.

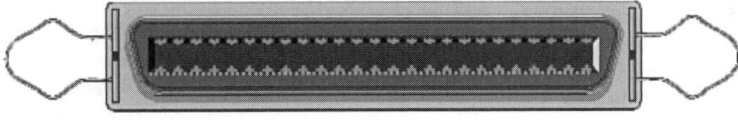

FIGURE 10.12

The 50-place external shielded connector alternative 1.

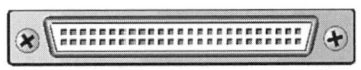

As with the nonshielded 50-pin connectors, shielded connector alternatives 1 and 2 differ in the functions assigned each pin. The pin-outs of the connector alternatives are the same as for the nonshielded versions. Because of the physical similarities and identical pin-outs, you can plug a raw drive into an external shielded alternative 1 connector (providing you don't mix the single-ended and differential signaling systems). The nonshielded and shielded versions of alternative 2 also share the same signal assignments with their pins, but the connectors are physically incompatible.

Some older external SCSI devices and host adapters used classic 50-pin D-shell connectors with the same signal assignments as the A connector. They never attracted a following because they were simply ungainly, about four inches long. These resemble the alternative 1 connectors but the pins are round rather than square, more widely spaced, and staggered. Figure 10.13 shows this large connector.

FIGURE 10.13

The nonstandardized 50-pin D-shell connector.

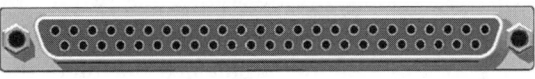

More popular was a design that trimmed the length of the D-shell connector in half by similarly trimming the pin count. These shorter, 25-pin D-shell connectors saved space and were popularized by Apple Computer for its Macintosh equipment. The connectors are identical to those used by most computer-makers for their parallel port connections. Despite the similarity, the signals on the SCSI and parallel ports are entirely different and should *never* be connected together.

To reduce the number of pins required, this style of connector eliminates many of the ground return signals used in single-ended SCSI. These connectors do not have enough connections for differential signals. Figure 10.14 shows this connector.

FIGURE 10.14
The female 25-pin D-shell connector used by some SCSI products.

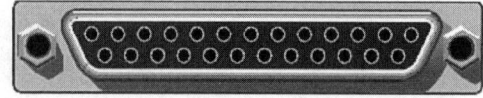

68-pin Connectors

Wide SCSI requires more connections than are possible with a 50-pin connector. To accommodate all the required signals, the SPI standards specify a set of 68-pin connectors. This connector system offers both nonshielded and shielded alternatives for internal and external devices.

Both the nonshielded and shielded versions use essentially the same design and the same signal assignments. The chief difference is the roughly D-shaped metal shield surrounding the contacts of both male and female connectors, with the shield also protecting the bare pins of the male connector, much as in a classic D-shell connector.

Both connectors are termed *alternative 3*. That is, the internal set make up *nonshielded connector alternative 3*, and the external set *nonshielded connector alternative 3*. Many sources refer to either the shielded or nonshielded connector simply as a *SCSI-3 connector*. Do not be misled by this label, which is best seen as an abbreviation for *SCSI alternative 3 connector*. All SCSI-3 systems do *not* use this connector system. In fact, the SCSI-3 standard allows any of the eight connector alternatives—as well as the connectors for the various other physical interconnection systems besides SPI.

The pins of the alternative 3 connectors are arranged in two rows of 34 male contacts. The pins within each row are located on 0.05-inch centers, and the two rows are spaced on 0.1-inch centers. Figure 10.15 shows the shielded version of this connector.

FIGURE 10.15
The 68-place shielded connector alternative 3.

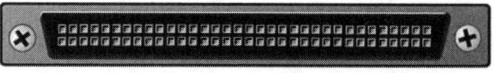

The SPI specifications allow for a second style of shielded 68-pin connector that looks like a miniaturized version of the classic 50-place external SCSI ribbon connector. Termed the *shielded connector alternative 4*, it uses the same pin-out as alternative 3. Instead of pins, it has two rows of ribbon contacts spaced at 0.0315-inch intervals. Figure 10.16 shows this connector.

80-pin SCA

Hot-swapping drives requires that both control signals and drive power be connected quickly and easily. To accommodate the needed power signals, drive-makers developed the 80-pin SCSI connector system. Under the SPI rubric, this is the *nonshielded connector alternative 4*. Figure 10.17 shows this connector.

FIGURE 10.16
Shielded connector
alternative 4.

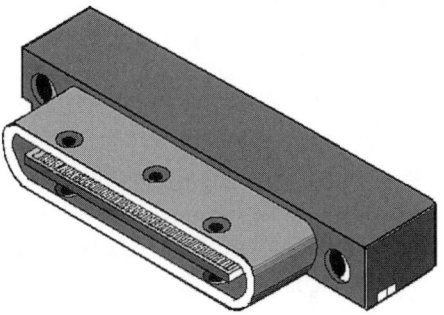

FIGURE 10.17
The 80-pin SCA con-
nector.

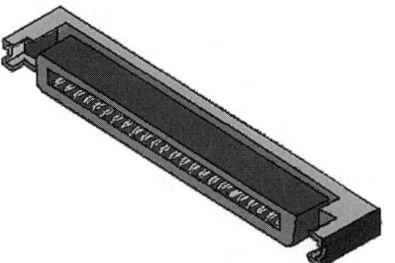

The SCA connector is designed chiefly for internal use—for sliding drives into racks. There is no external equivalent to the SCA connector.

All the pins on the connector on the SCA device are the same length. On the host end, however, several of the pins are extended so that they make contact first when the drive gets plugged in. These longer pins (numbers 1, 36–43, 45, 46, and 78–80) ground the drive, supply power to it, and set its SCSI ID number. The added length ensures that the drive powers up properly and is properly identified before it presents signals to the bus.

Mixing SCSI Standards

SCSI comes in so many flavors that you're likely to have devices that follow two or more standards that you'll want to hook together in a single chain. With modern host adapters that allow you to configure the transfer characteristics assigned to each SCSI ID, you can freely mix standards with a reasonable chance that you can get everything to work together. Better still, you can tune all devices to operate at their maximum transfer rate, with only a few exceptions.

In most cases, however, you can't just string together a mixed collection of SCSI peripherals with complete impunity. You still have to consider issues of bus width, signal type (single-ended or differential), and clock speed to make optimal connections. Some things just won't fit—and others you may not want to fit.

Bus Width

In theory, you can mix wide (16-bit) and narrow (8-bit) SCSI devices in a single chain. However, you must follow some rules.

With an *internal* chain of mixed devices, the wide ribbon cable carries the full compliment of signals to all the devices in the chain. The last device in the chain (the one that provides the termination) should be wide. You may need an adapter for each *narrow* SCSI device you want to plug into the wide chain.

To mix wide and narrow SCSI devices together in an *external* SCSI daisy-chain, you need to follow one rule: Wide goes first. The most important rule is that you must chain *all* of the wide devices together, plugged into the host adapter, then chain the narrow devices after the wide chain. A narrow device won't pass through the signals of a wide device, so any wide device after a narrow one in the chain will lose its wide-bus option.

Signaling System

The original SCSI specifications allowed for two types of SCSI buses: single-ended and differential. These quite different signaling systems are inherently incompatible. Although adapters help mate them together, dangers remain. For example, connecting a single-ended device such as a CD-ROM drive to a differential host adapter or a differential drive to a single-ended host adapter may physically damage both the host adapter and the drive. Because the SCSI connector system does not distinguish between signal types, you must be sure of the signal types used by all the devices in your SCSI system before making the first connection.

The single-ended and high-voltage differential signaling systems are incompatible and cannot be used on the same bus. In addition, high-voltage and low-voltage differential signaling types are also incompatible. Connecting a single HVD device to an LVD system could damage all the LVD devices in the system. In theory, single-ended and LVD devices can be chained together, but you need to be sure the full array of differential signals get to the LVD devices—which means not only differential signals but also the wide bus signals for Ultra160 and Ultra320 SCSI, which demand a wide bus for proper operation.

Clock Speed

Although the different top speeds of SCSI devices might appear to be a problem and limit all the devices, no matter how fast, to the speed constraints of the slowest, the issue never arises. The SCSI host adapter only communicates with a single device at a time, and those communications monopolize the SCSI bus while they are taking place. In today's SCSI systems, transfers do not go directly between devices but instead must travel through the host adapter. For example, to back up a hard disk, the disk first sends a block of data to the host adapter, which temporarily stores the data in system memory. When the disk finishes sending its block, the host adapter moves the data from memory to the tape drive. Consequently, the two SCSI devices—hard disk and tape drive—communicate with the host adapter independently of one another and may operate at different speeds.

A modern host adapter can adjust its speed to suit whatever devices with which it communicates. In general, it will set itself to transfer data to each device at the top speed at which that device can operate.

The one big exception to the "any speed" rule is Ultra2 SCSI. Put simply, you cannot attach an ordinary SCSI device to an Ultra2 SCSI port and expect Ultra2 SCSI peripherals to operate at top speed. The issue is not really speed, however. All Ultra2 SCSI devices use LVD signaling. Most ordinary SCSI devices use single-ended (SE) signaling. When you plug an SE device into the Ultra2 bus, the bus reverts to SE operation; otherwise, damage would result. The SCSI host adapter would send the negative-going differential voltages into a direct short-circuit because the associated signal pins are grounded in the single-ended device. Although reverting to single-ended operation minimizes the chance for damage, it also limits the speed potential to ordinary Ultra SCSI because the highest speeds of Ultra2 SCSI require the added integrity of differential signaling.

Operation and Arbitration

All devices connected to a single SCSI bus function independently, under the control of the host system through the SCSI adapter. Rather than just using signals on dedicated conductors on the bus that can be understood by devices as dumb as a light bulb, SCSI presupposes a high degree of intelligence in the devices it connects and provides its own command set—essentially, its own computer language—for controlling these devices.

Boot Up

Most software drivers search for their target devices when they are booted into your system. Consequently, all your external SCSI devices should be running when you switch on your computer. Turn on your SCSI devices before you switch on your computer, or use a power director (outlet box) that ensures that your entire computer system—computer and SCSI peripherals—switch on simultaneously.

Arbitration

Not only is SCSI more like an expansion bus of a computer than a traditional hard disk interface, but it also resembles today's more advanced Micro Channel and NuBus designs. Like the latest computer buses, SCSI provides an arbitration scheme. *Arbitration* enables the devices connected to the bus to determine which of them can send data across the bus at a given time. Instead of being controlled by the host computer and suffering delays while its microprocessor does other things, the arbitration of the SCSI bus is distributed among all the devices on the bus.

Arbitration on the SCSI bus is handled by hardware. Each of the up to seven SCSI devices is assigned a unique identifying number, usually by setting jumpers or DIP switches on the drive in a manner similar to the Drive Select jumpers on an ST506 device.

When a device, called the *initiator*, wants to access the SCSI bus, it waits until the bus is free and then identifies itself by sending a signal down one of the SCSI data lines. At the same time, it transmits a signal down another SCSI data line corresponding to the other SCSI device, called the *target*, that it wants to interact with. The eight data lines in the SCSI connection allow for the unique identification of seven SCSI devices and one host.

Note that SCSI devices can initiate arbitration on their own, independent of the host. Two SCSI devices also can transfer information between one another without host intervention. A SCSI hard disk, for example, may back itself up to a SCSI tape drive without requiring the attention of (and thus robbing performance from) its host computer. Better than background operation, this form of backup represents true parallel processing in the computer system.

In addition, SCSI provides for reselecting. That is, a device that temporarily does not need bus access can release the bus, carry out another operation, and then resume control. You can command a disk drive to format, and it can carry out that operation without tying up the bus, for example. The net result is, again, true parallel processing.

Because SCSI is a high-level interface, it also isolates the computer from the inner workings of the peripherals connected to it. The SCSI standard allows hard disks to monitor their own bad tracks independently from the computer host. The disk drive reassigns bad tracks and reports back to its computer host as if it were a perfect disk. In addition, hard disk drives can be designed to automatically detect sectors that are going bad and reassign the data they contain elsewhere, all without the host computer or the user ever being aware of any problems.

Sanctioning Organization

The American National Standards Institute (ANSI) maintains the official SCSI standards. SCSI standards in their final, published form are available only from ANSI.

The SCSI T10 Committee actively develops the various SCSI standards. It provides recommendations to ANSI, which, on its approval, sanctions the specifications as industry standards. The committee acts as a forum for introducing and discussing proposals for the standards. The committee maintains a Web address at `www.symbios.com/t10`.

The SCSI Trade Association promotes the use of SCSI and devices that adhere to that standard. The association maintains a Web site at www.scsita.org.

Fibre Channel

At one time, some engineers regarded Fibre Channel as the successor to the SCSI Parallel Interface for high-performance disk drives. Although it has been used successfully in many drive products, it has yet to earn the following of the other interfaces. The steady advance in the speeds of other interfaces has severely eroded its edge in performance. Both AT Attachment and the latest versions of parallel SCSI outrace Fibre Channel's 100MBps capabilities. Among personal computers, it remains a viable, but not popular, interface.

The current implementation of Fibre Channel used for mass storage systems is actually a specialized derivative subset of the technology called *Fibre Channel Arbitrated Loop* (FC-AL). Although even this slice of the standard allows a variety of cabling options, including twinaxial, coaxial, and optical connections, its chief use in mass storage currently is as a backplane interface. That is, FC-AL drives link directly to printed circuit boards in their computer hosts without any cabling between.

At that level, you don't have to understand FC-AL to use it. If you are physically capable of putting a drive in a bay, you've mastered all you need to know. In modern computers, the drives and interface are self-configuring and should require no intellectual intervention on your part.

Development of FC-AL began in 1992 with the creation of the Fibre Channel Systems Initiative, a group of three leading workstation manufacturers (Hewlett-Packard, IBM, and Sun Microsystems) with the specific goal of overcoming the inherent problems with the SCSI Parallel Interface.

As with all modern serial systems, Fibre Channel is packet based. The same circuit and protocol that carry the data also handle all control information. Commands to retrieve a particular block from a disk drive, for example, are carried through the system as data in the form of standard SCSI-3 commands. The drive collects the packets sent for it, interprets them, and carries out the commands. It sends data back, when requested to, in the same data packet form.

Although with hard disk drives you'll probably only have to deal with the backplane connector, the Fibre Channel Arbitrated Loop specifications allow for a great variety of wiring systems. All FC-AL systems take the form of a loop, even the backplane connection. Each device in the loop has separate input and output connections. The output of one device connects to the next device in the loop, until the last device, which connects back to the first and completes the loop. Disconnecting a device from the loop may interrupt communications. Consequently, systems such as drive arrays that permit hot-swapping of devices have built-in *port bypass circuits* that route the loop signaling around the removed device.

The principal body governing the promotion and development of Fibre Channel standards is the Fibre Channel Association. You can get in-depth information about Fibre Channel, products using it, and meeting schedules, from the association at the following address:

Fibre Channel Association

12407 MoPac Expressway North 100-357

P.O. Box 9700

Austin, TX 78766-9700

Phone: 800-272-4618 or 512-328-8422

Fax: 512-328-8423

E-mail: fca@fibrechannel.com

The Fibre Channel Loop Community, a working group that's part of the association, is focused on the FC-AL standard. The address of the Fibre Channel Loop Community is as follows:

Fibre Channel Loop Community

P.O. Box 2161

Saratoga, CA 95070

Phone: 408-867-6630

Web site: www.symbios.com/fclc/fclcmain.htm

Floppy Disk Interface

Some things are immutable, changing not at all as the years pass—the constellations in the sky, the crags and rocks of tall mountains, your credit card balance. The floppy disk interface fits in there pretty well, too. It's basically the same connection used on the first personal computer more than two decades ago. It sits there, waiting for you to slide in a boot disk so it can show you all of its stuff.

Part of the reason for this immutability is that the function of the floppy disk hasn't changed over the years. The floppy disk remains a boot device, a data-exchange system, and a backup system—although an increasingly feeble one. At one time, however, it was your only choice for each of these functions. The world has, of course, changed in the intervening years, and the floppy disk is at best the fallback choice for each of these functions. Your needs and the rest of your computer hardware have long passed by floppy technology. In the next few years, the floppy disk and its interface may be left behind.

But the floppy disk interface is not as unchangeable as you might think. During its short history, its speed has notched up twice, its connectors have changed, and the range of devices linking to it has broadened. And its role has changed. CDs have replaced the floppy disk for just about every purpose except emergencies. You could live without a floppy disk drive. Many sub-notebook computers get along perfectly well without them. Every once in a while, though, the need for a floppy arises, and the interface proves useful.

Controller

The floppy disk controller brings the interface to life. Its basic purpose is to convert the requests from the BIOS or operating system, couched in terms of track and sector numbers, into the pulses that move the head to the proper location on the disk. In this translation function, the controller must make sense from the stream of unformatted pulses delivered from the drive. It first must find the beginning of each track from the Index pulse and then mark out each sector from the information embedded in the data stream. When it identifies a requested sector, it must then read the information it contains and convert that information from serial to parallel form so that it can be sent through the computer bus. In writing, the controller must first identify the proper sector to write to—which is a read operation—and then switch on the write current to put data into that sector before the next sector on the disk begins.

Most of the hard work of the controller is handled by a single integrated circuit, the 765 controller chip, or rather the equivalent of its circuitry inside your computer's chipset. The 765 circuitry works much like a microprocessor, carrying out certain operations in response to commands it receives through registers connected to your computer's I/O ports. This programmability makes floppy disk controllers extremely versatile, able to adapt to changes in media and storage format as the computer industry has evolved. None of the essential floppy disk drive parameters are cast in stone or the silicon on the controller. The number of heads, tracks, and sectors on a disk are set by loading numbers into the registers of the 765 circuitry. The values that the controller will use are normally loaded into the controller when you boot up your computer.

Special software can reprogram your controller to make it read, write, and format floppy disks that differ from the computer standard. The most common alternate format is the Distribution Media Format used by Microsoft to stuff extra information on floppy disks used for distributing software in the years before programs came on CD.

Operation

In its heart and in operation, the floppy disk interface is a glorified serial port to which Dr. Frankenstein's son, the mad engineer, grafted a cable and drive. The control electronics help the drive keep spinning at the right speed and know where to move its head.

It's so simple that if two drives get connected to a floppy disk controller, they get all the same signals all the time, except for one. Two Drive Select signals are used to individually select either the first or second drive, usually drives A or B. If the signal assigned to a particular drive is not present, all the other input and output circuits of the drive are deactivated, except for those that control the drive motor. In this way, two drives can share the bulk of the wires in the controller cable without interference. However, this control scheme also means that only one drive in a pair can be active at a time.

Two signals in the floppy disk interface control the head position of each of the attached drives. One, Step Pulse, merely tells the stepper motor on the drive with its Drive Select active to move one step (that's exactly one track) toward or away from the center of the disk. The Direction signal controls which way the pulses move the head. If this signal is active, the head moves toward the center.

To determine which of the two sides of a double-sided disk to read, one signal, called Write Select, is used. When this signal is active, it tells the disk drive to use the upper head. When no signal is present, the disk drive automatically uses the default (lower) head.

Writing to disk requires two signals on the interface. Write Data contains the information that's actually to be written magnetically onto the disk. It consists of nothing but a series of pulses corresponding exactly to the flux transitions that are to be made on the disk. The read/write head merely echoes these signals magnetically. As a fail-safe that precludes the possibility of accidentally writing over valuable data, a second signal called Write Enable is used. No write current is sent to the read/write head unless this signal is active.

Four signals are passed back from the floppy disk drive to the controller through the interface. Two of these help the controller determine where the head is located. Track 0 indicates to the controller when the head is above the outermost track on the disk so that the controller knows from where to start counting head-moving pulses. Index helps the drive determine the location of each bit on a disk track. One pulse is generated on the Index line for each revolution of the disk. The controller can time the distance between ensuing data pulses based on the reference provided by the Index signal.

In addition, the Write Protect signal is derived from the sensor that detects the existence or absence of a write-protect tab on a floppy disk. If a tab is present, this signal is active. The Read Data signal comprises a series of electrical pulses that exactly matches the train of flux transition on the floppy disk.

Cabling

The original computer floppy system is the standard for nearly all floppy disk systems. It was designed so that you can install floppy disk drives with a minimum of thought—which gives you an idea of what manufacturers think of their assembly line workers. Once you understand a few simple rules, you can do as good a job as they can—or even better.

Drive Select Jumpers

New floppy disk drives simply plug into a floppy drive cable with no changes or settings. Old drives, however, had drive-select jumpers or switches that allowed you to adjust a given drive as unit zero or one. These settings allowed you to adjust a drive to suit systems that did not follow the current fashion (it's not really a standard) in personal computers. When you install one of these older drives, you must adjust the switches or jumpers to identify the drive as unit one rather than zero. Typically you install a jumper on the pins marked DS1 (for Drive Select One).

Terminations

Similarly, older systems required the last drive (the one at the end of the cable) to be terminated with a small chip full of resistors. The second drive (if installed) was left unterminated. For practical reasons, termination is no longer a concern. The problems of improper drive termination have proven minimal; manufacturers simply include a termination on all drives and design floppy disk controllers to work adequately whether they have one or two terminations on a given cable.

Drive Cabling

The cable used by your floppy disk system is key to its proper operation. A twist in the cable actually sets how the two drives get identified. The twist occurs in five conductors in the ribbon cable between the two drive connectors. This twist reverses the drive-select and motor-control signals in the cable as well as rearranges some of the ground wires in the cable.

Because all drives are set up as the second drive, this reversal makes the drive attached to the cable after the twist the first drive, drive A. In other words, drive A is attached to the connector at the end of the cable, the one where the wire twist takes place. Drive B is attached to the connector in the middle of the length of the cable. The third connector, at the end of the cable with no twist, goes to the floppy disk controller or host adapter. Figure 10.18 illustrates the floppy disk cable and the proper connections.

FIGURE 10.18
Classic floppy drive cable showing proper connections.

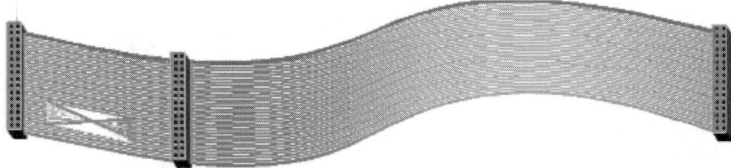

A: Drive   **B: Drive**   **Host Adapter**

Connectors

Physical aspects of the floppy disk interface have changed subtly over the years. The original computer floppy disk controller used an *edge connector* to attach to the floppy disk cable. Since about 1984, controllers generally have used *pin connectors*, although edge-connector products appeared into the 1990s. Similarly, the connectors on floppy disks migrated from edge connectors to pin connectors. With older computers, this difference can be critical when you need to get the correct cable. With modern computers, you'll want a cable that uses only pin connectors. Figure 10.19 contrasts the two connector styles.

FIGURE 10.19

Floppy disk cable connectors—edge connector (left) and pin connector.

Ports

No computer has everything you need built in to it. The computer gains its power from what you connect to it—its peripherals. Somehow your computer must be able to send data to its peripherals. It needs to connect, and it makes its connections through its ports.

Today's computers include two or three of these modern interfaces. Those that you're likely to encounter include *Universal Serial Bus (USB)*, today's general-purpose choice; *FireWire*, most popular as a digital video interface; *IrDA*, a wireless connection most often used for beaming data between handheld computers; *Bluetooth*, a radio-based networking system most suited for voice equipment; legacy *serial ports*, used by a variety of slower devices such as external modems, drawing tablets, and even PC-to-PC connections; and legacy *parallel ports*, most often used by printers. Table 11.1 compares these port alternatives.

TABLE 11.1 A Comparison of Serial Interfaces

Standard	Data Rate (Current)	Medium	Devices per Port
ACCESS.bus	100Kbps	Four-wire shielded cable	125
Bluetooth	723Kbps	Radio	8
FireWire (IEEE-1394)	400Mbps	Special six-wire cable	63
IrDA	4Mbps	Optical	126
Parallel (IEEE-1284)	2Mbps	25-conductor cable	1
Serial (RS-232C)	115,200bps	Twisted-pair	1
USB	480Mbps	Special four-wire cable	127

If you were only to buy new peripherals to plug into your computer, you could get along with only USB ports. Designed to be hassle-free for installing new gear, USB is fast enough (at least in its current version 2.0) that you need not consider any other connection. You can consider all the other ports special-purpose designs—the legacy pair (parallel and serial) for accommodating stuff that would otherwise be gathering dust in your attic; FireWire for plugging in your digital camcorder; IrDA for talking to your notebook computer; and Bluetooth for, well, you'll think of something.

Universal Serial Bus

In 1995, Compaq, Digital, IBM, Intel, Microsoft, NEC, and Northern Telecom, determined to design a better interface, pooled their efforts and laid the groundwork for the *Universal Serial Bus*, better known as *USB*. Later that year, they started the Universal Serial Bus Implementers Forum and in 1996 unveiled the new interface to the world. The world yawned.

Aimed at replacing both legacy serial and parallel port designs, the USB design corrected all three of their shortcomings. To improve performance, they designed USB with a 12Mbps data rate (with an alternative low-speed signaling rate of 1.5Mbps). To eliminate wiring hassles and worries about connector gender, crossover cables, and device types, they developed a strict wiring system with exactly one type of cable to serve all interconnection needs. And to allow one jack on the back of a computer to handle as many peripherals as necessary, they designed the system to accommodate up to 127 devices per port. In addition, they built in Plug-and-Play support so that every connection could be self-configuring. You could even hot-plug new devices and use them immediately without reloading your operating system.

On April 27, 2000, a new group, led by Compaq, Hewlett-Packard, Intel, Lucent, Microsoft, NEC, and Philips, published a revised USB standard, version 2.0. The key change was an increase in performance, upping the speed from 12Mbps to 480Mbps. The new system incorporates all the protocols of the old and is fully backward compatible. Devices will negotiate the highest common speed and use it for their transfers. Connectors and cabling remained unchanged.

Background

Designed for those who would rather compute than worry about hardware, the premise underlying USB is the substitution of software intelligence for cabling confusion. USB handles all the issues involved in linking multiple devices with different capabilities and data rates with a layer-cake of software. Along the way, it introduces its own new technology and terminology.

USB divides serial hardware into two classes: hubs and functions. A USB *hub* provides jacks into which you can plug functions. A USB *function* is a device that actually does something. USB's designers imagined that a function may be anything you can connect to your computer, including keyboards, mice, modems, printers, plotters, scanners, and more.

Rather than a simple point-to-point port, the USB acts as an actual bus that allows you to connect multiple peripherals to one jack on your computer with all the linked functions (devices) sharing exactly the same signals. Information passes across the bus in the form of packets, and all functions receive all packets. Your computer accesses individual functions by adding a specific address to the packets, and only the function with the correct address acts on the packets addressed to it.

The physical manifestation of USB is a port—a jack on the back of your computer or in a hub. Although your computer's USB port can handle up to 127 devices, each physical USB port connects to a single device. To connect multiple devices, you need multiple jacks. Typically, a new computer comes equipped with two USB ports. When you need more, you add a *hub*, which offers multiple jacks to let you plug in several devices. You can plug one hub into another to provide several additional jacks and ports to connect more devices.

The USB design envisions a hierarchical system with hubs connected to hubs connected to hubs. In that each hub allows for multiple connections, the reach of the USB system branches out like a tree—or a tree's roots. Figure 11.1 gives a conceptual view of the USB wiring system.

FIGURE 11.1

The USB hierarchical interconnection scheme.

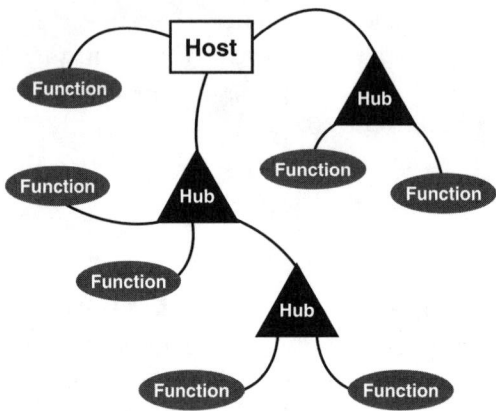

Your computer acts as the base hub for a USB system and is termed the *host*. The circuitry in your computer that controls this integral hub and the rest of the USB system is called the *bus controller*. Each USB system has one and only one bus controller.

Under USB 2.0, a device can operate at any of three speeds: *Low speed* is 1.5Mbps. *Full speed* is 12Mbps, and *high speed* is 480Mbps.

USB 2.0 is backward compatible with USB 1.1—all USB 1.1 devices will work with USB 2.0 devices, and vice versa, but USB 1.1 will impose its speed limit on USB 2.0 devices. The mixing of speeds makes matters complicated. If you plug both a USB 2.0 and a USB 1.1 device into a USB 2.0 hub, both devices will operate at their respective top speeds. But if a USB 1.1 hub appears in the chain between USB 2.0 devices, the slower hub will limit the speed of the overall system. Plug any USB 2.0 device into a USB 1.1 hub—even a USB 2.0 hub—and it will degrade to USB 1.1 operation (and if it's a hub, so will all the devices connected to that hub).

Other than this speed issue, the USB system doesn't care which device you plug into which hub or how many levels down the hub hierarchy you put a particular device. All the system requires is that you properly plug everything together following its simple rule: Each device must plug into a hub. The USB software then sorts everything out. This software, making up the *USB protocol*, is the most complex part of the design. In comparison, the actual hardware is simple—but the hardware won't work without the protocol.

The wiring hardware imposes no limit on the number of devices/functions you can connect in a USB system. You can plug hubs into hubs into hubs, fanning out into as many ports as you like. You do face limits, however. The protocol constrains the number of functions on one bus to 127 because of addressing limits. Seven bits are allowed for encoding function addresses, and one of the potential addresses (128) is reserved.

In addition, the wiring limits the distance at which you can place functions from hubs. The maximum length of a USB cable is five meters. Because hubs can regenerate signals, however, your USB system can stretch out for greater distances by making multiple hops through hubs.

As part of the Plug-and-Play process, the USB controller goes on a device hunt when you start up your computer. It interrogates each device to find out what it is. It then builds a map that locates each device by hub and port number. These become part of the packet address. When the USB driver sends data out the port, it routes that data to the proper device by this hub-and-port address.

USB requires specific software support. Any device with a USB connector will have the necessary firmware to handle USB built in. But your computer will also require software to make the USB system work. Your computer's operating system must know how to send the appropriate signals to its USB ports. All Windows versions starting with Windows 98 have USB support. Windows 95 and Windows NT do not. In addition, each function must have a matching software driver. The function driver creates the commands or packages the data for its associated device. An overall USB driver acts as the delivery service, providing the channel—in USB terminology, a *pipe*—for routing the data to the various functions. Consequently, each USB you add to your computer requires software installation along with plugging in the hardware.

Connectors

The USB system involves four different styles of connectors—two chassis-mounted jacks and two plugs at the ends of cables. Each jack and plug comes in two varieties: A and B.

Hubs have *A jacks*. These are the primary outward manifestation of the USB port—the wide, thin USB slots you'll find on the back of your computer. The matching *A plug* attaches to the cable that leads to the USB device. In the purest form of USB, this cable is permanently affixed to the device, and you need not worry about any other plugs or jacks.

This configuration may someday become popular when manufacturers discover they can save the cost of a connector by integrating the cable. Unfortunately, too many manufacturers have discovered that by putting a jack on their USB devices they save the cost of the cable by not including it with the device.

To accommodate devices with removable cables (and manufacturers that don't want the add the expense of a few feet of wire to their USB devices), the USB standard allows for a second, different style of plug and jack meant only to be used for inputs to USB devices. If a USB device (other than a hub) requires a connector so that, as a convenience, you can remove the cable, it uses a USB *B jack*, which is a small, nearly square hole into which you slide the mating *B plug*.

The motivation behind this multiplicity of connectors is to prevent rather than cause confusion. All USB cables will have an A plug at one end and a B plug at the other. One end must attach to a hub and the other to a device. You cannot inadvertently plug things together incorrectly.

Because all A jacks are outputs and all B jacks are inputs, only one form of detachable USB cable exists—one with an A plug at one end and a B plug at the other. No crossover cables or adapters are needed for any USB wiring scheme.

Cable

The USB system uses two kinds of cable—that meant for low-speed connections and that meant for full- and high-speed links. But you only have to worry about the higher-speed variety. Low-speed cables, those capable of supporting only 1.5Mbps signaling rates, must be permanently attached to the equipment using them. Higher-speed cables can be either permanently attached or removable.

Both speeds of physical USB wiring use a special four-wire cable. Two conductors in the cable transfer the data as a differential digital signal. That is, the voltage on the two conductors is of equal magnitude and opposite polarity so that when subtracted from one another (finding the difference) the result cancels out any noise that ordinarily would add equally to the signal on each line. In addition, the USB cable includes a power signal, nominally five-volts DC, and a ground return. The power signal allows you to supply power for external serial devices through the USB cable. The two data wires are twisted together as a pair. The power cables may or may not be.

The difference between low- and higher-speed cables is that the capacitance of the low-speed cable is adjusted to support its signaling rate. In addition, the low speed does not need twisted-pair wires, and the standard doesn't require them.

All removable cables must be able to handle both full-speed and high-speed connections. To achieve its high data rate, the USB specification requires that certain physical characteristics of the cable be carefully controlled. Even so, the maximum length permitted for any USB cable is five meters.

One limit on cable length is the inevitable voltage drop suffered by the power signal. All wires offer some resistance to electrical flow, and the resistance is proportional to the wire gauge. Hence, lower wire gauges (thicker wires) have lower resistance. Longer cables require lower wire gauges. At maximum length, the USB specification requires 20-gauge wire, which is one step (two gauge numbers) thinner than ordinary lamp cord.

The individual wires in the USB cable are color-coded. The data signals form a green-white pair, with the +Data signal on green. The positive five-volt signal rides on the red wire. The ground wire is black. Table 11.2 sums up this color code.

TABLE 11.2   USB Cable Color Code

Signal	Color
+Data	Green
-Data	White
VCC	Red
Ground	Black

Normally, you cannot connect one computer to another using USB. The standard calls for only one USB controller in the entire interconnection system. Physically the cabling system prevents you from making such a connection. The exception is that some cables have a *bridge* built in that allows two USB hosts to talk to each other. The bridge is active circuitry that converts the signals.

Protocol

As with all more recent interface introductions, the USB design uses a packet-based protocol using No Return-to-Zero Inverted (NRZI) data coding. All message exchanges require the swapping of three packets. The exchange begins with the host sending out a *token packet*. The token packet bears the address of the device meant to participate in the exchange as well as control information that describes the nature of the exchange. A *data packet* holds the actual information that is to be exchanged. Depending on the type of transfer, either the host or the device will send out the data packet. Despite the name, the data packet may contain no information. Finally, the exchange ends with a *handshake packet*, which acknowledges the receipt of the data or other successful completion of the exchange. A fourth type of packet, called *Special*, handles additional functions.

Each packet starts with two components—a Sync Field and a Packet Identifier—each one byte long. The *Sync Field* is a series of bits that serves as a consistent burst of clock pulses so that the devices connected to the USB bus can reset their timing and synchronize themselves to the host. The Sync Field appears as three on/off pulses followed by a marker two pulses wide. The *Packet Identifier* byte includes four bits to define the nature of the packet itself and another four bits as check-bits that confirm the accuracy of the first four. The four bits provide a code that allows for the definition of 16 different kinds of packets.

USB uses the 16 values in a two-step hierarchy. The two more significant bits specify one of the four types of packets. The two lesser significant bits subdivide the packet category. Table 11.3 lists the PIDs of the four basic USB packet types.

TABLE 11.3   USB Packet Identifications

Bit-Pattern	Packet Type
XX00XX11	Special packet
XX01XX10	Token packet
XX10XX01	Handshake packet
XX11XX00	Data packet

Token Packets

Only the USB host sends out token packets. Each token packet takes up four bytes, which are divided up into five functional parts. Figure 11.2 graphically shows the layout of a token packet.

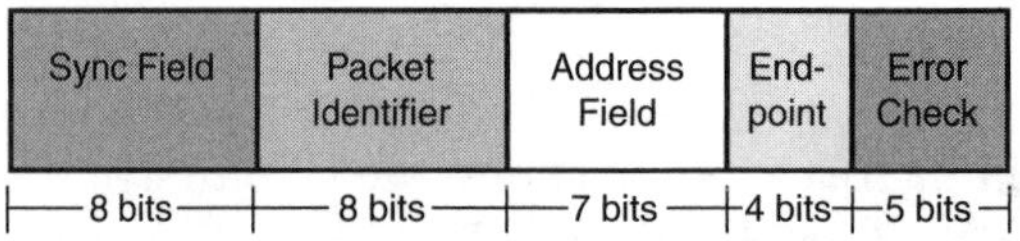

FIGURE 11.2

Functional parts of a USB Token Packet.

The two bytes take the standard form of all USB packets. The first byte is a Sync Field that marks the beginning of the token's bit-stream. The second byte is the *Packet Identifier*.

The PID byte defines four types of token packets. These include an Out packet that carries data from the host to a device; an In packet that carries data from the device to the host; a Setup packet that targets a specific endpoint; and a Start of Frame packet that helps synchronize the system.

Data Packets

The actual information transferred through the USB system takes the form of *data packets*. As with all USB packets, a data packet begins with a one-byte Sync Field followed by the Packet Identifier. The actual data follows as a sequence of 0 to 1,023 bytes. A two-byte cyclic redundancy check verifies the accuracy of only the Data Field, as shown in Figure 11.3. The PID field relies on its own redundancy check mechanism.

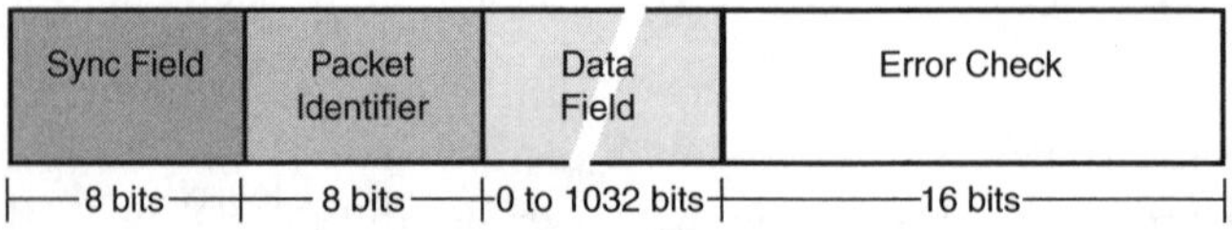

FIGURE 11.3

Constituents of a USB data packet.

Handshake Packets

Handshake packets handle flow-control in the USB system. All are two bytes long, comprised of nothing more than the Sync Field and a Packet Identifier byte that acknowledges proper receipt of a packet, as shown in Figure 11.4.

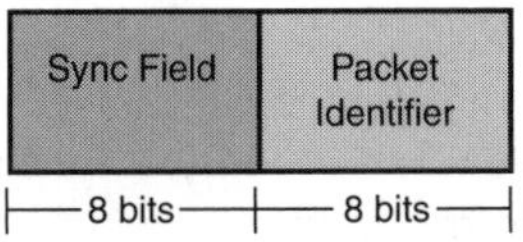

FIGURE 11.4
Constituents of a USB handshake packet.

Standard

The USB standard is maintained by USB Implementers Forum. You can download a complete copy of the current version of the specifications from the USB Website.

USB Implementers Forum

5440 SW Westgate Dr., Suite 217

Portland, OR 97221

Phone: 503-296-9892

Fax: 503-297-1090

Web site: www.usb.org

FireWire

Also known as *IEEE-1394*, *I.link*, and *DV*, FireWire is a serial interface that's aimed at high-throughput devices such as a hard disk and tape drives, as well as consumer-level multimedia devices such as digital camcorders, digital VCRs, and digital televisions. Originally it was conceived as a general-purpose interface suitable for replacing legacy serial ports, but with blazing speed. However, it has been most used in digital video—at least so far. Promised new performance and a choice of media may rekindle interest in FireWire as a general-purpose, high-performance interconnection system.

For the most part, FireWire is a hardware interface. It specifies speeds, timing, and a connection system. The software side is based on SCSI. In fact, FireWire is one of the several hardware interfaces included in the SCSI-3 standards.

As with other current port standards, FireWire continues to evolve. Development of the standard began when the Institute of Electrical and Electronic Engineers (IEEE) assigned a study group the task of clearing the murk of thickening morass of serial standards in September 1986. Hardly four months later (in January 1987), the group had already outlined basic concepts underlying FireWire, some of which still survive in today's standard—including low cost, a simplified wiring scheme, and arbitrated signals supporting multiple devices. The IEEE approved the first FireWire standard (as IEEE 1394-1995) in 1995, based on a design with one connector style and two speeds (100 and 200Mbps).

In the year 2000, the institute approved the standard IEEE 1394a-2000, which boasts a new, miniaturized connector, a higher speed (400Mbps), and streamlined signaling that makes connections quicker (because of reduced overhead) and more reliable.

As this is written, the engineers at the institute are developing a successor standard, IEEE 1394b, that will quadruple the speed of connections, add both fiber-optic and twisted-pair wiring schemes, and add a new, more reliable transport protocol.

For now, FireWire is best known as a 400Mbps connection system for plugging digital camcorders into computers, letting you capture video images (live or tape), edit them, and publish them on CD or DVD.

Overview

FireWire differs from today's other leading port standard, USB, in that it is a point-to-point connection system. That is, you plug a FireWire device directly into the port on your computer. To accommodate more than one FireWire device (the standard allows for a maximum of 63 interconnected devices), the computer host may have multiple jacks or the FireWire device may have its own input jack so that you can daisy-chain multiple devices to a single computer port.

Although FireWire does not use hubs in the network or USB sense, in its own nomenclature it does. In the FireWire scheme, a device with a single FireWire port is a *leaf*. A device with two ports is called a *pass-through*, and a device with three ports is called a *branch* or *hub*. Pass-through and branch nodes operate as *repeaters*, reconstituting the digital signal for the next hop. Each FireWire system also has a single *root*, which is the foundation around which the rest of the system organizes itself.

You can daisy-chain devices with up to 16 links to the chain. After that, the delays in relaying the signals from device to device go beyond those set in the standard. Accommodating larger numbers of devices requires using branches to create parallel data paths.

Under the current standard (1394a), FireWire allows a maximum cable length of 4.5 meters (about 15 feet). With 16 links to a daisy-chain, two FireWire devices could be separated by as much as 72 meters (almost 200 feet).

Each FireWire cable contains two active connections for a full-duplex design (signals travel both ways simultaneously in the cable on different wire pairs). Connectors at each end of the cable are the same, so wiring is easy—you just plug things together. Software takes care of all the details of the connection. The exception is that the 1394a standard also allows for a miniaturized connector to fit in tight places (such as a camcorder).

FireWire also allows for engineers to use the same signaling system for *backplane* designs. That is, FireWire could be used as an expansion bus inside a computer as well as the port linking to external peripherals. Currently, however, FireWire is not used as a backplane inside personal computers.

The protocol used by FireWire uses 64-bit addressing. The 63 device limitation per chain results from only six bits being used for node identification. The rest of the addressing bits provide for large networks and the use of direct memory addressing—10 bits for network identifications and 48 bits for memory addresses (the same as the latest Intel microprocessor, enough for uniquely identifying 281TB of memory per device). A single device may use multiple identifications.

Signaling

To minimize noise, data connections in FireWire use differential signals, which means it uses two wires that carry the same signal but of opposite polarity. Receiving equipment subtracts the signal on one wire from that on the other to find the data as the difference between the two signals. The benefit of this scheme is that any noise gets picked up by the wires equally. When the receiving equipment subtracts the signals on the two wires, the noise gets eliminated—the equal noise signals subtracted from each other equals zero.

The original FireWire standard used a patented form of signal coding called *data strobe coding*, using *two* differential wire pairs to carry a single data stream. One pair carried the actual data; the second pair, called the *strobe lines*, complimented the state of the data pair so that one and only one of the pairs changed polarity every clock cycle. For example, if the data line carried two sequential bits of the same value, the strobe line reversed polarity to mark the transition between them. If a sequence of two bits changed the polarity of the data lines (a one followed by a zero, or zero followed by a one), the strobe line did not change polarity. Summing the data and strobe lines together exactly reconstructed the clock signal of the sending system, allowing the sending and receiving devices to precisely lock up.

FireWire operates as a two-way channel, with different pairs of wire used for sending and receiving. When one pair is sending data, the other operates as its strobe signal. In receiving data, the pair used for strobe in sending contains the data, and the other (data in sending) carries the receive strobe. In other words, as a device shifts from sending and receiving, it shifts which wire pairs it uses for data and strobe.

The 1394b specification alters the data coding to use a system termed *8B/10B* coding, developed by IBM. The scheme encodes eight-bit bytes in 10-bit symbols that guarantee a sequence of more than five identical bits never occurs and that the number of ones and zeros in the code balance—a characteristic important to engineers because it results in no shift of the direct current voltage in the system.

Configuration

FireWire allows you to connect multiple devices together and uses an addressing system so that the signals sent through a common channel are recognized only by the proper target device. The linked devices can independently communicate among themselves without the intervention of your computer. Each device can communicate at its own speed—a single FireWire connection shifts between speeds to accommodate each device. Of course, a low-speed device may not be able to pass through higher-speed signals, so some forethought is required to put together a system in which all devices operate at their optimum speeds.

FireWire eliminates such concern about setting device identifications with its own automated configuration process. Whenever a new device gets plugged into a FireWire system (or when the whole system gets turned on), the automatic configuration process begins. By signaling through the various connections, each device determines how it fits into the system, either as a root node, a branch, a pass-through, or a leaf. The node also sends out a special clock signal. Once the connection hierarchy is set up, the FireWire devices determine their own ID numbers from their location in the hierarchy and send identifying information (ID and device type) to their host.

You can hot-plug devices into a FireWire tree. That is, you can plug in a new device to a group of FireWire devices without switching off the power. When you plug in a new device, the change triggers a bus reset that erases the system's stored memory of the previous set of devices. Then the entire chain of devices goes through the configuration process again and is assigned an address. The devices then identify themselves to one another and wait for data transfers to begin.

Arbitration

FireWire transfers data in packets, a block of data preceded by a header that specifies where the data goes and its priority. In the basic cable-based FireWire system, each device sharing a connection gets a chance to send one packet in an arbitration period that's called a *fairness interval*. The various devices take turns until all have had a chance to use the bus. After each packet gets sent, a brief time called the *sub-action gap* elapses, after which another device can send its packet. If no devices start to transmit when the sub-action gap ends, all devices wait a bit longer, stretching the time to an arbitration reset gap. After that time elapses, a new fairness interval begins, and all devices get to send one more packet. The cycle continues.

To handle devices that need a constant stream of data for real-time display, such as video or audio signals, FireWire uses a special isochronous mode. Every 125 microseconds, one device in the FireWire that needs isochronous data sends out a special timing packet that signals that isochronous devices can transmit. Each takes a turn in order of its priority, leaving a brief isochronous gap delay between their packets. When the isochronous gap delay stretches out to the sub-action gap length, the devices using ordinary asynchronous transfers take over until the end of the 125-microsecond cycle when the next isochronous period begins.

The scheme guarantees that video and audio gear can move its data in real time with a minimum of buffer memory. (Audio devices require only a byte of buffer; video may need as many as six bytes.) The 125-microsecond period matches the sampling rate used by digital telephone systems to help digital telephone services.

The new 1394b standard also brings a new arbitration system called *Bus Owner/Supervisor/Selector* (BOSS). Under this scheme, a device takes control of the bus as the BOSS by being the last device to acknowledge the receipt of a packet sent to it (rather than broadcast over the entire tree) or by receiving a specific grant of control. The BOSS takes full command of the tree, even selecting the next node to be the BOSS.

Connectors

In the original FireWire version only a single, small, six-pin connector was defined for all purposes. Each cable had an identical connector on each end, and all FireWire ports were the same. The contacts were arranged in two parallel rows on opposite sides inside the metal-and-plastic shield of the connector. The asymmetrical "D" shape of the active end of the connector ensured that you plugged it in properly. Figure 11.5 shows this connector.

FIGURE 11.5
A FireWire connector.

The revised 1394a standard added a miniaturized connector. To keep it compact, the design omitted the two power contacts. This design is favored for personal electronic devices such as camcorders. Figure 11.6 shows this connector.

FIGURE 11.6
A miniaturized FireWire connector.

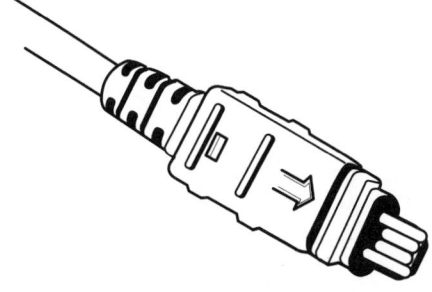

The 1394b standard will add two more connectors to the FireWire arsenal, each with eight contacts. The *Beta* connector is meant for systems that use only the new 1394b signaling system and do not understand the earlier versions of the standard. In addition, the new standard defines a *bilingual* connector, one that speaks both the old and new FireWire standards. The new designs are keyed so that while both beta and bilingual connectors will fit a bilingual port, only a beta connector will fit a beta-only port. Figure 11.7 shows this keying system.

FIGURE 11.7
The IEEE 1394b connector keying.

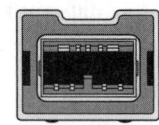

IEEE 1394B Beta jack   IEEE 1394B Bilingual jack

Cabling

In current form, FireWire uses ordinary copper wires in a special cable design. Two variations are allowed—one with solely four signal wires and one with the four signal wires and two power wires. In both implementations, data travels across two shielded twisted pairs of AWG 28 gauge wire, with a nominal impedance of 110 ohms. In the six-wire version, two AWG 22 gauge wires additionally carry power at 8 to 33 volts with up to 1.5 amperes to power a number of peripherals. Another shield will cover the entire collection of conductors.

The upcoming IEEE 1394b standard also allows for two forms of fiber optical connection—glass and plastic—as well as ordinary Category 5 twisted-pair network cable. The maximum length of plastic fiber optical connections is 50 meters (about 160 feet); for glass optical fiber, the maximum length is 100 meters (about 320 feet). Either style of optical connection can operate at speeds of 100 or 200Mbps. Category 5 wire allows connections of up to 100 meters but only at the lowest data rate sanctioned by the standard, which is 100Mbps.

All FireWire cables are crossover cables. That is, the signals that appear on pins 1 and 2 at one end of the cable "cross over" to pins 3 and 4 at the other end. This permits all FireWire ports to be wired the same and serve both as inputs and outputs. The same connector can be used at each end of the cable, and no keying is necessary, as is the case with USB.

The FireWire wiring scheme depends on each of the devices that are connected together to relay signals to the others. Pulling the plug to one device could potentially knock down the entire connection system. To avoid such difficulties and dependencies, FireWire uses its power connections to keep in operation the interface circuitry in otherwise inactive devices. These power lines could also supply enough current to run entire devices. No device may draw more than three watts from the FireWire bus, although a single device may supply up to 40 watts. The FireWire circuitry itself in each interface requires only about two milliwatts.

The FireWire wiring standard allows for up to 16 hops of 4.5 meters (about 15 feet) each. As with current communications ports, the standard allows you to connect and disconnect peripherals without switching off power to them. You can daisy-chain FireWire devices or branch the cable between them. When you make changes, the network of connected devices will automatically reconfigure itself to reflect the alterations.

IrDA

The one thing you don't want with a portable computer is a cable to tether you down; yet most of the time you have to plug into one thing or another. Even a simple and routine chore like downloading files from your notebook machine into your desktop computer gets tangled in cable trouble. Not only do you have to plug in both ends, reaching behind your desktop machine is only a little more elegantly done than fishing into a catch basin for a fallen quarter—and, more likely than not, unplugging something else that you'll inevitably need later only to discover the dangling cord—but you've got to tote that writhing cable along with you wherever you go. There has to be a better way.

There is. You can link your computer to other systems and components with a light beam. On the rear panel of many notebook computers, you'll find a clear LED or a dark red window through which your system can send and receive invisible infrared light beams. Although originally introduced to allow you to link portable computers to desktop machines, the same technology can tie in peripherals such as modems and printers, all without the hassle of plugging and unplugging cables.

History

On June 28, 1993, a group of about 120 representatives from 50 computer-related companies got together to take the first step in cutting the cord. Creating what has come to be known as the *Infrared Developers Association (IrDA)*, this group aimed at more than making your computer more convenient to carry. It also saw a new versatility and, hardly incidentally, a way to trim its own costs.

The idea behind the get together was to create a standard for using infrared light to link your computer to peripherals and other systems. The technology had already been long established, not only in television remote controls but also in a number of notebook computers already on the market. Rather than build a new technology, the goal of the group was to find common ground, a standard so that the products of all manufacturers could communicate with the computer equivalent of sign language.

Hardly a year later, on June 30, 1994, the group approved its first standard. The original specification, now known as *IrDA version 1.0*, essentially gave the standard RS-232C port an optical counterpart, one with the same data structure and, alas, speed limit. In August 1995, IrDA took the next step and approved high-speed extensions that pushed the wireless data rate to 4Mbps.

Overview

More than a gimmicky cordless keyboard, IrDA holds an advantage that makes computer manufacturers—particularly those developing low-cost machines—eye it with interest. It can cut several dollars from the cost of a complex system by eliminating some expensive hardware, a connector or two, and a cable. Compared to the other wireless technology, radio, infrared requires less space because it needs only a tiny LED instead of a larger and more costly antenna. Moreover, infrared transmissions are not regulated by the FCC as are radio transmissions. Nor do they cause interference to radios, televisions, pacemakers, and airliners. The range of infrared is more limited than radio and restricted to the line of sight over a narrow angle. However, these weaknesses can become strengths for those who are security conscious.

The original design formulated by IrDA was for a replacement for serial cables. To make the technology easy and inexpensive to implement with existing components, it was based on the standard RS-232C port and its constituent components. The original IrDA standard used asynchronous communication using the same data frame legacy serial ports as well as its data rates from 2400 to 115,200 bits per second.

To keep power needs low and prevent interference among multiple installations in a single room, IrDA kept the range of the system low, about one meter (three feet). Similarly, the IrDA system concentrates the infrared beam used to carry data because diffusing the beam would require more power for a given range and be prone to causing greater interference among competing units. The laser diodes used in the IrDA system consequently focus their beams into a cone with a spread of about 30 degrees.

After the initial serial-port replacement design was in place, IrDA worked to make its interface suitable for replacing parallel ports as well. That goal led to the creation of the IrDA high-speed standards for transmissions at data rates of 0.576, 1.152, and 4.0Mbps. The two higher speeds use a packet-based synchronous system that requires a special hardware-based communication controller. This controller monitors and controls the flow of information between the host computer's bus and communications buffers.

Consequently, a watershed of differences separate low-speed and high-speed IrDA systems. Although IrDA designed the high-speed standard to be backward compatible with old equipment, making the higher speeds work requires special hardware. In other words, although high-speed IrDA devices can successfully communicate with lower-speed units, such communications are constrained to the speeds of the lower-speed units. Low-speed units cannot operate at high speeds without their hardware being upgraded.

IrDA defines not only the hardware but also the data format used by its system. The group has published six standards to cover these aspects of IrDA communications. The hardware itself forms the *physical layer*. In addition, IrDA defines a link access protocol termed *IrLAP* and a link management protocol called *IrLMP* that describe the data formats used to negotiate and maintain communications. All IrDA ports must follow these standards. In addition, IrDA has defined an optional transport protocol and optional Plug-and-Play extensions to allow for the smooth integration of the system into modern computers. The group's IrCOMM standard describes a standard way for infrared ports to emulate conventional computer serial and parallel ports.

Infrared Light

Infrared light is invisible electromagnetic radiation that has a wavelength longer than that of visible light. Whereas you can see light that ranges in wavelength from 400 angstroms (deep violet) to 700 angstroms (dark red), infrared stretches from 700 angstroms to 1000 or more. IrDA specifies that the infrared signal used by computers for communication has a wavelength between 850 and 900 angstroms.

Data Rates

All IrDA ports must be able to operate at one basic speed—9600 bits per second. All other speeds are optional.

The IrDA specification allows for all the usual speed increments used by conventional serial ports, from 2400bps to 115,200bps. All these speeds use the default modulation scheme, Return-to-Zero Inverted (RZI). High-speed IrDA version 1.1 adds three additional speeds, 576Kbps, 1.152Mbps, and 4.0Mbps, based on a pulse-position modulation scheme.

Regardless of the speed range implemented by a system or used for communications, IrDA devices first establish communications at the mandatory 9600bps speed using the Link Access Protocol. Once the two devices establish a common speed for communicating, they switch to it and use it for the balance of their transmissions.

Pulse Width

The infrared cell of an IrDA transmitter sends out its data in pulses, each lasting only a fraction of the basic clock period or bit-cell. The relatively wide spacing between pulses makes each pulse easier for the optical receiver to distinguish.

At speeds up to and including 115,200 bits per second, each infrared pulse must be at least 1.41 microseconds long. Each IrDA data pulse nominally lasts just 3/16th of the length of a bit-cell, although pulse widths a bit more than 10 percent greater remain acceptable. For example, each bit cell of a 9600bps signal would occupy 104.2 microseconds (that is, one second divided by 9600). A typical IrDA pulse at that data rate would last 3/16th that period, or 19.53 microseconds.

At higher speeds, the minimum pulse length is reduced to 295.2 nanoseconds at 576Kbps and to only 115 nanoseconds at 4.0Mbps. At these higher speeds, the nominal pulse width is one-quarter of the character cell. For example, at 4.0Mbps, each pulse is only 125 nanoseconds long. Again, pulses about 10 percent longer remain permissible. Table 11.4 summarizes the speeds and pulse lengths.

TABLE 11.4   IrDA Speeds and Modulation

Signaling Rate	Modulation	Pulse Duration
2.4Kbps	RZI	78.13 microseconds
9.6Kbps	RZI	19.53 microseconds
19.2Kbps	RZI	9.77 microseconds
38.4Kbps	RZI	4.88 microseconds
57.6Kbps	RZI	3.26 microseconds
115.2Kbps	RZI	1.63 microseconds
0.576Mbps	RZI	434.0 nanoseconds
1.152Mbps	RZI	217.0 nanoseconds
4.0Mbps	4PPM, single pulse	125 nanoseconds
4.0Mbps	4PPM, double pulse	250.0 nanoseconds

Modulation

Depending on the speed at which a link operates, it may use one of two forms of modulation. At speeds lower than 4.0Mbps, the system employs *Return-to-Zero Invert (RZI)* modulation.

At the 4.0Mbps data rate, the IrDA system shifts to *pulse position modulation*. Because the IrDA system involves four discrete pulse positions, it is abbreviated 4PPM.

IrDA requires data to be transmitted only in eight-bit format. In terms of conventional serial-port parameters, a data frame for IrDA comprises a start bit, eight data bits, no parity bits, and a stop bit, for a total of 10 bits per character. Note, however, that zero insertion may increase the length of a transmitted byte of data. Any inserted zeroes are removed automatically by the receiver and do not enter the data stream. No matter the form of modulation used by the IrDA system, all byte values are transmitted with the least significant bit first.

Note that with RZI modulation, long sequences of logical ones will suppress pulses for the entire duration of the sequence. To prevent such a lengthy gap from appearing in the signal and causing a loss of sync, moderate speed IrDA systems add extra pulses to the signal with *bit-stuffing* (as discussed in Chapter 8).

Format

The IrDA system doesn't deal with data at the bit or byte level but instead arranges the data transmitted through it in the form of packets, which the IrDA specification also terms *frames*. A single frame can stretch from 5 to 2050 bytes (and sometimes more) in length. As with other packetized systems, an IrDA frame includes address information, data, and error correction, the last of which is applied at the frame level. The format of the frame is rigidly defined by the IrDA Link Access Protocol standard, discussed later.

Aborted Frames

Whenever a receiver detects a string of seven or more consecutive logical ones—that is, an absence of optical pulses—it immediately terminates the frame in progress and disregards the data it received (which is classed as invalid because of the lack of error-correction data). The receiver then awaits the next valid frame, signified by a start-of-frame flag, address field, and control field. Any frame that ends in this summary manner is termed an *aborted frame*.

A transmitter may intentionally abort a frame or a frame may be aborted because of an interruption in the infrared signal. Anything that blocks the light path will stop infrared pulses from reaching the receiver and, if long enough, abort the frame being transmitted.

Interference Suppression

High-speed systems automatically mute lower-speed systems that are operating in the same environment to prevent interference. To stop the lower-speed link from transmitting, the high-speed system sends out a special *Serial Infrared Interaction Pulse (SIP)* at intervals no longer than half a second. The SIP is a pulse 1.6 microseconds long, followed by 7.1 microseconds of darkness, parameters exactly equal to a packet start pulse. When the low-speed system sees what it thinks is a start pulse, it automatically starts looking for data at the lower rates, suppressing its own transmission for half a second. Before it has a chance to start sending its own data (if any), another SIP quiets the low-speed system for the next half second.

Bluetooth

Radio yields the most versatile connection system: no wires and no worries. Because radio waves can slip through most office walls, desktop ornaments, office supplies, and even employees, radio-based links eliminate the line-of-sight requirements of optical links such as IrDA. Linking devices with radio waves consequently yields the most convenient connection for workers to free their peripherals from the chains of interconnecting cables. A radio link can provide a reliable, cord-free connection that eliminates the snarl on the rear of every desktop PC. It also allows you to link your wireless devices—in particular, your cell phone—to your PC and *keep everything wireless*. Hardly a novel idea, of course, but one that has been a long time coming for practical connections.

Finally, a single standard may bring the wireless dream to life. To provide common ground and a standard for radio-based connections between PCs, their peripherals, and related communications equipment, several major corporations worked together to develop the *Bluetooth* specification. They designed the standard for the utmost in convenience, coupled with low cost but sacrificing range—Bluetooth is a short-range system suitable for linking devices in an office suite rather than across miles like a cell phone.

Originally conceived as a way to link cellular devices to PCs, the actual specification transcends its origins. Bluetooth makes possible not only cell phone connections but also could allow you to use your keyboard or mouse without a physical connection to your PC and without fretting about office debris blocking optical signals. But Bluetooth is more than a simple interface. It can become a small wireless network of intercommunicating devices, handling both voice and data with equal ease. Although not a rival to traditional networking systems—its speed limitations alone see to that—Bluetooth adds versatility that combines cell phone and PC technology.

The Bluetooth promoters refer to its multidevice links as a *piconet* (smaller than even a micronet), able to link up to eight devices. Bluetooth allows even greater assemblages of equipment by linking piconets together and accommodating temporarily inactive equipment within its reach.

On the other hand, the data speed of the Bluetooth system is modest. At most, Bluetooth can move bits at a claimed rate of about 723Kbps asymmetrically—that is, the high rate is in one direction; the return channel is slower, about one-fifth that rate. Moreover, Bluetooth slows to accommodate bidirectional data and phone conversations. Despite the modest data rate, however, the Bluetooth bit-rate is high enough to handle three simultaneous telephone conversations or a combination of voice and data simultaneously.

Good as it sounds, Bluetooth currently has a number of handicaps to overcome. It is not supported by any version of Microsoft Windows in current release (including the initial release of Windows XP). Microsoft, however, promises to add its own native support for Bluetooth in subsequent releases of Windows.

History

Certainly Bluetooth was not the first attempt at creating radio-based data links for computers. Wireless schemes for exchanging data have been around longer than personal computers. But Bluetooth differs from any previous radio-based data-exchange system in that it was conceived as an open standard for the computer and communications industries to facilitate the design of compatible wireless hardware.

As with so many modern standards, Bluetooth represents the work of an industry consortium. In May 1998, representatives from five major corporations involved with PCs, office equipment, and cellular telephones jointly conceived the idea of Bluetooth and began working toward creating the standard. The five founders were Ericsson (Telefonaktiebolaget LM Ericsson), International Business Machines Corporation, Intel Corporation, Nokia Corporation, and Toshiba Corporation. Together they formed the Bluetooth Special Interest Group (SIG) and started work on the standard and the technologies needed to make it a reality. The SIG released the first version of the specification, Bluetooth 1.0, on July 24, 1999. A slightly revised version was released in December 1999.

Membership in the Bluetooth SIG grew to nine on December 1, 1999, when 3Com Technologies, Lucent Technologies, Microsoft Corporation, and Motorola, Inc., joined the group. In addition, over 1,200 individuals and companies have adopted the technology by entering an agreement with the SIG that allows them to use the standard and share the intellectual property required to implement it.

Although support for Bluetooth has been slow in coming, manufacturers have adapted the technology for low-speed computer peripherals (such as wireless keyboards and mice). Owing to the success of other wireless technologies, most successful applications of Bluetooth are in communications products.

Overview

Bluetooth is a wireless packetized communications system that allows multiple devices to share data in a small network. Heir to both cell phone and digital technologies, it nestles between several existing standards, embracing them. It can link to your PC using a USB connection, and it shares logical layers with IrDA. It not only handles data like a traditional serial port but also can carry more than 60 RS-232C connections.

In theory, a Bluetooth system operates entirely transparently. Devices link themselves together without you having to do anything. All you need to do is turn on your Bluetooth devices and bring them within range of one another. For example, available devices should automatically pop up on your Windows desktop—at least once Windows gains Bluetooth support. You can then drag files to and from the device as if it were a local Windows resource.

Behind the scenes, however, things aren't quite so simple. The Bluetooth system must accommodate a variety of device and data types. It needs to keep in constant contact with each device. It must be able to detect when a new device appears and when other devices get switched off or venture out of range. It has to moderate the conversations between units, ensuring they don't all try to talk at the same time and interfere with one another.

Software Side

As an advanced interface, Bluetooth heavily processes the raw data it transmits. It repackages serial data bits into packets with built-in error control. It then combines a series of packets of related serial data into *links*. It further processes the links through multiplexing so that several serial streams can simultaneously share a single Bluetooth connection.

Bluetooth packetizes data, breaking a serial input stream into small pieces, each containing address and optional error-correction information. A series of packets that starts as a single data stream and is later reconstructed into a replica of that stream is a *link*.

The Bluetooth standard supports two kinds of data links: synchronous and asynchronous. Synchronous data is typically voice information, such as audio from telephone conversations. Asynchronous data is typically computer data. The chief difference is that synchronous data is time dependent, so synchronous packets get transmitted once without regard to their reception. If a synchronous packet gets lost during transmission, it is forever lost.

Synchronous links between Bluetooth devices provide a full-duplex channel with an effective data rate of 64Kbps in each direction. In effect, a synchronous link is a standard digital telephone channel with eight-bit resolution and an 8-KHz sampling rate. The Bluetooth standard allows for two devices to simultaneously share three such synchronous links, the equivalent of three real-time telephone conversations. All links begin asynchronously because commands can only be sent in asynchronous packets. After the link is established, the master and slave can negotiate to switch over to a synchronous link for voice transfers or to move data asynchronously.

Each piconet has a single master and, potentially, multiple slaves. Each piconet shares a single communications channel with all the devices (master and slave) locked together on a common frequency and using a common clock, as discussed later. The single channel is subdivided into one or more links—asynchronous and/or synchronous.

To handle contention between multiple links on its single channel, Bluetooth uses time-division multiplexing. That is, each separate packet of a link gets a time period for transmission. The standard divides the communications channel into time *slots*, each 625 microseconds long. The shortest single packet fits a single slot with room to spare, although Bluetooth allows packets to stretch out for up to five slots. Bluetooth allows a maximum length of single-slot packets of 366 microseconds. The system accommodates larger packets by letting them extend through up to five slots, filling the entire time of four of the slots and part of the fifth.

In the Bluetooth system, each packet also defines a *hop*. That is, after each packet is sent, the Bluetooth system switches to (or hops to) another carrier frequency. As noted later, frequency-hopping helps ensure the integrity of Bluetooth transmissions. The minimum hop length corresponds to a single slot, although a hop can last for up to five slots to accommodate a long packet.

The time division duplexing of the Bluetooth system works by assigning even-numbered slots to the master and odd-numbered slots to the slaves. Masters can begin their transmissions only in even-numbered slots. If a packet lasts for an even number of slots (two or four), no slave can begin until the next odd-numbered slot. In effect, then, packets use an odd number of slots even if they use only a shorter, even number of slots.

Hardware Side

Bluetooth hardware provides the connection that carries the processed and packetized data. Although in that Bluetooth makes a wireless connection, its hardware is essentially invisible—the system requires a collection of circuits to transmit and receive the data properly.

As with all radio systems, Bluetooth starts with a carrier wave and modulates it with data. Unlike most common radio systems, however, Bluetooth does not use a single fixed carrier frequency but rather hops to different frequencies more than a thousand times each second. As a serial transmission system, time is important to Bluetooth to sort out data bits. Each Bluetooth device maintains a clock that helps it determine when each bit in its serial stream appears. Bluetooth cleverly combines these necessary elements to make a wireless communications network.

Clocks

Each Bluetooth device has its own internal clock that paces its communications. The clock of each device operates independently at approximately the necessary rate.

For the Bluetooth signals to be effectively demodulated, the clocks of the master and slaves must be synchronized. The master device sets the frequency for all the slaves with which it communicates. The slaves determine the exact frequency of the clock from the packet data. The preamble of each packet contains a predetermined pattern of several cycles, which the slaves can use to achieve synchrony. The Bluetooth system does not alter the operation of the clock of the slaves, however. Instead, it stores the difference between the master and slave clocks and uses this difference value to maintain its lock on the master.

When another master takes control during a communication session, each slave readjusts the stored difference value to maintain its precise frequency coordination.

Topology

Bluetooth is designed to handle a variety of connection types. The basic link is *point-to-point*, two devices communicating only with one another. In such a link, one device operates as the *master* and the other as the *slave*. In a piconet configuration, a single master can communicate with up to seven active slaves (a total of eight devices intercommunicating). In addition, other slaves may lock on to the master's signal and be ready to communicate without sending out active signals. Such inactive slaves are said to be in a *parked* state.

The master in the piconet determines which devices can communicate (that is, which slaves are active or parked). In addition, several piconets can be linked together into a *scatternet*, with the master of one piconet communicating to a master or slave in another.

Frequencies

Bluetooth operates at radio frequencies assigned to industrial, scientific, and medical devices; a range termed the *ISM band*. This range of frequencies in the UHF (Ultra High Frequency) band has been set aside throughout most of the world for unlicensed, low-power electronic equipment. Near the top of the UHF range, the ISM band uses frequencies about twice that of the highest UHF television channel.

The exact frequencies available vary somewhat in North America, Europe, and Japan. In addition, France and Spain differ from the rest of Europe (although both countries are working on moving to the standards used throughout the rest of Europe).

Bluetooth uses channels one megahertz wide for its signals. Rather than operating on a single channel, a Bluetooth system uses them all. It uses the channels one at a time but switches between them to help minimize interference and fading. It can also help keep communications secure. Only the devices participating in a piconet know which channel they will hop to next.

In Europe (except France and Spain) and North America, the Bluetooth system can hop between 79 different channels. Elsewhere, the choices are limited to 23 channels. The available frequencies and number of channels available are summarized in the Table 11.5.

TABLE 11.5   Frequencies and Channels Available to Bluetooth

Location	Frequency Range	Channels Available
North America	2.400 to 2.4835GHz	79
Europe (except Spain and France)	2.400 to 2.4835GHz	79
Spain	2.445 to 2.475GHz	23
France	2.4465 to 2.4835GHz	23
Japan	2.471 to 2.497GHz	23

A given Bluetooth system does not operate on one frequency but rather uses them all, hopping from one channel to another, up to 1,600 times per second. If a given asynchronous packet does not get through on one frequency due to interference (and is therefore not acknowledged), the next hop will send out a duplicate packet at a different frequency.

Unfortunately, Bluetooth does not have the entire 2.4GHz band to itself. The IEEE 802.11 wireless-networking standard currently uses the same frequencies, and interference between the two systems (where both are active) is inevitable. Although in the long term IEEE 802.11 will migrate to the 5GHz frequency range, at present the only way to entirely prevent interference between the two systems is to use one or the other, not both.

Power

The Bluetooth specification defines three classes of equipment based on transmitter power. Class 1 devices are the most powerful and can transmit with up to 100 milliwatts of output power. Class 3 devices transmit with less than 1 milliwatt. Table 11.6 lists the maximum and minimum output powers for each power class.

TABLE 11.6   Powers Assigned to Bluetooth Power Classes

Power Class	Maximum Output Power	Minimum Output Power
1	100 mW	1 mW
2	2.5 mW	0.25 mW
3	1 mW	Not specified

As with any radio-based system, greater power increases the coverage area, so a Class 1 device will have greater range than a Class 3 device (about 10 times greater because radio propagation follows an inverse-square law). On the downside, greater output power means the need for greater input power, which directly translates into battery drain. That 100 mW of output power will require about 100 times the battery power as a 1-mW device. Fortunately, even Class 1 devices are modest power consumers compared to other facets of notebook computers. For example, the power needs of a Class 1 device are less than one-tenth the demand of a typical display screen.

Modulation

Bluetooth uses Gaussian frequency shift keying (FSK)—that is, the presence of a data bit alters (or *shifts*) the frequency of the carrier wave. Bluetooth specifies the polarity of the FSK modulation. It represents a binary one with a positive deviation of the carrier wave and a binary zero with a negative deviation. The raw data rate is 1Mbps (one million symbols per second).

Because of how the digital code affects the frequency shift keying modulation, the information content of the modulation affects the deviation of the signal. The Bluetooth standard specifies that the minimum deviation should never be smaller than 115KHz. The maximum deviation will be between 140 and 175KHz.

Components

Bluetooth architecture builds a system from three parts: a radio unit, a link control unit, and a support unit that provides link management and the host terminal interface. These are functional divisions, and all will be integrated into most handheld Bluetooth devices. In your PC, all three will likely reside on a Bluetooth interface card that installs like any other expansion board in a standard PCI slot.

The radio unit implements the hardware aspects of Bluetooth described earlier. It determines the power and coverage of the Bluetooth device, and its circuitry creates the carrier wave (altering its frequency for each hop), modulates it, amplifies it, and radiates it through an antenna. The ultra-high frequencies used by the Bluetooth system have a short wavelength that allows the antenna to be integrated invisibly into the cases of many mobile devices.

The link control unit is the mastermind of the Bluetooth system. It implements the various control and management protocols for setting up and maintaining the wireless connection. It searches out and identifies new devices wanting to join the piconet, tracks the frequency hopping, and controls the operating state of the device.

The support unit provides the actual interface between the logic of the host device and the Bluetooth connection. It adapts the signals of the host to match the Bluetooth system, both electrically and logically. For example, in a PC-based Bluetooth interface card, the support unit adapts the parallel bus signals of the PCI connection into the packetized serial form used by Bluetooth. It also checks data coming in from the wireless connection for errors and requests retransmission when necessary.

Standards and Coordination

The Bluetooth Special Interest Group promulgates the Bluetooth specifications. It also facilitates the licensing of Bluetooth intellectual property. You can obtain the complete specification from the SIG at www.bluetooth.com.

RS-232C Serial Ports

The day you win the vmega-lottery and instantly climb into wealth and social status, you may be tempted to leave your old friends to belch and scratch while drinking someone else's beer. But it's hard to leave old friends behind, particularly when you need someone to watch the house during your 'round-the-world cruise. So it is with the classic RS-232C port. It's got so many bad habits it's hard to talk about in polite company, but it's just too dang useful to forget about.

The serial port is truly the old codger of computer interfaces, a true child of the '60s. An industry trade group, the Electronics Industry Association (EIA) hammered out the official RS-232C specification in 1969, but the port had been in use for years at the time. It found ready acceptance on the first personal computer because no other electronic connection for data equipment was so widely used. The ports survive today because some folks still want to connect gear they bought in 1969 to their new computers.

Electrical Operation

RS-232C ports are asynchronous. They operate without a clock signal. But in order for two devices to communicate they need at least a general idea of what rate to expect data. Consequently, you must set the speed of each RS-232C port before you begin communicating, and the speeds of any two connected ports must match.

You have quite a wide variety to choose from. The serial ports in computers generally operate at any speed in the odd-looking sequence that runs 150, 300, 600, 1200, 2400, 4800, 9600, 19,200, 38,400, 57,600, and 115,200 bits per second.

The RS-232C moves data one byte at a time. To suit its asynchronous nature, each byte requires its own packing into a *serial frame*. In this form the typical serial port takes about a dozen bits to move a byte—a frame comprises two start bits, eight data bits, one parity bit, and one stop bit to indicate the end of the frame. As a result, a serial port has overhead of about one-third of its potential peak data rate. A 9600 bit per second serial connection actually moves text at about 800 characters per second (6400bps).

A basic RS-232C connection needs only three connections: one for sending data, one for receiving data, and a common ground. Most serial links also use hardware flow-control signals. The most common serial port uses eight separate connections.

RS-232C port use single-ended signaling. Although this design simplifies the circuitry to make the ports, it also limits the potential range of a connection. Long cable runs are apt to pick up noise and blur high-data-rate signals. You can probably extend a 9600bps connection to a hundred feet or more. At a quarter mile, you'll probably be down to 1200 or 300bps (slower than even cheap printers can type).

Because the RS-232C port originated in the data communications rather than computer industry, some of its terminology is different from that used to describe other ports. For example, the low and high logic states are termed *space* and *mark* in the RS-232C scheme. Space is the absence of a bit, and mark is the presence of a bit. On the serial line, a space is a positive voltage; a mark is a negative voltage.

In other words, when you're not sending data down a serial line, it has an overall positive voltage on it. Data will appear as a serial of negative-going pulses. The original design of the serial port specification called for the voltage to shift from a positive 12 volts to negative 12 volts. Because 12 volts is an uncommon potential in many computers, the serial voltage often varies from positive 5 to negative 5 volts.

Connectors

The physical manifestation of a serial port is the connector that glowers on the rear panel of your computer. It is where you plug your serial peripheral into your computer. And it can be the root of all evil—or so it will seem after a number of long evenings during which you valiantly try to make your serial device work with your computer, only to have text disappear like phantoms at sunrise. Again, the principal problem with serial ports is the number of options they allow designers. Serial ports can use either of two styles of connectors, each of which has two options in signal assignment. Worse, some manufacturers venture bravely in their own directions with the all-important flow-control signals. Sorting out all these options is the most frustrating part of serial port configuration.

25-Pin

The basic serial port connector is called a *25-pin D-shell*. It earns its name from having 25 connections arranged in two rows that are surrounded by a metal guide that roughly takes the form of a letter *D*. The male variety of this connector—the one that actually has pins inside it—is normally used on computers. Most, but hardly all, serial peripherals use the female connector (the one with holes instead of pins) for their serial ports. Although both serial and parallel ports use the same style 25-pin D-shell connectors, you can distinguish serial ports from parallel ports because on most computers the latter use female connectors. Figure 11.8 shows the typical male serial port DB-25 connector that you'll find on the back of your computer.

FIGURE 11.8

The male DB-25 connector used by serial ports on computers.

Although the serial connector allows for 25 discrete signals, only a few of them are ever actually used. Serial systems may involve as few as three connections. At most, computer serial ports use 10 different signals. Table 11.7 lists the names of these signals, their mnemonics, and the pins to which they are assigned in the standard 25-pin serial connector.

TABLE 11.7 25-Pin Serial Connector Signal Assignments

Pin	Function	Mnemonic
1	Chassis ground	None
2	Transmit data	TXD
3	Receive data	RXD

Pin	Function	Mnemonic
4	Request to send	RTS
5	Clear to send	CTS
6	Data set ready	RTS
7	Signal ground	GND
8	Carrier detect	CD
20	Data terminal ready	DTR
22	Ring indicator	RI

Note that in the standard serial cable, the signal ground (which is the return line for the data signals on pins 2 and 3) is separated from the chassis ground on pin 1. The chassis ground pin is connected directly to the metal chassis or case of the equipment, much like the extra prong of a three-wire AC power cable, and it provides the same protective function. It ensures that the case of the two devices linked by the serial cable are at the same potential, which means you won't get a shock if you touch both at the same time. As wonderful as this connection sounds, it is often omitted from serial cables. On the other hand, the signal ground is a necessary signal that the serial link cannot work without. You should never connect the chassis ground to the signal ground.

Nine-Pin

If nothing else, using a 25-pin D-shell connector for a serial port is a waste of at least 15 pins. Most serial connections use fewer than the complete 10; some as few as four with hardware handshaking, and three with software flow control. For the sake of standardization, the computer industry sacrificed the cost of the other unused pins for years until a larger—or smaller, depending on your point of view—problem arose: space. A serial port connector was too big to fit on the retaining brackets of expansion boards along with a parallel connector. In that all the pins in the parallel connector had an assigned function, the serial connector met its destiny and got miniaturized.

Moving to a nine-pin connector allowed engineers to put connectors for both a serial port and a parallel port on the retaining bracket of a single expansion board. This was an important concern because all ports in early computers were installed on expansion boards. Computer makers could save the cost of an entire expansion board by putting two ports on one card. Later, after most manufacturers moved to putting ports on computer motherboards, the smaller port design persisted.

As with the 25-pin variety of serial connector, the nine-pin serial jack on the back of computers uses a male connector. Figure 11.9 shows the nine-pin male connector that's used on some computers for serial ports.

FIGURE 11.9
*The male DB-9 plug
used by AT-class serial
devices.*

Nine-pin connectors necessarily have different pin assignments than 25-pin connectors. Table 11.8 lists the signal assignments on the most common nine-pin implementation of the RS-232C port.

TABLE 11.8   Nine-Pin Serial Connector

Pin	Function	Mnemonic
1	Carrier detect	CD
2	Receive data	RXD
3	Transmit data	TXD
4	Data terminal ready	DTR
5	Signal Ground	GND
6	Data set ready	DSR
7	Request to send	RTS
8	Clear to send	CTS
9	Ring indicator	RI

Other than the rearrangement of signals, the nine-pin and 25-pin serial connectors are essentially the same. All the signals behave identically, no matter the size of the connector on which they appear.

Signals

Serial communications is an exchange of signals across the serial interface. These signals involve not just data but also the flow-control signals that help keep the data flowing as fast as possible—but not too fast.

First, we'll look at the signals and their flow in the kind of communication system for which the serial port was designed—linking a computer to a modem. Then we'll examine how attaching a serial peripheral to a serial port complicates matters and what you can do to make the connection work.

Definitions

As with space and mark, RS-232C ports use other odd terminology. Serial terminology assumes that each end of a connection has a different type of equipment attached to it.

One end has a *data terminal* connected to it. In the old days when the serial port was developed, a terminal was exactly that—a keyboard and a screen that translated typing into serial signals. Today, a terminal is usually a computer. For reasons known but to those who revel in rolling their tongues across excess syllables, the term *Data Terminal Equipment* is often substituted. To make matters even more complex, many discussions talk about *DTE* devices, which means exactly the same thing as *data terminals*.

The other end of the connection has a *data set*, which corresponds to a modem. Often engineers substitute the more formal name *Data Communication Equipment* or talk about *DCE* devices.

The distinction between data terminals and data sets (or DTE and DCE devices) is important. Serial communications were originally designed to take place between one DTE and one DCE, and the signals used by the system are defined in those terms. Moreover, the types of RS-232 serial devices you wish to connect determines the kind of cable you *must* use. First, however, let's look at the signals; then we'll consider what kind of cable you need to carry them.

Transmit Data

The serial data leaving the RS-232 port travels on what is called the *Transmit Data* line, which is usually abbreviated *TXD*. The signal on it comprises the long sequence of pulses generated by the UART in the serial port. The data terminal sends out this signal, and the data set listens to it.

Receive Data

The stream of bits going the other direction—that is, coming in from a distant serial port—goes through the *Receive Data* line (usually abbreviated *RXD*) to reach the input of the serial port's UART. The data terminal listens on this line for the data signal coming from the data set.

Data Terminal Read

When the data terminal is able to participate in communications—that is, it is turned on and in the proper operating mode—it signals its readiness to the data set by applying a positive voltage to the *Data Terminal Ready* line, which is abbreviated *DTR*.

Data Set Ready

When the data set is able to receive data—that is, it is turned on and in the proper operating mode—it signals its readiness by applying a positive voltage to the *Data Set Ready* line, which is abbreviated *DSR*. Because serial communications must be "two way," the data terminal will not send out a data signal unless it sees the DSR signal coming from the data set.

Request to Send

When the data terminal is on and capable of receiving transmissions, it puts a positive voltage on its *Request to Send* line, usually abbreviated *RTS*. This signal tells the data set that it can send data to the data terminal. The absence of an RTS signal across the serial connection will prevent the data set from sending out serial data. This allows the data terminal to control the flow of the data set to it.

Clear to Send

The data set, too, needs to control the signal flow from the data terminal. The signal it uses is called *Clear to Send*, which is abbreviated *CTS*. The presence of the CTS signal in effect tells the data terminal that the coast is clear and the data terminal can blast data down the line. The absence of a CTS signal across the serial connection will prevent the data terminal from sending out serial data.

Carrier Detect

The serial interface standard shows its roots in the communication industry with the *Carrier Detect* signal, which is usually abbreviated *CD*. This signal gives a modem, the typical data set, a means of signaling to the data terminal that it has made a connection with a distant modem. The signal says that the modem or data set has detected the carrier wave of another modem on the telephone line. In effect, the carrier detect signal gets sent to the data terminal to tell it that communications are possible. In some systems, the data terminal must see the carrier detect signal before it will engage in data exchange. Other systems simply ignore this signal.

Ring Indicator

Sometimes a data terminal has to get ready to communicate even before the flow of information begins. For example, you might want to switch your communications program into answer mode so that it can deal with an incoming call. The designers of the serial port provided such an early warning in the *Ring Indicator* signal, which is usually abbreviated *RI*. When a modem serving as a data set detects ringing voltage—the low-frequency, high-voltage signal that makes telephone bells ring—on the telephone line to which it is connected, it activates the RI signal, which alerts the data terminal to what's going on. Although useful in setting up modem communications, you can regard the ring indicator signal as optional because its absence usually will not prevent the flow of serial data.

Signal Ground

All the signals used in a serial port need a return path. The signal ground provides this return path. The single ground signal is the common return for all other signals on the serial interface. Its absence will prevent serial communications entirely.

Flow Control

Serial ports can use both hardware and software flow control. *Hardware flow control* involves the use of special control lines that can be (but don't have to be) part of a serial connection. Your computer signals whether it is ready to accept more data by sending a signal down the appropriate wire. *Software flow control* involves the exchange of characters between computer and serial peripherals. One character tells the computer your peripheral is ready, and another warns that it can't deal with more data. Both hardware and software flow control take more than one form. As a default, computer serial ports use hardware flow control (or hardware handshaking). Most serial peripherals do, too. In general, hardware flow control uses the Carrier Detect, Clear to Send, and Data Set Ready signals.

Software flow control requires your serial peripheral and computer to exchange characters or tokens to indicate whether they should transfer data. The serial peripheral normally sends out one character to indicate it can accept data and a different character to indicate that it is busy and cannot accommodate more. Two pairs of characters are often used: XON/XOFF and ETX/ACK.

Cables

The design of the standard RS-232 serial interface anticipates that you will connect a data terminal to a data set. When you do, all the connections at one end of the cable that link them are carried through to the other end—pin for pin, connection for connection. The definitions of the signals at each end of the cable are the same, and the function and direction of travel (whether from data terminal to data set or the other way around) of each are well defined. Each signal goes straight through from one end to the other. Even the connectors are the same at either end. Consequently, a serial cable should be relatively easy to fabricate.

In the real world, nothing is so easy. Serial cables are usually much less complicated or much more complicated than this simple design. Unfortunately, if you plan to use a serial connection for a printer or plotter, you have to suffer through the more complex design.

Straight-Through Cables

Serial cables are often simpler than pin-for-pin connections from one end to the other because no serial link uses all 25 connector pins. Even with the complex handshaking schemes used by modems, only nine signals need to travel from the data terminal to the data set, computer to modem. (For signaling purposes, the two grounds are redundant— most serial cables do not connect the chassis ground.) Consequently, you need only make these 10 connections to make virtually any data terminal–to–data set link work. Assuming you have a 25-pin D-shell connector at either end of your serial cable, the essential pins that must be connected are 2 through 8, 20, and 22 on a 25-pin D-shell connector. This is usually called a *nine-wire serial cable* because the connection to pin 7 uses the shield of the cable rather than a wire inside. With nine-pin connectors at either end of your serial cable, all nine connections are essential.

Not all systems use all the handshaking signals, so you can often get away with fewer connections in a serial cable. The minimal case is a system that uses software handshaking only. In that case, you need only three connections: Transmit Data, Receive Data, and the signal ground. In other words, you need only connect pins 2, 3, and 7 on a 25-pin connector or pins 2, 3, and 5 on a nine-pin serial connector (providing, of course, you have the same size connector at each end of the cable).

Although cables with an intermediary number of connections are often available, they are not sufficiently less expensive than the nine-wire cable to justify the risk and lack of versatility. Therefore, you should limit your choices to a nine-wire cable for systems that use hardware handshaking or three-wire cables for those that you're certain use only software flow control.

Manufacturers use a wide range of cable types for serial connections. For relatively low data rates and reasonable lengths of serial connections, you can get away with just about anything, including twisted-pair telephone wire. To ensure against interference, you should use shielded cable, which wraps a wire braid or aluminum-coated plastic film around inner conductors to prevent signals leaking out or in. The shield of the cable should be connected to the signal ground. (Ideally, the signal ground should have its own wire, and the shield should be connected to the chassis ground, but most folks just don't bother.)

Adapter Cables

If you need a cable with a 25-pin connector at one end and a nine-pin connector at the other, you cannot use a straight-through design, even when you want to link a data terminal to a data set. The different signal layouts of the two styles of connectors are incompatible. After all, you can't possibly link pin 22 on a 25-pin connector to a nonexistent pin 22 on a nine-pin connector.

This problem is not uncommon. Even though the nine-pin connector has become a *de facto* standard on computers, most other equipment, including serial plotters, printers, and modems, has stuck with the 25-pin standard. To get from one connector type to another, you need an adapter. The adapter can take the form of a small assembly with a connector on each end of an adapter cable, typically from six inches to six feet long.

Crossover Cables

As long as you want to connect a computer serial port that functions to a modem, you should have no problem with serial communications. You will be connecting a data terminal to a data set, exactly what engineers designed the serial systems for. Simply sling a cable with enough conductors to handle all the vital signals between the computer and modem and—voilà—serial communications without a hitch. Try it, and you're likely to wonder why so many people complain about the capricious nature of serial connections.

When you want to connect a plotter or printer to a computer through a serial port, however, you will immediately encounter a problem. The architects of the RS-232 serial system decided that both computers and the devices are data terminal (DTE) devices. The designations actually made sense, at least at that time. You were just as likely to connect a serial printer (such as a teletype) to a modem as you were a computer terminal. There was no concern about connecting a printer to a computer because computers didn't even exist back then.

When you connect a plotter or printer and your computer—or any two DTE devices—together with an ordinary serial cable, you will not have a communication system at all. Neither machine will know that the other one is even there. Each one will listen on the serial port signal line that the other is listening to, and each one will talk on the line that the other talks on. One device won't hear a bit of what the other is saying.

The obvious solution to the problem is to switch some wires around. Move the Transmit Data wire from the computer to where the Receive Data wire goes on the plotter or printer. Route the computer's Receive Data wire to the Transmit Data wire of the plotter or printer. A simple *crossover cable* does exactly that, switching the Transmit and Receive signals at one end of the connection.

Many of the devices that you plug into a computer are classed as DTE (or data terminals), just like the computer. All these will require a crossover cable. Table 11.9 lists many of the devices you might connect to your computer and whether they function as data terminals (DTE) or data sets (DCE).

TABLE 11.9   Common Serial Device Types

Peripheral	Device Type	Cable Needed to Connect to PC
PC	DTE	Crossover
Modem	DCE	Straight-through
Mouse	DCE	Straight-through
Trackball	DCE	Straight-through
Digitizer	DCE	Straight-through
Scanner	DCE	Straight-through
Serial printer	DTE	Crossover
Serial plotter	DTE	Crossover

Note that some people call crossover cables *null modem cables*. This is not correct. A null modem is a single connector used in testing serial ports. It connects the Transmit Data line to the Receive Data line of a serial port as well as crosses the handshaking connections within the connector as described earlier. Correctly speaking, a null modem cable is equipped with this kind of wiring at both ends. It will force both serial ports constantly on and prevent any hardware flow control from functioning at all. Although such a cable can be useful, it is not the same as a crossover cable. Substituting one for the other will lead to some unpleasant surprises—such as text dropping from sight from within documents as mysteriously and irrecoverably as D. B. Cooper.

UARTs

A serial port has two jobs to perform. It must repackage parallel data into serial form, and it must send power down a long wire with another circuit at the end, which is called *driving the line*.

Turning parallel data into serial is such a common electrical function that engineers created special integrated circuits that do exactly that. Called *Universal Asynchronous Receiver/Transmitter* chips, or *UARTs*, these chips gulp down a byte or more of data and stream it out a bit at a time. In addition, they add all the other accouterments of the serial signal—the start, parity, and stop bits. Because every practical serial connection is bidirectional, the UART works both ways, sending and receiving, as its name implies.

Because the UART does all the work of serializing your computer's data signals, its operation is one of the limits on the performance of serial data exchanges. Computers have used three different generations of UARTs, each of which imposes its own constraints. Early computers used 8250 UARTs, and later machines shifted to the higher-speed 16450 UART. Both of these chips had one-byte buffers that were unable to keep up with normal communications when multitasking software came into use. The replacement was the 16550A UART (commonly listed as 16550AF and 16550AFN, with the last initials indicating the package and temperature rating of the chip), which has a 16-byte *First In, First Out* (FIFO) buffer.

To maintain backward compatibility with the 16450, the 16550 ignores its internal buffer until it is specifically switched on. Most communications programs activate the buffer automatically. Physically, the 16550 and 16450 will fit and operate in the same sockets, so you can easily upgrade the older chip to the newer one.

Modern computers do not use separate UARTs. However, all the UART circuitry—usually exactly equivalent to that of the 16550A—is built into the circuitry of nearly all chipsets. To your software, the chipset acts exactly as if your serial ports were on separate expansion boards, just as they were in the first personal computers.

Register Function

The register at the base address assigned to each serial port is used for data communications. Bytes are moved to and from the UART using the microprocessor's OUT and IN instructions. The next six addresses are used by other serial port registers. They are, in order, the Interrupt Enable register, the Interrupt Identification register, the Line Control register, the Modem Control register, the Line Status register, and the Modem Status register. Another register, called the Divisor Latch, shares the base address used by the Transmit and Receive registers and the next higher register used by the Interrupt Enable register. It is accessed by toggling a setting in the Line Control register.

This latch stores the divisor that determines the operating speed of the serial port. Whatever value is loaded into the latch is multiplied by 16. The resulting product is used to divide down the clock signal supplied to the UART chip to determine the bit rate. Because of the factor of 16 multiplication, the highest speed the serial port can operate at is limited to 1/16th the supplied clock (which is 1.8432MHz). Setting the latch value to its minimum, 1, results in a bit rate of 115,200.

Registers not only store the values used by the UART chip but also are used to report back to your system how the serial conversation is progressing. For example, the line status register indicates whether a character that has been loaded to be transmitted has actually been sent. It also indicates when a new character has been received.

Logical Interface

Your computer controls the serial port UART through a set of seven registers built in to the chip. Although your programs could send data and commands to the UART (and, through it, to your serial device) by using the hardware address of the registers on the chip, this strategy has disadvantages. It requires the designers of systems to allocate once and forever the system resources used by the serial port. The designers of the original IBM computer were loathe to make such a permanent commitment. Instead they devised a more flexible system that allows your software to access ports by name. In addition, they worked out a way that port names would be assigned properly and automatically, even if you didn't install ports in some predetermined order.

Port Names

The number of serial ports you can use in a computer varies with the operating system. Originally, personal computers could only use two, but in 1987 the designers of DOS expanded the possible port repertory to include COM3 and COM4. Under Windows 3.1, up to nine serial ports could be used. Windows versions since Windows 95 extend serial port support to 128.

Without special drivers, Windows recognizes four serial ports. When Windows checks your system hardware each time it boots up, it check the ranges of addresses normally used by the UART chips for serial ports. Each UART has seven registers that control it, and these are usually identified by a *base address*, the input/output port used by the first of these registers. The usual computer design allows for four base addresses for a serial port.

Current Windows versions search the nominal base addresses for serial ports and assign their serial port drivers to those that are active. Devices out of the normal range—including the serial ports built in to internal modems—require their own drivers to match their hardware.

Interrupts

Serial ports normally operate as interrupt-driven devices. That is, when they must perform an action immediately, they send a special signal called an *interrupt* to your computer's microprocessor. In the traditional computer design, only two interrupts are available for serial ports, as listed in Table 11.10.

TABLE 11.10   Default Settings for DOS and Windows Serial Ports

Port Name	Base Address	Interrupt
COM1	03F8(hex)	4
COM2	02F8(hex)	3
COM3	03E8(hex)	4
COM4	02E8(hex)	3

Systems with more than two serial ports (or oddly assigned interrupts) have to share two interrupts between these serial ports—one port is often assigned to two ports. This sometimes results in problems, particularly when a mouse is connected to a serial port. However, because all new computers have a dedicated mouse port, this problem no longer occurs.

Parallel Ports

The defining characteristic of the parallel port design is implicit in its name. The port is "parallel" because it conducts its signals through eight separate wires—one for each bit of a byte of data—that are enclosed together in a single cable. The signal wires literally run in parallel from your computer to their destination—or at least they did. Better cables twist the physical wires together but keep their signals straight (and parallel).

In theory, having eight wires means you can move data eight times as fast through a parallel connection than through a single wire. All else being equal, simple math would make this statement true. Although a number of practical concerns make such extrapolations impossible, throughout its life, the parallel port has been known for its speed. It beat its original competitor, the RS-232 port, hands down, outrunning the serial port's 115.2Kbps maximum by factors from two to five, even in early computers. The latest incarnations of parallel technology put the data rate through the parallel connection at over 100 times faster than the basic serial port rate.

In simple installations (for example, when used for its original purpose of linking a printer to your computer), the parallel port is a model of installation elegance. Just plug in your printer, and the odds are it will work flawlessly—or that whatever flaws appear won't have anything to do with the interconnection.

Despite such rave reviews, parallel ports are not trouble-free. All parallel ports are not created equal. A number of different designs have appeared during the brief history of the computer. Although new computers usually incorporate the latest, most versatile, and highest speed of these, some manufacturers skimp. Even when you buy a brand-new computer, you may end up with a simple printer port that steps back to the first generation of computer design.

A suitable place to being this saga is to sort out this confusion of parallel port designs by tracing the parallel port's origins. As it turns out, the history of the parallel port is a long one, older than even the personal computer, although the name and our story begin with its introduction.

History

Necessity isn't just the mother of invention. It also spawned the parallel port. As with most great inventions, the parallel port arose with a problem that needed to be solved. When IBM developed its first computer, its engineers looked for a simplified way to link to a printer, something without the hassles and manufacturing costs of a serial port. The simple parallel connection, already used in a similar form by some printers, was an elegant solution. Consequently, IBM's slightly modified version became standard equipment on the first computers. Because of its intended purpose, it quickly gained the "printer port" epithet. Not only were printers easy to attach to a parallel port, they were the only thing that you could connect to these first ports at the time.

In truth, the contribution of computer-makers to the first parallel port was minimal. They added a new connector that better fit the space available on the computer. The actual port design was already being used on computer printers at the time. Originally created by printer-maker Centronics Data Computer Corporation and used by printers throughout the 1960s and 1970s, the connection was electrically simple, even elegant. It took little circuitry to add to a printer or computer, even in the days when designers had to use discrete components instead of custom-designed circuits. A few old-timers still cling to history and call the parallel port a *Centronics* port.

The computer parallel port is not identical to the exact Centronics design, however. In adapting it to the computer, IBM substituted a smaller connector. The large jack used by the Centronics design had 36 pins and was too large to put where IBM wanted it—sharing a card-retaining bracket with a video connector on the computer's first Monochrome Display Adapter. In addition, IBM added two new signals to give the computer more control over the printer and adjusted the timing of the signals traveling through the interface. All that said, most Centronics-style printers worked just fine with the original computer.

At the time, the computer parallel port had few higher aspirations. It did its job, and did it well, moving data in one direction (from computer to printer) at rates from 50 to 150Kbps. The computer parallel port, or subtle variations of it, became ubiquitous if not universal. Any printer worth connecting to a computer used a parallel port (or so it seemed).

In 1987, however, IBM's engineers pushed the parallel port in a new direction. The motive behind the change was surprising—not a desire to improve communication but rather a band-aid solution for a temporary problem (for which it was hardly ever used). The company decided to adopt the 3.5-inch floppy disk drives for its new line of PS/2 computers at a time when all the world's computer data was mired on 5.25-inch diskettes. The new computers made no provision for building in the bigger drives. Instead, IBM believed that the entire world would instantly switch over to the new disk format. People would need to transfer their data once and only once to the new disk format. To make the transfer possible, the company released its *Data Migration Facility*, a fancy name for a cable and a couple disks. You used the cable to connect your old computer to your new PS/2 and software on the disks to move files through the parallel port from the old machine and disks to the new.

Implicit in this design is the ability of the PS/2 parallel port to receive data as well as send it out, as to a printer. The engineers tinkered with the port design and made it work both ways, creating a *bidirectional parallel port*. Because of the design's intimate connection with the PS/2, it is sometimes termed the *PS/2 parallel port*.

The Data Migration Facility proved to be an inspirational idea despite its singular shortcoming of working in only one direction. As notebook computers became popular, they also needed a convenient means to move files between machines. The makers of file transfer programs such as Brooklyn Bridge and LapLink knew a good connection when they saw it. By tinkering with parallel port signals, they discovered that they could make any parallel port operate in both directions and move data to and from computers.

The key to making bidirectional transfers on the old-fashioned one-way ports was to redefine signals. They redirected tours of the signals in the parallel connector that originally had been designed to convey status information back from the printer to your computer. These signals already went in the correct direction. All that the software mavens did was to take direct control of the port and monitor the signals under their new definitions. Of course, four signals can't make a byte. They were limited to shifting four bits through the port in the backward direction. Because four bits make a nibble, the new parallel port operating mode soon earned the name *nibble mode*.

This four-bits-at-a-time scheme had greater implications than just a new name. Half as many bits also means half the speed. Nibble mode operates at about half the normal parallel port rate—still faster than single-line serial ports but not full parallel speed.

If both sides of a parallel connection had bidirectional ports, however, data transfers ran at full speed both ways. Unfortunately, as manufacturers began adapting higher-performance peripherals to use the parallel port, what once was fast performance became agonizingly slow. Although the bidirectional parallel port more than met the modest data transfer needs of printers and floppy disk drives, it lagged behind other means of connecting hard disks and networks to computers.

Engineers at network adapter maker Xircom Incorporated decided to do something about parallel performance and banded together with notebook computer maker Zenith Data Systems to find a better solution. Along the way, they added Intel Corporation and formed a triumvirate called *Enhanced Parallel Port Partnership*. They explored two ways of increasing the data throughput of a parallel port. They streamlined the logical interface so that your computer would need less overhead to move each byte through the port. In addition, they tightly defined the timing of the signals passing through the port, minimizing wasted time and helping ensure against timing errors. They called the result of their efforts the *Enhanced Parallel Port* (EPP).

On August 10, 1991, the organization released its first description of what it thought the next generation of parallel ports should be and do. The organization continued to work on a specification until March 1992, when it submitted Release 1.7 to the Institute of Electrical and Electronic Engineers (IEEE) to be considered as an industry standard.

Although the EPP version of the parallel port could increase its performance by nearly tenfold, that wasn't enough to please everybody. The speed potential made some engineers see the old parallel port as an alternative to more complex expansion buses such as the SCSI system. With this idea in mind, Hewlett-Packard joined with Microsoft to make the parallel port into a universal expansion standard called the *extended capabilities port (ECP)*. In November 1992, the two companies released the first version of the ECP specification, aimed at computers that use the ISA expansion bus. This first implementation added two new transfer modes to the EPP design—a fast two-way communication mode between a computer and its peripherals, and another two-way mode with performance further enhanced by simple integral data compression—and defined a complete software control system.

The heart of the ECP innovation was a protocol for exchanging data across a high-speed parallel connection. The devices at the two ends of each ECP transfer negotiate the speed and mode of data movement. Your computer can query any ECP device to determine its capabilities. For example, your computer can determine what language your printer speaks and set up the proper printer driver accordingly. In addition, ECP devices tell your computer the speed at which they can accept transmissions and the format of the data they understand. To ensure the quality of all transmissions, the ECP specification included error detection and device handshaking. It also allowed the use of data compression to further speed transfers.

On March 30, 1994, the IEEE Standards Board approved its parallel port standard, *IEEE-1284-1994*. The standard included all the basic modes and parallel port designs, including both ECP and EPP. It was submitted to the American National Standards Institute and approved as a standard on September 2, 1994.

The IEEE 1284 standard marked a watershed in parallel port design and nomenclature. The standard defined (or redefined) all aspects of the parallel connection, from the software interface in your computer to the control electronics in your printer. It divided the world of parallel ports in two: *IEEE 1284-compatible devices*, which are those that will work with the new interface, which in turn includes just about every parallel port and device ever made; and *IEEE 1284-compliant devices*, which are those that understand and use the new standard. This distinction is essentially between pre- and post-standardization ports. You can consider IEEE 1284-*compatible* ports to be "old technology" and IEEE 1284-*compliant* ports to be "new technology."

Before IEEE 1284, parallel ports could be divided into four types: standard parallel ports, bidirectional parallel ports (also known as *PS/2 parallel ports*), enhanced parallel ports, and extended capabilities ports. The IEEE specification redefined the differences in ports, classifying them by the transfer mode they use. Although the terms are not exactly the same, you can consider a standard parallel port one that is able to use only nibble-mode transfers. A PS/2 or bidirectional parallel port from the old days is one that can also make use of byte-mode transfers. EPP and ECP ports are those that use EPP and ECP modes, as described by the IEEE 1284 specification.

EPP and ECP remain standards separate from IEEE 1284, although they have been revised to depend on it. Both EPP and ECP rely on their respective modes as defined in the IEEE specification for their physical connections and electrical signaling. In other words, IEEE 1284 describes the physical and electrical characteristics of a variety of parallel ports. The other standards describe how the ports operate and link to your applications.

Connectors

The best place to begin any discussion of the function and operation of the parallel port is the connector. After all, the connector is what puts the port to work. It is the physical manifestation of the parallel port, the one part of the interface and standard you can actually touch or hold in your hand. It is the only part of the interface that most people will ever have to deal with. Once you know the ins and outs of parallel connectors, you'll be able to plug in the vast majority of computer printers and the myriad of other things that now suck signals from what was once the printer's port.

Unfortunately, as with the variety of operating modes, the parallel port connector itself is not a single thing.

Parallel ports use three different connectors, called A, B, and C.

The A connector

The A connector appears only on computers as the output of a parallel port. Technically, it is described as a female 25-pin D-shell connector. Engineers chose this particular connector pragmatically—it was readily available and was the smallest connector that could handle the signals required in a full parallel connection. After it became ubiquitous, the IEEE adopted it as its 1284-A connector. Figure 11.10 shows a conceptual view of the A connector.

FIGURE 11.10

The IEEE-1284 A connector, a female 25-pin D-shell jack.

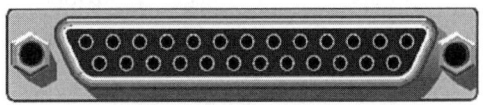

Of the 25 contacts on this parallel port connector, 17 are assigned individual signals for data transfer and control. The remaining eight serve as ground returns. Under the IEEE 1284 specification, the definition of each signal on each pin is dependent on the operating mode of the port. Only the definitions change; the physical wiring inside your computer and inside the cables does not change—if it did, shifting modes would be far from trivial. The altered definitions change the protocol, which is the signal handshaking that mediates each transfer.

A single physical connector on the back of your computer can operate in any of these five modes, and the signal definitions and their operation will change accordingly. Table 11.11 lists these five modes and their signal assignments.

TABLE 11.11   IEEE 1284-A Connector Signal Assignments in All Modes

Pin	Compatibility Mode	Nibble Mode	Byte Mode	EPP Mode	ECP Mode
1	nStrobe	HostClk	HostClk	nWrite	HostClk
2	Data 1	Data 1	Data 1	AD1	Data 1
3	Data 2	Data 2	Data 2	AD2	Data 2
4	Data 3	Data 3	Data 3	AD3	Data 3
5	Data 4	Data 4	Data 4	AD4	Data 4
6	Data 5	Data 5	Data 5	AD5	Data 5
7	Data 6	Data 6	Data 6	AD6	Data 6
8	Data 7	Data 7	Data 7	AD7	Data 7
9	Data 8	Data 8	Data 8	AD8	Data8
10	nAck	PtrClk	PtrClk	Intr	PeriphClk
11	Busy	PtrBusy	PtrBusy	nWait	PeriphAck
12	PError	AckDataReq	AckDataReq	User defined 1	nAckReverse
13	Select	Xflag	Xflag	User defined 3	Xflag
14	nAutoFd	HostBusy	HostBusy	nDStrb	HostAck
15	nFault	nDataAvail	nDataAvail	User defined 2	nPeriphRequest
16	nInit	nInit	nInt	nInt	nReverseRequest
17	nSelectIn	1284 Active	1284 Active	nAStrb	1284 Active
18	Pin 1 (nStrobe) ground return				
19	Pins 2 and 3 (Data 1 and 2) ground return				
20	Pins 4 and 5 (Data 3 and 4) ground return				
21	Pins 6 and 7 (Data 5 and 6) ground return				
22	Pins 8 and 9 (Data 7 and 8) ground return				

Pin	Compatibility Mode	Nibble Mode	Byte Mode	EPP Mode	ECP Mode
23	Pins 11 and 15 ground return				
24	Pins 10, 12, and 13 ground return				
25	Pins 14, 16, and 17 ground return				

Along with standardized signal assignments, IEEE 1284 also gives us a standard nomenclature for describing the signals. In Table 11.11, as well as all following tables that refer to the standard, signal names prefaced with a lowercase *n* indicate that the signal goes negative when active (that is, the absence of a voltage means the signal is present).

Mode changes are negotiated between your computer and the printer or other peripheral connected to the parallel port. Consequently, both ends of the connection switch modes together so that the signal assignments remain consistent at both ends of the connection. For example, if you connect an older printer that only understands compatibility mode, your computer cannot negotiate any other operating mode with the printer. It will not activate its EPP or ECP mode, so your printer will never get signals it cannot understand. This negotiation of the mode ensures backward compatibility among parallel devices.

The B Connector

The parallel port input to printers is quite a different connector from that on your computer. In fact, the design predates personal computers, having first been used by a printer company, Centronics, which gave the connector and parallel port its alternate name (now falling into disuse). The design is a 36-pin ribbon connector (the contacts take the form of thin metal ribbons) in a D-shell. Figure 11.11 shows this connector as a jack that would appear on the back of a printer.

FIGURE 11.11
The IEEE-1284 B connector, a 36-pin ribbon jack.

The assignment of signals to the individual pins of this connector has gone through three stages. The first standard was set by Centronics for its printers. In 1981, IBM altered this design somewhat by redefining several of the connections. Finally, in 1994, the IEEE published its standard assignments, which (like those of the A-connector) vary with operating mode.

The C Connector

Given a chance to start over with a clean slate and no installed base, engineers would hardly come up with the confusion of two different connectors with an assortment of different, sometimes-compatible operating modes. The IEEE saw the creation of the 1284 standard as such an opportunity, one they were happy to exploit. To eliminate the confusion of two connectors and the intrinsic need for adapters to move between them, they took the logical step: They created a third connector, IEEE 1284-C.

For the most part, the C connector is just the B connector with some of the air let out. Figure 11.12 shows a jack that you'd find on the back of equipment using C connectors.

FIGURE 11.12
Conceptual view of the 1284-C parallel port connector.

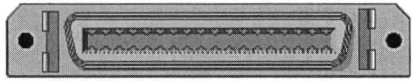

Adapters

The standard printer cable for computers is an adapter cable. It rearranges the signals of the A connector to the scheme of the B connector. Ever since the introduction of the first computer, you needed this sort of cable just to make your printer work. Over the years they have become plentiful and cheap.

To cut costs, many makers of adapter cables group all the grounds together as a single common line so that you need only 18 instead of 25 conductors in the connecting cable. Cheap adapters, *which do not meet the IEEE 1284 standard*, use this approach.

A modern printer cable should contain a full 25 connections with the ground signals divided up among separate pins. A true *IEEE 1284 printer cable* is equipped with an A connector on one end and a B connector on the other, with the full complement of connections in between.

As new peripherals with the 1284-C connector become available, you'll need to plug them into your computer. To attach your existing computer to a printer or other device using the C connector, you'll need an adapter cable to convert the A connector layout to the C connector design. On the other hand, if your next computer or parallel adapter uses the C connector and you plan to stick with your old printer, you'll need another variety of adapter—one that translates the C connector layout to that of the B connector.

Cable

The high-speed modes of modern parallel ports make them finicky. When your parallel port operates in EPP or ECP mode, cable quality becomes critical, even for short runs. Signaling speed across one of these interfaces can be in the megahertz range. The frequencies far exceed the reliable limits of even short runs of the dubious low-cost printer cables. Consequently, the IEEE 1284 specification precisely details a special cable for high-speed operation. Figure 11.13 offers a conceptual view of the construction of this special parallel data cable.

FIGURE 11.13
IEEE 1284 cable construction details.

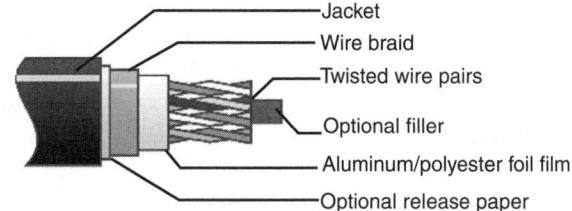

- Jacket
- Wire braid
- Twisted wire pairs
- Optional filler
- Aluminum/polyester foil film
- Optional release paper

Unlike standard parallel wiring, the data lines in IEEE 1284 cables must be double-shielded to prevent interference from affecting the signals. Each signal wire must be twisted with its ground return. Even though the various standard connectors do not provide separate pins for each of these grounds, the ground wires must be present and run the full length of the cable.

The differences between old-fashioned "printer" cables and those that conform to the IEEE 1284 standard are substantial. Although you can plug in a printer with either a printer or IEEE 1284–compliant cable, devices that exploit the high-speed potentials of the EPP or ECP designs may not operate properly with a noncompliant cable. Often, even when a printer fails to operate properly, the cable may be at fault. Substituting a truly IEEE 1284–compliant cable will bring reluctant connections to life.

Electrical Operation

In each of its five modes, the IEEE 1284 parallel port operates as if it were some kind of completely different electronic creation. When in compatibility mode, the IEEE 1284 port closely parallels the operation of the plain-vanilla printer port of bygone days. It allows data to travel in one direction only, from computer to printer. Nibble mode gives your printer (or more likely, another peripheral) a voice and allows it to talk back to your computer. In nibble mode, data can move in either of two directions, although asymmetrically. Information flows faster to your printer than it does on the return trip. Byte mode makes the journey fully symmetrical.

With the shift to EPP mode, the parallel port becomes a true expansion bus. A new way of linking to your computer's bus gives it increased bidirectional speed. Many systems can run their parallel ports 10 times faster in EPP mode than in compatibility, nibble, or byte mode. ECP mode takes the final step, giving control in addition to speed. ECP can do just about anything any other expansion interface (including SCSI) can do.

Because of these significant differences, the best way to get to know the parallel port is by considering each separately as if it were an interface unto itself. Our examination will follow from simple to complex, which also mirrors the history of the parallel port.

Note that IEEE 1284 deals only with the signals traveling through the connections of the parallel interface. It establishes the relationship between signals and their timing. It concerns itself neither with the data that is actually transferred, with the command protocols encoded in the data, nor with the control system that produces the signals. In other words, IEEE 1284 provides an environment under which other standards such as EPP and ECP operate. That is, ECP and EPP modes are not the ECP and EPP standards, although those modes are meant to be used by the parallel ports operating under respective standards.

Compatibility Mode

The least common denominator among parallel ports is the classic design that IBM introduced with its first computer. It was conceived strictly as a interface for the one-way transfer of information. Your computer sends data to your printer and expects nothing in return. After all, a printer neither stores information nor creates information on its own.

In conception, this port is like a conveyor that unloads ore from a bulk freighter or rolls coal out of a mine. The raw material travels in one direction. The conveyor mindlessly pushes out stuff and more stuff, perhaps creating a dangerously precarious pile, until its operator wakes up and switches it off before the pile gets much higher than his waist.

If your printer had unlimited speed or an unlimited internal buffer, such a one-way design would work. But like the coal yard, your printer has a limited capacity and may not be able to cart off data as fast as the interface shoves it out. The printer needs some way of sending a signal to your computer to warn about a potential data overflow. In electronic terms, the interface needs *feedback* of some kind—it needs to get information from the printer that your computer can use to control the data flow.

To provide the necessary feedback for controlling the data flow, the original Centronics port design and IBM's adaptation of it both included several control signals. These were designed to allow your computer to monitor how things are going with your printer—whether data is piling up, whether the printer has sufficient paper or ribbon, and even whether the printer is turned on. Your computer can use this information to moderate the outflowing gush of data or to post a message warning you that something is wrong with your printer. In addition, the original parallel port included control signals sent from your computer to the printer to tell it *when* the computer wanted to transfer data and to tell the printer to reset itself. The IEEE 1284 standard carries all these functions into compatibility mode.

Strictly speaking, then, even this basic parallel port is not truly a one-way connection, although its feedback provisions were designed strictly for monitoring rather than data flow. For the first half of its life, the parallel port kept to this design. Until the adoption of IEEE 1284, this was the design you could expect for the port on your printer and, almost as likely, those on your computer.

Each signal flowing through the parallel port in compatibility mode has its own function in handling the transfer of data.

Data Lines

The eight *data lines* of the parallel interface convey data in all operating modes. In compatibility mode, they carry data from the host to the peripheral on connector pins 2 through 9. The higher numbered pins are the more significant to the digital code. To send data to the peripheral, the host puts a pattern of digital voltages on the data lines.

Strobe Line

The presence of signals on the data lines does not, in itself, move information from host to peripheral. As your computer gets its act together, the pattern of data bits may vary in the process of loading the correct values. No hardware can ensure that all eight will always pop to the correct values simultaneously. Moreover, without further instruction your printer has no way of knowing whether the data lines represent a single character or multiple repetitions of the same character.

To ensure reliable communications, the system requires a means of telling the peripheral that the pattern on the data lines represents valid information to be transferred. The *strobe line* does exactly that. Your computer pulses the strobe line to tell your printer that the bit-pattern on the data lines is a single valid character that the printer should read and accept. The strobe line gives its pulse only after the signals on the data lines have settled down. Most parallel ports delay the strobe signal by about half a microsecond to ensure that the data signals have settled. The strobe itself lasts for at least half a microsecond so that your printer can recognize it. (The strobe signal can last up to 500 microseconds.) The signals on the data lines must maintain a constant value during this period and slightly afterward so that your printer has a chance to read them.

The strobe signal is "negative going." That is, a positive voltage (+5VDC) stays on the strobe line until your printer wants to send the actual strobe signal. Your computer then drops the positive voltage to near zero for the duration of the strobe pulse. The IEEE 1284 specification calls this signal *nStrobe*.

Busy Line

Sending data to your printer is a continuous cycle of setting up the data lines, sending the strobe signal, and putting new values on the data lines. The parallel port design typically requires about two microseconds for each turn of this cycle, allowing a perfect parallel port to dump out nearly half a million characters a second into your hapless printer. (As you will see, the actual maximum throughput of a parallel port is much lower than this.)

For some printers, coping with that data rate is about as daunting as trying to catch machine gun fire with your bare hands. Before your printer can accept a second character, its circuitry must do something with the one it has just received. Typically, the printer will need to move the character into its internal buffer. Although the character moves at electronic speeds, it does not travel instantaneously. Your printer needs to be able to tell your computer to wait for the processing of the current character before sending the next.

The parallel port's *busy line* gives your printer the needed breathing room. Your printer switches on the busy signal as soon as it detects the strobe signal and keeps the signal active until it is ready to accept the next character. The busy signal can last for a fraction of a second (even as short as a microsecond), or your printer could hold it on indefinitely while it waits for you to correct some error. No matter how long the busy signal is on, it keeps your computer from sending out more data through the parallel port. It functions as the basic flow-control system.

Acknowledge Line

The final part of the flow-control system of the parallel port is the *acknowledge line*. It tells your computer that everything has gone well with the printing of a character or its transfer to the internal buffer. In effect, it is the opposite of the busy signal, telling your computer that the printer is ready rather than unready. Whereas the busy line says, "Whoa," the acknowledge line says, "Giddyap!" The acknowledge signal is the opposite of the busy signal in another way: It is negative going whereas the busy signal is positive going. The IEEE 1284 specification calls this signal *nAck*.

When your printer sends out the acknowledge signal, it completes the cycle of sending a character. Typically the acknowledge signal on a conventional parallel port lasts about eight microseconds, stretching a single character cycle across the port to 10 microseconds. (IEEE 1284 specifies the length of nAck to be between 0.5 and 10 microseconds.) If you assume the typical length of this signal for a conventional parallel port, the maximum speed of the port works out to about 100,000 characters per second.

Select

In addition to transferring data to the printer, the basic parallel port allows your printer to send signals back to your computer so that your computer can monitor the operation of the printer. The original IBM design of the parallel interface includes three such signals that tell your computer when your printer is ready, willing, and able to do its job. In effect, these signals give your computer the ability to remotely sense the condition of your printer.

The most essential of these signals is *select*. The presence of this signal on the parallel interface tells your computer that your printer is online (that is, the printer is switched on and is in its online mode, ready to receive data from your computer). In effect, it is a remote indicator for the online light on your printer's control panel. If this signal is not present, your computer assumes that nothing is connected to your parallel port and doesn't bother with the rest of its signal repertory.

Because the rest state of a parallel port line is an absence of voltage (which would be the case if nothing were connected to the port to supply the voltage), the select signal takes the form of a positive signal (nominally +5VDC) that *in compatibility mode* under the IEEE 1284 specification stays active the entire period your printer is online.

Paper Empty

To print anything your printer needs paper, and the most common problem that prevents your printer from doing its job is running out of paper. The *paper empty* signal warns your computer when your printer runs out. The IEEE 1284 specification calls this signal *PError* for *paper error*, although it serves exactly the same function.

Paper empty is an information signal. It is not required for flow control because the busy signal more than suffices for that purpose. Most printers will assert their busy signals for the duration of the period they are without paper. Paper empty tells your computer the specific reason that your printer has stopped data flow. This signal allows your operating system or application to flash a message on your monitor to warn you to load more paper.

Fault

The third printer-to-computer status signal is *fault*, a catchall for warning of any other problems that your printer may develop—out of ink, paper jams, overheating, conflagrations, and other disasters. In operation, fault is actually a steady-state positive signal. It dips low (or off) to indicate a problem. At the same time, your printer may issue its other signals to halt the data flow, including busy and select. It never hurts to be extra sure. Because this signal is "negative going," the IEEE specification calls it *nFault*.

Initialize Printer

In addition to the three signals your printer uses to warn of its condition, the basic parallel port provides three control signals that your computer can use to command your printer without adding anything to the data stream. Each of these three provides its own hard-wired connection for a specific purpose. These include one to initialize the printer, another to switch it to online condition (if the printer allows a remote control status change), and a final signal to tell the printer to feed the paper up one line.

The *initialize printer* signal helps your computer and printer keep in sync. Your printer can send a raft of different commands to your printer to change its mode of operation, change font, alter printing pitch, and so on. Each of your applications that share your printer might send out its own favored set of commands. And many applications are like sloppy in-laws that come for a visit and fail to clean up after themselves. The programs may leave

your printer in some strange condition, such as set to print underscored boldface characters in agate size type with a script typeface. The next program you run might assume
some other condition and blithely print out a paycheck in illegible characters.

Initialize printer tells your printer to step back to ground zero. Just as your computer
boots up fresh and predictably, so does your printer. When your computer sends your
printer the initialize printer command, it tells the printer to boot up (that is, reset itself
and load its default operating parameters with its startup configuration of fonts, pitches,
typefaces, and the like). The command has the same effect as you switching off the printer
and turning it back on and simply substitutes for adding a remote control arm on your
computer to duplicate your actions.

During normal operation, your computer puts a constant voltage on the initialize printer
line. Removing the voltage tells your printer to reset. The IEEE 1284 specification calls
this negative-going signal *nInit*.

Select Input

The signal that allows your computer to switch your printer online and offline is called
select input. The IEEE 1284 specification calls it *nSelectIn*. It is active, forcing your printer
online, when it is low or off. Switching it to high deselects your printer.

Not all printers obey this command. Some have no provisions for switching themselves
on- and offline. Others have setup functions (such as a DIP switch) that allow you to
defeat the action of this signal.

Auto Feed XT

At the time IBM imposed its print system design on the rest of the world, different printers interpreted the lowly carriage return in one of two ways. Some printers took it literally. Carriage return means to move the printhead carriage back to its starting position on
the left side of the platen. Other printers thought more like typewriters. Moving the
printhead full left also indicated the start of a new line, so they obediently advanced the
paper one line when they got a carriage return command. IBM, being a premiere type-
writer-maker at the time, opted for this second definition.

To give printer developers flexibility, however, the IBM parallel port design included the
Auto Feed XT signal to give your computer command of the printer's handling of carriage
returns. Under the IEEE 1284 specification, this signal is called *nAutoFd*. By holding this
signal low or off, your computer commands your printer to act in the IBM and typewriter
manner, adding a line feed to every carriage return. Making this signal high tells your
printer to interpret carriage returns literally and only move the printhead. Despite the
availability of this signal, most early computer printers ignored it and did whatever their
setup configuration told them to do with carriage returns.

Nibble Mode

Early parallel ports used unidirectional circuitry for their data lines. No one foresaw the need for your computer to acquire data from your printer, so there was no need to add the expense or complication of bidirectional buffers to the simple parallel port. This tradition of single-direction design and operation continues to this day in the least expensive (which, of course, also means *cheapest*) parallel ports.

Every parallel port does, however, have five signals that are meant to travel from the printer to your computer. These include (as designated by the IEEE 1284 specification) nAck, Busy, PError, Select, and nFault. If you could suspend the normal operation of these signals temporarily, you could use four of them to carry data back from the printer to your computer. Of course, the information would flow at half speed, four bits at a time.

This means of moving data is the basis of nibble mode, so called because the computer community calls half a byte (the aforementioned four bits) a *nibble*. Using nibble mode, any parallel port can operate bidirectionally full speed forward but half speed in reverse.

Nibble mode requires that your computer take explicit command and control the operation of your parallel port. The port itself merely monitors all its data and monitoring signals and then relays the data to your computer. Your computer determines whether to regard your printer's status signals as backward-moving data. Of course, this system also requires that the device at the other end of the parallel port (your printer or whatever) know that it has switched into nibble mode and understand what signals to put where and when. The IEEE 1284 specification defines a protocol for switching into nibble mode and how computer and peripherals handle the nibble-mode signals.

The process is complex, involving several steps. First, your computer must identify whether the peripheral connected to it recognizes the IEEE standard. If not, all bets are off for using the standard. Products created before IEEE 1284 was adopted needed special drivers that matched the port to a specific peripheral. Because the two were already matched, they knew everything they needed to know about each other without negotiation. The pair could work without understanding the negotiation process or even the IEEE 1284 specification. Using the specification, however, allows your computer and peripherals to do the matching without your intervention.

Once your computer and peripheral decide they can use nibble mode, your computer signals to the peripheral to switch to the mode. Before the IEEE 1284 standard, the protocol was proprietary to the parallel port peripheral. The standard gives all devices a common means of controlling the switchover.

After both your computer and parallel port peripheral have switched to nibble mode, the signals on the interface get new definitions. In addition, nibble mode itself operates in two modes or phases, and the signals on the various parallel port lines behave differently in each mode. These modes include *reverse idle phase* and *reverse data transfer phase*.

In reverse idle phase, the PtrClk signal (nAck in compatibility mode) operates as an attention signal from the parallel port peripheral. Activating this signal tells the parallel port to issue an interrupt inside your computer, signaling that the peripheral has data available to be transferred. Your computer acknowledges the need for data and requests its transfer by switching the HostBusy signal (nAutoFd in compatibility mode) to low or off. This switches the system to *reverse data transfer phase*. Your computer switches the HostBusy signal to high again after the completion of the transfer of a full data byte. When the peripheral has mode data ready and your computer switches HostBusy back to low again, another transfer begins. If it switches to low without the peripheral having data available to send, the transition reengages reverse idle phase.

Because moving a byte from peripheral to computer requires two nibble transfers, each of which requires the same time as one byte transfer from computer to peripheral, reverse transfers in nibble mode operate at half speed at best. The only advantage of nibble mode is its universal compatibility. Even before the IEEE 1284 specification, it allowed any parallel port to operate bidirectionally. Because of this speed penalty alone, if you have a peripheral and parallel port that lets you choose the operating mode for bidirectional transfers, nibble mode is your *least* attractive choice.

Byte Mode

Unlike nibble mode, byte mode requires special hardware. The basic design for byte-mode circuitry was laid down when IBM developed its PS/2 line of computers and developed the Data Migration Facility. By incorporating bidirectional buffers in all eight of the data lines of the parallel port, IBM enabled them to both send and receive information on each end of the connection. Other than that change, the new design involved no other modifications to signals, connector pin assignments, or the overall operation of the port. Before the advent of the IEEE standard, these ports were known as *PS/2 parallel ports* or *bidirectional parallel ports*.

IEEE 1284 does more than put an official industry imprimatur on the IBM design, however. The standard redefines the bidirectional signals and adds a universal protocol for negotiating bidirectional transfers.

As with nibble mode, a peripheral in byte mode uses the PtrClk signal to trigger an interrupt in the host computer to advise that the peripheral has data available for transfer. When the computer services the interrupt, it checks the port nDataAvail signal, a negative-going signal that indicates a byte is available for transfer when it goes low. The computer can then pulse off the HostBusy signal to trigger the transfer using the HostClk (nStrobe) signal to read the data. The computer raises the HostBusy signal again to indicate the successful transfer of the data byte. The cycle can then repeat for as many bytes as need to be sent.

Because byte mode is fully symmetrical, transfers occur at the same speed in either direction. The speed limit is set by the performance of the port hardware, the speed at which the host computer handles the port overhead, and the length of timing cycles set in the IEEE 1284 specification. Potentially the design could require as little as four microseconds for each byte transferred, but real-world systems peak at about the same rate as conventional parallel ports (100,000 bytes per second).

Enhanced Parallel Port Mode

When it was introduced, the chief innovation of the Enhanced Parallel Port (EPP) was its improved performance, thanks to a design that hastened the speed at which your computer could pack data into the port. The EPP design altered port hardware so that instead of using byte-wide registers to send data through the port, your computer could dump a full 32-bit word of data directly from its bus into the port. The port would then handle all the conversion necessary to repackage the data into four-byte-wide transfers. The reduction in computer overhead and more efficient hardware design enabled a performance improvement by a factor of 10 in practical systems. This speed increase required more stringent specifications for printer cables. The IEEE 1284 specification does not get into the nitty-gritty of linking the parallel port circuitry to your computer, so it does not guarantee that a port in EPP mode will deliver all this speed boost. Moreover, the IEEE 1284 cable specs are not as demanding as the earlier EPP specs.

EPP mode of the IEEE 1284 specification uses only six signals in addition to the eight data lines for controlling data transfers. Three more connections in the interface are reserved for use by individual manufacturers and are not defined under the standard.

A given cycle across the EPP mode interface performs one of four operations: writing an address, reading an address, writing data, or reading data. The address corresponds to a register on the peripheral. The data operations are targeted on that address. Multiple data bytes may follow a single address signal as a form of burst mode.

nWrite

Data can travel both ways through an EPP connection. The *nWrite* signal tells whether the contents of the data lines are being sent from your computer to a peripheral or from a peripheral to your computer. When the nWrite signal is set to low, it indicates data is bound for the peripheral. When set to high, it indicates data sent from the peripheral.

nDStrobe

Soundboards are heavy feeders when it comes to system resources. A single soundboard may require multiple interrupts, a wide range of input/output ports, and a dedicated address range in High DOS memory. Because of these extensive resource demands, the need for numerous drivers, and often-poor documentation, soundboards are the most frustrating expansion products to add to a computer. In fact, a soundboard may be the perfect gift to surreptitiously gain revenge, letting you bury the hatchet with an estranged friend without the friend knowing you've sliced solidly into his back.

As with other parallel port transfers, your system needs a signal to indicate when the bits on the data lines are valid and accurate. EPP mode uses a negative-going signal called *nDStrobe* for this function in making data operations. Although this signal serves the same function as the strobe signal on a standard parallel port, it has been moved to a different pin, that used by the nAutoFd signal in compatibility mode.

nAStrobe
To identify a valid address on the interface bus, the EPP system uses the nAStrobe signal. This signal uses the same connection as nSelectIn during compatibility mode.

nWait
To acknowledge that a peripheral has properly received a transfer, it deactivates the negative-going *nWait* signal (making it a positive voltage on the bus). By holding the signal positive, the peripheral signals the host computer to wait. Making the signal negative indicates that the peripheral is ready for another transfer.

Intr
A peripheral connected to the EPP interface can signal to the host computer that it requires immediate service by sending out the *Intr* signal. The transition between low and high states of this signal indicates a request for an interrupt (that is, the signal is "edge triggered"). EPP mode does not allocate a signal to acknowledge that the interrupt request was received.

nInit
The escape hatch for EPP mode is the *nInit* signal. When this signal is activated (making it low), it forces the system out of EPP mode and back into compatibility mode.

Extended Capabilities Port Mode
When operating in ECP mode, the IEEE 1284 port uses seven signals to control the flow of data through the standard eight data lines. ECP mode defines two data-transfer signaling protocols—one for forward transfers (from computer to peripheral) and one for reverse transfers (peripheral to computer)—and the transitions between them. Transfers are moderated by closed-loop handshaking, which guarantees that all bytes get where they are meant to go, even if the connection is temporarily disrupted.

Because all parallel ports start in compatibility mode, your computer and its peripherals must first negotiate with one another to arrange to shift into ECP mode. Your computer and its software initiate the negotiation (as well as manage all aspects of the data transfers). Following a successful negotiation to enter into ECP mode, the connection enters its forward idle phase.

HostClk

To transfer information or commands across the interface, your computer starts from the forward idle phase and puts the appropriate signals on the data line. To signal to your printer or other peripheral that the values on the data lines are valid and should be transferred, your computer activates its *HostClk* signal, setting it to a logical high.

PeriphAck

The actual transfer does not take place until your printer or other peripheral acknowledges the HostClk signal by sending back the *PeriphAck* signal, setting it to a logical high. In response, your computer switches the HostClk signal to low. Your printer or peripheral then knows it should read the signals on the data lines. Once it finishes reading the data signals, the peripheral switches the PeriphAck signal to low. This completes the data transfer. Both HostClk and PeriphAck are back to their forward idle phase norms, ready for another transfer.

nPeriphRequest

When a peripheral needs to transfer information back to the host computer or to another peripheral, it makes a request by driving the *nPeriphRequest* signal low. The request is a suggestion rather than a command because only the host computer can initiate or reverse the flow of data. The nPeriphRequest signal typically causes an interrupt in the host computer to make this request known.

nReverseRequest

To allow a peripheral to send data back to the host or to another device connected to the interface, the host computer activates the *nReverseRequest* signal by driving it low, essentially switching off the voltage that otherwise appears there. This signals to the peripheral that the host computer will allow the transfer.

nAckReverse

To acknowledge that it has received the nReverseRequest signal and that it is ready for a reverse-direction transfer, the peripheral asserts its *nAckReverse* signal, driving it low. The peripheral can then send information and commands through the eight data lines and the PeriphAck signal.

PeriphClk

To begin a reverse transfer from peripheral to computer, the peripheral first loads the appropriate bits onto the data lines. It then signals to the host computer that it has data ready to transfer by driving the *PeriphClk* signal low.

HostAck

Your computer responds to the PeriphClk signal by switching the *HostAck* signal from its idle logical low to a logical high. The peripheral responds by driving PeriphClk high.

When the host accepts the data, it responds by driving the HostAck signal low. This completes the transfer and returns the interface to the reverse idle phase.

Data Lines

Although the parallel interface uses the same eight data lines to transfer information as do other IEEE 1284 port modes, it supplements them with an additional signal to indicate whether the data lines contain data or a command. The signal used to make this nine-bit information system changes with the direction of information transfer. When ECP mode transfers data from the computer host to a peripheral (that is, during a forward transfer), it uses the HostAck signal to specify a command or data. When a peripheral originates the data being transferred (a reverse transfer), it uses the PeriphAck signal to specify a command or data.

Logical Interface

Your computer controls each of its parallel ports through a set of three consecutive input/output ports. The typical computer sets aside three sets of these ports for three parallel ports, although most systems provide the matching hardware only for one. The base addresses used by parallel ports include 03BC(hex), 0378(hex), and 0278(hex).

When Windows boots up, it scans these addresses and assigns a logical name to each. These names are LPT1, LPT2, and LPT3. The name is a contraction of *Line Printer*, echoing the original purpose of the port. The port with the name LPT1 can also use the alias *PRN*. You can use these names at the system command prompt to identify a parallel port and the printer connected to it.

The computer printer port was designed to be controlled by a software driver. Your computer's BIOS provides a rudimentary driver, but most advanced operating systems similarly take direct hardware control of the parallel port through their own software drivers. Windows includes a parallel port driver of its own. You may need to install drivers for any device that connects to your parallel port. For example, every printer requires it own driver (many of which—but not all—are built in to Windows).

Control

Even in its immense wisdom, a microprocessor can't fathom how to operate a parallel port by itself. It needs someone to tell it how to move the signals around. Moreover, the minutiae of constantly taking care of the details of controlling a port would be a waste of the microprocessor's valuable time. Consequently, system designers created help systems for your computer's big brain. Driver software tells the microprocessor how to control the port, and port hardware handles all the details of port operation.

As parallel ports have evolved, so have these aspects of their control. The software that controls the traditional parallel port that's built in to the firmware of your computer has given way to a complex system of drivers. The port hardware, too, has changed to both simplify operation and to speed it up.

These changes don't follow the neat system of modes laid down by IEEE 1284. Instead, they have undergone a period of evolution in reaching their current condition.

Traditional Parallel Ports

In the original computer, each of its parallel ports linked to the computer's microprocessor through three separate I/O ports, each controlling its own register. The address of the first of these registers served as the base address of the parallel port. The other two addresses are next higher in sequence. For example, when the first parallel port in a computer has a base address of 0378 (hex), the other two I/O ports assigned it have addresses of 0379 (hex) and 037A (hex).

The register at the base address of the parallel port serves as a data latch, called the *printer data register*, which temporarily holds the values passed along to it by your computer's microprocessor. Each of the eight bits of this port is tied to one of the data lines leading out of the parallel port connector. The correspondence is exact. For example, the most significant bit of the register connects to the most significant bit on the port connector. When your computer's microprocessor writes values to the base register of the port, the register latches those values until your microprocessor sends newer values to the port.

Your computer uses the next register on the parallel port, corresponding to the next I/O port, to monitor what the printer is doing. Termed the *printer status register*, the various bits that your microprocessor can read at this I/O port carry messages from the printer back to your computer. The five most significant bits of this register directly correspond to five signals appearing in the parallel cable: Bit 7 indicates the condition of the busy signal; bit 6, acknowledge; bit 5, paper empty; bit 4, select; and bit 3, error. The remaining three bits of this register (bits 2, 1, and 0—the least significant bits) served no function in the original computer parallel port.

To send commands to your printer, your computer uses the third I/O port, offset two ports from the base address of the parallel port. The register there, called the *printer control register*, relays commands through its five least significant bits. Of these, four directly control corresponding parallel port lines. Bit 0 commands the strobe line; bit 1, the Auto Feed XT line; bit 2, the initialize line; and bit 3, the select line.

To enable your printer to send interrupts to command the microprocessor's attention, your computer uses bit 4 of the printer control register. Setting this bit to high causes the acknowledge signal from the printer to trigger a printer interrupt. During normal operation your printer, after it receives and processes a character, changes the acknowledge signal from a logical high to a low. Set bit 4, and your system detects the change in the acknowledge line through the printer status register and executes the hardware interrupt assigned to the port. In the normal course of things, this interrupt simply instructs the microprocessor to send another character to the printer.

All the values sent to the printer data register and the printer control register are put in place by your computer's microprocessor, and the chip must read and react to all the values packed into the printer status register. The printer gets its instructions for what to do from firmware that is part of your system's ROM BIOS. The routines coded for interrupt vector 017 (hex) carry out most of these functions. In the normal course of things, your applications call interrupt 017 (hex) after loading appropriate values into your microprocessor's registers, and the microprocessor relays the values to your printer. These operations are very microprocessor intensive. They can occupy a substantial fraction of the power of a microprocessor (particularly that of older, slower chips) during print operations.

Enhanced Parallel Ports

Intel set the pattern for Enhanced Parallel Port (EPP) by integrating the design into the 386SL chipset (which comprised a microprocessor and a support chip, the 386SL itself, and the 82360SL I/O subsystem chip, which together required only memory to make a complete computer). The EPP was conceived as a superset of the standard and PS/2 parallel ports. As with those designs, compatible transfers require the use of the three parallel port registers at consecutive I/O port addresses. However, EPP adds five new registers to the basic three. Although designers are free to locate these registers wherever they want because they are accessed using drivers, in the typical implementation, these registers occupy the next five I/O port addresses in sequence.

EPP Address Register

The first new register (offset three from the base I/O port address) is called the *EPP address register*. It provides a direct channel through which your computer can specify addresses of devices linked through the EPP connection. By loading an address value in this register, your computer could select from among multiple devices attached to a single parallel port, at least once parallel devices using EPP addressing become available.

EPP Data Registers

The upper four ports of the EPP system interface (starting at offset four from the base port) link to the *EPP data registers*, which provide a 32-bit channel for sending data to the EPP data buffer. The EPP port circuitry takes the data from the buffer, breaks it into four separate bytes, and then sends the bytes through the EPP data lines in sequence. Substituting four I/O ports for the one used by standard parallel ports moves the conversion into the port hardware, relieving your system from the responsibility of formatting the data. In addition, your computer can write to the four EPP data registers simultaneously using a single 32-bit double-word in a single clock cycle in computers that have 32-bit data buses. In lesser machines, the EPP specification also allows for byte-wide and word-wide (16-bit) write operations through to the EPP data registers.

Unlike standard parallel ports, which require your computer's microprocessor to shepherd data through the port, the Enhanced Parallel Port works automatically. It requires no other signals from your microprocessor after it loads the data in order to carry out a data transfer. The EPP circuitry itself generates the data strobe signal on the bus almost as soon as your microprocessor writes to the EPP data registers. When your microprocessor reads data from the EPP data registers, the port circuitry automatically triggers the data strobe signal to tell whatever device that's sending data to the EPP connection that your computer is ready to receive more data. The EPP port can consequently push data through to the data lines with a minimum of transfer overhead. This streamlined design is one of the major factors that enables the EPP to operate so much faster than standard ports.

Fast Parallel Port Control Register

To switch from standard parallel port to bidirectional to EPP operation requires only plugging values into one of the registers. Although the manufacturers can use any design they want, needing only to alter their drivers to match, most follow the pattern set in the SL chips. Intel added a software-controllable *fast parallel port control register* as part of the chipset. This corresponds to the unused bits of the standard parallel port printer control register.

Setting the most significant bit (bit 7) of the fast parallel port control register to high engages EPP operation. Setting this bit to low (the default) forces the port into standard mode. Another bit controls bidirectional operation. Setting bit 6 of the fast parallel port control register to high engages bidirectional operation. When low, bit 6 keeps the port unidirectional.

In most computers, an EPP doesn't automatically spring to life. Simply plugging your printer into EPP hardware won't guarantee fast transfers. Enabling the EPP requires a software driver that provides the link between your software and the EPP hardware.

Extended Capabilities Ports

As with other variations on the basic parallel port design, your computer controls an Extended Capabilities Port (ECP) through a set of registers. To maintain backward compatibility with products requiring access to a standard parallel port, the ECP design starts with the same trio of basic registers. However, it redefines the parallel port data in each of the port's different operating modes.

The ECP design supplements the basic trio of parallel port registers with an additional set of registers offset at port addresses 0400 (hex) higher than the base registers. One of these, the *extended control register*, controls the operating mode of the ECP port.

As with other improved parallel port designs, ECP behaves exactly like a standard parallel port in its default mode. Your programs can write bytes to its data register (located at the port's base address, just as with a standard parallel port) to send the bits through the data lines of the parallel connection. Switch to EPP or ECP mode, and your programs can write at high speed to a register as wide as 32 bits. The ECP design allows for transfers 8, 16, or 32 bits wide at the option of the hardware designer.

To allow multiple devices to share a single parallel connection, the ECP design incorporates its own addressing scheme that allows your computer to separately identify and send data to up to 128 devices. When your computer wants to route a packet or data stream through the parallel connection to a particular peripheral, it sends out a channel address command through the parallel port. The command includes a device address. When an ECP parallel device receives the command, it compares the address to its own assigned address. If the two do not match, the device ignores the data traveling through the parallel connection until your computer sends the next channel address command through the port. When your computer fails to indicate a channel address, the data gets broadcast to all devices linked to the parallel connection.

Local Area Networking

Computers are conspirators. They owe most of their success to deviously working together, subverting the established order like Bolsheviks plotting the overthrow of the Czar. Each computer by itself can be safely contained and controlled in a home or office. Linked together, however, and there's no telling what mischief they will get into. They might join together to pass subversive messages (which we call *email*). They might pool their resources so they can take advantage of powers beyond their capabilities and budgets (such as sharing a printer or a high-speed Internet connection). They can be each others' eyes and ears, letting them pry into affairs halfway around the world. They can gather information about you—even the most delicate personal matters, such as your credit card number—and share it with other conspirators (I mean "computers," of course) elsewhere in the world. They can just make your life miserable—oh wait, they did that when they weren't connected, too.

This computer conspiracy is the key to the power of the local area network and the Internet. It gives your computer more reach, more power, and more capabilities. It simply makes your life more convenient and your computer more connected. In fact, at one time local area networking was called *connectivity*.

Fortunately, computers themselves don't plot against you (although the people behind those computer may). Even when connected to a network, computers remain their obedient selves, ready to do your bidding.

The challenge you face in linking your computer to others is the same as faced by a child growing up with siblings—your computer has to learn to share. When kids share, you get more quiet, greater peace of mind, and less bloodshed. When computers share, you get the convenience of using the same files and other resources, centralized management (including the capability to back up all computers from one location or use one computer to back up others), and improved communication between workers in your business.

The drawback to connectivity is that computer networks are even more difficult to understand and manage than a platoon of teenagers. They have their own rules, their own value systems, their own hardware needs, and even their own language. Just listening in on a conversation between network pros is enough to make you suspect that an alien invasion from the planet Oxy-10 has succeeded. To get even a glimmer of understanding, you need to know your way around layers of standards, architectures, and protocols. Installing a network operating system can take system managers days; deciphering its idiosyncrasies can keep users and operators puzzled for weeks. Network host adapters often prove incompatible with other computer hardware, with their required interrupts and I/O addresses locking horns with SCSI boards, port controllers, and other peripherals. And weaving the wiring for a network is like threading a needle while wearing boxing gloves during a cyclone that has blown out the electricity, the candles, and your last rays of hope.

In fact, no one in his right mind would tangle with a network were not the benefits so great. File sharing across the network alone eliminates a major source of data loss, which is duplication of records and out-of-sync file updates. Better still, a network lets you get organized. You can put all your important files in one central location where they are easier to protect, both from disaster and theft. Instead of worrying about backing up half a dozen computers individually, you can easily handle the chore with one command. Electronic mail can bring order to the chaos of tracking messages and appointments, even in a small office. With network-based email, you can communicate with your coworkers without scattering memo slips everywhere. Sharing a costly laser printer or large hard disk (with some networks, even modems) can cut your capital cost of the computers' equipment by thousands or tens of thousands of dollars. Instead of buying a flotilla of personal laser printers, for example, you can serve everyone's hard copy needs with just one machine.

Concepts

Network designers get excited when someone expresses interest in their rather esoteric field, which they invariable serve up as a layer cake. Far from a rich devil's food with a heavy chocolate frosting (with jimmies), they roll out a network model, something that will definitely disappoint your taste buds because it's entirely imaginary. They call their cake the *Open Systems Interconnection Reference Model* (or the *OSI Model* for short), and it's a layer cake the way software is layered. It represents the structure of a typical network with the most important functions each given its own layer.

Although the discussion of networks usually begins with this serving of cake, the OSI Model does not represent any particular network. In fact, networks are by no means obliged to follow the model. Although most have layers of functions, they are often stacked differently. And while the OSI Model preaches a seven-layer model, even the foremost networkers in the world—the Institute of Electrical and Electronic Engineers—slip in one more layer for good measure. Table 12.1 highlights the equivalence of different layers in several common networking systems, including the OSI model.

TABLE 12.1   Approximate Equivalence of Network Layers

Layer	OSI Model	Internet Model	Windows Model	Real World
1	Physical	Not specified	Adapter	Twisted-pair
2	Data Link	Not specified		NIC
3	Network	Internet Protocol	Protocol	Network operating system
4	Transport	Transport Control Protocol (TCP)		
5	Session			Network driver
6	Presentation	FTP, HTTP	Service	Operating system
7	Application	Not specified	Client	Browser

What the OSI Model shows is how many different functions you need to make a network and how those functions interrelate to one another. It's a good place to begin, and it adds an academic aura to our network discussion, which just might make you believe you're learning something useful.

OSI Model

In 1984, the International Standards Organization laid out a blueprint to bring order to the nonsense of networking by publishing the Open Systems Interconnection Reference Model. You can imagine the bickering between hundreds of engineers trying to refine the right recipe for cooking up a network, then arguing over how many layers into which to divide their batter. The final, seven-layer model looks as if it might be the one and only way to build a network. These layers, ranging from the connecting wire to software applications, define functions and protocols that enable the wide variety of network hardware and software to work together. It just seems so logical, so compelling, that it is taught in most colleges and endorsed by major organizations such as IBM.

Regardless of where it fits in with your beliefs, philosophies, and diet, the OSI Model presents an excellent way to understand networks. The layering defined by the OSI Reference Model illustrates how the various elements of a network—from the wire running through your office ceiling to the Windows menu of your mail program—fit together and interact. Although few actual networks or network products exactly fit the model, the layers show how networks must be structured as well as the problems in building a network.

Physical

The first layer of the OSI Reference Model is the *Physical layer*. It defines the basic hardware of the network, which is the cable that conducts the flow of information between the devices linked by the network, or even the lack of a cable in wireless networking designs. This layer defines not only the type of wire (for example, coaxial cable, twisted-pair wire, and so on) but also the possible lengths and connections of the wire, the signals on the wire, and the interfaces of the cabling system—or the frequency and modulation of the radio devices that carry wireless network signals. This is the level at which the device that connects a computer to the network (the network host adapter) is defined.

Data Link

Layer 2 in a network is called the *Data Link layer*. It defines how information gains access to the wiring system. The Data Link layer defines the basic protocol used in the local network. This is the method used for deciding which computer can send messages over the cable at any given time, the form of the messages, and the transmission method of those messages.

This level defines the structure of the data that is transferred across the network. All data transmitted under a given protocol takes a common form called the *packet* or *network data frame*. Each packet is a block of data that is strictly formatted and may include destination and source identification as well as error-correction information. All network data transfers are divided into one or more packets, the lengths of which are carefully controlled.

Breaking network messages into multiple packets enables the network to be shared without interference and interminable waits for access. If you transfer a large file (say, a bitmap) across the network in one piece, you might monopolize the entire network for the duration of the transfer. Everyone would have to wait. By breaking all transfers into manageable pieces, everyone gets access in a relatively brief period, thus making the network more responsive.

Network

Layer 3 in the OSI Reference Model is the *Network layer*, which defines how the network moves information from one device to another. This layer corresponds to the hardware-interface function of the BIOS of an individual computer because it provides a common software interface that hides differences in underlying hardware. Software of higher layers can run on any lower-layer hardware because of the compatibility this layer affords. Protocols that enable the exchange of packets between different networks operate at this level.

Transport

Layer 4 controls data movement across the network. The Transport layer defines how messages are handled—particularly how the network reacts to packets that become lost as well as other errors that may occur.

Session

Layer 5 of the OSI Reference Model defines the interaction between applications and hardware, much as a computer BIOS provides function calls for programs. By using functions defined at this Session layer, programmers can create software that will operate on any of a wide variety of hardware. In other words, the Session layer provides the interface for applications and the network. Among computers, the most common of these application interfaces is IBM's Network Basic Input/Output System (NetBIOS).

Presentation

Layer 6, the *Presentation layer*, provides the file interface between network devices and the computer software. This layer defines the code and format conversions that must take place so that applications running under a computer operating system, such as DOS, OS/2, or Macintosh System 7, can understand files stored under the network's native format.

In classic networking, this function would be served by the computer's BIOS. The first personal computers lacked any hint of network connectivity, but in 1984 IBM introduced a trend-setting system called the *IBM PC Network*, which has been the foundation for small computer networking ever since. The critical addition was a set of new codes to the system BIOS developed by Sytek. This set of new codes—specifically, the Interrupt 5C(hex) routines—has become known as the Network BIOS, or *NetBIOS*.

The NetBIOS serves as a low-level application program interface for the network, and its limitations get passed on to networks built around it. In particular, the NetBIOS imposed requires that each computer on the network wear a unique name up to 15 characters long. This limits the NetBIOS to smaller networks. Today's operating systems use driver software that takes the place of the NetBIOS.

Application

Layer 7 is the part of the network that you deal with personally. The Application layer includes the basic services you expect from any network, including the ability to deal with files, send messages to other network users through the mail system, and control print jobs.

Internet Model

The Internet does not neatly fit the seven-layer OSI Model for the simple reason that the Internet is not meant to be a network. It describes a network of networks. Consequently, the Internet standards do not care about, nor do they describe, a "physical" layer or an "application" layer. (The World Wide Web standards arguably define a "presentation" layer.) When you use the Internet, however, the computer network you use to tie into the Internet becomes a physical layer, and your browser acts as an application layer.

Similarly, Ethernet does not conform to a seven-layer model because its concerns are at only the Physical through Session layers. Note that Ethernet breaks the Data Link layer into its own two-layer system.

Windows Model

When you work across a network using Windows, all the OSI layers come into play. Windows sees networks as layered somewhere between the two-tier practical approach and the seven layers of OSI. Microsoft assigns four levels of concern when configuring your network, using your network or operating system software. Under Windows, these levels include the adapter, protocol, service, and client software, as shown in the Windows Select Network Component Type dialog box (see Figure 12.1).

FIGURE 12.1

The Windows Select Network Component Type dialog box.

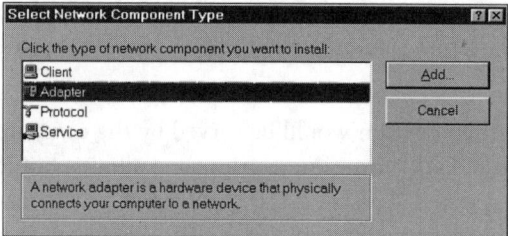

In this model, the network has four components—the client, the adapter, the protocol, and the service. Each has a distinct role to play in making the connection between computers.

Adapter

The *adapter* is the hardware that connects your computer to the network. The common term *network interface card*, often abbreviated as *NIC*, is one form of host adapter, a board you slide into an expansion slot. The host adapter function also can be integrated into the circuitry of the motherboard, as it often is in business-oriented computers.

No matter its form or name, the adapter is the foundation of the physical layer of the network, the actual hardware that makes the network work with your computer. It translates the parallel bus signals inside your computer into a serial form that can skitter through the network wiring. The design and standards that the adapter follows determine the form and speed of the physical side of the network.

From a practical perspective, the network adapter is generally the part of the network that you must buy if you want to add network capabilities to a computer lacking them. You slide a network host adapter or NIC into an expansion slot in your computer to provide a port for plugging into the network wire.

Protocol

The *protocol* is the music of the packets, the lyrics that control the harmony of the data traffic through the network wiring. The protocol dictates not only the logical form of the packet—the arrangement of address, control information, and data among its bytes—but also the rules on how the network deals with the packets. The protocol determines how the packet gets where it is going, what happens when it doesn't, and how to recover when an error appears in the data as it crosses the network.

Support for the most popular and useful protocols for small networks is included with today's operating systems. It takes the form of drivers you install to implement a particular networking system. Windows, for example, includes several protocols in its basic package. If you need to, you can add others as easily as installing a new software driver.

Service

The *service* of the network is the work the packets perform. The services are often several and always useful. Network services include exchanging files between disk drives (or making a drive far away on the network appear to be local to any or every computer in the network), sharing a printer resource so that all computers have access to a centralized printer, and passing electronic mail from a centralized post office to individual machines.

Most networking software includes the more useful services as part of the basic package. Windows includes file and printer sharing as its primary services. The basic operating system also includes e-mail support. Again, new services are as easy to add as new driver software.

Client

To the network, the client is not you but rather where the operating system of your computer and the network come together. It's yet another piece of software, the one that brings you the network resources so that you can take advantage of the services. The client software allows the network to recognize your computer and to exchange data packets with it.

Architecture

Now that we're done with the stuff that college professors want you to know to understand networks, let's get back to the real world and look at how networks are put together. Networks link computers, but a link can take many forms, which a visit to any sausage shop will readily confirm.

With networks, computers link together in many ways. The physical configuration (something those professors call a *topology*), describes how computers are connected, like the sausages that squirt out of the grinder. Sausages link in a straight line, one after another. Networks are more versatile.

Moreover, by their nature, networks define hierarchies of computers. Some networks make some computers more important than others. The terms describing these arrangements are often bandied about as if they mean something. The descriptions that follow should help you keep up with the conversation.

Topologies

In mathematics, *topology* is an elusive word. Some mathematicians see it as the study of geometry without shapes or distance. Some definitions call it the study of deformation. It is the properties of an object that survive when you change its size or shape by stretching or twisting it. A beach ball has the same topology with or without air. Concepts such as *inside* and *outside* survive the deformation, although they change physical places. It's a rich, rewarding, and fun part of mathematics.

Topology describes how the parts of an object relate to and connect with one another. The same word is applied to networks to describe how network nodes connect together. It describes the network without reference to distance or physical location. It shows the paths that signals must travel from one node to another.

Designers have developed several topologies for computer networks. Most can be reduced to one of four basic layouts: linear, ring, star, and tree. The names describe how the cables run throughout an installation.

Linear

A network with *linear* cabling has a single backbone, one main cable that runs from one end of the system to the other. Along the way, computers tap into this backbone to send and receive signals. The computers link to the backbone with a single cable through which they both send and receive. In effect, the network backbone functions as a data bus, and this configuration is often called a *bus topology*. It's as close as a network comes to the sausages streaming from the grinding machine. Figure 12.2 shows a network bus.

FIGURE 12.2
Simple bus network topology.

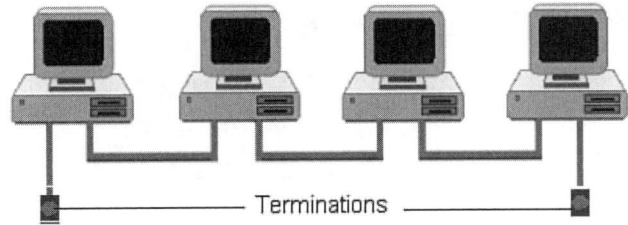

Terminations

In the typical installation, a wire leads from the computer to the backbone, and a T-connector links the two. The network backbone has a definite beginning and end. In most cases, these ends are terminated with a resistor matching the characteristic impedance of the cable in the background. That is, a 61-ohm network cable will have a 61-ohm termination at either end. These terminations prevent signals from reflecting from the ends of the cable, thus helping ensure signal integrity.

Ring

The ring topology looks like a linear network that's biting its own tail. The backbone is a continuous loop, a *ring*, with no end. But the ring is not a single, continuous wire. Instead, it is made of short segments daisy-chained from one computer to the next, the last connected, in turn, to the first. Each computer thus has two connections. One wire connects a computer to the computer before it in the ring, and a second wire leads to the next computer in the ring. Signals must traverse through one computer to get to the next, and the signals typically are listened to and analyzed along the way. You can envision it as a snake eating its own tail (or the first sausage swallowing the last link). If neither image awakens your imagination, Figure 12.3 also shows a network ring.

FIGURE 12.3
A simple network ring.

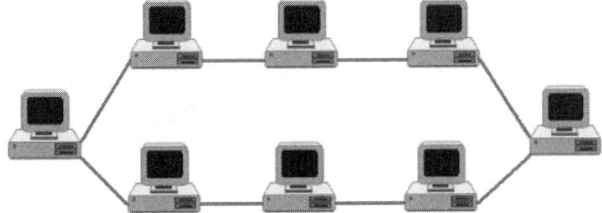

Star

Just as rays blast out from the core of a star, in the star topology, connecting cables emanate from a centralized location called a *hub*, and each cable links a single computer to the network. A popular image for the star topology is an old-fashioned wagon wheel—the network hub is the hub of the wheel, the cables are the spokes, and the computers are ignored in the analogy. Try visualizing them as clumps of mud clinging to the rim (which, depending on your particular network situation, may be an apt metaphor). Figure 12.4 shows a small network using the star topology.

FIGURE 12.4
Simple star network topology.

Star-style networks have become popular because their topology matches that of other office wiring. In the typical office building, the most common wiring is used by telephones, and telephone wiring converges at the wiring closet, which is the Private Branch Exchange, or PBX (the telephone switching equipment for a business). Star-style topologies require only a single cable and connection for each device to link to the central location where all cables converge into the network hub.

Tree

When multiple hubs are connected together, the result is a *tree*. More like a family tree than some great oak, the tree spreads out and, at least potentially, connects many more nodes than might a single hub. Figure 12.5 shows a small network tree.

FIGURE 12.5
A simple network tree.

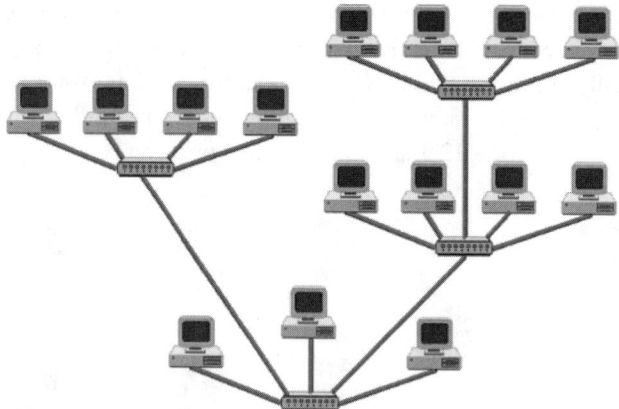

The typical home or small business network is a star, whereas large networks take the form of trees. (And network users eat the sausages.)

Hierarchies

Computers have classes—or at least a class system—in some networking schemes. Whereas some networks treat all computers the same, others elevate particular computers to a special, more important role as servers. Although the network performs many of the same functions in either case, these two hierarchical systems enforce a few differences in how the network is used.

Client/Server

In the *client/server* system, the shared resources of the network—files, high-speed connections with the Internet, printers, and the email system—are centralized on one or more powerful computers with very large disk storage capacity called *servers.* Individual workstation computers used by workers at the company are called *clients.*

Exactly what is on the server (or servers) and what is local to each client depends on the choices of the network manager. The server may host as little as a single shared database. The server may also host the data file used by each client. In extreme cases, programs used by each client load from a disk in the server.

As the network places more reliance on the server, the load on both the network and server increase. Because nearly every computer operation becomes a network operation, normal day-to-day use swallows up network bandwidth, and a slowdown in the network or the server slows work on every computer.

The strong point of the centralized client/server network is ease of administration. The network and all its connected clients are easier to control. Centralizing all data files on the server makes data and programs easier to secure and back up. Also, it helps ensure that everyone on the network is using the same programs and the same data.

When you surf the Internet, your computer becomes the client, and the computer that provides the Web pages you read is the server.

Peer-to-Peer

The client/server system is a royalist system, particularly if you view a nation's leader as a servant of the people rather than a profiteer. The opposite is the true democracy, in which every computer is equal. Computers share files and other resources (such as printers) among one another. They share equally, each as the peer of the others, so this scheme is called *peer-to-peer* networking.

Peer-to-peer means that there is no dedicated file server. All computers have their own, local storage, but each computer is (or can be) granted access to the disk drives and printers connected to the other computers. The peer-to-peer system is not centralized. In fact, it probably has no center, only a perimeter.

When you use the Internet to share files (say, downloading an MP3 file from someone else's collection), you're using peer-to-peer networking.

In a peer-to-peer network, no one computer needs to be particularly endowed with overwhelming mass storage or an incomprehensible network operating system. But all computers need not be equal. In fact, one peer may provide a network resource, such as a connection to a printer or the Internet. It may even have a large disk that's used to back up the files from other peers.

In other words, the line between client/server and peer-to-peer systems can be fuzzy, indeed. There is no electrical difference between the two systems. A peer-to-peer network and a client/server network may use exactly the same topology. In fact, the same network may take different characterizations, depending on how it is used.

Standards

A network is a collection of ideas, hardware, and software. The software comprises both the programs that make it work and the protocols that let everything work together. The hardware involves the network adapters as well as the wires, hubs, concentrators, routers, and even more exotic fauna. Getting it all to work together requires standardization.

Because of the layered design of most networks, these standards can appear at any level in the hierarchy; and they do. Some cover a single layer; others span them all to create a cohesive system.

Current technology makes the best small computer network a hub-based peer-to-peer design, cabled with twisted-pair wiring and running the software built in to your operating system. The big choice you face is the hardware standard. In the last few years, networks have converged on two basic hardware standards: 10Base-T and 100Base-T. Both are specific implementations of Ethernet.

Just as celebrities are people famous principally for being famous, 10Base-T and 100Base-T are popular because they are popular. They are well known and generally understood. Components for either are widely available and inexpensive. Setting them up is easy and support is widely available.

The distinguishing characteristic of network hardware is the medium used for connecting nodes. Small networks—the kind you might use in your home, office, or small business— most commonly use one of three interconnection types. They may be wired together in the classic style, typically using twisted-pair wires in a star-based topology. They may be linked wirelessly using low-powered radio systems, or their signals may be piggybacked on an already existing wiring system, such as telephone lines or utility power lines.

Ethernet

The elder statesman of networking is Ethernet. It still reigns as king of the wires, and wireless systems have appropriated much of its technology. It shows the extreme foresight of the engineers at Xerox Corporation's Palo Alto research center who developed it in the 1970s for linking the company's early Alto workstations to laser printers. The invention of Ethernet is usually credited to Robert Metcalf, who later went on to found 3Com

Corporation, an early major supplier of computer networking hardware and software. During its first years, Ethernet was proprietary to Xerox, a technology without a purpose, in a world in which the personal computer had not yet been invented.

In September, 1980, however, Xerox joined with minicomputer maker Digital Equipment Corporation and semiconductor manufacturer Intel Corporation to publish the first Ethernet specification, which later became known as E.SPEC VER.1. The original specification was followed in November, 1982, by a revision that has become today's widely used standard, E.SPEC VER.2.

This specification is not what most people call Ethernet, however. In January, 1985, the Institute of Electrical and Electronic Engineers published a networking system derived from Ethernet but not identical to it. The result was the IEEE 802.3 specification. Ethernet and IEEE 802.3 share many characteristics—physically, they use the same wiring and connection schemes—but each uses its own packet structure. Consequently, although you can plug host adapters for true Ethernet and IEEE 802.3 together in the same cabling system, the two standards will not be able to talk to one another. No matter. No one uses real Ethernet anymore. They use 802.3 instead and call it Ethernet.

Under the OSI Model, Ethernet provides the Data Link and Physical layers—although Ethernet splits the Data Link layer into two layers of its own: Media Access Control and the Logic Link Control layer (or the MAC-client layer). The Ethernet specifications define the cable, connections, and signals as well as the packet structure and control on the physical medium. Table 12.2 shows the structure of an IEEE 802.3 packet.

TABLE 12.2   Structure of an IEEE 802.3 (Ethernet) Packet

Function	Length	Comments
Preamble	Seven bytes	Each byte has the pattern 10101010.
Start frame delimiter	One byte	10101011 (for synchronization).
Destination address	Six bytes	Indicates where the packet is going.
Source address	Six bytes	Three-byte vendor ID, three-byte NIC ID.
Payload length	Two bytes	Number of bytes of data in the packet.
Data	As indicated above	Minimum length is 64 bytes; padded if shorter.
Frame check sequence	Four bytes	Error checking.

Data Link Layer

The basis of Ethernet is a clever scheme for arbitrating access to the central bus of the system. The protocol, formally described as *Carrier Sense, Multiple Access with Collision Detection* (CSMA/CD) is often described as being like a party line. It's not. It's much more like polite conversation. All the computers in the network patiently listen to everything that's going on across the network backbone. Only when there is a pause in the conversation will a new computer begin to speak. And if two or more computers start to talk at the same time, all become quiet. They will wait for a random interval (and because it is random, each will wait a different interval) and, after the wait, attempt to begin speaking again. One will be lucky and win access to the network. The other, unlucky computers hear the first computer blabbing away and wait for another pause.

Access to the network line is not guaranteed in any period by the Ethernet protocol. The laws of probability guide the system, and they dictate that eventually every device that desires access will get it. Consequently, Ethernet is described as a probabilistic access system. As a practical matter, when few devices (compared to the bandwidth of the system) attempt to use the Ethernet system, delays are minimal because all of them trying to talk at one time is unlikely. As demand approaches the capacity of the system, however, the efficiency of the probability-based protocol plummets. The size limit of an Ethernet system is not set by the number of computers but by the amount of traffic; the more packets computers send, the more contention, and the more frustrated attempts.

Physical Layer

The Ethernet packet protocol has many physical embodiments. These can embrace just about any topology, type of cable, or speed. The IEEE 802.3 specification defines several of these, and it assigns a code name and specification to each. Among today's Ethernet implementations, the most basic operates at a raw speed of 10MHz. That is, the clock frequency of the signals on the Ethernet (or IEEE 802.3) wire is 10MHz. Actual throughput is lower because packets cannot occupy the full bandwidth of the Ethernet system. Moreover, every packet contains formatting and address information that steals space that could be used for data.

Originally, Ethernet used coaxial cables, and two versions of the 10MHz IEEE version of Ethernet have proved popular: 10Base-5 (which uses thick coaxial cable, about one-half inch in diameter) and 10Base-2 (which uses a thin coaxial cable, about 2/10th inch in diameter).

Twisted-pair wiring is now used almost universally in Ethernet systems, except in special applications (for example, to link hubs together or to extend the range of connections). Basically the same kind of wire is used for speed that spans two orders of magnitude.

The base level for twisted-pair Ethernet is 10Base-T, which transfers the same signals as the coaxial systems onto two pairs of ordinary copper wires. Each wire pair carries a 10MHz balanced signal—one carrying data to the device and the other carrying it away (in other words, separate receive and transit channels) for full-duplex operation.

The next increment up is 100Base-T, which is likely today's most popular wired networking standard. The 100Base-T system operates at 100MHz, yielding higher performance consistent with transferring multimedia and other data-intensive applications across the network. Its speed has made it the system of choice in most new installations.

During its gestation, 100Base-T wasn't a single system but rather a family of siblings, each designed for different wiring environments. 100Base-TX is the purest implementation and the most enduring—but it's also the most demanding. It requires Class 5 wiring, shielded twisted-pair designed for data applications. In return for the cost of the high-class wiring, it permits full-duplex operation so that any network node can both send and receive data simultaneously. The signals on the cable actually operate at 125MHz but use a five-bit encoding scheme for every four bits. The extra code groups are used primarily for error control. The current 100Base-T standard is formalized in the IEEE 802.3u specification.

To make the transition from 10Base-T to higher speeds easier, 100Base-T4 was designed to work with shielded or unshielded voice-grade wiring, but it only allows for half-duplex operations across four wire pairs. In addition, 100Base-T2 uses sophisticated data coding to squeeze a 100Mbps data rate on ordinary voice-grade cables using one two-wire pair. Currently neither of these transitional formats is in general use.

At the highest-speed end, Gigabit Ethernet moves data at a billion bits per second. The first implementations used fiber optic media, but the most popular format is using the same Category 5 twisted-pair wires as slower versions of Ethernet. Commonly called 1000Base-T and officially sanctioned under the IEEE 802.3ab standard, Gigabit Ethernet's high speed is not a direct upward mapping of 100MHz technology. Category 5 cables won't support a 1GHz speed. Instead, 1000Base-T uses all four pairs in a standard Cat 5 cable, each one operating at 125MHz. To create a 1000Gbps data rate, the 1000Base-T adapter splits incoming data into four streams and then uses a five-level voltage coding scheme to encode two bits in every clock cycle. The data code requires only four levels. The fifth is used for forward error correction. The standard allows both half-duplex (four pairs) and full-duplex (eight pairs using two Cat 5 cables) operation.

Wireless

The problem with wiring together a network is the wiring, and the best way to eliminate the headaches of network wiring is to eliminate the wires themselves. True wireless networking systems do exactly that, substituting radio signals for the data line. Once an exotic technology, wireless networking is now mainstream with standardized components both readily available and affordable.

Wireless networking has won great favor, both in homes and businesses, because it allows mobility. Cutting the cable means you can go anywhere, which makes wireless perfect for notebook computers (and why many new notebooks come with built-in wireless networking). If you want to tote your computer around your house and work anywhere, wireless is the only way to go. Many airports and businesses also use standard wireless connections, so if you equip your portable computer with wireless for your home, you may be able to use it when you're on the move.

Moreover, wireless networks are easier to install, at least at the hardware end. You slide a PC Card into your notebook computer, plug the hub into a wall outlet, and you're connected. If you're afraid of things technical, that makes wireless your first choice. Of course, the hardware technology does nothing to make software installation easier, but wireless doesn't suffer any handicaps beyond all other network technologies.

On the other hand, wireless has a limited range that varies with the standard you use. Government rules restrict the power that wireless network systems can transmit with. Although equipment-makers quote ranges of 300 meters and more, that distance applies only in the open air—great if you're computing on the football field but misleading should you want to be connected indoors. In practical application, a single wireless network hub might not cover an entire large home.

All wireless networks are also open to security intrusions. Once you put your data on the air, it is open for inspection by anyone capable of receiving the signals. Encryption, if used, will keep your data reasonably secret (although researchers have demonstrated that resourceful snoops can break the code in an hour). More worrisome is that others can tap into your network and take advantage of your Internet connection. When you block them, you sacrifice some of the convenience of wireless.

Wireless networks endured a long teething period during which they suffered a nearly fatal malaise—a lack of standardization. Wireless systems were, at one time, all proprietary. But wireless technology proved so useful that the IEEE standardized it and keeps on adding new standards. Two are currently in wide deployment, and several others are nearing approval. Table 12.3 summarizes the current standards situation.

TABLE 12.3	Wireless Networking Standards			
Standard	*Common Name*	*Frequency*	*Data Rate*	*Status*
802.11a	WiFi-5	5.2GHz	54Mbps	Official
802.11b	WiFi	2.4GHz	11Mbps	Official
802.11b+		2.4GHz	22Mbps	Proprietary/Pending
802.11g		2.4GHz	54Mbps	Pending

The following discussion covers today's wireless networking standards and those likely to become standards in order of adoption or introduction.

802.11b

Through the year 2001, IEEE 802.11b was the most popular wireless standard on the market, popularized under the name Wireless Fidelity (WiFi), given to it by the industry group, the Wireless Ethernet Compatibility Alliance. That group now uses the name WiFi Alliance. WiFi equipment is also sometimes called *2.4MHz wireless networking* because of the frequency band in which it operates.

Until October 2001, WiFi was the *only* official wireless networking standard. Despite its "b" designation, 802.11b was the first official wireless networking standard to be marketed. Its destiny was set from its conception. It was the one IEEE wireless standard with acceptable performance that could readily be built.

The range of 802.11b is usually given as up to 300 meters—nearly 1000 feet—a claim akin to saying that you're up to 150 feet tall. Anything that gets in the way—a wall, a drapery, or a cat—cuts down that range. Moreover, the figure is mostly theoretical. Actual equipment varies widely in its reach. With some gear (such as the bargain models I chose), you'll be lucky to reach the full length of your house.

Moreover, range isn't what you might think. 802.11b is designed to gracefully degrade. What that engineering nonsense means is that the farther away you get, the slower your connection becomes. When you're near the limits of your system, you'll have a 2Mbps connection.

Note that the range is set by the least powerful transmitter and weakest receiver. In most cases, the least powerful transmitter is in the PC Card adapter in your notebook computer. Power in these is often purposely kept low to maintain battery life and to stay within the engineering limits of the card housing. You can often achieve longer distances with an external adapter, such as one that plugs into your computer's USB port.

802.11b is less than ideal for a home wireless network for more reasons than speed. Interference is chief among them. The 2.4GHz band within which 802.11b works is one of the most popular among engineers and designers. In addition to network equipment, it hosts cordless telephones and the Bluetooth interconnection system. Worse, it is close to the frequency used by consumer microwave ovens. Because the band is unlicensed, you can never be sure what you'll be sharing it with. Although 802.11b uses spread-spectrum modulation, which makes it relatively immune to interference, you can still lose network connections when you switch on your cordless phone.

802.11a

The place to start with 802.11a is with the name. Back-stepping one notch in the alphabet doesn't mean moving down the technological ladder, as it does with software revisions. When the standards-makers at the IEEE put pen to paper for wireless standards, 802.11a did come first, but it was the dream before the reality. The high speed of 802.11a was what they wanted, but they amended their views to accommodate its slower sibling, which they knew they could deliver faster. When manufacturers introduced equipment following the 802.11a standard, they initially promoted it as WiFi-5 because of the similarity with the earlier technology. The "5" designated the higher frequency band used by the newer system. In October, 2002, however, the WiFi Alliance decided to drop the WiFi-5 term—mostly because people wondered whatever happened to WiFi-2, 3, and 4.

From the beginning, 802.11a was meant by its IEEE devisors as the big brother to 802.11b. It is designed to be faster and provide more channels to support a greater number of simultaneous users. The bit-rate of the system is 54Mbps, although in practical application actual throughput tops out at about half that rate. In addition, as the distance between the computers and access points increase, the 802.11a system is designed to degrade in speed to ensure data integrity, slowing down to about 6Mbps at the farthest reaches of its range.

802.11a fits into the UN-II (Unlicensed National Information Infrastructure) band that's centered at about 5.2GHz, a band that's currently little used by other equipment and services. The design of 802.11a provides for eight channels, allowing that number of access points to overlap in coverage without interference problems.

The higher frequency band has a big advantage—bandwidth. There's more room for multiple channels, which means more equipment can operate in a given space without interference.

But the UN-II band occupied by 802.11a isn't without its problems. The biggest is physics. All engineering rules of thumb say the higher the frequency, the shorter the range. The 5.2GHz operating frequency puts 802.11a at a severe disadvantage, at least in theory.

Practically, however, the higher intrinsic speed of 802.11a not only wipes out the disadvantage but also puts the faster standard ahead. Because of the digital technology used by the common wireless networking systems, weaker signals mean lower speed rather than an abrupt loss of signal. The farther away from the access point a user ventures, the lower the speed his connection is likely to support.

Although physics doesn't favor 802.11a's signals, mathematics does. Because 802.11a starts out faster, it maintains a performance edge no matter the distance. For example, push an 802.11b link to 50 feet, and you can't possibly get it to operate faster than 11Mbps. Although that range causes some degradation at 802.11a's higher frequency, under that standard you can expect about 36Mbps, according to one manufacturer of the equipment.

Raw distance is a red herring in figuring how many people can connect to a wireless system. When the reach of a single access point is insufficient, the solution is to add another access point rather than to try to push up the range. Networks with multiple access points can serve any size campus. The eight channels available under 802.11a make adding more access points easier.

The security weakness is part of the plan. 802.11a is designed to match 802.11b at the software level.

802.11b+

There is no such thing as an 802.11b+ standard, at least a standard adopted by some official-sounding organization such as the IEEE. But you'll find a wealth of networking gear available that uses the technology that's masquerading under the name. Meant to fill the gap between slow-but-cheap 802.11b and faster-but-pricier 802.11a, this technology adds a different modulation system to ordinary 802.11b equipment to gain double the speed and about 30 percent more range. Because the technology is, at heart, 802.11b, building dual-mode equipment is a breeze, and most manufacturers do it. As a result, you get two speeds for the price of one (often less, because the 802.11b+ chipset is cheaper than other 802.11b chipsets).

The heart of 802.11b+ is the *packet binary convolutionary coding system* developed by Texas Instruments (TI) under the trademark PBCC-22. (A convolutionary code encodes a stream of data in which the symbol encoding a given bit depends on previous bits.) The "22" in the name refers to the speed. The only previous version was PBCC-11, the forerunner of PBCC-22 and also developed by TI.

PBCC-22 is a more efficient coding system than that used by ordinary 802.11b. In addition, the TI system uses eight-phase shift keying instead of 802.11b quadrature phase shift keying, but at the same data rate (11Mbps). The result is that the system fits twice the data in the same bandwidth as 802.11b. At the same time, the signal stands out better from background noise, which, according to TI, produces 30 percent more linear range or coverage of 70 percent more area. The same technology could be used to increase the speed of the 802.11b signaling system to 33MHz, although without benefit of the range increase. This aspect of PBCC-22 is not part of the TI chipset now offered for 802.1b+ components and has not received FCC approval.

802.11b+ can be considered a superset of 802.11b. Adapters and hubs meant for the new system also work with all ordinary 802.11b equipment, switching to their high speed when they find a mate operating at the higher speed.

Texas Instruments makes the only chipset to use 802.11b+ technology, so all equipment using the technology uses the TI chipset. TI often prices this chipset below the price of ordinary 802.11b chipsets, so the higher speed of 802.11b+ often is less expensive than the performance of equipment strictly adhering to the official 802.11b standard.

802.11g

As this is written, 802.11g is a proposal rather than an official standard, although its approval is expected in 2003. In effect a "greatest hits" standard, 802.11g combines the frequency band used by 802.11b with the modulation and speed of 802.11a, putting 54Mb operation in the 2.4GHz Industrial-Scientific-Medical (ISM) band.

Because of the lower frequency of the ISM band, 802.11g automatically gets an edge in range over 802.11a. At any given speed, 802.11g nearly doubles the coverage of 802.11a.

In addition, promoters cite that the ISM band is subject to fewer restrictions throughout the world than the 5GHz band, part of which is parceled out for military use in many countries. Of course, the opposite side of the coin is that the ISM band is more in demand and subject to greater interference. It also does not allow for as many channels as the 5GHz band.

Many of its promoters see 802.11g as a stepping stone to 802.11a. It allows engineers to create dual-speed equipment more easily because the two speeds (11Mbps and 54Mbps) will be able to share the same radio circuits.

Dual-Standard Systems

Nothing restricts a network or its equipment to using only one standard. To ease people who have already installed WiFi equipment into the higher-performance WiFi-5 standard, many manufacturers offer dual-standard equipment, including hubs that can recognize and use either standard to match the signals it receives. They also offer dual-standard network adapters capable of linking at the highest speed to whatever wireless signals are available. Nothing in the WiFi and WiFi-5 standards requires this interoperability.

Other high-speed standards do, however, guarantee interoperability. The proprietary 802.11b+ system is built around and is compatible with standard WiFi. Equipment made to one standard will operate with equipment made to the other, at the highest speed both devices support.

Similarly, 802.11g promises interoperability. In fact, at the time this is written, 802.11b+ has been proposed as an addition to 802.11g, making the proprietary standard official.

Sanctioning Organization

The various 802.11 standards are promulgated by the IEEE but are promoted by the WiFi Alliance. The organization maintains a Web site at www.weca.net.

HomePNA

One of the original design goals of the 10Base-T wiring scheme was for it to use the same kind of wires as used by ordinary telephones. Naturally, some people thought it would be a great idea to use the same wires as their telephones, but they were unwilling to give up the use of their phones when they wanted to network their computers.

Clever engineers, however, realized that normal voice conversations use only a tiny part of the bandwidth of telephone wiring—and voices use an entirely different part of that bandwidth than do computer networks. By selectively blocking the network signals from telephones and the telephone signals from networking components, they could put a network on the regular telephone wiring in a home or office while still using the same wiring for ordinary telephones.

Of course, there's a big difference between wiring a network and wiring a telephone system. A network runs point to point, from a hub to a network adapter. A telephone system runs every which way, connecting telephones through branches and loops and often leaving stubs of wire trailing off into nowhere. Telephone wiring is like an obstacle course to network signals.

History

Tut Systems devised a way to make it all work by developing the necessary signal-blocking adapters and reducing the data rate to about a megabit per second, to cope with the poor quality of telephone wiring. Tut Systems called this system *HomeRun*.

In June, 1998, eleven companies, including Tut (the others being 3Com, AMD, AT&T Wireless, Broadcom, Compaq, Conexant, Hewlett-Packard, IBM, Intel, and Lucent Technologies) formed the Home Phoneline Networking Alliance (HomePNA) to promote telephone-line networking. The alliance chose HomeRun as the foundation for its first standard, HomePNA version 1.0

In September, 2000, the alliance (which had grown to over 150 companies) kicked up the data rate to about 10Mbps with a new HomePNA version—Version 2.0.

On November 12, 2001, HomePNA released market (not technical) specifications for the next generation of telephone-line networking, HomePNA Version 3.0, with a target of 100Mbps speed. The new standard will be backward compatible with HomePNA 1.0 and 2.0 and won't interfere with normal and advanced telephone services, including POTS, ISDN, and xDSL. A new feature, Voice-over-HomePNA, will allow you to send up to eight high-quality telephone conversations through a single pair of ordinary telephone wires within your home. According to the association, the HomePNA Version 3.0 specification will be released by the end of 2002 and was not available as this is being written.

Version 1.0

Version 1.0 is a fairly straightforward adaptation of standard Ethernet, with only the data rate slowed to accommodate the vagaries of the unpredictable telephone wiring environment. The system does not adapt in any way to the telephone line. It provides its standard signal and that's that. Low speed is the only assurance of signal integrity. When a packet doesn't get through, the sending device simply sends it again. The whole system is therefore simple, straightforward, and slow.

The design of Version 1.0 allows for modest-sized networks. Its addressing protocol allows for a maximum of 25 nodes networked together. The signals system has a range of about 150 meters (almost 500 feet), although its range will vary with the actual installation—some telephone systems are more complex (and less forgiving) than others.

Version 2.0

Although HomePNA Version 1.0 is capable of most routine business chores, such as sharing a printer or DSL connection, it lacks the performance required for the audio and video applications that are becoming popular in home networking systems. Version 2.0 combines several technologies to achieve the necessary speed. It has two designated signaling rates: 2 million baud and 4 million baud (that's 2MHz and 4MHz, respectively). The signal uses quadrature amplitude modulation (the same technology of 28.8Kbps modems), but it can use several coding schemes, from 4 to 256 symbols per baud. As a result, the standard allows for actual data rates from 4Mbps (2 Mbaud carrier with 4 QAM modulation) to 32Mbps (4 Mbaud at 256 QAM modulation). The devices negotiate the actual speed.

Compared to ordinary 10Base-T Ethernet systems, HomePNA Version 2.0 suffers severely from transmission overhead, cutting its top speed well below its potential. To ensure reliability, HomePNA uses its highest speeds only for the data part of its packets (if at all). The system sends the header and tailer of each data frame, 84 bytes of each frame, at the lowest rate (4Mbps) to ensure that control information is error free. As a consequence, in every frame, overhead eats almost one-third of the potential bandwidth at the 32Mbps data rate, about 80 percent at the 16Mbps data rate, and correspondingly less at lower rates.

Equipment

HomePNA is a peer-to-peer networking system. It does not use a special hub or server. Each computer on the network plugs into a HomePNA adapter (usually through a USB port), which then plugs into a telephone wall jack. If you do not have a wall jack near your computer, you can use extension telephone cables to lengthen the reach of the adapter. No other hardware is required. Once all your computers are plugged in, you set up the network software as you would for any wired network.

Sanctioning Organization

The HomePNA specification is maintained by the Home Phoneline Networking Alliance. The group maintains a Web site at www.homepna.org.

HomePlug

The underlying assumption of the HomePlug networking system is that if you want to network computers in your home, you likely already have power wiring installed. If not, you don't likely need a network because you don't have any electricity to run your computers. Those big, fat, juicy electrical wires whisking dozens of amps of house current throughout your house can easily carry an extra milliwatt or two of network signal. In that the power lines inside your walls run to every room of your house, you should be able to plug your network adapter into an outlet and transport the signals everywhere you need them.

You'll want to be careful if you try such a thing. Unlike computer signals, house current can kill you—and the circuitry of your network adapter. House current is entirely different stuff from network signals. That's bad if you stick your fingers into a light socket, but it's good if you want to piggyback network signals on power lines. The big difference between the two means that it's relatively easy for a special adapter (*not* an ordinary network adapter!) to separate the power from the data.

On the other hand, although those heavy copper wires are adept at conducting high-current power throughout your home, they are a morass for multimegahertz data signals. At the frequencies needed for practical network operation, home wiring is literally a maze, with multiple paths, most of which lead into dead-ends. Some frequencies can squeak through the maze unscathed, whereas others disappear entirely, never to be seen again. Motors, fluorescent lights, even fish-tank pumps add noise and interference to your power lines, not to mention stuff that sneaks in from the outside, such as bursts of lightning. Radio frequency signals like those a network uses bounce through this booby-trapped electrical maze like a hand grenade caught in a pinball machine.

Transmission Method

The HomePlug solution is to try, try again. Rather than using a single technology to bust through the maze, HomePlug uses several. It is adaptive. It tests the wiring between network nodes and checks what sort of signals will work best to transport data between them. It then switches to those signals to make the transfer. Just in case, everything that HomePlug carries is doused with a good measure of error correction. The result is a single networking standard built using several technologies that seamlessly and invisibly mate, so you can treat your home wiring as a robust data communications channel.

The basic transmission technique in the HomePlug system is called *orthogonal frequency division multiplexing* (OFDM), similar to that used in some telephone Digital Subscriber Lines. The OFDM system splits the incoming data stream into several with lower bit rates. Each stream then gets its own carrier to modulate, with the set of carriers carefully chosen so that the spacing between them is inversely proportional to the bit-rate of each carrier (this is the principle of *orthogonality*). Combining the modulated carriers of different frequencies together results in the frequency division multiplexing. In the resulting signal, it is easy to separate out the data on each carrier because the data on one carrier is easily mathematically isolated from the others.

Each isolated carrier can use a separate modulation scheme. Under HomePlug, *differential quarternary phase shift keying* (DQPSK) is the preferred method. It differs from conventional QPSK in that the change in the phase of the carrier, not the absolute phase of the carrier, encodes the data. Alternately, the system can shift to *differential binary phase shift keying* (DBPSK) for lower speed but greater reliability when the connection is poor. DQPSK shifts between four phases, whereas DBPSK shifts between two. The data streams use a convolutionary code as forward error correction. That is, they add extra bits to the digital code, which help the receiver sort out errors.

In the ideal case, with all carriers operating at top speed, the HomePlug system delivers a raw data rate of about 20Mbps. Once all the overhead from data preparation and error correction gets stripped out, it yields a clear communication channel for carrying data packets with an effective bit-rate of about 14Mbps.

If two devices cannot communicate with the full potential bandwidth of the HomePlug system, they can negotiate slower transmissions. To best match line conditions, they can selectively drop out error-plagued carrier frequencies, shift from DQPSK to more reliable DBPSK modulation, or increase the error correction applied to the data.

The HomePlug system uses a special *robust mode* for setting up communication between channels. Robust mode activates all channels but uses DBPSK modulation and heavy error correction. Using all channels ensures that all devices can hear the signals, and the error correction ensures messages get through, if slowly. Once devices have negotiated the connection starting with robust mode, they can shift to higher-speed transmissions.

The HomePlug system selects its carriers in the range between frequencies of 4.5 and 21MHz, operating with reduced power in the bands in which it might cause interference with amateur radio transmissions. In addition, HomePlug transmits in bursts rather than maintaining a constant signal on the line.

Protocol

The HomePlug system moves packets between nodes much like the Ethernet system with a *Carrier Sense Multiple Access with Collision Avoidance* (CSMA/CA) protocol. That is, each device listens to the power line and starts to transmit only when it does not hear another device transmitting. If two devices accidentally start transmitting at the same time (resulting in a collision), they immediately stop, and each waits a random time before trying again. HomePlug modifies the Ethernet strategy to add priority classes, greater fairness, and faster access.

All packets sent from one device to another must be acknowledged, thus ensuring they have been properly received. If a packet is not acknowledged, the transmitting device acts as if its packet had collided with another, waiting a random period before retransmitting. An acknowledgement sent back also signals to other devices that the transmission is complete and that they can attempt to send their messages.

According to the HomePlug alliance, the protocol used by the system results in little enough delay that the system can handle time-critical applications such as streaming media and Voice-over-Internet telephone conversations.

To prevent your neighbors from listening in on your network transmissions or from sneaking into your network and stealing Internet service, the HomePlug system uses a

56-bit encryption algorithm. The code is applied to packets at the Protocol layer. All devices in a given network—that is, the HomePlug adapters for all of your computers—use the same key, so all can communicate. Intruders won't know the key and won't be recognized by the network.

With HomePlug, such intrusions are more than theoretical. Anyone sharing the same utility transformer with you—typically about six households tap into the same utility transformer—will share signals on the power line. Your HomePlug networking signals will consequently course through part of your neighborhood. That's bad if you want to keep secrets, but it could allow you and a neighbor share a single high-speed Internet connection (if your Internet Service Provider allows you to).

Equipment

HomePlug is a peer-to-peer networking system. It does not use a special hub or server. Each computer on the network plugs into a HomePlug adapter (usually through a USB port), which then plugs into a wall outlet. No other hardware is required. Once all your computers are plugged in, you set up the network software as you would for any wired network.

Sanctioning Organization

The specifications for the HomePlug networking system are maintained by the HomePlug Powerline Alliance.

HomePlug Powerline Alliance, Inc.
2694 Bishop Drive, Suite 275
San Ramon, CA 94583

Homeplug.org
Phone: 925-275-6630
Fax: 925-275-6691

Hardware

To make a network operate under any standard requires actual hardware—pieces of equipment that plug into each other to make the physical network. Most of today's networking systems require three different kinds of hardware. Network interface cards link your computer to the network wiring system (or wireless signaling system). A hub or access point brings the signals from all the computers and other devices in the network together. And a medium (such as wires or radio waves) links these two together. You build a network using these three components from one network standard.

Network Interface Cards

The *network interface card* (NIC) and its associated driver software have the most challenging job in the network. The NIC takes the raw data from your computer, converts it into the proper format for the network you're using, and then converts the electrical signals to a format compatible with the rest of the network. If it doesn't work properly, your data would be forever trapped in your computer.

Because it converts the stream of data between two different worlds (inside your computer and the outside world of the network), it needs to match two standards: a connection system used by your computer and the connection system used by the network.

Traditionally, a network adapter has plugged into the expansion bus of the host computer. No other connection could provide the speed required for network use. Desktop computers used internal NICs that slid into expansion slots. Portable computers used NICs in the form of PC Cards.

With the advent of USB, however, that situation has changed. Although expansion bus–based NICs remain important, many networks are shifting to NICs that plug into USB ports. The primary reason for this is that USB-based NICs are easier to install. Plug in one connector, and you're finished. Although early USB-based NICs gave up speed for this convenience, a USB 2.0 port can handle the data rates required even by 100Base-T networking.

The simplified piggyback networking systems HomePlug and HomePNA rely on USB-based NICs for easy installation. In wireless networking, USB-based NICs often have greater range than their PC Card–based peers because they can operate at higher power and with more sophisticated antennae. Compared to installing a PC Card adapter in your desktop computer and then sliding a wireless NIC into the adapter, the USB-based NIC makes more sense, both for the added range as well as the greater convenience and lower cost.

The NIC you choose must match the standard and speed used by the rest of your network. The exception is, of course, that many NICs operate at more than one speed. For example, nearly all of today's 100Base-T NICs slow down to accommodate 10Base-T networks. Dual-speed 802.11b+ wireless NICs will accommodate either 11 or 22MHz operation.

Most dual-speed NICs are *autosensing*. That is, they detect the speed on the network wire to which they are connected and adjust their own operating speed to match. Autosensing makes a NIC easier to set up, particularly if you don't know (or care) the speed at which your network operates. You can just plug in the network wire and let your hardware worry about the details.

Some network adapters allow for optional boot ROMs, which allow computers to boot up using a remote disk drive. However, this feature is more applicable to larger businesses with dedicated network servers rather than a home or small business network.

Hubs and Access Points

A network *hub* passes signals from one computer to the next. A network *access point* is the radio base station for a wireless network. Piggyback networks such as HomePlug and HomePNA do not use dedicated hubs, although one of the computers connected to the network acts like a hub.

Hubs

The most basic hub for a wired network has two functions. It provides a place to plug in the network wire from each computer, and it regenerates the signals to ensure against errors.

The design of Ethernet requires all the signals in the network loop to be shared. Every computer in the loop—that is, every computer connected to a single hub—sees exactly the same signals. The easiest way to do this would be to short all the wires together. Electrically, such a connection would be an anathema.

The circuitry of the hub prevents such disasters. It mixes all the signals it receives together and then sends out the final mixture in its output.

To make the cabling for the system easy, the jacks on a hub are wired the opposite of the jacks on NICs. That is, the send and receive connections are reserved—the connections the NIC uses for sending, the hub uses for receiving.

Inexpensive hubs are distinguished primarily by the number and nature of the ports they offer. You need one port on your hub for each computer or other device (such as a network printer or DSL router) in your network. You may want to have a few extra ports to allow for growth, but more ports cost more, too. Some hubs include a crossover jack or coaxial connection that serves as an *uplink* to tie additional hubs into your network.

Expensive hubs differ from the economic models chiefly by their management capabilities—things such as remote monitoring and reconfiguration, which are mostly irrelevant to a small network.

As with NICs, hubs can operate at multiple speeds. Although some require each network connection to be individually configured for a single speed (some are even physically set only at one speed), most modern dual-speed hubs are autosensing, much like NICs. Coupling a low-cost autosensing NIC and low-cost autosensing hub can sometimes be problematic with marginal wiring. The hub's sense may negotiate the highest-speed signals on the network, even though many packets fail to negotiate the wiring at higher speeds. In such instances, performance can fall below that of a low-speed-only network.

Some hubs are called *switches*; others have internal switches. A switch divides a network into segments and shifts data between them. Most dual-speed hubs actually act as switches when passing packets between 10Base-T and 100Base-T devices.

When used on a single-speed network, a switch can provide faster connections because the full bandwidth of the network gets switched to service each NIC. When several NICs contend for time on the network, however, the switch must arbitrate between them, and in the end, they share time as they would on a hub-based network.

Switches usually have internal buffers to make it easier to convert between speeds and arbitrate between NICs. In general, the larger the buffer the better, because a large buffer helps the switch operate at a higher speed more of the time.

Access Points

Access points earn their name because they provide access to the airwaves. Although in theory you could have a wireless-only hub to link together a small network of computers, such a network would shortchange you. You could not access the Internet or any devices that have built-in wired-networking adapters, such a network printers. In other words, most wireless networks also require a wired connection. The access point provides access to the airwaves for those wired connections.

The centerpiece of the access point is a combination of radio transmitter and receiver (which engineers often talk about simply as the *radio*). Any adjustment you might possibly make to the radio is hidden from you, so you don't have to be a radio engineer to use one. The access point's radio is both functionally and physically a sealed box, permanently set to the frequencies used by the standard used by the networking system supported by the access point. Even the power at which the access point operates is fixed. All access points use about the same power because the maximum limit is set by government regulations.

Access points differ in several ways, however. Because every access point has a wired connection, they differ just as wired network do—they may support different speed standards. In fact, most access points have multiple wired connections, so they are effectively wired hubs, too. The same considerations that apply to wired hubs therefore apply to the wired circuitry of access points.

Access points also differ in the interface between their radios and the airwaves—namely, their antennae. Lower-cost access points have a single, permanently attached antenna. More expensive hubs may have two or (rarely) more antennae. By using diversity techniques, multiple-antenna access points can select which of the antennae has the better signal and use it for individual transmissions. Consequently, dual-antennae access points often give better coverage.

Some access points make their antennae removable. You can replace a removable antenna with a different one. Some manufacturers offer *directional* antennae, which increase the range of an access point in one direction by sacrificing the range in all other directions. In other words, they concentrate the radio energy in one direction. Directional antennae are particularly useful in making an access point into a radio link between two nearby buildings.

Routers

When you want to link more than one network together—for example, you want to have both wired and wireless networks in your office—the device that provides the necessary bridge is called a *router* because it gives the network signals a route from one system to another. When you want to link a home network to the Internet through a DSL line, you need a router. Routers are more complex than hubs because they must match not only the physical medium but also the protocols used across the different media.

Sometimes what you buy as a hub actually functions as a router. Most wireless access points include 10Base-T or 100Base-T connections to link with a wired network. Many DSL adapters are sold as hubs and have multiple network connections (or even a wireless access point), even though they are, at heart, routers.

Cabling

Network wires must carry what are essentially radio signals between NICs and hubs, and they have to do this without letting the signals actually become radio waves—broadcasting as interference—or finding and mixing with companion radio waves, thus creating error-causing noise on the network line. Two strategies are commonly used to combat noise and interference in network wiring: shielding the signals with coaxial cable and preventing the problem with balanced signaling on twisted-pair wiring.

Coaxial Cables

Coaxial cables get their name because they all have a central conductor surrounded by one or more shields that may be a continuous braid or metalized plastic film. Each shield amounts to a long, thin tube, and each shares the same longitudinal axis—the central conductor. The surrounding shield typically operates at ground potential, which shields stray signals from leaking out of the central conductor or prevents noise from seeping in. Figure 12.6 shows the construction of a simple coaxial cable.

Coaxial cables are tuned as transmission lines—signals propagate down the wire and are completely absorbed by circuitry at the other end—which allows them to carry signals for long distances without degradation. For this reason, they are often used in networks for connecting hubs, which may be widely separated.

Twisted-Pair Wires

The primary alternative is twisted-pair wiring, which earns its name from being made of two identical insulated conducting wires that are twisted around one another in a loose double-helix. The most common form of twisted-pair wiring lacks the shield of coaxial cable and is often denoted by the acronym UTP, which stands *unshielded twisted pair*. Figure 12.7 shows a simplified twisted-pair cable.

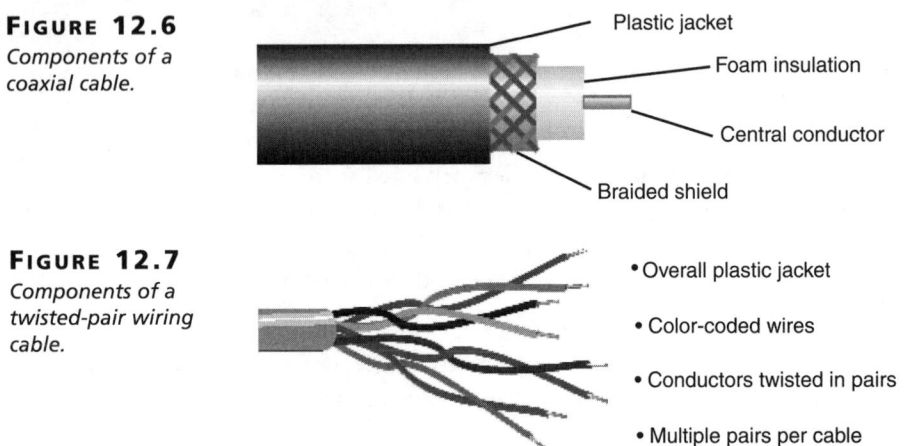

FIGURE 12.6
Components of a coaxial cable.

Plastic jacket
Foam insulation
Central conductor
Braided shield

FIGURE 12.7
Components of a twisted-pair wiring cable.

• Overall plastic jacket
• Color-coded wires
• Conductors twisted in pairs
• Multiple pairs per cable

Manufacturers rate their twisted-pair cables by category, which defines the speed of the network they are capable of carrying. Currently standards define six categories: 1 through 5 and 5e (which stands for 5 *enhanced*). Two higher levels, 6 and 7, exist on the periphery (proposed but not official standards). As yet, they are unnecessary because Gigabit Ethernet operates with Category 5 wiring. Note that, strictly speaking, until the standards for Levels 6 and 7 get approved, wires of these quality levels are not termed *Category 6* and *Category* 7, because the categories are not yet defined. Instead, they are termed *Level 6* and *Level* 7.

Those in the know don't bother with the full word *Category*. They abbreviate it *Cat*, so look for Cat 5 or Cat 5e wire when you shop. Table 12.4 lists the standards and applications of wiring categories.

TABLE 12.4　Standard Wire Categories

Category	Frequency Rating	Typical Application
1	None	Telephone and general wiring
2	4	Low-speed (1MHz) data
3	10	10Base-T
4	20	16Mbps token-ring networks
5	100	100Base-T networks
5e	100	100Base-T networks

Most UTP wiring is installed in the form of multipair cables with up to several hundred pairs inside a single plastic sheath. The most common varieties have 4 to 25 twisted pairs in a single cable. Standard Cat 5 wire for networking has four pairs, two of which are used by most 10Base-T and 100Base-T systems.

The pairs inside the cable are distinguished from one another by color codes. The body of the wiring is one color alternating with a thinner band of another color. In the two wires of a given pair, the background and banding color are opposites—that is, one wire will have a white background with a blue band, and its mate will have a blue background with a white band. Each pair has a different color code.

To minimize radiation and interference, most systems that are based on UTP use differential signals. For extra protection, some twisted-pair wiring is available with shielding. As with coaxial cable, the shielding prevents interference from getting to the signal conductors.

The specifications for most UTP networking systems limit the separation between any NIC and hub to no more than 100 meters (about 325 feet). Longer runs require repeaters or some other cabling system.

Telecommunications

Until the invention of the telegraph, no reliable communications traveled long distance faster than via a human letter carrier. That didn't stop people from trying, so in the pre-telegraph days a lot of exciting technologies promised to revolutionize communications—smoke signals, semaphore flags, and carrier pigeons were all attempts to break the bond between messenger and message.

The telegraph was able to let the messenger rest his feet and put pigeons back where they belong, atop the heads of dignitaries' statues in the park. With the advent of the telegraph, messages finally were able to travel at the ultimate speed limit of the universe—the speed of light.

Well, not quite. The telegraph only changed the speed of the messenger. It let the pony express rider exchange his steed for Pegasus, but the content of those messages never reached the speed of light. They were also slowed by the interface technology—the telegraph key in the hands of a human being. With fast fingers and a good ear, a 19th-Century telegrapher might squeeze ten words a minute down the wire, equivalent to a bit rate of less than ten per second. At that rate, sending a snapshot home from summer camp might take a month.

Since the advent of the telegraph, technology has concentrated on this other side of the speed issue, making the message move through the data channel faster. Using essentially the same wires as Samuel Morse, you can move data roughly 100,000 times faster through the telephone system and ten million times faster through your home network.

Getting there isn't always easy. The analog nature of your telephone line challenges data signals and imposes strict limits on how fast information can move through the system. The telephone line is an arcane world of strange technologies, all meant to get more speed from the simple telephone wire. It has been a long, hard battle, but one that has paid off. Today's modems now race ahead of the theoretical speed of which information can move through a telephone line. (They can do that because they're no longer really modems, but we're getting ahead of ourselves.)

You can do better. Digital services promise to deliver data 20 times faster than the best modem. Although people aren't switching over to the new, high-speed connections any-where near as fast as once predicted (that's one of the big reasons the telecommunications industry crashed in 2002), you can be sure someday you will have an all-digital connection.

Analog Services

A modem is standard equipment in every new computer—and with good reason. It's what most people use to connect to the Internet. Consider a computer without a modem, and you might as well buy a vacuum cleaner.

Today's modem is a world apart from those of only a few years ago, and the difference is speed. Nearly every new modem sold operates at a top speed of 56,000bps—fast enough that most people refuse to pay the higher charges demanded for faster-still all-digital ser-vices. Today's modems are fast enough for e-mail and most surfing. They falter only when you want an edge in playing online games, want to download streaming video, or want to exchange photos with relatives and friends.

Background

A true modem is a necessary evil in today's world of telecommunications because we still suffer from a telephone system that labors under standards devised even before electronics were invented, at a time when solid-state digital circuitry lay undreamed, almost a hun-dred years off. The telephone system was designed to handle analog signals only because that's all that speaking into a microphone creates. Over the years, the telephone system has evolved into an elaborate international network capable of handling millions of these analog signals simultaneously and switching them from one telephone set to another, any-where in the world.

In the last couple decades, telephone companies have shifted nearly all their circuits to digital. Most central office circuitry is digital. Nearly every long distance call is sent between cities and countries digitally. In fact, the only analog part of most telephone con-nections is the *local loop*, the wires that reach out from the telephone exchange to your home or office (and likewise extend from a distant exchange to the telephone of whomever you're calling).

The chief reason any analog circuitry remains in the telephone system is that there are hundreds of millions of plain-old telephone sets (which the technologically astute call simply *POTS*) dangling on the ends of telephone wires across the country. As long as people depend on POTS, they need an analog network to connect to.

Modem Technology

Of all modern communications systems, the one with the most severe limits on bandwidth is the telephone channel. Instead of the full frequency range of a good-quality stereo system (from 20 to 20,000Hz), a telephone channel only allows frequencies between 300 and 3000Hz to freely pass. This very narrow bandwidth works well for telephones because frequencies below 300Hz contain most of the power of the human voice but little of its intelligibility. Frequencies above 3000Hz increase the crispness of the sound but don't add appreciably to intelligibility.

What works well for voice is horrible for data. Although intelligibility is the primary concern with voice communications (most of the time), data transfer is principally oriented to bandwidth. The comparatively narrow bandwidth of the standard telephone channel limits the bandwidth of the modulated signal it can carry, which in turn limits the amount of digital information that can be squeezed down the phone line by a modem. The result is that dial-up telephone lines are poor data channels—but too often they are the only ones we have.

Shannon's Limit

Engineers can use a variety of technologies to squeeze more data into a narrow-bandwidth channel, but they still face an ultimate limit on the amount of data they can squeeze through a tight channel such as an analog telephone line. This ultimate limit combines the effects of the bandwidth of the channel and the noise level in the channel. The greater the noise, the more likely it will be confused with the information that has to compete with it. This theoretical maximum data rate for a communication channel is called *Shannon's Limit*. This fundamental law of data communications, discovered by Claude L. Shannon working at Bell Labs in 1948, states that the maximum number of digital bits that can be transmitted over a given communication path in one second can be determined from the bandwidth (W) and signal-to-noise ratio (S/N, expressed in decibels) by using the following formula:

Maximum data rate = W log (1 + S/N)

In telephone circuits, the analog-to-digital converters used in telephone company central offices contribute the noise that most limits modem bandwidth. In creating the digital pulse-coded modulation (PCM) signal, they create *quantization distortion*, which produces an effective signal-to-noise ratio of about 36 dB. Quantization distortion results from the inability of the digital system with a discrete number of voltage steps (256 in the case of telephone company A/D converters) to exactly represent an analog signal that has an infinite number of levels. At this noise level, Shannon's Limit for analog data on telephone lines is about 33,600 bits per second. Modern modems for dial-up data communications can be faster only by sidestepping some of the bandwidth issues.

Channels

Communications are supposed to be a two-way street. Information is supposed to flow in both directions. You should learn something from everyone you talk to, and everyone should learn from you. Even if you disregard the potential for success of such two-way communication, one effect is undeniable: It cuts the usable bandwidth of a data communication channel in one direction in half because the data going the other way requires its own share of the bandwidth.

Duplex

With modems, such a two-way exchange of information is called *duplex communications*. Often it is redundantly called *full-duplex*. A full-duplex modem is able to simultaneously handle two signals, usually (but not necessarily) going in opposite directions, so it can send and receive information at the same time. Duplex modems use two carriers to simultaneously transmit and receive data, each of which has half the bandwidth available to it and its modulation.

Half-Duplex

The alternative to duplex communications is *half-duplex*. In half-duplex transmissions, only one signal is used. To carry on a two-way conversation, a modem must alternately send and receive signals. Half-duplex transmissions allow more of the channel bandwidth to be put to use but slow data communications because often a modem must switch between sending and receiving modes after every block of data crawls through the channel.

Echoplex

The term *duplex* is often mistakenly used by some communications programs for computers to describe *echoplex* operation. In echoplex mode, a modem sends a character down the phone line, and the distant modem returns the same character, echoing it. The echoed character is then displayed on the originating terminal as confirmation that the character was sent correctly. Without echoplex, the host computer usually writes the transmitted character directly to its monitor screen. Although a duplex modem generates echoplex signals most easily, the two terms are not interchangeable.

With early communications programs, echoplex was a critical setup parameter. Some terminal programs relied on modem echoplex to display your typing on the screen. If you had echoplex off, you wouldn't see what you typed. Other terminal programs, however, displayed every character that went through the modem, so switching echoplex on would display two of every letter you typed, lliikkee tthhiiss. Web browsers don't bother you with the need to select this feature. Most, however, work without echoplex.

Switching Modems

To push more signal through a telephone line, some modems attempt to mimic full-duplex operation while actually running in half-duplex mode. Switching modems are half-duplex modems that reverse the direction of the signal at each end of the line in response to the need to send data. This kind of operation can masquerade as full-duplex because most of the time communications go only in one direction. You enter commands into a remote access system, and only after the commands are received does the remote system respond with the information you seek. Although one end is sending, the other end is more than likely to be completely idle.

On the positive side, switching modems are able to achieve a doubling of the data rate without adding any complexity to their modulation. However, the switching process itself is time-consuming and inevitably involves a delay because the modems must let each other know that they are switching. Because transmission delays across long-distance circuits are often a substantial fraction of a second (most connections take at least one trip up to a satellite and back down, a 50,000 mile journey that takes about a quarter of a second even at the speed of light), the process of switching can eat huge holes into transmission time.

Most software modem protocols require a confirmation for each block of data sent, meaning the modem must switch twice for each block. The smaller the block, the more often the switch must occur. Just one trip to a satellite would limit a switching modem with an infinitely fast data rate, using the 128-byte blocks of some early modem protocols, to 1024 bits per second at the two-switches-per-second rate.

Asymmetrical Channels

Because of this weakness of switching modems, *asymmetrical modems* cut the waiting by maintaining a semblance of two-way duplex communications while optimizing speed in one direction only. These modems shoehorn in a lower speed channel in addition to a higher speed one, splitting the total bandwidth of the modem channel unequally.

Early asymmetrical modems were able to flip-flop the direction of the high-speed communications, relying on algorithms to determine which way is the best way. The modern asymmetrical technologies have a much simpler algorithm. Designed for Internet communications, they assume you need a greater data rate downstream (to you) than upstream (back to the server). This design is effective because most people download blocks of data from the Internet (typically Web pages rife with graphics) while sending only a few commands back to the Web server.

The latest V.90 modems operate asymmetrically at their highest speed. Cable modems and satellite connections to the Internet also use a variation on asymmetrical modem technology. These systems typically provide you with a wide bandwidth downlink from a satellite or cable system to permit you to quickly browse pages but rely on a narrow-channel telephone link—a conventional modem link—to relay your commands back to the network.

Connection-Enhancing Technologies

Getting the most from your modem requires making the best match between it and the connection it makes to the distant modem with which you want to communicate. Although you have no control over the routing your local phone company and long distance carrier give to a given call (or even whether the connection remains consistent during a given call), a modem can make the best of what it gets. Using *line compensation*, it can ameliorate some problems with the connection. Fallback helps the modem get the most from a substandard connection or one that loses quality during the modem link-up. *Data compression* helps the modem move more data through any connection, and *error correction* compensates for transitory problems that would result in minor mistakes in transmissions.

Line Compensation

Although a long-distance telephone connection may sound unchanging to your ear, its electrical characteristics vary by the moment. Everything, from a wire swaying in the Wichita wind to the phone company's automatic rerouting of the call through Bangkok when the direct circuits fill up, can change the amplitude, frequency, and phase response of the circuit. The modem then faces two challenges: not to interpret such changes as data and to maintain the quality of the line to a high-enough standard to support its use for high-speed transmission.

Under modern communications standards, modems compensate for variations in telephone lines by equalizing these lines. That is, two modems exchange tones at different frequencies and observe how signal strength and phase shift with frequency changes. The modems then change their signals to behave in the exact opposite way to cancel out the variations in the phone line. The modems compensate for deficiencies in the phone line to make signals behave the way they would have in absence of the problems. If, for example, the modems observe that high frequencies are too weak on the phone line, they will compensate by boosting high frequencies before sending them.

Modern modems also use echo cancellation to eliminate the return of their own signals from the distant end of the telephone line. To achieve this, a modem sends out a tone and listens for its return. Once it determines how long the delay is before the return signal occurs and how strong the return is, the modem can compensate by generating the opposite signal and mixing it into the incoming data stream.

Echo Cancellation

When satellite rather than fiber optic technology dominated the long-distance telephone market, the half-second delay imposed by the long distance the signals traveled from earth to satellite and back created annoying "echoes" on the line. You spoke, and a fraction of a second later, you heard your own voice, delayed by the satellite hop, as it looped through the entire connection.

Switching to fiber optic long-distance connections minimizes the problem, at least to your ears. But modems can be confused even with the resulting short-delay echoes. A delayed pulse or phase-shift can sound like good data to a modem. To prevent such problems, modern modems use *echo cancellation*, which automatically subtracts the original signal from what the modem hears after the echo delay, thus canceling out the echo. To properly cancel the echo, the modem must be trained—during the initial handshake with a distant modem, it checks for echo and measures the delay. It later uses the discovered values for its echo cancellation.

Fallback

Most modems use at most two carriers for duplex communications. These carriers are usually modulated to fill the available bandwidth. Sometimes, however, the quality of the telephone line is not sufficient to allow reliable communications over the full bandwidth expected by the modem, even with line compensation. In such cases, most high-speed modems incorporate fallback capabilities. When the top speed does not work, they attempt to communicate at lower speeds that are less critical of telephone line quality. A pair of modems might first try 56,000bps and be unsuccessful. They next might try 53,000 or switch from high-speed to conventional modem technology with a fallback to 33,600bps.

Most modems fall back and stick with the slower speed that proves itself reliable. Some modems, however, constantly check the condition of the telephone connection to sense for any deterioration or improvement. If the line improves, these modems can shift back to a higher speed.

Multiple-Carrier Modems

Most modems rely on a relatively complex form of modulation on one or two carriers to achieve high speed. However, one clever idea (now relegated to a historical footnote by the latest modem standards) is the multiple-carrier modem, which uses relatively simple modulation on several simultaneous carrier signals. One of the chief advantages of this system comes into play when the quality of the telephone connection deteriorates. Instead of dropping down to the next incremental communications rate, thus generally cutting data speed in half, the multiple-carrier modems just stop using the carriers in the doubtful regions of the bandwidth. The communication rate may fall off just a small percentage in the adjustment. (Of course, it could dip by as much as a normal fallback modem as well.)

Data Compression

Although there's no way of increasing the number of bits that can cross a telephone line beyond the capacity of the channel, the information-handling capability of the modem circuit can be increased by making each bit more meaningful. Many of the bits that are sent through the telecommunications channel are meaningless or redundant—they convey no additional information. By eliminating those worthless bits, the information content of the data stream is more intense, and each bit is more meaningful. The process of paring the bits is called *data compression*.

The effectiveness of compression varies with the type of data that's being transmitted. One of the most prevalent data-compression schemes encodes repetitive data. Eight recurrences of the same byte value might be coded as two bytes, one signifying the value and the second the number of repetitions. This form of compression is most effective on graphics, which often have many blocks of repeating text. Other compression methods may strip out start, stop, and parity bits.

At one time, many modem manufacturers had their own methods of compressing data so that you needed two matched modems to take advantage of the potential throughput increases. Today, however, most modems follow international compression standards so that any two modems using the same standards can communicate with one another at compressed-data speeds. The most efficient of these international standards is called *V.44*.

These advanced modems perform the data compression on the fly in their own circuitry as you transmit your data. Alternately, you can precompress your data before sending it to your modem. Sort of like dehydrating soup, *precompression* (also known as *file compression*) removes the unnecessary or redundant parts of a file, yet allows the vital contents to be easily stored and reconstituted when needed. This gives you two advantages: The files you send and receive require less storage space because they are compressed, and your serial port operates at a lower speed for a given data throughput.

Note that once a file is compressed, it usually cannot be further compressed. Therefore, modems that use on-the-fly compression standards cannot increase the throughput of pre-compressed files. In fact, using one on-the-fly modem data-compression system (MNP5) actually can increase the transmission time for compressed files as compared to not using modem data compression.

Error Checking and Error Correction

Because all high-speed modems operate closer to the limits of the telephone channel, they are naturally more prone to data errors. To better cope with such problems, nearly all high-speed modems have their own built-in error-checking methods (which detect only transmission errors) and error-correction methods (which detect data errors and correct the mistakes before they get passed along to your computer). These error-checking and error-correction systems work like communications protocols, grouping bytes into blocks and sending cyclical redundancy checking information. They differ from the protocols used by communications software in that they are implemented in the hardware instead of your computer's software. That means they don't load down your computer when it's straining at the limits of its serial ports.

It can also mean that software communications protocols are redundant and a waste of time. As mentioned before, in the case of switching modems, using a software-based communications protocol can be counterproductive with many high-speed modems, slowing the transfer rate to a crawl. Most makers of modems using built-in error-checking advise against using such software protocols.

All modem error-detection and error-correction systems require that both ends of the connection use the same error-handling protocol. In order that modems can talk to one another, a number of standards have been developed. Today, the most popular are MNP4 and V.42. You may also see the abbreviations LAPB and LAPM describing error-handling methods.

LAPB stands for *Link Access Procedure, Balanced,* an error-correction protocol designed for X.25 packet-switched services such as Telebit and Tymnet. Some high-speed modem makers adapted this standard to their dial-up modem products before the V.42 standard (described later) was agreed on. For example, the Hayes Smartmodem 9600 from Hayes Microcomputer Products included LAPB error-control capabilities.

LAPM is an acronym for *Link Access Procedure for Modems* and is the error-correction protocol used by the CCITT V.42 standard, described later in the chapter.

Combining Voice and Data

Having but a single telephone line can be a problem when you need to talk as well as send data. In the old days, the solution was to switch. You'd type a message to the person at the other end of the connection, such as "Go voice," pick up the telephone handset, and tell your modem to switch back to command mode so you could talk without its constant squeal.

In the early 1990s, several manufacturers developed the means of squeezing both data and voice down a single telephone line at the same time using special modem hardware. Three technologies—VoiceView, VoiceSpan, and DSVD—vied for market dominance.

Internet technology has made all three irrelevant. Instead of combining data and voice in modem hardware, the modern alternative is to combine them using software inside your computer. Your computer captures your voice with a microphone and digitizes it. Web software packages the voice information into packets that get sent to an ordinary modem exactly like data packets. At the other end of the connection, the receiving computer converts the voice packets back to audio to play through the computer's speakers. The modem connection doesn't care—or even know—whether its passing along packets of data or digitized audio.

Analog Standards

Neither men nor modems are islands. Above all, they must communicate and share their ideas with others. One modem would do the world no good. It would just send data out into the vast analog unknown, never to be seen (or heard) again.

But having two modems isn't automatically enough. Like people, modems must speak the same language for the utterances of one to be understood by the other. *Modulation* is part of the modem language. In addition, modems must be able to understand the error-correction features and data-compression routines used by one another. Unlike most human beings, who speak any of a million languages and dialects, each somewhat ill-defined, modems are much more precise in the languages they use. They have their own equivalent of the French Academy: standards organizations.

In the United States, the first standards were set long ago by the most powerful force in the telecommunications industry, which was the telephone company. More specifically, the American Telephone and Telegraph Company was the telephone company prior to is breakup announced on January 8, 1982, which resulted in seven local operating companies (in addition to AT&T). Before then, the Bell System created nearly all U.S. telephone standards, including two of the historically most important modem standards, Bell 103 and Bell 212A.

With the globalization of business and technology, communication standards have become international, and the onus to set new standards has moved to an international standards organization that's part of the United Nations, the International Telecommunications Union (ITU) Telecommunications Standards Sector, which was formerly the Comite Consultatif International Telegraphique et Telephonique (in English, that's International Telegraph and Telephone Consultative Committee). All the current standards for modems fall under the aegis of the ITU. You can purchase copies of the ITU standards from the organization's Web site at www.itu.org.

Standards are important when buying a modem because they are your best assurance that a given modem can successfully connect with any other modem in the world. In addition, the standards you choose will determine how fast your modem can transfer data and how reliably it will work. The kind of communications you want to carry out will determine what kind of modem you need. If you're just going to send files electronically between offices, you can buy two nonstandard modems and get more speed for your investment. But if you want to communicate with the rest of the world, you will want to get a modem that meets the international standards. Table 13.1 summarizes major modem speed standards.

TABLE 13.1   Modem Speed Standards

Standard	Organization	Introduction	Baud Rate	Data Speed	Details
103	Bell	1963	300	300bps	FSK
V.21	CCITT	1965	300	300bps	International version of Bell 103 using different carrier frequencies
212A	Bell	1979	600	1200bps	QDPSK
V.22	CCITT	1980	600	1200bps	QDPSK, International version of Bell 212A
V.22bis	CCITT	1984	600	2400bps	QAM
V.32	CCITT	1984	2400	9600bps	QAM
V.32bis	CCITT	1991	2400	14,400bps	QAM
V.34	CCITT	1998	3429	33,600bps	QAM, highest true analog speed
V.90	ITU	1999	8000	56,000bps up, 33,600bps down	Level-sensitive digital encoding
V.92	ITU	2000	8000	56,000bps up, 48,000 down	Level-sensitive digital encoding

Nearly all new modems now sold operate at a top speed set by the V.92 modem standard, the international standard for modem communications at 56,000 bits per second (or 56Kbps) across dial-up telephone lines. It is the highest speed modem standard in use today and possibly the highest speed true modems will ever achieve. Note that this standard is essentially the same as ITU V.90. The new designation does not indicate an increase in speed. The chief changes between V.90 and V.92 include improved connection setup and handshaking, so it takes a modem less time to set up a V.92 connection. The V.92 standard includes (and is compatible with) the V.90 standard, and modems matching the two standards will interconnect using V.90 technology.

Strictly speaking, V.92 is not a modem standard because, at its top speeds, it involves no modulation or demodulation. When line conditions are not favorable, however, it shifts back to analog technology to cope.

It is an asymmetrical standard, with a maximum upstream data rate of 48,000bps and a maximum downstream data rate of about 56,000bps. It uses switching technology and cannot send and receive simultaneously. In theory, in many connections, its downstream falls short of its maximum rate because of line conditions. In addition, telephone regulations at one time prohibited the V.92 top operating speed because the last bit of speed pushed the power level on the telephone line above the allowed standards. Most sources listed a top practical speed of 53,000 bits per second, but your actual connection speed is now determined by line conditions and not law.

V.92 takes advantage of the digital technology already in use to shift voice calls across long-distance digital lines. The telephone standard for voice is to sample analog signals 8000 times a second using an eight-bit digital code. V.92 translates the digital code into voltage levels on the telephone line from your local phone company's digital switch to your home or office. Encoding digital information as voltage levels is a technology called *pulse amplitude modulation* (PAM). Because the V.92 standard requires modems to operate at frequencies in excess of normal voice circuits, its range is limited—V.92 connections require your modem to have no more than three miles of telephone wire between it and your telephone company's switch.

It should take 256 voltage levels, which are technically called *quantization levels*, to encode the eight-bit data stream. However, noise and line conditions can often mask changes of 1/256th of the voltage on an ordinary telephone line. To avoid problems with noise, the V.92 system uses only 128 quantization levels to encode data, allowing a seven-bit digital code with an 8000Hz sampling rate or a 56,000bps data rate.

As originally developed as the V.90 standard, modems used the PAM system only for downstream communications (that is, from the telephone company's switch to your modem). Upstream data (from your modem back to the phone company) relied on conventional modem technology under the V.34 standard, although limited to 31,200bps. The underlying assumption was that the phone company was better able to control digital signals and keep them within the required limits. Moreover, only the telephone company had direct access to the digital connection with long-distance trunk lines.

With the advent of the V.92 standard, this situation changed. Under V.92, modems use a technology called *V.PCM upstream* to let you use PAM to send data to other modems and services at a rate of 48,000 bits per second. The only difference between upstream and downstream is that the upstream signal is limited to only 64 quantization levels, thus allowing a six-bit code. The fewer voltage levels means that modem manufacturing inconsistencies and installation differences are less likely to cause signals exceeding the levels allowed by law.

To reduce the time needed for modems to connect, V.92 uses a technology called *QuickConnect* that takes advantage of the digital nature of the telephone system from the central office onward. The only part of the connection that needs line compensation is the local phone loop between where you use your modem and the telephone company's central office. Unless you're traveling with a notebook computer, this connection doesn't often change (and even when you're traveling, you're likely to use the same hotel phone for several connections at a time). Consequently, QuickConnect checks and remembers the settings for the local telephone loop and tries to reuse them if possible.

In truth, QuickConnect does not reduce the time required to determine the quality of a connection and compensate for it. Rather, it remembers the quality of your last connection under the assumption that you'll use the same telephone line for consecutive calls. The QuickConnect system stores in nonvolatile memory the equalizer and echo-cancellation settings as well as the digital characteristics of the line. When you place a subsequent call, your modem first examines the tone from the distant modem and compares it to the setting in memory. In case of a match, the modem starts with the stored settings to make a fast connection. If the modem detects a substantial change (such as you're using a notebook computer in a different hotel room), it walks through the standard V.90 handshaking procedure. The first time you use a V.92 modem in a given location, it will use the standard V.90 handshaking, requiring 20 to 30 seconds to adjust for the local phone line. Subsequent QuickConnect handshaking usually takes about half as long.

Recognizing how modems are used in normal telephone systems, V.92 explicitly recognizes the need to be able to pause modem communications so you can take another call. A feature called *Modem-on-Hold* lets you suspend data transfer without looking at your modem connection. In effect, you can put your modem on hold, take another call, and then return to your modem connection.

The V.92 standard is regarded as a refinement of V.90, which evolved out of two competing 56Kbps systems. *K56flex* is a proprietary technology that was independently developed and initially marketed as two different and incompatible systems by Rockwell and Lucent Technologies. In November, 1996, the two companies agreed to combine their work into a single standard. *x2* is a proprietary technology developed by U.S. Robotics. Both K56flex and x2 used the same PAM digital encoding as was adopted for V.90 and V.92. They differed from each other (and the standard) only in the handshaking used to set up the connection.

In addition to speed standards, several other standards have been used for data compression and error correction. Before the widespread adoption of international standards, many U.S. companies used technologies developed by Microcom Corporation and formalized as Microcom Networking Protocol Standards Levels 1 through 9. Currently, however, the dominant modem compression and error-control standards are those set by the ITU. These include V.42, a world-wide error-correction standard (which also incorporates MNP4 as an "alternative" protocol), V.42bis (data compression that can yield compression factors up to four, potentially quadrupling the speed of modem transmissions), and V.44, an improved compression system.

Modem Hardware

A modem is a signal converter that mediates the communications between a computer and the telephone network. In function, a modern computer modem has five elements: interface circuitry for linking with the host computer; circuits to prepare data for transmission by adding the proper start, stop, and parity bits; modulator circuitry that makes the modem compatible with the telephone line; a user interface that gives you command of the modem's operation; and the package that gives the modem its physical embodiment.

Computer Interface

For a modem to work with your computer, the modem needs a means to connect to your computer's logic circuits. At one time, all modems used a standard or enhanced serial port to link to the computer. However, because the standard serial port tops out at a data rate that's too slow to handle today's fastest modems—the serial limit is 115,200 bits per second, whereas some modems accept data at double that rate—modem-makers have developed parallel-interfaced modems.

All modems, whether installed outside your computer, in one of its expansion slots, or in a PCMCIA slot, make use of a serial or parallel communications port. In the case of an internal computer modem, the port is embedded in the circuitry of the modem, and the expansion bus of the computer itself becomes the interface.

With an external modem, this need for an interface (and the use of a port) is obvious because you fill the port's jack with the plug of a cable running off to your modem. With an internal modem, the loss is less obvious. You may not even detect it until something doesn't work because both your modem and your mouse (or some other peripheral) try to use the same port at the same time.

In the case of serial modems, this interface converts the parallel data of your computer into a serial form suitable for transmission down a telephone line. Modern modems operate so fast that the choice of serial port circuitry (particularly the UART) becomes critical to achieving the best possible performance.

The serial and parallel ports built into internal modems are just like dedicated ports of the same type. They need an input/output address and an interrupt to operate properly. The Plug-and-Play system assigns these values to the modem during its configuration process. (Older modems required you to select these values with jumpers or switches.)

Ordinarily you don't need to know or bother with these values. Some communications software, however, may not mesh perfectly with the Windows system. It may demand you tell it the port used by your modem. The modem's properties sheet lists this value. You can check it under Windows by clicking the modem icon in Control Panel and then clicking the Properties tab.

Data Preparation

Modern modem communications require that the data you want to send be properly prepared for transmission. This pre-transmission preparation helps your modem deliver the highest possible data throughput while preventing errors from creeping in.

Most modem standards change the code used by the serial stream of data from the computer interface into code that's more efficient (for example, stripping out data-framing information for quicker synchronous transfers). The incoming code stream may also be analyzed and compressed to strip out redundant information. The modem may also add error-detection or error-correction codes to the data stream.

At the receiving end, the modem must debrief the data stream and undo the compression and coding of the transmitting modem. A micro controller inside the modem performs these functions based on the communications standard you choose to use. If you select a modem by the communications standards it uses, you don't have to worry about the details of what this micro controller does.

Modulator

The heart of the modem is the circuitry that actually converts the digital information from your computer into analog-compatible form. Because this circuitry produces a modulated signal, it is called a *modulator*.

User Interface

The fourth element in the modem is what you see and hear. Most modems give you some way of monitoring what they do either audibly with a speaker or visually through a light display. These features don't affect the speed of the modem or how it works but can make one modem easier to use than another. Indicator lights are particularly helpful when you want to troubleshoot communication problems.

Line Interface

Finally, the modem needs circuitry to connect with the telephone system. This line interface circuitry (in telephone terminology, a *data access arrangement*) boosts the strength of the modem's internal logic-level signals to a level matching that of normal telephone service. At the same time, the line interface circuitry protects your modem and computer from dangerous anomalies on the telephone line (say, a nearby lightning strike), and it protects the telephone company from odd things that may originate from your computer and modem (say, a pulse from your computer in its death throes).

From your perspective, the line interface of the modem is the telephone jack on its back panel. Some modems have two jacks so that you can loop through a standard telephone. By convention, the jack marked "Line" connects with your telephone line; the jack marked "Phone" connects to your telephone.

Over the years, this basic five-part modem design has changed little. But the circuits themselves, the signal-processing techniques that they use, and the standards they follow have all evolved to the point that modern modems can move data as fast as the theoretical limits that telephone transmission lines allow.

Packaging

Internal modems plug into an expansion slot in your computer. The connector in the slot provides all the electrical connections necessary to link to your computer. To make the modem work, you only need to plug in a telephone line. The internal modem draws power from your computer, so it needs no power supply of its own. Nor does it need a case. Consequently, the internal modem is usually the least expensive at a given speed. Because internal modems plug into a computer's expansion bus, a given modem is compatible only with computers using the bus for which it was designed. You cannot put a computer's internal modem in a Macintosh or workstation.

External modems are self-contained peripherals that accept signals from your computer through a serial or parallel port and also plug into your telephone line. Most need an external source of power, typically a small transformer that plugs into a wall outlet and—through a short, thin cable—into the modem. At a minimum, then, you need a tangle of three cables to make the modem work. You have two incentives to put up with the cable snarl. External modems can work with computers that use any architecture as long as the computer has the right kind of port. In addition, external modems usually give you a full array of indicators that can facilitate troubleshooting.

Pocket modems are compact external modems designed for use with notebook computers. They are usually designed to plug directly into a port connector on your computer, eliminating one interface cable. Many eliminate the need for a power supply and cable by running from battery power or drawing power from your computer or the telephone line.

PC Card modems plug into that PCMCIA slots that are typically found in notebooks. They combine the advantage of cable-free simplicity of internal modems with the interchangeability of external modems (the PCMCIA interface was designed to work with a variety of computer architectures). The confines of the PCMCIA slot also force PC Card modems to be even more compact than pocket modems. This miniaturization takes its toll in higher prices, however, although the ability to quickly move one modem between your desktop and portable computer can compensate for the extra cost.

The confines of a PCMCIA slot preclude manufacturers from putting a full-size modular telephone jack on PC Card modems. Modem-makers use one of two workarounds for this problem. Most PC Card modems use short adapter cables with thin connectors on one end to plug into the modem and a standard modular jack on the other. Other PC Card modems use the X-Jack design, developed and patented by Megahertz Corporation (now part of 3Com). The X-Jack pops out of the modem to provide a skeletal phone connector into which you can plug a modular telephone cable. The X-Jack design is more convenient because you don't have to carry a separate adapter with you when you travel. On the other hand, the X-Jack makes the modem more vulnerable to carelessness. Yank on the phone cable, and it can break the X-Jack and render the modem useless. Yanking on an adapter cable will more likely pull the cable out or damage only the cable. On the other hand, the connectors in the adapter cables are also prone to invisible damage that can lead to unreliable connections.

Indicators

The principal functional difference between external (including pocket) and internal (including PC Card) modems is that the former have indicator lights that allow you to monitor the operation of the modem and the progress of a given call. Internal modems, being locked inside your computer, cannot offer such displays. Some software lets you simulate the lights on your monitor, and Windows will even put a tiny display of two of these indicators on your task bar. These indicators can be useful in troubleshooting modem communications, so many computer people prefer to have them available (hence, they prefer external modems).

The number and function of these indicators on external modems vary with the particular product and the philosophy of the modem-maker. Typically you'll find from four to eight indicators on the front panel of a modem, as shown in Figure 13.1.

FIGURE 13.1
Typical indicators on an external modem's front panel.

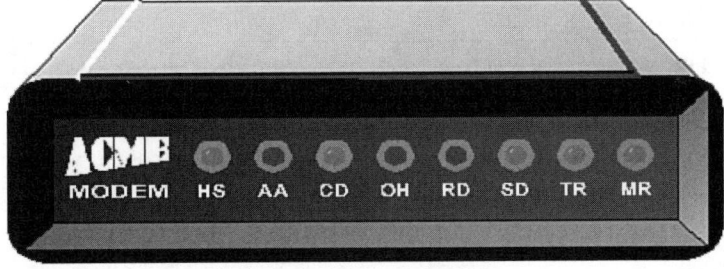

The most active and useful of these indicators are *Send Data* and *Receive Data*. These lights flash whenever the modem sends out or receives in data from the telephone line. They let you know what's going on during a communications session. For example, if the lights keep flashing away but nothing appears on your monitor screen, you know you are suffering a local problem, either in your computer, its software, or the hardware connection with your modem. If the Send Data light flashes but the Receive Data light does not flicker in response, you know that the distant host is not responding.

Carrier Detect indicates that your modem is linked to another modem across the telephone connection. It allows you to rule out line trouble if your modem does not seem to be getting a response. This light glows throughout the period your modem is connected.

Off-Hook glows whenever your modem opens a connection on your telephone line. It lights when your modem starts to make a connection and continues to glow through dialing, negotiations, and the entire connection.

Terminal Ready glows when the modem senses that your computer is ready to communicate with it. When this light is lit, it assures you that you've connected your modem to your computer and that your computer's communications software has properly taken control of your serial port.

Modem Ready glows whenever your modem is ready to work. It should be lit whenever your modem is powered up and not in its test state.

High Speed indicates that the modem is operating at its fastest possible speed. Some modems have separate indicators for each speed increment they support. Others forego speed indicators entirely.

Auto Answer lights to let you know that your modem is in its answer mode. If your telephone rings, your modem will answer the call (at least if its connected to the line that is ringing).

Table 13.2 summarizes the mnemonics commonly used for modem indicators and their functions.

TABLE 13.2   Modem Indicator Abbreviations and Definitions

Mnemonic	Spelled Out	Meaning
HS	High Speed	Modem is operating at highest speed.
AA	Auto Answer	Modem will answer phone.
CD	Carrier Detect	Modem is in contact with remote system.
OH	Off Hook	Modem is off hook, using the phone line.
RD	Receive Data	Modem is receiving data.
SD	Send Data	Modem is transmitting data.
TR	Terminal Ready	PC is ready to communicate.
MR	Modem Ready	Modem is ready to communicate.

Digital Services

Today, all of the international telephone network is digital, with the exception of one wire—the one running from the telephone company central office to your home. This local loop, sometimes called *the last mile*, is the same stuff that Alexander Graham Bell experimented with and uses the same technology he developed—a pair of copper wires designed to carry analog voice signals. Eventually, this local loop will be replaced with a newer connection technology, such as coaxial cable or fiber optics carrying only digital data.

Businesses already have this option available to them. Modern cable television systems offer digital data communications capabilities as well, although dial-up voice circuits remain the province of the telephone company (mostly for legal reasons). Even so, there's little doubt you'll eventually shift from analog to digital services for all of your telecommunications needs.

You can already get all-digital circuits for your data. The only question is who will provide the connection. Three technologies can provide you with a high-speed all-digital link—telephone, cable, and satellite.

All three work. All three deliver speeds that make modem connections seem like they are antiquated. In fact, the most important limiting factor is availability. Only satellite services can promise a link in any part of the United States (and most of the world). The others depend on your local telephone company or cable provider upgrading its facilities to handle digital subscriber services.

Telephone Services

One key player in the supply of digital telecommunications services is quite familiar—the telephone company. Beyond traditional POTS, telephone companies have developed a number of all-digital communication services. Some of these have been around for a while, aimed at business users with heavy data needs. Several new, all-digital services are aimed directly at you as an individual consumer.

The range of digital services supplied by telephone companies is wide and spans a range of data rates. Table 13.3 lists many of these and their maximum data rates.

TABLE 13.3   Maximum Data Rates of Digital Telecommunications Standards

Standard	Connection Type	Downstream Rate	Upstream Rate
V.34	Analog	33.6Kbps	33.6Kbps
V.90	Digital/analog	56Kbps	33.6Kbps
V.92	Digital	56Kbps	48Kbps
SDS 56	Digital	56Kbps	56Kbps
ISDN	Digital	128Kbps	128Kbps

continues

TABLE 13.3	Continued		
Standard	*Connection Type*	*Downstream Rate*	*Upstream Rate*
SDSL	Digital	1.544Mbps	1.544MBps
T1	Digital	1.544Mbps	1.544MBps
E1	Digital	2.048Mbps.	2.048Mbps
ADSL	Digital	9Mbps	640Kbps
VDSL	Digital	52Mbps	2Mbps

You will still talk on the telephone for ages to come (if your other family members give you a chance, of course), but the nature of the connection may finally change. Eventually, digital technology will take over your local telephone connection. In fact, in many parts of America and the rest of the world, you can already order a special digital line from your local telephone company and access all-digital switched systems. You get the equivalent of a telephone line, one that allows you to choose any conversation mate who's connected to the telephone network (with the capability of handling your digital data, of course), as easily as dialing a telephone.

T1

The basic high-speed service provided by the telephone company is called *T1*, and its roots go back to the first days of digital telephony in the early 1960s. The first systems developed by Bell Labs selected the now-familiar 8KHz rate to sample analog signals and translate them into eight-bit digital values. The result was a 64Kbps digital data stream. To multiplex these digital signals on a single connection, Bell's engineers combined 24 of these voice channels together to create a data frame 193 bits long, the extra bit length defining the beginning of the frame. The result was a data stream with a bit rate of 1.544Mbps. Bell engineers called the resulting 24-line structure *DS1*. AT&T used this basic structure throughout its system to multiply the voice capacity of its telephone system, primarily as trunk lines between exchanges.

As telephone demand and private business exchanges (PBXs) became popular with larger businesses, the telephone company began to offer T1 service directly to businesses. As digital applications grew, T1 became the standard digital business interconnect. Many Web servers tie into the network with a T1 line.

A key feature of the DS1 format was that it was compatible with standard copper telephone lines, although requiring repeaters (booster amplifiers) about every mile. The signal itself is quite unlike normal analog telephone connections, however, and that creates a problem. Its signal transmission method is called Alternate Mark Inversion (AMI), a formatting code for T1 transmissions over twisted-pair copper cable. T1 transmissions are in bipolar form. AMI represents a zero (or space) by the absence of a voltage; a one (or mark) is represented by a positive or negative pulse, depending on whether the preceding one was negative or positive (that is, marks are inverted on an alternating basis). This encoding system generates a signal with a bandwidth about equivalent to its data rate, 1.5MHz. This high-speed signal creates a great deal of interference, so much that two T1 lines cannot safely cohabitate in the 50-pair cables used to route normal telephone services to homes.

Outside of the United States, the equivalent of T1 services is called *E1*. Although based on the same technology as T1, E1 combines 30 voice channels with 64Kbps bandwidth to create a 2.048Mbps digital channel.

Serious Web surfers dream of having a dedicated T1 line. The cost, however, is prohibitive. Installation is often thousands of dollars and monthly charges may be a thousand dollars, sometime more. Typically, your Internet Service Provider has an T1 (or better) connection and divides it up, giving each customer a single modem-slice.

T3 is a synonym for DS3 service, which is approximately 45Mbps, and OC-3 is approximately 155Mbps fiber interface.

The primary problem with T1 is the interference-causing modulation system it uses, one based on 1960s technology. Using the latest modulation techniques, the telecommunications industry has developed a service called *High data rate Digital Subscriber Line* (HDSL) that features the same data rate as T1 or E1 but requires a much narrower bandwidth, from 80 to 240KHz. One basic trick to the bandwidth-reduction technique is splitting the signal across multiple phone lines. For T1 data rate, the service uses two lines; for E1, three. Besides reducing interference, the lower data rate allows longer links without repeaters, as much as 12,000 feet.

HDSL delivers high-speed data networking, up to 1.544Mbps over two copper pairs and up to 2.048Mbps over three pairs, at a maximum range of 20,000 feet (about 3.8 miles or 6.1 km) from a central office. It is similar to Symmetrical Digital Subscriber Line (discussed later) and has symmetrical transmission capabilities. Most T1 lines installed today utilize this technology.

Unfortunately the "subscriber" in the name of the standard was not meant to correspond to you as an individual. It fits into the phone company scheme of things in the same place as T1—linking businesses and telephone company facilities.

DSL

The service you're most likely to buy from your telephone company goes under the name *Digital Subscriber Line*. It uses your ordinary telephone wires to carry high-speed digital signals. In fact, today's technologies let you use both the analog phone service and the digital capacity of the same wires at the same time. The high frequencies of the digital signal are easily split from the low frequencies of the analog signal, so one wire can do double duty. When telephone companies first introduced this piggyback service, they called it *G.Lite*, but it has become the standard for residential DSL.

G.Lite is a special case of a more generalized service called Asymmetrical Digital Subscriber Line or ADSL. It is asymmetrical because it offers a higher downstream data rate from the server compared to its upstream rates, from you back to the server.

When telephone companies first offered DSL services, they needed to send out a technician on each job to install the splitters required to separate the analog and digital signals. The need for a technician added hundreds of dollars to the cost of setting up an ADSL connection. To eliminate the need for the splitter and create a common consumer standard for ADSL, several manufacturers in the telecommunications industry banded together to create the *Universal ADSL Working Group*, the organization that defined the G.Lite standard under the formal designation G.992.2.

ADSL can move downstream data at speeds up to 8Mbps. Upstream, however, the maximum rate is about 640Kbps to 1Mbps. ADSL doesn't operate at a single rate as does T1. Its speed is limited by distance, with longer distances imposing greater constraints. It can push data downstream at the T1 rate for up to about 18,000 feet from the central office. At half that distance, its downstream speed potential approaches 8.5Mbps. To distinguish the more general form of ADSL from G.Lite, this full-fledged ADSL is sometimes called *ADSL Full Rate* or *G.dmt*. Its official designation is G.992.1.

G.Lite is one variety of ADSL. G.Lite allows for a bandwidth downstream of up to 1.544Mbps. Upstream the asymmetrical system allows for a bandwidth of up to 512Kbps. The maximum length of a G.Lite connection stretching between the central office and your home or business is 18,000 feet.

Table 13.4 summarizes the downstream speeds and maximum distances possible with ADSL technology.

TABLE 13.4 ADSL Downstream Data Rates

Equivalent Service	Downstream Data Rate	Distance
G.Lite	1.544Mbps	18,000 feet
T1	1.544Mbps	18,000 feet
E1	2.048Mbps	16,000 feet
DS1	6.312Mbps	12,000 feet
ADSL	8.448Mbps	9000 feet

Another kind of DSL offers the same speed in both the upstream and downstream directions. Termed *Symmetrical Digital Subscriber Line* (SDSL), this kind of service is best suited
for companies offering Web services from their own servers. The data speed of the SDSL
system ranges from 160Kbps up to 1.544Mbps. The maximum usable rate depends on the
distance of the subscriber from the central office. The lowest speed occurs at a maximum
range of the SDSL system, which is 24,000 feet (about 4.5 miles or 7.2 km).

The acronym SDSL has been used in the past to describe another service called *Single-line
Digital Subscriber Line*, which was an alternative to multiline data services for high-speed
operation.

The modulation system used by all DSL services operates at frequencies above the base-
band used by the ordinary telephone service, which is why a single line can carry high-
speed digital signals and ordinary telephone signals simultaneously. In typical DSL
implementations, the DSL signals start at about 50KHz, leaving the lower frequencies for
carrying conventional voice signals.

The splitter that divides the signal between voice and data on the subscriber's premises is
the equivalent of a stereo speaker's crossover; the splitter combines a high-pass filter to
extract a data-only signal and a low-pass filter to extract the voice-only signal. Using the
G.Lite system, you install the required splitters (sometimes called *filters*) by simply plugging them in using modular plugs and jacks like ordinary telephone equipment.

VDSL

The next step above ADSL is the *Very-high-data-rate Digital Subscriber Line* (VDSL). A
proposal only, the service is designed to initially operate asymmetrically at speeds higher
than ADSL but for shorter distances, potentially as high as 51.84Mbps downstream for
distances shorter than about 1000 feet, falling to one-quarter that at about four times the
distance (12.86Mbps at 4500 feet). Proposed upstream rates range from 1.6Mbps to
2.3Mbps. In the long term, developers hope to make the service symmetrical. VDSL is
designed to work exclusively in an ATM network architecture. As with ADSL, VDSL can
share a pair of wires with an ordinary telephone connection or even ISDN service.

SDS 56

Switched Data Services 56 (sometimes shortened to *Switched-56*) is an archaic connection
system that yielded a single digital channel capable of a 56Kbps data rate—the same as
with a modem but with true digital signals. The Switched-56 signals traveled through
conventional copper twisted-pair wiring (the same old stuff that carries your telephone
conversations). For most telephone companies, it was an interim service to bridge the gap
between POTS and ISDN service areas.

With Switched-56 you needed special head-end equipment—the equivalent of a modem—to link the wire to your computer. To take advantage of the connection, you also needed to communicate with someone who also had SDS 56 service.

In some locales, SDS 56 was no more expensive than an ordinary business telephone line. Installation costs, however, could be substantially higher (PacBell, for example, at one time charged $500 for installation), and some telephone companies added extra monthly maintenance charges in addition to the normal dial-up costs. With modern modems promising the same speed with no extra charges, little wonder Switched-56 gets discussed in the past tense.

ISDN

The initials stand for *Integrated Services Digital Network*, a first attempt at bringing true digital communications to the home through existing telephone lines. Although the service is still available, it's essentially irrelevant because DSL offers more speed at about the same cost.

ISDN predates DSL. Its start came in November 1992 when AT&T, MCI, and Sprint embraced a standard they called *ISDN-1*. Today, two versions of ISDN are generally available. The simplest is the *Basic Rate Interface* (BRI), which takes advantage of the copper twisted-pair wiring that's already in place, linking homes and offices to telephone exchanges. Instead of a single analog signal, an ISDN line uses what is called "2B1Q line coding" to carry three digital channels: two B (for *Bearer*) channels that can carry any kind of data (digitally encoded voice, fax, text, and numbers) at 64,000bps, and a D (or *Delta*) channel, operating at 16,000bps, that can carry control signals and serve as a third data channel. The three channels can be independently routed to different destinations through the ISDN system.

The maximum distance an ISDN line can stretch from the central office is 18,000 feet (about 3.4 miles or 5.5 km). To accommodate longer runs, this distance can be doubled by adding a *repeater* in the middle of the line. A repeater is an amplifier that regenerates the digital signals, erasing the signal distortion that arises on long lines.

A single BRI wire enables you to transfer uncompressed data bidirectionally at the 64,000bps rate, exactly like a duplex modem today but with higher speed and error-free transmission, thanks to its all-digital nature. Even during such high-speed dual-direction connections, the D channel would still be available for other functions.

The more elaborate form of ISDN service is called the *Primary Rate Interface* (PRI). This service delivers 23 B channels (each operating at 64,000 bits per second) and one D channel (at 16,000 bits per second). As with normal telephone service, ISDN service is billed by time in use, not the amount of data transmitted or received.

The strength of BRI service is that it makes do with today's ordinary twisted-pair telephone wiring. Neither you nor the various telephone companies need to invest the billions of dollars required to rewire the nation for digital service. Instead, only the central office switches that route calls between telephones (which today are mostly plug-in printed circuit boards) need to be upgraded.

Cable Services

The chief performance limit on telephone service is the twisted-pair wire that runs from the central office to your home or business. Breaking through its performance limits would require stringing an entirely new set of wires throughout the telephone system. Considering the billions of dollars invested in existing twisted-pair telephone wiring, the likelihood of the telephone company moving into a new connection system tomorrow is remote.

Over the past two decades, however, other organizations have been hanging wires from poles and pulling them underground to connect between a third to a half of the homes in the United States—cable companies. The coaxial cables used by most such services have bandwidths a hundred or more times wider than twisted pair. They regularly deliver microwave signals to homes many miles from their distribution center.

Tapping that bandwidth has intrigued cable operators for years, and the explosive growth of the Internet has set them salivating. The advent of digital cable has made Web connections an option for most cable subscribers.

Architecture

The cable television system differs from the international telephone system in several ways. Most cable television systems are local. They are meant to cover only a limited geographic range. Cable systems do not interconnect. Each cable operator plucks the signals it needs from the air, either from distant broadcast stations or from satellite. There is no great cable web that allows you to directly link with another cable user anywhere in the world.

Moreover, cable systems are designed differently. Telephone systems are point to point, caller to caller, one on one. Cable systems are designed for broadcast in a one-to-many fashion. Cable systems send the same signals to each of their subscribers. The wiring for telephone systems resembles a star with a center hub (the central office) and individual nodes, each connected directly to the hub with its own (albeit low bandwidth) wire. The cable system is a spine—one big, wide bandwidth wire carrying signals for all subscribers, each of which taps into the same spine for the same signals.

The essence of the cable design is that all users share the same bandwidth. The cable is piled with as many as 500 television channels—that's a full 3GB of bandwidth-ignoring guard bands. When operators put Internet signals on the cable system, users have to share that bandwidth, too. How wide a slice of bandwidth each user gets depends primarily on how many users are sharing. If you're the only one to log on to the Internet on your cable system, you can get speeds that T1 users would envy. Log on when Microsoft offers free downloads of a new version of Internet Explorer or a beer company runs an online bikini competition, and you're apt to get more free beer than bandwidth through the cable (that is, about zero). With a high-speed DSL telephone line, you are guaranteed bandwidth. With cable, you share and take your chances. You could do better—or much, much worse. In technical terms, the telephone system guarantees *Quality of Service* (QoS). The cable system may not (although some operators are making QoS guarantees to lure you over to coaxial cable).

Cable systems allow for individual addressing of subscribers' equipment. Each cable box has an electronic serial number that the cable operator's equipment can address individually (for example, to alter the services you are authorized to receive). But this individual addressing does not provide an individual channel to your home. The signals to control your cable box are broadcast to all subscribers on the cable system. Only your box with the correct serial number responds to commands sent to it.

Standards

During the first few years of cable-based data services, the one element lacking was standardization. Each cable operator used its own equipment designs to adapt data signals to the cable medium. The adapters used by different cable operators were incompatible, as were the data signals from the *head-end*, the cable company's equivalent of the telephone company's central office. Although such proprietary designs gave cable companies a measure of security—they helped thwart widespread hacking—they also made equipment more expensive and employee training more difficult.

Several efforts at developing cable standards started in the mid–1990s. The first major effort started at the IEEE, which formed a new working group called the *Cable TV Media Access Control and Physical Protocol Working Group* in May 1994, to define a standard for cable modems. The IEEE group members had difficulty agreeing to any single standard, however, and the group missed its original target of December 1995, for publishing a specification.

An impatient cable industry got tired of waiting for engineers to come up with a standard, so a group of cable television operators, including such major players as Comcast, Cox, MSOs, TCI, and Time Warner, started their own standardization effort. The companies formed an independent limited partnership called *Multimedia Cable Network System Partners, Ltd.* (usually shortened to MCNS), which Continental Cablevision and Rogers Cablesystems then joined. In little more than a year, the partnership sifted through 12 proposals to produce a draft standard that it published as the *Data Over Cable Service*

Interface Specification (DOCSIS) in March, 1997. The industry research organization CableLabs took over the administration of the specification and developed a compliance program. By March 1998, the group had developed an interoperability certification program and, in March 1998, the ITU endorsed the DOCSIS standard as an official standard ITU J.112.

A revised version of the DOCSIS specification, version 1.1, was released in April 1999. The new standard better defined signal parameters to guarantee the bandwidth of the signal and minimize delays. In addition, the revision added standards for new services, including voice-over-Internet telephones and constant bit-rate services. A European version of DOCSIS, called EuroDOCSIS, is used with the different television standards prevailing there. Another update, to DOCSIS 2.0, is in the works. The complete DOCSIS specification is available online at www.cablemodem.com/specification.

DOCSIS fits data onto cable by taking over a single television channel for downstream data and a second channel for upstream data. Each television channel has a bandwidth of 6MB. In general, the system can use any channel in the VHF or UHF ranges (from 50 to 864MHz) for downstream data, but upstream data is restricted to lower frequencies (5 to 42MHz), which makes the adapters less expensive to manufacturer.

The DOCSIS standard allows cable operators flexibility in choosing either 64- or 256-state quadrate amplitude modulation for the downstream data signals they provide. Typically cable operators use 64-state QAM, with which a single 6MHz downstream television channel can carry data at a rate of about 27Mbps. Upstream, most cable operators have a choice of 16-state QAM or quadrature phase-shift keying, a more robust but slower modulation scheme most choose to ride over the higher noise levels prevalent at lower frequencies on cable. In this asymmetrical system, cable operators often limit upstream bandwidth from individual users, often to as little as 320Kbps, although the standard allows upstream rates as high as 10Mbps. At low-demand times, you might score downstream bandwidth approaching the full 27Mbps rate. Typically, however, cable services deliver downstream data at 1 to 3Mbps.

To allow multiple users to share the same bandwidth, DOCSIS uses time division multiple access (TDMA) technology. That is, each user gets a fraction of the total bandwidth in which to transmit and receive data. To gain access to the cable, DOCSIS uses the Ethernet MAC (Media Access Control) layer.

DOCSIS includes provisions for each user to have a 14-bit *subscriber ID*, which allows cable operators to individually tailor service much as they do premium cable television channels. For example, individual users may be assigned different bandwidths.

Before the wide adoption of DOCSIS, some cable companies deployed *telco-return modems*, which used the cable company's high-speed coaxial cable for downstream data but made the upstream link through a conventional phone line (with all its bandwidth constraints). With the move to DOCSIS, most cable modems now use only a cable connection.

Because all signals ride across the same coaxial cable, all your neighbors have access to the packets of data you send and receive. To maintain privacy, your cable modem automatically encrypts everything you send and receive using the Data Encryption Standard (DES) algorithm.

Satellite Services

The same technology used by direct-broadcast satellite television, through which you can grab viewable video directly from orbiting satellites, also works for data. Using a small parabolic antenna pointed at a geosynchronous satellite orbiting about 24,000 miles away, you can tap into the Internet at speeds well beyond the capabilities of dial-up telephone connections. Instead of television signals, the satellite simply beams a stream of data down to earth.

The leading satellite service, DirecPC from Hughes Electronics, initiated service in 1997. It bills itself as the fastest Internet service available nationwide. Although slower than either DSL or cable modems, it holds the advantage of availability—anywhere you can see the southern sky, you can make a connection to DirecPC.

Satellite systems are inherently asymmetrical. You don't transmit your needs to the satellite—doing so would require an uplink and a much larger antenna. Instead, you use the satellite connection only for a downlink, to receive data. To send data, your computer connects to the Web through a conventional dial-up modem. The satellite-based downlink operates at 400Kbps while your phone-based uplink struggles along at modem speed, 14.4 to 56Kbps.

Satellites best fit a broadcast model. That is, they dump out their signals across wide areas for consumption by the multitudes rather than directly targeting individuals. By limiting the downlink bandwidth to 400Kbps, they maximize the number of subscribers that can share the system. In addition, DirecPC attempts to maximize the speed and usefulness of its product using push technology. The system pushes out selected Web and newsgroup information, and your computer captures it as it is sent out, spooling the data to disk. When you want to access one of the pushed Web sites or newsgroups, you can read it almost instantly from the cache. So your computer won't clog up by trying to cache the entire Internet, the system allows you to choose which sites and groups to cache locally.

Digital Services

DirecPC uses a 21-inch elliptical antennae designed for roof mounting. The DirecPC antenna is a single-purpose device and can be used only for data, not satellite television reception. The system also requires a receiver (sometimes called a *modem*) that may be installed as an expansion board inside your computer or as a standalone external peripheral.

Internet

Surfing's a breeze—and I do mean riding the Web and not a wave. Just point and click, and you can visit any Web site, anywhere in the world, in microseconds (or a few minutes, if you have a dial-up line). About the only thing easier is being dead, and that's not nearly as much fun (or so I've been told).

The Web is easy to use because, believe it or not, it was designed that way. Scientists working around huge particle accelerators—the kind that smash the tiniest pieces of matter into one another at nearly the speed of light to create huge research budget deficits—spent a bit of their spare time developing the idea. Basically, they decided to put a pretty face on the work of the military-educational complex that let college professors in Berkeley play Pong with researchers at Princeton.

But what's easy for you to use isn't necessarily easy for your computer. And it's not just your computer. Beneath all the fun and games is a snarl of cables more tangled than a planet-size bowl of spaghetti, millions of computers, and an assortment of hardware stranger than the collection of an alien zoo (routers, switchers, multiplexers, and demultiplexers), and some things so esoteric no one knows what to call them. That easy point-and-click interface of the Web covers up an international conspiracy of computers working together to put pop-up ads atop your every click.

As with any conspiracy, getting to the bottom of the Internet requires getting the answers to a couple of questions: What does your computer know, and when does it know it? The answers tell how the complex web of the Internet really operates.

Actually, getting to the bottom of the Internet is easy. You're already there. The computer sitting in front of you is considered the lowest of the low, a mere client to the millions of servers on the Web. At the far end is a hallowed space—actually a super-superstitious 13 of them—housing the true masterminds of the Web, the 13 *root name servers*, the machines that are the ultimate organizers of the Web.

In between is the Internet. But it's nothing you can get your hands on. It's nothing real. Although the Internet is built using hardware, it is not hardware itself. Similarly, you need hardware to connect to the Internet, but that hardware only serves as a means to access what you really want: the information that the Internet can bring to your computer. Without the right hardware, you could not connect to the Internet, but having the hardware alone won't make a new World Wide Web.

Despite its unitary name, there is no giant Internet in the sky or in some huge office complex somewhere. In fact, the Internet is the classic case of "there is no there there," as Gertrude Stein observed in her book *Everybody's Autobiography* (impress your friends with that gem). Like an artichoke, if you slice off individual petals or pieces of the Internet, you'll soon have a pile of pieces and no Internet anywhere, and you won't find it among the pieces. Rather, like the artichoke, the Internet is the overall combination of the pieces.

Those pieces are tied together both physically and logically. The physical aspect is a collection of wires, optical fibers, and microwave radio links that carry digital signals between computers. The combination of connections forms a redundant network. Computers are linked to one another in a web that provides multiple signal paths between any two machines.

The logical side is a set of standards for the signals that travel through that network. The Internet uses various protocols, depending on what kind of data is being transferred. The chief protocol and the defining standard of the Internet is TCP/IP, discussed in this chapter.

To work properly, the TCP/IP system requires every computer (or device) connected to the Internet have a unique address, the *IP address*. Although simple in concept—the IP address is nothing more than a 32-bit binary number, at least for now—what that number means and the future of the entire addressing system are two of the most complex issues regarding the Internet.

Of course, 32-bit binary numbers probably don't roll off your tongue, and remembering one for each Web site you want to visit sounds about as fun as an overnight study session with too much coffee and stress. Thankfully, the developers of the Web concocted the *Domain Name System* (DNS), which assigns somewhat more memorable names to every Web site. Making the DNS system work, however, is one of the great challenges of the Internet.

The most visible piece of the Web is content. After all, if there weren't anything worth surfing for, you'd probably turn your attention to something else—say, surfing for real when the tsunami warnings go out. Every Web page is, surprisingly, a computer program written in unique languages understood by your Web browser.

And finally, you've somehow got to make a connection with the Internet. That's what you pay for.

History

The place to begin is the beginning—and with the Internet, we need to go way back. Although the Web is the medium of the moment, the Internet has a long history, and locating its origins depends on how primitive an ancestor you seek.

The thread of the development of the Internet stretches all the way back to 1958, if you pull on it hard enough. The Internet's mother—the organization that gave birth to it— was itself born in the contrail of Sputnik. In October, 1957, the USSR took the world by surprise by launching the first artificial satellite and made the U.S. suddenly seem techno-logically backward. In response, President Dwight D. Eisenhower launched the Advanced Research Project Agency (ARPA) as part of the Department of Defense in January, 1958.

Then, as now, ARPA's work involved a lot of data processing, much of it at various university campuses across the country. Each computer, like the college that hosted it, was a world unto itself. To work on the computer, you had to be at the college. To share the results of the work on the computer, you needed a letter carrier with biceps built up from carrying stacks of nine-track tapes from campus to campus. Information flowed no faster between computers than did the mail.

Bob Taylor, working at ARPA in 1967, developed the idea of linking together into a redundant, packet-based network all the computers of major universities participating in the agency's programs. In October, 1969, the first bytes crossed what was to become ARPAnet in tests linking Stanford Research Institute and the University of California at Los Angeles. By December, 1969, four nodes of the fledgling internetworking system were working.

The system began to assume its current identity with the first use of the Transmission Control Protocol in a network in July, 1977. As a demonstration, TCP was used to link together a packet radio network, SATnet, and ARPAnet. Then, in early 1978, the Transmission Control Protocol was split into a portion that broke messages into packets, reassembled them after transmission, kept order among the packets, and controlled error control, called *TCP*, and a second protocol that concerned itself with the routing of packets through the linkage of the network, called the *Internet Protocol* (IP). The two together made TCP/IP, the fundamental protocol of today's Internet.

If the Internet actually has a birthday, it's January 1, 1983, when ARPAnet switched over from the Network Control Protocol to TCP/IP. (By that time, ARPAnet was only one of many networks linked by TCP/IP.) To give a friendlier front end to communications with distant computer systems, Tim Berners-Lee, working at CERN in Geneva in 1990, invented the World Wide Web.

The final step in the development of today's Internet came in 1991. In that year the National Science Foundation, which was overseeing the operation of the Internet, lifted its previous restrictions on its commercial use. The free-market free-for-all began.

Addressing

If you want to go to a store, it's useful to know where it's at. You could cruise for hours or days looking for the store you want—and you might never find it. But once you have an address, you have an anchor. You know where to go, and you should be able to quickly figure out how to get there.

Although mindless cruising is one of the delights of the Web (after all, isn't that what surfing really is?), when you're more directed in your search (when you know what you're looking for), having an address can be helpful. Even if you surf, you may want to return to the same page you've visited before, and knowing where to find it will shorten your journey back (but maybe make it less fun).

Just like physical stores, the Internet uses an *address* to anchor Web sites. In fact, not only sites but every device that connects to the Internet gets its own, unique address. The Internet Protocol itself defines the addressing scheme that's used, so the addresses are naturally called *IP addresses*.

IP Addresses

Under the Internet Protocol, an address is four bytes, a 32-bit binary number. Usually you'll find it expressed as a series of four numbers called *octets*. The value of each octet is expressed in decimal notation, and the individual octets are separated by periods. Hence, an Internet address looks like this:

```
162.233.12.148
```

Every device gets its own, unique address. Do the math, and you'll see this scheme allows for 4,294,967,296 unique devices (which is simply 2 to the 32nd power, exactly what a 32-bit binary address means).

Dividing IP addresses into octets is more than a matter of readability. By design, the IP address is structured to help make finding any given computer easier. The address has two parts: The first identifies a network connected to the Internet, and the last part identifies a specific computer attached to the network.

For example, the computer with the IP address of `192.168.132.1` actually is computer number 1 attached to the network named `192.168.132.0`.

Structuring IP addresses in this way makes routing packets and messages across the Internet easier for the routers charged with the job. They only need to find the network and dump the packets on it. The network then routes the packets to the computer designated in the IP address.

Subnet Masks

You may detect the one small flaw in this addressing system—the IP address by itself does not indicate where the split between the network address and the device address occurs. Although it would be easy to define the last octet as the device address, that was too arbitrary and limiting for the folks who developed the Internet. Such a scheme would limit any network to only 256 addresses. The Internet designers preferred to permit greater versatility in configuring networks. After all, the Internet was specifically meant to allow colleges to exchange information, and most colleges now have substantially more than 256 students, each with his or her own computer tied into the network and Internet.

Instead of fixing the division between network and device addresses, the Internet designers chose to use a second number that defined the boundary. This second number is the *subnet mask*. You'll encounter it nearly every time you tangle with IP addresses.

The subnet mask takes the same form as an IP address, four octets in dotted-decimal format. Unlike IP addresses, however, which allow full variation to yield more than four billion distinct numbers, only 32 different subnet masks are allowed in the IP scheme of things. Once you think about it, this number makes sense because there are only 32 places to draw the line between network and device addresses. Table 14.1 lists all the valid subnet masks.

TABLE 14.1 Subnet Masks

Mask in Hex	Mask in Decimal	Number of Available Addresses
80.00.00.00	128.0.0.0	2,147,483,648
C0.00.00.00	192.0.0.0	1,073,741,824
E0.00.00.00	224.0.0.0	536,870,912
F0.00.00.00	240.0.0.0	268,435,456
F8.00.00.00	248.0.0.0	134,217,728
FC.00.00.00	252.0.0.0	67,108,864

continues

TABLE 14.1   Continued

Mask in Hex	Mask in Decimal	Number of Available Addresses
FE.00.00.00	254.0.0.0	33,554,432
FF.00.00.00	255.0.0.0	16,777,216
FF.80.00.00	255.128.0.0	8,388,608
FF.C0.00.00	255.192.0.0	4,194,304
FF.E0.00.00	255.224.0.0	2,097,152
FF.F0.00.00	255.240.0.0	1,048,576
FF.F8.00.00	255.248.0.0	524,288
FF.FC.00.00	255.252.0.0	262,144
FF.FE.00.00	255.254.0.0	131,072
FF.FF.00.00	255.255.0.0	65,536
FF.FF.80.00	255.255.128.0	32,768
FF.FF.C0.00	255.255.192.0	16,384
FF.FF.E0.00	255.255.224.0	8192
FF.FF.F0.00	255.255.240.0	4096
FF.FF.F8.00	255.255.248.0	2048
FF.FF.FC.00	255.255.252.0	1024
FF.FF.FE.00	255.255.254.0	512
FF.FF.FF.00	255.255.255.0	256
FF.FF.FF.80	255.255.255.128	128
FF.FF.FF.C0	255.255.255.192	64
FF.FF.FF.E0	255.255.255.224	32
FF.FF.FF.F0	255.255.255.240	16
FF.FF.FF.F8	255.255.255.248	8
FF.FF.FF.FC	255.255.255.252	4
FF.FF.FF.FE	255.255.255.254	2
FF.FF.FF.FF	255.255.255.255	1

Understanding why these particular masks are the only ones allowed and why they were chosen requires examining the IP address and subnet mask numbers in their native binary form.

Although most network administrators look at IP addresses in the dotted-decimal format, computer equipment sees them as a series of 32 ones and zeros. For example, what you see as the IP address 192.168.132.1 looks like this to your computer:

11000000101010001000010000000001

Divided into octets, this number becomes the following:

11000000.10101000.10000100.00000001

In this format, the number of the subnet mask makes more sense, at least if you look at it with an engineer's eyes. The number allows subnet mask numbers resulting in a dotted-decimal format that is all ones on the left and zeros on the right. For example, the subnet mask expressed as 255.255.255.128 can also be represented in binary as follows:

11111111.11111111.11111111.10000000

In this form, the columns filled with the ones represent the digits of the IP address that designate the network. The columns filled with zeros are the digits of the valid computer identification numbers.

Don't bother memorizing the table of subnet masks. If all you're going to do is home networking, you only need to deal with one subnet mask: 255.255.255.0. You'll find that this is Microsoft's default when you set up TCP/IP on your system, and it is both necessary and sufficient for most home network setups.

Network Classes

Subnet masks move into prominence when you venture into serious networking. That is, when you move your network onto the Internet and have your own galaxy of computers linking into workgroups. To accommodate the really big kids with prodigious needs, the Internet was designed to be divvied up among governments and businesses in chunks that depended on need and, more likely, lobbying.

Some organizations need more Internet space than others. Some are able to demand more space than others. And some are able to use whatever forms of legal blackmail are available to extort more network space than others. In the days that InterNIC (the organization charged with administering the Internet at that time) assigned blocks of Internet addresses, it followed a classification scheme with five levels: Classes A through E. Although this scheme is no longer used, the addresses assigned under it remain. You can classify it as interesting Internet trivia that still creeps into our lives when we least expect it.

In any case, in each of the first three classes defined under the InterNIC scheme, the number of addresses available to an organization was defined by the subnet mask. In addition, InterNIC defined two more classes for special purposes: multicasting (sending packets to multiple computers but not all on the Internet) and experimental purposes. These classes were assigned their own ranges of special IP addresses. The five classes are as follows:

- **Class A**—These Internet addresses use a subnet mask of `255.0.0.0`. The first bit in a Class A address is always zero, so Class A addresses always start with the first octet in the range of 0 to 126, inclusive. This classification leaves seven bits to identify the network and 24 bits to identify individual devices.

- **Class B**—These Internet addresses use a subnet mask of `255.255.0.0`. The first two bits of a Class B address are a one followed by a zero, so the first octet of a Class B address always falls in the range 128 to 191, inclusive. This classification leaves 14 bits to identify the network and 16 bits to identify individual devices.

- **Class C**—These Internet addresses use a subnet mask of `255.255.255.0`. The first three bits of a Class C address are always two ones followed by a zero, so Class C addresses always fall in the range with the first octet of 192 to 223, inclusive. This classification leaves 21 bits to identify the network and eight bits to identify individual devices.

- **Class D**—These addresses always start with binary addresses of three ones followed by a zero, which translates into a first octet in dotted-decimal notation in the range 224 to 239, inclusive. The remaining 28 bits in the address identify the group of computers for which the multicast is meant.

- **Class E**—These addresses always start with a binary address of four ones, which translates into a first octet in dotted-decimal notation in the range 240 to 255, inclusive. As with Class D, the remaining 28 bits in the address identify the group of computers for which the multicast is meant.

CIDR

Subnet masks are cumbersome in everyday use on the Internet. To help make routing messages between computer networks more efficient, Internet workers developed *Classless Inter-Domain Routing* (CIDR) to provide more flexibility than was possible with the subnet mask scheme. The CIDR system is now used by virtually every computer on the Internet's backbone to route messages to their destinations.

Basically, the CIDR system distills the four-byte subnet mask into a single number appended to an IP address called a *network prefix*. The number in the network prefix describes the number of bits in the address that constitute the network designation part of the address, much as the subnet mask does. For example, in the CIDR network address

192.168.132.7/24

the first 24 bits indicate the address of a network, and the last eight bits identify an individual computer.

IPv6

Although four billion is a lot of computers for a network, the Internet's administrators see the reserve of IP addresses quickly disappearing. They fear that sometime soon the world will run out of them and no new computer can connect.

They haven't been asleep, however. They have developed a revised version of the Internet Protocol to accommodate longer addresses to break through the 32-bit addressing limit. Called *Internet Protocol Version 6* (we used version 4 today), the revision allows for IP addresses 128-bits long. The result is that IPv6 accommodates more addresses than it is convenient to write down. Every person in the world could have four billion computers, each with its own IPv6 address, and there would still be 16 sextillion times more addresses available.

The revisions of IPv6 don't stop with longer addresses. Under IPv6, the packet header allows messages to be identified as part of a particular *flow*, such as a stream of audio or video. Properly identified, the packets can be routed to follow the same path to help them get reconstructed as a real-time stream. The header also includes extensions for authentication, error control, and privacy.

The IPv6 spec is designed to allow compatibility with today's IP addressing system. The lowest 32 bits of the IPv6 address can function as a current IP address and routed appropriately.

What Address to Use

When setting up a home or small office network, at some time or another you will be confronted with the choice of IP addresses to use—it's one of those unwelcome choices that is given every network administrator. As far as I can tell, no readily available source even hints at what IP address you should use. But the choice is critical, and the people who govern such things in the Internet publish the addresses you should use.

In fact, the Internet Assigned Numbers Authority (IANA, which you can find on the Web at www.iana.org) reserves three blocks of IP addresses for use by private networks—that is, those that don't intend on directly connecting to the Web. Because it's likely you will connect only through a gateway at your ISP, your home network falls into the private network class, and these reserved addresses are the ones you should choose from. Table 14.2 lists the addresses IANA reserves for private networks.

TABLE 14.2   Address Ranges Reserved for Private Networks

Start Address	End Address	Addresses in Range
10.0.0.0	10.255.255.255	16,777,216
172.16.0.0	172.31.255.255	1,048,576
192.168.0.0	192.168.255.255	65,536

Clearly, any of these three ranges will have more than enough room for any conceivable home network. Microsoft uses the last of these, the range starting at 192.168.0.0, for the private networks it automatically sets up for home use.

Certainly you're not limited to these values for your own private network. You could simply create your own IP address. If you're not too clever for you own good, you may get away with it. Coming up with a valid address is not difficult—but it's not a good idea either. Internet addresses are assigned, and the Internet governing bodies go to lengths to be sure there's no conflicts.

Addresses You Cannot Use

The IP naming rules dictate that you cannot use certain addresses for computers on a network. These fall at the two ends of the number range in the fourth octet. That is, addresses ending in zero, such as 192.168.155.0, and those ending in 255, such as 192.168.154.255, cannot be used as addresses for computers or other devices connected to a network. These addresses have a specifically defined meaning in the IP system.

Addresses ending in a zero refer to the network itself rather than any specific computer or device connected to it. Addresses ending in 255 are used to broadcast messages to all devices in the network, so all devices in a network will receive packets with the network address and a 255 at its end.

The rule is simple: *Never* use these addresses when assigning IP addresses to any device in your network.

DHCP

If you find IP addresses confusing, you're not the only one. Keeping track of all the addresses used by a network can be confusing, indeed. What you really need is someone who excels at organization, who rigidly assigns addresses and keeps track of every detail as if he were a machine. In fact, a machine such as a computer would be a good choice to take over the job.

Using the *Dynamic Host Configuration Protocol* (DHCP), you can move the responsibility for assigning and organizing the IP addresses your network uses to one of its servers.

DHCP is an automatic method for assigning addresses to devices. When a device wants to join the network, it queries the DHCP server, and the server sends back a unique IP address for the device.

Not just any address will do. In the Microsoft scheme of things, the addresses assigned by a server are drawn from within a *scope*, a range of no more than 255 contiguous addresses. All the devices in a workgroup must be within the same scope, although a network may have many intercommunicating scopes.

Setting up a DHCP server usually is more work than most normal people want to do. That's why it's usually left to network administrators. But if you buy an inexpensive router in order to share a high-speed Internet connection, odds are it has a DHCP server built in to it. When you log in to your network in preparation for sharing your connection, the DHCP server automatically sends your computer its own unique IP address so it can join the network.

Note that you should have only one DHCP server in a network. If you install a dedicated server to act as your DHCP server *and* you install a router for Internet sharing, the two DHCP servers may come into conflict, possibly preventing your network from operating, or just preventing some computers from seeing others on the network. To avoid problems, make sure you have only one DHCP server.

Domain Name System

Although DHCP does a good job of hiding your own computer's IP address from you, it does nothing to make IP addresses manageable on the Web. So that you don't have to type into your browser the IP address of each computer you want to visit on the Web (you can if you want, by the way), the Web's creators developed the *Domain Name System* (DNS).

From your perspective, DNS works by assigning a structured name to every Web site, the familiar whatever-dot-com you use every day. In the language of the Internet, that dot-com is called the *domain name* of the Web site.

Most domain names take the form of a word, a period, and another few letters. Those letters after the period comprise the *top-level domain*, the primary organizing structure of the Web. You can't use just anything as a top-level domain. The organization charged with administering Web names, the Internet Corporation for Assigned Names and Numbers (ICANN), maintains tight control of top-level domains.

There are two kinds of top-level domains: organizational and national. Originally, only six organizational top-level domains were allowed, but on November 16, 2000, ICANN added seven more. Table 14.3 lists the currently recognized top-level domains.

TABLE 14.3   Currently Recognized Top-Level Domains

TLD	Use
Original Top-Level Domains	
.com	Commercial use
.edu	Educational institutions
.gov	Government
.mil	Armed forces
.net	Service providers
.org	Organizations
Added November 18, 2000	
.aero	Air-transport industry
.biz	Businesses
.coop	Cooperatives
.info	Anything
.museum	Museums
.name	Individuals
.pro	Professionals

In addition, each nation in the world is also given its own top-level domain, a two-character country code. These are listed in Table 14.4.

TABLE 14.4   Internet Country Code Top-Level Domains

Country Code	Nation
.ad	Andorra
.ae	United Arab Emirates
.af	Afghanistan
.ag	Antigua and Barbuda
.ai	Anguilla
.al	Albania
.am	Armenia
.an	Netherlands Antilles
.ao	Angola

Domain Name System

Country Code	Nation
.aq	Antarctica
.ar	Argentina
.as	American Samoa
.at	Austria
.au	Australia
.aw	Aruba
.az	Azerbaijan
.ba	Bosnia and Herzegovina
.bb	Barbados
.bd	Bangladesh
.be	Belgium
.bf	Burkina Faso
.bg	Bulgaria
.bh	Bahrain
.bi	Burundi
.bj	Benin
.bm	Bermuda
.bn	Brunei Darussalam
.bo	Bolivia
.br	Brazil
.bs	Bahamas
.bt	Bhutan
.bv	Bouvet Island
.bw	Botswana
.by	Belarus
.bz	Belize
.ca	Canada
.cc	Cocos (Keeling) Islands
.cd	Democratic People's Republic of Congo

continues

TABLE 14.4   Continued

Country Code	Nation
.cf	Central African Republic
.cg	Republic of Congo
.ch	Switzerland
.ci	Cote d'Ivoire
.ck	Cook Islands
.cl	Chile
.cm	Cameroon
.cn	China
.co	Colombia
.cr	Costa Rica
.cu	Cuba
.cv	Cap Verde
.cx	Christmas Island
.cy	Cyprus
.cz	Czech Republic
.de	Germany
.dj	Djibouti
.dk	Denmark
.dm	Dominica
.do	Dominican Republic
.dz	Algeria
.ec	Ecuador
.ee	Estonia
.eg	Egypt
.eh	Western Sahara
.er	Eritrea
.es	Spain
.et	Ethiopia
.fi	Finland

Domain Name System

Country Code	Nation
.fj	Fiji
.fk	Falkland Islands (Malvinas)
.fm	Federal State of Micronesia
.fo	Faeroe Islands
.fr	France
.ga	Gabon
.gd	Grenada
.ge	Georgia
.gf	French Guiana
.gg	Guernsey
.gh	Ghana
.gi	Gibraltar
.gl	Greenland
.gm	Gambia
.gn	Guinea
.gp	Guadeloupe
.gq	Equatorial Guinea
.gr	Greece
.gs	South Georgia and the South Sandwich Islands
.gt	Guatemala
.gu	Guam
.gw	Guinea-Bissau
.gy	Guyana
.hk	Hong Kong
.hm	Heard and McDonald Islands
.hn	Honduras
.hr	Croatia/Hrvatska
.ht	Haiti
.hu	Hungary

continues

TABLE 14.4   Continued

Country Code	Nation
.id	Indonesia
.ie	Ireland
.il	Israel
.im	Isle of Man
.in	India
.io	British Indian Ocean Territory
.iq	Iraq
.ir	Iran (Islamic Republic of)
.is	Iceland
.it	Italy
.je	Jersey
.jm	Jamaica
.jo	Jordan
.jp	Japan
.ke	Kenya
.kg	Kyrgyzstan
.kh	Cambodia
.ki	Kiribati
.km	Comoros
.kn	Saint Kitts and Nevis
.kp	Democratic People's Republic of Korea
.kr	Republic of Korea
.kw	Kuwait
.ky	Cayman Islands
.kz	Kazakhstan
.la	People's Democratic Republic of Laos
.lb	Lebanon
.lc	Saint Lucia
.li	Liechtenstein

Country Code	Nation
.lk	Sri Lanka
.lr	Liberia
.ls	Lesotho
.lt	Lithuania
.lu	Luxembourg
.lv	Latvia
.ly	Libyan Arab Jamahiriya
.ma	Morocco
.mc	Monaco
.md	Republic of Moldova
.mg	Madagascar
.mh	Marshall Islands
.mk	Macedonia
.ml	Mali
.mm	Myanmar
.mn	Mongolia
.mo	Macau
.mp	Northern Mariana Islands
.mq	Martinique
.mr	Mauritania
.ms	Montserrat
.mt	Malta
.mu	Mauritius
.mv	Maldives
.mw	Malawi
.mx	Mexico
.my	Malaysia
.mz	Mozambique
.na	Namibia

continues

TABLE 14.4 Continued

Country Code	Nation
.nc	New Caledonia
.ne	Niger
.nf	Norfolk Island
.ng	Nigeria
.ni	Nicaragua
.nl	Netherlands
.no	Norway
.np	Nepal
.nr	Nauru
.nu	Niue
.nz	New Zealand
.om	Oman
.pa	Panama
.pe	Peru
.pf	French Polynesia
.pg	Papua New Guinea
.ph	Philippines
.pk	Pakistan
.pl	Poland
.pm	St. Pierre and Miquelon
.pn	Pitcairn Island
.pr	Puerto Rico
.ps	Palestinian Territories
.pt	Portugal
.pw	Palau
.py	Paraguay
.qa	Qatar
.re	Reunion Island
.ro	Romania

Country Code	Nation
.ru	Russian Federation
.rw	Rwanda
.sa	Saudi Arabia
.sb	Solomon Islands
.sc	Seychelles
.sd	Sudan
.se	Sweden
.sg	Singapore
.sh	St. Helena
.si	Slovenia
.sj	Svalbard and Jan Mayen Islands
.sk	Slovak Republic
.sl	Sierra Leone
.sm	San Marino
.sn	Senegal
.so	Somalia
.sr	Suriname
.st	Sao Tome and Principe
.sv	El Salvador
.sy	Syrian Arab Republic
.sz	Swaziland
.tc	Turks and Caicos Islands
.td	Chad
.tf	French Southern Territories
.tg	Togo
.th	Thailand
.tj	Tajikistan
.tk	Tokelau
.tm	Turkmenistan
.tn	Tunisia

continues

TABLE 14.4   Continued

Country Code	Nation
.to	Tonga
.tp	East Timor
.tr	Turkey
.tt	Trinidad and Tobago
.tv	Tuvalu
.tw	Taiwan
.tz	Tanzania
.ua	Ukraine
.ug	Uganda
.uk	United Kingdom
.um	US Minor Outlying Islands
.us	United States
.uy	Uruguay
.uz	Uzbekistan
.va	Holy See (City Vatican State)
.vc	Saint Vincent and the Grenadines
.ve	Venezuela
.vg	Virgin Islands (British)
.vi	Virgin Islands (USA)
.vn	Vietnam
.vu	Vanuatu
.wf	Wallis and Futuna Islands
.ws	Western Samoa
.ye	Yemen
.yt	Mayotte
.yu	Yugoslavia
.za	South Africa
.zm	Zambia
.zr	Zaire
.zw	Zimbabwe

To the left of the period is the name of the actual domain assigned the Web site through a registry. If there is more than one period in the name, the leftmost portion is a subdomain of the next domain name to the right. The DNS system allows for multiple subdomains. Each subdomain (or domain, if there are no subdomains) specifies an actual server on the network.

To the right of the top-level domain is the directory path to a particular file on the designated server containing a Web page or other data. In Internet lingo, this composite construction of the domain name and directory path is called a *Uniform Resource Locator*, because the name itself holds all the information computers on the Web need in order to find a particular page or file.

The best view of the Internet comes with following a packet sent from your computer. When you log in to a Web site, you actually send a command to a distant server telling it to download a page of data to your computer. Your Web browser packages that command into a packet labeled with the address of the server storing the page that you want. Your computer sends the packet to your modem (or terminal adapter), which transmits it across your telephone or other connection to your *Internet Service Provider* (ISP).

How DNS Works

The instant you press your mouse button with the cursor pointing at a particularly juicy image on your monitor, your computer drops everything to obey your command. The mouse sends your microprocessor an *interrupt* to make it pay immediate attention. The mouse driver checks to see whether a signal has come in saying you've pressed the mouse button. The driver passes this vital information to your operating system, which takes a peek into its private memory to see what location value it has stored for the location of your mouse's cursor on the screen. The operating system then checks to see whether the mouse location corresponds to a *hotspot* on the Web page you're viewing, indicating to your browser that there is a *hyperlink* instruction to send you to a new location on the Web. When there is, the fun on the Web begins.

Your browser has no idea where to find the page you want on the Web. All it has is a name—it's sort of like finding an isolated name on a message pad when you awake from a drunken stupor. You recognize it as a name, but you don't know why you wrote down the name or how to get in touch with the person to find out.

You might start with the white pages of your telephone book, but your computer can't even open a book, let alone look something up. The only thing it can do is send out an electrical signal down the connection with the Internet. It doesn't send out just any signal. It sends out the name of the Web site you're looking for in a special data packet. Rather than the white pages, the name goes to a *resolver*.

A resolver is not a special machine. Rather, the term *resolver* defines a particular function of a special kind of server on the network, called a *name server*. The resolver does what its name says—it tries to resolve the address of a site on the Web. It looks at the name your computer has sent to it in a standard form known as a *Uniform Resource Locator* (URL).

Like a mailman sorting mail and looking at the bottom of the address first (for the ZIP Code and state), the resolver examines the last part of the URL first—the part of the name to the right of the rightmost period—the familiar `.com`, `.org`, or `.edu`. This portion of the name is the *top-level domain*, which tells the resolver how to find the location of the Web site. In Internet terms, the top-level domain is about as general as describing a creature as being in the animal kingdom.

The top-level domain doesn't tell the resolver where to look for the Web site. Rather, it tells the resolver where to look for a list of site names in the top-level domain. Resolvers aren't stupid. If they've looked up a top-level domain before, they probably already know where to look. If not, however, they call on one of the 13 root name servers to tell them which servers store the information about each top-level domain.

The root name server, or, more likely, the resolver, passes your request for the Web site to one of the name servers assigned to the top-level domain of the URL you're looking for. Hundreds of thousands of servers may track this information. It's kept in multiple copies for speed and reliability. Speed because one server is not burdened with finding every requested URL in its domain, and reliability because if one server becomes unavailable, there are hundreds of others that can take its place.

This server matches your requested URL with the *domain name server* (also abbreviated DNS) that handles the Web site. The server sends the requested URL to the IP address—a block of four bytes of binary code—of the DNS. The DNS knows all the names of the Web sites it serves. It passes the IP address of the Web site you want back to your computer so it can use this address to find the page you want.

When your computer signals to the IP address, it sends a request for the page listed in the hotspot you clicked. The server at the Web site diligently finds the page and passes it back to your computer. Your operating systems passes it to your browser, which formats the page for the screen and passes it back to your operating system, which sends it, in turn, to your display driver and then your monitor screen.

All these requests travel from server to server with light speed, so everything happens fast. Your computer should know the IP address of the page you want and start loading the page in a fraction of a second. Meanwhile, you've probably become impatient and clicked on something else, starting the whole process over again.

Root Name Servers

The part of the Web in charge of identifying each site and getting its address to you is called the *Root Name Server System*. The master plan that makes it work is the DNS protocol, which describes the packets that need to be exchanged and provides the roadmap for them to follow. The *root name servers* hold the key to locating the indexes containing the IP addresses you need. The *root zone file* is the index itself.

The root name servers are arguably the most important computers on the World Wide Web. Only they store the official records of the locations of the registries for each *top-level domain*, the rightmost part of each Web address. Because this information is so vital to the operation of the Web, it's stored not in triplicate but in 13 duplicate copies in separate computers spread across the world.

Well, not quite. The 13 root name servers actually represent only six distinct geographic locations. Six are clustered around Washington, D.C., two are co-located (and co-operated) in Marina Del Ray, California, two are in the Silicon Valley area, one is in Japan, one is in the U.K., and one is in Sweden. Table 14.5 lists the 13 root name servers.

TABLE 14.5   The 13 Root Name Servers of the World Wide Web

Name	Organization	City, State/Province	Country	URL
A	Network Solutions, Inc.	Herndon, VA	USA	http://www.netsol.com
B	Information Sciences Institute, University of Southern California	Marina Del Rey, CA	USA	http://www.isi.edu
C	PSINet	Herndon, VA	USA	http://www.psi.net
D	University of Maryland	College Park, MD	USA	http://www.umd.edu
E	National Aeronautics and Space Administration	Mountain View, CA	USA	http://www.nasa.gov
F	Internet Software Consortium	Palo Alto, CA	USA	http://www.isc.org
G	Defense Information Agency Systems	Vienna, VA	USA	http://nic.mil
H	Army Research Laboratory	Aberdeen, MD	USA	http://www.arl.mil
I	NORDUNet	Stockholm	Sweden	http://www.nordu.net
J	Network Solutions, Inc.	Herndon, VA	USA	http://www.netsol.com
K	RIPE NCC (Réseaux IP Européens)	London	UK	http://www.ripe.net

continues

TABLE 14.5   Continued

Name	Organization	City, State/Province	Country	URL
L	University of Southern California	Marina Del Rey, CA	USA	http://www.isi.edu
M	WIDE	Tokyo	Japan	http://www.wide.ad.jp

WINS

There's another piece to the IP naming system: the names your computers wear when you access them over your own network using the networking capabilities of Windows. You assign these names using the *Windows Internet Name System* (WINS). This system is responsible for converting the names you assign to IP addresses for routing messages through networks using the Internet Protocol. In effect, WINS works like DNS at the local level.

In the WINS system, you assign your computer a name when you set up networking on that machine. The computer then sends its name to the server, and the server stores the names you assign in a database, which the server references to resolve requests for IP addresses.

Routing

An address does you no good if you have no way of getting there. You need wheels (and likely gas money).

The "wheels" of the Internet is the *Transport Control Protocol/Internet Protocol*, or as it is more commonly known, *TCP/IP*.

TCP/IP sees everything in terms of *packets*. Instead of moving data in a long stream like unraveling a roll of movie film, the protocol breaks it into pieces. Having a bunch of short chunks automatically ensures that there will be breaks in the flow of data during which other computers can negotiate for time to send their own packets. At the distant end of the connection, the packets get reassembled to put the data back into its original form.

Each has a predefined structure, with a header that contains address, routing, and control information and a payload of data. The payload moves through the network intact and unexamined, so its content is irrelevant to the network. Packets might contain anything, from program code for Unix computers, to bits of video images, to cream cheese on celery (if you could fit that into computer data).

Moving packets around the Internet is a lot like modern psychotherapy. It is nondirected. The packets simply ramble around until they happen upon the place where they are going. They may follow any one of a near infinite number of paths between the two communicating computers. The Internet imposes no fixed structure. That's one of its greatest strengths—because messages don't have an assigned path, an interrupt of any path won't stop data from flowing. It simply finds another path to its destination.

Of course, having packets floating all over the Internet is not the most efficient way of moving information. Consequently, servers build tables of paths to send the messages along, routing them according to IP address. When a message first goes to an IP address, an Internet server checks the path it followed and can reuse the same path (or start the packet along its way using the same path) for subsequent packets.

The wonderful thing about TCP/IP is that any computer system can use it. Microprocessor types, architectures, and programming languages mean nothing to TCP/IP. Think of TCP/IP packets as being the shipping containers of the Internet. A computer at one end of the connection fills a packet up, and another machine at the far end of the connection empties it out. It doesn't matter to the freight line what's inside (although customs may take a peek if it crosses borders—the Internet's equivalent of customs is the *firewall*). Using TCP/IP, the Internet will carry anything. It doesn't matter whether it's useful or even compatible with the recipient system. That's a matter left to the two communicating systems. The network doesn't care.

Web Pages

The World Wide Web is the most visually complicated and compelling aspect of the Internet. Despite its appearances, however, the Web is nothing more than another file transfer protocol. When you call up a page from the Web, the remote server simply downloads a file to your computer. Your Web browser then decodes the page, executing commands embedded in it to alter the typeface and to display images at the appropriate place. Most browsers cache several file pages (or even megabytes of them) so that when you step back, you need not wait for the same page to download once again.

The commands for displaying text use their own language, called the Hypertext Markup Language (HTML). As exotic and daunting as HTML sounds, it's nothing more than a coding system that combines formatting information in textual form with the readable text of a document. Your browser reads the formatting commands, which are set off by a special prefix so that the browser knows they are commands, and organizes the text in accordance with them, arranging it on the page, selecting the appropriate font and emphasis, and intermixing graphical elements. Writing in HTML is only a matter of knowing the right codes and where to put them. Web authoring tools embed the proper commands using menu-driven interfaces so that you don't have to do the memorization.

Service Providers

In truth, the Internet was not designed to link *computers* but rather to tie together *computer networks*. As its name implies, the Internet allows data to flow between networks. Even if you only have a single computer, when you connect with the Internet, you must run a network protocol the same as if you had slung miles of Ethernet cable through your home and office. Whether you like it or not, you end up tangled in the web of networking when you connect to the Internet.

The ISP actually operates as a message forwarder. At the ISP, your message gets combined with those from other computers and sent through a higher-speed connection (at least you should hope it is a high-speed connection) to yet another concentrator that eventually sends your packet to one of five regional centers (located in New York, Chicago, San Francisco, Los Angeles, and Maryland). There, the major Internet carriers exchange signals, routing the packets from your modem to the carrier that will haul them to their destination based on their Internet address.

Performance Limits

Linking to the Internet requires both hardware and software. The hardware runs a wide gamut. Most people connect through standard telephone lines using a modem.

Okay, so your Internet access through your modem or digital connection isn't as fast as you'd like. Welcome to the club. As the Duchess of Windsor never said, "You can never be too rich or thin or have an Interconnection that's fast enough." Everyone would like Web pages to download instantly. Barring that, they'd like them to load in a few seconds. Barring that, they'd just like them to load before the next Ice Age.

The most tempting way to increase your Internet speed is to update your modem—move from dial-up to a broadband service such as DSL, cable, or satellite. Once you do, you may discover the dirty secret of the Internet: You're working on the wrong bottleneck. You may have a high-speed connection, but the server you want to download pages from may be someone's ten-year-old computer hogtied by a similar-vintage 9600bps modem. Or a server with heady-duty equipment may be overwhelmed by more requests than it can handle. Remember, your packets may get slowed anywhere along their way through the Web.

You can easily check your Internet bottleneck and see what you can do about it. Pick a large file and download it at your normal online time. Then, pry yourself out of bed early and try downloading the same file at 6 a.m. EST or earlier when Internet traffic is likely to be low. If you notice an appreciable difference in response and download times, a faster modem won't likely make your online sessions substantially speedier. The constraints aren't in your computer but in the server and network itself.

Another way to check is with one of the many services designed for checking DSL speed. To find one, simply perform a Web search for "DSL speed test." One choice is `www.dslreports.com`.

Security

As originally conceived, the Internet is not just a means for moving messages between computers. It was designed as a link between computer systems that allowed scientists to share machines. One researcher in Boston could, for example, run programs on a computer system in San Francisco. Commands for computer systems move across wires just as easily as words and images. To the computer and the Internet, they are all just data.

Much of the expense businesses put into connecting to the Internet involves undoing the work of the original Internet creators. The first thing they install is a *firewall*, which blocks outsiders from taking control of the business's internal computer network. They must remain constantly vigilant that some creative soul doesn't discover yet another flaw in the security systems built into the Internet itself.

Can someone break into your computer through the Internet? It's certainly possible. Truth be told, however, rummaging through someone's computer is about as interesting as burrowing into his sock drawer. Moreover, the number of computers out there makes it statistically unlikely any given errant James Bond will commandeer your computer, particularly when there's stuff much more interesting (and challenging to break into) such as the networks of multibillion dollar companies, colleges, government agencies, and the military.

The one weakness to this argument is that it assumes whoever would break into your computer uses a degree of intelligence. Even a dull, uninteresting computer loaded with naught but a two-edition-old copy of Office can be the target of the computer terrorist. Generally, someone whose thinking process got stalled on issues of morality, the computer terrorist doesn't target you as much as the rest of the world that causes him so much frustration or boredom. His digital equivalent of a bomb is the computer virus.

A computer virus is program code added to your computer without your permission. The name, as a metaphor for human disease, is apt. As with a human virus, a computer virus cannot reproduce by itself—it takes command of your computer and uses its resources to duplicate itself. Computer viruses are contagious in that they can be passed along from one machine to another. And computer viruses vary in their effects, from deadly (wiping out the entire contents of your hard disk) to trivial (posting a message on your screen). But computer viruses are nothing more than digital code, and they are machine specific. Neither you nor your toaster nor your PDA can catch a computer virus from your computer.

Most computer viruses latch onto your computer and lie in wait. When a specific event occurs—for example, a key date—they swing into action, performing whatever dreadful act their designers got a chuckle from. To continue infecting other computers, they also clone themselves and copy themselves to whatever disks you use in your computer. In general, viruses add their code to another program in your computer. They can't do anything until the program they attach themselves to begins running. Virus writers like to attach their viruses to parts of the operating system so that the code will load every time you run your computer. Because antivirus programs and operating system now readily detect such viruses, the virus terrorists have developed other tactics. One of the latest is the macro-virus, which runs as a macro to a program. In effect, the virus is written in a higher-level language that escapes detection by the antivirus software.

Viruses get into your computer because you let them. They come through any connection your computer has with the outside world, including floppy disks and going online. Browsing Web pages ordinarily won't put you at risk because HTTP doesn't pass along executable programs. Plug-ins may, however. Whenever you download a file, you run a risk of bringing a virus with it. Software and drivers that you download are the most likely carriers. Most Webmasters do their best to ensure that they don't pass along viruses. However, you should always be wary when you download a program from a less reputable site. The same warning applies to e-mail from unknown senders.

There is no such thing as a sub-band or sub-carrier virus that sneaks into your computer through a "sub-band" of your modem's transmissions. Even were it possible to fiddle with the operation of a modem and add a new, invisible modulation to it, the information encoded on it could never get to your computer. Every byte from an analog modem must go through the UART in the modem or serial port, then be read by your computer's microprocessor. The modem has no facility to link a sideband signal (even if there were such a thing) to that data stream.

PART 4
Storage

The difference between genius and mere intelligence is *storage*. The quick-witted react fast, but the true genius can call upon memories, experiences, and knowledge to find real answers—the difference between pressing a button fast and having the insight to know which button to press.

Computers are no different. Without memory, a computer is nothing more than a switchboard. All its reactions would have to be hard-wired in. The machine could not read through programs or retain data. It would be stuck in a persistent vegetative state, kept alive by electricity but able to react only autonomously.

The technology for remembering did not originate with computers. Ever since people had thoughts they deemed worth preserving, they have used mechanical means for aiding their memories. When early humans first took charcoal and ochre to sketch on the walls of their ritual caves, they were making mechanical memories of hunts and ceremonies, of men, bison, and mastodons. Primitive, perhaps, but even with all our modern technologies, we have yet to make a record of ourselves that has lasted as long as cave drawings.

Perhaps inadvertently, those drawings have survived for the long term. But we, as thinking people, rely on another kind of memory—short term. When you're working on a problem, you have to hold a piece of it in your mind—say, the one to carry when you're adding a column of numbers or the telephone number you looked up and need to dial.

Computers have the same need for two kinds of memory—both long term and short term. Long-term storage holds the stuff you hope your computer never forgets—your operating system, your programs, your data, and the MP3 music you've acquired. Your computer also needs short-term memory while it works on your programs.

Unlike human beings, whose memory is not understood well enough to distinguish the different processes required for the long and short term, computers use widely different but well-understood technologies for their long- and short-term storage. This part of the book will examine how the two kinds of memory fit and work together. We'll also look at the individual technologies involved in short-term and long-term storage.

Principles: Freezing Time

The term *memory* covers a lot of territory, even when confined to the computer field. Strictly speaking, memory is anything that holds data, even a single bit. That memory can take a variety of forms. A binary storage system, the kind used by today's computers, can be built from marbles, marzipan, or metal-oxide semiconductors. Not all forms of memory work with equal efficacy (as you'll soon see), but the concept is the same with all of them—preserving bits of information in a recognizable and usable form. Some forms of memory are just easier for an electronic microprocessor to recognize and manipulate. On the other hand, other sorts of memory may roll or taste better.

When discussing the remembering capabilities of computers, engineers usually distinguish between memory and storage. Although both let your computer recall details and data, the two have different purposes and use different technologies—and a raft of different terminologies. Although the two concepts can be distinguished (and named) in many ways, the most useful is as primary and secondary storage.

Defining Memory

The stuff that most people call "computer memory" in a specific sense functions as your computer's *primary storage*. That is, the contents of the storage system are in a form that your computer's microprocessor can immediately access, ready to be used. It can be accessed using only electricity at the speed of electricity (which can be nearly the speed of light). It is the memory used by your computer's microprocessor to hold the data and program code that's used during the active execution of programs, the microprocessor's main job. For this reason, primary storage is sometimes called *working memory*.

The immediacy of primary memory requires that your microprocessor be able to find any given value without poring through huge blocks of data. The microprocessor must access any value at random. Consequently, most people refer to the working memory in their computers as *random access memory*, or RAM, although RAM has a more specific definition when applied to memory technologies, as you'll see later on.

No matter the name you use for it, primary storage is in effect the short-term memory of your computer. It's easy to get at but tends to be limited in capacity—at least compared to other kinds of storage.

The alternate kind of storage is termed *secondary storage*. In most computers, disks and tape systems serve as the secondary storage system. They function as the machine's long-term memory. Not only does disk and tape memory maintain information that must be kept for a long time, but it also holds the bulk of the information that the computer deals with. Secondary storage may be tens, hundreds, or thousands of times larger than primary storage. Secondary storage is often termed *mass storage* because of its voluminous capacity: It stores a huge mass of data.

Secondary storage is one extra step away from your computer's microprocessor. Your computer must transfer the information in secondary storage into its primary storage system in order to work on it. Secondary storage also adds a complication to the hardware. Most secondary storage is electromechanical. In addition to moving electrical signals, it also involves physically moving a disk or tape to provide access to information. Because mechanical things generally move slower than electrical signals (except in science fiction), secondary storage is slower than primary storage, typically by a factor of a thousand or more.

In other words, the most important aspect of the primary storage system in your computer is access speed, although you want to have as much of it as possible. The most important aspect of secondary storage is capacity, although you want it to be as fast as possible.

Why does your computer need two kinds of memory? The role of secondary storage is obvious. It's the only place that the computer can keep things without worrying about a power glitch making its memory disappear. It's the only kind of storage that allows you to freely exchange blocks of data, such as distributing programs.

The need for primary storage may not seem as obvious. The reason is purely speed. As a microprocessor operates, it needs a constant stream of instructions—the program that it executes as it operates—and data that the instructions tell it to manipulate. That stuff has to come from somewhere. If it were on disk, the microprocessor might have to wait for each byte to be found before it could carry out its operation. On the average, that would take about nine milliseconds per instruction. Today's microprocessors can run through instructions and data about twenty million times faster than that. Looking stuff up on disk would clearly slow things down.

Electronic memory bridges the gap. Your computer, under the direction of its operating system, copies the instructions and data that are recorded on your disk to solid-state memory. Your microprocessor can then operate at full-speed (or nearly so), millions of times faster than if it had to move bytes between disk and its registers.

Your computer never knows where its next byte is coming from. The microprocessor might need to read or write any byte in the program or the mass of data it is working with. If you're running several programs and shift between them, the need for bytes can be far ranging indeed. To prevent the million-fold slowdown of the microprocessor, modern computer systems are designed to keep all (or most) of each program and its data in solid-state primary storage. That's why you need dozens or hundreds of megabytes of primary storage in a modern computer equipped with Windows.

Volatility

In all all-too-human memories, one characteristic separates out short-term and long-term memories. The former are fleeting. If a given fact or observation doesn't make it into your long-term memory, you'll quickly forget whatever it was—for example, the name that went with the face so quickly introduced to you at a party.

A computer's primary storage is similar. The contents can be fleeting. With computers, however, technology rather than attention determines what gets remembered and what is forgotten. For computers, the reaction to an interruption in electrical supply defines the difference between short- and long-term remembering capabilities. The technical term used to describe the difference is memory *volatility*. Computer memory is classed either as nonvolatile or volatile.

Volatile memory is, like worldly glory, transitory. It lasts not the three score years and ten of human existence or the fifteen minutes of fame. It survives only as long as does its source of power. Remove power from volatile memory, and its contents evaporate in microseconds. The main memory system in nearly every computer is volatile.

Nonvolatile memory is exactly what you expect memory to be, forever. Once you store something in nonvolatile memory, it stays there until you change it. Neither rain, nor sleet, nor dark of night, nor a power failure affects nonvolatile memory. Types of nonvolatile memory include magnetic storage (tape and disk drives) and special forms of memory chips (read-only memory and Flash memory).

Nonvolatile memory can be simulated by providing backup power to volatile memory systems—a technology commonly used in the CMOS configuration memory systems used in most computers—but this memory remains vulnerable to the vagaries of the battery.

Should the battery die or slip from its connection even momentarily, the contents of this simulated nonvolatile memory may be lost.

Given the choice, you'd of course want the memory of your computer to be nonvolatile. The problem is that nearly all memory systems based solely on electricity and electronic storage are volatile. Those all-electric memory systems that are nonvolatile are cursed with a number of drawbacks. Most are substantially slower than volatile memory (rewriting a block of Flash memory can take seconds compared to the microseconds required by most kinds of volatile memory). The common nonvolatile memory systems also have limited lives. Flash memory typically can be rewritten a few hundred-thousand times. Volatile memory might get rewritten hundreds of thousands of times in less than a second.

Measurement

The basic form of computer memory is the *cell*, which holds a single bit of data. The term *bit* is a contraction of *binary digit*. A bit is the smallest possible piece of information. It doesn't hold much intelligence; it only indicates whether something is or isn't (on or off), is up or down, is something (one) or nothing (zero). It's like the legal system: Everything is in black and white, and there are no shades of gray (at least when the gavel comes down).

When enough bits are taken collectively, they can code meaningful information. A pattern of bits can encode more complex information. In their most elementary form, for example, five bits could store the number 5. Making the position of each bit in the code significant increases the amount of information a pattern with a given number of bits can identify. (The increase follows the exponential increase of powers of two—for n bits, 2 to the nth power of unique patterns can be identified.) By storing many bit-patterns in duplicative memory units, a storage system can retain any amount of information.

Measuring Units

People don't remember the same way computers do. For us human beings, remembering a complex symbol can be as easy as storing a single bit. Although two choices may be enough for a machine, we prefer a multitude of selections. Our selection of symbols is as broad as our imaginations. Fortunately for typewriter-makers, however, we've reserved just a few characters as the symbol set for our language—26 uppercase letters, a matching number of lowercase letters, ten numerals, and enough punctuation marks to keep grammar teachers preoccupied for entire careers.

Representing these characters in binary form makes computers wonderfully useful, so computer engineers tried to develop the most efficient bit-patterns for storing the diversity of symbols we finicky humans prefer. If you add together all those letters, numbers, and punctuation marks, you'll find that the lowest power of two that could code them all is two to the seventh power, or 128. Computer engineers went one better: By using an eight-bit code, yielding a capacity of 256 symbols, they found that all the odd diacritical marks of foreign languages could be represented by the same code. The usefulness of this eight-bit code has made eight bits the standard unit of computer storage, a unit called the *byte*.

Half a byte (a four-bit storage unit) is called a *nibble* because, at least in the beginning of the personal computer revolution, engineers had senses of humor. Four bits can encode 16 symbols—enough for ten numerals and six operators (addition, subtraction, multiplication, division, exponents, and square roots), making the unit useful for numbers-only devices such as handheld calculators.

The generalized term for a package of bits is the digital *word*, which can comprise any number of bits that a computer might use as a group. In the world of Intel microprocessors, however, the term *word* has developed a more specific meaning—two bytes of data, or 16 bits.

In the Intel scheme, a *double-word* comprises two words, or 32 bits; a *quad-word* is four words, eight bytes, or 64 bits.

The most recent Intel microprocessors are designed to handle data in larger gulps. To improve performance, they feature wider internal buses between their integral caches and processing circuitry. In the case of the current Intel microprocessors, this bus is 128-bits wide. Intel calls a single bus-width gulp a *line* of memory.

Because the designations *word* and *double-word* sometimes vary with the register width of microprocessors, the Institute of Electrical and Electronic Engineers (IEEE) developed a nomenclature system that's unambiguous for multiple-byte widths: *doublet* for two bytes, *quadlet* for four, and *octlet* for eight. Table 15.1 summarizes the common names and the IEEE standard designations for the sizes of primary storage units.

TABLE 15.1 Primary Intel Memory Storage Unit Designations

Unit	IEEE Standard Notation	Bits	Bytes
Bit		1	0.125
Nibble	Nibble	4	0.5
Byte	Byte	8	1
Word	Doublet	16	2
Double-word	Quadlet	32	4
Quad-word	Octlet	64	8
Line		128	16

The Multimedia Extensions (MMX) used by all the latest computer microprocessors introduced four additional data types into computer parlance. These repackage groups of smaller data units into the 64-bit registers used by the new microprocessors. The new units are all termed *packed* because they fit (or *pack*) as many smaller units as possible into the larger registers. These new units are named after the smaller units comprising them. For example, when eight bytes are bunched together into one 64-bit block to fit an MMX microprocessor register, the data is in *packed byte* form. Table 15.2 lists the names of these new data types.

TABLE 15.2   New 64-Bit MMX Storage Designations

Name	Basic Units	Number of Units
Packed byte	Byte (8 bits)	8
Packed word	Word (16 bits)	4
Packed double-word	Double-word (32 bits)	2
Quad-word	64 bits	1

Today's applications demand thousands and millions of bytes of memory. The basic measuring units for memory are consequently large multiples of the byte. Although they wear common Greek prefixes shared by units of the metric system, the computer world has adopted a slightly different measuring system. Although the Greek prefix *kilo* means thousand, computer people assign a value of 1024 to it, the closest round number in binary, 2^{10} (two to the tenth power). Larger units increase by a similar factor so that a megabyte is actually 2^{20} bytes and a gigabyte is 2^{30} bytes. Table 15.3 summarizes the names and values of these larger measuring units.

TABLE 15.3   Names and Abbreviations of Large Storage Units

Unit	Abbreviation	Size in Units	Size in Bytes
Kilobyte	KB or K	1024 bytes	1024
Megabyte	MB or M	1024 kilobytes	1,048,576
Gigabyte	GB	1024 megabytes	1,073,741,824
Terabyte	TB	1024 gigabytes	1,099,511,627,776
Petabyte	PB	1024 terabytes	1,125,899,906,843,624
Exabyte	EB	1024 petabytes	1,152,921,504,607,870,976
Zettabyte	ZB	1024 exabytes	1,180,591,620,718,458,879,424
Yottabyte	YB	1024 zettabytes	1,208,925,819,615,701,892,530,176

Access

Memory works like an elaborate set of pigeonholes used by post office workers to sort local mail. A memory location called an *address* is assigned to each piece of information to be stored. Each address corresponds to one pigeonhole, unambiguously identifying the location of each unit of storage. The address is a label, not the storage location itself (which is actually one of those tiny electronic capacitors, latches, or fuses).

Direct Access

Because the address is most often in binary code, the number of bits available in the code determines how many such unambiguous addresses can be directly accessed in a memory system. As noted before, an eight-bit address code permits 256 distinct memory locations ($2^8 = 256$). A 16-bit address code can unambiguously define 65,536 locations ($2^{16} = 65,536$). The available address codes generally correspond to the number of address lines of the microprocessor in the computer, although strictly speaking they need not.

The amount of data stored at each memory location depends on the basic storage unit, which varies with the design of the computer system. Generally, each location contains the same number of bits that the computer processes at one time. Although today's Pentium-class microprocessors have 32-bit registers and 64-bit data buses, the smallest unit of memory they can individually address is actually four double-words (16 bytes). Smaller memory units cannot be individually retrieved because the four least-significant address lines are absent from these microprocessors. Because the chips prefer to deal with data one line at a time, greater precision in addressing is unnecessary.

In writing to memory, where a microprocessor might need to change an individual byte but can only address a full line, the chip uses a technology termed *masking*. The mask preserves all the memory locations in the line that are not to be changed. Although they address the byte by the chunk it lies within, the mask prevents overwriting the bytes of memory that do not need to change.

Memory chips do not connect directly to the microprocessor's address lines. Instead, special circuits that comprise the memory controller translate the binary data sent to the memory address register into the form necessary to identify the memory location requested and retrieve the data there. The memory controller can be as simple as address-decoding logic circuitry or an elaborate application-specific integrated circuit that combines several memory-enhancing functions.

To read memory, the microprocessor activates the address lines corresponding to the address code of the wanted memory unit during one clock cycle. This action acts as a request to the memory controller to find the needed data. During the next clock cycle, the memory controller puts the bits of code contained in the desired storage unit on the microprocessor's data bus. This operation takes two cycles because the memory controller can't be sure that the address code is valid until the end of a clock cycle. Likewise, the microprocessor cannot be sure the data is valid until the end of the next clock cycle. Consequently, all memory operations take at least two clock cycles.

Writing to memory works similarly: The microprocessor first sends off the address to write to, the memory controller finds the proper pigeonhole, and then the microprocessor sends out the data to be written. Again, the minimum time required is two cycles of the microprocessor clock.

Reading or writing can take substantially longer than two cycles, however, because microprocessor technology has pushed into performance territory far beyond the capabilities of today's affordable DRAM chips. Slower system memory can make the system microprocessor—and the rest of the computer—stop while it catches up, extending the memory read/write time by one or more clock cycles.

Bank-Switched Memory

In some applications, a computer or piece of electronic gear has more memory than addresses available for storing it. (Such address shortfalls were admittedly more common in the past than today, when microprocessor's can address terabytes of memory.) For example, the telephone company long ago—back when there was but one telephone company—faced its own addressing shortage when the number of phones in use exceeded the ten million distinct seven-digit telephone numbers. The telephone company's solution was to break the nation (and the world) into separate ranges, what we know now as *area codes*. Each area code has the full ten million phone numbers available to it, expanding the range of available telephone numbers by a factor equal to the number of area codes.

When computers were limited to a few dozen kilobytes by the addressing range of their microprocessors, clever engineers developed their own version of the area code. They divided memory into *banks*, each of which individually fit into the address range of the microprocessor. Using the computer equivalent of a giant channel selector knob, engineers enabled the computer to switch any one of the banks into the addressing range of the microprocessor while removing the rest from the chip's control. The maximum addressable memory of the system becomes the product of the addressing range of the chip and the number of banks available. Because the various banks get switched in and out of the system's limited addressing range, this address-extension technique is usually called *bank-switching*.

The bank-switching technique was once used to extend the addressing range of personal computers, creating what was called *expanded memory*. Bank-switching is still sometimes used in video display systems, especially in older display modes.

The memory banks on the motherboards of most modern computers have nothing to do with bank switching. In this context, a *bank* of memory is any size block of memory that is arranged with its bits matching the number of data connections to your microprocessor. That is, a bank of memory for a Pentium 4 is a block of memory arranged 64 bits wide.

True bank-switching requires a special memory board that incorporates data registers that serve as the actual bank switches. In addition, programmers must specifically write their applications to use bank-switched memory. The program (or operating system that it runs under) must know how to track every switch and turn off memory to be sure that the correct banks are in use at any given moment.

Solid-State Memory

To remember a single bit—whether alone or as part of a nibble, byte, word, or double-word—computer memory needs only to preserve a single state (that is, whether something is true or false, positive or negative, or a binary one or zero). Almost anything can suffice to remember a single state—whether a marble is in one pile or another, whether a dab of marzipan is eaten or molding on the shelf, whether an electrical charge is present or absent. The only need is that the memory unit has two possible states and that it will maintain itself in one of them once it is put there. Should a memory element change on its own, randomly, it would be useless because it does not preserve the information that it's supposed to keep.

Although the possibilities of what can be used for remembering a single state are nearly endless, how the bits are to be used makes some forms of memory more practical than others. The two states must be both readily changeable and readily recognizable by whatever mechanism is to use them. For example, a string tied around your finger will help you remember a bit state but would be inconvenient to store information for a machine. Whatever the machine, it would need a mechanical hand to tie the knot and some means of detecting its presence on your finger—a video camera, precision radar set, or even a gas chromatography system.

True old-timers who ratcheted themselves down into computers from the mainframe computers that ran rampant in business and industry in the 1950s, 60s, and 70s sometimes use the term *core* when speaking of a computer's memory system. The term doesn't derive from the centrality of memory to the operation of the computer but rather from one of the first memory technologies used by ancient computers—a fabric of wires with a ferrite doughnut, called a *core*, woven into (literally) each intersection of the warp and woof. Although today the term *core* is but a memory, all current memory technologies share with it one important characteristic: Electricity is able to alter its contents. After all, today's computers think with electricity.

In digital computers, it is helpful to store a state electrically so the machine doesn't need eyes or hands to check for the string, marble, or marzipan. Possible candidates for electrical state-saving systems include those that depend on whether an electrical charge is present or whether a current will flow. Both of these techniques are used in computer memories for primary storage systems.

The analog of electricity, magnetism, can also be readily manipulated by electrical circuits and computers. Core memory, in fact, used the magnetic fields of the ferrite cores to store bits. Today, however, magnetic storage is mostly reserved for secondary storage because magnetism is one step removed from electricity. Storage devices have to convert electricity to magnetism to store bits and convert magnetic fields to electrical pulses to read them. The conversion process takes time, energy, and effort—all of which pay off for long-term storage, at which magnetism excels, but are unnecessary for the many uses inside the computer.

The vast majority of memory used in computers is based on storing electrical charges rather than magnetic fields. Because all the other signals inside a computer are normally electronic, the use of electronic memory is only natural. It can operate at electronic speed without the need to convert technologies. Chip-makers can fabricate electronic memory components exactly as they do other circuits, even on the same assembly lines. Best of all, electronic memory is cheap. In fact, it's the most affordable of all direct-access technologies.

Modern memory circuits are made from the same silicon semiconductors as other electronic circuits such as microprocessors. In other words, most primary storage in today's computers uses *solid-state* semiconductor technology.

Read-Write Memory

In this post-modern age, we want—we *expect*—everything to be recyclable. We want whatever we use to be used again rather than used once and thrown away. It's one of the most ecologically sound policies (although using less would be even better).

Computers prefer to treat their memory the same way and for a similar reason. They don't worry about physical waste. They don't worry at all. But they can run out of resources. If a computer could only use memory once, it would quickly use up all its addresses. As it has new things to store, it would slide each bit into a memory address until it ran out of places to put them. At that point, it would no longer be able to do anything new, at least until you added more memory.

In computer terms, people don't talk about using memory, nor do they use the mechanical terms of *recording* and *playing back*. Rather, they use terms of authorship. When a computer remembers something, it *writes* it to memory. To recall something is to *read* it from memory. Reusable memory that can be written to and read from whenever the computer wants or needs to is called *read-write memory*.

As straightforward as it sounds, the term *read-write memory* is almost never used. Instead, engineers have called the read-write memory of most computers *RAM*, the familiar *random-access* term. They use the fast random-access capability of primary storage to distinguish it from slower secondary storage, which confusingly is also mostly random access.

They also use *RAM* to distinguish read-write memory from *read-only* memory (which we will talk about next), even though ROM is also random access. About the best that can be said is that when someone says "RAM," what he usually means is read-write memory.

The electronic circuits that make random-access read-write memory possible take two forms: dynamic and static.

Dynamic Memory

The most common design that brings memory to life inside computers uses minute electrical charges to remember memory states. This form of memory stores electrical charges in small *capacitors*.

The archetypical capacitor comprises two metal plates separated by a small distance that's filled with an electrical insulator. A positive charge can be applied to one plate and, because opposite charges attract, it draws a negative charge to the other nearby plate. The insulator separating the plates prevents the charges from mingling and neutralizing each other. It's called a *capacitor* because it has the capacity to store a given amount of electricity, measured as its *capacitance*.

The capacitor can function as memory because a computer can control whether the charge is applied to or removed from one of the capacitor plates. The charge on the plates can thus store a single state and a single bit of digital information.

In a perfect world, the charges on the two plates of a capacitor would forever hold themselves in place. One of the imperfections in the real world results in no insulator being perfect. There's always some possibility that a charge will sneak through any material (although better insulators lower the likelihood, they cannot eliminate it entirely). Think of a perfect capacitor as being like a glass, holding whatever you put inside it (for example, water). A real-world capacitor inevitably has a tiny leak through which the water (or electrical charge) drains out. The leaky nature of capacitors themselves is made worse by the circuitry that charges and discharges the capacitor because it, too, allows some of the charge to leak off.

This system seems to violate the primary principle of memory—it won't reliably retain information for very long. Fortunately, this capacitor-based system can remember long enough to be useful—a few or a few dozen milliseconds—before the disappearing charges make the memory unreliable. Those few milliseconds are sufficient that practical circuits can be designed to periodically recharge the capacitor and refresh the memory.

Refreshing memory is akin to pouring extra water into a glass from which it is leaking out. Of course, you have to be quick to pour the water while there's a little left so you know which glass needs to be refilled and which is supposed to be empty.

To ensure the integrity of their memory, computers periodically refresh memory automatically. During the refresh period, the memory is not available for normal operation. Accessing memory also refreshes the memory cell. Depending on how a chip-maker has designed its products, accessing a single cell also may refresh the entire row or column containing the accessed memory cell.

Because of the changing nature of this form of capacitor-based memory and its need to be actively maintained by refreshing, it is termed *dynamic memory*. Integrated circuits that provide this kind of memory are termed *dynamic RAM* (DRAM) chips.

In personal computer memories, special semiconductor circuits that act like capacitors are used instead of actual capacitors with metal plates. A large number of these circuits are combined together to make a dynamic memory-integrated circuit chip. As with true capacitors, however, dynamic memory of this type must be periodically refreshed.

Static Memory

Whereas dynamic memory tries to trap evanescent electricity and hold it in place, *static memory* allows the current flow to continue on its way. It alters the path taken by the power, using one of two possible courses of travel to mark the state being remembered. Static memory operates as a switch that potentially allows or halts the flow of electricity.

A simple mechanical switch will, in fact, suffice as a form of static memory. It, alas, has the handicap that it must be manually toggled from one position to another by a human or robotic hand.

A switch that can itself be controlled by electricity is called a *relay*, and this technology was one of the first used for computer memory. The typical relay circuit provided a latch. Applying a voltage to the relay energizes it, causing it to snap from not permitting electricity to flow to it. Part of the electrical flow could be used to keep the relay itself energized, which would, in turn, maintain the electrical flow. Like a door latch, this kind of relay circuit stays locked until some force or signal causes it to change, thus opening the door or the circuit.

Transistors, which can behave as switches, can also be wired to act as latches. In electronics, a circuit that acts as a latch is sometimes called a *flip-flop* because its state (which stores a bit of data) switches like a political candidate who flip-flops between the supporting and opposing views on sensitive topics. A large number of these transistor flip-flop circuits, when miniaturized and properly arranged, together make a static memory chip. Static RAM is often shortened to *SRAM* by computer professionals. Note that the principal operational difference between static and dynamic memory is that static RAM does not need to be periodically refreshed.

Read-Only Memory

Not all memory must be endowed with the ability to be changed. Just as there are many memories you would like to retain—your first love, the names of all the constellations in the zodiac, the answers to the chemistry exam—a computer is better off when it can remember some particularly important things without regard to the vagaries of the power line. Perhaps the most important of these more permanent rememberings is the program code that tells a microprocessor that it's actually part of a computer and how it should carry out its duties.

You can render a simple memory system, such as a light switch, unchangeable by carefully applying a hammer. With enough assurance and impact, you could guarantee that the system would never forget. In the world of solid-state, the principle is the same, but the programming instrument is somewhat different. All that you need is switches that don't switch—or, more accurately, that switch once and jam. This permanent kind of memory is so valuable in computers that a whole family of devices called *read-only memory* (ROM) chips has been developed to implement it. These devices are called *read-only* because the computer that they are installed in cannot store new code in them. Only what is already there can be read from the memory.

Just as RAM isn't really RAM, most ROM isn't really ROM. The only true ROM is called *mask ROM* because its storage contents get permanently set in place when the chip is fabricated. When the circuits of the chip are laid out using a mask, they already reflect the information stored in the chip.

Most kinds of ROM chips can have their contents altered. They differ from RAM chips in that they cannot be written to in the normal operation of the computer. That is, nothing the computer normally does can change the contents of these almost-ROM chips. Their contents can be changed only using special equipment—or special programming routines inside the computer.

Errors

No memory system is perfect. Certainly your computer's memory won't mislay its gloves or forget your birthday, but it can suffer little slips, an errant bit here and there. Although one bit in a few million might not seem like a big deal, it's enough to send your system into a tailspin, or worse, alter the answer to some important calculation, jogging the decimal point a few places to the left.

Causes

The memory errors that your computer is likely to suffer fall into two broad classes: soft errors and hard errors. Either can leave you staring at an unflinching screen, sometimes but not always emblazoned with a cryptic message that does nothing to help you regain the hours' work irrevocably lost. The difference between them is *transience*. Soft errors are little more than disabling glitches that disappear as fast as they come. Hard errors linger until you take a trip to the repair shop.

Soft Errors

For your computer, a soft memory error is an unexpected and unwanted change. Something in memory might turn up different from what it's supposed to be. One bit in a memory chip may suddenly, randomly change state. Or a glitch of noise inside your system may get stored as if it were valid data. In either case, one bit becomes something other than what it's supposed to be, thus possibly changing an instruction in a program or a data value.

With a soft error, the change appears in your data rather than hardware. Replace or restore the erroneous data or program code, and your system will operate exactly as it always has. In general, your system needs nothing more than a reboot—a cold boot being best to gain the assurance of your computer's self-test of its circuits (including memory). The only damage is the time you waste retracing your steps to get back to the place in your processing at which the error occurred. Soft errors are the best justification for the sage advice, "Save often."

Most soft errors result from problems either within memory chips themselves or in the overall circuitry of your computer. The underlying mechanism behind these two types of soft errors is entirely different.

Chip-Level Errors

The errors inside memory chips are almost always a result of radioactive decay. The problem is not nuclear waste (although nuclear wastes *is* a problem) but something even more devious. The culprit is the epoxy of the plastic chip package, which like most materials may contain a few radioactive atoms. Typically one of these minutely radioactive atoms will spontaneously decay and shoot out an alpha particle into the chip. (There are a number of radioactive atoms in just about everything—they don't amount to very much, but they are there. And by definition, a radioactive particle will spontaneously decay sometime.) An alpha particle is a helium nucleus, two protons and two neutrons, having a small positive charge and a lot of kinetic energy. If such a charged particle hits a memory cell in the chip, the charge and energy of the particle can cause the cell to change state, blasting the memory bit it contains to a new and different value. This miniature atomic blast is not enough to damage the silicon structure of the chip itself, however.

Whether a given memory cell will suffer this kind of soft error is unpredictable, just as predicting whether a given radioactive atom will decay is unpredictable. When you deal with enough atoms, however, this unpredictability becomes a probability, and engineers can predict how often one of the memory cells in a chip will suffer such an error. They just can't predict which one.

In the early days of computers, radioactive decay inside memory chips was the most likely cause of soft errors in computers. Thanks to improved designs and technology, each generation of memory chip has become more reliable, no matter whether you measure per bit or per chip. For example, any given bit in a 16KB chip might suffer a decay-caused soft error every billion or so hours. The likelihood of any given bit in a modern 16MB chip will suffer an error is on the order of once in two trillion hours. In other words, modern memory chips are about 5000 times more reliable than those of first generation computers, and the contents of each cell is about five *million* times more reliable once you take into account that chip capacities have increased a thousand-fold. Although conditions of use influence the occurrence of soft errors, the error rate of modern memory is such that a typical computer with 8MB of RAM would suffer a decay-caused soft error once in 10 to 30 years. The probability is so small that many computer-makers now ignore it.

System-Level Errors

Sometimes the data traveling though your computer gets hit by a noise glitch—on the scale of memory cells, a little glitch can be like you getting struck by lightning. Just as you might have trouble remembering after such a glitch, so does the memory cell. If a pulse of noise is strong enough and occurs at an especially inopportune instant, it can be misinterpreted by your computer as a data bit. Such a system-level error will have the same effect on your computer as a soft error in memory. In fact, some system-level errors may be reported as memory errors (for example, when the glitch appears in the circuitry between your computer's memory chips and the memory controller).

The most likely place for system-level soft errors to occur is on your computer's buses. A glitch on a data line can cause your computer to try to use or execute a bad bit of data or program code, thus causing an error. Or your computer could load the bad value into memory, saving it to relish (and crash from) at some later time. A glitch on the address bus will make your computer similarly find the wrong bit or byte, and the unexpected value may have exactly the same effects as a data bus error.

The probability of a system-level error occurring depends on the design of your computer. A careless designer can leave your system not only susceptible to system-level errors but even prone to generating the glitches that cause them. Pushing a computer design to run too fast is particularly prone to cause problems. You can do nothing to prevent system-level soft errors other than to choose your computer wisely.

Hard Errors

When some part of a memory chip actually fails, the result is a *hard error*. For instance, a jolt of static electricity can wipe out one or more memory cells. As a result, the initial symptom is the same as a soft error—a memory error may cause an error in the results you get or a total crash of your system. The operative difference is that the hard error doesn't go away when you reboot your system. In fact, your machine may not pass its memory test when you try to start it up again. Alternately, you may encounter repeated, random errors when a memory cell hovers between life and death.

Hard errors require attention. The chip or module in which the error originates needs to be replaced.

Note, however, that operating memory beyond its speed capability often causes the same problem as hard errors. In fact, operating memory beyond its ratings causes hard errors. You can sometimes clear up such problems by adding wait states to your system's memory cycles, a setting many computers allow you to control as part of their advanced setup procedure. This will, of course, slow down the operation of your computer so that it can accommodate the failing memory. The better cure is to replace the too-slow memory with some that can handle the speed.

Detection and Prevention

Most computers check every bit of their memory for hard errors every time you switch your system on or perform a cold boot, although some computers give you the option of bypassing this initial memory check to save time. Soft errors are another matter entirely. They rarely show up at boot time. Rather, they are likely to occur at the worst possible moment—which means just about any time you're running your computer.

Computer-makers use two strategies to combat memory errors: parity and detection/correction. Either one will ensure the integrity of your system's memory. Which is best—or whether you need any error compensation at all—is a personal choice. Manufacturers consider the memory systems in most modern computers so reliable that they opt to save a few bucks and omit any kind of error detection. Where accuracy really counts, in servers, network managers usually insist their computers have the best error prevention possible by using memory that supports error-correction code.

Parity

When memory chips were of dubious reliability, computer manufacturers followed the lead of the first computer and added an extra bit of storage to every byte of memory. The extra bit was called a *parity check bit*, and it allows the computer to verify the integrity of the data stored in memory. Using a simple algorithm, the parity check bit permits a computer to determine that a given byte of memory has the right number of binary zeros and ones in it. If the count changes, your computer knows an error occurred.

When a microprocessor writes a byte to memory, the value stored in the parity check bit is set either to a logical one or zero in such a way that the total of all nine bits storing the byte is always odd. Every time your computer reads a given portion of memory, the memory controller totals up the nine bits storing each byte, verifying that the overall total (including the parity check bit) remains odd. Should the system detect a total that's even, it immediately knows that something has happened to cause one bit of the byte to change, making the stored data invalid.

The philosophy behind parity memory is that having bad data is worse than losing information through a system crash. One bad bit results in a halt to all computing. You won't make a mistake—and you won't like it when your computer's memory does. Although parity errors happened rarely, when they did, most people questioned the value of parity checking. Consequently, few people minded when manufacturers started omitting it from their designs.

Fake Parity

Fake parity memory is a means of cutting the cost of memory modules for computers with built-in parity checking. Instead of actually performing a parity check of the memory on the module, the fake parity system always sends out a signal indicating that memory parity is good. No extra bits of memory means the vendors of "fake parity" chips don't have to pay the extra bucks for extra memory.

Fake parity has two downsides. The cost savings often are not passed down to you, at least explicitly. The fake parity modules are often sold as ordinary parity modules with no indication of the underlying shortchange on technology. Moreover, a fake parity module does not offer protection against parity errors causing erroneous data in your computer. One fake parity module defeats the operation and purpose of the parity memory system in your computer. Fortunately, with the decline in the use of actual parity memory, the incentive to sell fake parity memory has disappeared.

Detection/Correction

Parity checking can only locate an error of one bit in a byte. More elaborate error-detection schemes can detect larger errors. Better still, when properly implemented, these schemes can fix single-bit errors without crashing your system. Called *error-correction code* (ECC), this scheme in its most efficient form requires three extra bits per byte of storage. The additional bits allow your system not only to determine the occurrence of a memory error but also to locate any single bit that changed so that the error can be reversed. Some people call this technology *Error Detection and Correction* (EDAC).

Most server computers use ECC memory. In fact, many desktop machines also allow you to use ECC. Support for ECC is built into many chipsets. If your BIOS allows you to turn this facility on, you can use ECC, but you'll also need ECC memory modules (which means tossing out the ones that you have).

Server-makers have another reason for shifting from parity to ECC memory. As the width of the data bus increases, error correction memory become less expensive to implement. In fact, with today's Pentium computers—which have 64-bit data buses—the cost of extra memory for parity checking and full error correction are the same. Table 15.4 summarizes the penalty required by parity and ECC technology for various bus widths.

TABLE 15.4   Comparison of Parity and ECC Memory

	Extra Bits Required		Cost Increase	
Bus Width	Parity	ECC	Parity	ECC
8	1	5	12.5%	62%
16	2	6	12.5%	38%
32	4	8	12.5%	25%
64	8	8	12.5%	12.5%

Parity and ECC memory are technologies for people who want or need to take every possible precaution. They are the kind of people who check the weather report, then put on their galoshes and carry an umbrella even when the prediction is 100 percent in favor of sun. They are the folks who get the last laugh when they are warm and dry after a once-in-a-century freak thunderstorm rumbles through. These people know that the best solution to computer and memory problems is *prevention*.

Mass Storage Systems

Secondary storage is essentially an electronic closet, a place where you put information that you don't want to constantly hold in your hands but that you don't want to throw away, either. As with the straw hats, squash rackets, wallpaper tailings, and all the rest of your dimly remembered possessions that pile up out of sight behind the closet door, retrieving a particular item from mass storage can take longer than when you have what you want at hand.

Access

Mass storage takes two forms: *online* storage, which is instantly accessible by your microprocessor's commands, and *offline* storage, which requires some extra, possibly human, intervention (such as you sliding a cartridge into a drive) for your system to get the bytes that it needs. Sometimes, the term *near-line* storage is used to refer to systems in which information isn't instantly available but can be put into instant reach by a microprocessor command. The jukebox—an automatic mechanism that selects CD-ROM cartridges, and sometimes tape cartridges—is the most common example.

Moving bytes from mass storage to memory determines how quickly stored information can be accessed. In practical online systems, the time required for this access ranges from less than 0.01 seconds in the fastest hard disks to 1000 seconds in some tape systems, spanning a range of 100,000 or five orders of magnitude.

By definition, the best offline storage systems have substantially longer access times than the quickest online systems. Even with fast-access disk cartridges, the minimum access time for offline data is measured in seconds because of the need to find and load a particular cartridge. The slowest online and the fastest offline storage system speeds, however, may overlap because the time to ready an offline cartridge can be substantially shorter than the period required to locate needed information written on a long online tape.

Data Organization

Computer mass storage systems differ in the way they organize and allow access to the information that they store. Engineers class the storage systems in modern computers as either *sequential* or *random access*. From a practical standpoint, the difference is functional—how the computer system finds the information it needs. But it also has a historic dimension—sequential computer mass storage predates random access. You can also look at the difference topographically. Sequential storage is one dimensional, whereas random access has two (or possibly more) dimensions.

Neither technology is inherently better. Both are used in modern computers. For a given application, of course, one of the two is typically more suitable. But because each has its own strengths, both will likely persist as long as computers populate desktops, if not longer.

Sequential Media

A fundamental characteristic of tape recording is that information is stored on tape one-dimensionally—in a straight line across the length of the tape. This form of storage is called *sequential* because all the bits of data are organized one after another in a strict sequence, like those paper-based dots. In digital systems, one bit follows after the other for the full length of the tape. Although in multiple-track and helical recording systems, bits may also spread across the width of the tape, conceptually these, too, store information in one dimension only.

CDs and DVDs designed for audio and video applications (that is, CD-DA, CD-Video, DVD-Video, and DVD-Audio) are designed to work best as one-dimensional media as well. They record data as a continuous stream meant to be displayed (or listened to) in the same sequential order it was recorded. However, the two-dimensional nature of the disc (a disc is a two-dimensional plane, after all) allows these media to transcend some of the limitations of sequential recording.

In the Newtonian universe (the only one that appears to make sense to the normal human mind), the shortest distance between two points is always a straight line. Alas, in magnetic tape systems, the shortest distance between two bits of data on a tape may also be a long time. To read two widely separated bits on a tape, all the tape between them must be passed over. Although all the bits in between are not to be used, they must be scanned in the journey from the first to second bits. If you want to retrieve information not stored in order on a tape, the tape must shuttle back and forth to find the data in the order that you want it. All that tape movement to find data means wasted time.

In theory, there's nothing wrong with sequential storage schemes—depending on the storage medium that's used, they can be very fast. For example, one form of solid-state computer memory, the all-electronic shift register, moves data sequentially at nearly the speed of light.

The sequential mass storage systems of today's computers are not so blessed with speed, however. Because of their mechanical foundations, most tape systems operate somewhat slower than the speed of light. For example, although light can zip across the vacuum of the universe at 186,000 miles per second (or so), cassette tape crawls along at one and seven-eighths inches per second. Although light can get from here to the moon and back in a few seconds, moving a cassette tape that distance would take about ten billion times longer, several thousand years.

Although no tape stretches as long as the 238,000 mile distance to the moon, sequential data access can be irritatingly slow. Instead of delivering the near-instant response most of today's impatient power users demand, picking a file from a tape can take as long as ten minutes. Even the best of today's tape systems require 30 seconds or more to find a file. If you had to load all your programs and data files from tape, you might as well take up crocheting to tide you through the times you're forced to wait.

Most sequential systems store data in *blocks*, sometimes called exactly that, and sometimes called *records*. The storage system defines the structure and contents of each block. Typically, each block includes identifying information (such as a block number) and error-control information in addition to the actual data. Blocks are stored in order on tape. In some systems, they lie end to end while others separate them with blank areas called *inter-record gaps*.

Most tape systems use multiple tracks to increase their storage (some systems spread as many as 144 tracks across tape just one-quarter inch wide). The otherwise stationary read-write head in the tape machine moves up and down to select the correct track. This multi-track design also improves the access speed of the medium. With multiple tracks, the drive doesn't have to scan the whole tape to get at a particular block. With 144 tracks, a drive needs only to scan 1/144th the length of the tape to find a particular block. Sequential

CDs and DVDs provide a greater speed-up because they can select among thousands of radial positions along the disc to read.

To take advantage of the speed-up afforded by multiple tracks, the drive needs to know on which track to find the block you're seeking. Old tape systems didn't keep track of location information, so they would scan back and forth along the tape, one track after another, to find the blocks you wanted. New tape standards put a directory on the tape that holds the location of information on the tape. By consulting the directory, the drive can determine which track holds the information you want and zero in on the correct track to trim the response time of the tape system.

Random-Access Media

On floppy and most hard computer disks, as well as some CD and DVD formats, the recorded data is organized to take advantage of the two-dimensional aspect of the flat, wide disk surface to give even faster access than is possible with the directory system on tape. Instead of being arranged in a single straight line, disk-based data is spread across several concentric circles like lanes in a circular racetrack or the pattern of waves rolling away from a splash. Some optical drives follow this system, but many other optical systems modify this arrangement, changing the concentric circles into one tightly packed spiral that continuously winds from the edge to the center of the disk. But even these continuous-data systems behave much as if they had concentric circles of information.

The mechanism for making this arrangement is quite elementary. The disk moves in one dimension under the read/write head, which scans the tape in a circle as it spins and defines a track, which runs across the surface of the disk much like one of the lanes of a racetrack. In most disk systems, the head can move as well; otherwise, the read/write head would be stuck forever hovering over the same track and the same stored data, making it a sequential storage system that wastes most of the usable storage surface of the disk.

In most of today's disks systems, the read/write moves across a radius of the disk, perpendicular to a tangent of the tracks. The read/write head can quickly move between the different tracks on the disk. Although the shortest distance between two points (or two bytes) remains a straight line, to get from one byte to another, the read/write head can take shortcuts across the lanes of the racetrack. After the head reaches the correct track, it still must wait for the desired bit of information to cycle around under it. However, disks spin relatively quickly—300 revolutions per minute for most floppy disks and up to 7200 rpm for some hard disks—so you only need to wait a fraction of a second for the right byte to reach your system.

Because the head can jump from byte to byte at widely separated locations on the disk surface and because data can be read and retrieved in any order or at random in the two-dimensional disk system, disk storage systems are often called *random-access devices*, even though they fall a bit short of the mark with their need to wait while hovering over a track.

The random-access capability of magnetic disk systems makes the combination much faster than sequential tape media for the mass storage of data. Disks are so superior and so much more convenient than tapes that tape is almost never used as a primary mass storage system. Usually, tape plays only a secondary role as a backup system. Disks are used to store programs and files that need to be loaded on a moment's notice.

Magnetic Storage

The most popular mass storage systems in modern computers are based on magnetism. Hard disks use magnetic storage, as do floppy disks and tape drives. Magnetic storage is one of the oldest storage mediums used by computers (only punch cards predate its application), and it ranks as one of the most reliable. It also yields systems with the lowest cost per byte of storage.

Magnetic systems are popular both because of the unique properties of magnetism and because of its heritage. It has been used so long that its operating principles are well understood. It gives engineers a head start when they look for ways to improve the technology—and improve it they have. In 20 years, the typical capacity of a hard disk system has grown by a factor of 10,000, while the disk mechanism itself has actually shrunk. Every time some new breakthrough technology threatens to beat the storage capabilities of magnetic media, engineers simply roll out a refinement or two that lets the old medium easily eclipse the new.

The original electronic mass storage system was magnetic tape—that thin strip of paper (in the United States) upon which a thin layer of refined rust had been glued. Later, the paper gave way to plastic, and the iron oxide coating gave way to a number of improved magnetic particle based on iron, chrome dioxide, and various mixtures of similar compounds.

The machine that recorded upon these rust-covered ribbons was the Magnetophon, the first practical tape recorder, created by the German division of the General Electric Company, Allgemeine Elektricitaets Gesellschaft (AEG) in 1934. Continually improved but essentially secret through the years of World War II, despite its use at German radio stations, the Magnetophon was the first device to record and play back sound indistinguishable from live performances. After its introduction to the United States (in a demonstration by John T. Mullin to the Institute of Radio Engineers in San Francisco on May 16, 1946), tape recording quickly became the premiere recording medium and within a decade gained the ability to record video and digital data. Today, both data cassettes and streaming tape systems are based on the direct offspring of the first Magnetophon.

The principle is simple. Some materials become magnetized under the influence of a magnetic field. Once the material becomes magnetized, it retains its magnetic field. The magnetic field turns a suitable mixture or compound based on one of the magnetic materials into a permanent magnet with its own magnetic field. A galvanometer or similar device can later detect the resulting magnetic field and determine that the material has been magnetized. The magnet material remembers.

Magnetism

Key to the memory of magnetism is *permanence*. Magnetic fields have the wonderful property of being static and semi-permanent. On their own, they don't move or change. The electricity used by electronic circuits is just the opposite. It is constantly on the go and seeks to dissipate itself as quickly as possible. The difference is fundamental. Magnetic fields are set up by the spins of atoms physically locked in place. Electric charges are carried by mobile particles—mostly electrons—that not only refuse to stay in place but also are individually resistant to predictions of where they are or where they are going.

Given the right force in the right amount, however, magnetic spins can be upset, twisted from one orientation to another. Because magnetic fields are amenable to change rather than being entirely permanent, magnetism is useful for data storage. After all, if a magnetic field were permanent and unchangeable, it would present no means of recording information. If it couldn't be changed, nothing about it could be altered to reflect the addition of information.

At the elemental particle level, magnetic spins are eternal, but taken collectively, they can be made to come and go. A single spin can be oriented in only one direction, but in virtually any direction. If two adjacent particles spin in opposite directions, they cancel one another out when viewed from a larger, macroscopic perspective.

Altering those spin orientations takes a force of some kind, and that's the key to making magnetic storage work. That force can make an alteration to a magnetic field, and after the field has changed, it will keep its new state until some other force acts upon it.

The force that most readily changes one magnetic field is another magnetic field. (Yes, some permanent magnets can be demagnetized just by heating them sufficiently, but the demagnetization is actually an effect of the interaction of the many minute magnetic fields of the magnetic material.)

Despite their different behavior in electronics and storage systems, magnetism and electricity are manifestations of the same underlying elemental force. Both are electromagnetic phenomena. One result of that commonalty makes magnetic storage particularly desirable to electronics designers—magnetic fields can be created by the flow of electrical energy. Consequently, evanescent electricity can be used to create and alter semi-permanent magnetic fields.

When set up, magnetic fields are essentially self-sustaining. They require no energy to maintain, because they are fundamentally a characteristic displayed by the minute particles that make up the entire universe (at least according to current physical theories). On the submicroscopic scale of elemental particles, the spins that form magnetic fields are, for the most part, unchangeable and unchanging. Nothing is normally subtracted from them—they don't give up energy, even when they are put to work. They can affect other electromagnetic phenomena (for example, they can be used in mass to divert the flow of electricity). In such a case, however, all the energy in the system comes from the electrical flow—the magnetism is a gate, but the cattle that escape from the corral are solely electrons.

The magnetic fields that are useful in storage systems are those large enough to measure and effect changes on things that we can see. This magnetism is the macroscopic result of the sum of many microscopic magnetic fields, many elemental spins. Magnetism is a characteristic of submicroscopic particles. (Strictly speaking, in modern science magnetism is made from particles itself, but we don't have to be quite so particular for the purpose of understanding magnetic computer storage.)

Magnetic Materials

Three chemical elements are magnetic—iron, nickel, and cobalt. The macroscopic strength as well as other properties of these magnetic materials can be improved by alloying them, together and with nonmagnetic materials, particularly rare earths such as samarium.

Many particles at the molecular level have their own intrinsic magnetic fields. At the observable (macroscopic) level, they do not behave like magnets because their constituent particles are organized—or disorganized—randomly so that in bulk, the cumulative effects of all their magnetic fields tend to cancel out. In contrast, the majority of the minute magnetic particles of a permanent magnet are oriented in the same direction. The majority prevails, and the material has a net magnetic field.

Some materials can be magnetized. That is, their constituent microscopic magnetic fields can be realigned so that they reveal a net macroscopic magnetic field. For instance, by subjecting a piece of soft iron to a strong magnetic field, the iron will become magnetized.

Magnetic Storage

If that strong magnetic field is produced by an electromagnet, all the constituents of a magnetic storage system become available. Electrical energy can be use to alter a magnetic field, which can be later detected. Put a lump of soft iron within the confines of an electromagnet that has not been energized. Any time you return, you can determine whether the electromagnet has been energized in your absence by checking for the presence of a magnetic field in the iron. In effect, you have stored exactly one bit of information.

To store more, you need to be able to organize the information. You need to know the order of the bits. In magnetic storage systems, information is arranged physically by the way data travels serially in time. Instead of being electronic blips that flicker on and off as the milliseconds tick off, magnetic pulses are stored like a row of dots on a piece of paper—a long chain with a beginning and end. This physical arrangement can be directly translated to the temporal arrangement of data used in a serial transmission system, just by scanning the dots across the paper. The first dot becomes the first pulse in the serial stream, and each subsequent dot follows neatly in the data stream as the paper is scanned.

Instead of paper, magnetic storage systems use one or another form of media—generally a disk or long ribbon of plastic tape—covered with a magnetically reactive mixture. The form of medium directly influences the speed at which information can be retrieved from the system.

In operation, the tape moves from left to right past a stationary read/write head. When a current is passed through an electromagnetic coil in this head, it creates the magnetic field needed to write data onto the tape. When the tape is later passed in front of this head, the moving magnetic field generated by the magnetized particles on the tape induces a minuscule current in the head. This current is then amplified and converted into digital data. The write current used in putting data on the tape overpowers whatever fields already exist on the tape, both erasing them and imposing a new magnetic orientation to the particles representing the information to be recorded.

No matter whether it's tape or disk, when a magnetic storage medium is blank from the factory, it contains no information. The various magnetic domains on it are randomly oriented. Recording on the medium reorients the magnetic domains into a pattern that represents the stored information, as shown in Figure 15.1.

After you record on a magnetic medium, you can erase it by overwriting it with a strong magnetic field. In practice, you cannot reproduce the true random orientation of magnetic domains of the unused medium. However, by recording a patter with a frequency out of the range of the reading or playback system—a very high or low frequency—you can obscure previously recorded data and make the medium act as if it were blank.

Digital Magnetic Systems

Computer mass storage systems differ in principle and operation from tape systems used for audio and video recording. Whereas audio and video cassettes record analog signals on tape, computers use digital signals.

FIGURE 15.1
Orientation of magnetic domains in blank and recorded media.

Blank magnetic medium

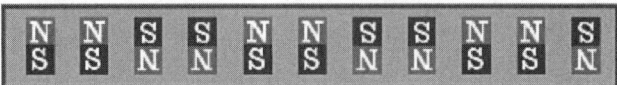

Digitally recorded magnetic medium

In the next few years, this situation will likely change as digital audio and video tape recorders become increasingly available. Eventually, the analog audio and video tape will become historical footnotes, much as the analog vinyl phonograph record was replaced by the all-digital compact disc.

In analog systems, the strength of the magnetic field written on a tape varies in correspondence with the signal being recorded. The intensity of the recorded field can span a range of more than six orders of magnitude. Digital systems generally use a code that relies on patterns of pulses, and all the pulses have exactly the same intensity.

The technological shift from analog to digital is rooted in some of the characteristics of digital storage that make it the top choice where accuracy is concerned. Digital storage resists the intrusion of noise that inevitably pollutes and degrades analog storage. Every time a copy is made of an analog recording, the noise that accompanies the desired signal essentially doubles because the background noise of the original source is added to the background noise of the new recording medium; however, the desired signal does not change. This addition of noise is necessary to preserve the nuances of the analog recording—every twitch in the analog signal adds information to the whole. The analog system cannot distinguish between noise and nuance.

In digital recording, however, there's a sharp line between noise and signal. Noise below the digital threshold can be ignored without losing the nuances of the signal. Consequently, a digital recording system can eliminate the noise built up in making copies. Moreover, noise can creep into analog recordings as the storage medium deteriorates, whereas the digital system can ignore most of the noise added by age. In fact, properly designed digital systems can even correct minor errors that get added to their signals.

Saturation

Digital recordings avoid noise because they ignore all strength variations of the magnetic field except the most dramatic. They just look for the unambiguous "it's either there or not" style of digital pulses of information. Analog systems achieve their varying strengths of field by aligning the tiny molecular magnets in the medium. A stronger electromagnetic field causes a greater percentage of the fields of these molecules to line up with the field, almost in direct proportion to the field strength, to produce an analog recording. Because digital systems need not worry about intermediate levels of signal, they can lay down the strongest possible field that the tape can hold. This level of signal is called *saturation* because much as a saturated sponge can suck up no more water, the particles on the tape cannot produce a stronger magnetic field.

Although going from no magnetic field to a saturated field would seem to be the widest discrepancy possible in magnetic recording—and therefore the least ambiguous and most suitable for digital information—this contrast is not the greatest possible or easy to achieve. Magnetic systems attempt to store information as densely as possible, trying to cram the information in so that every magnetic particle holds one data bit. Magnetic particles are extremely difficult to demagnetize, but the polarity of their magnetic orientation is relatively easy to change. Digital magnetic systems exploit this capability to change polarity and record data as shifts between the orientations of the magnetic fields of the particles on the tape. The difference between the tape being saturated with a field in one direction and the tape being saturated with a field in the opposite direction is the greatest contrast possible in a magnetic system and is exploited by nearly all of today's digital magnetic storage systems.

Coercivity

One word that you may encounter in the description of a magnetic medium is *coercivity*, a term that describes how strongly a magnetic field resists change, which translates into how strong of a magnetic field a particular medium can store. Stronger stored fields are better because the more intense field stands out better against the random background noise that is present in any storage medium. Because a higher coercivity medium resists change better than a low coercivity material, it also is less likely to change or degrade because of the effects of external influences. Of course, a higher coercivity and its greater resistance to change means that a recording system requires a more powerful magnetic field to maximally magnetize the medium. Equipment must be particularly designed to take advantage of high-coercivity materials.

With hard disks, which characteristically mate the medium with the mechanisms for life, matching the coercivity of a medium with the recording equipment is permanently handled by the manufacturer. The two are matched permanently when a drive is made. Removable media devices—floppy disks, tape cartridges, cassettes, and so on—pose more of a problem. If media are interchangeable and have different coercivities, you face the possibility of using the wrong media in a particular drive. Such problems often occur with floppy disks, particularly when you want to skimp and use cheaper double-density media in high-density or extra-density drives.

Moreover, the need for matching drive and medium makes upgrading a less-than-simple matter. Obtaining optimum performance requires that changes in media be matched by hardware upgrades. Even when better media are developed, they may not deliver better results with existing equipment.

The unit of measurement for coercivity is the *Oersted*. As storage media have been miniaturized, the coercivity of the magnetic materials as measured in Oersteds has generally increased. The greater intrinsic field strength makes up for the smaller area upon which data is recorded. With higher coercivities, more information can be squeezed into the tighter confines of the newer storage formats. For example, old 5.25-inch floppy disks had a coercivity of 300 Oersteds. Today's high-density 3.5-inch floppies have coercivities of 750 Oersteds. Similarly, the coercivities of the tapes used in today's high-capacity quarter-inch cartridges are greater than those of the last generation. Older standards used 550 Oersted media; data cartridges with capacities in excess of 1.5GB and minicartridges with capacities beyond 128MB require 900-Oersted tape. Although invisible to you, the coercivities of tiny modern hard disk drives are much higher than big old drives.

Coercivity is a temperature-dependent property. As the temperature of a medium increases, its resistance to magnetic change declines. That's one reason you can demagnetize an otherwise permanent magnet by heating it red hot. Magnetic media dramatically shift from being unchangeable to changeable—meaning a drop in coercivity—at a material-dependent temperature called the *Curie temperature*. Magneto-optical recording systems take advantage of this coercivity shift by using a laser beam to heat a small area of magnetic medium that is under the influence of a magnetic field otherwise not strong enough to affect the medium.

At room temperature, the media used by magneto-optical systems have coercivities on the order of 6000 Oersteds; when heated by a laser, that coercivity falls to a few hundred Oersteds. Because of this dramatic change in coercivity, the magnetic field applied to the magneto-optical medium changes only the area heated by the laser above its Curie temperature (rather than the whole area under the magnetic influence). Because a laser can be tightly focused to a much smaller spot than is possible with traditional disk read/write heads, using such a laser-boosted system allows data to be defined by tinier areas of a recording medium. A disk of a given size thus can store more data when its magnetic storage is optically assisted. Such media are resistant to the effects of stray magnetic fields (which may change low coercivity fields) as long as they are kept at room temperature.

Retentivity

Another term that appears in the descriptions of magnetic media is *retentivity*, which measures how well a particular medium retains or remembers the field that it is subjected to. Although magnetic media are sometimes depended upon to last forever—think of the master tapes of phonograph records—the stored magnetic fields begin to degrade as soon as they have been recorded. A higher retentivity ensures a longer life for the signals recorded on the medium.

No practical magnetic material has perfect retentivity, however; the random element of modern physical theories ensures that. Even the best hard disks slowly deteriorate with age, showing an increasing number of errors as time passes after data has been written. To avoid such deterioration of so-called permanent records, many computer professionals believe that magnetically stored recordings should be periodically refreshed. For example, they exercise tapes stored in mainframe computer libraries periodically (in intervals from several months to several years, depending on the personal philosophy and paranoia of the person managing the storage). Although noticeable degradation may require several years (perhaps a decade or more), these tape caretakers do not want to stake their data—and their jobs—on media written long ago.

Disk-makers view such precautions as verging on paranoia. The magnetic medium used in modern disk drives is nothing like that in the old, self-erasing tapes. Their plated media (see Chapter 17, "Magnetic Storage") have much higher retentivities. Moreover, new technologies such as S.M.A.R.T. let drives detect any degradation in the magnetic medium and warn you before you stand a chance of losing your data.

Old floppy disks and backup tapes are another matter. They are likely to deteriorate with time, enough so that the data on decade-old disks and tapes may be at risk. If you have old records on old media, for safety's sake you should consider copying the records to fresher media or a newer technology, such as an optical disc.

Optical Storage

Today the chief alternative to magnetic media in mass storage system is optical technology. Cheap and easy duplication has made computer optical disc storage an ideal distribution medium. Its versatility (the same basic technology stores data, sound, and video) came about because all engineers eagerly search for big, cheap storage. Both the Compact Disc (CD) and Digital Versatile Disc (DVD) have both of those virtues by design. In addition, because the discs both systems use for storage are removable and interchangeable, CD and DVD systems can serve as both online and offline storage.

Engineers made optical media into true mass storage systems by adding writing capabilities to both the CD and DVD designs. By altering the materials used in the discs, they were able to allow the same equipment that read data to write it as well.

One of the great virtues of any kind of optical storage is data density—little discs mean a lot of megabytes. By using light beams provided by lasers, optical storage earns several advantages. Lenses can focus a beam of light—particularly the coherent beam of a laser—

to a tiny spot smaller than the most diminutive magnetic domain writable on a hard disc drive. Unlike the restricted magnetic fields of hard discs that have to be used within a range of a few millionth of an inch, light travels distance with ease. Leaping along some 5.9 trillion miles in a year, some beams have been traveling since almost the beginning of the universe, 10 to 15 billion years ago. A small gap between the source and storage medium is consequently no problem. The equipment that generates the beam of light that writes or reads optical storage need not be anywhere near the medium itself, which gives equipment designers more freedom than they possibly deserve.

The basic idea behind optical disc storage is that you can encode binary data as a pattern of black and white splotches just as on and off electrical signals can. You can make your mark in a variety of ways. The old reliable method is plain, ordinary ink on paper. The bar codes found universally on supermarket products do exactly that.

Reading the patterns of light and dark takes only a *photo-detector*, an electrical component that reacts to different brightness levels by changing its resistance. Light simply allows electricity to flow through the photo-detector more easily. Aim the photo-detector at the bar code, and it can judge the difference in reflected light between the bars and background as you move it (or move the product along in front of it). The lasers that read bar-codes in the supermarket checkout line quicken the scan. The photo-detector watches the reflections of the red laser beam and patiently waits until a recognizable pattern—the bar code as the laser scans across it—emerges from the noise.

You could store the data of a computer file in one gigantic bar code and bring back paper tape as a storage medium—one long strip of bars that stretches past the horizon. Even if you were willing to risk your important data to a medium that turns yellow and flakes apart under the unblinking eye of the sun like a beach bum with a bad complexion, you'd still have all the joy of dealing with a sequential storage medium. That means renew your subscription to your favorite magazines because you'll have a lot of waiting to do.

The disc, with its random-access capabilities, is better suited as a storage system. Its two-dimensional storage makes randomly accessing a particular block of data a matter of milliseconds rather than miles. The choice of a fast-spinning disc was obvious even to the audio-oriented engineers who put the first compact disc systems together. They had a successful pattern to follow: the old black vinyl phonograph record. The ability to drop a needle on any track of a record had become ingrained in the hearts and minds of music lovers for over 100 years. Any new music storage system needed equally fast and easy access to any selection. The same fast and easy access suits computer storage equally well.

Optical storage brings another benefit. The optical patterns that encode data in both the CD and DVD systems can be formed mechanically. Both systems use physical pits that show up as small black holes against a shiny silver background as the dark and bright spots for optically coding data. The pits are mechanical features that can be duplicated mechanically. The process is inexpensive and fast. Machines can flawlessly mold multiple copies in a few seconds, and with multiple master molds, a factory can crank out a million copies in a few days. In other words, optical technology allows for duplicating megabytes, even gigabytes, *en masse*. Magnetic media, on the other hand, can duplicate data only byte by byte.

Virtual Memory

Even before anyone conceived the idea of the first personal computer, mainframe computer designers faced the same tradeoff between memory and mass storage. Mass storage was plentiful and cheap; memory was expensive, so much so that not even large corporations could afford as much as they wanted. In the early years of computers, engineers tried to sidestep the high cost of memory by faking it, making computers think they had more memory than they actually did. With some fancy footwork and a lot of shuffling around of bytes, they substituted mass storage for memory. The engineers called the memory the computer thought it had but in reality didn't exist *virtual memory*. Although the cost of memory has fallen by a millionfold, memory use has risen even faster. Programs' need for memory still outpaces what any reasonable person or organization can afford (or wants to pay for), so virtual memory not only exists but is flourishing.

Microprocessors cannot ordinarily use disk storage to hold the data they work on. Even if they could, it would severely degrade the performance of the system because the access time for disk storage is thousands of times longer than for solid-state memory. To prevent performance problems and keep active programs in solid-state memory where your computer's microprocessor can use them, virtual memory systems swap blocks of code and data between solid-state and disk storage.

Demand Paging

Most modern computers take advantage of a feature called *demand paging* that has been part of all Intel microprocessors since the 386. These chips are able to track memory content as it is moved between disk and solid state memory in 4K blocks. The microprocessor assigns an address to the data in the block, and the address stays constant regardless of where the data actually gets stored.

Once solid-state memory reaches its capacity, the virtual memory system copies the contents of one or more pages of memory to disk as the memory space is required. When the system needs data that has been copied to disk, it copies the least recently used pages to disk and refills their space with the disk-based pages it needs. When your system attempts to read from a page with an address that's not available in solid-state memory, it creates a *page fault.* The fault causes a virtual memory manager routine to handle the details of exchanging data between solid-state and disk storage.

This reactive kind of control is called *demand paging* because it swaps data only when the microprocessor demands unavailable addresses. It makes no attempt to anticipate the needs of the microprocessor.

Virtual memory technology allows your computer to run more programs than would be otherwise possible given the amount of solid-state memory in your system. The effective memory of your system approaches the spare capacity of your disk. The downside is that it takes away from the capacity of your hard disk (although disk storage is substantially less expensive than solid-state memory by about two orders of magnitude). In addition, performance slows substantially when your system must swap memory.

Virtual memory is an old technology, harking back to the days of mainframe computers when, as now, disk storage was cheaper than physical memory. Many DOS applications took advantage of the technology, and it has been part of every version of Windows since Windows 386—which means not only before Windows 95 but also Windows 3.1.

Windows uses a demand-paging system that's based on a least-recently used algorithm. That is, the Windows virtual memory manager (VMM) decides which data to swap to disk based on when it was last used by your system. The Windows VMM also maintains the virtual memory page table, which serves as a key to which pages are used by each application, which are kept in solid-state storage, and which are on disk.

Windows decides which pages to swap to disk using two flags for each page. The *accessed* flag indicates that the page has been read from or written to since the time it was loaded into memory. The *dirty* flag indicates the page has been written to.

When Windows needs more pages in solid-state memory, it scans through its page table looking for pages showing neither the accessed flag nor the dirty flag. As it makes its scan, it resets the accessed flag but not the dirty flag. If it does not find sufficient unflagged pages, it scans through the page table again. This time, more pages should be unflagged because of the previous resetting of the accessed flags. If it still cannot find enough available pages, the Windows virtual memory manager then swaps pages regardless of the flags.

Swap Files

The disk space used by a virtual memory system usually takes the form of an ordinary file, though one reserved for its special purpose. Engineers call the virtual memory file a *swap file* because the memory system swaps data to and from the file as the operating system requires it. Although earlier versions of Windows had several options you could choose for swap files—primarily the choice between a temporary file that swelled as you used it and a permanent file that forever stole disk space—Windows 95 erased such complications.

Under Windows 95 as well as Windows 98, the swap file mixes together features of temporary and permanent swap files. Like a temporary swap file, the current Windows swap file is dynamic, expanding as your system demands virtual memory and contracting when it does not. In addition, it can shuffle itself into the scatter clusters of a fragmented hard disk. It can even run on a compressed hard disk.

Windows gives you full menu control of its swap file. You can start the virtual memory control system by clicking the Virtual Memory button in the Performance tab of Device Manager. (You start the Device Manager by clicking the System icon in Control Panel.) Once you click the Virtual Memory button, you should see a dialog box like the one shown in Figure 15.2.

FIGURE 15.2

The Virtual Memory dialog box for controlling Windows 95 (and Windows 98) swap files.

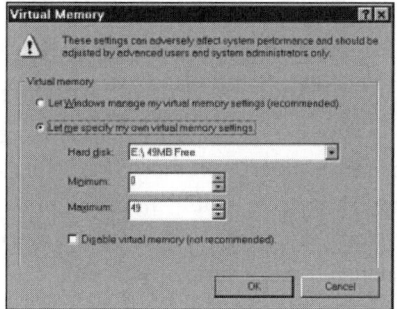

You can opt to let Windows choose the size and place of your swap file or take direct control. By default, Windows puts your swap file in the Windows directory of your C: drive. By selecting the appropriate box, you can tell Windows the disk and directory in which to put your swap file and set minimum and maximum limits for its size.

Data Compression

Just as virtual memory can stretch the capacity of your primary storage system, data compression can boost the capacity of your secondary storage system. Compression eliminates the waste in a storage system. It seeks to put every bit of information in the smallest possible space. In effect, the compression system squeezes the air out of the data stream. Data compression can reduce fat files into their slimmest possible representation, which can later, through a decompression process, be reconstituted into their original form.

Most compression systems work by reducing recurrent patterns in the data stream into short tokens. For example, the two-byte pattern "at" could be coded as a single byte, such as "@", thus cutting the storage requirement in half. Most compression systems don't permanently assign tokens to bit patterns but instead make the assignments on the fly. They work on individual blocks of data, one at a time, starting afresh with each block. Consequently, the patterns stored by the tokens of one block may be entirely different from those used in the next block. The key to decoding the patterns from the tokens is included as part of the data stream.

Disk compression systems put data compression technology to work by increasing the apparent capacity of your disk drives. Generally, they work by creating a virtual drive with expanded capacity, which you can use as though it were a normal (but larger) disk drive. The compression system automatically takes care of compressing and decompressing your data as you work with it. The information is stored in compressed form on your physical disk drive, which is hidden from you.

The compression ratio compares the resultant storage requirements to those required by the uncompressed data. For example, a compression ratio of 90 percent would reduce storage requirements by 90 percent. The compressed data could be stored in 10 percent of the space required by its original form. Most data-compression systems achieve about a 50-percent compression ratio on the mix of data that most people use.

Because the compression ratio varies with the kind of data you store, the ultimate capacity of a disk that uses compression is impossible to predict. The available capacity reported by your operating system on a compressed drive is only an estimate based on the assumed compression ratio of the system. You can change this assumption to increase the reported remaining capacity of your disk drive, but the actual remaining capacity (which depends on the data you store, not the assumption) will not change.

Most compression systems assume that you want to get back every byte and every bit you store. You don't want numbers disappearing from your spreadsheets or commands from your programs. You assume that decompressing the compressed data will yield everything you started with—without losing a bit. The processes that deliver that result are called *lossless* compression systems.

Sometimes, however, your data may contain more detail than you need. For example, you might scan a photo with a true-color 24-bit scanner and display it on an ordinary VGA system with a color range of only 256 hues. All the precise color information in your scan is wasted on your display, and the substantial disk space you use for storing it could be put to better use.

Analog images converted to digital form and analog audio recordings digitized often contain subtle nuances beyond the perception of most people. Some data-reduction schemes called *lossy* compression systems ignore these fine nuances. The reconstituted data does not exactly replicate the original. For viewing or listening, the restored data is often good

Data Compression

enough. Because lossy compression systems work faster than lossless schemes and because their resultant compression ratios are higher, they are often used in time- and space-sensitive applications, such as digital image and sound storage.

Compression has proved to be such a valuable technology that it is used in other ways besides increasing disk storage. For example, advanced modem protocols often include data compression to increase throughput levels. In addition, file-archiving software, such as the popular program PKZip, also takes advantage of compression to more effectively use your disk's space.

File-compression and file-archiving software differs from ordinary disk compression in several ways. It works on a file-by-file basis rather than across a complete disk. It is not automatic; you manually select the files you want to archive and compress. The archiving software does not work on the fly but instead executes upon your command. It compresses files individually but can package several files together into a single archive file. Archive files are stored as ordinary Windows files but can be read or executed only after they have been uncompressed.

Because these archiving systems do not compress on the fly, they can spend extra time to optimize their compression (for example, trying several compression algorithms to find the most successful one). They can often achieve higher compression ratios than standard disk-compression software. (Because they are time insensitive, these programs can try more complex compression methods and avoid the rule that a compressed file can be compressed no further.) Your disk compression software, however, can't squeeze their contents any tighter.

Perhaps the most popular application for file-compression software is preparing files for transmission by modem. It allows you to package together a group of related files, shrink them to the minimal possible size, and conveniently ship them off with a single send command. Of course, the resultant files will not be further compressible, so your modem will apparently operate at a slower speed, passing along the compressed data, byte for byte.

All compression systems use essentially the same compression methods, even the same algorithms. As a result, using more than one of these methods is counterproductive. After you have compressed data, you cannot squeeze it again (at least using the same algorithm). Layering multiple levels of compression won't yield more space and may in fact waste space—and it definitely impacts performance.

Memory

About the only time most people think about the memory in their computers is when they don't have enough. And all they care to learn about it is how to add more—or, better still, get someone else to do it for them.

They've got the right idea. With modern computers, memory isn't that big of a deal. In the past, you had to worry about all sorts of different kinds of memory with odd names and obscure functions. Now you can be safe in dealing with memory. Just go to the store, hand over your plastic, and take home all the memory you need.

Well, it's not quite that easy. What you don't know about memory can be a big handicap and can lead to your buying a handful of unusable chips and even a computer that no longer works. Moreover, if you have too little memory installed in your computer, there may be no overt symptoms—except your computer runs a lot more slowly than it could. You'll never see a warning that says, "Slowdown ahead. Add more megabytes." Windows and your programs leave you on your own to guess whether you have enough or too little or too much.

Modern computers make adding memory as easy as sliding a small card called a *memory module* into a slot. Usually you have nothing more to adjust. You system comes to life with more memory and greater capabilities—if it comes to life again at all. Adding the wrong kind of memory can, in fact, stop it from booting up. Even the relatively benign mistake of adding memory with too low of a rated speed can compromise your system's performance. A fast computer can lose a big fraction of its performance when you slide in a module with the wrong rating.

Dig a bit deeper into your computer, and you'll discover that there's a lot more to memory than just quantity, however. Memory is storage, certainly, but it is also a portal into your display. Your computer's operating system slices and dices it to suit its needs, storing vital data here and there and stealing blocks of memory addresses for the interfaces it uses.

Memory is more than modules, too, because the same stuff (or at least a close cousin) of the stuff that makes your programs run also has become a convenient secondary storage medium for applications "on the go." Solid-state memory makes digital cameras and MP3 workable and convenient. Without it, you'd need a handful of floppy disks for every song you want to play or picture you've taken.

We'll start our tour of electronic storage technology with a practical look at how much memory you need, why you come up short even when you have enough, and how much is enough. From there, we'll look at the technologies involved in different memory types so you can understand the differences in the kinds of memory available—and the kind you might want to install to increase your system's memory capacity. After an examination of memory modules—what your computer uses for its basic memory needs—we'll look at other memory packages: the cards, chips, and sticks that serve MP3 players and digital cameras as a mass storage and exchange medium.

Requirements

How much memory you actually need in a computer depends on what you want to do. If all you want to do is boot up your computer, you need amazingly little memory. The very first IBM personal computer could boot up with 16 kilobytes of memory—that's about 1/100th of what your computer uses for a typical full-screen display on your monitor. Loading an operating system and the programs you want to run takes more. With the latest of Microsoft's Windows operating systems, you need about 4000 times more.

Minimums

The big numbers reflect big changes in computer software. Most people would never want to tangle with the black screen with a few characters in green pasted on it that the first computers beckoned with. Adding the friendly and familiar face of Windows (it's at least familiar by now) required about 8MB in its first modern incarnation, Windows 95. Since then, every major new version of Windows has required about double the previous version. Table 16.1 summarizes the minimal memory requirements of the various versions of Windows.

TABLE 16.1 Memory Requirement of Various Windows Versions

Windows Version	Minimum Memory	Recommended Memory
Windows 95	8MB	16MB
Windows 98	16MB	32MB
Windows Me	32MB	64MB
Windows NT	32MB	64MB
Windows 2000	64MB	128MB
Windows XP	128MB	256MB

Once Windows loads, it can cope with almost any program—even one that uses more memory than you have in your system. When Windows runs out of physical memory in your computer, it dips into virtual memory and uses part of your hard disk to simulate extra solid-state memory. Because virtual memory relies on your hard disk with its physical speed limits, its use slows your system dramatically. You can avoid such slowdowns by adding memory above the listed minimum to your system. Doubling the memory minimum usually provides enough memory if you mostly rely on running a single application. If you're seriously into multitasking and regularly switch between applications, or if you regularly edit large images or videos, you'll want even more memory—up to the maximum allowed by your system (if you can afford it).

System Resource Memory

If you run an early version of Windows on your computer, you can often run into out-of-memory errors, even when you have sufficient memory in your computer and even after you install more memory. This problem arises because Windows internally allocates blocks of memory to specific purposes. Windows calls these blocks *heaps*, and together they make up system resource memory. For reasons reaching back into the history of the Windows environment, these blocks are fixed in size and can impose severe limits on the operation of your computer. You may have dozens of megabytes available in your computer, but Windows will issue an out-of-memory error when one of these heaps approaches its capacity. It may also tell you to unload some of your applications to free up memory, although this rarely helps. Windows just doesn't deal with depleted resources well, and the best cure is usually a reboot.

For example, if you try to put too many icons on the screen at once, you may run out of memory in a heap. Windows will report too little memory and fail to rasterize the icons, leaving them as black boxes, even though you have multiple megabytes of free memory in your system. Free up some memory, and the icons will come back, but whatever problem caused the shortfall—typically a poorly designed program—will still nibble away at your resources, often even after you unload the errant application.

This problem is particularly acute with Windows 95. With Windows 98, Microsoft increased the storage allocated to system resources, although the problem can still occur (even with Windows Me). The Windows NT family (including Windows 2000 and Windows XP) uses a different structure that makes such errors unlikely.

You can check the available system resources in a Windows 95 or 98 system by choosing the System icon from the Control Panel window. Select the Performance tab, and Windows will list its memory and system resource usage, as shown in Figure 16.1.

FIGURE 16.1
The Windows Performance tab.

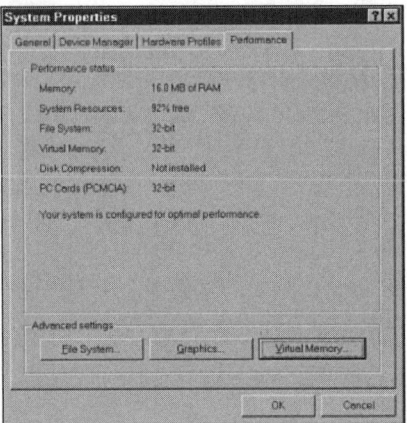

Maximum Usable Memory

You face four limits to the maximum amount of memory you can install in a computer. Two are imposed by hardware, one by Windows, and one by your budget.

The physical design of your computer limits the number of memory modules you can install. You cannot fit more memory into your system than will fit into its memory sockets. The specification of most computers will state this memory maximum. Usually it is listed as the number of slots for memory modules and the maximum size of module supported. For example, a computer with three slots each allowing a 512MB memory module has a maximum capacity of 1.5GB.

The chipset in your computer also limits the amount of memory you can install. Although today's microprocessors readily handle 64GB or more, most chipsets are more severely constrained. Again, the chipset limits the number of slots for adding modules and maximum module size. These numbers typically match or exceed the physical spaces available in your computer.

Each version of Windows has its own addressing limit. Add more memory—even when space is available in your computer—and the excess will be unusable. In some cases, too much memory can even stop your programs and computer from working.

In DOS-based versions of Windows—that is, Windows 95, 98 and Me—you will run into a roadblock if you install more than 512MB of memory. Your system may erroneously report that it does not have enough memory to run a specific application or even Windows itself, refusing to run the operating system. The problem arises from the 32-bit cache driver used by these versions of Windows. This driver automatically sets its size based on the amount of memory it detects in your system. If you have more than 512MB, it can steal memory from the Windows system area, leaving none for such functions as loading a DOS prompt.

To use more than 512MB memory with these versions of Windows, you must adjust the size of vcache in the `system.ini` file. This is a text file that you can view and modify with any text editor, such as Notepad (which is included with Windows). But be careful when editing any system file—a mistake can cause programs, and Windows itself might not to work properly. Find the entry `[VCache]` and adjust the `MaxFileCache` setting to 512MB or less. The entry is in kilobytes rather than megabytes, so you need to specify 524,288 kilobytes or less, as shown here:

```
[VCache]
    MinFileCache=51200
    MaxFileCache=524288
```

In general, the addressing limits of the Windows NT family exceed the physical capacity of most of today's computers. Earlier Windows versions may, however, constrain the amount of useful memory you can install in your computer. Table 16.2 summarizes the maximum memory usable by popular versions of Windows.

TABLE 16.2 Windows Addressing Limits

Windows Version	*Maximum Addressable Memory*
Windows 95	768MB*
Windows 98	768MB*
Windows Millennium Edition	768MB*
Windows NT	4GB
Windows 2000 Professional	4GB
Windows 2000 Server	4GB
Windows 2000 Advanced Server	8GB

continues

TABLE 16.2 Continued	
Windows Version	*Maximum Addressable Memory*
Windows XP Home Edition	4GB
Windows XP Professional	4GB
Windows XP 64-Bit Edition	16GB

Logical Organization

Some people fall into the egregious habit of thinking all memory is alike. Nefarious computer vendors are particular culprits. They are likely to lump together anything inside a computer involving memory chips as memory, implying that you can use it for running your programs. To them memory is memory, and that's that. But all memory is not the same. The random access memory used for running software gets divvied up among multiple functions inside your computer, putting it off-limits to your applications. You often end up with less usable memory than you might think you have inside your computer.

Some of your computer's RAM is compartmentalized for special functions. Computers with Intel microprocessors reserve a megabyte simply for getting started. Windows assigns other chunks for its own functions. Engineers describe this compartmentalization of RAM with a *memory map*, a graphic representation of the addresses of memory reserved for particular purposes.

In addition to RAM, most computers have other kinds of memory that's physically distinct and dedicated to specific purposes. This memory often is not within the contiguous addressing range of your computer's microprocessor. For example, the primary and secondary caches in your computer's microprocessor are chunks of memory, and each has its own dedicated purpose. High-performance interface cards may also include a megabyte or more of cache. The video systems of most computers also include a block of memory reserved as a frame buffer.

The result is that computers are stuck with a hierarchy of memory types, each with different capabilities and compatibilities—some useful to some applications, some useless to all but a few. Rather than improving with age, every advance adds more to the memory mix up. The classification of memory depends, in part, on the operating system that you run. Part of modern operating systems is memory management software that smoothes over the differences in memory type.

Real Mode Memory

The basic memory in any Intel-architecture computer is that which can be addressed by your computer's microprocessor while it is running in real mode—a special limited operating mode that's chiefly used today as your computer boots up. All Intel-architecture microprocessors start up in real mode.

For today's microprocessors based on the Intel design to be backward compatible and able to run other software, they must mimic the memory design of the original 8086 family. The hallmark of this design is the real operating mode in which they must begin their operation. Because of the original Intel 8086 microprocessor design, real mode only allows for 1MB of memory. Because it serves the host microprocessor operating in its real mode, this starting memory is termed *real mode memory*.

The address range used by real mode memory starts at the very beginning of the address range of Intel microprocessors—zero. The last address is one shy of a megabyte because counting starts at zero instead of one (that is 1,048,575 in decimal, expressed in hexadecimal as 0FFFFF). Because this memory occurs at the base or bottom of the microprocessor address range, it is also called *base memory*.

The first 640KB of real-mode memory is sometimes called *lower memory* or *DOS* memory, because only this small chunk was usable by programs running under DOS, the early personal computer operating system. The rest of the real mode addressing range above lower memory is called, logically enough, *upper memory*. In most computers, the top 32KB of upper memory addresses are occupied by the ROM holding the BIOS code of the system.

The BIOS uses the first kilobyte of space for remembering information about the system and the location of certain sections of code that are executed when specific software interrupts are made. Among other functions, this memory range holds data used by BIOS functions, and it is consequently called the *BIOS data area*.

A design quirk in Intel microprocessors allows them to address extra memory, a total of 64KB minus 16 bytes, above the real mode memory area. Called the *high memory area*, this memory cannot be used by ordinary DOS programs but was exploited by the operating system before today's versions of Windows (which run in protected mode) became popular.

Protected Mode Memory

The rest of the memory that can be addressed by modern microprocessors is termed *protected mode memory*. As the name implies, this memory can be addressed only when the microprocessor is running in its protected mode. The address range of protected mode memory stretches from the top of real mode memory to the addressing limit of your microprocessor. In other words, it starts at 1MB—1,048,576 or 100000(hex)—and extends to 16MB for 286 microprocessors, to 4GB for 386 through Pentium Pro and Celeron microprocessors, and to 64GB with the Pentium II, III, and 4 microprocessors (including the Xeon offshoots). Contrasted with base memory, protected mode memory is sometimes called *extended memory*.

Frame Buffer Memory

Computer video systems are *memory mapped*, which means the color of every pixel on your monitor gets stored in a memory location that your computer's microprocessor can directly alter, the same way it writes data into memory. Your computer holds a complete image frame in memory. Your video system scans the memory address by address to draw an image frame on your monitor screen. The memory that holds a complete image frame is termed a *frame buffer*.

Although the frame buffer in most video adapters is physically distinct from ordinary system RAM, it is usually mapped into a block of addresses in the range used by RAM. This mapping affords the microprocessor the fastest possible access to video memory.

A *memory aperture* is the address range used by computer peripherals for memory-mapped input/output operation and control, with one of the most common uses being to reach the frame buffer. That is, your computer sends data to the frame buffer by writing to the range of addresses in the aperture. The video controller picks up the data there, converts it to video, and passes it along to your monitor.

Unified Memory Architecture

Some computers do not use physically distinct frame buffers. Instead, they use a block of system RAM as the frame buffer, a design called *Unified Memory Architecture*, sometimes abbreviated as *UMA*. This design unifies the memory in a computer by moving the video frame buffer from its privileged position, connected through a bus to the video controller, to part of the main memory of the computer. In other words, part of the memory of the system gets allocated for storing video images. Because both the microprocessor and video controller have access to this memory, it is sometimes called *shared memory architecture*.

The chief attraction of this design is that it cuts the cost of a computer. Manufacturers no longer need to pay for video board memory. But because some of the memory in a UMA system must be given over to the video buffer, it is not available to your applications. Hence, a UMA system acts as if its has less memory than the specification sheet implies.

To the digital logic of your computer's microprocessor, the UMA design appears no different from a conventional video system. The frame buffer appears in the same logical location as always. If it did not, your applications would not be able to access it.

Shadow Memory

Although microprocessors used 64-bit data buses, most ROM chips allowed only an eight-bit connection. Consequently, microprocessors would slow down to about one-eighth speed to access code in ROM, which includes the system BIOS. Before Windows was widely adopted, the BIOS code was some of the most used by computer operations, so the slow access to ROM severely slowed system operations.

To break through this speed barrier, computer designers created *shadow memory*, a block of system RAM containing a copy of the contents of the eight-bit BIOS. The software controlling the shadow memory rerouted calls to the BIOS to the fast-memory copy, speeding up system operation. Although the BIOS is essentially ignored by all recent versions of Windows, most systems retain shadow memory capabilities. Most BIOS setup procedures allow you to switch on or off the shadowing of various memory ranges. Switching on shadowing brings no benefit when running Windows and can interfere with the operation of some programs. Consequently, shadow memory is best left off.

Technologies

Just as some kinds of memory play different roles in the operation of your computer, the various kinds of memory work differently and are made differently. Read-write memory is optimized for speed. It has to run as fast as it can to try to keep up with the high speeds of modern microprocessors—and it inevitably loses the race. Read-only memory, on the other hand, takes a more leisurely look at what it remembers, opting for intransigence instead of incandescent speed.

Both major divisions of the memory world have also endured a long and twisted evolution. Read-only memory has quested ever-higher speed by dashing from one technology to the next. The old withers and dies, soon forgotten—and when not forgotten, expensive. Older technology memory quickly becomes rare, and with that its price becomes dear. Unfortunately, you can rarely substitute faster, new technology memory for the slower, older kind. (Here's a buying tip: When a new technology appears ready to ascend to dominance, you're well advised to stock up on the old—buy all you think you'll ever need.)

With read-only memory, the improvements come mostly in convenience and versatility. You can do more with newer kinds of read-only memory, but the old types remain useful. Nearly all kinds of read-only memory remain in production. Although that's good if you ever need to replace some, you almost never need to replace some. But you do stand to reap the benefits of newer technologies. For example, without Flash memory, you'd have to stick a battery-hungry disk drive or some other primitive storage device in your digital camera or MP3 player.

Read-Only Memory

Although read-only memory is usually made from the same silicon stuff as other memory circuits, silicon is merely a matter of convenience, not a necessity. After all, you can make read-only memory with a handful of wires and a soldering iron. (Okay, maybe only someone who knows what he is doing could, but you get the idea.) Any electrical circuit that can be permanently changed can be read-only memory.

The challenge for engineers has been to design read-only memory that's easier to change. That seeming contradiction has a practical basis. If someone had to solder a handful of wires every time a circuit needed ROM, a computer would be a complicated rat's nest of circuits just waiting for an unpropitious moment to fail. If that doesn't sound too different from the system on your desk, a machine with wires instead of silicon ROM would likely be as expensive as a battleship and about as easy to maneuver around your desk. If you wanted to change a bit of ROM—say, to make an upgrade so your system doesn't crash whenever AOL delivers your mail—you'd have to call a service technician to lug over his soldering iron and schematic diagrams.

Changeable ROM is upgradeable ROM. And engineers have made steady progress to make your upgrades easier. The first ROM was as unchangeable as your grandfather's mind. Then engineers developed chips you could change in special machines. After that they created chips that could be changed by special circuits inside your computer. Today, you can update read-only memory in a flash—and that's what they call it.

Mask ROM

If ROM chips cannot be written by the computer, the information inside must come from somewhere. In one kind of chip, the mask ROM, the information is built into the memory chip at the time it is fabricated. The mask is a master pattern that's used to draw the various circuit elements on the chip during fabrication. When the circuit elements of the chip are grown on the silicon substrate, the pattern includes the information that will be read in the final device. Nothing, other than a hammer blow or its equivalent in destruction, can alter what is contained in this sort of memory.

Mask ROMs are not common in personal computers because they require their programming be carried out when the chips are manufactured; changes are not easy to make, and the quantities that must be created to make things affordable are daunting.

PROM

One alternative is the *programmable read-only memory* chip, or *PROM*. This style of circuit consists of an array of elements that work like fuses. Too much current flowing through a fuse causes the fuse element to overheat, melt, and interrupt the current flow, thus protecting equipment and wiring from overloads. The PROM uses fuses as memory elements. Normally, the fuses in a PROM conduct electricity just like the fuses that protect your home from electrical disaster. Like ordinary fuses, the fuses in a PROM can be blown to stop the electrical flow. All it takes is a strong enough electrical current, supplied by a special machine called a PROM programmer or PROM burner.

PROM chips are manufactured and delivered with all their fuses intact. The PROM is then customized for its given application using a PROM programmer to blow the fuses, one by one, according to the needs of the software to be coded inside the chip. This process is usually termed *burning the PROM*.

As with most conflagrations, the effects of burning a PROM are permanent. The chip cannot be changed to update or revise the program inside. PROMs are definitely not something for people who can't make up their minds—or for a fast changing industry.

EPROM

Happily, technology has brought an alternative—the *erasable programmable read-only memory* chip, or *EPROM*. Sort of like self-healing semiconductors, the data inside an EPROM can be erased and the chip reused for other data or programs.

EPROM chips are easy to spot because they have a clear window in the center of the top of their packages. Invariably this window is covered with a label of some kind, and with good reason. The chip is erased by shining high-intensity ultraviolet light through the window. If stray light should leak through the window, the chip could inadvertently be erased. (Normal room light won't erase the chip because it contains very little ultraviolet. Bright sunshine does, however, and can erase EPROMs.) Because of their versatility, permanent memory, and easy reprogrammability, EPROMs are ubiquitous inside personal computers.

EEPROM

A related chip is called *electrically erasable programmable read-only memory*, or *EEPROM* (usually pronounced *double-E PROM*). Instead of requiring a strong source of ultraviolet light, EEPROMs need only a higher than normal voltage (and current) to erase their contents. This electrical erasability brings an important benefit—EEPROMs can be erased and reprogrammed without popping them out of their sockets. EEPROM gives electrical devices such as computers and their peripherals a means of storing data without the need for a constant supply of electricity. Note that whereas EPROM must be erased all at once, each byte in EEPROM is independently erasable and writable. You can change an individual byte if you want. Consequently, EEPROM has won favor for storing setup parameters for printers and other peripherals. You can easily change individual settings yet still be assured the values you set will survive switching the power off.

EEPROM has one chief shortcoming—it can be erased only a finite number of times. Although most EEPROM chips will withstand tens or hundreds of thousands of erase-and-reprogram cycles, that's not good enough for general storage in a computer that might be changed thousands of times each second you use your machine. This problem is exacerbated by the manner in which EEPROM chips are erased—unlike ordinary RAM chips in which you can alter any bit whenever you like, erasing an EEPROM means eliminating its entire contents and reprogramming every bit all over again. Change any one bit in an EEPROM, and the life of every bit of storage is shortened.

Flash Memory

Today's most popular form of nonvolatile memory—the stuff that makes the memory cards in your camera and MP3 player work—is *Flash memory*. Although strictly speaking, Flash is a kind of EEPROM, it earns its distinction (and value) by eliminating special circuits for reprogramming. Instead of requiring special, higher voltages to erase it contents, Flash memory can be erased and reprogrammed using the normal voltages inside a computer. Normal read and write operations use the standard power (from 3.3 to 5 volts) that is used by the rest of the computer's logic circuits. Only erasing requires a special voltage, one higher than usual called a *super-voltage*, which is typically 12 volts. Because the super-voltage is out of the range of normal memory operations, the contents of Flash memory remain safe whether the power is off or your computer is vigorously exercising its memory.

For system designers, the electrical reprogrammability of Flash memory makes it easy to use. Unfortunately, Flash memory is handicapped by the same limitation as EEPROM—its life is finite (although longer than ordinary EEPROM), and it must be erased and reprogrammed as one or more blocks instead of individual bytes.

The first generation of Flash memory made the entire memory chip a single block, so the entire chip had to be erased to reprogram it. Newer Flash memory chips have multiple, independently erasable blocks that may range in size from 4KB to 128KB. The old, all-at-once style of Flash ROM is now termed *bulk erase* Flash memory because of the need to erase it entirely at once.

New multiple-block Flash memory is manufactured in two styles. *Sectored-erase* Flash memory is simply divided up into multiple sectors that your computer can individually erase and reprogram. *Boot block* Flash memory specially protects one or more blocks from normal erase operations so that special data in it—such as the firmware that defines the operation of the memory—will survive ordinary erase procedures. Altering the boot block typically requires applying the super-voltage to the reset pin of the chip at the same time as performing an ordinary write to the boot block.

Although modern Flash memory chips can be erased only in blocks, most support random reading and writing. Once a block is erased, it will contain no information. Each cell will contain a value of zero. Your system can read these blank cells, though without learning much. Standard write operations can change the cell values from zero to one but cannot change them back. Once a given cell has been changed to a logical one with a write operation, it will maintain that value until the Flash memory gets erased once again, even if the power to your system or the Flash memory chip fails.

Flash memory is an evolving technology. The first generation of chips required that your computer or other device using the chips handle all the minutiae of the erase and write operations. The current generation of chips have their own onboard logic to automate these operations, making Flash memory act more like ordinary memory. The logic controls the timing of all the pulses used to erase and write to the chip, ensures that the proper voltages reach the memory cells, and even verifies that each write operation was carried out successfully.

On the other hand, the convenience of using Flash memory has led many developers to create disk emulators from it. For the most effective operation and longest life, however, these require special operating systems (or, more typically, special drivers for your existing operating system) that minimize the number of erase-and-reprogram cycles to prolong the life of the Flash memory.

Read-Write Memory

In the single-minded quest for speed, engineers have developed and cast away a variety of technologies. Certainly faster chips almost automatically result when they design smaller chips to fit more megabytes on a silicon sliver, but making chips faster is a lot easier said than done. By carefully designing chips to trim internal delays and taking advantage of the latest fabrications technologies, chip-makers can squeeze out some degree of speed improvement, but the small gains are hard won and expensive.

By altering the underlying design of the chips, however, engineers can wring out much greater performance increases, often with little increase in fabrication cost. In a quest for quicker response, designers have developed a number of new memory chip technologies. To understand how they work and gain their edge, you first need to know a bit about the design of standard memory chips.

The best place to begin a discussion of the speed limits and improvements in Dynamic Random Access Memory (DRAM) is with the chips themselves. The critical issue is how they arrange their bits of storage and allow it to be accessed.

The traditional metaphor for memory as the electronic equivalent of pigeonholes is apt. As with the mail sorter's pigeonholes, memory chips arrange their storage in a rectangular matrix of cells. A newer, better metaphor is the spreadsheet, because each memory cell is like a spreadsheet cell, uniquely identified by its position, expressed as the horizontal row and vertical column of the matrix in which it appears. To read or write a specific memory cell, you send the chip the row and column address, and the chip sends out the data.

In actual operation, chips are somewhat more complex. To keep the number of connections (and thus, cost) low, the addressing lines of most memory chips are *multiplexed* (that is, the same set of lines serve for sending both the row and column addresses to the chip).

To distinguish whether the signals on the address lines mean a row or column, chips use two signals. The Row Address Strobe signal indicates that the address is a row, and the Column Address Strobe signal indicates the address is a column. These signals are most often abbreviated as RAS and CAS, respectively, with each acronym crowned with a horizontal line indicating the signals are inverses (logical complements), meaning that they indicate "on" when they are "off." Just to give engineering purists nightmares (and to make things typographically easier and more understandable, this book uses a slightly different convention, putting a minus sign in front of the acronyms for the same effect). Multiplexing allows 12 address lines plus the -CAS and -RAS signals to encode every possible memory cell address in a 4Mb chip (or 4MB memory module).

In operation, the memory controller in your computer first tells the memory chip the row in which to look for a memory cell and then the column the cell is in. In other words, the address lines accompanied by the -RAS signal select a memory bank; then a new set of signals on the address lines accompanied by the -CAS signal selects the desired storage cell.

Even though electricity travels close to the speed of light, signals cannot change instantly. Changing all the circuits in a chip from row to column addressing takes a substantial time, at least in the nanosecond context of computer operations. This delay, together with the need for refreshing, is the chief limit on the performance of conventional memory chips. To speed up memory performance, chip designers have developed a number of clever schemes to sneak around these limits.

These memory technologies have steadily evolved. When ordinary DRAM chips proved too slow to accommodate microprocessor needs, chip-makers first tried static column memory before hitting on fast page mode DRAM chips (which proved the industry stalwart through 1995). Next, they tinkered with addressing cycles to create Extended Data Out (EDO). They even tried to improve EDO with a burst-mode version. But these conventional technologies proved too slow to keep up with gigahertz and faster microprocessors.

The current kinds of memory take different strategies. Lower-cost systems use SDRAM chips (discussed later in this chapter) to coax more speed from the conventional memory design. The quickest memory systems of the fastest computers break with all the past technologies to use a new form of memory addressing, commonly called *Rambus*.

Fast Page-Mode RAM

The starting point for discussions of modern memory is *fast page-mode RAM*, which was still an alternative for computers about five years ago. (Other kinds of memory preceded FPM chips, but the machines using it are obsolete today.)

FPM earns its name by allowing repeated access to memory cells within a given page to occur quickly. The memory controller first sends out a row address and then activates the -RAS signal. While holding the -RAS signal active, it then sends out a new address and the -CAS signal to indicate a specific cell. If the -RAS signal is kept active, the controller can then send out one or more additional new addresses, each followed by a pulse of the -CAS, to indicate additional cells within the same row. In memory parlance, the row is termed a *page*, hence, the name of the chips.

The chief benefit of this design is that your computer can rapidly access multiple cells in a single memory page. With typical chips, the access time within a page can be trimmed to 25 to 30 nanoseconds, fast enough to eliminate wait states in many computers. Of course, when your computer needs to shift pages, it must change both the row and column addresses with the consequent speed penalty.

Extended Data Out Memory

Rather than a radical new development, *Extended Data Out* (EDO) is a variation on fast page-mode memory (which allows waitless repeated access to bits within a single page of memory). The trick behind EDO is elegant. Whereas conventional memory discharges after each read operation and requires recharging time before it can be read again, EDO keeps its data valid until it receives an additional signal. EDO memory modifies the allowed timing for the -CAS signal. The data lines remain valid for a short period after the -CAS line switches off (by going high). As a result, your system need not wait for a separate read cycle but can read (or write) data as fast as the chip will allow address access. It doesn't have to wait for the data to appear before starting the next access but instead can read it immediately. In most chips, a 10-nanosecond wait period is normally required between issuing the column addresses. The EDO design eliminates this wait, allowing the memory to deliver data to your system faster. Standard page-mode chips turn off the data when the -CAS line switches off. For this system to work, however, your computer has to indicate when it has finished reading the data. In the EDO design, the memory controller signals with the Output Enable signal.

In effect, EDO can remove additional wait states, thereby boosting memory performance. In theory, EDO could give a performance boost as high as 50 to 60 percent over FPM. In reality and the latest computers, the best EDO implementations boosted performance by 10 to 20 percent.

Physically, EDO chips and SIMMs appear identical to conventional memory. Both use the same packaging. You can't tell a difference just by looking—unless you're intimately famil-iar with the part numbers. Telling the difference is important, however. You can't just plug EDO into any computer and expect it to work. It requires a completely different manage-ment system, which means the system (or at least its BIOS) must match the memory technology. Although you can install EDO SIMMs in most computers, they will work, if at all, as ordinary memory and deliver no performance advantage.

Note that the speed ratings of EDO chips are given in nanoseconds, much like page-mode chips. For a given nanosecond rating, however, EDO memory will act as if it is about 30 percent faster. For example, whereas a 70 ns page-mode chip can deliver zero wait state operation to a 25MHz memory bus, a 70 ns EDO chip can operate at zero wait states on a 33MHz bus.

Burst EDO DRAM

To gain more speed from EDO memory, Micron Technology added circuitry to the chip to make it match the burst mode used by Intel microprocessors since the 486. The new chips, called *Burst EDO DRAM* (BEDO), perform all read and write operations in four-cycle bursts. The same technology also goes by the more generic name *pipeline nibble mode DRAM*, because it uses a data pipeline to retrieve and send out the data in a burst.

The chips work like ordinary EDO or page-mode DRAM in that they send out data when the -CAS line goes active. However, instead of sending a single nibble or byte of data (depending on the width of the chip), a two-bit counter pulses the chip internally four times, each pulse dealing out one byte or nibble of data.

Although BEDO was relatively easy and inexpensive to fabricate, because it requires a minimum of changes from ordinary EDO or page-mode DRAM, it never caught on with computer-makers. They opted to leapfrog the design and move to far faster technologies.

Synchronous DRAM

Because of their multiplex operation, ordinary memory chips cannot operate in lock-step with their host microprocessors. Normal addressing requires alternating cycles. By redesigning the basic chip interface, however, memory chips can make data available every clock cycle. Because these resulting chips can (and should) operate in sync with their computer hosts, they are termed *synchronous DRAM* (SDRAM).

Although altering the interface of the chip may remove system bottlenecks, it does nothing to make the chip perform faster. To help SDRAM chips keep up with their quicker interface, a pipelined design is used. As with pipelined microprocessors, SDRAM chips are built with multiple, independently operating stages so that the chip can start to access a second address before it finishes processing the first. This pipelining extends only across column addresses within a given page.

Some SDRAM memory is *registered*, which means that the memory controller on the motherboard relies on the memory modules themselves to drive and synchronize their own memory control signals. Nonregistered modules get the required synchronizing signals from the memory controller. Through some strange quirk in engineering language, nonregistered memory is generally called *unbuffered*, whereas buffered memory is termed *registered*.

All SDRAM chips suffer from a delay between when your computer makes its request to read memory and the time valid memory becomes available. Engineers call this delay *CAS latency*, because it is the measure of time between when your computer applies the Column Address Strobe signal and when data becomes available. They measure the delay in clock cycles. With today's memory products, the CAS latency is typically two or three, and it is a function of the memory chips themselves. Chips and memory modules are rated as to their CAS latency (although you may need to be an engineer to dig the information out of a product's data sheet). Knowing the CAS latency of memory is useful because it is one of the parameters you can adjust with some BIOS setup procedures to speed up your computer.

Single Data-Rate Memory

Ordinary SDRAM memory is often called *single data-rate* (SDR) memory in the modern world to contrast it with, well, double data-rate (DDR) memory. It earns its new name because SDR memory modules transfer data at the same rate as the system bus clock rate. On each clock pulse, SDR transfers a single bit down each line of its bus.

SDR memory is rated by the speed of the system bus to which it attaches, although only two speeds are commonly recognized and sold: PC100 for computers with 100MHz system buses, and PC133 for computers with 133MHz system buses. You can assume that unrated SDR memory is meant for 66MHz system buses, although the designation PC66 appears sometimes.

Double Data-Rate Memory

Memory chips that use DDR technology are rated by their effective data speed (that is, twice their actual clock speed). Three speed ratings of chips are available. They are designated DDR 200, DDR 266, and DDR 333.

The speed ratings on DDR memory *modules* are based on peak bandwidth rather than bus speed. The result is a much more impressive number. For example, a DDR module on a 100MHz bus transfers data at 200MHz, but its peak bandwidth is 1.6GBps. A module at this speed becomes a PC1600 memory module. These large figures serve to distinguish DDR from SDR modules, so you are less likely to confuse the two. Table 16.3 lists the rated speeds and bus speeds of DDR modules.

TABLE 16.3   DDR Memory Speed Ratings

DDR Speed Rating	Module Peak Bandwidth	Data Rate	System Bus Speed
PC1600	1.6GBps	200MHz	100MHz
PC2100	2.1GBps	266MHz	133MHz
PC2700	2.7GBps	333MHz	166MHz

Note that both SDR and DDR memory have two buses—one for addressing and one for transferring data. In DDR, only the data bus operates at double speed. The address bus still works at the standard clock speed. Consequently, DDR memory only speeds up part of the memory cycle, the part when data actually moves. Because most memory transfers now occur in bursts, this handicap is not as substantial as it might seem—for some requests, DDR memory may need only one address cycle for a burst of a full page of memory, so the overhead is only one slow cycle for 4096 DDR memory transfers.

Quad Data-Rate Memory

The next generation of SDRAM is exactly what you might expect—*quad data-rate* (QDR) memory. This new technology has already been developed through the joint efforts of Cypress, Hitachi, IDT, Micron, NEC, and Samsung. Chips using QDR have already been developed, but they have not been applied to memory modules. Currently there are not even specifications for QDR modules.

Rather than doubling up the data speed once again, QDR uses a double-ported design. Each chip has an input and an output port that can operate simultaneously, and each port uses double-clocking to transfer data. The result is that information can move through a QDR chip four times faster than ordinary SDRAM, hence the "quad" in the name. According to the QDR promoters, the double-ported design eliminates even the possibility of contention between the memory chip and its controller. In addition, QDR boosts the speed of the address bus to the same double rate as used by the data bus, giving QDR an automatic edge on DDR.

The developers of QDR maintain an informational Web site in support of the technology at www.qdrsram.com.

Rambus DRAM

The next step up in memory speed comes from revising the interface between memory chips and the rest of the system. The leading choice is the Rambus design, developed by the company with the same name. Intel chose Rambus technology for its fastest systems designs. An earlier incarnation of the technology was used in the Nintendo 64 gaming system.

The Rambus design has evolved since its beginnings. Rambus memory chips use an internal 2048-byte static RAM cache that links to the dynamic memory on the chip through a very wide bus that allows the transfer of an entire page of memory into the cache in a single cycle. The cache is fast enough that it can supply data at a 15-ns rate during hits. When the cache misses, the chip retrieves the request data from its main memory and at the same time transfers the page containing it into the cache so that it is ready for the next memory operation. Because subsequent memory operations will likely come from the cache, the dynamic portion of the chip is free to be refreshed without stealing system time or adding wait states.

The Rambus operates like a small network, sending data in packets that can be up to 256 bytes long. The system uses its own control language to control memory and steer bytes around. The overhead from this system saps about 10 percent of the bandwidth from the peak transfer rate of the system.

You won't ordinarily deal with individual Rambus chips but rather complete memory modules. Because of the different technology used by Rambus chips, the modules work differently with your system, too. Whereas with conventional memory it is important to match the width of the memory bus to that of the rest of your computer, such matches are unnecessary with Rambus. The memory controller reorganizes the data it pulls from Rambus memory to make it fit the bus width of the host computer. Consequently, a Rambus module with a 16-bit bus works in a computer with a 64-bit bus. Usually, however, Rambus systems put two or more modules in parallel. The goal of this design is to increase memory speed or bandwidth.

Rambus modules don't link to a computer system like standard memory. Instead, the design uses a special high-speed bus (hence, the origin of the Rambus name). In current Rambus modules, memory connects to the chipset in your computer through two high-speed buses. One of them, called the *request bus*, is used to send control and address information to memory. This bus uses an eight-bit connection. In addition, the *data bus* is a 16-bit-wide channel that transfers the data for reading from and writing to memory. The two buses are synchronized, although the data bus transfers bits on both edges of the clock, much as is done with DDR memory. The speed rating of Rambus modules is usually given by the data rate on the data bus—twice the actual clock frequency of the overall memory system. Rambus modules also have a third, low-speed bus that's used only for initialization and power management.

The Rambus itself—the lines that carry the request bus, data bus, and timing signals—is designed as a transmission line like those carrying radio signals. Transmission lines are sensitive to changes in tuning, much like the rabbit-ear antennae on portable televisions that, if not perfectly adjusted, make a scene look like a blizzard across the prairie. The Rambus transmission line loops through each module in a Rambus circuit before stopping at the line termination at its end (which "terminates" the signal by absorbing it all and not letting any reflect back down the transmission line to interfere with other signals).

This design has important practical implications. Because the Rambus signals loop through each module, in current computers all Rambus sockets must be filled with memory modules. Most computer-makers design their systems to accommodate two Rambus modules per Rambus circuit. Typically, computer-makers install one memory module at the factory to allow you a socket for future memory expansion. Because even the Rambus signal must loop through unused sockets, the second socket in each Rambus circuit in most new computers gets filled with a "dummy" module. The memory system will not work unless dummy modules (or memory upgrades) are properly installed.

To increase memory speed and capacity, most of today's computers use two Rambus circuits. This doubles both the total bandwidth of the memory system and the potential total memory in the system. As a consequence, computers that use today's 16-bit Rambus modules must expand their memories two modules at a time.

In the future, Rambus modules will use both 32-bit and 64-bit bus widths in addition to the 16-bit modules currently in use. Modules with 32-bit buses will be essentially the same as two 16-bit modules on one card with two request buses and two data buses. The 32-bit modules will use a different design with a single shared request bus and four data buses. These wider bus modules are incompatible with today's computers and their memory systems. Consequently, Rambus designed the module connectors to be physically incompatible, too, so you cannot inadvertently slide the wrong kind of Rambus module into your computer.

Current Rambus modules for personal computers are designed to operate at 800MHz or 1066MHz. Because of the double clocking of the data buses in the modules, 800MHz modules perfectly match 400MHz system buses, and 1066MHz modules match 533MHz system buses. In older computers using Rambus, 100MHz system buses are best matched by 800MHz modules, and 133MHz system buses best match 1066MHz modules.

Video Memory

Memory access problems are particularly prone to appear in video systems. Memory is used in display systems as a frame buffer, where the onscreen image is stored in digital form with one unit of memory (be it a bit, byte, or several bytes) assigned to each element of the picture. The entire contents of the frame buffer are read from 44 to 75 times a second as the stored image is displayed on the monitor screen. All the while, your computer may be attempting to write new picture information into the buffer to appear on the screen.

With normal DRAM chips, these read and write operations cannot occur simultaneously.

One has to wait for another. The waiting negatively affects video performance, your system's speed, and your patience.

The wait can be avoided with special memory chips that have a novel design twist—two paths for accessing each storage location. With two access paths, this memory acts like a warehouse with two doors—your processor can push bytes into the warehouse through one door while the video system pulls them out through another. Strictly speaking, this memory can take two forms: True dual-ported memory allows simultaneous reading and writing; video memory chips (often called *VRAM* for video random access memory) give one access port full read and write random access, while the other port only allows sequential reading (which corresponds to the needs of scanning a video image).

The chief disadvantage of VRAM technology is that it is more expensive because it requires more silicon (about 20 percent more area on the chip die). It more than makes up for its higher cost with its speed advantage. Using VRAM can speed up video systems by as much as 40 percent.

Packaging

Most memory comes in the form of *chips*, individual integrated circuits meant for permanent installation on a printed circuit board. The capacity of each chip is measured in bits—or, as is more likely in the modern world, *megabits*. The first chips had narrow, one-bit-wide data buses, so they moved information one bit at a time. To achieve a byte-wide data bus, eight chips had to be used together (under the coordination of the memory controller). Most modern chips use wider data buses—four or eight or more bits—but none comes close to matching the 64-bit data buses of modern computers.

To make memory more convenient to install and upgrade in practical computers, memory-makers package several memory chips on a small circuit board to make a *memory module*. Despite the added circuit board, modules provide a more compact memory package because the chips are soldered to the modules, thus eliminating space-wasting sockets. Soldering the chips down also allows them to be installed closer together (because no individual access is required). Moreover, because the discrete chips that are installed in the memory module never need to be individually manipulated except by a machine, they can use more compact surface-mount packages. A single memory module just a few inches long can thus accommodate a full bank of hundreds of megabytes of memory.

Memory modules are the large economy size—RAM in a bigger package to better suit the dietary needs of today's computers. Besides the more convenient package that allows you to deftly install a number of chips in one operation, the memory module also better matches the way your computer uses memory. Unlike most chips, which are addressed at the bit level, memory modules usually operate in bytes. Whereas chip capacities are measured in kilobits and megabits, memory modules are measured in megabytes.

The construction of a memory module is straightforward; it's simply a second level of integration above the basic memory chip. Several chips are brought together on a small glass-epoxy circuit board with their leads soldered down to the circuit traces and the entire assembly terminated in an external connector suitable for plugging into a socket or soldering to another circuit board.

Memory modules come in a variety of types, many of which are no longer common. *Single Inline Memory Modules*, which are commonly called *SIMMs*, connect the contacts on the opposite sides of the board together so that each pair provides a single signal contact. *Single Inline Pin Package* modules, or *SIPPs*, have a row of pins projecting from the bottom of the module instead of edge connectors. Both of these packages are no longer used in new computers.

Several designs are in current use. *Dual Inline Memory Modules*, called *DIMMs*, put separate signals on each contact so that the contacts on each side of the board serve different purposes. *Small Outline DIMMs*, termed *SoDIMMs*, shrink the package to fit more compact computers. *Rambus Inline Memory Modules*, or *RIMMs*, basically follow the DIMM design but use Rambus instead of SDRAM memory.

Dual Inline Memory Modules

Engineers created the DIMMs to accommodate the needs of Pentium computers. Earlier module designs—in particular SIMMs—had 8- or 32-bit data buses. As a consequence, a single bank of 64-bit Pentium memory required several modules. Not only were multiple modules a pain when you wanted to upgrade, they took up valuable motherboard space. Moreover, the many sockets they required were incompatible with the high-speed needs of modern memory systems. With more sockets and longer circuit traces, the more difficult it is to achieve high-frequency operation. Figure 16.2 shows a typical DIMM.

FIGURE 16.2

A 168-pin DIMM module showing components.

All DIMMs provide a 64-bit data bus that exactly matches the needs of Pentium-class computers. Practical module capacity now ranges from 64MB to 512MB. Larger capacity modules often put memory chips on both sides of the circuit board. To fit even more memory on each module, one manufacturer (Kingston Technology) has developed a stacking scheme that piggybacks a physically larger chip over a smaller package, thus doubling the holding capacity of a single module.

DIMMs come in three types: Those using old-technology (FPM or EDO memory) chips, those for SDR DRAM memory, and those for DDR memory. In size, the three types of modules are identical. They are 5.25 inches wide and (usually) 1 or 1.5 inches tall, although modules with unusually large memory endowments often are taller. Figure 16.3 shows the dimensions of a typical DIMM. To prevent you from sliding a DDR module into a slot meant for a SDR module, the two designs use different connector designs that are keyed to be incompatible.

FIGURE 16.3

Dimensions of a typical 168-pin DIMM.

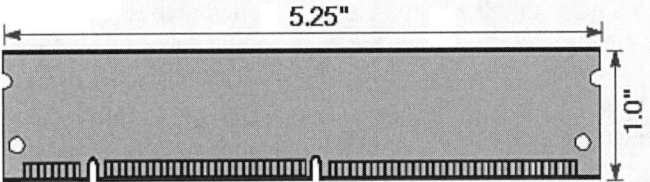

DIMMs can be equipped with non-parity, parity, or error-correction code (ECC) memory. The packages look identical and slide into the same sockets. Old-technology memory modules use signals on several connector contacts called *presence detect pins* to indicate these parameters. SDR and DDR modules use a more sophisticated design that is sometimes called *serial presence detect*. Each module is equipped with 2048 bytes of onboard nonvolatile memory that your computer can read and use to identify the module memory type. After reading this information, your computer can then configure itself appropriately.

Old Technology DIMMs

Memory modules that use old memory technology have edge connectors with 168 separate contacts arrayed on both sides of their small circuit boards. Eight of these contacts are reserved for presence-detect indications. In particular, these presence-detect signals indicate the speed rating of the module. Four of these contacts indicate the organization and addressing characteristics of the memory on the module. One pin, PD5, indicates whether the module contains FPM or EDO memory. Two, PD6 and PD7, indicate the speed rating of the chip, as indicated by the code listed in Table 16.4. (Note the rating in nanoseconds does not correspond to today's PC66/100/133 nomenclature because these modules are not used in modern computers.) The eighth contact indicates whether the module uses parity or ECC technology. In addition to the eight presence-detect indicators, two other contacts carry module ID signals that describe the module type and refresh mode used by the chip.

TABLE 16.4   Old-Technology (FPM and EDO) 168-Pin DIMM Speed Code

Signal	Pin Number	60 ns	70 ns	80 ns
PD6	165	H	L	H
PD7	82	H	H	L

SDR DIMMs

SDR modules have 168 pins on their bottom edge. They are keyed with two notches, dividing the contacts into three groups with short gaps between. The first group runs from pin 1 to pin 10; the second group from pin 11 to pin 40; and the third group from pin 41 to pin 84. Pin 85 is opposite pin 1. The notches are designed to prevent you from sliding a smaller SIMM with fewer connections into a DIMM socket—the longest space between two notches is shorter than the shortest SIMM. The asymmetrical arrangement of the notches on the DIMM prevent its inadvertent improper insertion into its socket—turn a DIMM end-for-end and it won't fit into a socket. Some DIMMs have holes to allow you to latch the modules into their sockets, although some DIMMs lack these holes.

DDR DIMMs

The standard DIMM for DDR memory has a connector with 184 pins. It bears a single notch near the center of the connector. Otherwise, DDR modules look much the same as SDR modules and can be handled similarly.

Rambus Inline Memory Modules

Because of the radical interface required by Rambus memory, memory-makers redesigned individual modules to create a special Rambus Inline Memory Module (RIMM) to accommodate the technology. The basic module appears similar to a standard DIMM, with individual memory chips soldered to a printed circuit board substrate that links to a socket using a conventional edge connector. Despite the relatively narrow bus interface used by the Rambus systems (16 bits), the RIMM package pushes its pin count to 184, partly because alternate pins are held to ground potential as a form of shielding to improve stability and decrease interference at the high clock frequency for which the modules are designed (800MHz).

RIMMs also differ in their operating voltage. The Rambus standard calls for 2.5-volt operation, as opposed to the 3.3 volts standard with DIMMs. Future RIMMs may operate at 1.8 volts.

The standard 184-pin design supports both non-parity and error-correction RIMMs, with bus widths of 16 and 18 bits, respectively. Figure 16.4 shows a RIMM package.

FIGURE 16.4
A RIMM package.

Small Outline DIMMs

Although convenient for desktop computers, full-size memory modules are unnecessarily large for notebook machines. Consequently, the makers of miniaturized computers trimmed the size of ordinary memory modules about in half to create what they called the *Small Outline DIMM* (SoDIMM).

The first SoDIMMs were offshoots of the 72-pin SIMMs used for FPM and EDO memory. They had the same 72 contacts as full-size SIMMs but arrayed them on both sides of the module (making it "dual inline"). In a SIMM, the contacts on opposite sides of the module's circuit board are electrically connected together. On a SoDIMM, each has a different function, putting the connection space to more efficient use and allowing the smaller size. Figure 16.5 illustrates a Small Outline Dual Inline Memory Module of this design.

FIGURE 16.5
A 72-pin Small Outline Dual Inline Memory Module package.

As you would expect, a 72-pin SoDIMM is about half the length of a 72-pin SIMM, measuring about 2.35 inches long. As with other module styles, a notch at one end of a 72-pin SoDIMM prevents you from latching it into its socket with the wrong orientation. The notch is on your left when you look at the chip side of the SoDIMM. Figure 16.6 shows the dimensions of a typical SoDIMM.

FIGURE 16.6
Dimensions of a typical 72-pin Small Outline Dual Inline Memory Module.

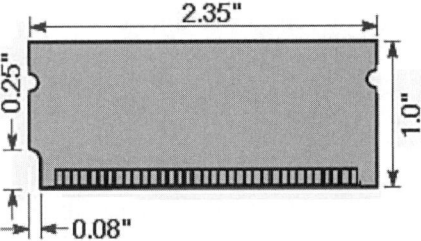

The SoDIMM package proved so compelling it has been adapted for SDRAM modules. The SDRAM SoDIMMs are slightly longer than those used by older technologies, measuring 2.67 inches (67.6 millimeters) long.

As with full-size DIMMs, SDRAM SoDIMMs come in two physically incompatible styles for SDR and DDR.

SDR SoDIMMs have 144 contacts on their edge connectors. DDR modules have 200. Each style of SoDIMM has a single notch, but the position of the notch is different for SDR and DDR modules. With SDR modules, the notch is only slightly offset from the center; with DDR modules, the notch is near one edge (the pin 1 side) of the module. Figure 16.7 shows the difference in the notches used by the two varieties of SDRAM modules.

FIGURE 16.7
The difference between the SDR and DDR SoDIMM notches.

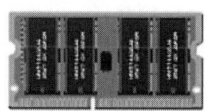   

SDR SoDIMM   DDR SoDIMM

Installation

In general, the memory of your computer will work throughout the life of the machine without requiring any attention. Memory has no moving parts that require service or lubrication. The only time you're likely to tangle with memory is when you decide to add to your computer's native endowment, either by adding to its main memory on the motherboard or by adding an expansion board to enhance the size of a disk cache or video frame buffer.

Memory installation is a process that requires care but does not demand expertise or extreme precision. You can usually add a few megabytes in a few minutes without worrying about damaging the memory, your computer, or yourself.

The care required involves taking simple precautions. Avoid static electricity, which can damage *any* solid state circuitry, including memory chips. The most cautious sources usually recommend that you ground yourself to a cold water pipe before you dig into the circuitry of your computer. Most people just plug in chips or modules without a thought to static. Unless you draw sparks when you touch things on your workbench, you're probably safe to install memory modules.

In that one of the primary design goals of memory modules is simplified installation, modules make expanding the memory of your computer easy—or at least easier than it would be with a box full of discrete chips. Modules do not, however, make memory installation or expansion "trouble free." You still must match modules with your computer and insert them in their sockets properly.

Memory Speed

Memory speed is one of the most critical factors in computer performance. Faster memory can move data to the microprocessor faster. Today's microprocessors are so fast that they outrace any kind of memory, so anything you do to make your system's memory faster can help performance.

Most of what you can do to speed up memory requires an advanced degree in tinkering. You can experiment with the advanced setup adjustments in your computer's BIOS (if it affords you such adjustments) to see how many corners you can cut before your computer freezes up and dies.

Mostly what you do with memory makes your computer slower. The design of your computer limits the top speed at which its memory can operate (even though faster memory might benefit your computer). Adding faster memory won't break through this speed limit. On the other hand, add memory that's too slow when you expand your system, and your whole system might shift into low gear. Modern memory systems can detect the speed rating of memory modules, and they will slow down their operation to match the slowest memory in your computer.

The best strategy when adding memory to your computer is to duplicate what you already have. If your system has PC100 memory installed, always install more PC100 memory.

Mixing Modules

Modern memory module design precludes you from using the wrong kind of memory in your computer. Because memory modules are made from discrete chips, they use the same underlying technologies. SIMMs made using static, dynamic, video, and page-mode RAM technologies are available. As with discrete chips, different module technologies are not completely interchangeable, so you need to specify the correct type when ordering memory for your computer.

At one time, however, the different memory types—fast page-mode, EDO, and Burst EDO—all used exactly the same style of module: the standard SIMM. In general, a computer designed for fast page-mode SIMMs could use other SIMM technologies but derives no benefit from doing so. Similarly, the higher speed of the more advanced memories could be wasted. Sliding a fast page-mode SIMM into an EDO socket would slow your entire system down to the fast page-mode speed.

With DIMMs, you ordinarily do not need to match modules. Each one constitutes a full bank of memory. You should be able to mix different sizes and install modules in any order. Mixing module speeds will only result in your system operating at the speed of the slower module (if it doesn't reject the laggardly memory as too slow). In reality, you may find slight differences between modules and motherboards. (A motherboard can sometimes be persnickety about where you put the modules.) That said, upgrading memory is much easier than it used to be, and you're much less likely to encounter problems if you just slide modules into the sockets that they fit into.

Contact Material

At one time, the contacts used by memory modules sometimes came plated with tin and sometimes with gold. The purpose of this plating is to prevent oxidation or corrosion that would increase the resistance of the contact and lower the reliability of the connection. In the abstract, gold is the preferred material because it oxidizes less readily. Gold also costs substantially more, encouraging manufacturers to opt for tin.

One manufacturer of electronic component sockets, AMP, points out that the material is not so important as the match. You should choose memory modules with contacts plated with the same material as used in the sockets in your computer. The explanation goes deeper than the plating.

According to AMP, putting tin in contact with gold and exerting pressure on the contact results in a problem called *fretting*. Part of the tin rubs off, attaches to the gold, and oxidizes there, thus building up a thin layer of tin oxide. The longer the two materials contact one another, the thicker the oxide build up.

Gold is not the only material susceptible to this oxide buildup. It can develop when tin contacts nearly any dissimilar metal. The problem does not arise when tin-plated contacts press against other tin-plated contacts. Of course, the tin surface will naturally oxidize on the tin-plated contacts, but when you insert a tin-plated edge connector into a tin-plated socket, the soft tin gives way. Pushing the contacts together squeezes or wipes the tin oxide away from the contact area so that tin presses against tin.

Today, nearly all DIMMs and their sockets use gold plating, so you're unlikely to encounter problems with modern computers. With older SIMMs, however, you'll find both contact materials are prevalent. Matching material is the best bet. If you have an older computer with a metals mismatch in its sockets and memory errors, you may be able to correct the problem by cleaning the contacts on the memory modules. Although special contact cleaners are available, you will get good results wiping the contacts clean with an ink eraser (the kind that is slightly abrasive). Don't clean too hard, though, because you may wipe the contact material entirely off.

Orientation

When installing memory modules, remember that their orientation is important. In general, all modules in a computer will face in the same direction. Of course, with two-sided modules with components on both sides, you can't easily tell which direction anything is facing. The key is to look at the notches in the edge connector at the bottom of the module. You'll see the notches line up with tabs in the socket when the module is oriented in only one direction—the right way. Should you try to insert a module and discover that it refuses to fit, you probably have it in the wrong orientation or improperly seated.

Memory Cards

Computers don't have a monopoly on memory. Today's high-tech toys such as MP3 players and digital cameras also need memory for storing their software—the music you play on your MP3 player and the pictures you take with your digital camera.

The requirements for this memory differs from that you install in your computer. Although you want computer memory to be as fast as possible, speed is not as important as permanence for other electronics. You want your music and pictures to always be there when you want them, not subject to the vagaries of your batteries or utility electricity supply. In a word, cameras and MP3 players want *nonvolatile* memory.

In addition, you want to be able to quickly add to or exchange the contents of the memory in your camera or MP3 player or to interchange blocks of memory. To allow you to make such exchanges quickly and easily, memory-makers have developed a wide array of memory cards. They work like a PC Card designed to the PCMCIA standard (we considered a PC Card as an expansion bus, which it really is, in Chapter 9, "Expansion Buses"). You simply slide them in, and they work. But, thanks to the benefit of more refined technologies and less need to accommodate non-memory devices such as network adapters and modems, memory cards can be smaller. Some, in fact, are hardly bigger than memory chips.

The first two designs, CompactFlash and SmartMedia, came from two different but well-established directions. CompactFlash simply put the PC Card interface on a smaller card. SmartMedia did little more than repackage Flash memory chips. The latest additions to the memory card zoo all add copy management provisions so that music publishers can control what you put on cards and whether (or even how many times) you duplicate copyrighted material.

The question as to which is better often is meaningless. The best card is the one that your camera or music player uses. However, the medium used may influence your choice of camera or player. A device using CompactFlash gives you more storage and versatility, although other cards yield more compact storage.

CompactFlash

Sometimes, even a PC Card is too big, so in a quest for miniaturization, the electronics industry, led by Intel, developed a yet-smaller standard. Appropriately called *Miniature Card*, it was designed as a reduced-size version of a PC Card aimed particularly at memory devices. Although it never caught on, its heir, CompactFlash, has found wide application in digital cameras. Although engineers designed the Miniature Card to be a general-purpose expansion format, one application dominated the minds of designers eyeing the small cards: memory. A variety of electronic devices have a need for compact and removable memory, perhaps the most important of which initially was the digital camera.

Intel developed Miniature Card and released the initial version (logically enough, version 1.0) on February 29, 1996. Envisioned as the perfect memory solution for digital cameras and miniaturized digital audio recorders, Miniature Cards measured less than an inch and a half square but could store up to 64MB using any standard memory technology. The limit was imposed by the bus design, pure PC Card.

In 1994, PC Card maker SanDisk developed a new small card design as CompactFlash. As the name implies, the company aimed the product specifically at accommodating Flash memory in a format small enough to fit into a digital camera that wouldn't require a mule team to transport.

The CompactFlash specification is now governed by the CompactFlash Association (CFA), founded in 1995 by Apple Computer, Canon, Eastman Kodak, Hewlett-Packard, LG Semicon, Matsushita, Motorola, NEC, Polaroid, SanDisk, Seagate, and Seiko Epson. The organization maintains a Web site at `www.compactflash.org`.

An early promoter of the various PCMCIA specifications, SanDisk patterned the signals used by CompactFlash cards on the PC Card bus design. Logically, the interface conforms to the AT Attachment specifications, and software accesses the memory on the card as if it were a disk drive.

Electrically, CompactFlash cards act much like full-size PC Cards. As a result, each card must include its own control logic and conform to the logical format standards promulgated by PCMCIA. This makes the cards more complex than the competing tiny-card format SmartMedia, discussed next. Although the larger amount of circuitry also adds to the cost of producing the cards, large-scale integration and high volumes hold the potential of minimizing any such handicap. In fact, the prices of the two media are comparable, although the edge usually goes to SmartMedia.

The added complexity of PC Card compatibility has one big benefit. It allows CompactFlash cards to be readily adapted to full-size PC Card slots. The required adapter card need not contain any electronics, thus making it inexpensive. The only need is to make the small card physically fit into a larger socket, rerouting its circuits to fit the larger connector used by the PC Card standard.

Standard CompactFlash cards measure 43 mm (1.7 in) by 36 mm (1.4 in) by 3.3 mm (0.13 in), the same thickness as a PC Card and about one-quarter the size. To increase physical capacity, the CFA has designed a slightly thicker format, designated CompactFlash Type II. At 5 mm thick, the new format conforms to the thickness of Type II CardBus and PC Cards.

Unlike physical disk drives, however, CompactFlash cards can withstand more physical abuse (about 2000 Gs) and wider temperature ranges (-25° C to +75° C for CompactFlash compared to +5° C to +55° C for typical disk drives). The expected life of the medium is in excess of 100 years, with data integrity protected by both built-in dynamic defect management and error correction.

CompactFlash capacities start at 2MB. Currently the largest capacity per card is 512MB. Up to 1GB is available in the same package using a micro hard disk drive. Systems can double the data storage of any card using compression software, although digital cameras use JPEG compression, which ordinarily cannot be further compressed by standard software-compression algorithms.

The CompactFlash design requires dual-voltage operation. All cards are completely compatible with both 5.0- and 3.3-volt systems. Any card will work in any system, regardless of its operating voltage.

Most operating systems support the PCMCIA logical interface used by CompactFlash cards through software drivers. CompactFlash cards can be used with DOS, Windows 95 and 98, OS/2, Apple Macintosh, and most flavors of Unix.

SmartMedia

SmartMedia is the pioneering minimal memory format, at one time (but no longer) the thinnest and smallest type of removable Flash memory card. About one-third the size of a PC Card, a SmartMedia chip (there's no better description) measures 45 millimeters (mm) by 37 mm by 0.76 mm. It appears like a monolithic slice of plastic, and that's almost what it is. Its "overmolded" thin package (OMTP) simply encases one or more memory chips with a solid protective outer shell. Two rows of a total of 22 surface contacts provide the necessary connections for an eight-bit interface.

Originally developed under the name *Solid-State Floppy Disk Card* (SSFDC), a name that still rules over its supporting body's Web site (www.ssfdc.com), its original creator (Toshiba) has trademarked the name *SmartMedia* for the format. The SmartMedia format is currently used by the makers of many digital cameras, including nearly all Japanese brands as well as Agfa and Apple.

The small size of the SmartMedia cards does not stand in the way of large capacities. Although originally introduced only in sizes from 2MB to 8MB, Toshiba has developed a high-density connection and packaging system to increase the potential storage of the SmartMedia format. Current specifications allow cards storing up to 128MB.

The total capacity of each card is arrayed in blocks of about 16KB, each block comprising 32 pages of 528 bytes each. Because the memory is solid-state, access time is brief, rated at only 7 microseconds. Transferring a bit through the serial interface requires only 50 nanoseconds, an effective clock speed of 20Mbps. In actual operation, transfer speeds of 0.5 to 1.0Mbps can be achieved. Writing is slower—about two milliseconds to erase a 16KB block of memory and 200 microseconds to write it again.

The heart of each SmartMedia card is one or more NAND Flash EEPROM (electrically erasable programmable read-only memory) chips embedded in the plastic shell. The NAND Flash memory technology used by SmartMedia provides fast write and erase functions plus high-speed read with minimal power consumption.

This simple electrical design is key to the low-cost potential of SmartMedia. Despite the name, the cards are not very intelligent. They contain only memory. The controller is in the host. To work in a PC Card slot, an adapter for a SmartMedia card must itself contain a controller. Adapters are consequently more expensive than slot adapters for PC Cards.

The SmartMedia logical data format is based on the AT Attachment and DOS file standards and is compatible with computers running Windows 95, Windows 98, Windows NT, or OS/2 Warp. It also works on Apple Macintosh computers.

Both 5.0-volt and 3.3-volt cards are permitted under the SmartMedia specification. A notch codes the voltage used by each card to prevent you from putting a board in a host supplying the wrong voltage. A right notch indicates 3.3-volt cards; a left notch, 5.0-volts cards.

The SmartMedia standards are administered through the SSFDC Forum, which you can access on the Web at `www.ssfdc.or.jp/english/`.

Memory Stick

Sony Corporation developed the Memory Stick package as a proprietary technology. Sony uses Memory Stick as a cross-platform package. The same stick fits digital cameras, digital video recorders, and MP3 players.

Memory Sticks resemble an old-fashioned stick of chewing gum, about 2 inches long (50 millimeters), 0.85 inches wide (21.45 millimeters), and a bit more than 1/10th inch (2.8 millimeters) thick. For applications demanding even smaller media, Sony offers the Memory Stick Duo, which measures 1.25 inches (31 millimeters) by 0.75 inches (20 millimeters) and 1/16th inch (1.6 millimeters) thick.

The plastic package of each Memory Stick comes in one of two colors. The basic Memory Stick is blue. It is meant for general-purpose storage and holds nothing but memory and interfacing circuitry. A white Memory Stick has Sony's Magic Gate copy-management protocol.

Sony calls Memory Stick the *de facto* standard for digital networks. What that means is that Memory Stick does not bear the imprimatur of a recognized standards organization but lots of companies use the same design (under license from Sony). Currently five manufacturers offer Memory Stick products: Apacer Technology, Hagiwara Sys-Com Co. Ltd., I-O Data Device, Lexar Media, SanDisk, and Sony.

At one time, the Memory Stick format was more expensive than competing card formats. Now, Sony has licensed other manufacturers to make and sell Memory Sticks, and the price is competitive with other packages. Two Web sites are meant to provide information about Memory Sticks. The general public can access www.memorystick.com. Memory Stick licensees can access www.memorystick.org.

Multimedia Cards

Almost as a response to SmartMedia's claims to be the smallest, SanDisk Corporation and Siemens AG/Infineon Technologies AG developed the MultiMedia Card, which is less than half the size of the SmartMedia card (although twice as thick). According to its promoters, a MultiMedia Card is about the size of a postage stamp. That's true in a way (some commemorative postage stamps are nearly the size of envelopes). The MultiMedia Card (MMC) actually measures a little more than an inch square, at 24 by 37 mm and 1.4 mm thick (big for a stamp but small for a memory and exchange medium).

Designed specifically for memory, MultiMedia Cards were originally designed with a 64MB maximum capacity. Cards come in two types: ROM-based for prerecorded music (you cannot record on ROM), and Flash memory for recording your own music and photos.

The one-piece molded plastic package has seven gold pins on one edge to provide a serial interface.

To promote MultiMedia Card technology, 14 companies founded the MultiMedia Card Association in 1998. It has since grown to host over 100 members. The MultiMedia Card Association maintains a Web site at www.mmca.org.

Secure Digital

Derived from the MultiMedia Card, you can consider the Secure Digital card to be MMC with copy protection. The Secure Digital design is an obvious rethinking of the MultiMedia Card concept.

The Secure Digital card uses a nine-pin serial interface, similar to that of the MultiMedia Card. In fact, the two extra pins are grafted on to the layout of the older card design, with a small pin 8 crammed between pin 7 and the edge of the card. Pin 9 resides at the opposite side, adjacent to pin 1 but in the notch area.

The initial design of the Secure Digital card was thicker than the MultiMedia Card to allow the most complex circuitry required by its serial copy management electronics. The Secure Digital specifications also describe a "thin" card, one with the same 1.4 mm thickness of the MMC.

The Secure Digital card also incorporates a write-protect tab. By sliding the tab up the side of the card, you can prevent compliant electronic gear from disturbing the contents of the card. The specification also allows for a read-only card without a sliding tab.

The current designs of the Secure Digital card accommodates capacities from 32MB to 256MB.

Secure Digital Association
719 San Benito Street, Suite C
Hollister, CA 95023

Phone: 831-636-7322 (SDCA)
Fax: 831-636-2522
Email: sda@hollinet.com

xD Picture Card

The latest player in the memory card game is the xD Picture Card, announced July 30, 2002. Jointly developed by Olympus and Fuji Photo Film Company, this card is about the size of a postage stamp, as described by news releases from each company. In fact, the xD Picture Card is actually the smallest of the memory card formats. The standard card dimensions are 20 by 25 mm and 1.7 mm thick.

According to the developers, the name is taken from the phrase "Extreme Digital." Initially, Toshiba will manufacture the cards.

The card design allows for capacities up to 8GB per card, but initial real-world implementations store only 16 to 128MB.

Although only Fuji and Olympus cameras are initially slated to use the xD Picture Card, with an adapter it can also be used in place of PC Cards. A card reader with a USB interface was also introduced at the same time as the first cards, and a Compact Flash adapter is under development.

Magnetic Storage

If you've ever seen a punch card, much less had to work with them, you know why computer workers joyously sang the praises of magnetic storage. When all the world and computers were young, the long-term memory of the best computer systems was entrusted to 3.5×8.5-inch sheets of cardboard, punched with rectangular holes, each one storing a single code symbol, a whole card holding about a sentence. A program took a file drawer filled with them. Cardiac arrest required only dropping the drawer, because the order in which the cards were arranged was crucial.

Magnetic storage is faster, more compact, and more permanent. Although magnetic media appear vulnerable (especially if you've had or heard of a disk crash), magnetic records are among the longest-lived of any storage method. In fact, magnetic records store the itinerary of the drifting continents, preserving the details of their shifts in data back at least 250 million years.

In your computer, three different storage systems use magnetism as their working medium, none of them quite as permanent as hot magma but with the potential to outlast you. The most important is your hard disk, without which you simply could not run modern software. The other two magnetic systems are incidental, at least these days. You could live without them, and an increasing number of people do. The teetering twosome includes the floppy disk, as much a vestige of our past as is continental drift (even though most computers still come with a floppy disk drive), and tape, which has declined in importance as people put more faith in the integrity of their hard disk systems.

Hard Disks

People who think they know such things often liken a computer's hard disk to a filing cabinet. Such folk really don't know much about hard disks—or the way real people store information. A hard disk is more like the desk and office of a writer, who in his few lucid moments between delirium tremens and alcoholic stupor crafts work of unparalleled insight and beauty from the scribbled notes, torn-out newspaper stories, yellowing magazines, and broken-back books stacked everywhere in piles that defy both organizational sense and the law of gravity. (Think Poe with the benefit of modern chemistry.)

Your computer's hard disk only looks organized, an illusion as compelling as your own feelings of prowess and courage that arise after you've drunk a meal with your friend, the alcoholic writer. In reality, it's much more like the pack rat's stash the writer calls an office, with uncountable snippets of thoughts, beat-up old photographs, and little bright shiny things all heaped together, some worth keeping, some that should have been tossed long ago, and a trash bag full of things that were thrown away but haven't yet been carried out.

Your hard disk holds everything you work with on your computer as well as a surprising amount of stuff that you'll never use again. It is your computer's long-term memory, but on the disk, the information is confounded into pieces much like a messy desk or your own mind. Unlike your mind or mess, however, the disk has an organizing aid, the operating system. All the neatly arranged files you store on your disk owe their existence to the operating system. Dig deep into your hard disk and you'll see it's nothing but a receptacle—or a giant collection of receptacles—for storing blocks of information. The disk's job is simply to put the information into the receptacles, preserve it, and retrieve it in the off-chance that you need it again. As with everything else, the hard work of the hard disk is in the details.

The hard disk is actually a combination device, a chimera that's part electronic and part mechanical. Electrically, the hard disk performs the noble function of turning evanescent pulses of electronic digital data into more permanent magnetic fields. As with other magnetic recording devices—from cassette recorders to floppy disks—the hard disk accomplishes its end using an electromagnet, its read/write head, to align the polarities of magnetic particles on the hard disk itself. Other electronics in the hard disk system control the mechanical half of the drive and help it properly arrange the magnetic storage and locate the information that is stored on the disk.

History

Because of their ability to give nearly random access to data, magnetic disk drives have been part of computing since long before there were personal computers. The first drives suffered from the demands of data processing, however, and quickly wore out. Their heads ground against their disks, leaving dust where data had been. For fast access, some lined dozens of heads along the radius of the disk, each sweeping its own dedicated range of disk and data. Such designs had fast access speeds, dependent only on the speed of the spin of the disk (which is still an issue, even today), and minimal maintenance worries because they had a minimum of moving parts. But the size of the heads and the cost of arraying a raft of them meant such drives were inevitably expensive. Though not a major problem with mainframe computers priced in the millions, pricing a computer with such a drive would put the computer within the budgets solely of those with personal Space Shuttles in their garages.

The breakthrough came at IBM's Hursley Labs near Winchester in England. Researchers there put a single head to work scanning across the disk to get at every square inch (England had not yet gone metric) of its surface. Their breakthrough, however, totally eliminated the wear of head against disk and was destined to set the standard for computer storage for more than three decades. By floating—actually flying—the read/write head on a cushion of air, the head never touched the disk and never had a chance to wear it down. Moreover, the essentially friction-free design allowed the head to move rapidly between positions above the disk.

This original design had two sections: a "fixed" drive that kept its disk permanently inside and a removable section that could be dismounted for file exchange or archiving. Each held 30MB on a platter about 14 inches across. During development, designers called the drive a 30/30 to reflect its two storage sections. In that Remington used the same designation for its most famous repeating rifle—the gun that won the West—this kind of drive became known as a *Winchester disk drive*.

The name *Winchester* first referred to the specific drive model. Eventually it was generalized to any hard disk. In the computer industry, however, the term was reserved for drives that used that same head design as the original Winchester. New disk drives—including *all* those now in computers—do not use the Winchester head design.

Besides Winchester, you may also hear other outdated terms for what we today call a *hard disk*. Many folks at IBM still refer to them as *fixed disks*. When computer people really want to confound you, they sometimes use another IBM term from the dark ages of computing, *DASD*, which stands for Direct Access Storage Device. No matter the name, however, today all hard disks are essentially the same in principle, technology, and operation.

Mechanism

The mechanism of the typical hard disk is actually rather simple, comprising fewer moving parts than such exotic devices as the electric razor and pencil sharpener. The basic elements of the system include a stack of one or more platters—the actual hard disks themselves. Each of these platters serves as a substrate upon which is laid a magnetic medium in which data can be recorded. Together the platters rotate as a unit on a shaft, called the *spindle*. Typically the shaft connects directly to a spindle motor that spins the entire assembly.

Rotation

Hard disks almost invariably spin at a single, constant rate measured in revolutions per minute (RPM). This speed does not change while the disk is in operation, although some disks may stop to conserve power. Storing information using this constant spin is technically termed *constant angular velocity recording*. This technology sets the speed of the disk's spin at a constant rate so that, in any given period over any given track, the drive's read/write head hangs over the same-length arc (measured in degrees) of the disk. The actual length of the arc, measured linearly (in inches or centimeters) varies depending on the radial position of the head. Although the tiny arc made by each recorded bit has the same length when measured angularly (that is, in degrees), when the head is farther from the center of the disk, the bit-arcs are longer when measured linearly (that is, in inches or millimeters). Despite, or because of, the greater length of each bit toward the outer edge of the disk, each spin stores the same number of bits and the same amount of information. Each spin at the outer edge of the disk stores exactly the same number of bits as those at the inner edge.

Constant angular velocity equipment is easy to build because the disk spins at a constant number of RPM. Old vinyl phonograph records are the best example of constant angular velocity recording—the black platters spun at an invariant 33 1/3, 45, or 78 RPM. Nearly all hard disks and all ISO standard magneto-optical drives use constant angular velocity recording.

A more efficient technology, called *constant linear velocity recording*, alters the spin speed of the disk depending on how near the center tracks the read/write head lies, so that in any given period, the same length of track passes below the head. When the head is near the outer edge of the disk, where the circumference is greater, the slower spin allows more bits and data to be packed into each spin. Using this technology, a given-size disk can hold more information.

Constant linear velocity recording is ill-suited to hard disks. For the disk platter to be properly read or written, it must be spinning at the proper rate. Hard disk heads regularly bounce from the outer tracks to the inner tracks as your software request them to read or write data. Slowing or speeding up the platter to the proper speed would require a lengthy wait, perhaps seconds because of inertia, which would shoot the average access time of the drive through the roof. For this reason, constant linear velocity recording is used for high-capacity media that don't depend so much on quick random access. The most familiar is the Compact Disc, which sacrifices instant access for sufficient space to store your favorite symphony.

Figure 17.1 illustrates the on-disk difference between the two methods of recording. The sector length varies in constant angular velocity but remains constant using constant linear velocity. The number of sectors is the same for each track in constant angular velocity recording but varies with constant linear velocity recording.

FIGURE 17.1
Comparison of constant angular and line velocity recording methods.

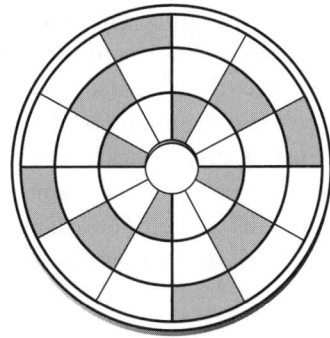
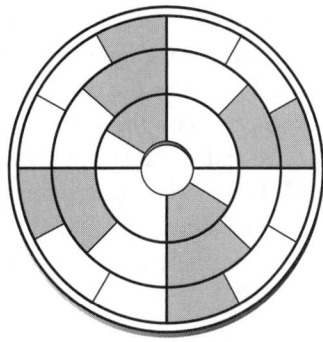

Constant Angular Velocity   Constant Linear Velocity

Modern hard disks compromise between constant angular velocity and constant linear velocity recording. Although they maintain a constant rotation rate, they alter the timing of individual bits depending on how far from the center of the disk they are written. By shortening the duration of the bits (measured in microseconds) over longer tracks, the drive can maintain a constant linear length (again, measured in inches or whatever) for each bit. This compromise technique underlies *multiple zone recording* technology, which we will more fully discuss later.

Speed

The first disk drives (back in the era of the original IBM Winchester) used synchronous motors. That is, the motor was designed to lock its rotation rate to the frequency of the AC power line supplying the disk drive. As a result, most motors of early hard disk drives spun the disk at the same rate as the power line frequency, 3600 revolutions per minute, which equals the 60 cycles per second of commercial power in the United States.

Synchronous motors are typically big, heavy, and expensive. They also run on normal line voltage—117 volts AC—which is not desirable to have floating around inside computer equipment where a couple of errant volts can cause a system crash. As hard disks were miniaturized, disk-makers adopted a new technology—the servo-controlled DC motor—that eliminated these problems. A servo-controlled motor uses feedback to maintain a constant and accurate rotation rate. That is, a sensor in the disk drive constantly monitors how fast the drive spins and adjusts the spin rate should the disk vary from its design specifications.

Because servo motor technology does not depend on the power-line frequency, manufacturers are free to use any rotation rate they want for drives that use it. Early hard disks with servo motors stuck with the standard 3600 RPM spin to match their signal interfaces designed around that rotation rate. Once interface standards shifted from the device level to the system level, however, matching rotation speed to data rate became irrelevant. With system-level interfaces, the raw data is already separated, deserialized, and buffered on the drive itself. The data speeds inside the drive are entirely independent from those outside. With this design, engineers have a strong incentive for increasing the spin rate of the disk platter: The faster the drive rotates, the shorter the time that passes between the scan of any two points on the surface of the disk. A faster spinning platter makes a faster responding drive and one that can transfer information more quickly. With the design freedom afforded by modern disk interfaces, disk designers can choose any spin speed without worrying about signal compatibility. As a result, the highest performing hard disks have spin rates substantially higher than the old standard—some rotate as quickly as 10,000 or 15,000 RPM.

Note that disk rotation speed cannot be increased indefinitely. Centrifugal force tends to tear apart anything that spins at high rates, and hard disks are no exception. Disk designers must balance achieving better performance with the self-destructive tendencies of rapidly spinning mechanisms. Moreover, overhead in computer disk systems tends to overwhelm the speed increases won by quickening disk spin. Raising speed results in diminishing returns.

Today, most of the spins of hard disks fit a three-tier hierarchy. The slowest, turning 4200 RPM, are used only in notebook computers. Disks running at 5400 RPM are general-purpose consumer drives, although a few newer "high-performance" drives for notebook machines now reach this speed. Faster drives are used in network servers and high-performance workstations. This high-performance category itself has three speed levels: 7500, 10,000, and 15,000 RPM.

Latency

Despite the quick and constant rotation rate of a hard disk, it cannot deliver information instantly on request. There's always a slight delay that's called *latency*. This term describes how long after a command to read from or write to a hard disk the disk rotates to the proper angular position to locate the specific data needed. For example, if a program requests a byte from a hard disk and that byte has just passed under the read/write head, the disk must spin one full turn before that byte can be read from the disk and sent to the program. If read and write requests occur at essentially random times in regard to the spin of the disk (as they do), on the average the disk has to make half a spin before the read/write head is properly positioned to read or write the required data. Normal latency at 3600 RPM means that the quickest you can expect your hard disk—on the average—to find the information you want is 8.33 milliseconds. For a computer that operates with nanosecond timing, that's a long wait, indeed.

The newer hard disks with higher spin speeds cut latency. The relationship between rotation and latency is linear, so each percentage increase in spin pushes down latency by the same factor. A modern drive with a 5400 RPM spin achieves a latency of 5.56 milliseconds. Table 17.1 lists the latency of disks based on rotation rate.

TABLE 17.1   Average Latency at Common Drive Rotation Rates

Rotation Rate	Average Latency	Typical Application
3600 RPM	8.33 ms	Obsolete
4500 RPM	6.67 ms	Notebook computers
5400 RPM	5.56 ms	Consumer computers
7200 RPM	4.17 ms	Servers and workstations
10,000 RPM	3.00 ms	Servers
15,000 RPM	2.00 ms	High-performance servers

Standby Mode

During operation, the platters in a hard disk are constantly spinning because starting and stopping even the small mass of a two-inch drive causes an unacceptable delay in retrieving or archiving your data. This constant spin ensures that your data will be accessible within the milliseconds of the latency period.

In some applications, particularly notebook computers, the constantly spinning hard disk takes a toll. Keeping the disk rotating means constant consumption of power by the spindle motor, which means shorter battery life. Consequently, most hard disks are designed to be able to cease spinning when they are not needed. Typically, the support electronics in the host computer determine when the disk should stop spinning. Current versions of Windows make this feature optional (you'll find the controls in the Power Option section of Control Panel). When the feature is activated (as it is by default in most notebook computers), it means that if you don't access the hard disk for a while, the computer assumes you've fallen asleep, died, or had your body occupied by aliens and won't be needing to use the disk for some time. When you do send out a command to read or write the disk, you then will have to wait while it spins back up to speed—possibly as long as several seconds. Subsequent accesses then occur at high hard disk speeds until the drive thinks you've died again and shuts itself down.

The powering down of the drive increases the latency from milliseconds to seconds. It can be a big penalty. Consequently, most notebook computers allow you to adjust the standby delay. The longer the delay, the more likely your drive will be spinning when you want to access it—and the quicker your computer's battery will discharge. If you work within one application, a short delay can keep your computer running longer on battery power. If you shift between applications when using Windows or save your work often, you might as well specify a long delay because your disk will be spinning most of the time, anyway. Note, too, that programs with auto-saving defeat the purpose of your hard disk's standby mode, particularly when you set the auto-save delay to a short period. For optimum battery life, you'll want to switch off auto-saving—if you have sufficient faith in your computer.

Data-Transfer Rate

The speed of the spin of a hard disk also influences how quickly data can be continuously read from a drive. At a given storage density (which disk designers try to make as high as possible to pack as much information in as small a package as possible), the quicker a disk spins, and the faster information can be read from it. As spin rates increase, more bits on the surface of the disk pass beneath the read/write head in a given period. This increase directly translates into a faster flow of data—more bits per second.

The speed at which information is moved from the disk to its control electronics (or its computer host) is termed the *data-transfer rate* of the drive. Data-transfer rate is measured in megabits per second, megahertz (typically these two take the same numeric value), or megabytes per second (one-eighth the megabit per second rate). Higher is better.

The data-transfer rates quoted for most hard disks are computed values rather than the speeds you should expect in using a hard disk drive in the real world. A number of factors drive down the actual rate at which information can be transferred from a disk drive.

The measure of the actual amount of useful information that moves between a disk drive and your computer is called the *throughput*. It is always lower—substantially lower—than the disk's data-transfer rate. The actual throughput achieved by a drive system varies with where the measurement is made because each step along the way imposes overhead. The throughput between your drive and controller is higher than between drive and memory. And the actual throughput to your programs—which must be managed by your operating system—is slower still. Throughput to your operating system on the order of a few hundred kilobytes per second is not unusual for hard disk drives that have quoted transfer rates in excess of 10 or 20 megabytes per second.

Read/Write Heads

Besides the platters, the only other moving part in most hard disk drives is the head system. In nearly all drives, one read/write head is associated with each side of each platter and flies just above or below its surface. Each of these read/write heads is flexibly connected to a more rigid arm, which supports the flying assembly. Usually several of these arms are linked together to form a single moving (usually pivoting) unit.

Physical Design

The head is loosely connected to the actuator so that it can minutely rise or fall. When the hard disk drive is turned off or in sleep mode so that its platters are not spinning, the head rests lightly against them by a slight spring force. The physical design of the head makes it into an airfoil much like an airplane wing. As the platters spin, they drag the air in contact with them along for the ride. The moving air creates a slight breeze, which, like the air whisking past the airplane wing, generates lift on the hard disk head's airfoil. The head rises, flying a few millionths of an inch above the spinning surface of the platter.

The height at which the read/write head of a hard disk flies is one factor in determining the ultimate storage capacity of the drive. Magnetic fields spread out with distance, so the farther the head is from the disk, the larger the apparent size of the field that's generated by a flux transition on the disk. Moving the head closer shrinks the apparent size of the flux transitions, allowing them to be packed closely together on the disk surface and increasing the capacity of the disk. The typical first-generation hard disk head flew about 10 to 12 micro-inches (millionths of an inch) above the surface of the platter. Modern disk drive heads fly closer, five or fewer micro-inches. These lower heights are possible thanks to smoother platters and smooth thin-film media.

Electrical Design

Flying is a means to an end, not the ultimate purpose of the read/write head. The real job of the head is to create or detect the magnetic pulses on the disk platter that correspond to the data you store there. Modern hard disks use one of two basic designs to accomplish this design purpose: inductive or magneto-resistive.

Inductive Read/Write Heads

An *inductive read/write head* is nothing more than a miniature electromagnet akin those of childhood experimentation. Wrap a long length of wire around and around a nail, connect the two ends of the wire to the positive and negative terminals of a battery, and the nail becomes a magnet. The electricity flowing through the wire *induces* a magnetic field in the nail. In the inductive read/write head, the wire is called the *coil* and the part that acts as the nail is the *core*. The principle is the same. The disk drive electronics send a current through the read/write head coil, which induces a magnetic field in the core. The magnetic field alters the orientation of the magnetic particles on the nearby platter. The read process simply reverses the relationship. The magnetic fields of the particles on the platter slightly magnetize the core, which, in turn, induces a small voltage in the coil. The disk drive electronics detect the small voltage fluctuations in the coil and interpret them as data.

The physical design of the core allows the focusing of the head's read and write capabilities into a small area. Instead of a long, thin nail, the core is folded so that its two poles (ends) are not quite touching, separated by a thin gap. This design concentrates the magnetic field into the tiny gap. The first practical read/write heads, those in vintage tape recorders, had nothing more than air in the gap. Basic disk drive read/write heads fill the gap with a nonmagnetic metal. Such designs are termed *metal-in-gap heads*. Modern read/write heads replace the coil of wire with a thin layer of copper deposited in coil form as a film. Called *thin-film heads*, their technology allows for finer, lower-mass coils that are easier and less expensive to fabricate.

Magneto-Resistive Heads

The latest trend in head design is *magneto-resistive read/write heads*. These heads work on an entirely different physical principle from inductive heads. They measure the change in electrical resistance that a magnetic field causes in some materials. The disk drive electronics send a small, constant current through the magneto-resistive material (usually an alloy of iron and nickel) and measure the change in voltage across the head—as the resistance of the head goes up, the voltage goes down. The change is minuscule but easily detectable by modern precision electronics.

The magneto-resistive action is one-way. It can be used only to detect changes in magnetic fields. It cannot create the fields. In other words, the magneto-resistive principle works only for read operations. Consequently, disk drives with magneto-resistive heads actually have combination heads—a magneto-resistive read head combined with an inductive write head. Dividing the functions of a read/write head into separate elements allows each to be tailored to best operation. The magneto-resistive design allows for higher frequency operation, which equates to greater storage densities and operating speeds.

Write Precompensation

Constant angular velocity recording has another drawback: The shorter sectors closer to the spindle require data to be packed into them more tightly, squeezing the magnetic flux reversals in the recording medium ever closer together. The ability of many magnetic media to hold flux transitions falls off as the transitions are packed more tightly—pinched together, they produce a feebler field and induce a lower current in the read/write head.

One way of dealing with this problem is to write on the disk with a stronger magnetic field as the sectors get closer to the spindle. By increasing the current in the read/write head when it writes nearer the center of the disk, the on-disk flux transitions can be made stronger. They can then induce stronger currents in the read/write head when that area of the disk is read.

This process is called *write precompensation* because the increased writing current compensates for the fall off in disk responses nearer its center at a place logically before the information is stored on the disk. The electronics of modern hard disk drives automatically make the necessary compensation.

Partial Response Maximum Likelihood

Although group-coding techniques have served well through the evolution of the computer hard disk, another technique called *Partial Response Maximum Likelihood* (PRML) technology works in the opposite direction. Instead of modifying the data—essentially expanding it to make it work better with existing hardware—PRML modifies the read electronics of the disk drive so they can better sort through densely recorded data. IBM first introduced PRML electronics in 1990, and the technology found its way into computer hard disk drives a few years later.

PRML works only during reading the disk. Its specific goal is to compensate for *intersymbol interference*, a kind of distortion that appears when a drive packs data densely. As the read/write head scans the disk, it produces an analog signal. Conventional disk read electronics detect the peaks of the analog pulses and translate them into digital bits. At high bit-rates, which occur when flux transitions are packed densely and the disk spins rapidly, the peaks can blur together. The electronics can readily mistake two bits for one or make similar errors. PRML read electronics can better sort through the analog signals and more reliably translate the signals into data.

The first step in the PRML process is to filter the signal from the read/write head using digital techniques, shaping it with a partial response characteristic by altering its frequency response and timing characteristics. Using digital processing, the PRML system then detects where signals from flux transitions are most likely to occur. The PRML system uses a sequence-detection algorithm that accurately sorts through the data.

The chief advantage of PRML is that it ensures data integrity with high bit densities and faster data rates between head and electronics. PRML does not require special coding during recording. In fact, one of its advantages is that it sidesteps the increase in bit-count that arises with group-coding techniques. Because fewer bits must be written to disk, PRML allows more data to fit on a given disk. Because PRML allows higher disk densities, it can increase the read rate of a disk without altering its mechanical rate of rotation.

Head Actuators

Each read/write head scans the hard disk for information. Were the head nothing more than that, fixed in position as is the head of a tape recorder, it would only be able to read a narrow section of the disk. The head and the entire assembly to which it is attached must be able to move in order to take advantage of all the recordable area on the hard disk. The mechanism that moves the head assembly is called the *head actuator*. Usually the head assembly is pivoted and is swung across the disk by a special head actuator solenoid or motor.

The first head actuators were *open loop*. That is, the actuator moved the head to a preset position and hoped it was right. Modern actuators are *closed loop*. They move the head, check its position over the disk (by reading magnetically coded identification from the disk), and readjust the position until they get it right. Closed-loop actuators are more accurate and quicker.

The closed-loop system gets a constant stream of information regarding the head position from the disk, so it always knows exactly where the head is. The system determines the location of the head by constantly reading from a special, dedicated side of one platter—the servo surface—that stores a special magnetic pattern that allows the drive mechanism to identify each storage location on the disk. Some more recent magnetic hard disks put the servo information on the same recording surface as the stored data. This combined data-and-servo system is called *embedded servo technology*.

The most common of the closed-loop actuator systems uses a voice coil mechanism that operates like the voice coil in a loudspeaker and is therefore called a *servo-voice coil actuator*. In this design, a magnetic field is generated in a coil of wire wrapped around part of the actuator (making it a solenoid) by the controlling electronics, and this field pulls the head mechanism against the force of a spring. By varying the current in the coil, the head mechanism is drawn farther from its anchoring spring, and the head moves across the disk. The voice coil mechanism connects directly to a pivoting arm, which also supports the read/write head above the platter. The varying force of the voice coil swings the head in an arc across the platter surface.

Landing Zone

Hard disks are most vulnerable to head crash damage when they are turned off. As soon as you flick the off switch on your computer, the platters of its hard disk must stop spinning, and the airflow that keeps the heads flying stops. Generally, the airflow decreases gradually, and the head slowly progresses downward, eventually landing like an airplane on the disk media.

In truth, however, any head landing is more of a controlled crash and holds the potential for disk damage. Consequently, most hard disks—even those with thin-film media—have a dedicated *landing zone* reserved in their media in which no data can be recorded. This landing zone is usually at the inner edge of the actual data storage area.

Park-and-Lock

Usually a software command is necessary to bring the head to the landing zone and hold it there while the disk spins down. This process is called *head parking*. The first hard disks had no special provisions for parking their heads and required a specific software command to move their heads to the landing zone. All modern hard disks are designed so that whenever their power is switched off, the head automatically retracts to the landing zone before the disk spins down. Such drives are said to have *automatic head parking*. In addition, the most modern drives latch their heads in the landing zone after power is removed. The latch prevents an impact or other shock to the system from jarring the head out of the landing zone and, in the process, bouncing it across the vulnerable medium. This feature is generally termed *automatic park-and-lock*. All drives now incorporate it.

Thermal Compensation

All materials expand and contract as temperatures change, and the metals used in constructing hard disk drives are no exception. As a drive operates, it generates heat from the motors that spin its platters, the actuator that moves the heads, and the electronics that control its operation. This heat causes the various components of the drive to expand slightly, changing its dimensions slightly but measurably. Because of the miniaturization of modern hard disks that packs thousands of tracks in an inch, even this slight thermal expansion can alter the geometry of the drive sufficiently that heads and tracks can move from their expected positions.

To compensate for such changes, most hard disk drives periodically perform a *thermal calibration*, or *T-cal*. The disk moves its heads to read special calibration tracks to reestablish a proper reference for head positioning. Drive manufacturers developed their own algorithms for determining when their drives would perform thermal calibration (for example, at fixed intervals or upon the occurrence of seek errors). In general, the thermal compensation takes priority over normal read operations and sometimes imposes a delay when you request data. The delay can amount to several dozen milliseconds because the drive's heads must move to the calibration tracks before fulfilling any data requests.

To avoid the delays imposed by thermal calibration, many high-performance drives have the ability to delay the calibration until the completion of a read operation to avoid the interrupt of the delivery of prolonged sequential data streams, such as those that might occur in playing back a video clip. Most drives calibrate all heads simultaneously, which results in the drive being unavailable for reading or writing data for the milliseconds required by the recalibration. A few drives can now recalibrate heads individually, allowing the other heads to retrieve data at the same time.

Medium

The disk spinning inside the hard disk drive is central to the drive—in more ways than one. The diameter of this platter determines how physically large a drive mechanism must be. In fact, most hard disk drives are measured by the size of their platters. When the computer first burst upon the scene, makers of hard disks were making valiant attempts at hard disk platter miniaturization, moving from those eight inches in diameter (so-called *eight-inch disks*) to 5.25-inch platters. Today the trend is toward ever-smaller platters. Most large-capacity drives bound for desktop computer systems now use 3.5-inch platters. Those meant for computers in which weight and size must be minimized (which means, of course, notebook and smaller computers) have platters measuring 2.5, 1.8, or 1.3 inches (currently the smallest) in diameter. (See Chapter 32, "Cases," for form-factor details.)

To increase storage capacity in conventional magnetic hard disk storage systems, both sides of a platter are used for storing information, each surface with its own read/write head. (One head is on the bottom, where it must fly below the platter.) In addition, manufacturers often put several platters on a single spindle, making a taller package with the same diameter as a single platter. The number of platters inside a hard disk also influences the speed at which data stored on the hard disk can be found. The more platters a given disk drive uses, the greater the probability that one of the heads associated with one of those platters will be above the byte that's being searched for. Consequently, the time to find information is reduced.

Substrates

The platters of a conventional magnetic hard disk are precisely machined to an extremely fine tolerance, measured in micro-inches. They have to be—remember, the read/write head flies just a few micro-inches above each platter. If the disk juts up, the result is akin to a DC-10 encountering Pike's Peak—a crash that's good for neither airplane nor hard disk. Consequently, disk-makers try to ensure that platters are as flat and smooth as possible.

The most common substrate material is aluminum, which has several virtues: It's easy to machine to a relatively smooth surface. It's generally inert, so it won't react with the material covering it. It's nonmagnetic, so it won't affect the recording process. It has been used for a long while (since the first disk drives) and is consequently a familiar material. And above all, it's cheap.

A newer alternative is commonly called the *glass platter*, although the actual material used can range from ordinary window glass to advanced ceramic compounds akin to Space Shuttle skin. Glass platters excel at exactly the same qualities as do aluminum platters, only more so. They can be smooth and allow read/write heads to fly lower. They are also less reactive than aluminum and, with the right choice of material, can be lighter.

Areal Density

The smoothness of the substrate affects how tightly information can be packed on the surface of a platter. The term used to describe this characteristic is *areal density*—that is, the amount of data that can be packed onto a given area of the platter surface. The most common unit for measuring areal density is megabits per square inch. The higher the areal density, the more information that can be stored on a single platter. Smaller hard disks require greater areal densities to achieve the same capacities as larger units.

Areal density is generally measured in megabytes per square inch of disk surface, and current products achieve values on the order of 500 to 1000 megabits per square inch.

A number of factors influence the areal density that can be achieved by a given hard disk drive. The key factor is the size of the magnetic domain that encodes each bit of data, which is controlled in turn by several factors. These include the height at which the read/write head flies and the particle (grain) size of the medium.

Manufacturers make read/write heads smaller to generate smaller fields and fly them as closely to the platter as possible without risking the head running into the jagged peaks of surface roughness. The smoothness of the medium determines the lowest possible flying height—a head can fly closer to a smoother surface.

The size of magnetic domains on a disk is also limited by the size of the magnetic particles themselves. A domain cannot be smaller than the particle that stores it. At one time, ball mills ground a magnetic oxide medium until the particle size was small enough for the desired application. Platters were coated with a slurry of the resulting magnetic material. Modern magnetic materials minimize grain size by electroplating the platters.

Media

The first magnetic medium used in hard disks was made from the same materials used in conventional audio recording tapes—ferric or ferrous oxide compounds (essentially fine grains of rather exotic rust). As with recording tape, the oxide particles are milled in a mixture of other compounds, including a glue-like binder and often a lubricant. The binder also serves to isolate individual oxide particles from one another. This mud-like mixture is then coated onto the platters. But this coating is rather rough, too rough for today's high-capacity, small-size hard disks. Moreover, it is soft and prone to damage should the read/write head touch it, resulting in a *head crash* that may render part of the disk unusable. As a result, although once an important technology, oxide media have been abandoned by drive-makers.

In all current hard disk drives, drive-makers have replaced oxide coatings with thin-film magnetic media. As the name implies, a thin-film disk has a microscopically skinny layer of a pure metal, or mixture of metals, mechanically bound to its surface. These thin-films can be applied either by plating the platter, much the same way chrome is applied to automobile bumpers, or by *sputtering*, a form of vapor-plating in which metal is ejected off a hot electrode in a vacuum and electrically attracted to the disk platter.

The very thinness of thin-film media allows higher areal densities because the magnetic field has less thickness in which to spread out. Because the thin-film surface is smoother, it allows heads to fly closer. Thin-film media also have higher coercivities, which allow smaller areas to produce the strong magnetic pulses needed for error-free reading of the data on the disk.

One reason that thin film can be so thin and support high areal densities is that, as with chrome-plated automobile bumpers and faucets, plated and sputtered media require no binders to hold their magnetic layers in place. Moreover, as with chrome plating, the thin films on hard disk platters are genuinely hard, many times tougher than oxide coatings. That makes them less susceptible to most forms of head crashing—the head merely bounces off the thin-film platter just as it would your car's bumpers.

Contamination

Contaminants such as dust and air pollution particles stuck to the media surface can cause problems. With older oxide media drives, contaminants could result in a head crash. With plated media, contaminants aren't as likely to cause damage, but they can interfere with the proper read/write operation of the drive.

To help guard against contamination of the platter surface with dust, hair, and other floating gunk, most hard disks keep all their vulnerable parts in a protective chamber. In fact, this need to avoid contamination is why nearly all computer hard disks use nonremovable media, sealed out of harm's way.

The disk chamber is not completely airtight. Usually a small vent is designed into the system to allow the air pressure inside the disk drive to adjust to changes in environmental air pressure. Although this air exchange is minimal, a filter in this vent system traps particles before they can enter the drive. Microscopic pollutants, such as corrosive molecules in the air, can seep through the filter, however, potentially damaging the disk surface. Although the influx of such pollutants is small—the hard disk vent does not foster airflow, only pressure equalization—it is best not to operate a hard disk in a polluted environment. You wouldn't want to be there to use it, anyhow.

Geometry

The geometry of a hard disk expresses the physical arrangement on the platters inside the drive. Today it is an issue for engineers only because the logical block addressing used by all new hard disk drives effectively hides the drive geometry from you and your operating system. As long as a drive has all the blocks it advertises, they could be laid out like a Jackson Pollock painting, and your operating system wouldn't know the difference.

If you accidentally enter the netherworld of your computer's BIOS setup and jog your hard disk away from automatic configuration, you likely will be confronted with a *disk parameter table* that requests you enter the number of heads, cylinders, and sectors of your drive. The best strategy is to notch the settings back to "Auto." But the drive parameters put you squarely in geometry territory.

Tracks

No matter the type of magnetic media or style of head actuator used by a disk, the read/write head must stop its lateral motion across the disk whenever it reads or writes data. While it is stationary, the platter spins underneath it. Each time the platter completes one spin, the head traces a full circle across its surface. This circle is called a *track*.

A disk drive stores the data-bits of a given track sequentially, as if it were a strip of tape spliced end to end. With every spin, the same data passes by the head, as long as the drive holds in the same place. The electronics of the drive select which portion of the track to read (or write) to find a random block of data.

Cylinders

Each head traces out a separate track across its associated platter. The head actuator locks all the heads together so that all are at the same position from the center of the disk along a given radius. Because the combination of all the tracks traced out at a given head actuator position forms the skeleton of a solid cylinder, such a vertical stack of tracks is often termed exactly that—a *cylinder*.

The number of cylinders in a drive is the same as the number of tracks on a platter in that drive. Both numbers are permanently determined when the manufacturer makes the drive.

In most drives, the number of cylinders is set by a magnetic pattern called a *servo pattern*. Older hard disks dedicated one surface of a platter to this servo information. Most modern disks put the servo information on the same surface as the stored data. The servo information gets read along with the data, and the drive electronics sort everything out—using the servo information to find its place and sending the data to your applications. This kind of hard disk is called an *embedded servo drive*.

The more cylinders in the drive, the more data the drive can store. The maximum number of cylinders is limited by physical factors inherent in the technology used by the drive. More tracks on each platter means the tracks are squeezed closely together, forcing them to be smaller. The minimum width of a track is set by the size of the head but is limited by other factors—such as how closely the head flies to the disk surface—that also limit the amount of information that the drive can fit into each track. Once hard disk drives had as few as 312 cylinders. Modern drives have thousands.

Sectors

Most hard disk systems further divide each track into short arcs termed *sectors*, and the sector is the basic storage unit of the drive. Some operating systems use the sector as their basic storage unit, as does the NTFS system used by Windows NT and Windows 2000, for example. Under the VFAT system of Windows 95 and Windows 98, however, the operating system gathers together several sectors to make its basic unit of storage for disk files—the *cluster*.

Sectors can be soft, marked magnetically with bit-patterns embedded in the data on the track itself, or hard, set by the drive mechanism itself. Soft sectors are demarcated using a low-level format program, and their number can vary almost arbitrarily depending on the formatting software and the interface used for connecting the disk. Disks with device-level interfaces are essentially soft-sectored. For all practical purposes, disks with system-level interfaces are hard-sectored because their sector size is set by the servo information encoded on the drive platters, which cannot be changed once the drive leaves the factory. Magneto-optical cartridges are hard-sectored by an embedded optical format prerecorded on the medium.

In the computer hard disk industry, the size of a sector is, by convention, almost universally 512 bytes. The number of sectors per track depends on the design of the disk. The sector count on any given track of older hard disks is the same as every other track because of their use of constant angular velocity recording. Most modern hard disk drives use a technique called *multiple zone recording* (MZR), which puts variable numbers of sectors on each track. MZR allows the drive-maker to use the storage capacity of the magnetic medium more efficiently.

A disk with a fixed number of sectors per track stores data at lower densities in its outer tracks than it does in its inner tracks. Only the innermost tracks pack data at the highest density allowed by the medium. All the other tracks must be recorded at a lower density, an inevitable result of the constant angular velocity recording used by the hard disk and the fixed frequency of the data signals.

Multiple zone recording allows the drive to maintain a nearly constant data density across the disk by dividing it into zones. The drive alters the frequency of the data signals to match each zone. Using higher frequencies in the zones near the outer tracks of a disk increases their data density to about that of the inner tracks. This, in turn, can substantially increase overall disk capacity without compromising reliability or altering the constant spin needed for quick access.

Sometimes MZR technology is described as *zoned constant angular velocity* (ZCAV) recording, a term which confirms that the spin rate remains the same (constant angular velocity) but the platter is divided into areas with different recording densities (zones). Seagate Technologies uses a proprietary form of MZR called *zone-bit recording*—different name, same effect.

Physical Format

The geometry of a disk drive describes only the numbers of the various drive parameters—cylinders, heads, and sectors. The drive *format* describes the arrangement and alignment of these parameters.

Disk geometry fixes the tracks as concentric circles, with the sectors as small arcs within each track. The format defines the location of the sectors in regard to one another—that is, the order in which they are read. Sectors need not be read one after another in a given track. Moreover, their starting edges need to exactly align on the disk.

Neither tracks nor sectors are engraved on the surface of individual platters. They are instead defined magnetically by coded bit-patterns recorded on the disk. Before data can be written on such a disk, the sectors have to be marked to serve as guideposts markers so that the information can later be found and retrieved. The process by which sectors are defined on the hard disk is called *low-level formatting* because it occurs at a control level below the reaches of normal Windows commands.

Three methods have found general application in defining tracks: simply by the count of the stepper motor in the oldest band-stepper drives, by the permanently recorded track servo data on the dedicated servo surface of old servo-voice coil drives, and by embedded servo data in modern drives.

In classic hard disk drives, special bit-patterns on the disk serve as sector-identification markings. The patterns indicate the start of the sector and encode an ID number that gives the sector number within the track. The sector ID precedes each sector; error-correction data typically follows each sector. In normal operation, the disk servo system seeks a particular track, then the drive begins to read sector IDs until it finds the sector that your computer has requested.

The sector ID can consume a significant portion of the available space on each disk track, about 10 percent. Consequently, manufacturers have sought means to eliminate it. For example, the *No-ID Format* developed by IBM eliminates sector IDs by putting a format map in RAM. The map tells the drive where on each track each sector is located and which sectors have been marked bad. The map, for example, tells the drive how many sectors are on a track in a zoned recording system and where each begins in reference to the track servo information embedded on the disk. This format also improves access speed because the drive can immediately locate a given sector without detours in chasing replacements for defective sectors.

File System

To store a file on disk, the FAT file system breaks it down into a group of clusters, perhaps hundreds of them. Each cluster can be drawn from anywhere on the disk. Sequential pieces of a file do not necessarily have to be stored in clusters that are physically adjacent.

The earliest—and now obsolete—versions of the FAT file system followed a simple rule in picking which clusters are assigned to each file. The first available cluster, the one nearest the beginning of the disk, is always the next one used. Therefore, on a new disk, clusters are picked one after another, and all the clusters in a file are contiguous.

When a file is erased, its clusters are freed for reuse. These newly freed clusters, being closer to the beginning of the disk, are the first ones chosen when the next file is written to disk. In effect, a FAT-based file system first fills in the holes left by the erased file. As a result, the clusters of new files may be scattered all over the disk.

The earliest versions of the FAT file system used this strange strategy because they were written at a time when capacity was more important than speed. The goal was to pack files on the disk as stingily as possible. For more than a decade, however, the FAT system has used a different strategy. Instead of immediately trying to use the first available cluster closest to the beginning of the disk, the file system attempts to write on never-before-used clusters before filling in any erased clusters. This helps ensure that the clusters of a file are closer to one another, a technique that improves the speed of reading a file from the disk.

File Allocation Table

To keep track of which cluster belongs in which file, the default file system of consumer Windows (including 95, 98, Me, and XP) uses a *file allocation table* (FAT), essentially a map of the clusters on the disk. When you read to a file, the FAT-based file system automatically and invisibly checks the FAT to find all the clusters of the file; when you write to the disk, it checks the FAT for available clusters. No matter how scattered over your disk the individual clusters of a file may be, you—and your software—only see a single file.

FAT-based file systems simply number all the clusters in a manner similar to the way a disk drive numbers logical blocks. The operating system keeps track of the cluster numbers and in what order clusters have been assigned to a given file. The operating system stores most of the cluster data in the file allocation table.

The FAT file system works by chaining together clusters. The directory entry of a file or subdirectory contains several bytes of data in addition to the file's name. Along with the date the file was last changed and the file's attributes is the number of the first cluster used to store the file or subdirectory.

When the operating system reads a file, it first checks the directory entry to find the first cluster number. In addition to reading the data from the cluster from the disk, the operating system also checks the file allocation table for the entry with the number corresponding to the first cluster number. This FAT entry indicates the number of the *next* cluster in the file. After reading that cluster, the operating system checks the entry corresponding to that cluster number to find the next cluster. If the file has no additional clusters, the cluster entry has a value of 0FF(hex). The operating system assigns unused clusters—those available for adding to files to store data—the value of zero.

When the standard FAT-based computer operating system erases a file, it merely changes the first character of the filename in the directory entry to 0E5(hex) and changes all the FAT entries of the file to zero. Because the rest of the directory information remains intact (at least until the file system runs out of space for directory information and overwrites the entries of erased files), it can be recovered to help reconstruct accidentally erased files. An unerase or undelete utility checks the directory for entries with the first character of 0E5(hex) and displays what it finds as candidates for recovery. From the remaining directory data, the unerasing program can locate the first cluster of the file. Finding the remaining clusters from the FAT is a matter of making educated guesses.

The FAT of a disk is so important that Windows guards against losing its data by putting two complete (and identical) copies of the FAT end to end on the disk.

Clusters

As clever as using clusters to allocate file data may be, the technique has its drawback. It can be wasteful. Disk space is divvied up in units of a cluster. No matter how small a file (or a subdirectory, which is simply a special kind of file) may be, it occupies at minimum one cluster of disk space. Larger files take up entire clusters, but any fractional cluster of space that's left over requires another cluster. On average, each file on the disk wastes half a cluster of space. The more files, the more waste. The larger the clusters, the more waste. Unless you work exclusively with massive files, increasing cluster size to increase disk capacity is a technique to avoid whenever possible.

The first versions of DOS used FATs with 12-bit entries for cluster numbers, which allowed a total of 4096 uniquely named clusters. Later, Microsoft updated the FAT to use 16-bit entries, and this FAT structure, usually called *FAT16*, was used through Windows 95. By that time, however, disks had become larger than a 16-bit structure could reasonably handle. Microsoft introduced a new 32-bit FAT with the second edition of Windows 95. The new system, commonly called *FAT32*, reserves 4 of its 32 bits for future purposes, so each cluster is actually identified with a 28-bit value. Using FAT32, recent Windows versions can accommodate drives up to 2048GB and on smaller disks store files more efficiently with smaller clusters (see Table 17.2).

TABLE 17.2   Drive Capacity Versus Cluster Size in 32-Bit FAT Systems

Drive Capacity	*Cluster Size*
0 up to 6GB	4K
6GB up to 16GB	8K
16GB up to 32GB	16K
32GB up to 2048GB	32K

FAT32 is the most recent version, and drivers for it ship with all current Windows versions. If you choose to use a FAT-based file system, Windows will ask if you want large disk support and automatically install FAT32.

Compression

Microsoft includes a disk-compression system with many Windows versions that the company calls *DriveSpace*. The file system takes uncompressed data one cluster at a time and maps it in compressed form into sectors in the compressed volume file. To locate which sector belongs to each file, the file system uses a special FAT called the *Microsoft DoubleSpace FAT* (or MDFAT, with DoubleSpace being the DriveSpace predecessor) that encodes the first sector used for storing a given cluster, the number of sectors required for coding the cluster, and the number of the cluster in the uncompressed volume that's stored in those sectors. When the operating system needs the data from a file, the file system first searches for the clusters in the main disk FAT and then looks up the corresponding starting and length values in the MDFAT. With that information, the operating system locates the data, uncompresses it, and passes it along to your applications.

To speed up operations when writing compressed data to disk, the operating system uses a second kind of FAT in the compressed volume file. Called the *BitFAT*, this structure reports which sectors reserved in the compressed volume file hold active data and which are empty. The BitFAT uses only one bit for each sector as a flag to indicate whether a sector is occupied.

New Technology File System

Windows NT, Windows 2000, and Windows XP give you two choices for your file system: the same old FAT-based system used since time began and the newer Windows NT File System, usually termed *NTFS*.

The centerpiece of the NTFS is the *master file table* (MFT), which stores all the data describing each directory and file on a given disk. The basic data about each file is contained in a file record in the master file table. These file records may be two, four, or eight sectors long (that is, 1KB, 2KB, or 4KB). The first 16 records are reserved for system use to hold data of special metadata files, the first of which stores the attributes of the master file table itself.

To NTFS, a file is a collection of *attributes*, each of which describes some aspect of the file. One of the attributes is the name of the file, another is the data contained in the file. Others may include who worked on the file and when it was last modified. The master file table tracks these attributes. To identify attributes, the file system assigns each file a unique ID number, a 48-bit value (allowing for nearly 300 trillion entries).

Instead of the clusters used by the FAT system, NTFS uses the sector as its basic unit of storage. Sectors on a disk or partition are identified by relative sector numbers, each of which is 32 bits long—sufficient to encode 4,294,967,296 sectors or a total disk space of 2048GB. Sectors are numbered sequentially, starting with the first one in the partition. Files are allocated in multiples of single sectors; directories, however, are made from one or more blocks of four sectors.

Each file or directory on the disk is identified by its *File NODE*, which stores descriptive data about the file or directory. This information includes file attributes, creation date, modification dates, access dates, sizes, and a pointer that indicates in which sector the data in the file is stored. Each File NODE is one sector (512 bytes) long. Up to 254 bytes of the File NODE of a disk file store an extended filename, which can include upper- and lowercase characters, some punctuation (for example, periods), and spaces.

An NTFS disk organizes its storage from a root directory. In an NTFS system, however, the root directory does not have a fixed location or size. Instead, the root directory is identified by reference to the disk *super block*, which is a special sector that is always kept as the 16th sector from the beginning of the HPFS partition. The 12th and 13th bytes— that is, at an offset of 0C(hex) from the start of the block—of the super block point to the location of the root directory File NODE. Free space on the disk is identified by a bitmapped table.

As with other FNODEs, a pointer in the root directory FNODE stores the location of the first block of four sectors assigned to the root directory. The root directory is identical to the other directories in the HPFS hierarchy, and like them it can expand or shrink as the number of files it contains changes. If the root directory needs to expand beyond its initial four sectors, it splits into a tree-like structure. The File NODE of the root directory then points to the base File NODE of the tree, and each pointer in the tree points to one directory entry and possibly a pointer to another directory node that may in turn point to entries whose names are sorted before the pointer entry. This structure provides a quick path for finding a particular entry, along with a simple method of scanning all entries.

NTFS can accommodate any length file (that will fit in the partition, of course) by assigning multiple sectors to it. These sectors need not be contiguous. NTFS, however, preallocates sectors to a file at the time it is opened, so a file may be assigned sectors that do not contain active data. The File NODE of the file maintains an accurate total of the sectors that are actually used for storing information. This preallocation scheme helps prevent files from becoming fragmented. Normally, the block of sectors assigned to a file will be contiguous, and the file will not become fragmented until all the contiguous sectors have been used up.

Two types of sectors are used to track the sectors assigned a given file. For files that have few fragments, the File NODE maintains a list of all the *relative sector numbers* of the first sector in a block of sectors used by the file, as well as the total number of sectors in the file before those of each block. To capture all the data in a file, the operating system finds the relative sector number of the first block of sectors used by the file and the total number of sectors in the block. It then checks the next relative sector number and keeps counting with a running total of sectors in the file.

If a file has many fragments, it uses a tree-style table of pointers to indicate the location of each block of sectors. The entry in the file's File NODE table then stores pointers to the sectors, which themselves store pointers to the data. Each of these sectors identifies itself with a special flag, indicating whether it points to data or to more pointers.

Besides its huge capacity, NTFS has significant advantages when dealing with large hierarchies of directories, directories containing large number of files, and large files. Although both the NTFS and FAT use tree-structured directory systems, the directories in the NTFS are not arranged like a tree. Each directory gets stored in a tree-like structure that, coupled with the presorting of entries automatically performed by the NTFS, allows for faster searches of large directories. NTFS also arranges directories on the disk to reduce the time required to access them—instead of starting at the edge of the disk, they fan out from the center.

The master file table attempts to store all the attributes of a file in the record it associates with that file. When the attributes of a file grow too large to be held in the MFT record, the NTFS just spreads the attribute data across as many additional disk clusters' records to create as many *nonresident attributes* as are needed to hold the file. The master file table keeps track of all the records containing the attributes associated with a given file by the file's ID number.

This system allows any file to grow as large as the complete storage space available while preserving a small allocation unit size. No matter how large a disk or partition is, NTFS never allocates space in increments larger than 4KB.

Performance Issues

When shopping for hard disks, many people become preoccupied with disk performance. They believe that some drives find and transfer information faster than others. They're right. But the differences between state-of-the-art hard disk drives are much smaller than they used to be, and in a properly set-up system, the remaining differences can be almost completely equalized.

The performance of a hard disk is directly related to design choices in making the mechanism. The head actuator has the greatest effect on the speed at which data can be retrieved from the disk, with the number of platters exerting a smaller effect. Because the head actuator designs used by hard disk–makers have converged, as have the number of platters per drive because of height restrictions of modern form factors, the performance of various products has also converged.

Clearly, however, all hard disks don't deliver the same performance. The differences are particularly obvious when you compare a drive that's a few years old with a current product. Understanding the issues involved in hard disk performance will help you better appreciate the strides made by the industry in the last few years and show you what improvements may still lie ahead.

Average Access Time

You've already encountered the term *latency*, which indicates the average delay in finding a given bit of data imposed because of the spin of the disk. Another factor also influences how long elapses between the moment the disk drive receives a request to reveal what's stored at a given place on the disk and when the drive is actually ready to read or write at that place—the speed at which the read/write head can move radially from one cylinder to another. This speed is expressed in a number of ways, often as a *seek time*. Track-to-track seek time indicates the period required to move the head from one track to the next. More important, however, is the average access time (sometimes rendered as *average seek time*), which specifies how long it takes the read/write head to move on the average to any cylinder (or radial position). Lower average access times, expressed in milliseconds, are better.

The type of head actuator technology, the mass of the actuator assembly, the physical power of the actuator itself, and the width of the data area on the disk all influence average access time. Smaller drives have some inherent advantages in minimizing average access time. Their smaller, lighter head and actuators have less inertia and can accelerate and settle down faster. More closely spaced tracks mean the head needs to travel a shorter distance in skipping between them when seeking data.

Real-world access times vary by more than a factor of ten. The first computer-size hard disks had access times hardly better than floppy disks, sometimes as long as 150 milliseconds. The newest drives are usually below ten milliseconds; some are closer to six milliseconds.

How low an average access time you need depends mostly on your impatience. Quicker is always better and typically more costly. You can feel the difference between a slow and fast drive when you use your computer, particularly when you don't have sufficient memory to hold all the applications you run simultaneously. Once access time is below about ten microseconds, however, you may be hard pressed to pay the price of improvement.

Disk-makers have explored all sorts of exotic technologies to reduce access time. Some primeval hard disks had a dozen or more fixed heads scanning huge disks. Because the heads didn't move, the access time was close to zero—more correctly, half the latency of the drive. About a decade ago, drive-makers experimented with dual-actuator drives—two heads mean less than half the waiting because with an intelligent controller the drive could overlap read and write requests. None of these technologies made it into the computer mainstream because an even better idea—one much simpler and cheaper—has taken the forefront: the disk array (discussed later). Instead of multiple actuators in a single drive, arrays spread the multiple actuators among several drives.

Advanced disk controllers, particularly those used in disk arrays, are able to minimize the delays caused by head seeks using a technique called *elevator seeking*. When confronted with several read or write requests for different disk tracks, the controller organizes the requests in the way that moves the head the least between seeks. Like an elevator, it courses through the seek requests from the lower-numbered tracks to the higher-numbered tracks and then goes back on the next requests, first taking care of the higher-numbered tracks and working its way back to the lower-numbered tracks. The data gathered for each individual request is stored in the controller and doled out at the proper time.

Data-Transfer Rate

Once a byte or record is found on the disk, it must be transferred to the host computer. Another disk system specification—the data-transfer rate—reflects how fast bytes are batted back and forth, effecting how quickly information can shuttle between microprocessor and hard disk. The transfer rate of a disk is controlled by a number of design factors completely separate from those of the average access time.

The transfer rate of a hard disk is expressed in megahertz (MHz) or megabytes per second (or MBps, which is one-eighth the megahertz rate). The figure is invariably the *peak transfer rate*, the quickest that a single byte can possibly move, at least in theory, when all conditions are the most favorable and there's a strong tailwind. In truth, information *never* moves at the peak transfer rate—only the signals containing the data switch at the peak rate. The actual flow of data is burdened by overhead of various sorts, both in the hardware interface and the software data exchange protocol. That said, although the actual number expressed in the peak transfer rate is purely bogus if you want to count how fast data moves, such numbers do allow you to compare interfaces. Transferring information in modern systems requires about the same overhead, notwithstanding the interface standard (although there are differences). Therefore, a disk that has a peak transfer rate of 320MBps is faster than one with a rate of 133MBps, regardless of how fast each can actually move bytes.

In modern usage, the peak transfer rate is often reserved for discussions of disk interfaces. Disks themselves are constrained by their physical nature. How fast they can produce information is governed by how closely the information is linearly packed and how fast it moves under the read/write head. The faster it moves, the more data the head sees in a second.

The biggest factor in determining this speed is the spin rate of the disk. A faster spinning disk reveals more flux transitions to the read/write head. As a result, today most people focus on the spin rate of the disk to measure its data-transfer performance.

Disk Caching

The ultimate means of isolating your computer from the mechanical vagaries of hard disk seeking is *disk caching*. Caching eliminates the delays involved in seeking when a read request (or write request in a system that supports write caching) involves data already stored in the cache—the information is retrieved at RAM speed. Similarly, the cache pushes the transfer rate of data stored in the cache up to the ceiling imposed by the slowest interface between the cache and host microprocessor. With an on-disk cache, the drive interface will likely be the primary constraint; with a hardware cache in the disk controller or host adapter, the bus interface is the limit; with a software cache, microprocessor and memory-access speed are the only constraints.

AV Drives

Drive-makers have tailored a special breed of hard disk to suit the needs of audio and video recording and editing. Called *AV drives* because their primary application is audio and video, these drives are optimized for transferring large blocks of data sequentially (unlike normal hard disks, which must provide instant access to completely random data). Audio and video files tend to be long and linear and therefore read sequentially for long periods. Fast access time is not as important for such applications as is a high sustained data-transfer rate. For example, most video production today requires data rates of 27MBps but uses compression ratios averaging about ten to one to produce a data stream of about 2.7MBps that needs to be stored and retrieved. Most modern hard disks can achieve the performance required by audio and video applications, but hard disk–makers still offer a number of drives specially tailored to AV use.

To achieve the highest possible performance, these AV drives add extensive buffering and may sacrifice or delay some data-integrity features. For example, they trade off absolute data security to eliminate interruptions in the high-speed flow of information. The hard disk industry rationale for this design is that video data, unlike spreadsheets or databases, tolerates errors well, so a short sequence of bad data won't hurt anything. After all, a single sector isn't even a third of a line of uncompressed video. The video subsystem can correct for such one-time errors in part of a line, masking them entirely.

One way to prevent interruptions in the flow of data is to alter error handling. Engineers usually require that most hard disk drives attempt to reread the disk when they encounter an error. Most manufacturers use elaborate algorithms to govern these rereads, often minutely changing the head position or performing an entire thermal calibration. If these are not successful, the drive may invoke its error-correction code to reconstruct the data. AV drives alter these priorities. Because error correction is entirely electronic and imposes no mechanical delays, AV drives use it first to attempt error recovery. Only after error correction fails may the drive try to reread the data, often for a limited number of retries.

Advanced hard disks log the errors that they encounter so that they may be used later for diagnostics. The logging operation itself takes time and slows disk performance. AV drives delay error logging until it does not interrupt the data stream.

One feature that slows down conventional drives is *sector remapping*, which AV drives avoid to sidestep its performance penalties. The remapping process imposes delays on the flow of data because the read/write head of the drive must jump from one place to another to write or retrieve the data from the remapped sector at the time of the data access. AV drives often avoid auto-relocation to prevent interruption of the flow of high-speed data.

Drive Arrays

When you need more capacity than a single hard disk can provide, you have two choices: Trim your needs or plug in more disks. But changing your needs means changing your lifestyle—foregoing instant access to all your files by deleting some from your disk, switching to data compression, or keeping a tighter watch on backup files and intermediary versions of projects under development. Of course, changing your lifestyle is about as easy as teaching an old dog to change its spots. The one application with storage needs likely to exceed the capacity of today's individual hard disks—200GB and climbing—is a network server, and a total lifestyle change for a network server is about as probable as getting a platoon of toddlers to clean up a playroom littered with a near-infinite collection of toys.

Consequently, when the bytes run really low, you're left with the need for multiple disks. In most single-user computers, each of these multiple drives acts independently and appears as a separate drive letter (or group of drive letters) under common Windows. Through software, such multiple-drive systems can even be made to emulate one large disk with a total storage capacity equal to that of its constituent drives. Because Windows 95 and Windows 98 handle I/O serially—they can do only one I/O task at a time—such a solution is satisfactory, but it's hardly the optimum arrangement where reliability and providing dozens of users instant access is concerned. Instead of operating each disk independently, you can gain higher speeds, greater resistance to errors, and improved reliability by linking the drives through hardware to make a drive array—what has come to be known as a *Redundant Array of Inexpensive Disks*, or *RAID*.

Principles

The premise of the drive array is elementary—combine a number of individual hard disks to create a massive virtual system. But a drive array is more than several hard disks connected to a single controller. In an array, the drives are coordinated, and the controller specially allocates information between them using a program called *Array Management Software* (AMS). The AMS controls all the physical hard disks in the array and makes them appear to your computer as if they were one logical drive. For example, in some drive arrays, the AMS ensures that the spin of each drive is synchronized and divides up blocks of data to spread among several physical hard disks.

The obvious benefit of the drive array is the same as any multiple-disk installation—capacity. Two disks can hold more than one, and four more than two. But drive array technology can also accelerate mass-storage performance and increase reliability.

Data Striping

The secret to both of these innovations is the way the various hard disks in the drive array are combined. They are not arranged in a serial list, where the second drive takes over once the capacity of the first is completely used up. Instead, data is split between drives at the bit, byte, or block level. For example, in a four-drive system, two bits of every byte might come from the first hard disk, the next two bits from the second drive, and so on. The four drives could then pour a single byte into the data stream four times faster—moving all the information in the byte would only take as long as it would for a single drive to move two bits. Alternatively, a four-byte storage cluster could be made from a sector from each of the four drives. This technique of splitting data between several drives is called *data striping*.

At this primitive level, data striping has a severe disadvantage: The failure of any drive in the system results in the complete failure of the entire system. The reliability of the entire array can be no greater than that of the least reliable drive in the array. The speed and capacity of such a system are greater but so are the risks involved in using it.

Redundancy and Reliability

By sacrificing part of its potential capacity, an array of drives can yield a more reliable, even fault-tolerant, storage system. The key is redundancy. Instead of a straight division of the bits, bytes, and blocks each drive in the array stores, the information split between the drives can overlap.

For example, in the four-drive system, instead of each drive getting two bits of each byte, each drive might store four. The first drive would take the first four bits of a given byte, the second drive the third, fourth, fifth, and sixth bits; the third drive, the fifth, sixth, seventh, and eighth bits; and the fourth drive, the seventh, eighth, first, and second bits. This digital overlap allows the correct information to be pulled from another drive when one encounters an error. Better yet, if any single hard disk should fail, all the data it stored could be reconstituted from the other drives.

This kind of system is said to be *fault tolerant.* That is, a single fault—the failure of one hard disk—will be tolerated, meaning the system operates without the loss of any vital function. Fault tolerance is extremely valuable in network applications because the crash of a single hard disk does not bring down the network. A massive equipment failure therefore becomes a bother rather than a disaster.

The sample array represents the most primitive of drive array implementations, one that is particularly wasteful of the available storage resources. Advanced information-coding methods allow for higher efficiencies in storage, so a strict duplication of every bit is not required. Moreover, advanced drive arrays even allow *hot-swapping*, a feature that permits a failed drive to be replaced and the data that was stored upon it reconstructed without interrupting the normal operation of the array. A network server with such a drive array need not shut down even for disk repairs.

Implementations

In 1988, three researchers at the University of California at Berkeley—David A. Patterson, Garth Gibson, and Randy H. Katz—first outlined five disk array models in a paper titled *A Case for Redundant Arrays of Inexpensive Disks.* They called their models *RAID Levels* and labeled them as RAID 1 through 5, appropriately enough. Their numerical designations were arbitrary and were not meant to indicate that RAID 1 is better or worse than RAID 5. The numbers simply provide a label for each technology that can be readily understood by the cognoscenti.

In 1993, these levels were formalized in the first edition of the RAIDBook, published by the RAID Advisory Board, an association of suppliers and consumers of RAID-related mass storage products. The book is part of one of the RAID Advisory Board's principle objectives—the standardization of the terminology of RAID-related technology. Although the board does not officially set standards, it does prepare them for submission to the recognized standards organizations. The board also tests the function and performance of RAID products and verifies that they perform a basic set of functions correctly.

The RAID Advisory Board currently recognizes nine RAID implementation levels. Five of these conform to the original Berkeley RAID definitions. Beyond the five array levels described by the Berkeley group, several other RAID terms are used and acknowledged by the RAID Advisory Board. These include RAID Level 0, RAID Level 6, RAID Level 10, and RAID Level 53.

The classification system is nonhierarchical—a higher number does not imply a better or more advanced technology. The numbers are no more than labels for quickly identifying the technologies used. Because the common perception—really a misperception—is that the numbers *do* imply a ranking and that higher is better, some manufacturers have developed proprietary labels (RAID 7) or exploited non-Berkeley definitions (RAID 10 and 53) with high numbers that hint they are somewhat better than the lower-numbered systems. Although each level has its unique advantages (and disadvantages), no one RAID technology is better than any of the others for all applications.

In an attempt to avoid such confusion, the RAID Advisory Board now classifies disk array products by what they accomplish in protecting data rather than by number alone. The board's Web site includes both a description and listing of classified products.

RAID Level 0

Early workers used the term *RAID Level 0* to refer to the absence of any array technology. According to the RAID Advisory Board, however, the term refers to an array that simply uses data striping to distribute data across several physical disks. Although RAID Level 0 offers no greater reliability than the worst of the physical drives making up the array, it can improve the performance of the overall storage system. For example, reading data in parallel from two drives can effectively double throughput.

RAID Level 1

The simplest of drive arrays, RAID Level 1, consists of two equal-capacity disks that mirror one another. One disk duplicates all the files of the other, essentially serving as a backup copy. Should one of the drives fail, the other can serve in its stead.

This reliability is the chief advantage of RAID Level 1 technology. The entire system has the same capacity as one of its drives alone. In other words, the RAID Level 1 system yields only 50 percent of its potential storage capacity, making it the most expensive array implementation. Performance depends on the sophistication of the array controller. Simple systems deliver exactly the performance of one of the drives in the array. A more sophisticated controller could potentially double data throughput by simultaneously reading alternate sectors from both drives. Upon the failure of one of the drives, performance reverts to that of a single drive, but no information (and no network time) is lost.

RAID Level 2

The next step up in array sophistication is RAID Level 2, which interleaves bits or blocks of data as explained earlier in the description of drive arrays. The individual drives in the array operate in parallel, typically with their spindles synchronized.

To improve reliability, RAID Level 2 systems use redundant disks to correct single-bit errors and detect double-bit errors. The number of extra disks needed depends on the error-correction algorithm used. For example, an array of eight data drives may use three error-correction drives. High-end arrays with 32 data drives may use seven error-correction drives. The data, complete with error-detection code, is delivered directly to the array controller. The controller can instantly recognize and correct for errors as they occur, without slowing the speed at which information is read and transferred to the host computer.

The RAID Level 2 design anticipates that disk errors occur often, almost regularly. At one time, mass storage devices might have been error prone, but no longer. Consequently, RAID Level 2 can be overkill except in the most critical of circumstances.

The principal benefit of RAID Level 2 is performance. Because of their pure parallel nature, RAID Levels 2 and 3 are the best-performing array technologies, at least in systems that require a single, high-speed stream of data. In other words, RAID Level 2 yields a high data-transfer rate. Depending on the number of drives in the array, an entire byte or even a 32-bit double-word could be read in the same period it would take a single drive to read one bit. Normal single-bit disk errors don't hinder this performance in any way because of RAID Level 2's on-the-fly error correction.

The primary defect in the RAID Level 2 design arises from its basic storage unit being multiple sectors. As with any hard disk, the smallest unit each drive in the array can store is one sector. File sizes must increase in units of multiple sectors—one drawn from each drive. In a ten-drive array, for example, even the tiniest two-byte file would steal ten sectors (5120 bytes) of disk space. (Under the Windows VFAT system, which uses clusters of four sectors, the two-byte file would take a total of 20,480 bytes!) In actual applications this drawback is not severe because systems that need the single-stream speed and instant error correction of RAID Level 2 also tend to be those using large files (for example, mainframes).

RAID Level 3

This level is one step down from RAID Level 2. Although RAID Level 3 still uses multiple drives operating in parallel, interleaving bits or blocks of data, instead of full error correction it allows only for *parity checking*. That is, errors can be detected but without the guarantee of recovery.

Parity checking requires fewer extra drives in the array—typically only one per array—making it a less expensive alternative. When a parity error is detected, the RAID Level 3 controller reads the entire array again to get it right. This rereading imposes a substantial performance penalty—the disks must spin entirely around again, yielding a 17 millisecond delay in reading the data. Of course, the delay appears only when disk errors are detected. Modern hard disks offer such high reliability that the delays are rare. In effect, RAID

Level 3 compared to RAID Level 2 trades off fewer drives for a slight performance penalty that occurs only rarely.

RAID Level 4

This level interleaves not bits or blocks but sectors. The sectors are read serially, as if the drives in the array were functionally one large drive with more heads and platters. (Of course, for higher performance, a controller with adequate buffering could read two or more sectors at the same time, storing the later sectors in fast RAM and delivering them immediately after the preceding sectors have been sent to the computer host.) For reliability, one drive in the array is dedicated to parity checking. RAID Level 4 earns favor because it permits small arrays of as few as two drives, although larger arrays make more efficient use of the available disk storage.

The dedicated parity drive is the biggest weakness of the RAID Level 4 scheme. In writing, RAID Level 4 maintains the parity drive by reading the data drives, updating the parity information, and then writing the update to the parity drive. This read-update-write cycle adds a performance penalty to every write, although read operations are unhindered.

RAID Level 4 offers an extra benefit for operating systems that can process multiple data requests simultaneously. An intelligent RAID Level 4 controller can process multiple input/output requests, reorganize them, and read its drives in the most efficient manner, perhaps even in parallel. For example, while a sector from one file is being read from one drive, a sector from another file can read from another drive. This parallel operation can improve the effective throughput of such operating systems.

RAID Level 5

This level eliminates the dedicated parity drive from the RAID Level 4 array and allows the parity-check function to rotate through the various drives in the array. Error checking is thus distributed across all disks in the array. In properly designed implementations, enough redundancy can be built in to make the system fault tolerant.

RAID Level 5 is probably the most popular drive array technology currently in use because it works with almost any number of drives, including arrays as small as two, yet permits redundancy and fault tolerance to be built in.

RAID Level 6

To further improve the fault tolerance of RAID Level 5, the same Berkeley researchers who developed the initial five RAID levels proposed one more, now known as RAID Level 6. This level adds a second parity drive to the RAID Level 5 array. The chief benefit is that any two drives in the array can fail without the loss of data. This enables an array to remain in active service while an individual physical drive is being repaired, yet still remain fault tolerant. In effect, a RAID Level 6 array with a single failed physical disk becomes a RAID Level 5 array. The drawback of the RAID Level 6 design is that it requires two parity blocks to be written during every write operation. Its write performance is extremely low, although read performance can achieve levels on par with RAID Level 5.

RAID Level 10

Some arrays employ multiple RAID technologies. RAID Level 10 represents a layering of RAID Levels 0 and 1 to combine the benefits of each. (Sometimes RAID Level 10 is called RAID Level 0&1 to more specifically point at its origins.) To improve input/output performance, RAID Level 10 employs data striping, splitting data blocks between multiple drives. Moreover, the Array Management Software can further speed read operations by filling multiple operations simultaneously from the two mirrored arrays (at times when both halves of the mirror are functional, of course). To improve reliability, the RAID level uses mirroring so that the striped arrays are exactly duplicated. This technology achieves the benefits of both of its individual layers. Its chief drawback is cost. As with simple mirroring it doubles the amount of physical storage needed for a given amount of logical storage.

RAID Level 53

This level represents a layering of RAID Level 0 and RAID Level 3—the incoming data is striped between two RAID Level 3 arrays. The capacity of the RAID Level 53 array is the total of the capacity of the individual underlying RAID Level 3 arrays. Input/output performance is enhanced by the striping between multiple arrays. Throughput is improved by the underlying RAID Level 3 arrays. Because the simple striping of the top RAID Level 0 layer adds no redundant data, reliability falls. RAID Level 3 arrays, however, are inherently so fault tolerant that the overall reliability of the RAID Level 53 array far exceeds that of an individual hard disk drive. As with a RAID Level 3 array, the failure of a single drive will not adversely affect data integrity.

Which implementation is best depends on what you most want to achieve with a drive array: Efficient use of drive capacity, fewest number of drives, greatest reliability, or quickest performance. For example, RAID 1 provides the greatest redundancy (thus reliability), and RAID 2 the best performance (followed closely by RAID 3).

Parallel Access Arrays

In *parallel access arrays*, all the individual physical drives in the array participate in every input and output operation of the array. In other words, all the drives operate in unison. Systems that correspond to the RAID Level 2 or 3 design fit this definition. The drives in *independent access arrays* can operate independently. In advanced arrays, several individual drives may perform different input and output operations simultaneously, filling multiple input and output requests at the same time. Systems that follow the RAID Level 4 or 5 design fit this definition. Although RAID Level 1 drives may operate either as parallel access or independent access arrays, most practical systems operate RAID Level 1 drives independently.

Interfacing

Just connecting four drives to a SCSI controller won't create a drive array. An array requires special electronics to handle the digital coding and control of the individual drives. Usually these special electronics take the form of a *RAID controller.* The controller may be part of a standalone disk array in its own cabinet, in which case the array attaches to the host computer as a single SCSI device. Alternatively, the RAID controller may be a single expansion board that resembles a host adapter for a SCSI or AT Attachment interface but incorporates RAID electronics and usually megabytes of cache or buffer memory. The disk drives for the array may be installed inside the computer host or in a separate chassis.

Most disk arrays use SCSI hard disks because that interface allows multiple drives to share a single connection. A growing number of manufacturers now offer AT Attachment (IDE) array controllers, which allow you to take advantage of lower cost ATA hard disks. The earliest of these supported only the four drives normally allowed in a single computer system under the ATA specifications. These typically allow you your choice of a RAID Level 0 or RAID Level 1 configuration. At least one manufacturer now offers a RAID Level 5 controller for ATA hard disk drives.

Floppy Disks

Since the first computer booted up, the floppy disk has been a blessing and a curse, subject of the same old saying usually reserved for kids, spouses, and governments: "You can't live with them, and you can't live without them." They were the first storage system for personal computers, and they've remained relatively unchanged ever since. Microprocessors might be 10,000 times faster than they used to be. Hard disks might hold 10,000 times more bytes. But today's basic floppy disk hardly holds about the same amount of data as the very first. Although the floppy disk has shrunk from eight inches to three-and-a-half and grown a hard turtle-like shell, the basic disk still holds little more than a megabyte, truly puny in a world of giga-everything.

Despite the best efforts of computer-makers, floppy disks aren't dead yet. You can still depend on them in the vilest of emergencies, when nothing else works to bring your computer to life. You (or a technician) can still troubleshoot your computer using its floppy disk drive. And you can still exchange files with friends on the cheap, even disposable, floppy disk medium. The floppy disk still has a role, although a modest one, in the life of your computer.

The floppy disk provides a recording medium that has several positive qualities. The flat disk surface allows an approximation of random access. As with hard disks, data is arranged in tracks and sectors. The disk rotates the sectors under a read/write head, which travels radially across the disk to mark off tracks. More importantly, the floppy disk is a removable medium. You can shuffle dozens of floppies in and out of drives to extend your storage capacity. The floppy disk in the drive provides online storage. Offline, you can keep as many floppy disks as you want.

The term *floppy disk* is one of those amazingly descriptive terms that abound in this age of genericisms. Inside its protective shell, the floppy disk medium is both a floppy (flexible) and wide, flat disk. To protect it, the floppy resides in a shell. The first floppies had a truly floppy protective shell, one made out of thicker but still flexible Mylar. Today, the floppy fits into a hard case and overall is not very floppy. The disk inside, the one made from the media, remains floppy so the name remains the same—uniquely accurate in a world of computers inhabited by spinning fixed disks and recordable read-only memory.

History

When the floppy was first conceived, personal computers didn't exist. Its creator, IBM, first used the floppy disk to store diagnostic programs and microcode for its large computer system—instead of tape (too cumbersome, and many applications didn't require such a large capacity) or memory chips (too expensive). It was the Dark Ages equivalent of a CD-ROM. It was also big, about eight inches square, but for the time had a large capacity—about 100KB—and random-access capabilities.

By 1973, engineers had adapted the eight-inch floppy to a convenient read/write medium suitable for both the original application and for storage for data-entry systems, such as IBM's DisplayWriter word processing system. The 8-inch floppy disk had a number of features going for it that made it desirable as a computer data-storage medium. The floppy disk was compact (at least compared to the ream of paper that could hold the same amount of information), convenient, and standardized. Above all, it was inexpensive to produce and reliable enough to depend on.

In 1976, Shugart Associates introduced the 5.25-inch floppy disk, a timely creation that exactly complimented the first commercial personal computers, introduced at about the same time. (Both Apple Computer and Microsoft Corporation were founded in 1976, although fledgling Microsoft offered a BASIC interpreter as its first product—its operating system for floppy disks did not arrive until 1981.) Because these were smaller than the older eight-inch variety, these 5.25-inch floppies were called *diskettes* by some. The irregularly used name later spread to even smaller sizes of the floppy disk.

In 1980, Sony Corporation introduced the 3.5-inch floppy disk of the same mechanical construction that we know it today. After a lukewarm reception, the little disks gained a foothold when Apple adopted them for its initial Macintosh in 1984. Portable computers added more incentive for the move to 3.5-inch disks, as did IBM's adoption of the format in 1987. The standard floppy disk has remained unchanged since then, despite further attempts to improve it (such as the "quad-density" disks with double the normal capacity).

The first appearance of Mount Rainier technology in CD-RW drives (see Chapter 18, "Optical Storage (CD and DVD)") in late 2002 likely marked the end-of-the-line for the floppy disk. This new industry initiative endows the CD with all the capabilities of a floppy disk, in addition to its much greater capacity. As Mount Rainier drives become widespread, floppy disk drives will become truly obsolete.

Medium

The traditional floppy disk medium itself is the thin, flexible disk inside the protective shell. This disk is actually a three-layer sandwich, the meat of which is a polyester substrate that measures about 3.15 mils (thousandths of an inch), or 80 micrometers thick. The bread is the magnetic recording medium itself, a coating less than one-thousandth of an inch thick on each side of the substrate.

The floppy disk medium starts out as vast rolls of the substrate that are coated in a continuous process at high speed. The stamping machine cuts individual disks from the resulting roll, or *web*, of medium, like a cookie cutter. After some further mechanical preparation (for example, a metal hub is attached to the cookies of 3.5-inch disks), another machine slides the disks into their protective shells.

Although retailers sell some floppy disks as "single sided," a mixture of magnetic oxide and binder coats both sides of the substrate of all floppy disks. Those sold as single sided are only tested on one side, and their manufacturers only certify that one side for storing data. By convention, the bottom surface of the disk is used in single-sided floppy disk drives.

Magnetic Properties

The thickness of the magnetic coating on the floppy disk substrate varies with the disk type and storage density. In the most common disk types, it measures from 0.035 mil to 0.1 mil (that is, 0.9 to 2.5 micrometers). In general, the higher the storage density of the disk, the thinner the magnetic coating. The individual particles are also finer grained. Table 17.3 lists the coating thicknesses for both current and obsolete floppy disk types.

TABLE 17.3   Floppy Disk Media Characteristics

Disk Type	Coating Thickness	Coercivity
5.25-inch double-density	2.5 micrometers	290 oersteds
5.25-inch high-density	1.3 micrometers	660 oersteds
3.5-inch double-density	1.9 micrometers	650 oersteds
3.5-inch high-density	0.9 micrometers	720 oersteds

Although all common floppy disk coatings use ferric oxide magnetic media, engineers have tailored the magnetic particles in the mix to the storage density at which the disks are used. The higher storage density media generally have higher coercivities, as shown in Table 17.3.

Despite the names used by various floppy disk types, all floppy disk drives use Modified Frequency Modulation (MFM) recording, which produces double-density recording. In other words, both normal and high-density disks are double-density, even though many manufacturers reserve the *double-density* term for lower-capacity disks.

Extra-high-density disks (that is, the 2.88MB floppies still occasionally sold) use a novel technology called *perpendicular recording*. In conventional floppy disks, the grains of magnetic medium are aligned flat against the substrate, and the write process aligns them along a radius of the disk. The particles of the medium used in perpendicular recording are arranged vertically so that one end of each particle points toward the substrate. A special read/write head in the disk drive changed the vertical orientation of the magnetic field of the media particles. In addition, extra-high-density disks use a high-coercivity barium-ferrite recording medium.

Shell

The chief difference between a modern 3.5-inch floppy disk and the earliest disks is the hard plastic shell. Magnetically and logically, the disks work the same as the first 8-inch floppies. Drives, too, are basically the same, only miniaturized to suit the medium and modern computers.

The shell protects the magnetic medium inside from whatever terrors lurk in your world, be they teething infants, churning chair casters, or simple carelessness. The tough shell allows you to put a label on the disk and then write whatever identification you want on it, even with a ballpoint pen. The thinner shells of earlier disks could not protect the media within from pen points, so writing on a label already affixed to an early floppy could crease the medium and make it unreadable. Figure 17.2 shows the shell of a 3.5-inch floppy disk and its notable external features.

FIGURE 17.2

Layout of 3.5-inch floppy disk.

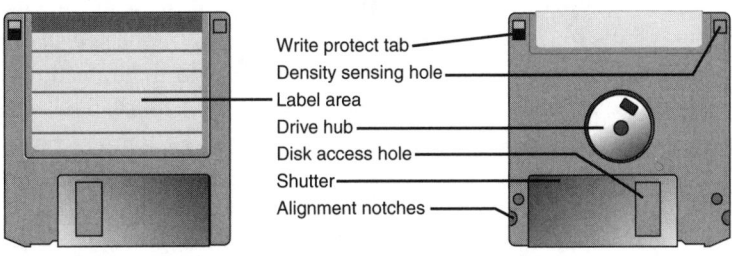

The shell of a 3.5-inch floppy disk measures 3.7 inches (94 millimeters) front to back, and just over 3.5 inches (90 millimeters) wide. Each disk is a little more than one-eighth inch (3.3 millimeters) thick. A single disk weighs just over three-quarters of an ounce, about

22 grams. Despite its 3.5-inch name, the media disk inside the shell actually measures about 3.4 inches (nominally 86 millimeters) across.

To protect the medium inside from dirt, dust, and fingerprints, the head access opening on a 3.5-inch floppy disk is covered with a spring-loaded sliding metal shield or *shutter*. It opens automatically only when you insert a disk into a drive and slides closed when you pop the disk from the drive. The shutter is an effective dust shield that prevents contaminants from collecting on the medium surface whenever the disk is out of its drive. This protection means that 3.5-inch disks include all the protection they need and don't need an additional sleeve or shuck that older floppy disks required.

Liners

As protective as the hard shell of 3.5-inch floppies may be, the medium needs protection from it as well. A thin sheet of unwoven cloth akin a loose-woven paper towel cushions each side of the medium from rubbing against the shell. The interlocked threads of the liner serve as a slip-sheet and dust collector. Light contact with the strands of the liner let the medium slide with little friction. At the same time, the material sweeps dust and particles from the surface of the medium so that it doesn't scrape against the read/write head of the drive.

Hub

The creators of the 3.5-inch floppy disk learned that the one area of older floppies that sustained the most damage was the hub hole. Every time you slide a disk into a drive, drive hubs clamp onto the disk to hold and spin it. The hub entered the drive hole and forced the entire disk into the proper position for proper reading and writing. At times, the hub clamping down damaged the edges of the hole. After a disk suffered enough damage, it could become unreliable or unusable. The only protection to the hub hole offered by older floppy disks was an optional reinforcing ring some manufacturers elected to add to the perimeter of the hub hole.

The 3.5-inch floppy eliminates such problems by using a sturdy metal hub with a square center spindle hole, which mates with the mechanism of the disk drive. The stamped steel hub resists damage. The single rectangular cutout in the hub allows the drive mechanism to unambiguously identify the radial alignment of the disk. The cutout serves as a mechanical reference for the position of data on the disk. The hub itself is glued to the disk media.

Insertion Key

A 3.5-inch floppy disk has four edges and two sides, giving you eight possible ways to try to slide it into your disk drive, only one of which is correct. Although the over-square design of the floppy shell prevents you from sliding a disk in sideways, you can still shove one in backward or upside down. To ensure that you don't damage your disk drive by improperly inserting a disk, the shell of 3.5-inch floppies is keyed by a notch in one corner. A tab in the drive blocks this corner, so if the notch is not present you cannot slide the disk all the way into the drive. The last few millimeters of sliding in the disk open the shutter and load the heads against the disk, so the notch prevents the heads from ramming against the floppy's shell instead of the access area.

Molded into the plastic of the shell is a small arrow that serves as a visual reminder to you. It points to the edge of the disk that you should slide into your disk drive, just in case the shutter is not enough guidance.

Write Protection

The fundamental design of the floppy disk is to serve as a read/write medium so that you can store information on it and read it back. Sometimes, however, you might want to protect the data on a floppy disk from change. For example, you might back up your archives to floppy disk. Software vendors prefer protection against writing to the distribution disks holding their programs so that you don't accidentally erase the code and become a support problem for them.

The 3.5-inch floppy design incorporates a *write-protect tab* that allows you to make any floppy disk a read-only medium. The design uses a hole and a plastic slider. When the slider blocks the hole, you can read, write, and format the disk. When the slider is moved back to reveal the hole, an interlock on the drive prevents you from writing to the disk. You can move the slider back and forth to write-protect a disk and then make it writable again as often as you want.

Software vendors often remove the slider entirely. Without the slider, the write-protected hole cannot be covered and the disk is permanently write-protected. You can, however, circumvent even this "permanent" form of write-protection by blocking off the write-protect hole. The easiest way is to cover both sides of the hole with opaque tape to make a distribution disk writable. This method is not without its dangers, however. If the tape does not stick tightly to the disk, it can jam the drive mechanism, likely preventing you from popping or pulling the disk out of the drive.

Density Key

In order for your disk drive to determine the type of magnetic medium on your disk so that its electronics can be adjusted to match the disk's coercivity, 3.5-inch floppy disks incorporate a *density key*. This key is actually the presence or absence of a hole in one corner of the disk shell. Double-density disks lack a hole. High-density disks have a hole. An extra-high-density notch marks disks with 2.88MB capacity. Higher-density disks also have a visual indication of their capacity—for example, the stylized "HD" silk-screened near the shutter of high-density disks.

The connections between many floppy disk drives and the host computer often do not properly relay the density key information to the computer and its operating system.

When the density key information is not available, you can format a double-density disk as high density. In years gone by, some enterprising manufacturers also offered hole-punches designed to add a density-key hole to double-density disks so that you could format them as high density. Although the difference in coercivities between double- and high-density media is modest, there are other differences in the formulation of the media that make double-density disks unreliable at high-density capacities. Moreover, the hole-punches often left residue in the form of small particles of plastic to contaminate the disks (at the factory the density key is molded rather than punched). These contaminants can shorten the life of the medium or damage your disk drive.

Format

Four formats are commonly used for 3.5-inch floppy disks, three of which are supported on computers. (Computers do not support single-sided 3.5-inch floppy disk formats.) Your disks drives and operating system automatically adjust to the format of the disks you attempt to read, providing your drive is capable of reading the format. All higher-capacity drives can read formats of lower capacity. Table 17.4 summarizes the essential characteristics of these four formats for 3.5-inch floppy disks.

TABLE 17.4   The Characteristics of a 3.5-inch Floppy Disk

Capacity	Units	360KB	720KB	1.44MB	2.88MB
Sides	Number	1	2	2	2
Tracks	Number	80	80	80	80
Sectors per track	Number	9	9	18	36
Sector size	Bits	512	512	512	512
Rotation rate	RPM	300	300	300	300
Data-transfer rate	Kbps	500	500	500	1000
Bit density (max)	BPI	8717	8717	17,434	34,868
Track density	TPI	135	135	135	135
Coercivity	Oersteds	650	650	720	1200

The capacity of a floppy disk is set when the disk is formatted. Using the Format option from the Windows menu associated with your floppy disk drive, you can select the capacity of new floppy disks (or reformat floppies to change their capacity). Preformatted disks relieve you of the chore of formatting floppies yourself, although you can always format over the factory format to change the capacity of a disk.

Double density is the starting format for 3.5-inch floppy disks. It uses 80 tracks with nine sectors per track. The tracks are spaced 135 to the inch (about 5.3 to the millimeter). The small diameter disk only allows a swath about 0.6 inch (15 millimeters) wide around the disk for reading and writing. The high-density format merely doubles the number of sectors per track, packing the data in twice as tightly.

Because 3.5-inch floppy disks spin at a fixed speed of 300 RPM, doubling the density of the data on each track also boosts the speed at which the information is read from the disk. The basic reading speed of 250Kbps for double-density is doubled to 500Kbps with high-density disks.

Extra-high-density disks again double the sector count on each track, to 36 sectors per track, without changing the number of tracks or their spacing. Again, this increase in storage density also increases the reading and writing speed to 1000Kbps.

Note that the capacities of *all* floppy disks are given with the format in place. The formatting data steals away some of the usable storage area of the disk. Floppy disk–makers occasionally list the unformatted capacities of their products. The unformatted capacity of a double-density (720KB formatted) disk is 1MB; that of a high-density (1.44MB formatted) disk is 2MB; that of an extra-high-density (2.88MB formatted) disk is 4MB.

Before CD-ROM media took over the job of program distribution, software publishers sought and developed ways of shoehorning more data onto every floppy disk. The leading extra-capacity alternative was Microsoft's *Distribution Media Format* (DMF). This variation in the high-density design allowed Microsoft to fit 1,720,320 bytes on a standard high-density 3.5-inch floppy disk in place of the more normal 1,474,560 bytes (nominal 1.44MB). The DMF format differed from the standard format in that it used 21 sectors per track instead of the normal 18. DMF squeezed more sectors on each track by reducing the interrecord gap (the space between sectors) down to nine bytes.

The differences went deeper, however. Each track used a 2:1 interleave factor so that sectors did not appear in order. This interleaving resulted in slower reading because the disk had to spin around twice for each track to be read. The DMF format also skewed the sectors on adjacent tracks by three sectors so that Sector 1 on Track 4 sat next to Sector 1 on Track 2.

The small interrecord gap made DMF disks difficult to write to with normal floppy disk drives. In fact, Microsoft called DMF a read-only format. In any case, you cannot write to DMF disks using ordinary software. However, several special utilities are available for copying and even creating DMF disks. Note that Microsoft enforces a limit of 16 entries in the root directory of a DMF disk by only allocating a single cluster to service as the root, so DMF-formatted disks usually use a subdirectory structure for their contents.

Microsoft operating systems cannot ordinarily read DMF floppies. Consequently, DMF floppies were used only when software required multiple floppy disks for its installation. The first disk of the installation package—usually called the *setup disk*—loaded software to reprogram your floppy disk controller to read the DMF disks.

Zip Disks

The Zip disk, developed and first marketed by Iomega Corporation in 1995, was the first floppy disk system with a capacity larger than 100MB. Although initially a proprietary system, Iomega has licensed Zip to other companies. Both drives and media are now available from multiple sources, although the format is totally under the control of Iomega.

To gain its large capacity, the Zip system uses optical technology that was first applied to a little-remembered 20MB floppy disk system called *Floptical*. The Zip medium uses an optically read servo track to allow repeatable head positioning in fine increments.

The first generation of Zip disks had listed nominal capacities of either 25MB (25,107,968 actual bytes) or 100MB (actually 100,431,872 bytes) per disk.

By increasing the density of storage on slightly modified media, in 1998 Iomega was able to boost the capacity of the Zip system by a factor of two and a half without major modifications to the drive mechanism. As a result, Iomega was able to offer an improved system with 250MB capacity at the same initial price as the original Zip drive.

Thanks to the increased lineal density of data on the 250MB Zip tracks, the data throughput of the new system is more than two times greater than the old, although access time remains comparable. Actual data throughput often is limited by the drive interface. High-capacity Zip drives use the same interfaces as the old, and performance through parallel ports is compromised.

The shell of the Zip disk makes it a true cartridge. To achieve speeds in the hard disk range, the medium must spin at a high rate, and the friction from rubbing against a liner is an anathema to speed. The thicker cartridge gives the Zip disk spinning room and enables it to rotate at 2968 RPM. In addition, the Zip disk drive has hard disk–like access speeds, with the first generation of drives having a 26 millisecond average access time. The disk requires about three seconds to spin up to speed or spin down, which becomes a factor only when you're exchanging cartridges.

The actual Zip media disk inside a cartridge measures true 3.5-inches across. Consequently, the cartridge must be larger than conventional 3.5-inch floppies and MO cartridges, measuring 3.7 inches (94 millimeters) square and a quarter-inch (6.35 millimeters) thick. These dimensions alone make the Zip disk incompatible with traditional floppy disks.

Instead of using a mechanical write-protect mechanism on the cartridge shell, Zip disks are write-protected electronically. The Iomega system provides three protection modes with optional password access limits as part of its ZipTools software. The three modes include conventional write protection that prevents the inadvertent alteration of data on the disk; read/write protection, which requires a password to access data on the disk; and unprotect until eject, which lets you work with the data on the disk but protects the disk when you remove it from the drive. The same software that adds write protection is required to remove it. Passwords, however, are not recoverable—even by Iomega.

Zip disk drives read only Zip disks. Iomega has manufactured products using any of four interfaces or ports—AT Attachment (IDE), parallel port, SCSI, and USB. IDE is now favored for internal drives, and USB 2.0 is favored for external drives.

The move to 250MB required changes to both the medium and drives, although superficially high-capacity Zip disks look almost identical to their older, low-capacity forebears. The drive electronics were adapted to accommodate the higher read and write rates required by the new media, and the magnetic medium has a higher coercivity to improve high-density storage. As a consequence, older drives cannot be upgraded, and disks with 250MB capacity are rejected outright by older drives as incompatible.

Because of the laser/mechanical formatting of the disks and the differing media, low-capacity Zip disks cannot be reformatted to higher capacities. In fact, the servo tracks cannot be erased by any means that would not destroy the cartridge.

On the other hand, high-capacity Zip drives are fully backward compatible with old media. New 250MB drives can read and write 100MB disks. Old drives, however, can neither read nor write 250MB media.

In 2002, Iomega further refined the Zip drive to increase its capacity to 750MB per disk. The chief trick was simply to increase the storage density, resulting in 4,780 tracks per inch with data squeezed into each track at 137Kb per inch. The disk itself spins at 3676 RPM. The drives use the USB 2.0 interface and feature a data-transfer rate that peaks at 7.5Mbps. Although compatible with USB 1.0 connections, using the older interface will severely degrade the performance of the drive.

The new 750MB disks can only be read and written by matching 750MB drives. However, the drives are backward compatible with earlier Zip disk formats. A 750MB drive can both read and write 250MB disks and read 100MB disks. It cannot write 100MB disks.

SuperDisks

Jointly developed by Compaq Computer Corporation, the storage products division of 3M Company (now Imation Corporation), Matsushita-Kotobuki Electronics Industries, Ltd., and O. R. Technology, parent company of Optics Research, Inc., the *SuperDisk* was supposed to be the next generation of floppy disk drive. First marketed in March, 1996 as the *LS-120* system, the first drives were made by MKE, installed in Compaq computers, and used media manufactured by 3M. The optical technology used by the drives was developed by ORT.

Outwardly a SuperDisk resembles an ordinary 3.5-inch floppy diskette. The only obvious difference is the shape of the shield over the head slot. Instead of rectangular, the SuperDisk wears a roughly triangular shield. Figure 17.3 shows an LS-120 diskette.

FIGURE 17.3
An LS-120 diskette.

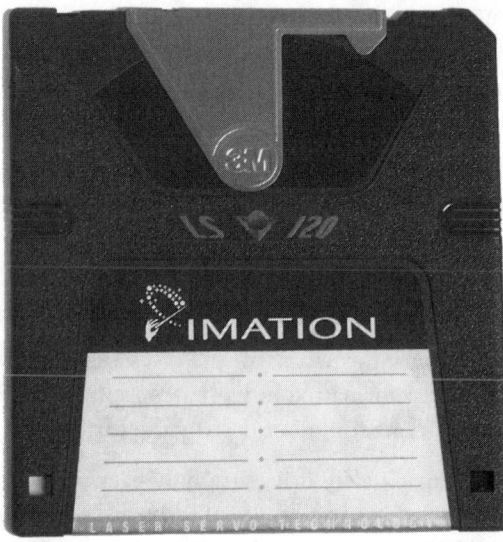

Inside, however, the SuperDisk system uses a thinner substrate (2.5 mils) than traditional floppies, one that is cut from a different plastic, polyethylene terathalate (PET). This substrate is more flexible than the traditional polyester to give the SuperDisk medium better bend around the head for more reliable contact.

Format

Each SuperDisk diskette can store up to 125,829,120 bytes, or 120MB, accounting for the designation of the drive. Not all of that capacity is usable. As with conventional floppy disks, part of the total capacity must be devoted to the FAT and directory data.

The SuperDisk drive combines two technologies to increase its capacity: an opto-mechanical laser servo system and zoned recording.

The major increase comes from increasing the track density to 2490 per inch, achieved using the laser servo system. The small diameter of the disk only allows 1736 tracks per side at this density. Even so, it requires a special medium, a two-layer metal particle compound.

For compatibility with computer hardware and software, the track layout of the SuperDisk medium is mapped to a logical format (the way the drive appears to your computer), having 960 tracks per side. This mapping results in the drive—which has two heads, one for each disk side—appearing to your system as if it has eight heads.

The SuperDisk system uses zoned recording with 55 different zones across the radius of each disk. The number of sectors per track varies from 51 on the innermost tracks to 92 at the outer edge. Table 17.5 lists the physical and logical formats of an LS-120/SuperDisk diskette.

TABLE 17.5   LS-120 Disk Format

Format Type	Cylinders	Heads	Sectors
Physical	1736	2	51 to 92 (zoned recording)
Logical	960	8	32

The SuperDisk medium spins at a constant 720 revolutions per minute. As a result of the constant spin and varying sector count, a SuperDisk drive reads data from the disk at a rate that changes with the track position of the read/write head. Near the center of the disk, the transfer rate is lowest, about 400KBps. At the outer edge, the transfer rate reaches 665KBps. Initial SuperDisk drives had an average access time of about 70 milliseconds. Table 17.6 lists the specifications of the SuperDisk medium and its format.

TABLE 17.6   LS-120 Specifications

Feature	Specification
Media diameter	3.5 inches
Recording medium	Metal particle
Capacity (formatted)	120MB
Bytes per sector	512
Sectors per track	51–92 (ZBR)
Track data capacity	26,112–47,616KB
Tracks per surface	1736
Track density	2490 tracks per inch
Areal density	33,660 flux changes/inch
Recording surfaces (sides)	2
Track pitch	10.2 μm
Peak transfer rate	3.20 to 5.33MBps
Throughput	313–571
Estimated life	5 million passes

Technology

The stepper-motor-based open-loop mechanisms used by conventional floppy disk drives cannot correctly position a read/write head with sufficient precision to reliably locate the fine tracks used by the SuperDisk system. To achieve the necessary track density, the SuperDisk system used an embedded-servo system. Servo data is etched into the disk during factory preparation. The SuperDisk drive then uses a laser to detect and read the etched servo information from the disk and align the read/write head properly on each track. In fact, the "LS" designation is an abbreviation for *laser servo*.

The read/write head has two gaps—one used for the fine tracks used in high-density recording and one used for working with conventional double-density and high-density floppy disk media. The laser servo design does not increase the capacity of conventional floppy disk media.

Compatibility

All SuperDisk drives are backward compatible with standard 1.44MB floppy disks. The drives can both read and write standard floppies, and the 1.44MB floppies written on a SuperDisk drive are readable by conventional floppy disk drives. Because of the higher spin speed of the SuperDisk drive, however, it can achieve a higher transfer rate with a 1.44MB floppy—approximately 2.5 times higher—than a conventional floppy disk drive.

The SuperDisk media are designed to appear as write-protected to conventional 1.44MB floppy disk drives by virtue of a cutout that corresponds to the write-protect hole in a conventional floppy. Consequently, there is no risk of damage to data by inadvertently sliding an LS-120 disk into a conventional floppy disk drive.

The SuperDisk media are beyond the control capabilities of the chip on the controllers for conventional floppy disk drives. The initial SuperDisk drives instead used an IDE interface.

Mechanisms

As computer equipment goes, floppy disk drives are simple devices. The essential components are a *spindle motor*, which spins the disk, and a stepper-motor, which drives a metal band in and out to position the read/write heads, and an assembly that is collectively called, as with hard disks, the *head actuator*. A spring-loaded latch locks the disk in place and ejects it when you press the button on the front of the drive.

After more than two decades of development, about the only refinement made to the conventional floppy disk system has been miniaturization. Drives now can be less than one-third the height of the first. No matter their size, however, all conventional floppy disk drives work in essentially the same way.

To carry out their design purpose, all floppy disk drive mechanisms must be able to carry out a few basic tasks. They have to spin the disks at a uniform speed. They must also move their read/write heads with sufficient precision to locate each and every data track on a given disk. And the open-loop head-positioner design requires a known starting place, an index, which the drive must be able to locate reliably.

Speed Control

All the electronics packed onto the one or more circuit boards attached to the drive unit merely control those simple disk drive operations. A servo system keeps the disk spinning at the correct speed. Usually an optical sensor looks at a stroboscopic pattern of black dots on a white disk on the spindle assembly. The electronics count the dots that pass the sensor in a given period to determine the speed at which it turns, adjusting it as necessary. Some drives use similar sensors based on magnetism rather than optics, but they work in essentially the same way—counting the number of passing magnetic pulses in a given period to determine the speed of the drive.

Head Control

Other electronics control the radial position of the head assembly to the disk. The stepper-motor that moves the head reacts to voltage pulses by moving one or more discrete steps of a few degrees (hence, the descriptive name of this type of motor). Signals from the floppy disk controller card in the host computer tell the disk drive which track of the disk to move its head to. The electronics on the drive then send the appropriate number of pulses to the stepper-motor to move the head to the designated track.

The basic floppy disk mechanism receives no feedback on where the head is on the disk. It merely assumes it gets to the right place because of the number of steps the actuator makes. Because the drive does its best to remember the position of the head, hard reality can leave the head other than in its expected place. For instance, you can reach in and manually jostle the head mechanism. Or you might switch off your computer with the head halfway across the disk. Once the power is off, all the circuitry forgets, and the location of the head becomes an unknown.

Head Indexing

So that the head can be put in the right place with assurance, the floppy disk drive resorts to a process called *indexing*. That is, it moves the head as far as it will go toward the edge of the disk. Once the head reaches this index position, it can travel no farther, no matter how hard the actuator tries to move it. The drive electronics make sure that the actuator moves the head a sufficient number of steps (a number greater than the width of the disk) to ensure that the head will stop at the index position. After the head has reached the index position, the control electronics can move it a given number of actuator steps and know exactly where on the radius of the disk the head is located.

Tape

Tape was the first magnetic mass storage system used in computers, harking back to the days of room-size Univacs and vacuum tubes. It first proved itself as a convenient alternative to punched cards and punched paper tape—the primary storage system used by mainframe computers. Later, information transfer became an important use for tape. Databases could be moved between systems as easily as carting around one or more spools of tape. After magnetic disks assumed the lead in primary storage, tape systems were adapted to backing them up.

As a physical entity, tape is both straightforward and esoteric. It is straightforward in design, providing the perfect sequential storage medium—a long, thin ribbon that can hold orderly sequences of information. The esoteric part involves the materials used in its construction.

The tape used by any system consists of two essential layers—the backing and the coating. The backing provides the support strength needed to hold the tape together while it is flung back and forth across the transport. Progress in the quality of the backing material mirrors developments in the plastics industry. The first tape was based on paper. Shortly after the introduction of commercial tape recorders at the beginning of the 1950s, cellulose acetate (the same plastic used in safety film in photography for three decades previously) was adopted. The state-of-the-art plastic is polyester, of double-knit leisure-suit fame. In tape, polyester has a timeless style of its own—flexible and long-wearing with a bit of stretch. It needs all those qualities to withstand the twists and turns of today's torturous mechanisms, fast shuttle speeds, and abrupt changes of direction. The typical tape backing measures from one-quarter mil (thousandth of an inch) to one mil thick, about 10 to 40 microns.

The width of the backing varies with its intended application. Wider tapes offer more area for storing data but are most costly and, after a point, become difficult to package. The narrowest tape in common use, cassette tape, measures 0.150 inches (3.8 millimeters) wide. The widest in general use for computing measures 0.5 inches (12.7 millimeters). Equipment design and storage format determine the width of tape to be used.

Coatings have also evolved over the decades, as they have for all magnetic media. Where once most tapes were coated with doped magnetic oxides, modern coatings include particles of pure metal in special binders and even vapor-plated metal films. Tape coatings are governed by the same principles as other magnetic media; the form is different but the composition remains the same. As with all magnetic storage systems, modern tape media have higher coercivities and support higher storage densities.

Taken by itself, tape is pretty hard to get a handle on. Pick up any reasonable length of tape, and you'll have an instant snarl on your hands. The only place that tape is used by itself is in endless loops (one end spliced to the other) in special bins used by audio and video duplicating machines. In all other applications, the tape is packaged on reels or in cartridges.

Reels came first. A simple spool onto which a length of tape gets wound, the reel is the simplest possible tape carrier. In this form, tape is called *open reel*. Putting tape in a cartridge adds a permanent package that both provides protection to the delicate medium and makes it more convenient to load. The most basic cartridge design simply packages a reel of tape in a plastic shell and relies on an automatic threading mechanism in the drive itself. All current computer-size tape systems use a more sophisticated design—cassette-style cartridges that include both the supply and take-up reels in a single cartridge.

The basic cassette mechanism simply takes the two spools of the open-reel tape transport and puts them inside a plastic shell. The shell protects the tape because the tape is always attached to both spools, eliminating the need for threading across the read/write heads and through a drive mechanism. The sides of the cassette shell serve as the sides of the tape reel—holding the tape in place so that the center of the spool doesn't pop out. This function is augmented by a pair of Teflon slip-sheets, one on either side of the tape inside the shell, that help to eliminate the friction of the tape against the shell. A clear plastic window in either side of the shell enables you to look at how much tape is on either spool—how much is left to record on or play back.

The reels inside the cassette are merely hubs that the tape can wrap around. A small clip that forms part of the perimeter of the hub holds the end of the tape to the hub. At various points around the inside of the shell, guides are provided to ensure that the tape travels in the correct path.

More recent tape cartridges have altered some of the physical aspects of the cassette design but retain the underlying technologies.

Technologies

Tape systems are often described by how they work—that is, the way they record data onto the tape. For example, although the term *streaming tape* that's appended to many tape drives may conjure up images of a cassette gone awry and spewing its guts inside the dashboard of your card (and thence to the wind as you fling it out the window), it actually describes a specific recording mode that requires an uninterrupted flow of data. At least four of these terms—start-stop, streaming, parallel, and serpentine—crop up in the specifications of common tape systems for computers.

Start-Stop Tape

The fundamental difference between tape drives is how they move the tape. Early drives operated in *start-stop mode*—they handled data one block (ranging from 128 bytes to a few kilobytes) at a time and wrote each block to the tape as it was received. Between blocks of data, the drive stopped moving the tape and awaited the next block. The drive had to prepare the tape for each block, identifying the block so that the data could be properly recovered. Watch an old movie with mainframe computers with jittering tape drives, and you'll see the physical embodiment of start-stop tape.

Streaming Tape

When your computer tape drive gets the data diet it needs, bytes flow to the drive in an unbroken stream and the tape runs continuously. Engineers called this mode of operation *streaming tape*. Drives using streaming tape technology can accept data and write it to tape at a rate limited only by the speed the medium moves and the density at which bits are packed—the linear density of the data on the tape. Because the tape does not have to stop between blocks, the drive wastes no time.

Parallel Recording

Just as disk drives divide their platters into parallel tracks, the tape drive divides the tape into multiple tracks across the width of the tape. The number of tracks varies with the drive and the standard it follows.

The first tape machines used with computer systems recorded nine separate data tracks across the width of the tape. The first of these machines used *parallel recording*, in which they spread each byte across their tracks, one bit per track, with one track for parity. A tape was good for only one pass across the read/write head, after which the tape needed to be rewound for storage. Newer tape systems elaborate on this design by laying 18 or 36 tracks across a tape, corresponding to a digital word or double word, written in parallel.

Parallel recording provides a high transfer rate for a given tape speed because multiple bits get written at a time but makes data retrieval time consuming—finding a given byte might require fast forwarding across an entire tape.

Serpentine Recording

Most computer tape systems use multitrack drives but do not write tracks in parallel. Instead, they convert the incoming data into serial form and write that to the tape. Serial recording across multiple tracks results in a recording method called *serpentine recording*.

Serpentine cartridge drives write data bits sequentially across the tape in one direction on one track at a time, continuing for the length of the tape. When the drive reaches the end of the tape, it reverses the direction the tape travels and cogs its read/write head down one step to the next track. At the end of that pass, the drive repeats the process until it runs out of data or fills all the tracks. Figure 17.4 shows the layout of tracks across a tape using four tracks of serpentine recording.

FIGURE 17.4

Layout of four tracks using serpentine recording.

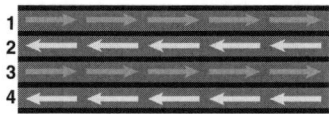

A serpentine tape system can access data relatively quickly by jogging its head between tracks, because it needs to scan only a fraction of the data on the tape for what you want. Additionally, it requires only a single channel of electronics and a single pole in the read/write head, thus lowering overall drive costs. Modern serpentine systems may use over 50 tracks across a tape.

Helical Recording

The basic principle of all the preceding tape systems is that the tape moves past a stationary head. In a *helical scan recording system*, both the head and tape move. Usually multiple rotating heads are mounted on a drum. The tape wraps around the drum outside its protective cartridge. Two arms pull the tape out of the cartridge and wrap it about halfway around the drum (some systems, like unlamented Betamax, wrap tape nearly all the way around the drum). So that the heads travel at an angle across the tape, the drum is canted at a slight angle, about five degrees for eight-millimeter drives and about six degrees for DAT. The result is that a helical tape has multiple parallel tracks that run diagonally across the tape instead of parallel to its edges. These tracks tend to be quite fine—some helical systems put nearly 2000 of them in an inch.

In most helical systems, the diagonal tracks are accompanied by one or more tracks parallel to the tape edge used for storing servo control information. In video systems, one or more parallel audio tracks may also run the length of the tape. Figure 17.5 shows how the data and control tracks are arranged on a helical tape.

FIGURE 17.5

Helical scan recording track layout.

Data tracks

Control track

Helical scan recording can take advantage of the entire tape surface. Conventional stationary-head recording systems must leave blank areas—guard bands—between the tracks containing data. Helical systems can and do overlap tracks. Although current eight-millimeter systems use guard bands, DAT writes the edges of tracks over one another.

This overlapping works because the rotating head drum actually has two (or more) heads on it, and each head writes data at a different angular relationship (called the *azimuth*) to the tracks on the tape. In reading data, the head responds strongly to the data written at the same azimuth as the head and weakly at the other azimuth. In DAT machines, one head is skewed 20 degrees forward from perpendicular to its track; the other head is skewed backward an equal amount.

Formats

Each of these various recording methods, along with physical concerns such as tape width and cartridge design, allow for a nearly infinite range of tape-recording systems. When you try to make sense of backup systems, it often seems like all the possibilities have been tried in commercial products.

Linear Recording Tape Systems

The most straightforward tape systems use simple linear recording. That is, they move the tape past a stationary head just like the very first audio tape recorders. Linear recording is the old reliable in tape technology. The process and methods have been perfected (as much as that is possible) over more than five decades of use.

Open-reel tape is still used in computer systems, but most personal computers use more modern, more compact, and more convenient cassette-style cartridges. The most common of these are patterned after a design the 3M Company first offered using quarter-inch tape as a data-recording medium. First put on the market in 1972, these initial quarter-inch cartridges were designed for telecommunications and data-acquisition applications calling for the storage of serial data, such as programming private business telephone exchanges and recording events. Compared to the cassette, the tape cartridge requires greater precision and smoother operation. To achieve that end, a new mechanical design was invented by Robert von Behren of the 3M Company, who patented it in 1971—the quarter-inch cartridge mechanism.

Instead of using the capstan drive system like cassettes, the quarter-inch cartridge operates with a belt drive system. A thin, isoelastic belt stretches throughout the cartridge mechanism, looping around (and making contact with) both the supply and take-up spools on their outer perimeters. The belt also passes around a rubber drive wheel, which contacts a capstan in the tape drive.

The capstan moves the belt but is cut away with a recess that prevents it from touching the tape. The friction of the belt against the outside of the tape reels drives the tape. This system is gentler to the tape because the driving pressure is spread evenly over a large area of the tape instead of pinching the tape tightly between two rollers. In addition, it provides for smoother tape travel and packing of the tape on the spools. The tape is wound, and the guide and other parts of the mechanism arranged so that the fragile magnetic surface of the tape touches nothing but the read/write head (see Figure 17.6).

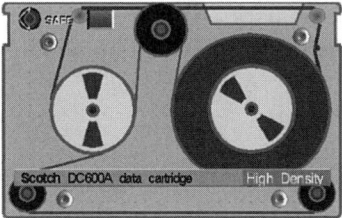

FIGURE 17.6

Quarter-inch cartridge mechanisms (DC-600 style cartridge is shown; the DC2000 is similar but smaller).

For sturdiness, the cartridge is built around an aluminum baseplate. The rest of the cartridge is transparent plastic, allowing the condition of the tape and the mechanism to be readily viewed.

To try to lessen the chaos in the tape cartridge marketplace, a number of tape drive manufacturers—including DEI, Archive, Cipher Data, and Tandberg—met together at the National Computer Conference in Houston in 1982. They decided to form a committee to develop standards so that a uniform class of products could be introduced. The organization took the name, Working Group for Quarter-Inch Cartridge Drive Compatibility, often shortened into QIC committee. In November, 1987, the organization was officially incorporated as Quarter-Inch Cartridge Standards, Inc.

QIC developed a number of standards for data cartridges. But as personal computers became popular, most tape companies realized that the cartridges were just too big. Squeezing a drive to handle a six-by-four cartridge into a standard 5.25-inch drive bay is a challenge; fitting one in a modern 3.5-inch bay is impossible. Seeking a more compact medium, quarter-inch cartridge makers cut their products down to size, reducing tape capacity while preserving the proven drive mechanism. The result was the mini-cartridge. QIC quickly developed standards for the new cartridge.

Because the 3M Company introduced the first mini-cartridge with the designation DC2000, many people in the computer industry persist in calling all mini-cartridges "DC2000-style" cartridges. Mini-cartridges actually come in a variety of designations. As with the current model numbers of DC600-size cartridges, the model designations of most mini-cartridges encode the cartridge capacity as their last digits. For example, a DC2080 cartridge is designed for 80MB capacity; a DC2120 for 120MB.

One big advantage of the smaller cartridges is that drives for them easily fit into standard 3.5-inch bays. The mini-cartridge package measures just under 3.25×2.5×0.625 inches. As originally developed, it held 205 feet of tape with the same nominal quarter-inch width used by larger cartridges, hence the initial "2" in the designation.

After trying to exploit the compact size of the mini-cartridge for years, media-makers decided they had gone too far. They cut too much capacity from their cartridges.

Therefore, they added some extra inches back on the back of the cartridges so that the cartridges would still slide into smaller drives but could hold more tape. Two formats developed: Travan and QIC-EX.

Travan

In 1995, tape- and drive-makers pushed mini-cartridges to yet higher capacities with the simple expedient of making the cartridges bigger so that they could hold more tape. The fruit of the labors of an industry group comprising Conner, Iomega, HP, 3M Company, and Sony was called *Travan* technology.

The increase in cartridge size appears in three dimensions. The cartridges are both wider, deeper, and taller. The added height allows the use of wider tape, the same eight-millimeter (0.315-inch) tape used by the QIC-Wide format, the format pioneered by Sony. The wider tape permits an increase in track count by about 30 percent (from 28 to 36 in the initial Travan format).

In addition, Travan adds an extra half-inch to the width and depth of cartridges. The Travan cartridge measures 0.5×3.6×2.8 inches (HWD), smaller in the front (3.2 inches) than the rear, where the tape spools reside. Internally, the Travan cartridge uses the same 3M mechanism as other quarter-inch cartridges and must be formatted before use.

Although the increase seems modest, it allows the tape capacity to more than double, from 307 feet in a DC2120 cartridge to 750 feet in the Travan. The extra size gives Travan a distinctive shape, basically rectangular with two corners curved in to make sliding in a cartridge easier. Figure 17.7 shows a Travan cartridge.

FIGURE 17.7
A Travan tape cartridge.

The combination of more tracks and greater tape length was sufficient to boost single cartridge capacity to 400MB (uncompressed) in the initial Travan implementation. Nothing about the Travan design impairs making further improvements, so whatever developments add to the capacity of standard mini-cartridges can be directly reflected in increased Travan capacities. In fact, since its introduction, Travan has been improved three times, each change about doubling single-cartridge capacities.

The first change, creating TR-2, boosted the coercivity of the medium and allowed for a 50-percent increase in data density, both in a greater number of tracks and a higher linear density on each track. The next change doubled linear density again, without altering the track count, to create TR-3. Another increase in linear density and matching increase in track count boosted the TR-4 Travan implementation to 4GB per cartridge. Table 17.7 summarizes the characteristics of the various Travan implementations.

TABLE 17.7 Travan Tape Cartridge Specifications

Model	TR-1	TR-2	TR-3	TR-4
Capacity, uncompressed	400MB	800MB	1.6GB	4GB
Capacity, compressed	800MB	1.6GB	3.2GB	8GB
Minimum transfer rate	62.5KBps	62.5KBps	125KBps	567KBps
Maximum transfer rate	125KBps	125KBps	250KBps	567KBps
Media length	750 ft.	750 ft.	750 ft.	740 ft.
Media width	0.315 in.	0.315 in.	0.315 in.	0.315 in.
Media coercivity	550 Oe	900 Oe	900 Oe	900 Oe
Tracks	36	50	50	72
Data density	14,700 ftpi	22,125 ftpi	44,250 ftpi	50,800 ftpi
Interface	Floppy	Floppy	Floppy	SCSI/E-IDE
Read/write compatibility	QIC-80	QIC-3010	3020/3010	3080/3095
Read-only compatibility	QIC-40	QIC-80	QIC-80	QIC-3020

Perhaps the most notable part of the Travan design is its compatibility: A Travan drive accepts standard DC2000 cartridges and QIC-Wide cartridges as well as its own native media—that's two different cartridge sizes and tape widths in one drive. Compatibility extends to both reading and writing all three cartridge styles. The various Travan implementations also feature backward compatibility. The more recent standards can read tapes made under the earlier Travan standards.

QIC-EX

As long as the cartridge in a QIC drive sticks out like Travan, you might as well let it all hang out. That dated cliché underlies the philosophy of QIC-EX. By allowing a cartridge to stick nearly three inches out of the drive, QIC-EX accommodates up to 1000 feet of tape in the QIC format. That's more than double the capacity of ordinary mini-cartridges.

Increase the tape width to QIC-Wide's eight millimeters, and you can fit gigabytes onto a standard tape cartridge, as shown in Figure 17.8.

FIGURE 17.8

*Dimensions of a
QIC-EX tape cartridge.*

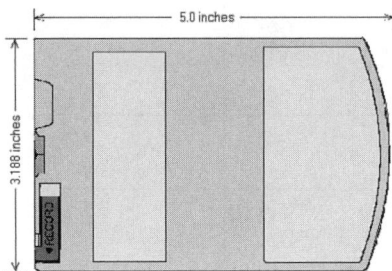

Unlike Travan, which requires a wider drive with a wider throat to accommodate the wider cartridges, the QIC-EX design is the same width as standard mini-cartridges. QIC-EX tapes consequently fit into most mini-cartridge drives to give an instant capacity increase.

Helical-Scan Systems

Although helical-scan recording was originally designed for video signals, it is also an excellent match for digital data. The high tape-to-head speed can translate to high data-transfer rates. Although the narrow data tracks devote but a small area of recording medium to storing information, so small that it increases the noise content of the recorded signal, digital technology handily avoids the noise. As with all digital signals, the electronics of the helical-scan tape system simply ignore most of the noise, and error correction takes care of anything that can't be ignored.

Helical-scan systems are the children of the digital age. They trade the mechanical precision required in the linear-scan systems for servo-controlled designs. Servo-mechanisms in the helical-scan recorder control both the tape speed and head speed to ensure that the read/write head exactly tracks the position of the tracks on the tape. Although servo-electronics can be built with other technologies, digital electronics and miniaturization make the required circuitry trivial, a single control chip. Moreover, servo-control automatically compensates for inaccuracies in the operation and even construction of the tape-transport system. This design allows manufacturers to use less expensive fabrication processes and helps the mechanism age gracefully, adjusting itself for the wear and tear of old age.

Three different helical-scan systems are currently used in tape systems for digital data: eight-millimeter tape, four-millimeter tape (which is formally called the Digital Data Standard), and a proprietary system sold by Pereos.

Eight Millimeter

Probably the most familiar incarnation of eight-millimeter tape is in miniaturized camcorders. Sony pioneered the medium as a compact, high-quality video-recording system. The same tapes were later adapted to data recording by Exabyte Corporation and first released on the computer market in 1987.

In the original Exabyte eight-millimeter digital recording system, the head drum rotated at 1800 revolutions per minute while the tape traveled past it at 10.89 millimeters per second to achieve a track density of 819 per inch and a flux density of 54 kilobits per inch—enough to squeeze 2.5MB on a single cartridge. Improvements extended the capacity to 5MB without compression and up to 10GB with compression. The tape can be rapidly shuttled forward and backward to find any given location (and block of data) within about 15 seconds.

Eight-millimeter drives tend to be quite expensive. Complete systems cost thousands of dollars. A raw drive alone starts at over one thousand dollars. Its primary market is backing up file servers, machines that can benefit from its huge capacity.

Advanced Intelligent Tape

Sony developed an alternative eight-millimeter technology. By incorporating nonvolatile RAM memory into the shell of an eight-millimeter tape, a tape drive can quickly retrieve directory information without the need to scan the tape. It doesn't have to read the tape at all to find out what's there.

This memory is what makes Sony's *Advanced Intelligent Tape* so smart. Each cartridge has 16KB for storing table of contents and file-location information. Each cartridge can store 25MB of uncompressed data. With data compression the AIT system can achieve transfer rates of 6MBps and a capacity of 50MB per cartridge.

Despite being based on eight-millimeter technology, AIT is not backward compatible with the older medium. AIT drives reject conventional eight-millimeter tapes as unsupported media, and hardware write-protection prevents older drives from altering AIT tapes.

Digital Data Storage

Developed originally as a means to record music, the *Digital Data Storage* first saw commercial application as *Digital Audio Tape* (DAT), a name sometimes applied to the system even when it is used for storing computer data. The technology was first released as a computer storage medium in 1989. Using a tape that's nominally four millimeters wide (actually 3.81 mm or 0.150 in, the same as cassette tape), the system is sometimes called *four-millimeter tape*. The thin tape fits into tiny cartridges to store huge amounts of data.

The first DAT system could pack 1.3GB into a cassette measuring only 0.4 × 2.9 × 2.1 inches (HWD). The result was, at the time, the most dense storage of any current

computer tape medium, 114 megabits per square inch on special 1450 oersted metal particle tape (the same material as used by eight-millimeter digital tape systems). A cassette
held either 60 or 90 meters of this tape. The shorter tapes stored 1.3GB; the longer
tapes, 2.0GB.

Under the aegis of Hewlett-Packard and Sony Corporation, in 1990 this format was formalized as DDS, sometimes listed as DDS-1 (to distinguish it from its successors). The
same format underlies DDS-DC, which adds *data compression* to the drive to increase
capacity. Although DDS at first was listed in some literature (and in an earlier edition of
this book) as an abbreviation for Digital Data Standard, the DDS organization that coordinates the specification renders it officially as *Digital Data Storage*.

In 1993, the same companies updated the standard to DDS-2, doubling both the data-
transfer speed and capacity of the system as well as introducing new 120-meter cassettes
using a tape coated with a metal powder medium.

In 1995, the standard got upped again to DDS-3, which can pack up to 12GB on each
cartridge or 24GB of compressed data. In addition, the DDS-3 standard allows for transfers at double the DDS-2 rate with speed potential of up to 1.5 megabits per second (dis-
counting the effects of compression). DDS-3 uses the same tape media as its predecessor
format but increases the data density to 122 kilobits per inch. The key to this higher density is a new technology termed *Partial Response Maximum Likelihood* (PRML).

Announced in 1998, DDS-4 further enhances the four-millimeter format to provide 20GB
of storage on a single tape. Part of the capacity increase results from longer tapes, up to
155 meters per cartridge. In addition, DDS-4 reduces track width by 25 percent. Because
of its higher data density, DDS-4 also gains a bit of speed. The standard allows for transfer rates from 1 to 3Mbps.

DDS-5, originally planned for the year 2001, aimed for a native capacity of 40GB per cartridge but has yet to be formally released. The DDS Web site has not been updated since
1999. Table 17.8 summarizes the various DDS implementations.

TABLE 17.8 Summary of DDS Specifications

Format	DDS	DDS-DC	DDS-2	DDS-3	DDS-4	DDS-5
Year introduced	1989	1991	1993	1995	1999	2001
Cartridge capacity	1.3GB	2.0GB	4.0GB	12GB	20GB	40GB
Transfer rate	183Kbps	183Kbps	360 to 750Kbps	720Kbps to 1.5Mbps	1 to 3Mbps	1 to 6Mbps
Tape length	60 m	90 m	120 m	125 m	155 m	N/A

In a DDS drive, the tape barely creeps along, requiring about three seconds to move an inch—a tape speed of 8 millimeters per second. The head drum, however, spins rapidly at 2000 revolutions per minute, putting down 1869 tracks across a linear inch of tape with flux transitions packed 61 kilobits per inch.

The first DAT systems shared tapes with audio DAT recorders. Since that time, however, the later DDS standards have required improved magnetic media with higher coercivities. As a result, to get the highest reliability you must use a tape made to the standard that matches your drive. Although you may be able to read older tapes in a later DDS drive, successful writing (where coercivity comes into play) is less probable. Similarly, DDS tape will not work in your DAT recorder. The DDS Manufacturers Group, the organization that coordinates DDS activities, has also developed a technology called *Media Recognition System* that is able to detect audio DAT tapes. The DDS organization has developed distinctive logos for each level of the DDS hierarchy so that you can readily distinguish tapes and drives. Figure 17.9 shows the logos for DDS-2 through DDS-4.

FIGURE 17.9
The official DDS-2, DDS-3, and DDS-4 logos.

DDS-2

DDS-3

DDS-4

Hewlett-Packard and Sony hold intellectual property rights to DDS technology, and all drives using DDS must be licensed by them. The DDS Manufacturers Group maintains a Web site at `www.dds-tape.com`.

Alas, all tape technologies have lost their luster. They are all hard-pressed to keep up with the huge increases in disk storage densities and capacities. The tape systems with adequate capacity for backing up today's hard disk drives cost more than most personal computers. Consequently, most individual users prefer other backup methods, such as extra hard disks, networked storage (including backing up over the Internet), DVD recorders, and simply ignoring the need for backing up. Data centers rely on a few super-capacity backup systems that are priced well beyond the reach of individuals. Tape is therefore not quite dead. You can use either a mini-cartridge or DDS system for backing up a few gigabytes (about 20GB without compression with today's drives). That should be sufficient for keeping a spare copy of your personal files (including such megabyte-hogs as Computer-Aided Design drawings, graphics, and videos). However, DVD is probably the best, lowest-cost bet for backup today.

Optical Storage (CD and DVD)

Optical media are today's most important software distribution method, for both computer programs and entertainment such as music and videos. Add writing capabilities, and your optical drive can also back up your hard disk or make discs to send files to friends or production houses. You can even make your own CDs for your stereo system or turn home movies into private-label DVDs. And a read/write optical drive can even substitute as your primary mass storage system should your hard disk fail and you have patience even a saint would envy. When the new Mount Rainier system makes its way into operating systems, your CD drive will likely fully take over the role formerly assigned to floppy disks.

Although the CD and DVD are often treated as two different systems, they share a common heritage and technology. The DVD is really only the second generation of optical disc storage for computers. The major technical differences are a result of improvements in technology over the nearly two-decade history of the CD medium. No revolutionary changes separate the two. In fact, the biggest changes only reflect new formats created to take advantage of the larger capacity the technical refinements permit.

History

Developed by the joint efforts of Philips and Sony Corporation in the early 1980s, when the digital age was taking over the stereo industry, the Compact Disc was first and foremost a high-fidelity delivery medium. The CD was initially released in the United States in 1983 (in Japan the

CD got a one-year head start, officially released in 1982 according to Sony), and within five years it had replaced the vinyl phonograph record as the premiere stereophonic medium because of its wide range, lack of noise, near invulnerability to damage, and long projected life.

The CD was designed chiefly for capacity and real-time playback of music. Engineers set many of the practical aspects of the CD around the requirements of music recording. For example, they selected the 70 or so minutes of music capacity as one of the core specifications in designing the system, because a primary design goal was to fit the entire Beethoven's Ninth Symphony, without interruption, on a single disc. As originally conceived, its storage was not reliable enough for computers. And computers had little use for it. At the time, they were choking when confronted with a few megabytes. CDs wielded hundreds of them.

But as the CD rose to prominence as the primary distribution medium for prerecorded music, computer engineers began to look at the shiny medium with a covetous gleam in their eyes. They saw the digital storage provided by the disc as a repository for more megabytes than anyone had reason to use. After all, data is data (okay, data *are* data) regardless of whether the bytes encode a symphony or an operating system. When someone got the idea that a plastic puck that cost a buck to make and retailed for $16.99 could be filled with last year's statistics and marketed for $249, the rush was on. The Compact Disc became the CD-ROM (which stands for Compact Disc, Read-Only Memory), and megabytes came to the masses.

Soon sound became only one of the applications of the Compact Disc medium. The original name had to be extended to distinguish musical CDs from all the others. To computer people, the CD of the stereo system became the CD-DA, Compact Disc, Digital Audio.

Engineers tinkered with the storage format of the CD to stuff the discs with other kinds of data. Philips optimized the medium for interactive applications—multimedia presentations and games—to create CD-I, which stands for *Compact Disc Interactive*. Some even thought that compression—a lot of it—could fit video on the discs. *Compact Disc-Video* succeeded in squeezing video on the little discs, but not very much and not very well. Viewable video had to await another string of developments and the new generation of optical storage.

DVD was the needed innovation. The initials stand for Digital Versatile Disc, although the system was first termed the Digital Video Disc before the adoption of the current technical standards.

The roots of DVD go back to two competing proposals, both of which had the primary intent of storing video on a disc the same size as a CD. The original developers of the Compact Disc, Philips and Sony, backed a format they called MMCD for *Multimedia Compact Disc* (they owned the CD name so they took advantage of it). The other camp, led by Matsushita, Time Warner, and Toshiba, developed their own, incompatible format they called *SD*.

For a while, the industry appeared poised for a repeat of the Beta/VHS debacle that put two mutually incompatible videotape cassette formats on the market for nearly a decade. In September, 1995, the industry appeared to come to its senses, hammering out a single standard agreeable to both camps. To distinguish it from the earlier efforts and reflect the expanded range of possibilities afforded by the new medium, the format was rechristened with *Versatile* replacing the *Video* of the earlier proposals. Credit for developing the initial standard is generally given to an industry consortium that included Hitachi, JVC, Matsushita, Mitsubishi, Philips, Sony, Thompson, Time Warner, and Toshiba.

As with CDs, each application format for the DVD has its own subdesignation. These include DVD-Video for video applications, such as the distribution of motion pictures; DVD-Audio, as a high-quality audio disc with capabilities far beyond today's 16-bit discs; and DVD-ROM for the distribution of computer software and other data.

When it came to developing a recordable format for DVD, however, the consensus fell apart. As this is written, promoters advocate three read-only formats under the names DVD-R(A), DVD-R(G), and DVD+R. Read/write systems are equally confused with four competing standards, including DVD-Multi, DVD-RAM, DVD-RW, and DVD+RW.

Although the differences between these recordable standards is blurring—each one now boasts a full 4.7 gigabytes-per-disc capacity as well as some degree of compatibility with home DVD players—the animosity is not fading. The industry is split into two camps, the "plus" camp and the "hyphen" camp. The former, the promoters of the "plus" systems of DVD+R and DVD+RW, include Dell, Hewlett-Packard, Mitsubishi, Philips, Ricoh, Sony, and Thomson. The "hyphen" camp promotes the DVD-Multi format, which brings together DVD-R(A) and DVD-R(G) as well as DVD-RAM and DVD-RW. The DVD Forum, an organization that includes nearly all consumer electronics manufacturers (with the notable exceptions of Dell and Hewlett-Packard but including the other "plus" camp members), maintains the official standards.

Despite the wide variety of formats now used in computer optical storage systems, the underlying technology for all remains the same—a spinning disc is the target for the laser beam.

Medium

The heart of both the Compact Disc and Digital Versatile Disc systems is the disc medium itself. Its design, based on a pattern of dots that can be read optically but mass-produced mechanically, makes optical storage the fastest and least expensive medium for duplicating hundreds of megabytes of data.

The flat disc shape also offers a distinct advantage. Machines can mold copies of discs by stamping them between dies instead of filling a three-dimensional mold with a casting liquid. This stamping process has a long history. It has been used for over a century in duplicating recorded music—first with shellac and clay to copy Emil Berliner's first phonograph records, then with vinyl for old-fashioned record albums. Duplicating CDs and DVDs requires extra precision and a few extra steps, but it remains essentially the same stamping process.

The disc-duplicating process begins with a disc master. A mastering machine equipped with a high-powered laser blasts the pits in a blank disc—the recording master—to make an original mechanical recording. Then the master is made into a mold called a *stamper*. A negative copy is electroplated onto the master, then separated from it, leaving the master unscathed. One master can make many duplicate molds, each of which is then mounted in a stamping machine. The machine heats the mold and injects a glob of plastic into it. After giving the plastic a chance to cool, the stamping machine ejects the disc and takes another gulp of plastic.

In making a CD or DVD, another machine takes the newly stamped disc and aluminizes it so that it has a shiny, mirror-like finish. To protect the shine, the disc is laminated with a clear plastic cover that guards the mechanical pattern from chemical and physical abuse (oxidation and scratches). Finally, another machine silk-screens a label on the disc. It is packaged, shrink-wrapped, and sent off to a warehouse or store.

The DVD process differs in that a disc can have multiple layers. In the current process, a separate master is made for each layer. The layers are stamped out separately, each only half as thick as a complete disc. The two complete layers are then fastened together with a special transparent glue.

In theory, a disc could be any size, and setting a standard is essentially an exercise in pragmatism. Size is related to playing time. The bigger the disc, the more data it holds, all else being equal. If you want to store a lot of data, a big disc has its allure. On the other hand, a platter the size of a wading pool would win favor with no one but plastics manufacturers. You can also increase the capacity of a disk by shrinking the size of every stored bit of digital code, but the practical capabilities of technology limit how small you can make a bit. In trying to craft a standard, engineers have to balance the convenience of small size, the maximum practical storage density, and a target for the amount of information they need to store.

In the late 1970s when Philips and Sony were developing the CD, the maximum practical storage density of the then-current technology was about 150 megabytes per square inch. The arbitrary design goal of about 70 minutes per disc side (enough room for Beethoven's Ninth) dictated about 650MB at the data rate selected (which itself was a tradeoff between data requirements and sound quality). The result was that the design engineers found a

120-millimeter (that's about 4.6 inches) platter to be their ideal compromise. A nice, round 100 millimeters was just too small for Beethoven.

For portable applications, the engineers came up with a smaller form factor for discs, 80 mm (about 3.1 inches). Once plated and given its protective plastic coating, either size of CD is about 1.2 mm (about 0.05 inch) thick.

For DVDs, the same sizes have been retained. This expedient allows the same equipment used to make CDs with only minor modification to stamp out DVDs. In addition, the same drives that read and write can also use CDs, whether in your home entertainment system or inside your computer.

The DVD medium differs from conventional CDs in that discs can use both sides for recording data and have multiple layers on each side. (Although two-sided CDs are possible, they have been commercially produced only rarely.) As noted earlier, current technology fabricates each DVD in two pieces, each 0.6 mm thick, which are later cemented together. Cemented back-to-back, the disc gains two sides. Cemented so the face of one butts the back of the other, the disc gains two layers. The latter configuration allows you to play both recorded surfaces without flipping the disc over. To shift between layers, the DVD player needs only to refocus its laser beam. The process is fast—it takes only milliseconds—and, with adequate buffering, can be completely invisible to your computer and its software. There's no pause in the data streaming from the drive.

Under the DVD standards, eight possible types of disc are currently defined, depending on the size, number of sides, and number of layers. Table 18.1 summarizes the various DVD disc types and their storage capacities.

TABLE 18.1   DVD Disc Types and Capacities

Name	Diameter	Capacity	Sides	Layers
DVD-1	8 cm	1.36GB	1	1
DVD-2	8 cm	2.48GB	1	2
DVD-3	8 cm	2.72GB	2	1
DVD-4	8 cm	4.95GB	2	2
DVD-5	12 cm	4.38GB	1	1
DVD-9	12 cm	7.95GB	1	2
DVD-10	12 cm	8.75GB	2	1
DVD-18	12 cm	15.9GB	2	2

Almost all discs made thus far conform to the DVD-5 standard. This format was tailored to the needs of the motion picture and videocassette industry. It allows a standard

Hollywood-style movie to fit on a single disc. Unlike videocassettes, however, the movie will have digital quality images and sound—and not just stereo sound but full eight-channel surround. In that the cost of duplicating DVDs is a fraction of that of videocassettes, the software industry will be urging you into the new medium as fast as it can. In that you should easily be able to see and hear the difference, you shouldn't need too much encouragement.

The DVD format allows your disc drive to read the two layers in either of two ways, determined when the disc is recorded. Parallel tracking path (PTP) tracks are read in *parallel*. Your drive reads both layers at nearly the same time, in parallel. In practice, the two tracks may contain the same material in different formats—one might hold a standard aspect-ratio image and the other a widescreen image—allowing you to switch between them instantly. Opposite tracking path (OTP) tracks are read sequentially. The drive reads one layer to its end, then reverses and reads the second layer in the *opposite* direction. To minimize changeover time when the read head reverses direction, the drive starts reading the bottom layer from the inside out and then switches to reading the inside layer from the outside in. Discs that use OTP tracks are sometimes describe as *reverse-spiral dual-layer* (RSDL) discs. Some disc producers prefer them because they offer a longer (nearly) continuous playing time.

The first DVDs were mostly two-sided, single-layer DVD-10 discs, usually a motion picture in full-frame format on one side and widescreen on the other. One reason was that drives capable of reading two-layer discs required more development, but all DVD drives can handle two-sided discs, providing you physically flip the disc to access the other side.

A modern DVD drive distinguishes the separate layers of a multiple-layer disc by selective focus. To read the bottom layer, it simple focuses on its pits. To read the upper layer, it focuses through the semitransparent lower layer to the upper layer. The separation between the two layers, about 20 to 70 microns, is sufficient for each layer to have a distinct-enough focus for them to be distinguished. The pattern in the layer that is out of focus blurs together so that individual bits blur together and don't register.

Four-layer DVDs, which have two layers of data on each of their two sides, require a not-quite-perfected manufacturing process that writes two layers simultaneously on each of the two halves that are cemented to make the completed disc.

Materials

The recording materials used by read-only, recordable, and rewritable optical disc systems are quite different because each system operates on different physical principles. Read-only media depend on fast, mechanical reproduction of discs. Recordable media require a one-use material with a long life. Rewritable media require a recording material that can be cycled between states so that it can be erased and reused.

Read-Only

Every Compact Disc is a three-layer sandwich. The bulk of the disc is a transparent poly-carbonate plastic substrate called the *carrier*. It is made from the material injected into the stamping press—the machine smashes a warm glob of raw plastic flat and embosses the spiral pattern of pits encoding the digital data into one of its surfaces. The aluminum coating that makes the disc reflective (except for the data pits) is vapor-plated on the poly-carbonate substrate to a thickness of about one-tenth micron. To protect the aluminum from oxidation (which would darken it and make the pattern of pits difficult or impossible to read), it is protected with a final layer of lacquer about 200 microns thick.

The laser in a disc drive reads from the *reflective* side of the disc. That is, the laser reads through the thick carrier to the aluminized layer. The label of the disc gets silk-screened onto the thin protective lacquer coating. Note that the coating is about one thousand times thinner than the carrier on the reflective side. As a result, a compact disc is more vulnerable to damage on the label side. Although a scratch here may not interfere with the reading of the disc, it may allow air to come into contact with the aluminize layer and oxidize it, thus ruining the disc.

The construction of multilayer DVDs is similar, except the polycarbonate carrier is only half as thick. Double-sided and double-layer discs cement two half-thickness discs together. DVD-5 discs (single-sided, single-layer) cement a dummy half-thickness disc to the back of the one active layer. In any case, in the center of the disk, the protective plastic layer is replaced with a transparent plastic cement, which seals the aluminize layer on the lower half of the disc and binds the upper half to it.

Compared to vinyl phonograph records or magnetic discs, CDs and DVDs offer a storage medium that is long-lived and immune to most abuse. The protective clear plastic layer resists physical tortures (in fact, Compact Discs and one-sided DVDs are more vulnerable to scratches on their label side than the side that is scanned with the playback laser). The data pits are sealed within layers of the disc itself and are never touched by anything other than a light beam. These discs never wear out and acquire errors only when you abuse them purposely or carelessly (for example, by scratching them against one another when not storing them in their plastic jewel boxes). Although error correction prevents errors from showing up in the data, a bad scratch can prevent a disc from being read at all. The smaller features used by the DVD system for storing data are more vulnerable (one scratch can wipe out more stored data), but the DVD system has a more robust error-correction system that more than compensates.

Recordable

Discs used in CD recorders differ in two ways from those used by conventional CD play-ers—besides being blank when they leave the factory. CD-R discs require a recordable surface, something that the laser in the CD recorder can alter to write data. This surface takes the form of an extra layer of dye on the CD-R disc. Recordable CDs also have a formatting spiral permanently stamped into each disc.

As with other CDs, a recordable disc has a protective bottom layer or carrier of clear polycarbonate plastic that gives the disc its strength. A thin reflective layer is plated on the polycarbonate to deflect the CD beam back so that it can be detected by the drive. Between this reflective layer and the normal protective top lacquer layer of the disc, a CD-R disc has a special dye layer. The dye is photoreactive and changes its reflectivity in response to the high-power mode of the CD recorder's laser. Figure 18.1 shows a cross-section of a typical CD-R disc.

FIGURE 18.1

Cross-section of recordable CD media using cyanine dye (not to scale).

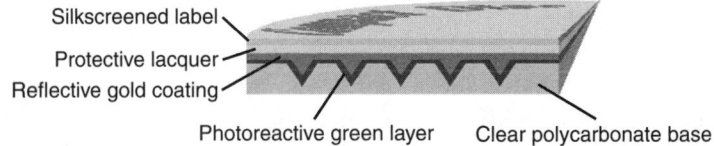

Silkscreened label

Protective lacquer

Reflective gold coating

Photoreactive green layer   Clear polycarbonate base

The CD-R medium records information by burning the dye layer in the disc. By increasing the power of the laser in the drive from 4 to 11 milliwatts, its beam heats the dye layer to about 250 degrees (Celsius). At this temperature, the dye-layer melts and the carrier expands to take its place, creating a nonreflective pit within the disc.

Colored Substrate CD-Rs, sometimes simply called *Color CD-Rs*, dye the polycarbonate substrate a pleasing tint. The most popular colors include black, blue, orange, purple, and red. The dye has absolutely no effect on the digital code that's written to the disc, so it does not affect the data or music stored on a CD.

The color of the substrate should not be confused with the color of the recording medium. Three different compounds are commonly used for photoreactive dyes used by CD-R discs, and each of these dyes has a characteristic color. These include green, gold, and blue.

- **Green**. The dye used in green CD-R discs is based on a cyanine compound. The Taiyo Yuden company developed this photoreactive dye, which was used for the first CD-R discs, including those used during the development of the CD-R standards. Even now green CD-R discs are believed to be more forgiving laser power variations during the read and write processes. The green cyanine dye is believed to be permanent enough to give green CD-R discs a useful life of about 75 years. In addition to Taiyo Yuden, several companies including Kodak, Ricoh, TDK, and Verbatim make or have made green CD-R discs.

- **Gold**. Gold CD-R discs used a phthalocyanine dye developed by Mitsui Toatsu Chemicals. The chief advantage of gold over green discs is longer life, because the dye is less sensitive to bleaching by ambient light. If it were on a dress or shirt, it would be more colorfast. Gold CD-R discs are believed to have a useful life of about 100 years. Some people believe that gold discs are also better for high-speed (2× or 4×) recording than are green discs. Mitsui Toatsu and Kodak manufacture most gold CD-R discs.

- **Blue**. The most recent of the CD shades is blue, a color that results from using cyanine with an alloyed silver substrate. The material is proprietary and patented by Verbatim. According to some reports, it is more resistant to ultraviolet radiation than either green or gold dyes and makes reliable discs with low block error rates.

Some manufacturers use multiple layers of dyes on their discs, sometimes even using two different dyes. The multiple-layer CD-R discs are often described as green-green, gold-gold, or green-gold, depending on the colors of the various layers.

Additionally, the reflective layers of recordable CDs also vary in color. They may be silver or gold, which subtly alters the appearance of the dye. The basic reflective layer looks silver because it is made from aluminum. Gold discs have actual gold added to the mix to increase the lifespan of the medium, which also makes the discs look better—golden.

 **NOTE** At one time, manufacturers believed gold discs could endure for 100 years, compared to 30 years for mere silver. The makers of silver-based discs now also claim a 100-year span. In that the medium itself is less than 20 years old, no one knows for sure.

With current CD drives, there is no functional difference between the different CD-R colors, be they a result of tinting the substrate, the dye, or the reflective layer—all appear the same hue to the monochromatic laser of a CD drive that glows at a wavelength of 780 nanometers. All the current CD-R materials reliably yield approximately the same degree of detectable optical change. In the past, however, early CD-ROM readers had varying sensitivities to the materials used in CD-R discs and would reliably read one color but not another. Consequently, lore about one color or kind of disc being better overall than the others arose. The major differences in discs result from mechanical tolerances (how well the manufacturer maintains the perfect spiral of the track) than they do from the color of the disc. Poorly performing discs are simply badly made, regardless of color.

No matter the dye used, recordable CD media are not as durable as commercially stamped CDs. They require a greater degree of care. They are photosensitive, so you should not expose them to direct sunlight or other strong light sources. The risk of damage increases with exposure. The label side of recordable CDs is often protected only by a thin lacquer coating. This coating is susceptible to damage from solvents such as acetone (finger nail polish remover) and alcohol. Many felt-tip markers use such solvents for their inks, so you should never use them for marking on recordable CDs. The primary culprits are so-called permanent markers, which you can usually identify by the strong aroma of their solvents. Most fine-point pen-style markers use aqueous inks, which are generally safe on CD surfaces. Do not use ballpoint pens, fountain pens, pencils, or other sharp-tipped markers on recordable CDs because they may scratch through the lacquer surface and damage the data medium.

The safest means of labeling a recordable CD is using a label specifically made for the recordable CD medium. Using other labels is not recommended because they may contain solvents that will attack the lacquer surface of the CD. Larger labels may also unbalance the disc and make reading it difficult for some CD players. In any case, once you put a label on a recordable CD, do not attempt to remove it. Peeling off the label likely will tear off the protective lacquer and damage the data medium.

Eraseable/Rewritable

The CD-RW system is based on *phase-change* media. That is, the reflective layer in the disc is made from a material that changes in reflectivity depending on whether it is in an amorphous or crystalline state. The most common medium is an alloy of antimony, indium, silver, and tellurium, which has an overall silver color.

In its crystalline state, the medium has a reflectivity of about 15 to 25 percent. In its amorphous state, the reflectivity falls a few percent—enough to be reliably detected by the laser-based disc-reading system.

A blank disc has all its reflective medium in its crystalline state. To record data, the drive increases laser power to between 8 and 15 milliwatts and heats the medium to above its 500 to 700-degree (Celsius) melting point. The operating is straightforward and equivalent to the CD-R writing process, except for laser power.

CD-RW discs typically use a fine metal alloy for their phase-change medium, coating it on the substrate in 8 to 12 layers. Some sources state that the phase-change media are more stable than the one-use CD-R media and therefore can preserve your data for decades longer.

Erasing the CD-RW disc complicates the recording process. To completely erase a disc and restore it to its original crystalline state, the disc must be annealed. The reflective layer is heated to about 200 degrees Celsius and held at that temperature while the material recrystallizes. The first CD-RW systems required that you entirely erase a disc to reuse it, a time-consuming process. Although the heating and recrystallization took only a tiny fraction of a second for each spot of data, erasing an entire disc required about 37 minutes. Most modern drives use on-the-fly erasing, selectively annealing small areas of the disc with the laser at moderate power as they need to be reused. The annealed areas may be rewritten with higher laser power.

Physical Format

The medium provides space to store information, but a complete storage system requires something more. It needs a standardized method of organizing that information. That organization may take several levels—a physical level and one or more logical levels. The physical level or format determines how densely information fits onto the medium and how it is accessed. The logical level determines how it is addressed and used.

The physical format of the Compact Disc and Digital Versatile Disc shares a characteristic with hard disks that's the same with most disc-based media—the information is arranged *around* the disc in long arcs. But whereas hard disks and floppy disks make those arcs into concentric tracks, the CD and DVD turn the arc into a long spiral. As a result, CDs don't have tracks like hard disks. They have one continuous track. DVDs have a multiple tracks but only one on each layer.

The difference is that hard disks are meant to be a random-access medium. CDs and DVDs are designed for sequential access. The CD was optimized for storing music, which usually is a continuous and uninterrupted stream of data. The DVD was primarily optimized for video, which also requires a continuous and uninterrupted stream. In scanning a single spiral track, the reading mechanism never has to pause to jog to a new position. As long as it follows the track, it's where it needs to be.

CDs and DVDs also differ from hard and floppy disks in that they do not spin at a constant rate. Drives adjust the speed of the spin so that they read the same number of data pits of the same size in any given period. Technically speaking, hard and floppy disks spin with *constant angular velocity*. In any given period (say, a millisecond), the disk always rotates by the same-size angle. In contrast, CDs and DVDs are a *constant linear velocity medium*. In any given period, they spin the same linear length of track past the reading mechanism. As a result, near the center of a CD or DVD, where the diameter is small, the disc must spin faster to present the same length of track to the reading mechanism.

The actual linear velocity used by the original Compact Disc system was 1.2 meters per second. As a result, the spin varied from about 400 revolutions per minute (RPM) at the inner diameter to about 200 RPM at the outside edge. Higher-speed drives, discussed later, spin at multiples of this rate. Under the basic Digital Versatile Disc standard, a single-layer disc spins at a constant linear velocity of 3.49 meters per second. As a result, a disc's spin rate must vary from 600 RPM at the outer edge to about 1200 RPM at the inner edge of the recordable area. Multilayer discs spin somewhat faster, 3.68 meters per second. Although DVD drives in computers may spin at faster rates, the DVD players you connect to your video system are locked to this speed.

With each spin of a disc, the track advances outward from the center of the disc, a distance called the *track pitch*. In the case of CDs, the track pitch is 1.6 micrometers. The individual pits on the track that encode data bits are at least 0.83 micrometers long. The raw data rate at the basic speed of the CD system is 4.3218 megabits per second. In original form as an audio playback device, the actual data throughput was 150 kilobytes per second (1.2 megabits per sec) after demodulating, decoding, error-correcting, and formatting the raw signal.

DVD storage is considerably denser. Most significantly, all measurements can be smaller because the DVD system uses a shorter wavelength laser (650 to 680 nanometers compared to 780 nanometers used by CDs). The standard DVD track pitch measures 0.74 microns. On a single-layer disc, each data pit is about 0.40 micron long. On double-layer discs, pits measure 0.44 micron. The basic data rate for DVD is 26.16 megabits per second. Subtract out the overhead, and the net rate is about 11.08 megabits per second. Table 18.2 summarizes the physical format of CDs and DVDs.

TABLE 18.2   CD and DVD Physical Formats

	CD	Single-Layer DVD	Double-Layer DVD
Disc diameter	120 or 80 mm	120 or 80 mm	120 or 80 mm
Track pitch	1.6 nm	0.74 nm.	0.74 nm
Standard read velocity	1.2 m/sec	3.49 m/sec	3.68 m/sec
Minimum pit length	0.83 micron	0.4 micron	0.44 micron
Laser wavelength	780 nm	680 nm	680 nm
Basic read rate	4.3218Mbits/sec	26.16Mbits/sec	26.16Mbits/sec

Both CD-R and CD-RW blank discs (as well as their DVD equivalents) have a physical format already laid down on them. Each has one continuous spiral track at the standard pitch (1.6 microns for CDs). In addition, this track *wobbles* with a period of 22.05 kilohertz and an excursion of 0.3 microns. That is, the smooth spiral actually acts as a superimposed S-shape. The CD drive detects this wobble and uses it to control the rotation rate of the disc. The wobble is frequency-modulated by a one kilohertz signal that provides an absolute timebase for the drive.

Drives

The hundreds or thousands of megabytes on your CDs and DVDs would do you no good without a means for reading them. That means is the optical disc drive. A CD drive or CD-ROM reader gives you access only to CDs, be they audio or data discs. All DVD drives can read both CD and DVD discs, although early drives often cannot read discs written with CD-R and CD-RW drives.

With the price difference between CD and DVD drives disappearing, there's less reason than ever to consider a CD drive. A DVD drive will do everything the CD drive does (but likely better). Performance and compatibility are no longer issues. Consequently, in any new computer, a DVD drive is the preferred option.

All optical disc drives in computers can play back audio CDs. The multimedia standards require that CD-ROM drives on multimedia computers have both a front panel headphone jack and volume control. Of course, the multimedia PC standards date back to a time when decent speakers connected to a computer were as rare as bagpipes in a symphony. Today's drives get around needing the extra jacks because all drives have an audio connector on their rear panels for linking to your computer's sound system. This connector provides analog audio—that is, the sound from a disc that has already been decoded from its original digital format. Drives also have standard mass storage interface jacks (typically AT Attachment or SCSI) to send digital data to your computer.

In theory, you can recover digital audio through this connection. Drives differ in their ability to deliver usable audio in digital form, however, a feature called *digital audio extraction* (DAE). For example, if you wanted to capture a track from an audio CD to convert into an MP3 file, you would need a drive that supports digital audio extraction. All current drives support DAE. Older CD drives with the AT Attachment interface often had difficulty with DAE (if they supported the feature at all). You may encounter problems if you try to use one of these older drives to capture audio.

Dedicated home DVD players have video jacks but the DVD drives in computers do not. At one time, decent video playback in your computer required that the DVD reader plug into an *MPEG decoder* that slid into an expansion slot and directly linked to your computer's video system. As the microprocessors and video systems in computers gained speed, however, the complex decoding job was readily assumed by software, a special MPEG video codec.

Speed

When Philips and Sony originally propounded the Compact Disc system, memory was expensive and computers were only for hobbyists. Players had to read audio data from each disc at the same rate as it was to be played. Higher speeds were irrelevant. Once computers adopted the CD, however, audio speed became a horrendous holdup. Audio CD speed was lower than a modern floppy disk, and floppy disks were too slow.

Data, unlike music, need not abide by the constraints of real-time playback. It wasn't long before computer engineers took advantage of a simple expedient to speed up the CD drives connected to computers. They made the discs spin faster...and faster...and faster. From humble beginnings of only twice as fast as ordinary audio CDs, they have revved up to as high as 50 times faster.

Drive-makers describe the speed of their products using the x-factor. The base speed of an audio CD drive is 1×. A 2× drive spins twice as fast. A 12× drive spins 12 times faster, and so on.

After about 12×, the rotation rates for CDs become awesome. When reading from the inside of the disk, a 12× rate amounts to about 3600 RPM. At the outer edge, the disc spins at half that rate. Higher speed factors (for example, 20×, 36×, or 50×) are comparably faster. Not only is spinning the disc at these rates a challenge, altering the spin speed from the inner to outer reaches of the disc is tricky and time consuming. The need to change speeds can really slow down random access.

In data applications, a constant data rate is unnecessary. With that gem of wisdom in mind, drive-makers developed CD players with a constant spin rate that, with a logic peculiar to the computer market, are known as *variable-speed drives*. Although the spin rate is constant, the data rate the drives deliver is not. It is twice as high at the outer edge of the disc as it is at the inner edge. The x-factor of the drive varies with the data rate.

As any cynic would expect, drive manufacturers invariably quote the *fastest* speed that variable-speed drives can possibly deliver. In practical use, drives almost never achieve this rate. Because these "multispeed" drives actually spin their discs at a constant rate (that is, at a constant *angular* velocity), at smaller diameters, the data rate (and the x-factor) is lower than at larger diameters near the outside edge of the disc. But the data on optical discs starts at the inside of the track spiral and continues to the outside. Consequently, variable-speed drives read (or write) at their top speed only at the very end of a completely full disc. Most discs aren't filled to capacity, so the highest speed areas of the disc aren't often used—and variable speed drives rarely achieve the high speed at which they are rated. A few more reputable computer-makers describe variable-speed drives by listing both their slowest and fastest speed, such as 12/24×.

On the other hand, variable-speed drives have an advantage in random access. Because they spin your discs at a constant rate, you don't have to wait for the drive to alter its speed to match the rate required at a particular place on the disc.

Note, too, that high-speed drives impose an access penalty. Drives with faster speed ratings require more time to spin your discs up to the proper speed. That means you have to wait longer after you slide a disc into the drive before you can read it. The problem is particularly severe with portable computers, which stop their discs from spinning after a minute or so to conserve power. Each time the drive powers down, you have to wait for it to spin the disc back up to speed before you can read from it.

The x-factor for DVD drives is not the same as for CD drives. As with the CD, the DVD speed ratings are pegged to the base data rate of the original video-only DVD system. The linear velocity of the DVD system is about 2.98 times faster than the linear velocity of the CD. But drive electronics don't care about linear speed. They lock onto the data rate. The data format of the CD has larger features than those of DVDs. The minimum pit length, for example, is 0.83 microns for CDs and only 0.4 for DVDs. For a given data rate, the CD must spin about twice as fast as a DVD to produce the same data rate, the 26.16Mbps basic read rate of DVDs. Add the increased linear velocity to the change required by feature size and read rate, and the result is that a 1× DVD drive best reads data at about six times the base CD rate. Consequently, every DVD "×" is worth about six "×" from a CD drive. Table 18.3 gives a comparison of some common CD and DVD speeds (assuming a constant data rate).

TABLE 18.3   Comparison of CD and DVD Drive Speed Factors

CD Factor	DVD Factor	Raw Data Rate
1×	0.17×	4.32Mbits/sec
2×	0.33×	8.64Mbits/sec
4×	0.67×	17.3Mbits/sec
6×	1×	26.2Mbits/sec
12×	2×	52.4Mbits/sec
18×	3×	78.6Mbits/sec
20×	3.3×	86.4Mbits/sec
24×	4×	105Mbits/sec
30×	5×	131Mbits/sec
36×	6×	157Mbits/sec
40×	6.7×	173Mbits/sec

Because the coding system used by DVDs is more efficient than that used by CDs, a DVD drive extracts more information at a given raw data rate. The user data rate from a 1× DVD drive *reading a DVD* is about nine times that of a 1× CD drive *reading a CD*.

In general, a faster drive is a better drive—providing you can put up with the extended spin-up times of really quick disc drives. Some software makes particular speed demands from CD drives. The minimum speed requirement usually is in the range of 4× to 6×. All CD drives in new computers deliver at least 12×, so you should encounter no problem with software speed compatibility. Similarly, the base DVD rate is fast enough for most applications, although you may prefer the quicker load times afforded by a 4× or faster DVD drive.

When you play audio from CDs or movies from DVDs, high drive speeds and x-factors make no difference. A faster drive will not produce a higher-quality signal from these isosynchronous sources. Only when you read computer data from disc do the x-factors matter. For example, play a CD so you can listen to it, and your drive will operate at 1×. When you attempt to extract digital data from the same audio CD to create an MP3 file, however, the drive may shift to a higher speed—if your computer can process the data fast enough. Extraction need not occur in real time.

Access Time

Compared to magnetic hard disks, all optical disc readers are laggardly beasts. Mass is the reason. The read head of an optical drive is substantially more massive than the flyweight mechanisms used in hard disks. Instead of a delicate read/write head, the CD or DVD drive has a large optical assembly that typically moves on a track. The assembly has more mass to move, which translates into a longer wait for the head to settle into place. Optical drives consequently have hefty access times—where the typical hard disk drive now has an average access time of 9 milliseconds or less, a quick optical drive is about one-tenth the speed (with an average access time about 90 to 100 milliseconds).

As noted earlier, the constant linear velocity system used by some drives also slows the access speed. Because the spin rate of the disc platter varies depending on how far the read/write head is located from the center of the disc, as the head moves from track to track, the spin rate of the disc changes. With music, which is normally played sequentially, that's no problem. The speed difference between tracks is tiny, and the drive can quickly adjust for it. Make the optical drive into a random-access mechanism, and suddenly speed changes become a big issue. The drive might have to move its head from the innermost to outermost track, requiring a drastic speed change. The inertia of the disc spin guarantees a wait while the disc spins up or down.

Controls

Nearly all optical disc drives have an eject button on the front panel. Pressing this button causes the drive to spin down the disc inside the drive (if there is one) and then slide out the tray or pop out the caddy should one be used. Pressing the button again slides the tray back in. Usually pressing on the tray open will also trigger the drive to slide it all the way in.

The various Multimedia PC (MPC) specifications require a volume control on the front panel of any CD-ROM drive you have in your multimedia computer. This control is useful if you decide to use your drive for playing back music while you work. You can plug headphones into the jack on the front of the drive (also required by the MPC standards) and use the volume control to adjust the loudness of the playback independent of the CD control software you run on your computer. The front panel volume control usually does not control the output on the audio connector on the rear of the drive.

Some CD and DVD drives have extended control panels, usually with the standard motion controls as found on dedicated disc players: stop, play, fast forward, rewind, track forward, and track back. Although these controls are not required, they can be handy when you use the DVD player in your computer for playing video through an external monitor.

With the exception of the volume control, all the front panel control functions (including eject) can be operated through suitable software.

Compatibility

DVD drives are required to be able to play back audio CDs made under the Red Book standard. Although as a digital system that can read CD-ROM data, DVD could be compatible with any CD, this is not always the case. Most DVD systems cannot handle interactive Green Book CDs. The dye used in many CD-R media is invisible to DVD wavelengths, so early DVD drives may be unable to read the CD-R discs you make. Drive-makers have adopted a number of strategies to enable their newer DVD drives to read CD-Rs properly. Of course, different CD-R media use different dyes, so you might find your DVD drive works with some CD-Rs and not with others. CD-RW media complicate matters because the medium is not as reflective as that used by prerecorded CDs and DVDs. Manufacturers have developed a "MultiRead" label to assure you that the drive will read CD-ROM, CD-R, and CD-RW media. DVD drives are not required to be able to read CD-Video disc (White Book), but most can—it takes no great technical feat because the DVD drive can read the CD medium, and the MPEG-2 circuitry in the DVD drive also handles the MPEG-1 of CD-Video. DVD players can read data from Enhanced CDs made under the Blue Book standard, including music CDs.

Standards

Because both the Compact Disc and Digital Versatile Disc were conceived as distribution media for software—in this case, *software* meaning audio for the CD and video for the DVD—standardization has been of the utmost importance. Without hard and fast standards, you cannot be sure that the disc you buy will play back in your drive. Consequently, every format of disc has an official standard that guides both drive- and disc-makers so their products can be compatible.

The Sony-Philips standards are published in books that are commonly referred to by the colors of their covers. This small rainbow covers all currently recognized CD standards and was enlarged to embrace the new Super Audio CD. The DVD standards, promulgated by the DVD Forum and published by Toshiba, wear more prosaic identifying names based on a simple letter designation. The five standards recognized at the time of this writing include those for audio, video, read-only data, write-once data, and read/write data. Table 18.4 summarizes these standards.

TABLE 18.4   CD and DVD Standards

Book	Name	Application	Standard
Book A	DVD-ROM	Data distribution	
Book B	DVD-Video	Consumer video playback	
Book C	DVD-Audio	Consumer audio playback	
Book D	DVD-WO (DVD-R)	Write-one data storage	
Book E	DVD-E (DVD-RW)	Rewritable data storage	
Red Book	CD-DA	Consumer audio playback	ISO-10149
Scarlet Book	SA-CD	Super Audio CD	Pending
Orange Book	CD-R, CD-RW	Writable and rewritable datastorage	
Yellow Book	CD-ROM	Data distribution	ISO 10149:1989 (E)
Green Book	CD-i	Interactive CDs	
Blue Book	CD-Extra, CD-Plus	Stamped multisession CDs	
White Book	CD-V	Consumer video playback	

The primary DVD standard is maintained by Toshiba Corporation. It is freely available but hardly free. Anyone can obtain a copy from the DVD Forum at `http://www.dvdforum.org` after paying a $5,000 fee and signing a nondisclosure agreement.

Each of the most widely used of the CD and DVD standards is separately discussed in the following sections.

Note that the original format for CDs was audio. The data format, CD-ROM, was separately developed around the audio parameters. In DVD, the original format was DVD-ROM, with the first application, DVD-Video, being a subset of the DVD-ROM format.

CD-DA

CD-DA, which stands for Compact Disc, Digital Audio, is standardized in the Red Book. It was the original Compact Disc application, storing audio information in digital form. The name *Red Book* refers to the international standard (ISO 10149), which was published as a book with a red cover and specifies the digitization and sampling rate details, including the data-transfer rate and the exact type of pulse code modulation used.

Under the standard, a CD-DA disc holds up to 74 minutes of stereo music with a range equivalent to today's FM radio station—the high end goes just beyond 15KHz (depending on the filtering in the playback device); at the low frequency end, nearly to DC, zero hertz. The system stores audio data with a resolution of 16 bits, so each analog audio level is quantified as one of 65,536 levels. With linear encoding, that's sufficient for a dynamic range of 96 decibels. To accommodate an upper frequency limit of 15KHz with adequate roll-off for practical antialiasing filters, the system uses a sampling rate of 44.1KHz.

Under the Red Book standard, this digital data is restructured into 24-byte blocks, arranged as six samples, each of a pair of stereophonic channels (each of which has a depth of 16 bits). These 24 bytes are encoded along with control and subchannel information into the 588 optical bits of a small frame, each of which stores about 136 microseconds of music. Ninety-eight of these small frames are grouped together in a large frame, and 75 large frames make one second of recorded sound.

In CD-DA systems, the large frame lacks the sync field, header, and error-correction code used in CD-ROM storage, discussed later. Instead, the error-correction and control information is encoded in the small frames. The necessary information to identify each large frame is spread through all 98 bits of subchannel Q in a given large frame. One bit of the subchannel Q data is drawn from each small frame.

From the subchannel Q data, a sector is identified by its ordinary playing time location (in minutes, seconds, and frame from the beginning of the disc). The 98 bits of the subchannel Q signal spread across the large frame is structured into nine separate parts: a two-bit synchronization field; a four-bit address field to identify the format of the subchannel Q data; a four-bit control field with more data about the format; an eight-bit track number; an eight-bit index number; a 24-bit address, counting up from the beginning of the track (counting down from the beginning of the track in the pre-gap area); eight reserved bits; a 24-bit absolute address from the start of the disc; and 16 bits of error-correction code. At least nine of ten consecutive large frames must have their subchannel Q signals in this format.

In the remaining large sectors, two more subchannel Q formats are optional. If used, they must occur in at least 1 out of 100 consecutive large frames. One is a disc catalog number that remains unchanged for the duration of the disc; the other is a special recording code that is specific and unchanging to each track.

Super Audio CD

The Scarlet Book covers the Super Audio CD, the DVD/CD hybrid developed jointly by Philips and Sony to compete with DVD-Audio. The format specifications were first released in March 1999.

The standard allows for three forms—a single-layer disc that only supports Super Audio, a disc with two Super Audio layers, and a *hybrid* disc that mates a Super Audio layer with a conventional CD-A layer for compatibility with old equipment. A hybrid disc works and sounds like a conventional CD in a conventional CD drive but plays back Super Audio in an SA drive.

To store all the data necessary for Super Audio, all Super Audio layers use basic DVD technology. The data on these layers takes the form of Sony's proprietary Direct Stream Digital (DSD) encoding technology (discussed later). The CD layer uses conventional CD technology (16-bit audio sampled at 44.1KHz).

The DSD encoding system provides frequency response to 100KHz and a dynamic range in excess of 120 dB. Although few people can hear anything beyond 20KHz, the highest quality analog master tapes recorded at a speed of 30 inches per second often have information out to 50KHz. The high-frequency range of DSD will finally put to rest complaints that digital doesn't sound as good as analog.

The DSD system uses one-bit sampling at a 2.8224MHz rate, the same as used in a high-quality pulse-code modulation (PCM) encoding system that uses 64× oversampling. Instead of converting the resulting code to PCM, the DSD system records the one-bit sample values. *Delta sigma modulation* determines the one-bit value for each sample—that is, the sample represents the sum (sigma) of the changes (delta) of the signal. The system maintains a running total of the bits representing the strength of the analog waveform. At each sampling interval, it compares the present value with the previous value. If the new value is higher than the previous value, the system adds a logical "1" to the code stream. If the current value is lower than the previous value, the system adds a logical "0" to the code stream. If a value does not change, it is nevertheless evaluated and will produce an alternating pattern of 1's and 0's that correct one another.

The overall result is that a rising (positive) waveform will be a dense string of 1's, and a full falling (negative) waveform will be a dense string of 0's. Consequently, this form of modulation is often termed *Pulse Density Modulation* (PDM). As with all digital signals, the PDM output is resistant to noise and distortion—and alteration to the signal smaller than an entire pulse will be ignored in processing and excluded from the reconstructed signal. Unlike coded digital signals, however, PDM signals (and the signals of a similar digital modulation system, called *Pulse Width Modulation*) are closely allied to their analog equivalent. The pulses in the signal mimic the analog signal in strength and frequency. In fact, a simple low-pass filter can convert the digital signals into analog form.

In the case of Sony's DSD, the simple analog conversion isn't very good. Digital artifacts make the simple conversion noisy. The Sony system uses high-order filtering to move the noise out of the audio band.

The CD-compatible layer of a Super Audio CD is created during mastering through a process Sony calls *super bit mapping direct* downstream conversion. It is essentially the same process used in mastering ordinary audio CDs from 64× oversampled masters.

Although the standard Super Audio CD format uses two audio channels of DSD signals, the specification allows for up to six such channels for future applications. In addition, storage space on the outside of the audio signal area is reserved for text, graphics, or videos—for example, to accompany the audio presentation.

The Super Audio CD also includes provisions for watermarking (invisibly indicating the origin of the media) discs through coding embedded in the wobble of the track. This feature can be used for tracking the origins of a particular disc (for example, for controlling disc piracy) or in copy-protection schemes.

According to Sony, a hybrid Super Audio CD will play in any drive—CD, DVD, or SA-CD. In a CD drive, it will deliver better than CD quality thanks to the super bit mapping downstream conversion. Current DVD drives will also play the discs with CD quality. The true beauty of the disc will come out only on special SA-CD players or a future generation of DVD drives that have the proper playback algorithms.

CD-ROM

The Yellow Book, first introduced in 1984, describes the data format standards for CD-ROM discs and includes CD-XA, which adds compressed audio information to other CD-ROM data. The Yellow Book divides CD-ROM operation into two modes. Mode 1 is meant for ordinary computer data. Mode 2 handles compressed audio and video data. Because Yellow Book discs can contain audio, video, and data in their two modes, they are often termed *mixed mode* discs. Yellow Book is the standard that first enabled multimedia CDs. It is now an internationally recognized standard as ISO 10149:1989 (E).

As the full name implies, Compact Disc Read-Only Memory is fundamentally an adaptation of the Compact Disc for storing digital information—Rock and Roll comes to computer storage. Contrary to the implications of the name, however, you can write to CD-ROM discs with your computer, providing you buy the right (which means *expensive*) equipment. For most applications, however, the CD-ROM is true to its designation—it delivers data from elsewhere into your computer. Once a CD-ROM disc is pressed, the data it holds cannot be altered. Its pits are present for eternity.

In the beginning, CD-ROM was an entity into itself, a storage medium that mimicked other mass storage devices. It used its own storage format. The kind of data that the CD-ROM lent itself to was unlike that of other storage systems, however. The CD-ROM supplied an excellent means for distributing sounds and images for multimedia systems, consequently engineers adapted its storage format to better suit a mixture of data types. The original CD-ROM format was extended to cover these additional kinds of data with its Extended Architecture. The result was the Yellow Book standard.

Logical Format

As with other disc media, the CD's capacity is divided into short segments called *sectors*. In the CD-ROM realm, however, these sectors are also called *large frames* and are the basic unit of addressing. Because of the long spiral track, the number of sectors or large frames per track is meaningless—it's simply the total number of sectors on the drive. The number varies but can reach about 315,000 (for example, for 74 minutes of music) or about 340,000 for newer, 80-minute discs.

Large frames define the physical format of a Compact Disc and are defined by the CD-ROM media standards to contain 2352 bytes. (Other configurations can put 2048, 2052, 2056, 2324, 2332, 2340, or 2352 bytes in a large frame.) The CD-ROM media standards allow for several data formats within each large frame, dependent on the application for which the CD-ROM is meant. In simple data-storage applications, Data Mode 1, 2048 bytes in a 2352-byte large frame actually store data. The remaining 304 bytes are divided among a synchronization field (12 bytes), a sector address tag field (4 bytes), and an auxiliary field (288 bytes). In Data Mode 2, which was designed for less critical applications not requiring heavy-duty error correction, some of the bytes in the auxiliary field may also be used for data storage, providing 2336 bytes of useful storage in each large frame. Other storage systems allocate storage bytes differently but in the same large-frame structure.

The four bytes of the sector address tag field identify each large frame unambiguously. The identification method hints at the musical origins of the CD-ROM system—each large frame bears an identification by minute, second, and frame, which corresponds to the playing time of a musical disc. One byte each is provided for storing the minute count, second count, and frame count in binary coded decimal (BCD) form. BCD storage allows up to 100 values per byte, more than enough to encode 75 frames per second, 60 seconds per minute, and the 74 minute maximum playing time of a Compact Disc (as audio storage). The fourth byte is a flag that indicates the data storage mode of the frame.

In Data Mode 1, the auxiliary field is used for error detection and correction. The first four bytes of the field store a primary error-detection code and are followed by eight bytes of zeros. The last 276 hold a layered error-correction code. This layered code is sufficient for detecting and repairing multiple-bit errors in the data field.

Extended architecture rearranges the byte assignment of these data modes to suit multi-session applications. In XA Mode 2 Form 1, the 12 bytes of sync and four of header are followed by an eight-byte subheader that helps identify the contents of the data bytes, 2048 of which follow. The frame ends with an auxiliary field storing four bytes of error-detection code and 276 bytes of error-correction code. In XA Mode 2 Form 2, the auxiliary field shrinks to four bytes; the leftover bytes extending the data contents to 2324 bytes.

Data Coding

The bytes of the large frame do not directly correspond to the bit-pattern of pits that are blasted into the surface of the CD-ROM. Much as hard discs use different forms of modulation to optimize both the capacity and integrity of their storage, the Compact Disc uses a special data-to-optical translation code. Circuitry inside the Compact Disc system converts the data stream of a large frame into a bit-pattern made from 98 small frames.

Each small frame stores 24 bytes of data (thus 98 of them equal a 2352-byte large frame) but consists of 588 optical bits. Besides the main data channel, each small frame includes an invisible data byte called the *subchannel* and its own error-correction code. Each byte of this information is translated into 14 bits of optical code. To these 14 bits, the signal-processing circuitry adds three merging bits, the values of which are chosen to minimize the low-frequency content of the signal and optimize the performance of the phase-lock loop circuit used in recovering data from the disc.

The optical bits of a small frame are functionally divided into four sections. The first 27 bits comprise a synchronization pattern. They are followed by the byte of subchannel data, which is translated into 17 bits (14-bit data code plus three merging bits). Next comes the 24 data bytes (translated in 408 bits), followed by eight bytes of error-correction code (translated into 136 bits).

The subchannel byte actually encodes eight separate subchannels, designated with letters *P* through *W*. Each bit has its own function. For example, the P subchannel is a flag used to control audio muting. The Q subchannel is used to identify large frames in audio recording.

As with a hard disk, this deep structure is hidden from your normal application software. The only concern of your application is to determine how the 2048 (or so) bytes of active storage in each large frame are divided up and used. The CD-ROM drive translates the block requests made by the SCSI interface (or other interface) into the correct values in the synchronization field to find data.

Sessions

A *session* is a single recorded segment on a CD and may comprise multiple tracks. The session is normally recorded all at once in a single session, hence the name. Under the Orange Book standard, a session can contain data, audio, or images.

On the disc, each session begins with a lead-in, which provides space for a table of contents for the session. The lead-in length is fixed at 4500 sectors, equivalent to one minute of audio or 9MB of data. When you start writing a session, the lead-in is left blank and is filled in only when you close the session.

At the end of the session on the disc is a lead-out, which contains no data but signals to the CD player that it has reached the end of the active data area. The first lead-in on a disc measures 6750 sectors long, the equivalent of 1.5 minutes of audio or 13MB of data. Any subsequent lead-outs on a single disc last for 2250 sectors (half a minute, or about 4MB of data).

Addressing

The basic addressing scheme of the Compact Disc is the track, but CD tracks are not the same as hard disk tracks. Instead of indicating a head position or cylinder, the track on a CD is a logical structure akin to the individual tracks or cuts on a phonograph record.

A single Compact Disc is organized as one of up to 99 tracks. Although a single CD can accommodate a mix of audio, video, and digital data, each track must be purely one of the three. Consequently, a disc mixing audio, video, and data would need to have at least three tracks.

The tracks on a disc are contiguous and sequentially numbered, although the first track containing information may have a value greater than one. Each track consists of at least 300 large frames (that's four seconds of audio playing time). Part of each track is a transition area called pre-gap and post-gap areas (for data discs) or pause areas (for audio discs).

Each disc has a lead-in area and a lead-out area corresponding to the lead-in and lead-out of phonograph records. The lead-in area is designated track zero, and the lead-out area is track 0AA(hex). Neither is reported as part of the capacity of the disc, although the subchannel of the lead-in contains the table of contents of the disc. The table of contents lists every track and its address (given in the format of minutes, seconds, and frames).

Tracks are subdivided into up to 99 indices by values encoded in the subchannel byte of nine out of ten small frames. An index is a point of reference that's internal to the track. The number and location of each index is not stored in the table of contents. The pre-gap area is assigned an index value of zero.

Capacity

The nominal maximum capacity of a CD amounts to 74 minutes of music recording time or about 650MB when used for storing data. With 80-minute discs, the data capacity extends to about 700MB. These capacities are only approximate, however. A number of factors control the total capacity of a given disc. For example, mass-produced audio CDs sometimes contain more than 74 minutes of sound because disc-makers can cram more onto each disc by squeezing the track on the glass master disc into a tighter, longer spiral. This technique is the secret to extending the playing time 80-minute discs.

The special CDs that you can write on with your computer cannot benefit from this tighter-track strategy because their spiral is put in place when the discs are manufactured. The standard formats yield four capacity levels on two different sizes of disc, as discussed in the upcoming CD-R section. In any case, these numbers represent the maximum storage capacity of a recordable CD. Nearly anything you do when making a CD cuts into that capacity.

Format

The Yellow Book describes how to put information on a CD-ROM disc. It does not, how-ever, define how to organize that data into files. In the DOS world, two file standards have been popular. The first was called High Sierra format. Later this format was upgraded to the current standard, the ISO 9660 specification.

The only practical difference between these two standards is that the driver software sup-plied with some CD-ROM players, particularly older ones, meant for use with High Sierra–formatted discs may not recognize ISO 9660 discs. You're likely to get an error message that says something like "Disc not High Sierra." The problem is that the old ver-sion of the Microsoft CD-ROM extensions—the driver that adapts your CD-ROM player to work with DOS—cannot recognize ISO 9660 discs.

To meld CD-ROM technology with DOS, Microsoft Corporation created a standard bit of operating code to add onto DOS to make the players work. These are called the *DOS CD-ROM extensions*, and several versions have been written. The CD-ROM extensions before Version 2.0 exhibit the incompatibility problem between High Sierra and ISO 9660, noted earlier. The solution is to buy a software upgrade to the CD-ROM extensions that came with your CD-ROM player from the vendor who sold you the equipment. A better solution is to avoid the problem and ensure any CD-ROM player you purchase comes with Version 2.0 or later of the Microsoft CD-ROM extensions.

ISO 9660 embraces all forms of data you're likely to use with your computer. Compatible discs can hold files for data as well as audio and video information.

For Windows 95, Microsoft created another set of extensions to ISO 9660. Called the *Joliet CD ROM Recording Specification*, these extensions add support for longer file names—but to 128 characters instead of the 255-character maximum of Windows 95—as well as nesting of directories beyond eight levels, allowing directory names to use extensions, and broadening the character set. To maintain compatibility with ISO 9660, the extra Joliet data must fit in a 240-character limit, foreclosing on the possibility of encoding all Windows 95 directory data.

CD-Recordable

The Orange Book is the official tome that describes the needs and standards for Compact Disc-Recordable (CD-R) systems. It turns the otherwise read-only medium into a write-once medium so that you can make your own CDs. Introduced in 1992, the Orange Book standard introduced multisession technology. A multisession disc can contain blocks of data written at different times (sessions). Each session has its own lead-in track and table of contents.

Developed jointly by Philips and Sony (sound familiar?), the Orange Book defines both the physical structure of recordable CDs and how various parts of the data area on the disc must be used. These include the *program area*, which holds the actual data the disc is meant to store; the *program memory area*, which records the track information for the whole disc and all the sessions it contains; the *lead-in* and *lead-out areas*; and a *power calibration area* that's used to calibrate the power of the record laser.

The nature of the CD-ROM medium and the operation of CD recorders make the creation and writing of a CD-ROM a more complex operation than simply copying files to a hard disk drive. Because CD-ROMs are essentially sequentially recorded media, the CD recorder wants to receive data and write it to disc as a continuous stream. In most CD recorders, the stream of data cannot be interrupted once it starts. An interruption in the data flow can result in an error in recording. Moreover, to obtain the highest capacity possible from a given CD, you want to limit the number of sessions into which you divide the disc. As noted earlier, each session steals at least 13MB from disc capacity for the overhead of the session's lead-in and lead-out.

If your system cannot supply information to your CD recorder fast enough, the result is a *buffer underrun error*. When you see such an error message on your screen, it means your CD recorder has exhausted the software buffer and run out of data to write to the disc. You can prevent this error by increasing the size of the buffer if your software allows it. Or you can better prepare your files for transfer to CD. In particular, build a CD image on a hard disk that can be copied on the fly to the CD.

The best strategy is to give over your computer to the CD-writing process, unloading any TSR programs, background processes, or additional tasks in a multitasking system. Screensavers, pop-up reminders, and in-coming communications (your modem answering the phone for data or a fax) can interrupt your CD session and cause you to waste your time, a session, or an entire disc.

Your system needs to be able to find the files it needs to copy to your CD-ROM as efficiently as possible. Copying multiple short files can be a challenge, particularly if your hard disk is older and slower or fragmented. CD recorder–makers recommend discs with access times faster than about 19 milliseconds. An AV-style hard disk is preferable because such drives are designed for the smooth, continuous transfer of data and don't interrupt the flow with housekeeping functions, such a thermal calibration. You'll also want to be sure your files are not fragmented before transferring them to CD. Run your defrag utility before writing to your CD.

Depending on the manufacturer of your CD recorder and the software accompanying it, you may have a choice of more than one mode for copying data to CD. In general, you have two choices: building a CD image on your hard disk and copying that image intact to your CD. Some manufacturers call this process "writing on the fly." From a hardware standpoint, this is the easiest for your system and CD recorder to cope with because the disc image is already in the form of a single huge file with all the directory structures needed for the final CD in their proper places. Your system needs to only ready your hard disk and send a steady stream of data to the CD recorder.

The alternative method is to create the CD structure in its final form on the CD itself. Some manufacturers call this "writing a virtual image." In making a CD by this method, your CD recorder's software must follow a script or database to find which files it should include on the disc and locate the files on your hard disk. The program must allocate the space on your CD, dividing it into sectors and tracks, while at the same time reading the hard disk and transferring the data to the CD.

Capacity Issues

With a read-only medium, you normally don't have to concern yourself with the issue of storage capacity. That's for the disc-maker to worry about—the publisher has to be sure everything fits. With about 650 megabytes of room on the typical CD and many products requiring only a few megabytes for code, the big problem for publishers is finding enough stuff to put on the disc so that you think you're getting your money's worth.

The advent of recordable CDs changes things entirely. With CDs offering convenient long-term storage for important files such as graphic archives, you'll be sorely tempted to fill your CDs to the brim. You'll need to plan ahead to make all your files fit.

CD-ROMs have substantial overhead that cuts into their available capacity. If you don't plan for this overhead, you may be surprised when your files don't fit.

Raw Capacity

CD-ROM capacities are measured in minutes, seconds, and sectors, based on the audio format from which engineers derived the medium. Recordable CDs come in five capacities: 18- and 21-minute discs are 80 millimeters in diameter; 63-, 74-, and 80-minute discs are 120 millimeters in diameter.

Two kinds of file overhead affect the number of bytes available on a given recordable CD, which can actually be used for storage. One is familiar from other mass storage devices, resulting from the need to allocate data in fixed-size blocks. The other results from the format structure required by the CD standards.

Logical Block Padding

As with most hard and floppy discs, CD-ROMs allocate their storage in increments called *logical blocks*. Although logical block sizes of 512, 1024, and 2048 bytes are possible with today's CD drives, only the 2048-byte logical block format is in wide use. If a file is smaller than a logical block, it is padded out to fill a logical block. If a file is larger than one logical block, it fills all its logical blocks except the last, which is then padded out to be completely filled. As a result of this allocation method, all files except those that are an exact multiple of the logical block size require more disc space than their actual size. In addition, all directories on a CD require at least one logical block of storage.

Format Overhead
In addition to the block-based overhead shared with most mass storage devices, CD-ROMs have their own format overhead that is unique to the CD system. These are remnants of the audio origins of the CD medium.

Because audio CDs require lead-in and lead-out tracks, the Yellow Book standard for CD-ROM makes a similar allowance. The specifications require that data on a CD-ROM begin after a two-second pause, followed by a lead-in track 6500-sectors long. Consequently, the first two seconds of storage space and the lead-in area on a CD are not usable for data. These two seconds comprise a total of 150 sectors, each holding 2048 bytes, which trims the capacity of the disc by 307,200 bytes. The 6500-sector lead-in consumes another 13,312,000 bytes. The lead-out gap at the end of a storage session and the pre-gap that allows for a subsequent session consume another 4650 sectors or 9,523,200 bytes.

The ISO 9660 file structure also eats away at the total disc capacity. The standard reserved the first 16 sectors of the data area—that's 32,768 bytes—for system use. Various elements of the disc format also swallow up space. The root file, primary volume descriptor, and volume descriptor set terminator each require a minimum of one sector. The path tables require at least two sectors. The required elements consequently take another five sectors or 10,120 bytes of space. Discs with complex file structures may exceed these minima and lose further storage space.

The more sessions you divide a given CD into, the less space that will be available for your data. Each session on a multisession CD requires its own lead-in. Consequently, each session requires at least 13MB of space in addition to the file structure overhead.

Operation
Creating a CD is a complete process. The drive doesn't just copy down data blocks as your computer pushes them out. Every disc, even every session, requires its own control areas to be written to the disc. Your CD-R drive doesn't know enough to handle these processes automatically because the disc data structure depends on your data and your intentions. Your CD-R drive cannot fathom either of these. The job falls to the software you use to create your CD-R discs.

Your CD-creation software organizes the data for your disc. As it sends the information to your CD-R drive, it also adds the control information required for making the proper disc format. After you've completed writing to your disc, the software fixates the disc so that it can be played. The last job is left to you—labeling the disc so you can identify the one you need from a stack more chaotic than the pot of an all-night poker game.

Speed

As with ordinary CD-ROM, the speed of CD-R drives is the transfer rate of the drive measured in multiples of the basic audio CD speed, 150KBps. The very first CD recorders operated at 1× speed, and each new generation has doubled that speed. The fastest drives currently operate at 4×, although technical innovation can increase that just as it has improved basic CD speed.

Most CD recorders have two speed ratings—one for writing and one for reading. The writing speed is invariably the same or less than the reading speed. Advertisements usually describe drives using two numbers, the writing speed (lower number) first. The most common speed combinations are 1×1, single-speed read and write; 1×2, single-speed write and double-speed read; 2×2 double-speed writing and reading; 2×4 double-speed writing and quadruple-speed reading; and 4×4 quadruple-speed in both writing and reading.

How fast a CD recorder writes is only one factor in determining how long making one or more CDs will take. Other variables include your system, writing mode (whether you try to put files together for a CD session on the fly or try to write a disc image as one interrupted file), and the number of drives.

Your system and writing mode go hand in hand. As noted later in this section, a CD recorder requires a constant, uninterrupted stream of data to make a disc. The speed at which your computer can maintain that data flow can constrain the maximum writing speed of a CD-R drive. Factors that determine the rate of data flow include the speed of the source of the data (your hard disk), the fragmentation of the data, and the interfaces between the source disc and your CD recorder.

Most CD recorders have built-in buffers to bridge across temporary slowdowns in the data supply, such as may be involved when your hard disk's read/write head repeatedly moves from track to track to gather a highly fragmented file or when an older, non-A/V drive performs a thermal calibration. Even with this bridge action, however, such hard disk slowdowns reduce the net flow of data to the CD recorder. If you try to create a CD by gathering together hundreds of short hard disk files on the fly, your hard disk may not be able to keep up with the data needs of a 4× CD recorder. In fact, if the files are many and small, the hard disk may not even be able to maintain 1× speed, forcing you to resort to making an image file before writing to the disc.

On the other hand, one manufacturer (Mitsumi) reports that higher writing speeds produce more reliable CDs. At the 1× writing speed, the laser remains focused on a given disc area longer, possibly overheating it. In other words, you may want to avoid 1× speed unless the performance of your system and its software requires it. Although early software, drives, and computers often could not keep up with speeds in excess of 1×, most current products do not have difficulties at higher speeds.

When you have to produce a large number of CDs quickly, one of the best strategies is to use multiple drives. Five drives writing simultaneously cuts the net creation time of an individual CD by 80 percent. For moderate-volume applications, stacks of CD writers can make a lot of sense—and CDs. For large-volume applications (generally more than a few hundred), pressing CDs is the most cost-effective means of duplication, albeit one that requires waiting a few days for mastering and pressing.

Disc-Writing Modes

Depending on your CD-R drive and your CD-creation software, you may have your choice of the mode you use for writing to your CD. The mode determines what you can write to your discs and when. Typically you don't have to worry about the writing mode because your software takes care of the details automatically. However, some drives and software may be limited to the modes under which they can operate.

The basic CD-writing modes are four: track-at-once, multisession, disc-at-once, and incremental writing. Each has its own requirements, limitations, and applications. A new standard, Mount Rainier, discussed separately, ensures compatible on incrementally written discs.

Track-at-Once

The most basic writing method for CDs is the creation of a single track. A track can be in any format that your CD-R drive can write (for example, a CD-ROM compatible disc or a CD-DA disc for your stereo system). The track-at-once process writes an entire track in a single operation. A track must be larger than 300 blocks and smaller than the total capacity of the disc minus its overhead.

Writing track-at-once requires only that you designate what files you want to put on a CD. Your CD-creation software takes over and handles the entire writing process.

Originally the big limitation of track-at-once writing was that you could write only one track on a disc in a single session. Consequently, unless you had a lot to write to your disc already prepared beforehand, this process was wasteful of disc space. Some modern CD systems can add one track at a time to a disc within a single session, even allowing you to remove the disc from the drive and try it in another in the middle of the process.

Each track has overhead totaling 150 blocks for run-in, run-out, pre-gap and linking. CD standards allow 99 tracks per disc. Consequently, if your tracks are small, you may waste substantial capacity. Writing the maximum number of blocks of minimal size (300 blocks plus 150 blocks of overhead each) will only about half-fill the smallest, 18-minute CD disc (44,550 blocks on a 81,000 block disc).

Track Multisession

Sometimes called *track incremental* mode, *track multisession* mode is the most common means of allowing you to take advantage of the full capacity of CDs. Track multisession writing allows you to add to CDs as you have the need for it by dividing the capacity of the disc into multiple sessions, up to about 50 of them. Each session has many of the characteristics of a complete CD, including its own lead-in and lead-out areas as well as a table of contents.

In fact, the need for these special formatting areas for each session is what limits the number of sessions on the disc. The lead-in and lead-out areas together require about 13.5MB of disc space. Consequently, CDs with a total capacity of 680MB can hold no more than about 50 sessions.

When the CD standards were first created, engineers didn't even consider the possibility that individual consumers would ever be able to write their own discs. Consequently, they assumed that all discs would be factory mastered in a single session. They designed early CD drives to recognize only one session on a disc. Many older CD-ROM drives (particularly those with 1× and 2× speed ratings) were single-session models and cannot handle multisession discs written in track multisession mode. Single-session drives generally read only the first session on a disc and ignore the rest.

Another problem that may arise with multisession discs is the mixing of formats. Many CD players are incapable of handling discs on which CD-ROM Mode 1 or 2 sessions are mixed with XA sessions. The dangerous aspect of this problem is that some CD-mastering software (and CD drives) allow you to freely mix formats in different sessions. You may create a disc that works when you read it on your CD drive that cannot function in other CD drives. The moral is not to mix formats on a disc. (Don't confuse format with data type. You can freely mix audio, video, and pure data as long as they are written in the same format, providing the one you choose is compatible with all three data types.)

Most modern CD-R machines allow you to write more than one track in a given session. The advantage of this technique is the elimination of most of the 13.5MB session overhead. Instead of lead-in and lead-out tracks, each pair of tracks is separated by 150 blocks (two seconds) of pre-gap—overhead of only about 300KB. The entire session must, of course, be framed by its own lead-in, table of contents, and lead-out areas.

In multisession discs, the drive writes to the lead-in area after it finishes with the data on the disc. The lead-in contains the table of contents for the session as well as an indication of the remaining writable area on the disc. The lead-in of the last session on the disc indicates that no more sessions are present, closing the disc.

Disc-at-Once

Old-fashioned vinyl phonograph records were cut as a single, continuous process. From the moment the cutting stylus plunked down on the master disc until it finished the disc, spinning around in the capture track, the mastering process had to be free of interruptions. After all, any gap in the spiral track of the phonograph record would stall your record player. To cut a master record, the engineers prepared a master tape that was complete in every detail of everything that was to go on the final disc, including blank tape for the gaps between cuts on the final disc.

The CD equivalent to making such a master disc is the disc-at-once process. As with cutting a master record, the disc-at-once process must be completely free from interruption from the beginning of the lead-in area to the completion of the lead-out area. The table of contents, all tracks, and the Q channel must all be prepared before the writing process begins. The entire disc will be written in one swoop so that the formatting data will appear on the disc (for example, the lead-in will be written before the data). Typically, to make a CD using disc-at-once writing, you'll prepare an exact image of the CD and store it on a hard disc. The hard disc must be A/V rated so that it does not interrupt the data stream for thermal calibration or other housekeeping and thus cause buffer underrun (see the section titled "Underrun," later in the chapter).

In effect, disc-at-once is a combination of track-at-once and multisession writing that simply extends across the entire CD (or as much of it as will ever be used).

Disc-at-once is the recording method that must be used when you prepare a disc to serve as the master for making mass-produced CDs. Because the laser never turns off, a disc recorded using the disc-at-once mode contains no link blocks.

Packet Writing

If you could make a CD-R work like a conventional hard disc, it would be capable of *incremental writing*. That is, you could add data to your disc whenever you needed to simply by saving a file. In CD terminology, this is called *packet writing*. With appropriate software drivers, you can drag and drop files to your CD recorder as if it were a hard disk drive.

In this context, a packet is a block of data smaller than a track. Your drive accepts the packet and writes it to the disc, identifying it with four blocks of run-in information, two of run-out information, and a link block. Each packet thus suffers seven blocks or about 15KB of overhead in addition to that required for directory information.

The ISO 9660 file system comes up short in packet writing. It requires that all the file information be written in the table of contents when you create a session. Multisession discs sidestep this problem by creating a new file system every time you write a new session, with all the overhead of a complete file system (whoops, there goes another 13.5MB). Packet writing therefore requires drives and software that follow the Universal Data Format (UDF) system, discussed under "DVD-ROM," later in the chapter.

Mount Rainier

Whereas packet writing requires software added as an application on top of an operating system, the Mount Rainier standard incorporates the same functionality (and more) within the operating system. Jointly developed by Compaq (now Hewlett-Packard), Microsoft,

Philips Electronics, and Sony, the Mount Rainier specification obsoletes packet writing with a similar drag-and-drop interface to allow random writing to CD and DVD drives. In addition, the specification requires that drives be able to access data in 2KB allocation units, like those used on magnetic disks.

One of the most important parts of the Mount Rainier specification is shifting responsibility for managing disc defects from the packet-writing software to the disc drive itself. The drive maintains a map of bad sections of the disc in a special table carved from the user data area of the disc. Using the table, the drive can skip over bad areas of the disc when writing data without any intervention from the operating system—without the operating system even knowing the bad areas exist.

This feature alone requires new drive designs. Conventional CD and DVD drives cannot be upgraded to Mount Rainier technology. On the other hand, conventional media work with Mount Rainier drives, and Mount Rainier drives can read discs written under earlier standards.

Mount Rainier eliminates much of the hassle of formatting CDs by moving the process to the background. Although you can use preformatted discs with a Mount Rainier drive, using unformatted discs imposes no penalty. Slide a new disc in the drive, and the drive automatically starts formatting it even as you write data.

Discs created using Mount Rainier technology cannot be read by conventional drives without special software drivers. Make a Mount Rainier disc in one computer, and you won't be able to read it on another machine that does not have a driver that supports the technology. You can enable an older system to read (but not write) Mount Rainier discs by installing new driver software (when it becomes available).

The common name for Mount Rainier is *EasyWrite* technology. The promoters of the new format have developed a certification program and a logo that lets you quickly identify drives that correctly implement the technology.

The Mount Rainier specification was first published on July 30, 2002. The Web site www.mt-rainier.org provides access to the full specification.

Underrun

No matter the mode, the CD-writing process is continuous, start to finish. The laser switches on at the beginning of a session and remains in continuous operation until that session is finished. The CD format requires the interleaving of data between blocks during the writing process to help ensure data integrity. To properly sort the interleaved data, the drive needs an overview of the data. To gain this overview, the drive has a data buffer from which it draws the data to write.

For the laser in a CD-R drive to operate continuously, it must have a continuous supply of data to keep its buffer filled with enough information to properly perform the interleaving. If at any time it runs out of data to write, the writing process is interrupted. Unlike hard disks, the CD drive can't pick up where it left off on the next spin of the disc. The error resulting from the interruption of the data flow is termed *buffer underrun*.

CD players see the interrupted session as an error (which it is) that may render the disc unplayable. In other words, buffer underrun ruins a disc. Better CD-R drives allow you to close the interrupted session and recover the remaining space on the disc for other sessions.

Testing

To prevent you from wasting discs with inadvertent data underruns, most CD-R mastering software makes a trial run or test of the recording session before actually committing your data to disc. The test involves performing exactly the same steps as the actual write operation—including operating the laser in the drive in its write mode—but keeps the power of the laser at read level. The CD-R drive runs through the entire write operation, but the lower power of the laser prevents it from affecting (and potentially ruining) a disc.

If the recording software discovers a problem during recording that would cause an underrun or other problem, it will advise you how to sidestep the problem, typically by stepping down to a lower writing speed on your CD-R drive or, as a last resort, defragmenting your hard disk.

The only problem with pre-write testing is that the trial run takes as long as writing everything to your disc, essentially doubling the write time of every disc you make. Most CD-mastering programs allow you to switch off this pre-write testing. Although you do this at your own peril (and the expense of ruined CDs), if you're making a batch of discs it is a viable timesaving option. In general, if you can write the first disc successfully, you can run through dozens of additional copies without worry.

Fixation

Before a CD that you write can be read by a CD-ROM drive or the audio CD player in your stereo system, it must have an overall table of contents that follows the ISO 9660 standard. The process of finishing the disc for reading is termed *fixation*. In the process of fixation, the disc is *finalized* when your CD-R drive writes an overall *absolute lead-in area* and *absolute lead-out area* for the entire disc.

Multisession drives also can create discs that are *fixated for appending*. The individual sessions each have their own table of contents that reflects the sessions actually written on the disc, but the disc lacks the overall lead-in and lead-out areas. When you've added the last session to the disc, the *finalization* process writes an indication on the disc that no further sessions are present, then writes the overall disc lead-in and lead-out areas, completing a table of contents compatible with the ISO 9660 standard. Most CD-mastering programs refer to this finalization process as *closing the disc*.

Software that performs packet writing—for example, Sony's Compact Disc Recordable File System (CDRFS)—may require a process termed *freezing the disc* before you can use packet-written discs in ordinary CD players. The freezing process writes lead-in and lead-out areas on the disc. After a disc has been frozen, you can still write additional sessions onto it, providing, of course, additional capacity is available. The freeze process only subtracts from the available capacity, draining away the 13MB of overhead required by any single session.

CD-Rewritable

CD-RW stands for CD-Rewritable, meaning that these drives can create new CDs that you can erase and use again. In fact, you can treat a rewritable CD as if it were a big floppy disk drive or slow hard disk drive. All CD-RW drives also function as CD-R drives, and they are standardized under the Orange Book just as are CD-R drives.

The difference between CD-R and CD-RW is in the media. Put a blank CD-R disc in a CD-RW drive, and you make a permanent record that you cannot change. With a CD-RW disc, you can rewrite and reuse disc space thanks to its phase-change medium.

CD-RW drives are actually the third incarnation of phase-change technology. The first drives, under the Phase Change Recordable banner (or PCR), were made by Toray Industries. It used a medium slightly larger than CDs, 130 millimeters in diameter as opposed to the CD's 120 mm, that was consequently physically incompatible with CD drives. Both sides of the disc had a recordable surface, allowing for a total capacity of 1.5GB per disc. Panasonic's PD discs reduced the size of the disc to the same as CDs and modified the storage format. The actual writing format uses sectors of 512 bytes versus the 2048 byte or larger sectors used by CD, so PD discs are also logically incompatible with CDs. You cannot duplicate a CD on the PD medium. Moreover, the logical format of the PD system limits its capacity to 650MB per disc, as opposed to the 680MB total of CDs. Further, the phase-change material used by the Panasonic PD drives is not compatible with the optical heads and electronics of CD drives. Although the electronics of the Panasonic drives adapted to handle either phase-change or conventional CD media, PD discs work only in PD drives.

Because of the lower reflectivity of CD-RW media, phase-change discs often are unreadable in early (pre-1998) CD-ROM and CD-R drives. Newer drives have compensatory circuitry built in called *automatic gain control*.

In operation, a CD-RW drive can function more like a conventional hard disk than a CD-R. The drive can update the disc table of contents at any time, so you can add files and tracks without additional session overhead. Under Windows, you typically drag and drop files to your CD-RW drive just like you would with any other disk. The Mount Rainier standard, discussed earlier, formalizes a system with this capability and more.

Discs written by CD-RW drives made before the Mount Rainier standard are not entirely compatible with all CD drives. The format used during CD-RW operation in pre–Mount Rainier drives is usually different from that of conventional CDs. To read a CD-RW disc in a CD-ROM or CD-R drive, the disc must be closed, an operation that effectively reorganizes its format. In the typical implementation, the reorganization process requires blank space on the disc, so you cannot fill one of these CD-RW discs with data and expect to later use it in another drive.

DVD-ROM

To your computer, the storage on a DVD looks much like that of any disk system. Information is organized into 2KB blocks that correspond to the clusters on disk systems. The file structure takes the form of the Micro UDF/ISO Bridge format. In effect it bridges two storage formats.

Universal Data Format (UDF) was designed by the Optical Storage Technology Association (OSTA), a group of companies involved in optical data storage, to make data stored on optical discs independent of any operating system (hence, *universal*). The goal was to allow you to write an optical disc on your computer and read it on any other computer in the world, regardless of operating system, microprocessor, or even whether it was powered by electricity or steam. UDF defines the data structures (partitions, files, sectors), error correction, character sets, and read/write method of the DVD system. ISO 9660 defines the tree-oriented directory structure (the same as on computer CDs) compatible with Windows and other popular operating systems. The overall structure of the disc fits the UDF format with the ISO 9660 structure on top, the intent being to eventually eliminate ISO 9660 support.

The UDF specification has incremented up to version 2.01, the level that OSTA recommends DVD-ROM publishers follow. DVD-Video discs and players are locked to the UDF version 1.02 specifications. You can download both versions of the specification in their entirety from www.osta.org.

The Micro UDF/ISO Bridge format imposes some limits on DVDs. One oft-quoted limit is a maximum file size of 1GB. This constraint applied only to DVD-Video discs. Although it seems incompatible with two hours of continuous video playback, the DVD system was designed to agglomerate multiple small files (including video, audio, and control information), process them together, and output a single continuous video stream.

On the disc itself, the block is chopped and scattered to help in error recovery. The tiny size of the pits on the disc means that a splotch or scratch will likely span a considerable storage area. Spreading the data out scatters potential read errors into small pieces in different storage units so that they can be more readily detected and corrected.

Each 2KB block is translated into a 2064-byte physical sector for storage on the disc. The sector gets further subdivided into 12 rows of 172 bytes each. The central ten rows store only data. The first starts with a 12-byte sector header to identify the storage unit. Four bytes provide the actual ID information with two additional bytes used for error correction dedicated to the ID data. The remaining six bytes in the header are reserved. The following 160 bytes in the first row contain data. The last row of each sector ends with four bytes of error-detection and error-correction information for the data area of the sector.

Sixteen sectors are then interleaved together to form a larger storage unit, the *block*. Ten bytes of error-correction code are added to each row in the block, and the resulting overall block gains another 16 rows of error-correction code. The result is a block that's 37,856 bytes, with about 15 percent of its contents devoted to error-correction information. These blocks are then written sequentially to the disc.

The DVD-ROM format allows for both constant linear velocity and constant angular velocity recording. The former favors capacity in sequential access applications (audio and video). The latter improves random access speed for data applications but reduces the capacity of each layer. Although it is an inherent part of the DVD-ROM specification, the chief application of CAV recording in DVD has been the various rewritable formats.

The required support to read UDF-based DVD-ROM discs is built in to Windows 98 and later Windows versions. Earlier Windows versions will require add-on drivers, which are usually included with DVD drives. In addition to decoder software, playback of DVD-Video requires DirectShow 5.2 or newer, which is included with Windows 98. More recent versions can be downloaded from Microsoft's Web site at www.microsoft.com. Again, DVD drives usually include the necessary decoder (as software or as a separate hardware MPEG-decoder board) as well as DirectShow.

DVD-Video

The DVD-Video system devotes one track to video information that may use either MPEG-1 or MPEG-2 encoding. All commercial discs use MPEG-2 because it simply looks (and works) better. A dedicated DVD player can render either into video for your television or monitor. With current technologies, a DVD-ROM player in a computer works best with a separate hardware-based MPEG-2 decoder. Only the fastest computer processor can decode MPEG-2 in real time, and even these don't work as well as dedicated hardware decoders. Moreover, because your computer must devote nearly all its power to decoding the video, there's little left for doing other work at the same time.

DVD-Video would not be possible without compression (nor would any other digital video system be practical). DVD-Video data originates with a bit-rate of 124Mbps, and it must be compressed down to the maximum rate permitted under the DVD standard, 9.6Mbps. The average bit rate is about 3.5Mbps. Despite the heavy-duty compression,

DVD still delivers about twice the resolution of VHS videocassettes. A typical DVD-Video system produces horizontal resolution of about 500 lines, compared to less than 240 lines for a VHS tape.

DVD-Video goes far beyond today's VHS and CD-Video systems. It allows both conventional-style images with the 4:3 aspect ratio as well as those with the 16:9 ratio favored by High-Definition Television systems. DVD players are required to have built-in filters to translate 16:9 images into the full-width of a 4:3 aspect ratio screen—in other words, built-in letterbox format translation. The DVD players will also allow you to zoom in to fill the screen height with a 16:9 image and pan to either side of the picture. The MPEG-2 encoding delivers about four times the spatial resolution as MPEG-1 (used by some CD systems) and allows a high-quality display with 480 lines of 720 pixels, each to fit into a 4MBps data stream. As with any video-compression technique, the exact data rate depends on the complexity of the image. Typically a high-quality image requires *less* data than a low-quality one plagued by noise. The onscreen resolution produced by a DVD system is in the range of 480–500 horizontal lines. Unlike other video systems—VCRs and laserdisc systems—DVD stores video images in component format (separate red, green, and blue images). Other consumer formats use composite video.

DVD-Video also introduces the concept of *subpictures*, which are additional images of limited color depth that can be multiplexed with the main audio and video data. The DVD standard allows for up to 32 subpictures, which typically will be menus for control systems, subtitles for foreign language films, or production credits. Each subpicture can measure as large as 720 by 480 pixels in four colors.

Note that DVD-Video is not High-Definition Television (HDTV). About the only thing in common between the two is the 16:9 aspect ratio supported by both. DVD-Video is more closely aligned with standard NTSC video, offering quality similar to that in the television studio. An HDTV image has about five times the number of pixels as the DVD-Video format. Its compressed format requires about twice the data rate (about 19.4Mbps). Certainly the DVD-18 medium has enough capacity to store HDTV, but it will require a new storage and playback format to cope with the HDTV data rate.

DVD mimics HDTV by offering a wide aspect ratio format. The DVD standard allows for both the old television and video aspect ratio of 4:3 and the HDTV aspect ratio of 16:9. The wide aspect ratio images have the same number of pixels as 4:3 images. The image is compressed anamorphically to fit. On playback the ostensibly square pixels get stretched horizontally to the wider aspect ratio. The standard allows the display of wide aspect ratio images in three different ways, which you can select when playing back a disc. These include the following:

- **Letterbox mode**. This mode fills the width of the screen with the full width of the image, leaving bands 60 lines high at the top and bottom of the screen black.

- **Pan and Scan mode**. This mode fills the full narrow screen with a window into the wide image. The window is dynamic. The disc stores cues determined by the director of the film or producer of the DVD that guide the window to follow the action in the image.

- **Widescreen mode**. This mode provides a full-width image on a 16:9 aspect ratio screen.

The audio accompanying DVD-Video can take any of many forms. The most common (used on nearly all releases of theatrical movies) is Dolby Digital. Although the Dolby Digital system can accommodate up to 5.1 channels of PCM audio, the standard embraces lesser configurations as well—including simple monophonic and stereophonic recordings. In other words, a label proclaiming "Dolby Digital" on a movie box does not guarantee anything in the way of true multichannel sound.

The required audio support depends on the standard followed by the recorded video. Discs containing NTSC video (the standard in North America and Japan) are required to use Dolby Digital. Discs containing PAL video (Europe and most of the rest of the world) must use MPEG-2 audio. Other audio formats may optionally accompany either video standard.

The DVD-Video standard accommodates eight tracks of audio, each track being a single data stream that may comprise one or more audio channels. Each of these channels may use any of five encoding systems. In addition to Dolby Digital (with up to 5.1 channels per track), all DVD drives must also be able to decode PCM audio, up to eight channels per track (potentially 64 channels per disc, but real data rates ordain the channel count be lower), and MPEG audio (up to 7.1 channels per track). Optional decoding systems—which may or may not be included within the circuitry of a given DVD drive but can be attached as an accessory—include Digital Theater Sound (DTS) and Sony Dynamic Digital Sound (SDDS). Chapter 25, "Audio Systems," discusses these systems in more detail.

Video DVDs are burdened with several layers of copy protection that are entwined both with hardware and operating system software. Copy-protection occurs at three levels:

- **Analog copy protection.** Alters the video output so that the signal appears corrupted to VCRs when you attempt to record it. The current *Analog Protection System* (APS) adds a rapid modulation to the colorburst signal (called a *colorstripe*) and pulses in the vertical blanking signal (termed *AGC* because it is meant to confuse the *automatic gain control* of VCRs). Computer video boards with conventional analog video outputs (composite or S-video) must incorporate APS. DVD-Video discs themselves control whether the APS system is used on playback by signaling to the disc player to switch APS on or off.

- **Serial copy protection**. Protects by encoding control information in the signal that determines whether it can be copied. The *copy generation management system* adds information to line 21 of the NTSC video signal to tell equipment whether copying is permitted. Although DVD-Video encodes line 21 differently, the information is regenerated into the analog video output of DVD players and computer video boards.

- **Digital encoding.** Encrypts the digital form of media files requiring the video player to know the key necessary for decrypting the code. The DIVX licensing system (abandoned as a DVD format on June 16, 1999) works through digital encoding.

In addition, DVDs are marked with a regional code, a number that specifies the part of the world in which playback of the DVD's content is permitted. The DVD player checks to see whether a region code on the software matches that encoded into its hardware. If the two don't match, the disc won't play. DVD media boxes are marked with the region code as a number on a globe icon, the number corresponding to one of six regions, as listed in Table 18.5.

TABLE 18.5   DVD Regional Codes

Code Number	Region
1	Canada and United States (including U.S. territories)
2	Egypt, Europe, Japan, Middle East, and South Africa
3	East and Southeast Asia
4	Central and South America, Caribbean, Australia, New Zealand, and Pacific Islands
5	Africa, Former Soviet Union, Indian subcontinent, Mongolia, and North Korea
6	China

DVD-Audio

Ever since the introduction of the CD-DA format, audio purists have insisted that it was not good enough. They could hear a definite digital sound (whatever that might be) that interfered with their enjoyment of music. They were quick to point out that tradeoffs made in the design of the CD-DA format slighted sound quality. The relatively low sampling rate required to pack enough information on a disc required high-order low-pass filtering to keep digital artifacts out of the audio, and even then the upper cutoff frequency must be too low to accommodate everything that old analog tape recorders could capture.

The huge capacity of the DVD system eliminates the need for the tradeoffs of the CD-DA system and unleashes the potential for superb audio quality—good enough to satisfy listeners with 24-karat ears. The audio-only implementation of DVD—termed *DVD-Audio*—isn't just for purists, however. The system can use the multigigabyte storage of the medium for super-quality audio, additional channels, or both.

Whereas CDs are built around a 44.1KHz sampling rate, DVD supports both this rate (and the whole Red Book standard) as well as 48KHz, the same as professional audio systems, and a super-high quality 96KHz sampling rate. In addition to today's 16-bit digital audio, DVD will also support 24-bit audio as well as several compressed multichannel formats to accompany video. The multichannel audio standards vary with the video standard used, with Dolby AC-3 (eight-channel audio) for NTSC video.

The options allowed the producer for linear PCM are wide. The systems support up to six channels with bit-depths of 16, 20, and 24. Recording may use either of two bit-rate families—the 44.1KHz of Red Book audio, supplemented by 88.2 and 176.4KHz multiples, or a 48KHz base rate supplemented by 96 and 192KHz multiples. The highest sampling rate and bit-depth (192KHz at 24 bits) allows response to nearly 96KHz, with a dynamic range approaching 144 dB. The maximum data rate of the system, 9.6Mbps, constrains the system to two channels of these highest-quality signals, and the storage capacity of the DVD system limits playing time (at this quality level) to about 67 minutes.

To extend playing time, the DVD-Audio standard allows for data compression of various sorts, including MPEG. Most intriguing is MLP, which stands for *Meridian Lossless Packing*. As the name implies, this system works like file compression and reduces data redundancies in the digital audio but allows the original signal to be perfectly reconstructed during decoding. Compression extends playing time enough to allow up to about 135 minutes of six-channel 24-bit audio sampled at the 96KHz rate.

To make six-channel audio compatible with two-channel stereo sound systems, DVD-Audio incorporates a special *System-Managed Audio Resource Technique*, or *SMART* (entirely different from the S.M.A.R.T. hard disk failure-prediction technology). This system allows the producer of an audio DVD to determine the optimum mix-down that combines the channels together for each selection on each disc. The mixdown information is stored as a table of coefficients—the level assigned to each channel in the mix—and each selection on the disc can have a particular table assigned to it. Each disc can accommodate up to 16 tables.

DVD-Audio discs also accommodate other kinds of data in addition to digital audio. The standard allows for including up to 16 still images in each track and for synchronizing a display of lyrics with the music. In addition, the DVD-Audio system provides for computer-style navigation through a screen-oriented menu system (or a simplified control system for audio players without computer displays).

Write-Once DVD Formats

The three write-once DVD systems are all based on the same technology as CD-R discs. They use an organic-dye medium that is essentially burnt by a high-power laser to create darkened pits on a disc.

DVD-R(A)

The *A* in the name stands for *authoring*. DVD-R(A) was the first rewritable DVD format, marketed by Pioneer in 1997. The initial drive stored only 3.95GB per disc and was priced at $17,000—hardly a mass-market item. The format was revised in 1999 to accommodate the full 4.7GB of other DVD systems. Both the 3.95GB and 4.7GB formats remain in use.

The DVD-R system is aimed at professional applications. It has been widely deployed to store images of documents used in commerce and for mastering DVDs, where it replaces the Digital Linear Tape systems once widely used for the purpose. Using the new Cutting Master Format on 4.7GB discs allows the use of part of the lead-in track to hold the Disc Description Protocol header information that was used on DLT tapes.

The DVD-R(A) system is centered around a 635-nanometer laser that's used for writing discs. The dye media are tuned to this wavelength, so only discs designed for DVD-R(A) can be recorded in DVD-R(A) writers. The resulting discs can, however, be read by most DVD players, including both DVD-R(A) and DVD-R(G) drives.

The DVD-R(A) standard is sanctioned by the DVD Forum and is an official standard of ECMA International (which changed its name from the European Computer Manufacturers Association in 1994) titled ECMA-279.

DVD-R(G)

The *G* in the name stands for *general purposes*. DVD-R(G) is both an offshoot and refinement of the older DVD-R(A) technology. The chief change is the substitution of a less-expensive 650-nanometer laser for the shorter wavelength used in the DVD-R(A) system. This laser allows for less expensive drives and media but inhibits compatibility. DVD-R(G) discs can be written only in DVD-R(G) drives, although they can be read in almost any DVD player, including those designed for DVD-R(A) discs. The change in laser does not affect capacity. DVD-R(G) discs hold up to 4.7GB.

Because DVD-R(G) is a consumer-level medium, it incorporates content protection to the extent that a DVD-R(G) drive cannot make a copy of an ordinary DVD—for example, a motion picture—that uses CSS encryption. Moreover, the DVD-R(G) system does not support the CRF system used in mastering DVDs. The DVD-R(G) standard is sanctioned by the DVD Forum and is part of the DVD-Multi specification.

DVD+R

DVD+R is a relatively recent addition to the write-once repertory. An offshoot of DVD+RW technology (hence the use of the plus sign in the name), DVD+R discs can be created in any DVD+RW drive manufactured since the introduction of the format in April 2002.

As with CDs, the write-once DVD+R media are less expensive than the rewritable media, so DVD+R is a more affordable way of making permanent records. In addition, the dye-based medium is more reflective than the rewritable medium, making it more easily read in commercial DVD players. Whereas DVD+RW playback may be marginal in some early DVD players, DVD+R discs will likely work better.

The foremost consideration in developing the DVD+R format was compatibility with both DAT drives and video drives. As a consequence, the media hold the same 4.7GB as commercial DVDs, and there are no plans for alternate formats. The DVD+R specifications do allow for two-sided media, but the technology precludes the use of multilayer discs.

The DVD+R specification is sanctioned by the DVD+RW Alliance, and the official standard is published (along with DVD+RW) as ECMA-274.

Rewritable DVD Formats

The same phase-change technology that makes CD-RW possible has been applied to DVD to make a number of rewritable formats. The first of these came from the DVD Forum (and all were delivered months later than promised).

DVD-RAM

The first rewritable format, DVD-RAM, was aimed particularly at data applications. It uses a combination of phase-change and magneto-optical technologies to produce a long-life medium with the ruggedness further enhanced by putting each disc in its own cartridge/carrier, much like a floppy disk shell. As a result, the DVD-RAM system produces discs projected not only to be reliable data archives for more than 30 years, but also the medium itself should endure more than 100,000 write/rewrite cycles.

When DVD-RAM drives first appeared in June, 1998 each disc packed only 2.6GB per side. Two-sided discs doubled that capacity but added the need to flip the cartridge over to access the second side. By October 1999, the specification had been extended to a capacity of 4.7GB per disc side with the first drives arriving in June 2000. The revised specification also included cartridges using discs 80 millimeters in diameter, aimed particularly at high-end digital video camcorders.

The DVD-RAM system uses a wobbled groove to generate the clock used for synchronizing data writing with the spin of the disc. The wobble, a periodic side-to-side twist of the spiral track, is pressed into the blank disc along with fixed sector headers during manufacture. Initially all DVD-RAM discs were encased in cartridges, but the latest design makes the disc removable from the cartridge so you can use it in other formats of DVD drive. Drives can write only on discs encased in their cartridges. Most sources list the DVD-RAM system as incompatible with most other drive formats. DVD-RAM drives write only DVD-RAM discs, and reading the discs in other kinds of drives is chancy. DVD-RAM drives, on the other hand, readily read all other DVD formats.

DVD-RAM drives have built-in defect management, making them the best choice for computer data. In professional camcorders, DVD-RAM has proved impressive, and the defect-management system built in to the drives makes them a good choice for random-access use, their original design intent. The chief handicap of the DVD-RAM system is its inability to make discs that are playable on other kinds of DVD drives.

The DVD-RAM specification is maintained by the DVD Forum, and the standard is published by ECMA as ECMA-272 and ECMA-273.

DVD-RW

Developed originally as a companion to and offshoot of the DVD-R(A) format, DVD-RW is the DVD Forum's choice for a sequential read/write DVD medium. It uses about the same track pitch, data length, and speed control (constant linear velocity) as both DVD-R formats and differs chiefly in medium. DVD-RW uses a phase-change medium, which has somewhat less reflectivity than do the write-once dyes, 18 to 30 percent for DVD-RW, compared to 45 to 80 percent for single-layer DVD-ROM. As a consequence, DVD-RW's initial slow start was further impeded by incompatibilities. Ordinary DVD drives had difficulty reading DVD-RW discs, often mistaking the lower reflectivity as two-layer media in that the disc's 18-to-30-percent reflectivity is the same as that of two-layer DVD-ROMs.

Blank DVD-RW discs actually have two kinds of data prewritten to them. To synchronize the spinning disc with data being written, the disc has address information written on the land area between the grooves of the spiral. In addition, each disc has a prewritten lead-in track that's used by copy-protection systems to prevent the pirating of movies. This lead-in data takes three forms:

- Version 1.0 discs have it physically embossed on the disc during manufacturing

- Version 1.1 discs (the most common) have the data written normally (that is, by a special DVD-RW drive) on the lead-in

- Variation "B" of Version 1.1 discs also have a unique 64-bit disc identification barcode etched near the hub (in the burst cutting area) that's required by some serial copy management systems.

The first DVD-RW systems were designed specifically for recording video. They operated as sequential media and supported only disc-at-once writing. Although editing was possible, it was cumbersome because the entire disc required rewriting for a single simple change. Initial drives operated only in real time—that is, 1× speed—although faster drives are now available. Discs must be formatted before use, although preformatted discs and a quick-format process help minimize the pain.

The expected lifetime of a DVD-RW disc is about 1000 write/rewrite cycles. DVD-RW is sanctioned by the DVD Forum and is part of the DVD-Multi specification.

DVD+RW

From the start, DVD+RW was designed to be a random-access data medium. At the same time, the system was designed to be capable of producing discs compatible with most DVD players. The DVD+RW format is compatible with standard DVDs, and the same 650-nanometer laser reads and writes the medium. The only significant difference is the medium itself, a phase-change compound with somewhat lower reflectivity than standard DVD discs, comparable to that of DVD-RW. As a result, some older DVD players may mistake DVD+RW media for two-layer discs.

Although DVD+RW discs are compatible during reading, the system incorporates a number of enhancements to make DVD+RW useful in data storage. The standard allows drives to use constant linear velocity recording (as with DVD-RW) as well as constant angular velocity recording (constant spin rate) for faster random access. Discs made with either spin-control method are playable on standard DVD players (which use CLV).

For synchronizing disc spin and writing speed, DVD+RW uses wobble tracks—a periodic radial shift to the spiral groove. The wobble produces a frequency of 817KHz during 1× recording, correspondingly higher at faster write speeds. The wobble clock provides four addresses for each 32KB block of data on the disc, allowing the drive to accurately locate any 2KB data cluster. This addressability allows for *lossless linking*, a term used by the DVD+RW promoters to describe the ability of a DVD+RW drive to resume writing within one micron of the place it left off whenever it is interrupted for whatever reason.

This ability to locate accurately any 2KB block of data makes the DVD+RW system truly random access. It can change any data cluster independently of the others without the need to rewrite the entire disc. This ability fits with the Mount Rainier drag-and-drop writing process, so making Mount Rainier DVD+RW drives requires little more than new firmware and certification.

Initially DVD+RW allowed for only one kind of disc, a 12-centimeter disc holding 4.7GB. The same disc can be used both in computer drives for storing data and in dedicated DVD recorders for motion pictures. In August, 2002, the DVD+RW alliance approved 8-centimeter discs holding 1.46GB for applications such as digital camcorders.

DVD+RW discs require formatting before use, but the DVD+RW system supports automatic background formatting. As soon as you insert a new disc into a drive, it starts formatting the lead-in. This way, the drive is immediately ready to use the disc. If you interrupt the formatting process (for example, by removing a partially formatted disc), the drive will resume formatting the disc the next time you insert it. DVD+RW drives support automatic defect management, hiding bad storage areas from your computer and operating system.

The DVD+RW system allows for standalone DVD video recorders. In such applications, it supports four writing modes or quality levels, differing chiefly by bit-rate and playing time. Table 18.6 summarizes these speeds.

TABLE 18.6   DVD+RW Video Recorder Quality Levels

Designation	Name	Recording Time	Data Rate	Resolution
HQ	High Quality	1 hour	9.72Mbits/sec	720 × 480 pixels
SP	Standard Play	2 hours	5.07Mbits/sec	720 × 480 pixels
LP	Long Play	3 hours	3.38Mbits/sec	360 × 480 pixels
EP	Extended Play	4 hours	2.64Mbits/sec	360 × 480 pixels

Initial DVD+RW drives for computers operated at up to 2.4× normal DVD speed and allowed writing at their highest speeds. In August 2002, the DVD+RW Alliance announced the approval of 4× drives.

Although not supported by the DVD Forum, the DVD+RW format is standardized at ECMA-247.

Blu-ray

In February 2002, a consortium of nine electronics firms (none American—the list includes Hitachi, LG Electronics, Matsushita, Philips Electronics, Pioneer, Samsung, Sharp, Sony, and Thomson Multimedia) announced it had agreed on the specifications for the successor to the DVD. Called the *Blu-ray Disc*, the innovation resembles nothing more than a DVD—it's the same size and color and uses the same basic technology. The disc spins in a drive and a laser reads tiny digital spots to play back movies or music. The difference is capacity. The initial Blu-ray discs will be able to store up to 27GB of data, about 5.75 times more than today's DVDs. Moreover, plans include more than doubling that capacity with two-layer discs (a technology already used by DVDs). The specification also allows for discs holding 25 or 23.3GB with relaxed pit-length requirements.

Although initial products will likely only play commercially recorded material, Blu-ray technology allows for erasing and rewriting discs, much as computers already do with

CDs. Existing DVD drives will not be able to play Blu-ray media, although Blu-ray drives should be backward compatible with current formats.

The Blu-ray name explains the secret to the new technology. The laser that reads the disc uses shorter wavelengths (at 405 nanometers, it's closer to violet than blue) that can pick out digital dots that are closer together than can the yellowish laser used by DVDs or the red laser used by CDs. The tracking pitch—the distance between adjacent grooves in the single-track spiral—is only 0.32 micrometers, and the shortest data pits are only 0.138 micrometers long.

All Blu-ray discs use a phase-change medium coated with a 0.1 millimeter optical trans-mittance protection layer. To further "ruggedize" the discs, they are housed in a tough plastic cartridge that measures 5.1 by 5.2 inches and about one-quarter-inch thick. (Exact dimensions: 129 by 131 by 7 millimeters.)

Blu-ray is specifically aimed at putting high-definition television onto DVD-style discs. The system encodes video into MPEG-2 data streams and writes data at 36Mbps. A single disc can hold over two hours of HDTV or 13 hours of VHS-quality video at a 3.8Mbps rate.

As of this writing, Blu-ray is not yet an official standard. The optical community is cur-rently exploring an alternate blue-laser system that uses a 0.8-millimeter protective layer.

PART 5
Human Interface

Cyborgs—creatures half man, half machine that inhabit the nether reaches of space and the imaginations of viewers of *Star Trek: The Next Generation*—differ from the union of you and your computer only in a matter of degree. They represent the intimate interconnection of human neurons and post-silicon circuitry, where human-like bodies receive direct signals from a master wireless network, including modest directives of the nature to subjugate, enslave, assimilate, or destroy Earth. Cyborgs are most scary because they are imaginable, understandable, and—we shudder with growing awareness—possible sooner than we think.

Scary, too, because you're already directly communicating with your computer. You've used your thoughts to guide and control your computer, to tell it what to do. And it commands you, too. Think of that last trip you took when you surfed over to Mapquest.com for directions. A giant computer network told you what to do. Although you were free to ignore the commands, you probably followed them for fear of hearing your wheels slowly grinding themselves down to the axles in mud, lost in a world so dark, gloomy, and far from civilization that even your cell phone won't work.

The difference between you at your computer and a cyborg is only the communication channel and code. The cyborg technology of science fiction has mastered the interface between biological electrical circuitry and electronics, and it has cracked the code your body uses for nerve impulses and the thoughts inside your brain.

The first time you tried to communicate with your computer such a direct connection probably sounded pretty good, especially if you had no previous skills with a keyboard. Direct thought control of your computer would eliminate all of that finger-torture and even speed everything up—at least until some of your inner thoughts started to muck things up. Worse yet, your brain would be flooded by the computer's responses to your commands directly altering your own thoughts. Certainly it would be great for the computer to fill your brain with the right directions when you want to go someplace, but the computer might just as well flood your gray matter with the belief that you actually wanted to go somewhere. It might even make you think you're already there or create a world of entire fantasy. Such ideas have given science fiction writers a field day—and a wealth of plots to explore—which would be wonderful if you weren't the subject of the experiments.

In other words, the interface between you and your computer is yet another case of "be careful what you wish for." Today's communications systems are primitive, indeed, but they work, and what you really want may not be what you really want. You may long for something better—the grass is always greener in the other guy's photo-editing program—but today's connections between you and your computer do a pretty good job of bringing disparate worlds together.

Principles: Connecting to You

Chapter 1, "Computers," noted that programmability is one of the defining features of a computer. But you need some way of getting a program into your computer. After all, the program is how you take command and control your computer.

Engineers programmed the first computers with wires and plug-boards. The wiring defined patterns that formed the digital code of the program. Although such hard-wired programs are the ultimate in nonvolatile memory, they are a bit inconvenient. Each bit in a program is a connection you have to make by hand, and all too often you're apt to make a few mistakes as you plug in thousands of wires.

Next, engineers tried banks of switches to enter programs. Although switches are a bit easier to change than hard wiring, they are just as prone to error, and it's time consuming to have to enter each bit, one at a time.

Teletypes

Banks of switches were hardly the way to get big programs of hundreds or thousands of bytes into a computer. What engineers longed for was a device that could directly generate digital codes with a familiar interface, a familiar means for people to use it. Fortuitously, exactly what they needed was already widely used in the communications industry. The *teletype machine* traces its roots back to 1902 when researchers finally cracked one of the toughest problems plaguing the printing telegraph since Samuel Morse created the first one in 1845. With the creation of the start-stop code (which lives on today in the RS-232C port, see

Chapter 11, "Ports") in 1908, Charles and Howard Krum produced the first practical automatic printer connected to a telegraph line.

In 1919, the father-son duo created a keyboard-based transmitter, and the foundation for the teletype system was in place. In 1925, they merged their interests with those of a rival developer, Edward Kleinschmidt, and the company took the name Teletype Corporation in 1929 and was purchased by the Bell System a year later.

Although the printer was the most important side of the invention for its creators, computer designers eagerly adapted the transmitter to their machines. The transmitter became what is essentially the first computer keyboard—you typed into a typewriter-style keyboard and produced digital code (in the form of a five-bit international code invented by Emile Baudot in 1870 and named after him).

Keypresses on the teletype keyboard produced punched tape that, when fed into a reader, generated the Baudot code. Makers of tabulators, such as IBM, found the same technology could make the punch-cards they used. This punch-card technology became the input and output system of the first commercial computer, ENIAC. Two years later, the Binac computer used an electrically controlled typewriter keyboard to write magnetic code on tape.

By 1964, Bell Laboratories and General Electric created the first electronic computer terminal for the Multics computer system. With the introduction of this first *video data terminal* (VDT), all the intermediary steps between the keystrokes and final digital code disappeared. Each keypress produced a code in electronic form that could be immediately processed by the computer.

Regardless of whether punched tape serves as an intermediary or a terminal creates digital codes directly, all these technologies owe one particular bit of heritage to the teletype. You need to type in each letter the computer receives in exactly the same order you want the computer to receive it. The stream of characters is a serial sequence. Communication is reduced to a single, unidirectional stream, much like telling a story in a novel.

From the cyborg viewpoint, all this text comes from the language processing part of your brain. Your ideas must be fully digested and turned into words, and the words into text, before you communicate them with your computer.

This same technology survives today in all computers. The interface between man and machine in this process is your computer's keyboard. The first major personal computer operating system used the keyboard as its primary (and only) input device. Your only means of control and data input was the keyboard. Even the longest, most intricate programs required that someone, somewhere, enter all the commands and data used in writing them through the keyboard.

Pointing Devices

To many people, the keyboard is the most formidable and forbidding aspect of a computer. The keys might as well be teeth ready to chomp down on their fingers as soon as they try to type. Typing just isn't something that comes naturally to most people. Learning to type takes months or years of practice—practice that's about as welcome as a piano lesson on a sunny afternoon when the rest of the neighborhood kids are playing in the pool outside.

Imagine trying to drive your car by typing in commands—turn right 15 degrees, increase speed to 55 miles per hour, stop before driving off that cliff—oh, well. Brace yourself for the landing. Although the keyboard provides an excellent way to move your properly formatted language-based thoughts into your computer, it is inefficient at more sophisticated means of control. Even if you could type with your fingers moving at the speed of light, control through the keyboard would still be slow because your brain needs to perform some heavy-duty processing of the data first, at biologic rather than electronic speeds.

Teletype-style input poses another problem. Control systems built from it are *command driven*. You have to type in individual commands, which in turn requires that you know which commands to type. If you don't know the commands, you sit there with your fingers knotted and nothing happening.

One of Douglas C. Engelbart's jobs at the Stanford Research Institute between 1957 and 1977 was to find ways of making computers more accessible and usable by ordinary people. One of his ideas was to put graphics on the computer screen and use a handheld device that would point at different places on the screen as you moved the device across your physical desktop. He made his first model of the device in 1964 and received a patent in 1970 for the first computer mouse. He called it that because it had a tail coming out the end, the interface wire.

Engelbart's concept of combining the pointing device coupled with a graphical/menu-driven onscreen user interface was later developed at the Palo Alto Research Laboratory of Xerox Corporation in its Alto workstation in 1973. Xerox first commercially offered these concepts in its 1981 Star workstation, which inspired the Apple Lisa and Macintosh computers but was in itself not a marketing success.

The underlying concept was to allow you to indicate what function you want your computer to carry out by selecting from a list of commands presented as a menu. You point at the menu selection by physically moving the pointing device, which causes a corresponding onscreen movement of the cursor. One or more buttons atop the device enable you to indicate that you want to select a menu item—a process much easier to do than describe. The mouse was meant to be small enough to fit under the palm of a hand with the button under a fingertip. The whole process of moving the mouse and its onscreen representation is termed *dragging the mouse*.

Apple Computer, understanding the achievements made at SRI and Xerox with the mouse and graphical interface, incorporated both into its Macintosh computer in 1984. Although you could obtain a mouse and software to use it for Intel-architecture computers at about the same time, widespread use of a graphical interface did not become popular with Intel machines until the introduction of Windows 95.

Graphic Input Devices

A mouse is an indicator rather than a full-fledged input device. When you want to put graphic images into your computer, a mouse works only if you want to draw them anew. Capturing an existing image is more complex because your computer needs a way to represent it.

That need had already been filled by bitmapped display systems (see "Two-Dimensional Graphics," later in the chapter), which break an image into visual units small enough that they blend together in the eye to form a single, solid image. The units used to represent the image are termed *pixels*, short for picture elements. The process of converting an image or the representation of an object into pixels is called *pixelization*.

The process is not easy because it must deal with two worlds, the optical and electronic, converting the optical representation of an image or object into an electronic signal with a recognizable digital format. Several devices can make this conversion, including the scanner and digital camera.

The scanner can convert anything you have on paper—or for that matter, anything reasonably flat—into computer-compatible electronic form. Dot by dot, a scanner can reproduce photos, line drawings, even collages in detail, sharper than your laser printer can duplicate. Better yet, equip your computer with optical character recognition software, and the images your scanner captures of typed or printed text can be converted into ASCII files for your word processor, database, or publishing system. Just as the computer opened a new world of information management to you, a scanner opens a new world of images and data to your computer.

The digital camera captures what you see in the real world. It grabs a view of not only three-dimensional objects but also entire scenes in their full splendor. As the name implies, the digital camera is the computer equivalent of that old Kodak, one that produces files instead of film. It captures images in a flash—or without one in bright daylight—and requires no processing other than what you do with your photo-editing software. It tops the list of most wanted computer peripherals because it's not only a useful tool but also a neat toy that turns anyone into an artist and can add a good dose of fun to an otherwise drab day at the computer.

Output

At the other end of the computer, its output, where it needs to communicate to you, the history is much the same as the input side. The first computers used hardcopy printed output to express their answers or displeasure. Even Charles Babbage envisioned printed paper as the basic output for his Analytical Engine. After all, paper has an enduring advantage. You can see your results for as long as you want, and more importantly, you can see your mistakes. When you can hold the evidence of your mistakes in your hand, you can repair your errors more quickly.

But putting all output on paper has a big disadvantage. If you've ever waited for an important job to print, you know the frustration of watching each line slowly appear down the paper. Printing is a slow, mechanical process. Trying to run an interactive computing session while relying on your printer for output would be like running a relay race with a glacier anchoring your team.

Much as the video data terminal changed computer input, it revolutionized computer output. Without it, interactive computing would be no more than a dream. But the computer terminal didn't appear on the market like Athena, fully armed and prepared for battle. It entered this world as a teletype machine that wrote with lighted phosphors instead of ink (and at the same speed). Over the years, the computer terminal picked up momentum, graphics, colors, and finally windows.

At first, the personal computer simply split the video system from the keyboard and inserted the computer in the middle. Communications with the display followed the same routine as the terminal and the teletype—the slow, serial stream of text characters. In a quest for speed, engineers sidestepped their own best plans and revealed the magic of direct access and painting pictures directly on the screen. Today's systems add a second computer to your computer, one solely aimed at making images on your screen faster than you can blink.

Teletype to Terminal

When engineers ushered in Harvard Mark I in 1943, television was little more than a bluish dream in the minds of broadcasters, barely off to a flickery black-and-white start. The first commercial licenses went into effect in July, 1941, and then went on hold for the years of World War II. Putting text on the screen meant holding up a printed card. The only output devices available to the first computer were mechanical, and the one most readable by humans was printed paper, courtesy of the teletype machine.

The early connection between computer and teletypes lingers on in the lingo. Even today, the data that's sent by a computer to its output device as a string of printable characters is still termed *teletype output*. The character string, if converted to the correct code, would run a mechanical teletype happily through reams of coarse paper.

The first terminals were little more than teletypes that printed on the screen instead of onto paper. Essentially the same minimal design survives today at the *dumb terminal*, named not for the engineers who design it but for how it processes what you see. A dumb terminal is not smart enough to do data processing on its own. It puts each character on its screen exactly as it is received through the umbilical cable linking it to its computer host. Compared to the mechanical teletype, refinements are few. Instead of rattling off the edge of the paper, a too-long electronic line more likely will "wrap" or scroll down to the line below. The terminal never runs out of paper—it seemingly has a fresh supply of blank screen below, rolling upward as necessary to receive each additional line. But the output it generates is even more tenuous than the flimsiest tissue and disappears at the top of the screen, perchance never to be seen again.

In the electronic form of the computer terminal, the teletype method of text-handling means that when one character changes on the screen, a whole new screen full of text must be generated and sent to the terminal. The system cannot back up to change the one character, so it must rush headlong forward, reworking the whole display along the way.

Add brains to a dumb terminal and you get a *smart terminal*. A microprocessor inside lets the smart terminal recognize special commands for formatting its display and may even be able to do some computer-like functions on its own.

BIOS Support

Computers act like dumb terminals in their most basic display functions. They put characters on the screen like teletypes to produce teletype output under the guidance of their BIOSs. In fact, the basic computer BIOS gives several layers of teletype output. In the most primitive, a program must load one character at a time into a microprocessor register and issue a *video interrupt*—specifically, interrupt 010(hex). The BIOS then takes over, instructing the microprocessor to check where to put the character (a several-step process in itself) and then pushing the character into the appropriate place in memory. The BIOS then returns control back to the program to process the next character. The most advanced teletype mode lets a program put an entire line of text on the screen through a similar, equally cumbersome process.

In basic teletype mode, characters are written on the screen from left to right, from screen top to bottom, merely scrolling after each line is full or ended with a carriage return. More advanced display technologies are able to write anywhere on the monitor screen using formatting instructions much as smart terminals do. For example, commands in the computer BIOS let your programs locate each character anywhere on the screen.

HTML

The great advance made in communications by the Internet has at its heart teletype technology. Your computer displays basic Web text in teletype style—one character at a time as if it came as part of a string from a teletype. The chief difference between what came across the teletype wire and what comes through your Internet connection is the code. Teletypes used Baudot; the Web uses *Hypertext Markup Language* (HTML), layered upon the ordinary ASCII code that specifies individual letters.

HTML uses the processing power of the computer to improve on basic teletype technology. Certainly it's quieter. Unlike a teletype machine, your screen does not chatter like the teeth of a freezing epileptic. More importantly, the HTML character stream includes formatting codes that allow it to specify type size and faces, even colors. Although your computer still pops each character on your screen in the order it appears in the HTML string, it can make changes in the appearance of each character based on the in-stream codes.

The codes act as switches. When one appears in the data stream, it switches on a text feature—for example, turning the text red. All later text gets displayed in red until another HTML code turns it off or sets another color.

Some HTML codes affect the formatting of characters displayed on your computer's screen (for example, indenting lines). This formatting is relative rather than absolute. Its effects vary depending on the size and shape of your Web display. For example, a simple tab might take up half a column on a narrow window or a few character widths in a wide one. In this way, HTML operates like a teletype—the characters in the HTML stream come out without regard to the size or shape of the display medium.

More recent revisions to HTML allow the Web to go beyond minimally formatted text. Tables allow you to create more structure in your text displays. In addition, you can embed streams of images with your text characters. Even these elements, however, are handled like the letters and numbers relayed to an old teletype display. In other words, old ideas don't die. They just go online.

Character Technologies

The most notable aspect of teletype technology, be it on your screen or on the Web, is that it is *character oriented*. The smallest unit of information it deals with is a text character. At the times when your computer steps back to this technology of yesteryear—for example, the first few moments of booting up, before it spins its disks to load the basic code of your operating system, or when you read your email—your computer lets you see its world only in terms of letters and numbers.

Somehow your computer must organize the characters it wants to display. Teletype machines handle this matter mechanically. They simply stamp each character on a piece of paper. The typing automatically organizes the text and the inky image preserves it. Your computer isn't so lucky. It has to organize the text in electronic form, it has to be able to move the character representations around inside its circuitry, and it has to keep the characters you see glowing on a screen that would rather remain permanently black.

Your system has two alternative ways of dealing with the characters it wants to put on your screen. It can store and manipulate them in the form of individual characters, or it can break the characters down into tiny pieces called a *bitmap*, in which each piece representing one of the bright dots appearing on your computer display. Your computer uses both of these technologies every day. Although Windows treats your entire display screen as one giant bitmap, applications running under Windows often send information to the operating system to display in character form.

Character-Mapping

When your computer deals with characters as a fixed unit, one code per indivisible character, it uses a technology termed *character-mapping*. The name refers to the *character map*, a special range of addresses that's sometimes called *screen memory* or *display memory*. The memory of the character map is reserved for storing the characters that will appear on the screen. Simple programs such as your computer's bootup BIOS routines write text on the screen by pushing bytes into the proper places in that memory. Just as a street on a roadmap corresponds to the location of a real street, each byte of display memory corresponds to a character position on the screen.

The most common operating mode of the character-mapped display systems used by computers when they boot up divides the screen into a matrix (essentially a set of pigeon-holes, with each hole corresponding to one position on the screen) that measures 80 characters wide and 25 high. To display a character on the screen, a program loads the corresponding code into the memory location associated with its matrix cell. To put the image on the screen, the display system reads the entire matrix, translates into a serial data stream that scans across the monitor screen, and moves the data to the video output. In other words, it creates the exact bit-pattern that will appear on the screen on the fly, computing each nanosecond of the video signal in real time. From there, the signal is the monitor's problem.

For your programs, writing characters to the screen is simply a matter of writing directly to screen memory. Consequently, this display technique is often called *direct writing*. It is the fastest way to put information on a computer screen. Character-mapping is also more versatile than teletype technology. Programs can push characters into any screen location in any order they please—top, bottom, left, or right, even lobbing one letter atop another, overwriting the transitory existence of each.

Once an advanced operating system such as Windows loads, however, your computer steps away from character-mapping. The operating system imposes itself between your programs and the BIOS. The operating system captures the characters your text-oriented programs attempt to fling directly at the screen. The operating system can then recompute the map, making it larger or smaller and, in the latter case, moving it to a designated area of the screen.

Direct Writing

This quick way of putting characters on the screen is often termed *direct writing*, because programs simply move the code assigned to a character directly to the memory location corresponding to that character's screen position—a one-step process that requires only one microprocessor instruction.

Direct writing makes a specific demand from programs using it: They need to know the exact location of each screen memory address. For all applications to work on all computers, the addresses used by each system must be the same—or your software needs some means of determining what addresses your computer uses. In the first personal computers, the design engineers reserved two memory areas to serve as character buffers, one for color text and one for monochrome. These memory areas became standard for all computers, and your system still uses them for the text it displays on the screen while it is booting up. To determine which character buffer to use, your software can check the *video mode flag* at a special location in memory, which indicates the proper buffer. Although this dual-buffer feature remains part of every personal computer, it's hardly necessary because of the universal use of color display systems.

Character Boxes

In text modes, the display memory addresses hold codes that have nothing to do with the shapes appearing on the monitor screen except as a point of reference. The actual patterns of each character that appears on the screen are stored in a special ROM chip called the *character ROM* that's part of the video circuitry of the computer. The code value that defines the character is used by the video circuitry to look up the character pattern that matches it. The bit-pattern from the character ROM is scanned and sent to the screen to produce the final image.

Modern display adapters allow you to download your own fonts (typefaces) into onboard RAM that's reserved from the same block that would serve as the character map. These downloaded fonts can be used as if they were located in ROM with the same ease of manipulation as ROM-based fonts. Downloaded fonts appear just the same, whether pushed on the screen through the teletype or direct-access technique.

Each onscreen character is made from an array of dots, much like the text output of a teletype or dot-matrix printer. Computer and display adapter manufacturers use several video standards to build individual characters out of different size dot arrays. The framework in which the dots of an individual character are laid out, called the *character box*, is a matrix like a crossword puzzle. The character box is measured by the number of dots or cells composing its width and its height. For example, Figure 19.1 shows a series of characters formed in character boxes measuring 15 by 9 cells.

The text modes used by various early display standards all had their own, distinctive character boxes. The standard Video Graphics Array (VGA) text screen uses a 16-by-9 character box. Each character takes up a space on the screen measuring 16 dots high and 9 dots wide.

FIGURE 19.1

Characters formed in 15-by-9-cell boxes.

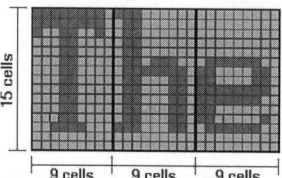

The last vestige of character mode display technology that remains under Windows is the DOS box, or *command mode*. You can select the height and width of the character box used in the command mode to adjust the size of the windows in which your character-based applications run in text mode using the properties sheet for command mode.

The size of the character box does not exactly describe how large each character is or how many dots are used in forming it. To improve readability, individual characters do not necessarily take up the entire area that a character box affords. For instance, text characters on most monochrome displays keep one row of dots above and one below those used by each character to provide visible separation between two adjacent lines of text on the screen.

Video Attributes

The character-mapped displays of most computer video systems do not store each letter adjacent to the next. Instead, each onscreen character position corresponds to every other byte in screen memory; the intervening bytes are used as *attribute bytes*. Even-numbered bytes store character information; odd bytes, attributes.

The attribute byte determines the highlighting or color of a displayed character that's stored in the preceding memory byte. The codes used in monochrome and color displays are different. Monochrome characters are allowed the following attributes: normal, highlighted (brighter onscreen characters), underlined, and reverse-video characters (dark on light instead of the normal light on dark). The different attributes can be combined, although in the normal scheme of things highlighted reverse-video characters make the character background brighter instead of highlighting the character shape itself. These monochrome display attributes are listed in Table 19.1.

TABLE 19.1   Monochrome Display Attributes

Byte Value	Attribute
00	Non-display
01	Underline
07	Normal
09	Intensified underline
0F	Intensified
71	Reverse video underline
77	Reverse video
79	Reverse video intensified underline
7F	Reverse video intensified
81	Blinking underline
87	Blinking normal
89	Blinking intensified underline
8F	Blinking intensified
F1	Blinking reverse video underline
F7	Blinking reverse video
F9	Blinking intensified reverse video underline
FF	Blinking intensified reverse video

Color systems store two individual character hues in the attribute byte. The first half of the byte (the most significant bits of the digital code of the byte) code the color of the character itself. The latter half of the attribute (the least significant bits) code the background color. Because four bits are available for storing each of these colors, this system can encode 16 foreground and 16 background colors for each character (with black and white considered two of these colors). In normal operation, however, one bit of the background color code indicates a special character attribute—blinking. This attribute allows any color combination to blink, but it also cuts the number of hues available for backgrounds in half (to eight colors, with all intensified color choices eliminated). When you or your software needs to be able to display all 16 background colors, a status bit allows the character-flashing feature to be defeated. Color display attributes are shown in Table 19.2.

TABLE 19.2   Color Display Attributes

Nibble Value	Foreground Color	Background Color	Flashing
0	Black	Black	No
1	Blue	Blue	No
2	Green	Green	No
3	Red	Red	No
4	Cyan	Cyan	No
5	Magenta	Magenta	No
6	Brown	Brown	No
7	Light gray	Light gray	No
8	Dark gray	Black	Yes
9	Bright blue	Blue	Yes
A	Bright green	Green	Yes
B	Pink	Red	Yes
C	Bright cyan	Cyan	Yes
D	Bright magenta	Magenta	Yes
E	Yellow	Brown	Yes
F	White	Light gray	Yes

Because each character on the screen requires two bytes of storage, a full 80-character column by 25-character row of text (a total of 2000 characters) requires 4000 bytes of storage. In the basic computer monochrome video system, 16KB are allotted to store character information. The basic (and basically obsolete) color system reserves 64KB for this purpose.

Video Pages

The additional memory does not go to waste, however. It can be used to store more than one screen of text at a time, with each separate screen called a *video page*. Either basic video system is designed to quickly switch between these video pages so that onscreen images can be changed almost instantly. Switching quickly allows a limited degree of animation. The technique is so useful that even today's most advanced 3D graphics boards use it, although with pictures instead of text.

Two-Dimensional Graphics

The only graphics available on the first computers were block graphics, akin in more than name to the first toys of toddlers, mere playthings that you wouldn't want to use for serious work. The first computer graphics systems made television look good, which in any other context would be an insurmountable challenge to the imagination. The foundation of the new display systems—called *bitmapped graphics*—proved powerful enough that in a few years computer display quality not only equaled that of television, but computers were also used in *making* television images. The modern computer graphics system has taken a further step beyond and attempts to build a real (or real-looking) three-dimensional reality.

The development of computer graphics is best described as accumulation rather than evolution. Each new system builds upon the older designs, retaining full backward compatibility. Even the latest 3D graphics systems retain the ability to work with the first rudimentary block graphics. Just as you share genes with some of the lowest forms of life, such as bacteria, planaria, and politicians, your sleek new computer comes complete with state-of-the-art 1981 graphics technology.

Block Graphics

You don't need a lot of computer power and an advanced operating system to put graphics on your screen, which is good because in the early years computers didn't have a lot of power or decent operating systems. In fact, even teletypes that are able only to smash numbers and letters on paper can print primitive graphic images. By proper selection of characters, standing far from printouts, and squinting, you could imagine you saw pictures in some printouts (a triangle of text might vaguely resemble a Christmas tree, for example).

When computers operate like teletypes, their graphic output faces the same limitations as printouts—characters can only approximate real-world images. To try to improve matters, the designers of the original computer took advantage of the extra potential of storing characters as byte values. Because one byte can encode 256 different characters, and the alphabet and other symbols total far short of that number, the first computer's designers assigned special characters to some of the higher-numbered bytes in its character set. Beyond dingbats and foreign language symbols, a few of the extra characters were reserved for drawing graphic images from discrete shapes and patterned blocks that partly or entirely fill in the character matrix.

When your computer is operating in text mode, such as in command mode, you can still create rough graphic images by strategically locating these character blocks on the screen so that they form larger shapes. Other extra characters comprise a number of single and double lines as well as corners and intersections of them to draw borders around text areas. The characters are building blocks of the graphic images, and consequently this form of graphics is termed *block graphics*. Figure 19.2 shows the block graphic characters in the standard computer character set.

FIGURE 19.2
Standard computer block graphic characters.

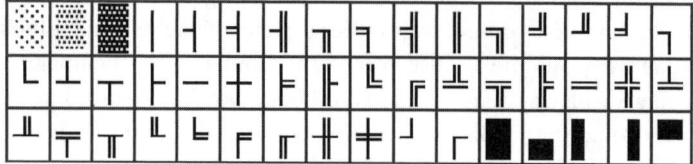

To a computer display system, block graphics are considered text and are handled exactly like ordinary text characters. All the text attributes are available to every character of block graphics, including all the available text colors, highlighting, and reverse video characteristics. The characters are also pushed onto the screen in text mode, which gives them high-speed potential, but they are available only in text mode or the Windows DOS box. Because they use the high-order ASCII characters—foreign territory for most seven-bit email systems—you cannot ordinarily use them for images in ordinary email.

Bitmapped Graphics

Windows marked the transition of the primary operating mode of computer display systems. From character-based displays, Windows ushered in the age of the bitmapped display. *Bitmapped graphics* improve the poor quality of block graphics by making the blocks smaller. The smaller the blocks making an image, the finer grain that can be shown, and therefore more detail. Physical aspects of the display system impose a distinct and unbreakable limit on how small each block can be—the size of the individual dots that make up the image on the video screen. The sharpest and highest-quality image that could be shown by any display system would individually control every dot or pixel on the screen.

The most straightforward way of handling the information to be displayed on such a screen is to assign some part of memory to each pixel, just as two bytes are given over to each character of a character-mapped display. In the computer scheme of things, because the data controlling each pixel is stored as one or more memory bits, this kind of display system is often called *bitmapped graphics*. Alternately, because each pixel or point on the video screen can be separately addressed through memory, this method of controlling the video display is often called *all points addressable* graphics or an *APA display*.

In the bitmapped graphics system, display memory stores an exact electronic representation of the onscreen image. It's actually a time-slice of what you see—the software running on your computer is constantly sending new data into display memory to update the screen image. The memory temporarily stores or buffers the changes' frame until they are read out as a complete image frame dozens of times per second. Because of this function, graphics display memory is often called the *frame buffer*.

As with character-mapped memory, programmers have their choice of methods to write bitmapped graphics to your monitor screen. The BIOS can do it, but Windows substitutes its own drivers for the purpose. Programs can also write directly to memory, but modern video systems make that chancy because each display system uses its own memory locations, display modes, and resolutions. Video drivers bridge these differences.

Bitmapped graphics hold the potential for being much sharper than block graphics. More pixels mean more detail. The number of dots on a screen and the ultimate number of pixels are many times the number of characters that are displayed on that same screen, from 64 to 126 times greater. However, bitmapped graphics imposes its own, interrelated penalties—memory usage and speed.

The amount of memory required by a graphics display system depends on two factors: the sharpness of the display image and the number of colors (or gray levels) to be displayed. Each increase in sharpness and number of colors means that your computer is putting more detail (more information) on its screen and storing more information in its display buffer. As a result, it must move around more information (more bytes), which means more work. And the harder your computer works, the longer it takes to complete its job.

Vector Graphics

Bitmapped graphics are sometimes termed *raster graphics* because the technology organizes the screen into a series of lines called a *raster* that's continually scanned dozens of times a second. Although raster graphics are the basis of all computer displays—as well as today's television and video systems—this is not the only way to put a computer image on a monitor. A completely different technique does not regularly scan the screen at all. Instead, it precisely controls the circuitry operating the horizontal and vertical deflection yokes. It doesn't trace scan lines but instead draws figures the same way you would as a series of strokes of a paintbrush. To keep the screen lit, it constantly retraces the figures.

Because the signals controlling the monitor drive the electron beam in the CRT as a series of vectors, this image-making technique is usually termed *vector graphics*. Alternately, this kind of display system is sometimes called a *stroker* because of the kinship to drawing brushstrokes. Although not used on computers, the term pops up occasionally in the descriptions of expensive computerized workstations.

Resolution

The number that quantifies the possible sharpness of a video image is called *resolution*. It indicates how many individual pixels an image contains that your display system will spread across the width and height of the screen. Because your computer generates the image as an electrical signal completely independent from your computer monitor (it would make the same image even if your monitor wasn't connected to the computer at all), physical properties of the monitor (such as its physical dimensions) play no part in resolution measurements. In other words, the number of pixels in an image does not vary with the size of the screen that it is displayed upon. Resolution is expressed without reference to units of linear measurement—resolution is described in pixels or dots rather than dots per inch. For example, the computer minimal resolution mode display—called VGA (for the circuitry of the first display system to use it, the *Video Graphics Array*)—has a resolution of 640 pixels horizontally by 480 pixels vertically in its native graphics mode. Today's typical display has at least 1024 pixels horizontally and 768 pixels vertically.

Dots per inch is a measure of actual onscreen sharpness, and it depends both on resolution and the size of the resulting image. At the same resolution, a larger screen has less sharpness than a smaller screen—all else being equal.

The higher the resolution of an image, the more pixels it will contain. The more pixels, the more memory needed to store them.

Graphic Attributes

How much memory is required for a given resolution depends on a second factor in addition to the number of pixels—the number of bits assigned to each pixel. At minimum, each pixel requires a single bit of storage. That bit can be used to code either of two conditions—whether the pixel is illuminated on the screen or invisibly dark. In the simplest bit-image graphics system, one bit of memory would then be used to map the condition of each pixel in the video display.

What's lacking from this primitive mapping system is contrast and color. All bits are treated the same and their associated pixels look about the same, either on or off. The result is a single-hued picture with no variation or shading, essentially the same sort of an image as a line drawing. Although that may be sufficient for some purposes (for instance, the display of a chart or graph that mimics the monochrome look of ink on paper), color and contrast can add impact.

The way to add color to bitmapped images is much the same as adding color to character-based displays—adding attribute information. Additional memory is devoted to storing the attribute of each bit. The bitmapped system works somewhat differently from the character-based mode, however. All the memory devoted to a pixel is used to describe it. No information needs to be devoted to identifying a character or pattern for each picture element because each one is essentially a featureless dot.

Color Planes

A single bit per pixel results in what graphics folk call a *two-color system*, because it puts everything in black and white—each pixel is either on or off. Putting more color in the image requires encoding more information—more bits and more memory. Adding a second bit per pixel doubles the number of possible displayable colors. (Shades—degrees of darkness or light—are considered different colors in the terminology of computer graphics.) Every additional bit assigned to each pixel likewise doubles the number of possible colors. Hence, with n bits, $2n$ colors are possible.

In computer graphics, the number of bits assigned to coding color information is sometimes described as the number of *color planes*. This term relates to the organization of display memory. The memory map of the graphic image can be visualized much like a Mercator projection of the world, with latitude and longitude lines corresponding to the different positions of the bits corresponding to pixels in the image. Additional bits per each pixel add a third dimension, much like layers of maps stacked atop one another, a series of flat planes containing the color information.

With more colors used in an image, the better the apparent image-quality and the more life-like its appearance. For this reason, the temptation is to increase the bit-depth of each pixel as high as possible. However, the more colors or color planes, the more storage is needed for encoding each pixel. Moreover, much to the dismay of purveyors of video memory, the human eye is limited in its ability to resolve individual colors—most people can distinguish only a few million distinct colors. Color monitors are even more limited in the number of colors they can display. Most monitors top out at about 262,144 colors, corresponding to the capabilities of an 18-bit display system. Once these limits are reached and enough memory is assigned each pixel, further "improvements" do not improve appearances.

The practical limit on color is a bit-depth of 24 bits, which allows a system to store and theoretically display any of 16,777,216 hues. Display systems with this bit-depth are termed *24-bit color* or *True Color* systems, because they can store sufficient information to encode more colors than anyone could possibly see—they hold a truly accurate representation of any color.

Although some of the capabilities of True Color display systems are superfluous because they exceed the human ability to distinguish colors, True Color is a convenient system for designers because it assigns one byte of storage for each of the three additive primary colors (red, green, and blue) to each pixel. Before memory became cheap and processors raced beyond a gigahertz, this three-byte-per-pixel memory requirement was a burden on computer systems, straining both speed and storage.

Some newer display systems have a 32-bit color mode. Instead of allocating the additional byte of storage to color information, however, most of these 32-bit systems put the extra bits to work as an alpha channel. The bits in the alpha channel hold control rather than color information. In effect, the alpha channel provides a storage place for special-effects information. The bits in the alpha channel normally are not tallied in counting color planes.

The newest scanners may have 48-bit color capabilities. The extra bits are for colors you cannot see but could. When you want to adjust an image (for example, to brighten a dark scene), the extra bits ensure that even dark shadows have color differences. Brighten the image, and the shadows will have detail instead of being big, black blobs.

The math for finding the amount of memory required to display a color graphics screen is straightforward. Simply multiply the number of pixels on the screen—that is, the resolution—by the bit-depth of each pixel. Then divide by eight to translate bits into bytes. For example, an XGA screen with 1024 by 768 pixels comprises exactly 786,432 pixels. If you want True Color (one byte of storage per color, or a total of 24-bits per pixel), you need 18,874,368 bits to store the image data—that's 2,359,296 bytes. A display adapter with only 2MB won't handle that combination of colors and resolution, but (rounding up to the next generally available increment) a board with 4MB will do nicely.

Table 19.3 summarizes the memory required for common resolutions at various bit-depths for standard business graphics.

TABLE 19.3   Display Memory Required for Given Resolutions and Color Depths

Resolution	Mono	16 Colors	256 Colors	High Color	True Color
Bits per pixel	1	4	8	16	24
Bytes per pixel	0.125	0.5	1	2	3
640×480	38,400	153,600	307,200	614,400	921,600
800×600	60,000	240,000	480,000	960,000	1,440,000
1024×768	98,304	393,216	786,432	1,572,864	2,359,296
1152×864	124,416	497,664	995,328	1,990,636	2,985,984
1280×1024	163,840	655,360	1,310,720	2,621,440	3,932,160
1600×1200	240,000	960,000	1,920,000	3,840,000	5,760,000
1920×1340	321,600	1,286,400	2,572,800	5,145,600	7,718,400
2048×1536	393,216	1,572,864	3,145,728	6,291,456	9,437,184

The values shown in this table refer only to two-dimensional display systems. The three-dimensional systems that are becoming popular gorge themselves on memory. Most have two frame buffers to take advantage of the double-buffering and use additional memory in rendering the image—for example, to serve as a z-buffer. (Double-buffering and z-buffering are both discussed in the section later in this chapter titled "Three-Dimensional Graphics.") More memory is required for describing objects and even stuff you never see.

Color Coding

The best and worst display systems assign the same number of bits to each of the three primary colors—a bit or an entire byte. For intermediary color depths, however, the base-2 digital nature of the computer and the three-fold nature of color vision come into direct collision. For example, if you want to assign a single byte to store the colors of each pixel, how can you evenly allocate eight bits among three colors? With two bytes per pixel, how do you divide 16 by 3 evenly?

You don't. But you don't have to. You don't even have to code colors as a mix of red, green, and blue.

Because the human eye is most sensitive to green and its shadings (probably something to do with primitive humans living in an environment lush with chlorophyll-green plants), some color-coding systems split their bit assignments evenly and assign the odd bit to green. For example, when the first computer engineers designed a 16-bit VGA color system, they assigned five bits to red and blue and gave six to green.

Color Spaces

In mixing colors to produce a full spectrum, the number of hues any system can produce is limited by the range of its medium. Because most systems of colors involve three signals, such as the three primary colors of light, mapping them requires three dimensions, which in turn defines a volume or space. The range of colors that a specific system can handle is consequently called the *color space*. In the RGB system used by computer monitors, the range of red, green, and blue signals define the three dimensions of the color space, but the RGB system is only one possible color space.

Other image systems encode colors in an entirely different manner. One of the most common is to encode colors by brightness (technically called *luminance* and abbreviated as Y) and two color (or chromaticity) values (abbreviated C1 and C2) that essentially correspond to coordinates on a map of colors. In more general form, the signals used are termed Y, Cr, and Cb. In effect, Y is the luminance or overall image brightness, derived by totaling together all three of the RGB signals. Cr represents the difference between the red and luminance signal. Cb represents the difference between the blue and the luminance signal. Subtract Cr from Y and you get the red signal. Subtract Cb from Y and you get blue. Subtract both the resulting red and blue signals from Y and you get green.

A related system used by composite video signals transforms the YCrCb signals into intensity, hue, and saturation. In the intensity/hue/saturation color space, intensity describes one axis of the color space. Saturation is defined as the distance from the intensity axis, and hue is the direction from the axis. Together these three measures—two distances and an angle—define the three dimensions of the space. In effect, hue is represented as an angle in the phase relationship between two signals.

In conventional video signals, as used by televisions, VCRs, and other video equipment, the intensity information is called the *luminance signal*, and it takes the form of a standard black-and-white television signal. The saturation information is represented as the corresponding amplitude of an added signal called the *color burst*. The phase relationship between the luminance signal and the color burst defines the hue. In this way, the three dimensions of the video color space are cleverly encoded in two signals.

Commercial printers use a different color scheme to start, the so-called *process colors* of cyan, magenta, yellow, and black (often abbreviated as CMYK). These colors correspond to the ink colors used in the four-color printing process. The black adds depth to the printed colors.

These different color spaces and coding methods are useful to particular output devices—CMYK colors for storing images that eventually will be printed and published; luminance and chrominance coding for images that will eventually be used in broadcast-style (as opposed to computer) video systems. To be displayed by normal computer monitors, they must be translated from their native format to the RBG signals used by computer monitors.

Color-Mapping

Another method of encoding colors in memory that requires translation has found greater use in computers, particularly when a manufacturer wants to scrimp on video memory. A technique called *color-mapping* stores only code numbers for colors, allowing each code number to stand for almost any color. One code number gets stored in video memory for each onscreen pixel. The display system matches the stored numeric code values to a Color Look-Up Table (CLUT) that tells which color corresponds to each number; then that color is sent along to the monitor. Because of the nature of colors in the real world, color-mapping can lead to substantial economies in display memory.

When the values stored in screen memory directly indicate what color appears on the screen, as they do in the preceding example, the colors are said to be *direct mapped*.

Direct mapping allows any pixel to be any color, but most images are made from far fewer colors. By mapping the colors, you can trim the amount of memory used to store an image. Although memory is not so much an issue with computers as it used to be, file size remains a consideration when shipping images across the Internet. Consequently, most images use some kind of mapping when they are stored. Most image-compression schemes use some form of color-mapping. The GIF (which stands for *Graphic Interchange Format*) files widely used on the Web are color-mapped to use only eight bits of storage for each pixel.

Graphic Commands

The secret weapon of achieving high speed in any graphics system is the high-level graphic command. By combining all the tiny steps of complex screen operations into a single routine, some of the most intricate onscreen images can be encoded as a few commands. Not only do high-level graphic commands make programs more compact, they allow your computer's microprocessor to offload the work of building images in the frame buffer.

Your microprocessor uses the high-level graphic commands to send instructions to a graphics subsystem. In today's computers, that means a graphics accelerator chip or a 3D accelerator. The accelerator executes the commands to move pixels around in the frame buffer.

The range of these graphic commands is large. Each accelerator chip has it own repertory of them. The most common among them are detailed in the following subsections.

Bit-Block Transfers

Bit-block transfers are instructions that tell the graphics chip to move data from one place to another in display memory. Instead of moving each byte of screen data through memory, the microprocessor only needs to tell the graphics chip what block to move (the source of the data) and where to put it (the destination). The graphics chip then carries out the entire data-transfer operation on its own.

Often shortened to *BitBlt*, bit-block transfers are most commonly used for scrolling an image up the screen. You can easily see the effect the command makes in video performance. When you scroll a bit-image up the screen using a graphics chip, the top part of the image often snaps into its new position, leaving a black band at the bottom of the screen that slowly fills with the remainder of the image. The initial quick move of the top of the image is made entirely in display memory using BitBlts. The rest of the image must be brought into display memory through the I/O bus or local bus, thus resulting in delays.

Drawing Commands

Drawing commands tell the graphics chip how to construct part of an image on the screen—drawing a line, rectangle, or arc, or filling a closed figure with a solid color or pattern. Often called *graphic primitives*, these commands break the image into its constituent parts that can be coded digitally to build a shape on the screen.

Before your computer's microprocessor puts a line on the screen, it first has to compute where each bit of the line will appear. It must compute the coordinates of each pixel to appear on the screen and then transfer the change into display memory across the bus. With a graphics chip, the microprocessor only needs to indicate the starting and ending points of a line to the chip. The graphics chip then computes the pixels and puts the appropriate values in display memory.

Sprites

Sprites are small images that move around the screen as a unit, much like an onscreen mouse pointer. General-purpose microprocessors have no provisions for handling sprites, so they must compute each bit of the sprite image anew every time the sprite moves across the screen. Many graphic chips have built-in capabilities to handle sprites. They store the bit-pattern of the sprite in memory and only need instructions telling them where to locate the sprite on the screen. Instead of redrawing the sprite, the graphics chip need only change the coordinates assigned its onscreen image, essentially only remapping its location.

Windowing

Windowing is one of the most common features of today's graphic operating systems. Each task is given an area of the screen dedicated to its own operations and images. Keeping straight all the windows used by every task is a challenge for a general-purpose microprocessor. Graphics chips and 3D accelerator chips, however, are usually designed to manage windows using simple commands. Once an onscreen window is defined, it can be manipulated as a single block rather than moving individual bytes around. The windowing operations can be strictly software manipulations, or the graphics chip may include special hardware provisions for streamlining the control of the windows.

In a conventional windowing system, software controls the display of each window. The layout of the screen is calculated, and the proper values for each pixel are plugged into the appropriate locations in the memory map. The image is generated by reading each memory location in sequence and using the information it contains to control the intensity of the electron beam in the display as it sweeps down the screen. Every memory location is scanned sequentially in a rigid order.

Hardware windowing works by slicing up the frame buffer. Although each dot on the screen has one or more bits of memory assigned to it, the map no longer needs to be an exact coordinate-for-coordinate representation of the screen. The video chip no longer scans each memory location in exact sequential order as the video beam traces down the screen. Instead, the memory scanned to control the beam is indicated by pointers, which guide the scan between different memory areas. Each memory area pointed to represents an onscreen window.

Each window can be individually manipulated. The memory used by a window can even be mapped into the address range of the system microprocessor while the rest of the screen is handled separately. As a consequence, most of the calculating normally required to change a window is eliminated. Therefore, screen updates speed up substantially.

Panning

Hardware panning takes advantage of the some of the memory in the video system that's not needed as a frame buffer. For example, your video board may have 2MB of memory but uses only 1.5MB to store a full 1024-by-768-pixel image with 16-bit color. The extra half megabyte of memory can hold an image that's bigger than that displayed on the monitor screen—the monitor image essentially becomes a window into display memory. Instead of stretching out for 1024-by-768 pixels, for example, the extra display memory might allow the filling of an 1152-by-864-pixel map. To pan the onscreen image one way or another on the screen, the display circuits only need to change the address of the area routed through the output of the board.

Changing addresses is much faster than moving blocks of bytes with BitBlt instructions, so hardware panning takes place very quickly—as long as the video board's memory holds the entirety of the image to be displayed. This technique is most useful when you have an older monitor that's not quite up to today's high scan rates—you put as much image on your screen as your monitor can tolerate while organizing your work across a larger desktop.

Depending on the hardware and drivers you've installed in your computer, Windows allows you to adjust the size of your desktop and onscreen display independently through the Settings tab of Display Properties.

Three-Dimensional Graphics

All the latest display adapters claim to have the capacity to display three-dimensional images. In other words, they claim to be *3D boards*. In terms of a display adapter, 3D means more and less than it seems. 3D does not mean what it did in the 1950s when your parents or grandparents put on blue-and-red glasses with cardboard frames to watch *The Creature from the Black Lagoon* jump out of the movie screen at them. In computer terms, that kind of 3D is a *stereoscopic display*.

In computer terms, 3D means adding simulated depth to the flat images on a monitor screen. But a 3D graphics adapter does more than add the appearance of a third dimension. It also gives 3D motion to your images to add excitement to games and give attention-grabbing effects to your presentations.

Indeed, the motion part of the 3D board's job is its toughest assignment. Not only must it make 3D images, but it also has to make them fast enough (at least 15 frames per second) that you think they are moving rather than just flashing at you.

Generating those images takes more processing power than was available in a computer a few years ago. The 3D boards have to move megabytes, even hundreds of them, every second. They have to cope with mathematical functions you probably never knew existed in high school—and frightened you into an Arts degree once in college. Yet they now encapsulate all the power they need in today's graphics accelerators. Better still, most of the math is gone. When developers write programs, they only need to call the advanced functions built in to programming interfaces such as Microsoft's DirectX.

No matter what you use your 3D board for, it needs to handle a few basic functions to generate its illusion of 3D reality. These functions can take place in hardware or software—that is, your graphics accelerator can take care of the heavy-duty computing itself or rely on your computer's microprocessor to do the hardware and merely pass along conventional two-dimensional functions to your 3D board. Obviously, a 3D board is supposed to do all the 3D work itself, but DirectX will take over if your board doesn't have the hardware functions it needs.

Tessellation

Computers face a problem in creating and manipulating three-dimensional objects. Because a computer works only with numbers, objects must be mathematically described for the computer to have any idea of how to deal with them. Finding a set of equations to describe a complex object is a daunting task—so daunting that programmers don't dare face it. Instead, they break complex objects into easily describable pieces and use the computer to manipulate those pieces. What they do is make their images the same way a mosaic artist makes a picture from small tiles.

The process of breaking the image into tile-like pieces is termed *tessellation*. The term comes from the name given to one of the mosaic artist's tiles, *tessera* (the plural form is *tesserae*).

In 3D graphics, the computer manipulates each tessera individually. When its transformation is complete, the computer recombines all the tesserae to create the original object. To eliminate the seams between the individual tessera and other artifacts of the manipulation, the graphics system *filters* the resulting image combination.

In practical 3D display systems, the tesserae are polygons, usually triangles. The performance of 3D processors is often expressed in the number of polygons (or triangles) that can be rendered in a second. The number has to be prodigious. A complex object may require 20,000 or more polygons. Rotate it with 15 updates per second, and your graphic chip has to render 300,000 polygons per second.

The polygons per second description of a product really doesn't reveal a lot. The rendering time for any polygon depends on its shading, texture, and other attributes. Chipmakers rate their products with their theoretical capabilities, and you can guess whether they would use best-case (monochrome, smooth surface triangles) or worst-case (True Color, polygons with complex textures, filtering, and antialiasing) conditions.

Texture-Mapping

At this level, the individual tesserae of the image would have the appearance of armor plates or a stealth fighter. Each one would be a single, solid, unrelieved color. Outside of jousts and midnight bombings, reality rarely looks so armor plated. Real objects have shading and texture that makes them look, well, realistic.

To add realism to the 3D objects your computer generates, the graphics system adds texture. Through a process called *texture-mapping*, a two-dimensional texture is applied to the surface of each tessera, making up the image. In effect, the texture is glued to each surface of the image.

In the texture-mapping process, the computer starts out with an image of the texture. The complete texture is broken into small constituent parts, similar to the pixels in a video image. Each of these pieces is termed a *texel*. The computer manipulates the texture by rotating and scaling it and applying perspective techniques to make it correspond to the manipulations performed on the tessera to which it is applied. The computer then maps the texels to pixels.

Because of the manipulations of the tesserae and texture, one pixel does not always correspond to one texel. Typically, the position of a given pixel appears between texels. Simply applying the color of the closest texel to the pixel results in an unrealistic image. The image may get blocky as multiple pixels take on the same color, or it may shimmer with slight movements as pixel values shift dramatically between texel values. To prevent these effects, the graphics system may apply *bilinear filtering* during the texture-mapping process. The pixel color takes on a value intermediate between the colors of the four adjacent texels. The result is a more realistic appearance of the texture color, particularly as the image is moved or rotated.

Most 3D systems store their textures in several different levels of detail for situations requiring different 3D depths and resolutions. Typically, each level is designed for half the resolution of the preceding one, so a collection would include textures at resolutions of 100, 50, 25, and 12.5 percent. Each texture level is prefiltered and tuned to best appearance at its resolution level. Taken together, the stored collection of a single texture at various levels of detail is termed a *mipmap*.

Objects can appear at any depth in the image, but the mipmap stores only discrete levels of detail. At some depths the texture applied to a polygon will require a level of detail between those in the mipmap. The 3D processor interpolates an intermediate texture using a technique termed *trilinear filtering*. The processor first performs bilevel interpolation (bilevel filtering) and a further linear interpolation between the detail levels applicable on either side of the polygon's depth.

Texture-mapping is one of the most complex of the operations required in three-dimensional graphics systems. Making the necessary calculations for mapping and filtering may take up half or more of the processing time for the image. Consequently, texture-mapping benefits greatly from hardware acceleration.

Depth Effects

What separates ordinary graphics displays from 3D displays is the appearance of depth to the image. In a 3D image, some objects appear closer than others. The difference in depth is, of course, an illusion because the face of the picture tube or LCD remains flat. The 3D display system must fool the eye into believing it perceives depth.

The problem is not new to 3D display systems. Ever since the first cavemen scratched walls with charcoal and ochre, artists have attempted to add depth to their paintings and drawings. Over the years they discovered (and often rediscovered) the techniques of perspective and other means that take advantage on the depth cues the human eye uses to put distant objects in their places.

Recession

One of the primary depth cues to the human eye is image size. The smaller an object of a known size appears to be, the farther away it seems. Three-dimensional graphics systems use a technique termed *perspective divide* to simulate this effect. To make a distant object smaller, the graphics system scales distances in the x and y coordinates of the image by a factor that is proportional to the z coordinate. In simplest form, distances in the x/y coordinate system are divided by the z value—the larger the z value, the smaller the object becomes.

The effect is the same as one-point perspective in the art world. Parallel lines, such as railroad tracks, converge at a single point in the distance—as z approaches infinity, the values of x and y approach zero and the coordinates collapse into a point.

Atmospheric Perspective

Artists have long used the technique of *atmospheric perspective* to add depth to paintings. Because of the effects of looking through a long reach of atmosphere, which isn't perfectly clear because of the haze of dust and water vapor suspended in it, distant objects appear paler and bluer than nearer objects. Artists capitalize on this visual effect and mix white and a trace of blue with the color of objects that are supposed to appear in the distance in their paintings.

The corresponding technique in three-dimensional computer graphics is termed *fogging*. To make an object appear more distant, the graphic system adds a fixed color called the *fog color* to the hue of the object. The amount of fog color added in increases with the apparent distance of the object. Because the fogging technique corresponds to the appearance of natural haze, the technique is sometime called by that name, *haze*. This technique is also called *depth cueing*.

Lighting Effects

Photographers and artists quickly learn that lighting is the key to making their two-dimensional images appear to represent three dimensions. The pattern and depth of bright areas and shadows allow the human eye to determine depth and the relative locations of objects. When an object sits between another object and the light source, the first object is brightly lit and the second object is in shadow. The technique of rendering images using the effects of light and shadow is called *chiaroscuro*, from the Italian for "clear-dark." *Chiaroscuro* rendering is one of the great challenges facing the 3D graphics system.

Ray-Tracing

The most powerful and compelling way to render the lighting of a three-dimensional scene uses the technique of *ray-tracing*. The computer follows, or *traces*, the path of every light ray that impinges on the scene. The process is complex. The computer determines which object each ray strikes based on the direction of the origin of the ray. After the ray strikes the object, the computer determines how much of the ray illuminates the object and is reflected. Based on the angle of the object surface to the light beam, the computer determines a new path for the reduced beam and plots it to the next object, continuing until the beam is so diminished it has no further effect. Once all the rays have been traced, the computer sums up the amount of light that has struck each surface. Those surfaces with the most rays are the brightest; those with few rays are in shadow.

Of course, to make the math tractable, the computer deals with only a reduced set of rays (the more, the better the rendering). The math is so complex that computers cannot perform ray-tracing on reasonably sized images in real time. The technique works extremely well for static images (if you're patient) but requires each frame of an animation to be individually rendered, taking perhaps a minute per frame. The ray-tracing technique consequently is not suitable to generating compelling 3D animations in real time.

Shading

Computer graphics systems use a simplified means of creating the chiaroscuro effect called *shading*. In the simplest form, the computer determines the angle of a surface to the light source and, using the reflectivity of the surface, computes how bright the surface should be rendered. *Gouraud shading*, also known as *smooth shading*, takes an additional step. It interpolates lighting values across the face of a surface to give gradual color transitions from a bright edge to a dim edge.

Z-Buffering

One way to eliminate the display of hidden surfaces is to track the depth of picture elements. The depth—or the distance away from you the element is supposed to appear—is assigned a value. This value corresponds to the position of the element on the z-axis of the three-dimensional coordinate system. In the *z-buffering* technique, this depth value gets stored in a special z-buffer. As the graphic chip updates the image, it compares the z value of each pixel to that stored in the z-buffer. When the z value in the buffer is less than that of the newly rendered pixel, the old value is nearer and would obscure the new value, so the new value is discarded. If the new value is lower and would thus appear in front of the old value, the old value gets discarded, replaced by the new value.

Transparency

Objects in the real world are not always opaque; otherwise, seeing through the windshield of your car would be a much greater challenge. To account for the effects of a transparent object sitting in front of another object, many 3D imaging systems store a transparency attribute for colors in addition to the normal red, green, and blue values. The storage for this additional attribute data is termed the *alpha channel*. Commonly the alpha channel is an extra eight bits added to the 24 bits used to store True Color pixel data, resulting in a 32-bit storage system (or four bytes per pixel). Most systems assign higher values to greater opacity, so 255 would be totally opaque and 0 totally transparent.

When calculating the appearance of a given pixel, the graphics processor uses the alpha channel values to determine its resulting color through a process termed *alpha-blending*. The processor adds an fraction of the color of the transparent object set by the alpha channel value to the color of the background object. Mixing the colors together gives the appearance that the background color is seen through a layer of the transparent object.

By itself, of course, alpha-blending only changes the color of pixels. You need more to give the true illusion of transparency. The viewer's eye also takes cues from the shape of the transparent object (defined by the color change made by the alpha-blending) as well as the difference between the background color seen with and without the transparent mask. The programmer must take all of these factors into account to produce a compelling three-dimensional image.

Double-Buffering

To create smooth animation, 3D display adapters use the technique of *double-buffering*. As the name implies, this technology puts two frame buffers in control of the graphics chip.

The *front buffer* corresponds to the traditional display buffer, connected to the rasterization circuitry that reads it sequentially and sends the video data to the screen. While the front buffer is scanned, the graphics chip draws in the *back buffer*, where the rendering operation is hidden and access is not limited by the timing of the rasterization process. Once the graphics chip completes its drawing, the two buffers are switched—the back buffer becomes the front buffer and the image drawn in it gets sent to the display. The graphics chip can then begin drawing in the new back buffer.

By cycling between the two buffers, double-buffering allows a fast but limited form of animation. It also achieves the same end as double-ported video RAM without using expensive, specialized memory chips. At the same time, it eliminates the appearance of the drawing process on the screen.

Image Creation

The various hardware technologies are only tools used by your computer's display system in creating a bitmap of the screen image. Your software—that is, your computer game—first must generate the scene that will be displayed and make a new one as often as 30 times each second.

Generating the 3D images used in today's games is the most computationally intense task your computer faces. In fact, the work involved in creating and updating all the information in a 3D graphic scene in real time is beyond the capabilities of even today's most powerful microprocessors and display systems. That's not to say the images you see on your screen today are impossible—it's just that they are not all they seem to be.

Of the many lessons the designers of 3D graphics have learned from Hollywood, the art of building sets is probably the most important. Watch any movie epic, and you'll see lavish scenes of grand structures, huge crowds, and endless panoramas, none of which ever really existed. The panoramas may be painted, projected, or matted into the scene. The crowds are photographed to make a few people seem like a mass, or the same supernumeraries are shot two or four times in every scene. And the huge sets and extravagant buildings are mere facades, a pretty face with nothing behind but bare two-by-fours propping everything up. The important lesson is that *only what shows counts.*

That's the secret that makes today's 3D graphics look as good as they do. When confronted with an overwhelming calculating chore, your graphics hardware does exactly what any high-school student would do in the situation. It ignores most of it. But far from blaming what it doesn't do on the errant ways of the family canine, it takes the approach of the Hollywood set builder. It assesses exactly what will show in the final image and concentrates its work on that. As far as the behind-the-scenes stuff goes, the software only does what's necessary so that the whole set doesn't collapse around the stars. In other words, writing good 3D graphics software is the art of knowing what *not* to do. Engineers call this strategy *culling*, which means picking the best or most important.

Spaces

Unlike two-dimensional display software, which creates each scene exactly as you see it on the screen, a 3D display system images a scene as objects. An object is anything that can be manipulated—moved, rotated, stretched, or squashed—as a single entity. The software describes each object numerically and transforms it from frame to frame using mathematics. Each object defines its own *model space* with its own coordinate system for these manipulations.

The objects are mapped into the coordinate system of the world in which they act, corresponding to the Hollywood sound stage or location set. All objects in this *world space* use the same coordinate system that defines exactly where they appear in the scene.

Once the software has put all the objects into place, it can generate a camera's-eye view of the scene, like dropping the tripod legs of a Panavision camera to film the scene. The camera sees the scene from its own coordinates, creating what engineers call the *camera space* or *view space*. At this point, the software can trace the path of light rays from the camera to distant parts of the scene. This view lets the software begin cheating. When a ray hits a solid (as opposed to transparent) object, it can go no further. The software knows that it can ignore anything from that point on, so it does not have to calculate other objects or background textures that lie beyond that point.

This view space is actually encompassing a solid volume, a pyramid with the camera at its apex, called the *view frustum*. The software transforms this view into *clip space* by distorting the frustum into a cube. That is, it mathematically spreads out the pyramid. This process distorts the objects in the scene, making those closer to the camera larger, which makes the more distant objects appear smaller. This transformation yields perspective and a distance effect.

Finally, the software squashes the clip space cube into a two-dimensional view of the scene that corresponds to what you would see on your video display, the *screen space*. The object descriptions that survive culling and have been transformed into screen space get loaded into the frame buffer and passed along to your computer display for your viewing.

3D Pipeline

Most 3D display systems process scenes in a *3D pipeline*, much as a microprocessor executes programs. The pipeline allows the 3D accelerator to work on several steps of display processing at the same time to speed up its operation. It starts out in software, typically the game you are playing. The software defines the objects and whatever transformations they require from one frame to the next. The software describes an object as a set of points representing the vertices of triangles (triangles, because the three points making up the vertices uniquely describe a plane surface). At this point, the object is nothing more than a few points describing a *wireframe* made up of triangles. Even so, the software can start the culling process, identifying the triangles on the back of the object, those that won't appear in the final view.

The software can put the objects at this stage into their world space and construct a view space, again culling the areas that will be in view. It will also define the lighting of the scene and where shadows will fall.

At this point, the software is ready to develop the screen space. It now fills in the rectangles with the proper shades and textures. To add aerial perspective, it may also add fog to distant objects. It may also smooth out jagged outlines. The software then moves the rendered image into the frame buffer (alternately, it may render the image directly in the frame buffer). At that point, the image need only be rasterized by the video controller and sent on its way to the monitor and then to your eyes.

Keyboards

The primary input device for most computer systems is the keyboard, and until voice-recognition systems are perfected to the point that they can recognize continuous speech, the dominance of the keyboard is not likely to change. Even then the keyboard will probably remain unapproachable for speed and accuracy for years to come. The keyboard also is more suited to data entry in open offices, airplanes, and anywhere your privacy is not ensured and your sanity not beyond reproach.

When you're buying a new computer, the keyboard is the least of your worries. After all, the manufacturer takes care of it for you. Nearly every desktop computer comes completely equipped with a keyboard (otherwise the computer wouldn't be much good for anything). Notebook computers have their keyboards completely built in. Moreover, keyboards are pretty much all the same these days—or at least they all look the same. Over the last decade, the key layout has become almost completely standardized, the one true keyboard design that might have been ordained by God. With a desktop machine, you get 101 keys on a surfboard-size panel that monopolizes your desktop or overflows your lap. With a notebook computer, you're stuck with whatever the computer-maker thought best for you and the market value of its executive stock options.

The default keyboard that comes with your computer is more variable than you might think, however. Underneath all those keys you might find one or another exotic technology that would seem best left to the realm of engineers. But the technology used by your keyboard determines not only how it works but also how long it works and how much you will enjoy working with it. It may even influence whether keyboarding is a time of pleasure or pain. The underlying differences are enough to make you consider casting aside the (usually) cheap, default keyboard the maker of your desktop computer packed in the box and getting something more suitable to your fingers and your work. When you consider a notebook computer, a difference in keyboards might be enough to make you favor one machine over another, particularly when the rest of the two systems are well matched.

Technologies

The keyboard concept—a letter for every pushbutton—is almost ancient, dating back to the days of the first typewriter. The design seems fixed in stone. Actually, it's the product of something even more immovable—human inertia. The basic layout and function of the keyboard has changed little since the last half of the 19th century, and the mold for the computer refinement was first cast in 1987. No matter what computer you buy today, you're almost certain to get a keyboard that follows the now industry-standard design. That's good because you can confront any computer and start working in seconds. But that's also bad when those seconds stretch to hours of uninterrupted typing.

All keyboards have the same function: detecting the keys pressed down by your fingers and relaying that information to your computer. Even though two keyboards may look identical, they may differ considerably in the manner in which they detect the motion of your fingers. The technology used for this process—how the keyboard works electri-cally—can affect the sturdiness and longevity of the keyboard. Although all operate in effect as switches by altering the flow of electricity in some way, the way those changes are detected has evolved into an elaborate mechanism. The way that technology is put into action affects how pleasant your typing experience is.

Nearly every technology for detecting the change in flow of electricity has been adapted to keyboards at one time or another. The engineer's goal has been to find a sensing mech-anism that combines accuracy—detecting only the desired keystroke and ignoring errant electrical signals—with long life (you don't want a keyboard that works for six words) and with the right "feel," the personal touch. In past years, keyboard designers found promise in complex and exotic technologies such as Hall-effect switches, special semiconductors that react to magnetic field changes. The lure was the wonder of magnetism—nothing needs to touch to make the detection. A lack of contact promised a freedom from wear, a keyboard with endless life.

In the long run, however, the quest for the immortal keyboard proved misguided. Key-boards rated for tens of millions of keypresses met premature ends with a splash from a cup of coffee. In the end, manufacturers opted for the simplest and least expensive, hard-contact technology, as close to a plain switch as you can get without a wall plate. The chief alternative, capacitive technology, led the pack at the start. It was more reliable, longer lived, more complicated—and for a long while, more popular. It was also more expensive. In today's dollars, the keyboard of the first computer cost more than an entire current computer system. Something had to give.

Contact

The direct approach in keyboards involves using switches to alter the flow of electricity. The switches in the keyboard do exactly what all switches are supposed to do—open and close an electrical circuit to stop or start the flow of electricity. Using switches requires simpler (although not trivial) circuitry to detect each keystroke, although most switch-based computer keyboards still incorporate a microprocessor to assign scan codes and serialize the data for transmission to the system unit.

Design simplicity and corresponding low cost have made switch-based keyboards today's top choice for computers. These keyboards either use novel technology to solve the major problem of switches—a short life—or just ignore it. Cost has become the dominant factor in the design and manufacture of keyboards. In the tradeoff between price and life, the switch-based design is the winner.

Three switch-based keyboard designs have been used in computers: mechanical switches, rubber domes, and membrane switches.

Mechanical Switches

Mechanical switches use the traditional switch mechanism, precious metal contacts forced together. In the *discrete switch* design, the switch under each keyboard station is an independent unit that can be individually replaced. Alternatively, the entire keyboard can be fabricated as one assembly. Although the former might lend itself to easier repair, the minimum labor charge for computer repair often is higher than the cost of a replacement keyboard.

The contact in a mechanical switch keyboard can do double-duty, chaperoning the electrical flow and positioning the keycaps. Keyboard contacts can operate as springs to push the keycaps back up after they have been pressed. Although this design is compelling because it minimizes the parts needed to make a keyboard, it is not suited to computer-quality keyboards. The return force is difficult to control, and the contact material is apt to suffer from fatigue and break. Consequently, most mechanical switch keyboards incorporate springs to push the keycaps back into place as well as other parts to give the keyboard the right feel and sound.

Although several manufacturers have built keyboards with mechanical switches, the design has fallen from favor. Probably less than two percent of all keyboards use discrete switches.

Rubber Dome

Rubber dome keyboards combine the contact and positioning mechanisms into a single piece. A puckered sheet of elastomer—a stretchy, rubber-like synthetic—is molded to put a dimple or dome under each keycap, the dome bulging upward. Pressing on the key pushes the dome down. Inside the dome is a tab of carbon or other conductive material that serves as one of the keyboard contacts. When the dome goes down, the tab presses against another contact and completes the circuit. Release the key, and the elastomer dome pops back to its original position, pushing the keycap back with it.

The rubber dome design initially won favor on notebook computers, where its resistance to environmental stress (a euphemism for "spilled coffee") was a major strength. The design also is inexpensive to manufacture. The switches for the entire keyboard can be molded as one piece about as easily as making a waffle. The design was readily adapted to desktop keyboards and provides the foundation for many inexpensive, lightweight models.

Properly designed, a rubber dome keyboard has an excellent feel—the give of the individual domes can be tailored to enable you to sense exactly when the switch makes contact. A poor design, however, makes each keypress feel rubbery and uncertain. Moreover, some elastomers have a tendency to become stiff with age, and as a result, some keys can become recalcitrant.

Membrane Keyboards

Membrane keyboards are similar to rubber domes except they use thin plastic sheets—the membrane—printed with conductive traces rather than elastomer sheets. Most designs use a three-sheet sandwich—top and bottom sheets with printed contacts and a central insulating sheet with holes at each key position to hold the contacts apart. The top sheet is dimpled, and pressing down on the dimple pushes the top contact down to meet the bottom contact. The dimple snaps from one position to another, giving distinct tactile feedback that indicates when you've pressed a key.

The membrane design often is used for keypads to control calculators and printers because of its low cost and trouble-free life. The materials making contact can be sealed inside the plastic, impervious to harsh environments.

By itself, the membrane design makes a poor computer keyboard because its contacts require only slight travel to actuate. However, an auxiliary key mechanism can tailor the feel (and key travel) of a membrane keyboard and make typing on it indistinguishable from working with a keyboard based on another technology.

Non-Contact

The biggest problem with all contact keyboards is the contacts themselves. Although switches work well for room lights, they are fickle when it comes to the minuscule voltages and currents used by computer systems. At a microscopic (and microtemporal) level, making a contact is an entire series of events—tiny currents start and stop flowing until finally good contact is made and the juice really gets going. The brief little pulses that precede making final contact aren't apparent when you throw a light switch, but a computer can detect each little pulse as a separate keystroke. Keyboards have special circuits called *debouncers* that make your keypresses unambiguous. However, as contacts age, they oxidize. Oxidation puts a less-conductive layer of oxide on the contacts and makes your keypresses even less reliable—to the point they cannot be unambiguously detected.

Early in the history of the computer, manufacturers scorned contact keyboards because they knew traditional contact materials were fated to short lives, not the tens of millions of keystrokes they expect from keyboards. Modern keyboards use ceramics and exotic metals that, resistant to oxidation, can achieve the required life.

The most popular of the non-contact designs is the *capacitive* keyboard. *Capacitance* is essentially a stored charge of static electricity. Capacitors store electricity as opposite static charges in one or more pairs of conductive plates separated by a nonconductive material. The opposite charges create an attractive field between one another, and the insulating gap prevents the charges from coming together and canceling out one another. The closer the two charged plates are, the stronger the field and the more energy that can be stored. Moving the plates in relation to one another changes their capacity for storing a charge, which in turn can generate a flow of electricity to fill up the increased capacity or drain off the excess charge as the capacity decreases. These minute electrical flows are detected by the circuitry of a capacitive keyboard. The small, somewhat gradual changes of capacity are amplified and altered so that they resemble the quick flick of a switch.

The first computer keyboards and some of the more robust designs of the past all used capacitive technology. The best of these designs could work reliably for 100 million keystrokes compared to 10 to 15 million for most contact designs. Although that extended life may be commendable, most people never typed even 10 million keystrokes during the lifetime of their computers. They usually move on to another computer well before the keyboard wears out. The added cost of the capacitive design consequently yields no additional useful life, and the design has fallen from favor. The last capacitive keyboard from a major manufacturer rolled out of the Key Tronic Corporation factory in early 1999.

Touch

Today the principal dividing line between keyboards is not technology but touch—what typing actually feels like. A keyboard must be responsive to the touch of your fingers—when you press down, the keys actually have to go down. More than that, however, you must feel like you are typing. You need tactile feedback, sensing through your fingers when you have activated a key.

The most primitive form of tactile feedback is the hard stop—the key bottoms out and stops moving at the point of actuation. No matter how much harder you press, the key is unyielding, and that is the problem. To assure yourself that you are actuating the key, you end up pressing harder than necessary. The extra force tires you out more quickly.

One alternative is to make the key actuate before the end of key travel. Because the key is still moving when you realize that it registered your keystroke, you can release your finger pressure before the key bottoms out. You don't have to expend as much effort, and your fingers don't get as tired.

The linear travel or linear touch keyboard requires that you simply press harder to push a key down. In other words, the relationship between the displacement of the key and the pressure you must apply is linear throughout the travel of the key. The chief shortcoming of the linear touch keyboard is that your fingers have no sure way of knowing when they have pressed down far enough. Audible feedback, a click indicating that the key has been actuated, can help, as does the appearance onscreen of the character you typed. Both slow you down, however, because you are calling more of your mind into play to register a simple keystroke. If your fingers could sense the actuation of the keys themselves, your fingers could know when to stop reflexively.

Better keyboards provide this kind of tactile feedback by requiring you to increase pressure on the keyboard keys until they actuate and then dramatically lower the force you need to press down farther until you reach the limit of travel. Your fingers detect the change in effort as an over-center feel. Keyboards that provide this positive over-center feel are generally considered to be the best for quick touch-typing.

A spring mechanism, carefully tailored to abruptly yield upon actuation of each key, is the classic means of achieving a tactile feel and can be adapted to provide an audible "click" with every keypress. The spring mechanism also returns the key to the top of its travel at the end of each keystroke. The very first computer keyboards were elaborate constructions that used a separate spring assembly for each key. Modern keyboards use a single overall spring assembly or, more likely, an elastic rubber dome that pops between positions. Dome-based keyboards give satisfying tactile feedback, but individual keys may sporadically require increased force for a stroke or two, thus subverting their smooth operation. Nevertheless, the low cost and good reliability make dome technology popular among keyboard-makers.

Soft-touch keyboards use a compressible foam to work as the spring mechanism as well as to cushion the end of each keystroke. Soft-touch keyboards give a more linear feel but are preferred by some people for exactly the same reason others dislike them—their lack of snap and quiet operation.

Another influence on the feel of a keyboard is the force required to actuate a key. Some keyboards require you to press harder than others. In general, however, most keyboards require between 1.9 and 2.4 ounces of pressure to actuate the key. Stiff keyboards can require as much as three ounces.

On March 22, 1999, Key Tronic Corporation introduced the first varied key-feel keyboard, one that required differing amounts of pressure to activate its keys. Called *ErgoForce* by its developer, the varied key pressures are tailored to the fingers expected to activate them. For example, the "A" key, which is usually operated by the left little finger, requires only 1.25 ounces (35 grams) of force to activate, whereas the spacebar requires 2.3 ounces (80 grams). Depending on the location of each key, it requires one of five levels of effort to activate—35, 45, 55, 65, or 80 grams. According to the manufacturer, the tailored effort makes typing easier and improves the level of typing comfort for people using a keyboard for long periods.

Keyboards also differ in how far you must press down on a key to actuate it. Full-travel keyboards require your fingers to move down between 0.14 and 0.18 of an inch to actuate a key. Studies show that the full-travel design helps typists achieve high speeds and lower error rates. In laptop and notebook computers, where every fraction of an inch counts, however, keyboards sometimes are designed with less than full travel. A short-travel keyboard actuates with less than about 0.10 inch of key travel. Whether you can live with—or even prefer—a short-travel keyboard is a personal issue.

Legends

Each key on a keyboard bears a legend identifying the letter, symbol, or function it activates. These legends are usually applied using one of three technologies:

- **Double-shot keycaps have the legend molded in**. Making each keycap is a two-step process. Black plastic is molded into the inner shape of the keycap that attaches to the switch mechanism. The legend protrudes from the top of this inner cap. Then light plastic is molded over and around the inner cap with the legend showing through the top.

  Using the double-shot technique, each keycap for each key is a separate and different part that must be individually installed in the correct position on the keyboard as the final step in the production process. Assembly is complex, and stock-keeping of parts and completed keyboards can be costly. Although once popular, this technology has fallen from favor.

- **Pad-printed keycaps have their legends stamped into place**. A machine inks on the legends on all the keys on a fully manufactured keyboard at one swoop. Then a transparent protective layer is applied over the ink and is baked to a permanent finish. Notebook computers and keyboards with light legends over dark caps often have their keys pad-printed. In the case of notebooks, the assembled keyboard gets baked before the keyboard is installed on the computer.

- **Laser-marked keycaps have their legends burned into place with a laser**. The process is akin to a laser printer that operates on keycaps rather than plastic. The complete keyboard is put into a big machine with a laser and mirrors, and the laser burns the legends into all the keycaps in one operation. The advantage of the process is that the legends only need to be applied at the last moment, right before the keyboard is shipped out with a new computer, and the language and layout of the keyboard need not be set until then. The process is fast, the legends are long lived, and stock-keeping is simplified. Most new keyboards are now laser-marked.

Layouts

On a full-size keyboard, the spacing between the keycaps for individual character keys is 0.75 inch (19 millimeters), center to center. The keycaps themselves are about 0.5 inch (12.5 millimeters) across at the top, dished to help you place your fingers. The shape of this curve is somewhat arbitrary. Most American designs put a concave cylindrical curve (it's curved only around the longitudinal axis) at the top of the keys; some European designs use a concave spherical curve.

QWERTY

The one unvarying aspect of keyboards also seems the most odd—the nonalphabetical arrangement of the alphabet keys. Anyone new to typing will be amazed and perplexed at the seemingly nonsensical arrangement of letters on the keys of the typical computer keyboard. Even the name given to this esoteric layout has the ring of some kind of black magic or odd cabala—QWERTY. Simply a list of the first six characters of the top row of the nominal arrangement, the absurdity harks back to the keyboard of the first practical typewriter.

There is no doubt that the standard arrangement is not the only possible ordering of the alphabet—in fact, there are 26! (or 26 factorial, exactly 403,291,461,126,605,635,584,000,000) different possible arrangements of letters alone, not to mention the further complications of using rows of different lengths and nonalphabetic keys. QWERTY is not the only possible layout, and it's probably not the best. Nor is it the worst. But it is the standard that millions of people have spent years mastering.

A legend surrounds the QWERTY key arrangement. The typewriter was invented in 1867 by Christopher Sholes, and his very first keyboard had its letter keys arranged alphabetically. Within a year of his invention, however, Sholes discovered what he viewed as a superior arrangement, QWERTY.

According to the common myth, Sholes created QWERTY because typists pounded on keys faster than the simple mechanisms of the first typewriters could handle their strokes. The keys jammed. The odd QWERTY arrangement slowed down the typists and prevented the jams.

Sholes left no record of how he came upon the QWERTY arrangement, but it certainly was not to slow down speedy typists. High typing rates imply modern-day touch typing, ten fingers flying across the keyboard. This style of typing did not arise until about ten years after Sholes had settled on the QWERTY arrangement. Typewriter development was indeed slow—the Shift key wasn't added to the basic design to permit lowercase characters until 1878!

Other hypotheses about the QWERTY placement also lead to dead-ends. For example, breaking a strict alphabetic order to separate the keys and prevent the type bars (the levers that swing up to strike letters on paper) from jamming doesn't make sense, because the arrangement of the type bars has no direct relationship to the arrangement of keys.

Dvorak-Dealey

The most familiar challenger to QWERTY, one that crawls in a distant second in popularity and use, is the Dvorak-Dealey letter arrangement, named for its developers, August Dvorak and William L. Dealey. The name is often shortened to Dvorak. Figure 20.1 shows the Dvorak layout applied to a typical keyboard.

FIGURE 20.1
Dvorak-Dealey key layout.

The Dvorak-Dealey design incorporates several ideas that should lead to faster typing. A basic goal is to foster the alteration of hands in typing. After you strike one letter with a key under a finger of your left hand, the next key you'll want to press likely is under a right-hand finger. This hand alteration is a faster typing strategy. To make hand alteration more likely, the Dvorak-Dealey arrangement places all vowels in the home row under the left hand's fingertips and the consonants used most often in the right hand's home row. Note that the Dvorak-Dealey arrangement was developed for speed and does nothing to make the keyboard more alphabetic or easier to learn to use.

The first publication of the Dvorak-Dealey keyboard was in the 1936 book *Typewriting Behavior*, authored by the developers of the new letter arrangement. To back up the philosophic and theoretical advantages attributed to the Dvorak-Dealey arrangement, tests were conducted in the 1930s on mechanical typewriters, amounting to typing races between the QWERTY and Dvorak-Dealey key arrangements. Dvorak and Dealey ran the tests, and—not surprisingly—they came out the winner by factors as large as 30 percent.

Dvorak believed in both his keyboard and his test results and wrote papers promoting his ideas. Alas, the more he wrote, the greater his claims became. Articles such as "There Is a

Better Typewriter Keyboard" in the December 1943 issue of *National Business Education Quarterly* has been called by some experts "full of factual errors." Tests run by the United States Navy and the General Accounting Office reported much more modest results for Dvorak.

Notwithstanding the exaggerated claims, the Dvorak layout does offer some potential advantages in typing speed, at least after you become skilled in its use. The penalty for its increased typing throughput is increased difficulty in typing when confronted with a QWERTY keyboard.

The design of the computer makes converting to Dvorak relatively easy. Whereas typewriters have to be redesigned for the new key arrangement, you can just plug a new keyboard into your computer. Commercial Dvorak keyboards often are available by special order.

In fact, if you don't mind your keytop legend bearing no likeness to the characters that actually appear on your screen (and in your files), you can simply reprogram your computer to think that it has a Dvorak keyboard by intercepting the signals sent by the keyboard to your computer and converting them on the fly.

Windows makes specific provisions for the Dvorak key arrangement. The standard keyboard driver allows you to select the Dvorak option. From Windows Control Panel, select the Keyboard icon. Next, select the Language tab, on which you'll find a Properties button. Clicking this button will reveal a screen like that shown in Figure 20.2, one that allows you to choose the keyboard language. The Dvorak layout is available as an option in the United States layout, as shown in the figure.

FIGURE 20.2

Selecting the Dvorak layout in Windows.

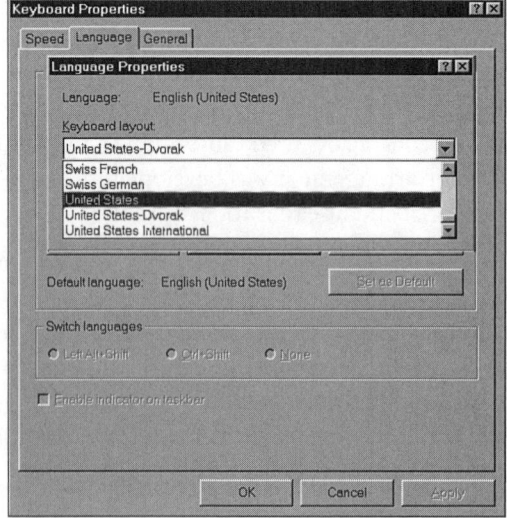

Control and Function Keys

The classic key layouts fail when it comes to computer keyboards. The array of keys they offer simply doesn't match the needs of a computer control system. Certainly the alphabet hasn't changed—at least over the 125-year history of the QWERTY arrangement. But computers have needs not addressed by the letters of the alphabet or basic numerals. They require navigation keys and buttons to control system functions. Even that's not enough to provide an easy-to-use control system for applications and operating systems. In addition (as well as subtraction and other math operations), a dedicated numeric keypad can help immensely when your work involves entering a lot of numbers.

Each additional key adds another option in laying out the keyboard. Another word for it is potential chaos. Although computer manufacturers have exploited some of the opportunities to craft their own, peculiar keyboards—particularly in notebook computers—the basic design has gravitated toward a single standard.

A common design for all keyboards seems an obvious idea, but it didn't arise spontaneously. After a short, wrenching evolution between 1981 and 1987 involving three major design changes, the layout has remained subject to tinkering. The last significant change came when Microsoft added three keys tied specifically to functions in the Windows operating system. Although most keyboard-makers stick to this arrangement, they sometimes alter the size and shapes of some keys—just enough to frustrate you during your first attempts at using an unfamiliar computer.

As with QWERTY, the arrangement of auxiliary keys is quite arbitrary, to the point of defying explanation. As personal computers were emerging as a technology, the Video Data Terminal with a detached keyboard was still a relatively new concept, as were function keys. The first personal computer keyboard appeared to be designed by programmers rather than typists—it had a small Enter/Return key but placed the function keys handily left of the alphabetic keys, just a pinkie-touch away. Experienced typists—many of the early adopters of personal computers, and the most vociferous of them were writers—complained, and the engineers complied, enlarging the Enter key to make the 84-key AT keyboard (named after the 1984 IBM Personal Computer AT, which originated it).

The next wave of new users, more interested in mastering software and entering numbers, complained that the left-hand function keys didn't correspond to the help legends that sometimes appeared in a row at the bottom of the screen. As a result, in its next generation of personal computers, the Personal Systems/2 of 1987, IBM created a third design. It was one of those attempts to satisfy everyone that leaves everyone dissatisfied. To add extra features, IBM's engineers added keys, making a total of 101. Termed the *Advanced Keyboard* by IBM, it is also commonly called the *Enhanced Keyboard*. Figure 20.3 illustrates the United States layout of the Advanced Keyboard.

FIGURE 20.3
The IBM Advanced Keyboard layout.

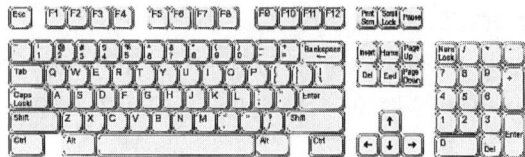

The key additions were several. A new, dedicated cursor control pad was provided separate from the combined numeric and cursor pad, and several other control keys were duplicated in another small pad. Two new function keys (F11 and F12) were added, and the whole dozen were moved to a top row, above and slightly separated from the alphanumeric area. Duplicate Ctrl and Alt keys were provided at either side of the spacebar, and Caps Lock was moved to the former location of the Ctrl key.

A few functions of Windows don't fall readily under the caps of 101-key keyboards. To better match the operation of Windows, many keyboard-makers now add three additional keys—two Windows keys and a pop-up menu key—in the otherwise vacant area around the spacebar, which has also shrunk to provide more room. The two Windows keys, identified by the zooming window logo on their caps, serve as attention keys to pop you into the Windows Task Manager. One is located on the left of the space bar between the Ctrl and Alt keys. The other fits on the right side, just right of the right Alt key. The third key serves to select the item at which the mouse cursor points. It is located to the right of the right Windows key.

Most makers of Windows keyboards also modify other keys for easier typing. In particular, they enlarge the Enter key to the size used by the lamented 84-key design. To provide the extra key area, the backslash shrinks and moves upward, sandwiched between a shortened Backspace key and the plus/equals key. Figure 20.4 illustrates the most common form of the 104-key Windows keyboard.

FIGURE 20.4
Layout of the 104-key Windows keyboard.

To distinguish their products and make computers easier to use, some keyboard-makers have added *application pushbuttons* to their keyboards that are keyed to particular software features. In most cases, these added controls take the form of round, rubberized pushbuttons in a line above the function keys. Popular Microsoft keyboards, for example, provide pushbuttons for commonly used Internet functions, such as triggering your browser forward and back as well as entering your email system.

The functions of these added buttons are defined by the keyboard driver software. The keyboard simply passes a code to your computer indicating you've pressed one of the buttons. The driver software then checks which button you've pressed and passes a predefined command along to your software. If your software differs from what Microsoft expects, the keys might not work properly. If you have installed the keyboard properly, you can adjust its settings through the Keyboard Properties menu in Windows Control Panel.

Ergonomic Designs

No one likes to type, except possibly masochists and men from Mars. For most people typing is a pain. In fact, extended typing without taking a break can cause pain and worse, occupational ailments such as Carpal Tunnel Syndrome. The best way to avoid such problems is to avoid typing—yet another good reason to quit early each day. When you can't avoid pounding on the keyboard all day long, the next best choice is to find a keyboard that minimizes the pain.

Human factors specialists who deal in the science of how people relate to the workplace and machines, called *ergonomics*, point out that the keyboard was not designed with human beings in mind. The original layout of keys in four (or five or six) rows was a mix of the arbitrary and the needs of the original lever-operated typewriter mechanism. As good as straight rows are for pounding on paper, they are an anathema for most human hands. Normal typing forces you to splay your hands apart, bending them at the wrists and keeping them in that position while you type away. The bend stresses the ligaments in your wrist and squeezes the nerves that lead into your hand through the carpal tunnel (essentially a hole in the bones of your wrist). Over time the stress adds up and may eventually impair the functioning of your hands.

Computer keyboards do not suffer the same constraints as the keyboards of mechanical typewriters. Designers can put the key switches in any position they choose. Some of the more imaginative designs result in *ergonomic keyboards*. These split the alphanumeric keypad in two and angle the two halves in respect to one another. The result is an odd-looking keyboard—at least to the eyes of those long used to the mechanical typewriter design—that's supposed to make typing less painful.

The theory underlying the ergonomic design is that the typing position of your hands on the split keypad lets you keep your wrists straight. Your hands follow more of the natural position they would assume when hanging down from your sides (hence the name of Microsoft's *Natural Keyboard*). Because there is less stress, prolonged typing should be less painful on a split-pad keyboard.

With old-fashioned keyboards, and especially those of mechanical typewriters, you must bend your wrists in another direction, vertically, for normal typing. When your arm lies flat on your desk, you must angle your hands upward to reach the keys of a keyboard lying atop your desk. When you use the little feet at the back of your keyboard to angle your keyboard further, you must bend your wrists even more.

As with the horizontal bending of your wrists, these vertical bends can also cause stress and, possibly, carpal tunnel syndrome or other occupational ailments. Consequently, many keyboards have extended wrist rests that force you to minimize the bending of your wrists.

Unlike changes to the layout of key caps, these ergonomic designs require a brief (if any) training period in which to accustom yourself to them. They might seem odd at first, but you can quickly start using them effectively. The choice of a regular or ergonomic design is simply a matter of your own preference.

Electrical Function

In the macroscopic world in which we live, switches operate positively without hesitation or doubt. Switch on a light, and it comes on like, well, a light. In the realm of microelectronics, however, switches are not so certain in their first steps toward changing state. As a switch makes contact, it hesitates, letting tiny currents flow and then halting them; then letting more flow. These initial jitters are called *switch bounce*, and they result from a number of causes. The contact materials of most switches are far from perfect. They may become coated with oxidation or other impurities, and they often don't mesh together perfectly. The contacts touch, bounce, cut through the crud, and finally mate firmly together. In the process, many tiny pulses of electricity can slip through. These pulses aren't enough to affect a light bulb but can be more than sufficient to confuse a semiconductor circuit.

For use in computer circuits, switches require special electronics to remove the jitters, to "debounce" their contacts. Such debouncing circuits monitor the switch contacts and change the hesitating initial stabs at changing state into a sharp, certain switch. Unfortunately, each switch contact requires its own debouncer. This is not much of a concern with a single switch, but it can be a nightmare for the designer who must debounce the 101 switches in a typical keyboard.

Instead of individual debouncing, computer keyboards use a different process for eliminating the hesitation from keyboard switches. The keyboard electronics do not detect when each switch changes but rather check periodically to see whether a switch has changed. When the electronics note a change in the state of a switch corresponding to the press of a key, they generate an indication of the switch switching that is sent along to your computer.

This process has its own shortcomings. The go-and-look method of detection adds a brief wait to signaling each keypress. Moreover, each and every key must be individually checked. But the high speed of today's computer circuits makes this system entirely workable. The process is reduced to a routine—the keyboard electronics scan each key at rates approaching a million times every second, looking for a change in the state of any key. In general, a microprocessor (an 8048-series device in the most popular keyboards) scans the keyboard for current changes every few microseconds, and the minute current flow caused by a keystroke can be detected. Because a slight chance exists that random noise—the stuff that must be debounced away—could cause a current pulse similar to that generated by a keystroke, keyboards may require that the increased current flow be detected during two or more consecutive scans of the keyboard.

In today's computers, the keyboard can use either of two technologies to relay the effects of your keypresses to your computer. In the traditional design, used in systems since the first computers, the keyboard sends data to your computer in the form of scan codes. The personal computer industry is making an effort to shift keyboard communications from scan codes to formatted data sent through the USB port.

Keyboard Port

In the traditional (legacy) keyboard design, the keyboard connects to your computer and sends its codes, called *scan codes*, through a specialized serial port. A microprocessor in the keyboard assigns a code of pulses to your every keypress, and a second processor called a *keyboard controller* converts the scan code pulses into bus-compatible data using a hexadecimal code.

When it receives a scan code, the keyboard controller chip issues an interrupt to notify your computer's microprocessor that you've pressed a key and it had better do something about it. To service the interrupt, your computer sorts through the scan codes and figures out which keys are pressed and in which combination. The program code for doing this is part of your system's BIOS. The computer remembers the condition of the locking shift keys by changing special memory locations, called *status bytes*, to reflect each change made in their condition.

Each press of a key generates two different scan codes—one when the key is pushed down and another when it pops back up. The two-code technique allows your computer system unit to tell when a key is pressed and held down—for example, when you hold down the Alt key while pressing a function key.

Rather than a single standard for scan codes, there are three. These comprise three operating modes and correspond to the three generations of keyboard development. Mode 1 is the system used by the original 83-key keyboard of the first computers. Mode 2 is the system used by the 84-key keyboard of the computer AT. Mode 3 is the system introduced with the 101-key keyboard design that's now ubiquitous among computers. In general, more modern keyboards can emulate older models by shifting their operating modes based on commands sent to the keyboard by your computer.

In any given operating mode, each key generates a unique scan code. Even if the same legend appears on two keys, such as the duplicate number keys in the alphanumeric and numeric/cursor keypads, the individual keys generate the same codes. The code for a given key is determined by its position and is not affected when the Caps Lock or other shift key is in effect. In Mode 1, all scan codes are single bytes, and the make and break codes of individual keys are different. In Modes 2 and 3, scan codes may be one or more bytes. In general, the make code is a single byte and the break code is two bytes, the byte F0(hex) followed by the make code.

Although scan codes were originally fixed to key positions rather than characters, when manufacturers alter the arrangements of their auxiliary keys they maintain the same scan codes for the characters as in the basic design. Otherwise, every key layout would generate different scan codes and confuse both your computer and you as you type. Foreign languages have their own scan code mappings. Each different keyboard design for a specific language puts different characters on punctuation keys, so the scan codes elicited by these characters will vary in languages other than English.

Modern 101-key and 104-key keyboards have two Enter keys, one on the alphanumeric keypad, the scan code for which is listed with the rest of the keys in this pad, and a second one in the numeric/cursor keypad. This second Enter key—as well as the duplicate number and math function keys on the numeric/cursor keypad—has its own scan code. As a result, your computer can distinguish *which* Enter or number key (or whatever) you press, just as it can distinguish between left and right Shift keys. Although for most operations the two keys work identically, in some cases they do not. For example, hotkey sequences often make use of one or the other of the Shift keys but not both.

All computer keyboards have dedicated *function keys* that have no predefined role. What they do often changes with each application you run, although some programmers strive for a bit of consistency (such as making F1 elicit help and F10 exit). The function keys may be arrayed in two vertical rows of five on an 83-key or 84-key keyboard or as a single horizontal row of 12 on 101-key and 104-key keyboards. In either arrangement, the scan codes of these keys are the same, although the scan codes of F11 and F12 won't be available from keyboards with only ten function keys.

Each key of the dedicated cursor keypad that's interposed between the alphanumeric and numeric/cursor keypads on 101-key and 104-key keyboards also generates a scan code distinct from the keys with duplicate functions located elsewhere.

Normally you do not have to deal with scan codes. The computer makes the translation to numbers and letters automatically and invisibly. The converted information is used in generating the information that appears on your monitor screen, and it is also made available to the applications you run and even the programs you write. Sometimes, however, when you write your own programs, it is useful to detect every key change. You may, for example, want to cause something to happen when a certain key combination is pressed. Your program need only read the keyboard input port and compare what it finds there to a scan code table.

Your computer receives these scan codes at a special I/O port that operates much like a serial port without explicitly following the RS-232 standard. Instead of an array of data and handshaking signals, the keyboard uses only two. By activating or deactivating these two signals in combinations, the system manages communications both from the keyboard and, in all but the initial computer keyboard design, from the host system. Although the very first computers used a one-way flow of data from the keyboard to the computer, current keyboards use a bidirectional interface with its own command protocol.

Protocol

Keyboards use different serial codes for bytes depending on operating mode. In Mode 1, the standard protocol uses nine bits per byte. The first bit is a start bit, which must be a logical one (1). The eight data bits follow in sequence, ordered from least significant to most. In Modes 2 and 3, keyboards use an 11-bit protocol. Each byte begins with a start bit, but a logical 0. Next, the eight data bits follow in sequence, least to most significant. Next comes a parity bit. All keyboards use odd parity, so this bit is set to a logical one or zero so that an odd number of logical ones appears in the combination of eight data bits and one parity bit. The protocol ends with a stop bit, which is always a logical one. Table 20.1 lists the details of this protocol.

TABLE 20.1   Standard Keyboard Serial Byte Protocol

Bit Number	Function	Mode 1	Modes 2 and 3
1	Start bit	1	0
2	Data bit 0	Least significant bit	Least significant bit
3	Data bit 1		
4	Data bit 2		
5	Data bit 3		
6	Data bit 4		
7	Data bit 5		
8	Data bit 6		
9	Data bit 7	Most significant bit	Most significant bit
10	Parity	Not used	Depends on data
11	Stop bit	Not used	1

Handshaking

The signaling and handshaking system is quite elaborate. The keyboard uses the clock line to send out signals that synchronize the bits on the data line with the receiver in your computer. In addition, the computer uses the clock line to throttle the flow of data from the keyboard. The clock line uses *tri-state logic*, which allows both ends of the connection to alter the signal. Normally the keyboard supplies a voltage to the clock line and interrupts it to provide the synchronizing signal. Your computer can also pull down the voltage—essentially shorting it out without harm to the keyboard—as a means to signal its data needs. The data line also uses tri-state logic.

The keyboard monitors the status of both the data and clock lines to determine when it can send information to your computer. Only when both the clock and data lines are high, not pulled low by your computer, will the keyboard send character data to your computer. When the clock line is low, the keyboard holds any characters it wants to send in its buffer. If the clock line is high but the data line is held low by your computer, the keyboard waits to receive a command sent from your computer. The keyboard monitors the clock line throughout the transmission of each byte, and if your computer pulls the line low before your keyboard sends off the parity bit, the keyboard stops its transmission and holds the character in its buffer, waiting until the clock line going high signals that it can retry its transmission.

To send a command byte to the keyboard, your computer first checks to see whether any data is coming its way. To immediately stop the data flow, it pulls the clock line low. Then, by letting the clock line go high again and pulling the data line low, it signals the keyboard that it will send data. The keyboard then counts the bits on the data line. If it receives the correct number, it sends an acknowledgment byte, FA(hex), back to the computer. If the bit count is wrong, it asks for a retransmission with the FE(hex) command.

Software Commands

Your computer has a modest repertory of commands that it can issue to the keyboard to adjust its internal operation. It can alter the operating mode of the keyboard (and hence, which scan codes it sends out) with the command F0(hex) followed by the mode number. It can also alter the typematic rate using the command F3(hex) or alter the status of the locking key indicators with the command ED(hex). Table 20.2 summarizes the commands that your computer can send your modern keyboard. Very old keyboards, such as the 83-key models accompanying the first computers, cannot receive these instructions because of their unidirectional interface. When in Mode 1, keyboards only respond to the Reset command FF(hex), but they then can switch to another mode to act upon other instructions.

TABLE 20.2 Commands Sent to the Keyboard from the Host PC

Byte Value	Command Definition
ED	Change keyboard indicators (bitmapped).
	Bit 0, Scroll Lock.
	Bit 1, Num Lock.
	Bit 2, Caps Lock.
EE	Echo.
EF	Invalid command.
F0	Set keyboard mode to byte following (1, 2, or 3).
	00 = Keyboard sends out current setting.
	01 = Switch to Mode 1.
	02 = Switch to Mode 2.
	03 = Switch to Mode 3.
F1	Invalid command.
F2	Send keyboard I.D.
F3	Set repeat delay and rate to bit-coded value.
	Format 0ddbbaaa.
	Delay = (dd+1) 8 250 msec.
	Rate = (8 + aaa) * 2 ^{bb} * 4 msec.
F4	Clear buffer.
F5	Restore default settings and wait for enable.
F6	Restore default settings.
F7	Set all keys typematic.
F8	Set all keys make/break.
F9	Set all keys make.
FA	Set all keys typematic/make/break.
FB	Set key type typematic.
FC	Set key type make/break.
FD	Set key type make.
FE	Error; requests retransmission.
FF	Reset keyboard.

In addition to its scan codes, the keyboard has a modest range of commands and status information it can relay back to your computer. For example, it can tell your computer that it has too many characters in its in-board buffer, whether it has properly received a command from the computer, and the status of its internal self-test. Table 20.3 lists these commands and status signals.

TABLE 20.3 Commands Sent from the Keyboard to the Host PC

Byte Value	Command Definition
00	Buffer overflow (Modes 2 and 3).
AA	Self-test passed.
F0	Byte that follows is break code.
FA	Acknowledge last command.
FD	Self-test failed.
FC	Self-test failed.
FE	Last command in error; resend.
FF	Buffer overflow (Mode 1).
E0	Byte that follows is scan/release code Mode 2.

To start communications, the keyboard starts by sending a series of the self-test passed character—AA(hex)—to your computer using the wrong parity to indicate that it has not been initialized. When your computer has gone through the boot process sufficiently to be ready to accept data, it sends an error acknowledgment to the keyboard—FE(hex). The keyboard responds by correcting the parity and sending the self-test passed character, providing of course it passed its internal self-test. At this point, the keyboard and computer are ready for normal operation.

Host Interface

The keyboard interface inside your computer is a complete subsystem with its own dedicated microprocessor. The original design used an Intel 8042 microprocessor for handling keyboard communications, but in modern computers, circuitry equivalent to such a microprocessor is typically built in to the chipset. This microprocessor monitors the data and clock lines linking it to the computer, deciphers the serial code, and repackages it in parallel form for passing to your computer.

Your computer receives data from the keyboard interface and sends data to it through a pair of I/O ports. When the ports receive a byte and have it ready for processing by your computer, they generate a hardware interrupt.

In modern computers, the location of keyboard ports and the interrupt generated by the controller may vary with the hardware design and BIOS of your computer. If you are curious, you can check the ports used from the Windows Control Panel by selecting the Keyboard icon and then the Resources tab. You'll see a display like that shown in Figure 20.5.

FIGURE 20.5

A Windows display of the resources used by the keyboard sub-system.

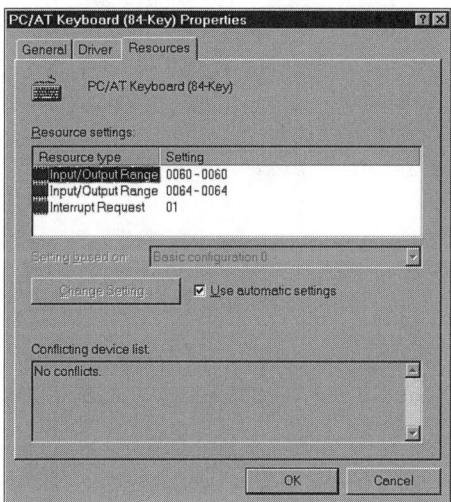

At this point, the keyboard controller passes a scan code sent from the keyboard to your system, and the keyboard BIOS routine determines the character to be sent to your operating system. The standard BIOS interrupt–processing routine generates a second interrupt that permits a subroutine to process the scan code before it gets processed into a character. Under Windows, these BIOS routines are replaced by keyboard drivers that perform the same functions. By default, current consumer versions of Windows install two keyboard drivers—a real-mode driver (keyboard.drv) and a protected-mode driver (vkd.vxd). You can see the drivers installed in your system or change the drivers using the Drivers tab of the Keyboard Properties dialog box in Windows, as shown in Figure 20.6.

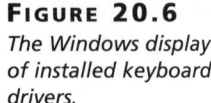

FIGURE 20.6

The Windows display of installed keyboard drivers.

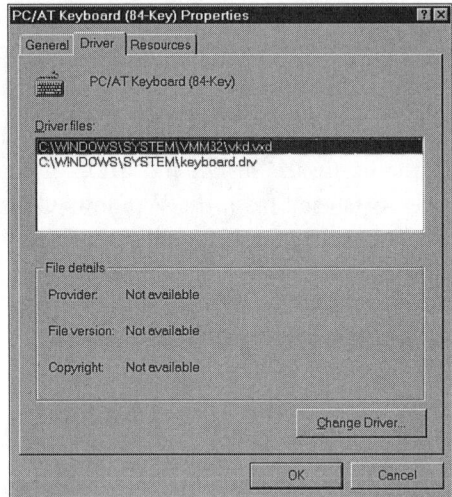

Compatibility

The vast majority of today's keyboards use the same interfaces, protocols, and scan codes and are essentially interchangeable at the electrical and logical level. Because key layouts often differ, however, your fingers might find some compatibility problems, especially when confronted with the layout of the keys on a new notebook computer.

You may encounter compatibility problems in two cases, however. Very old computers and keyboards used a one-way, send-only keyboard design that's different from current designs. Most of these predated the current 101-key design. In the transition period between the acceptance of the two designs, many aftermarket keyboards were switchable between two operating modes. The old, one-way mode was designated XT (or rarely, PC) mode. The modern mode is distinguished as AT (or rarely, PS/2) mode. Very old computers require XT mode keyboards.

The connectors used by very old keyboards also differ from the current design, using a large five-pin plug, as discussed later. Note that the connector is not a reliable guide to the operating mode of the keyboard. Keyboards using the large, old, five-pin connector may operate as either XT or AT keyboards. All keyboards using the modern, miniaturized connector operate in the AT mode (although some old models may have switches allowing support of XT mode).

Another compatibility issue affects keys beyond the 101 defined for the PS/2 keyboard design. Your computer needs a software driver to recognize these additional keys. Windows generally can identify your keyboard when it scans your hardware and set itself up accordingly with the correct driver (or it will ask you for a disk).

If you have reason to believe that its choice was incorrect or if you want to install a keyboard manually into Windows for any reason, Windows gives you that option. You access the keyboard selection in the General tab of the Keyboard Properties dialog box. To open the Keyboard Properties dialog box, select the Keyboard icon in Control Panel.

If the keyboard Windows displays is not the one you want, click the Change button. Windows will respond with a list of keyboards it inherently knows how to manage, as shown in Figure 20.7.

FIGURE 20.7

Selecting a keyboard in Windows.

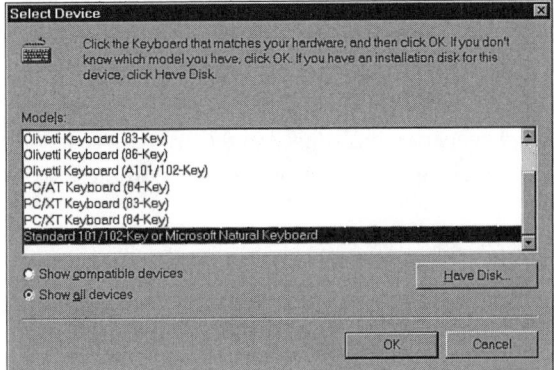

As with installing any hardware on your computer, Windows allows you to install a keyboard without built-in Windows support using a driver supplied by the keyboard-maker. If the keyboard you want to use is not listed as one of those directly supported, click the Have Disk button and slide the floppy disk or CD supplied by your keyboard vendor into the appropriate drive slot when Windows instructs you to. You specify a disk location and complete the installation process as you would with any other hardware device.

Connections

The scan-code system and serial signaling simplify the connection scheme used by computer keyboards. Scan codes are sent from the keyboard to the computer serially so that only one wire conductor is needed to convey the keyboard data information. A second conductor is required to serve as a return path for the data signal; as a ground, it serves as a common return for all other circuits in the keyboard cable. To synchronize the logic in the keyboard with that in the computer, a separate wire is used for a keyboard clock signal. A fourth and final wire is used to supply the keyboard with the five-volt direct current power it needs to operate. These four conductors are all that is necessary to link keyboard to computer.

The physical embodiment of those signals is the keyboard connector. Nearly all keyboards now use a miniature six-pin DIN connector. This design is usually called *PS/2-style* because IBM introduced it with its PS/2 computers in 1987, and it has served every since.

The six pins are arrayed in a circle around a rectangular plastic tab that, along with three guides in the shield, keys the connector against improper insertion. As with the five-pin connector, the pin numbers follow an irregular pattern. Figure 20.8 shows the six-pin miniature DIN keyboard connector and its signal layout.

FIGURE 20.8

The six-pin minia-ture DIN keyboard connector.

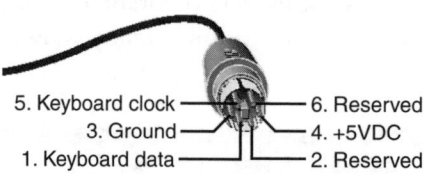

5. Keyboard clock ——— 6. Reserved
3. Ground ——— 4. +5VDC
1. Keyboard data ——— 2. Reserved

Only four pins are significant to keyboard use: Pin 1 is assigned keyboard data; pin 3, ground; pin 4, five volts; pin 5, keyboard clock. Pins 2 and 6 are reserved, and the shield is attached as a chassis ground. Table 20.4 lists the signal assignments on the PS/2-style keyboard connector.

TABLE 20.4   Six-Pin Miniature DIN Keyboard Connector Pinout

Pin	Description	Direction
1	Data	In
2	Reserved	N/A
3	Ground	N/A
4	+5 V	Out
5	Clock	In
6	Reserved	N/A
Shield	Ground	N/A

Older keyboards use a five-pin plug—a standard, as opposed to miniature, DIN connector. Because the five-pin and six-pin keyboard connectors use the same signals with only a slight rearrangement, a simple adapter will convert one style of connector to another. These keyboard adapters are readily available on the computer parts market. If you're so inclined, you can make your own using the interconnection guide given in Table 20.5.

TABLE 20.5   Keyboard Connector Adapter Wiring Scheme

PC Connector Five-Pin DIN Six-Pin Mini-DIN	PS/2 Connector Signal Function
1	5 Clock
2	1 Data

PC Connector Five-Pin DIN Six-Pin Mini-DIN	PS/2 Connector Signal Function
3	2 Reserved
4	3 Ground
5	4 +5 V
NC	6 Reserved

In some computers, the keyboard cable can be disconnected from the keyboard itself. This detachable design makes the cable easy to service (by replacing it) and a single keyboard adaptable between five-pin and six-pin cabling standards. The keyboard-to-cable connection uses a modular (AMP) jack on the rear of the keyboard with a matching plug on the cable, as shown in Figure 20.9.

FIGURE 20.9

The modular keyboard connector and signal assignments.

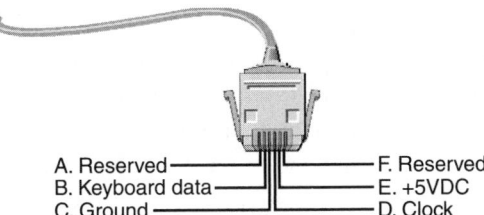

In some computers, As shown in the figure, this modular connector has the following signal assignments: A, reserved; B, keyboard data; C, ground; D, keyboard clock; E, five volts; F, reserved. When looking at the gold contacts of the connector, the contacts are labeled in reverse alphabetical order from left to right. Table 20.6 summarizes these signal assignments.

TABLE 20.6   Modular Keyboard Connector Pinout

Pin	Description	Direction
A	Reserved	N/A
B	Data	Out
C	Ground	N/A
D	Clock	Out
E	+5 V	In
F	Reserved	N/A
Shield	Ground	N/A

USB Port

In the long run, computer-makers hope to make the keyboard port as obsolete as steam-powered personal computers. The alternative is the Universal Serial Bus (USB), which computer-makers hope will replace all the other ports on the back of your computer.

As computers shift to the use of the Universal Serial Bus, keyboard connections will move to this high-speed interface. USB-based keyboards were displayed as early as February, 1996, but the early introduction proved premature. Even in 2003, computer-makers prefer the conventional keyboard interface because it is cheap and reliable, despite admonitions from Intel and Microsoft to move to USB. As the interface matures, however, USB keyboards are destined to become more popular.

Because USB is designed and designated a universal interface, one that will link devices other than keyboards, it is treated in a separate chapter devoted to ports, Chapter 10.

The inner workings of USB keyboards are immaterial to your computer. It just looks for data packets received through the USB port. Any packets containing keyboard data get routed by the USB driver to the keyboard driver of the operating system. Then the operating system pulls the data from the packets to see what you've typed. If your computer wants to send a command to the keyboard, it notifies the keyboard driver, which generates the code of the command and passes it along to the USB driver, which routes it out the port and to your keyboard as another packet on the USB circuit.

The flaw in this design is that it doesn't work until the operating system and its USB drivers load. Before then, the keyboard driver has no route through which to get keystroke codes. That's all right, because if the operating system hasn't loaded, the keyboard driver won't have loaded, either. With neither the USB nor keyboard driver running, your computer faces a problem if it needs to read the keyboard while booting up—for example, to step through the setup menu.

Your computer's BIOS makes up for this flaw. It patches together the old and new keyboard systems.

Wireless

As computers merge into entertainment systems, you're apt to sit farther and farther away from the display screen. A home entertainment computer, for example, fits into your living room more like a television set, at one end of the room with you at the other. Just as a wireless remote control has become *de rigueur* for your television, a wireless keyboard gives you the same flexibility when the computer takes over.

Wireless keyboards are two-piece systems. Each involves the keyboard itself, which functions as a transmitter, and a base station, which acts as the receiver. (Keyboard communications are actually a two-way street, but the transmitter/receiver distinction is valid as a view of the data you generate by typing.) A single base station can serve both a wireless keyboard and wireless mouse (or other pointing device).

The first wireless keyboards used infrared technology (similar to, but predating, IrDA), with the interface (a little red optical sensor) built in to the host computer. Today, however, wireless systems are add-ons that plug into conventional interfaces—either the keyboard port or USB port. The connection between the base station and your computer is completely conventional. Your computer receives exactly the same scan codes or USB packets it would expect from a plug-in keyboard.

All the magic is in the wireless link. And wireless links might as well be magic because they need to follow no standards other than the Federal Communications Commission's limits on unlicensed radiation. That is, as long as they don't use too much power—definitely less than what is apt to cause interference—and stick to the authorized frequency bands, wireless keyboard-makers are free to do whatever they want with their signals.

The range of these wireless systems stretch from about 5 feet to more than 30 feet. Unfortunately, the only guidance available as to the range of a particular keyboard is the claim of its manufacturer.

Pointing Devices

Your mom probably told you that it's impolite to point, but your mom probably wasn't trying to move a mouse cursor across her computer screen at the time. Trying to navigate through Windows with nothing but keyboard commands is like threading a needle in boxing gloves, only more frustrating. (It is Windows, after all.) You could point at the screen and show Windows where to put the [expletive deleted] cursor, but you could shout four-letter words until your face was as red as the nose of a career politician to no avail. (Maybe that's why they call it a cursor.) You need a method to point out to Windows where to move the cursor—namely, a pointing device.

As with any problem, technology has brought us not one, but several, solutions. When you sit at your desk, mice and trackballs fall naturally to hand for pointing your intentions to Windows. Go mobile, and you might use a TouchPad or TrackPoint to indicate cursor moves. Although each achieves the same result, each uses a different set of technologies.

Mice

The computer mouse was the first computer pointing device, developed concurrently with the graphic environment—the problem and solution created together. Through its near 40 years of evolution, the mouse has changed surprisingly little. Today's mice take the same basic form as the original—made to fit the hand—with the same control layout of buttons at your fingertips. Over so long a period, however, species naturally diverge, and so have mice. Where once there was only one breed of computer mouse, a mechanical creation wearing a single switch, now there are several.

Mice can be distinguished by five chief differences: the technology they use to detect motion (mechanical or optical), the number of buttons they have, the presence of a scroll wheel, the manner in which they connect with their computer hosts, and the protocol or language they use to encode the information they send to your computer. The last two of these differences also apply to other pointing devices, so we'll hold back on our discussion of them until we've looked at mouse alternatives.

As a mechanical transducer, a mouse somehow has to be able to detect its motion across your work surface. Although engineers have a wide range of position-sensing technologies to choose from—they could even use the satellite-based Global Positioning System to determine the absolute location of the mouse and then deduce changes you make in its position—only two techniques have actually been used in practice. These are mechanical sensing and optical sensing.

Mechanical Mice

The first mouse was a mechanical design based on a small ball that protruded through its bottom and rotated as the mouse was pushed along a surface. Switches inside the mouse detected the movement and relayed the direction of the ball's rotation to the host computer.

Although the ball is free to rotate in any direction, only four directions are detected, corresponding to two axes of a two-dimensional coordinate system. The movement in each of the four directions is quantified (in hundredths of an inch) and sent to the host as a discrete signal for each discrete increment of movement.

The mechanical mouse works on just about any surface. In general, the rotating ball has a coarse texture and is made from a rubbery compound that even gets a grip on smooth surfaces. In fact, you can even turn a mechanical mouse upside down and spin the ball with your finger (although you'll then have difficulty fingering the pushbuttons!).

On the other hand, the mechanical mouse requires that you move it across a surface of some kind, and all too many desks do not have enough free space to give the mouse a good run. (Of course, if all else fails, you can run a mechanical mouse across your pant leg or skirt, but you're likely to get some odd looks.) In addition, mechanical parts can break. A mechanical mouse tends to pick up dirt and lint, which can impede its proper operation. You should therefore regularly clean your mechanical mouse even if you think your desktop is spotless. Cleaning is easy, if bothersome. Twist the ring on the bottom of the mouse that retains the ball counterclockwise to release the ball. Remove both ring and ball. With a Q-tip dampened with rubbing alcohol, scrub off the residue you find inside, particularly that on the small rubber rollers (you may need to use your fingernail to pry loose some of the more tenacious grime). After the alcohol evaporates—usually after a few dozen seconds—reassemble your mouse.

Inside the mechanical mouse, the ball rolls against two perpendicular sensors. These sensors generate electrical pulses as they rotate, and the mouse sends the pulses to your computer. By counting the number of pulses in each direction, your computer can calculate the movement of the mouse.

The sensors can use various technologies. For example, the wheel may be optically encoded with an alternating pattern of black and white (or clear and opaque), and a photo-detector senses the changes. Alternatively, the sensor may use electromagnetic technology, sensing as a pattern of magnetic material passes a detector.

Optical Mice

The alternative to the mechanical mouse is the optical mouse. Instead of a rotating ball, the optical mouse uses a light beam to detect movement across your desk surface. Because no moving parts are involved, there's less inside an optical mouse to get dirty and break.

Original Design

The first optical mouse required special patterned mouse pads to operate properly and used two pairs of LEDs and photodetectors on its bottom, one pair oriented at right angles to the other. Its matching mouse pad was coated with an overlapped pattern of blue and yellow grids. Each pair of LEDs and photodetectors detected motion in either direction across one axis of the grid. A felt-like covering on the bottom of the mouse made it easy to slide across the plastic-coated mouse pad.

The big disadvantage of the optical mouse was that it required that you use its special mouse pad and put the pad somewhere. The pad itself could get dirty, be damaged, or simply get lost. On humid days, the plastic coating of the pad might stick to your bare forearm and lift off in sheets. For these and other reasons, this form of optical technology has fallen from favor in mouse design despite its simplicity and low cost.

Current Design

Today's optical mice bear little resemblance to the original optical designs. Comparing the two is like comparing an abacus to a computer. The original optical mouse only had to be smart enough to count lines as they rippled past a sensor. The current design uses a pattern-recognition system in a digital processor that in itself is more powerful than a complete computer of only a few years ago. The sophisticated pattern-processing capabilities of the modern optical mouse frees the critter from the tyranny of the mouse pad. Instead of following the preprinted pattern on the pad, today's optical mice detect the minuscule variations in the brightness of whatever surface you run them across. They rely on the texture that's present on most surfaces as the pattern they require to sense motion.

The modern optical system has several advantages. As with older optical mice, no moving parts are required to sense motion, so the mice require no maintenance. They don't get dirty, and they do not wear out. Moreover, optical mice can work on surfaces that cause mechanical mice to falter, such as soft fabric or curved hard surfaces. On the other hand, current optical technology has a few shortcomings. The optical sensors do not work well on surfaces such as glass that lack visible detail or are reflective. In addition, surfaces can be *too* patterned. A highly repetitive pattern such as the screens applied to photos to print them in newspapers and magazines can confuse modern optical sensors.

A current optical mouse has three functional parts: an illumination system, a sensor that's essentially a small video camera, and a digital signal processor for pattern recognition.

The optical mouse includes its own illumination for the surface over which it operates, generally an inexpensive red light emitting diode (LED). The self-contained light source is more than a means to operate the mouse when you turn the lights low. It's key to creating a pattern on the work surface that the mouse can identify. When the light source is kept at an oblique angle, close to the surface and sharply focused, it can create a pattern of bright areas and shadows even on seemingly smooth surfaces.

The sensor detects the light-and-shadow pattern created by the illumination system on the work surface. Like a miniature video camera, the sensor comprises a lens and photodetector array. The lens focuses the pattern on the photodetector array, a matrix of light-sensitive CMOS elements. In today's optical mice, this camera system is small and accurate enough to resolve details measuring about 800 to the inch.

The digital signal processor (DSP) samples the output of the sensor about several thousand times each second. It compares each image to the previous one, looking for changes in the light-and-shadow pattern. The processor can detect both the direction and magnitude in the shift in the pattern, which directly correspond to any movement of the mouse. Because the sampling occurs so often, sequential images overlap and changes are apt to be small, which allow relatively simple algorithms to suffice for detecting changes.

The choice of algorithm is the choice of the mouse's designer. DSPs make brute-force methods easy. The DSP samples the brightness at every pixel of the sensor of the previous sample to the current sample. It then shifts the current sample one pixel in an arbitrary direction and checks the match. It tries every direction in turn, then shifts another pixel and tries each direction. Once it has measured the difference between all of these, it knows the one showing the least difference is the one that reflects the most likely movement of the mouse. Designers can simplify and quicken this procedure by adding more intelligence. For example, when the DSP finds an exact match, there's no reason for it to keep checking. Or rather than choosing an arbitrary direction for its first test, it could start in the same direction as the last movement.

The sampling rate determines the maximum speed at which you can move your mouse and expect it to reliably indicate the motion. The slowest-sampling mice capture about 1500 images per second; the fastest, about 6000 images per second. According to

Microsoft, a 2500-samples-per-second rate is sufficient to handle a mouse that moves at a physical rate of 11 inches per second. At 6000 samples per second, a mouse can track movement made at speeds up to 37 inches per second. Even the most rapid mouse movements rarely exceed 30 inches per second.

After the processor has detected the motion of the mouse, a modern optical mouse functions much like a mechanical mouse, relaying position information to the host computer through a serial or USB port.

Buttons

In its purest form, as envisioned by the inventor of the mouse, Douglas Engelbart, a mouse has exactly one pushbutton. Movement of the mouse determines the position of the onscreen cursor, but a selection is made only when that button is pressed, preventing any menu selections that the mouse has inadvertently dragged across from being chosen.

One button is the least confusing arrangement and the minimum necessary to carry out mouse functions. Operating the computer is reduced to nothing more than pressing the button. Carefully tailored menu selections allow the single button to suffice in controlling all computer functions. The Apple Macintosh uses this kind of mouse with one button.

As Microsoft developed Windows, however, its engineers opted instead for two buttons next to each other in place of one. Two buttons allow designers more flexibility—for example, one can be given a "Do" function, and a second, an "Undo" function. In a drawing program, one might "lower" the pen analog that traces lines across the screen while the other button "lifts" the pen.

Of course, having three buttons would be even better. The programmer would have still more flexibility. Even a fourth button could be added—but as the number of mouse buttons rises, the mouse becomes increasingly like a keyboard. It becomes a more formidable device with a more rigorous learning curve. A profusion of mouse buttons is counterproductive.

Three buttons would appear to be the practical limit, because three positions are available for the index, middle, and ring fingers while the thumb and pinkie grab the sides of the mouse. Designers have, however, created mice that are little more than miniaturized keyboards with dozens of buttons. Five-button mice are in current production.

In general, having three or more buttons is superfluous. Most Windows applications are designed to recognize only the two standard mouse buttons. Special applications may take advantage of additional buttons. Moreover, the driver software for most multibutton mice lets you decide the function to assign to each button. The software makes the button functions *programmable*, allowing you to make each button mimic your press of a series or combination of keystrokes on your keyboard.

The technology behind the buttons is simple, no matter the number of buttons. Each button presses down on an electrical switch or contact. The circuitry inside the mouse detects your press as the closure of an electrical circuit and then relays a digital code to your computer to indicate the button has been pressed. When you release the button, the circuitry responds with a different code that indicates you've let go. Each of the buttons has its own code value for its press and release.

Wheels

In 1997, Microsoft added a new feature to the design of its first Intellimouse, a rubber wheel nestled between its two pushbuttons. This *scroll wheel* allows you to scroll the screen without clicking on scroll bars.

Actually, the mouse's wheel puts only about one-sixth of the circumference of a rubber tire under your finger's control, the rest is hidden inside the mouse. You recognize it as a wheel only by its feel. The tire, about three-eighths inch across and made from textured rubber to give your fingers a better grip, fits a small plastic wheel-and-axle that's molded as a single piece.

Inside the mouse, the wheel is connected to a rotary motion sensor. In fact, the wheel may be part of the sensor itself. As with the motion sensors of mechanical mice, the one used by the wheel may be based on optical or magnetic technology. The optical sensor detects the movement of a black-and-white pattern on the wheel, counting the stripes to detect how many degrees you've turned the wheel. Magnetic sensors detect a grooved or notched texture to the magnetic material on the wheel to count the degrees you spin the wheel. The electronics of the mouse send out codes corresponding to the wheel's motion that are recognized by the mouse's driver software.

The wheel should smoothly spin but doesn't by design. To prevent you from inadvertently scrolling with every brush of the wheel, mechanical resistance is added to the wheel. Most often it takes the form of detents—the mouse notches from one position to the next as it rotates. A spring-loaded stop lodges its circular base into a matching notch or pit in the wheel. As you rotate the wheel, you force the stop upward, and it pushes itself back down into the next notch. The action is purely mechanical and independent of the motion sensing.

Resolution

Mice are sometimes rated by their resolution—the number of counts per inch (CPI) that they can detect. When a mouse is moved, it sends out a signal indicating each increment of motion it makes as a single count. The number of these increments in an inch of movement equals the mouse's CPI rating.

The higher the CPI, the finer the detail in the movement the mouse can detect. Unless the mouse driver compensates, higher resolution has an odd effect. More resolution translates into faster movement of the mouse pointer onscreen because the screen pointer is controlled by the number of counts received from the mouse, not the actual distance the mouse is moved. Consequently, a higher-resolution mouse is a faster mouse, not a more precise mouse.

The true limit on how precisely you can position your mouse cursor is your own hand. If you want to be more accurate with your mouse, you can compensate for your human limitations by opting for less resolution from your mouse. Because you have to move your mouse physically farther for each onscreen change, a lower mouse resolution helps you put the cursor where you want it.

Trackballs

Just like its namesake in the Rodentia, the computer mouse needs room to roam and ends up almost anywhere. A mouse does not stay put because moving around is in its nature—and that's how you use it.

The problem is that many folks do not have room for a roaming rodent. Their desks are just too cluttered or they are traveling with a laptop and neglected to carry a desk along with them into the coach-class cabin. More insidious issues also involve mice. Pushing a plastic rodent requires clumsy, wasteful, and tiring whole-arm movements. Mice are inefficient and exhausting.

The leading mouse alternative, the trackball, eliminates these problems. Essentially a mouse turned upside down, the trackball is much like it sounds—an often big ball that, when rotated, causes the screen pointer (mouse cursor) to track its movements. The trackball spins in place and requires no more desk space than its base, a few square inches.

Switches

As with mice, trackballs also require switches so that you can indicate when the cursor is pointing to what you want. Most trackballs have two or three pushbuttons that duplicate the selection functions of mouse buttons. Although some trackballs boast four buttons, the foursome typically functions as two duplicate pairs—mirror images—so that one trackball can serve either a right or left hand.

No standard exists for switch placement on trackballs because no consensus exists on how you are supposed to operate a trackball. Some are designed so that you spin the ball with your fingers. Others prefer that your thumb do the job. Which is better depends on whom you believe and how you prefer to work.

According to one theory, your fingers are more agile than your thumb and therefore more precise at spinning the ball, so you should get a trackball that you operate with your fingers. A competing theory holds that the thumb has more muscle control than the fingers, so a thumb-operated trackball makes more sense. Some trackball-makers wisely avoid such issues and make trackballs that can be used equally adeptly by the posed or opposed digit. In truth, which design and how you use a trackball is a matter of preference rather than hard science.

Ball Size

Another trackball design choice is the size of the ball itself and how it is retained inside the mechanism. Various products range in dimensions from the size of a shooter marble to those equaling cue balls. Bigger once was thought to be better, but the trackballs built into laptop and notebook computers are making smaller sizes popular.

Because no definitive study has shown the superiority of any particular size for a trackball, the best advice is to select one that feels best to you—or the one that comes already attached to your computer.

As with the balls in mechanical mice, trackballs naturally attract dirt. Although the trackball doesn't pick up dirt from rolling around, dust does fall upon the ball and the oils from your fingers collect there, too. A readily removable ball can be quickly and easily cleaned. This sort of serviceability is absent from many trackball designs—something to consider if you plan on using your trackball for a long time.

Optical trackballs are growing in popularity. Most work like old-fashioned optical mice, only the pattern used for recognition is part of the ball itself. If you look closely at the big red ball that these optical trackballs use, you can see the faint lines that sensors inside the trackball mechanism detect. Optical trackballs require less maintenance than the mechanical kind, although if they get really dirty you'll need to swab off their optical sensors, which are readily visible once you remove the ball. Use a Q-tip dampened with plain water. Resort to window cleaner only if using water alone is not successful.

Handedness

Most mice are symmetrical. Although two- and three-button mice define different functions for their left- and right-side buttons, most enable you to flip the functions of the buttons to suit right- or left-hand operation if what button falls under a given finger is important to you.

Trackballs, however, are sometimes asymmetrical. In itself, that can be good. An asymmetrical trackball can better fit the hand that it is designed for, right or left. But this handedness among trackballs poses a problem when you make your purchase—you have to determine whether you want a right- or left-handed trackball. Which you need does not necessarily correspond to the way you write. Some left-handed people prefer right-handed trackballs (and some righties like lefties). Consequently, a right-handed trackball isn't always the best choice for a right-handed person. Before you buy a one-handed trackball, make sure you know which hand you will favor in using it. If you switch hands when you tire from using one hand for spinning your trackball all day long, you may not want a product with definite handedness at all.

Resolution

Somewhere buried in the specification of a trackball, you may find a resolution rating, either as the number of counts per inch (CPI) of movement or as DPI (as with mice). These figures are rarely published anymore because today's driver software makes them irrelevant. Trackball resolution indicates how much you have to spin a ball to move the cursor on the screen—higher resolution requires more spin to move the cursor. Software drivers allow trackball manufacturers to give you several choices for the effective resolution of their products so that you can tailor their actions and reactions to match the way you work. In addition, most trackball-makers offer ballistic operation in which the translation of ball movement to onscreen cursor change varies with the speed of the ball's spin. This yields fast positioning without loss of precision. The only problem is getting used to such nonlinear control in which the speed at which you spin the trackball has as much (and sometimes more) effect as how far you spin it.

Unlike most other peripherals, no one trackball is objectively better than the rest. Operating any of them is an acquired talent like brain surgery, piano-playing, or hair-combing. Any judgment must be subjective, and which is better suited a particular user depends most on personal preference and familiarity.

TouchPads

In their developmental years, notebook computers used a variety of pointing devices. Several tried integrated trackballs. The designer's whims determined placement—sometimes at the corner of the screen, sometimes below the keypad. In any case, the balls were small (they had to be to fit in a portable system), and the perfectly located trackball was rare, indeed.

Hewlett-Packard developed a pop-out mouse tethered to the right side of the system. The system detected mouse movement through the thin, flat tether, so you could hold the mouse in the air and its movements would nevertheless register. The downside was the need for space on the right, either air or desktop, a requirement not easily met in crowded aircraft.

The notebook industry needed a better alternative for a pointing device and found it in the TouchPad (the name is a trademark of Synaptics Corporation). Almost by default the

TouchPad became the most popular pointing device for notebook systems. It wasn't that the TouchPad necessarily was so good. All the alternatives were worse. Figure 21.1 shows a TouchPad.

FIGURE 21.1
A TouchPad on a notebook computer.

The TouchPad detects the location of your finger on the pad by detecting the electrical capacitance of your finger. Your finger attracts a minute static electrical charge, which causes a small current flow in the circuitry of the TouchPad. The electronics associated with the TouchPad detects this minute current from two adjacent edges of the pad, so it can precisely locate your finger in two dimensions. By following changes in the current, it can determine the motion of your finger across the pad.

Mechanically, the foundation of the TouchPad is a printed circuit board. The top of the board holds a pattern of conductive sensor lines etched into place. The bottom of the board holds the electronics that make the pad work. A layer of Mylar covers the top of the board to protect it and gives your finger a smooth surface to trace across. Current designs are capable of resolving 1000 points per inch (40 points/mm).

A TouchPad is inherently an absolute position detector. The electronics of the pad converts the absolute location information it determines into mouse-like relative motion that can be sent to your computer in standard mouse protocol.

The TouchPad can be completely sealed from any kind of contamination, so it is an excellent choice as a pointing device for a machine that has to operate in a hostile environment. On the other hand, useful TouchPads must be large enough to conveniently register your finger movements. That means they steal space from the top of your notebook computer. Most notebook computer–makers take advantage of this space requirement to give you a hand rest below the keyboard—and to give the manufacturer more room for the components inside the computer.

Computer-makers can choose from several sizes of TouchPads for their products. Typically the active pad surface measures 62 by 46.5 millimeters, although larger (90.6 by 72.1 millimeters) and smaller (55.9 by 32.9 millimeters or less) versions are also readily available.

Most manufacturers locate the TouchPad just below the space bar on their keyboards. This location allows you to use your thumbs to move the mouse so you don't have to take your hands from the home row when typing, an important consideration if you touch-type on your computer. Notebook computers differ in the height and sensitivity of their TouchPads. Although the differences are subtle, they affect usability. If the TouchPad height is wrong for your typing system, you're likely to inadvertently move the mouse, or even activate it. You'll want to try out the keyboard and the TouchPad of any portable computer that has one before you commit to buying it.

TrackPoint

Invented by IBM, which has trademarked the name and patented the technology, the TrackPoint system was developed by Ted Selker and Joseph D. Rutledge of IBM's Thomas J. Watson Research Center and first used in IBM notebook computers. In principle, the pointing stick is a miniature joystick that's stuck between the G and H keys of a conventional keyboard. The pointing stick protrudes just two millimeters above the normal typing surface. Its position enables you to maneuver it with either index finger while the rest of your fingers remain in the home row. Because in normal touch-typing your fingers should never cross the G/H boundary, it does not interfere with normal typing. The selection function of mouse buttons is given over to bar keys at the lower edge of the keyboard, adjacent to the spacebar. Figure 21.2 shows the placement of the TrackPoint.

FIGURE 21.2
A TrackPoint device in its native environment.

The nub—which typically is removable in case you wear it smooth—mechanically connects to a pair of solid-state pressure sensors mounted at right angles to one another. When you press against one side of the TrackPoint device, it senses the pressure you apply even though the nub itself does not move. The TrackPoint electronics and software driver convert this pressure data into an indication of relative motion. The harder you press, the greater the signal the pressure sensor generates and the faster it tells your computer to move the mouse pointer. The paired sensors give you two axes of control corresponding to moving the mouse along its X and Y axes.

The TrackPoint system has several advantages in addition to its favorable typing location. It is entirely solid state and sealed so it, like a TouchPad, is environmentally rugged. It has no moving parts to wear out, except for the pointing nub, which you can readily replace. The disadvantage is that many people find it unnatural to use until they have acquired experience using it.

Game Controllers

When you drive your car, you don't use a keyboard and mouse—at least not yet. When you're racing along Santa Monica Boulevard in a round of *Grand Theft Auto 3*, you probably don't want to type in commands to mash the accelerator through the floor and hang a flying Louie. You want the experience and the control system to be as real as possible without live ammunition. You want a real steering wheel, real pedals, and the real aroma of searing rubber and SAE30 motor oil flaming out your exhaust pipe.

So far electronic devices aren't very adept at generating odors (although bad software really does stink), but some special hardware can help make you more adept in playing games—mechanisms that give you better control. Computer people have a clever name for the devices that help you control games. They call them *game controllers*.

The history of game controllers goes back to the first personal computers and beyond. As soon as computers graduated from the workbench to the television set, people played games on them. For control, they used *joysticks*. Even the business-oriented IBM Personal Computer made provisions for joysticks and a two-player option called *game paddles* using a special interface called the *game port*. But such primitive control systems are as passé as *Pong*, the first real video game.

Today's elaborate wheel-and-pedal combinations are possible thanks to the architectural changes made by Windows. The game port hardware interface defined the control afforded by joysticks—two position sensors and a single pushbutton. Thanks to an additional layer of interface abstraction (driver software) and a better connection system (USB), designers are free to create any kind of control system they want when working with Windows.

The essential part of any game controller is one or more *sensors* or *transducers*. A sensor samples a physical measurement—be it brightness, distance, direction, or weight. A transducer converts or translates a physical property or change into an electrical signal. (The line between them is hard to draw—transducers are sensors, but not all sensors are transducers.) A pressure sensor, for example, is a transducer that varies its output with how hard you press on it (say, by hammering the accelerator). The magnetic or optic motion sensors in mice are not generally considered transducers.

The difference isn't what matters. Rather, the game controller depends on being able to sense what you do—push a pedal, spin a wheel, pull back on a throttle or stick—and quantify it. The controller then takes the result of that quantification, translates it into a digital code, packages the information in a data packet, and whisks it out to your computer through its interface. The driver software in your computer receives the packet from the interface and translates its content into a form compatible with your game (or other program) and passes it along through the program's Application Program Interface (API). Your game then decides what to do with the control data.

There's no limit to the number of controls possible using this system. You could have a game controller as complex as the bridge of the Starship Enterprise. (Actually, that's easy because the bridge is just a set, and none of the controls really work.) The controller designer is free to create anything imaginable (but technically and economically feasible, of course). Moreover, the system works both ways, so designers can put feedback mechanisms—for example, controllers that shake you up so you know when you're really applying power—to make games more realistic. The only essential element is that the game software understand the information sent by the controller. Controller designers must match the requirements of game APIs. The software driver and interface are simply the glue that holds everything together.

Interfaces

To communicate its codes to your computer, any pointing device needs to be connected in some way. Notebook computers have it easy—signals can take the direct route because they are built in. Desktop systems require some kind of port to which you can connect your mouse or other pointing device. Most systems today have a dedicated mouse port. But the industry-wide push to eliminate legacy ports of any kind, as well as the need for alternative pointing devices, are making the USB interface popular (at least among computer-makers). A few mice using the legacy RS-232C serial port are also available.

Mouse Port

The most popular way to connect a mouse to a desktop computer is via the *mouse port*. Physically the mouse port resembles a keyboard jack. Both use a six-pin miniature DIN connector. The design owes its heritage to the first IBM Personal Systems/2 (PS/2) and consequently is sometimes termed a *PS/2 mouse port.* The only lasting change affected by the computer industry on this port design has been color-coding. To distinguish a mouse port from a keyboard port, the mouse port jack and connector are colored aqua, a bluish green. (Keyboard ports are purple.)

Electrically the mouse port is also similar to a keyboard port, using low-speed serial technology to send signals from mouse to computer using its own interrupt to avoid conflicts with other devices. This design limits the use of the mouse port because it is not fast enough to handle the needs of more sophisticated pointing devices.

USB Port

True to the "universal" in its name, the USB port accommodates mice and any other kind of pointing device. The port, even in its early Version 1.0 form, offers enough speed for the most elaborate pointing devices. Moreover, because pointing devices are not used during bootup before the operating system and its drivers load, there's no need for special BIOS provisions for handling USB mouse control. The hardware installation of a USB-based pointing device requires only plugging it in, which is why this connection system is preferred.

Serial Mice

The serial port was the first connection system used by mice, and its shortcomings provided the incentive to develop the dedicated mouse port. In general, mice make no onerous demands on the serial port. They operate at a low communication rate (1200 bits per second) and adapt to any available port thanks to driver software. But putting a mouse on a serial port is hardly trouble-free. Because every mouse movement generates a serial-port interrupt, if your system has more than two serial ports, you can easily generate interrupt conflicts with a mouse. Because serial ports 1 and 4 (that is, the ports that DOS calls COM1 and COM4) share interrupt 4, and serial ports 2 and 3 (COM2 and COM3) share interrupt 3, a mouse can conflict with another device connected to the other port sharing its interrupt. If you have a serial mouse, it's always best to plug your mouse into the port that does not have to share its interrupt (for example, COM1 if your computer has three serial ports) to avoid surprises—the kind that can crash your computer. Better still, use a mouse port or USB mouse.

Wireless

The most irksome trait of the mouse is the tail that inspired its name. The cord dangling from the far end of the mouse is a desktop hazard, liable to snag whatever you're working on. Thank goodness that inkwells are about as likely as chimera on modern desks; otherwise, you could count on your mouse making your work a uniform ink-stained blue at least once a day. Mice consequently benefit from wireless technology even more than key-boards.

Making a mouse wireless is much the same as cutting the keyboard cord. The wireless link operates between the mouse and a base station, which connects to your computer through one of the aforementioned standard mouse interfaces. The wireless link is proprietary, allowing the manufacturer to chose whatever technology and design best fits the purpose and price of the product.

Infrared (IR) technology, although chosen by some manufacturers, does not mate with the typical cluttered desktop environment. The IR sensor in the base station must be able to see the mouse—literally—and any object in the way can create errors of omission, unde-tected mouse movements. If you confine your mouse to a pad, you can put the base sta-tion adjacent to the pad without risk of losing communication. But with today's optical mouse technologies, the temptation is to move your mouse on any suitable desktop bare spot, which may not be near the base station.

Radio technology is a better match for the lifestyle of the modern mouse, and most manu-facturers have shifted to it. Because radio waves penetrate most desktop objects, you can put the base station almost anywhere and still expect your mouse to work.

If you're thinking of going wireless, a better choice is to buy a wireless keyboard and mouse as a package so you need only one base station for both.

Protocols and Drivers

Mice convert the motions they detect into a digital code that can be processed or analyzed by your computer. The only loose end is what code the mouse uses. A standard mouse code would help software writers craft their products to better take advantage of mice. A standard mouse code would be so useful, in fact, that the industry has come up with four distinct standards, called *mouse protocols*, all of which were in use at one time. These stan-dards were developed by four of the major forces in the mouse industry, and each bore its originator's name. These include Microsoft, Mouse Systems Corporation (for a period known as MSC Corporation), Logitech, and IBM Corporation. The first three were designed for individual mouse products created by the respective companies. The IBM protocol was introduced with the PS/2 series of computers, which came equipped with a built-in jack that accepted a mouse. Other pointing devices use their own protocols, com-plicating matters further.

In truth, you don't need to know the details of any of these protocols. That's the challenge handled by the software driver used by your pointing device. And that's why you must match the right driver software to your pointing device.

Today, the Microsoft mouse protocol is the most prevalent. Most generic mice will work as a Microsoft mouse if you don't have a specific driver for your mouse. But the generic Microsoft mouse protocol does not take advantage of the specific features of the products of other manufacturers.

In normal circumstances, Windows will find and recognize your mouse or other pointing device and install the proper driver software for it. Because Windows has a large repertory of built-in drivers, you may not need a specific driver for your device. You can also install a new mouse manually. Windows gives you at least two ways of accomplishing the installation: through the Add New Hardware icon in Control Panel or the Mouse icon in Control Panel (using the General tab and clicking the Change button).

Scanners

The scanner is a science-fiction aficionado's dream, a device that shifts between dimensions. It takes three-dimensional objects—your artwork, pages from books and magazines, even small objects such as coins—and reduces them to two-dimensional images by looking at them one dimension at a time. Without a trace of the alien technology or the supernatural, the scanner converts images you see in the real world and hold in your hand into the flatland of graphics, ready to adorn your documents or edit into arresting artwork.

The essence of any scanner is elementary. As you would expect, it scans. That is, it uses a long array of light sensors to scan across whatever you put into its range of sight. Each light sensor detects the differences in the brightness of reflections off a tiny spot of the object or image you scan.

In the typical scanner, the light sensors comprise a linear (hence, one-dimensional) array of charge-coupled devices (CCDs), squeezed together hundreds per inch in a narrow strip that stretches across the full width of the largest image that can be scanned. The width of each scanning element determines the smallest area that can be individually judged, thus the finest resolution the scanner can detect within a single line. The narrower each scanning element and the closer they are all packed together, the higher the resolution and the finer the detail the scanner can capture.

Circuitry inside the scanner reads each sensing element in the line, one by one, and in order. From that data, it creates a string of serial data representing the brightness of each point in each individual scan line. Once the scanner has collected and arranged the data from each dot on the line, it advances the sensing element to read the next line.

Types

How the view of the scanning sensor moves to that following line is the fundamental design difference between scanners. Somehow the long line of sensing elements must shift their attention with extreme precision over the entire surface of the image to be captured. Nearly all scanners require a mechanical sweep of the sensors across the image, although a few low-resolution scanners use video technology to sweep their view electronically.

To make a sweep in a mechanical scanner, engineers have devised two primary strategies. One requires the image sensor to move across a fixed original, like you examining a statue in a museum by walking around it. The other moves the original in front of a fixed scanner the same way you might examine an apple for intruders that have bored inside, by holding it in your hand and turning it around in front of your eyes. With a video scanner, nothing moves except an electron beam.

Drum Scanners

The very first scanners helped newspapers and wire services send images across the country with the ease of telegraphing messages. Someone in one newspaper office wrapped a photo around a metal cylinder or drum, and the scanner spun the drum around while a single light sensor checked the brightness of the photo at a single spot—which became a chain of observations as the drum continually spun the image under the watchful photo-eye. With every spin of the drum, the light detector moved slightly down the photo until it got to see the entire image. A matching spinning drum covered with light-sensitive paper (like photographic film) at the other end of the connection created the image by scanning it with a light beam.

Engineers adapted this same moving-cylinder approach into the *drum scanner.* Instead of a single photo-eye, the drum scanner uses a linear array so that a single spin of the drum covers the entire image.

Operationally, the drum scanner works like a printing press in reverse. You feed a piece of paper that bears the image you want to capture into the scanner, and the paper wraps around a rotating drum that spins the image past a sensor string that's fixed in place inside the machine.

The drum design lends itself to document processing. The mechanism puts the paper being scanned in motion, so adding a page feeder is a relatively simple addition. Because of their orientation to scanning printed pages, drum scanners are sometimes termed *page scanners.*

Today, most consumer-model drum scanners lack the drum that gave them their name. Instead of wrapping each sheet of paper around a drum, most scan each sheet as it slides through their mechanisms flat. The image sensor peers through a narrow slit across the paper path, recording line after line as the paper rushes through. Expensive, precision scanners used in the graphic arts industry still cling to the classic drum design because of its precision and simplicity.

The drum scanner mechanism imposes a stiff penalty—it allows only thin, flexible images to be scanned. In general, a drum scanner accepts only sheets of normal paper. Books (at least while intact) and solid objects are off limits. Moreover, most drum scanners accept only a few sizes of paper, typically the 8.5-by-11-inch sheets of business documents. Consequently, drum-scanning technology today is restricted to high-volume (and expensive) document processing systems used in big businesses.

Flatbed Scanners

The *flatbed scanner* takes the opposite tack. Instead of moving the paper to scan it, the flatbed scanner moves its line-up of sensors down the sheet. It earns its "flatbed" name from the flat glass surface, the bed upon which you must place the item to be scanned, face down. In most flatbeds, the linear array of scanning sensors is mounted on a bar that moves under the glass, automatically sweeping across the image. The clear glass lets the sensors see up to the image. In addition, the glass protects the sensors and gives them a target fixed in place at a preset distance from the scanner, which keeps things in focus.

Flatbed scanners have precision mechanisms that step the sensors or image a small increment at a time, each increment representing a single scan line. The movement of the mechanism, which is carefully controlled by the electronics of the scanner, determines the width of each line (and thus the resolution of the scanner in that direction).

Flatbed scanners are like copying machines in that anything you can lay flat on their glass faces can be scanned—books, magazines, sections of poster, even posteriors and other parts of your anatomy if you get imaginative, bored, or drunk. Of course, the scanned image can be no larger than the scanner bed.

In the past, the chief drawback of the flatbed scanner has been price. But manufacturers have refined flatbed technology to the point flatbed scanners are sometimes given away free to entice you to buy a particular computer. Although top-quality flatbed scanners for graphic arts professionals still demand hefty prices, you can buy an entirely satisfactory flatbed scanner for little more than $50. Those prices have made scanners that use other technologies scarce.

Hand Scanners

Hand scanners are a variation on the flatbed design (believe it or not!) that make *you* the motive force that propels the sensor over the image. You hold the T-shape hand scanner in the palm of your hand and drag it across the image you want to scan. A string of sensors peers through a plastic window in the bottom of the hand scanner to register the image.

Hand scanners must cope with the vagaries of the sweep of your all-too-human hand. If you move your hand at a speed other than that at which the scanner expects, lines will be scanned as too wide or too narrow, resulting in image distortion—at best the aspect ratio may be off, at worse the scanned image will look as wavy as the Atlantic under the influence of an errant typhoon. To avoid such disasters, the hand scanner uses a feedback mechanism that tracks the position of the image. Most have a roller that presses down against the image you're scanning to sense how fast you drag the scanner along. The rate at which the roller spins gives the scanner's electronics the feedback it needs about scanning speed. From this information, the software that controls the hand scanner can give each scanned dot its proper place.

At one time, hand scanners were a low-cost alternative to flatbed designs. Because they omitted the most expensive parts of most scanners—the precision mechanism for moving the paper or sensor—they had an automatic edge in price. With the plummet in prices of flatbed scanners, however, hand scanners were hard-pressed to keep up. A low-cost flatbed is now likely to be less expensive than a hand scanner. Consequently, few hand scanners are left on the market.

Those remaining have survived because of the chief remaining advantage of the hand scanner—portability. Hand scanners are compact and easy to carry. You could plug one into your notebook computer and carry the complete system to the neighborhood library to scan from books in its collection.

In addition, using a hand scanner can be quicker than using a flatbed because you can make fast sweeps of small images instead of waiting for the lumbering mechanism of a flatbed to cover a whole sheet. Hand scanners may also adapt to some nonflat surfaces and three-dimensional objects. For example, most will easily cope with the pages of an open atlas or gothic novel—although few can do a good job on a globe or watermelon.

On the downside, the small size of the hand scanner means a single pass of the scanner will cover an image no more than about four inches wide. Although that's enough for a column of text (and most scanners offer a means of pasting together parallel scans of larger drawings and photos), the narrow strips of scan make dealing with large images inconvenient. On the other hand (and in the other direction), because a hand scanner is not limited by a scanning mechanism, it can allow you to make absurdly long scans, typically limited only by the scanning software you use.

Note that hand-scanning is like typing—it's a learned skill. To use a hand scanner effectively, you'll have to practice until you learn to move the scanner smoothly and at the proper speed, which means very slowly at high resolutions.

Video Scanners

A *video scanner* is the electronic equivalent of a photographic copy stand. That is, the scanner operates like a camera, taking in a view of the entire image in a single look. That makes a video scanner fast—capturing an image takes a fraction of a second. You'll spend more time setting up the image or object to be scanned than the scanner needs to scan.

Typically a video scanner uses a conventional video camera to capture an image. Most video scanners permanently mount the camera on a stand and give you a stage on which you put the item to be scanned. The stage may have a backlight to allow you to scan photographic slides or negatives, or it may be a large bed for sheets of paper or even three-dimensional objects.

Video scanners avoid all the problems and inaccuracies imposed by mechanical scans. They have the potential for the greatest precision. Typically, however, video scanners yield the lowest quality. Like a video camera, video scanners require a CCD element for every pixel they scan, and affordable two-dimensional CCD arrays have only a few hundred thousand pixels. Because video scanners use the same CCD arrays as video cameras, they have the same resolution as video cameras, not measured in dot per inch but in pixels across the entire image. They are suited to snapshots and catalog illustration but not high-quality scans.

Photo Scanners

As their name implies, *photo scanners* are special-purpose devices aimed at capturing digital images from photographic prints. Most use an adaptation of drum-scanner technology. They move the original rather than the sensor, sliding the photo past the image sensor, flat.

Photo scanners can be quicker to use because you only need to slide your snapshots in like you're feeding dollar bills into a vending machine. Because their mechanisms are inherently less complex than those of flatbed scanners, at one time dedicated photo scanners had a price edge. With the current generation of low-cost flatbed scanners, however, that advantage has vanished. A flatbed can do everything a photo scanner can—and more—but if all you need to scan is photos, you'll have a quicker and easier time with the dedicated device.

Slide Scanners

The *slide scanner* is not a special technology but rather a special implementation of flatbed or video scanner technology. A slide scanner is a *transmissive* scanner rather than reflective. That is, it registers the light that is transmitted through an image rather than the light reflected from the image. The source of illumination is on one side of the image, and the image sensor is on the other. The image must be on a transparent medium.

A flatbed-style slide scanner is optimized for the higher-resolution needs of scanning small photographic transparencies or negatives but relies on a modified flatbed scanner mechanism. It needs only more precision in its control because of the smaller size of the scanned area of negatives and slides (and the correspondingly high resolution required). A video slide scanner is subject to the same limitations as any video scanner—chiefly, low resolution—but gives you an inexpensive means of capturing limited-resolution snapshot-quality images from slides and negatives.

Features

Beside their basic mechanism, scanners are distinguished by their features. Among these are whether the scanner can produce color images, its scanning speed, the dynamic range it can handle, its resolution, and whether it can recognize text characters and translate them into character rather image data. The availability of options such as transparency adapters, sheet feeders, and optical character recognition software also makes one model more suited to some applications than others.

Scanning Speed

Early color scanners give monochrome models a hefty edge in performance. The earliest color scanners were *three-pass* machines. That is, they required three passes to make a complete image, one pass for each of the primary colors. These ancient scanners used three separate light sources of different colors and took a full scan in each color. Nearly all modern scanners use *one-pass* designs. They have a single light source and rely on filtering in their photodetectors to sort out the colors. One-pass color scanners can operate just as quickly as monochrome models, although transferring a large color image measuring dozens of megabytes still takes longer than moving a monochrome image one-third its size.

The speed at which the scanning CCD moves across the image area is only one factor in the total time required to make a scan. Most scans require at least two separate passes. First, you command the scanner to make a *pre-scan*, which is a relatively quick, low-resolution pass across the image that helps you establish its brightness range and also lets you target a specific area for scanning. Then you make the actual scan at the resolution you want.

In addition, the interface used by a scanner influences the speed of scans, as noted later in the chapter. The high-resolution bit-images produced by the scanner represent a huge amount of data—megabytes—and a slow interface constricts this data's flow.

If the scan you want to make is large, you also have to wait for image processing, both in the scanning software and in the host application. Very large scans can add minutes or more to the total scan time if you exceed the memory capabilities of your computer. Although Windows can take advantage of virtual memory to let you capture images of nearly any size, this technology uses your disk drive for extra storage space, which adds the seeking, writing, and reading times to the total time of your scan. If you plan to regularly make large scans, you'll speed things up more by adding memory to your computer—in the dozens of megabytes—rather than looking for a faster scanner.

Dynamic Range

At one time, the base-level distinction between scanners was like that of television sets—color or monochrome. And, as with televisions, the monochrome variety is almost extinct. But color scanners aren't all equally colorful. Some recognize more hues than others.

The compass of colors a scanner can discern is termed the scanner's *dynamic range*. The most common means of expressing dynamic range is bit-depth, the number of bits needed to digitally encode the total color capacity. Most common scanners can distinguish 256 (8-bit), 1024 (10-bit), or 4096 (12-bit) brightness levels in each primary color. Just to make their scanners seem more capable, scanner manufacturers add up the total number of colors within the scanner repertory, so you'll see 24-bit, 30-bit, and 36-bit color scanners.

The actual dynamic range and the bit-depth of a scanner are not necessarily the same. A high-quality scanner will be able to resolve the number of brightness levels its bit-depth implies. The bit-depth actually specifies the range of the analog-to-digital converters that convert the level detected by the scanner's CCD sensors into digital signals. Taking advantage of that bit-depth requires that the scanned image be properly focused on the CCD sensor under optimal illumination. If the focus of the scanner's optics is off, pixels will blur into one another, which lowers image contrast and the dynamic range of the scanner. Similarly, if the illumination provided for the image during the scan is uneven, the variations will wipe out some of the available brightness levels of the dynamic range. Consequently, two scanners with the same number of bits quoted for their dynamic range may, in fact, have different actual dynamic ranges.

Most computers can, of course, display from 256 to 16.7 million different hues (that is, 8-bit to 24-bit color). When that is more than you or your software wants to manage, the scanner's palette can easily be scaled back, either through hardware controls or through software, to an even smaller bit-depth. With even a minimal 24-bit scanner capable of giving your software more than enough color, the extra bits of higher-cost scanners might seem superfluous.

Those extra bits are very useful, however, when the scanner preprocesses image data before passing it along to your computer. A scanner with 36-bit dynamic range can capture all the shades and hues of an image and let you process them down into 24-bit color for your computer to use. You get to choose how to handle the conversion, compressing the dynamic range or cutting off colors you don't want to use. The extra bits ensure that your scanner can capture all the detail in the darkest shadows and brightest highlights. When you use a transparency adapter, greater dynamic range helps you compensate for thinner or denser originals, potentially yielding workable scans from transparencies you can barely see through.

The trend among high-end scanners is toward a dynamic range of 48 bits, giving you a greater range of manipulation. Note, however, that most existing software for image manipulation cannot yet handle 48-bit images (although the current release of Adobe Photoshop can).

Many scanners have automatic modes through which they determine the proper brightness and contrast ratios to take best advantage of the translation of the scanner's dynamic range into the 24-bit level of color (or other level of color) used by your computer. The most common means of making this optimization is to pre-scan the image. The scanner then checks the brightest and darkest points of the scanned area. Using these values to establish the actual range of brightness and color in the image, the scanner can adjust its transformation to yield the image with the greatest tonal range to your applications.

D-max

With slide scanners, another factor influences your ability to work with marginal slides and negatives—the maximum image density, usually abbreviated as *D-max*, that the scanner can handle. A more dense image is darker—there's more dye or silver in the image. Because slide scanners work by shooting light through the slide or negative, a very dense image may prevent any light from getting through at all. The D-max indicates how dense an image can be before the scanner can no longer distinguish the light shining through it. Any part of an image that's more dense than the scanner's D-max rating blocks up as solid black (or, if you're scanning a negative, solid white).

Technically speaking, the *density* of a photographic negative or slide is the ratio of the intensity of light shining through the image over the intensity of light that actually gets through, expressed as a logarithm. The scientific formula for density is as follows:

Density = log (incident light/transmitted light)

As a practical matter, the best of today's slide scanners cope with a D-max of about 4.2. That means they can detect light that's diminished by a factor of more than 10,000. A scanner with a D-max of less than 3 will have difficulty dealing with the full range of image brightnesses, even on properly exposed film.

Resolution

Scanners differ in the resolution at which they can capture images. All scanners have a maximum mechanical limit on their resolution. It's equal to the smallest step that their sensor can be advanced; typically a minimal scanner will start with about 300 dots per inch and go up from there in regular steps such as 600, 1200, then 2400 dots per inch. Special-purpose slide scanners achieve resolutions as high as 10,000 dots per inch. Because it represents the limit of the quality the scanner hardware is able to resolve, this measurement is often termed the *hardware resolution* of the scanner. Another term for the same value is *optical resolution.*

Beyond the mechanical resolution of a given scanner, the control software accompanying the scanner often pushes the claimed resolution even higher, to 4800 or even 9600 dots per inch, even for an inexpensive scanner. To achieve these higher-resolution figures, the control software *interpolates* dots. That is, the software computes additional dots in between those that are actually scanned.

This artificial enhancement results in a higher resolution value quoted for some printers as *interpolated resolution.* Although interpolating higher resolution adds no more information to a scan—which means it cannot add to the detail—it can make the scan look more pleasing. The greater number of dots reduces the jaggedness or stair-stepping in the scan and makes lines look smoother.

The new dots created by interpolation add to the size of the resulting scanned file, possibly making a large file cumbersome indeed. In that interpolation adds no new information, it need not be done at the time of scanning. You can store a file made at the mechanical resolution limit of your scanner, then later increase its apparent resolution through interpolation without wasting disk space storing imaginary dots.

As with colors and shades of gray, a scanner can easily be programmed to produce resolution lower than its maximum. Lower resolution is useful to minimize file size, to match your output device, or simply to make the scanned image fit on a single screen for convenient viewing. Although early scanners and their control software shifted their resolution in distinct increments—75, 150, and 300 dpi, for example—modern scanner-plus-software combinations make resolution continuously variable within wide limits.

The actual hardware resolution of a scanner is fixed across the width of the image by the number of elements in the CCD sensor that determines the brightness of each pixel. The hardware resolution along the length of the scan is determined by the number of steps the CCD sensor takes as it traverses the image area. The size of these steps is also usually fixed. Scanning software determines lower as well as higher resolution values by interpolating from the hardware scan. Consequently, even when set for 50 dpi, a scanner will sense at its hardware resolution level, deriving the lower-resolution figure through software from its higher capabilities.

Transparency Adapters

As with people, scanners are not blessed with the ability to see in the dark. To make a proper scan—that is, one that doesn't resemble a solar eclipse in a coal mine—the scanner needs a light source. All scanners have their own built-in and usually calibrated light sources. In drum and flatbed scanners, the light sources are inside the mechanism, typically one or three cold cathode tubes that glow brightly. Handheld scanners often use light emitting diodes (LEDs) as their illumination source. In any case, in normal operation the light *reflects* from the material being scanned, and the CCD sensors in the scanner measure the brightness of the reflected light.

Some source materials fail to reveal their full splendor under reflected light. The most important of these are transparencies such as photographic slides or presentation foils. These are designed to have light shine through them (that is, transmitted light).

To properly scan these media, the scanner must put the media between its light source and its sensor. Slide scanners have the source for transmitted light built in. Most other desktop scanners have an optional secondary source for transmitted light called a *transparency adapter*. The secondary light source tracks the CCD sensor as it scans across the image, but from the opposite side of the original.

Most commonly the transparency adapter takes the form of a thicker cover over the glass stage on which you lay your originals to be scanned. A few scanners have add-on arms that scan over the top of the transparencies you lay on the stage. The latter style works well but does not hold original transparencies as flat against the stage as do the former.

Optical Character Recognition

Scanners don't care what you point them at. They will capture anything with adequate contrast, drawing or text. However, text captured by a scanner will be in bit-image form, which makes it useless to word processors, which use ASCII code. You can translate text in graphic form into ASCII codes in two ways—by typing everything into your word processor or by Optical Character Recognition (OCR). Add character-recognition software to your scanner, and you can quickly convert almost anything you can read on your screen into word processor, database, or spreadsheet files. Once the realm of mainframe computers and special hardware costing tens of thousands of dollars, OCR is now within the reach of most computers and budgets.

Early OCR software used a technique called matrix matching. The computer would compare small parts of each bit-image it scanned to bit-patterns it had stored in a library to find what character was the most similar to the bit-pattern scanned. For example, a letter A would be recognized as a pointed tower 40 bits high with a 20-bit wide crossbar.

Matrix matching suffers a severe handicap—it must be tuned to the particular typeface and type size you scan. For example, an italic letter A has a completely different pattern signature from a roman letter A, even within the same size and type family. Consequently, a matrix-matching OCR system must have either an enormous library of bit-patterns (requiring a time-consuming search for each match) or the system must be limited to matching a few typestyles and fonts. Even then, you will probably have to tell the character-recognition system what typeface you want to read so it can select the correct pattern library. Worse, most matrix-matching systems depend on regular spacing between characters to determine the size and shape of the character matrix, so these systems work only with monospaced printing, such as that generated by a typewriter.

Most of today's OCR systems use *feature matching*. Feature-matching systems don't just look and compare; they also analyze each bit-pattern that's scanned. When it sees the letter A, it derives the essential features of the character from the pattern of bits—an up-slope, a peak, and a down-slope with a horizontal bar across. In that every letter A has the same characteristic features—if they didn't your eyes couldn't recognize each one as an "A," either—the feature matching system doesn't need an elaborate library of bit-patterns to match nearly any font and type size. In fact, feature-matching recognition software doesn't need to know the size or font of the characters it is to recognize beforehand. Even typeset text with variable character spacing is no problem. Feature-matching software can thus race through a scan very quickly while making few errors.

Sheet Feeders

The typical OCR application involves transferring the information content of multiple pages into electronic form. You must, of course, scan each page separately to derive its information content. With long documents, the chore is time consuming and usually not the most productive way to spend your working hours.

A sheet feeder automatically runs each sheet of a multiple-page document through a scanner. Although a sheet feeder is easiest to implement with a drum scanner, because the scanner has to put the paper in motion anyway, some flatbed scanners have built-in or optional sheet feeders as well.

Sheet feeders are useful primarily for OCR applications. Graphic scanning usually involves individual setup of each page or image. Actually loading a page into the scanner is a trivial part of the graphic scan. Adding a sheet feeder to a scanner used primarily for graphics is consequently not cost effective.

Sheet feeders require loose sheets. They cannot riffle through the pages of a book or other bound document. When a job requires high productivity and the information is more valuable than the printed original, some people cut apart books and similar materials for scanning using a sheet feeder. In any case, you'll probably find a staple-puller to be a worthy accessory to your sheet feeder.

Electrical Interfacing

At least six different interfaces designs are or have been used by scanners: Small Computer System Interface (SCSI), General-Purpose Interface Bus (GPIB), standard serial, parallel, USB, and proprietary. Almost all current products rely on parallel, SCSI, or USB connections.

Parallel models plug into legacy printer ports. Most have special cables or connectors that allow you to link your printer to the same port used by the scanner. With modern port/driver software, parallel-interfaced scanners are the easiest to get running—they come to life almost as soon as you plug them in (and install the drivers). The parallel interface is also inexpensive.

The downside of the parallel connection is performance. It is the slowest of the scanner links, and it may double the scan time of a typical page.

The SCSI interface, on the other hand, is fast—the fastest scanner connection in use. The penalty is, of course, the need to tangle with a SCSI connection. This need not be a problem. When the SCSI-based scanner is the only device plugged into a SCSI port, getting the scanner to work is about as easy as with a parallel port. Adding a scanner to a long SCSI chain is as fraught with problems as linking any additional SCSI device.

The other problem with SCSI-based scanners is that they require a SCSI port. Most SCSI-based scanners come with their own SCSI host adapters and cables. (This is one reason the SCSI interface adds to the cost of a scanner.) Installing the adapter in an expansion slot complicates the installation process. Worse, if you want to use a SCSI scanner with a notebook computer, you'll need to purchase a PC Card SCSI adapter.

USB scanners fit in the middle. Although they require a free USB port, nearly all new computers (including notebooks) have at least one. Most have at least two. Scanners fit readily into USB's Plug-and-Play system, but they suffer from the same teething difficulties as other USB products. Although USB scanning is quicker than parallel, it is not as faster as SCSI scanning.

Application Interfacing

As with other input devices, scanners have their own control and signaling systems that must link to your software to be used effectively (or at all). Early scanners used their own proprietary application interfaces to relay commands and data. Consequently, each scanner required its own software or drivers. Oftentimes you could only use the scanner manufacturer's own software to grab images.

Thanks to a concerted effort by the scanner industry, that situation has changed. Now you can expect any scanner to work with just about any graphics program. Moreover, scanning is consistent across applications. The same screens that control your scanner in PhotoShop appear in Corel Photo-Paint.

Central to this standardization is Twain. First released in early 1992, Twain is a scanner software interface standard developed by a consortium of scanner and software makers called (in its final form) the Working Group for Twain. The primary companies involved in forming the working group included Aldus Corporation, Caere Corporation, Eastman Kodak Company, Hewlett-Packard, and Logitech.

The Twain name requires some explanation. Twain is not an acronym, so only its initial letter needs to be capitalized. Rendering Twain in all capital letters is a typographic error. That said, the promoters of the standard usually write it in all capital letters as if it were an acronym.

Officially, the Twain developers have explained that the name is a reference to the purpose of the interface. Not an acronym, it derives from making the twain (an archaic word for *two*) meet, the two of the twain being applications and scanners. However, a few wags insist that Twain stands for "Technology Without An Interesting Name."

When the Twain interface was being developed, it wore a number of different names. The most common of these were *Direct-Connect* and *CLASP*, the latter of which stands for the Connecting Link for Applications and Source Peripherals. The developers of Twain considered these and others as the formal names of the interface. After searching through lists of trademarks in use, however, they found so many conflicts they felt that lawsuits would be a distinct possibility if any of the developmental names were to be used. Instead they chose the name Twain to, in the words of one of the developers, "describe this interface which brings together two entities, applications and input devices."

Twain links programs and scanner hardware, giving software writers a standard set of function calls by which to control the features of any scanner. One set of Twain drivers will handle any compatible scanning device. Because the Twain connection has two ends—your scanner and your software—both need to be Twain compatible for you to take advantage of the connection.

Twain defines its hardware interface as its *Source*. The Source is hardware or firmware in a scanner that controls the information that flows from the scanner into Twain. The scanner-maker designs the Source to match its particular hardware and interface. Your software links to the Twain Source through a *Source Manager*, which is essentially a set of program calls.

Twain takes the form of a software driver. The original driver was written in 16-bit code and takes the name `TWAIN.DLL`. The working group has also created a fully 32-bit version of the driver called `TWAIN32.DLL`. Both the 16- and 32-bit versions work with all versions of Windows since 95 (including 32-bit versions such as NT, 2000, and XP).

Digital Cameras

Forget the yellow or green boxes and snub your nose at the one-hour photo place. A digital camera doesn't need film—that's the whole point of it—and it doesn't need a film company. No need for the photofinisher any more, either. The digital camera is a revolution in photography. Better than Polaroid, you don't have to wait to see what develops or suffer the agonizing wait as colors fill in through the fog. Instantly you know what went wrong (and with photography, something *always* goes wrong—the challenge is finding the least-wrong image) and whether you need to snap again. You can review a half dozen shots at a time *in the camera*, choose the ones you want, and take some more without wasting an inch of film. When you're done, you download everything into your computer, where you can digitally edit and enhance your images until everything is perfect. And, finally, you can put to work that photo-quality printer that came with your computer, electronically paste snapshots into your digital documents, or illustrate your Web site with your own photos.

The digital camera is the facilitating device for *digital photography*, often called *non-silver photography* because of its lack of reliance on conventional photographic film. Film depends on the photosensitivity of silver salts and the chemical reaction—using chemicals that are known carcinogens—called development. Digital photography is much more environmentally friendly. In digital photography, photons are detected electrically by an *image sensor* that's so sensitive there's no need for the chemical amplification of the film developer. And once you tally up the cost of the film you don't need and the photofinishing you won't use, it's wallet friendly, too.

The digital images created by digital cameras are perfect for posting on the Web, pasting into newsletters and catalogs, cataloging on CD, and printing in full color on an inexpensive inkjet printer. You can edit the images yourself to eliminate the plague of red-eye in flash photographs or an ex-spouse in family photographs.

The Big Three

There are three kinds of camera that capture digital images. In theory, you can use any of the three to make digital images, although some work better for specific purposes.

Still Cameras

When anyone talks about digital cameras, they mean *digital still cameras*. That is, handheld cameras designed like the film cameras of old. You peer through a viewfinder, push a button, and take a picture.

The most important characteristic of digital still cameras is *high resolution*. The images they capture contain as much image information—detail—as the photographs taken by classic film cameras. The high-resolution images are suitable for printing as conventional photographs. Their quality is high enough you can even publish them in print magazines and books. But you can also take lower-resolution images—or reduce the resolution of high-resolution images—to make pictures for the Web and electronic publications. Depending on the memory you have available to your digital still camera, you can cram from a dozen to more than a hundred images into a single session.

To match their high resolution, digital still cameras have top-quality lenses characterized by their sharpness. Most digital still camera lenses also have optical zooming capabilities, ranging from 2× zooming in inexpensive cameras to a maximum (currently) of about 10×.

Digital still cameras are meant to work like their film-based counterparts—handheld or on a tripod—by using the available light or a flash. But most offer additional features. Some capture short video clips. Most have video outputs so you can plug them into your computer and capture moving images, just as you would with a video camera. You can also use this video output as a Web cam (providing your computer has a video input).

Video Cameras

Digital video cameras are made for capturing movies digitally. They are characterized by their fast capture rate. They have to snap at least 30 frames every second. But they do not need to have as much resolution as digital still cameras. Most have resolution that matches that of your computer's most basic display mode, VGA. That means resolution of 640-by-480 pixels.

Because of the low resolution of digital video cameras, their lenses need not be as sharp as those of digital still cameras. On the other hand, to give you more versatility in movie-making, digital video cameras usually have extended zoom ranges, often higher than 30×.

Most digital video cameras also have single-shot modes in which they operate as digital still cameras—but with a difference. They produce video-like resolution rather than still-camera resolution when taking snapshots. You can also used a digital video camera for a Web camera if your computer has the proper input and software.

Web Cameras

Web cameras are the low end of the digital-photo spectrum. They have about the same resolution capabilities as a digital video camera (sometimes less) but skimp on the lens. Most have a fixed focus lens without zoom—which means low-cost, at least to manufacturers. Their low resolution level is tailored to match the needs of Webcasting and video messaging.

Most Web cameras have USB outputs inside of standard video outputs so you can plug them into computers that don't have video inputs. With the right software, however, you can use a Web cam to make low-grade movies or still images. In fact, the quality you get from a Web cam may be enough for posting on the Web (what did you expect?) or even for putting images into electronic publications.

Imaging Sensors

The heart of any digital camera is its *image sensor*, which actually captures the image, registering it in a form that can later be used. It detects photons and translates their energy into a minute electrical current that computer circuits can sense, amplify, digitize, and store.

Many people call image sensors *CCDs*, the name of the technology used by most digital camera image-sensing devices (charge coupled devices). Although CCDs are used in most cameras, some companies have adopted a similar technology that's usually termed *CMOS*. Yes, it's the same name as the memory used for system-configuration data in your computer, because the image sensors and the memory use the same semiconductor technology—Complimentary Metal-Oxide Semiconductor technology. Because of the use of garden-variety circuit technology, CMOS sensors tend to be less expensive, although they typically are not as sensitive as CCDs.

Although the term *CCD* usually is used in the singular, the actual image sensor of a digital camera requires an array of CCDs. The mere presence of light is not as important as its pattern, which makes up the actual image. A single CCD (or CMOS sensor) element registers only a single point. Consequently, image sensors are an array of individual CCD elements. In video cameras, the CCD elements get arranged as a matrix. Camera circuitry samples each element in turn to scan an image frame.

Size

Image sensors come in various sizes. Typically they measure one-quarter, one-third, or one-half inch (diagonally). All else equal, the larger the CCD, the greater the number of elements that can be packed into the array. The number of elements determines the resolution of the image signal produced by the CCD. This number is related to, but is not the same as, the number of pixels in an image.

The size of the sensor affects other elements of the camera design. For example, the coverage of the lens usually is tailored to match the sensor size. (That's one reason why camera-makers cannot simply put CCDs inside ordinary 35 mm cameras—today's practical sensors are substantially smaller than 35 mm film and would only register a fraction of the image from the lens.) Because most image sensors are smaller than the film used in ordinary cameras, interchangeable lenses often act "longer" on digital cameras. That is, a 50 mm lens from a standard film-based SLR might give the view of a 65 mm lens when twisted onto a digital camera. The sensor sees only the central part of the image from the lens. With many of today's high-end digital cameras with interchangeable lenses, 35 mm lenses act as if their focal length were 1.3 times longer than on a film camera.

Resolution

The maximum possible resolution is set by the number of pixels that the CCD can sense. The keyword in digital photography currently is *megapixel*—that is, a million pixels. At one time photographers used the million-pixel mark as distinguishing good cameras from bad. Today the best consumer-model digital cameras have about five megapixels of resolution, which results in images comparable to 35 mm film.

The number of total pixels is directly related to the resolution of the image sensor. If you know the number of elements in an image sensor (video cameras are sometimes described by this figure), you can determine its highest possible resolution using these formulae:

Horizontal resolution = 4 * sqr(number of pixels/12)

Vertical resolution = 3 * sqr(number of pixels/12)

Unlike the measure of resolution of other computer peripherals, where each pixel requires an individual sensor for each color (three sensor elements equal one pixel), digital camera makers exaggerate their resolutions by using the total number of pixels for all colors to come up with a resolution figure. Most digital cameras use an array of sensors that alternate green with each of the other two colors. Using interpolation algorithms, the camera calculates three individual color values at each element position, regardless of its color sensitivity; in effect, creating three virtual pixels (one of each color) for each image sensor element. A megapixel camera thus has only one million sensing elements.

Sensitivity

Image sensors vary in their sensitivity to light. The best can detect a single photon. Those in digital cameras require dozens of photons to make a detected signal. It is similar to the rating of film speed. In fact, to give film photographers a better feel for their digital cameras, many digital cameras allow you to adjust their sensitivities to the equivalent of an ASA or ISO film speed rating (typically the ASA 100 or ASA 400 rating of the most popular films).

The inherent sensitivity of the image sensor is not, however, directly relevant to practical photography. Other aspects of the design of the camera overwhelm concerns about the native sensitivity of image sensors. The most important of these is the lens.

Lenses

The lens determines the quality of the images that are formed inside a camera. The lens and its quality determine what kind of image your camera can collect and to a great degree set the ultimate quality of picture you can hope to take.

You can take photographs without a lens—that's the principle behind pinhole photography. But nearly all cameras have lenses for one very good reason: A lens collects a lot of light. It captures more photons. That gives the camera more light to work with and makes exposures quicker. The lens also affects the view, what the camera sees. It even alters the aesthetics of the image you make.

Aperture

Literally speaking, an *aperture* is nothing more than a hole, and that's what it means for cameras. The aperture is the hole in the lens through which light can get to the image sensor. In photography, digital or otherwise, the aperture is more important than a mere hole. It's a variable hole, one you can make larger or smaller to let more or less light reach the film or sensor. A larger aperture lets more light in; smaller lets in less.

Varying the size of the aperture helps a camera of any kind cope with light conditions. When light is too bright, it can overwhelm the image sensor; too dim, and the image sensor might not be able to find enough photons to make an image. To prevent these problems, most cameras use wider apertures in dim light and smaller apertures in bright light.

The mechanism for setting the aperture is termed the *iris* of the camera, and it corresponds to the iris of the human eye. By sliding thin plates called *iris blades*—in manual mode typically by rotating a ring around the lens termed, appropriately enough, the *aperture ring*—you can adjust the size of the hole between the blades and thus the aperture.

The size of the aperture is measured as an *f-stop*. Most commonly, the f-stop is a number in the geometric series 1.4, 2.0, 2.8, 4.0, 5.6, 8.0, 11.0, 16.0, 22, 32. The series is designed so that the next higher stop cuts the light transmitted through the lens to half the value of the previous stop. An f-stop setting of 8.0 allows half as much light into the camera as a setting of 5.6. (The sequence is simpler than it looks. Each f-stop differs from its predecessor by the square root of two, the results rounded.) Table 23.1 lists the ISO standard (nominal) f-stops, the actual (computed) f-stops, and relative light values.

TABLE 23.1 F-Stops

Nominal Stop (ISO)	Actual Stop and Half-Stop	Light Value (Relative f/1.0)
1	1.00	1.00
	1.19	1.41
1.4	1.41	2.00
	1.68	2.83
2	2.00	4.00
	2.38	5.66
2.8	2.83	8.00
	3.36	11.31
4	4.00	16.00
	4.76	22.63
5.6	5.66	32.00
	6.73	45.25
8	8.00	64.00
	9.51	90.51
11	11.31	128.00
	13.45	181.02
16	16.00	256.00
	19.03	362.04
22	22.63	512.00
	26.91	724.08
32	32.00	1024.00
	38.05	1448.15
45	45.25	2048.00
	53.82	2896.31
64	64.00	4096.00

Although the sequence of numbers is now an arbitrary sequence, the value of the f-stop is scientifically defined. It is the focal length of the lens divided by the apparent aperture of the lens (not the actual size of the hole in the iris but the size of the hole visible through the lens—the glass in the lens can magnify the aperture or even make it appear smaller). For example, a lens with a 50-millimeter focal length set at f-stop 4 would have a visible aperture of 12.5 millimeters. This relationship leads to the common way of writing f-stop settings. A setting of four is usually written as f/4. In other words, it is the focal length divided by four.

Lenses are usually described by the widest aperture at which they can be set (for example f/1.4 or f/2.8). Sometimes the widest aperture setting falls between the numbers of the standard f-stop sequence (for example f/2.3), but the value represents the same concept.

Many zoom lenses are marked with two f-stops (for example f/2.8–4.3). The two values do not represent the total range of stops available from the lens. Rather, they represent the range of minimum f-stop values. The formula for determining the f-stop of a lens requires the size of the aperture to vary with the focal length of the lens at a constant f-stop setting. A longer lens requires a wider aperture for the same f-stop setting.

Zoom lenses are able to vary their focal lengths to change the size of the image they make in your camera. Nearly all zoom lenses automatically change the aperture as you zoom to maintain a constant f-stop setting. The physical diameter of the lens limits its maximum aperture—the hole in the iris can't be bigger than the lens itself. When the focal length is set shorter, however, the largest possible aperture represents a wider (lower value) f-stop, which is desirable because it allows more light into the lens so that you can take photographs in dimmer light. Consequently, lens-makers let you take advantage of the wider f-stop settings at shorter focal lengths, and the minimum f-stop value varies with the focal length setting of the lens. The highest f-stop number represents the widest setting at the longest focal length setting of the lens. The lower value represents the widest f-stop setting possible at the most favorable focal length setting.

When using a lens, the aperture or f-stop setting can have a dramatic effect on the final image beyond setting exposure. The f-stop determines the *depth of field* (more correctly, the depth of *focus*) in the image.

Focal Length

Technically speaking, the *focal length* of a lens is the distance from its nodal point to the plane of focus of its image of an object an infinite distance from the lens (that is, where the image appears sharpest). Although this highly technical concept appears to have no practical value in judging cameras or lenses, focal length has an important ramification. It determines the field of view a lens provides or, the corollary, the size of the image. As a practical matter, a lens with a short focal length provides a wide field of view and makes things look smaller and farther away. A long lens provides a narrow field of view and large images that look closer. There are other aesthetic considerations we'll discuss in the chapter about using a camera.

Wider, smaller, larger, and closer are all relative concepts. With lenses, such terms relate to a "normal" lens. For some reason not readily apparent, the photographic world has decided a normal lens has a field of view of 46 degrees. That is, the angle between the camera and the left side of what it sees is 46 degrees from a line drawn to the rightmost side of the image. On a 35 mm camera, that means a 50 mm lens is "normal."

Zoom

Technically speaking, a zoom lens is one that allows you to change its focal length within a given range. For most people, however, the results of the zooming process are more important. Zooming lets you change the size of the image in your viewfinder and in your files. You zoom in to make things bigger, as if you had stepped closer to whatever you're photographing. Zooming out makes things smaller so you can fit more of your subject into the frame. Zooming also has aesthetic effects, such as changing the depth of field and compressing distance.

Optical Zooming

The classic zoom is *optical*. The lens creates the entire zoom effect by changing the path light beams take through the lens. The optical principle is actually simple. A zoom lens has an extra internal element that acts as a magnifier, increasing the size of the image by apparently increasing the focal length of the original lens. The magnifying effect changes as the magnifier moves with respect to the other elements of the lens. Therefore, by sliding the magnifier, you can continuously change the focal length of the original lens.

In practice, zoom lenses are not so simple. They are among the most complex optical devices in common use. They have multiple lens elements to correct for image problems and distortions added by the zoom process—for example, maintaining that constant f-stop setting as the focal length of the lens changes.

Maintaining the quality of the image produced by a lens throughout its zoom range has always been a challenge for optical designers. Thanks to modern computers, however, they have become adept at creating superb zoom lenses. The designs are complex, however, and that means they can be costly to produce. That's the chief disadvantage of the optical zoom.

The quality—meaning the sharpness, contrast, and color saturation—of the image produced by a modern zoom lens does not change as you zoom through the entire range of the lens. Keep that in mind. It's the chief advantage of the optical zoom.

Digital Zooming

Optical zooming works on the image before it is actually formed on the image sensor inside a digital camera. Digital zooming, in contrast, manipulates the image after it is registered by the sensor. In effect, digital zooming is nothing more than interpolating the image to a different size. The process is exactly the same as you can do with image-editing software inside your computer. It's called *digital zooming* only because it takes place within the digital camera with the results showing in the camera's viewfinder.

As with any interpolation, quality can suffer. The interpolation process cannot create image data that's not there to start with. Because the zooming process typically fills the entire frame with an image taken from a fractional part of the frame and discards the rest, the zoomed image inevitably is of lower quality than the full-frame image.

Zoom Range

The zooming range of a lens is measured in its own x-factor. The "×" number represents the longest focal length of the zoom lens divided by its shortest focal length. For example, a 50 to 150 mm zoom lens is described as a 3× zoom (150 divided by 50). At that, the x-factor describes the power of the zoom to increase the linear dimensions of the images it produces. With a 3× zoom, for example, the greatest magnification of an image will be three times taller and three times wider than at its least magnification.

A larger zoom range is better than a small one and, of course, typically more costly. Be alert that sometimes camera-makers publish the total zoom capabilities of their cameras as a single figure that's a product of both optical (useful) and digital (doubtful) zoom capabilities. For example, a camera advertised with 6× zoom capabilities often has a 3× optical zoom and a 2× digital zoom. For most practical purposes, you can consider such a camera to have merely 3× capabilities.

Supplemental Lenses

Just as modern lenses are made from multiple elements, you can add additional elements to a lens to change its fundamental characteristics. For example, put a positive (convex) element in front of a camera lens, and you will change its focus—it will focus nearer. Additional elements that you can attach to the basic lens of your camera are called *supplemental lenses*. Some digital camera makers call them *conversion lenses*.

Four types of supplemental lenses are sometimes available. These include the following:

- **Telephoto converters**. These lenses make distant images closer and larger without affecting the camera's ability to focus a faraway object.
- **Close-up converters**. These lenses allow your camera to fill its frame with the image of a nearby object. You can photograph things closer to your camera but, when using the converter, you can no longer focus on faraway objects.

- **Wide-angle converters**. These lenses allow your camera to take in more panoramic views. This type of converter will add drama to landscape photos but can be even more useful indoors when you can't otherwise get far enough from large subjects (for example, groups of people) to fit them entirely in the frame.
- **Fisheye converters**. These lenses take wide-angle to the extreme, giving you a 180-degree view by bending the straight lines of the image to fit the frame.

Which of these four types of converters are available to you depends on what your camera-maker offers or whether aftermarket products fit the camera you choose. If you want to experiment with additional telephoto reach or wide-angle panoramas, check to see which options you can buy before you purchase a new digital camera.

Shutters

The role of the shutter in a camera is to *limit* the amount of light getting in. Certainly too much light will overexpose film and overwhelm image sensors, but constraining the quantity of light isn't the only function of the shutter. After all, reducing the aperture will similarly prevent overexposure. The shutter controls exposure by its duration, the period during which light is allowed into the camera. Images often change over time—people blink, horses gallop, racecars race, grass grows, and paint peels. By limiting the time during which light is gathered, the shutter can capture a small slice of the image during which movement is minimal, even invisible. A fast shutter can simply stop motion—more correctly, stop the blurring effects of motion on captured images.

With a digital camera, the shutter speed is the period over which the image sensor captures photons. The longer the period, the more photons the sensor will capture.

Shutter Speeds

Over the years, shutter speeds have been standardized in a sequence in which each speed is one-half the next fastest, effectively cutting the light that passes through by one half. Consequently, each step in shutter speed alters the amount of light reaching the film or image sensor by the same amount as the change in one standard f/stop. Here's a list of the standard shutter speeds:

- 1 second
- 1/2 second
- 1/4 second
- 1/8th second
- 1/15th second

- 1/30th second
- 1/60th second
- 1/125th second
- 1/250th second
- 1/500th second
- 1/1000th second
- 1/2000th second
- 1/4000th second
- 1/8000th second

Shutter speed settings are typically displayed on conventional cameras without the "1/" indication. Consequently, the notch for a shutter speed of 1/125th second will be identified as simply 125.

Cameras differ in the speeds they make available to you. Only more expensive, professional-grade cameras offer the highest speeds, 1/2000th second and greater.

Choosing a shutter speed is not arbitrary. You (or the program of an automatic camera) must consider several issues. The two most important are proper exposure and the minimization of the effect of camera shake.

With 35 mm cameras, the oft-stated rule for the slowest shutter speed that will yield sharp images when the camera is handheld is one over the focal length of the lens (or shorter). For example, with a standard 50 mm lens the slowest speed recommended for handheld exposures is 1/60th second. Some people are able to make sharp exposures at speeds a notch or two slower than the general rule. But when you need to make an exposure longer than these recommendations, you should mount your camera on a tripod to prevent shake. A tripod is not a cure-all, however. Even a tripod won't prevent the image blurring because of subject movement.

Shutter Delay

Mechanical cameras don't take a picture the instant you push the shutter release. All sorts of cams, gears, and levers swing into action as soon as you press, but light cannot peep through the shutter for several milliseconds as everything comes up to speed. This slight wait is called *shutter lag*. With a digital camera, there's no mechanical inertia to slow the taking of a picture, but most digital cameras impose their own shutter delay penalties that are substantially longer than those of mechanical cameras. With some digital cameras, you may wait more than half a second between the instant you press the button and when the camera actually makes an exposure. If you don't properly anticipate the action, you may be as surprised as your images. Between the press and the exposure, smiles of surprise melt into shock and anger, high divers disappear into the deep, UFOs accelerate into the ether, and Bigfoot shuffles back into the wilderness. Strangely, longer delays arise most often with more expensive digital cameras.

The cause of the lag is twofold: mechanical and electronic. Even though digital cameras take electronic pictures, they are still dependent on mechanical processes for the optics and focusing. The auto-focusing systems of many digital cameras, especially higher-end cameras that do a better job of it, may require several hundred milliseconds to lock on a subject. You can often eliminate this part of the lag by prefocusing or by focusing manually. The electronic delays are imposed in setting up the electronics to actually capture the image. The time required often increases with the resolution of the camera because there's more to do with more pixels to capture. You can't do anything about the electronic lag except learn to live with it and anticipate action. Newer digital cameras are notably faster than their forebears, but the lag can still be bothersome. Avoid surprises and check the shutter lag of any digital camera before you buy it.

Exposure

The lens aperture and shutter can control the light striking the light sensor, but to do the job properly, they need to be carefully controlled. A sunny day may be 10,000 times brighter than a dark room, yet the camera's light sensor is called upon to register minute differences in each. At one time, photographers had to guess at the correct aperture and shutter speed settings. *Light meters* that measure the brightness of individual scenes gave them a tool to objectively evaluate the proper shutter and aperture settings. *Automatic exposure systems* directly link the light meter to the exposure-regulating controls of the camera so you don't have to worry about adjusting the settings at all.

Sensing

Making an automatic exposure system work requires the camera measure the brightness of the scene you want to photograph. So you need to measure the brightness of the scene. However, brightness is a property not of each scene but of each part of a scene. As long as the world isn't a uniform gray, some parts of a scene will be brighter than others. This inevitable difference in brightness is good—without it we wouldn't see anything. But it poses a difficult question for exposure metering: Where should you measure brightness?

Answering that question is tough because it has no one correct answer. Certainly there are obvious choices: Measure everything, measure the brightest spot, average the brightest and darkest areas, measure only the center, and so on. Although almost any strategy results in an image, often acceptable, none will always produce the best possible image. Finding a way of evaluating image brightness in the greatest number of situations has challenged camera designers since they first glued selenium cells on the fronts of their products to make automatic exposure systems.

The advent of the digital camera alters only the mechanics of the situation. Digital cameras (and video cameras, for that matter) can, in theory, measure the brightness at every pixel in an image. But the camera designer must choose how to combine those signals to control the aperture and shutter.

The issue is not only which pixels to sample but what importance to assign to the signal from each one—that is, the *weighting* to assign to each of potentially a few million brightness measurements. The guiding factor is as much aesthetic as engineering, however. Through the years, a number of schemes have been tried, increasing in complexity as technology has allowed. The primary choices are three (in order of introduction): full-scene, spot, and matrix, lumped together as metering patterns.

Full-scene is simply an average of the brightness of the entire scene, which works in a surprisingly large number of cases. But it's also fooled into the wrong setting in many cases. Backlighting—when a person faces the camera with the sun *behind* him—usually results in a silhouette, leaving the subject's smile lost in the darkness.

Spot metering looks only at a central spot of the image, usually the most important part of the image. By measuring only the face in a backlit scene, for example, it ignores the bright sun and lets you see the expression on your subject's face. But a bright or dark spot in the center of the image can fool the spot meter. (Most spot-based systems let you compensate by making a measurement on the most important part of your subject, locking the setting, and then letting you compose the image and make the exposure.

Matrix metering subdivides the image into several areas of importance, applies a weight to each, and then integrates the values to come up with an exposure setting. The most advanced form of matrix metering uses computer-based intelligence to deduce what you're trying to photograph—not quite a canned aesthetic sense but no more than a step away. Camera-makers have discovered that certain patterns of brightness—for example, bright around the edges but dark in the center—are trademarks of common photographic situations. The example would indicate a backlit subject, which the camera can identify and compensate for. The best digital cameras use matrix metering. Each camera-maker has developed its own set of patterns and algorithms that it believes best cover most photographic situations.

Control

Metering only creates information. The next issue is what to do with the information that the metering system develops. The shutter speed and aperture interact, so you have to choose the best setting of each for your particular photographic situation. You have two ways of dealing with the choices—let the camera deal with them or do it yourself (in other words, automatic or manual exposure control).

Manual

Manual exposure is the old-fashioned way. You read the meter (which may be inside the camera and displayed in the viewfinder of a modern digital camera) and then adjust both the shutter speed and lens aperture to match its recommendations. Old match-needle metering requires you simply to adjust the camera so that the needle of its light meter moves to the center of its display; newer cameras may ask you to make adjustments until a red LED turns green, or some such nonsense.

For the most part, manual exposure systems existed because camera-makers had not yet learned how to make them automatic. Manual exposure still gives you the utmost in control, however. It allows you to control the "depth of field" of your photographs, the amount of blurring from image movement, and similar aesthetic pictorial features. If you have the least pretense toward making artistic photographs, you'll want a camera that allows you to step backward to manual exposure control.

Automatic

Automatic exposure is not a single miracle, it's several. Auto-exposure systems may operate in any of three distinct modes and may even allow you to choose which to use. These modes include the following:

- **Aperture priority**. This mode asks that you set the lens aperture and automatically adjusts the shutter speed for proper exposure.

- **Shutter priority**. This mode asks that you set the shutter speed, and the camera automatically adjusts the aperture for proper exposure.

- **Programmed**. This mode asks only that you point the camera in the general direction of what you want to photograph, and the camera adjusts both shutter speed and lens aperture according to a stored program.

  The programs used by programmed exposure systems vary at the discretion of the camera manufacturer. Some favor shorter exposures to lessen the chance of blurring with long lenses. Some favor smaller apertures to yield more depth of field to simplify the job of auto-focus systems. More expensive cameras allow you to select from different programs to match the photographic situation you face. Some cameras even let you tailor your own programs or select from more exotics programs stored on removable memory cards.

In any case, most cameras set off flashing lights, beeps, or sirens to warn when you try to photograph a scene out of the range of the automatic exposure system's capabilities to ensure a proper exposure. (A few snotty cameras may even prevent you from taking a photo that they think they cannot properly expose.) Usually adjusting the parameter that's left to manual control (the aperture or shutter that has priority) will resolve these difficulties unless the scene is just too dark.

The compromise between automatic and manual exposure is to handle things automatically but give you a veto. That is, let the camera find its own way but allow you to take over when things get too challenging.

To allow you to override the automatic exposure system and fine-tune the exposure of your images, most cameras provide *exposure-compensation controls*. These are also called *backlight switches* or something similar in recognition of the situation most often requiring compensation: when the source of light is behind the actual subject, making the background substantially brighter than the foreground. The exposure-compensation control simply tells the camera to overexpose the overall image to bring the actual subject into the proper exposure range. This overexposure control is also useful for other special situations, such as snowy ski scenes and bright sandy beaches. Although advanced matrix metering systems supposedly cope with this sort of lighting, a camera with exposure compensation gives you a degree of control without sacrificing general automatic operation.

Flash

No matter how sensitive a light sensor is, none can find an image in absolute darkness. When it's truly dark, there are no photons available to register on it. To allow you to take photographs even when insufficient light is available, most digital cameras incorporate their own photon source—a *flash*. As the name implies, a flash unit makes a flash of bright light. Although once based on contained explosions sealed inside small light bulbs, today's flash units rely on the excitation of xenon gas to produce a brief but bright pulse of light. The brevity of the flash allows the near-instant illumination to stop motion (the object illuminated can't move far during the brief pulse during which it is illuminated), much like a mechanical stroboscope apparently stops motion. Repeating flashes can thus operate as stroboscopes, too, and consequently some old-time photographers call their xenon-based flash units *strobes*. Another common term is *speedlight*, probably created by anxious marketeers wanting consumers to disregard the lengthy period required by their products to recharge between flashes.

When one is judging flash units or the flash incorporated into a camera, several issues are important. These include the guide number, exposure control, red-eye reduction, and the possibility of external connections.

The *guide number* of a flash unit allows you to determine the aperture setting of your camera for proper exposure using the flash. Guide numbers depend on film speed, so you'll see them listed as something like "Guide number 50 with ASA 100 film." The guide numbers for the built-in flashes of digital cameras are calibrated to the sensitivity of the camera's image sensor, so they don't have to include an ASA number, although some manufacturers note the ASA equivalent. The guide number represents the maximum distance away a subject can be for a proper flash exposure multiplied by the aperture of the camera lens you want to use. For example, a guide number of 80 indicates that, at an f-stop setting of f/8, your subject should be no more than ten feet away.

Most of the time you don't have to bother with guide numbers. All digital camera flashes are automatic. They are designed to provide just the right amount of light to properly illuminate your subject when taking a picture. But the guide number does tell you the maximum distance at which the automatic flash exposure system will work. Some manufacturers simply list this maximum distance and forego guide numbers entirely so you don't have to bother with the math.

Focusing

All lenses must be focused to present a sharp image. At the point of focus, the light rays emanating from any point on the subject are brought back together again as a single point in the resulting image—or as close as possible to a single point. Rays of light (photons) leave the subject in many directions. A few of them strike the lens. The wider the lens aperture, the more of them the lens can collect. Then the job of the curved surface of the lens is to nudge the photons in a new direction. The curve of the lens varies the nudging for the different angles at which the photons left the subject. The problem is that once the lens nudges the photons, they keep traveling straight. The photons from any given point will converge on a point at a distance from the lens. At greater or lesser distances than the point at which they all meet, they may be close together but are still spread apart in the shape of the aperture. When you focus a lens, you move the lens closer to or farther from the film or image sensor to make the distance proper. Only when the lens is set properly will the image be sharp or "in focus."

You might think that you'd be able to set the focus once and forget it. Light, alas, isn't so cooperative. Proper focus depends on the distance between subject to lens and lens to image sensor. When one changes, you have to change the other to keep the image sharp. You and your camera must compensate for the different distances between the camera and its subject by "focusing" the lens. *Conventional focusing*, the traditional way, is to move the lens closer to or farther from the image sensor—when you focus on a more distant image, the front of the image may extend. A more modern technique is *internal focusing*, which alters elements within the lens to change its focusing distance by changing the power of the lens. Either technique works. It's the lens designer's choice.

From a more practical standpoint, the *means* by which the focus gets changed is more important. Three different types of focusing systems are possible, and all are used on digital cameras. These include fixed focus, manual focus, and auto-focus.

Fixed Focus

Fixed focus actually means no focusing at all. The distance between lens and sensor is physically fixed. Nothing moves. That's good because there's nothing for you to adjust. But it's bad, too, because a fixed-focus lens creates a sharp image at only one distance from its subject. Everything else (and often just plain everything) is a bit bleary, out of focus.

Although this situation would seem highly undesirable and even unacceptable in a camera, fixed focus often works and is popular in inexpensive cameras. Fixed focus works best when its shortcomings are hidden by other shortcomings in the camera system. If a lens never produces a truly sharp image, you'll never be able to tell when it is out of focus. If an image sensor only produces 320-by-240 pixel resolution, any loss of sharpness may be lost in the jaggies of the big pixels. Consequently, the limitations of inexpensive lenses cover up the lack of true focus.

The fixed-focus system takes advantage of another optical property. Wide-angle lenses make focusing less critical, so most fixed-focus lenses are a bit wider than "normal." In addition, a smaller aperture makes focusing less critical, so fixed focus lens have relatively small apertures and work only outdoors or with flash.

Manual Focus

A manual focus camera puts you in charge. Typically you twist the lens to move it closer to or farther from the film to compensate for subjects at different distances. The twist gives you finer control compared to sliding the lens directly like a trombone. You have to monitor sharpness by eye, either through the viewfinder or display screen. It's not always easy to do (especially in dim lighting).

Although most cameras use auto-focusing (discussed next) to relieve you of the chore, sometimes manual focusing can be preferable. Manual focusing lets you control the "look" of the image so you can exploit techniques such as selective focus or intentional blurring. You can also use manual focus when auto-focusing fails. Although mid-range auto-focusing cameras may not offer you the manual option, you'll want to look for the option if you're serious about photography.

Auto-Focus

A good auto-focus system is more accurate than most people at adjusting the focus of a camera. Auto-focus systems are generally faster at focusing than are mere human beings.

And auto-focus systems are more reliable. They do not forget to focus the camera before that once-in-a-lifetime shot.

Auto-focus systems come in either of two types: passive or active. *Passive* auto-focus systems look at a scene and attempt to figure out what the correct focus is by making edges as sharp as possible. *Active* auto-focus systems work like radar or sonar. They send out a signal, usually infrared, watch for its reflections, and judge from the time elapsed between transmission and reception how far the signal has traveled.

Both sorts of auto-focus achieve their intended purpose, at least most of the time. Active systems can be fooled more easily, however. With sonar-based systems, for example, when your subject is behind a window, the sound waves from the sonar system bounce off the glass rather than the subject. As a result, the camera focuses on the window and leaves the subject a blur. Moreover, active auto-focus systems have a finite range. The sound or light they send out is effective only for a limited distance. For normal length lenses, that distance is the equivalent of infinity focus, so this shortcoming poses no problem. With long telephoto lenses, however, the active auto-focus system may run out of range before the lens.

Passive auto-focus systems work like the human visual system by trying to make lines sharp. To do so, the passive auto-focus system requires something to focus on, a subject with a definite outline in high contrast. Without adequate image contrast, the passive auto-focus system won't work. It is particularly susceptible to darkness because low light levels usually reduce contrast (less light means less overall range in brightness, which means less contrast). Passive systems don't work at all in the dark. Active systems have no problem with darkness.

Most auto-focus systems for cameras don't bring objects into absolute focus. Rather, they have a *stepped focus* system that adjusts the lens to accommodate a range of distances for the subject. Cameras may have as few as three focus ranges or *steps*. More is better, but infinity is unnecessary.

White Balance

The white balance control of a camera allows you to adjust it for the varying *color temperature* of the scene you wish to photograph. (You'll find a full discussion of color temperature in Chapter 24, "Video Systems.") Although color temperature is a complex concept, the effect of white balance is easy to judge—scenes taken under incandescent lighting look abnormally orange. Whereas adjusting for color temperature with chemical cameras meant toting around a set of color correction filters, most digital cameras have automatic white balance systems that adjust to the available light. Some digital cameras also let you make manually settings for sunny, cloudy, incandescent, fluorescent, and flash lighting conditions.

Image Storage

Film combines two discrete functions—it is both a sensing and storage medium. A digital camera separates the two functions, leaving you with the need for a storage system. Most digital cameras use flash memory to store the images they capture.

Inexpensive cameras have only built-in memory, which allows them to hold a finite number of images—typically about a dozen—before you need to *download* them to a computer or printer.

Better digital cameras use a memory card of some type. These cards are removable so that you can quickly exchange cards to take more pictures, much like loading a new roll of film. In fact, some vendors of memory cards call them *digital film*, which they are not. You can also slide out a memory card and slide it into a dedicated card reader to transfer the images into your computer. Chapter 16, "Memory," describes the various card types.

To increase the capacity of each card, most digital cameras give you the option of storing your images at two or more quality levels, which trade good looks for more compact storage. (Almost no one uses native or uncompressed mode to store digital camera images—with only a couple of shots, a memory card is full.) Although some early digital cameras distinguished their quality levels by their actual resolution, more modern cameras operate at one or two basic resolutions and trade off higher compression for greater storage capacity. When decoded, the more highly compressed images yield lower quality—they typically look fuzzier—but nevertheless display at the basic resolution level of the camera.

The compression method of choice is JPEG, which stands for the *Joint Photographic Experts Group*, a committee that hammered out standards for the algorithms. JPEG uses *lossy* compression, which means that some information gets sacrificed in the effort to shrink file size. The lost information can never be regained, so once an image is compressed, its original quality can never be restored.

At moderate levels of compression, the losses made by JPEG compression show up as a loss of image sharpness. However, if you examine a reconstructed JPEG image at high magnification, you can see patterns that arise from the compression algorithm. As you increase the JPEG compression ratio, these artifacts become obvious, the image loses definition, and it finally falls apart so that your eye can no longer make sense from it.

The storage or operating modes of most modern digital cameras correspond to the degree of JPEG compression used. The best quality mode—often called exactly that—uses the least compression, typically file size reduction by about a factor of four. The next increment down may compress by a factor of 12. Economy or low-quality mode may compress by a factor of 36 or more. Sometimes a camera's economy mode ratchets resolution down by one giant notch—for example, to VGA resolution, 640 by 480 pixels.

Viewfinders

The *viewfinder* is named after its function: It helps you find the view that you want to photograph. A plain viewfinder does nothing but give you a view. It can be as simple as two frames that you line up to locate the image that the camera will picture. Most digital cameras elaborate on the basic viewfinder design.

Optical viewfinders use a combination of lenses that work like a telescope, giving you a view at a glance so you don't have to line up frames. The lenses are small and separate from the lens in the camera used to take the actual picture. The least expensive digital cameras use simple optical viewfinders.

Many cameras have *reflex viewfinders*, which use the camera lens as part of the viewfinder. Through the use of a mirror or prisms, you can see the actual image seen by the lens. A mirror reflects the lens image up into the viewfinder, the reflection being the camera's reflex. The most expensive professional digital cameras use true reflex viewfinders (as do a few lesser expensive models).

A reflex viewfinder allows you to see the effects of zooms. Moreover, the reflex viewfinder gives you a detailed color image without the need for using a power-hungry (and battery-draining) LCD panel. But because you don't see how the camera's electronics are affecting the image, you can only guess at how the camera's electronics are dealing with the image.

Digital cameras add *video viewfinders* or *LCD panels* that allow you to see exactly the image seen by the camera lens after it's processed by the camera's circuitry. In addition to letting you preview the image before you capture it, the LCD panel also lets you *review* the images you've already captured.

Big-screen or *view-screen viewfinders* give you a larger LCD display meant to be watched like a television set instead of a pirate's telescope. It gives the best possible view of the image before and after recording. Using big-screen viewfinders can seem unnatural to anyone accustomed to the peepshow method of previewing images in other camera formats.

Some digital cameras give you what looks to be a conventional optical viewfinder at the back of the camera—you peer through it with one eye—but put a small LCD panel at the other end to create an *electronic view finder* (EVF). The EVF gives you a preview like an LCD panel at the back of the camera but is smaller and dimmer (it doesn't have to over-power daylight as does the panel on the back of the camera), so it uses substantially less power than the big panel on the back.

Some digital cameras switch their EVFs to black-and-white in dimly lit situations to help you focus more easily. Note, too, that the frame rate of the EVF, often slower than conventional video systems, may distort smooth motion. It's something you have to get used to.

View Panels

In framing a shot, the only image you need to see displayed on the LCD view panel on the back of your camera is a full-screen look through the lens. For the review of photos you've previously captured, however, most digital cameras offer additional modes. Some of these include single-image mode, multiple-image mode, slideshow mode, and zoom mode.

Single Image

In single-image mode, that's all you see—a one-shot view. Most cameras will let you step through all the images you've exposed so that you can look at them one at a time. Although you can't compare shots (except in your mind), you will see the greatest possible level of detail. Single-image mode is the basic viewing mode for digital cameras in review mode, and usually the only preview view.

Multiple Image

In multiple-image mode—sometimes called *thumbnail* mode—your camera breaks its viewfinder into a matrix of individual images, typically an array of four or nine. Although each image is a fraction of its individual size (say one-quarter or one-ninth), this mode allows you to make side-by-side comparisons. You can pick out an image to keep or trash in one quick glance. This mode is particularly useful when you urgently need more memory and want to eliminate wasted shots to gain memory space.

Slideshow

Long before we had home videos to bore our friends and neighbors through wintry evenings, God gave us the slideshow. You'd drag out a rolled-up screen that never properly unrolled, plug in the projector, and flash side after slide, one at a time, on the screen. The slideshow mode of a digital camera's electronic viewfinder operates similarly, a one-after-another display of the images in its memory. This mode allows you to briefly view all the photos you've captured before deciding to chuck them all and start over.

The slideshow lets you assess the mass of your work in full detail. At that, it can be quite useful in making a quick evaluation of your technical prowess. As with the presentation of single images, it does not allow you to make quick comparisons.

Zoom

The small screen and low pixel count in digital camera LCD displays can make checking image details difficult. Consequently, many cameras incorporate an electronic zoom mode in their viewfinder systems. Typically this mode will let the LCD panel display one pixel for each pixel in the captured image, which magnifies the image by a factor of two to four. Although you cannot see the entire image at one time, you can usually pan across its width and height to check each pixel. If you're critical about the images you take, you'll want zoom mode. For ordinary snapshots, however, you may find it unnecessary and may not miss the feature in a camera that lacks it.

If you plan only to use your LCD panel to review images, you don't much care about where it is on your camera. You can just tilt the camera to the viewing angle you prefer. If, however, you want to use the panel as a viewfinder, the mounting of the LCD is decidedly important. It must be located so you can view it conveniently while pointing the camera lens at your subject. Not all digital cameras have LCD panels that let you do this conveniently.

Adjustable panels allow you to swivel the LCD to whatever position is most comfortable for you to view it. In particular, you can tilt it upward so that it functions as a waist-level viewfinder, which many professional photographers prefer, particularly for portrait photography.

Connections

Downloading images from camera to computer requires some kind of connection. Among current digital cameras, four interfaces are popular—standard serial, optical, USB serial, and FireWire. The technical aspects of each are described in Chapter 11, "Ports."

The standard serial connection accommodates the widest range of computers but is also the slowest connection in general use. A so-called "high-speed" serial interface in the computer realm operates at a speed of 115,200 bits per second, a rate that may demand ten minutes to download the contents of a modest-size camera memory unit. (The Apple Macintosh fares a bit better—its standard serial interface can accept information about eight times faster, 921 kilobits per second.) Older digital cameras relied on serial connections, as do some inexpensive, low-resolution models. But serial connections are too slow to handle today's large image sizes.

Optical connections use the IrDA interface. Although serial in nature, an IrDA connection can handle data speeds up to 4Mbps. The chief shortcoming of optical links is the need for an IrDA interface at both ends of the connection. Although at one time every notebook computer had an IrDA interface, the interface is uncommon in desktop computers. Many manufacturers are omitting them from their notebook machines as well. Although the IrDA interface is fast and convenient, you'll want to ensure your computer can deal with it.

Most newer digital cameras take advantage of the Universal Serial Bus port design. The latest should use USB Version 2.0. This interface combines high speed with connection convenience. Even USB 1.0, which operates at about 12 megabits per second, is fast enough to empty a digital camera's memory card in a minute.

Digital video cameras usually use FireWire connections, which provided the only consumer-level connection system capable of handling video before the advent of USB 2.0. The FireWire connection has not caught on among makers of still cameras.

Analog Video Output

Better digital cameras have analog video outputs, which you can use for image preview or as a video source. For example, you can set your digital camera up in a studio and use a conventional television monitor for big-screen previews of your shots. Or you can record images from your digital still camera on a VCR or, with a video input, on your computer. Note that you cannot get video images at the full resolution of your camera.

Analog video outputs of digital cameras typically follow the standards for the part of the world in which the cameras are marketed. The standards in Europe, most of Asia, Africa, and South America differ from those of North America and Japan. Buy a camera meant for the wrong market, and you may not be able to use the analog video outputs. The analog video outputs of digital cameras meant for North America and Japan usually follow the National Television Standards Committee (NTSC) video standard, which is fully described in Chapter 24, "Video Systems."

Power

Digital cameras are electronic devices and consequently need a steady supply of electricity. With today's technologies, their needs border on the prodigious and often sneak to the far side of the border. That power has to come from somewhere, and the places of choice are two—from self-contained batteries or from utility-supplied electricity through an external transformer, the ubiquitous power brick.

Batteries

Unlike camcorders, the batteries for most digital cameras are standard sizes. Most digital cameras use standard AA or AAA batteries, typically about four (the number needed to get enough voltage for conventional logic circuits). Most manufacturers generously include batteries with their products.

Digital cameras are high-current devices. They cannot use standard or heavy-duty batteries based on carbon-zinc technology. They require alkaline or rechargeable cells. In fact, some manufacturers warn to use their products only with rechargeable batteries, such as nickel-cadmium cells or nickel-metal hydride (NiMH) cells. Chapter 31, "Power," discusses these battery technologies in detail.

Batteries may seem to behave strangely under the high-current demands of digital cameras. For example, while alkaline cells may last long enough to capture a dozen images, rechargeable cells of the same size may work for 100 images or more. Subtle differences in battery construction used by different brands can have a big effect on battery capacity. Some manufacturers' cells may appear to fail after only a few exposures. Such batteries are far from dead, but they can no longer generate the high current your digital camera requires.

The high-current demand also makes battery life unpredictable. You'll always want to carry spares.

When loading fresh batteries in your camera, never mix battery technologies or even battery brands. Different battery brands may use slightly different physical constructions or even different chemical mixes with the possible result of the internal resistance of the brands of cells being different, resulting in some cells working harder (and draining faster) than others. In other words, make sure the cells you use are identical.

AC Power

Nearly all digital cameras make provisions for plugging in an AC adapter. Many, however, make the AC adapter an option. If you work primarily in a studio, the AC adapter is a worthwhile expense because it will save you the cost of batteries and the time needed to change them.

You can substitute a generic AC adapter for the official one offered by the camera manufacturer. Check your camera's specification sheet to determine the current your camera requires as well as the voltage and polarity of the AC adapter. Often polarity is described graphically with a plus or minus sign pointing to a dot inside a circle. The dot corresponds to the central conductor of the power connector. The only important issue is that the diagram that's shown in your camera's specifications match that of the AC adapter you choose.

Display Systems

Seeing is believing. If you couldn't see the results of your calculations or language manipulations, the personal computer would be worthless as a tool. You need some way of viewing the output of the computer system to know what it has done and why you're wasting your time feeding it data.

Out of all potential technologies for giving you feedback about what your computer is doing, the one almost universal choice is the one you see on your screen. But it's what goes on behind the screen that really counts. The screen just shows you the results of a lot of technologies and systems working together.

The total entity made from these technologies is your computer's *display system*. At the hardware level, it comprises two distinct parts. The *display* is the screen you see, either as a separate monitor or as a panel that's a permanent part of your computer. The *display adapter*, which may be a separate expansion board or built in to your system's motherboard, converts the logical signals in your computer to the form digestible by the display.

The first display systems used by personal computers were based on television sets. In fact, many were television sets, adapted to the job with a *modulator* that turned video signals from your computer into Channel 3 or 4. Today's display systems are vastly more sophisticated than mere television sets, often having greater resolution than is promised by even High Definition Television (HDTV) systems. But at heart, computer display systems remain video systems, based on the same technologies as the lowly TV.

Video Technology

As far as most of your computer is concerned, its job is done when it writes an image to the frame buffer. After all, once you've got all the pixels arranged the way you want them in memory, shipping them off through a cable to your display should be a simple matter. It isn't. The image must be transformed from its comparatively static position in screen memory to a signal that can traverse a reasonable interface—after all, the cable alone for a parallel interface capable of moving data for nearly a million pixels would likely be thicker than the average computer. Consequently, the frame-buffer image must be converted into a stream of serial data for transmission.

The need for this kind of image transformation became evident when television was invented. The system developed by Philo T. Farnsworth (one of several folks credited with inventing television) relied on scanning images that naturally produced a serial data stream. Although television has improved somewhat since the 1920s when Farnsworth was developing it (at least technical standards have improved—the quality of entertainment is another matter entirely), the transmission system remains essentially the same for today's analog television signals as well as the connections between computers and their displays.

Scanning

Serializing images for the first television system was inherent in the way the cameras captured the images using the technique of *raster scanning*. The first television cameras traced an electron beam across the projection of an image on a special material that changed its electrical characteristics in response to the bright and dark areas of a scene. By focusing the electron beam, the camera could detect the brightness of a tiny spot in the scene. By dividing the scene into dots the size of its sensing spot and rapidly examining each one, the camera could gather all the data in the image.

Although there's no naturally required order to such an examination, the inventors of television looked to what we humans have been doing for centuries—reading. We read text one line at a time, progressing from left to right across each line. The various inventors of television (and there are many competing claims to the honor) followed the same pattern, breaking the image into lines and scanning the dots of each line from left to right.

To make a scan in a classic television camera, the electron beam sweeps across the image under the control of a combination of magnetic fields. One field moves the beam horizontally, and another vertically. Circuitry in the camera supplies a steadily increasing voltage to two sets of deflection coils to control the sweep of the beam. These coils are electromagnets, and the increasing voltage causes the field strength of the coils to increase and deflect the beam further. At the end of the sweep of a line, the field that controls the horizontal sweep of the electron beam is abruptly switched off, returning the beam to the starting side of the screen. Likewise, when the beam reaches the bottom of the screen, the field controlling the vertical sweep switches off. The result is that the electron beam follows a tightly packed zigzag path from the top of the screen to the bottom.

The primary difference between the two sweeps is that several hundred horizontal sweeps take place for each vertical one. The rate at which the horizontal sweeps take place is called the *horizontal frequency*, or the *line rate*, of the display system. The rate at which the vertical sweeps take place is called the *vertical frequency*, or *frame rate*, of the system because one complete image frame is created every time the beam sweeps fully down the screen.

The television receiver scans the inside of the cathode ray tube (CRT) in exactly the same fashion. In fact, its electron beam is precisely synchronized to that of the camera. The one-line-at-a-time, left-to-right scan nicely accomplishes the required dimensional conversion.

The video circuits of your computer have to carry out a similar conversion. The only difference is that the image is laid out in a logical two-dimensional array in memory instead of a physical two-dimensional array on a photosensitive layer inside the camera tube (or more likely today, a *charge coupled device*, or *CCD*).

To make a scan of the video buffer is a lot easier than sweeping an electron beam. Your computer need only read off addresses in the video buffer in sequential order, one row at a time. To carry out this task, your computer uses a special electronic circuit called the *video controller*, which scans the memory addresses, reads the data value at each address, and sends the data out in one serial data stream.

Synchronizing Signals

In television, the biggest complication of the scanning systems is ensuring that the camera and television set displaying the image both scan at exactly the same position in the image at exactly the same time. The frequencies used by horizontal and vertical scanning must exactly match. In addition, the camera and television must use exactly the same starting position.

To keep the two ends of the system locked together, television systems use *synchronizing signals*. They take the form of sharp pulses, which the circuitry inside your monitor converts to the proper scanning signals. The television camera generates one special set of pulses at the beginning of each line and another at the start of each image frame. The television knows to start each line when it receives the pulses.

In your computer, the video controller generates similar synchronizing signals for exactly the same purpose. It sends out one (the horizontal synchronizing signal) before each line in the image and one (the vertical synchronizing signal) at the beginning of each frame. The monitor uses the pulses to trigger its sweep of each line and to reset to the top of the image to start the scan of the next frame.

The video controller doesn't scan at just any frequency. It uses standard frequencies, which vary with the geometry of the image—its height and width along with the frame rate. The monitor is tuned to expect these frequencies, using the synchronizing signals only to achieve a precise match.

In conventional television, the synchronizing signals were designed to sit invisibly in the same single data stream that conveyed the picture information. In modern production studios and the connection between your computer and monitor, however, the synchronizing signals are usually kept separate from the picture information. Actually, there are four common ways of combining or not combining video data and synchronizing signals. These include the following:

- **Composite video**. The all-together-now television approach that puts all video data and the two required synchronizing signals into one package for single-wire or single-channel transmission systems.

- **Composite sync**. Combines the horizontal and vertical synchronizing signals together and puts them on one wire. Another, separate wire carries the image data.

- **Separate sync**. Gives a separate wire and connection to the image data, the horizontal, and the vertical synchronizing signals.

- **Sync-on-green**. Combines the vertical and horizontal synchronizing signals together and then combines them with the data for the green data channel.

In any of these four systems, the relative timing of the synchronizing and data signals is the same. The chief difference is in the wiring. A composite video system requires only one wire. The other systems use three wires for data (one for each primary color). Sync-on-green therefore requires only three connections, composite sync requires four (three colors, one sync), and separate sync requires five (three colors, two sync). The standard video system in most computers uses composite sync—the signal monitor cable has four separate connections for image data and synchronizing signals.

Retrace

In a television signal, the data corresponding to the dots on the screen doesn't fill a video signal wall-to-wall. The physics of the first television systems saw to that. To make the image you see, the electron beam in a conventional television picture tube traces a nearly horizontal line across the face of the screen then, in an instant, flies back to the side of the screen from which it started but lower by the width of the line it already traced out. This quick zipping back is termed *horizontal retrace*, and although quick, it cannot take place instantly because of the inertia inherent in electrical circuits. Consequently, the smooth flow of bytes must be interrupted briefly at the end of each displayed line (otherwise the video information would vanish in the retrace). The video controller must take each retrace into account as it serializes the image.

In addition, another variety of retrace must occur when the electron beam reaches the bottom of the screen when it has finished painting a screen-filling image: *vertical retrace*. The beam must travel as quickly as possible back up to its starting place, and the video controller must halt the flow of data while it does so.

Blanking

During retrace, if the electron beam from the gun in the tube were on, it would paint a bright line diagonally across the screen as the beam returns to its proper position. To prevent the appearance of this distracting line, the beam is forcibly switched off not only during retrace but also during a short interval on either side to give the beam time to stabilize. The interval in which the beam is forced off and cannot be turned on by any degree of programming is called *blanking* because the electron beam can draw nothing but a blank on the screen.

The classic television signal cleverly combines synchronization, retrace, and blanking together. The horizontal synchronizing signal is a strong pulse of the opposite polarity of the image data that lasts for the retrace period. The negative nature of the signal effectively switches off the electron beam, and the frequency of the signal effectively synchronizes the image.

Front and Back Porches

Most computer monitors don't fill their entire screens with data. They center (or try to) the image within darkened borders to minimize the image distortions that sneak in near the edges of the screen. To produce these darkened, protected areas, the electron beam is held at the level that produces a black image for a short while before and after the data of each image line is displayed. The short interval before the data of a line begins is termed the *front porch* of the signal. The interval after the end of the data but before the synchronizing signal is called the *back porch*. If you examined the signal, you'd see that it dips down for blanking and pops up to an intermediate height (called *black level* by broadcasters) to create the porches between blanking and data. Use your imagination and the black-level signals look like shelves—or porches.

Vertical Interval

The period during which the screen is blanked during the vertical retrace is called, appropriately, the *vertical interval*. Its physical manifestation is the wide black horizontal bar that's visible between image frames when your television screen or computer monitor picture rolls and requires adjustment of the vertical hold control. The big black bar corresponds to the time during which the signal carries no video information.

The vertical interval is a carryover from the early days of television when vacuum tube electronics needed time to "recover" between fields and frames. This allowed voltages inside the circuitry of the TV set to retreat to the proper levels to begin the next field. Modern electronics—say, for example, those of televisions made in the last 30 years—don't really require the long duration of the vertical interval. Consequently, broadcasters have found the time devoted to it useful for stuffing in extra information. Television stations add a *vertical interval test signal* (VITS) to monitor operation of their transmitters and associated equipment. The text for the closed captioning system is also encoded during the vertical interval, as is all sorts of other miscellaneous data.

Video Integration

The signals between computers and their monitors don't follow the same standards used by broadcast television and studio video systems. Nevertheless, these standard video signals have become an intrinsic part of both what computers do and what you expect from your computer. After all, computers are now regularly used to produce videos, including those for presentation on television, even on networks. At the other end of the channel, computers display video images—from a television using a TV adapter board or from a DVD drive. Video images inevitably confront the computer display system, and dealing with them can be a challenge.

Many display adapters make conventional video signals along with those meant for your computer display. Add a video-capture board to your computer, and you can turn conventional video signals into digital form so you can edit home movies or package them on CD or DVD. You can even watch television on your computer monitor using a technique called *video overlay*.

Standards

When it comes to images, the standard most widely used stares you in the face, literally, for several hours a day. The unblinking eye of the television set defines the most widely used image communication system in the world. Considering when the basic television standards were created, their longevity has been amazing, particularly compared to the short tenure of computer standards—the basic television signal was defined half a century ago. Only recently has it come under threat by digital and high-definition technologies. (The Federal Communications Commission hopes to turn off all conventional television signals by 2007, substituting a new all-digital television standard.)

First a bit of definition. The word *video* means "I see" in Latin. The word *television* is a hodge-podge derived from the Greek for "distant" and Latin for "sight." Television is what is broadcast or transmitted over a distance. Video is up close and personal, the signals inside a studio or your home.

When we talk of "video" among computers, however, we mean an electrical signal that encodes an image in raster form, hence the term *video board* that's often used instead of *graphics adapter*. When people involved with television speak of video, they mean a particular form of this signal, one with well-defined characteristics. A television transmitter modulates a carrier wave with this video signal to make the broadcasts to which you tune in. Video signals range in frequency from zero to a half-dozen megahertz. Television signals start out at 60MHz and extend upward to nearly ten times that. Television sets tune in television signals, receiving them on their antenna inputs. Monitors display video signals.

Although one standard currently dominates video signals in the United States and Japan, other standards are used elsewhere in the world. In addition, a secondary standard termed *S-video* appears in high-quality video applications.

NTSC

The most common form of video wears the designation NTSC, which stands for *National Television Standards Committee*, an industry organization formed in the early 1950s to create a single signal standard for color television. At the time, CBS had been broadcasting for over a year with an electromechanical color system that essentially spun a color wheel in front of the camera and a matching wheel in front of the monitor. RCA, owner of rival NBC, proposed an all-electronic alternative. The RCA system had the advantage that it was backwardly compatible with black-and-white television sets, whereas the CBS system was not. The NTSC was formed chiefly to put an impartial stamp of approval on the RCA system.

In the RCA/NTSC system, each pixel gets scanned in each of the three primary colors. Although studio equipment may pass along the three colors separately like the RGB signals in computers, for broadcast they are combined together with synchronizing signals to create NTSC video.

The magic is in the combining process. The NTSC system packages three channels of color into one using some clever mathematical transformations.

First, it transforms the color space. For compatibility with monochrome, NTSC combines all three color signals together. This produces a signal called *luminance*, which encodes all the brightness information in a television image. The luminance signal is essentially a monochrome signal and produces an image entirely compatible with black-and-white television sets. The name of the luminance signal is often abbreviated as Y.

Next, the NTSC system creates two signals encoding color, or rather the differences between the color signals and the luminance signal. One signal (called I in the NTSC system) encodes the difference between luminance and the red signal, and another (called Q) encodes the difference between luminance and the blue signal. Subtract the first from luminance, and you get red again. Subtract the other, and you get blue. Subtract both, and the remainder is green.

Next, the NTSC system combines the two difference signals into a single signal that can carry all the color information, called *chrominance* (abbreviated as *C*). Engineers used quadrature modulation to combine the two signals into one. The result was that colors were encoded into the chrominance signal as different phase angles of the signal.

Together the luminance and chrominance signals provided a guide to a map of colors, a polar chart. The chrominance encodes the angle between the color and the X-axis of the chart, and the luminance indicates the distance from the origin to the color.

Finally, to fit the chrominance signal in where luminance should only fit, the NTSC engineers resorted to putting chrominance on a subcarrier. That is, they modulated a carrier wave with the chrominance signal and then added it to the luminance signal. Although the subcarrier had much less bandwidth than the main luminance channel, the process was effective because the human eye is less sensitive to color differences than brightness differences.

The NTSC chose a frequency of 3.58MHz as the color subcarrier frequency. The chrominance is an amplitude modulated signal on a 3.58MHz carrier. To avoid interference with the luminance signal, the NTSC process eliminates the carrier and lower sideband of the chrominance signal after the modulation process.

The NTSC process has two drawbacks: The luminance signal must be cut off before it reaches 3.58KHz to avoid it interfering with the subcarrier. This frequency cap limits the highest possible frequencies in the luminance signal, which means that the sharpness of the image is reduced from what it would be when using the full bandwidth (4.5MHz for the video signal) of the channel. Chrominance carries even less detail.

The basic frame rate of a color video signal is about 29.97 per second. Each frame is made from two interlaced fields, so the field rate is 59.94Hz. Each frame is made from 525 lines, of which about 480 are visible, and the rest are devoted to vertical retrace. Ideally, a studio image would have about 640 pixels across a line. However, the 3.58MHz bandwidth imposed by the NTSC color process constrains the luminance signal bandwidth to 400 to 450 pixels horizontally. Although that might sound paltry, a good home VCR may be able to store images with only about half that resolution.

Black-and-white signals are different. They use a 30Hz frame rate (each with two fields) and lack the color subcarrier. As a result, they can be sharper than color signals because the entire 4.5MHz bandwidth can be devoted to the image.

Instead of NTSC, most of the world uses a color system called PAL, which stands for *Phase Alternating Line*. France and most of the nations that once formed the USSR, such as Russia and Ukraine, use a system called SECAM, which stands for *Sequence Couleur à Memoire* (in English, sequential color with memory). These video standards—and the equipment that follows them—are mutually incompatible.

S-Video

The constraints of NTSC color are required because of the need for backward compatibility. The color signal had to fit into exactly the same bandwidth as black and white. In effect, NTSC gives up a bit of black-and-white resolution to fit in the color information.

Video signals that never make it to the airwaves need not suffer the indignities required by the NTSC broadcast standard. Studio signals have always transcended broadcast standards—studio RGB signals have full-bandwidth, high-resolution (640-pixel) images in each of their three colors. To raise home viewing quality, VCR designers came up with a way to get more quality in color signals by avoiding the NTSC process.

The part of the NTSC process that most limits visual quality is the squeezing of the color signal onto its subcarrier. By leaving the video in two parts, separate luminance and color signals, the bandwidth limitation can be sidestepped. This form of video is termed *S-video*, short for *separate video*. High-end VCRs, camcorders, and monitors use often use S-video signals.

Other than not modulating chrominance onto a subcarrier, the color-encoding method used by S-video is identical to that of NTSC. The three RGB color signals are combined into luminance and chrominance using exactly the same formulae. Although you cannot substitute one signal for the other, the innards of S-video monitors need not be radically different from those of NTSC displays. The level of quality is often quite visibly different. S-video components may have twice the horizontal resolution as composite video.

Note that once a signal is encoded as NTSC, information is irretrievably lost. There's no point to decoding an off-the-air television signal to S-video. The only time S-video helps is when you have a source of the signals that has never been NTSC encoded.

Video Overlay

To put active video in a window on your computer screen, many graphics adapters use a technique called *video overlay*, which allows them to do most of the image processing in hardware rather than software (where it would slow down the rest of your system).

The video overlay process borrows from an old television technology called *chroma keying*. This process works by substituting one image for a key part of another image. Typically the key—an area in the image being shown on the screen—would be identified by its color or *chroma*. Hardware then substitutes another image for the key color. In computers, the graphics adapter paints the television image into the key area, the windows, on the screen. Traditionally in television, the color of choice is a sky blue. This color is preferred because it's optically the opposite of average Caucasian flesh tones, so it's least apt to make parts of people disappear on the screen. Sometimes the process is used in reverse—for example, a weather reporter stands in front of a chroma-key blue screen, and the background gets filled with a weather map or satellite photo. Television people call this technique *blue screening*.

In video overlay, the driver software uses standard Windows instructions to paint a window on the screen, keyed to a special value (it need not be blue). The graphics adapter intercepts the signals destined for your monitor and substitutes the video signal where it finds the keyed windows. Your software and even your computer's microprocessor never need to deal with processing the video. In fact, the video never even makes it as far as the expansion bus. It is isolated on the overlay board. You get full-motion video on your screen with virtually no impact on the performance of your computer.

Video Capture

Gathering up video images so that they can be used by your programs—*video capture*—requires hardware that combines aspects of a more traditional video board and a digital video camera. Traditional video images are analog signals and require an *analog-to-digital converter* (A-to-D converter) to put them in a form usable by your computer.

The A-to-D converter works by sampling the voltage level of the video at each pixel position of the video image and assigning a digital value to it. In most systems, the signal is first decoded into your computer's standard RGB format to determine the strengths of individual colors before sampling. Typically the image gets stored in a buffer and is sampled from the buffer rather than from the real-time video signal. The buffer helps bridge between the different timings and formats of the video signal and its target digital form.

Today's video-capture systems can snag active video in real time. Most can also snatch a single frame to use as a still image. In single-frame mode, the board operates as a *video-frame grabber*.

Image Compression

Nothing eats memory and storage faster than full-motion, full-color video. The math is enough to make the manufacturers drool. Full-color video, which requires three bytes per pixel, at 640×480 resolution, equals nearly 1MB of digital data per frame. At the 30 frames per second used in the United States and most of the Western Hemisphere (or even the 25 frames per second standard in Europe and elsewhere), a video producer would easily use up 1GB of hard disk space in storing less than one minute of uncompressed digital video information.

Digital video systems with reasonable storage needs are possible only because of *video compression*, much as digital photographs are made more compact with image compression. Video compression takes the next step and analyzes not only the image data but the changes in sequential images. Unlike data-compression systems, which reduce the size of a file without losing any information, image- and video-compression systems are *lossy*. That is, they throw away information—usually the part that is least perceptible—that is lost and can never be recovered.

Normal still-image compression programs work two dimensionally, analyzing areas and reducing the data required for storing them. The most popular is called JPEG, which stands for the *Joint Photographic Experts Group*, the group that developed the standard. Video compression works three dimensionally—in addition to compressing individual areas, it processes changes that occur between images in the time dimension. It takes advantage of how little actually changes from frame to frame in a video image. Only the changes get stored or transmitted; the static parts of the image can be ignored. For example, when someone moves against a backdrop, only the pixels in the moving character need to be relayed to the data stream. The most popular form is called MPEG, for the *Motion Picture Experts Group*, an organization similar to JPEG (part of the same overall body) but separate from it.

Filters and Codecs

Compressing still- and video-image data streams is so different that developers use distinct terminologies when speaking of the conversion process. Moreover, they even handle the conversion software differently.

The program routines that compress still images are usually termed *filters*. Most graphic applications have several filters built in to handle a variety of different compression systems and file formats.

Video compression requires either a software- or hardware-based processor that is termed a *codec*, short for coder/decoder. The most efficient software codecs are proprietary designs that rely on patented technology. Each has its own advantages (such as speed of processing, high compression ratio, or good image quality) that make it best suited for a given type of application. Consequently, many codecs remain in common use. Most multimedia applications include the appropriate codec in their playback software or work with those assumed to be installed in your operating system.

JPEG

JPEG is at its best compressing color images, because it relies on psycho-visual perception effects to discard image data that you might not be able to perceive. It also works on grayscale images but yields lower compression ratios at a given quality level. It does not work well on monochrome (two-tone or black-and-white) images and requires that color-mapped images be converted to a conventional, continuous-tone color format before processing—which, of course, loses the compression effect of the color mapping.

JPEG processing involves several steps, some of which are optional. Several of these steps may reduce the amount of detail in the image and therefore its quality. The JPEG standard allows you to select the amount of information that's thrown away in these steps so you can control how well an image reconstructed from the compressed data will resemble the original. One option is *lossless*, which throws away no information other than that which would be redundant. This typically compresses an image file to 50 percent of its original size. Even invoking lossy compression, you can reconstruct an image visually indistinguishable from the original with a reduction to 33 percent of the original. The loss becomes apparent somewhere around reductions of 5 to 10 percent of the original data size. You can brute-force the image data down to 1 percent of the original size, although the results will resemble more a mew work of computer art than whatever masterpiece you started with.

MPEG

The videos that you're most likely to display on your computer use MPEG compression. As with JPEG, MPEG is a committee working under the joint direction of the International Standards Organization (ISO) and the International Electro-Technical Commission (IEC). The formal name of the group is ISO/IEC JTC1 SC29 WG11—the stuff after the organization simply further delineates the organization (JTC stands for Joint Technical Committee, Subcommittee 29, Work group 11). It began its life in 1988 under the leadership of Leonardo Chiariglione and Hiroshi Yasuda.

Despite the similarity of names, the JPEG and MPEG groups are separate and share few members. Some of the technologies used by the two compression systems are similar, but they are meant for different kinds of data. The most prominent point of divergence is that MPEG achieves most of its data reduction by compressing in the time dimension, encoding only differences between frames in video data.

MPEG includes multiple standards for encoding not only video but also the accompanying audio. Over the years it has progressed through several levels with increasing sophistication and quality.

MPEG-1

The first MPEG standard, now usually called *MPEG-1* but formally titled "Coding of Moving Pictures and Associated Audio for Digital Storage Media at up to about 1.5 MBit/s," became an international standard in October, 1992. It has four parts. The actual compression of video and video signals is covered under International Standard 11172-2. Related parts describe the compression of audio signals, synchronizing audio and video, and testing for compliance with the standard.

MPEG-1 is used by CD-i (interactive compact discs) because it achieves a data rate that is within the range of CD drives. To get down that low with the technology existing at the time the standard was developed, the system had to sacrifice resolution. At best, an MPEG-1 image on CD-i has about one-quarter the pixels of a standard TV picture. MPEG also requires hefty processing power to reconstruct the moving image stream, which is why CD-i players can display it directly to your TV or monitor, but only the most powerful computers can process the information fast enough to get it to your display without dropping more frames than an art museum in an earthquake. If you're used to the stuff that pours out of a good VCR, this early MPEG looks marginal, indeed.

MPEG-2

MPEG-2 was meant to rectify the shortcomings of MPEG-1, at least in regard to image quality. The most apparent difference appears on the screen. The most common form of MPEG-2 extends resolution to true TV quality (720 pixels horizontally and 480 vertically) while allowing for both standard and wide-screen formats (4:3 and 16:9 aspect ratios, respectively). Although MPEG-2 benefits from advances in compression technology, this higher quality also demands more data. The TV-quality image format requires a bandwidth of about 4Mbps. Beyond that, the MPEG-2 standard supports resolutions into ionspheric levels. All MPEG-2 chips are also required to step back and process MPEG-1 formats.

In addition to high-quality video, MPEG-2 allows for 5.1 audio channels—that is, left and right main channels (front), left and right rear channels (surround), and a special effects channel for gut-thumping rumbles limited to no higher than 100Hz. (The ".1" in the channel description refers to the 100Hz limit.) MPEG-1 only allows for a single stereo pair.

MPEG-3

What was initially MPEG-3 has been incorporated into MPEG-2. The concept behind MPEG-3 was to make a separate system for High Definition TV for images with resolutions up to 1920 by 1080 pixels with a 30Hz frame rate. Fine-tuning the high levels of MPEG-2 worked well enough for HDTV images that there was insufficient need to support a separate standard.

MPEG-4

Adopted as ISO/IEC 14496 in early 1999, MPEG-4 defines a standard for *interactive media*. Although it incorporates a compression scheme (actually, several), it looks at images entirely differently than does MPEG-2. Instead of compressing an entire scene as an image, MPEG-4 makes the scene from *video* objects, each of which the standard allows to be independently defined and manipulated. A single scene may incorporate several video objects as well as a background. The standard also allows for conventional rectangular images such as movie frames as a special class of video objects. Its compression is optimized for low rates suited to moving images through conventional modems for video-phones or small-screen video conferencing. For example, such images may have low resolution (about 176×144 pixels) and a low frame rate, on the order of 10Hz.

In effect, MPEG-4 is a standardization of many of the features of a 3D accelerator (an unremarkable convergence in that both are designed for the same purpose—the effective presentation of action video). It provides compression algorithms for video, textures, and wire-frames as well as a system for manipulating objects, scenes, and sequences. In addition, it incorporates MPEG-J, an application program interface that allows combining MPEG-4 data with Java code to make a cohesive multimedia playback environment.

Other MPEGs

MPEG-7 is a content-retrieval standard rather than a compression or storage standard, called a *Multimedia Content Description Interface*. It will provide a standard for describing different types of multimedia information that links the description to the content itself. By searching the description, the link will allow you to quickly and efficiently find the material that interests you. MPEG-7 is designed to let you search any kind of medium from still images and graphics to audio to conventional and 3D movies. Its designers even envision its extension to classifying facial expressions and personal characteristics.

MPEG-5 and MPEG-6 are not defined.

Computer Display Standards

The display systems used by today's computers follow several standards that dictate key aspects of their signals, including the onscreen resolution, the number of colors on the screen, and the signals used to connect monitors to your computer.

The starting point in a modern computer display is called *VGA*, named after IBM's pioneering Video Graphics Array, which was introduced in 1987. This little bit of history remains the default mode of nearly every computer video system. Switch on your computer, and it begins life as a VGA system. Only after your operating system loads its video drivers does it switch to the resolution you set. The first screen you see, usually the Windows splash screen announcing your investment in making Bill Gates' fortune, pops on your monitor courtesy of VGA. When you can't get anything to work and your Windows-based computer snarls into service in safe mode, VGA is what you see. Much as you might want, you can't get away from VGA.

But VGA is still just for starters. Except for the lowliest of notebook systems, every computer today strives higher. The best display systems put more than six times as much detail on your screen in more colors than you can name (or even distinguish). At one time, standards were important for properly displaying these higher resolution modes. But because the use of driver software has removed the need for hardware to exactly match any set configuration, most of the older standards survive only as names that identify onscreen resolutions or operating modes. Table 24.1 lists the most popular display standards for personal computers.

TABLE 24.1	Computer Video Standards		
Designation	*Name*	*Resolution*	*Maximum Colors*
MDA	Monochrome Display Adapter	720 by 350	3
CGA	Color Graphics Adapter	640 by 200	16
EGA	Enhanced Graphics Adapter	640 by 350	256
VGA	Video Graphics Array	640 by 480	256/65,536
SVGA	SuperVGA	800 by 600	16.7 million
XGA	Extended Graphics Array	1024 by 768	16.7 million
SXGA	SuperXGA	1280 by 1024	16.7 million

Display Adapters

The hardware that changes your pulsing digital computer's thoughts into the signals that can be displayed by a monitor is called the *display adapter*. Over the years, the display adapter has itself adapted to the demands of computer users, gaining color and graphics capabilities as well as increasing its resolution and range of hues. In most machines, the display adapter is a special expansion board that serves primarily to make graphic images; hence, the display adapter is often called a *graphics board*. Because the graphics board sends out signals in a form that resembles (but is not identical to) that of your home video system, it is often termed a *video board*. Notebook computers lack video boards—they typically lack any conventional expansion boards at all—but all of them also include display adapter circuitry on their motherboards.

No matter its name, the function of display adapter circuitry is the same—control. The adapter controls every pixel that appears on your computer display. But there is one more essential element. Just any control won't do. Give a room full of monkeys control of a million light dimmers (you'll need a mighty large room or a special breed of small, social simians), and the resulting patterns might be interesting—and might make sense at about the same time your simians have completed duplicating the works of Shakespeare. The display adapter circuitry also organizes the image, helping you make sense from the chaos of digital pulses in your computer. It translates the sense of your computer's thoughts into an image that makes sense to you.

The video circuitry of your computer, whether on a dedicated display adapter or part of the motherboard circuitry in the chipset, performs the same functions. In its frame buffer (or in main memory in systems using Unified Memory Architecture), it creates the image your computer will display. It then rasterizes the memory-mapped image and converts the digital signals into an analog format compatible with your monitor.

The modern video board usually has five chief circuits that carry out these functions, although some boards lack some of these elements. A *graphics accelerator* chip builds the image, taking commands from your software and pushing the appropriate pixel values into the frame buffer. *Memory* forms the frame buffer that stores the image created on the board. A *video controller* reads the image in the frame buffer and converts it to raster form. A *RAMDAC* then takes the digital values in the raster and converts them into analog signals of the proper level. Finally, a *video BIOS* holds extension code that provides the video functions your system needs as it boots up.

Accelerator Chips

Of all the chips on a video board, the most important is the graphics accelerator. The chip choice here determines the commands the board understands—for example, whether the board carries out 3D functions in its hardware or depends on your computer to do the processing of 3D effects. The speed at which the accelerator chip operates determines how quickly your system can build image frames. This performance directly translates into how quickly your system responds when you give a command that changes the screen (for example, dropping down a menu) or how many frames get dropped when you play back a video clip. The accelerator also limits the amount and kind of memory in the frame buffer as well as the resolution levels of the images your computer can display, although other video board circuits can also impose limits. In short, the graphics accelerator is the most important chip in the entire video system.

That said, the accelerator is optional, both physically and logically. The oldest display adapters lack accelerators; hence, they are not "accelerated," which means your computer's microprocessor must execute all drawing instructions. In addition, even boards with accelerators may not accelerate all video operations. The board may lack the knowledge of a specific command to carry out some video task, or the board's driver software may not take advantage of all its features. In such circumstances, the drawing functions will be emulated by a Hardware Emulation Layer (often abbreviated HEL) in your operating system—which means your microprocessor gets stuck with the accelerator's drawing work.

As computers have evolved, the need for graphics processing has shifted back and forth between the accelerator and your system's microprocessor. For example, the MMX instructions of newer Pentium microprocessors overlap the functions of graphics accelerators. Streaming SIMD extensions add performance to most graphics operations, complementing MMX. In Unified Memory Architecture (UMA) computers, these technologies can take the place of a dedicated graphics accelerator. In computers with frame buffers, these features work in conjunction with the graphics accelerator. They speed up your computer's ability to calculate what images look like—for example, decompressing stored images or calculating wire-frames for your drafting program. But the final work, actually painting the images that will appear on your screen, relies on the graphics accelerator.

The graphics accelerator is an outgrowth of an older chip technology—the *graphics coprocessor*. An early attempt to speed up the display system, the graphics coprocessor was introduced as a supplemental microprocessor optimized for carrying out video-oriented commands.

The graphics coprocessor added speed in three ways. By carrying out drawing and image-manipulation operations without the need for intervention by the microprocessor, the coprocessor freed up the microprocessor for other jobs. Because the graphics coprocessor was optimized for video processing, it could carry out most image-oriented operations faster than could the microprocessor, even if the microprocessor was able to devote its full time to image processing. The graphics coprocessor also broke through the bus bottleneck that was (at the time of the development of graphics coprocessor technology) choking video performance. When the microprocessor carried out drawing functions, it had to transfer every bit bound for the monitor through the expansion bus—at the time, the slow ISA bus. The coprocessor was directly connected to the frame buffer and could move bytes to and from the buffer without regard to bus speed. The microprocessor only needed to send high-level drawing commands across the old expansion bus. The graphics coprocessor would carry out the command through its direct attachment to the frame buffer.

The workstation market triggered the graphics coprocessor. Microprocessor-makers altered their general-purpose designs into products that were particularly adept at manipulating video images. Because the workstation market was multifaceted, with each different hardware platform running different software, the graphics coprocessor had to be as flexible as possible—programmable just like its microprocessor forebears.

These coprocessors joined the computer revolution in applications that demanded high-performance graphics. But the mass acceptance of Windows made nearly every computer graphics intensive. The coprocessor was left behind as chipmakers targeted the specific features needed by Windows and trimmed off the excess—programmability. The result was the fixed-function graphics coprocessor, exactly the same technology better known now as the *graphics accelerator*.

The most recent evolution of graphics acceleration technology has produced the *3D accelerator*. Rather than some dramatic breakthrough, the 3D accelerator is a fixed-function graphics coprocessor that includes the ability to carry out the more common 3D functions in its hardware circuitry. Just as an ordinary graphics accelerator speeds up drawing and windowing, the 3D accelerator gives a boost to the 3D rendering. Nearly all of today's video boards are equipped with a 3D accelerator. The technology is even built in to many motherboard chipsets.

As with the microprocessors, graphics and 3D accelerators come in wide varieties with different levels of performance and features. Each maker of graphics accelerators typically has a full line of products, ranging from basic chips with moderate performance designed for low-cost video boards to high-powered 3D products aimed at awing you with benchmark numbers far beyond the claims of their competitors (and often, reality).

The performance and output quality of a graphics accelerator depends on a number of design variables. Among the most important of these are the width of the registers it uses for processing video data, the amount and technology of the memory it uses, the ability of the chip to support different levels of resolution and color, the speed rating of the chip, the bandwidth of its connection to your computer and display, and the depth and extent of its command set, as well as how well those commands get exploited by your software.

Graphics accelerators work like microprocessors dedicated to their singular purpose, and internally they are built much the same. The same design choice that determines microprocessor power also affects the performance of graphics accelerator chips. The internal register width of a graphics accelerator determines how many bits the chip works with at a time. As with microprocessors, the wider the registers, the more data that can be manipulated in a single operation.

The basic data type for modern graphics operations is 32 bits—that's the requirement of 24-bit True Color with an alpha channel. Many accelerators at least double that and can move pixels two (or four) at a time in blocks. Today's best are full 128-bit processors, able to operate on multiple pixels at a time.

Because the graphics or 3D accelerator makes the video circuitry of your computer a separate, isolated system, concerns about data and bus widths elsewhere in your computer are immaterial. The wide registers in graphic accelerators work equally well regardless of whether you run 16-bit software (Windows 95 through Windows Me) or 32-bit software (Windows NT, Windows 2000, and Windows XP), no matter what microprocessor you have or what bus you plug your video board into.

The design of a graphics accelerator also sets the maximum amount of memory that can be used in the frame buffer, which in turn sets upper limits on the color and resolution support of a graphics accelerator. Other video board circuit choices may further constrain these capabilities. In general, however, the more memory, the higher the resolution and the greater the depth of color the accelerator can manage.

The same graphics or 3D accelerator chip may deliver wildly different performance when installed in different video boards, even boards with substantially similar circuitry. One of the chief reasons for performance differences among different brands of video board is not in the hardware but the software support. Drivers can radically alter the performance of a given accelerator chip. After all, the chip only processes instructions. If the instructions are optimized, the performance of the chip will be optimum. To be useful at all, a video board must have drivers to match the operating system you want to use.

Video Controllers

The primary job of the video controller in desktop computers that use picture tubes is to serialize the data in display memory. The conversion often is as convoluted as a video game maze. The resemblance between the memory map and the onscreen image is only metaphoric. The rows and columns by which the frame buffer is organized have no relationship to the rows and columns of pixels on your monitor screen. The bytes of video information are scattered between a handful of memory chips or modules, sliced into several logical pages, and liberally dosed with added-in features such as cursors and sprites. Somehow, all the scattered bytes of data must get organized and find their way to the monitor. In addition, the monitor itself must be brought under the control of the computer, synchronized in two dimensions.

The video controller generates the actual scanning signals. Using the regular oscillations of a crystal, the controller generates a *dot clock*, a frequency corresponding to the rate at which it will scan the data for the pixels to appear on the screen. The controller divides down this basic operating frequency to produce the horizontal synchronizing frequency, and from that, the vertical synchronizing frequency. From these frequencies, the controller can create a monitor signal that lacks only image data. In real time, the controller scans through the memory addresses assigned to each pixel on the screen in the exact order in which each pixel will appear on the screen. The time at which each address gets read exactly matches the time and position the pixel data appears in the final video output signal.

In modern analog computer video systems, the controller doesn't read memory directly. Rather, the digital data scanned by the controller from memory gets routed first through the RAMDAC, which converts the data from digital to analog form. The video controller then adds the analog data to the scanning signals to create the video signal that gets passed along to your monitor.

The video controller may draw pixel data from places other than the frame buffer. The circuits used by computers generate the cursor that appears on the screen in text modes. Or it may add in the bit-values associated with a sprite. By rerouting its scan, it can make hardware windows.

In the language of computer engineering, the part of the video circuitry that performs the actual scanning operation is called the *CRT controller*, because the signals it generates actually control the sweep of the electron beam in the CRT or picture tube of your monitor.

In the first computers, the CRT controller was a separate integrated circuit, the 6845 made by Motorola. This chip originally was not designed for computers but as a generalized scan-maker for any sort of electronic device that might plug in to a television set or monitor. The engineers who designed the first computers chose it because it was a readily available, off-the-shelf product that made the development of video boards relatively easy and cheap. Long ago most video board manufacturers switched to custom-designed and manufactured CRT controllers, often part of other computer video circuitry. Even the most advanced of these chips emulate the 6845 in their basic operating modes. When software calls upon the video system to operate in one of the original computer's modes to display text or low-resolution graphics, all CRT controllers react the same way to basic hardware instructions.

RAMDACs

Modern computer monitors use analog signals so that the signals supplied them do not limit the range of color they can display. The data stored in your computer's frame buffer is digital because…well, everything in your computer is digital. Moreover, no convenient form of analog memory is available. As a result of this divergence of signal types—digital in and analog out—your video board must convert the digital data into analog form compatible with your monitor. The chip that performs this magic is termed a *digital-to-analog converter*. Sometimes it may be referred to as a *RAMDAC*—RAM for *random access memory*—because its digital data originates in memory.

RAMDACs are classified by the number of digital bits in the digital code they translate. The number of bits translates into the number of signal levels that can appear in its output signal. For example, an eight-bit RAMDAC converts the levels encoded in eight-bit digital patterns into 256 analog levels. In a monochrome system, each one of those levels represents a shade of gray.

In color systems, each primary color or channel requires a separate DAC, a total of three. Video RAMDACs usually put all three converter channels into a single package, although some older video boards may use separate DAC chips for each color channel. Total up the number of bits across all three channels of each RAMDAC, and you'll get the number of bit-planes of color a system can display—its *palette*. Most of the RAMDACs in today's video systems have three eight-bit channels, allowing them to generate the 16.7 million hues of True Color.

RAMDACs are also speed rated. The RAMDAC chip must be fast enough to process each pixel that is to be displayed on the screen. The higher the resolution of the image you want to display, the higher the speed required from your RAMDAC. The required speed corresponds directly to the *dot-clock* (the number of pixels on the screen times the refresh rate). To accommodate high-resolution displays, some RAMDACs are rated 200MHz and higher. They don't have to enter the gigahertz stratosphere inhabited by microprocessors, because such speeds are well beyond the needs of any practical video resolution.

Memory

On a video board, memory mostly means *frame buffer*. Every video board includes a good dose of some kind of RAM for holding the bitmap of the image that appears on the screen. In addition, 3D accelerators need memory for their special operations. *Double-buffering*, as the name implies, doubles the memory needs by putting two separate frame buffers to work. Z-buffering and working memory for the calculations of the 3D accelerator also increase the memory needs of the video board.

The requirements of the graphics or 3D accelerator determine the type of memory required. The manufacturer of the video board sets the amount actually included on the board. Some manufacturers provide sockets to allow you to later upgrade to increase the resolution or color depth capabilities of your video system. As memory prices have fallen to the point that sockets are an appreciable fraction of the cost of adding memory, manufacturers have resorted to providing separate board models with differing memory dosages, all soldered down and not upgradable.

Because of the low prices of memory, most display adapters include substantially more memory than even the largest frame buffers require. The memory on display adapters no longer limits the resolution capabilities of the board. But more memory allows the display adapter to implement more speed-enhancing technologies. In other words, a display adapter with more memory generally will be faster.

Displays

You cannot see data. The information that your computer processes is nothing but ideas, and ideas are intangible—no matter whether in your mind or your computer's. Whereas you can visualize your own ideas, you cannot peer directly into the pulsing digital thought patterns of your computer. You probably have no right to think that you could—if you can't read another person's thoughts, you should hardly expect to read the distinctly non-human circuit surges of your computer.

The display is your computer's line of communication to you, much as the keyboard enables you to communicate with it. Like even the best of friends, the display doesn't tell you everything, but it does give you a clear picture, one from which you can draw your own conclusions about what the computer is doing.

Background

Although the terms are often used interchangeably, a display and a monitor are distinctly different. A *display* is the image-producing device itself, the screen that you see. The *monitor* is a complete box that adds support circuitry to the display. This circuitry converts the signals set by the computer (or some other device, such as a videocassette recorder) into the proper form for the display to use. Although most monitors operate under principles like those of the television set, displays can be made from a variety of technologies, including liquid crystals and the photon-glow of some noble gases.

Because of their similar technological foundations, monitors to a great extent resemble the humble old television set. Just as a monitor is a display enhanced with extra circuitry, the television is a monitor with even more signal-conversion electronics. The television incorporates into its design a tuner or demodulator that converts signals broadcast by television stations or a cable television company into about the same form as those signals used by monitors. Beyond the tuner, the television and monitor work in much the same way. Indeed, some old-fashioned computer monitors work as televisions as long as they are supplied the proper signals.

New monitors have developed far beyond their television roots, however. They have greater sharpness and purity of color. To achieve these ends, they operate at higher frequencies than television stations can broadcast.

Computer displays and monitors use a variety of technologies to create visible images. A basic bifurcation once divided the displays of desktop computers and those of laptop machines. All notebook computers and a growing number of desktop machines use the new technology, the flat-panel display. Most use large liquid crystal displays (LCDs). The remaining desktop computers use monitors based on cathode ray tube (CRT) technology. The old-technology monitors earn their desktop home with low prices, higher resolution, and bigger screens than their LCD counterparts.

The glaringly apparent difference between thin LCD panels and fat cathode ray tubes hides far greater internal dissimilarities. About the only characteristic the two technologies share is that they make images. CRTs and LCDs differ not only in how they form images but also how they are viewed and how they are best connected to your computer.

Cathode Ray Technology

The oldest electronic image-generating system still in use is the *cathode ray tube*. The name is purely descriptive. The device is based on a special form of vacuum tube—a glass bottle that is partially evacuated and filled with an inert gas at very low pressure. The tube of the CRT is hardly a tube but more flask-shaped, with a thin neck that broadens like a funnel into a wide, nearly flat face. Although CRTs appear to be made like simple bottles—in fact, people in the monitor business sometimes refer to CRTs as *bottles*—their construction is surprisingly complex and involves a variety of glasses of many thicknesses. The face of the typical CRT, for example, often is about an inch thick.

The *cathode* in the CRT name is a scientific term for a negatively charged electrode. In a CRT, a specially designed cathode shoots a beam or ray of electrons toward a positively charged electrode, the anode. (Electrons, having a negative charge, are naturally attracted to positive potentials.) Because it works like a howitzer for electrons, the cathode of a CRT is often called an *electron gun*.

The electrons race on their way at a substantial fraction of the speed of light, driven by the high-voltage potential difference between the cathode and anode, sometimes as much as 25,000 volts.

At the end of their flight to the anode, the electrons crash into a layer of a coating made from phosphor compounds that has the wondrous property of converting the kinetic energy of the electrons into visible light.

Physical Characteristics

The CRT is a physical entity that you can hold in your hand, drop on the floor, and watch shatter. Little of its design is by chance—nearly every design choice in making the CRT has an effect on the image you see.

Four elements of the CRT exert the greatest influence on the kind and quality of image made by a monitor. The phosphors chosen for the tube affect the color and persistence of the display. The electron guns actually paint the image, and how well they work is a major factor in determining image sharpness. In color CRTs, the shadow mask or aperture grille limits the ultimate resolution of the screen. The face of the screen and the glare reflected from it affect both image contrast and how happy you will be in working with a monitor.

Phosphors

At the end of the electrons' short flight, from the gun in the neck of a CRT to the inside of its wide, flat face, lies a layer of a phosphor-based compound with a wonderful property—it glows when struck by an electron beam. The image you see in a CRT is the glow of the electrically stimulated phosphor compounds, simply termed *phosphors* in the industry. Not all the phosphorous compounds used in CRTs are the same. Different compounds and mixtures glow in various colors and for various lengths of time after being struck by the electron beam.

The type of phosphor determines the color of the image on the screen. Several varieties of amber, green, and whitish phosphors are commonly used in monochrome displays. Color CRT displays use three different phosphors painted in fine patterns across the inner surface of the tube. The patterns are made from dots or stripes of the three additive primary colors—red, green, and blue—arrayed next to one another. A group of three dots is called a *color triad* or *color triplet*.

One triad of dots makes up what's called a *picture element*, often abbreviated as *pixel* (although some manufacturers prefer to shorten picture element to *pel*).

The makers of color monitors individually can choose each of the three colors used in forming the color triads on the screen. Most monitor-makers have adopted the same phosphor family, which is called P22 (or B22, which is the same thing with a different nomenclature), so the basic color capabilities of most multihued monitors are the same.

The color monitor screen can be illuminated in any of its three primary colors by individually hitting the phosphor dots associated with that color with the electron beam. Other colors can be made by illuminating combinations of the primary colors. By varying the intensity of each primary color, the tube can display a nearly infinite spectrum.

Monochrome displays have their CRTs evenly coated with a single, homogenous phosphor so that wherever the electron beam strikes, the tube glows in the same color. The color of the phosphors determines the overall color that the screen glows.

Just as important to screen readability as the phosphor colors is the background color of the display tube. The background area on a color screen—that is, the space in between the phosphor dots—is called the *matrix*. It is never illuminated by the electron beam. The color of the matrix determines the color screen's background color (usually termed *matrix color*)—what it looks like when the power is off, either pale gray, dark green-gray, or nearly black. Darker and black matrixes give an impression of higher contrast to the displayed images. Lighter-gray matrixes make for purer whites. The distinctions are subtle, however, and unless you put two tubes side-by-side, you're unlikely to appreciate the difference.

Color Temperature

If your work involves critical color matching, the color temperature of your monitor can be an important issue. White light is not white, of course, but a mixture of all colors. Alas, all whites are not the same. Some are richer in blue, some in yellow. The different colors of white are described in their color temperature, the number of kelvins (degrees Celsius above absolute zero) that a perfect luminescent body would need to be to emit that color.

Like the incandescence of a hot iron horseshoe in the blacksmith's forge, as its temperature gets higher the hue of a glowing object shifts from red to orange to yellow and on to blue-white. Color temperature simply assigns an absolute temperature rating to these colors. Figure 24.1 shows the effect of color temperature.

FIGURE 24.1

The color temperatures associated with various conditions.

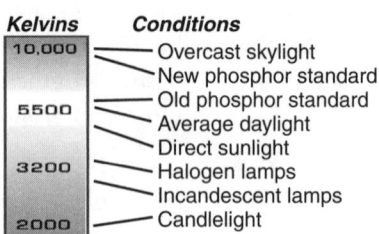

Kelvins	Conditions
10,000	Overcast skylight
	New phosphor standard
	Old phosphor standard
5500	Average daylight
	Direct sunlight
3200	Halogen lamps
	Incandescent lamps
2000	Candlelight

For example, ordinary light bulbs range from 2,700 to 3,400 kelvins. Most fluorescent lights have noncontinuous color spectra rich in certain hues (notably green) while lacking others, which makes assigning a True Color temperature impossible. Other fluorescent lamps are designed to approximate daylight with color temperatures of about 5,000 kelvins.

Monitors are designed to glow with the approximate color temperature of daylight rather than incandescent or fluorescent light. Unfortunately, not everyone has the same definition of daylight. Noonday sun, for instance, ranges from 5,500 to 6,000 kelvins. Overcast days may achieve a color temperature of 10,000 kelvins because the scattered blue glow of the sky (higher color temperature) dominates the yellowish radiation from the sun.

The colors and blend of the phosphors used to make the picture tube screen and the relative strengths of the electron beams illuminating those phosphors determine the color temperature of a monitor. Some engineers believe the perfect day is a soggy, overcast afternoon suited only to ducks and Englishmen and opt to run their monitors with a color temperatures as high as 10,000 kelvins. Others, however, live in a Kodachrome world where the color temperature is the same 5,300 kelvins as a spring day with tulips in the park.

Many monitors now add color temperature to their setup menus, so you can choose whether you want 5000-kelvin or 8500-kelvin white—or something else entirely. Unless you have a need to make precise color matches, the temperature setting you use is only a matter of personal preference.

Electron Guns

To generate the beams that light the phosphors on the screen, a CRT uses one or more electron guns. An electron gun is an electron emitter (a cathode) in an assembly that draws the electrons into a sharp, high-speed beam. To move the beam across the breadth of the tube face (so that the beam doesn't light just a tiny dot in the center of the screen), a group of powerful electromagnets arranged around the tube, called the *yoke*, bend the electron beam in the course of its flight. The magnetic field set up by the yoke is carefully controlled and causes the beam to sweep each individual display line down the face of the tube.

Monochrome CRTs have a single electron gun that continuously sweeps across the screen. Most color tubes have three guns, although some color televisions and monitors boast "one-gun" tubes, which more correctly might be called "three guns in one."

The gun count depends on the definition of a gun. Like all color CRTs, the one-gun tubes have three distinct electron-emitting cathodes that can be individually controlled. The three cathodes are fabricated into a single assembly that allows them to be controlled as if they were generating only a single beam.

In a three-gun tube, the trio of guns is arranged in a triangle. So-called "one-gun" tubes arrange their cathodes in a straight line, often earning the epithet *inline guns*. In theory, inline guns should be easier to set up, but as a practical matter, excellent performance can be derived from either arrangement.

The three guns in a color CRT emit their electrons simultaneously, and the three resulting beams are steered together by force of a group of electromagnets around the neck of the tube called the *yoke*. Monitors provide individual adjustments, both mechanical and electrical, for each of the three beams to ensure that each beam falls exactly on the same triplet of color dots on the screen as the others. Because these controls help the three beams converge on the same triad, they are called *convergence controls*. The process of adjusting them is usually termed color *alignment*.

Convergence

The three electron beams inside any color monitor must converge on exactly the right point on the screen to illuminate a single triad of phosphor dots. If a monitor is not adjusted properly—or if it is not designed or made properly—the three beams cannot converge properly to one point. Poor convergence results in images with rainbow-like shadows and a loss of sharpness and detail. Individual text characters no longer appear sharply defined but become two- or three-color blurs. Monochrome monitors are inherently free from such convergence problems because they have but one electron beam. Figure 24.2 shows the difference between good and poor convergence.

FIGURE 24.2
Excellent (left) and poor convergence on a monitor screen.

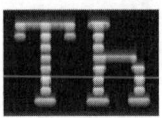 

Convergence problems are a symptom rather than a cause of monitor deficiencies. Convergence problems arise not only from the design of the display but also from the construction and setup of each individual monitor. It can vary widely from one display to the next and may be aggravated by damage during shipping.

The result of convergence problems is most noticeable at the screen periphery because that's where the electron beams are the most difficult to control. When bad, convergence problems can be the primary limit on the sharpness of a given display, having a greater negative effect than wide dot-pitch or low bandwidth (discussed later).

Many monitor-makers claim that their convergence is a given fraction of a millimeter at a particular place on the screen. If a figure is given for more than one screen location, the center of the screen invariably has a lower figure—tighter, better convergence—than a corner of the screen.

The number given is how far one color may spread from another at that location. Lower numbers are better. Typical monitors may claim convergence of about 0.5 (one-half) millimeter at one of the corners of the screen. That figure often rises 50 percent higher than the dot-pitch of the tube, making the convergence the limit on sharpness for that particular monitor.

Misconvergence problems often can be corrected by adjustment of the monitor, usually using the monitor's internal convergence controls. A few, high-resolution (and high-cost) monitors even have external convergence adjustments. But adjusting monitor convergence is a job for the specialist—and that means getting a monitor converged can be expensive, as is any computer service call.

Many monitor-makers now claim that their products are converged for life. Although this strategy should eliminate the need to adjust them, it also makes it mandatory to test your display before you buy it. You don't want a display that's been badly converged for life.

Purity

The ability of a monitor to show you an evenly lit screen that does not vary in color across its width is termed *purity*. A monitor with good purity will be able to display a pure white screen without a hint of color appearing. A monitor with poor purity will be tinged with one color or another in large patches. Figure 24.3 illustrates the screens with good and poor purity.

FIGURE 24.3
Comparison of good and bad monitor purity.

Excellent purity

Poor purity

Poor purity often results from the shadow mask or aperture grille of a cathode ray tube becoming magnetized. Degaussing the screen usually cures the problem. Most larger monitors have built-in automatic *degaussers*.

You can degauss your monitor with a degaussing loop designed for color televisions or even a bulk tape eraser. Energize the degaussing coil or tape eraser in close proximity to the screen, then gradually remove the coil to a distance of three or more feet away before switching it off. The gradually declining alternating magnetic field will overpower the static field on the mask, and the gradual removal of the alternating field prevents the strong field from establishing itself on the mask.

Shadow Masks

Just pointing the electron beams at the right dots is not enough, because part of the beam can spill over and hit the other dots in the triplet. The result of this spillover is a loss of color purity—bright hues become muddied. To prevent this effect and make images as sharp and colorful as possible, most color CRTs used in computer displays and televisions alike have a *shadow mask*—a metal sheet with fine perforations in it—located inside the display tube and a small distance behind the phosphor coating of the screen.

The shadow mask and the phosphor dot coating on the CRT screen are critically arranged so that the electron beam can only hit phosphor dots of one color. The other two colors of dots are in the "shadow" of the mask and cannot be seen by the electron beam.

The spacing of the holes in the shadow mask to a great degree determines the quality of the displayed image. For the geometry of the system to work, the phosphor dots on the CRT screen must be spaced at the same distance as the holes in the mask. Because the hole spacing determines the dot spacing, it is often termed the *dot-pitch* of the CRT.

The dot-pitch of a CRT is simply a measurement of the distance between dots of the same color. It is an absolute measurement, independent of the size of the tube or the size of the displayed image.

The shadow mask affects the brightness of a monitor's image in two ways. The size of the holes in the mask limits the size of the electron beam getting through to the phosphors. Off-axis from the guns—that is, toward the corners of the screen—the round holes appear oval to the gun and less of the beam can get through. As a result, the corners of a shadow mask screen are often dimmer than the center, although the brightness difference may not be distinguishable.

The mask also limits how high the electron beam intensity can be in a given CRT. A stronger beam—which makes a brighter image—holds more energy. When the beam strikes the mask, part of that energy is absorbed by the mask and becomes heat, which raises the temperature of the mask. In turn, this temperature rise makes the mask expand unpredictably, distorting it minutely and blurring the image. To minimize this heat-induced blur, monitor-makers are moving toward making shadow masks from materials that have a low coefficient of thermal expansion. That is, they change size as little as possible with temperature. The alloy Invar is favored for shadow masks because of its capability to maintain a nearly constant size as it warms.

Aperture Grilles

With all the problems associated with shadow masks, you might expect someone to come up with a better idea. Sony Corporation did exactly that, inventing the Trinitron picture tube.

The Trinitron uses an *aperture grille*—slots between a vertical array of wires—instead of a mask. The phosphors are painted on the inner face of the tube as interleaved stripes of the three additive primary colors. The grille blocks the electron beam from the wrong stripes, just as a shadow-mask blocks it from the wrong dots. The distance between two sequential stripes of the same color is governed by the spacing of the slots between the wires—the slot-pitch of the tube. Because the electron beam fans out as it travels away from the electron gun and because stripes are farther from the gun than is the mask, the stripes are spaced a bit farther apart than the slot-pitch. Their spacing is termed *screen-pitch*. For example, a 0.25-millimeter slot-pitch Trinitron might have a screen-pitch of 0.26 millimeters. Figure 24.4 shows how dot-pitch and slot-pitch are measured.

FIGURE 24.4
Measuring dot-pitch and slot-pitch.

Dot-pitch

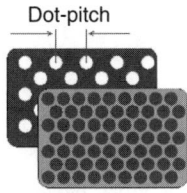

Shadow mask

Slot-pitch

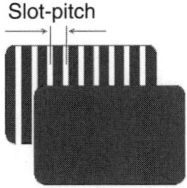

Aperture grille

The wires of the aperture grille are quite thick, about two-thirds the width of the slot-pitch. For example, in a Trinitron with a 0.25-millimeter slot-pitch, the grille wires measure about 0.18 millimeters in diameter because each electron beam is supposed to illuminate only one-third of the screen. The wires shadow the other two-thirds from the beam to maintain the purity of the color.

The aperture grille wires are held taut, but they can vibrate. Consequently, Trinitron monitors have one or two thin tensioning wires running horizontally across the screen. Although quite fine, these wires cast a shadow on the screen that is most apparent on light-colored screen backgrounds. Some people find the tensioning wire shadows objectionable, so you should look closely at a Trinitron before buying.

Trinitrons hold a theoretical brightness advantage over shadow-mask tubes. Because the slots allow more electrons to pass through to the screen than do the tiny holes of a shadow mask, a Trinitron can (in theory) create a brighter image. This added brightness is not borne out in practice. However, Trinitrons do excel in keeping their screens uniformly bright. The aperture grille wires of a Trinitron block the beam only in one dimension, and they don't impinge as much on the electron beam at the screen edges.

Required Dot-Pitch

Regardless of whether a monitor uses a shadow mask with a dot-pitch or an aperture grille with a slot-pitch, the spacing of image triads on the screen is an important constituent in monitor quality. A monitor simply cannot put dots any closer together than the holes in the mask or grille allow. It's easy to compute the pitch necessary for a resolution level in a computer system. Just divide the screen size by the number of dots required to be displayed.

For example, a typical small display measures 14 inches diagonally. A horizontal line stretching across the full width of such a screen would measure 11.2 inches or about 285 millimeters. To properly display an SVGA image (800 pixels by 600 pixels) would require a dot-pitch of 0.36 millimeters or smaller (that is, 285/800 of a millimeter or less). Often a monitor's image is somewhat smaller than full screen width and such displays require an even finer dot-pitch. The larger the display, the coarser the dot-pitch can be for a given level of resolution.

Line Width

Another factor limits the sharpness of monitor images: the width of the lines drawn on the screen. Ideally, any vertical or horizontal line on the screen will appear exactly one pixel wide, but in practical monitors, the width of a line may not be so compliant. If lines are narrower than one pixel wide, thin black lines will separate adjacent white lines and wide white areas will be thinly striped in black. If the line width exceeds the size of a pixel, the display's ability to render fine detail will be lost.

The ideal line width for a monitor varies with the size of the screen and the resolution displayed on the screen. As resolution increases, lines must be narrower. As screen size goes up (with the resolution constant), line width must increase commensurately. You can calculate the required line width the same way as for the preceding dot-pitch example. The line width should equal the maximum dot-pitch you calculate. In other words, for the preceding 14-inch screen at SVGA resolution, you'd want a line width of 0.36 millimeters.

Several factors influence the width of lines on the screen. The monitor must be able to focus its electron beam into a line of ideal width. However, width also varies with the brightness of the beam—brighter beams naturally tend to expand out of focus. Consequently, when you increase the brightness of your monitor, the sharpness of the image may decline. For this reason, test laboratories usually make monitor measurements at a standardized brightness level.

Screen Curvature

Most CRTs have a distinctive shape. At one end, a narrow neck contains the electron gun or guns. Around the neck fits the deflection yoke, an external assembly that generates the magnetic fields that bend the electron beams to sweep across the inner surface of the wide face of the tube. The tube emerges from the yoke as a funnel-like flaring, which enlarges to the rectangular face of the screen itself. This face often (but becoming much less common) is a spherically curving surface.

The spherical curve of the face makes sense for a couple of reasons. It makes the distance traveled by the electron beam more consistent at various points on the screen, edge to center to edge. A truly flat screen would require the beam to travel farther at the edges than at the center and would require the beam to strike the face of the screen obliquely, resulting in image distortion. Although this distortion can be compensated for electrically, the curving screen helps things along.

In addition, the CRT is partly evacuated, so normal atmospheric pressure is constantly trying to crush the tube. The spherical surface helps distribute this potentially destructive force more evenly, making the tube stronger.

Screen curvature has a negative side effect. Straight lines on the screen appear straight only from one observation point. Move your head closer, farther away, or to one side, and the supposedly straight lines of your graphic images will bow this way and that.

Technology has made the reasons underlying spherical curved screens less than compelling. The geometry of inline guns simplifies tube construction and alignment sufficiently that cylindrically curved screens are feasible. They have fewer curvilinear problems because they warp only one axis of the image. Trinitrons characteristically have faces with cylindrical curves. Most shadow-mask tubes have spherical faces.

In the last few years, the technical obstacles to making genuinely flat screens have been surmounted. Besides the easier geometry offered by true flat-screen CRTs, they bring another benefit. The curved screen on conventional tubes reflects light from nearly the entire area in front of the tube. No matter where you point the display, it's sure to pick up some glare. True flat-screen tubes reflect glare over a very narrow angle. If you point a flat-screen display slightly downward, most of the room glare will reflect down onto your keyboard and away from your eyes.

Resolution Versus Addressability

The resolution of a video system refers to the fineness of detail that it can display. It is a direct consequence of the number of individual dots that make up the screen image and is therefore a function of both the screen size and the dot-pitch.

Because the size and number of dots limit the image quality, the apparent sharpness of screen images can be described by the number of dots that can be displayed horizontally and vertically across the screen. For example, the resolution required by the Video Graphics Array system in its standard graphics mode is 640 dots horizontally by 480 vertically. Modern display systems may produce images with as many as 1600×1200 dots in their highest resolution mode.

Sometimes, however, the resolution available on the screen and that made by a computer's display adapter are not the same. For example, a video mode designed for the resolution capabilities of a color television set hardly taps the quality available from a computer monitor. On the other hand, the computer-generated graphics may be designed for a display system that's sharper than the one being used. You might, for instance, try to use a television in lieu of a more expensive monitor. The sharpness you actually see would then be less than what the resolution of the video system would have you believe.

Resolution is a physical quality of the video display system—the monitor—that's actually being used. It sets the ultimate upper limit on the display quality. In color systems, the chief limit on resolution is purely physical—the convergence of the system and the dot-pitch of the tube. In monochrome systems, which have no quality-limiting shadow masks, the resolution is limited by the bandwidth of the monitor, the highest frequency signal with which it can deal. (Finer details pack more information into the signals sent from computer system to monitor. The more information in a given time, the higher the frequency of the signal.)

Addressability is essentially a bandwidth measurement for color monitors. It indicates how many different dots on the screen the monitor can point its electron guns at. It ignores, however, the physical limit imposed by the shadow mask. In other words, addressability describes the highest quality signals the monitor can handle, but the full quality of those signals is not necessarily visible to you onscreen.

Anti-Glare Treatment

Most mirrors are made from glass, and glass tries to mimic the mirror whenever it can. Because of the difference between the index of refraction of air and that of glass, glass is naturally reflective. If you make mirrors, that's great. If you make monitors—or worse yet, use them—the reflectivity of glass can be a big headache. A reflection of a room light or window from the glass face of the CRT can easily be brighter than the glow of phosphors inside. As a result, the text or graphics on the display tend to "wash out" or be obscured by the brightness.

The greater the curvature of a monitor screen, the more apt it is to have a problem with reflections. You can't change the curve of your monitor's face, but anti-glare treatments can reduce or eliminate reflections from the monitor face. Several glare-reduction technologies are available, and each varies somewhat in its effectiveness.

Mesh

The lowest tech and least expensive anti-glare treatment is simply a fabric mesh, usually nylon. The mesh can either be placed directly atop the face of the screen or in a removable frame that fits about half an inch in front of the screen. Each hole in the mesh acts like a short tube, allowing you to see straight in at the tube, but cutting off light from the sides of the tube. Your straight-on vision gets through unimpeded, while glare that angles in doesn't make it to the screen.

As simple as this technique is, it works amazingly well. The least expensive after-market anti-glare system uses mesh suspiciously similar to pantyhose stretched across a frame. Unfortunately, this mesh has an unwanted side effect. Besides blocking the glare, it also blocks some of the light from the screen and makes the image appear darker. You may have to turn the brightness control up to compensate, which may make the image bloom and lose sharpness.

Mechanical

Glare can be reduced by mechanical means—not by a machine that automatically intercepts glare before it reaches the screen, but by mechanical preparation of the screen surface. By lightly grinding the glass on the front of the CRT, the face of the screen can be made to scatter rather than reflect light. Each rough spot on the screen that results from the mechanical grinding process reflects light randomly, sending it every which direction. A smooth screen reflects a patch of light all together, like a mirror, reflecting any bright light source into your eyes. Because the light scattered by the ground glass is dispersed, less of it reaches your eyes and the glare is not as bright. However, because the coarse screen surface disperses the light coming from inside the tube as well as that reflected from the tube face, it also lessens the sharpness of the image. The mechanical treatment makes text appear slightly fuzzier and out of focus, which to some manufacturers is a worse problem than glare.

Coating

Engineers can reduce the glare reflected from a CRT screen by applying a coating with dispersive or interference properties to the screen. A dispersive coating forms a rough film on the face of the CRT. This rough surface acts in the same way as a ground-glass screen would, scattering light that would otherwise reflect back as glare. An optical interference coating cancels out reflections.

Interference coatings work by reflecting light between multiple thin layers of a compound, such as magnesium fluoride. By precisely controlling the thickness of this coating, light can be made to reflect in such a way its waves cancel out. The fluoride coating is made to be a quarter the wavelength of light (usually of light at the middle of the spectrum). Light going through the fluoride and reflecting from the screen thus emerges from the coating out of phase with the light striking the fluoride surface, visually canceling out the glare. Multiple layers are tuned to the different frequencies of the colors of visible light. Camera lenses are coated to achieve exactly the same purpose, the elimination of reflections. A proper interference coating can minimize glare without affecting image sharpness or brightness.

Polarization

Light can be *polarized*—that is, its photons can be restricted to a single plane of oscillation. A polarizing filter allows light of only one polarization to pass. Two polarizing filters in a row can be arranged to allow light of only one plane of polarization to pass (by making the planes of polarization of the filters parallel), or the two filters can stop light entirely when their planes of polarization are perpendicular.

The first filter lets only one kind of light pass; the second filter lets only another kind of light pass. Because none of the second kind of light reaches the second filter, no light gets by.

When light is reflected from a surface, its polarization is shifted by 90 degrees. This physical principle makes polarizing filters excellent reducers of glare.

A sheet of polarizing material is merely placed a short space in front of a display screen. Light from a potential source of glare goes through the screen and is polarized. When it strikes the display and is reflected, its polarization is shifted 90 degrees. When it again reaches the filter, it is out of phase with the filter and cannot get through. Light from the display, however, only needs to go through the filter once. Although this glow is polarized, there is no second screen to impede its flow to your eyes.

Every anti-glare treatment has its disadvantage. Mesh makes an otherwise sharp screen look fuzzy, because smooth characters are broken up by the cell structure of the mesh. Mechanical treatments are expensive and tend to make the screen appear to be slightly fuzzy or out of focus. The same is true of coatings that rely on the dispersion principle. Optical coatings, polarizing filters, and even mesh suffer from their own reflections. The anti-glare material itself may add its own bit of glare. In addition, all anti-glare treatments—polarizing filters in particular—tend to make displays dimmer. The polarizing filter actually reduces the brightness of a display to one-quarter its untreated value.

Even with their shortcomings, however, anti-glare treatments are amazingly effective. They can ease eyestrain and eliminate the headaches that come with extended computer use.

Deflection Angle

Another difference between CRTs is their *deflection angle*, which measures the maximum degree the tube allows its electron beam to bend. This corresponds to the angle at which the tube flares out. A tube with a narrow deflection angle will be long with a small screen. A wide deflection angle permits large screens with shorter tubes. Ideally, the best tube would be the shortest, but as the deflection angle increases, it becomes more difficult to control the electron beam and make a perfect image. Consequently, lower deflection angles usually produce better images. Improved technology has allowed deflection angles to increase while maintaining image quality. This allows monitors to be shorter and take up less desk space.

A monitor can deflect the electron beam inside its CRT both left and right of the centerline path the beam would take without deflection. By custom, the deflection angle listed for a given CRT is the total deflection from maximum left to maximum right. Until the late 1990s, nearly all computer monitors used CRTs with deflection angles of 90 degrees. Television sets, which can get by with less image quality, typically use 110-degree tubes. In 1999, computer monitors with 100-degree tubes began to enter the market.

Image Characteristics

The electronics of a monitor control the size, shape, and other aspects of the image displayed on a monitor's screen. The image qualities are defined and characterized in a number of ways. The most rudimentary is screen size—the bigger your monitor screen, the larger the images it can make. Because of the underscanning common among computer monitors, however, the actual image size is almost always smaller than the screen. The aspect ratio of the image describes its shape independent of its size. Most monitors give you a variety of controls to alter the size and shape of the image, so you are the final arbiter of what things look like on your monitor screen.

Screen Size

The most significant measurement of a CRT-based monitor is the size of its screen. Although seemingly straightforward, screen size has been at best an ambiguous measurement and at worst downright misleading.

The confusion all started with television, where confusion often begins. The very first television sets had round CRTs, and their size was easy to measure—simply the diameter of the tube. When rectangular tubes became prevalent in the 1950s, the measurement shifted to the diagonal of the face of the tube. The diagonal was, of course, the closest equivalent to the diameter of an equivalent round tube. It was also the largest dimension that a television manufacturer could reasonably quote.

Unlike television images, which usually cover the entire face of the CRT, computer monitors limit their images to somewhat less. The image is most difficult to control at the edges of the screen, so monitor-makers maintain higher quality by restricting the size of the image. They mask off the far edges of the CRT with the bezel of the monitor case.

That bezel means that no image can fill the entire screen—at least no image that you can entirely see. The tube size becomes irrelevant to a realistic appraisal of the image. Some monitor-makers persisted in using it to describe their products. Fortunately most of the industry recognized this measuring system as optimistic exaggeration and began using more realistic diagonal measurement of the actual maximum displayable image area.

VESA adopted the diagonal of the maximum image area as the measurement standard in its Video Image Area Definition standard, version 1.1, which it published on October 26, 1995. This standard requires that the screen image area be given as horizontal and vertical measurements of the actual active image area when the monitor is set up by the manufacturer using the manufacturer's test signals. The dimensions must be given in millimeters, with an assumed maximum variance of error of plus or minus two percent. Wider tolerances are allowed but must be explicitly stated by the manufacturer. In no case can the expressed image dimensions exceed the area visible through the monitor bezel.

Because the aspect ratio of computer monitor displays is 4:3, computation of the horizontal and vertical screen dimensions from the diagonal is easy. The diagonal represents the hypotenuse of a 3-4-5 right triangle, and that ratio applies to all screen sizes. Table 24.2 lists the dimensions for the most common nominal screen sizes.

TABLE 24.2 Nominal CRT Screen Dimensions

Diagonal	Horizontal Millimeters	Vertical Inches	Horizontal	Vertical
14 inches	284	213	11.2	8.4
15 inches	305	229	12	9
16 inches	325	244	12.8	9.6
17 inches	345	259	13.6	10.2
20 inches	406	305	16	12
21 inches	427	320	16.8	12.6

Portrait displays, which are designed to give you a view more like the printed sheets that roll out of your laser printer and into envelopes, merely take an ordinary CRT and turn it on its side. The market is not large enough to justify development of custom CRTs for portrait applications. Moreover, the 4:3 aspect ratio works fine because the "active" image on a sheet of letterhead—the space actually occupied by printing once you slice off the top, bottom, left, and right margins—is about eight by ten inches, a nearly perfect fit on a standard picture tube. When measuring the images on these portrait displays, horizontal becomes vertical, and all measurements rotate 90 degrees.

Overscan and Underscan

Two monitors with the same-size screens may have entirely different onscreen image sizes. Composite monitors are often afflicted by *overscan*—they attempt to generate images larger than their screen size, and the edges and corners of the active display area may be cut off. (The overscan is often designed in so that as the components inside the monitor age and become weaker, the picture shrinks down to normal size—likely over a period of years.) *Underscan* is the opposite condition—the image is smaller than nominal screen size. For a given screen size, an overscanned image will appear larger at the expense of clipping off the corners and edges of the image as well as increasing distortion at the periphery of the image. Underscanning wastes some of the active area of the monitor screen. Figure 24.5 illustrates the effects of underscanning and overscanning on the same size screen.

FIGURE 24.5
Underscan and over-scan compared.

Underscan is perfectly normal on computer displays and does not necessarily indicate any underlying problems unless it is severe—for example, when it leaves a two-inch black band encircling the image. Underscanning helps keep quality high because image geometry is easier to control nearer to the center of the screen than it is at the edges. Pulling in the reigns on the image can ensure that straight lines actually are displayed straight. Moreover, if you extend the active image to the very edge of the bezel and you change your viewing position so that you are not facing the screen straight on, the edge of the image may get hidden behind the bezel. The glass in the face of the screen is thicker than you might think, on the order of an inch (25 millimeters), enough that the third dimension will interfere with your most careful alignment.

On the other hand, whereas overscan gives you a larger image and is the common display mode for video systems, it is not a good idea for computer monitor images. Vital parts of the image may be lost behind the bezel. You may lose the first character or two from each line of type of one edge of a drafting display to overscan. With video, however, people prefer to see as big an image as possible and usually pay little attention to what goes on at the periphery. Broadcasters, in fact, restrict the important part of the images they deal with to a "safe area" that will be completely viewable, even on televisions with substantial overscan.

Aspect Ratio

The relationship between the width and height of a monitor screen is termed its *aspect ratio*. Today, the shape of the screen of nearly every monitor is standardized, as is that of the underlying CRT that makes the image. The screen is 1.33 times wider than it is high, resulting in the same 4:3 aspect ratio used in television and motion pictures before the wide-screen phenomenon took over. Modern engineers now prefer to put the vertical number first to produce aspect ratios that are less than one. Expressed in this way, video has a 3:4 aspect ratio, a value of 0.75.

The choice of aspect ratio is arbitrary and a matter of aesthetics. According to classical Greek aesthetics, the *Golden Ratio* with a value of about 0.618 is the most beautiful. The exact value of the Golden Ratio is irrational, (SQRT(5)-1)/2. Its beauty is mathematical as well as aesthetic, the solution to the neat little equation x+1 = 1/x. (Hardly coincidental, expressed as a ratio of horizontal to vertical, the Golden Ratio becomes 1.618, the solution to x-1 = 1/x.)

Various display systems feature their own aspect ratios. The modern tendency is toward wider aspect ratios. For example, High Definition Television (HDTV) stretches its aspect ratio from the 3:4 of normal video and television to 9:16. The normal negatives you make with your 35 mm camera have a 4:6 aspect ratio. (These numbers are often reversed—for example, 16:9 for HDTV—but they refer to the same screen shape, which has a longer horizontal axis than vertical axis.) The reason video is so nearly square carries over from the early days of television when cathode ray tubes had circular faces. The squarer the image, the more of the circular screen was put to use. Figure 24.6 compares the aspect ratios of three common display systems.

FIGURE 24.6
Aspect ratios of display systems.

The image on your monitor screen need not have the same aspect ratio as the tube, however. The electronics of monitors separate the circuitry that generates the horizontal and vertical scanning signals and results in their independent control. As a result, the relationship between the two can be adjusted, and that adjustment results in an alteration of the aspect ratio of the actual displayed image. For example, by increasing the amplification of the horizontal signal, the width of the image is stretched, thus raising the aspect ratio.

Image Sizing

Normally you set up your monitor to display the best possible image at the resolution you use most often. Most people leave their monitors locked at one resolution level.

Those who change resolution settings often run into a problem—the monitor produces different size images at different resolution levels. Images with more dots are larger than those with fewer.

Monitor-makers developed *autosizing* technology to compensate for changes in resolution. Autosizing works by examining the video signal and automatically adjusting the monitor to compensate for different line widths and screen heights. True autosizing works regardless of the signal going to the monitor and scales the image to match the number of display lines.

Image Distortion

Between the electron guns and the phosphors in a cathode ray tube, the electron beam passes through an electronic lens and deflection system that focuses and steers the beam to ensure that its path across the screen is the proper size and in the proper place. The electronics of the monitor control the lens and deflection system, adjusting it throughout the sweep of the electron beam across the screen. In addition to other chores, the electronics must compensate for the difference in the path of the electron beam at different screen positions. Modern monitors do a magnificent job of controlling beam placement.

When the control system is not properly adjusted, however, the image may exhibit any of a number of defects. Because these defects distort the image from its desired form, they are collectively called *image distortion*.

The two most common forms of image distortion are barrel distortion and pincushion distortion. *Barrel distortion* causes vertical or horizontal lines in the image to bow outward so that the center of the lines lies closer to the nearest parallel edge of the screen. *Pincushion distortion* causes the vertical or horizontal lines in the image to bow inward so that the center of the lines is closer to the center of the screen. Figure 24.7 shows these two kinds of image distortion.

FIGURE 24.7
Barrel and pincushion distortion.

  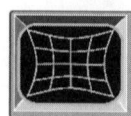

No distortion   Barrel   Pincushion

Barrel and pincushion distortion arise from the same cause—improper image compensation—and are essentially opposites of one another. Overcompensate for pincushion distortion and you get barrel distortion. Collectively, the two are sometimes simply called *pincushioning*, no matter which way the lines bow.

Pincushioning is always worse closer the edges of the image. All monitors have adjustments to compensate for pincushioning, although these adjustments are not always available to you. They may be hidden inside the monitor. Other monitors may include pincushioning adjustments in their control menus. Technicians usually use test patterns that display a regular grid on the screen to adjust monitors to minimize pincushioning. You can usually use a full-screen image to adjust the pincushioning controls so that the edges of the desktop background color are parallel with the bezel of your monitor.

Less common is *trapezoidal distortion*, which leaves lines at the outer edge of the screen straight but not parallel to the bezel. In other words, instead of your desktop being a rectangle, it is a trapezoid with one side shorter than its opposite side. As with pincushioning, all monitors have controls for trapezoidal distortion but not all make them available to you as the user of the monitor. If your monitor does have an external control for trapezoidal distortion, you adjust it as you do for pincushioning.

Image Controls

A few monitors (far from a majority) make coping with underscan, overscan, and odd aspect ratios simply a matter of twisting controls. These displays feature horizontal and vertical size (or gain) controls that enable you to adjust the size and shape of the image to suit your own tastes. With these controls—providing they have adequate range—you can make the active image touch the top, bottom, and sides of the screen bezel, or you can shrink the bright area of your display to a tiny (but geometrically perfect) patch in the center of your screen.

Size and position controls give you command of how much screen the image on your monitor fills. With full-range controls, you can expand the image to fill the screen from corner to corner or reduce it to a smaller size that minimizes the inevitable geometric distortion that occurs near the edges of the tube. A full complement of controls includes one each of the following: horizontal position (sometimes termed *phase*), vertical position, horizontal size (sometimes called *width*), and vertical size (or *height*).

A wide control range is better than a narrow one. Some monitors skimp on one or more controls and limit you in how large you can make the onscreen image. Worse, sometimes a monitor-maker doesn't include a control at all. For example, some monitors have no horizontal size controls. As a result, you cannot adjust both the size and aspect ratio of the image.

The optimum position for these controls is on the front panel, where you can adjust them and view the image at the same time. Controls on the rear panel require you to have gorilla-like arms to reach around the monitor to make adjustments while checking their effect.

Image controls come in two types: analog and digital. Analog controls are the familiar old knobs like you find on vintage television sets. Twist one way and the image gets bigger; twist the other and it shrinks. Analog controls have one virtue—just by looking at the knob you know where they are set, whether at one or the other extreme of their travel. The control itself is a simple memory system; it stays put until you move it again. Analog controls, however, become dirty and wear out with age, and they usually enable you to set just one value per knob—one value that must cover all the monitor's operating modes.

Digital controls give you pushbutton control over image parameters. Press one button, and the image gets larger or moves to the left. Another compensates in the opposite direction. Usually digital controls are linked with a microprocessor, memory, and mode-sensing circuitry so that you can preset different image heights and widths for every video standard your monitor can display.

Digital controls don't get noisy with age and are more reliable and repeatable, but you never know when you are approaching the limit of their travel. Most have two-speed operation—hold them in momentarily and they make minute changes; keep holding them down and they shift gears to make gross changes. Of course, if you don't anticipate the shift, you'll overshoot the setting you want and spend a few extra moments zeroing in on the exact setting.

Most CRT-based displays also carry over several controls from their television progenitors. Nearly every computer monitor has a brightness control, which adjusts the level of the scanning electron beam; this in turn makes the onscreen image glow brighter or dimmer. The contrast control adjusts the linearity of the relationship between the incoming signal and the onscreen image brightness. In other words, it controls the brightness relationship that results from different signal levels—how much brighter high-intensity is. In a few displays, both the brightness and contrast functions are combined into a single "picture" control. Although a godsend to those who might get confused by having to twiddle two knobs, the combined control also limits your flexibility in adjusting the image to best suit your liking.

Flat-Panel Display Technology

Throughout the age of television, predictions of the future have almost universally included big, flat TV screens. Almost as soon as the first CRTs cast their blue spells in living rooms across the world, everyone knew they were only temporary technology.

Something better would soon come along. Of course, at the same time pundits predicted an autogyro in every garage.

Although engineers never pursued the dream of the personal autogyro, they have attacked the flat-screen challenge with verve and a variety of approaches. None of the results quite takes television to reaches, along with that autogyro, that are still whispering siren-like from the land of to-be. CRTs are impractical for portable computers, as anyone who has toted a forty-pound first-generation portable computer knows. The glass in the tube itself weighs more than most of today's portable machines, and running a CRT steals more power than most laptop or notebook machines budget for all their circuitry and peripherals.

LCD

The winner in the display technology competition was the liquid crystal display, the infamous LCD. Unlike LED and gas-plasma displays, which glow on their own emitting photons of visible light, LCDs don't waste energy by shining. Instead, they merely block light otherwise available. To make patterns visible, they either selectively block reflected light (reflective LCDs) or the light generated by a secondary source either behind the LCD panel (backlit LCDs) or adjacent to it (edgelit LCDs). The backlight source is typically an electroluminescent (EL) panel, although some laptops use cold-cathode fluorescent (CCF) panels for brighter, whiter displays with the penalty of higher cost, greater thickness, and increased complexity.

Nematic Technology

A number of different terms describe the technologies used in the LCD panels themselves, terms such as supertwist, double-supertwist, and triple-supertwist. In effect, the twist of the crystals controls the contrast of the screen, so triple-supertwist screens are "contrastier" than ordinary supertwist.

The history of laptop and notebook computer displays has been led by innovations in LCD technology. Invented by RCA in the 1960s (General Electric still receives royalties on RCA's basic patents), LCDs came into their own with laptop computers because of their low power requirements, light weight, and ruggedness.

An LCD display is actually a sandwich made from two plastic sheets with a very special liquid made from rod-shaped or nematic molecules. One important property of the nematic molecules of liquid crystals is that they can be aligned by grooves in the plastic to bend the polarity of light that passes through them. More importantly, the amount of bend the molecules of the liquid crystal give to the light can be altered by applying an electrical current through them.

Ordinary light has no particular orientation, so liquid crystals don't visibly alter it. But polarized light aligns all the oscillations of its photons in a single direction. A polarizing filter creates polarized light by allowing light of a particular polarity (or axis of oscillation) to pass through. Polarization is key to the function of LCDs.

To make an LCD, light is first passed through one polarizing filter to polarize it. A second polarizing filter, set to pass light at right angles to the polarity of the first, is put on the other side of the liquid crystal. Normally, this second polarizing filter stops all light from passing. However, the liquid crystal bends the polarity of light emerging from the first filter so that it lines up with the second filter. Pass a current through the liquid crystal and the amount of bending changes, which alters in turn the amount of light passing through the second polarizer.

To make an LCD display, you need only to selectively apply current to small areas of the liquid crystal. The areas to which you apply current are dark; those that you don't are light. A light behind the LCD makes the changes more visible.

Over the past few years, engineers have made several changes to this basic LCD design to improve its contrast and color. The basic LCD design outlined thus far is technically termed *twisted nematic* (TN) technology. The liquid molecules of the TN display in their resting state always bend light by 90 degrees, exactly counteracting the relationship between the two polarizing panels that make up the display.

By increasing the bending of light by the nematic molecules, the contrast between light and dark can be increased. An LCD design that bends light by 180 to 270 degrees is termed a *supertwist nematic* (or simply *supertwist*) display. One side effect of the added twist is that the appearance of color artifacts results in the yellowish green and bright blue hues of many familiar LCD displays.

This tinge of color can be canceled simply by mounting two supertwist liquid crystals back-to-back so that one bends the light the opposite direction of the other. This design is logically termed a *double-supertwist nematic* (or simply *double-supertwist*) display. This was once used for laptop computers but is not currently used for several reasons—not the least of which is the lack of color. In addition, because two layers of LCD are between you and the light source, double-supertwist panels appear darker or require brighter backlights for adequate visibility. That's why most notebook computers need backlights for their screens.

Triple-supertwist nematic displays instead compensate for color-shifts in the supertwist design by layering both sides of the liquid crystal with thin polymer films. Because the films absorb less light than the twin panels of double-supertwist screens, less backlight—and less backlight power—is required for the same screen brightness.

Cholesteric Technology

In 1996, the Liquid Crystal Institute of Kent State University developed another liquid crystal technology into a workable display system and began its commercial manufacture. Termed *cholesteric LCDs*, this design uses crystals that switch between transmissive and reflective states instead of twisting. These changes are more directly visible and require no polarizers to operate. In that polarizing panels reduce the brightness of nematic displays by as much as 75 percent, cholesteric LCDs can be brighter. Early screens are able to achieve high contrast ratios without backlights.

Cholesteric screens have a second advantage. They are bi-stable. That is, maintaining a given pixel in either the transmissive or reflective phase requires no energy input. Once switched on, a pixel stays on until switched off. The screen requires power only to change pixels. In fact, a cholesteric screen will retain its last image even after it is switched off. Power usage in notebook computer applications are likely to be as low as 10 percent of nematic panels.

Passive Matrix

Nematic LCDs also come in two styles, based on how the current that aligns their nematic molecules is applied. Most LCD panels have a grid of horizontal and vertical conductors, and each pixel is located at the intersection of these conductors. The pixel is darkened simply by sending current through the conductors to the liquid crystal. This kind of display is called a *passive matrix*.

Active Matrix

The alternate design, the *active matrix*, is more commonly referred to as *Thin Film Transistor* (TFT) technology. This style of LCD puts a transistor at every pixel. The transistor acts as a relay. A small current is sent to it through the horizontal and vertical grid, and in response the transistor switches on a much higher current to activate the LCD pixel.

The advantage of the active matrix design is that a smaller current needs to traverse the grid, so the pixel can be switched on and off faster. Whereas passive LCD screens may update only about half a dozen times per second, TFT designs can operate at ordinary monitor speeds—ten times faster. That increased speed equates to faster response—for example, your mouse won't disappear as you move it across the screen.

The disadvantage of the TFT design is that it requires the fabrication of one transistor for each screen pixel. Putting those transistors there requires combining the LCD and semiconductor manufacturing processes. That's sort of like getting bricklayers and carpenters to work together. Even so, manufacturers have lowered production costs so that nearly all LCDs in new computers and monitors use active matrix designs.

Double-Scanned Displays

To achieve the quality of active matrix displays without paying the price, engineers at one time opted to up the scan on passive panels. Double-scanned passive displays work exactly like the name says: They scan their screens twice in the period that a normal screen is scanned only once. Rather than go over each pixel two times, a double-scanned display divides its screen into two halves and scans the two halves at the same time. The idea is something like the interlacing of CRT screens, lowering the required scanning frequency, but the arrangement and effect are different. Double-scanned displays split the screen in the middle into upper and lower halves. The split means that each pixel gets twice as long for updates as would be the case if the whole screen were scanned at the same frequency. As a result, double-scanning can eke out extra brightness, contrast, and speed. These screens do not, however, reach the quality level set by active matrix screens. Consequently, they have dropped from favor in step with the drop in active-matrix pricing.

Sometimes manufacturers use the abbreviation *DSTN* to indicate double-scanned displays. It is an acronym for *double-scanned supertwist nematic*. HPA, which stands for *high performance addressing*, is an improved double-scanned technology. Note that both DSTN and HPA display systems use passive matrix technology.

Response Time

The LCD panel equivalent of persistence is *response time*. Charging and discharging individual pixels requires a finite period, and the response time measures this period. The time to charge and the time to discharge a given pixel can be, and often are, different, and they're typically individually specified. For example, the off times of some active screens may be twice that of the on time.

The ambient temperature can have dramatic effects on the response time of an LCD panel. At freezing, the response time of a panel may be three times longer (slower) than at room temperature.

At room temperature, an active matrix display pixel has a response time on the order of 10 to 50 milliseconds.

Bad Pixels

One of the major issues in making LCD panels is *yield*. That is, the number of good, fully functional panels that can be made in each batch. Out of 100 screens manufactured, for example, 30 may work properly, resulting in a yield of 30 percent. Early in production, yield might not be any higher than that, although as the technology matures, yields have been improving.

One way of improving yields is to lower the standard for what you call "fully functional." Some manufacturers believe that a screen with a few pixels that do not work properly still is a usable—and more importantly, *salable*—screen. These bad pixels may remain constantly lit or may never light. In any case, you get a screen with a few dots that persistently stay one color.

Constantly lit pixels of a single color appears to be the most common defect. Although these one-color pixels stand out against an overall black screen, they disappear against the default white Windows background.

Color Issues

The displayable range of colors of today's LCD panels is more limited than that of CRT displays. Although the color shortfall recommends against using a desktop LCD panel in color-critical applications such as prepublishing, the range is more than broad enough to present realistic full-color images. In fact, unless you need to do Pantone matching, you're unlikely to notice the lack of color range.

A related problem with LCD panels has been control of color temperature. Early LCD panels have had almost random color temperatures—they were set at whatever the commonly available backlights would permit. Modern displays have advanced to the point that many now offer selectable color temperatures, typically a daylight value (in the range of 5000 kelvins), a "bluish" hot temperature (in the 9000-kelvin range), and an adjustable user-defined temperature.

Transmissive Displays

Most of today's LCD panels are *transmissive*—that is, light is transmitted through the entire sandwich that makes up the panel. The light has to come from somewhere, and that source usually takes the form of an EL panel called a *backlight*. Although EL panels are more efficient than incandescent lights, they still consume a substantial amount of power. In notebooks computers, for example, the EL panel may require about one-third of the entire energy budget of the computer. For this reason, most notebook computer manufacturers restrict the brightness of the display when a computer operates from batteries. Dimming the screen can greatly increase battery life.

Most display manufacturers make the EL panel a separately replaceable element of their computer monitors (although most displays require a service technician to replace the backlight panel). These panels dim with age (at least early models do), making the overall display dimmer. Such displays can often be rejuvenated by replacing the backlight.

Even the brightest backlights pale in comparison to daylight. Consequently, transmissive displays do not work well outdoors. Although you can work with one in the shade, you'll end up raising the backlight brightness to a level that will quickly consume your battery reserves.

Reflective Displays

A reflective display reflects ambient light from the crystals in the screen. The brighter the ambient light, the brighter the screen. Reflective screens are at their best outdoors and are almost impossible to read in dim light. Reflective screens are more energy efficient because they have no need for a power-hungry backlight.

Reflective technology is mostly reserved for the small displays of toys and appliances and are often monochrome. The technology does not work well for large color computer displays.

A half-bred technology called *transflective* combines both transmissive and reflective qualities. In bright light, the screen acts as a reflective display but allows a backlight to takeover and make the screen operate in transmissive mode. Although still in the developmental stage, transflective screens hold promise for extending battery life for computers used in outdoor environments because the backlight serves only part-time.

Some handheld computers and Personal Digital Assistants attempt to bridge the gap between battery-saving reflective technology and power-draining transmissive technology by sidelighting their small screens. These machines use a reflective screen augmented by a light shining through its edge. Although the technology does not yield a bright screen, the sidelit screens are readable and long battery life compensates for some of the squinting.

Electronics

The image you see onscreen is only part of the story of a complete display system. The video signals from your computer must be amplified and processed by the electronics inside the monitor to achieve the right strength and timing relationships to put the proper image in view.

The basic electronic components inside a monitor are its *video amplifiers*. As the name implies, these circuits simply increase the strength (amplify) of the approximately one-volt signals they receive from your computer to the thousands of volts needed to drive the electron beam from cathode to phosphor. Monochrome monitors have a single video amplifier; color monitors, three (one for each primary color).

In an analog color monitor, these three amplifiers must be exactly matched and absolutely linear. The input and output of each amplifier must be precisely proportional, and they must be the same as the other two amplifiers. The relationship between these amplifiers is called *color tracking*. If it varies, the color of the image on the screen won't be what your software had in mind.

The effects of poor color tracking are all bad. You lose precision in your color control. This is especially important for desktop publishing and presentation applications. With poor color tracking, the screen can no longer hope to be an exact preview of what eventually appears on paper or film. You may even lose a good fraction of the colors displayable by your video system.

What happens is that differences between the amplifiers cause one of the three primary colors to be emphasized at times and de-emphasized at others, casting a subtle shade on the onscreen image. This shading effect is most pronounced in gray displays—the dominate color or colors tinge the gray.

Although you don't have to worry about color tracking in a monochrome display, the quality of the amplifier nevertheless determines the range of grays that can be displayed. Aberrations in the amplifier cause the monitor to lose some of its grayscale range.

The relationship between the input and output signals of video amplifiers is usually not linear. That is, a small change in the input signal may make a greater than corresponding change in the output. In other words, the monitor may exaggerate the color or grayscale range of the input signal—contrast increases. The relationship between input and output is referred to as the *gamma* of the amplifier. A gamma of one would result in an exact correspondence of the input and output signals. However, monitors with unity gammas tend to have washed out, pastel images. Most people prefer higher gammas, in the range 1.5 to 1.8, because of their "contrastier" images.

Synchronizing Frequency Range

At one time, engineers locked computer monitors to one standard, much as video monitors lock to standard NTSC or PAL video signals. In order to access higher resolutions, however, monitor-makers abandoned such *fixed frequency* monitors and opted for *multiscanning monitors* that could lock on a wide range of signals. Almost all new computer monitors use multiscanning technology.

Coping with today's variety of signal standards makes mandatory a monitor's ability to synchronize with the widest possible range of synchronizing frequencies. You have two frequencies to worry about. The *vertical synchronizing frequency*, sometimes called the *refresh rate* or *frame rate*, determines how often the complete screen is updated. The *horizontal synchronizing frequency* (or *horizontal scan rate*) indicates the rate at which the individual scan lines that make up the image are drawn. These frequency ranges are important to you because they determine with which video standards the monitor can work.

The starting point for the scan rate of a modern monitor is the 31.5KHz used by the VGA system. All current monitors require compatibility with this scan rate to make legible displays when your computer boots up. (Under the DVI standard, discussed later, new digitally interfaced monitors can emulate this mode, although DVI itself will make scan rate issues irrelevant.) A higher maximum scan rate is always better.

The lowest frame rate normally required is the 59Hz used by some early VESA modes, although today you'll only run into such low refresh rates with old display adapters. You'll want a new monitor that supports the highest possible frame rate, as high as 85Hz under some VESA standards.

Scan rate, refresh rate, and resolution interact. Table 24.3 lists the scanning frequencies of most common computer display systems.

TABLE 24.3   Scanning Frequencies Specified by Monitor Standards

Standard	Resolution	Vertical Sync (Frame Rate)	Horizontal Sync (Line Rate)
MDA	720×350	50Hz	18.3KHz
CGA	640×200	60Hz	15.75KHz
EGA	640×350	60Hz	21.5KHz
MCGA (Graphics)	640×480	60Hz	31.5KHz
MCGA (Text)	720×400	70Hz	31.5KHz
VGA (Graphics)	640×480	60Hz	31.5KHz
VGA (Text)	720×400	70Hz	31.5KHz
Macintosh	640×480	67Hz	35.0KHz
XGA-2	640×480	75Hz	39.38KHz
VESA	640×480	75Hz	37.5KHz
Apple Portrait	640×870	76.5Hz	70.19KHz
VESA guideline	800×600	56Hz	35.5KHz
VESA guideline	800×600	60Hz	37.9KHz
VESA standard	800×600	72Hz	48.1KHz
VESA standard	800×600	75Hz	46.875KHz
RasterOps	1024×768	75.1Hz	60.24KHz
Supermac	1024×768	75.1Hz	60.24KHz
VESA guideline	1024×768	60Hz	48.3KHz
VESA standard	1024×768	70.1Hz	56.5KHz
VESA standard	1024×768	75Hz	60KHz
8514/A	1024×768	44Hz *	35.5KHz
XGA	1024×768	44Hz *	35.5KHz
XGA-2	1024×768	75.8Hz	61.1KHz
Apple 2-page	1152×870	75Hz	68.68KHz
VESA standard	1280×1024	75Hz	80KHz

Note that two old standards (the legacy 8514/A and XGA systems) have very low frame rates, 44Hz, because they are interlaced systems (discussed next). To properly display these signals, a monitor must have sufficient range to synchronize with the *field rate* of these standards, which is twice the frame rate.

Interlacing

Most computer display systems use *progressive scanning*. That is, the system starts by displaying the first (top) line in the video image and then displays each subsequent line, one after the other down the screen. Televisions and video systems use *interlaced scanning*. Instead of scanning lines sequentially from top to bottom, each frame of the image is broken in half into two fields. One field consists of the odd-numbered lines of the image; the other the even-numbered lines. The electron beam sweeps across and down, illuminating every other line, and then starts from the top again and finishes with the ones it missed on the first pass.

This technique achieves an apparent doubling of the frame rate. Instead of sweeping down the screen 30 times a second (the case of a normal television picture), the top-to-bottom sweep occurs 60 times a second. Whereas a 30-frames-per-second rate would noticeably flicker, the ersatz 60-frames-per-second rate does not—at least not to most people under most circumstances. Some folks' eyes are not fooled, however, so interlaced images have earned a reputation of being flickery. Figure 24.8 compares progressive and interlaced scanning.

FIGURE 24.8
Progressive versus interlaced scanning.

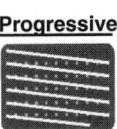

Progressive	Interlaced	
Frame	First field	Second field

Interlacing is used on computer display signals to keep the necessary bandwidth down. A lower frame rate lowers the required bandwidth of the transmission channel. Although interlaced scanning should have been forgotten along with the 8514/A and original XGA display systems, it occasionally pops up in computer displays—typically low-priced monitors that claim high resolutions. Be wary of any monitor that specifies its maximum resolution as interlaced.

Bandwidth

Perhaps the most common specification usually listed for any sort of monitor is bandwidth, which is usually rated in megahertz. Common monitor bandwidths stretch across a wide range—figures from 12 to 200MHz are sometimes encountered.

In theory, the higher the bandwidth, the higher the resolution and sharper the image displayed. In the case of color displays, the dot-pitch of the display tube is the biggest limit on performance. In a monochrome system, however, bandwidth is a determinant of overall sharpness. The computer display standards do not demand extremely wide bandwidths. Extremely large bandwidths are often superfluous.

The bandwidth necessary in a monitor is easy to compute. A system ordinarily requires a bandwidth wide enough to address each individual screen dot plus an extra margin to allow for retrace times. (Retrace times are those periods in which the electron beam moves but does not display—for instance, at the end of each frame when the beam must move from the bottom of the screen at the end of the last line of one frame back up to the top of the screen for the first line of the next frame.)

A typical color display operating under the VGA standard shows 288,000 pixels (a 729×400-pixel image in text mode) 70 times per second, a total of 20.16 million pixels per second. An 800×600-pixel Super VGA display at 75Hz must produce 36 million pixels per second.

Synchronizing signals require their own slice of monitor bandwidth. Allowing a wide margin of about 25 percent for retrace times, it can thus be seen that for most computer applications, a bandwidth of 16MHz is acceptable for TTL monitors, and 10MHz of bandwidth is sufficient for sharp composite video displays and figures well within the claims of most commercial products. For VGA, 25MHz is the necessary minimum.

Multiplying the dot-clock by 25 percent yields an acceptable estimate of the bandwidth required in a monitor. For the standards IBM promulgated, the company listed actual bandwidth requirements. Table 24.4 summarizes these requirements and calculated estimates for various computer display standards.

TABLE 24.4   Dot-Clocks and Recommended Bandwidths for Video Standards

Video Standard	Dot-Clock	Recommended Bandwidth
MDA	12.6MHz	16.3MHz
CGA	7.68MHz	14.3MHz
EGA	13.4MHz	16.3MHz
PGC	18.4MHz	25MHz
VGA (350- or 480-line mode)	18.4MHz	25MHz
VGA (400-line mode)	20.2MHz	28MHz
8514/A	34.6MHz	44.9MHz
VESA 800×600, 75Hz	36MHz	45MHz
VESA 1024×768, 75Hz	60MHz	75MHz
VESA 1280×1024, 75Hz	100MHz	125MHz

Although these estimates are calculated using the dot-clock of the display, the relationship between dot-clock and bandwidth is not as straightforward as the calculations imply. Because in real-world applications the worst-case display puts an illuminated pixel next to a dark one, the actual bandwidth required by a display system should be the dot-clock plus system overhead. A pair of on/off pixels exactly corresponds to the up and down halves of a single cycle. The higher bandwidth you calculate from the dot clock allows extra bandwidth that gives greater image sharpness—sharply defining the edges of a pixel requires square waves, which contain high-frequency components. Consequently, the multiplication of the dot-clock by display overhead offers a good practical approximation of the required bandwidth, even though the calculations are on shaky theoretical ground.

Energy Star

Compared to some of the things you might connect to your computer, a monitor consumes a modest amount of electricity. A laser printer can draw as much as a kilowatt when its fuser is operating. A typical computer requires 100 to 200 watts. A typical monitor requires only about 30 watts. Unlike the laser fuser, however, your monitor may stay on all day long, and an office may have hundreds of them, each continually downing its energy dosage. Those watts add up, not just in their power consumption but also their heat production that adds to the load on the office air conditioning.

To help cut the power used by computer equipment, the Environmental Protection Agency started the Energy Star program, which seeks to conserve power while computers and their peripherals are in their idle states. For monitors, Energy Star means that the monitor powers down to a one of two lower power conditions or shuts off entirely when its host computer has not been used for awhile.

Energy Star–compliant monitors have four operating modes: on, standby, suspend, and off. During normal operation when the monitor displays an active image generated by your computer, it is on. In standby mode, the monitor cuts off the electron beam in its CRT and powers down some of its electronics. It keeps the filament or heat of the CRT (the part that has to warm up to make the tube work) hot so that the monitor can instantly switch back to its on state. In suspend mode, the filament and most of the electronics of the monitor switch off. Only a small portion of the electronics of the monitor remain operational to sense the incoming signals, ready to switch the monitor back on when the need arises. This conserves most of the power that would be used by the monitor but requires the CRT to heat up before the monitor can resume normal operation. In other words, the monitor trades rapid availability for a reduction in power use. In off mode, the monitor uses no power but requires you to manually switch it on.

To enable your computer to control the operating mode of your monitor without additional electrical connections, VESA developed its Display Power Management Standard (DPMS). This system uses the two synchronizing signals your video board supplies to your monitor to control its operating mode. To signal the monitor to switch to standby operation, your video card switches off only its horizontal sync signal. To signal the monitor to switch to suspend mode, your video board cuts both the video signal and the vertical sync but leaves the horizontal sync on. In off mode, all signals are cut off. Table 24.5 summarizes these modes.

TABLE 24.5   VESA Display Power Management Summary

Monitor State	Video	Vertical Sync	Horizontal Sync	DPMS	Recovery Time	Power Savings
On	On	On	On	Mandatory	None	None
Standby	On	On	Off	Optional	Short	Minimal
Suspend	Off	Off	On	Mandatory	Longer	Substantial
Off	Off	Off	Off	Mandatory	Warm-up	Maximum

Advanced operating systems monitor your system usage and send out the standby and/or suspend signals when you leave your system idle for a predetermined time. Your video driver software controls the DPMS signals. Note that screensaver software defeats the purpose of DPMS by keeping your system active even when it is not in use. You can trim your power usage by relying on DPMS rather than a screensaver to shut down your monitor.

Many monitors made before the DPMS standard was created often incorporate their own power-saving mode that's initiated by a loss of the video signal for a predetermined time. In other words, these monitors sense when your screen is blank and start waiting. If you don't do something for, say, five minutes, the monitor switches to standby or suspend mode, no matter the state of the synchronizing signals. The DPMS system is designed so that these monitors, too, will power down (although only after the conclusion of both the DPMS and their own internal timing cycles).

To enable the DPMS system under Windows, you must tell the operating system that your monitor is Energy Star compliant. If your monitor is in the Windows database, Windows will know automatically whether the monitor is compliant. You can also check the Energy Star compliance in the Change Display Settings screen. You must also activate the DPMS screen blanker from the Screen Saver tab of your Display Properties screen.

Identification

The prevalence of multiscanning monitors with wildly different capabilities makes getting the most from your investment a challenge. You must be able to identify not only the display capabilities of the monitor, but also those of your video board, and then make the best possible match between them. If you're wrong, you won't get everything that you've paid for. Worse, you might not see anything intelligible on your screen. Worse still, you face a tiny chance of actually harming your monitor or video board.

Hard-Wired Coding

The problem is neither new nor one that arose with multiscanning systems. When the VGA system was new, IBM developed a rudimentary system for letting its computers determine the type of monitor that was connected—limited, of course, to the monitors IBM made. The system had limited capabilities. It could identify whether the monitor was monochrome or color and whether it met merely the VGA standard or advanced into higher-resolution territory. At the time, IBM only offered four monitors, and that modest range defined the extent of the selection.

The IBM scheme was to use three of the connections between the monitor and the video board to carry signals identifying the monitor. These first signals were crude—a simple binary code that put the signal wire either at ground potential or with no connection. Table 24.6 lists this coding system.

TABLE 24.6   Monitor-Identification Coding Used by IBM

Display Type	Size	IBM Model	ID 0	ID 1	ID 2
Monochrome	12 inch	8503	NC	Ground	NC
Color	12 inch	8513	Ground	NC	NC
Color	14 inch	8512	Ground	NC	NC
Hi-resolution	15 inch	8514	Ground	NC	Ground

Display Data Channel

This rudimentary standard was not up to the task of identifying the wide range of monitor capabilities that became available in the years after the introduction of VGA. Yet adding true Plug-and-Play capabilities to your computer requires automatically identifying the type of monitor connected to your computer so that the display adapter (and the rest of the system) can be properly configured. To meet this challenge, VESA developed the *Display Data Channel* (DDC), an elaborate monitor-identification system based on the same connections as the early IBM system but with greatly enhanced signals and capabilities.

Through the DDC, the monitor sends an *Extended Display Identification* (EDID) to your computer. In advanced form, the DDC moves data both ways between your monitor and your computer using either the I^2C or ACCESS.bus serial interfaces. The DDC2B standard uses I^2C bus signaling on two of the wires of the monitor connection to transfer data both ways between monitor and its attached video board. DDC2AB uses a full ACCESS.bus connection and protocol, which allow you to connect other computer peripherals (for example, your keyboard) to your monitor rather than the system unit.

All levels of the DDC system gain information about your monitor in the same way. The monitor sends out the EDID as a string of serial bits on the monitor data line, pin 12. Depending on the level of DDC supported by the monitor, the EDID data stream is synchronized either to the vertical sync signal generated by the video board present on pin 14 of 15-pin video connectors or to a separate serial data clock (SCL) that's on pin 15 in DDC2 systems. One bit of data moves with each clock cycle. When the system uses vertical sync as the clock, the data rate will be in the range of 60 to 85Hz. With DDC-compliant monitors, your video board can temporarily increase the vertical sync frequency to up to 25KHz to speed the transmission of this data. Using the SCL signal when both the video board and monitor support it, data rates as high as 100KHz are possible.

The serial data takes the form of nine-bit sequences, one per byte. The first eight bits encode the data, the most significant bit first. The last bit can be either a zero or one, at the choice of the monitor manufacturer. The only restriction is that the ninth bit must have the same value for every byte.

The DDC system sends data from the monitor to your display adapter in 128-byte blocks. The first of these is the Extended Display Identification or EDID block. It is optionally followed by an Extended EDID block or additional proprietary manufacturer data blocks. Table 24.7 lists the structure of the basic EDID.

TABLE 24.7   Basic EDID Structure

Start Byte	Length	Description
0	8 bytes	Header
8	10 bytes	Vendor/product identification
18	2 bytes	EDID version/revision
20	15 bytes	Basic display parameters/features
35	19 bytes	Established/standard timings
54	72 bytes	Timing descriptions × 4 (18 bytes each)
126	1 byte	Extension flag
127	1 byte	Checksum

The header is always the same data pattern and serves to identify the EDID information stream. The vendor identification is based on EISA manufacturer identifications. The product identification is assigned by the manufacturer. It includes the month and year of manufacture of the monitor.

The basic display parameters that EDID relays to your system include the maximum size of your monitor's display, expressed as the largest width and height of the image area. Your applications or operating system can use this information to automatically set the proper scaling for fonts displayed on the screen. The timing data includes a bit representing the ability to support each of the various VESA standards so that your system can determine the possible modes and frequencies your monitor can use.

In addition to basic DDC support, VESA provides for two higher levels of standardization. The DDC2B system uses the Philips I^2C signaling system to transfer data bidirectionally across the interface. The DDC2AB system includes full ACCESS.bus support that supplies a low-speed serial interconnection bus suitable for linking such peripherals as keyboards and pointing devices through the monitor.

Because standard expansion buses do not provide suitable connections for routing ACCESS.bus signals, VESA has defined an auxiliary connector for the purpose, a five-pin "Berg" connector. Table 24.8 lists the signal assignments of this connector.

TABLE 24.8   Access Bus Connector Signal Assignments

Pin	Function
1	Ground
2	Mechanical key
3	Serial data (SDA)
4	+5V ACCESS.bus supply voltage
5	Serial data clock (SCL)

Monitors that are compliant with DDC use the same connectors as ordinary VGA displays. All the active video and synchronizing signals are located on the same pins of the connector, no matter the DDC level the monitor uses (or even if it doesn't use DDC at all). The only difference is the definition of the monitor-identification signals. DDC1 video boards sacrifice the Monitor ID Bit 1 pin, number 12, as a channel to receive identification data from your monitor. DDC2 systems make this signal bidirectional and take over pin 15 for use carrying the clock signal. In any case, pin 9 may be used to supply five volts for running accessory devices. Table 24.9 lists the signal assignments of the VGA 15-pin connector under DDC.

TABLE 24.9   VESA Display Data Channel Signal Assignments

Pin	DDC1 Host	DDC2 Host	DDC1/2 Display
1	Red video	Red video	Red video
2	Green video	Green video	Green video
3	Blue video	Blue video	Blue video
4	Monitor ID bit 2	Monitor ID bit 2	Optional
5	Return	Return	Return
6	Red video return	Red video return	Red video return
7	Green video return	Green video return	Green video return
8	Blue video return	Blue video return	Blue video return
9	+5V (optional)	+5V (optional)	+5V load (optional)
10	Sync return	Sync return	Sync return
11	Monitor ID bit 0	Monitor ID bit 0	Optional
12	Data from display	Bidirectional data	Bidirectional data
13	Horizontal sync	Horizontal sync	Horizontal sync
14	Vertical sync	Vertical sync	Vertical sync
15	Monitor ID bit 3	Data clock (SCL)	Data clock (SCL)

Manual Configuration

If your monitor or video board does not support any level of the DDC specification, you will be left to configure your system on your own. In general, you won't need to perform any special configuration to a multiscanning monitor to match it to your video board if the signals from the video board are within the range of the monitor. That's the whole point of the multiscanning display—it adjusts itself to accommodate any video signal.

That said, you may not get the most from your monitor. You might slight its refresh rate and quickly tire your eyes with a flickering display. Worse, you might exceed its capabilities and end up with a scrambled or blank screen.

Windows includes its own configuration process that attempts to optimize the signals of your compliant video adapter with your monitor type. Windows already knows what video board you have—you have to tell it when you install your video drivers. Without a DDC connection, however, Windows is cut off from your monitor, so you must manually indicate the brand and model of monitor you're using.

You make these settings by clicking the Change Display Type button in the Settings tab of your Display properties menu. Click the button, and you see a dialog box like that shown in Figure 24.9.

FIGURE 24.9
The Change Display Type dialog box in Windows.

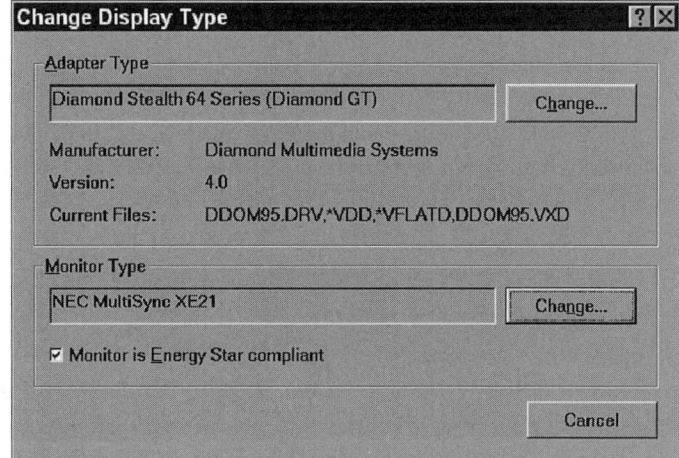

Interfaces

The video system in your computer must somehow link up with the rest of its circuitry. In most display systems, the connection is intimate. It gives your computer's microprocessor the power to directly intervene and inject data, such as an image bitmap, right into the frame buffer. In nearly all of today's computers, the necessary link is an accelerated graphics port (AGP).

Although based on the PCI expansion bus, AGP delivers substantially higher performance because it incorporates dedicated pipelined access to main memory. Thanks to its wide bandwidth, the design allows an accelerator chip on an AGP expansion board to use main memory for video functions such as z-buffering, texture-mapping, and alpha-blending.

The AGP may be embedded and hidden in the circuitry of your computer when the display system is part of the motherboard or chipset. Otherwise, AGP takes the form of a single special slot on your desktop computer's motherboard.

Accelerated Graphics Port

The AGP design originated in Intel Labs and was officially released as a standard (version 1.0) on July 31, 1996. As you might expect from a new bus design from Intel, it is based on the PCI design and follows basic PCI protocol and signaling. Because of its high speed—potentially four times that of today's PCI—it uses its own, incompatible connector design and imposes tight restrictions on design layouts. On May 4, 1998, Intel revised the AGP design to version 2.0. The improvements were twofold. By adding a transfer mode, Intel created a new quadruple-speed mode for AGP. In addition, the new specification allows for lower-voltage operation. In addition to the 3.3-volt design of AGP 1.0, the revision allows for 1.5-volt operation as well.

Although based on revision 2.1 of the PCI specifications, the AGP design goes beyond them with three innovations: pipelined memory that eliminates wait states, separate address and data lines on the bus to cut the necessary number of cycles per transfer, and a timing specification allowing operation at 133MHz across a 32-bit bus, thus allowing for throughput on the order of 500MBps. The actual clock speed of the AGP bus is 66MHz, matching the PCI 2.1 specs. To achieve the higher data rates, the AGP system relies on more exotic technologies, discussed in the 2× transfer mode and 4× transfer mode sections, later.

The AGP shares the same physical address space for memory with the PCI system and microprocessor. It uses a 32-bit address bus that can handle up to a 4GB address range. Matching its 32-bit data bus, AGP transfers always move data in eight byte blocks, double the granularity of standard PCI transfers (which slices data into four bytes blocks). To accommodate smaller data types, the AGP interface can also use PCI transfer modes.

Despite its PCI foundation, AGP has its own set of commands and transfer protocol. The AGP interface hardware supports both the AGP transfers and traditional PCI transfers as separate modes.

Unlike PCI, where address and data cycles are intimately linked, the AGP modes disconnect them. This allows other data to intervene in between. This design allows the system to keep the pipeline filled. Each access request across the AGP is sent to a queue while it awaits the transfer of its associated data. The AGP devices track the access requests and data in their hardware. Access requests in the queue are prioritized into high- and low-priority subqueues. PCI transfers have their own queue.

The AGP design allows for a maximum of 256 transactions in the pipeline at once, although hardware capabilities will further constrain the pipeline. When the Plug-and-Play system sets up the AGP board, the AGP hardware reports the maximum depth that the pipeline can support in its host computer.

On the other hand, the AGP transfer modes allow access only to memory. They do not link to input/output ports or configuration memory. In addition, to help the AGP achieve its high speed, its design cuts it free from cache snooping, so changes made through AGP are not necessarily reflected in the memory cache.

Architecture

AGP clearly shows the new role of video in the future of the computer. Through AGP, video is given its own dedicated interface and connection. It does not share a bus with expansion boards or even memory. It has a direct reach to the high holy sanctum of the computer, the microprocessor and chipset.

In effect, the AGP is a fourth bus in a modern computer, added to the expected compatibility bus (ISA), high-speed expansion bus (PCI), and memory bus. The signals for AGP arise in the same system-control logic that links to the PCI bridge and main memory in the computer. As shown in Figure 24.10, the AGP design gives the graphics chip of a computer the same direct connection with the chipset as honors the microprocessor, PCI bridge, and memory system.

FIGURE 24.10

Block diagram showing the role of AGP in modern system architecture.

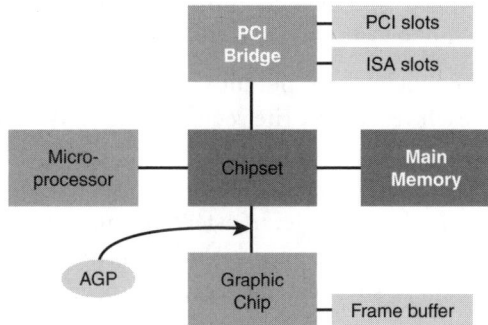

AGP operates solely between two devices. By design, one of these must be the system memory controller, which is normally part of the computer's chipset. To the AGP system, the chipset is the target device, and AGP transfers are controlled by the graphics board at the other end of the connection, which is the master. In PCI transfer modes, the host chipset operates as a PCI sequencer, which is capable of service as both master and target. The video board only needs to operate as a PCI target, although it may also have master functions as well.

Operation

Intel envisioned that the AGP would be used in two different ways. Its DMA model pictured AGP would be used as a fast channel for moving large blocks of data between a dedicated frame buffer and main system memory. Your computer's graphic chip would work conventionally, working in the memory on the expansion board, carrying out most operations directly in the frame buffer. The system would use DMA transfers across the AGP to move bit-image data from system memory to the frame buffer. The execute model sees the AGP as a means of connecting the graphics accelerator to main memory. The accelerator chip on the video board can use main memory for execution of high-level functions such as antialiasing and 3D rendering. The graphics chip would use the AGP to draw data from system memory and hold intermediate results, loading the final data of the image into the local frame buffer.

In either case, transfers are mediated in the same way. First, either end of the connection negotiates to use the interface.

When operating in its native AGP mode, the graphics controller starts each transaction by making an access request to the system board chipset. The chipset then schedules its action on the request, working around other tasks that involve the bus. The chipset can accumulate several graphics requests and begin to process them while waiting for the actual data transfer to take place. In effect, the processing steps involved in the transfer requests are pipelined much like instructions in an advanced microprocessor.

The transfer requests in the pipeline are split into two queues, one with high priority and one with low priority, for each read and write request. The AGP system puts the responsibility for tracking the status of all the transfers on the graphics controller requesting them, and the controller determines the number of requests waiting in each queue. The chipset processes the request—for example, transferring data from system memory to the frame buffer—as free time in the system allows it. It can process requests from the various queues as system resources allow, so it may interleave the processing of read and write requests.

When operating in its PCI mode, the graphics controller acts like any PCI device. However, the PCI transfers are not pipelined like the native AGP transactions.

The signals used for AGP transfers are built on a foundation of the PCI bus. The AGP standard augments the PCI standard with special control signals Intel terms *sideband signals*. They alter the timing of the PCI bus to allow higher data throughput. The PCI data and bus control lines still channel information during AGP transfers, but a new signal termed *PIPE#* defines the AGP transfer, much as the FRAME# signal defines PCI transfers.

When the PIPE# signal is active, the system operates in the AGP 2× transfer mode and moves data across the bus twice during each cycle. Request queuing, pipelining, parallel execution, and the double-time transfer cycle all contribute to the higher throughput of the AGP interface.

AGP-defined protocols (for example, pipelining) are overlaid on the PCI bus at a time and in a manner that a PCI bus agent (non-AGP) would view the bus as idle. Both pipelined access requests (read or write) and resultant data transfers are handled in this manner. The AGP interface uses both PCI bus transactions without change, as well as AGP pipelined transactions as defined herein. Both of these classes of transactions are interleaved on the same physical connection. The access request portion of an AGP transaction (bus command, address, and length) is signaled differently than is a PCI address phase. The information is still transferred on the AD and C/BE# signals of the bus, as is the case with PCI 6, but is identified or framed with a new control signal, PIPE#, in a similar way to which PCI address phases are identified with FRAME#.

2× Transfer Mode

For high-performance systems in which the 266MBps potential of basic AGP is inadequate, the original AGP specification allowed for higher-speed transfers in its *2× transfer mode*. Using the proven technique called *double-clocking*, 2× mode pushes the maximum potential throughput of the AGP system to 533MBps.

Double-clocking makes the clock signal do double duty, keying transfers to both its leading and trailing edges. That is, the transition marking the beginning of the clock signal triggers one transfer across the bus, and the transition ending the clock pulse triggers another. In most logic systems and basic AGP mode, only the leading edge of the clock signals valid data, allowing the making of a transfer.

To improve the reliability of 2× transfer mode, it uses three *strobe* signals rather than the clock itself. The clock signal originates in your computer as part of its array of PCI signals. In contrast, the device sending data generates the strobe signals. When your computer sends data to the AGP board, it creates the strobes. When the AGP board sends data to your computer, it creates the strobes. Because the sending device generates both the data and strobe signals, the timing relationship between the two can be more precisely controlled.

The strobe signals appear only within the interconnection between the AGP transmitting and receiving circuits and the hardware connection between them. In AGP terminology, this is the *inner loop*. The rest of the AGP system is the *outer loop*.

The specification defines individual strobe signals for the low and high 16 bits of the AGP bus as well as the sideband. The AGP circuitry issues the strobe signals at the same frequency as the AGP clock, but the specification more rigidly defines the timing of the strobes. The high and low phases of the strobe signal are equal, so leading and trailing edges of the signals are evenly spaced and transfers keyed to the edges occur uniformly.

4× Transfer Mode

In enhancing the performance of AGP, the Intel engineers faced a major problem. The original design already strained at the high-frequency limit of the connector system. Increasing the speed of AGP would require a redesign with expensive new technologies. To avoid most of these issues, the Intel engineers kept their changes inside the inner loop, designing a more elaborate strobe system.

To create 4× transfer mode, Intel's engineers doubled the frequency of the strobe signals and double-clocked the data keyed to them. This change again doubles the potential throughput of the system, yielding a maximum rate of 1066MBps.

With the increase in strobe frequency comes a need for a tighter definition of the timing of the signals. Intel created the necessary precision by adding three more strobe signals. Each one is paired with one of the 2× transfer mode signals but is the opposite polarity, turning each strobe into a differential pair. When one of the strobes in a pair transitions from high to low, the other moves from low to high. At one instant during the paired transitions, at approximately midway between them, the voltage values of the two signals are equal—on a timing chart, the values cross. The 4× transfer mode keys each transfer to one of these crossings. Because these crossings occur twice in each strobe cycle and the strobe frequency is twice the basic AGP clock frequency, transfers occur at four times the basic AGP rate.

Intel took another step to help AGP achieve the speed required by 4× transfer mode. It lowered the voltage of the signals, which helps deal with the capacitance inherent in any bus system. All AGP boards that operate in AGP 4× transfer mode must use 1.5-volt signaling.

UMA

Unified Memory Architecture (UMA) is an alternate way to design a computer for lower-cost construction. It actually can have a beneficial effect on video performance. Because the frame buffer is integrated into the main memory of the computer, bitmaps don't have to cross any I/O bus at all. Of course, the memory used by the frame buffer cannot also be used by programs, but today's memory prices make this loss of storage almost inconsequential.

To provide a common standard to which designers could create the electrical and logical interface between the video system using UMA and the core logic of a computer, VESA developed its own standard called *VESA Unified Memory Architecture* (VUMA). First published in March, 1996, VUMA allows for adding external devices to your computer that can share direct access to its main memory system to use it as a frame buffer. Although UMA has become popular in low-cost computers, even with this standard, add-on devices that use the technology have not become popular.

Monitor Interfacing and Connectors

The video connection carries the image between your video board and monitor.

Monitors can be grouped by the display standard they support, mostly based on the display adapter card they are designed to plug into. One basic guide that helps you narrow down the compatibility of a display just by inspecting its rear panel is the input connector used by the monitor. After all, if you cannot plug a monitor into your computer, odds are it is not much good to you.

You'll likely encounter one of three styles of connector on the back of your computer. These include legacy connectors used by display systems too ancient to worry about, analog system used by the majority of today's display systems, and new digital interfaces that are beginning to appear on the market and mark the look (and connection) of things to come.

Legacy Connectors

The first video connector used by computers was the nine-pin D-shell connector, as shown in Figure 24.11. It is now used only by legacy video systems and serves mostly as a warning that you may encounter trouble in trying to match your video system to a monitor.

FIGURE 24.11

A nine-pin D-shell jack used by legacy video systems.

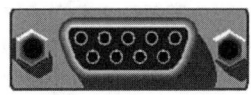

Analog Connection Systems

Three styles of connectors are shared by different computer video standards. By name, these three connectors are the RCA-style pin jack, the nine-pin D-shell, and the 15-pin "high-density" D-shell. In addition, some high-resolution monitors use three or more BNC connectors for their input signals.

Pin Jacks

The bull's-eye jack used on stereo and video equipment is used by most manufacturers for the composite video connections in computer display systems, although a wealth of monitors and television sets made by innumerable manufacturers also use this connector. This connector does give you many choices for alternate displays—that is, if you don't mind marginal quality.

Composite monitors (those dealing with the composite video and NTSC color only) rank among the most widely available and least expensive in both color and monochrome. Even better quality television sets have such jacks, shown in Figure 24.12, available.

FIGURE 24.12

A pin jack used by composite video signals.

Although you can use any composite video display with a CGA or compatible color card, the signal itself limits the possible image quality to okay for monochrome, acceptable for 40-column color, and unintelligible for 80-column color. Nevertheless, a composite video display—already a multipurpose device—becomes even more versatile with a computer input.

Daisy-Chaining

A side benefit of pin plug/composite video displays is that most have both input and output jacks. These paired jacks enable you to daisy-chain multiple monitors to a single video output. For example, you can attach six composite video monitors to the output of your computer for presentations in the classroom or boardroom.

In many cases, the jacks just loop through the display (that is, they connect together). The display merely bridges the input video signal and alters it in no other manner. You can connect a nearly unlimited number of monitors to these loop-through connections with no image degradation. Some monitors, however, buffer their outputs with a built-in video amplifier. Depending on the quality of the amplifier, daisy-chaining several of these monitors can result in noticeable image degradation.

One way to tell the difference is by plugging the output of the display into the output of your computer. Most amplifiers don't work backwards, so if the display has a buffering amplifier, nothing appears onscreen. If you do get an image comparable to the one you get when plugging into the input jack, the signal just loops through the display.

Analog Voltage Level

The specifications of composite monitors sometimes include a number describing the voltage level of the input signal. This voltage level can be important when selecting a composite display because all such monitors are essentially analog devices.

In analog monitors, the voltage level corresponds to the brightness the electron beam displays onscreen. A nominal one-volt peak-to-peak input signal is the standard in both the video and computer industries and should be expected from any composite monitor. The VGA system requires a slightly different level—0.7 volts.

Termination

For proper performance, a composite video signal line must be terminated by an impedance of 75 ohms. This termination ensures that the signal is at the proper level and that aberrations do not creep in because of an improperly matched line. Most composite input monitors (particularly those with separate inputs and outputs) feature a termination switch that connects a 75-ohm resistor across the video line when turned on. Only one termination resistor should be switched on in any daisy-chain, and it should always be the last monitor in the chain.

If you watch a monitor when you switch the termination resistor on, you'll notice that the screen gets dimmer. That's because the resistor absorbs about half the video signal. Because composite video signals are analog, they are sensitive to voltage level. The termination cuts the voltage in half and consequently dims the screen by the same amount. Note that the dim image is the proper one. Although bright might seem better, it's not. It may overload the circuits of the monitor or otherwise cause erratic operation.

Composite monitors with a single video input jack and no video output usually have a termination resistor permanently installed. Although you might try to connect two or more monitors to a single CGA composite output (with a Y cable or adapter), doing so would be unwise. With each additional monitor, the image gets dimmer (the signal must be split among the various monitors), and the CGA adapter is required to send out increasing current. The latter could cause the CGA to fail.

VGA Connectors

The most common connector on computer monitors is the *15-pin high-density D-shell* connector. Originally put in use by IBM for its first VGA monitors, this connector has become adopted as an industry standard for all but the highest performance computer displays.

Because the signals generated by VGA are so different from those of previous IBM display systems, IBM finally elected to use a different, incompatible connector so the wrong monitor wouldn't be plugged in with disastrous results. Although only nine connections are actually needed by the VGA system (11 if you give each of the three video signals its own ground return as IBM specifies), the new connector is equipped with 15 pins. It's roughly the same size and shape as a nine-pin D-shell connector, but before IBM's adoption of it, this so-called high-density 15-pin connector was not generally available. Figure 24.13 shows this connector.

FIGURE 24.13
A 15-pin mini D-shell connector used by VGA and similar video systems.

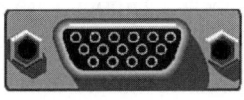

In addition, to allow for four video signals (three primary colors and separate sync) and their ground returns, the VGA connector provides a number of additional functions. In the original VGA design, it enabled the coding of both monitor type and the line count of the video signal leaving the display adapter. The modern adaptation of the connector to the VESA DDC standard redefines several pins for carrying data signals, as noted earlier. Table 24.10 lists the signal assignments of the VGA connector.

Table **24.10**	VGA and SuperVGA Connector Pinout
Pin	*Function*
1	Red video
2	Green video
3	Blue video
4	Reserved
5	Ground
6	Red return (ground)
7	Green return (ground)
8	Blue return (ground)
9	Composite sync
10	Sync return (ground)
11	VESA display data channel
12	Reserved
13	Horizontal sync
14	Vertical sync
15	VESA display data channel

IBM's 8514 and 8515 displays as well as 8514/A and XGA display adapters also use the same connector, even though they at times use different signals. Again, however, IBM has incorporated coding in the signals to ensure that problems do not arise. The 8514/A and XGA adapters can sense the type of display connected to them and do not send out conflicting signals. The 8514 and 8515 monitors operate happily with VGA signals, so problems do not occur if they are plugged into an ordinary VGA output.

The advantage of the 15-pin connector is convenience. One cable does everything. On the downside, the connector is not arranged for proper high-speed operation, and its deficiencies can limit high-frequency performance, which in video terms equates to sharpness when operating at high resolutions and refresh rates. Consequently, the highest resolution systems often forego the 15-pin connector for separate BNC connectors for each video channel.

BNC Connectors

True high-resolution systems use a separate coaxial cable for every signal they receive. Typically, they use BNC connectors to attach these to the monitor. They have one very good reason: Connectors differ in their frequency-handling capabilities, and capacitance in the standard 15-pin high-density D-shell connector can limit bandwidth, particularly as signal frequencies climb into the range above 30MHz. BNC connectors are designed for frequencies into the gigahertz range, so they impose few limits on ordinary video signals.

Monitors can use either three, four, or five BNC connectors for their inputs. Figure 24.14 shows an array of five BNC connectors on the rear of a monitor.

FIGURE 24.14

A monitor with five BNC connectors for input.

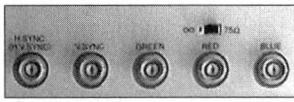

A three-connector system integrates both horizontal and vertical synchronizing signals with the green signal. The resulting mix is called *sync-on-green*. Others use three connectors for red, green, and blue signals and a fourth for the horizontal and vertical sync signals combined together. This scheme is called *composite sync*. Five-connector systems use three color signals, one for horizontal sync, and one for vertical sync. These are called *separate sync systems*.

Digital Video Interface

Flat-panel displays made the need for a high-performance digital display interface obvious. Analog-interface flat panels work but are only an interim solution.

Among the other problems with the standard analog links so popular on today's monitors, one stands in the way of getting truly high-resolution images on your monitor—limited bandwidth. The now-dominant VGA connector has a maximum bandwidth of about 150MHz, so it already constrains the quality of some display systems. Conventional high-frequency video connectors (primarily BNC) require a separate cable for each video signal and allow no provisions for auxiliary functions such as monitor identification.

Achieving a single standard has been problematic for the industry, however. In the last few years, various groups have developed at least three specifications, all promoted as "standards." Despite the infighting among the promoters of each, the three are not in competition, however, but represent the evolution of what will likely be the dominant standard for the future, the *Digital Video Interface* (DVI).

In late 1998, Intel rounded up the usual suspects to work on yet another digital display standard. The result was the Digital Display Working Group, initially comprising representatives from both the Plug and Display and Digital Flat Panel (DFP) connector camps—Intel, Compaq, Fujitsu, Hewlett-Packard, IBM, NEC, and Silicon Image.

The working group took the better features of each of the two earlier standards and developed the Digital Video Interface as kind of the "greatest hits" of monitor connectors.

The standard was adopted and published by VESA as DVI version 1.0 on April 2, 1999. Number Nine Visual Technology demonstrated the first product to use the interface, the SR9 graphics adapter, on May 19, 1999.

DVI shares the connector design and some of the non-video data signals with Plug and Display, but it breaks off the integral USB port from the connector. Although the DVI standard does not preclude USB in displays, to do so a separate connection must be used for the USB signals.

Although DVI uses the same Transition Minimized Differential Signaling (TMDS) signals as Plug and Display and DFP, it doubles the effective bandwidth of these signals with the simple expedient of using two of them. Both are locked to the single clock channel provided by the interface, so they are automatically synchronized to each other. Each color signal has two signals, which are interleaved so that data is spread between the two channels of a given color, creating what is essentially a parallel connection. Display systems may use either the one-channel system or the two-channel system, but the DVI specification draws a hard line between the two. Signals requiring a bandwidth of less than 165MHz must use the single-channel system. Systems requiring larger bandwidths must use two channels.

The three signal paths of DVI are not named with colors, although they correspond to red, green, and blue data. Each signal path actually carries three interleaved channels of data. The signal path used by blue data, for example, also carries a horizontal synchronizing signal and a vertical synchronizing signal. The two channels in the remaining pair of signal paths are currently reserved and have no assigned function.

Analog video is an optional part of DVI. Rather than shape, the DVI connector uses the cross-pin in the connector as a key for the presence of analog signals. The same connector can be used for all-analog or all-digital systems. Analog signals, when present, are located in the four quadrants around the keying cross in the connector.

Audio Systems

Of the five senses, most people only experience personal computers with four: touch, smell, sound, and sight. Not that computers are tasteless—although a growing body of software doesn't even aspire that high—but most people don't normally drag their tongues across the cases of their computers.

Touch is inherent in typing and pushing around a mouse or digitizer cursor.

Smell is more limited still—what you appreciate in opening the box holding your new computer or what warns you when the fan in the power supply stops, internal temperatures rise, and roasting resistors and near "inflammatory" components begin to melt.

Most interactions with computers involve sight: What you see on the monitor screen and, if you're not a touch-typist, a peek down at the keyboard. High-resolution graphics make sight perhaps the most important part of interacting with any computer—or at least the most expensive.

To really experience your computer, however, you need to get aural with it. You need an added sensual dimension—sound. In fact, top-quality sound distinguishes today's computers from previous generations (at least those modern computers meant for home use rather than as office workstations).

Today, a computer can generate sounds on its own, acting like a music synthesizer or noise generator, and it can control external devices that do the same thing through a MIDI interface. It can record or sample sounds on any standard computer medium (the hard disk being today's preferred choice) with sonic accuracy every bit as good (even better) than commercial stereo CDs. It can file all of your music and dole it out to your MP3 player. Moreover, all the sounds it makes and stores can be edited and manipulated: Tones can be stretched; voices shifted; noises combined; music mixed. It can play back all the sounds it makes and records with the same fidelity, pushing the limits of even the best stereo systems.

Sound

Sound is different from what your computer normally deals with. The electrical signals inside and at its ports, even the light from your monitor, are electro-magnetic phenomena. Sound is purely physical. It is simply the rapid change in air pressure.

When a physical object vibrates, it forces air to move along its undulations. After all, air and the object cannot take up the same place at the same time. Air is pushed away from the place the object bows out and rushes into the empty place where it bends in. The movements are tiny to your eye, but on the molecular level, they are huge.

Air, being made from physical molecules, has its own inertia. It can't immediately move out of the way of a vibrating object but instead gets squeezed, which raises the pressure between molecules. Where the air gets sucked toward the vibrating object, the pressure goes down. Consequently, the air around a vibrating object is repeatedly squeezed and expanded as the object moves. The pressure changes affect the adjoining air, so the changes in pressure move away from the vibrating object as a series of high-and-low pressure waves. Your ear detects the changes in air pressure as sound.

Unlike light, which happily traverses the vacuum of space, sound requires a medium (usually air) for transmission. The speed of sound depends not on the moving object but on the density of the medium. The higher the density, the faster the sound moves—for example, sound propagates faster in water than air.

Because the waves of sound spread out as they move away from a vibrating object, the intensity of the sound pressure declines with distance. Unconstrained, this decline would follow the famous inverse-square law, because as the sound travels in one dimension, it must spread over two. By confining or directing the air channel, however, you can alter the rate of this decay.

Fitting its digital signals into this world of pressure waves is a challenge for the computer in several ways. The computer needs a convenient form for manipulating sound. Fortunately, sound has an analog in the electronic world called *analog audio*, which uses electrical signals to represent the strengths of the pressure waves. Computers turn these electrical signals into *digital audio* that's compatible with microprocessors, other digital circuits, and sound systems. Of course, the computer is not limited to sounds supplied by others—it can create the digital signals itself, a process termed *synthesis*. To turn those digital signals into something that approaches sound—back to audio again—your computer uses its own audio circuitry or a *soundboard* that includes both a digital-to-analog converter and an amplifier. Finally, your computer plugs into *loudspeakers*, which convert the audio into pressure waves once again.

Analog Audio

As a human sensation, sound is an analog phenomenon. It has two primary characteristics—loudness (or amplitude) and frequency—that vary over a wide range with an infinite range of variations between its limits. Sounds can be loud or soft or any gradation in between. Frequencies can be low or high or anything in between.

Frequency

Sound frequencies are measured in *hertz*, just like the frequencies of computer clocks or radio signals. The range of frequencies that a human being can hear depends on age and sex. Younger, female ears generally have wider ranges than older, male ears—maybe that's why some older adults miss the nuances of rap music. Maybe not. In any event, most sources ignore individual differences and list the range of human hearing as being from 20 hertz to 15,000 hertz (or as high as 20,000 hertz if your ears are particularly good).

Lower frequencies correspond to bass notes in music and the thumps of explosions in theatrical special effects such as exploding spaceships and particularly tenacious indigestion. High frequencies correspond to the "treble" in music, the bright, even harsh sounds that comprise overtones in music—the brightness of strings, the tinkle of bells, the sharp edge of crashing glass—as well as hissy sounds, such as sibilants in speech, the rush of waterfalls, and overall background noise.

Low frequencies have long wavelengths, in the range of ten feet (three meters) for middle bass notes. The long wavelengths allow low frequencies to easily bend around objects and, from a single speaker, permeate a room. Moreover, human hearing is not directionally sensitive at low frequencies. You cannot easily localize a low frequency source. Acoustical designers exploit this characteristic of low frequencies when they design low-frequency loudspeakers. For example, because you cannot distinguish the locations of individual low-frequency sources, a single speaker called a *subwoofer* is sufficient for very low frequencies, even in stereo and multichannel sound systems.

High frequencies have short wavelengths, measured in inches or fractions of an inch (or centimeters). They can easily be blocked or reflected by even small objects. Human hearing is acutely sensitive to the location of higher frequency sources.

Amplitude

Amplitude describes the strength or power of the sound. The amplitude of sound traveling through the air is usually expressed as its *sound pressure level* (SPL). The threshold of human hearing is about 0.0002 microbars—which means a pressure change of

1/5,000,000,000th (one five-billionth) of normal atmospheric pressure. In other word, the ear is a sensitive detector of pressure changes. Were it any more sensitive, you might hear the clink of Brownian motion as dust particles ricochet through the air.

In audio systems, electrical signals take the place of sound pressure waves. These signals retain the characteristic frequencies of the original sounds but their amplitude refers to variations in electrical strength. Usually the *voltage* in an audio system represents the amplitude of pressure of the original sound waves.

Decibels

A term that you'll usually see engineers use in measuring amplitude loudness is the *decibel* (dB). Although the primary unit is actually the *bel*, named after Alexander Graham Bell, the inventor of the hydrofoil (and yes, the telephone), engineers find units of one-tenth that quantity to be more manageable.

The decibel in itself represents not a true measuring unit but a relationship between two measurements. The bel is the ratio between two powers expressed as a logarithm. For example, a loud sound source may have an acoustic power of one watt, whereas a some-what softer source may only generate one milliwatt of power, a ratio of 1000:1. The loga-rithm of 1000 is 3, so the relationship is 3 bels or 30 decibels—one watt is 30 decibels louder than one milliwatt.

In addition to reducing power relationships to manageable numbers, decibels also approx-imately coincide with the way we hear sounds. Human hearing is also logarithmic, which means that something twice as loud to the human ear does not involve twice the power. For most people, for one sound to appear twice as loud as another, it must have ten times the power. Expressed as dB, this change is an increase in a level of three dB because the logarithm of 10 is 0.3, so the relationship is 0.3 bels or 3 decibels.

Engineers also use the decibel to compare sound pressures and voltages. Because sound pressures represent power, the math is the same as for electrical power. But for voltages, the decibel relationship is different. Power varies as the square of the voltage, so a dou-bling in voltage results in four times more power (four is two squared). With logarithms, increasing a quantity by the power of two doubles a logarithm. Consequently, a doubling of voltage represents not a 3 dB change but one of 6 dB.

Most commonly you'll see dB used to describe signal-to-noise ratios and frequency response tolerances. The unit is apt in these circumstances because it is used to reflect relationships between units. Sometimes, however, people express loudness or signal levels as a given number of "dB." This usage is incorrect and meaningless because it lacks a ref-erence value. When the reference unit is understood or specified, however, dB measure-ments are useful.

Any unit may be used as a reference for measurements expressed in dB. Several of these have common abbreviations, as listed in Table 25.1.

TABLE 25.1   Reference Units in dB Measurements

Abbreviation	Reference Unit
0 dBj	1 millivolt
0 dBv	1 volt
0 dBm	1 milliwatt
0 dBk	1 kilowatt

In sound systems, the dBm system is most common. The electronic industry adopted (in May, 1939) a power level of one milliwatt in a 600 ohm circuit as the standard reference for zero dBm.

You'll also encounter references to *volume units* (VU), as measured by the classic VU meter. A true VU meter is strictly defined, and the zero it indicates reflects a level 4 dB above 0 dBm. The meters on tape and cassette recorders have VU designations but are not, strictly speaking, VU meters. They are usually referenced to a specific recording level on the tape. Similarly, meters on radio transmitters are often calibrated in VU, but zero corresponds not to the input line level but the output modulation level—0 VU usually means 100-percent modulation.

Distortion

No one is perfect, and neither are audio amplifiers. All analog audio amplifiers add subtle defects to the sound called *distortion*. In effect, distortion adds unwanted signals—the defects—to the desired audio. The most common way to express distortion is the ratio between the unwanted and wanted signals expressed as a percentage. In modern low-level circuits, the level of added distortion is vanishingly small, hundredths of a percent or less, and is often lost in the noise polluting the signal. Only if your hearing is particularly acute might you be able to detect the additions.

In power amplifiers, the circuits that produce the high-level signals used to operate non-powered loudspeakers, the addition of distortion can rise to levels that are not only noticeable but also objectionable, from one-tenth to several percent. Power amplifier distortion also tends to increase as the level increases—as you turn the volume up.

Better amplifiers produce less distortion. This basic fact has a direct repercussion when it comes to getting the best sound quality from a computer. The soundboards typically found in computers produce a lot of distortion. You can often get appreciably better audio quality by plugging your stereo system (which is designed for low distortion even at high power levels) into the low-level outputs of your soundboard so that the audio signal avoids the soundboard's own power amplifier. In fact, better-quality soundboards often lack power amplifiers in the recognition that any included circuitry is apt to be of lower sound quality due to the restrictions of installing them on a circuit board with limited power supply capacity.

Digital Audio

Computers, of course, use digital signals, as do many modern stereo components such as Compact Disc players and Digital Audio Tape systems. Once a sound signal has been translated from analog into digital form, it becomes just another form of data that your computer can store or compute upon. Digital technology adds new terms to the audio vocabulary and raises new concerns.

Digital recording of sound turns music into numbers. That is, a sampling circuit examines audio waveforms thousands of times every second and assigns a numerical value to the strength of the sound every time it looks; it then records the numbers. To reproduce the music or noise, a computer's sound system works backward. It takes the recorded numbers and regenerates the corresponding signal strength at intervals exactly corresponding to those at which it examined the original signal. The result is a near-exact duplication of the original audio.

The digital recording process involves several arbitrary variables. The two most important are the rate at which the original audio signal is examined—called the *sampling rate*—and the numeric code assigned to each value sampled. The code is digital and is defined as a given number of bits, the *bit-depth* or *resolution* of the system. The quality of sound reproduction is determined primarily by the values chosen for these variables.

Sampling Rate

The sampling rate limits the frequency response of a digital recording system. The highest frequency that can be recorded and reproduced digitally is half the sampling frequency. Why? Start by taking the worst case, when the sampling frequency and the frequency being sampled are the same. The sample would then occur at exactly the same place in the audio wave with each sample. The numbers in the digital code would be the same, and when reproduced the system would not produce a tone but a constant, unvarying voltage—direct current. The sampling frequency thus acts like an audio stroboscope. As the frequency being sampled goes up past half the sampling frequency, the tone reconstructed from the digital code actually goes down, reaching zero at the sampling frequency. Go even higher and the regenerated tone starts increasing again—from zero.

This top frequency that can be sampled (that is, half the sampling frequency) is often called the *Nyquist frequency*, after Harry Nyquist, a Swedish-born American scientist working at Bell Labs who first published the explanation of the limit in 1928. Higher frequencies become ambiguous and can be confused with lower frequency values, producing distortion. To prevent problems, frequencies higher than half the sampling frequency must be eliminated—filtered out—before they are digitally sampled. Because frequencies beyond the Nyquist frequency masquerade as lower frequencies when they get regenerated, the regenerated tones are said to *alias*, and filters that remove the high frequencies before sampling are called *antialiasing filters*.

Because no audio filter is perfect, most digital audio systems have antialiasing filters with cutoff frequencies somewhat lower than the Nyquist frequency. The Compact Disc digital audio system is designed to record sounds with frequencies up to about 15KHz, and it uses a sampling rate of 44.1KHz and a Nyquist frequency of 20.05Hz. Table 25.2 lists the sampling rates in common use in a variety of applications.

TABLE 25.2 Common Digital Sampling Rates	
Rate (Hz)	*Application*
5563.6	Apple Macintosh, lowest quality
7418.3	Apple Macintosh, low quality
8000	Telephone standard
8012.8	NeXT workstations
11,025	PC, low quality (1/4th CD rate)
11,127.3	Apple Macintosh, medium quality
16,000	G.722 compression standard
18,900	CD-ROM/XA long-play standard
22,050	PC, medium quality (1/2 CD rate)
22,254.5	Basic Apple Macintosh rate
32,000	Digital radio, NICAM, long-play DAT, HDTV
37,800	CD-ROM/XA higher-quality standard
44,056	Professional video systems
44,100	Basic CD standard
48,000	DVD, Audio Codec '97, Professional audio recording
96,000	DVD at highest audio quality

The odd numbers used by some of the standards are often less arbitrary than they look. For example, the 22,254.5454 Hz rate used by Apple Macintosh system matches the horizontal line rate of the video display of the original 128K Macintosh computer system.

For Mac people, that's a convenient number. The 44,056 rate used by some professional video systems is designed to better match the sampling rate to the video frame rate.

Resolution

The number of bits in a digital code or *bit-depth* determines the number of discrete values it can record. For example, an eight-bit digital code can represent 256 distinct objects, be they numbers or sound levels. A recording system that uses an eight-bit code can therefore record 256 distinct values or steps in sound levels. Unfortunately, music and sounds vary smoothly rather than in discrete steps. The difference between the digital steps and the smooth audio value is heard as distortion. This distortion also adds to the noise in the sound recording system. Minimizing distortion and noise means using more steps. High-quality sound systems—that is, CD-quality sound—require a minimum of a 16-bit code. High-quality systems use 20- or 24-bit codes.

Bandwidth

Sampling rate and resolution determine the amount of data produced during the digitization process, which in turn determines the amount that must be recorded. In addition, full stereo recording doubles the data needed because two separate information channels are required. The 44.1KHz sampling frequency and 16-bit digital code of stereo CD audio result in the need to process and record about 150,000 bits of data every second, about 9MB per minute.

For full CD compatibility, most newer soundboards have the capability to digitize at the CD level. Intel's Audio Codec '97 specification requires a bit more, a 48K sampling rate, and undoubtedly stereophiles will embrace the extraordinarily high optional 96K sampling rate allowed by the DVD standard. For most computer operations, however, less can be better—less quality means less data to save in files and ship across the Internet. The relatively low quality of loudspeakers attached to computers, the ambient background noise in offices, and the noise the computer and its fan and disks make themselves make the nuances of top-quality sound inaudible anyways.

To save disk space and processing time, computer sound software often gives you the option of using less resource-intensive values for sampling rate and bit-depth. Most computer sound systems support 22 and 11KHz sampling; some offer other intermediate values, such as 8, 16, or 32KHz. You can trim your data needs in half simply by making system sounds monophonic instead of stereo. (Note that such savings are not quite so straightforward once audio is compressed, such as when using MP3.)

If you are making original recordings of sounds and music, you will want to use as high a rate as is consistent with your computer's resources. Often the application will dictate your format. For example, if you want to use your CD-R drive to master audio CDs, you'll need to use the standard CD format, stereo 16-bit quantization at a 44.1KHz sampling rate. On the other hand, the best tradeoff between quality and bandwidth for Internet-bound audio is 11KHz sampling with 8-bit quantization. If you have an eye to the future and an ear of gold, go for 96KHz sampling (if your computer allows it).

Note that the format of the data sets a limit on quality without determining the actual quality of what you will hear. In other words, you cannot do better than the quality level you set through choice of bit-depth and sampling rate. The shortcomings of practical hardware, particularly inexpensive sound systems and loudspeakers, dictate that the quality of the sound that actually makes it into the air will be less realistic than the digital format may allow.

Transmission

Moving digital audio around is the same as sending any digital signal. You can move files through any convenient port.

You can usually move CD-quality audio through a 10Base-T network with no problem. For example, you can put WAV files on a server and play them back smoothly on any computer connected to the network. That is, unless you put your computer to work on other jobs that are extremely resource intensive or your network bears heavy traffic.

USB provides a quick and easy connection and is coming into use for digital recording and editing. The bandwidth of USB is, however, constrained. After allowing for hand-shaking and other transmission overhead, you can expect to route about six CD-quality digital audio signals simultaneously through a USB 1.0 connection.

The Web provides a big challenge for audio. Real-time audio playback across the Web is inevitably a big compromise, one that relies on heavy compression that restricts band-width, which in turn limits frequency response and guarantees a high noise level.

If you don't need real-time audio playback—if you are collecting music rather than listen-ing to it—you can move any kind of digital audio through any channel. Ordinary tele-phone connections make the time involved prodigious, especially if you want to move raw CD-quality audio for an album collection. Compressing audio files trims the time to transmit them through such connections, which is why most music now moves through the Internet in compressed form using aurally friendly algorithms such as MP3 (discussed next) and newer, related systems.

Compression

The Internet is not the only place where the size of digital audio files becomes oppressive. At about 10MB per minute, audio files quickly grow huge. Archiving more than a few sound bites quickly becomes expensive in terms of disk space.

To squeeze more sound into a given amount of storage, digital audio can be compressed like any other data. Actually, audio lends itself to compression. The more efficient algorithms take into account the special character of digital sound. The best rely on psycho-acoustic principles, how people actually hear sound. They discard inaudible information, not wasting space on what they cannot hear.

The algorithms for compressing and decompressing digital audio are called *codecs*, short for coder/decoder. Several have become popular for different applications. Windows includes several, invisibly selecting the proper one when necessary to play back an audio file. When recording, your software will prompt you to select the codec to use if a selection is available.

The Internet has brought other compression systems to the forefront. Although nothing inherent in the Web requires them, because they reduce the size of audio files (and hence their transmission time), they have made audio distribution through the Web practical. More than that, high-quality compressed audio and the Web are revolutionizing how music gets distributed.

As excitement about the Web was reaching its peak in the year 2000, developing a new audio compression system spurred more investment than perhaps any other area of Web development. Every promoter had a new and better system that he hoped to make a new industry standard. Although most of these efforts claimed high degrees of compression (and thus small file sizes), the chief ingredient in each was *rights management*, the ability to control duplication of music files to protect publishers' copyrights. Some systems (such as RealAudio) allow you to listen from the Web without the ability to save music. Others only let you play downloaded files on a single system after you've paid for them. All these rights-management systems are based on digital encryption. The Digital Millennium Copyright Act makes breaking these codes or even publishing how to break the codes illegal.

The most important open standard—and the one that inspired the newer compression systems—is MP3, shorthand for MPEG, Level 3. (It does not stand for MPEG-3—there is no such standard, at least not yet). Although usually regarded as a video standard, the MPEG standards discussed in Chapter 24, "Display Systems," also describe the audio that accompanies the moving images. The applications of MPEG audio are widespread—its compression system is used by Digital Compact Cassettes, digital broadcasting experiments, and the DVD.

MPEG audio is not one but a family of audio coding schemes based on the human perception of sound. The basic design has three *layers* that translate directly into sound quality. The layers, numbered 1 through 3, form a hierarchy of increasing complexity that yield better quality at the same bit-rate. Each layer is built on the previous one and incorporates the ability to decode signals coded under the lower layers. Table 25.3 summarizes the MPEG audio layers.

TABLE 25.3   MPEG Layers and Bit-Rates Compared

Layer	Allowed Range	Target or Optimum	Sample Application
1	32 to 448Kbps	192Kbps	Digital Compact Cassette
2	32 to 384Kbps	128Kbps	MUSICAM (Broadcasting)
3	32 to 320Kbps	64Kbps	DVD and Internet sound

As the layer number increases, the encoding becomes more complex. The result is a greater amount of compression. Because greater compression requires more processing, there is apt to be more latency (signal delay) as the layer number increases.

The layer number does not affect perceived sound quality. All layers permit sampling frequencies of 32, 44.1, or 48Kbps. No matter the layer, the output quality is dependent on the bit-rate allowed—the higher the bit-rate, the higher the quality. The different standards allow higher quality to be maintained at lower bit-rates. At their target bit-rates, all three layers deliver sound quality approaching that of CDs.

Unlike other standards, MPEG does not define compression algorithms. Instead, the layers provide standards for the data output rather than how that output is achieved. This descriptive approach allows developers to improve the quality of the algorithms as the technology and their discoveries permit. Header information describes the level and methodology of the compression used in the data that follows.

MPEG is asymmetrical in that it is designed with a complex encoder and a relatively simple decoder. Ordinarily you will decode files. Only the producer or distributor of MPEG software needs an encoder. The encoding process does not need to (and often does not) take place in real time. All layers use a polyphase filter bank with 32 sub-bands. Layer 3 also adds a modified discrete cosine transform (MDCT) that help increase its frequency resolution.

MP3 takes advantage of the high compression afforded under the MPEG audio standard and uses it as the basis for a file system, which serves as a basis for today's MP3 hardware. The advantage of MP3 is simply compression. It squeezes audio files into about one-twelfth the space raw digital audio data would require. As a result, music that would nominally require a 50MB file under the WAV format only takes about 4MB. Smaller files means less transmission time so that cuts and entire albums can reasonably be sent across the Internet. This also allows a substantial length of music (an hour or more) to be encoded into solid-state memory and carried about in a no-moving-parts player.

Better still, by squeezing the size of the MP3 file, the data rate required for playing back a file in real time can be similarly reduced. Instead of requiring approximately 1.2Mbps to move two CD-quality audio channels, MP3 files need only 64Kbps for near-CD-quality playback. Although that's not slow enough for real-time playback through a 56K modem (remember, MP3 files are already compressed so modem-based compression cannot appreciably speed up transfer rates), real-time playback is possible with ISDN terminal adapters (with a good 128K connection and fast server), cable "modems," and ADSL connections. With light network traffic and a 56K modem, you can expect to download an MP3 file from the Web in two to four times its actual playing time.

Because MP3 is part of the MPEG-1 standard, it accommodates only stereo. MPEG-2 is designed for surround sound using up to eight channels. In the works is a new level of compression, often referred to as *MP4*, which will extend MP3-like compression to surround sound systems.

The tradeoff with gaining the compactness of MP3 files is data processing. Decoding the audio data from an MP3 file requires a substantial amount of microprocessor power, so you can't use a vintage computer you stuck on your shelf a decade ago as an audio component. Machines more than a couple of generations old can't process MP3 in real time. Typically, you'll need at least a 100MHz Pentium microprocessor, although a 300MHz Pentium II system make a great audio-playback (and MP3-encoding) computer. In other words, save your old computer for your stereo system.

You can recognize MP3 files by their filename extension of MP3. Note that some encoding programs that generate MP3 files allow you to choose the "level" of processing— typically Level 1, 2, or 3. These selections correspond to the levels under the MPEG standard and represent higher degrees of compression (smaller files and lower data rates) as the numbers ascend, but only Level 3 creates true MP3 files. Nearly all MP3 decoders will handle whatever level you choose, so go for the lower numbers if you want the highest quality and don't mind giving up more disk space.

Looped Sound

When you want to include sound as a background for an image that your audience may linger over for a long but predetermined amount of time (for example, to add background sounds to a Web page), you can minimize the storage and transmission requirements for the audio by using *looped sound*. As the name implies, the sound forms an endless loop, the end spliced back to the beginning. The loop can be as short as a heartbeat or as long as several musical bars. The loop simply repeats as long as the viewer lingers over the Web page. The loop only requires as much audio data as it takes to code a single pass, no matter how long it plays.

No rule says that the splice between the end and beginning of the loop must be inconspicuous, but if you want to avoid the nature of the loop becoming apparent and distracting, it should be. When looping music, you should place the splice so that the rhythm is continuous and regular. With random sounds, you should match levels and timbre at the splice.

Most computer sound editors will allow you to finely adjust the splice. Most Internet sound systems support looped sounds.

Internet Sound Systems

Go online and you'll be confronted with a strange menagerie of acronyms describing sound systems promising everything from real-time delivery of rock concerts, background music from remote radio stations a zillion miles away, and murky audio effects percolating in the background as you browse past pages and pages of uninteresting Web sites. All this stuff is packaged as digital audio of some kind; otherwise, it could never traverse the extent of the Internet. Rather than straight digital audio, however, it is processed and compressed into something that fits into an amazingly small bandwidth. Then, to get it to you, it must latch on to its own protocol. It's amazing that anything gets through at all, and, in truth, some days (and connections) are less amazing than others.

The biggest hardware obstacle to better Internet sound is bandwidth. Moving audio digitally consumes a huge amount of bandwidth, and today's typical communications hardware is simply not up to the chore. A conventional telephone conversation with a frequency response of 300 to 3000 hertz—hardly hi-fi—gets digitized by the telephone system into a signal requiring a bandwidth of 64,000 bits per second. That low-fidelity data is a true challenge to cram through a modem that has but a 28,800 or even a 33,400 bits per second data rate. As a result, all Internet sound systems start with data compression of some kind to avoid the hardware-imposed bandwidth limits.

The Internet poses another problem for audio systems—the Web environment itself is rather inhospitable to audio signals. From its inception, the Net was developed as an asynchronous packet-switched network. Its primary protocol, TCP, was not designed for the delivery of time-critical isosynchronous data such as live audio. When you're downloading a file (or a Web page, which is essentially a file as well), it doesn't matter whether a packet gets delayed, but a late packet in an audio stream is less than worthless—it's an interruption that can ruin whatever you're listening to. Some Internet sound systems abandon TCP for audio transfer and use the UDP protocol instead, which can complicate matters with systems and firewalls designed expressly for TCP. Other Internet sound systems rely on TCP, citing that it ensures top audio quality in transferred files.

Several streaming audio players are available for download from the Web. The three most popular are the audio side of Apple's QuickTime (`www.apple.com/quicktime/`), RealAudio from Real.com (`www.real.com`), and Microsoft's Windows Media Player (included with current versions of Windows and available from `www.microsoft.com/windows/windowsmedia/`).

Multichannel Sound

When sound recording first became possible, people were so thrilled to hear anything at all that small issues such as sound quality were unimportant to them. A tiny voice against a scratchy background sounded as real as a loving coo whispered in their ears. As new technologies such as electronic recording processes brought more life-like qualities to reproduced sound, people discovered that recordings had a missing dimension. In real life, they could hear depth, but the single horn on top of the old Victrola compressed the sound down to a single point.

Trying to recover the depth of sound recording has occupied the minds of engineers and researchers almost since the advent of electronic recording in the 1920s. Their aim has been to reproduce the entire listening experience so that you don't just hear the music but feel like you are immersed in it, sitting in a concert hall rather than your living room.

Stereo

The most natural improvement was stereophonic recording. The idea was simple, even intuitive. Scientists knew that people were able to localize sound because they had two ears. At the time, they didn't know exactly what allowed human hearing to determine locations, but they found that reproducing music through two-speaker systems with separately recorded signals created a miraculous effect: Instead of hearing sound from one speaker or the other, the ears of the listeners were fooled into hearing sounds coming from the entire space *between* the speakers.

Binaural

Closely related to stereo is *binaural* recording. As with stereo, binaural uses two recording channels, but binaural requires a special recording method for creating those signals that uses tiny microphones placed inside the ears of a dummy head. Playback, too, differs from ordinary stereo. In its purest form, a binaural system requires headphones instead of loud-speakers. In effect, the binaural system records the sounds that reach the dummy's ears directly into your ears.

The difference between stereo and binaural is astounding. Unlike simple stereo systems, binaural creates a convincing illusion of three-dimensional space. Listen to a conventional stereo recording on headphones, and all the sounds appear to emanate from inside your head. The only spread is between your ears. With a binaural recording, the sound appears to come from all around, outside your head, surrounding you. You are convincingly transported to the place and position of the dummy head used in making the original recording.

Without headphones, the binaural illusion disappears. To most people, a binaural recording played through loudspeakers sounds like a conventional stereophonic recording.

The development of binaural recording paralleled conventional stereo. Although initially more a laboratory curiosity, in the 1960s and early 1970s record companies released a few commercial binaural discs and radio stations transmitted a few binaural broadcasts of classical music and, rarely, rock concerts. Unfortunately, the artificial head recording technique was incompatible with the multitrack studio tapes used for the vast majority of popular and rock discs, so the technology never transcended its status as a laboratory curiosity.

Quadraphonic

An abortive attempt at creating a three-dimensional sound stage appeared in the form of quadraphonic recording in the early 1970s. The idea was simple: To create listening space around and behind the listener, two recording channels and speakers dedicated to them were added behind the listener—essentially it was stereo squared.

The problem with quad was not the concept but the available technology for broadcasting and recording discs. At the time, quad was invariably a compromise. Because of the limitations of analog technology, engineers were invariably forced to squeeze in four channels where only two were meant to fit. The most common method involved a sacrifice in channel separation. To achieve compatibility with conventional stereo, the engineers combined the front and back information for each of the two stereo channels. They then piggybacked difference information—the back channel minus the front channel—on top of the front-plus-back signal using a form of phase modulation (quadrature modulation, which, despite the similarity of names, is not related to the quadraphonic concept). These systems provided a front-to-back channel separation of about six decibels—much less than the 20 to 30 dB of separation for the front channels but sufficient (or so the engineers said) for providing the illusion of depth.

Only tape systems could provide four full-bandwidth and completely separate audio channels. At the time, however, the only legitimate tape systems with quality suitable for music recording used cumbersome open-reel tape. The audio cassette was still in its infancy.

Although the Compact Disc would have permitted true quadraphonic recording with four equal channels (although with a halving of playing time), it came too late. By the time of the introduction of the CD, consumer-level quad was long a dead issue. It had never made it into Disco let alone the 1980s. Worse, quad bore the stigma of unfulfilled promises along with skepticism about its origins. Many people suspected the stereo industry introduced and promoted quad solely to sell more stereo equipment at a time when hardware sales were flagging. Because of its bad name, the advent of technology capable of handling quad was not sufficient to resurrect it, and modern systems carefully avoided any association with it. Note that no new technology professing to be "surround sound" uses four speakers.

3D Sound

The notion that two channels of sound are all that you need for two ears is hard to shake. Somehow with just two ears most people are able to perceive sound in three dimensions—you can tell not only whether a sound source is left or right of you but also whether it is above, below, or anywhere else. Two ears shouldn't be sufficient for 3D, but (obviously) they are. Binaural recording and playback shouldn't work.

As early as the first studies of stereo sound, scientists have puzzled over this anomaly. They discovered that two ears alone aren't enough. The ears had to be coupled to a powerful computer—the human brain. The brain exploited subtle differences in the signals received in each ear, differences caused by the odd shape of the human ear (in some people odder than others), and extracted enough information not only for depth but height and everything else.

Once they figured out how people could deduce depth from the signals from two ears, engineers went to work reversing the process. They figured if they altered the signal before it was played back, they could add cues that would fool listeners into thinking they heard sound in three dimensions when played through two speakers.

Surround Sound

Although surround sound is a relatively new innovation for home listening, it actually predates two-channel stereo by decades. The first commercial presentation of surround sound came with Walt Disney's animated feature film, *Fantasia*, released in 1941 with a six-channel soundtrack. Although not known then as "surround," similar multichannel formats became popular in cinematic productions during the 1950s as movie producers attempted to fight the defection of their audience to the small screens of television sets. They stretched their already-giant movie screens with Cinerama and Cinemascope and filled the auditoriums with six or more sound channels. Although these systems were formally classed as "stereo," industry insiders began to refer to the speakers in the sides and rear of the auditoriums as "surrounds," and soon the technology became *surround sound*.

Although "surround sound" does not inherently imply any specific number of channels, the most popular format made four the basic standard. In 1976, Dolby Laboratories introduced Dolby optical stereo sound, a system that used noise reduction to coax high-quality sound from optical sound tracks. Until then, most movies with surround sound used magnetic soundtracks, a technology that adds to the cost and complication of printing films. Optical soundtracks are printed in the same operation as the images. Fitting four channels into the optical soundtrack required matrixing, the same technique that put quadraphonic sound on vinyl phonograph discs.

The difference between this four-channel form of surround sound and quad is the arrangement of channels. Quad uses four equal speakers in the corners of the listening space—a square. Surround uses a diamond arrangement with two primary speakers—one left, one right—a center speaker, and a rear speaker. Not only is this arrangement effective in producing an illusion of an all-encompassing sound field, it is also more amenable to the matrixing technique that combines four channels into two. Videocassettes labeled "Dolby Surround" use this technology.

Dolby Pro Logic adds signal steering to the basic surround sound arrangement. That is, it is able to emphasize (or exaggerate) the surround sound effect by selectively altering the balance between channels in response to coding in the original two-channel signal. Both Dolby Surround and Dolby Pro Logic are analog technologies, although the latter uses digital logic to control the balance between channels.

In discussing surround sound, the arrangement of speakers is often abbreviated in what looks like a fraction—two numbers separated by a slash. The first number represents the speakers in front of the listener; the latter number, the speakers behind the listener. Table 25.4 lists the common surround sound configurations.

TABLE 25.4 Surround Sound Channel Configurations

Designation	Common Name	Speakers Used							
		Front Left	Front Mid Left	Front Front Center	Mid Right	Front Right	Rear Left	Rear Center	Rear Right
1/0	Mono	o	o	X	o	o	o	o	o
2/0	Stereo	X	o	o	o	X	o	o	o
3/0	Center-channel stereo	X	o	X	o	X	o	o	o
2/1	Three-channel surround	X	o	o	o	X	o	X	o
2/2	Quadra-phonic	X	o	o	o	X	X	o	X
3/2	Standard surround	X	o	X	o	X	X	o	X
5/2	Enhanced surround	X	X	X	X	X	X	o	X

Further complicating the designations is a decimal component sometimes listed in the count of channels (for example, 5.1 or 7.1). The decimal indicates an additional sound source that doesn't quite reach to being a full-range channel because of limited bandwidth. Sometimes this extra channel is termed the *low frequency effects* (LFE) channel. Its frequency range is limited to that of nondirectional low frequencies (below 100 to 150 Hz), as would be used to power a subwoofer. Nearly all theater-style surround sound systems use an LFE channel to accentuate explosions and other impacts so that their low-frequency components might be felt as readily as they are heard.

AC-3

More commonly known as Dolby Digital (Dolby Labs holds patents on the perceptual encoding system it uses), AC-3 is a 5.1 channel sound system. In other words, it uses five full-bandwidth (20 Hz to 20KHz) channels along with one reduced-bandwidth

(20 Hz to 120 Hz) channel dedicated to low frequency effects. Speakers for a full-fledged AC-3 system are arrayed in the 3/2 configuration with three in front (left, center, and right) and two in the rear (left and right). The subwoofer can be put in any convenient location. AC-3 also allows for other configurations, including plain mono and stereo.

AC-3 is the standard sound format of movies distributed on DVD, having been approved for that purpose in December, 1995. In the DVD system, all six channels of AC-3 are discrete, separately recorded and isolated from the others. The full-bandwidth channels are encoded with a sampling rate of 48KHz and a depth of 16 bits.

In operation, AC-3 compresses the raw audio data encompassing all the channels down to a bit-rate that can range from 64Kbps to 448Kbps. Typically, in stereo the bit-rate will be 192Kbps. In full 5.1 channel configuration, the bit-rate runs about 384Kbps.

AC-3 is the standard for sound on NTSC-based DVD-Video discs. In addition, it has also been adopted as the sound system for the American digital television transmission standard (ATSC). As such, the full text of the AC-3 standard is available from the ATSC Web site at www.atsc.org.

DTS

Digital Theater Systems (DTS) began as a proprietary system for providing top-quality digital surround sound to motion picture theaters. Using the same encoding and compression system as it applied to professional applications, DTS created an alternative audio format for digital source material. The DTS system is an option for both audio and video DCDs. Nearly all DVD players lack the facility for decoding DTS signals, although you can usually connect an auxiliary processor to handle them.

As with most of the sound formats for DVD, the DTS system began as an enhancement for theatrical films. The professional DTS system syncs a CD-based digital playback system with movie projectors using a timecode encoded along with conventional sound tracks on the film itself. The timecode allows the digital audio source to be exactly locked to the film even after editing or repair (cutting and splicing) of the film.

In DVD form, the DTS sound stream encodes up to 5.1 channels sampled at 48KHz with a depth of up to 20 bits. It allows all standard channel combinations from mono to 3/2 surround with an LFE channel. The chief advantage of DTS is that it uses a lower compression ratio (about 4 to 1) than does Dolby Digital. As a result, it holds the potential of delivering higher-quality audio. The bit stream may have a data rate from 64Kbps to 1536Kbps.

SDDS

By acquiring Columbia Pictures, Sony became a major player in the motion picture business. The company is active not only in software but has also developed its own high-quality digital surround system called Sony Dynamic Digital Sound (SDDS). Based on the same compression system used by the zombie Minidisc system, SDDS can encode up to eight channels in a 1280Kbps stream. Typically it samples 5.1 or 7.1 channels at 48KHz and a depth of 16 bits. SDDS is an optional DVD format.

Capturing Sounds

If you're not content using the sound given you by others and don't want to go to the trouble of synthesizing your own, you may look longingly at all the noises already available to you that just aren't in computer-compatible form. You might have a stack of old vinyl albums you want to transfer to CD; you might want to move a cut from a CD into an MP3 file for more compact listening on your notebook computer while your travel; or you may want to steal a sound from a television program or movie to spice up your computer's otherwise drab responses (my system has Homer Simpson crying "Doh!" every time I hit the wrong key). Equipped with a modern soundboard and suitable software, your computer can readily capture any audio source you have for whatever purpose you want.

As with most computing matters, however, you have several choices in capturing sounds. You can directly transfer the digital data from CD, you can digitize analog data from conventional audio sources, or you can make original recordings. Each technique has its own methodology and produces different results.

CD-Ripping

Audio Compact Discs already contain digital audio information, so you might think that capturing the data would be easy. After all, your computer already can tap its built-in CD drive to get the data it needs to set up programs. Matters are not quite so simple, however. The format for audio CDs is substantially different from the Yellow Book standard used by digital data CDs. The differences extend to formatting and error correction. Simply put, your ears tolerate audio errors much better than digital systems tolerate errors in code. Although a data error may be inaudible to you when you listen to a CD playing back, the data stream may include errors that will send digital circuits into conniptions. If your computer cannot detect the audio errors, they will be faithfully encoded as digital data in the proper format but with the wrong value. Transient audio errors become a permanent part of the data—and the digitally encoded audio that you listen to.

The ability for a CD to deliver audio in digital form to your computer is called *digital audio extraction*. The process requires special software that has come to be known as the *CD ripper*. Similarly, the extraction process is often called *CD-ripping*.

CD drives differ widely in their ability to yield up pure audio data. Most early drives cannot faithfully extract audio data. They are unable to properly frame that audio data into digital form, resulting in jitter. The aural result is distortion in the digital audio, most often in the form of loud clicks that repeat throughout a transfer, sort of like someone has thoroughly rubbed 80-grit sandpaper over your favorite vinyl album.

Note that the quality of digital audio extraction is primarily dependent on the CD drive that you use. Older ATAPI-based (IDE) CD drives were poor at digital audio extraction. Music ripped using them contained numerous objectionable clicks and pops, if you could rip from them at all. Today's drives do a much better job. The only time you're likely to encounter clicks and pops is when ripping copy-protected commercial CDs. The noise is intentional.

CD-ripping is fast. With a fast microprocessor your computer will likely rip through CDs at the fastest speed at which your CD drive is capable. In other words, you may be able to rip CD files in from one-sixth to one-thirty-second the time it would take the cut to play back.

Analog Capture

The alternative to ripping digital audio is to capture audio in analog form and convert it to digital. All soundboards have analog-to-digital converter circuits that carry out this process, which is nothing more than ordinary audio sampling. You only need supply the analog source to your soundboard and specify the parameters of the sample—bit-rate and bit-depth.

Internal CD

If your source material is CD, you can use the internal CD drive of your computer for analog capture even if it is not capable of digital audio extraction. Use the mixer software supplied with your soundboard to specify the CD drive as the source and then mute or switch off other sources. Your soundboard will then sample only the audio from your CD.

The quality you get from analog capture will be lower than with direct extraction. Your samples will pick up all noise and distortion present in the analog circuitry of your soundboard, which can be substantial. For example, while the noise floor of CD audio is about 96 dB below peak level, going through the analog audio circuitry of both the CD drive and soundboard may increase the noise so that it is only 60 to 70 dB below peak audio. This level of noise is often not objectionable and can actually sound superior to audio extracted from a marginal CD drive that is rife with clicks and pops. In fact, this noise level is comparable with optimum FM radio reception. If you are a purist, you can remove most of the residual noise with the digital noise–reduction functions available in some audio-editing programs.

Another disadvantage of analog capture of CD audio is speed. Analog capture is a real-time process. Sampling a cut from a CD will require precisely the playback time of the cut. In addition, you may need to edit what you've captured, trimming the silence from the beginning and end of the cut.

External Components

You can also capture sounds from external components using the Auxiliary Input that's available on most (but not all) soundboards. The Auxiliary Input functions exactly like the input to a cassette recorder. The audio signals you plug in there are routed through the mixer function of the soundboard to its analog-to-digital converter to be sampled. Once the audio signals are digitized, you can use the audio data exactly like that ripped from CD.

You can plug an external audio CD player directly into the Auxiliary Input of your soundboard. Better still, you can connect the recorder outputs of your receiver to the Auxiliary Input of your soundboard and use your computer as if it were a cassette recorder, using the receiver to select the external audio source you want to record.

The mixer software supplied with most soundboards also has a MIDI input that allows you to translate MIDI files—both those you make and those you obtain elsewhere—into digital audio files that you can play back like any other music file. You can make recordings by selecting the MIDI source and using any sound-recording software. Note, however, that most soundboards use their own MIDI circuitry to synthesize the sounds, so the capabilities and idiosyncrasies of your soundboard will determine the musical voices in the MIDI recordings that you make.

Microphone Inputs

The worst way to try to capture audio from a CD is to shove a microphone in front of a speaker. Not only does the quality suffer the indignity of conversion from digital to analog format, but it also suffers the substantial shortcomings of both the speaker and the microphone. You might just as well listen to a friend play the CD over the telephone.

Using microphones is the only way to capture live sounds, be it your own speech or the band infesting your garage that no amount of warfarin will deter. Most soundboards have microphone inputs that allow you to plug directly in and start recording simply by selecting the microphone (or mic) source in your soundboard's mixer program.

That said, you should be aware that most soundboard microphone inputs are designed primarily for speech. Although they are able to accept a wide frequency range, they have a high noise level because their circuits are immersed inside the noisy electronics of your computer. You can obtain better quality recordings by using an external microphone pre-amplifier such as that in a mixing console (or "board").

Note that most soundboard microphone inputs are stereophonic and use stereophonic miniature jacks with three connections—tip, ring, and sleeve. A single monophonic microphone with a standard miniature plug (tip and sleeve) usually won't work with these inputs. Adapters are readily available to let you use a single microphone with a stereo input or to combine the signals from two microphones into a single plug to match your soundboard. Modern microphones designed for computer applications are usually equipped with stereo plugs to match the inputs of soundboards.

Legal Issues

Commercial recordings—in general that means all the CDs that you've bought—are protected by copyright laws. You should not post what you've captured or sampled on the Internet. You should not use material in a production (for example, a slideshow, training video, or simply as background sound) without the permission of the copyright holder. You should never sell a copy of anything that you've sampled from a copyrighted source such as a CD.

You can *back up* a CD that you have bought to an MP3 file for your personal use (for example, to make an MP3 file that you can listen to on a portable MP3 player). Current copyright law allows you to make a single *backup* of copyrighted software that you have bought. It's no different than making a copy of a disk on a cassette to play in your car (although some folks question the legality of making such copies, as long as you only make one copy and do it for personal use only, you won't have to worry about the copyright police pounding on your door). On the other hand, it is both illegal and immoral to copy tracks from discs that you have borrowed from a friend or library.

Hardware

The job of the audio circuitry in your computer is to set the air in motion, making sounds that you can hear to alert you, to entertain you, and to amaze you. Computers have had sound circuitry from the very beginning. But in the beginning of computers, as in the beginning of life on earth, things were primitive, about the audio equivalent of amoebic blobs bobbing along *en masse* in black swamps. From humble beginnings, however, computer sound systems have evolved to parity with the stuff in all but the best and most esoteric stereo systems.

From the standpoint of a computer, sound is foreign stuff. Indeed, it's something that happens to stuff—air—while the computer deals with the non-stuff of logical thoughts. Video images are much more akin to computer electronics—at least the photons that you see are electromagnetic. Sound is purely mechanical, and that makes the computer's job of dealing with it tough. To make sound audible, it somehow has to do something mechanical. It needs a transducer, a device that transmits energy from one system to another—from the electrical computer to the kinetic world sound.

Basic Sound System

Although the audio capabilities of some computers rival the best stereo systems, the least common denominator among them is low indeed. The basic sound system that you're assured of finding in all computers is exactly the same primitive design that IBM bolted into its original Personal Computer.

To be charitable, the basic computer sound system wasn't designed for high fidelity. In fact, it was conceived as a beeper. Its goal was to generate pure, if harsh, tones to alert you to events occurring in your computer (for example, the beep code of the BIOS). After all, in 1981 computers didn't sing opera.

This basic sound system has three components—a tone generator, an amplifier, and a loudspeaker—all of which must be called rudimentary because there's nothing lower on the scale. When all worked together, you could make your computer beep as easily as typing Ctrl+G in DOS (this won't work in Windows). The frequency and amplitude of the tone was predetermined by the designers of the first IBM Personal Computer. You were lucky to get any noise at all, let alone a choice.

Clever programmers quickly discovered that they could easily alter the tone, even play short ditties with their data. As programmers got clever, they found they could modulate the primitive sound system and indeed make the computer sing. Considering the standard equipment, you can make your computer sound surprisingly good just by adding the right driver to Windows.

Tone Generator

The fundamental tone-generation circuit is the oscillator, the same as the clock that generates the operating frequency of your computer's microprocessor. The only difference is that the tone generator operates at lower frequencies, those within the range of human hearing (once they are translated into sounds).

The first computers used one of the channels of their computer's 8253 or 8254-2 timer/counter integrated circuit chips as the required oscillator. Modern computers integrate the same functions into their chipsets.

No matter the implementation, the circuits work the same. The timer develops a train of pulses by turning a voltage on and off. The timing of these cycles determines the frequency of the tone the circuit produces.

The computer timer/counter chip starts with a crystal-controlled fixed frequency of 1.19MHz and divides it down into the audio range. A register in the timer chip stores a 16-bit divisor, by which value the timer reduces the oscillator frequency. Loading the highest possible value into the divisor register (65,535) generates the lowest possible tone the basic computer sound system can produce, about 18 Hz, low enough to strain the limits of normal hearing were the computer's speaker able to reproduce it. Divisor values above about 64 produce tones beyond the upper range of human hearing.

Because of the circuit design of the computer, these tones are produced as square waves, which means they are not pure tones but are rich in overtones or harmonics. Musically they sound harsh—exactly what the doctor (or engineer) ordered for warning tones.

In this basic operating mode, the dynamics of the signal are limited. The output of the timer/oscillator chip is set at a constant level—the standard digital signal level—so the sound level produced by the speaker does not vary. All the sounds produced by the computer's motherboard have the same level. Some tones generated by the computer timer sound louder than others primarily because they are more obnoxious. They are made from the exact right combination of frequencies to nag at the aesthetic parts of your brain. That's about all they were designed to do. Listen long enough and you'll agree that the computer's designers succeeded beyond their wildest dreams at creating obnoxious sound.

Using a technique called *pulse-width modulation*, programmers discovered they could use even this primitive control system to add dynamics to the sounds they generated. Pulse-width modulation uses the duty cycle of a high-frequency signal coupled with a low-pass filter to encode the loudness of an analog signal equivalent. The loudness of a sound corresponds to the length of a signal pulse of a high-frequency carrier wave. A soft sound gets a brief pulse whereas loud sounds are full-strength square waves. The low-pass filter eliminates the high carrier frequency from the signal and leaves a variable-strength audio signal (the modulation).

Amplifier

The output of the tone-generator chip is too weak for sounding a speaker at a listenable level. The chip simply cannot supply enough current. The standard way to boost signal strength is with an amplifier. The basic computer sound system uses a simple operational amplifier. Modern systems incorporate this circuitry into the basic motherboard chipset. In any case, even with the boost, the signal amounts to only about 100 to 200 milliwatts, not enough to shake a theater with THX.

The standard computer design also adds a low-pass filter and a current limiting resistor between the driver and the loudspeaker. The low-pass filter eliminates frequencies higher than normal hearing range (and some in the upper ranges that you probably can readily hear). Computers often use higher, inaudible frequencies as pieces that can be put together to make audible sounds, and the low pass filter prevents artifacts from these high frequencies from leaking into the speaker. In other words, it smoothes things out.

A resistor (typically about 33 ohms) in series with the loudspeaker prevents the internal loudspeaker of a computer from drawing too much current and overloading the driver circuit. A resistor also lowers the loudness of the speaker because it absorbs some power as part of the current-limiting process. Although some circuit-tinkerers bypass this resistor to make their computers louder, doing so risks damage to the driver circuit.

Loudspeaker

The actual noisemaker in the computer's basic sound system is a small, two-to-three-inch dynamic loudspeaker. To most computer designers, the internal loudspeaker is an obligatory headache. They have to put one somewhere inside the computer no matter how inconvenient. Usually the speaker gets added almost as an afterthought. After all, all you have to do is hear it. You don't have to hear it well.

Because computer designers make no effort at optimizing the quality of the sound of the basic speaker, it is usually unbaffled, meaning it is open to the air on both sides (which ruins whatever ability it has to produce bass notes). Its small size and acoustics prevent it from generating any appreciable sound at low frequencies, anyway. Its physical mounting and design limit is high frequency range as well. Outside of replacing the loudspeaker with something better, you cannot do anything to break through these limits.

In most computers, the speaker connects to the motherboard using a simple, short two-wire twisted-pair cable. The motherboard usually, but not always, includes a four-pin loudspeaker connector. In many computers, one of the pins is removed for keying the polarity of the speaker connection. One matching hole in the speaker cable connection often is blocked. Only two of the four pins of the motherboard connector are active, the two at the ends of the connector. The center one or two pins aren't connected to anything. Figure 25.1 shows this connection.

FIGURE 25.1
Basic computer speaker connections.

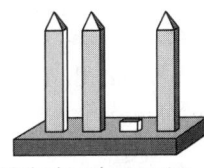

Motherboard connector

Speaker connector

In most computers, the loudspeaker is electrically floating. That is, neither of its terminals is connected to the chassis or any other computer wiring except for the short to which it is soldered. When the speaker is electrically floating, the polarity of its connection is irrelevant, so the keying of the connection is essentially meaningless. In other words, if the speaker connector on your computer is not keyed—if all four pins are present in the motherboard connector and none of the holes in the speaker connector are plugged—don't worry. The speaker will operate properly no matter how you plug it in.

Drivers

Other than beeping to indicate errors, the basic sound system in a computer has a life of leisure. If left to its own devices, it would sit around mute all the while you run your computer. Applications can, however, take direct hardware control and use the basic sound system for audible effects. For example, text-to-speech converters can use the basic sound system with pulse-width modulation techniques to simulate human speech.

Under all versions of Windows, only the native tone-generating capabilities of the basic sound system get used, again just to beep warnings. Microsoft and some others have developed speaker drivers that allow the built-in basic sound system to play more elaborate noises, such as the "Windows sound" when the operating system starts. These drivers let you play WAV files only. They do not synthesize sounds, so they cannot play MIDI files (discussed later) nor do they work with most games.

Some business systems still lack high-quality sound (perhaps as a way for managers dissuading employees from playing computer games on company time). A speaker driver can sidestep the issue, adding some more advanced capabilities to the tiny internal speaker.

The prototype of these drivers is called the *Windows speaker driver* and was developed by Microsoft strictly for Windows 3.1. The speaker driver has not been updated for more recent versions of Windows. In fact, the history of the speaker driver is even more checkered—it was included with the beta test versions of Windows 3.1 but not the release version. During the development of Windows 3.1, Microsoft found that this driver sometimes misbehaved with some programs. To avoid support headaches, Microsoft elected not to include the driver in the basic Windows 3.1 package. The driver is included in the Microsoft Driver Library and Microsoft does license it to developers to include with their products. It remains available from a number of sources, as are other, similar drivers.

These drivers will work under Windows 95 and some later versions, although Microsoft offers no explicit support of such operation. The official Microsoft strategy is to require a real sound system in your computer if you want to hear anything beyond simple beeps. If you're used to simple beeps, these drivers sound amazingly convincing. They are not, however, a substitute for a real sound system.

Sound Systems

Clearly the basic sound system in computers is inadequate for the needs of modern multimedia. Getting something better requires additional circuitry. Traditionally, all the required electronics get packaged on a single expansion card termed a *soundboard*. Higher quality audio has become such a necessity in modern computers that most new notebook machines include all the circuitry of a soundboard on their motherboards or an audio riser board (which simply extends the motherboard another level). Many new desktop computers and replacement motherboards also make all the functions of a soundboard an integral part of their designs. The physical location of the circuits is irrelevant to their normal operation. Electrically and logically, they are equivalent.

To cope with the needs of multimedia software and the demands of human hearing and expectation, the sound system needs to carry out several audio-related functions using specific hardware features. Foremost is the conversion of digital sound data into the analog form that speakers can shake into something that you can hear using a *digital-to-analog* converter. In addition, most sound systems sample or record sounds for later playback with a built-in *analog-to-digital* converter. They also create sounds of their own using built-in *synthesizers*. Sound systems include *mixer* circuits as well that combine together audio from all the sources available to your computer—typically a microphone, the output of the sound system's digital-to-analog converter (which itself combines the synthesizer, WAV files read from disk, and other digital sources), the analog audio output of your computer's CD player, and an auxiliary input from whatever audio source tickles your imagination. Finally, the sound system includes an *amplifier* that takes this aural goulash and raises it to ear-pleasing volume.

Soundboards may include additional functions, one of which is required by the various multimedia computer specifications—a MIDI interface. This additional connection lets you link your computer to electronic musical instruments—for example, allowing your computer to serve as a sequencer or, going the other way, connecting a keyboard to control the sound system's synthesizer. Some makers of soundboards want their products to act as single-slot multimedia upgrades, so they include CD drive interfaces on their soundboards. With the trend for incorporating audio onto motherboards, however, MIDI has been left behind. Few computers with built-in audio offer built-in MIDI as well. In general, to integrate your computer with external musical keyboards and synthesizers, you'll have to add a dedicated MIDI interface on an expansion board.

Soundboards can be distinguished in several ways. The most important of these divisions are the three C's of soundboards—compatibility, connections, and quality. Compatibility determines the software with which a given soundboard will work. The connections the board supports determines what you can plug in—usually MIDI and CD devices. Quality influences how satisfied you will be with the results, essentially whether you will be delighted or dismayed by your foray into multimedia.

Compatibility

Compatibility often is the more important, because if your software can't coax a whimper from your sound system, you won't hear anything no matter what you plug in or how well the circuitry on the board might be able to do its job. Compatibility issues arise at two levels: hardware and software. More practically, you can regard these levels as DOS and Windows compatibility (or games and Windows, if DOS is foreign to your nomenclature).

For the most part, compatibility refers to the synthesizer capabilities of a sound system. For your games to make the proper noises, it must be able to tell the sound system exactly what to do, when and whether to belch and boom. Your software needs to know which ports to access the functions of the sound system. With today's sound systems, this compatibility is ensured through Windows and the driver software associated with your sound system.

If you want to play old games that sidestep Windows, compatibility becomes an issue. Most old games and other software require compliance with two basic *de facto* industry standards: Ad Lib and SoundBlaster.

Beyond synthesis capabilities, the reigning standard for computer sound systems is *Audio Codec '97*, a set of specifications published by Intel that documents an audio architecture originally designed around two separate chips—a controller that handles all digital operations and an analog chip that turns the computer signals into audio. The two are connected by a five-wire serial connection termed the *AC link*.

The heart of the Audio Codec '97 design are two digital-to-analog converters (DAC) capable of operating at a 48 kilohertz sampling rate to generate a pair of stereo audio channels. The specification requires that the controller be able to simultaneously process four signals: two inputs and two outputs. Each channel must be able to translate the signals to or from at least six sampling rates to the 48 kilohertz basic rate of the system. These include 8.0, 11.025, 16.0, 22.05, 32.0, and 44.1 kilohertz. To maintain true hi-fi quality, the specification requires a signal-to-noise ratio of 90 dB.

The DACs are fed by a mixer that accepts inputs from all the digital sources in the computer, including the synthesizer section of the Intel codec chipset. For inputs, the system includes a pair of analog-to-digital converters that also operate at 48 kilohertz as well as an optional third, matching channel dedicated as a microphone input. Nearly all computers sold today meet or exceed the requirements of this standard.

Control

Sound systems provide important control functions for music-making and audio playback. The mixer circuitry in the sound system serves as a volume control for each of the various sources that it handles.

An audio *mixer* combines several signals into one—for example, making the distinct signals of two instruments into a duet in one signal. Most audio mixers allow you to individually set the volume levels of each of the signals that they combine.

Mixers work by summing their input signals. *Analog mixers* work by adding together their input voltages. For example, an analog mixer would combine a 0.3 volt signal with a 0.4 volt signal to produce a 0.7 volt signal. *Digital mixers* combine digital audio signals by adding them together mathematically using their digital values. The results are the same as in analog mixing, only the type of audio signal differs.

In your computer, however, the difference is significant. The sound system performs analog mixing in real time in its onboard circuitry. Most computers use their microprocessors to do digital mixing, and they usually don't make the mix in real time. For example, your computer may mix together the sounds from two files and let you later play back the combination.

All sound systems incorporate mixer circuitry that lets you combine all the analog signals the board works with. The resulting audio mixture goes to your speakers and the analog-to-digital converter on the board so that you can record it into a file.

To control the relative volume levels of the various mixer inputs, most soundboard-makers provide mixer software that gives you an onscreen slider to adjust each input interactively.

Quality

In sound systems, quality wears more than one face. Every board has designed-in capabilities and, likewise, limits that control what the board might possibly do. Lurking beneath, however, is the quality that a given board can actually produce. Dreams and reality being as they are, most sound systems aspire higher than they perform. This difference is hardly unexpected and would not be an issue were not the difference so great. A sound system may have specifications that put it beyond Compact Disc quality and yet perform on par with an ancient AM radio crackling away in a thunderstorm.

In general, most sound systems list their "quality" capabilities in the range of the digital signals they manage. That is, a given sound system may support a range of sampling frequencies and bit-depths. Nearly any modern sound system worth considering for your computer will list capabilities at least as good as the 44.1KHz sampling and 16-bit resolution of the CD medium. Newer boards should accommodate the 48KHz sampling of professional audio and the DVD system.

In terms of digital quality, the CD rates should be good for a flat frequency response from DC to 15 kilohertz with a signal-to-noise ratio of about 96 decibels. Commercial sound systems miss both of those marks.

The shortfalls arise not in the digital circuitry—after all, *any* change in a digital signal, including those that would degrade sound quality, are errors, and no modern computer should let errors arise in the data it handles. Rather, the analog circuitry on the sound system teases, tortures, and truncates the signals that travel through it. Both frequency response and dynamic range suffer.

Most of the time, man-handling audio signals makes little difference. When sounds play through typical computer loudspeakers, you probably won't hear the deficiencies. Most inexpensive computer speakers (which means most computer speakers) are so bad that they mask the signal shortfalls. Listen through headphones or through a good stereo system, however, and the problems become readily apparent.

Many computer sound systems shortchange you on *frequency response*. Certainly the sampling rate of a digital system automatically imposes a limit on the high frequencies that the system can handle. At the other end of the sound spectrum, there should be no such limitation. A digital system should easily be capable of encoding, storing, and reproducing not only the lowest frequencies that you can hear but also sounds lower than you can hear and even levels of direct current. Less expensive sound systems do not dip so low, however. In fact, many boards cannot process low-frequency sounds within the range of human ears, often missing the fundamental frequencies of bass notes and the stomach-wrenching rumbles of computer game special effects. These limits arise in the analog circuitry on the board from the coupling of AC signals through the various amplifier stages.

Most common analog systems require coupling capacitors between amplifier stages (and in the output) to block both supply voltages and direct current errors from interfering with the amplified audio signal. The size of the capacitor (its rating in *microfarads*, a unit of measure of electrostatic capacity) determines the low-frequency limit of the overall system. Larger capacitors are more expensive and harder to place on compact circuit boards, so manufacturers of budget products are apt to skimp on capacitor size. Better audio circuits use larger capacitors that pass lower frequencies or direct-coupled designs that totally eliminate their need (and push response down to DC).

The size of any capacitor in the amplifier output is particularly critical because, as the power level increases, the required capacity to pass a given frequency increases. Consequently, the first place the low-frequency limit of a sound system suffers usually is in its power amplifier, the part that provides a high-level signal suitable for unpowered speakers. It is not unusual for low-priced sound systems to cut off sounds below 150 Hz, which means few bass frequencies get through. Because the low frequencies are not present as the speaker jacks of such sound systems, plugging in better amplified speakers or even your stereo system will do nothing to ameliorate the low frequency deficiencies. Line-level outputs, as opposed to speaker outputs, are more likely to preserve low frequencies, and they should be preferred for quality connections.

The other signal problem with inexpensive sound systems is *noise*. The noise level in any digital system is constrained by the bit-depth, and in the typical 16-bit system, the noise floor is pushed down below that of many stereo components. Listen critically to the sounds from many sound systems and CD-ROM drives, however, and you'll hear squeaks and peeps akin to the conversations of Martians, as well as more mundane sounds such as swooshes and hisses. Most of these sounds are simply extraneous signals intercepted by the sound system, mixed with the sounds you want to hear and amplified to offend your ears. Not only do these arcane sounds interfere with your listening enjoyment, but they may also make their imprint on the sounds you digitize and store, forever preserving the marginal quality of your poor choice of sound system for posterity. Most sound systems keep the level of these noises below that which you can hear through inexpensive speakers, but listen to soft music from your CD drive, and you may find your peace shattered by Martian madness.

Better sound systems incorporate shielding to minimize the pickup of extraneous noises. For example, the circuit traces on the boards will be shielded by *ground planes*, extra layers of circuit traces at ground potential covering the inner traces of multilayer printed circuit boards. Only the best sound systems can digitize analog signals without raising the overall noise level well above the 92 to 96 dB promised by good CD drives.

If you plan on using a sound system for transferring analog audio to digital form (for example, to back up your old vinyl phonograph records to CD), you will want a sound system that guarantees low noise and low-frequency response extending down to 20 Hz.

Digital Audio Output Systems

To avoid the problems inherent in using low-level audio signals inside noisy digital machines, the makers of computers and audio equipment are increasingly moving the sensitive analog circuitry out of the computer itself. For example, professional recording systems may put both analog input and output circuits in an external box connected through a digital port. Consumer-level devices such as USB speakers and MP3 players adopt the same strategy, although for different reasons.

The underlying idea is to eliminate the need for almost any analog circuitry inside your computer and cut the interference from the digital signals, which may be a thousand times louder than the audio, thus making *crosstalk* (the leakage of an undesired signal into the desired signal) almost inevitable. The result is that the low-level noises you can hear through your speakers when your hard disk rattles into action (as well as any strange sounds that appear when your computer engages in heavy-duty processing) disappear. Your computer becomes a truly hi-fi sound system.

USB Speakers

USB speakers look like ordinary loudspeakers, usually a pair of small desktop speakers or a three-piece system with a subwoofer and two satellites. The only difference between USB speakers and conventional speakers is the connection. As you might guess, the USB speakers use an all-digital USB link with your computer instead of an analog connection. The necessary analog-to-digital conversion circuitry is built in to the speakers.

In theory, USB speakers can eliminate the need for a soundboard or sound system in your computer, at least if you only want to play back sounds. In addition, the speaker-maker can tailor the D-to-A converter and amplifier to exactly match the speaker. It also eliminates a confusing jack from the back of your computer and integrates all your computer's wiring into the USB system. Because the signals used by USB speakers remain digital at all times, both inside your computer and through the cable that transports them into the speakers, they are not subject to noise or the degradation that analog signals suffer. The speakers reproduce the sounds encoded in your audio files in pure, unadulterated form.

In theory, USB speakers should sound better than ordinary analog speakers. But the sound quality of any speaker system mostly depends on the transducers rather than the signals. Small speakers cannot produce room-filling bass notes, for example.

USB speakers have shortcomings, too. Digital audio eats a big chunk from the available USB bandwidth—as a practical matter, once you account for overhead, the speaker connection swallows up about one-third of a USB version 1.0 channel's bandwidth, limiting the number of other devices that can share the USB port. Load the port too heavily, and the sound is likely to drop out for long, irritating gaps. With the introduction of the USB 2.0 interface and its wide bandwidth, such problems are unlikely (but both speakers and your computer's USB port should follow the USB 2.0 standard).

Remember, too, the speaker connection is only one function of a sound system. USB speakers do nothing to assume the other sound system functions. For example, they provide no microphone input. Although you could, in theory, link your microphone to your computer with a USB connection, too, USB mics are as rare as unicorns or dot-com success stories.

Although USB speakers have strong theoretical advantages over conventional analog speakers, in current applications the benefits accrue mostly to the computer-maker. Designing a computer system that relies on USB speakers shifts the costs of the analog circuitry to the speaker manufacturer.

On the other hand, using the high speed of USB 2.0, some multimedia developers are creating entire external sound systems for computers. These have the advantage of moving the low-level audio circuitry out of the noisy system unit. In theory, external sound systems can delivery better overall audio quality.

MP3 Players

One of the truly revolutionary products of digital audio technology, the MP3 player is the ultimate portable music machine. Because it has no moving parts, it holds two key advantages over other portable music systems. No discs or tapes to shake, rattle, or roll ensures that jogging or even leaping hurdles won't cause your music to warble, skip, or entirely stop. No motor to move any parts means that an MP3 player doesn't waste energy battling friction and spinning its wheels during every song you play. The MP3 player therefore needs less power for a given playing time.

At heart, a portable MP3 player is little more than a USB speaker with memory. It downloads digital code, typically through a USB port, and decodes the digits into analog format that you can hear through headphones or speakers. The difference is that USB speakers play back in real time, but the MP3 player remembers and plays on demand.

An MP3 player requires prodigious memory, enough to hold all the songs you want to hear. That's why the "MP3" in the name is so important. Without MP3 compression, the typical player would be able to store little more than a single song. The monotony would make you want to cut any exercise short. With MP3 technology, however, you can put an hour of music in the palm of your hand—or even a day's worth, if you opt for a "jukebox" player with a built-in hard disk drive.

MP3 players also incorporate a control system that, at an invisible level, allows the player to manage its memory and keep tabs on the songs it stores. On the visible level, it lets you organize your music and play the selections you want.

Memory and compression determine how much music you can fit into any given player. Most MP3 players have built-in memory, although many supplement their native endowments with memory cards or Memory Sticks. The minimum in any current player is 32MB of native RAM. At the typical rate of music downloaded from the Internet, 64 kilobits per second, that's enough for about an hour of music—67 minutes. More memory increases playing time commensurately; high data rates for better quality playback cuts playback time. Table 25.5 is a matrix showing playing time for various combinations of memory and quality.

TABLE 25.5 MP3 Playing Times Versus Memory Capacity and Data Rate

	Data Rate			
Memory	*64Kbps*	*128Kbps*	*256Kbps*	*320Kbps*
16MB	33 min	17 min	8 min	7 min
32MB	1 hr 7 min	33 min	17 min	13 min
64MB	2 hr 13 min	1 hr 7 min	33 min	27 min
128MB	4 hr 27 min	2 hr 13 min	1 hr 7 min	53 min
256MB	8 hr 53 min	4 hr 27 min	2 hr 13 min	1 hr 47 min
512MB	17 hr 47 min	8 hr 53 min	4 hr 27 min	3 hr 33 min
1GB	35 hr 33 min	17 hr 47 min	8 hr 53 min	7 hr 7 min

Transducers

The bridge between the electronic world of audio (both analog and digital) and the mechanical world of sound is the acoustic transducer. The *microphone* converts sound into audio, and the *loudspeaker* converts audio into sound.

Microphones

All sound systems have microphone inputs to enable you to capture your voice into the digital medium. You can use digital transcriptions of your voice to annotate reports, spreadsheets, and other files or incorporate them into multimedia presentations. With a suitable sound system, you can even connect high-quality microphones to your computer and make digital recordings of music, edit them, and write them to CDs to play in your stereo system.

The job of the microphone is simple: to translate changes in air pressure into voltage changes. The accuracy of the microphone's translation determines the quality of the sound that can be recorded. No microphone is perfect. Each subtly distorts the translation, not making the results unidentifiable but minutely *coloring* the captured sound. One side of the microphone designer's art is to make these colorations as pleasing as possible. Another side of the art is to attempt to make the microphone work more like the human ear, tuning in only to what you want to hear, rejecting unwanted sounds.

Technologies

Engineers can use any of several technologies to build microphones. The microphones you're most likely to connect to a sound system to capture your voice are *dynamic*. A dynamic microphone acts like a small electrical generator or dynamo, using a moving magnetic field to induce a current in a coil of wire. To detect changes in air pressure, a dynamic microphone puts a *diaphragm* into the path of sound waves. The diaphragm is typically made from lightweight plastic and formed into a domed shape, or something even more elaborate, to stiffen it. The diaphragm connects to a lightweight coil of wire called a *voice coil* that's wrapped around a small, usually cylindrical, permanent magnet. The voice coil is suspended so that it can move across the magnet as the diaphragm vibrates. The moving coil in the permanent magnetic field generates a small voltage, which provides the signal to the microphone input of your sound system.

Most microphones used for recording music today use a different operating principle. Called *condenser microphones* (or sometimes, *capacitor microphones*), they modify an existing voltage instead of generating a new one. In a classic condenser microphone, the diaphragm acts as one plate of an electrical capacitor (which, in the days of vacuum tubes was often called a *condenser*, hence the name of the microphone). As the diaphragm vibrates, the diaphragm capacitance changes, which in turn modifies the original voltage.

Directionality

Microphones are often described by the *directionality*, how they respond to sounds coming from different directions. An *omnidirectional microphone* does not discriminate between sounds, no matter what direction they come from. This type of microphone hears everything the same in a full circle around itself. A *unidirectional microphone* has one preferred direction in which it hears best. It partially rejects sounds from other directions. Most unidirectional microphones are most sensitive to sounds directly in front of them. Sounds in the preferred direction are called *on-axis sounds*. Those that are not favored are called *off-axis sounds*. The most popular unidirectional microphone is called the *cardioid microphone* because of the heart-like shape of its pattern of sensitivity (*kardia* being Greek for *heart*). Hypercardioid microphones focus their coverage more narrowly while maintaining the basic cardioid shape. *Bidirectional microphones* are, as the name implies, sensitive to sounds coming from two directions, generally the front and rear of the microphone, which resembles the numeral 8. Consequently, bidirectional microphones are sometimes called *figure-eight microphones*. This design is chiefly used in some special stereophonic recording techniques. Figure 25.2 illustrates the major types of microphone directional patterns.

FIGURE 25.2
Microphone directional patterns.

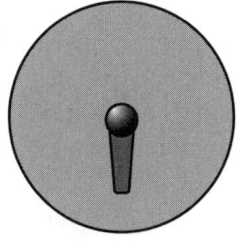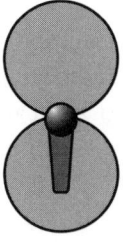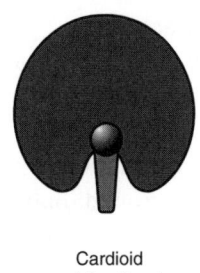

Omnidirectional   Bidirectional   Cardioid
                                                unidirectional

The inexpensive microphones that accompany cassette tape recorders and some sound systems are typically omnidirectional dynamic microphones. If you want to minimize external noises or office commotion when annotating documents, a better unidirectional microphone will often make a vast improvement in sound quality.

Electrical Characteristics

The signals produced by microphones are measured in several ways. The two most important characteristics are impedance and signal level.

Microphones are known as low impedance (from 50 to 600 ohms) and high impedance (50,000 and more ohms). Some microphones have switches that allow you to change their impedance. Plugging a microphone of one impedance into a circuit meant for another results in low power transfer—faint signals. Nearly all professional microphones and most other microphones now operate at low impedance, as do most microphone inputs. If your microphone has an impedance switch, you'll usually want it set to the low (150 ohm) position.

The signal levels produced by microphones are measured in millivolts or dB (decibels) at a given sound pressure level. This value is nominal. Loud sounds produce higher voltages. Most microphones produce signals described as –60 to –40 dBv, and they will work with most microphone inputs. If you shout into any microphone, particularly one with a higher output (closer to –40 dB), its output level may be too high for some circuits to process properly, particularly those in consumer equipment—say, your computer's sound system. The high level may cause distortion. Adding an *attenuator* (or switching the microphone with output level switches to a lower level) will eliminate the distortion.

Microphone signals can be balanced or unbalanced. Balanced signals require two wires and a ground; unbalanced, one wire and a ground. Balanced signals are more immune to noise. Unbalanced signals require less sophisticated electronic input circuitry. Most sound systems use unbalanced signals. Most professional microphones produce balanced signals.

You can often convert a balanced signal into an unbalanced one (so you can connect a professional microphone to your sound system) by tying together one of the two signal wires of the balanced circuit with the ground. The ground and the other signal wire then act as an unbalanced circuit.

Connectors

Both inexpensive microphones and sound systems use the same kind of connector, known as a *miniature phone plug*. Better quality professional microphones with balanced signals typically use XLR connectors (named after the model designation of one of the original designs) with three pins for their two signals and ground. In these connectors, pin 1 is always ground. In balanced circuits, pin 2 carries the positive signal; pin 3, the negative. When used in unbalanced circuits, pins 1 and 3 are usually connected together.

Phone plugs have two or three connections. The end of the plug is called the *tip*, and the shaft of the connector is called the *sleeve*. Some connectors have a third contact in the form of a thin ring between the tip and the sleeve. This ring is called the *ring*. Figure 25.3 illustrates a typical phone plug.

FIGURE 25.3

Components of a typical phone plug.

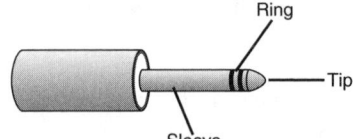

In unbalanced audio circuits, the tip is always connected to the hot or positive signal wire, and the sleeve is connected to the shield or ground. With balanced signals, positive still connects to the tip, negative connects to the ring, and the shield or ground goes to the sleeve. In stereo connections, the left channel goes to the tip, the right channel to the ring, and the common ground or shield goes to the sleeve.

Loudspeakers

From the standpoint of a computer, moving air is a challenge as great as bringing together distant worlds, the electronic and the mechanical. To make audible sounds, the computer must somehow do mechanical work. It needs a *transducer*, a device that transmits energy from one system to another—from the electrical computer to the kinetic world of sound. The device of choice is the dynamic *loudspeaker*, invented in 1921 by Kellogg Rice.

The dynamic loudspeaker reverses the dynamic microphone design. An electrical current activates a *voice-coil* (a solenoid or coil of wire that gives the speaker its voice) that acts as an electromagnet, which is wrapped around a permanent magnet. The changing current in the voice-coil changes its magnetic field, which changes its attraction and repulsion of the permanent magnet, which makes the voice-coil move in proportion to the current change. A diaphragm called the *speaker cone* is connected to the voice-coil and moves with the voice-coil to create the pressure waves of sound. The entire assembly of voice-coil, cone, and supporting frame is called a speaker *driver*.

The art of loudspeaker design only begins with the driver. The range of human hearing far exceeds the ability of any driver to reproduce sound uniformly. Accurately reproducing the full range of frequencies that you can hear requires either massive electronic compensation (called *equalization* by audio engineers) or using multiple speaker drivers, with each driver restricted to a limited frequency range.

Commercial speaker systems split the full audible frequency range into two or three ranges to produce *two-way* and *three-way* speaker systems. Modern systems may use more than one driver in each range, so a three-way system may actually have five drivers.

Woofers operate at the lowest frequencies, which mostly involve bass notes, usually at frequencies of 150 hertz and lower. *Tweeters* handle the high frequencies associated with the treble control, frequencies that start somewhere in the range of 2000 to 5000 hertz and wander off to the limits of human hearing. *Midrange* speaker drivers take care of the range in between. A *crossover* divides the full range of sound into the individual ranges required by the specialized speaker drivers.

The term *subwoofer* is also used to describe a special, auxiliary baffled speaker system meant to enhance the sound of ordinary speakers by extending their low-frequency range. Because the human ear cannot localize low-frequency sounds, you can place this subwoofer anywhere in a listening room without much effect on stereophonic imaging. The other, smaller speakers are often termed *satellite speakers*.

Baffles and Enclosures

The low-frequency range is particularly difficult for speaker systems to reproduce. The physics of sound require that more air move at lower frequencies to achieve the same pressure changes or loudness, so larger speakers do a better job generating low frequency sounds. But the packaging of the speaker also influences its low-frequency reproduction. At low frequencies, the pressure waves created by a loudspeaker can travel a substantial distance in the time it takes the speaker cone to move in and out. In fact, when frequencies are low enough, the air has time to travel from the high pressure area in front of the speaker to the low pressure area behind an outward-moving speaker cone. The moving air cancels out the air pressure changes and the sound. At low frequencies—typically those below about 150 Hz—a loudspeaker in free air has little sound output. The small size and free-air mounting of the loudspeakers inside computers severely constrain their ability to reproduce low frequencies.

To extend the low-frequency range of loudspeakers, designers may install the driver in a cabinet that blocks the air flow from the front to the back of the speaker. The cabinet of a speaker system is often termed a *baffle* or *enclosure*. Strictly speaking, the two terms are not equivalent. A *baffle* controls the flow of sound, whereas an *enclosure* is a cabinet that encircles the rear of the speaker.

Not just any cabinet will do. The design of the cabinet influences the ultimate range of the system as well as its ability to deliver uniform frequency response. As with any enclosed volume, the speaker enclosure has a particular resonance. By tuning the resonance of the enclosure, speaker system designers can extend the frequency range of their products. Larger enclosures have lower resonances, which helps accentuate the lowest frequencies speaker drivers can produce.

Most speaker enclosures use one of two designs. *Acoustic suspension* speaker systems seal the low-frequency driver in a cabinet, using the confined air to act as a spring (which in effect "suspends" the speaker cone in its resting position). A *ducted* speaker or *tuned-port* speaker or *bass reflex* speaker puts a vent or hole in the cabinet. The vent both lowers the resonance of the enclosure and, when properly designed, allows the sound escaping from the vent to reinforce that produced by the speaker driver. Ducted speakers are consequently more efficient, producing louder sounds for a given power, and they can be smaller for a given frequency range.

Although tuning a speaker cabinet can extend its frequency range downward, it can't work magic. The laws of physics stand in the way of allowing a speaker of a size that would fit on your desk or bookshelf or inside a monitor from reproducing bass notes at levels you can hear. For most business applications, reproducing low frequencies isn't necessary and may even be bothersome to coworkers in adjacent cubicles when you start blasting foreign agents and aliens.

Subwoofers and Satellites

A *subwoofer* extends the low-frequency capabilities of your computer's sound system for systems that need or require it. The distinguishing characteristic of the subwoofer is that it is designed to supplement other speaker systems and reproduce only the lowest audible frequencies, typically those from 20 to 100 hertz. Because these low frequencies are essentially nondirectional (your ear cannot tell where they are coming from), a single subwoofer suffices in stereo and multichannel sound systems.

The classic speaker system puts all the drivers for various frequency ranges in a single cabinet to produce a *full-range speaker system*. One major trend in speaker design is to abandon the full-range layout and split the cabinetry. Designers put the midrange speakers and tweeters into small cabinets called *satellite speakers* and rely on one or two subwoofers to produce the low frequencies. Practical considerations underlie this design. The small size of the satellites allows you to place them where convenient for the best stereo imaging, and you can hide the nondirectional subwoofers out of sight. Figure 25.4 shows a satellite-subwoofer combination.

FIGURE 25.4
Satellite speakers combined with a subwoofer.

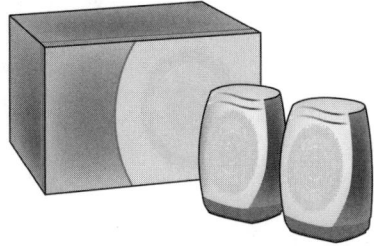

Passive and Active Systems

The speakers you add to your computer typically come in one of two types: active or passive. The difference is that *active speakers* have built-in amplifiers whereas *passive speakers* do not.

Most speaker systems designed for stereo systems are passive. They rely on your receiver or amplifier to provide them with the power they need to make sound. Most computer speakers are active, with integral amplifiers designed to boost the weak output of the typical sound system to the level required for filling a room with sound.

The amplifiers in active speakers are like any other audio amplifiers, with output power measured in watts (and in theory matched to the speakers) and quality measured in terms of frequency response and distortion. The big difference is that most active speakers, originally designed for portable stereos, operate from battery power. If you plan to plug active speakers into your desktop computer, ensure that you get a battery eliminator power supply so you can plug them into a wall outlet. Otherwise, if you're serious about multimedia, you'll be single-handedly supporting the entire battery industry.

Most sound systems produce sufficient power to operate small passive speaker systems. Their outputs are almost uniformly about four watts because all use similar circuitry to generate the power. This level is enough even for many large stereo-style passive speaker systems. Most active speakers work with these higher-powered sound systems and, in many cases, deliver better (if just louder!) sound through their own amplifiers.

Printers

Printing, reduced to its basics, is the art of moving ink from one place to another. Although that definition likely will please only a college instructor lost in his own vagueness, any more precise description fails in the face of a reality laced with printouts of a thousand fonts and far fewer thoughts. A modern computer printer takes ink from a reservoir and deposits it on paper or some other medium in patterns determined by your ideas and computer. In other words, a printer makes your thoughts visible.

Behind this worthy goal is one of the broadest arrays of technology in data processing, including processes akin to hammers, squirt guns, and flashlights. The range of performance is wider than with any other peripheral. Various printers operate at speeds from lethargic to lightning-like, from slower than an arthritic typist with one hand tied behind his back to faster than Speedy Gonzales having just munched tacos laced with amphetamines. They are packaged as everything from one-pound toteables to truss-stressing monsters and look like anything from Neolithic bricks to Batman's nightmares. Some personal-size printers dot paper with text quality that rivals that of a professional publisher and chart out graphics with speed and sharpness that puts a plotter to shame. Some make a two-year-old's handiwork look elegant.

Printer technology predates the video display system. In fact, printing is far older than the personal computer, computers in general, or even electronics. It can trace its inky roots back at least as far as Johannes Gutenberg, who first slathered ink on slugs of lead and squeezed it onto paper over 500 years ago (he printed his famous *42-Line Bible* in Mainz, in what is now Germany, in 1455).

Gutenberg didn't invent the ink-transfer process. His insight was to subdivide the woodblocks used for making page-size prints of pictures into reusable pieces. Instead of wood, with its limited life, he cast his characters out of rot-free metal. Each alphabetic letter became its own metal printing block. In effect, Gutenberg invented character-based technology that served the first generation of computer printers so well.

The latest printing technologies simply take Gutenberg to the extreme, subdividing the printed character and producing the ink-equivalent of video's all-points-addressable graphics. The technology divides each character into a matrix of minuscule dots and prints them individually. The arrangement of dots makes each character—or forms the bright and dark parts of a graphic image. The dots have gotten smaller and the detail produced greater as computer technology and the ability to control the placement of individual dots has improved.

Thirty years ago, about the best printing technology had mastered the ability to place an entire character as a single piece on paper, squeezing ink out all at once, much like Gutenberg, as the *fully formed character printer*. Today, a character made by a laser printer may comprise 10,000 dots, each one individually controlled.

At one time, printing had two faces. Commercial printing was Gutenberg's offspring, the process of making multiple copies by mass production. Computer printing was more concerned with making individual copies. Computer printers, like the first typewriters (raise your hand if you remember what a typewriter is), used mechanical means to make each page look more readable, translating electronic data into ink form.

Today, however, the lines are blurring. The personal printers you attach to your computer are just as apt to be publishing engines that crank out pamphlets, fliers, and newsletters as they are individual page-makers. Commercial printing presses are going electronic and are just as capable of printing single pages as any desktop machine. Commercial printing presses may, in fact, use the same technologies as the desktop printer, though on a more massive scale.

Print Engines

The challenge faced by any printer is how to get ink (or something that looks like ink but isn't) onto paper—and keep it there. The actual mechanism that handles this job and forms an image on paper is called the *print engine*. Engineers have developed a number of technologies for print engines, and each uses a somewhat different physical principle to form an image on paper. Although each technology has its strengths, weaknesses, and idiosyncrasies, you might not be able to tell the difference between the pages they print. Careful attention to detail has pushed quality up to a level where the paper rather than the printer is the chief limit on resolution, and color comes close to photographic, falling short only on the depth that only a thick gelatin coating makes possible.

In making those images, however, the various print engine technologies work differently at different speeds, at different noise levels, and with different requirements. These differences can make one style of print engine a better choice for your particular application than the others.

Impact Dot-Matrix

Today's computer printer evolved from a brash, noisy creation called the *impact dot-matrix printer*. Although only a few models persist on the market, impact printers once were the mainstay of the industry, and their method of forming characters, from a matrix of dots one line at a time, survives to this day in nearly all low-cost printers.

The heart of the dot-matrix printer is a mechanical printhead that shuttles back and forth across the width of the paper. A number of thin print wires act as the hammers that squeeze ink from a fabric or Mylar ribbon to paper. Once the mainstay of computer printing, the classic dot-matrix printer is now an endangered species. It remains noteworthy, however, as the progenitor of the computer printer.

In most impact dot-matrix printers, a seemingly complex but efficient mechanism controls each of the print wires. The print wire normally is held away from the ribbon and paper, and against the force of a spring, by a strong permanent magnet. The magnet is wrapped with a coil of wire that forms an electromagnet, wound so that its polarity is the opposite of that of the permanent magnet. To fire the print wire against the ribbon and paper, this electromagnet is energized (under computer control, of course), and its field neutralizes that of the permanent magnet. Without the force of the permanent magnet holding the print wire back, the spring forcefully jabs the print wire out against the ribbon, squeezing ink onto the paper. After the print wire makes its dot, the electromagnet is de-energized and the permanent magnet pulls the print wire back to its idle position, ready to fire again. Figure 26.1 shows a conceptual view of the mechanism associated with one printhead wire.

FIGURE 26.1

Conceptual view of the impact dot-matrix printhead mechanism.

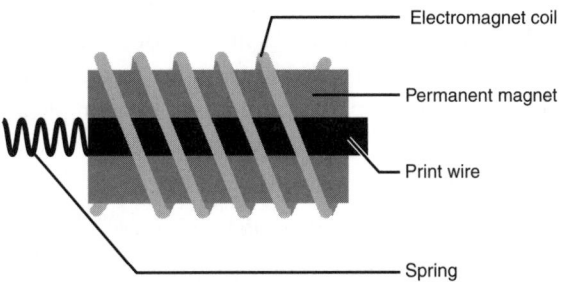

Electromagnet coil

Permanent magnet

Print wire

Spring

The two-magnets-and-spring approach is designed with one primary purpose—to hold the print wire away from the paper (and out of harm's way) when no power is supplied to the printer and the printhead. The complexity is justified by the protection it affords the delicate print wires.

The printhead of a dot-matrix printer is made from a number of these print wire mechanisms. Most first-generation personal computer printers and many current machines use nine wires arrayed in a vertical column. To produce high quality, the second generation of these machines increased the number of print wires to 18 or 24. These often are arranged in parallel rows with the print wires vertically staggered, although some machines use different arrangements. Because the larger number of print wires fit into the same space (and print at the same character height), they can pack more detail into what they print. Because they are often finer than the print wires of lesser endowed machines, the multitude of print wires also promises higher resolution.

No matter the number of print wires, the printhead moves horizontally as a unit across the paper to print a line of characters or graphics. Each wire fires as necessary to form the individual characters or the appropriate dots for the graphic image. The impact of each wire is precisely timed so that it falls on exactly the right position in the matrix. The wires fire on the fly—the printhead never pauses until it reaches the other side of the paper.

A major factor in determining the printing speed of dot-matrix machines is the time required between successive strikes of each print wire. Physical laws of motion limit the acceleration that each print wire can achieve in ramming toward the paper and back. Therefore, the time needed to retract and reactuate each print wire puts a physical limit on how rapidly the printhead can travel across the paper. It cannot sweep past the next dot position before each of the print wires inside it is ready to fire. If the printhead travels too fast, dot-positioning (and character shapes) would become rather haphazard.

Adding color to an impact dot-matrix printer is relatively straightforward. The color that the impact printer actually prints is governed by the ink in or on its ribbon. Although some manufacturers build color impact printers using multiple ribbons, the most successful (and least expensive) design uses special multicolored ribbons lined with three or four bands corresponding to the primary colors. To change colors, the printer shifts the ribbon vertically so that a differently hued band lies in front of the print wires. Most of the time the printer will render a row in one color, shift ribbon colors, and then go across the same row in a different color. The extra mechanism required is simple and inexpensive, costing as little as $50 extra. (Of course, the color ribbon costs more and does not last as long as its monochrome equivalent.)

Although the ribbons used by most of these color printers are soaked with three or four colors of ink, they can achieve seven colors on paper by combining color pairs. For example, laying a layer of blue over a layer of yellow results in an approximation of green.

Most impact printers can spread their output across any medium that ink has an affinity for, including any paper you might have lying around your home, from onion skin to thin cardstock. Although both impact and non-impact technologies have been developed to the point that either can produce high-quality or high-speed output, impact technology takes the lead when you share one of the most common business needs: making multipart forms. Impact printers can hammer an impression not just through a ribbon but through several sheets of paper as well. Slide a carbon between the sheets, or better yet, treat the paper for noncarbon duplicates, and you get multiple, guaranteed-identical copies with a single pass through the mechanism. For a number of business applications—for example, the generation of charge receipts—exact carbon copies are a necessity and impact printing is an absolute requirement.

But impact printers have fallen from favor for several reasons. The primary one is, as always, cost. That marvelous printhead is a complicated mechanism with many parts to manufacturer and many areas to develop problems. Today's leading printer technologies have cut the number of moving parts in a printer (and thus its cost) dramatically. Moreover, because the wires are mechanical constructions, making them smaller is a tough engineering problem. Compared to other technologies, the size of the dots made by impact printers is huge and the quality is low. Impact printouts look like, well, old-fashioned computer printouts.

Impact printers reveal their mechanical heritage in other ways. The hammer bashing against the ribbon and paper makes noise, a sharp staccato rattle that is high in amplitude and rich in high frequency components, penetrating and bothersome as a dental drill or angry horde of giant, hungry mosquitoes. Typically, the impact printer rattles and prattles louder than most normal conversational tones, and it is more obnoxious than an argument. The higher speed the impact printer, the higher the pitch of the noise and the more penetrating it becomes. What's more, printheads wear out. Nothing can take a constant beating without suffering, and tiny printhead wires are no different.

Engineers discovered how to duplicate the work of the impact dot-matrix printer, only do it better, sharper, and with fewer moving parts and noise. The result was the inkjet printer, today's low-cost, mass-market leader.

Inkjets

Today's most popular personal printers use inkjet print engines. The odd name, *inkjet*, actually describes the printing technology. If it conjures up images of the Nautilus and giant squid or a B-52 spraying out blue fluid instead of a fluffy white contrail, your mind is on the right track. Inkjet printers are electronic squids that squirt out ink like miniature jet engines fueled in full color. Although this technology sounds unlikely—a printer that sprays droplets of ink onto paper—it works well enough to deliver image sharpness on par with most other output technologies.

In essence, the inkjet printer is a line printer, little more than a dot-matrix printer with the hammer impact removed. Instead of a hammer pounding ink onto paper, the inkjet flings it into place from tiny *nozzles*, each one corresponding to a print wire of the impact dot-matrix printer. The motive force can be an electromagnet or, as is more likely today, a piezoelectric crystal (a thin crystal that bends when electricity is applied across it). A sharp, digital pulse of electricity causes the crystal to twitch and force ink through the nozzle in its flight to paper.

Today's inkjet printers are able to make sharper images than impact dot-matrix technology because they do not use ribbons, which would blur their images. The on-paper quality of an inkjet can equal and often better that of more expensive laser printers. Even inexpensive models claim resolution as high or higher than laser printers, say about 1200 or 1440 dots per inch.

Another advantage of the inkjet is color. Adding color is another simple elaboration. Most color impact printers race their printheads across each line several times, shifting between different ribbon colors on each pass—for example, printing a yellow row, then magenta, then cyan, and finally black. Inkjet printers typically handle three or four colors in a single pass of the printhead, although the height of colored columns often is shorter.

The liquid ink of inkjet printers can be a virtue when it comes to color. The inks remain fluid enough even after they have been sprayed on paper to physically blend together. This gives color inkjet printers the ability to actually mix their primary colors together to create intermediary tones. The range of color quality from inkjet printers is wide. The best yield some of the brightest, most saturated colors available from any technology. The vast majority, however, cannot quite produce a True Color palette.

Because inkjets are non-impact printers, they are much quieter than ordinary dot-matrix engines. Without hammers pounding ink onto paper like a bunch of myopic carpenters chasing elusive nails, inkjet printers sound almost serene in their everyday work. The tiny droplets of ink rustle so little air they make not a whisper. About the only sound you hear from them is the carriage coursing back and forth.

As mechanical line printers, however, inkjet engines have an inherent speed disadvantage when compared to page printers. Although they deliver comparable speeds on text when they use only black ink, color printing slows them considerably, to one-third speed or less.

The underlying reason for this slowdown is that most color inkjets don't treat colors equally and favor black. After all, you'll likely print black more often than any color or blend. A common Lexmark color inkjet printhead illustrates the point. It prints columns of color only 16 dots high while printing black columns 56 dots high (see Figure 26.2). Printing a line of color the same height as one in black requires multiple passes, even though the printer can spray all three colors with each pass.

FIGURE 26.2
Printheads from a color inkjet printer showing nozzle placement.

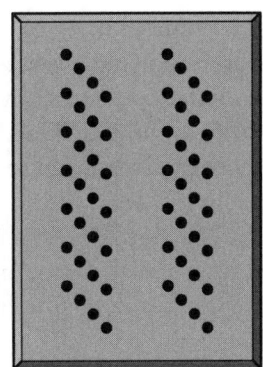 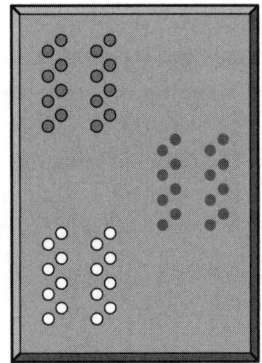

Black ink nozzle plate   Color ink nozzle plate

Inkjet technology also has disadvantages. Although for general use you can consider them to be plain-paper printers, able to make satisfactory images on any kind of stock that will feed through the mechanism, to yield their highest quality inkjets require special paper with controlled absorbency. Although plain paper produces printouts adequate for business letters and other public disclosures, inkjet paper delivers the last iota of sharpness. You also have to be careful to print on the correct side of the paper because most paper stocks are treated for absorption only on one side. If you try to get by using cheap paper that is too porous, the inks wick away into a blur. If the paper is too glossy, the wet ink can smudge.

Early inkjet printers also had the reputation, often deserved, of clogging regularly. To avoid such problems, better inkjets have built-in routines that clean the nozzles with each use. These cleaning procedures do, however, waste expensive ink. Most nozzles now are self-sealing, so when they are not used, air cannot get to the ink. Some manufacturers even combine the inkjet and ink supply into one easily changeable module. If, however, you pack an inkjet away without properly purging and cleaning it first, it is not likely to work when you resurrect it months later.

Inkjet printers commonly use two different technologies, thermal and piezo-electric. (A third inkjet technology, phase-change, is distinct enough to have entirely different printing qualities.) At heart, the basic technology of both kinds of inkjets is the same. The machines rely on the combination of the small orifice in the nozzle and the surface tension of liquid ink to prevent a constant dribble from the jets. Instead of oozing out, the ink puckers around the hole in the inkjet the same way that droplets of water bead up on a waxy surface. The tiny ink droplets scrunch together rather than spread out or flow out the nozzle, because the attraction of the molecules in the ink (or water) is stronger than the force of gravity. The inkjet engine needs to apply some force to break the surface tension and force the ink out, and that's where the differences in inkjet technologies arise.

Thermal Inkjets

The most common inkjet technology is called *thermal* because it uses heat inside its print-head to boil a tiny quantity of water-based ink. Boiling produces tiny bubbles of steam that can balloon out from the nozzle orifices of the printhead. The thermal mechanism carefully controls the bubble formation. It can hold the temperature in the nozzle at just the right point to keep the ink bubble from bursting. Then, when it needs to make a dot on the paper, the printhead warms the nozzle, the bubble bursts, and the ink sprays from the nozzle to the paper to make a dot. Because the bubbles are so tiny, little heat or time is required to make and burst the bubbles—the printhead can do it hundreds of times in a second.

This obscure process was discovered by a research specialist at Canon way back in 1977, but developing it into a practical printer took about seven years. The first mass-marketed computer inkjet printer was the Hewlett-Packard ThinkJet, introduced in May, 1984, which used the thermal inkjet process (which HP traces back to a 1979 discovery by HP researcher John Vaught). This single-color printer delivered 96 dot per inch resolution at a speed of 150 characters per second, about on par with the impact dot-matrix printers available at the same time. The technology—not to mention the speed and resolution—has improved substantially since then. The proprietary name, *BubbleJet*, used by Canon for its inkjet printer derives from this technology, although thermal-bubble design is also used in printers manufactured by Hewlett-Packard, Lexmark, and Texas Instruments.

The heat that makes the bubbles is the primary disadvantage of the thermal inkjet system. It slowly wears out the printhead, requiring that you periodically replace it to keep the printer working at its best. Some manufacturers minimize this problem by combining their printers' nozzles with their ink cartridges so that when you add more ink you auto-matically replace the nozzles. With this design you never have to replace the nozzles, at least independently, because you do it every time you add more ink.

Because nozzles ordinarily last much longer than the supply in any reasonable inkjet reservoir, other manufacturers make the nozzles a separately replaceable part. The principal difference between these two systems amounts to nothing more than how you do the maintenance. Although the combined nozzles-and-ink approach would seem to be more expensive, the difference in the ultimate cost of using either system is negligible.

Piezoelectric Inkjets

The alternative inkjet design uses the squirt gun approach—mechanical pressure to squeeze the ink from the printhead nozzles. Instead of a plunger pump, however, these printers generally use special nozzles that squash down and squeeze out the ink. These nozzles are made from a *piezoelectric crystal*, a material that bends when a voltage is applied across it. When the printer zaps the piezoelectric nozzle with a voltage jolt, the entire nozzle flexes inward, squeezing the ink from inside and out the nozzle, spraying it out to the paper. This piezoelectric nozzle mechanism is used primarily by Epson in its Stylus line of inkjet printers.

The chief benefit of this design, according to Epson, is a longer-lived printhead. The company also claims it yields cleaner dots on paper. Bursting bubbles may make halos of ink splatter, whereas the liquid droplets from a piezoelectric printer form more solid dots.

Phase-Change Inkjets

Closely related to inkjet machines are *phase-change printers*. These printers are actually a derivation on inkjet technology that concentrates on the ink more than its motion. Instead of using solvent-based inks that are fixed (that is, that dry) by evaporation or adsorption into the print medium, the phase-change printer uses inks that harden, changing phase from liquid to solid. Scientifically speaking, the hardening process is a change in the state or phase of the ink, hence the name of the technology.

The ink of the phase-change printer starts as solid sticks or chunks of specially dyed wax. The printhead melts the ink into a thin liquid that is retained in a reservoir inside the printhead. The nozzles mechanically force out the liquid and spray it on paper. The tiny droplets, no longer heated, rapidly cool on the medium, returning to its solid state. Because of the use of solid ink, this kind of printer is sometimes called a *solid inkjet* printer.

The first printer to use phase-change technology was the Howtek Pixelmaster in the late 1980s. Marketed mostly as a specialty machine, the Howtek made little impression in the industry. Phase-change technology received its major push from Tektronix with its introduction of its Phaser III PXi in 1991. Tektronix, which was acquired by Xerox in 2001, refined phase-change technology to achieve smoother images and operation. Whereas the Pixelmaster used plastic-based inks that left little lumps on paper and sometimes clogged the printhead, the Phaser III used wax-based inks and a final processing step—a *cold fuser*—that flattened the cold ink droplets with a steel roller as the paper rolled out of the printer.

Phase-change printers are less sensitive to media than ordinary inkjet printers. They are also renown for the bright, saturated colors of their wax-based inks.

Laser

The one revolution that has changed the faces of both offices and forests around the world is the photocopier. Trees plummet by the millions to provide fodder for the duplicate, triplicate, *mega*plicate. Today's non-impact, bit-image laser printer owes its life to this technology.

At heart, the laser printer principle is simple. Some materials react to light in strange ways. Selenium and some complex organic compounds modify their electrical conductivity in response to exposure to light. Both copiers and laser printers capitalize on this photo-electric effect by focusing an optical image on a photoconductive drum that has been given a static electrical charge. The charge drains away from the conductive areas that have been struck by light but persists in the dark areas. A special pigment called a *toner* is then spread across the drum, and the toner sticks to the charged areas. A roller squeezes paper against the drum to transfer the pigment to the paper. The pigment gets bonded to the paper by heating or "fusing" it.

The laser printer actually evolved from the photocopier. Rather than the familiar electro-static Xerox machine, however, the true ancestor of the laser printer was a similar compet-ing process called *electrophotography*, which used a bright light to capture an image and make it visible with a fine carbon-based toner. The process was developed during the 1960s by Keizo Yamaji at Canon. The first commercial application of the technology, called *New Process* to distinguish it from the old process (xerography), was a Canon photo-copier released in 1968.

The first true laser printer was a demonstration unit made by Canon in 1975 based on a modified photocopier. The first commercial computer laser printer came in 1984 when Hewlett-Packard introduced its first LaserJet, which was based on the Canon CX engine. At heart, it and all later laser printers use the same process, a kind of heat-set, light-inspired offset printing.

The magic in a laser printer is forming the image by making a laser beam scan back and forth across the imaging drum. The trick, well known to stage magicians, is to use mir-rors. A small, rotating mirror reflects the laser across the drum, tracing each scan line across it. The drum rotates to advance to the next scan line, synchronized to the flying beam of laser light. To make the light-and-dark pattern of the image, the laser beam is modulated on and off. It's rapidly switched on for light areas, off for dark areas, one minuscule dot at a time to form a bit-image.

The major variations on laser printing differ only in the light beam and how it is modu-lated. *LCD-shutter printers*, for example, put an electronic shutter (or an array of them) between a constant light source (which need not be a laser) and the imaging drum to modulate the beam. *LED printers* modulate ordinary light-emitting diodes (LEDs) as their optical source. In any case, these machines rely on the same electrophotographic process as the laser printer to carry out the actual printing process.

The basic laser printer mechanism requires more than just a beam and a drum. In fact, it involves several drums or rollers, as many as six in a single-color printer and more in color machines. Each has a specific role in the printing process. Figure 26.3 shows the layout of the various rollers.

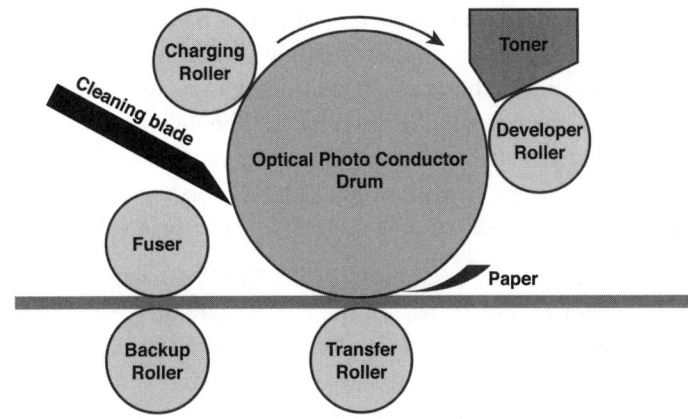

FIGURE 26.3
Conceptual view of the laser printer mechanism.

The imaging drum, often termed the *OPC* for optical photoconductor, first must be charged before it will accept an image. A special roller called the *charging roller* applies the electrostatic charge uniformly across the OPC.

After the full width of an area of the OPC gets its charge, it rotates in front of the modulated light beam. As the beam scans across the OPC drum and the drum turns, the system creates an electrostatic replica of the page to be printed.

To form a visible image, a *developing roller* then dusts the OPC drum with particles of toner. The light-struck areas with an electrostatic charge attract and hold the toner against the drum. The unexposed parts of the drum do not.

The printer rolls the paper between the OPC drum and a *transfer roller*, which has a strong electrostatic charge that attracts the toner off the drum. Because the paper is in between the transfer roller and the OPC drum, the toner collects on the paper in accord with the pattern that was formed by the modulated laser. At this point, only a slight electrostatic charge holds the toner to the paper.

To make the image permanent, the printer squeezes the paper between a *fuser* and *backup roller*. As the paper passes through, the printer heats the fuser to a high temperature—on the order of 350 degrees Fahrenheit (200 degrees Celsius). The heat of the fuser and the pressure from the backup roller melt the toner and stick it permanently on the paper. The completed page rolls out the printer.

Meanwhile, the OPC drum continues to spin, wiping the already-printed area against a *cleaning blade* that scrapes any leftover toner from it. As the drum rotates around to the charging roller again, the process repeats. Early lasers used OPC drums large enough to hold an entire single-page image. Modern machines use smaller rollers that form the image as a continuous process.

Although individual manufacturers may alter this basic layout to fit a particular package or to refine the process, the technology used by all laser machines is essentially the same. At a given resolution level, the results produced by most mechanisms is about the same, too. You need an eye loupe to see the differences. The major difference is that manufacturers have progressively refined both the mechanism and electronics to produce higher resolutions. Basic laser printer resolution starts at 300 dots per inch. The mainstream is now at the 600 dpi level. The best computer-oriented laser printers boast 1200 dpi resolution.

In most laser printers, the resolution level is fixed primarily by the electronics inside the printer. The most important part of the control circuitry is the *raster image processor*, also known as the *RIP*. The job of the RIP is to translate the string of characters or other printing commands into the bit-image that the printer transfers to paper. In effect, the RIP works like a video board, interpreting drawing commands (a single letter in a print stream is actually a drawing command to print that letter), computing the position of each dot on the page and pushing the appropriate value into the printer's memory. The memory of the printer is arranged in a raster just like the raster of a video screen, and one memory cell—a single bit in the typical black-and-white laser printer—corresponds to each dot position on paper.

The RIP itself may, by design, limit a laser printer to a given resolution. Some early laser printers made this constraint into an advantage, allowing resolution upgrades through after-market products that replaced the printer's internal RIP and controlled the printer and its laser through a *video input*. The video input earns its name because its signal is applied directly to the light source in the laser in raster scanned form (like a television image), bypassing most of the printer's electronics. The add-in processor can modulate the laser at higher rates to create higher resolutions.

Moving from 300 dpi to 600 dpi and 1200 dpi means more than changing the RIP and adding memory, however. The higher resolutions also demand improved toner formulations because, at high resolutions, the size of toner particles limits sharpness, much as the size of print wires limits impact dot-matrix resolution. With higher-resolution laser printers, it becomes increasingly important to get the right toner, particularly if you have toner cartridges refilled. The wrong toner limits resolution just as a fuzzy ribbon limits the quality of impact printer output.

Adding color to a laser printer is more than dumping a few more colors of toner. The laser must separately image each of its three or four primary colors and transfer the toner corresponding to each to the paper. The imaging process for each color requires forming an entire image by passing it past the OPC drum. Forming a complete image consequently requires three or four passes of the drum.

Exactly what constitutes a pass varies among manufacturers. Most color laser printers use three or four distinct passes of each sheet of paper. The paper rolls around the drum and makes four complete turns. Each color gets images separately on the drum, then separately transferred to the sheet. The printer wipes the drum clean between passes.

So-called "one-pass" printing, pioneered by Hewlett-Packard, still requires the drum to make four complete passes as each color gets separately scanned on the drum and toner is dusted on the drum separately for each color. The paper, however, only passes once through the machine to accept the full-color image at once and then to have all four colors fused together onto the paper. The first three colors merely transfer to the drum. After the last color—black—gets coated on the drum, the printer runs the paper through and transfers the toner to it. The paper thus makes a single pass through the printer, hence the "one-pass" name.

This single-pass laser technology yields no real speed advantage. The photoconductor drum still spins around the same number of times as a four-pass printer. The speed at which the drum turns and the number of turns it makes determines engine speed, so the one-pass process doesn't make a significant performance increase.

The advantage to one-pass color laser printing comes in the registration of the separate color images. With conventional color laser systems, the alignment of the paper must be critically maintained for all four passes for all the colors to properly line up. With the one-pass system, paper alignment is not a problem. Only the drum needs to maintain its alignment, which is easy to do because it is part of the mechanism rather than an interloper from the outside world.

No matter the number of passes, adding color in laser printing subtracts speed. In general, color laser speed falls to one-quarter the monochrome speed of a similar engine because of the requirement of four passes. (With three-pass printing, speed falls to one-third the monochrome rate). For example, a printer rated at 12 pages per minute in monochrome will deliver about 3 ppm in color. Even allowing for this slowdown, however, color lasers are usually faster than other color page printers. They are also often quieter. Compared to thermal wax transfer printers, a popular high-quality color technology, they are also economical because a laser uses toner only for the actual printed image. Thermal wax machines need a full page of ink for each page printed regardless of the density of the image.

Direct Thermal

A printer that works on the same principle as a wood-burning set might seem better for a Boy Scout than an on-the-go executive, but today's easiest-to-tote printers do exactly that—the equivalent of charring an image on paper. Thermal printers use the same electrical heating of the wood-burner, a resistance that heats up with the flow of current. In the case of the thermal printer, however, the resistance element is tiny and heats and cools quickly, in a fraction of a second. As with inkjets, the thermal printhead is equivalent to that of a dot-matrix printer, except that it heats rather than hits.

Thermal printers do not, however, actually char the paper on which they print. Getting paper that hot would be dangerous, precariously close to combustion (although it might let the printer do double-duty as a cigarette lighter). Instead, thermal printers use special, thermally sensitive paper that turns from white to near-black at a moderate temperature.

Thermal technology is ideal for portable printers because few moving parts are involved—only the printhead moves, nothing inside it. No springs and wires means no jamming. The tiny, resistive elements require little power to heat, actually less than is needed to fire a wire in an impact printer. Thermal printers can be lightweight, quiet, and reliable. They can even run on batteries.

The special paper they require is one drawback. Not only is it costly (because it is, after all, special paper), but it feels funny and it is prone to discoloration if it is inadvertently heated to too high a temperature. Paper cannot tell the difference between a hot printhead and a cozy corner in the sun.

Thermal printers have become special application machines. Inkjets have many of the same virtues and more reasonable paper; therefore, low-cost inkjets dominate the printer market.

Thermal Transfer

Engineers have made thermal technology more independent of the paper or printing medium by moving the image-forming substance from the paper to a carrier or ribbon. Instead of changing a characteristic of the paper, these machines transfer pigment or dyes from the carrier to the paper. The heat from the printhead melts the binder holding the ink to the carrier, allowing the ink to transfer to the paper. On the cool paper, the binder again binds the ink in place. In that the binder is often a wax, these machines are often called *thermal wax transfer* printers.

These machines produce the richest, purest, most even and saturated color of any color print technology. Because the thermal elements have no moving parts, they can be made almost arbitrarily small to yield high resolutions. Current thermal wax print engines achieve resolutions similar to those of laser printers. However, due to exigencies of printhead designs, the top resolution of these printers extends only in one dimension (vertical). Top thermal wax printers achieve 300 dots per inch horizontally and 600 dots per inch vertically.

Compared to other technologies, however, thermal wax engines are slow and wasteful. They are slow because the thermal printing elements must have a chance to cool off before advancing the 1/300th of an inch to the next line on the paper. And they are wasteful because they use wide ink transfer sheets, pure colors supported in a wax-based medium clinging to a plastic film base—sort of like a Mylar typewriter ribbon with a gland condition. Each of the primary colors to be printed on each page requires a swath of inked transfer sheet as large as the sheet of paper to be printed—that is, nearly four feet of transfer sheet for one page. Consequently, printing a full-color page can be expensive, typically measured in dollars rather than cents per page.

Because thermal wax printers are not a mass market item and each manufacturer uses its own designs for both mechanism and supplies, you usually are restricted to one source for ink sheets—the printer manufacturer. Although that helps ensure quality (printer-makers pride themselves on the color and saturation of their inks), it also keeps prices higher than they might be in a more directly competitive environment.

For color work, some thermal wax printers give you the choice of three- or four-pass transfer sheets and printing. A three-pass transfer sheet holds the three primary colors of ink—red, yellow, and blue—whereas a four-color sheet adds black. Although black can be made by overlaying the three primary colors, a separate black ink gives richer, deeper tones. It also imposes a higher cost and extends printing time by one-third.

From these three primary colors, thermal wax printers claim to be able to make anywhere from seven to nearly 17 million colors. That prestidigitation requires a mixture of transparent inks, dithering, and ingenuity. Because the inks used by thermal wax printers are transparent, they can be laid one atop another to create simple secondary colors. They do not, however, actually mix.

Expanding the thermal wax palette further requires pointillistic mixing, laying different color dots next to each other and relying on them to visually blend together in a distant blur. Instead of each dot of ink constituting a picture element, a group of several dots effectively forms a super pixel of an intermediate color.

The penalty for this wider palette is a loss of resolution. For example, super pixels measuring five by five dots would trim the resolution of a thermal wax printer to 60 dots per inch. Image quality looks like a color halftone—a magazine reproduction—rather than a real photograph. Although the quality is shy of perfection, it is certainly good enough for a proof of what is going to a film recorder or the service bureau to be made into color separations.

A variation of the thermal wax design combines the sharpness available from the technology with a versatility and cost more in line with ordinary dot-matrix printers. Instead of using a page-wide printhead and equally wide transfer sheets, some thermal wax machines use a line-high printhead and a thin transfer sheet that resembles a Mylar typewriter ribbon. These machines print one sharp line of text or graphics at a time, usually in one color—black. They are quiet as inkjets but produce sharper, darker images.

Dye-Diffusion

For true photo-quality output from a printer, today's stellar technology is the thermal dye-diffusion process, sometimes called *thermal dye-sublimation*. Using a mechanism similar to that of the thermal wax process, dye-diffusion printers are designed to use penetrating dyes rather than inks. Instead of a dot merely being present or absent, as in the case of a thermal wax printer, diffusion allows the depth of the color of each dot to vary. The diffusion of the dyes can be carefully controlled by the printhead. Because each of the three primary colors can have a huge number of intensities (most makers claim 256), the palette of the dye-diffusion printer is essentially unlimited.

What is limited is the size of the printed area in some printers. The output of most dye-diffusion printers looks like photographs in size as well as color. In fact, dye-diffusion printing doesn't merely look like a photograph, many of your photos are actually made using a dye-diffusion printer. Kodak, for example, uses dye-diffusion for the color prints that it processes.

Characteristics

On paper, you may be challenged to determine what printer technology created an image. Although an old dot-matrix printout is distinctive, modern printers have converged on a uniform, high-quality level of output. That's not to say that printer technologies are interchangeable. Laser printers excel at everyday black-and-white business work, producing pages at high speed and low cost. Inkjets trade their low acquisition cost for a higher cost per page (mostly because of the absurdly high cost of ink) with the ancillary benefit of color. They are consequently the top choice for home printing.

But at a deeper level, printers differ in a number of aspects. These include printing speed, on-paper quality, color capabilities, the print engine, media-handling, and the cost of various consumables. Although many of these issues seem obvious, even trivial, current printer technologies—and hype—add some strange twists. For example, speed ratings may be given in units that can't quite be compared. Quality is more than a matter of dots per inch. And color can take on an added dimension—black.

Speed

No one wants to wait. When you finish creating a report or editing a picture, you want your hardcopy immediately—you've finished, and so should your computer. The ideal printer would be one that produces its work as soon as you give the "print" command—all fifty thousand pages of your monthly report in one big belch.

No printer yet has achieved instantaneous operation. In fact, practical machines span a wide range of printing speeds.

Engineers divide computer printers into two basic types: line printers and page printers. A *line printer*, as its name implies, works on text one line at a time. It usually has a printhead that scans across the paper one line of characters at a time. These printers earn their name because they think of printing in terms of the line. Most line printers start printing each line as soon as all the character data to appear in that line is received. Inkjet printers are today's preeminent line printers. On the other hand, a *page printer* rasterizes a full page image in its own internal memory and prints it one line of dots at a time. It must receive all the data for a full page before it begins to print the page. Laser printers are page printers.

Line printers and page printers produce equivalent results on paper. For engineers, the chief difference is what gets held in the printer's memory. For you, the chief difference is how the engineers specify the speed of the two kinds of printer.

Measuring Units

The two most common measurements of printer speed are characters per second and pages per minute. Both should be straightforward measures. The first represents the number of characters a printer can peck out every second, and the second represents the number of completed pages that roll into the output tray every minute. In printer specification sheets, however, both are theoretical measures that may have little bearing on how fast a given job gets printed.

Line printer speed is usually measured in characters per second. Most printer manufacturers derive this figure theoretically. They then take the time the printhead requires to move from the left side of a page to the right side and divide it into the number of characters that might print on the line. This speed is consequently dependent on the width of the characters, and manufacturers often choose the most favorable value.

The highest speed does not always result from using the narrowest characters, however. The rate at which the printhead can spray dots of ink (or hammer print wires) is often fixed, so to print narrower characters the printer slows its printhead.

Characters per second does not directly translate into pages per minute, but you can determine a rough correspondence. On a standard sheet of paper, most line printers render 80 characters per line and 60 lines per page, a total of 4800 characters per page. Because there are 60 seconds in every minute, each page per minute of speed translates into 80 characters per second. Or you can divide the number of characters per second by 80 to get an approximate page per minute rating.

This conversion can never be exact, particularly on real-world printing chores. Few documents you print will fill every line from left to right with dense text. A line printer uses time only to work on lines that are actually printed. Modern printers have sufficient built-in intelligence to recognize areas that will appear blank on the printed sheet and don't bother moving their printheads over these empty spaces. Page printers, on the other hand, must scan an entire page even if it only has a single line of text on it. A line printer, on the other hand, dispenses with a single-line page in a few seconds.

Engine Speed Versus Throughput

Even within a given family of printers, ratings do not reflect real-world performance. The characters per second or pages per minute rating usually given for a printer does not indicate the rate at which you can expect printed sheets to dribble into the output tray. These speed measurements indicate the *engine speed*, the absolute fastest the mechanism of the printer allows paper to flow through its path. A number of outside factors slow the actual *throughput* of a printer to a rate lower—often substantially so—than its engine speed.

With line printers, the speed ratings can come close to actual throughput. The major slow-downs for line printers occur only when lines are short and the printhead changes direction often and when the printhead travels long distances down the sheet without printing.

With page printers, the difference between theory and reality can be dramatic. Because of their high resolutions, line printers require huge amounts of data to make bit-image graphics. The transfer time alone for this information can be substantial. Page printers suffer this penalty most severely when your computer rasterizes the image and sends the entire page as a bit-image to the printer. On the other hand, if the printer rasterizes the image, the processing time for the rasterization process adds to the print time. In either case it is rare, indeed, for pages to be prepared as quickly as the engine can print them when graphics are involved. Instead of pages per minute, throughput may shift to minutes per page.

Modes

Some printers operate in a number of different modes that trade off print quality for speed. These modes vary with the technology used by the printer.

Older impact printers often had several other modes. In *draft mode*, they blackened only every other dot. The thinly laid dots gave text and graphics a characteristic gray look. *Near letter quality mode* slowed the printhead so that text characters could be rendered without the machine-gun separated-dots look of draft mode. Because the dot density is higher, characters appear fully black and are easier to read. *Letter quality mode* slowed printing further, often using two or more passes to give as much detail as possible to each individual character.

Inkjet printers aren't bothered by the mechanical limitations of impact printers, so you need not worry so much about dot density at higher speeds. Nevertheless, the time required to form each jet of ink they print constrains the speed of their printheads. Most inkjet printers operate at the maximum speed the jet-forming process allows at the time. However, some offer the choice of higher quality modes keyed to different paper types. An inkjet printer may slow down to render characters with greater quality on better paper. Although it may not indicate separate printing modes, you can often see a speed difference when you shift between types of paper and resolution levels.

When it comes to choosing between color and black-and-white printing, speed differences can be substantial. Most color inkjet designs have fewer nozzles for color ink than they do for black ink. Typically, each of the three primary colors will have one-third the number of nozzles as black. As a result, the printhead must make three times as many passes to render color in the same detail as black, so color mode is often one-third the speed as black-and-white printing.

The speed relationship between color and black-and-white printing varies widely, however. In comparing the speeds of two printers, you must be careful to compare the same mode. The most relevant mode is the one you're likely to use most. If you do mostly text, then black-and-white speed should be the most important measure to you. If you plan to do extensive color printing, compare color speeds.

Although many bit-image printers don't allow you to directly alter their resolution, you can accelerate printing by making judicious choices through software. A lower resolution requires less time for rendering the individual dots, so in graphics mode, choosing a lower resolution can dramatically accelerate print speed. The speed gain isn't only mechanical. When you select a lower resolution, you also reduce rendering time. Fewer dots means less data to manipulate. At low resolutions, graphics printing speed can approach engine speed. The downside is, of course, you might not like the rough look of what you print.

Quality

The look of what you get on paper isn't completely in your control. By selecting the resolution your printer uses, you can raise speed and lower quality. But every printer faces a limit as to the maximum quality it can produce. This limit is enforced by the design of the printer and its mechanical construction. The cause and measurement of these constraints vary with the printer technology.

As with computer displays, the resolution and addressability of any kind of printer are often confused. *Resolution* indicates the reality of what you see on paper; *addressability* indicates the more abstract notion of dot placement. When resolution is mentioned, particularly with impact dot-matrix printers, most of the time addressability is intended. A printer may be able to address any position on the paper with an accuracy of, say, 1/120th of an inch. If an impact print wire is larger than 1/120th of an inch in diameter, however, the machine never is able to render detail as small as 1/120th of an inch. Inkjet printer mechanisms do a good job of matching addressability and resolution, but those efforts easily get undone when you use the wrong printing medium. If inkjet ink gets absorbed into paper fibers, it spreads out and obscures the excellent resolution many of these machines can produce.

Getting addressability to approach resolution was often a challenge for the designers of the impact dot-matrix printer (and one of the many reasons this technology has fallen from favor). The big dots made by the wide print wires blurred out the detail. Better quality impact dot-matrix printers had more print wires, and they were smaller. Also, the ribbon that is inserted between the wires and paper blurred each dot hammered out by an impact dot-matrix printer. Mechanical limits also constrained the on-paper resolution of impact machines.

With non-impact bit-image printers, resolution and addressability usually are the same, although some use techniques to improve apparent resolution without altering the number of dots they put in a given area.

Resolution Enhancement Technology (ReT) improves the apparent quality of on-paper printing within the limits of resolution—it can make printing look sharper than would ordinarily be possible. The enhancement technology, introduced by Hewlett-Packard in March, 1990, with its LaserJet III line of printers, works by altering the size of toner dots at the edges of characters and diagonal lines to reduce the jagged steps inherent in any matrix bit-image printing technique. Using ReT, the actual on-paper resolution remains at the rated value of the print engine—for example, 300 or 600 dpi—but the optimized dot size makes the printing appear sharper.

Increasing resolution is more than a matter of refining the design of print engine mechanics. The printer's electronics must be adapted to match, including adding more memory—substantially more. Memory requirements increase as the square of the linear dot density. Doubling the number of dots per inch quadruples memory needs. At high resolutions, the memory needs for rasterizing the image can become prodigious—about 14MB for a 1200 dpi image. Table 26.1 lists the raster memory needs for common monochrome printer resolutions.

TABLE 26.1   Raster Memory Size for Monochrome Printer Resolutions

Resolution	Dots	Bytes
75 dpi	450,000	56,250
150 dpi	1,800,000	225,000
300 dpi	7,200,000	900,000
360 dpi	10,368,000	1,296,000
600 dpi	28,800,000	3,600,000
720 dpi	41,472,000	5,184,000
1200 dpi	115,200,000	14,400,000

Adding color, of course, increases the memory requirements. Fortunately, the color bit-depth used by common printer technologies doesn't impose the same extreme demands as monitors. A printer has only a few colors corresponding to the hues of its inks and, except for continuous-tone technologies such as dye-diffusion, the range of each color usually is limited to on or off. Thankfully, color resolutions are generally substantially lower than monochrome, defined by the size of the color super-pixels rather than individual dots. In any case, the raster memory requirements of a color printer are substantially higher than monochrome.

Note that when printing text, page printers may operate in a character-mapped mode, so memory usage is not as great. Even with minimal memory, a printer can store a full-page image in ASCII or a similar code, one byte per letter, as well as the definitions for the characters of several fonts. In this mode, it generates the individual dots of each character as the page is scanned through the printer.

Moving to higher resolutions makes other demands on a printer as well. For example, in laser printers, finer resolutions require improved toner formulations because, at high resolutions, the size of toner particles limits sharpness, much as the size of print wires limits impact dot-matrix resolution. With higher-resolution laser printers, it becomes increasingly important to get the right toner, particularly if you have toner cartridges refilled. The wrong toner limits resolution just as a fuzzy ribbon limits the quality of impact printer output.

Color

Printers start with the primaries when it comes to color. They start with inks corresponding to the three primary colors—red, yellow, and blue. If you want anything beyond those, the printer must find some way of mixing them together. This mixing can be physical or optical.

The physical mixing of colors requires that two or more colors of ink actually mix together while they are wet. Printer inks are, however, designed to dry rapidly, so the colors to be mixed must be applied simultaneously or in quick succession. Few printers rely on the physical mixing of inks to increase the number of colors they produce.

Optical mixing takes place in either of two ways. One color of ink can be applied over another (that has already dried) or the colors can be applied adjacent to one another.

Appling multiple layers of color requires that the inks be to some degree transparent, because a truly opaque ink would obscure the first color to be applied. Most modern printer inks are transparent, which allows them to be used on transparencies for overhead projection as well as on paper. The exact hue of a transparent ink is, of course, dependent on the color of the medium it is applied to.

Optical mixing also takes place when dots of two or more colors are intermixed. If the dots are so close together that the eye cannot individually resolve each one, their colors blend together on the retina, mixing the individual hues together. Most computer color printers take advantage of this kind of optical mixing by dithering.

Three-, Four-, and Six-Color Printers

Color primaries in printing aren't so simple as the familiar threesome. To achieve better color reproduction, printers use a skewed set of primary colors—magenta instead of red, cyan instead of blue, and plain-old ordinary yellow. Even this mix is so far from perfect that, when all are combined, they yield something that's often far from black. Consequently, better printers include black in their primary colors.

Black, in fact, may play two roles in a color printer. A few inkjet printers allow you to choose between black-and-white and color operation as simply as swapping ink cartridges. In these machines, black is treated as a separate hue that cannot be mixed in blends with the three color primaries. These *three-color printers* render colors only from the three primaries even though some machines can print pure black when using a suitable black-only ink cartridge. The approximation of black made from the three primaries is termed *composite black* and often has a off-color cast. Four-color printers put black on the same footing as the three primary hues and mix with all four together. This four-color printing technique gives superior blacks, purer grays, and greater depth to all darker shades.

To further increase the range of pure colors possible with a printer, manufacturers are adding more colors of ink. The most common addition is two extra ink colors beyond the standard four, generally orange and violet, which extend the spectrum that the printer can render. This greater range in primaries translates into more realistic reproduction of photographs with less need for other color-enhancing techniques, such as dithering.

Dithering

Color televisions do an excellent job with their three primaries and paint a nearly infinite spectrum. But the television tube has a luxury most printers lack. The television can modulate its electron beam and change its intensity. Most printers are stuck with a single intensity for each color. As a result, the basic range of most printers is four pure colors and seven when using mixtures, blending magenta and blue to make violet, magenta and yellow for orange, and blue and yellow for green. Count the background color of the paper being printed upon, and the basic range of most color printers is eight hues.

Commercial color printing faces the same problem of trying to render a wide spectrum from four primary colors. To extend the range of printing presses, graphic artists make color halftones. They break an image into dots photographically using a screen. Using special photographic techniques (or, more often today, a computer), they can vary the size of the dot with the intensity of the color.

Most computer printers cannot vary the size of their dots. To achieve a halftone effect, they use *dithering*. In dithering, colors beyond the range of pure hues of which a printer is capable are rendered in patterns of primary-colored dots. Instead of each printed dot representing a single pixel of an image, dithering uses a small array of dots to make a single pixel. These multiple-dot pixels are termed *super-pixels*. By varying the number of dots that actually get printed with a given color of ink in the super-pixel matrix, the printer can vary the perceived intensity of the color.

The problem with dithering is that it degrades the perceived resolution of the color image. The resolution is limited by the size of the super-pixels rather than the individual dots. For example, to attempt to render an image in True Color (eight bits per primary), the printer must use super-pixels measuring eight by eight dots. The resolution falls by an equivalent factor. A printer with 600 dpi resolution yields a color image with 75 dpi resolution.

Drivers

Getting good color with dithering is more art than science. The choice of dithering pattern determines how smooth colors can be rendered. A bad choice of dithering pattern often results in a moiré pattern overlaid on your printed images or wide gaps between super-pixels. Moreover, colors don't mix the same on screen and on paper. The two media often use entirely different color spaces (RGB for your monitor, CYMK for your printer), thus requiring a translation step between them. Inks only aspire to be pure colors. The primary colors may land far from the mark, and a color blended from them may be strange, indeed.

Your printer driver can adjust for all these issues. How well the programmer charged with writing the driver does his job is the final determinant in the color quality your printer produces. A good driver can create photo-quality images from an inkjet printer, whereas a bad driver can make deplorable pictures even when using the same underlying print engine. Unfortunately, the quality of a printer's driver isn't quantified on the specifications sheet. You can only judge it by looking at the output of a printer. For highest quality, however, you'll always want driver software written for your particular model of printer, not one that your printer emulates. Moreover, you'll want to get the latest driver. You may want to periodically cruise the Web site of your printer-maker to catch driver updates as they come out.

Permanence

Most inks fade. The ultraviolet energy in daylight attacks many pigments, breaking the molecular bonds that give a dye or pigment its color. With enough light, the color changes, shifting in hue, or fades until it is invisible on paper. Light is not the only culprit. Airborne chemicals (such as pollution) also react with dyes and pigments and can change their colors. Pigments sometimes even react with each other when they are mixed—a problem for painters that's rarely encountered in printing.

Of all ink colors, black is usually the most permanent, at least when it is made using carbon as a pigment. This black does not fade in light and, except for fire, rarely reacts with chemicals in the air. The black toner used by most laser printers is therefore among the most color-permanent of printing. The conventional commercial printing ink that's used for books usually is based on carbon pigments.

Colors, however, vary in their permanence. Many of the brightest hues fade quickly, while a few hues are immutable as black. The color inks used by most computer printers are designed to last only for a few years. For most business documents, this impermanence is no problem. It may even save you a trip to the shredder. But if you want to print artwork or a family photo, having it turn green or fade to white after a few months of display is far from ideal. To help prevent problems with fading, some printer manufacturers (particularly those offering photo printers) have begun to manufacture permanent inks rated for more than 100 years of display.

Permanence has another aspect. Some inks are water soluble. When a printout made using soluble ink get soaked or even damp, the colors can run like a bad tie-dye job. The somewhat psychedelic effect can be interesting, but it also interferes with legibility. Most inkjet printer inks are water soluble. For more permanent printouts, some manufacturers offer nonsoluble inks and special papers that help fix the soluble inks and prevent their running.

Paper-Handling

Key to the design of all printers is that their imaging systems operate in only one dimension, one line at a time, be it the text-like line of the line printer or the single raster line of the page printer. To create a full two-dimensional image, all printers require that the printing medium—typically paper—move past the print mechanism. With page printers, this motion must be smooth and continuous. With line printers, the paper must cog forward, hold its position, and then cog forward to the next line. Achieving high resolutions without distortion requires precision paper movement with a tolerance of variation far smaller than the number of dots per inch the printer is to produce.

Adding further complexity, the printer must be able to move paper or other printing media in and out of its mechanism. Most modern printers use sheet feeders that can pull a single page from a stack, route it past the imaging mechanism, and stack it in an output tray. Older printers and some of the highest speed machines use continuous-form paper, which trades a simplified printer mechanism for your trouble in tearing sheets apart. Each paper-handling method has its own complications and refinements.

The basic unit of computer printing is the page, a single sheet of paper, so it is only natural for you to want your printer to work with individual sheets. The computer printing process, however, is one that works with volume—not pages but print jobs, not sheets but reams.

The individual sheet poses problems in printing. To make your ideas, onscreen images, and printed hardcopy agree, each sheet must get properly aligned so that its images appear at the proper place and at the proper angle on every sheet. Getting perfect alignment can be vexing for both human and mechanical hands. Getting thousands into alignment is a project that might please only the Master of the Inquisition. Yet every laser printer, most inkjet printers, and a variety of other machines face that challenge every time you start a print job.

To cope with this hardcopy torture, the printer requires a complex mechanism called the *cut-sheet feeder*, or simply the *sheet feeder*. You'll find considerable variation in the designs of the sheet feeders of printers. All are complicated designs involving cogs, gears, rods, and rollers, and every engineer appears to have his own favorite arrangement. The inner complexity of these machines is something to marvel at but not dissect, unless you have too much time on your hands. Differences in the designs of these mechanisms do have a number of practical effects: the capacity of the printer, which relates to how long it can run without your attention; the kinds and sizes of stock that roll through; how sheets are collated and whether you have to spend half an afternoon to get all the pages in order; and duplex printing, which automatically covers both sides of each sheet.

No matter the details, however, all sheet feeders can trace their heritage back to one progenitor design—the basic friction feed mechanism.

Friction Feed

When you load a single sheet of paper into a modern inkjet printer, it reverts to *friction feed*, which uses the same technology as yesteryear's mechanical typewriter. It moves paper through its mechanism by squeezing the paper against a rubber drive roller. The first inkjet printers actually used the large rubber roller of the typewriter, called a *platen*, and smaller drive rollers. Friction between the rubber and the paper or other printing media gives the system a positive grip that prevents slipping and ensures each sheet gets where it's suppose to. This friction also gives the technology its name.

In modern printers, the friction feed mechanism often goes by other names, such as *cut-sheet feeder* and *bin feed mechanism*. All rely on the friction between paper and rubber rollers.

The mechanism also relies on the lack of friction to operate properly. To feed individual sheets, the friction feed mechanism must grasp only a single sheet, which must slide against all the others. If there's too much friction between individual sheets of paper, they may stick together. Several may go through the printer at once, or you may seem to print on every other sheet. Many factors in the production and packaging of paper affect whether sheets stick to one another. In addition, the environment exerts its own effect—according to Hewlett-Packard, humidity can cause paper jams. When paper is too damp, sheets can stick together. When it is too dry, paper may develop a static charge, which also makes sheets stick together. Most laser printers have some means of draining the static from paper, but sometimes it is not successful.

If you cannot change the humidity around your printer and its paper, you can ward off the effects of sticky sheets by choosing a different kind or brand of paper. Some people recommend riffling through the paper before you load it into your printer to separate the sheets. Riffling each ream also helps avoid the other causes of sheets sticking together.

Modern printers integrate the feed mechanism with the rest of the printer drive system. You load cut sheets into a bin or removable tray, and the printer takes over from there. The mechanism is reduced to a number of rollers chained, belted, or geared together that pull the paper smoothly through the printer. This integrated design reduces complexity, increases reliability, and often trims versatility. Its chief limitations are in the areas of capacity and stock-handling.

Capacity

The most obvious difference between sheet feed mechanisms of the printer is capacity. Some machines are made only for light, personal use and have modestly sized paper bins that hold 50 or fewer sheets. In practical terms, this means that every 10 to 15 minutes, you must attend to the needs of the printer, loading and removing the wads of paper that course through it. Larger trays require less intervention. Printers designed for heavy network use may hold several thousand sheets at a time.

The chief enemy of capacity is size. A compact printer must necessarily devote less space—and therefore less capacity—to stocking paper. A tray large enough to accommodate a ream (500 sheets) of paper would double the overall volume of some inkjet printers. In addition, larger tray capacities make building the feed mechanism more difficult. The printer must deal with a larger overall variation in the height of the paper stack, which can challenge both the mechanism and its designer.

A printer needs at least two trays or bins—one to hold blank stock waiting to be printed upon and one to hold the results of the printing. These need not be, and often are not, the same size. Most print jobs range from a few to a few dozen sheets, and you will usually want to grab the results as soon as the printing finishes. An output bin large enough to accommodate your typical print job usually is sufficient for a personal printer. The input tray usually holds more so that you need to load it less frequently—you certainly don't want to deal with the chore every time you make a printout.

Media-Handling

Most printers are designed to handle a range of printing media, from paper stock and cardboard to transparency acetates. Not all printers handle all types of media. Part of the limitation is in the print engine itself. Many constraints arise from the feed mechanism, however.

With any cut-sheet mechanism, size is an important issue. All printers impose minimum size requirements on the media you feed them. The length of each sheet must be long enough so that one set of drive rollers can push it to the next. When too short sheets slide between rollers, nothing except your intervention can move them out. Similarly, each sheet must be wide enough that the drive rollers can get a proper grip. The maximum width is dictated by the width of the paper path through the printer. The maximum length is enforced by the size of paper trays and the imaging capabilities of the printer engine.

In any case, when selecting a printer you must be certain that it can handle the size of media you want to use. Most modern printers are designed primarily for standard letter-size sheets; some, but not all, accommodate legal-size sheets. If you want to use other sizes, take a close look at the specifications. Table 26.2 lists the dimensions of common sizes of paper.

TABLE 26.2 Dimensions of Common Paper Sizes

Designation	Height Millimeters	Width Millimeters	Height Inches	Width Inches
A9	37	52	1.5	2.1
B9	45	64	1.8	2.5
A8	52	74	2.1	2.9
B8	64	91	2.5	3.6
A7	74	105	2.9	4.1
B7	91	128	3.6	5.0
A6	105	148	4.1	5.8
B6	128	182	5.0	7.2
A5	148	210	5.8	8.3
Octavo	152	229	6	9
B5	182	256	7.2	10.1
Executive	184	267	7.25	10.5
A4	210	297	8.3	11.7
Letter	216	279	8.5	11
Legal	216	356	8.5	14
Quarto	241	309	9.5	12
B4	257	364	10.1	14.3
Tabloid	279	432	11	17
A3	297	420	11.7	16.5
Folio	309	508	12	20
Foolscap	343	432	13.5	17
B3	364	515	14.3	20.3
A2	420	594	16.5	23.4
B2	515	728	20.3	28.7
A1	594	841	23.4	33.1
B1	728	1030	28.7	40.6
A0	841	1189	33.1	46.8
B0	1030	1456	40.6	57.3

Most sheet-fed printers cannot print to the edges of any sheet. The actual image area is smaller because drive mechanisms may reserve a space to grip the medium, and the engine may be smaller than the sheet to minimize costs. If you want to print to the edge of a sheet, you often need a printer capable of handling larger media and then must trim each page when it is done. Printing to (and beyond) the edge of a sheet is termed *full-bleed* printing. Only a few sheet-fed printers are capable of managing the task.

Printing media also differ in weight, which roughly corresponds to the thickness of paper. In general, laser printers are the most critical in regard to media weight. The capabilities of a given printer are listed as a range of paper weights the printer can handle—in the case of laser printers, typically from 16 to 24 pounds (most business stationery uses 20- or 24-pound stock). If you want to print heavier covers for reports, your printer needs to be able to handle 70-pound paper. Similarly, printer specifications will reveal whether the mechanism can deal with transparency media and label sheets.

Laser printers impose an additional specification on paper stock—moisture content. The moisture content of paper affects more than whether sheets stick together. It also changes the conductivity of the paper. The laser printing process is based on carefully controlled static charges, including applying a charge to the paper to make toner stick to it. If paper is too moist or conductive, the charge and the toner may drain away before the image is fused to the sheet. In fact, high humidity around a laser printer can affect the quality of its printouts—pale printouts or those with broken characters can often be traced to paper containing too much moisture or operating the printer in a high-humidity environment (which in turn makes the paper moist).

Most modern printers readily accommodate envelopes, again with specific enforced size restrictions. As with paper, envelopes come in standard sizes, the most common of which are listed in Table 26.3.

TABLE 26.3   Common Envelope Sizes (Flap Folded)

Designation	Height in Millimeters	Width in Millimeters	Height in Inches	Width in Inches
6 3/4	91.4	165	3.6	6.5
Monarch	98.4	190.5	3.875	7.5
Com-10	195	241	4.125	9.5
DL	110	220	4.33	8.66
C5	165	229	6.5	9.01

With a modern computer printer, you should expect to load envelopes in the normal paper tray. Be wary of printers that require some special handling of envelopes—you may find it more vexing than you want to deal with.

Collation

The process of getting the sheets of a multipage print job in proper order is called *collation*. A printer may take care of the process automatically or leave the chore to you.

When sheet-fed printers disgorge their output, it can fall into the output tray in one of two ways—face up or face down. Although it might be nice to see what horrors you have spread on paper immediately rather than saving up for one massive heart attack, face down is the better choice. When sheets pile on top of one another, face down means you do not need to sort through the stack to put everything in proper order.

Most printers now automatically collate by stacking sheets face down. A few have selectable paths that give you the choice of face-up or face-down output.

Duplex Operation

A *duplex* printer is one that automatically prints on both sides of each sheet when you want it to. The chief advantage of double-sided printing is, of course, you use half as much paper, although you usually need thicker, more expensive stock so that one side does not show through to the other.

You can easily simulate duplex printing by printing on one side, turning each sheet over, and printing on the other. When you have a multipage print job, however, it can be daunting to keep the proper pages together. A single jam can ruin the entire job.

With laser printers, you should *never* try to print on both sides of a sheet except when using a duplex printer. When printing on the second side, the heat of the second fusing process can melt the toner from the first pass. This toner may stick to the fuser and contaminate later pages. With sufficient build-up, the printer may jam. Duplex printers eliminate the problem by fusing both sides of the sheet at once.

Consumables

Consumables are those things that your printer uses up, wears out, or burns through as it does its work. Paper is the primary consumable, and the need for it is obvious with any printer. Other consumables are less obvious, sometimes even devious in the way they can eat into your budget.

You probably think you are familiar with the cost of these consumables. A couple months after the old dot-matrix ribbon starts printing too faintly to read, you finally get around to ordering a new $5 ribbon to hold you through for the rest of the decade. But if you buy one of today's top-quality printers—laser, thermal wax, or dye-diffusion—you may be in for a surprise. When the toner or transfer sheet runs out, the replacement may cost as much as your old dot-matrix printer.

The modern trend in printer design and marketing is to follow the "razor blade" principle. The marketers of razors (the nonelectric shavers) discovered they could make greater profits selling razor blades by offering the razors that use them at a low price, even a loss. After all, once you sell the razor you lock in repeat customers for the blades.

Similarly, the prices of many inkjet and laser printers have tumbled while the consumables remain infuriatingly expensive, often a good fraction (such as one-third) of the cost of the printer itself. This odd situation results from the magic of marketing. By yourself you can't do anything about it, but you must be aware of it to buy wisely.

If you truly want to make the best buy in getting a new printer, you must consider its overall *cost of ownership*. This total cost includes not only the purchase price but the cost of consumables and service over the life of the printer. Take this approach and you'll discover a more expensive printer is often less expensive in the long run.

When you have a small budget, however, the initial price of a printer becomes paramount because it dictates what you can afford. Even in this situation, however, you should still take a close look at the price of consumables. Two similarly priced printers may have widely varying costs for consumables.

Cartridges

Laser printers use up a bit of their mechanism with every page they print. The organic photoconductor drum on which images are made gradually wears out. (A new drum material, silicon, is supposed to last for the life of the printer, but few printer models currently use silicon drums.) In addition, the charging corona or other parts may also need to be periodically replaced. And, of course, you need toner.

Laser printer manufacturers have taken various approaches to replacing these consumables. Hewlett-Packard's LaserJet printers, for example, are designed with one-piece cartridges that contain both the drum and toner. The whole assembly is replaced as a single unit when the toner runs out. Other laser printers are designed so that the toner, drum, and sometimes the fuser, can be replaced individually.

The makers of the latter style of printer contend that the drum lasts for many times more copies than a single shot of toner, so dumping the drum before its time is wasteful. On the other hand, the all-in-one cartridge folks contend that they design their drums to last only as long as the toner.

Surprisingly, from a cost standpoint, the choice of technology does not appear to make a difference. (From an ecology standpoint, however, the individual replacement scheme still makes more sense.)

A similar situation reigns among inkjet printers. Some designs incorporate the printhead nozzles into the ink cartridge. Others make the nozzles a separately replaceable item. Although the latter should have a cost advantage and a convenience disadvantage, as a practical matter the differences are not significant.

A more important issue to consider with inkjets is single versus separate cartridges for ink colors. Many printers—typically the less expensive models—use a single cartridge for all three primary ink colors. If you use all three colors equally, this is a convenient arrangement. Most of the time, however, one color will run out before another and force you to scrap a cartridge still holding a supply of two colors of rather expensive ink. If you are frugal or simply appalled at the price of inkjet ink, you'll want a separate cartridge for each ink color.

Refilling

One way to tiptoe around the high cost of laser printer consumables is to get toner or ink cartridges refilled. Most manufacturers do not recommend this—because they have no control over the quality of the toner, they can't guarantee that someone else's replacement works right in their machines. Besides, they miss the profits in selling the toner or ink.

Quality really can be an issue, however. The Resolution Enhancement Technology of the HP LaserJet III-series, for example, requires toner with a particle size much smaller than that of toner used by other printers. You cannot tell the difference in toner just by looking at it—but you can when blotchy gray pages pour out of the printer. When you get cartridges refilled, you must be sure to get the proper toner quality.

Paper

When comparing the costs of using different printer technologies, do not forget to make allowances for machines that require special paper. In most cases, approved media for such printers is available only from the machine's manufacturer. You must pay the price the manufacturer asks, which, because of the controlled distribution and special formulation, is sure to be substantially higher than buying bond paper at the office supply store.

With inkjet printers, paper is another profit area for machine-makers. Getting the highest quality from an inkjet requires special paper. Inkjet ink tends to blur (which reduces both sharpness and color contrast) because it dries at least partly by absorption into paper. Most inkjet printers work with almost any paper stock but produce the best results—sharpest and most colorful—with specially coated paper that has controlled ink absorption. On nonabsorbent media (for example, projection acetates), the ink must dry solely by evaporation, and the output is subject to smudging until the drying process completes. Of course, the treated paper is substantially more expensive, particularly if you restrict yourself to buying paper branded by the printer-maker. For printing photos, gelatin-coated papers yield glossy images with great color depth—at a price that can reach 50 cents to a dollar a sheet. Fortunately, inkjet printing has become so pervasive that every paper-maker offers tailored inkjet papers and competition is driving down prices to the range of ordinary copier paper.

Interfacing

The hardware connection between your computer and printer may be the easiest to manage among all computer peripherals. Most printers, still, use the vintage printer port. A few (and soon, more than a few) printers use a USB connection. Both of these connection systems are covered in Chapter 11, "Ports." In either case, you need do little more than plug in the printer. All the details of the linkup are automatically taken care of—or passed off to software.

And with the software, the interface gets interesting. The interface doesn't just have to get signals to the printer (the hardware does take care of that), but it must ensure that the right signals, those that the printer understands, get there. Modern software considers every dot on the page individually and has to tell the printer what to do with it. Your computer, through its operating system and printer driver, describes what the printer should put on paper using a command language or by sending a bit-image of the entire page to print.

At one time the control language used by a printer determined what applications could take advantage of all the features and the quality the printer had to offer. You had to match your software to the *command set* the printer understood.

Modern operating systems have eliminated this concern. Instead, the chief issue is the *printer driver*. The driver matches the printer's native commands to the operating system and *all* the applications that run under it. Once you install a driver, the printer's command set doesn't matter.

That said, printers usually fit three classes: Windows GDI, PCL, or PostScript.

Windows GDI printers have drivers that directly mate with the Windows Graphic Device Interface. They use proprietary commands for eliciting each printer's features. In most cases, graphics and even the entire page may be sent through the GDI to the printer as a bit-image. In most cases, the GDI is the fastest way of communicating with a printer. The computer, with its powerful processor, does all the work of rasterizing the image. Most Windows printer drivers now use the GDI.

PCL is the abbreviation for *Printer Control Language*, a command system originally developed by Hewlett-Packard for its inkjet printers and later adapted to laser machines as well. The commands in PCL tell a specific printer what to do to make an image on a page of paper. PCL thus focuses on *how* to draw the image on the page.

Although PCL is now a common language used by a wide variety of printers, it is a *device-dependent* language. That is, the driver for a printer may send out somewhat different codes for another output device, even if it is another printer.

Through the years, PCL has gone through six distinct versions (four that apply to laser printers), each building on the features of the earlier versions. PCL ships the information to be printed as a combination of characters and graphics commands, relying on a raster image processor in the printer.

PostScript is a *page-description language* developed by Adobe Systems, now in its third major revision (PostScript 3). It describes every dot that appears on a printed page. The language is intended to be device independent. That is, the PostScript code that yields a printed page will be the same for all devices that understand PostScript, and not necessarily only printers. PostScript focuses on the final output, what the image on paper looks like. *How* that image gets drawn doesn't matter to PostScript.

This device independence is a blessing when you need to preview something on a draft-quality machine before sending it out to a production house—both the draft printer and the production house's typesetting equipment work from the same code. At the same time, PostScript attaches a penalty. It requires substantial processing to convert the language commands into a raster image of a page. Using PostScript usually results in slower throughput from the printer.

Fax

Fax, short for *facsimile transmissions*, gives the power of *Star Trek*'s transporter system (usually without the aliens and pyrotechnics) to anyone who needs to get a document somewhere else in the world at the speed of light. Although fax doesn't quite dematerialize paper, it does move the images and information a document contains across continents and reconstructs them at the end of its near-instantaneous travels. The recipient gets to hold in his own hands a nearly exact duplicate of the original, the infamous *reasonable facsimile*.

From that angle, fax is a telecopier—a Xerox machine with a thousand miles of wire between where you slide the original in and the duplicate falls out. In fact, a product called the Telecopier was once offered by Xerox Corporation and was the progenitor of today's fax machines.

From a computer perspective, however, fax operates as a *teleprinter* rather than a telecopier, a printer that operates by remote control miles away from your computer. You create documents using Word or some other word-processing program and, instead of printing them on paper, send them half a world away. In fact, if you don't have a real printer installed in your computer, Windows assumes you'll use fax as your primary output system. You can imagine fax working like a 1200-mile printer cable.

For Windows, fax is just another way of printing. Just as the Windows GDI rasterizes images bound for laser printers, fax drivers (much like printer drivers) rasterize them for fax transmission. Windows, using fax drivers, calculates every dot that will appear on a sheet of paper and then sends them out—but, instead of using the control code for a printer and the printer interface, Windows uses standardized fax codes and your telephone line.

At one time, computer-based fax was a hot new technology bound to change the world. Although the technology has cooled—or at least the excitement has died down—computer-based fax remains alive and well, still carrying out its job, only now far from the limelight, hidden in the shadow of the Internet. Although manufacturers no longer need fax out datasheets when they are posted on the Web, contracts and updates to blueprints still need the fast, remote replication that only fax can provide. Although even a $500 computer is not cost competitive with a $50 standalone fax machine, no mere fax machine has the programmable features of a computer to handle mailing lists and get the word out with a fax blitz. Nor can a mere fax machine save and edit fax pages.

Fax and computers aren't just friends—they're coworkers. Together they expand the capabilities of both fax and computer technologies.

Technology

In a classic fax system, you start using fax by dialing up a distant fax system using a touch pad on your fax machine, just as you would any other telephone. You slide a sheet of paper into the fax's scanner, and the page curls around a drum in front of a photodetector. Much as a television picture is broken into numerous scan lines, a fax machine scans images as a series of lines, takes them one at a time, and strings all of the lines scanned from the document into a continuous stream of information. The fax machine converts the data stream into a series of modulated tones for transmission over the telephone line. After a connection is made at the receiving end, another fax machine converts the data stream into black and white dots representing the original image, much as a television set reconstructs a TV image. A printer puts the results on paper using either thermal or laser printer technology.

Computer-based fax systems can do away with the paper. Fax software can take the all-electronic images you draw or paint with your graphics software and convert them into the standard format that's used for fax transmissions. A fax modem in your computer can then send that data to a standard fax machine, which converts the data into hard-copy form. Alternatively, your computer fax system can receive a transmission from a standard fax machine and capture the image into a graphics file. You can then convert the file into another graphic format using conversion software, edit the image with your favorite painting program, or turn its text contents into ASCII form using optical character recognition (OCR) software. You can even turn your computer into the equivalent of a standard fax machine by adding a scanner to capture images from paper. Your printer will turn fax reception into hard copy, although at a fraction of the speed of a standalone fax machine.

Computer-based fax beats standalone fax with its management capabilities. Computer fax software can broadcast fax messages to as wide a mailing list as you can accommodate on your hard disk, waiting until early morning hours when long-distance rates are cheapest to make the calls. You can easily manage the mailing list as you would any other computer database.

The concept of facsimile transmissions is not new. As early as 1842, Alexander Bain patented an electromechanical device that could translate wire-based signals into marks on paper. Newspaper wire photos, which are based on the same principles, have been used for generations.

Hardware

The first fax machines looked much like current models only bigger—and usually smellier. Each had a telephone handset and a touch-tone keypad for dialing a distant machine. Each had a slot to slide in documents and another where received pages slid out, often a bit damp from the primitive chemical-based printing technology. Today, the fax machine combines several other office functions—a fax modem with a scanner, printer, and telephone set—that would tempt you to tie in your computer, but the standalone fax machine puts all its goodies out of the reach of your computer and its applications.

Today, standalone fax machines survive because, compared to computers, they are easier to use—they have no need for the hassle of clicking through windows or even booting up a computer to simply dial the telephone. Moreover, most fax machines are designed as—and perceived as by office workers—ordinary business machines, nothing so exotic or esoteric as a computer. They are seen more as a telephone with a paper slot than a brain-draining thinking machine. Even unskilled office workers are unfazed by a stand-alone fax machine.

A document whisking its way across the country is nothing more than digital data. Once that simple fact registered on computer engineers, they figured out ways of linking that data with the day's best data manipulator—the personal computer. The solution was the *fax modem*. Briefly, a small industry flourished making modems that could give your computer fax capabilities. Then the technology went mainstream, and the fax modem became a *de rigueur* part of every computer.

Fax machine–makers got another idea that they could give you the best of both worlds with standalone fax machines that accepted data such as telephone lists through a cable connection with your computer. Modern technology has done those simple connections one better—maybe four better. *Multifunction printers* often start with an ordinary fax machine but give your computer direct access to individual fax functions. The one multifunction printer can also serve as both a printer and a scanner for your computer—at least if you don't demand graphic arts-quality scanning. Or you can slide a sheet of paper in, press a button, and have a digital copier. At a more mundane level, you can pick up the receiver and use the multifunction printer as an ordinary telephone. One manufacturer has even added an answering machine to its fax printers.

Modems

In the computer realm, the term *fax modem* means an expansion board that slides into a vacant slot inside your computer to give it the capability of sending and receiving fax transmissions. Although at one time it took a specialized product to handle faxes, even the least expensive of modern modems include fax capabilities.

The fax modem converts rasterized documents and page scans into a form compatible with the international telephone system. Nearly every high-speed modem sold today has built-in fax capabilities. This bonus results from the huge demand for fax in the business world, coupled with the trivial cost of adding fax capabilities to chips used to build modern modems. Everything that's necessary for fax comes built in to the same chipsets that make normal high-speed modem communications possible.

Multifunction Printers

The fax sections of multifunction printers are little more than ordinary standalone fax machines. Nearly all commercial products use the same chipsets as fax modems. They differ chiefly in the capability of their standalone functions: how many numbers they remember and organize.

The printer sections of multifunction machines vary widely, nearly as widely as ordinary printer technology. The least expensive multifunction machines use inkjet printers. Although at one time the bargain-basement machines got away with including only monochrome printing, nearly all inkjet-based multifunction printers now have color capabilities. That doesn't mean the machines can send and receive color images. The color serves only the computer printer function, so you have the full spectrum available to you when want you want to print, for example, a page from the Web.

Nothing precludes a multifunction printer from using other technologies, and a few more expensive machines do use laser engines. You get all the advantages of a laser printer—fast, sharp images on plain paper—along with the ability to send fax directly from the printer or through your computer. As with other general-purpose laser printers, you're restricted to monochrome printing, both for fax and general computer output. (No manufacturer has adapted color laser technology to fax printing.) Fax standards limit the resolution of documents received by fax to 200 dots per inch. Scans and copies are limited by the resolution of the scanner section. Output from your computer, however, prints at the hardware resolution of the print engine.

Most multifunction printers use drum scanner technology. It is less expensive to move paper than it is to move an internal scanner. Drum technology also permits more compact machines and makes adding document feeders for multipage faxes much easier. A few multifunction printers use flatbed scanners. Although these are not as useful for faxing (document feeders for them are expensive add-ons), they add versatility to the scanning function.

As with other flatbeds, they allow the use of small and odd-shaped documents as well as three-dimensional objects (such as books) that would be off limits to a drum scanner.

The scanners in multifunction printers are optimized for fax use and do not pretend to compete with dedicated scanners for producing high-quality graphics. They often have limited resolution (some as low as 200 dpi), limited dynamic range, and sometimes no color capabilities at all. Fax doesn't need color. The output is, however, sufficient for document processing and works well with OCR software on your computer.

To make copies, the multifunction printer manufacturers simply link the fax scanner to the printer. The connection is indirect, detouring through the microprocessor and memory, a scenic route that adds versatility. You can make multiple copies (up to 99 on each machine) and, with most machines, alter the size of the image. On the downside, quality is limited by scanner resolution (no chance of counterfeiting $20 bills with a multifunction machine), and speed is constrained by processing and the printer engine. Some machines take nearly a minute to copy a single page, although speeds are increasing.

Group Standards

The widespread use of fax in business is a more recent phenomenon, and its growth parallels that of the computer for much the same underlying reason. Desktop computers did not take off until the industry found a standard to follow—the IBM computer. Similarly, the explosive growth of fax began only after the CCITT adopted standards for the transmission of facsimile data.

Analog

The original system, now termed *Group 1*, was based on analog technology and used frequency shift keying, much as 300 baud modems do, to transmit a page of information in six minutes. Group 2 improved upon that analog technology and doubled the speed of transmission, up to three minutes per page.

Group 3

The big break with the past was the CCITT's adoption in 1980 of the Group 3 fax protocol, which is entirely digitally based. Using data compression and modems that operate at up to 14,400 bits per second, full-page documents can be transmitted in 20 to 60 seconds using the Group 3 protocol. New transmission standards promise to pump up the basic Group 3 data rate to 28,800 bits per second.

Resolution

Under the original Group 3 standard, two degrees of resolution or on-paper sharpness are possible: standard, which allows 1728 dots horizontally across the page (about 200 dots per inch) and 100 dots per inch vertically, and fine, which doubles the vertical resolution to achieve 200 by 200 dpi and requires about twice the transmission time. Fine resolution also approximately doubles the time required to transmit a fax page because it doubles the data that must be moved.

Revisions to the Group 3 standard have added more possible resolutions. Two new resolutions compensate for the slight elongation that creeps into fax documents when generated and transmitted in purely electronic form. New fax products may optionally send and receive at resolutions of 204 by 98 pixels per inch in standard mode or 204 by 196 pixels per inch in fine mode. Two new high-resolution modes of 300 by 300 pixels per inch and 400 by 400 pixels per inch were also established. The 300 by 300 mode enables fax machines, laser printers, and scanners to share the same resolution levels for higher quality when transferring images between them. To take advantage of these resolutions, both sending and receiving fax equipment must support the new modes.

Data Rates

The basic speed of a Group 3 fax transmission depends on the underlying communications standard that the fax product follows. These standards are similar to data modem standards. With the exception of V.34, data and fax modems operate under different standards, even when using the same data rates. Consequently, data and fax modems are not interchangeable, and a modem that provides high-speed fax capabilities (say, 9600 bps) may operate more slowly in data mode (say, 2400 bps).

The Group 3 protocol does not define a single speed for fax transmissions but allows the use of any of a variety of transmission standards. At data rates of 2400 and 4800 bits per second, fax modems operate under the V.27 ter standard (note that *ter* stands for tertiary). At 7200 and 9600 bits per second, they follow V.29 (or V.17, which incorporates these V.29 modes). At 12,000 and 14,400 bits per second, fax modems follow V.17. The V.34 standard will take both fax and data modems up to 28,800 bits per second. New standards will allow the use of the Group 3 fax protocol over ISDN and other future digital telephone services.

Fax modems are typically described by the communications standards they support or by the maximum data rate at which they can operate. Most modern fax modems follow the V.17 standard, which incorporates the lower V.29 speeds. Most will also fall back to V.27 ter to accommodate older, slower fax products.

Compression

In a typical fax machine, you slide a page into the machine, place the call, and the machine calls a distant number. Once the connection is negotiated, the fax machine scans the page with a photodetector inside the machine, which detects the black and white patterns on the page one line at a time at a resolution of 200 dots per inch. The result is a series of bits with the digital ones (1) and zeros (0) corresponding to the black and white samples each 1/200th of an inch. The fax machine compresses this raw data stream to increase the apparent data rate and shorten transmission times.

Data compression makes the true speed of transmitting a page dependent on the amount of detail that each page contains. In operation, the data-compression algorithm reduces the amount of data that must be transferred by a factor of five to ten. On the other hand, a bad phone connection can slow fax transmissions, as fax modems automatically fall back to lower speeds to cope with poor line quality.

Group 3 fax products may use any of three levels of data compression, designated as MH, MR, and MMR. The typical Group 3 fax product includes only MH compression. The others are optional, and MMR is particularly rare. To be sure that a given fax product uses MR or MMR, you will need to check its specifications.

MH stands for *Modified Huffman* encoding, which is also known as one-dimensional encoding. MH was built in to the Group 3 standard in 1980 so that a fax machine could send a full page in less than one minute using a standard V.27 ter modem that operated at 4800 bits per second. With 9600 bps modems, that time is cut nearly in half.

MR, or *Modified Read* encoding, was added as an option shortly after MH encoding was adopted. MR starts with standard MH encoding for the first line of the transmission but then encodes the second line as differences from the first line. Because with fine images, line data changes little between adjacent lines, usually little change in information is required. To prevent errors from rippling through an entire document, at the third line, MR starts over with a plain MH scan. In other words, odd-numbered scan lines are MH and even lines contain only difference information from the previous line. If a full line is lost in transmission, MR limits the damage to, at most, two lines. Overall, the transmission time savings in advancing from MH to MR amounts to 15 to 20 percent, the exact figure depending on message contents.

MMR, or *Modified Modified Read* encoding, foregoes the safety of the MR technique and records the entire page as difference data. Using MMR, the first line serves as a reference and is all white. Every subsequent line is encoded as the difference from the preceding line until the end of a page. However, an error in any one line will repeat in every subsequent line, so losing one line can garble an entire page. To help prevent such problems, MMR can incorporate its own error-correction mode (ECM) through which the receiving fax system can request the retransmission of any lines received in error. Only the bad lines are updated, and the rest of the page is reconstructed from the new data. MMR with ECM is the most efficient scheme used for compressing fax transmissions and can cut the time needed for a page transmission with MH in half.

Instead of individual dots, under MH (and therefore MR and MMR) the bit-pattern of each scan line on the page is coded as short line segments, and the code indicates the number of dots in each segment. The fax machine sends this run-length coded data to the remote fax machine. Included in the transmitted signal is a rudimentary form of error protection, but missed bits are not reproduced when the receiving fax machine reconstructs the original page.

The exact code used by MH under Group 3 fax uses four code groups—two for sequences of white dots and two for sequences of black dots. Sequences from 0 to 63 dots long are coded using *terminating codes*, which express the exact number of dots of the given color in the segment. If the segment of like-color dots scanned from the paper is longer than 63 dots, MH codes it as two code groups—a terminating code and a make-up code. The *make-up code* value indicates the number of 64-dot blocks in the single-color segment.

Binary File Transfer

More than just following the same modem standard, the capabilities of fax service are merging with those of standard data communications. New fax modems, for example, incorporate Binary File Transfer (BFT) capabilities, which enable them to ship BFT files from one fax system to another as easily as document pages. You could, for example, send a file from your computer to a printer for a remote printout or to a computer where it could be received automatically. The receiving fax modem picks up the line, makes the connection, and records the file as dutifully as it would an ordinary fax page—without anyone standing around to control the modem.

Group 4

In 1984, the CCITT approved a super-performance facsimile standard called Group 4, which allows resolutions of up to 400 by 400 dpi as well as higher-speed transmissions of lower resolutions. Although not quite typeset quality (phototypesetters are capable of resolutions of about 1200 dpi), the best of Group 4 is about equal to the resolving capability of the human eye at normal reading distance. However, today's Group 4 fax machines require high-speed dedicated lines and do not operate as dial-up devices. Group 3 equipment using new, higher-resolution standards and coupled to digital services offers a lower-cost alternative to Group 4.

Interface Classes

As with data modems, fax modems must link up with your computer and its software. Unlike data modems, which were blessed with a standard since early on (the Hayes command set), fax modems lacked a single standard. In recent years, however, the Electronics Industry Association and the Telecommunications Industry Association have created a standard that is essentially an extension to the Hayes AT command set. The standard embraces two classes for support of Group 3 fax communications: Class 1 and Class 2.

Class 1 is the earlier standard. Under the Class 1 standard, most of the processing of fax documents is performed by computer software. The resulting fax data is sent to the modem for direct transmission. It includes requirements for autodialing; a GSTN interface; V-series signal conversion; HDLC data framing, transparency, and error detection; control commands and responses; and data commands and reception.

Class 2 shifts the work of preparing the fax document for transmission to the fax modem itself. The modem hardware handles the data compression and error control for the transmission. The Class 2 standard also incorporates additional flow-control and station-identification features, including T.30 protocol implementation, session status reporting, phase C data transfer, padding for minimum scan line time, quality check on received data, and packet protocol for the DTE/DCE interface.

These classes hint at the most significant difference between computer-based fax systems, which is software. Fax modem hardware determines the connections that can be made, but the software determines the ultimate capabilities of the system. A fax modem that adheres to various standards (classes as well as protocols) will open for you the widest selection of software and the widest range of features.

PART 6
Infrastructure

Imagine someone asking you if you'd like a Rolex for free. As soon as you nod your head and hold out your hands, he empties a box of tiny gears, levers, cams, and a pair of watch hands into your palms.

"It's kind of a kit," he laughs, like a mad hatter after a tea party.

That's where we've left your understanding of computer hardware. We've talked about all the parts but haven't bothered to put them all together. Worse, we haven't even discussed what holds them all together and gives them what they need to work.

It's not jam or jelly. In this book, we'll call it your computer's *infrastructure*, because it holds everything together and supplies what you need, much like the infrastructure of a city—the roads, utility wires, and water and sewer pipes that link you to civilization and civilized life. More than that, it's also the foundation that your computer is built upon, the metal and plastic that make up the computer that you can touch.

In the early chapters of this book, we looked at the pieces that make up the electronic circuits that actually make your computer work. We discussed printed circuit boards in the abstract— what they do and how they are made—but stopped short of the prevailing standards that dictate how big they are and how they plug together. That's because your computer would work no matter how engineers fit the pieces together. As long as they take care of their assigned functions, the computer will work.

But if they are not put together, if they lack what we're calling *infrastructure*, they cannot work, or at least they cannot work together. This infrastructure stuff is an afterthought, but one that's necessary to making things work.

The most important piece of this infrastructure is the *motherboard*. It holds all the essential circuitry of the computer. On it you'll find the microprocessor, memory, ports, and often the audio and often the video circuits of your computer. The motherboard is the centerpiece where everything comes together.

The circuits that don't fit on the motherboard reside on *expansion boards*, which plug into slots on the motherboard. The slots are the physical embodiment of the expansion bus. In addition, the motherboard provides the link between the power supply and the circuits of your computer.

The power supply is an essential element to any electronic device. It provides a steady, refined source of electricity for every component in your computer.

Holding all this together is your computer's case. Although seemingly the least-technical part of your high-tech computer, the simple case embodies a remarkable number of functions and technologies of its own. Not only is it tailored to fit the essential circuitry of your computer and its peripherals, it also matches your environment and how you use your computer. What's more, it protects your computer's circuits from that environment—and protects you from its circuits.

Put it all together, and you have a complete computer.

Principles: Hardware

Open your computer and you'll see the motherboard inside. It usually lines the bottom of a desktop system, covers one side of a tower or mini-tower system, or fills the center of a notebook machine like the meat of a sandwich or ham of a burger. It's the biggest circuit board inside the computer, likely the biggest circuit board in any electronic device you have around your home or office. Typically, the motherboard takes the form of a thick green sheet about the size of a piece of notebook paper and is decorated with an array of electronic components.

Although all motherboards look much the same, that similarity belies many differences in technologies and approaches to computer design. Some computer-makers strive to cram as much circuitry as possible on the motherboard. Others put as little as possible there. The difference affects both the initial cost of your computer and its future use and expansion.

Design Approaches

Nothing about computers requires a motherboard. You could build a computer without one—at least if you had sufficient knowledge of digital circuits and electronic fabrication, not to mention patience that would make Job seem a member of the television generation. Building a computer around a single centralized circuit board seems obvious, even natural, only because of its nearly universal use. Engineers designed the very first mass-market computers around a big green motherboard layout, and this design persists to this day.

Motherboards exist from more than force of habit, however. For the computer manufacturer, the motherboard design approach has immediate allure. Building a computer with a single large motherboard is often the most economical way to go, at least if your aim is soldering together systems and pushing them out the loading dock. There are alternatives, however, that can be more versatile and are suited to some applications. The more modular approach used in some of these alternatives allows you more freedom in putting together or upgrading a system to try to keep up with the race of technology.

The motherboard-centered design of most computers is actually a compromise approach between two diametrically opposed design philosophies. One approach aims at diversity, adaptability, and expandability by putting the individual functional elements (microprocessor, memory, and input/output circuitry) on separate boards that plug into connectors that link them together through a circuit bus. You can change the power and personality of such a computer as easily as swapping boards. Such machines are known as *bus-oriented computers* because everything connects through a bus, akin to an expansion bus. The alternative concentrates on economy and simplicity by uniting all the essential components of the computer on a single large board, thus making a *single-board computer*. Each of these designs has its strengths and weaknesses.

Bus-Oriented Computers

At the time the computer was developed, the bus-oriented design was the conservative approach. A true bus-oriented design seems the exact opposite of the motherboard. Instead of centralizing all circuitry, the bus-oriented design spreads it among multiple circuit boards. It's sort of the Los Angeles approach to computer design—it sprawls out all over without a distinct downtown. Only a freeway system links everything together to make a working community. In the bus-oriented computer, that freeway system is the *bus*.

The bus approach enabled each computer to be custom-configured for its particular purpose and business. You attached whatever components the computer application required to the bus. When you needed them, you could plug larger, more powerful processors, even multiple processors, into the bus. This modular design enabled the system to expand as business needs expanded. It also allowed for easier service. Any individual board that failed could be quickly removed and replaced without circuit-level surgery.

Actually, among smaller computers that preceded the introduction of the first IBM PC in 1981, the bus-oriented design originated as a matter of necessity simply because all the components required to make a computer would not fit on a circuit board of practical size. The overflowing circuitry had to be spread among multiple boards, and the bus was the easiest way to link them all. Although miniaturization has nearly eliminated such needs for board space, the bus-oriented design still occasionally resurfaces. You'll sometimes find special-purpose computers, such as numerical control systems and network servers, that use the bus-oriented approach for the sake of its modularity.

Single-Board Computers

The advent of integrated circuits, microprocessors, and miniaturized assemblies that put multiple electronic circuit components into a single package, often as small as a fingernail, greatly reduced the amount of circuit board required for building a computer. By the end of the 1970s, putting an entire digital computer on a single circuit board became practical.

Reducing a computer to a single circuit board was also desirable for a number of reasons. Primary among them was cost. Fewer boards means less fabrication expense and lower materials cost. Not only can the board be made smaller, but the circuitry that's necessary to match each board to the bus can be eliminated. Moreover, single-board computers have an advantage in reliability. Connectors are the most failure-prone part of any computer system. The single-board design eliminates the bus connectors as a potential source for system failure.

On the downside, however, the single-board computer design is decidedly less flexible than the bus-oriented approach. The single board has its capabilities forever fixed the moment it is soldered together at the factory. It can never become more powerful or transcend its original design. It cannot adapt to new technologic developments.

Modern technology has made most of us accept the inevitable obsolescence of computers, so the sting of the single-board approach now is much milder than with the first machines. Computers have almost reached the point of being throwaway devices. Locking a machine to a given level of technology is no hardship.

Notebook and sub-notebook computers all follow the single-board design for the sake of compactness. Squeezing everything onto a single board nearly eliminates the need for expansion boards sprouting up everywhere. By minimizing (or eliminating) connections between boards, the single-board design also improves the reliability of notebook machines—there's less to jostle and work itself loose.

But the single-board approach is also becoming more prevalent on the desktop. The motivation is mostly price. Putting everything on a single motherboard allows computer-makers to save the cost of extra boards and connectors, which helps pare down the retail price of machines. Many of today's computers are true single-board designs but still offer expansion slots for later adding options.

Some manufacturers have tried using today's high-speed ports in lieu of an expansion bus to make sealed-box computers, designed to make maintenance costs for businesses essentially zero. With nothing to service or upgrade inside, these machines have no service costs during their operating lifetimes. So far, however, such an approach has not been a marketplace success.

Compromise Designs

Until computers became true mass-market products, most followed a design compromise. Rather than strictly following either the single-board or bus-oriented approach, computer-makers brought the two philosophies together, mixing the best features of the single-board computer and the bus-oriented design in one box. This was the design that IBM chose for its first Personal Computer, which set the design for almost two decades of desktop computers. In it, one large board hosts the essential circuitry that defines the computer, but it relies on additional circuits on secondary circuit boards and provides further space for expansion and adaptability.

Throughout the history of the computer, functions have migrated from auxiliary circuit boards to the motherboard to bring desktop systems closer to the ideal single-board computer design. Early computers required extra circuit boards for their serial and parallel ports. Modern computers pack those ports and USB (and even FireWire) ports on the motherboard. At one time, most system memory, mass-storage interfaces, high-quality sound circuitry, network adapters, and video circuitry all required additional boards. Now many systems incorporate all these functions on their motherboards.

At least three motivations underlie this migration: expectations, cost, and capability. As the power and potential of personal computers have increased, people expect more from their computers. The basic requirements for a personal computer have risen so that features that were once options and afterthoughts are now required. To broaden the market for personal computers, manufacturers have striven to push prices down. Putting the basics required in a computer on the main circuit board lowers the overall cost of the system for exactly the same reasons that a single-board computer is cheaper to make than the equivalent bus-oriented machine. Moreover, using the most modern technologies, manufacturers simply can fit more features on a single circuit board. The original computer had hardly a spare square inch for additional functions. Today, all the features of a computer hundreds of times more powerful than the original IBM PC will fit into a couple of chips.

As with any trend, however, aberrant counter-trends in computer design appear and disappear occasionally. Some system designers have chosen to complicate their systems to make them explicitly upgradable by pulling essential features, such as the microprocessor, off the main board. The rationale underlying this more modular design is that it gives the manufacturer (and your dealer) more flexibility. The computer-makers can introduce new models as fast as they can slide a new expansion board into a box—motherboard support circuitry need not be reengineered. Dealers can minimize their inventories. Instead of stocking several models, the dealer (and manufacturer) need only keep a single box on the shelf, shuffling the appropriate microprocessor module into it as the demand arises. For you, as the computer purchaser, these modular systems also promise upgradability, which is a concept that's desirable in the abstract (your computer need never become obsolete) but often impractical (upgrading is rarely a cost-effective strategy).

Today, the compromise design survives in mainstream machines, although most motherboards delegate only their video circuitry to an expansion board—video being the one place where manufacturers are constantly adding improvements that benefit (mostly) game players. Most machines retain the capability for adding additional circuit boards, even though most people are not apt to bother.

Blade Servers

In the computer rooms of today's businesses, a further variation on motherboard design is making itself prominent. Called the *blade server*, this new design puts an entire computer—actually a powerful server computer—on a single board that's often the size of an expansion board (see "Expansion Boards," later). These motherboards earn their name because the boards are wide and flat like a knife blade. The blades slide into a large board in a rack-mounted chassis like component boards would slide into a bus-oriented computer. The bus, however, only provides power and, sometimes, a network connection between the blades.

Blade servers have become popular because they allow several computers to fit where only one used to. They lower costs because each server requires no cabinet or power supply of its own. Also, individual servers can be replaced almost instantly by sliding the bad board out and a replacement in should there be a failure.

Despite the new technology, each blade is simply a single-board computer. The only change is that microelectronics have made its circuits more compact.

Nomenclature

More confusing than board designs is the terminology used to describe the motherboard. The industry is rife with words that mean the same thing as "motherboard" or have subtle variations from that definition. Here are some of the most common:

- **System boards**. This term is little more than a desexed version of *motherboard*, introduced to the realm of personal computer by IBM when it introduced its first machine. At the time America was preoccupied with issues of sexual equality, and well-meaning but linguistically naive people confused issues of gender with sex. The term *system board* stands in its own right, however, because it indicates the role of the board as the centerpiece of the entire computer system. IBM continues to use the term to mean *motherboard*.

- **Planar boards**. Although *planar board* may seem simply another desexed word for *motherboard*, it bears a distinction. Although all modern circuit boards are planar in the sense they take the form of a flat plane, the planar board in a computer forms the mounting plane of the entire system.

- **Baseboards**. Intel often refers to the motherboard as the *baseboard* in many of its technical manuals. The company is not consistent about its usage—for example, the manual dated May, 1996, for Intel VS440FX lists the product as a "motherboard," whereas the manual for the Performance/AU, dated December 1995, terms the product a "baseboard." Again, there is a subtle distinction. A motherboard goes into a computer; a baseboard decorates the junction of a wall and the floor.

- **Main board**. Apparently contributed by offshore motherboard-makers, the term *main board* may be a result of translation, but it is actually a particularly appropriate term. The "main board" is the largest circuit board inside and the foundation for the computer system and, hence, it *is* the main board in a computer's case.

- **Logic board**. In the realm of the Apple Macintosh, the term *logic board* often refers to the equivalent of a computer's motherboard—notwithstanding, every printed circuit board inside a computer contains digital logic.

- **Backplane**. Another term sometimes used to describe the motherboard in computers is *backplane*. The name is a carryover from bus-oriented computers. In early bus-oriented design, all the expansion connectors in the machine were linked by a single circuit board. The expansion boards slid through the front panel of the computer and plugged into the expansion connectors in the motherboard at the rear. Because the board was necessarily planar and at the rear of the computer, the term *backplane* was perfectly descriptive. With later designs, the backplane found itself lining the bottom of the computer case.

Backplanes are described as *active* if, as in the computer design, they hold active logic circuitry. A *passive* backplane is nothing more than expansion connectors linked by wires or printed circuitry. The system boards of most personal computers could be described as active backplanes, although most engineers reserve the term *backplane* for bus-oriented computers in which the microprocessor plugs into the backplane rather than residing on it. The active circuitry on an active backplane under such a limited definition would comprise bus control logic that facilitates the communication between boards.

Expansion Boards

You know an expansion board as soon as you see one. It has an edge connector that fits only one place: on the motherboard made to accommodate it. But the reality of the expansion board is confused by issues of nomenclature and standards.

Nomenclature

Even the name *expansion board* holds a bit of confusion. Some people call them *expansion cards*. Is it a card or a board? In fact, the computer industry uses the two terms indiscriminately. This confused usage has a good precedent—long before computers, the electronics industry used the same terms for printed circuit assemblies. If there was any distinction, *board* was the generalized term (as in *printed circuit board*). Cards typically were smaller and usually plugged into a connector. Boards were usually screwed or bolted in place. No one cared, because both terms were generally understood.

However, the expansion boards used by notebook computers truly are cards, even though their printed circuit cards (or boards) are safely sealed inside their metal cases. They are called *cards* because of their similarity to credit cards. The names of the standards for them explicitly make them cards: PC Card and CardBus. These names and the similarity to credit cards were not accidental—the little expansion boards were designed to be a familiar and friendly credit-card size.

In the computer industry, several terms describe the boards used for expanding computers, sometimes with subtle differences in design or technology. Some of these terms include the following:

- **Expansion boards**. The smaller printed circuit boards that plug into your computer's motherboard are most often termed *expansion boards* because they provide you with the means of expanding the capabilities of your computer. As noted before, the expansion board is distinct from the expansion slot, the space inside the computer chassis the board occupies (or potentially occupies), and the expansion connector into which you plug the board.

  Expansion boards are often distinguished by the standard followed by their interface or the connector at the bottom of the board. For example, an *ISA board* follows the Industry Standard Architecture bus standard, and a *PCI board* follows the Peripheral Component Interconnect standard. We'll discuss these standards a bit later.

- **Option boards**. Some computer-makers prefer to describe expansion boards as *option boards*. You plug them into your system to add an optional feature. Strictly speaking, then, a standard equipment expansion board—for example, a graphics adapter—would not be an option board, but for consistency's sake (or maybe inconsistency), most manufacturers include such standard equipment among their options boards, perhaps to give you the idea you're getting options for free—just like that lunch.

- **Daughter boards**. Strictly speaking, any board that plugs into a motherboard should be a *daughter board*, but in the realm of the computer, the family relationship is not so straightforward. Many boards that plug into the motherboard of a computer have special names of their own—memory modules, microprocessor cartridges, and expansion boards are all daughter boards. However, most computer hardware–makers reserve the term *daughter board* for add-on circuit boards that attach as a second layer to their expansion boards.

This two-story form of packaging was prevalent when all the circuitry needed to build an expansion board just wouldn't fit in the space available in a single slot. The daughter board bought added square inches for circuitry. Today's circuits are so compact that this form of construction is rarely used. Most manufacturers don't even use the entire allowable size for their expansion board products.

- **Riser boards**. As noted previously, low-profile computers reduce their size by providing horizontal slots for their expansion boards. To connect these boards to the motherboard, most use a special board called a *riser board*. As with an ordinary expansion board, the riser board plugs into the motherboard, but its circuit endowment comprises little more than a set of connectors to accommodate your expansion boards.

Although computer expansion boards can all be considered daughter boards, not all daughter boards are expansion boards. For example, some computer expansion boards can themselves be expanded by plugging a daughter board onto them. Because such boards plug only into their host board, they are not true computer expansion boards. Most people call the circuit boards that plug into the motherboard the system's expansion boards. Circuit boards that plug into expansion boards are daughter boards. That convention at least relieves us of adding another generation and creating the *granddaughter board*.

Construction

As a concept, an expansion board might be almost anything as long as it can fulfill its purpose of enhancing the capabilities of the motherboard. As a practical matter, however, the expansion board has evolved to become a printed circuit board that fits into a connector in the motherboard and a space inside the computer chassis that makes up an *expansion slot*. This size and shape of an expansion board is entirely arbitrary. The expansion board could be as large as all creation or as small as a single chip.

Of course, expansion boards are not. Standards have been set on the size of expansion boards to make them interchangeable so that boards from different manufacturers will fit in as many computers as possible.

These standards are not entirely arbitrary. Several factors have influenced the choice of size. For example, an expansion board cannot be larger than the space provided by the expansion slot; otherwise, it would not fit and could hardly fulfill its expansion function. The board has to be large enough to hold the circuitry it needs to do what it has to do. Manufacturers prefer smaller boards because they cost less to make. However, the board can't be too small or it cannot hold the required expansion connector.

Several components define the physical reality of the standard computer expansion board. The board proper is an ordinary printed circuit board fabricated with pin-in-hole or surface-mount technology or a combination of both. An expansion connector connects the board to the electronic circuitry of your computer. A retaining bracket secures the board inside your computer and provides a place to put peripheral connectors.

Substrate

The substrate is the board itself, a slice of glass-epoxy upon which the various circuit components and connection traces are bonded. Computer-makers fabricate expansion boards using exactly the same technologies as motherboards.

The original design for expansion boards envisioned one end of each board sliding into a *card guide*, a thin slot at one end of the expansion slot, to stabilize the board inside the computer and keep it from bending or flapping in the breeze. These expansion boards that stretch from one end of the slot to the other are often called *full-length* expansion boards.

Most modern expansion board designs don't require all the area allowed for the substrate in the computer and are classed as *short cards*. Because of their diminutive dimensions and low mass, they are adequately secured in your computer by the expansion connector and their retaining brackets.

Retaining Bracket

Nearly all expansion boards have an L-shaped bracket attached at one end. Manufacturers use a number of terms for this bracket, perhaps the most colorful being "ORB," an acronym for *option retaining bracket*. The current trend is to refer to this bracket as the *bracket*.

In a computer, the bracket serves two functions. It secures and stabilizes the expansion board in its slot. It provides a mounting space for port connectors that may be required for connecting peripherals to the expansion board, and it helps shield your computer, keeping electrical interference inside your computer's case by plugging up the hole at the end of the expansion slot.

In most computers, a screw secures the bracket to the computer's chassis. When installing an expansion board, you should always ensure that this screw tightly holds each expansion board in place. Properly installing each board with a screw will prevent you from accidentally pushing the board out of the expansion connector when you plug into the connector on the board. (Tilting the expansion board can cause the contacts on its edge connector to bridge across several pins of the expansion connector, thus shorting them out and possibly crashing or even damaging your computer.) In addition, firmly screw-mounting the bracket ensures electrical continuity between the bracket and computer chassis.

Connector

The card-edge connector on each expansion board is little more than an extension of the etched copper traces of the printed circuits on the board substrate. The chief difference is that the connector pads are gold plated during the fabrication of the expansion board. The gold does not tarnish or oxidize, so it ensures that the edge connector will make a clean contact with the expansion connector on the motherboard.

The chief current expansion board standard uses the placement of pad areas and slots to key the board so that expansion boards fit only in slots designed for them.

Nearly all expansion standards for desktop computers use *edge connectors* for one very good reason: They are cheap. The connector's contacts get etched onto the board at the same time as the rest of its circuit traces. The only extra expense is the thin gold plating on the contact area to stave off the oxidation of the copper or lead-and-tin-coated traces.

After the pragmatic choice of an edge connector, the creator of an expansion standard still has a variety of choices. Most important is the spacing between contacts in the connector. The spacing, along with the number of contacts, determines the size. In a dream world— the one in which many designers operate—the size of the connector is no concern. In the real world, however, it has two dramatic effects. It determines how much space must be given up to connectors on the motherboard, and it governs the insertion force of an expansion board into the connector.

In true bus-style computers, the board space given up to the expansion bus is immaterial. The computer chassis is nothing but the bus, so there is no problem in devoting the whole back or bottom of the machine to the expansion bus. In the traditional computer design, however, the bus takes up space on the motherboard, which also has to provide the basic circuitry of the computer. The more motherboard space taken up by the bus, the less is available for building the basic computer. Consequently, the bus area must be as compact as possible to yield the largest possible circuit space on the motherboard.

The larger the connector, the more area of the expansion board that rubs against the contacts inside the socket when you plug the board in. To ensure a reliable electrical connection, the socket contacts must press forcefully against the contact tabs on the circuit board. Sliding an expansion board into a socket requires enough force to squeeze the board contacts between the socket contacts. The more area devoted to contacts, the greater the required *insertion force*. When a connector is too long, the insertion force may be greater than some people can comfortably apply, even greater than the automatic insertion machinery used by computer manufacturers can apply. Worse, if the insertion force is high enough, sliding in an expansion board may overly stress the motherboard, potentially cracking it or one of the conductive traces and putting it out of action.

Making the contact smaller shortens the connector, cutting down on the motherboard space required for the bus and reducing insertion force. It also requires greater precision in the manufacture of expansion boards. Nevertheless, newer expansion board standards are marked by closer spacing of their edge connector contacts—just compare an ISA board to a PCI board inside your computer.

More specialized bus standards, such as those for notebook computers and industrial computers, rely on *pin connectors*. These necessarily cost more because they add another part that must be soldered to each expansion board. But because the connector is a separate part, it can be manufactured with greater precision, and the greater precision allows for smaller, more compact connectors. Moreover, pin connectors can use more than two contact rows to further reduce the space that must be devoted to the bus. Pin connectors are also more reliable because they allow their contacts to mate on multiple sides. Pin connectors are also easier to shield, making them more desirable as concerns about emissions increase along with bus speeds.

Power

The infrastructure that makes a city includes not only highways and mass transportation but also utilities, which supply businesses and homes with what they need in the modern world: water, sewers, gas, and electricity.

Computers, too, need utility supplies to keep them going. As mere electronic beasts, however, they need neither water nor gas, and whatever sewage they create usually gets stored on their hard disks rather than carted away. Electricity is the sole necessity of the computer.

Not just any electricity will do. Computers have a definite and strict requirement for the power they use, which fortunately for us corresponds to ordinary utility power that you get at your wall outlet. The circuits inside your computer would disappear in a flash if utility power got to them, however. They require a special diet, one that the infrastructure of your computer must create for them.

The power supply inside your computer converts utility power into a form that's safe for computer circuitry. The infrastructure of your computer distributes this power, both to the motherboard and to the various disk drives you install inside your computer.

Cases

The final aspect of your computer's infrastructure is what truly holds everything together—its case. Although it appears to be nothing more than a box, the simple case has several complex functions. It is both the foundation for your computer and a protective shell that guards against both physical and invisible dangers. More importantly, the case is the one part of your computer that you see all the time. It is your pride and joy. The case is the physical embodiment of your computer.

In fact, the case is the body of your computer. It's a housing, vessel, and shield that provides the delicate electronics of the computer a secure environment in which to work. Cases come in various sizes, shapes, and effectiveness at their protective tasks to match your computer and the way you plan to use it.

In its protective role, the case guards the delicate circuitry inside your computer. Part of that protection is physical, guarding against physical dangers—forces that might act against its circuit boards, bending, stressing, even breaking them with deleterious results to their operation. It also prevents electrical short circuits that may be caused by the infall of the foreign objects that typically inhabit the office—paper clips, staples, letter openers, beer cans, and errant bridgework. The case also guards against invisible dangers, principally strong electrical fields that could induce noise that would interfere with the data handling of your system, potentially inducing errors that would crash your system.

The protective shield of the case works both ways. It also keeps what's inside your computer inside your computer. Among the wonders of the workings of a computer, two in particular pose problems for the outside world. The electrical voltages inside the computer can be a shocking discovery if you accidentally encounter them. And the high-frequency electrical signals that course through the computer's circuits can radiate like radio broadcasts and interfere with the reception of other transmissions—including everything from television to aircraft navigational beacons.

Your computer's case also has a more mundane role. Its physical presence gives you a place to put the things that you want to connect to your computer. *Drive bays* allow you to put mass-storage devices within ready reach of your computer's logic circuits while affording the case's protection to your peripherals. In addition, your computer's case provides the physical embodiment of the *expansion slot*, affording the boards that slide into the connectors of your computer's expansion bus protection with the same mechanical and electrical shelter as the rest of the system.

The case can play a more mundane role, too. It also can serve as the world's most expensive monitor stand, raising your screen to an appropriate viewing angle, elevated high above the clutter and confusion of your desktop. Or a tall, desk-side computer can be an impromptu stand for your coffee or cola cup or a more permanent residence for the papers that spillover from your desk. Appropriately chosen, the right notebook computer can be a gimmick pick-up device that can win you dates—providing you hang with the right (or wrong, depending on your perspective) crowd.

Compounding the function of your computer's case is the need to be selective. Some of what's inside your computer needs to get out—heat, for instance. And some of what's outside needs to get in—such as signals from the keyboard and power from your electrical outlets. In addition, the computer case must form a solid foundation upon which your system can be built. It must give disk drives a firm base and hold electrical assemblies out of harm's way. Overall, the simple case may not be as simple as you think.

WINN L. ROSCH
HARDWARE BIBLE,
SIXTH EDITION

CHAPTER

29

Motherboards

This is where it all comes together. Everything we've talked about so far in this book is either part of, connects to, or comes from the motherboard. Without a motherboard, you would not have a computer. You'd just have a box, a few leftover parts, and a high degree of frustration. You wouldn't even have a jack to plug into.

Not only does the motherboard make your computer, but it also defines it. The components and circuits on the motherboard determine exactly what your computer can do and how fast it runs.

Nearly all computers and compatible computers share one common feature: They are built with a single, large printed circuit board as their foundation. In many cases, the big board—usually called the *motherboard*—essentially is the entire computer. Almost completely self-contained, the one board holds the most vital electronic components that define the computer: its microprocessor, support circuitry, memory, and often video and audio functions. Anything you want to add to your computer plugs into the expansion bus that's part of the motherboard. As such a basic element, the motherboard defines both the computer and its capabilities. The circuitry it contains determines the overall performance of your system. Without the motherboard, you wouldn't have a computer.

In a modern computer, the motherboard is the big green centerpiece inside the case. Each computer-maker essentially builds the rest of its computer around the motherboard. On the motherboard, the computer-makers put all the most important electrical circuits that make up the computer. The expansion bus on the motherboard provides a foundation for future expansion, adding new features and capabilities to your computer.

Physical Requirements

Besides holding the essential circuitry of a computer, the motherboard of a computer must accommodate some form of expansion. In desktop computers, the motherboard is home to special electrical jacks called *expansion connectors* that allow you to plug in additional printed circuit boards. The space potentially occupied by an expansion board is an *expansion slot*, usually referred to simply as a *slot*.

Notebook computers and their ilk also incorporate expansion boards but in a different form. A protective shell, usually sheathed with aluminum, encases their circuit boards to make a near monolithic assembly that's termed a *PCMCIA card* or *PC Card*. PCMCIA stands for the organization that sets the standard for these cards, the Personal Computer Memory Card International Association. *PC Card* is actually a term of art that more particularly describes one of the interface standards used by these cards. Most people call the space potentially occupied by the cards a *PCMCIA slot* or simply a *card slot*.

Manufacturers cannot designate expansion areas on their motherboards willy-nilly. There is order and reason behind their designs—all backed by standards.

Beyond standardization, other concerns include the number, size, and arrangement of the slots. These considerations determine how expandable a given computer really is. In addition, the spacing of the bus connectors in the slots is a concern. Put them too close together, and you'll limit the designer's choice of circuit components to those that are short or force the designer to put the components flat against the board, thus wasting its expensive space. Even the number of expansion connectors may be set or limited by the bus standard.

Bus Standard

The basic characterization of motherboards is by the standard they follow for the physical and electrical characteristics of their expansion slots. The choice dictates which boards plug into the motherboard—in other words, which products you can use to upgrade your computer. Although the choice is no longer wide, variations remain.

Expansion standards for desktop computer motherboards have gone through a lengthy evolution, with a number of interesting but now essentially irrelevant side trips. Today, however, one standard (PCI) dominates, and the only option is whether a given motherboard or computer condescends to accommodate legacy (old) expansion boards that follow the ISA standard. The situation is simpler among notebook computers because their evolution has been shorter and they missed the chaotic early days of computer development. You'll find a complete discussion about the history of expansion standards in Chapter 9, "Expansion Buses."

Slot Number

The number of expansion slots in a given computer is a compromise with multiple considerations. More is better, but a computer with an infinite number of slots would be infinitely wide. The practical dimensions of the motherboard and case limit the space available for slots.

Electrical considerations also keep the slot count modest. The high-speed signals used by today's expansion buses are hard to control. The higher the speed, the fewer slots that are practical. Even at 33MHz, today's most popular expansion bus standard allows for only three slots per controller.

Adding more slots requires additional control circuitry, which adds to the price of the computer (as does the cost of the expansion connectors themselves). With manufacturers slugging it out over every penny of their prices, the tendency is to constrain costs and slot count.

How many expansion slots you need on a motherboard depends on how many functions the motherboard-maker has integrated into the board. Most practical computers fill one or more of their slots with standard equipment (such as a video board and modem). Over the three-to-five-year life of the typical computer, you're likely to add more than one new accessory to it, possibly something you might not have conceived of when you bought the machine. Therefore, you need to plan in advance for the need for expansion.

Notebook computers get away with two or fewer slots because they encapsulate all the normal functions of a computer on their motherboards. Nevertheless, two is still better than one, and you're likely to use what's available. Note, too, that super-thin computers, which are most likely to have single slots, are the ones that will more likely need two. For example, these machines may require a slot to run a CD drive that would otherwise be built in to a thicker system.

Slot Spacing

Expansion boards are three-dimensional objects (as is everything else in the real world). In addition to length and width, they also have thickness. PCMCIA explicitly gives all three dimensions of conforming cards. The thickness of desktop computer expansion boards is more implicit, determined by the spacing of the expansion slots. If slot spacing is too narrow, boards simply won't fit. Worse, one board might touch another and short-circuit a computer signal, leading to erratic operation or complete non-operation of the computer. If slot spacing is too wide, fewer will fit in a computer of reasonable size, thus limiting your expansion options.

A printed circuit board itself is quite thin, about one-eighth inch, and can be made even thinner when board dimensions become small. The thickness of most expansion boards and the requirement for adequate slot spacing arise from the components installed on the board—which may include another printed circuit board clinging to the first like a remora.

Surface-mounted components make thinner boards practical, but taller components remain prevalent enough that the spacing of slots has remained the same since 1982. On all motherboards, expansion connectors are located on 0.8-inch centers.

Not only does this standard set the maximum thickness of any expansion board, it also dictates the number of slots that may be available for a given size of motherboard. The board must be as least wide enough to accommodate all the slots it is to hold. Some motherboards are hardly wider than that.

In any case, the spacing of expansion slots was originally set arbitrarily. It represents what the developers of the first computers thought was the optimum compromise between compact layout and adequate allowance for the height of circuit components. The choice was wise enough that it still reigns today.

Slot Layout

In desktop computers, the layout of the slots is mostly a concern of the system designer. As long as your boards fit, you shouldn't have to worry. The designer, however, must fret about the electrical characteristics of signals that are close to invading the territory of microwave ovens. Some are purely electronic issues that cause high-speed buses to operate erratically and interact detrimentally with other electronic circuits by generating interference.

Expansion buses pose more engineering problems than other circuits because they require the balancing of several conflicting needs. The expansion bus must operate as fast as possible to achieve the highest possible transfer rate. The expansion bus also must provide a number of connectors for attaching peripherals, and these connectors must be spread apart to allow a reasonable thickness for each peripheral. In other words, the bus itself must stretch over several inches. The common solution is to use several short buses instead of one long one. Although the connectors on the motherboard may appear to link all expansion boards into a single bus, if your system has more than three high-speed expansion slots, it likely has multiple buses, each with its own controller, powering the slots.

There's another design consideration in desktop and tower computers—whether expansion boards slide into their slots vertically or horizontally. In full-size systems, expansion boards plug into the motherboard perpendicularly. The result is that the main plane of each expansion board is vertical in desktop computers and horizontal in tower-style machines. A few compact desktop computers, termed *low-profile* designs, align expansion boards parallel to the motherboard, horizontal in desktop systems.

Although alignment of the expansion slots appears to be only an aesthetic consideration, it also has a practical importance. Vertical boards cool naturally through convection. Air currents can rise across each board and cool its innermost components. Horizontal boards defeat convective cooling because the boards themselves block vertical air currents. In general, computers with horizontal expansion boards should have some kind of active cooling system—translated from technical language, that means they need a fan to blow a cooling breeze across them.

Slot layout is more complicated in notebook computers in which the layout of PCMCIA slots may determine what cards you can plug into your computer. Most notebook computers have two slots, and they are arranged like the barrels of a shotgun—either in a side-by-side or over-and-under fashion. These options are not functionally equivalent. PC Cards come in any of three thicknesses (discussed later), and most slots accommodate the two slimmer cards. An over-and-under arrangement of two slots will hold either two slim cards or one of the thickest sort. Although the over-and-under configuration gives you the largest number of expansion options, many of today's ultra-thin notebooks can only accommodate side-by-side slot mountings.

Standards

Modern motherboards can be any size or shape that suits the design of the computer. Only the need for standard-size expansion slot connectors limits the freedom of design. Many computers, however, are built around motherboards of a few standard sizes. This standardization is a matter of convenience. It allows a computer manufacturer flexibility in the choice of suppliers—standardized dimensions make motherboards interchangeable.

For you as the purchaser of a new computer, motherboard standardization has its downside. You face the problem of the computer manufacturer selling systems equipped with a motherboard *du jour*, whatever OEM motherboard was available cheapest on the day the computer was put together. On the other hand, a computer built around a standard-sized motherboard gives you upgrade freedom. Should you become dissatisfied in the performance of your computer, you can replace a standard-size motherboard with a more powerful one.

The earliest motherboard standards followed the leads set by IBM. They duplicated the physical dimensions of the motherboards used by the most popular IBM machines. Even when they lopped off vast areas of board to trim costs, most manufacturers retained compatibility with IBM's designs, keeping mounting holes in the same locations so that one board could be substituted for another. This heritage continues even in some of the latest designs.

After IBM ceded its influence as the setter of the standard dimensions of motherboards, the industry was essentially adrift. Major manufacturers developed their own designs without regard to older products, while smaller manufacturers clung to the old board layouts. The situation is changing, though, with new motherboards standards now promulgated by Intel. The most recent of these, the *ATX motherboard* design, goes further than ever before and specifies not only dimensions and mounting holes but also connector placement and even connector designs. To standardize the motherboards of more powerful computer workstations, the computer industry recently developed and then dropped the *WTX specification*.

Motherboard design divergence first arose among makers of small-footprint computers, machines designed with smaller dimensions to cover less of your desktop. These machines compromised expansion by reducing the number of expansion slots and drive bays to gain their more modest measurements. Many manufacturers developed *low-profile computers* that reduced system height by turning expansion boards on their sides. These designs necessitated changes from the more standardized motherboard layout. The computer industry has rallied around the low-profile design and produced two standards that support the concept. First came the *LPX motherboard*, and then came a smaller derivative, the *Mini-LPX*. To accommodate the needs of new microprocessor and memory technologies (and to add a wealth of other features), the industry adopted the *NLX motherboard*.

In general, smaller manufacturers are more likely to use standard-size motherboards. Larger manufacturers are better able to afford the price of custom-designing cases and motherboards to match. Even large computer-makers have moved to standard-size boards at least for their offerings that take advantage of the latest microprocessors. In truth, systems that use the latest microprocessors often all have exactly the same motherboard design inside, using a motherboard designed and manufactured by Intel. Even large manufacturers may rely on Intel motherboards until their engineers develop a familiarity with new chips. For example, all but a handful of the first Pentium Pro computer models uniformly used standard-size Intel-manufactured motherboards.

ATX

To bring a degree of uniformity to motherboard design, the computer industry created a new motherboard standard that roughly conforms to the Mini-AT board size but with a few design twists that result in lower-cost engineering. Called *ATX*, the standard is promulgated by Intel but is openly published. Intel released the most recent version, 2.1, in February 1996, fine-tuning the design based on industry feedback.

The ATX standard defines the number and position of the motherboard mounting holes and offers recommendations as to component, expansion board, and port connector placement. Although the standard does not demand any particular slot type or configuration, it's aimed primarily at ISA, PCI, and ISA/PCI combination designs. It also allows for both 5.0- and 3.3-volt system operation (or both simultaneously).

The odd orientation of the board facilitates port placement. It provides the maximum space for expansion boards and port connectors at the rear of the host computer chassis. The design also envisions that the microprocessor will be located near the right edge of the board, where it will be in close proximity to both the power supply and the cooling fan. In the recommended configuration, memory sockets can be readily accessed between the microprocessor and expansion slots.

The ATX board itself measures a maximum of 12 by 9.6 inches (305 by 244 millimeters). This size is not a random choice but, according to Intel, was selected to allow manufacturers to cut two boards from a standard-size 18-by-24-inch raw printed circuit panel. It provides sufficient space for about seven expansion slots, which are spaced at the conventional 0.8 inches apart. It incorporates nine mandatory and one optional mounting holes, most of which are in the same positions as the holes in a Mini-AT motherboard. Figure 29.1 shows the dimensions and mounting hole placement for an ATX motherboard.

FIGURE 29.1

Dimensions and hole placement of an ATX motherboard.

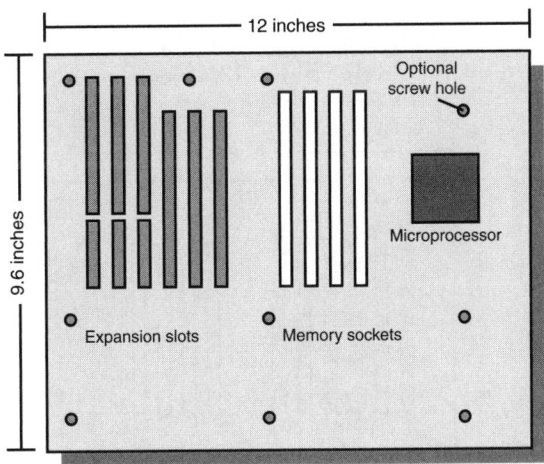

The ATX specification goes further than simply indicating mechanical board dimensions. The standard also embraces the PS/2 size of power supply and specifies a new motherboard power connector (see Chapter 31, "Power").

Besides uniformity, the ATX design aims at trimming costs for computer-makers. By putting port connectors on the motherboard, even in multiple layers, the cost of connecting cables as well as the labor required for assembly is eliminated. Eliminating cables also helps minimize potential radio frequency interference. In its recommended configuration, the ATX layout also allows the use of shorter floppy and hard disk connecting cables, with similar benefits. The power supply choice and location also trims cost for the computer manufacturer as well as helps the computer run cooler and even quieter.

Mini-ATX

The designers of the ATX board realized that the one certainty in computer circuit design is that functions get combined and made more compact. As more and more of the functions of a computer squeezed into one or two chips, the ATX designers imagined that soon much of the ATX real estate would be superfluous. In that one of the primary goals in the design of ATX was trimming costs, they figured that trimming motherboards to a size smaller than ATX as the technology permitted would reap savings in materials cost. Consequently, they included a standard size for Mini-ATX motherboards in the original ATX specification.

The Mini-ATX design chops the ATX motherboard down to 11.2 by 8.2 inches (284 by 208 millimeters). When installed in a computer, the Mini-ATX motherboard still sits at the rear edge of the chassis so that port connectors can be mounted directly to it without cables. In most chassis, the left edge still aligns with the left side of the case to allow space for a full complement of expansion boards. Because of this placement, the smaller size of the Mini-ATX board cuts off one row of ATX mounting holes. As a result, the lower row of mounting holes is displaced on the Mini-ATX design, as shown in Figure 29.2.

FIGURE 29.2
Mini-ATX motherboard dimensions and layout.

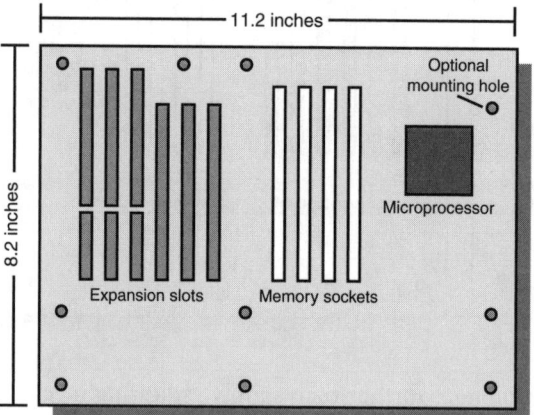

microATX

The Mini-ATX design has one chief benefit. It reduces the materials costs for a motherboard by about 30 percent when compared to a full-size ATX board. But that wasn't enough for the creators of the ATX specifications. They created another small-size motherboard called *microATX*, which took over the role of Mini-ATX. The current incarnation of the standard, version 1.0, was published in 1997.

The microATX specification represents more rethinking than a simple extra shrinking. The new design is actually a bit larger than Mini-ATX. A microATX motherboard measures 9.6 inches (244 millimeters) square.

The chief difference between Mini-ATX and microATX is how the two mate with the full-size ATX standard. Mini-ATX motherboards pay little heed to the larger standard; microATX boards fit neatly inside it. Although microATX motherboards are narrower than full-size ATX designs, they use nearly the same mounting scheme, so a microATX board will fit into a full-size chassis. Expansion slots appear in the same position, except microATX allows for fewer slots because of its reduced size—a maximum of four slots, typically three PCI and one AGP. (ISA slots are also allowed.) In addition, most of the screw holes used for mounting a microATX motherboard match the positions of those on a full-size ATX motherboard.

To mate with the conventional ATX chassis, the microATX motherboard reserves the same space for port connectors as does the full-size board, and the two boards use exactly the same power connectors. Figure 29.3 illustrates the microATX motherboard and compares it to its full-size sibling.

FIGURE 29.3

The microATX motherboard layout.

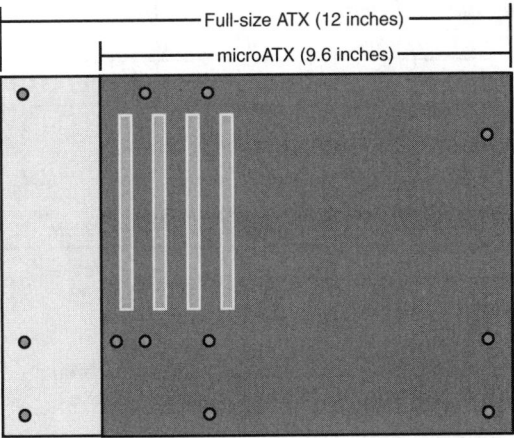

FlexATX

If small is good, even smaller is better. In 1999, Intel's engineers unveiled yet another motherboard format, *FlexATX*, which shaves inches off the microATX design. The name reflects the design goal: FlexATX is meant to be flexible and allows for the development of devices beyond the traditional personal computer (but based on the traditional personal computer motherboard). In the classification system of its promoters, FlexATX is not a standalone standard but an addendum to the microATX specification.

A FlexATX motherboard measures no more than 9 inches wide and 7.5 inches deep. It retains the same area (in both size and location) for ports and connectors as that used by ATX and microATX motherboards.

Seeing a wide application of compact motherboards, however, the FlexATX design fits inside the conventional ATX chassis. The placement of its mounting holes matches those of an ATX motherboard, although (as with microATX) two added holes provide mounting security on the edge adjacent to where excess glass-epoxy was pared off.

The FlexATX design does not specify the number and location of expansion slots because the creators of the standard envisioned its use in systems that provide no board-style expansion (although the standard does permit engineers to use their imagination and add slots to the design).

Table 29.1 lists the dimensions for ATX motherboards and those derived from that standard. The complete ATX specifications and those related to it are available on the Web at www.formfactor.org.

TABLE 29.1 Dimensions of Modern Motherboards

Motherboard	Width (in)	Length (mm)	Area (in)	Area (mm)	Area (Square in)	Area (Square cm)
ATX	12.0	305	9.6	244	115.2	744.2
Mini-ATX	11.2	284	8.2	208	91.8	590.7
microATX	9.6	244	9.6	244	92.2	595.4
FlexATX	9.0	229	7.5	191	67.5	437.4

NLX

Announced in September 1996, by Intel, the NLX motherboard design was a cooperative effort among several manufacturers, including IBM. At the time of its introduction, 12 computer-makers and one motherboard-only manufacturer (ASUStek) had announced support of the specification. The computer-makers included AST, Digital Equipment Corporation (now part of Compaq), Fujitsu, Gateway 2000, Hewlett-Packard, IBM, ICL Personal Computers, Micron Electronics, NEC Computer Systems, Sony, Toshiba, and Tulip Computers.

NLX is an improved low-profile layout. It was created specifically to overcome some shortcomings of earlier, no longer supported designs (LPX and its reduced-size version, Mini-LPX), in that those designs interfered with adapting to the latest technologies. NLX is meant to support all current Intel microprocessor designs and memory technologies as well as the advanced graphics port (AGP) for high-speed interconnections with video boards. In addition, the NLX design enhances the physical packaging of systems to allow greater mechanical integrity, better cooling, and more space for peripheral ports.

Key to the NLX design is the *riser* board. Although it's similar to the riser boards of LPX systems, because you plug expansion boards into it, under the NLX design the riser takes on a greater role. In effect, it operates as a backplane and the NLX motherboard itself is a glorified processor board. The riser board attaches permanently to the chassis of its host computer while the NLX motherboard readily slides in and out of the case like a steroid-enhanced expansion board. In purest form of the NLX implementation, all cables in the system—including the power supply—attach to the riser, and none attach to the motherboard. Typically the cables for the floppy disk and hard disk drives in a computer will plug into the riser.

Although the design of the NLX motherboard is fixed by the specification, the riser board is not. Computer-makers can customize its design to accommodate different system designs. Although the typical riser board has four expansion connectors, the NLX specification allows a great deal of freedom to accommodate not only low-profile computers but also tower-style systems. The specification describes signals for up to five PCI expansion slots and an unlimited number of ISA slots on a single riser. All boards slide into the riser parallel to the motherboard.

The one aberration in the NLX motherboard/riser design is its accommodation for AGP video boards. The specification reserves a special area on the left side of the motherboard, opposite the riser board, for a single AGP slot. The AGP board slides into the motherboard slot parallel to the riser board. Microprocessors (the NLX design accommodates up to two) and memory reside on the right side of the motherboard so that they do not interfere with expansion boards. Figure 29.4 shows the basic layout of this two-board system.

FIGURE 29.4
NLX motherboard layout.

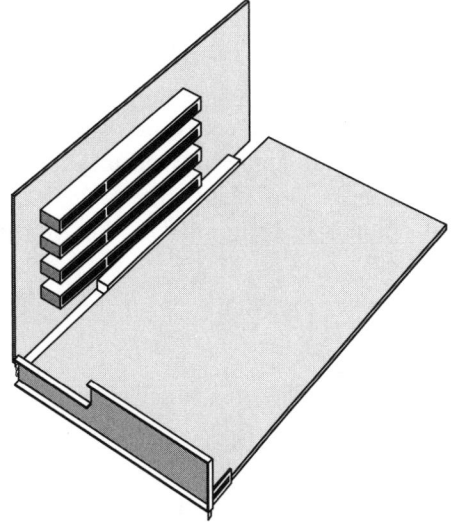

An L-shaped integral rear panel of the board provides space for peripheral connectors. The higher part of the panel allows designers to stack multiple connectors, one over the other, on the right side of the chassis, away from expansion boards. The NLX design envisions the motherboard to be readily removable without removing an expansion board (except the AGP board) from inside the computer case. In a typical computer, the motherboard slides out the side of the chassis, guided by rails at the bottom of the chassis. Four screws inside the computer secure the board to the chassis and electrically ground the two together. A latch that's part of the chassis and under the motherboard holds the board horizontally in place and also serves as a board ejector to aid in removing the motherboard. Spring-like contact fingers around the periphery of the rear panel shield electrically integrate the board with the rest of the chassis.

The mechanical specification of NLX motherboards allows for a small degree of freedom in their size. The specs allow any width between eight and nine inches (inclusive), except for systems integrating AGP video boards. These must be nine inches wide because the space reserved for the AGP connector is on the last inch of the board. NLX motherboards may be between 10.0 and 13.6 inches long. The smallest NLX motherboard is approximately the size of a mini-LPX motherboard; the largest about the size of an LPX board.

The NLX specifications provide for three different mounting screw patterns, depending on the length of the board. An NLX motherboard may use any of the three patterns, but each NLX chassis design must accommodate all three.

NLX uses a 340-pin connector between the motherboard and riser. This single connector carries signals for the ISA and PCI buses, IDE drives, and miscellaneous system functions. In addition, the specification reserves space for a larger connector to accommodate future, wider expansion buses and an optional connector for other system features.

WTX

Workstations require greater power and design flexibility from ordinary general-purpose computers, so in September, 1998, Intel introduced a new specification aimed at standardizing many aspects of workstation design. Under the specification, motherboards could be up to 14 by 16.75 inches or any size smaller. This design proved superfluous, however, and although the WTX specification is still published on the Web at www.wtx.org, its promoters no longer advocate its use.

Expansion Boards

The essence and key to success of expansion boards is standardization. By rigidly defining every dimension and contacts, expansion board standards allow you to plug almost any expansion board into almost any computer. But standardization is not a single issue. Expansion boards must be physically, electrically, and logically compatible with the motherboards with which they mate.

First of all, a board must fit into the computer for which it is designed. Consequently, today's expansion board standards dictate the physical size of expansion boards. In addition, the board must be able to send its signals to the motherboard and listen to those that the motherboard sends out. It must have some kind of electrical connection with the motherboard. Consequently, the physical standardization of expansion boards extends to their electrical connectors. Before signals can hope to get from one board to another, the connectors must mate together. They must match as to size, style, and placement so that they can properly fit together.

Although the physical size of an expansion board has no effect on its electrical compatibility, it is a major issue in compatibility. After all, an expansion board has to fit in the computer it is meant to expand. All expansion standards define the size of the circuit boards they use either as exact dimensions or as a set of maximum and, often, minimum dimensions.

Given his druthers—or even someone else's druthers—a circuit board designer would rather have more board space, acres upon acres of it stretching from here to the horizon to the limits of time and the universe. More space to work with makes the job easier. Unfortunately for the designer, practical concerns such as keeping the size of the computer manageable restrains his ambitions and board space.

On the other hand, smaller boards help manufacturers cut costs, at least after the price for developing new designs is paid. They require less in the way of the glass-epoxy base materials from which the boards are built. Consequently, setting the dimensions for an expansion board standard is always a compromise.

The prototype of all expansion boards was the card that fit into the original IBM computer of 1981. The bus and physical form of this board lurks behind all computer expansion to this day, evolving into Industry Standard Architecture and legacy expansion boards, now obsolete thanks to more modern designs.

The reigning standard is the physical size of the PCI bus standard, which specifies the slot and board size as well as other physical and electrical characteristics of expansion boards. Even though PCI electrically and logically differs markedly from the original legacy design, PCI still shows its heritage in several of its physical characteristics. The maximum board length and thickness both go back to the first days of the computer. The multipart basic design, too, harkens back to the first computer expansion cards. The same physical design also embraces the offshoots of PCI technology—PCI-X and PCI-Express.

Other expansion standards you're likely to encounter include the PC Card and CardBus standards, which from a physical perspective are identical (despite the electrical differences). Your desktop computer may also have a riser board for some of its features (such as sound and networking), which you may be able to upgrade or replace, much like an expansion board. Servers may use expansion boards based on the InfiniBand standard.

PCI Boards

The PCI specification defines several variations on the basic expansion board. The standard defines two official sizes of board, each with three connector arrangements (5 volt, 3.3 volt, and dual voltage). The dimensions of the two board sizes may seem arbitrary, but they owe their heritage to traditional ISA expansion boards. The similarity arose because early PCI-based computers also hosted ISA expansion boards for compatibility reasons. The ISA boards defined the size of the computer, and PCI boards were tailored to fit the space.

Dimensions

A full-size PCI expansion board measures 12.283 inches (312 mm) long. The main body of the board is about 3.875 inches high, although the expansion edge connector and a short skirt extend the width of the board to 4.2 inches (106.68 mm). The critical reference dimension is the centerline of the notch in the expansion connector, which is displaced

4.113 inches (104.47 mm) from the back edge (retaining bracket side) of the board. Figure 30.1 shows the dimensions of a full-size PCI board in 5-volt configuration. Cards designed for 3.3 volts or universal operation will differ in contact number and placement but not overall size.

FIGURE 30.1

Primary dimensions of a full-size 5-volt PCI expansion board.

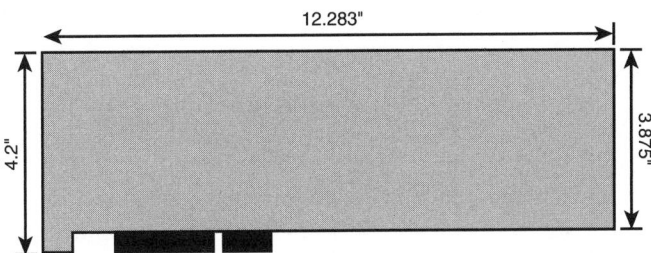

PCI also defines a short board, about half the length of a full-size board at 6.875 inches (174.63 mm) front to back. All other vital dimensions, including the distance from rear edge to the registration notch in the expansion connector, are identical to a full-size board. Figure 30.2 shows the dimensions of a PCI short card.

FIGURE 30.2

Primary dimensions of a 5-volt PCI short card.

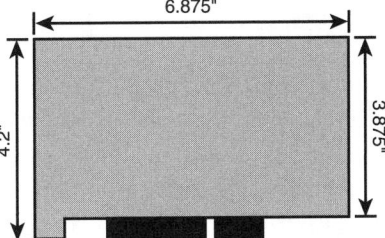

No matter the length of the board, PCI specifies a maximum thickness. The components on a PCI board can rise no more than 0.570 inches above the substrate. On the other side of the board, components can protrude no more than 0.105 inches. Add those heights to the nominal 0.100-inch thickness of the substrate, and PCI provides for 0.025 inches of safety gap between board components, with standard slot spacing of 0.800 inches.

Connectors

To accommodate the development of low-voltage "green" computers, PCI specifies two connector types and three different connector regimes: a 5-volt connector for today's prevailing circuit designs, a 3.3-volt connector for low-power designs, and the capability to combine both connectors on a single expansion board for a smooth transition between designs. A key on 5-volt sockets (blocking pins 50 and 51) prevents the insertion of 3.3-volt boards. (Five-volt boards have a slot corresponding to the key.) A key on 3.3-volt sockets (at pins 12 and 13) restricts the insertion to correspondingly slotted 3.3-volt boards. Boards capable of discriminating the two voltage regimes have slots in both places, as shown in Figure 30.3.

FIGURE 30.3

Edge connectors for 5 and 3.3 volt PCI cards (32 bit).

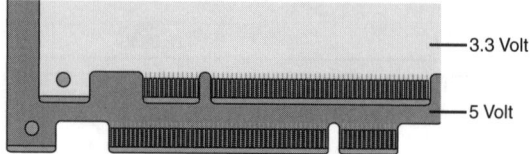

3.3 Volt

5 Volt

The 64-bit implementation of PCI extends the edge connector to accommodate the additional required signals. Figure 30.4 shows this extended connector and the full implementation of all of its options.

FIGURE 30.4

The 64-bit universal PCI edge connector.

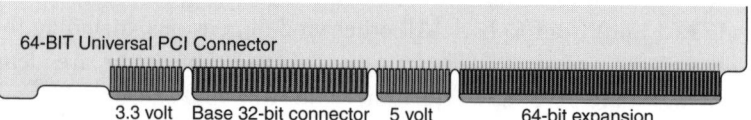

64-BIT Universal PCI Connector

3.3 volt   Base 32-bit connector   5 volt   64-bit expansion

Accelerated Graphics Port

Boards of the accelerated graphics port (AGP) design follow a physical standard derived from that of PCI, much as the AGP electrical interface is an offshoot of PCI. The AGP design assumes that the 3D accelerator chip and frame buffer will have a home on an expansion board rather than the motherboard, although nothing about the interface design precludes putting all the circuitry on the motherboard. In a typical computer, an expansion slot supporting the AGP connection fits on the motherboard like a PCI slot, with the same spacing and dimensional requirements. Although a given computer or motherboard may omit a PCI slot in favor of an AGP connection, AGP is electrically separate from the PCI slots and does not reduce the number of slots that may be connected to a single bridge.

Dimensions

The AGP circuit board design is built around a conventional PCI card, at least for use in full-size computers—those matching (or approximating) the ATX design. For these systems, the original AGP standard provides for the two sizes of card. A full-size AGP board measures 4.2 inches (107 millimeters) tall and 12.28 inches (312 millimeters) long. Short cards measure only 6.875 inches (175 millimeters) long. Figure 30.5 illustrates these principal dimensions.

Accelerated Graphics Port

FIGURE 30.5

Dimensions of an ATX-size AGP video board.

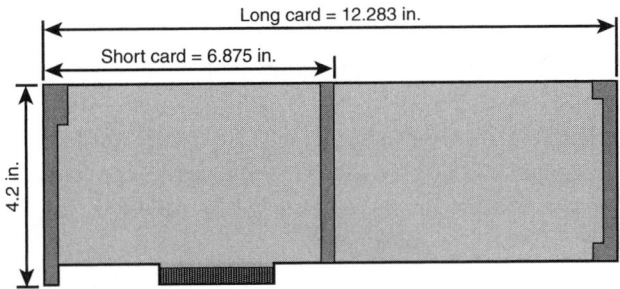

For low-profile computers that match the NLX standards, the revised AGP 2.0 standard provides a special, low-slung card form factor that allows the AGP-based graphics adapter to plug into the motherboard rather than the riser that accommodates other expansion boards. Figure 30.6 shows the dimensions of the NLX-style AGP board.

FIGURE 30.6

Dimensions of an NLX-style AGP video board.

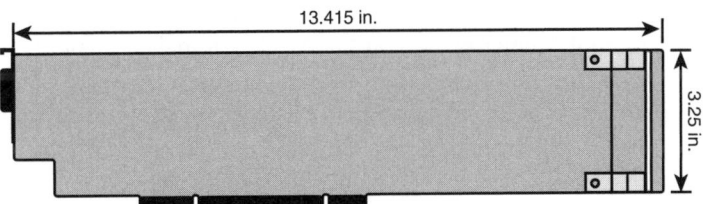

The slot spacing for AGP expansion boards in ATX computers is the same as for PCI and ISA boards, 0.8 inches. AGP boards in such systems use the same retaining bracket design as ordinary PCI boards. The NLX design, however, requires a specialb bracket, as shown in Figure 30.7.

FIGURE 30.7

The NLX-styleb AGP retaining bracket.

Connector

Although the AGP slot bin a computer uses an edge connector, it is an entirely different connector from those used in PCI slots. This physical difference ensures against inserting an expansion board in an inappropriate slot. Other aspects of AGP further constrained the design of the connector. The chosen design interleaves contacts at two depths inside the connector with the mating fingers on the edge connector arranged in a flip-flop pattern, as shown in Figure 30.8.

FIGURE 30.8
Layout of the high-density contacts on an AGP edge connector.

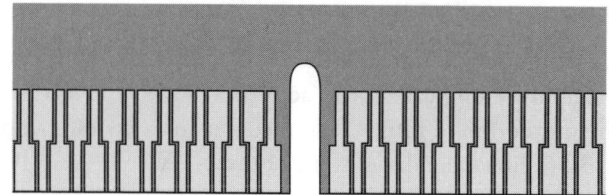

The interleaved contact fingers on the AGP card make hot-plugging AGP boards impossible. That is, you should not slide an AGP board into its slot when the power is on to your computer. When you slide a board into a slot, the contact fingers closest to the edge of the board are apt to wipe across the connector contacts for the deeper contacts. Even a quick wipe can send weird, even damaging signals through the card and your computer. Intel recommends that you slide AGP boards into their slots as straight as you can without rocking them back and forth to seat them in the connector. Even when the power is off, the side-to-side wiping action can damage the miniaturized contacts in the AGP connector.

Riser Boards

A riser board looks like an expansion board and works like an expansion board. Using the quack-standard—if it looks like a duck and quacks like a duck—a riser board *is* an expansion board. But really it's not, at least according to the people who have created the standards that make it possible to consider riser boards as being expansion boards. In its various riser board standards, Intel claims that its riser boards are not an expansion board standard.

Rest assured you're not the only one confused by riser boards. The concept underlying them is the same as an expansion board—put extra circuitry on a special card so that it can be easily removed and changed. The boards look like expansion boards, pegged at the same height and using similar expansion connectors. Risers slide into a motherboard slot placed adjacent to ordinary expansion boards so that, at least from the outside, they look like simply another expansion board.

Intel doesn't want you to think of riser boards as expansion boards because it doesn't want to confuse you with more than one expansion board standard. It doesn't want third-party manufacturers putting riser boards in boxes and selling them in retail stores. Likely the company fears someone will buy a riser and discover they can't slide it into a PCI slot, and the lonely worker handling support will get a barrage of telephone calls asking for help.

Functionally, a riser board is simply a bend in a motherboard. It rises perpendicularly from the motherboard (much like an expansion board) to hold circuitry that otherwise would not fit on the motherboard (much like an expansion board). Riser boards can even use a slot position, much like an expansion board, but they follow their own standards, which have absolutely nothing to do with PCI. This independence, in fact, is one of the graces of the riser board. It allows you to change or customize your system using a low-cost product that avoids the complications (and cost) of a full PCI interface. Moreover, the Audio Modem Riser (AMR) slot doesn't count against the tiny maximum number of PCI boards that can be connected to your computer's PCI bridge circuitry.

Put another way, riser boards offer a system designer three big benefits: space, timeliness, and isolation. The physical size of the riser board amounts to additional real estate on which to locate electronic circuitry, as well as bracket space at the back of the computer for extra connectors. Using a riser board, a motherboard can be more compact. In fact, Intel created the original standard riser, the Audio Modem Riser, as an adjunct to its small-footprint microATX motherboard.

Today, communication and networking standards change faster than most computer standards. Keeping up with these changes may require motherboard-makers to revise their designs more often than they would otherwise like (they would otherwise like never to change their designs, because each change racks up design expenses). By restricting the changes to a small riser board, the manufacturer trims the cost of keeping its motherboards timely.

There's another reason for putting audio circuits on a separate board. Audio circuits are the most prone to picking up interference from the rest of your computer. Analog audio uses signals that vary in a wide range, over more than three orders of magnitude. Interference typically produces tiny signals that are ignored by logic circuits but are amplified into bothersome noise by analog circuits. A signal one-thousandth the strength of a normal logic signal would have zero effect on the operation of your computer but would be audible in high-quality speakers attached to your computer. By putting the interference-prone circuits on a separate board, designers can physically isolate them from the other signals on the motherboard, which adds a degree of electrical isolation as well.

With these ideas in mind, Intel and other companies have created three standards for riser boards meant to work in modern computers. These include the original Audio Modem Riser standard, the Communications and Networking Riser standard, and the Advanced Communications Riser standard.

Audio Modem Riser

The first of the riser-board standards independent of a specific motherboard design was Intel's original Audio Modem Riser (AMR). The AMR specification was originally published on June 30, 1998, and updated to its final form (version 1.01) on September 10, 1998. It envisions a board capable of holding up to four audio codecs on a single board that's at most 6.875 inches long and 4.2 inches high. It uses a single 42-contact edge connector located between the AGP port and other port connectors on the motherboard. It takes the space of an ordinary expansion board but not the connector or the circuitry, so it doesn't count against the maximum number of PCI boards that can be inside a single computer.

The interface was designed to allow a great deal of flexibility. Not only does it allow for four codecs where two would typically be used—one to implement a modem, one for the equivalent of a soundboard—a special set of *split I/O signals* allows, for example, a sound system implementation on the motherboard to communicate with a modem on the riser board. These signals take the form of four separate serial data channels from the chipset (typically) to the audio circuitry on the riser board. The interface also provides the power and clock signals needed to make the audio circuits work, as well as signals for future applications (including the USB bus).

Although you'll still find some references to the AMR design, Intel has replaced it with the Communications Network Riser standard (discussed next) and has removed the AMR specification from its Web site.

Communications Network Riser

On February 7, 2000, Intel released its replacement for the AMR design, which it called the *Communications and Networking Riser* (*CNR*). The "networking" part of the name marks the major difference. CNR incorporates provisions for networking and USB interfaces as well as the audio and modem technologies of the earlier design. The full specification for the CNR board and its interfaces is available at the Intel Web site at www.intel.com.

The CNR design uses a new 60-pin connector with a preferred location at the edge of the motherboard: outboard of its normal PCI expansion slots, a position formerly used by a legacy ISA slot on many motherboards. Significantly, the new connector is incompatible with AMR boards.

Despite the physical incompatibility, the CNR standard starts with some of the basic functional compatibilities as with boards made for the AMR specification. At heart, CNR incorporates the Audio Codec (AC) '97 interface. Unlike AMR, which permits four AC '97 channels, the CNR specification originally allowed only two, although it was revised (to version 1.2) on November 8, 2001, to permit three.

The networking side of the CNR design defines two different board implementations, each using the same connector but with different pinouts. The "A" variation uses eight contacts for a platform LAN connection interface, meaning that the hard work of generating the network signals is on the motherboard. The riser only packages them, for example, putting them on the same RJ-11 jack as the modem signals. The "B" variation uses 17 contacts for a Media Independent Interface (MII, as defined under the IEEE 802.3u specification) bus, allowing the riser board circuitry to set up any kind of physical connection (which makes the riser board circuitry more complex). In other words, the "A" variation allows for less complex riser boards, whereas the "B" variation allows for greater versatility (for example, permitting the manufacturer to install different network interfaces by changing the riser board).

The CNR design also allows for the integration of a USB interface on the riser board. With the CNR version 1.1 revision of October 18, 2000, the specification added support for USB version 2.0 at 480Mbps.

So that the CNR board will be properly identified by the host computer, each board has five signal lines for a System Management Bus (SMBus) interface. The host computer can use the bus to interrogate ROM memory on the board to identify its function and its resource needs each time the host boots up. The CNR design also includes several lines to provide power to the circuitry on the riser board at 12, 5, and 3.3 volts (DC) as well as sleep-mode voltage so the circuitry of the CNR board may remain active while the host is in sleep mode. (This voltage allows the CNR circuitry to wake the host computer upon modem ring or network request.)

The physical specifications for the CNR board are similar to those of the AMR board. Both boards are limited to the same maximum height, 4.2 inches (106.68 millimeters), dictated by host height restrictions within the PCI standard. CNR boards have a slightly shorter maximum length than AMR boards, at 6.579 inches (167.11 millimeters). The connector is, of course, different, unique to the CNR board, although the pin spacing on its edge connector matches that of the standard PCI connector.

Advanced Communications Riser

This need for yet another new connector and other shortcomings of the CNR design led an industry group to design its own alternative to CNR on February 11, 2000. That organization, which called itself the *Advanced Communications Riser Special Interest Group* (ACR SIG), has grown to 55 members at the time of this writing, including, significantly, Advanced Micro Devices, but not Intel.

Working together, they created the Advanced Communications Riser (ACR) board to add network and Digital Subscriber Line (DSL) capabilities to simple add-on boards without losing compatibility with AMR boards or adding the need for a new connector.

Physically, the ACR slot uses a 120-pin PCI connector (for its ready availability), but the connector is reversed and offset in its position in its slot. This change in orientation and position makes it compatible with AMR boards. The first 42 contact positions on the ACR board have the same functions and signals as the AMR board. The ACR design envisions its slot position on the outside edge of the motherboard, replacing the legacy ISA slot in many motherboard designs.

An AMR board can slide directly into an ACR slot. An ACR board will, too, although it won't slide into an AMR slot because of the longer connector on the ACR board.

The electrical functions of the ACR board start with the four Audio Codec '97 channels of the AMR board and add two more AC '97 channels, for a total of six.

In addition, the ACR design provides two new pins as a serial data channel for board identification. Each ACR board includes an onboard ROM chip to identify the board and its capabilities to the host computer as part of the Plug-and-Play setup process.

One of the new sets of 14 signals is the Integrated Packet Bus, developed in conjunction with the ACR design to directly link the host microprocessor with the communications subsystem and control high-speed Internet connections. Two sets of 18 signals each provide a pair of channels that separately link your chipset to phone-line networking and ordinary twisted-pair networks following the 10Base-T or 100Base-T standards. The ACR specification reserves an additional eight contacts for future applications, such as wireless networking adapters.

The ACR design specifically recognizes home phone-line networking (HomePNA). It envisions modem-makers offering a single multifunction board that includes a V.92 modem, a HomePNA network adapter, and a DSL adapter. A single ACR card will link to your home phone-line network, your telephone line as a regular modem (for data as well as dialing and Internet phone service), and your DSL line, without the need for external adapters. All phone-line communications functions can then use a single RJ-11 jack on the ACR card.

Although the ACR SIG claims that its standard is open, the specification is available only to members of the group. Its Web site is located at www.acrsig.org.

PCMCIA Cards

Notebook computers use PCMCIA cards of two types for expansion: 18-bit PC Cards based on the ISA bus and 32-bit CardBus cards based on the PCI bus. No matter which standard a given card follows, however, it must follow exactly the same physical specifications as all PCMCIA cards. Every card will slide into every slot—well, almost. The standard allows for three thickness variations, but one of which is almost never found, and nearly all slots will accommodate the other two sizes. In other words, physically, PC Cards and CardBus cards are identical, and both use exactly the same connector.

Under the PCMCIA standard, PC Cards and CardBus cards come in three sizes, differing only in thickness. The basic unit of measurement—the size of the typical card slot—is based on the medium-thickness card, designated Type II. Measuring 54 by 85 millimeters (2.126 by 3.37 inches) and 5 mm (about three-sixteenths of a inch) thick.

PC Cards and CardBus cards physically follow the form factor of earlier memory cards (including the IC Card) standardized by JEIDA (the Japan Electronic Industry Development Association). The first release of the PCMCIA specification paired this single-size card with a Fujitsu-style 68-pin connector. Under the current PCMCIA specification, version 8.0 (and all versions since the 2.1 specification), this form factor is designated as the Type I PC Card.

The thinness of the Type I card proved an unacceptable limitation. Even without allowing for the PC Card packaging, some solid-state devices are themselves thicker than 3.3 mm. Most important among these "fat" devices are the EPROMs used for nonvolatile storage. (Most computers use EPROMs to store their system BIOS, for example.) Unlike ordinary, thin ROMs, EPROMs can be reprogrammed, but this requires a transparent window to admit the ultraviolet radiation used to erase the programming of the chip. The windowed packaging makes most EPROMs themselves 3.3 mm or thicker.

Fujitsu faced this problem when developing the firmware to be encoded on memory cards and therefore developed a somewhat thicker card that could be plugged into the same sockets as could standard memory cards. Modem and other peripheral makers found the Fujitsu fat card more suited to their purposes. To accommodate them, PCMCIA 2.0 standardized an alternative: the Type II PC Card. Essentially based on the old Fujitsu developmental EPROM form factor, Type II PC Cards are 5 mm thick but otherwise conform to the same dimensions as Type I cards.

The PCMCIA standard puts the extra thickness in a planar bulge, called the *substrate area*, in the middle of the card. This thicker area measures 48 mm wide and 75 mm long. Three millimeters along each side of the Type II card are kept to the thinness of the Type I standard so that the same card guides can be used for either card type. Similarly, the front 10 mm of a Type II card maintain the 3.3 mm thickness of the Type I standard so that the same connector can be used for either card type. Naturally, the actual card slot for a Type II card must be wide enough to accommodate the maximum thickness of the card.

In September 1992, PCMCIA approved a third (Type III) form factor for PC Cards. These still-thicker cards expand the bulge of Type II from 5 mm to 10.5 mm and are designed to accommodate miniaturized hard disks and similar mechanical components. As with Type II cards, Type III PC Cards remain thin at the edges to fit standard card guides and standard connectors. Although a number of hard disk drives appeared in this format, few are used today in notebook computers. However, high-capacity MP3 players have embraced the Type III card design.

In practical terms, a Type I card comes closest to being a truly flat, credit-card style card. Type II cards have small bulges at the top and bottom to accommodate circuitry. Type III cards have thick lumps to hold a disk drive. Figure 30.9 illustrates the apparent differences between the three card types.

FIGURE 30.9
The three PCMCIA card types vary in thickness from 3.3 mm to 10.5 mm.

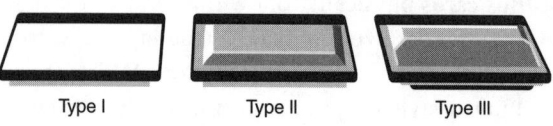

Type I   Type II   Type III

Note that many notebook computers lay out their endowment of two PCMCIA slots with one over the other and without a metal separator. This design allows the two slots to hold two individual Type II or a single Type III card. Nearly all current PCMCIA slots are wide enough to accommodate Type II cards. The only place you're likely to encounter a slot that will accept only Type I cards is equipment manufactured before 1992.

Under the current PCMCIA standard, both Type I and Type II cards can be implemented in extended form. That is, their depth can be increased by an additional 50 mm (to 135 mm) to hold additional componentry—for example, the antennae of WiFi network adapters. Such extended cards project about two inches more from standard PCMCIA slots.

To ensure that all cards easily and securely mate with their connectors, the PCMCIA standard requires that card guides be at least 40 mm long and that the PCMCIA card connector must engage and guide the connector pins for 10 mm before the connector bottoms out.

The layout of a PC Card or CardBus card is essentially symmetrical, meaning that it could inadvertently be inserted upside down. The PCMCIA design allows for such cases of brain fade by eliminating the risk of damage. Although the cards do not work while inverted, neither they nor the computers into which they are plugged will suffer damage.

Because the size and placement of labels on the cards is part of the standard, when you are familiar with the layout of one PC Card, you will know the proper orientation of them all, and CardBus cards as well. Moreover, other physical aspects of the cards—the position of the write-protect switch (if any) and battery (if needed)—are standardized as well. The PCMCIA standard also recommends that the batteries in all cards be oriented in the same direction (positive terminal up).

In addition to the physical measures that facilitate getting the cards into their sockets, two pins—one on each side of the connector—allow the computer host to determine whether the card is properly seated. If the signal (ground) from one is present and the other is not, the system knows that the card is skewed or otherwise improperly inserted in the connector.

Connector

All types of PCMCIA cards use the same 68-pin connector, whose contacts are arranged in two parallel rows of 34 pins. The lines are spaced at 1.27 mm (0.050 inch) intervals between rows and between adjacent pins in the same row. Male pins on the card engage a single molded socket on the host.

To ensure proper powering up of the card, the pins are arranged so that the power and ground connections are longer (3.6 mm) than the signal leads (3.2 mm). Because of their greater length, therefore, power leads engage first so that potentially damaging signals are not applied to unpowered circuits. The two pins (36 and 67) that signal that the card has been inserted all the way are shorter (2.6 mm) than the signal leads.

Power

All practical computers made today operate electronically. Moving electrons—electricity—are the media of their thoughts. Electrical pulses course from one circuit to another, switched off or on in an instant by logic chips. Circuits combine the electrical pulses together to make logical decisions and send out other pulses to control peripherals. The computer's signals stay electrical until electrons colliding with phosphors in the monitor tube push out photons toward your eyes or generate the fields that snap your printer into action.

Of course, your computer needs a source for the electricity that runs it. The power does not arise spontaneously in its circuits but rather must be derived from an outside source. Conveniently, nearly every home in America is equipped with its own electrical supply that the computer can tap into. Such is the wonder of civilization.

But the delicate solid-state semiconductor circuits of today's computers cannot directly use the electricity supplied by your favorite utility company. Commercial power is an electrical brute, designed to have the strength and stamina to withstand the miles of travel between generator and your home. Your computer's circuits want a steady, carefully controlled trickle of power. Raw utility power would fry and melt computer circuits in a quick flash of miniature lightning.

For economic reasons, commercial electrical power is transmitted between you and the utility company as alternating current, the familiar AC found everywhere. AC is preferred by power companies because it is easy to generate and adapts readily between voltages (including to very high voltages that make long distance transmission efficient). It's called *alternating* because it reverses polarity—swapping positive for negative—dozens of times a second (arbitrarily 60Hz in America; 50Hz in Europe).

The changing or oscillating nature of AC enables transformers to increase or decrease voltage (the measure of driving force of electricity), because transformers only react to electrical changes. Electrical power travels better at higher voltages because waste (as heat generated by the electrical current flowing through the resistance of the long-distance transmission wires) is inversely proportional to voltage. Transformers permit the high voltages used in transmitting commercial power—sometimes hundreds of thousands of volts—to be reduced to a safe level (nominally 117 volts) before it is led into your home.

As wonderful as AC is to power companies, it's an anathema to computer circuits. These circuits form their pulses by switching the flow of electricity tapped from a constant supply. Although computers can be designed that use AC, the constant voltage reversal would complicate the design so that juggling knives while blindfolded and riding a roller coaster would seem tame in comparison. Computers (and most electronic gear) use direct current (DC) instead. Direct current is the kind of power that comes directly from a primary source—a battery—a single voltage that stays at a constant level (at least constant as long as the battery has the reserves to produce it). Moreover, even the relatively low voltage that powers your lights and vacuum cleaner would be fatal to semiconductor circuits. Tiny distances separate the elements inside solid-state circuits, and high voltages can flash across those distances like lightning, burning and destroying the silicon along the way.

Power Supplies

The intermediary that translates AC from your electrical outlets into the DC that your computer's circuits need is called the *power supply*. As it operates, the power supply of your computer attempts to make the direct current supplied to your computer as pure as possible, as close to the ideal DC power produced by batteries. The chief goal is regulation, maintaining the voltage as close as possible to the ideal desired by the circuits inside your computer.

The power needs of the circuitry of desktop and notebook computers are the same. Both are built with the same circuitry with the same voltage and similar current requirements. Ultimately, both kinds of computers draw power from the same source—electric utilities. But they differ in how they handle the power between your outlet and their circuits. Desktop systems provide a direct route. Utility power gets converted to circuit power once and for all inside a little tin box called a *power supply*. Notebook computers add an auxiliary power source—their batteries—to the mix. In so doing, the power circuitry of the computer system is rearranged to suit the needs of both the logic circuitry of your computer and its batteries.

In effect, the notebook computer has two power sources: utility power when you're near an outlet (and plugged in) and battery power when you're in the field (or in an airplane). But they are not entirely independent. The same circuits regulate the voltage going to the logic of your computer whether your notebook machine is running from AC or battery power. In fact, should you remove its batteries and the charging and control circuits, the power functions of a notebook are the same as a desktop machine. Only the location of the power circuits has been rearranged to suit the system designers. The same technologies that bring a desktop power supply to life also are at work in notebook machines.

Desktop Power Supplies

Most computers package their power supplies as a subassembly that's complete in itself and simply screws into the chassis and plugs into the system board and other devices that require its electricity. The power supply itself is ensconced in a metal box perforated with holes that let heat leak out but prevent your fingers from poking in.

In fact, the safety provided by the self-contained and fully armored computer power supply is one of the prime advantages of the original design. All the life-threatening voltages—in particular, line voltage—are contained inside the box of the power supply. Only low, non-threatening voltages are accessible—that is, touchable—on your computer's system board and expansion boards. You can grab a board inside your computer even when the system is turned on and not worry about electrocution (although you might burn yourself on a particularly intemperate semiconductor or jab an ill-cut circuit lead through a finger).

Grabbing a board out of a slot of an operating computer is not safe for the computer's circuits, however. Pulling a board out is apt to bridge together some pins on its slot connector, if but for an instant. As a result, the board (and your computer's motherboard) may find unexpected voltages attacking, possibly destroying, its circuits. In other words, never plug in or remove an expansion board from a computer that has its power switched on. Although you may often be successful, the penalty for even one failure should be enough to deter your impatience.

In many desktop computers, the power supply serves a secondary function. The fan that cools the power supply circuits also provides the airflow that cools the rest of the system. This fan also supplies most of the noise that computers generate while they are running. In general, the power supply fan operates as an exhaust fan—it blows outward. Air is sucked through the other openings in the power supply from the space inside your system. This gives dust in the air taken into your computer a chance to settle anywhere on your system board before getting blown out through the power supply.

The prevailing standard for power supplies of today's computers is ATX. This standard defines not only the power supply itself but also the connectors and voltages available for the motherboard and devices inside the computer.

Technologies

In electronic gear, two kinds of power supplies are commonly used: linear and switching. The former is old technology, dating from the days when the first radios were freed from their need for storage batteries in the 1920s. The latter rates as high technology, requiring the speed and efficiency of solid-state electronic circuitry to achieve the dominant position it holds today in the computer power market. These two power supply technologies are distinguished by the means used to achieve their voltage regulation.

Linear Power Supplies

The design first used for making regulated DC from utility-supplied AC was the linear power supply. At one time, this was the only kind of power supply used for any electronic equipment. When another technology became available, it was given the linear label because it then used standard linear (analog) semiconductor circuits, although a linear power supply need not have any semiconductors in it at all.

In a linear power supply, the raw electricity from the power line is first sent through a transformer that reduces its voltage to a value slightly higher than required by the computer's circuits. Next, one or several rectifiers, usually semiconductor diodes, convert the now low-voltage AC to DC by permitting the flow of electricity in only one direction, blocking the reversals. Finally, this DC is sent through the linear voltage regulator, which adjusts the voltage created by the power supply to the level required by your computer's circuits.

Most linear voltage regulators work simply by absorbing the excess voltage made by the transformer, turning it into heat. A shunt regulator simply shorts out excess power to drive the voltage down. A series regulator puts an impediment—a resistance—in the flow of electricity, blocking excess voltage. In either case, the regulator requires an input voltage higher than the voltage it supplies to your computer's circuits. This excess power is converted to heat (that is, it's wasted). The linear power supply achieves its regulation simply by varying the waste.

Switching Power Supplies

The design alternative is the switching power supply. Although more complex, switching power supplies are more efficient and often less expensive than their linear kin. Although designs vary, the typical switching power supply first converts the incoming 60 hertz utility power to a much higher frequency of pulses (in the range of 20,000Hz, above the range of normal human hearing) by switching it on and off using a transistors.

At the same time, the switching regulator increases the frequency of the commercial power; it regulates the commercial power using a digital technique called *pulse width modulation* (PWM). That is, the duration of each power pulse is varied in response to the needs of the computer circuitry being supplied. The width of the pulses is controlled by the electronic switch; shorter pulses result in a lower output voltage. Finally, the switched pulses are reduced in voltage down to the level required by the computer circuits by a transformer and then turned into pure direct current via rectification and filtering.

Switching power supplies earn their efficiency and lower cost in two ways. Switching regulation is more efficient because less power is turned into heat. Instead of dissipating energy with a shunt or series regulator, the switching regulator switches all current flow off, albeit briefly. In addition, high frequencies require smaller, less expensive transformers and filtering circuits. For these two very practical reasons, nearly all of today's personal computers use switching power supplies.

Power Needs

Modern computer logic circuits operate by switching voltages with the two different logic states (true or false, one or zero, for example) coded as two voltage levels—high and low. Every family of logic circuits has its own voltage standards.

The primary consumers of power inside a computer are its logic circuits. At one time, nearly all logic circuits used five volts of direct current. This power level was set by the design of the electronic circuit components they used, based around the requirements of *transistor-transistor logic* (TTL). In a TTL design, *high* refers to voltages above about 3.2 volts, and *low* means voltages lower than about 1.8. The middle ground is undefined logically, an electrical guard band that prevents ambiguity between the two meaningful states.

To reduce the power needs of today's high-speed circuits, computer designs are shifting to 3.3-volt logic and require power supplies that deliver that voltage level (often in addition to 5-volt power). The ATX design and those derived from it (SFX and TFX) provide for both 5-volt and 3.3-volt supplies.

Some computer circuits, such as microprocessors, run at even lower voltages. The levels required by their circuits are not available from most computer power supplies. Instead, motherboard-makers use *voltage regulators* to reduce a 12-, 5-, or 3.3-volt power source to the level required by the chips. This design allows standard power supplies to work with chips rated for almost any voltage.

In addition to the basic logic voltage, computers often require other voltages as well. The motors of most disk drives (hard and floppy) typically require 12 volts to make them spin. Other specialized circuits in computers sometimes require bipolar electrical supplies. A serial port, for example, signals logic states by varying voltages between positive and negative in relation to ground. Consequently, the mirror image voltages (–5 and –12 volts) are usually available inside every computer.

In notebook computers, most of which have no room for generic expansion boards, all these voltages are often unnecessary. For example, many new hard disks designed for notebook computers use 5-volt motors, eliminating the need for the 12-volt supply. The custom-tailored power systems of notebook computers supply only the voltages required by circuits actually built in to the computer.

Voltages and Ratings

The power supplies you are most likely to tangle with are those inside desktop computers, and these must produce all four common voltages to satisfy the needs of all potential combinations of circuits. In older desktop computers, the power supply typically produces four voltages (+5, −5, +12, and −12) that are delivered in different quantities (amperages) because of the demands associated with each. A separate *voltage regulator* on the motherboard produces the lower voltage in the 3.3-volt range required by Pentium-level microprocessors and their associated circuitry. In some systems, the output voltage of this regulator may be variable to accommodate energy-saving systems (which reduce the speed and voltage of the microprocessor to conserve power and reduce heat dissipation). Newer power supplies, such as those that follow the ATX design standard, sometimes also provide a direct 3.3-volt supply.

The typical computer has a lot of logic circuitry, so it needs copious quantities of 5-volt power, often as much as 20 to 25 amperes). Many disk drives use 12-volt power; the typical modern drive uses an ampere or so. Only a few components require the negative voltages, so most power supplies only deliver a few watts of each.

Most power supplies are rated and advertised by the sum of all the power they can make available, as measured in watts. The power rating of any power supply can be calculated by individually multiplying the current rating of each of the four voltages it supplies and summing the results. (Power in watts is equal to the product of voltage times current in amperes.) Most modern full-size computers have power supplies of 150–220 watts. Notebook computers may use from 10 to 50 watts when processing at full speed.

Note that this power rating does not correspond to the wattage that the power supply draws from a wall outlet. All electronic circuits—and power supplies in particular—suffer from inefficiencies, linear designs more so than switching. Consequently, a power supply requires a wattage in excess of what it provides to your computer's circuits—at least when it is producing its full output. Computer power supplies, however, rarely operate at their rated output. As a result, efficient switching power supplies typically draw less power than their nominal rating in normal use. For example, a computer with a 220-watt power supply with a typical dosage of memory (say, 4MB) and one hard disk drive likely draws less than 100 watts while it is operating.

When you're selecting a power supply for your computer, the rating you require depends on the boards and peripherals with which you want to fill your computer. Modern computers are not nearly so power hungry as their forebears. Nearly all computer components require less power than the equivalents of only half a dozen years ago. The one exception is the microprocessor. Greater performance requires more power. Although Intel's engineers have done a good job at reducing the power needs of the company's products by shifting to lower-voltage technologies, the reductions have been matched by increasing demands. Chips need as much power as they ever have, sometimes more.

In a desktop computer, a 200-watt power supply essentially loafs along; most individual computers (as opposed to servers or workstations) could get along with 120 watts without straining. A system board may require 15–25 watts; a floppy disk drive, 3–20 (depending on its vintage); a hard disk, 5–50 (also depending on its vintage); a memory or multifunction expansion board, 5–10. Table 31.1 summarizes the needs of both vintage and modern computer components.

TABLE 31.1 Typical Device Power Demands

Device Class	Device Type	Power	Example
Floppy disk drive	Full height, 5.25 inch	12.6 watts	IBM PC diskette drive
	Half height, 5.25 inch	12.6 watts	QumeTrak 142
	One-inch high, 3.5 inch	1.4 watts	Teac FD-235J
Graphics board	Two-board old technology	16.2 watts	IBM 8514/A
	High performance, full length	13.75 watts	Matrox MGA
	Accelerated half-card	6.5 watts	ATI VGA Wonder, Graphics Ultra+
Hard disk	Full height, 5.25-inch	59 watts	IBM 10MB XT hard disk
	Half height, 5.25-inch	25 watts	[Estimated]
	One-inch high, 3.5 inch	12.25 watts (peak)	maxtor DiamondMax Plus 9
	2.5 inch	2.2 watts	Quantum Go-Drive 120AT
	PCMCIA card	3.5 watts	Maxtor MXL-131-III
	Full height, 3.5 inch	12 watts	Quantum ProDrive 210S
Memory	1MB SIMM	4.8 watts	Motorola MCM81000
	4MB SIMM	6.3 watts	Motorola MCM94000
	8MB SIMM	16.8 watts	Motorola MCM36800
	128MB SoDIMM	1.8 watts	Micron MT8LSD3264
Modem	PCMCIA card	3.5 watts	MultiTech MT1432LT
	Internal, half-card	1.2 watts	Boca V.32bis
Network adapter	Ethernet, half-card	7..9 watts	Artisoft AE-2/T
System board	286, AT size	25 watts	[Estimated]
	386, XT size	12 watts	Monolithic Systems MSC386 XT/AT
	486 or Pentium, AT size	25 watts	[Estimated]

Reserve power is always a good thing, and with switching power supplies, it comes without a penalty (except in the cost of making the power supply). In other words, although you could get along with a smaller power supply in your desktop computer, the quasi-standard 200 watts remains a good choice.

Supply Voltage

Most power supplies are designed to operate from a certain line voltage and frequency. In the United States, utility power is supplied at a nominal 115 volts and 60 hertz. In other nations, the supply voltage and frequency may be different. In Europe, for instance, a 230-volt, 50Hz standard prevails.

Most switching power supplies can operate at either frequency, so that shouldn't be a worry when traveling. (Before you travel, however, check the ratings on your power supply to be sure.) Linear power supplies are more sensitive. Because their transformers have less reactance at lower frequencies, 60Hz transformers draw more current than their designers intend when operating on 50Hz power. Consequently, they are liable to over-heat and fail, perhaps catastrophically.

Most computer power supplies are either universal or voltage selectable. A *universal power supply* is designed to have a wide tolerance for supply current. If you have a computer with such a power supply, all you need to do is plug the computer in, and it should work properly. Note that some of these universal power supplies accommodate any supply voltage in a wide range and will accept any standard voltage and a line frequency available in the world—a voltage range from about 100 to 250 volts and a line frequency of 50 to 60Hz. Other so-called universal supplies are actually limited to two narrow ranges, bracketing the two major voltage standards. Because you are unlikely to encounter a province with a 169.35-volt standard, these dual-range supplies are universal enough for worldwide use.

Voltage-selectable power supplies have a small switch on the rear panel that selects their operating voltage, usually in two ranges—115 and 230 volts. If your computer has a voltage-selectable power supply, make sure that the switch is in the proper position for the available power before you turn on your computer.

 **CAUTION** When traveling in a foreign land, always use this power supply switch to adjust for different voltages. Do not use inexpensive voltage converters. Often these devices are nothing more than rectifiers that clip half the incoming waveform. Although that strategy may work for light bulbs, it can be disastrous to electronic circuitry. Using such a device can destroy your computer. It's not a recommended procedure.

Standards

The metal modules that serve as power supplies for desktop computers were one of the first components to be standardized. The technology for building a power supply is common and straightforward, and reverse-engineering a power supply for given computer is almost trivial. There are no strange codes or complex logic signals coming from a power supply, just a few, easily measured voltages. Each popular case used a characteristic power supply that became a *de facto* industry standard, both in size (the power supply had to match the case mechanically) and connectors (to plug into motherboards and drives). The earliest of these matched models of IBM computers—PC, XT, and AT—the last being the reigning standard for a decade.

The standards used by modern computers arose when Intel standardized its motherboard offerings and inspired the industry to follow suit with its ATX design. The new motherboard broke with the past with a different physical layout that required a new case design, which in turn dictated a different size for the power supply. In addition, Intel chose to break with the past standards for power connectors to create a new one of its own for the ATX motherboard. The choice was more than Intel wishing to re-create the industry to suit itself. A new connector was overdue—the old design could not accommodate the 3.3-volt supplies that new logic designs required.

The result was the ATX power supply. Roughly patterned after previous designs, the ATX power supply is a steel-cased modular design that incorporates the computer's primary (and usually, only) external power connection. It supplies all the voltages required by both past and current logic circuitry: positive direct-current voltages of 5 and 12 volts in addition to the new 3.3-volt supply as well as negative supplies of 5 and 12 volts. But on its new 20-pin motherboard connector, the ATX design has added several signals aimed at the needs of modern computers:

- **Power Good**. This signal is a carryover from older designs. The power supply sends out the Power Good signal to indicate that its output voltages are at the correct level and safe for computer circuits. A computer won't turn on unless the Power Good signal is present. The technical designation of this signal under the ATX standard is PWR_OK.

- **On**. This is a signal from the motherboard telling the power supply to switch its main outputs on. This signal allows an external switch to control the computer power. More importantly, it allows the motherboard to control the power supply. The motherboard can shift the system to standby and cut its power consumption by switching off the On signal, and it can shift back to normal operation by restoring it. This mode of operation is essential for features such as wake-on-alarm, wake-on-modem, and wake-on-network that shift the system to standby awaiting a specific event (an alarm, incoming call, or network request). The engineering name for this signal is PS_ON#.

- **Standby Supply Voltage**. This is an auxiliary source of logic voltage that is not controlled by the On signal. It provides the power the motherboard needs when it is on standby and the main voltages from the power supply have been switched off. The engineering name for this signal is +5 VSB.

The ATX standard also defines an *auxiliary power connector* with six pins. This connector is aimed at high-current power supplies. It gives another channel to the main 5 and 3.3 volts when the current from the supply exceeds the safe carrying capacity of the 16-gauge wires recommended for the connections. This connector is used when the 3.3-volt output exceeds 18 amperes or the 5-volt output exceeds 24 amperes.

ATX power supplies also include several peripheral connectors for disk drives (and, sometimes, auxiliary fans and other accessories). Two styles are usually present: large four-pin Molex connectors to match hard disk drives and old floppy disks, and miniaturized four-pin connectors for modern floppy disk drives.

With the introduction of ATX version 2.0, Intel added a variation on the ATX power supply called *ATX12V*. The new design differs from ordinary ATX power supplies only in the presence of one or more new *+12V power connectors*. These four-pin connectors provide a high-current 12-volt supply designed to feed the voltage regulators of high-current processors or other demanding peripherals.

The ATX specification allows for two types of power supplies—those meant to cool not only themselves but also the microprocessor with their fans, and those with fans that cool only the power supply. The only difference between the two is the location of ventilation holes. Otherwise, all ATX power supplies look much the same and measure 5.8 inches (150 millimeters) wide, 5.5 inches (140 mm) long, and 3.4 inches (86 mm) thick.

The ATX design served as a pattern for two additional power supplies designed for cases more compact than those used by standard ATX motherboards. These include the SFX and TFX designs. No matter the physical package, these power supplies offer the same connectors and signals as the basic ATX power supply.

The SFX and SFX12V power supplies are *small form-factor* designs meant for smaller computers (hence the *SF* in the designation). The SFX power supply standard envisions computers needing from 90 to 180 watts. The standard defines two basic packages. One is called the *40-millimeter profile* design that's about 5 inches (125 mm) long, 4 inches (100 mm) wide, and 2 inches (50 mm rather than 40 mm) thick. In addition, the standard also allows for a *60-millimeter profile* version that's actually 63.5 millimeters (2.5 inches) thick. The standard also allows manufacturers to add external fans to the 60-millimeter profile power supplies either as external or internal fans. In either case, the fan adds about 17 millimeters to the thickness of the power supply. The SPX12V design provides one or more four-pin +12V power connectors, which the ordinary SPX does not.

The TFX12V is a *thin form-factor* design (hence the designation) made to match microATX and FlexATX motherboards and fit into low-profile chassis. Under the standard, a TFX12V power supply measures 6.9 inches (175 millimeters) long, 3 inches (75 mm) high, and 2.6 inches (65 mm) thick. The standard does not define the total output of the supply (or the current to be supplied at any of its output voltages) but rather envisions supplies with outputs in the range of 180 to 220 watts. The "12V" in the name indicates that each TFX12V power supply makes available one or more four-pin +12V power connectors.

The official specifications for ATX, SFX, and TFX power supplies are available on the Web at www.formfactors.org.

In modern computer designs, only the WTX power supply design does not follow the connector and signal standards popularized by ATX. WTX power supplies are meant to match WTX motherboards in workstations and servers, applications demanding more power than the ATX family can deliver.

WTX recognizes two sizes of power supply: single-fan power supplies capable of delivering from 400 to 460 watts, and a two-fan design meant to supply from 550 to 850 watts. In addition to harboring an additional fan, two-fan designs are physically larger. A single-fan WTX power supply measures 9.1 inches (230 mm) long, 5.8 inches (150 mm) wide, and 3.4 inches (86 mm) thick. A two-fan supply measures 9.1 inches (230 mm) long, 8.8 inches (224 mm) wide, and 3.4 inches (86 mm) thick.

Either size of WTX power supply offers five power connectors that do not match the ATX standard. These include a primary 24-pin connector that supplies most of the power, a 22-pin connector with control signals (as well as some power), an eight-pin connector meant to supply voltage converters for low-voltage memory and processors, and two six-pin connectors that supply high-current 12VDC to power pods for high-current processors and similar applications.

The complete WTX specification is available on the Web at www.wtx.org. This standard is now being phased out. The Server System Infrastructure group at www.ssi.org has developed a new set of specifications for servers and their power supplies.

Portable Computer Power

In comparison to desktop computers, notebook and subnotebook computers would seem to have it easy when it comes to power supplies. Notebooks work with battery power, which is generated inside the battery cells in exactly the right form for computer circuits—low voltage DC. But notebook computers actually have much more complex power systems, more complex than desktop computers because of their use of two power systems, utility and battery.

Even though battery power is smooth direct current, battery-powered computers require built-in voltage regulation because the voltage from batteries varies as cells discharge. In addition, most computer batteries are rechargeable, so they need to get electricity from somewhere. Moreover, most of the time laptop and notebook computers are close to electrical supplies when they are used, so it makes sense to use utility power rather than battery power—or charge batteries at the same time. Consequently, notebook computers also use power supplies, but such supplies have a significantly different design, one that splits the desktop power supply design into pieces.

The power supplies of most notebook computers have an external half that reduces utility voltage to a safe, near-battery level and rectifies it into DC. These external power supplies generally create only one voltage, one that will substitute for battery power. But that's not the end of it. Inside the notebook computer's case are several *voltage regulators* that keep these low voltages at the constant levels logic circuits require. These voltage regulators wallpaper over the wide variations that occur to the voltage output of a battery as it discharges. The regulators also ensure that the low-voltage power from the external power supply exactly matches battery power before it gets to critical circuits. In addition, notebook computers have another, specialized regulator that desktop computers lack, one that charges the notebook computer's battery reserves and keeps the batteries topped up when external utility power is available.

Unlike the power supplies and voltage regulators for desktop computers, those for notebooks do not follow any industry standards. Each make and model of machine is different. In general, the power circuitry isn't even in one place or one module (as with desktop computers) but rather spread throughout the computer system.

The notebook computer is more concerned with minimizing power waste rather than regulating. Today's power-management functions, which save energy in both desktop and notebook computers, had their origins in the power-saving features of notebook machines.

External Power Supplies

In essence and operation, the external power supply of a notebook computer is little more than a repackaged version of those inside desktop computers. Line voltage AC goes in, and low voltage DC (usually) comes out. The output voltage is close to that of the system's battery output, always a bit higher. (A slightly higher voltage is required so that the batteries are charged to their full capacity.)

In most rudimentary form, the external power supply is nothing more than a transformer that supplies low-voltage AC to a computer. This approach has two benefits. It moves the heaviest element of the power supply out of the computer, reducing its weight and making it more portable. In addition, it keeps dangerous high voltages out of the computer itself, not only making the computer inherently safer but also reducing the number of hurdles the manufacturer must leap to get regulatory approval for the entire computer package.

Current external power supply designs are more elaborate. Instead of AC, they supply DC to the computer. More importantly, they benefit from the latest power technologies and eliminate the large, heavy (and expensive) power transformers required by older designs. As a result, the external power supply weighs less and is more energy efficient.

Despite this design change, many people still call the external power supply a *transformer*. Another common name is *power brick* because of the shape of the supply (although the brick-like weight left the design along with the power transformer).

No standard exists for the external battery chargers/power supplies of notebook computers. Every manufacturer—and often every model of computer from a given manufacturer—uses its own design. They differ as to output voltage, current, and polarity. You can substitute a generic replacement only if the replacement matches the voltage used by your computer and generates at least as much current. Polarity matching gives you two choices—right and wrong—and the wrong choice is apt to destroy many of the semiconductors inside the system. In other words, make extra certain of power polarity when plugging in a generic replacement power supply. (With most computers, the issue of polarity reduces to a practical matter of whether the center or outer conductor of the almost-universal coaxial power plug is the positive terminal.)

Most external power supplies are designed to operate from a single voltage (a few are universal, but don't count on it). That means you are restricted to plugging in and charging your portable computer to one hemisphere (or thereabouts) or the other. Moving from a 117-volt to a 230-volt electrical system requires a second, expensive external charger. Experienced travelers often buy a second external supply/charger at travelling voltage.

Car and Airplane Adapters

Utility power is not the only external source available for powering computers. Both automobiles and airplanes have their own electrical systems that can be used as an external power source for notebook computers. However, you must still match the available power to the requirement of your computer.

Today, the standard power system in automobiles is direct current of approximately 12 volts. The 12-volt rating is only nominal, however. When your car is running and charging its battery, the voltage in the electrical system is often as high as 16 volts. When the car is starting, the available voltage may dip below 8 volts. In fact, even a so-called 12-volt car battery, when fully charged, actually delivers 13.2 volts.

A few computers managed to deal with the wide range of voltages in automotive electrical systems directly. They required only a simple cable with a plug that fit a cigarette lighter to operate from automotive power. But most current computers are more demanding in their power requirements, often needing voltages greater than available from standard 12-volt automotive systems. Although you can power these computers from an automobile cigarette lighter, you need a more costly kind of adapter called an *inverter*.

An inverter is a device that converts DC to AC and increases the voltage to that of utility-supplied power—inverting what you expect a power supply to do. You simply plug your notebook computer's external power supply into the inverter exactly as you would plug into utility power; then you plug your computer in normally.

In some commercial airplanes—primarily in first- and business-class sections but occasionally in economy—you'll find power jacks meant to supply electricity to portable computers. These jacks supply the equivalent of automobile power, regulated to a constant 15 volts of direct current (usually limited to about 75 watts per seat). This power is not meant to directly operate notebook computers but to supply an adapter, which in turn powers the computer. Each computer model is supposed to use its own adapter.

The airline jacks use a special connector manufactured by the Hypertronics Corporation but commonly referred to as an *Empower* connector or *ARINC 628* power connector. One exception is American Airlines, which uses an automotive-style cigarette lighter connector for in-seat power.

You can avoid the need for a special computer power adapter by using an inverter. Several manufacturers now offer small inverters with both airline-style and automotive connectors. The inverters produce the equivalent of normal house current into which you can plug your computer's standard AC adapter.

Note that these airplane power jacks are meant as a convenience for passengers. The main electrical power system of most airplanes does not operate at 15 volts nor is it compatible with house current.

Batteries

Outside of the physical difference in packaging, notebook computers differ from desktop machines most significantly in that they are designed with self-contained power systems. They hold their own electricity and can run on batteries. The power versatility is what gives the notebook machine the ability to compute anywhere.

But batteries play a larger role in modern computing. Wireless keyboards and mice, digital cameras, and MP3 players all rely on batteries as their primary source of power (as likely does your cell phone and a host of other electronic gadgets you take for granted). It's enough to make you want to buy stock in a battery company—and shudder to think what all those throw-away batteries are doing to landfills.

Batteries represent the primitive side of electricity, the chemical side. It's a territory strewn with things that get your hands dirty, including smudgy black carbon and a host of toxic materials you hope you never do get on your fingers. Batteries have stubbornly refused to give in to micro-miniaturization, yielding only small increases in capacity with every investment in research and development.

Electrical Characteristics

We often forget the chemical nature of batteries because the chemistry is all sealed away, usually permanently. To use the battery usually is a small cylinder that produces electricity (or, in the case of batteries for notebook computers, an expensive plastic shell that doesn't hold nearly enough electricity). In any case, the outward manifestations of the battery are physical and electrical. Its physical size and shape determine where it will fit. Its electrical ratings determine what it can run.

The most popular batteries for small electronic devices come in standard sizes. The battery packs for notebook computers are usually tailored to a specific model of machine, although many such packs comprise a set of standard batteries permanently connected together. All batteries produce the same kind of electricity—direct current—but they vary in the amount of energy they can store and several other electrical characteristics.

Cell Types

Batteries can be divided into two types: primary and secondary or storage. In primary batteries, the creation of electricity is irreversible; one or both of the electrodes is altered and cannot be brought back to its original state except by some complex process (such as re-smelting the metal). Secondary or storage batteries are rechargeable; the chemical reaction is reversible by the application of electricity. The electrons can be coaxed back from whence they came. After the battery is discharged, the chemical changes inside can be reversed by pumping electricity into the battery again. The chemicals revert back to their original, charged state and can be discharged to provide electricity once again.

In theory, any chemical reaction is reversible. Clocks can run backwards, too. And pigs can fly, given a tall enough cliff. The problem is that when a battery discharges, the chemical reaction affects the electrodes more in some places than others; recharging does not necessarily reconstitute the places that were depleted. Rechargeable batteries work because the chemical changes inside them alter their electrodes without removing material. For example, an electrode may become plated with an oxide, which can be removed during recharging.

Primary and secondary (storage) batteries see widely different applications, even in computers. Nearly every modern computer has a primary battery hidden somewhere inside, letting out a tiny electrical trickle that keeps the time-of-day clock running while the PC is not. This same battery also maintains a few bytes or kilobytes of CMOS memory to store system configuration information. Storage batteries are used to power just about every notebook computer in existence. (A few systems use storage batteries for their clocks and configuration memory.)

Voltage

The most important of these is *voltage*, which describes the electrical potential of a battery, the force with which the battery can move electrons through circuitry. The technical term is *electromotive force* (EMF), but most people usually talk about its direct measure, *volts*.

All batteries have a voltage rating that is both unchangeable and varying. That is, the voltage of a battery cell is characteristic of the cell design and the chemical reaction taking place inside, and this reaction does not change. But the voltage produced by the reaction varies with temperature (most batteries produce lower voltage as the temperature declines), the age of the cell (most batteries produce lower voltage as they age), and load (most batteries produce lower voltages when they are called upon to deliver more current).

These factors result in battery voltage varying widely from the nominal or rated voltage. Cells may start life producing 1.8 volts and remain useful until their output falls to half that. Because of the wide variance of cell voltage, most equipment that uses battery power is either insensitive to the exact voltage supplied or regulates the supplied voltages so that the internal circuitry of the equipment sees a constant voltage no matter the exact voltage produced by battery cells. Consequently, typical commercial cells that use carbon-zinc (nominally rated at 1.5 volts), nickel-cadmium (nominally rated at 1.2 volts), and lithium disulfide (nominally rated at 1.6 volts) are essentially interchangeable.

Depending on the chemistry used, a single cell can produce anywhere from a small fraction of a volt to somewhat more than three volts. Batteries rated with voltages higher than about three are composites of several cells linked together. (Technically, the term *battery* describes a collection of several individual electrochemical cells, although in common usage a commercial battery may only be a single cell.)

Current

Current describes the number of electrons the potential can push, the quantity of electricity. Current is measured in amperes (named after the French mathematician and physicist André Marie Ampére, 1775–1836), usually clipped to the term *amps*.

Battery cells are limited in the current they can produce by their designs and chemistries. In theory, if the entire chemical reaction in a battery cell occurred instantly, the cell would produce unlimited current—for an instant. Practical factors limit the chemical reaction rate and the current a cell can produce. Chief among these are the basic reaction rate of the chemicals, the design of the cell, and the area over which the reaction takes place. Consequently, some cells are inherently able to produce high currents. Others can only product weak currents. For example, the currents produced by lead-acid batteries and nickel-cadmium cells are so high, such batteries can melt metals and start fires when shorted out. Put an unpackaged ni-cad battery in your pocket, and it may short out against your keys and loose change. The high current and heat from the short circuit could start a fire. Consequently, these high-current cells often wear warning labels.

Cell size is also an important factor in determining the reaction area of the cell chemistry and consequently the current-creating capabilities of the cell. Making a cell larger increases the current it can produce, so heavy-duty applications often require large cells. "D" cells can produce more current than "AA" cells.

The various factors in cell design and chemistry essentially reduce to a single mathematical factor—the equivalent *internal resistance* of the cell, which determines current capabilities. A low internal resistance allows high currents.

Energy and Capacity

Voltage and current are instantaneous values that describe battery characteristics that are relevant when determining what kind of device the battery can power. Electrical circuits and motors vary in their voltage and current needs, and they must be tailored to match the battery used to power them.

The actual *power* that a battery can produce is the product of the voltage and current and is described in *watts* (named in honor of Scottish inventor and engineer James Watt, 1736–1819). A battery's power is independent of its size—a battery designed to produce a high current can generate tremendous power, although briefly. For example, even a small AA ni-cad battery can create enough current to melt metal, but it wouldn't last very long when challenged with the task of running a notebook computer.

A more relevant measure is the *energy* a given battery can produce. Energy is the amount of power a battery can produce over an extended period. A common measure is the *watt-hour*, the steady production of one watt of power for one hour.

The rated *capacity* of a cell or battery is the amount of electricity or electric charge it can produce when fully charged under specified conditions. As with voltage, the actual amount of charge the battery can produce varies with its temperature and the discharging current.

In science, the standard unit for measuring battery capacity is the *coulomb* (named after French physicist C. A. de Coulomb, 1736–1806), which describes the time the battery can produce a given current. One coulomb is one ampere produced for one second. In practice, however, cell or battery capacity is more commonly expressed in ampere-hours (AH) or milliampere-hours (mAH), equal to 3600 times the coulomb rating. The total energy in a battery is its capacity multiplied by its voltage (which results in a measurement of watt-hours).

Storage Density

The ratio of capacity to the weight (or size) of the battery is called the *storage density* of the battery. For you, as a battery user and the person charged with carrying around a notebook computer weighed down with batteries, this is a most important measure. The storage density of a battery determines how heavy a load of batteries your computer needs for a given runtime. The higher the storage density of a battery, the more energy that can be stored in a given size or weight of a cell and, hence, the more desirable the battery.

The chemistry used by a battery to store or produce electricity is the primary factor in determining the storage density of a battery. Table 31.2 lists the storage density of the major chemical systems used in storage batteries for personal computer and cell phone applications, expressed in watt-hours per kilogram of weight (Wh/kg).

TABLE 31.2   Storage Densities of Common Battery Technologies

Cell Type	Nominal Voltage	Storage Density
Lead-acid	2.1 volts	30 Wh/kg
Nickel-cadmium	1.2 volts	40 to 60 Wh/kg
Nickel-metal hydride	1.2 volts	60 to 80 Wh/kg
Circular lithium ion	3.6 volts	90 to 100 Wh/kg
Prismatic lithium ion	3.6 volts	100 to 110 Wh/kg
Polymer lithium ion	3.6 volts	130 to 150 Wh/kg

The storage density of each chemistry falls into a range of values because the actual construction of a battery cell—the materials used and the layout—also affects its storage density.

Shelf Life

No battery stores energy forever. The chemicals inside the cells inevitably react and slowly degrade. As a result, the charge stored by the battery degrades as well. The degradation takes two forms.

Some of the chemical reactions permanently affect the ability of the cell to store chemical energy. After a while, the battery loses its usefulness and becomes nothing more than a colorful piece of clutter. The period during which the cell remains useful is termed its *shelf life*. The chemistry and construction of the cell determine its shelf life, as do the conditions of storage. Some cells, such as modern lithium designs, have shelf lives in excess of ten years, whereas other cells may deteriorate in a matter of weeks (for example, zinc-air batteries once activated). Poor storage conditions—especially high temperatures—usually accelerate the degradation of cells, whereas refrigeration (and, with some chemistries, freezing) often prolongs shelf life.

In secondary cells, the reversible chemical reactions that produce electricity slowly take place even when the cell is not used. These reactions discharge the cell as if it were being used and are consequently called *self-discharge*. As with normal discharge of the cells, the reactions of self-discharge are reversible by simply recharging the cells. The self-discharge rates of batteries vary with the same factors affecting shelf life, although in modern cells the chemistry and cell design are the major determinants. Some chemistries lose as much as 10 percent of their charge in a day; others less than 1 percent.

Chemical Systems

The chemical reactions in the cell are the most important factor constraining energy density and the usefulness of batteries. In fact, the entire history of battery technology has been mostly a matter of finding and refining battery chemistries to pack more energy in ever-smaller packages. Today's batteries use a variety of chemical systems, some dating from the late 19th Century, as mentioned previously, and some hardly a decade old. The diversity results from each having distinct benefits for particular applications. The following battery chemistries are the most popular for portable computer, cell phone, power system, and peripheral applications.

Carbon-Zinc

The starting point for battery technology is the carbon-zinc cell, the heir of Georges Leclanché's 1866 invention of the wet cell for producing electricity. Carbon-zinc cells are probably the most common batteries in the world, known under a variety of names, including dry cell and flashlight battery. When you think of batteries, it's likely that carbon-zinc cells first come to mind. One company alone, Energizer, sells over six billion carbon-zinc cells each year. They are the lowest priced primary cells. They also have the lowest storage density of any common battery.

One reason carbon-zinc cells are so popular is that the name actually describes two or three different chemistry systems. These include Leclanché cells, zinc chloride cells, and alkaline batteries.

The name describes the basic chemistry of the cells. In the basic carbon-zinc cell, the "carbon" in the name is a cathode current collector—a carbon rod in the center of the cell. The actual material of the cathode is a mixture of manganese dioxide, carbon conductor, and electrolyte. The zinc serves as the anode and often serves as the metal shell of the battery. The electrolyte is a complex mixture of chemicals that typically includes ammonium chloride, manganese dioxide, and zinc chloride.

The electrolyte is the chief difference between Leclanché and zinc-chloride cells. The former use a slightly acidic mix of ammonium chloride and zinc chloride in water. The electrolyte in zinc-chloride cells is mostly zinc chloride. Zinc chloride cells produce a slightly higher open-circuit voltage than Leclanché cells (1.6 versus 1.55 volts).

Although zinc-chloride cells typically have a greater capacity than Leclanché cells, this difference shrinks under lighter loads, so zinc-chloride cells are often termed *heavy-duty*. In any case, the efficiency of any carbon-zinc cell decreases as the load increases—doubling the current drain more than cuts in half the capacity of the cell. The most efficient strategy is to use as large a cell as is practical for a given application. That's why power-hungry toys demand "D" batteries and low-drain transistor radios make do with "AA" cells.

Alkaline batteries, no matter the advertised claims, are little more than an enhancement of 19th Century carbon-zinc technology. The biggest change in chemistry is an alteration to the chemical mix in the electrolyte that makes it more alkaline (what did you expect?). This change helps to increase storage density and shelf life of the cells.

The construction (as opposed to chemistry) of alkaline cells differs significantly from ordinary carbon-zinc cells, however. Alkaline cells are effectively turned inside-out. The shell of the alkaline battery is nothing more than that—a protective shell—and it does not play a part in the overall chemical reaction. The anode of the cell is a gelled mixture of powered zinc combined with the electrolyte (itself a mixture of potassium hydroxide—a strong alkali—and water), and the combination is linked to the negative terminal of the cell by a brass spike running up the middle of the cell. The cathode, a mixture of carbon and manganese dioxide, surrounds the anode and electrolyte, separated by a layer of nonwoven fabric such as polyester.

Depending on the application, alkaline cells can last for four to nine times the life of more traditional carbon-zinc cells. The advantage is greatest under heavy loads that are infrequently used—that is, something that draws heavy current for an hour once a day rather than a few minutes of each hour.

Carbon-zinc cells nominally produce 1.5 volts, but this full voltage is available during the initial discharge of the cell. The voltage of the cell diminishes as the load to the cell increases and as the charge of the cell decreases.

Standard nine-volt batteries also use carbon-zinc chemistry. To produce the higher voltage, six separate carbon-zinc cells are stacked and connected in series inside each battery. Higher-voltage carbon-zinc cells can be made similarly, such as the "B" batteries of the 1950s, which stacked from 45 to 90 volts of cells to power vacuum-tube portable radios.

Ordinarily, alkaline batteries cannot be recharged because the chemical reactions in the cell cannot be readily reversed. If you attempt to recharge an ordinary carbon-zinc cell, it acts more like a resistor than a storage cell, turning the electricity you apply to it into heat. Apply too much power to a cell and it will heat up enough to explode—a good reason never to attempt to recharge carbon-zinc or alkaline batteries.

The exceptions to this rule are the Renewal batteries produced under license by Rayovac Corporation. The Renewal design relies on a two-prong attack on carbon-zinc technology. The Renewal cell is fabricated differently from a standard cell. More importantly, Renewal batteries are part of a system that requires a special battery charger. Instead of applying a nearly constant current to recharge the cells, the Renewal charger adds power in a series of pulses. A microprocessor in the charger monitors how each pulse affects the cell to prevent overheating. Even with the novel charger, however, Renewal cells have a limited life, typically between 25 and 100 charge/discharge cycles. In that Renewal cells cost only about twice as much as standard alkaline cells, they can be very cost-effective in some applications.

Lead-Acid

The most common storage batteries in the world are the lead-acid batteries used to start automobiles. Gaston Planté developed the first lead-acid cell in France in 1859, and the design remains virtually unchanged today. Lead-acid cells use anodes made from porous lead and cathodes made from lead oxide, both soaked in a sulfuric acid electrolyte.

The lead in the cells makes these batteries inherently heavy. Filled with highly corrosive acid (which is also heavy), they are cumbersome and dangerous. Not only can the acid and its fumes damage nearby objects (particularly metals), but overcharging cells also results in electrolysis of the water component of the internal acid. The hydrogen released by the electrolysis is highly combustible and, mixed with air and a spark, prone to a Hindenburg-like explosion.

The breakdown of the water in the cells also has another effect: It reduces the overall amount of water in the cell. Too little water reduces the reaction area inside the cell, reducing its capacity. It also allows the cells to deteriorate by atmospheric action. The electrodes can flake and possibly short out a cell entirely, reducing its capacity to zero. Early lead-acid cells consequently required regular maintenance to keep the water/acid inside the cell at the proper level. Only the water electrolyzes in the battery, so only it needs to be replaced. To avoid contaminating the battery chemistry, manufacturers recommend you use only distilled water to replenish the battery. Judging the proper amount to add requires only refilling the battery to its normal level. If the battery carries no mark as to the proper level, you should fill it so that the liquid in the battery just covers the electrode plates inside the cell.

In stationary applications, lead-acid batteries were once cased in glass. Not only would it resist the internal acid, but it also allowed maintenance workers to quickly assess the condition of the cells. Automotive applications required a more shatterproof case, for which engineers developed hard rubber or plastic enclosures.

The convenience of using lead-acid batteries is immensely increased by sealing the cells. The result is the so-called *maintenance-free battery*. Because the vapors within the cell cannot escape, electrolysis losses are minimized. The maintenance-free battery never needs water (or at least it shouldn't).

However, maintenance-free batteries are not entirely trouble free. They still have acid sloshing around inside them, after all, and it can leak out the battery vent, damaging the battery compartment or even the equipment in which the battery is located. Engineers developed two ways of eliminating the slosh. One keeps the liquid acid inside a plastic separator between cell electrodes (typically a micro-porous polyolefin or polyethylene). The other alternative chemically combines the liquid electrolyte with other compounds that turn it into a gel—a colloidal form like gelatin—which is less apt to leak out.

Lead-acid cells have several other drawbacks besides the cantankerous nature of their acidic contents. As noted before, they are heavy. The energy a lead-acid battery stores per pound of battery is lower than just about any technology short of a potato wired with zinc plates. This is the chief frustration of automotive engineers who would like to use low-cost lead-acid batteries to power electric cars. Once a sufficient number of lead-acid batteries to move the car a worthwhile distance get piled into the car, it weighs more like an electric truck.

On the other hand, besides being cheap, lead-acid batteries have over 150 years of technical development behind them. They can be custom-tailored to specific applications, such as those requiring deep discharge cycles (for example, where the batteries are used as the sole power source for electrical equipment) or for battery backup uses, such as in large uninterruptible power supply systems in data centers. Lead-acid cells also have a low internal resistance and therefore can produce enormous currents. They suffer no memory effect as do some more exotic cell designs, such as nickel-cadmium cells. (This effect, discussed in relation to nickel-cadmium batteries, reduces the capacity of a cell if it gets recharged before being fully discharged). The cells also have a moderately long, predictable life. And, of course, they are cheap.

Most uninterruptible power systems rely on gelled lead-acid cells for their power reserves. In this application, they require little maintenance. That is, you don't have to do anything to keep them going. The power system, however, must be tailored to the needs of the cells. Gel cells are degraded by the application of continuous low-current charging after they have been completely charged. (Most lead-acid batteries are kept at full capacity by such "trickle" charging methods.) Consequently, gel cells require special chargers that automatically turn off after the cells have been fully charged. The chargers switch back on when the battery discharges—either under load or by self-discharge—to a predetermined level. Uninterruptible power systems typically check their batteries periodically (usually weekly) to ensure they maintain a full charge.

Nickel-Cadmium

In consumer electronic equipment, the most popular rechargeable/storage batteries are nickel-cadmium cells, often called *ni-cads*. These batteries use cathodes made from nickel and anodes from cadmium, as the name implies. Their most endearing characteristic is the capability to withstand a huge number of full charge/discharge cycles, in the range of 500 to 1000, without deteriorating past the point of usefulness. Ni-cads are also relatively lightweight, have a good energy storage density (although about half that of alkaline cells), and tolerate trickle charging (when properly designed). On the downside, cadmium is toxic, thus the warning labels that implore you to be cautious with them and properly dispose of them.

The output voltage of most chemical cells declines as the cell discharges, because the reactions within the cell increase its internal resistance. Ni-cads have a very low internal resistance—meaning they can create high currents—which changes little as the cell discharges. Consequently, the ni-cad cell produces a nearly constant voltage until it becomes almost completely discharged, at which point its output voltage falls precipitously.

This constant voltage is an advantage to the circuit designer because fewer allowances need to be made for voltage variations. However, the constant voltage also makes determining the state of a ni-cad's charge nearly impossible. As a result, most battery-powered computers deduce the battery power they have remaining from the time they have been operating and known battery capacity rather than by actually checking the battery state.

Ni-cads are known for another drawback: memory. When some ni-cads are partly discharged and then later recharged, they may lose capacity. Chemically, recharging ni-cads before they are fully discharged often results in the formation of cadmium crystals on the anodes of the cell. The crystals act like a chemical memory system, marking a second discharge state for the cell. When the cell gets discharged to this secondary discharge state, its output abruptly falls despite further capacity being available within the cell. In subsequent cycles, the cell remembers this second discharge level, which further aggravates the situation by reinforcing the memory of the second discharge state. The full capacity of the cell can only be recovered by nudging the cell past this second discharge state. This will erase the memory and restores full cell capacity.

As a practical matter, the cure for the memory problem is deep discharge—discharging the battery to its minimum working level and then charging the battery again. Deep discharge does not mean totally discharging the battery, however. Draining nearly any storage battery absolutely dry will damage it and shorten its life. If you discharge a ni-cad battery so that it produces less than about one volt (its nominal output is 1.2 volts), it may suffer such damage. Notebook computers are designed to switch off before their batteries are drained too far, and deep discharge utilities do not push any farther, so you need not worry in using them. But don't try to deeply discharge your system's batteries by shorting them out—you risk damaging the battery and even starting a fire.

According to battery-makers, newer ni-cads and nickel-metal hydride cells are free from memory effects, although this has not been proven in practice. Some lithium battery–makers claim that the memory effect results from the use of nickel rather than cadmium (a view not supported by the chemistry), and some users also report contrary experiences with both nickel-based battery types. In any case, to get the longest life from ni-cads, the best strategy is to operate them between extremes—operate the battery through its complete cycle. Charge the battery fully, run it until it is normally discharged, and then fully charge it again.

As with lead-acid batteries, nickel-cadmium cells are also prone to electrolysis breaking down water in the electrolyte into potentially explosive hydrogen and oxygen. Battery-makers take great steps to reduce this effect. Commercially available ni-cads are sealed to prevent leakage. They are also designed so that they produce oxygen before hydrogen, which reacts internally to shut down the electrolysis reaction.

To prevent sealed cells from exploding should gas somehow build up inside them, their designs usually include resealable vents. You risk the chance of explosion if you encase a ni-cad cell in such a way it cannot vent. The vents are tiny and usually go unnoticed. They operate automatically. The warning against blocking the vents applies mostly to equipment-makers. Standard battery holders won't block the vents, but encapsulating the battery epoxy to make a solid power module certainly will.

Nickel-Metal Hydride

Chemically, one of the best cathode materials for battery cells would be hydrogen. But hydrogen is problematic as a material for batteries. At normal temperatures and pressures, hydrogen is a lighter-than-air gas, as hard to hold to as grabbing your breath in your hands.

In the late 1960s, however, scientists discovered that some metal alloys have the ability to store atomic hydrogen 1000 times their own volume. These metallic alloys are termed *hydrides* and typically are based on compounds such as $LiNi_5$ and $ZrNi_2$. In properly designed systems, hydrides can provide a storage sink of hydrogen that can reversibly react in battery cell chemistry.

The most common cells that use hydride cathodes carry over the nickel anodes from ni-cad cell designs. These cells typically have an electrolyte of a dilute solution of potassium hydroxide, which is alkaline in nature.

Substituting hydrides for cadmium in battery cells has several advantages. The most obvious is that such cells eliminate one major toxic material, cadmium. No cadmium also means that the cells should be free from the memory effect that plagues ni-cad cells. In addition, hydrogen is so much better as a cathode material that cells based on nickel and metal hydrides have a storage density about 50 percent higher than nickel-cadmium cells. In practical terms, that means cells of the same size and about the same weight can power a notebook computer for about 50 percent longer.

Cells based on nickel and metal hydrides—often abbreviated as NiMH cells—are not perfect. Their chief drawback is that most such cells have a substantially higher self-discharge rate than do ni-cad cells. Some NiMH cells lose as much as five percent of their capacity per day, although this figure is coming down with more refined cell designs.

As with ni-cads, NiMH cells have a nominal output voltage of 1.2 volts that remains relatively flat throughout the discharge cycle, falling precipitously only at the end of the useful charge of the cell. (Fully charged, a NiMH cell produces about 1.4 volts, but this quickly falls to 1.2 volts, where it remains throughout the majority of the discharge cycle.)

In many ways NiMH cells are interchangeable with ni-cads. They have a similar ability to supply high currents, although not quite as much as ni-cads. NiMH cells also endure many charge/discharge cycles, typically up to 500 full cycles, but they are not a match for ni-cads.

Although the discharge characteristics of NiMH and ni-cads are similar, the two cell types react differently during charging. Specifically, ni-cads are essentially endothermic while being charged, and NiMH cells are exothermic—they produce heat. As the NiMH cell approaches full charge, its temperature can rise dramatically. Consequently, chargers are best designed for one or the other type of cell. NiMH cells work best in chargers designed for them. NiMH cells do, however, readily accept trickle charging (discussed later).

Lithium Ion

Lithium is the most chemically reactive metal and provides the basis for today's most compact energy storage for notebook computer power systems. Nearly all high-density storage systems use lithium because it has an inherent chemical advantage. Lithium has a specific capacity to store 3860 ampere-hours per kilogram of mass, compared to 820 AH/kg for zinc and 260 AH/kg for lead.

Lithium is also very reactive. Depending on the anode, cells with lithium cathodes can produce anywhere from 1.5 volts to 3.6 volts per cell, higher voltage than any other chemistry.

The problem with lithium is that it is too reactive. It reacts violently with water and can ignite into flame. Batteries based on lithium metal were developed and manufactured in the 1970s, and in the 1980s some companies introduced commercial rechargeable cells based on metallic lithium. Such batteries quickly earned a reputation for doubtful safety.

To prevent problems caused by reactive metallic lithium, battery-makers refined their designs to keep the lithium in its ionic state. In this way, they were able to reap the electrochemical benefits of lithium-based cells without the safety issues associated with the pure metal. In lithium ion cells, the lithium ions are absorbed into the active material of the electrodes rather than being plated out as metal.

The typical lithium ion cells use carbon for its anode and lithium cobalt dioxide as the cathode. The electrolyte is usually based on a lithium salt in solution.

Lithium batteries offer higher storage densities than nickel-metal hydride cells, which equates to using them in notebook computer systems for about fifty percent longer without a recharge. Lithium ion cells also lack the memory effect that plagued early nickel-cad cells.

On the other hand, current lithium cells have a higher internal resistance than nickel-cadmium cells and consequently cannot deliver high currents. A ni-cad could melt a screwdriver, but a lithium cell cannot—that's why lithium cells don't wear the same warnings as ni-cads. The available power is sufficient for a properly designed notebook computer that minimizes surge requirements (meaning that certain devices, such as disk drives, may require a fair surge of power during certain phases of operation, notably spin-up). Moreover, the life of lithium cells is more limited than that of nickel-based designs, although lithium ion cells withstand hundreds of charge/recharge cycles.

Because lithium ion cells use a liquid electrolyte (although one that may be constrained in a fabric separator), cell designs are limited to the familiar cylindrical battery form. Although such designs are no more handicapped than they are with other battery chemistries, the lithium ion chemistry lends itself to other, space-saving designs based on polymerized electrolytes.

Lithium Polymer

A refinement of familiar lithium chemistry, called the *lithium solid polymer cell*, promises more power for portable applications, but through packaging rather than high-energy density. Whereas conventional lithium ion cells require liquid electrolytes, solid polymer cells integrate the electrolyte into a polymer plastic separator between the anode and cathode of the cell. As an electrolyte, lithium polymer cells use a polymer composite such as polyacrylonitrile containing a lithium salt. Because there's no liquid, the solid polymer cell does not require the chunky cylindrical cases of conventional batteries. Instead, the solid polymer cells can be formed into flat sheets or *prismatic* (rectangular) packages better able to fit the nooks and crannies of notebook computers.

Although the energy density of solid polymer cells is similar to ordinary lithium ion cells, computer manufacturers can shape them to better fit the space available in a notebook machine, squeezing more capacity into otherwise unused nooks and crannies. For example, simply by filling the empty space that would appear in the corners around a cylindrical cell, a solid polymer battery can fit in about 22 percent more chemistry and energy capacity. In addition, solid polymer batteries are environmentally friendly, lighter because they have no metal shell and safer because they contain no flammable solvent. Most battery-makers and computer-makers are switching to the lithium solid polymer cell design.

Lithium-Iron Disulfide

Unlike other lithium cells that have chemistries tuned to obtaining the greatest capacity in a given package, lithium-iron disulfide cells are a compromise. To match to existing equipment and circuits, their chemistry has been tailored to the standard nominal 1.5-volt output (whereas other lithium technologies produce double that). These cells are consequently sometimes termed *voltage-compatible lithium* batteries. Unlike other lithium technologies, lithium-iron disulfide cells are not rechargeable.

Internally, the lithium-iron disulfide cell is a sandwich of a lithium anode, a separator, and iron disulfide cathode with an aluminum cathode collector. The cells are sealed but vented.

Compared to the alkaline cells with which they are meant to compete, lithium-iron disulfide cells are lighter (weighing about 66 percent of same-size alkaline cells), higher in capacity, and longer in life. Even after ten years of shelf storage, lithium-iron disulfide cells still retain most of their capacity.

Lithium-iron disulfide cells operate best under heavier loads. In high-current applications, they can supply power for about 260 percent the time of a same-size alkaline cell. This advantage is less at lower loads, however, and at very light loads may disappear entirely. For example, under a 20 mA load, one manufacturer rates its AA-size lithium-iron disulfide cells as providing power for about 122 hours, whereas its alkaline cells will last for 135 hours. With a one-ampere load, however, the lithium-iron disulfide cells last for 2.1 hours versus only 0.8 for alkaline.

You can use lithium-iron disulfide cells wherever you might use zinc-carbon batteries, although they are cost-effective only under high-current loads—flashlights, motor-driven devices, and powerful electronics. They are not a wise choice for clocks and portable radios.

Zinc-Air

Of the current battery technologies, the one offering the densest storage is zinc-air. One reason is that one of the components of its chemical reaction is external to the battery. Zinc-air batteries use atmospheric oxygen as their cathode reactant, hence the "air" in the name. Small holes in the battery casing allow air in to react with a powered zinc anode through a highly conductive potassium hydroxide electrolyte.

Originally created for use in primary batteries, zinc-air batteries were characterized by their long stable storage life, at least when kept sealed from the air and thus inactive. A sealed zinc-air cell loses only about 2 percent of its capacity after a year of storage. Once air infiltrates the cell, zinc-air primary cells last only for months, whether under discharge or not.

Some battery-makers have adapted zinc-air technology for secondary storage. Zinc-air cells work best when frequently or continuously used in low-drain situations. The chief drawback of zinc-air batteries is, however, a high internal resistance, which means zinc-air batteries must be huge to satisfy high-current needs—for notebook computers that means an auxiliary battery pack about the size of the computer itself.

Standards

Contrary to appearances, most rechargeable batteries used by notebook computers are standard sizes. Computer manufacturers, however, package these standard-size batteries in custom battery packs that may fit only one model of computer. Usually you cannot change the batteries in the pack but must buy a new replacement if something goes awry.

Attempts at standardizing batteries for notebook computers have fallen flat, as witnessed by the near extinction of Duracell's "standard" designs. Computer-makers find proprietary cells more profitable. They can put a few dollars of individual cells in a cheap but odd plastic package and sell the assembly for a hundred dollars or more.

Anyone who has ever received a holiday gift and discovered the batteries weren't included knows the basic rule about the different standard sizes for batteries: The one you need is the one you don't have or cannot find. Frustrating as the multiplicity in standard sizes may be, the situation is better than having no existing standards. For example, nearly all battery packs for notebook computers are nonstandard and consequently very costly. You're captive to the manufacturer's pricing policy in many cases, although there are lower-cost second sources for batteries for various notebook computers, cellular phones, and other common portable electronic devices that use rechargeable batteries. Many people remain suspicious of the build quality, longevity, and safety of some of these second-source batteries, although most are likely fine for the majority of targeted applications. Standard batteries, on the other hand, are readily available from multiple sources and far less expensive than rechargeables.

The chief battery standards now in use originally applied to carbon-zinc cells, but other technologies (some varieties of lithium, nickel-cadmium, and nickel-metal hydride cells) now follow the same size standards. These standards specify the basic dimensions of the batteries, allowing many manufacturers to produce interchangeable cells. Table 31.3 lists the dimensions of many standard battery types.

TABLE 31.3 Dimension of Common Battery Types			
Cell Type	*Shape*	*Height*	*Diameter*
AAAA	Cylindrical	42.5 mm	8.3 mm
AAA	Cylindrical	44.5 mm	10.5 mm
AA	Cylindrical	50.5 mm	14.5 mm
C	Cylindrical	50.0 mm	26.2 mm
D	Cylindrical	61.5 mm	34.2 mm
J	Rectangular	48.5 mm	35.55 by 9.2 mm
N	Cylindrical	29.35 mm	11.95 mm
9 volt	Rectangular	48.5 mm	26.5 by 17.5 mm

Note that these sizes are a physical characteristic only. You might find any battery chemistry in any cell size, some of which might not be suited to a give application. In other words, just because a battery fits into a holder is no indication that it will work properly there.

Battery Charging

Just as your electronic gear is sensitive to the kind of electricity you supply it, battery chemistry is extremely sensitive to the electricity used for charging cells. If the voltage applied is too low, the cell will output current instead of accepting it—that is, discharging rather than charging. If the voltage is too high, undesirable reactions can take place that can destroy the cell. For example, raising the voltage inevitably raises the current, and too much current can cause the cell to overheat. In addition, trying to charge a cell beyond its capacity can result in the production of explosive gases—and an explosion itself.

Modern battery chargers are consequently sophisticated electronic devices with many different types of safety circuitry to protect both you and the batteries you want to charge. Most batteries require a specific charger tailored to their needs. Plug the wrong batteries into the wrong charger (or the wrong charger into your battery pack), and you may destroy the batteries, the charger, and even the equipment connected to the batteries.

The chief difference between battery chargers is the mode in which they operate. The choice is between constant voltage and constant current.

Constant voltage chargers are the simplest. They always produce a specific voltage level but deliver a current that depends on the charge level of the battery (and environmental factors). As the battery becomes charged, its voltage increases while that of the charger remains the same, so there is less difference in potential between the charger and battery. As a result, less current can flow through the system. When the two are equal, no current flows.

A constant-voltage charger requires little more than a transformer (to reduce line voltage to the level required for battery charging) and a rectifier (to change the alternating current of utility power into the direct current used to charge batteries). Such simple designs are often found in the battery chargers used for charging car and boat batteries.

The lead-acid cells used for cars and backup power systems typically use constant-voltage chargers. In addition, lithium ion cells often use constant-voltage systems, although these usually are more complex with added circuitry to protect both the batteries and your safety.

The alternate design for battery chargers maintains a constant current and alters the voltage applied to the batteries to maintain this current. These constant-current chargers vary the voltage they apply to the batteries to maintain a constant current flow, switching off when the voltage reaches the level of a full charge. (Remember, the voltage produced by any cell falls as it becomes discharged.) This design is usually used for nickel-cadmium and nickel-metal hydride cells or batteries.

In addition to charging cells at the proper rate, battery chargers also face another vital issue: the proper time to switch off. A charger can destroy a battery by overcharging it. Depending on the requirements of the battery to be charged and the sophistication of the charger, the charger may use any of several technologies to determine the proper time to turn off.

The most straightforward way of determining charge is by the voltage produced by the battery. The charger monitors the battery's voltage and switches off when it reaches the *cutoff voltage*. The voltage-sensing technique is not adequate for many kinds of batteries—

in particular, ni-cads have a very linear discharge curve that makes the cutoff voltage difficult to determine.

More advanced charging systems use *temperature cutoff*. That is, the charger monitors the temperature of the battery cells and switches off or reduces the charging rate when the battery begins to heat up (which indicates an overcharge condition). Typically battery packs using temperature cutoff have built-in thermometers that relay a control signal to the charger circuitry.

More sophisticated chargers combine the voltage and temperature cutoff (VTCO). Chargers using this technology may switch from high-current charging to a lower or maintenance charge rate using circuitry that senses both temperature and voltage.

Standard battery chargers supply less current than the battery's discharge rate. *High-current chargers* supply a current greater than the battery's nominal discharge rate. *Trickle chargers* supply a charging current at a rate so low it only compensates for the self-discharge of the battery (by definition, a trickle charger is one that compensates for self-discharge). The trickle charging rate typically is about one-twentieth to one-thirtieth the battery's nominal discharge rate. Modern battery chargers often operate at several charging rates, starting at high current and switching to low current as the battery nears full charge. If the battery is of a type that tolerates trickle charging (ni-cads, for example, do not), the charge will switch to a trickle rate at the end of the charging cycle.

Engineers design most chargers for computer and cell phone batteries. These chargers can be plugged into the batteries continuously without any detrimental effects on the batteries.

Smart Battery Specifications

Battery charging is actually an interaction between the battery and the charger. The charger must attend to the state of the battery if it is to avoid damaging the battery by overcharging the battery and damaging your state of mind by undercharging the battery so that you run out of power long before you run out of the need for your computer.

Charging and monitoring the charge of batteries has always been problematic. Both capacity and charge characteristics vary with the battery type and over the life of a given battery. The smartest conventional battery chargers monitor not the voltage but the temperature of their subjects, because a sharp rise in temperature is the best indication available to the charger of the completion of its work. Even this rise varies with battery chemistry, so ni-cad and NiMH batteries present different—and confusing—temperature characteristics that would lead to a charger mistaking one for the other, possibly damaging the battery.

The *Smart Battery* system, developed jointly by battery-maker Duracell and Intel and first published as the Smart Battery Data Specification, Version 1.0, on February 15, 1995, eliminates these problems by endowing batteries with enough brains to tell of their condition. When matched to a charger with an equivalent I.Q. that follows the Smart Charger specification, the Smart Battery gets charged perfectly every time with never a worry about overcharging.

The Smart Battery system defines a standard with several layers that distribute intelligence between battery, charger, and your computer. It provides for an inexpensive communication link between them and outlines the information that a battery can convey to its charger and the message format for doing so.

Among other data that the battery can relay are its chemistry, its capacity, its voltage, and even its physical packaging. Messages warn not only about the current status of the battery's charge but even how many charge/recharge cycles the battery has endured so that the charger can monitor its long-term prognosis. The specification is independent of the chemistry used by the battery and even the circuitry used to implement its functions.

The battery packs of nearly all new notebook computers follow the Smart Battery specifications or a similar replacement standard called the *Control Method Battery Interface*, because battery management is required for compatibility with the latest versions of Windows. Use of either of the two battery-management standards is required by the Advanced Configuration and Power Interface (ACPI). The Control Method Battery Interface is part of the ACPI standard and effectively supercedes Smart Battery.

Battery Safety

The maximum current any battery can produce is limited by its internal resistance. Zinc-carbon batteries have a relatively high resistance and produce small currents, on the order of a few hundred milliamperes. Lead-acid, nickel-cadmium, and nickel-hydride batteries have very low internal resistances and can produce prodigious currents. If you short the terminals of one of these batteries, whatever produces the short circuit—wires, a strip of metal, a coin in your pocket—becomes hot because of resistive heating. For example, you can melt a wrench by placing it across the terminals of a fully charged automotive battery. You can also start a fire with something inadvertently shorting the terminals of the spare nickel-cadmium battery for your notebook or subnotebook computer. Be careful and never allow anything to touch these battery terminals except the contacts of your notebook computer.

When a battery is charged, a process called *electrolysis* takes place inside. If you remember your high-school science experiments, electrolysis is what you did to break ordinary water into hydrogen and oxygen using electricity. Hydrogen is an explosive gas; oxygen is an oxidizer. Both are produced when charging batteries. Normally these gases are absorbed by the battery before they can do anything (such as explode), but too great a charging current (as results from applying too high a voltage) can cause them to build up. Trying to charge a primary battery produces the same gas build-up. As a result, the battery can explode from too great an internal pressure or from combustion of the gases. Even if the battery does not catastrophically fail, its life will be greatly reduced. In other words, use only the charger provided with a portable computer battery and never try to hurry things along.

Nearly all batteries contain harmful chemicals of some kind. Even zinc-carbon batteries contain manganese, which is regarded as hazardous. All batteries present some kind of environmental hazard, so be sure to dispose of them properly. Some manufacturers are beginning to provide a means of recycling batteries. Encourage them by taking advantage of their offers.

Power Management

With few advances in battery storage density expected in the near-term future, computer-makers have relied on reducing the power consumption of their notebook computers to extend the time a machine can operate between battery charges.

Engineers can use two basic strategies to reduce the power consumption of computers. They can design circuits and components to use less power, and they can manage the power used by the devices. Managing power needs usually means switching off whatever system components aren't being actively used. Although the two design methods can be used separately, they are generally used in tandem to shrink computer power needs as much as possible.

Microprocessors, the most power hungry of computer circuits, were among the first devices to gain built-in power management. *System Management Mode* endowed processors with the ability to slow down and shut off unnecessary circuits when they were idle. Similarly, makers of hard disk drives have added sleep modes to spin down their platters and reduce power needs. Most computers also incorporate timers to darken their screens to further conserve power.

Although these techniques can be successful in trimming power demands, they lack a unified control system. In response, the industry developed the Advanced Power Management (APM) interface to give overall control to the power-savings systems in computers. More recently, APM has been updated and augmented by the Advanced Configuration and Power Interface specification.

Advanced Power Management

The Advanced Power Management interface specification was jointly developed by Intel and Microsoft to integrate the control of hardware power-saving features with software control. First published in January 1992, as the APM BIOS Interface Specification, the current version, 1.2, was published in February 1996.

Although nominally a BIOS interface, the APM specification describes a layered control system that manages computer devices to reduce power consumption using both BIOS and API interfaces. To be fully functional, APM requires a compatible BIOS and hardware devices that recognize APM control. In addition, hardware devices may have their own built-in automatic power-management functions that are not controlled by your computer's software. For example, a hard disk drive may automatically power down after a given period without a specific command from your computer. The APM specification tolerates but does not affect these built-in functions.

States

APM is an overall system feature. Although it has the ability to individually control the features of each device it manages, the basic-design APM controls all devices together to conserve power. It manages system power consumption by shifting the overall operating mode of the computer, called *APM states*. APM shifts the operating state of the system based on the needs of the system as determined from a combination of software commands and events. The various APM states provide for power savings that occur in five levels (six, if you count normal power-hungry operation). The APM specification gives each of these levels a specific state name.

The first state, *Full On*, means that the system is operating at full power without any management at all. The APM software is not in control, and no power savings can be achieved. A system without APM or with its APM features disabled operates in Full On state.

When the APM system is active, all devices run in their normal, full-power consumption modes. The system is up and ready to do business, operating in what the specification calls the *APM Enabled* state.

In the *APM Standby* state, the microprocessor may stop, and many of the system devices are turned off or operate at reduced power. The system usually cannot process data, but its memory is kept alive and the status of all devices is preserved. When your activity or some other event requires system attention, the computer can rapidly shift from the APM Standby to the APM Enabled state.

In the *APM Suspend* state, the system shifts to its maximum power-savings mode—most devices that follow the APM standard are switched off, and the microprocessor switches to its lowest power state with its clock turned off. Your computer becomes a vegetable.

Hibernation is a special implementation of the APM Suspend state that allows the system to be switched entirely off and still be restored to the point at which it entered the APM Suspend state. When entering the APM Suspend state, the system saves all its operating parameters. In entering the Hibernation state, the system copies memory and other status data to nonvolatile storage, such as the hard disk, allowing you to switch off memory power. A system event can shift back to the APM Enabled state from APM Suspend or Hibernation, but changing modes from APM Suspend to APM Enabled takes substantially longer than from APM Standby to APM Enabled.

The *Off* state is exactly what the name implies. Power to the system is entirely off. The computer is more a mineral than vegetable. The only event that restores the system is turning it back on. If you enter the Off state directly—say, by switching your computer off—no status information or memory gets saved. The system must run through the entire boot-up process and starts with a clean slate.

Structure

APM adds a layered control system to give you, your software, and your hardware a mechanism to shift states manually or automatically.

The bottom layer of the system is the *APM BIOS*, which provides a common software interface for controlling hardware devices under the specification. APM specifies that the BIOS have at least a real-mode interface that uses interrupt 15(hex) to implement its functions. In addition, the APM BIOS may also use 16- or 32-bit protected mode using entry points that are returned from the protected-mode connection call using the real-mode interrupt.

The APM BIOS is meant to manage the power of the motherboard. Its code is specific to a given motherboard. Under the APM specification, the APM BIOS can operate independently of other APM layers to effect some degree of power savings in the system by itself. Your computer's operating system can switch off this internal BIOS APM control to manage system power itself, still using the APM BIOS interface functions to control hardware features.

Linking the APM BIOS to your operating system is the *APM driver*. The driver provides a set of function calls to the operating system, which it translates to BIOS interrupts. The driver is more than a mere translator, however. It is fully interactive with both the BIOS and operating system. For example, the BIOS may generate its own request to power down the system, and the driver then checks with the operating system to determine whether it should permit the power-down operation.

The APM system has a built-in failsafe. The APM driver must interact with the BIOS at least once per second. If it does not, after a second, the BIOS assumes the operating system has malfunctioned and takes self-contained control. The driver can regain control by sending the appropriate commands (interrupts) to the BIOS.

Certain system events termed *wake-up calls* tell the APM system to shift modes. Interrupts generated by events such as a press of the resume button, the modem detecting an incoming telephone ring, or an alarm set on the real-time clock can command the APM BIOS to shift the system from the APM Suspend to the APM Enabled state.

Advanced Configuration and Power Interface

Customizing the power use of your computer is a natural part of setting up your system. Understanding that, Intel, Microsoft, and Toshiba decided that the best way to integrate power management with your system was to combine it with the computer's setup facilities and to give both a common interface. The result is called the Advanced Configuration and Power Interface, a formal specification that was first published by the threesome as ACPI version 1.0 in December 1996.

ACPI is an integral part of the Microsoft-inspired *OnNow initiative*, which was created to minimize the delays inherent in starting up and shutting down a computer burdened with megabytes of operating system overhead, to let the computer run tasks while it appears to be off, and to lower the overall power requirement of the computer. At the time *OnNow* was proposed, operating systems required time to test the host computer, to check out Plug-and-Play devices, and to set up their structures. These functions required a lengthy period to carry out, so booting your system took so long it seemed to be warming up from absolute zero. OnNow was designed to eliminate that wait. The first inkling of OnNow appeared in Windows Me, and Windows XP continues to develop the concept.

OnNow also sought to integrate the power and configuration interfaces of modern (meaning Windows) operating systems so that programmers can write to a common standard.

To bring these features to life, the OnNow design moves the operating system to the center of power management using ACPI and builds a new table structure for storing and organizing configuration information.

As a power-management system, the ACPI specification can accommodate the needs of any operating system, integrating all the necessary power-management features required in a computer, from the application software down to the hardware level. It enables the operating system to automatically turn on and off and adjust the power consumption of nearly any peripheral, from hard disk drives to displays to printers. It can reach beyond the computer to other devices that may be connected into a single system some time in the future—televisions, stereos, VCRs, telephones, and even other appliances. Using the Smart Battery specification, under ACPI the operating system takes command of battery charging and monitoring. It also monitors the thermal operation of the system, reducing speed or shutting down a computer that might overheat.

The ACPI standard itself defines the interface for controlling device power and a means of identifying hardware features. The interface uses a set of five hardware registers that are controlled through a higher-level application programming interface through the operating system. The descriptive elements identify not only power management but also device features through a nested set of tables. The ACPI standard supplements Plug-and-Play technology, extending its existing structure with an architecture-independent implementation, and replaces the Plug-and-Play BIOS with a new ACPI BIOS.

Soft Off

The fundamental and most noticeable change made by ACPI is the power button on the front of new computers. In systems equipped to handle ACPI, this is a soft switch or set of two switches. Although one of these switches may be labeled "Power" and imply that it is an on/off switch, in the ACPI scheme of things the power switch does not actually switch the power to the system on and off. Rather, it sends a command to the system to shut itself off—and not exactly what you think is off.

Using the front panel Off button actually puts the computer in a new mode called *Soft Off*. In this mode, the computer acts like you've shut it off and requires rebooting to restart it. But it doesn't remove all power from the system. A slight bit of power continues to be supplied to the motherboard and expansion boards, enabling them to monitor external events. For example, a network board will still listen to network traffic for packets targeted at it. A modem or fax board may lie in wait for a telephone call. Or you may set a time (such as midnight) at which the tape backup system starts. When any of these designated external events occurs, the computer automatically switches itself back on to deal with it.

ACPI envisions that some manufacturers will also put a *sleep switch* (or standby button) on the front panel or on the keyboard. Pressing it puts the computer in a sleep mode that uses somewhat more power than Soft Off but allows the system to resume operation more quickly.

States

As with APM, the ACPI design works by shifting modes called *ACPI states*. The states differ substantially from those in APM. Under ACPI, four basic types of states are defined—Global, Special Sleep, Microprocessor, and Device—and these can be further subdivided. Most importantly, ACPI lets the operating system control all aspects of the power consumption of a computer by shifting the single devices or the entire system between these states.

The ACPI Global states most closely correspond to the APM modes, affecting the entire operation of the computer and how you deal with it. Formally, the states are termed G0 through G3, but they are effectively the same as the APM states, with the addition of Soft Off. The chief operational difference between them is how long it takes your computer to move from each state to normal operation, which can be instantaneous in Sleeping state (corresponding to Suspend), a bit longer in Soft Off (similar but not identical to Hibernation), and a full boot-up from Power Off. Table 31.4 lists the Global ACPI states.

	TABLE 31.4 ACPI States		
State	*Name*	*Appearance*	*Recovery Time*
G0	Working state	Normal execution	Zero
G1	Sleeping state	No activity	Fast
G2	Soft Off	No activity	Slow
G3	Power Off	No activity	Boot-up

Under ACPI, each device, such as your hard disk, modem, or display screen, operates under several similar states (but termed with the letter *D*) corresponding to various power-saving modes. Similarly, the microprocessor (designed with state names starting with *C*) can switch to various power-saving states. As a device is needed, your operating system can switch it on or off using the ACPI protocols. Most of these changes happen invisibly—you may only detect a slight (or longer) lag as a device powers up from a lower state.

Configuration

To handle its configuration function, ACPI must manage a tremendous amount of data, not only about the power needs and management capabilities of the system but also describing the features available for all the devices connected to the system. ACPI stores this information in a hierarchy of tables.

The overall master table is called the *Root System Description Table*. It has no fixed place in memory. Rather, upon booting up, the BIOS locates a pointer to the table during the memory scan that's part of the boot-up process. The Root System Description Table itself is identified in memory because it starts with the signature "RSDT." Following the signature is an array of pointers that tells the operating system the location of other description tables that provide it with the information it needs about the standards defined on the current system and individual devices.

One of these tables is called the *Fixed ACPI Description Table*. In it the operating system finds the base address of the registers used for controlling the power-management system. In addition, the Fixed ACPI Description Table also points to the Differentiated System Description Table, which provides variable information about the design of the base system. Some of the entries in this table are *differentiated definition blocks*, which can contain data about a device or even a program that sets up other structures and defines new attributes. ACPI defines its own languages for programming these functions.

Energy Star

Rather than a technology, the Energy Star standard is a goal. The Energy Star standard itself was created by the United States Environmental Protection Agency in 1992 with the goal of encouraging manufacturers to create business equipment that minimizes power consumption. Since then, the standard has been adopted by Japan, New Zealand, and Sweden.

Energy Star is a certification program that allows compliant computers and peripherals (as well as other devices unrelated to computers) to wear a certification badge. The program specifically covers computers, monitors, printers, fax machines, copiers, scanners, and multifunction devices—as well as telephones, home appliances (including washing machines), and even entire buildings. Equipment conforming to the Energy Star standard must meet strict guidelines on power consumption published by the Environmental Protection Agency.

Manufacturers have a strong incentive to embrace the Energy Star standard and put the label on their products—some businesses and many federal contracts require that new PC equipment meet the Energy Star standards.

All that said, the actual Energy Star standards for PCs are quite simple. Energy Star version 2.0, which applies to products shipped after October 1, 1995, asks only that a PC or monitor be able to switch to a low-power mode that consumes less than 30 watts after 15 to 30 minutes of inactivity (a default you are allowed to adjust). Combination monitor-and-PC units are allowed the full 60 watts. Printers able to generate seven or fewer pages per minute must reduce their drain to 15 watts after 15 minutes; 14 or fewer ppm, 30 watts after 30 minutes; faster or high-end color printers, 45 watts after an hour.

You can find out more about the Energy Star program at its Web site, www.energystar.gov.

Power Protection

Normal line voltage is often far from the 115-volt alternating current you pay for. It can be a rather inhospitable mixture of aberrations such as spikes and surges mixed with noise, dips, and interruptions. None of these oddities is desirable, and some can be powerful enough to cause errors in your data or damage to your computer. Although you cannot avoid them, you can protect your computer against their ill effects.

Power Line Irregularities

Power line problems can be broadly classed into three basic categories: over-voltage, under-voltage, and noise. Each problem has its own distinct causes and requires a particular kind of protection.

Over-Voltage

The deadliest power-line pollution is over-voltage—lightning-like high potential spikes that sneak into your computer and actually melt down its silicon circuitry. Often the damage is invisible—except for the very visible lack of image on your monitor. Other times, you can actually see charred remains inside your computer as a result of the over-voltage.

As its name implies, an over-voltage gushes more voltage into your computer than the equipment can handle. In general—and in the long run—your utility supplies power that's very close to the ideal, usually within about ten percent of its rated value. If it always stayed within that range, the internal voltage regulation circuitry of your computer could take its fluctuations in stride.

Short duration over-voltages larger than that may occur too quickly for your utility's equipment to compensate, however. Moreover, many over-voltages are generated nearby, possibly within your home or office, and your utility has no control over them. Brief peaks as high as 25,000 volts have been measured on normal lines, usually due to nearby lightning strikes. Lightning doesn't have to hit a power line to induce a voltage spike that can damage your computer. When it does hit a wire, however, everything connected to that circuit is likely to take on the characteristics of a flash bulb.

Over-voltages are usually divided into two classes by duration. Short-lived over-voltages are called *spikes* or *transients* and last from a nanosecond (billionth of a second) to a microsecond (one millionth of a second). Longer-duration over-voltages are usually termed *surges* and can stretch into milliseconds.

Sometimes power companies do make errors and send too much voltage down the line, causing your lights to glow brighter and your computer to teeter closer to disaster. The occurrences are simply termed *over-voltages*.

Most AC-power computers are designed to withstand moderate over-voltages without damage. Most machines tolerate brief surges in the range of 800 to 2,000 volts. On the other hand, power cords and normal home and office electrical wiring break (by arcing between the wiring conductors) at potentials between about 4,000 and 6,000 volts. In other words, electrical wiring limits the maximum surge potential your computer is likely to face to no more than about 6,000 volts. Higher voltage surges simply can't reach your computer.

Besides intensity and energy, surges also differ in their mode. Modern electrical wiring involves three conductors: a hot, neutral, and ground. Hot is the wire that carries the power; neutral provides a return path; and ground provides protection. The ground lead is ostensibly connected directly to the earth.

A surge can occur between any pairing of conductors: hot and neutral, hot and ground, or neutral and ground. The first pairing is termed *normal mode*. It reflects a voltage difference between the power conductors used by your computer. When a surge arises from a voltage difference between hot or neutral and ground, it is called *common mode*.

Surges caused by utility switching and natural phenomena—for the most part, lightning—occur in the normal mode. They have to. The National Electrical Code requires that the neutral lead and the ground lead be bonded together at the service entrance (where utility power enters a building) as well as at the utility line transformer, typically hanging from a telephone pole near your home or office. At that point, neutral and ground must have the same potential. Any external common mode surge becomes normal mode.

Common mode surges can, however, originate within a building because long runs of wire stretch between most outlets and the service entrance, and the resistance of the wire allows the potential on the neutral wire to drift from that of ground. Although opinions differ, recent European studies suggest that common mode surges are the most dangerous to your equipment. (European wiring practice is more likely to result in common mode surges because the bonding of neutral and ground is made only at the transformer.)

Under-Voltage

An under-voltage occurs when your equipment gets less voltage than it expects. Under-voltages can range from sags, which are dips of but a few volts, to complete outages or blackouts. Durations vary from nearly instantaneous to hours—or even days, if you haven't paid your light bill recently.

Very short dips, sags, and even blackouts are not a problem. As long as they are less than a few dozen milliseconds—about the blink of an eye—your computer should purr along as if nothing happened. The only exceptions are a few old computers that have power supplies with very sensitive Power Good signals. A short blackout may switch off the Power Good signal, shutting down your computer even though enough electricity is available.

Most computers are designed to withstand prolonged voltage dips of about 20 percent without shutting down. Deeper dips or blackouts lasting for more than those few milliseconds result in a shutdown. Your computer is forced to cold start, booting up afresh. Any work you have not saved before the under-voltage is lost.

Noise

Noise is a nagging problem in the power supplies of most electronic devices. It comprises all the spurious signals that wires pick up as they run through electromagnetic fields. In many cases, these signals can sneak through the filtering circuitry of the power supply and interfere with the signals inside the electrical device.

For example, the power cord of a tape recorder might act like an antenna and pick up a strong radio signal. The broadcast could then sneak through the circuitry of the recorder and mix with the music it is supposed to be playing. As a result, you might hear a CB radio maven croaking over your Mozart.

In computers, these spurious signals could confuse the digital thought coursing through the circuitry of the machine. As a practical matter, they don't. All better computers are designed to minimize the leakage of their signals from inside their cases into the outside world to minimize your computer's interfering with your radio and television. The same protection that prevents signals leaking out works well in warding off other signals from getting in. Personal computers are almost automatically well-protected against line noise. You probably won't need a noise filter to protect your computer.

Then again, noise filtering doesn't hurt. Most power-protection devices have noise filtering built in to them because it's cheap, and it can be an extra selling point (particularly to people who believe they need it). Think of it as a bonus. You can take advantage of its added protection—but don't go out of your way to get it.

Over-Voltage Protection

Surges are dangerous to your computer because the energy they contain can rush through semiconductor circuits faster than the circuits can dissipate them—the silicon junctions of your computer's integrated circuits fry in microseconds. Spike and surge protectors are designed to prevent most short-duration, high-intensity over-voltages from reaching your computer. They absorb excess voltages before they can travel down the power line and into your computer's power supply. Surge suppressors are typically connected between the various conductors of the wiring leading to your computer. Most short out surges that rise above a preset level.

The most important characteristics of over-voltage protection devices are how fast they work and how much energy they can dissipate. Generally, a faster response time or clamping speed is better. Response times can be as short as picoseconds—trillionths of a second. You get better protection from devices that have higher energy-handling capacities, which are measured in watt-seconds or joules. Devices claiming the capability to handle millions of watts are not unusual.

Four kinds of devices are most often used to protect against surges: metal-oxide varistors (MOVs), gas tubes, avalanche diodes, and reactive circuits. Of these, the MOVs dominate because the parts are inexpensive and they work effectively against most surges.

The MOV is a disc-shaped electronic component typically made from a layer of zinc-oxide particles held between two electrodes. The granular zinc oxide offers a high resistance to the flow of electricity until the voltage reaches a break-over point. The electrical current then forms a low-resistance path between the zinc-oxide particles that shorts out the electrical flow. The energy-handling capability can be increased simply by enlarging the device (typical MOVs are about an inch in diameter; high-power MOVs may be twice that). Figure 31.1 shows a typical MOV.

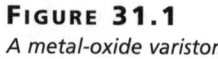

FIGURE 31.1
A metal-oxide varistor.

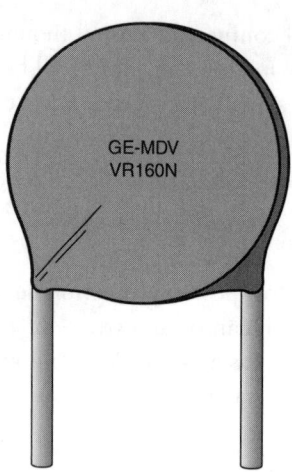

The downside to MOVs is that they degrade. Surges tend to form preferred paths between the zinc-oxide particles, reducing the resistance to electrical flow. Eventually, the MOV shorts out, blowing a fuse or (more likely) overheating until it destroys itself. The MOV can end its life in flames or with no external change at all—except that it no longer offers surge protection.

Thanks to the laws of thermodynamics, the excess energy in a surge cannot just disappear; it can only change form. With most surge suppression technologies (all except reactive devices), the over-voltage is converted into heat that's dissipated by the wiring between the device and the origin of the surge as well as inside the surge suppressor itself. The power in a large surge can destroy a surge suppressor so that it yields up its life to protect your computer.

Because they degrade cumulatively with every surge they absorb, MOVs are particularly prone to failure as they age. Eventually, an MOV will fail, sometimes in its own lightning-like burst. Although it's unlikely this failure will electrically damage the circuits of your computer, it can cause a fire—which can damage not just your computer, but your home, office, or self.

An MOV-based surge suppressor also can fail more subtly—it just stops sucking up surges. Unbeknownst to you, your computer can be left unprotected. Many commercial surge suppressors have indicators designed to reveal the failure of an internal MOV.

In any case, a good strategy is to replace MOV-based surge suppressors periodically to ensure that they do their job and to lessen the likelihood of their failure. How often to replace them depends on how dirty an electrical diet you feed them, but most MOV-based surge protectors should work effectively for a few years before needing replacement.

Blackout Protection

Protecting against total blackouts requires a local source of electricity, either a generator or storage batteries. A local generator is the choice when you want to continue to work as normal, running from local power for hours or days. Battery backup lasts only as long as the batteries, typically a few minutes to allow the orderly shutdown of your computer so you can start back up when normal utility power returns.

Battery backup systems are often called *uninterruptible power systems* (UPSs) because they supply power continuously, without interruption. UPSs are often used in conjunction with generators to bridge over the few seconds that power would otherwise not be available while the generator is starting. A battery backup system is built around powerful batteries that store substantial current. An inverter converts the direct current from the batteries into alternating current that can be used by your computer. A battery charger built in to the system keeps the reserve power supply fully charged at all times. *Long runtime* UPSs, which have extra batteries, sometimes substitute for generators, keeping computer servers (particularly those in remote locations where they are not readily accessible) running for hours.

Although the term *UPS* has become the industry standard for any kind of battery backup system, there are actually two kinds of UPSs, only one of which provides truly uninterruptible power. An *offline* or *standby* power system switches the input of your computer from utility power to backup power when the utility fails. An *online* power system keeps your computer constantly connected to the backup power source, so it never has to switch.

Offline Backup Systems

As the name implies, the standby power system constantly stands by, waiting for the power to fail so that it can leap into action. Under normal conditions—that is, when utility power is available—the battery is offline and its charger draws only a slight current to keep its source of emergency energy topped off. The AC power line from which the offline supply feeds is directly connected to its output, and thence to the computer. The batteries are out of the loop.

When the power fails, the offline supply switches into action—*switch* being the key word. The current-carrying wires inside the power supply that lead to your computer are physically switched (usually by a mechanical relay) from the utility line to the current coming from the battery-powered inverter.

Most offline power systems available today switch within one-half of one cycle of the AC current they are supplied—that's less than ten milliseconds, quick enough to keep nearly all computers running as if no interruption occurred. Although the standby power system design does not protect again spikes and surges, most offline power systems have other protection devices installed in their circuitry to ensure that your computer gets clean power.

Line-interactive power systems are offline designs with an added feature. They react to changes in line voltage and compensate when the voltage gets too high or too low. To change the voltage, they use multitap autotransformers. When the voltage falls low, the line-interactive UPS switches to a tap that *boosts* the voltage back to the appropriate level. When the voltage gets too high, it switches to a different tap that *bucks* the voltage down, reducing it. If the line voltage is too far from normal for the transformer taps to compensate, the UPS reacts as if it suffered a power failure, switching to battery power. The line-interactive design offers the big benefit of compensating for most brownouts without draining its battery reserves.

Online Backup Systems

Online backup systems use several designs to guarantee that there is never an interruption in their output power. The traditional design is the *double-conversion UPS*. These devices earn their name from converting the power twice. First, incoming utility power is transformed down to battery level and rectified to direct current. Then this direct current is inverted and transformed back up to utility voltage to be supplied to your computer. The process would seem to be wasteful and redundant except that a set of batteries connects in the middle. When utility power is available, the constant supply at low voltage keeps the batteries charged. When utility power fails, the batteries maintain the low voltage that feeds the inverter, so the power to your computer is never interrupted.

This traditional double-conversion design is wasteful and expensive. It requires two large transformers capable of carrying the entire load (your computer's and its peripherals), which are very costly and resistant to miniaturization technology. UPS-makers consequently have shifted to a slightly different design that eliminates the transformers. These newer double-conversion UPSs simply rectify the incoming utility voltage to DC and then send it to an inverter, which changes it back to AC. The batteries connect in the middle, but instead of a direct link, they couple through a DC-to-DC converter that matches their voltage to the power line. DC-to-DC converters are high-tech electronic devices that cost substantially less than conventional transformers. As a result, this kind of double-conversion UPS not only has replaced other online designs, but it can also be cost-competitive with offline designs.

In effect, a double-conversion UPS acts like your computer's own generating station, one that is only inches away from the machine it serves. It keeps your system safe from the polluting effects of lightning and load transients found on long-distance power lines. Moreover, dips and surges can never reach the computer. Instead, the computer gets a genuinely smooth, constant electrical supply, exactly like the one for which it was designed.

An alternate online design is more like an offline standby system but uses clever engineering to bridge over even the briefest switching lulls. These UPSs connect both the input power and the output of their inverters together through a special transformer, which is then connected to your computer or other equipment to be protected. Although utility power is available, this kind of UPS supplies it through the transformer to your computer. When the utility power fails, the inverter kicks in, typically within half a cycle. The inductance of the transformer, however, acts as a storage system and supplies the missing half-cycle of electricity during the switchover period.

The double-conversion UPS provides an extreme measure of surge and spike protection (as well as eliminating sags) because no direct connection bridges the power line and the protected equipment—spikes and their kin have no pathway to sneak in. Although the transformer in the new style of UPS absorbs many power-line irregularities, overall it does not afford the same degree of protection. Consequently, these newer devices usually have other protection devices (such as MOVs) built in.

Specifications

The most important specification to investigate before purchasing any backup power device is its capacity as measured in volt-amperes (VA) or watts. This number should always be greater than the rating of the equipment to which the backup device is to be connected.

In alternating current (AC) systems, watts do not necessarily equal the product of volts and amperes (as they should by the definition that applies in DC systems) because the voltage and current can be out of phase with one another. That is, when the voltage is at a maximum, the current in the circuit can be at an intermediary value. So the peak values of voltage and amperage may occur at different times.

Power requires both voltage and current simultaneously. Consequently, the product of voltage and current (amperage) in an AC circuit is often higher than the actual power in the circuit. The ratio between these two values is called the *power factor* of the system.

What all this means to you is that volt-amperes and watts are not the same thing. Most backup power systems are rated in VA because it is a higher figure thanks to the power factor. You must make sure the total VA used by your computer equipment is less than the VA available from the backup power system. Alternatively, you must make sure that the wattage used by your equipment is less than the wattage available from the backup power system. Don't indiscriminately mix the VA and watts in making comparisons.

To convert a VA rating to a watt rating, multiply the VA by the power factor of the backup power supply. To go the other way—watts to VA—divide the wattage rating of the backup power system by its power factor. (You can do the same thing with the equipment you want to plug into the power supply, but you may have a difficult time discovering the power factor of each piece of equipment. For computers, a safe value to assume is 2/3.)

Both online and offline backup systems also are rated as to how long they can supply battery power. This equates to the total energy (the product of power and time) that they store. Such time ratings vary with the VA the backup device must supply—because of finite battery reserves, it can supply greater currents only for shorter periods. Most manufacturers rate their backup systems for a given minutes of operation with a load of a particular size instead of in more scientific fashion using units of energy. For example, a backup system may be rated to run a 250 volt-ampere load for 20 minutes.

If you want an idea of the maximum possible time a given backup supply can carry your system, check the ratings of the batteries it uses. Most batteries are rated in ampere-hours, which describes how much current they can deliver for how long. To convert that rating to a genuine energy rating, multiply it by the nominal battery voltage. For example, a 12-volt, 6 amp-hour battery could, in theory, produce 72 watt-hours of electricity. That figure is theoretical rather than realistic because the circuitry that converts the battery DC to AC wastes some of the power and because ratings are only nominal for new batteries. However, the numbers you derive give you a limit. If you have only 72 watt-hours of battery, you can't expect the system to run your 250 VA computer for an hour. At most, you could expect 17 minutes; realistically, you might expect 12 to 15.

You probably will not need much time from a backup power system, however. In most cases, five minutes or less of backup time is sufficient because the point of a backup supply is not to keep a system running forever. Instead, the backup power system is designed to give you a chance to shut down your computer without losing your work. Shutting down shouldn't take more than a minute or two.

UPS-makers warn that no matter the rating of your UPS, you should never plug a laser printer into it. The fusers in laser printers are about as power hungry as toasters—both are resistive heaters. The peak power demand when the fuser switches on can overload even larger UPSs, and the continuing need for current can quickly drain batteries. Moreover, there's no need to keep a print job running during a power failure. Even if you lose a page, you can reprint it when the power comes back at far less expense than the cost of additional UPS power capable of handling the laser's needs. Some printers, such as inkjets, are friendlier to UPSs and can safely be connected, but you'll still be wasting capacity. The best strategy is to connect only your computer, your monitor, and any external disk drives to the UPS. Plug the rest of your equipment into a surge suppresser.

To handle such situations, many UPSs have both battery-protected outlets and outlets with only surge protection. Be sure to check which outlets you use with your equipment, making sure your computer has battery-backed protection.

Interfaces

An ordinary UPS works effectively if you're sitting at your computer and the power fails. You can quickly assess whether it looks like the blackout will be short or long (if the world is blowing away outside your window, you can be pretty sure any outage will be prolonged). You can save your work, haul down your operating system, and shut off your computer at your leisure. When a computer is connected to a network or is running unattended, however, problems can arise.

During a prolonged outage, a simple UPS only prolongs a disaster with an unattended computer—it runs another dozen minutes or so while the power is off, then the UPS runs out of juice and the computer plummets with it. Of course, if a server crashes without warning, no one is happy, particularly if a number of files were in the queue to be saved.

To avoid these problems, better UPSs include interfaces that let them link to your computer, usually through a serial port. Install an appropriate driver, supplied by the UPS-maker, and your computer can monitor the condition of your power line. When the power goes off, the software can send messages down the network warning individual users to save their work. Then, the UPS software can initiate an orderly shut down of the network.

Some UPSs will continue to run even after your network or computer has shut itself down. Better units have an additional feature termed *inverter shutdown* that automatically switches off the UPS after your network shuts down. This preserves some charge in the batteries of the UPS so that it can still offer protection if you put your computer or network back online and another power failure follows shortly thereafter. A fully discharged UPS, on the other hand, might not be ready to take the load for several hours.

Battery Life

The gelled electrolyte batteries most commonly used in uninterruptible power systems have a finite life. The materials from which they are made gradually deteriorate, and the overall system loses its ability to store electricity. After several years, a gelled electrolyte battery will no longer be able to operate a UPS, even for a short period. The UPS then becomes nonfunctional. The only way to revive the UPS is to replace the batteries.

Battery failure in a UPS usually comes as a big surprise. The power goes off and your computer goes with it, notwithstanding your investment in the UPS. The characteristics of the batteries themselves almost guarantee this surprise. Gelled electrolyte batteries gradually lose their storage capacity over a period of years, typically between three and five. Then, suddenly, their capacity plummets. They can lose nearly all their total storage capability in a few weeks. Figure 31.2 illustrates this characteristic of typical gelled electrolyte batteries.

FIGURE 31.2
UPS battery capacity slowly deteriorates, then suddenly plummets.

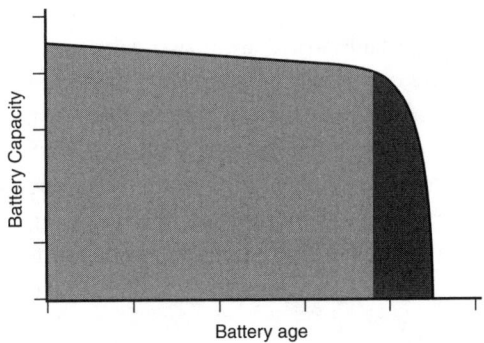

Battery Capacity

Battery age

Note that the deterioration of gelled electrolyte batteries occurs regardless of whether they are repeatedly discharged. They deteriorate even when not used, although repeated heavy discharges will further shorten their lives.

To guard against the surprise of total battery failure, better UPSs incorporate an automatic testing mechanism that periodically checks battery capacity. A battery failure indication from such a UPS should not be taken lightly.

Phone and Network Line Protection

Spikes and surges affect more than just power lines. Any wire that ventures outside holds the potential for attracting lightning. Any long wiring run is susceptible to induced voltages, including noise and surges. These over-voltages can be transmitted directly into your computer or its peripherals and cause the same damage as a power line surge.

The good news is that several important wiring systems incorporate their own power protection. For example, Ethernet systems (both coaxial and twisted pair) have sufficient surge protection for their intended applications. Apple LocalTalk adapters are designed to withstand surges of 2000 volts with no damage. Because they are not electrical at all, fiber-optical connections are completely immune to power surges.

The bad new is that two common kinds of computer wiring are *not* innately protected by surges. Telephone wiring runs long distances through the same environments as the power-distribution system and is consequently susceptible to the same problems. In particular, powerful surges generated by direct lightning hits or induction can travel through telephone wiring, through your modem, and into the circuitry of your computer. In addition, ordinary serial port circuitry includes no innate surge suppression. A long unshielded serial cable can pick up surges from other cables by induction.

The best protection is avoidance. Keep unshielded serial cable runs short whenever possible. If you must use a long serial connection, use shielded cable. Better still, break up the run with a short-haul modem, which will also increase the potential speed of the connection.

Modem connections with the outside world are unavoidable in these days of online connectivity and the Internet. You can, however, protect against phone-line surges using special suppressors designed exactly for that purpose. Better power-protection devices also have modem connections that provide the necessary safeguards. Standalone telephone surge suppressors are also available. They use the same technologies as power-line surge suppressors. Indeed, the voltage that rings your telephone is nearly the same as the 110–120 volt utility power used in the United States. Most phone-line suppressors are based on MOV devices. Better units combine MOVs with capacitors, inductors, and fuses.

Cases

The case is your computer. It's what you kick when it won't behave. It's the big, bulky box that makes too much noise and takes up too much space—except if you have a notebook computer. It's the thing that gets in the way, the thing you pay too much for. It's all the things that you hate about your computer.

The case is the most visible part of your computer. It's the most physical. But don't be misled. The physical side of your computer's case is almost trivial. It's almost all style. Although the substance of it is vital for holding your computer together, that's all blacksmith technology. The case is no mere shell. It is a sophisticated piece of engineering. In addition to its mechanical function, it also serves to keep your computer cool, thereby extending the life of its circuits. In addition, the case is a protective shield that looks after you as well as the delicate circuits inside. It even protects the world from the high-frequency (and low) signals inside.

Mechanical Construction

The obvious function of the case is mechanical—you can see it and touch it as a distinct object. And it steals part of your desktop, floor, or lap when you put it to work. It has a definite size—always too small when you want to add one more thing but too large when you need to find a place to put it (and particularly when that place happens to be inside your carry-on luggage). The case also has a shape, which may be functional to allow you the best access to all those computer accoutrements, such as the slot into which you shove your backup tapes. But shape and color also are part of your computer's style, which can set one system apart from the boring sameness of its computer kin.

Modern computers have wings, waves, and flares—all only aesthetics calculated to make a given manufacturer's machines stand out among the masses, style to make you think they are more modern and capable. The features, such as some of the more interesting paint shades with which some manufacturers have started experimenting, are design gimmicks, the tail-fins of the new century. There's nothing wrong with a computer that looks like you've stolen it from the deck of an aircraft carrier, but there's nothing inherently better about it, either. Beneath the plastic you'll find that same basic mechanical design and construction of systems built a decade ago.

When a computer is being built, two issues are paramount: how the case is put together and how a computer is put together inside it. In the first case, how the case gets constructed—whether with screws, rivets, or welds—is not so important as the size of the finished product. The size of the case determines what it can hold, which in turn limits how much you can expand the system to add all the features you want. How components install inside the case affect how much you want to expand your system. If sliding in an expansion board or just getting at a drive bay to install a new disk makes you think the system was designed by someone in league with the devil (or another employee of Microsoft), you're not going to look on expansion with much favor.

Some computer companies actually sympathize with your plight, knowing the happy customer brings goodwill, and a satisfied customer is less likely to make calls to the support staff that's so expensive to pay. Over the years, they have developed several schemes to make working on and expanding your computer easier—everything from cases you can open without tools to cases you cannot open at all, relying instead on external expansion.

In computers, form dictates function as much (if not more) than it does for any other type of office equipment. Computers have the shape they have so that they can hold what you want to put inside them—primarily all those expansion options that give your machine power and capabilities. It has to be large enough to accommodate the expansion boards you want to plug in as well as provide adequate space for all the disk drives your computer and life would not be complete without—hard, floppy, DVD, and the like.

For most manufacturers, the sizes of both boards and drives are preordained. Both are covered by industry standards that were set years ago and remain invariant. The case must be designed around these standards if it is to accommodate the generally available motherboards, expansion boards, and disk drives.

Standards

All current desktop computer cases follow the motherboard mounting dimensions laid down by the ATX motherboard standard, the microATX standard, or the NLX standard. These standards describe not only the minimum dimensions for a computer case but also the locations of mounting standards for the screws that hold the motherboard in place.

The guidance given by these standards is, in fact, minimal. The standards define only the footprint of the motherboard and a space on the rear panel of the case for port connectors. Even so, you can be sure that an ATX motherboard will fit into an ATX case.

With notebook computers, all bets are off. Despite attempts at defining a notebook motherboard standard, every manufacturer goes its own way—both in motherboard and case design.

Size

A computer can be any size to carry out its job. Thanks to miniaturization, even the smallest computers can rival the power of the largest—with one exception. You can stuff more stuff into a big box than you can a small one.

That's the essence of size differences among computers. Bigger means more expansion, more places to put power-enhancing accessories. As long as you don't need an extraordinary amount of expansion, even the physically smallest computer will suffice.

A number of terms are used to describe the size of computers, although none approaches being an official designation.

Compact

The basic computer—that is, the smallest with the least future potential—uses a compact device that's sometimes called a *small footprint computer*. In the jargon of the computer industry, the footprint is the space a computer occupies on your desk, so the small footprint steals less desk space, making it an ideal office companion. Compact desktop computers are sometimes called *low-profile computers* because they are short, usually as short as possible, and still hold a whole computer.

To achieve compact size, computer-makers must do some serious trimming from the designs of larger computers. The principal loss is in expansion. Compact systems have fewer slots and bays than other computers. They have a minimum of extra space for expansion—once filled with standard factory equipment, perhaps as little as a single open slot and a single unfilled bay. The underlying philosophy is that the compact computer comes with everything you need already installed, so there's no need to add anything more.

To shave down the height of low-profile cases while conserving the capability of handling tall expansion boards, compact machines move their options on edge. Instead of boards sliding into slots vertically, these tiny computers align them horizontally. The motherboard boards remain horizontal in the case and have a single master expansion slot. A special expansion board rises vertically with additional slot connectors on one side to allow you to slide in several ordinary expansion boards (typically three) parallel to the system board.

Although the exact assortment of drive possibilities varies with the design of compact systems, most small-footprint machines offer similar drive options. They are constrained by what you expect and need in any computer. A floppy disk drive and a CD or DVD drive leer out from the front panel, and a hard disk hides safely inside. If any drive expansion is available inside these systems, it comprises a single bay suitable for an inch-tall hard disk.

Desktop

At one time, *desktop* meant a particular case design—a low, flat cabinet meant to sit on a desk and hold a monitor on top. The basic configuration and even the standard dimensions carried over from the original IBM Personal Computer. The result was a case measuring 21 inches wide by 17 inches deep, designed to accommodate two large disk drives measuring 5.25 inches across, side by side. Its height, to allow for expansion boards and three-eighths inch feet underneath for airflow (just enough so you could lose a pencil—maybe the designers did have some kind of inspiration!), measured 5.5 inches.

Because few people need more than one large (5.25-inch) drive bay, most new desktop computers opt to shrink the other bay area to the 3.5-inch size, shaving about two inches of the computer in the process. This intermediate package, measuring about 5.5 by 19 by 17 inches is today's most popular in desktop systems.

Towers

Stand a conventional computer on edge and you get a tower. At least that's how the tower format evolved. The design has proved so popular that these days, one form of tower or another probably *is* the standard computer.

The upright design actually makes the ultimate small-footprint computer. It steals no space from your desk if you set it next to the furniture. A smaller footprint is hard to imagine.

Freed from restraints required when sharing a desktop, tower computers could expand to suit even the most fanciful dreams. The largest have nearly as many bays as the Eastern seaboard—as many as 11 in a single system. On the other hand, they usually do not extend the number of expansion slots over eight. The reason is not a spatial limitation but an economic one. Most towers use standard, off-the-shelf motherboards. Raising the slot number would involve expensive redesign (as well as more motherboard, circuitry, and assembly costs).

With modern components, vertically mounting computer components causes no problems. Electronic circuits don't know which way is up. Although mechanical devices such as disk drives may care, the only practical effects with current hardware are really your problem. Putting a CD drive on edge can turn loading a disc into a dash across your office floor and down the hallway as you race after the errant disc that dropped and rolled away. Most towers keep their bays horizontal to avoid the office chase scene. Compaq even developed a computer transformer—by remounting the drive bay and changing the front panel bezel, you can switch the Deskpro EP series from desktop to tower and back.

The tower design has been so successful, designers have fine-tuned the vertical package to meet a variety of expansion needs. *Mini-tower cases* are the most compact and usually accommodate only Mini-AT and smaller motherboards and a few drive options. *Full-size tower cases* hold full-size motherboards and more drive bays than most people know what to do with. Recently, *midi-tower cases*, with accommodation falling in-between, have become a popular option. There is no standardization of these terms. One manufacturer's *mini* is another's *midi*.

Choose a computer with a tower-style case for its greater physical capacity for internal peripherals and its flexibility of installation wherever there are a few vacant feet of floor space. You also need to be critical about the provisions for physically mounting mass-storage devices. Some towers provide only flimsy mounting means or require you to work through a Chinese puzzle of interlocking parts to install a drive. You need a system that provides sufficient drive-mounting options.

Notebook

Back in the days before micro-miniaturization, anything instantly became portable the moment you attached a handle. The first generation of portable televisions, for example, was eminently portable—at least for anyone accustomed to carrying a carboy of mineral water under each arm. The first generation of computers had similar pretenses of portability, challenging your wherewithal with a weighty bottle of gas and photons and a small but hardly lightweight picture tube. The typical weight of a first-generation portable computer was about 40 pounds—about the limit of what the market (or any reasonable human being) would bear. These portables were essentially nothing more than a repackaging that combined a conventional computer with an integral monitor.

Replacing the bottle with a flat-panel display gave designers a quick way to cut half the weight and repackage systems into *lunchbox* computers. The name referred to the slab-sided design with a handle on top, reminiscent of what every kid not party to the school lunch program toted to class. But with some weighing in at 20 to 25 pounds, these packages were enough to provide Paul Bunyan with his midday meal. The largest of these did allow the use of conventional motherboards with space for several conventional expansion slots. Overall, however, the design was one that only a mother could love, at least if she advocated an aggressive weight-training program.

The ultimate in computer compression is the notebook computer, machines shrunk as small as possible while allowing your hands a grip on their keyboards (and eyes a good look at the screen) and as thin as componentry allows. Manufacturers have managed to squeeze the typical notebook computer down to a little more than six pounds. Size is limited by the choice of display screen. With bleary-eyed users demanding the biggest possible screens—one manufacturer now offers a notebook computer with a 16-inch screen—cases have been tailored to match. Although easy on your eyes when you're work-ing or playing games, the big screens make today's notebook a bit more troublesome to carry and almost impossible to use in an economy-class airline seat.

The notebook design spawned the subnotebook for people on the move who want to carry the minimal computer. Typically, subnotebooks forgo several features, such as port connectors and optical drives, to achieve their smaller size. In general, a subnotebook is a portable computer weighing under four pounds, has a 12-inch or smaller LCD screen, and is a little larger than an inch-thick stack of writing tablets.

Fitting into the small notebook and subnotebook packages forces manufacturers to sacri-fice some degree of convenience. For example, a number of subnotebook machines have been developed with keyboards reduced to 80 percent of the standard size. Most people adapt to slightly cramped keyboards and continue to touch-type without difficulty. Smaller than that, however, and touch-typing becomes challenging. In other words, handheld computers are not for extensive data entry.

Besides length and width, notebook computer–makers also have trimmed the depth of their keyboards, reducing the height of keytops—not a noticeable change—as well as reducing key travel. The latter can have a dramatic effect on typing feel and usability. Although the feel and travel of a keyboard are mostly user preference, odds favor greater dissatisfaction with the shrunken, truncated keyboards in miniaturized computers com-pared to full-size machines.

Notebook computers have forced manufacturers to miniaturize a number of components that don't naturally lend themselves to miniaturization. Both CD and DVD-ROM drives now fit into a space one-third their desktop size, but they suffer the penalty of lower top speeds.

Hard disk drives suffer the same fate. Drive-makers have shrunk their products to fit a 2.5-inch form factor with little capacity penalty. Instead, they have sacrificed speed. Notebook drives spin more slowly than desktop models (which helps them gain some of the capacity they need).

Internal Access

Two philosophies surround the issue of access into your computer's case. One school of thought holds that it should be as easy as possible so that you can make upgrades quickly and easily. The other school believes that you can only get yourself into trouble inside your computer. Students of this school believe that the best case is one that's sealed against access. If they had their way, your computer would be embedded in a block of Lucite so you could see its pretty lights but not touch a thing inside.

The curriculum divides roughly on application lines. Computers used at home or in a small business—that is, one small enough that you're responsible for your own computer—are best with open access. Large businesses that have a unified Information Systems department headed by an all-powerful *fuehrer* want to keep in absolute control—which means keeping you out. The needs of these folks led the move to the Network Computer and other abortive attempts at electronic mind control.

Tool-free entry allows you to open and upgrade your system without special tools or any tools at all. You won't have to steal a knife from the silverware drawer to get into your computer or buy a special screwdriver to pull out an expansion board. In the ideal case, the lid unlatches and slides off your computer with minimum effort. Disk drives snap into place, and knurled posts that you can tighten with your fingers lock expansion boards into place. Some current systems approach this ideal, but few go all the way.

Bays

Bays come in two basic varieties: those with *front panel access* and those without. Front-panel-access bays are for devices using removable media. You have to have access to the front of the drive to slide in a disk or tape cartridge. Floppy disk drives, CD and DVD drives, and tape drives all must be mounted in bays with front panel access.

Internal bays lack front panel access. They may be tucked away inside the computer or just below the bays with front panel access. Internal bays suit devices that require no direct user interaction, those you don't have to see or touch. The chief occupant of an internal bay is the hard disk drive.

Form Factors

Disk drives come in a variety of heights and widths. The basic unit of measurement of the size of a drive is the *form factor*, which is simply the volume of a standard drive that handles a particular medium. Several form factors regularly find their way into discussions of personal computers, ranging in size from 8 inches to 1.3 inches, most of which allow for one or more device heights.

The full-size drive, the unit that defines the form factor and occupies all of its volume, is usually a first-generation machine. Its exact dimensions, chosen for whatever particular reason, seemed fitting, perhaps allowing for the mood of the mechanical engineer on the day he was drafting the blueprints. If the drive is a reasonable size and proves particularly successful—successful enough that other manufacturers eagerly want to cash in, too—others follow suit and copy the dimension of the product, making it a standard.

Device Heights

The second generation of any variety of hardware inevitably results in some sort of size reduction. Cost cutting, greater precision, experience in manufacturing, and the inevitable need to put more in less space gang up to shrink things down.

The succession of heights first appeared among 5.25-inch drives. At 5.25 inches, devices are measured in increments of the original full-height package. Devices that are two-thirds height, half-height, one-third, or quarter-height have all been manufactured at one time or another.

At the 3.5-inch form factor, sizes are more pragmatic, measured as the actual height in inches. The original 3.5-inch drives may be considered full height and typically measure about 1.6 inches high. The next most widely used size was an even inch in height (defining five-eighths height, for the fractious folk who prefer fractions). Sub-inch heights have been used for some devices, some as small as 0.6 inches.

At 2.5 inches, the size of most notebook computer drives, height is described as actually measured. Typical high-capacity drives measure 12.5 millimeters high (roughly half an inch) with 9.5 millimeters preferred for the drives in subnotebook computers.

Smaller drives have also been manufactured, although the one standard for tiny drives fits the CompactFlash package. These have superceded the 1.8-inch size that won particular favor for fitting into Type 3 PC Cards that follow the most recent standards promulgated by PCMCIA.

Racks

Most drive-mounting schemes are meant for permanent installations. Your hard disk drive is supposed to last for the life of your computer. In certain situations, however, you may want something less permanent.

If you deal in secrets or have valuable information that you store on your computer, you might not want to leave it out on your desk untended all night long. Although packing up and putting your computer away for the evening is more trouble than most people want to bother with, pulling out a disk drive and sliding it into a safe is not.

Although hard disks are quite reliable, every one you add to your system increases the chances that one will fail. Multiple disk drives and the need for reliable operation go hand-in-hand in RAID systems. To speed repairs, most RAID systems have moved to mounting drives for hot-swapping.

In either case, the choice is mounting your drive in a removable *rack*. The typical hot-swap rack allows you to install a 3.5-inch hard disk in a 5.25-inch bay. More than an adapter, it puts the drive on a submodule that slides into the rack, connects, and locks in place. You can remove a drive for the evening or swap a new drive for an old one at any time. Each rack manufacturer uses its own designs, so there's no intercompatibility among different rack systems.

Slots

All expansion slots are not the same. Put another way, a slot is not a slot is not a slot. Expansion slots differ in two primary ways—the standard followed and length.

To push up slot totals, many manufacturers also add that their systems (or motherboards) include an accelerated graphics port (AGP) slot. Technically they are correct. The AGP slot works exactly like an expansion slot. But it is irrelevant when analyzing the availability of expansion. Any computer with an AGP slot likely fills it with an AGP graphics adapter (why else would the slot be there?), so the AGP slot is never available for expansion (although it does allow you to upgrade your video system). Ordinary expansion boards—both PCI and ISA—will *not* fit into the AGP slot in a computer.

Slots also vary in length. A *full-size* slot allows you to install any length of expansion board. A *short slot* cannot hold a full-length expansion board. Although PCI describes the dimensions of a short card, computer-makers make short slots of any length that suits their designs. In general, these short slots are more than half the length of a full-size slot and will accommodate most short cards. Most modern expansion boards are short, so you ordinarily won't have problems matching slot length.

Cooling

A case can be confining. It can keep just about everything from escaping, including the heat that electronic circuits produce as a by-product of performing their normal functions. Some of the electricity in any circuit (except one made from superconductors) is turned into heat by the unavoidable electrical resistance of the circuit. Heat is also generated whenever an element of a computer circuit changes state. In fact, nearly all the electricity consumed by a computer eventually turns into heat.

Inside the protective (and confining) case of the computer, that heat builds up, thus driving up the temperature. Heat is the worst enemy of semiconductor circuits; it can shorten their lives considerably or even cause their catastrophic failure. Some means of escape must be provided for the excess heat. In truth, the heat build-up in most computers may not be immediately fatal to semiconductor circuits. For example, most microprocessors shut down (or simply generate errors that shut down your computer) before any permanent damage occurs to them or the rest of the components inside your computer. However, heat can cause circuits to age prematurely and can trim the lives of circuit components.

The design of the case of a computer affects how well the machine deals with its heat build-up. A case that's effective in keeping its internal electronics cool can prolong the life of the system.

Passive Convection

The obvious way to make a computer run cooler is to punch holes in its case to let the heat out—but to keep the holes small enough so that other things such as mice and milkshakes can't get in. In due time, passive convection—less dense hot air rising with denser cool air flowing in to take its place—lets the excess thermal energy drift out of the case.

Any impediment to the free flow of air slows the passive cooling effect. In general, the more holes in the case, the merrier the computer will be. Remove the lid, and the heat can waft away along with temperature worries.

Unfortunately, your computer's case should be closed. Keeping a lid on it does more than just restrict cooling—it is also the only effective way to deal with interference. It also keeps your computer quieter, prevents foreign objects and liquids from plummeting in, and gives your monitor a lift.

Moreover, passive cooling is often not enough. Only low-power designs (such as notebook and Green computers) generate little enough heat that convection can be entirely successful. Other systems generate more heat than naturally goes away on its own.

Active Cooling

The alternative to passive cooling is, hardly unexpectedly, *active* cooling, which uses a force of some kind to move the heat away from the circuits. The force of choice in most computers is a fan.

Usually tucked inside the power supply, the computer's fan forces air to circulate both inside the power supply and the computer. It sucks cool air in to circulate and blows the heated air out.

The cooling systems of early computers, however, were particularly ill-conceived for active cooling. The fans were designed mostly to cool off the heat-generating circuitry inside the power supply itself and only incidentally cooled the inside of the computer. Moreover, the chance design of the system resulted in most of the cool air getting sucked in through the floppy disk drive slots. Along with the air came all the dust and grime floating around in the environment, polluting whatever media you had sitting in the drive. At least enough air coursed through the machine to cool off the small amount of circuitry that the meager power supply of the computer could provide.

Modern computers do much better. Many have carefully designed air channels to route cooling air over the places most apt to get work (such as memory chips). Some manufacturers opt to put one or more additional fans (besides the one in the power supply) into their systems to keep the overall chassis cool.

Modern microprocessors generate so much waste heat that a single system fan can't keep them cool. They require an additional means to keep air circulating. Most microprocessors in desktop computers now use fans integrated into their heatsinks to keep the chips cool. Each heatsink design requires a fan custom tailored to it.

Large cooling fans make noise. Some computer manufacturers try to minimize this noise by making their fans thermostatically controlled. They switch on only when your computer needs cooling. Sometimes this feature is controlled through the BIOS; other times it is an invariant feature. If you suspect fan failure (discussed later in this chapter in more detail), be sure your system does not have a thermostatically controlled fan that simply has not switched on.

Many people believe you cannot overdo cooling—more fans is always better. In fact, the cooler you keep your chips, the longer they will last. Heat *is* their worst enemy. The only downside to blowing hurricanes through your computer is that air is inevitably fouled with dust and lint. A substantial amount of foreign material may accumulate inside your computer, and it may alter or stop airflow in some places in the system, causing them to overheat. To prevent such problems, fans may be equipped with filters. In any case, whenever a computer is operated in an environment likely to cause dust and lint contamination (say, for instance, you have a cat), you should vacuum the inside of your computer periodically to remove any accumulation.

Fan Failure

The fan inside a computer power supply is a necessity, not a luxury. If it fails to operate, your computer won't falter—at least not at first. But temperatures build up inside. The machine—the power supply in particular—may even fail catastrophically from overheating.

The symptoms of fan failure are subtle but hard to miss. You hear the difference in the noise your system makes. You may even be able to smell components warming past their safe operating temperature.

Should you detect either symptom, hold you hand near where the air usually emerges from your computer. (On most computers, that's near the big round opening that the fan peers through.) If you feel no breeze, you can be certain your fan is no longer doing its job.

A fan failure constitutes an emergency. If it happens to your system, immediately save your work and shut the machine off. Although you can safely use it for short periods, the better strategy is to replace the fan or power supply as soon as you possibly can.

Radiation

Besides heat, all electrical circuits radiate something else—electromagnetic fields. Every flow of electrical energy sets up an electromagnetic field that radiates away. Radio and television stations push kilowatts of energy through their antennae so that this energy (accompanied by programming in the form of modulation) radiates over the countryside, eventually to be hauled in by a radio or television set for your enjoyment or disgruntlement.

The electrical circuits inside all computers work the same way but on a smaller scale. The circuit board traces act as antennae and radiate electromagnetic energy whenever the computer is turned on. When the thinking gets intense, so does the radiation.

You can't see, hear, feel, taste, or smell this radiation, just as you can't detect the emissions from a radio station (at least not without a radio), so you would think there would be no reason for concern about the radiation from your computer. But even invisible signals can be dangerous, and their very invisibility makes them more worrisome—you may never know if they are there or not. The case of your computer is your primary (often only) line of defense against radiation from its electronic circuitry.

The problems of radiation are twofold: the radiation interfering with other, more desirable signals in the air, and the radiation affecting your health.

Radio Frequency Interference

The signals radiated by a computer typically fall in the microwatt range, perhaps a billion times weaker than those emitted by a broadcasting station. You would think that the broadcast signals would easily overwhelm the inadvertent emissions from your computer. But the strength of signals falls off dramatically with distance from the source. They follow the inverse-square law; therefore, a signal from a source a thousand times farther away would be a million times weaker. Radio and television stations are typically miles away, so the emissions from a computer can easily overwhelm nearby broadcast signals, turning transmissions into gibberish.

The radiation from the computer circuitry occurs at a wide variety of frequencies, including not only the range occupied by your favorite radio and television stations but also aviation navigation systems, emergency radio services, and even the eavesdropping equipment some initialed government agency may have buried in your walls. Unchecked, these untamed radiations from within your computer can compete with broadcast signals, not only for the ears of your radio but those of your neighbors. These radio-like signals emitted by the computer generate what is termed *radio frequency interference* (RFI), so called because they interfere with other signals in the radio spectrum.

The government agency charged with the chore of managing interference—the Federal Communications Commission—has set strict standards on the radio waves that personal computers can emit. These standards are complex, and ensuring your computer is actually in compliance would require expensive test equipment. The law does not require that you check—the burden is on the manufacturer. Moreover, at their hearts, the FCC standards simply enforce a good-neighbor policy. They require that the RFI from computers be so weak that it won't bother your neighbors, although it may garble radio signals in your own home or office.

The FCC sets two standards: Class A and Class B. Computer equipment must be verified to meet the FCC Class A standard to be legally sold for business use. Computers must be certified to conform with the more stringent FCC Class B standard to be sold for home use.

Equipment-makers, rather than users, must pass FCC muster. You are responsible, however, for ensuring that your equipment does not interfere with your neighbors. If your computer does interfere, legally you have the responsibility for eliminating the problem. While you can sneak Class A equipment into your home, you have good reasons not to. The job of interference elimination is easier with Class B certified equipment because it starts off radiating lower signal levels, so Class B machines give you a head start. Moreover, meeting the Class B standards requires better overall construction, which helps ensure that you get a better case and a better computer.

Minimizing Interference

Most television interference takes one of two forms: noise and signal interference.

Noise interference appears on the screen as lines and dots that jump randomly about. The random appearance of noise reflects its origins. Noise arises from random pulses of electrical energy. The most common source for noise is electric motors. Every spark in the brushes of an electric motor radiates a broad spectrum of radio frequency signals that your television may receive along with its normal signals. Some computer peripherals may also generate such noise.

Signal interference usually appears as a pattern of some sort on your screen. For example, a series of tilted horizontal bars or noise-like snow on the screen that stays in a fixed pattern instead of jumping madly about. Signal interference is caused by regular, periodic electrical signals.

Television interference most commonly occurs when you rely on a "rabbit ear" antenna for your television reception. Such antennae pull signals from the air in the immediate vicinity of the television set, so if your computer is nearby, its signals are more likely to be received. Moving to cable or an external antenna relocates the point your TV picks up its signals to a distant location and will likely minimize or eliminate interference from a computer near the TV set.

You can minimize the interference your computer radiates and improve your television reception by taking several preventive measures.

The first step is to make sure the lid is on your computer's case and that it and all expansion boards are firmly screwed into place. Fill all empty expansion slots with blank panels. Firmly affixing the screws is important because they ground the expansion boards or blank panels, which helps them shield your computer. This strategy also helps minimize the already small fire hazard your computer presents.

If the interference persists after you've screwed everything down in your computer, next check to see if you can locate where the interference leaks out of your computer. The most likely suspects are the various cables that trail out of your computer and link to peripherals such as your monitor, keyboard, and printer. Disconnect cabled peripherals one at a time and observe whether the disconnection reduces the interference.

Because it operates at the highest speed (and therefore the highest frequency), an external SCSI cable is most prone to radiating interference. All external SCSI cables should be shielded.

Your mouse is the most unlikely part of your computer to cause TV interference. The mouse operates at serial data rates, which are much too low to interfere even with VHF television.

If disconnecting a cable reduces onscreen TV interference, the next step is to get the offending signal out of the cable. The best way is to add a ferrite core around the cable. Many computer cables already have ferrite cores installed. They are the cylindrical lumps in the cable near one or the other connector. Install the ferrite core by putting it around the offending cable near where the cable leaves your computer. You can buy clamp-on ferrite cores from many electronic-parts stores.

Unplugging one cable—your computer's power cable—should completely eliminate the interference radiated by your computer. After all, the computer won't work without power and can't generate or radiate anything. You can reduce the interference traveling on the power line by adding a noise filter between your computer's plug and its power outlet. You can usually obtain noise filters from electronic-parts suppliers. Although a noise filter is not the same thing as a surge suppresser, most of the better surge suppressers also include noise filtering.

Health Concerns

Some radiation emitted by computers is of such low frequencies that it falls below the range used by any radio station. These *very low frequency* and *extremely low frequency* signals (often called *VLF* and *ELF*) are thought by some people to cause a variety of health problems.

Radiation

Your computer's case is the first line of defense against these signals. A metal case blocks low-frequency magnetic fields, which some epidemiological studies have hinted might be dangerous, and shields against the emission of electrical fields. Plastic cases are less effective. By themselves they offer no electrical or magnetic shielding. But plain plastic cases would also flunk the FCC tests. Most manufacturers coat plastic cases with a conductive paint to contain interference. However, these coatings are largely ineffective against magnetic fields. Most modern systems now use metal cases or internal metal shielding inside plastic cases to minimize radiation.

No matter the construction of your computer, you can minimize your exposure to radiation from its case by ensuring that it is properly and securely assembled. Minimizing interference means screwing in the retaining brackets of all the expansion boards inside your computer and keeping the lid tightly screwed into the chassis. Keeping a tight computer not only helps keep you safe, it also keeps your system safe and intact.

Index

airplane adapters,
1023-1024

algorithms, cyclical redundancy check (CRC) algo-
rithm, 304

alignment, color, 838

all points addressable
graphics (APA display),
706

Allgemeine Elektricitaets
Gesellschaft. *See* AEG

alpha channel, 719

alpha-blending, 719

Alternate Mark Inversion
(AMI), 468

alternating current. *See* AC

Alto workstation, 695

ALU (arithmetic/logic
unit), 84

AMD (Advanced Micro
Devices)
HyperTransport, 282
PowerNow!, 107-109

American digital television
transmission standard
(ATSC), 900

American National
Standards Institute. *See*
ANSI

American Telephone and
Telegraph Company, 458

AMI (Alternate Mark
Inversion), 468

AML (ACPI Machine
Language), 203

AMP (manufacturer of
electronic component
sockets), 574

Ampére, André Marie, 1026

amplification, 63

amplifiers, 906
gamma, 859
video, 858

amplitude
modulation, 233
sound, 885-886

AMR (audio modem riser),
1004

AMS (Array Management
Software), 610

analog audio, 884-885
amplitude, 885-886
decibels, 886-887
distortion, 887-888
frequencies, 885
voltage, 886

analog captures, 902-903

analog connection systems,
875-877

analog mixers, 910

Analog Protection System
(APS), 681

analog services
modems, 450-451
background, 450-451
channels, 452-454
*connection-enhancing tech-
nologies, 454-458*
hardware, 462-466
Shannon's Limit, 451-452
standards, 458
*ITU (International
Telecommunications
Union), 458*
*modem speed standards,
458-461*
telephone company, 458

analog standards, 961

analog video output, 809

analog voltage level, 876

analog-to-digital converters, 822, 908

Analytical Engine, 6

angular velocity, 656

ANSI (American National
Standards Institute), 320
ATA standards, 320
SCSI parallel interface,
344-345

ANSI T13 Technical
Committee, 307

anti-glare treatment, CRTs
(cathode ray tubes),
844-846

antialiasing filters, 889

APA display (all points
addressable graphics), 706

aperture
digital camera lenses, 791-793
grilles, 840-841

APIC (Advanced
Programmable Interrupt
Controller), 162

APIs (Application
Programming Interfaces),
51

APM (Advanced Power
Management), 1042-1043
ACPI (Advanced
Configuration and Power
Interface), 1045-1047
BIOS, 1044
driver, 1044
states, 1043-1044
structure, 1044

Apple
Lisa, 695
QuickTime, 895

applets, 38

application interfacing
(scanners), 782-784

Application layer (OSI
model), 421

application programming
interfaces (APIs), 51

applications, 8, 34-36
applets, 38
application suites, 37
databases, 36
digital electronics, 79-80
disassembling, 35
drawing/painting, 36
email, 36
Microsoft Office, 37
multimedia, 36

color temperature, 836-837
controllers, 831-832
convergence, 838-839
dot-pitch, 841
electron guns, 837-838
image controls, 851-852
image distortion, 850-851
image sizing, 850
line width, 842
monitors, 28
over scans, 848-849
phosphors, 835-836
purity, 839
resolution, 843-844
screen curvature, 842-843
screen size, 846-848
shadow masks, 839-840
under scans, 848-849
CSMA/CA (Carrier Sense Multiple Access with Collision Avoidance), 440
CSMA/CD (Carrier Sense, Multiple Access with Collision Detection), 429
CTS (clear to send), 384
Curie temperature, 538
currents
AC (alternating currents), 1012
batteries, 1026
DC (direct current), 1012
cut-sheet feeders, 946-947
cutoff voltage, 1039
CW (carrier wave) modulation, 231-232
Cycle Frame (FRAME#), 266
cycle shaving, 217
cyclical redundancy check (CRC) algorithm, 304
cylinders, hard disks, 598-599

D

D-max scanners, 778
DAC (digital-to-analog converter), 910
DAE (digital audio extraction), 655
daisy-chain wiring system, 876
FireWire, 362
SCSI
bus width, 342
connectors, 333-334
terminations, 334-336
DASD (Direct Access Storage Device), 585
DAT (Digital Audio Tape), 639
data access arrangements, 463
data area, BIOS, 199-200
data bits, 254
data buses, 85
data caches, 102
data coding, CD-ROMs, 664-665
Data Communication Equipment (DCE), 383
data compression, 456, 543-545
compression ratios, 544
disk compression systems, 544
file compression, 545
lossless compression systems, 544
data density, optical memory storage, 539
Data Encryption Standard algorithm. *See* **DES algorithm**
data integrity signals, PCI (Peripheral Component Interconnect), 267-268

data lines
expansion buses, 241
parallel ports, 401, 410
ports, 238-239
Data Link layer
Ethernet, 429-430
OSI model, 420
PCI Express, 275
Data Migration Facility, 392
data organization
Data Organization Layer, PC cards, 292
secondary storage (memory), 529
random-access media, 531-532
sequential media, 529-531
Data Over Cable Service Interface Specification. *See* **DOCSIS**
data packets, USB, 360
data preparation, as modem hardware, 463
data rates
Group 3, 961-962
Group 4, 964
IrDA, 369
Data Recording Format Layer, PC cards, 292
data registers (enhanced parallel ports), 412-413
data set ready (DSR), 383
data striping, 610
data strobe coding, 363
Data Terminal Equipment (DTE), 383
Data Terminal Ready (DTR), 383
data transfers
attribute phase, 273
hard disk mechanism, 590
hard disk performance, 607-608
non-cache coherent, 273
PC cards, 289
register-to-register transfers, 273

directional antennae

expansion buses

finalization process, 676

firewalls, 503-505

FireWire, 353, 361-363
  arbitration, 364-365
  cable, 366-367
  configuration, 364
  connectors, 365-366
  daisy-chaining, 362
  leaf, 362
  signaling, 363

firmware, BIOS, 176-177

first-in, first-out buffer, 388

Fisheye converters, 796

fixated for appending, 676

fixation, CD-Rs, 676-677

Fixed ACPI Description
  Table, 1047

fixed disk parameter table
  (FDPT), 202

fixed disks, 585

fixed focus, 803

flash digital cameras,
  801-802

Flash memory, 558-559

flat-panel displays, 834,
  852-853. *See also* LCDs

flatbed scanners, 773

Fleming, John, 65

FlexATX motherboards,
  991-992

flip-flop circuits, 522

flip-flop memory, 76

floating-point unit (microprocessors), 87-88

floppy disks, 346-347,
  616-617
  cable, 348-350
  chipsets, 173
  controllers, 347
  formats, 622-625
  history, 617-618
    density key, 621-622
    hubs, 620
    insertion key, 620-621

liners, 620
magnetic properties,
  618-619
medium, 618
shell, 619-620
writing protection, 621
mechanisms, 628-629
operation, 347-348
SuperDisks, 625-628

floppy drives, 24-25

flow control
  AT Attachment, 302
  expansion buses, 243
  ports, 239
  RS-232C ports, 385

flux transitions, 252

FNODEs (File NODE),
  604

focal length, digital camera
  lenses, 793-794

focus (cameras), 793,
  802-804

fog color, 718

fogging, 718

form factors, 1067

formats
  CD-ROMs, 667
  floppy disks, 622-625
  hard disks, 600-601
  IrDA, 371
  SuperDisks, 626-627

four-color printing, 944

FPM RAM (fast page-mode
  RAM), 560-561

frame buffer memory, 554

frames
  buffers, 51, 706
  group-coding, 254-256
  IrDA, 371
  rates, 815, 859

"freezing the disc", 677

frequencies
  Bluetooth, 376-377
  display systems, 815
  dividers, 160

LFE (low frequency effects),
  899
modulation, 233-234, 253
multipliers, 160
Nyquist, 888
response, 911
sound, 885
synchronizing, 859-861

frequency shift keying
  (FSK), 232, 377

fretting, 574

friction feeds, 947

front buffer, 720

front panel access, 1067

front porches, 817

front-side buses, 99-100,
  122

Frozen mode, AT
  Attachment security, 311

FSK (frequency shift key-
  ing), 232, 377

Full On state (APM), 1043

full-bleed printing, 950

full-duplex modems, 452

full-length expansion
  boards, 977

full-range speaker systems,
  920

full-size slot, 1069

full-size tower cases, 1065

fully formed character
  printers, 924

function keys (keyboards),
  735-737, 740

functions, 17-19
  BIOS, 177
    initialization, 179-188
    interface, 188-191, 195-198
    IPL (Initial Program Load),
      178, 183-184
    storage, 199-220
  chipsets, 155-156
  communications, 21, 225-226
    channels, 225-258
    expansion buses, 21-22

intersymbol interference, 592

Intr, 408

inverters, 1023, 1057

IP addresses, 480-483

IPL (Initial Program Load), 178, 183-184

IPv6 (Internet Protocol Version 6), 487

IR (Infrared) technology, 767

IrDA (Infrared Data Association), 22, 353, 367-369
> data rates, 369
> formats, 371
> frames, 371
> history, 367-368
> infrared light, 369
> modulation, 370-371
> pulse width, 369-370
> speed, 370

iris blades, 791

iron, as magnetic material, 534

ISA (Industry Standard Architecture), 30, 975

ISDN (Integrated Services Digital Network), 472-473
> BRI (Basic Rate Interface), 472
> PRI (Primary Rate Interface), 472

ISM band (Industrial-Scientific-Medical band), 376, 435

ISO (International Standards Organization), 824

isochronous communications, 248

isochronous mode (FireWire), 364

ISPs (Internet Service Providers), 499, 504
> performance limits, 504-505
> security, 505-506

Itanium microprocessors, 129, 142-143

ITU (International Telecommunications Union), 458

J

JEITIA (Japan Electronics and Information Technology Industries Association), 286-287

Joint Photographic Experts Group. *See* JPEGs

Joint Technical Committee (JTC), 824

Joliet CD-ROM Recording Specification, 667

JPEGs (Joint Photographic Experts Group), 805, 823-824

JTC (Joint Technical Committee), 824

jukeboxes, near-line storage, 528

K

K56flex, 461

kardia, 916

Katmai. *See* Pentiums

Katz, Randy H., 611

Key Tronic Corporation, 729-731

keyboards, 27, 695, 725-726
> Advanced Keyboard, 735-736
> capacitive, 729
> chipsets, 173

> control keys, 735-737
> controllers, 739
> debouncers, 729
> dome-based, 730
> electrical functions, 738-739
>> *compatibility, 746-747*
>> *connections, 747-749*
>> *host interface, 744-745*
>> *ports, 739-742*
>> *software commands, 742-744*
>> *USB port, 750*
> ergonomic designs, 737-738
> function keys, 735-740
> layouts, 732
>> *Dvorak-Dealey, 733-734*
>> *QWERTY, 732-733*
> legends, 731-732
> linear travel, 730
> modular keyboard connector, 749
> non-contact, 728-729
> PS/2-style, 747-749
> short-travel, 731
> soft-touch, 730
> stiff, 731
> switches, 727-728
> technologies, 726-727
> touch, 729-731
> transmitter, 694
> wireless, 750-751

keycaps, 731-732

keypresses, 694

Kleinschmidt, Edward, 694

Krum, Charles, 694

Krum, Howard, 694

L

lag, digital camera shutters, 797-798

landing zone, read/write heads, 594-595

MMCD

Motion Picture Experts Group. *See* MPEGs

Mount Rainier, 674-675

Mount Rainier drives, 618

mouse, 27, 753-758

MOVs (metal-oxide varistors), 1051-1052

MP3 players, 914-915

MPC (Multimedia PC), 658

MPEGs (Motion Picture Experts Group), 655, 823-826

MR (Modified Read) encoding, 963

Multi-Cavity Module. *See* MCM

multi-word DMA transfers, 303-304

multichannel sound, 895-896

multifunction fax printers, 959-961

multilayer circuit boards, 72

multimedia, software, 36

Multimedia Cable Network System Partners, Ltd.. *See* MCNS

MultiMedia Cards, 579

Multimedia Compact Disc (MMCD), 644

Multimedia Content Description Interface, 826

Multimedia Extensions. *See* MMX

Multimedia PC (MPC), 658

multiple zone recording (MZR), 587, 599-600

multiple-carrier modems, 455

multiple-image mode, 807

multiplexing
    expansion buses, 242
    memory chips, 559-560
    PCI (Peripheral Component Interconnect), 266

multipliers, 216

multiprocessors
    accumulators, 54
    logic gates, 75-76

multitasking, 79

MZR (multiple zone recording), 587, 599-600

N

N-channel Metal Oxide Semiconductor. *See* NMOS

N-type semiconductors, 67

nAckReverse, 409

name servers, 500

names, RS-232C, 389-390

NAND (Not AND), 75

nanoprocessors, 89

narrow SCSI, 342

nAStrobe, 408

National Business Education Quarterly, 734

National Television Standards Committee (NTSC), 819-820

Natural Keyboard, 737

nAutoFd, 404

nDStrobe, 407-408

Near letter quality mode, 940

near-line storage, 528

nematic technology, LCDs (liquid crystal displays), 853-855

NetBIOS (Network Basic Input/Output System), 421

network interface cards. *See* NICs

Network layer (OSI model), 420

networks, 417-418
    architecture, 424-428
    classes, 485-486
    connectivity, 21

    hardware, 441-445
    Internet model, 422
    LANs, 23
    Internet. *See* Internet
    OSI model, 418-421
    prefixes (CIDR), 486
    standards, 428-436
    WANs, 23
    Windows model, 422-423
    wireless, 23

New Process technology, 932

nFault, 403

ni-cad cells (batteries), 1032-1034

nibbles, 393, 405-406, 515

nickel, as magnetic material, 534

nickel-cadmiums. *See* ni-cad cells

nickel-metal hydrides (batteries), 1034-1035

NICs (network interface cards), 442-443

NiMH. *See* nickel-metal hydrides

nine-pin D-shell jacks, 875

nine-wire serial cable, 386

nInit signal, 408

NLX motherboards, 988, 992-994

NMOS (N-channel Metal Oxide Semiconductor), 67-68

No Return-to-Zero (NRZ), serial channels, 249

No Return-to-Zero Inverted (NRZI), serial channels, 249-250, 359

No-ID Format, 601

noise interference, 1073

noise protection, 1050-1051

nomenclature
    expansion boards, 974-976
    motherboards, 973-974

commands, keyboard,
742-744
databases, 36
disassembling programs, 35
drawing/painting, 36
email, 36
flow control, 385
interface, PC cards, 290-291
interrupts, 80, 191, 195
multimedia, 36
operating systems. *See* operating systems
spreadsheets, 36
utilities, 37-38
Web browsers, 36
Word processors, 36
Software Retriggerable Strobe mode (8253 Timer/Counter Chip), 165
solder-ball grid array, 112
solid inkjet printers, 931
solid-state electronics, 66
Solid-State Floppy Disk Cards. *See* **SSFDCs**
solid-state memory, 519-520
read-only memory, 523
read-write memory, 520-522
Sony Corporation
Dynamic Digital Sound (SDDS), 681, 900
floppy disks, 617
Memory Stick package, 578-579
sound, 884-885
analog audio, 885
amplitude, 885-886
decibels, 886-887
distortion, 887-888
frequencies, 885
voltage, 886
digital audio, 888
bandwidth, 890-891
capturing, 901-904
compression, 891-900
output systems, 913-915

resolution, 890
sampling rate, 888-890
transmission, 891
sound pressure level (SPL), 885
sound systems, 904-905, 908-909
amplifiers, 906
compatibility, 909-910
control, 910-911
drivers, 907-908
loudspeakers, 906-907
pulse-width modulation, 906
quality, 911-913
tone generators, 905-906
transducers, 915
loudspeakers, 918-921
microphones, 915-918
soundboards, 885, 908-909
compatibility, 909-910
control, 910-911
quality, 911-913
source code, 47
Source Manager, Twain, 783
Source-Synchronous Transfer, 134
Space, serial signal, 379
spacing
expansion slots, 985-986
image creation, 721-722
screen-pitch, 840
speakers
active systems, 921
bass reflec, 920
cones, 918
drivers, 908
ducted, 920
full-range speaker system, 920
loudspeakers. *See* loudspeakers
midrange, 919
passive systems, 921
satellite, 920-921
satellite speakers, 919
three-way, 919

tuned-port, 920
two-way, 919
USB, 913-914
Windows, 908
specifications, backup power devices, 1055-1056
speculative execution, 96
speed
CD-Rs, 671-672
clock, 94-95, 216-217
clocking, SCSI, 342-343
DDR memory (double data-rate memory), 563
digital camera shutters, 796-797
floppy disks, 629
hard disk mechanism, 587-588
IrDA, 370
optical media, 655-658
PCI (Peripheral Component Interconnect), 265-266
printers, 938-941
scanners, 776-777
USB, 356
speedlight, 801
SpeedStep, 107-108
SPGA (staggered pin grid array), 111
spikes, 1049
Spindle Sync/Cable Select signal, 317
spindles, 585, 628
SPL (sound pressure level), 885
split transactions
PCI (Peripheral Component Interconnect), 274
protocol, 122
spreadsheets, 36
sprites, 713
Square Wave mode (8253 Timer/Counter Chip), 165
SSE (Streaming SIMD Extensions), 92